Fodor's 06

W9-AYD-456

Bradbury

ITALY

**Where to Stay & Eat
for All Budgets**

**Must-See Sights
& Local Secrets**

Ratings You Can Trust

Fodor's Travel Publications   New York, Toronto, London, Sydney, Auckland
www.fodors.com

FODOR'S ITALY 2006
Editor: Matthew Lombardi

Editorial Production: Bethany Cassin Beckerlegge and Jacinta O'Halloran
Editorial Contributors: Peter Blackman, Mary Beth Bohman, Jeff Booth, Ryan Bradley, Linda Cabasin, Lisa Dunford, Elaine Eliah, Robert I. C. Fisher, Robin S. Goldstein, Cristina Gregorin, Valerie Hamilton, Roberta Kedzierski, Dana Klitzberg, Francesca Marretta, Ann Reavis, Chris Rose, Patricia Rucidlo, Pamela Santini, Maria Sophocles, Amanda Theunissen, Caroline Trefler, Mark Walters, Amy Wang
Maps: David Lindroth, *cartographer;* Bob Blake and Rebecca Baer, *map editors*. Additional cartography provided by Henry Colomb, Mark Stroud, and Ali Baird, Moon Street Cartography; and by Mapping Specialists Ltd.
Design: Fabrizio La Rocca, *creative director*, Chie Ushio, Guido Caroti, Siobhan O'Hare, Tina Malaney, Brian Ponto
Photography: Melanie Marin, *senior picture editor*
Production/Manufacturing: Colleen Ziemba
Cover Photo (Country road and house, Tuscany): Simon Des Rochers/Masterfile

ISBN 1–4000–1555–3

ISSN 0361–977X

SPECIAL SALES
This book is available for special discounts for bulk purchases for sales promotions or premiums. Special editions, including personalized covers, excerpts of existing books, and corporate imprints, can be created in large quantities for special needs. For more information, write to Special Markets/ Premium Sales, 1745 Broadway, MD 6-2, New York, New York 10019, or e-mail specialmarkets@ randomhouse.com.

AN IMPORTANT TIP & AN INVITATION
Although all prices, opening times, and other details in this book are based on information supplied to us at press time, changes occur all the time in the travel world, and Fodor's cannot accept responsibility for facts that become outdated or for inadvertent errors or omissions. So **always confirm information when it matters,** especially if you're making a detour to visit a specific place. Your experiences—positive and negative—matter to us. If we have missed or misstated something, **please write to us.** We follow up on all suggestions. Contact the Italy editor at editors@fodors. com or c/o Fodor's at 1745 Broadway, New York, NY 10019.

PRINTED IN THE UNITED STATES OF AMERICA

10 9 8 7 6 5 4 3 2 1

Be a Fodor's Correspondent

Your opinion matters. It matters to us. It matters to your fellow Fodor's travelers, too. And we'd like to hear it. In fact, we *need* to hear it.

When you share your experiences and opinions, you become an active member of the Fodor's community. That means we'll not only use your feedback to make our books better, but we'll publish your names and comments whenever possible. Throughout this guide, look for "Word of Mouth," excerpts of your unvarnished feedback.

Here's how you can help improve Fodor's for all of us.

Tell us when we're right. We rely on local writers to give you an insider's perspective. But our writers and staff editors—who are the best in the business—depend on you. Your positive feedback is a vote to renew our recommendations for the next edition.

Tell us when we're wrong. We're proud that we update most of our guides every year. But we're not perfect. Things change. Hotels cut services. Museums change hours. Charming cafés lose their charm. If our writer didn't quite capture the essence of a place, tell us how you'd do it differently. If any of our descriptions are inaccurate or inadequate, we'll incorporate your changes in the next edition and will correct factual errors at fodors.com *immediately.*

Tell us what to include. You're bound to have some fantastic experiences not mentioned in this guide—Italy's that kind of place. Why not share them with a community of like-minded travelers? Maybe you chanced upon a palazzo or a trattoria that you don't want to keep to yourself. Tell us why we should include it. And share your discoveries and experiences with everyone directly at fodors.com. Your input may lead us to add a new listing or highlight a place we cover with a "Highly Recommended" star or with our highest rating, "Fodor's Choice."

Give us your opinion instantly at our feedback center at www.fodors.com/feedback. You may also e-mail editors@fodors.com with the subject line "Italy Editor." Or send your nominations, comments, and complaints by mail to Italy Editor, Fodor's, 1745 Broadway, New York, NY 10019.

You and travelers like you are the heart of the Fodor's community. Make our community richer by sharing your experiences. Be a Fodor's correspondent.

Buon viaggio! (Or simply: Happy traveling!)

Tim Jarrell, Publisher

CONTENTS

ITALY IN FOCUS

CLOSEUPS

MAPS

Organization

The first part of this book is designed to give you the lay of the land and help you figure out where to go. Look to **What's Where** for descriptions of Italy's regions, including their pleasures and pitfalls for travelers. **If You Like** . . . identifies some classic Italian experiences and tells you where you to go to have them.

Next comes **Smart Travel Tips,** a section of nuts-and-bolts trip-planning information. Topics are arranged in alphabetical order. Some won't apply to you, but many will.

The remainder of the book consists of our region-by-region listings—the places to go and things to do—interlaced with history, background, and tips from our on-the-spot writers. Chapters appear in geographical order, beginning at the top of the boot and working south.

Our Ratings

Anything we list in this guide, whether it's a museum, a ruin, or a restaurant, has our recommendation. Naturally, not every place is going to be for everyone. Our goal is to provide the information you need to make choices that are right for you.

A black star next to a listing means it's **Highly Recommended.** Year in and year out, travelers of all stripes have great experiences at these spots.

Orange stars indicate our highest rating, **Fodor's Choice.** These are the places we think you'll be telling your friends about when you return home—places where you stand a good chance of making a memory. Some selections you'll expect, but others might surprise you. They're all truly special and uniquely Italian. When you have your own Fodor's Choice experience, let us know about it at www.fodors.com/feedback.

Deciphering the Listings

For the most part, our listings are self-explanatory, but a few details are worth mentioning.

For attractions, we give standard adult admission fees; reductions for children, students, and senior citizen are rare (unless you're an EU citizen). Hotel and restaurant price categories are defined on the charts found in each chapter. Unless otherwise indicated, restaurants are open for lunch and dinner daily. We mention dress at restaurants only when there's a specific requirement and reservations only when they're essential or not accepted. Hotels have private bath, phone, TV, and air-conditioning unless otherwise indicated. We list facil-

ities but not whether you'll be charged extra to use them, so when pricing accommodations, find out what's included.

Want to pay with plastic? **AE, DC, MC, V** following restaurant and hotel listings indicate whether American Express, Diner's Club, MasterCard, and Visa are accepted.

Many Listings

★	Fodor's Choice
★	Highly recommended
☺	Family-friendly
⊠	Physical address
⊠	Branch address
✛	Directions
⊕	Mailing address
☎	Telephone
🖷	Fax
⊕	On the Web
✉	E-mail
🖅	Admission fee
☉	Open/closed times
Ⓜ	Metro stations
▭	Credit cards
⇨	See also

Hotels & Restaurants

🏨	Hotel
⇥	Number of rooms
⚴	Facilities
⋓⊘⋓	Meal plans
✕	Restaurant
⚲	Reservations
🕮	Dress code
↘	Smoking
🍸	BYOB
✕🏨	Hotel with restaurant that warrants a visit

WHAT'S WHERE

VENICE

Venice is one of the world's most novel cities, with canals where streets should be and an atmosphere of faded splendor that practically defines the word *decadent*. Once a great seafaring power, Venice now lives for tourism, prompting detractors to compare it to Disneyland. It's true that Piazza San Marco, the magnificent main square, is often packed with sightseers, and there are plenty of kitschy souvenirs for sale in the heavily trafficked area around the Rialto Bridge. But Venice is no Mickey Mouse affair: it has a rich history, it's packed with artistic treasures accumulated over a thousand years, and despite the crowds it remains inescapably romantic. If you give the city a few days and spend time wandering the quieter neighborhoods, it's easy to succumb to Venice's allure.

THE VENETIAN ARC

The green plains stretching west of Venice hold three of northern Italy's most appealing midsize cities: Padua, Vicenza, and Verona. Each has notable artistic treasures and an attractive historic center; Padua is famous for its Giotto frescoes, Vicenza for its Palladian villas, and Verona for its ancient arena. Farther north, Alpine foothills are dotted with small, welcoming towns and some of Italy's most distinguished vineyards. To the east, the region of Friuli–Venezia Giulia has a split personality, half Italian and half Central European. In the main city, Trieste, you can feel the influences of both Venice and Vienna.

THE DOLOMITES

The Dolomites are Italy's finest mountain playground, with stupefying cliffs, curiously shaped peaks, charming meadows, and crystal-clear lakes. The skiing, hiking, and mountain drives are comparable to what you'll find in the Austrian Alps just to the north, at better prices and with an Italian sensibility. There's a definite Austrian influence here as well; most of the area is bilingual, with German sometimes prevailing. Notable cities are the lively university town of Bolzano, history-rich Trento, the spa center Merano, and the chic ski resorts of Cortina d'Ampezzo and Madonna di Campiglio.

MILAN, LOMBARDY & THE LAKES

The variety of natural beauty in Italy is remarkable, and the region of Lombardy makes a significant contribution to the mix with its gorgeous lakes, Como, Garda, and Maggiore. Their deep-blue, Alp-fed waters have been drawing accolades since the days of ancient Rome. In more recent times, regal villas, voluptuous gardens, and pretty resort towns have taken up positions along their shores. At the center of Lombardy is Milan, Italy's second-largest city and its business capital. The Milanese are criticized for being too businesslike—for not knowing how to relax and enjoy life the way their countrymen do. But the city's wealth has brought with it some sophisticated pleasures, including Italy's most renowned opera house and its most stylish shopping district.

PIEDMONT & VALLE D'AOSTA

On lists of Italian superlatives, these two regions in the northwest corner of the country almost always find themselves one spot down from the top. The mountains are unquestionably impressive, but for hiking and skiing they rate just below the Dolomites. The French-influenced cuisine is a pleasure, but isn't as heralded as Emilia-Romagna's. The city of Turin ranks second to Milan in urban sophistication and business clout. And the wine-producing hills aren't quite as alluring as their counterparts in Tuscany—though the wine itself is second to none. So, there are two reasons to visit this area: first, all those runner-up honors mean you can have a variety of great experiences; second, you'll be off the main tourist circuit—unless, that is, you're here in February 2006, when Turin is host city for the Winter Olympics.

THE ITALIAN RIVIERA

The region of Liguria (known to pleasure-seekers as the Italian Riviera) has northern Italy's most attractive stretch of coastline. Though there are some good beaches, the main appeal is the beauty of the seaside cliffs and coves, and of the small towns interspersed among them. The most celebrated is tiny but glamorous Portofino, though these days it gets competition from the even tinier villages of the Cinque Terre, famous for the hiking paths that run between them. Smack in the middle of the coast is Genoa, Italy's busiest port. It holds the region's main cultural attractions, intermixed with some port-city grit.

EMILIA-ROMAGNA

Emilia-Romagna doesn't have the striking natural beauty of its neighboring regions—instead, it wins your heart through your stomach. Many of Italy's signature food products come from here, including Parmigiano-Reggiano cheese (aka Parmesan), prosciutto di Parma, and balsamic vinegar. The pasta is

Italy

considered Italy's finest—a reputation the region's chefs earn every day. But food isn't Emilia-Romagna's be all and end all. Attractive cities dot the map: Bologna is the principal cultural and intellectual center, with rows of street arcades winding through grandiose towers. The mosaics in Ravenna are glittering treasures left from the era of Byzantine rule, and Ferrara, Parma, and Modena all reward you for your attention.

FLORENCE

It's hard to think of a place that's more closely linked to one specific historical period than Florence. In the 15th century the city was at the center of an artistic revolution, later labeled the Renaissance, that changed the way people see the world. Five hundred years later the Renaissance remains the reason people see Florence—the abundance of treasures is mind-boggling. Present-day Florentines have a somewhat uneasy relationship with their city's past; the neverending stream of tourists is something they seem to tolerate more often than embrace. Still, they pride themselves on living well, and that means you'll find exceptional restaurants and first-rate shopping to go with all that amazing art.

TUSCANY

Nature outdid herself in Tuscany, the central Italian region that has Florence as its principal city. Descriptions and photographs can't do the landscape justice—the hills, draped with woods, vineyards, and olive groves, may not have the drama of mountain peaks or waves crashing on the shore, yet there's any undeniable magic about them. Aside from Florence, Tuscany has several midsize cities that are well worth visiting, but the greatest appeal lies in the smaller towns, often perched on hilltops and not significantly altered since the Middle Ages. Despite its popularity with fellow travelers, Tuscany remains a place you can escape to.

**UMBRIA &
THE MARCHES**

Umbria was the first region in Italy to be dubbed by travel writers "the next Tuscany," a term that's since been applied to locations all up and down the boot. There's some sense to the comparison—like Tuscany, Umbria has beautiful rolling hills with attractive old towns sitting on top of them. There's no city with the size or significance of Florence, but a number of the smaller cities, particularly Assisi, Perugia, Spoleto, and Orvi-

ROME

eto, have lots to hold your interest. Umbria's Roman past is much in evidence—expect to see Roman villas, aqueducts, theaters, walls, and temples. To the east, in the region of the Marches, the main draw is the town of Urbino, where the Ducal Palace reveals more about the artistic energy of the Renaissance than a shelf of history books.

LAZIO

Rome is a large, busy city that lives in the here and now, yet there's no other place on earth where you'll encounter such powerful evocations of a long and spectacular past. Take a few steps from a piazza designed by Michelangelo and you're looking down upon the ruins of ancient Rome, with the Colosseum as your backdrop. Exit a church holding a masterpiece by Caravaggio, turn the corner, and find yourself face to face with the Pantheon. From there a short walk takes you across the River Tiber to the world headquarters of the Roman Catholic Church, with its grandest cathedral and a massive, spectacular art collection, topped off by the Sistine Chapel. If there's a down side to Rome's abundance, it's that you can find yourself feeling overwhelmed. It pays to prioritize, pace yourself, and accept the fact that you won't see it all.

NAPLES & CAMPANIA

The region surrounding Rome has appealing places to visit if you're looking for a break from the hubbub of the city. In fact, people have been doing just that for almost as long as Rome has existed. The worthwhile, generally undervisited sights include papal palaces, landscaped gardens, medieval hill towns, beaches, and antiquities both Etruscan and Roman.

Campania is the gateway to southern Italy—and as far south as many travelers get. The region's happy combination of spectacular geology and rich cultural heritage makes it a popular place both to unwind—on the pint-size island of Capri or the resorts of the Amalfi Coast—and to explore the past—at the archaeological ruins of Pompeii, Herculaneum, and Paestum. In the middle of everything is Naples, a chaotic metropolis that people love and hate in nearly equal measure, though after a decade of urban renewal the lovers now appear to be in the majority. On a good day it's Italy's most fun and friendly large city. On a bad one it's a giant traffic jam, filled with crooked cabbies and purse-snatching kids on scooters.

THE MEZZOGIORNO	
	The southernmost regions of the peninsula—Puglia, Basilicata, and Calabria—are known informally as the *mezzogiorno*. The name translates literally as "midday," and it's meant to evoke the blazing sun that presides over the medieval villages, shimmering seas, and varied landscapes. The coastline of Puglia, along the heel of Italy's boot, is popular with beachgoers, but for the most part you're off the beaten path here, with all the pleasures and challenges that entails. You'll find fewer English-speakers but more genuine warmth from the people you encounter. The most distinctive attractions are the *sassi* (cave dwellings in the Basilicata village of Matera) and *trulli* (mysterious conical-roofed dwellings found in abundance in the Puglia town of Alberobello). Both are UNESCO World Heritage sites.
SICILY	
	The architecture of Sicily reflects the island's centuries of successive dominion by the Greeks, Byzantines, Arabs, Normans, and Spaniards. Baroque church–hopping could be a sport in the cacophonous streets of Palermo and seafaring Siracusa. The breezes are sultry, and everyday life is without pretense, as witnessed in the workaday stalls of the fish markets all along the ports of the Tyrrhenian and Ionian coasts, bursting with tuna, swordfish, and sardines. Greek ruins stand sentinel in Agrigento's Valley of the Temples, blanketed in almond, oleander, and juniper blossoms. All over the island the ins and outs of life are celebrated each day as they have been for centuries— over a morning coffee, at the family lunch table, and in the evening *passeggiata*.
SARDINIA	
	Too distant from imperial and papal Rome to be influenced by the character of the mainland, Sardinia is as unique as its weather-worn landscape. Although the indigenous culture is one of Italy's most interesting, many travelers opt to explore the high-profile Costa Smeralda, a chic resort developed by the Aga Khan, who discovered its charms when his yacht took shelter from a storm. Intrepid travelers head for the *nuraghi,* cyclopean stone defensive structures that are among prehistory's enigmas. Severely beautiful Sardinia is a prime destination if you're looking for a vacation getaway—whether of the chic or rugged variety.

°F VENICE °C

°F FLORENCE °C

°F ROME °C

°F NAPLES °C

The main tourist season runs from April to mid-October. The so-called low season from fall to early spring may be cooler and rainier, but it has its rewards: less time waiting in line and more time for unhurried views of what you want to see.

Tourists crowd the major art cities at Easter, when Italians flock to resorts and to the country. From March through May, busloads of schoolchildren take cities of artistic and historical interest by storm. You don't want to be on an Italian beach in August because of the crowds. June and September are best; July can be crowded at the major resorts.

Climate

The best months for sightseeing are April, May, June, September, and October, when the weather is mild. The hottest months, July and August, can be unpleasant. Winters are relatively mild in most places on the main tourist circuit but always include some rainy spells.

In general, the northern half of the peninsula and the Adriatic Coast down to Puglia are rainier than elsewhere. Except for Taormina and some towns on the Italian Riviera, coastal resorts usually close up tight from October through Easter.

🗂 Forecasts **Weather Channel Connection** ☎ 900/932-8437 95¢ per minute ⊕ www.weather.com.

QUINTESSENTIAL ITALY

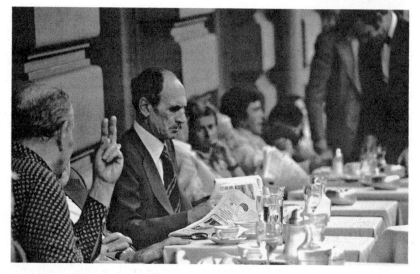

Il Caffè (Coffee)

The Italian day begins and ends with coffee, and more cups of coffee punctuate the time in between. To live like the Italians do, drink as they drink, standing at the counter or sitting at an outdoor table of the corner bar. (In Italy, a "bar" is a coffee bar.) A primer: *Caffè* means coffee, and Italian standard issue is what Americans call espresso—short, strong, and usually taken very sweet. *Cappuccino* is a foamy half-and-half of espresso and steamed milk; cocoa powder *(cacao)* on top is acceptable, cinnamon not. If you're thinking of having a cappuccino for dessert, think again—Italians drink only caffè or *caffè macchiato* (with a spot of steamed milk) after lunchtime. Confused? Homesick? Order *caffè americano* for a reasonable facsimilie of good old filtered joe.

Il Calcio (Soccer)

Imagine the most rabid of American football fans—the ones who paint their faces on game day and sleep in pajamas emblazoned with the logo of their favorite team. Throw in a dose of melodrama along the lines of a tear-jerking soap opera. Ratchet up the intensity by a factor of ten, and you'll start to get a sense of how Italians feel about their national game, soccer—known in the mother tongue as *calcio*. On Sunday afternoons throughout the long September-to-May season, stadiums are packed throughout Italy from tip to toe. Those who don't get to games in person tend to congregate around television sets in restaurants and bars, rooting for the home team with a passion that feels like a last vestige of the days when the country was a series of warring medieval city-states. How calcio mania affects your stay in Italy depends on how eager you are to get involved. At the very least, you may notice an eerie Sunday-afternoon silence

If you want to get a sense of contemporary Italian culture, and indulge in some of its pleasures, start by familiarizing yourself with the rituals of daily life. These are a few highlights—things you can take part in with relative ease.

on city streets, or erratic restaurant service around the same time, accompanied by occasional cheers and groans from a neighboring room. If you want a memorable, truly Italian experience, attend a game yourself. Availability of tickets may depend on the current fortunes of the team in the town where you're staying, but they often can be acquired with some help from your hotel concierge.

Il Gelato (Ice Cream)

During warmer months, *gelato*—the Italian equivalent of ice cream—is a national obsession. It's considered a snack rather than a dessert, bought at stands and shops in piazzas and on street corners, and consumed on foot, usually at a leisurely stroll. (See La Passeggiata below.) Gelato is softer, less creamy, and more intensely flavored than its American counterpart. It comes in simple flavors that capture the essence of the main ingredient. (You won't find

Chunky Monkey or Cookies 'n' Cream.) At most gelaterias standard choices include pistachio, nocciola (hazelnut), caffè, and numerous fresh-fruit varieties. Quality varies; the surest sign that you've hit on a good spot is a line at the counter.

La Passeggiata (Strolling)

A favorite Italian pastime is the *passeggiata* (literally, the promenade). In the late afternoon and early evening, especially on weekends, couples, families, and packs of teenagers stroll the main streets and piazzas of Italy's towns. It's a ritual of exchanged news and gossip, window-shopping, flirting, and gelato eating that adds up to a uniquely Italian experience. To join in, simply hit the streets for a bit of wandering. You may feel more like an observer than a participant, until you realize that observing is what la passeggiata is all about.

IF YOU LIKE . . .

Ancient Civilizations

Heavily colonized by the ancient Greeks, and then center of the Roman Empire, Italy has a wealth of classical sites, many of them in an excellent state of preservation. Rome was, of course, the capital of the Roman Empire, and a number of ancient sites remain there today, seemingly plunked down in the middle of the modern metropolis.

Campania, too, is full of important classical landmarks from both the Greek and Roman eras. Farther south, Sicily was a center of trade and culture in the Hellenic world, and the island is still richly blessed with remarkable Greek temples—and fantastic Roman mosaics too. Sardinia, meanwhile, is dotted with *nuraghi*, mysterious prehistoric stone fortresses. Italy's Classical highlights include:

- **Ancient Rome.** The Roman Forum, the Capitoline Hill, and the unforgettable Colosseum and Pantheon are the best-preserved ruins of the Empire's epicenter. At every turn you'll behold the crumbling remains of an ancient civilization—with motor scooters whizzing blithely past.

- **Pompeii and Herculaneum.** The eruption of Mount Vesuvius in AD 79 left these two Roman cities buried in the volcanic ash and mud that famously preserved buildings and objects of everyday life. To walk their streets is to travel back in time.

- **Valley of the Temples, Agrigento.** This valley on the southern coast of Sicily, awash in almond blossoms, is considered by many to have the finest and best-preserved Greek temples anywhere—including Greece.

Renaissance Art

Travel veterans will tell you that the seemingly countless masterpieces of Italian art can cause first-time visitors—eyes glazed over from a heavy downpour of images, dates, and names—to lean, Pisa-like, on their companions for support. After a surfeit of Botticellis and Raphaels, even the miracle of the High Renaissance may begin to pall. The secret is to act like a tortoise, not a hare, and take your sweet time.

Instead of trotting after brisk tour guides, allow the splendors of the age to unfold slowly. Don't stop at the museums; get out and explore the chapels, palaces, and town squares for which Italy's marvelous art was conceived centuries ago and where much of it remains. Take in Michelangelo's *David* in Florence's Accademia, but then meander down the nearby 15th-century street where the sculptor was born.

These caveats aside, here are the places to go when you're ready for an art feast:

- **Galleria degli Uffizi, Florence.** Allow the better part of a day to explore the world's greatest collection of Italian Renaissance art.

- **Musei Vaticani, Rome.** To gaze up at the impossible brushstrokes forming Michelangelo's Adam into muscular perfection at the zenith of the Sistine Chapel is to confront the divine—however you define it.

- **Basilica di San Francesco, Arezzo.** Piero della Francesa's *Legend of the True Cross* merits a pilgrimage to this Tuscan town.

Monumental Churches

Few images are more identifiable with Italy than the country's great churches, stunning works of architecture that often took one or even two centuries to build. And just as every Italian town has its main piazza, every town also has its duomo, often rising above that piazza.

Duomo literally means "dome," but is used to refer to the principal church of any given town or city. Generally speaking, the bigger the city, the more splendid its duomo. Still, some impressive churches inhabit some unlikely places—in the Umbrian hill towns of Assisi and Orvieto, for example.

Across the boot you'll find churches whose architecture ranges from flying-buttressed medieval Gothic to rococo and fanciful baroque. In Venice you'll see Byzantine influences, in Palermo you'll see Arab-Norman flair, and in Alto Adige (Südtirol) don't be surprised to see onion-bulb towers and Germanic spires.

- **Duomo, Milan.** The largest Gothic cathedral in Italy dates back to 1386; it is regal and arrogant, its spire rising high over fashionable Milan.

- **Duomo, Florence.** Brunelleschi's beautiful dome is the most recognizable in Italy, an unequalled feat of 15th-century.

- **Basilica di San Pietro, Rome.** You've probably seen the Catholic Church's mothership a thousand times on TV, but the imposing splendor of the Vatican can't be captured by the small screen.

- **Duomo, Siracusa.** Nowhere is Italy more in touch with its classical past than in this cathedral, which incorporates the columns of a 6th-century BC Greek temple.

Driving

If you associate Italian roads with unruly motorists and traffic nightmares, you're only partly right. You'll attract headlight-flashing tailgaters if you plod along at 120 kph in the left lane, but Italy's network of fast *autostrade* (toll highways) is well-maintained, with excellent service stations.

More rewarding, though, are the rural back roads, along which you might stop, on a lark, to take pictures of a crumbling farmhouse, have a coffee in a time-frozen hilltown, or enjoy an epic lunch at a rustic *agriturismo* inaccessible to public transportation. Driving, in short, is the best way to see Italy. Winding rural roads with beautiful scenery crisscross the country, but here are three of the most memorable drives:

- **SS 48 (Grande Strada delle Dolomiti).** This legendary mountain ascent takes you through the so-called "Heart of the Dolomites," the famous Passo di Sella, and into the Val Gardena, passing some of Europe's most unforgettable, craggy-peaked views.

- **SS 1 (Via Aurelia).** Every time the A1 autostrada tunnels through the mountains, this smaller road stays out on the jagged coastline of the Italian Riviera, passing palm-filled winter gardens, terraced vineyards, cliff-hanging villages, and shimmering seas.

- **SS 222 (Strada Chiantigiana).** This back road between Florence and Siena meanders through classic Tuscan landscapes: rolling hills and vineyards in the heart of the Chianti wine region. Take the drive slowly, stopping at wineries and local *enoteche*.

Rustic Cooking

Italian cuisine all comes back to *la cucina di casa* (home cooking). From Genoa's handmade pasta twists with garden-fresh pesto to a simply grilled whole fish drizzled with olive oil anywhere along Italy's coastline, the finest plates are often the simplest. The emphasis is on exceptionally good *materie prime* (primary ingredients) handled with skill and with respect for the foods themselves and for the traditional methods of preparing them.

Each region of Italy has its own distinct, time-tested cuisine that's a source of local pride, and even sophisticated restaurants often maintain an orthodox focus on generations-old recipes. Chefs revere even the most humble ingredients, devoting the same attention to day-old bread that they do to costly truffles. Here are a few places where the simplest food will take your breath away:

- **Da Michele, Naples.** There are only two items on the menu here—a margherita and a marinara—but the transcendent pizza at this 130-year-old establishment by itself justifies a trip to Italy.

- **Trattoria Casareccia, Lecce.** In Italy's warm and welcoming Deep South, this white-walled house could be your Italian grandmother's. Their *purè di fave e cicoria* (puree of fava bean with chicory) is peasant food at its best.

- **Su Gologone, Nuoro, Sardinia.** There is a deep commitment to centuries-old recipes at this rural guest house and restaurant strikingly situated within Sardinia's wild interior.

Alta Cucina

Even with the strong peasant traditions of Italian cooking, French-influenced haute cuisine, or *alta cucina* in Italian, has blossomed at certain top-end restaurants around the boot. Sophisticated recipes take traditional techniques and give them a creative twist that often shows influences from beyond Italian borders, but Italy's commitment to top primary ingredients remains a signature.

To partake of alta cucina, you should be prepared to journey off the beaten path. Many of Italy's most heralded—and best—restaurants are located in the countryside, in small, otherwise unexceptional towns. These are places of pilgrimage, where you can plan to escape the city and indulge in a long, opulent meal free from outside distractions. Here are a few:

- **Ambasciata, Quistello, Lombardy.** Chef Romano Tamani's food isn't just world-class—it's something unique in the world, deeply in touch with rural Italian tradition (and the town of Quistello is about as rural as it gets).

- **Ristorante San Domenico, Imola, Emilia-Romagna.** In the Italian region most dedicated to food worship, this is a gourmet's temple improbably located in a town known for auto racing.

- **Il Mulinazzo, Villafrati, Sicily.** Nino Graziano is the chef that put Sicily on the alta cucina map, and this is the groundbreaking restaurant in the countryside south of Palermo where he did it.

Hiking

Even if you don't fancy yourself a disciple of Reinhold Messner (the favorite son of the Dolomites and the first man to reach the peak of Everest without oxygen), you'll find great summer hiking aplenty all over Italy.

First and foremost is the mountainous region of Trentino-Alto Adige, whose Dolomites are striped with well-marked trails on every level. But it doesn't end there. The Apennines are a highlight further south. The well-established Club Alpino Italiano (CAI) is an excellent resource that can point you to mountain refuges all over Italy.

- **Vie Ferrate (Iron Ways), Trentino-Alto Adige.** Reinforced trails through the mountains, once forged by the Italian and Austro-Hungarian armies, feature ladders, bridges, and safety cables; they're a great way to get off the beaten path in the Dolomites.

- **Cinque Terre, Italian Riviera.** They're not undiscovered, as they once were—you'll hear English spoken everywhere—but these five villages clinging to the cliffs of the Riviera Levante are still spectacular, and they're all connected by invigorating hiking trails with memorable views of the towns, the rocks, and the Ligurian Sea.

- **The Paths of St. Francis, Umbria.** Outside Assisi, an easy half-hour walk takes you to the site of St. Francis's sermon to the birds. It takes a bit more effort to make the walk from Assisi to the Eremo delle Carceri; from there you can head up to the summit of Monte Subasio, where you have views for miles in every direction.

Shopping

"Made in Italy" is synonymous with style, quality, and craftsmanship, whether it refers to high fashion or Maserati automobiles. The best buys are leather goods of all kinds (from gloves to bags to jackets), silk goods, knitwear, ceramics, and, of course, the country's world-famous food products, from artisanal pasta sauces to world-class wine to extra-virgin olive oil.

Every region has its specialties. Venice is known for glassware, lace, and velvet; Milan and Como for silk; and the Dolomites and the mountains of Calabria and Sicily for hand-carved wooden objects. Bologna and Parma are known for their cheeses and hams; Modena for its balsamic vinegar; Florence for straw goods, gold jewelry, leather, and paper products (including beautiful handmade notebooks); Assisi for embroidery; and Deruta, Gubbio, Vietri, and many towns in Puglia and Sicily for ceramics.

- **Quadrilatero, Milan.** Italy's fashion capital is shop-happy, and the streets of the *quadrilatero* district display the cutting edge of European design—but come with a full wallet. End-of-season discounts go into effect in mid-January and mid-July.

- **Piazza di Spagna, Rome.** You can join the throngs shopping for high fashion in the shadow of the Spanish Steps—or hit the Via del Corso for more than a mile of stores of all varieties.

- **Tamburini, Bologna.** Be overwhelmed by the smells of all that is good about the legendary food of Emilia-Romagna—and of Italy. Then, vacuum-pack it all and take it home with you.

Nightlife

In the big cities, generic techno clubs hop with activity on Friday and Saturday. But the cutting-edge nightlife in Rome and Milan is exclusive, expensive, and evanescent. You'd do best to ask a model or soccer star where the scene is that particular week—then see if you can get in.

Outside the very largest cities, Italy is an eminently seasonable place, and partying happens mostly during *ferragosto* (August vacation), when Italians flock to beaches all over the country's extensive coastline and partake of up to a month of nonstop revelry that dwarfs the nightlife at any other time of year. Prominent party towns include:

- **Rimini, Emilia-Romagna.** It's not for everyone, but as far as many young Italians are concerned, this murky-water Adriatic beach town hosts the best summer party, anywhere, anytime.

- **Capri.** You may come to this island to admire its rocky cliffs and *grotta azzurra,* but the Italians come in August to admire each other. On a late summer evening the island's picture-perfect piazzas burst at the seams with beautiful young things.

- **Catania, Sicily.** Many tourists think of the island's youngest and liveliest city as dirty and dangerous, but it's neither. Catania has become a nerve center of youth culture in southern Italy, with an exploding live music scene, micro-brewed beer, and nightclubs to rival those of the cities of the north—without the exclusivity.

Wine

For years, most Italian wine production was mass-export jug wine, much of it from the flat southern vineyards. Unfortunately, many wine drinkers identified Italy more with this low-quality *vino sfuso* than with the country's prestigious D.O.C.G. ("Denominazione di Origine Controllata") appellations, which include Barolo and Barbaresco (tannic, age-worthy Piedmontese wines), Brunello di Montalcino (a Tuscan wine made with Sangiovese), and Amarone (the deep, dark pride of the Veneto).

Recent decades seen the emergence of the "Super Tuscans." Dubbed *vini di tavola* (table wines) or "I.G.T." *(indicazione geografica tipica),* these nontraditional blends have powerful flavors suited to the tastes of the modern wine world.

Regions such as Umbria and Sicily are following in the footsteps of the Super Tuscans, creating their own newfangled upscale blends at lower prices. Many results have been exciting. Wines to look for include:

- **Ca' del Bosco.** No winery in Italy has won more acclaim from the wine press than this Lombardy house, for both its bruts and reds.

- **Cerviolo.** One of the more affordable ways to taste a Super Tuscan, this wine is as interesting and potent as bottles costing two or three times as much.

- **Feudi di San Gregorio.** This winery has emerged as the pride of Campania, making fresh but complex whites and deep, dark, spicy, and full-bodied reds, including the masterful Patrimo.

Skiing

Italy may not have Europe's most challenging ski areas, but the views of the Alps and Dolomites along the slopes in the northern regions of Valle d'Aosta and Trentino-Alto Adige are peerless, and Italian ski passes are cheaper than Swiss or Austrian ones. There's little snowmaking here, so slopes are often not viable until mid-February—but thereafter they're frequently blanketed with wonderful fresh powder.

Italian recreational skiers favor a full-week stay (*settimana bianca*), during which they tend to keep a relaxed ski schedule—10 or 11AM until 3 or 4PM. (If you're an early riser, you'll have the snow to yourself.) Perhaps unsurprisingly, the Italians have perfected the art of après-ski; grappa, the king of Italian digestifs, is in its finest form when enjoyed in front of a ski-lodge fire after a day on the lifts.

- **Courmayeur, Valle d'Aosta.** Monte Bianco, or Mont Blanc, is one of Europe's most famous mountains, but Courmayeur's slopes are fairly tame. Take your passport for the jaw-dropping cable-car ride over to Chamonix on the French side of the mountain.

- **Cortina d'Ampezzo, Alto Adige.** Probably the best town in Italy for après-ski, Cortina is the grand old Dolomites resort town with the region's best hotels and liveliest bars. The nearby Sella Ronda is Italy's best ski circuit.

- **Mount Etna, Sicily.** Believe it or not, you can actually ski this active volcano, and while the trails are unremarkable, they make for great scenery—and a great story.

Il Dolce Far Niente

"The sweetness of doing nothing" has long been an art form in Italy. This is a country in which life's pleasures are warmly celebrated, not guiltily indulged. Of course, doing "nothing" doesn't really mean nothing. It means doing things differently. It means lingering over a glass of wine for the better part of an evening just to watch the sun slowly set. It means coming home from wherever you are at midday, whether you're a suited businessman or a third-grade schoolgirl, just to have lunch at the family table.

It means savoring a slow and flirtatious evening passeggiata along the main street of a little town, a procession with no destination other than the town and its streets. And it means making a commitment—however temporary—to thinking, feeling, and believing that there is nowhere that you have to be next, that there is no other time than the magical present.

- **Ravello.** This quiet, stunningly positioned hilltop village above the Amalfi Coast is the quintessential small Italian town—and a perfect place to gaze out at the Gulf of Salerno and *far niente.*

- **Bellagio.** Italy's enchanting Alpine lakes are icons of relaxation. Meander through stately villa gardens, dance on the wharf, or just watch the boats float by in the shadow of the Alps.

- **Gondola ride, Venice.** There is still nothing more romantic than a glide along Venice's canals in a gondola, your escorted trip to nowhere, watched over by Gothic palaces with delicately arched eyebrows.

GREAT ITINERARIES

A FIRST TRIP: HITTING THE MUST-SEES

This itinerary and the ones that follow are designed for maximum impact—they'll keep you moving. Treat them as rough outlines, and if you have more time, consider lingering longer in the places covered instead of adding more destinations.

Day 1: Venice

Arrive in Venice's Marco Polo Airport (there are some direct flights from the U.S.), take the boat across the lagoon to Venice, check into your hotel, then get out and get lost in the back canals for a couple of hours before dinner. Osteria da Fiore would make a memorable first meal in Italy; it's an unforgettable place for sweet, delicate Adriatic seafood.

Logistics: At the airport, follow signs for water transport and look for Alilaguna, which operates the soothing one-hour boat trip into Venice. The boats stop at the Lido and finally leave you near Piazza San Marco; from there you can get to your hotel on foot or by vaporetto. The water taxis are much more expensive and aren't really worth the cost, although they'll take you directly to your hotel.

Day 2: Venice

Begin by skipping the coffee at your hotel and have a real Italian coffee at a real Italian coffeeshop. Spend the day at Venice's top few sights, including the Basilica San Marco, Palazzo Ducale, and Galleria dell'Accademia. Stop for lunch, perhaps sampling Venice's traditional specialty, *sarde in saor* (grilled sardines in a mouthwatering sweet-and-sour preparation that includes onions and raisins), and be sure to check out the ancient fish market, Rialto

bridge, and sunset at the Zattere before dinner. Later, stop at one of the pubs around the Campo San Luca or Campo Santa Margherita, where you can toast to freedom from automobiles.

Logistics: Venice is best seen by wandering. The day's activities can be done on foot, with the occasional vaporetto ride.

Day 3: Ferrara/Bologna

Get an early start and head out of Venice on a Bologna-bound train. The ride to Ferrara—your first stop in Emilia-Romagna—is about an hour and a half. Visit the Castello Estense and Duomo before lunch; a panino and a beer at one of Ferrara's prim and proper cafés should fit the bill. Wander Ferrara's cobblestone streets before hopping on the train to Bologna (a ride of less than an hour). In Bologna, check into your hotel and take a walk around Piazza Maggiore before dinner. At night, you can check out some of northern Italy's best nightlife.

Logistics: In Ferrara, the train station lies a bit outside the city center, so you'll want to take a taxi into town (check your luggage at the station). Going out, there's a taxi stand near the back of the castle, toward Corso Ercole I d'Este. In Bologna the walk into town from the station is more manageable, particularly if you're staying along Via dell'Indipendenza.

Day 4: Bologna/Florence

After breakfast, spend the morning checking out some of Bologna's churches and piazzas, including a climb up the leaning Torre degli Asinelli for a red rooftop–studded panorama. After lunch, head back to the train station and take the short ride to Florence. You'll arrive in time for an afternoon siesta and an evening passeggiata.

Logistics: Florence's Santa Maria Novella train station is within easy access to some hotels, farther from others. Florence's traffic is legendary, but taxis are plentiful; make sure you get into a licensed, clearly marked car that's outside in line.

Day 5: Florence

This is your day to see the sights of Florence. Start with the Uffizi Gallery (reserve your tickets in advance), where you'll see Botticelli's *Primavera* and *Birth of Venus*. Next, walk to the Piazza Duomo, the site of Brunelleschi's spectacular dome, which you can climb for an equally spectacular view. By the time you get down, you'll be more than ready for a simple lunch at a laid-back café. Depending on your preferences, either devote the afternoon to art (Michelangelo's *David* at the Galleria dell'Accademia, the magnificent Medici Chapels, and perhaps the church of Santa Croce) or hike up to Piazzale Michelangelo, overlooking the city. Either way, finish the evening in style with a traditional *bistecca alla fiorentina* (a grilled T-bone steak with olive oil).

Day 6: Lucca/Pisa

After breakfast, board a train for Lucca. It's an easy hour-and-a-half trip on the way to Pisa to see this walled medieval city. Don't miss the Romanesque Duomo, or a walk in the park that lines the city's ramparts. Have lunch at a local trattoria before continuing on to Pisa, where you'll spend an afternoon seeing—what else—the Leaning Tower, along with the equally impressive Duomo and Battistero. Walk down to the banks of the Arno river, contemplate the majestic views at sunset, and have dinner at one of the many cheap local restaurants in the real city center—a bit away from the most touristy spots.

Logistics: Lucca's train station lies just outside the walled city, so hardier travelers may want to leave the station on foot; otherwise, take a taxi. Check your luggage at the station. Pisa's train station isn't far from the city center, although it's on the other side of town from the Campo dei Miracoli (site of the Leaning Tower).

Day 7: Orvieto/Rome

Three hours south of Pisa is Orvieto, one of the prettiest and most characteristic towns of the Umbria region, and conveniently situated right on the Florence-

Rome train line. Check out the memorable cathedral before a light lunch accompanied by one of Orvieto's famous white wines. Get back on a train bound for Rome, and in a little more than an hour you'll arrive in the Eternal City in time to make your way to your hotel and relax for a bit before you head out for the evening. When you do, check out Piazza Navona, Campo de' Fiori, and the Trevi fountain—it's best in the evening—and take a stand-up *aperitivo* (Campari and soda is the classic) at an unpretentious local bar before dinner. It's finally pizza time; you can't go wrong at any of Rome's popular local pizzerias.

Logistics: To get from Pisa to Orvieto, you'll first catch a train to Florence and then get on a Rome-bound train from there. Be careful at Rome's Termini train station, which is a breeding ground for scam artists. Keep your possessions close at hand, and only get into a licensed taxi at the taxi stand.

Day 8: Rome

Rome took millennia to build, but unfortunately on this whirlwind trip you'll only have a day and a half to see it. In the morning, head to the Vatican Museums to see the Michelangelo's glorious *Adam* at the Sistine Chapel. See St. Peter's Cathedral and Square before heading back into Rome proper for lunch around the Pantheon, followed by a coffee from one of Rome's famous coffeeshops. Next, visit ancient Rome—first see the magnificent Pantheon, and then head across to the Colosseum, stopping along the way along Via dei Fori Imperiali to check out the Roman Forum

from above. From the Colosseum, take a taxi to Piazza di Spagna, a good place to see the sunset and shop at stylish boutiques. Take another taxi to Piazza Trilussa at the entrance of Trastevere, a beautiful old working-class neighborhood where you'll have a relaxing dinner.

Day 9: Rome/Departure

Head by taxi to Termini station and catch the train to Fiumicino airport. Savor your last cup of the world's richest coffee at one of the coffee bars in the airport before boarding.

Logistics: The train from Termini station to the airport is fast, inexpensive, and easy—for most people, it's preferable to an exorbitantly priced taxi ride that, in bad traffic, can take twice as long.

TIPS

❶ The itinerary can also be completed by car on the modern autostrade, although you'll run into dicey traffic in Florence and Rome. For obvious reasons, pick up your car on day 3, when you leave Venice.

❷ Among trains, aim for the reservation-only Eurostar Italia—it's more comfortable and faster.

❸ The sights along this route are highly touristed; you'll have a better time if you make the trip outside the busy months of June, July, and August.

THE COURTLY NORTH

Day 1: Genoa

Fly into Genoa's pint-sized Aeroporto Cristoforo Colombo, pick up your rental car, and drive to your hotel (try to get a place near Piazza de Ferrari, the gateway to the *centro storico*). Leave your car there for the rest of the day. Spend the afternoon wandering the Old City's ancient streets— *vicoli*—some of which are so narrow that lovers on upper floors would leap across to each other's rooms. Don't miss the Porta Soprana, the fortified portal to Europe's largest medieval city; the black-and-white striped San Lorenzo cathedral; Via Garibaldi, lined with some of northern Italy's most impressive palazzos; and a ramble around the old port, site of Europe's largest aquarium. Do some window shopping during the evening passeggiata along Via XX Settembre, then sample the city's culinary delights—the fresh fish with a water view at Antica Osteria del Bai, for example (you'll want to take a taxi there), or *trofie al pesto* (stubby, dense pasta twists with pesto, potatoes, and green beans) anywhere in town. Genoa is the birthplace of pesto—and foccacia too.

Logistics: Alitalia's international flights to Genoa connect through Milan, Rome, or, if you're on a European carrier, other European cities including Zürich, Paris, London, and Munich. Try to get in as early in the morning as possible. Genoa is a vertical city, implausibly sandwiched between the mountains and the sea. Maps have a hard time conveying this third dimension, so be sure to ask your hotel for detailed driving and parking directions.

Day 2: Riviera di Levante/ Cinque Terre

Heading out of Genoa, cross you fingers for good weather, and spend the morning driving one of Italy's most scenic roads, the Via Aurelia, in the direction of La Spezia (along the Riviera Levante, or the "Riviera of the Rising Sun"). This road hugs the coast for hours. Stop for a brief wander around one or two of the many idyllic villages you pass; good candidates include Camogli and Santa Margherita Ligure, less than an hour outside of Genoa. Portofino is on a promontory framed by those two towns; it's a bit more of a detour, but its allure is unmistakable. When you arrive in the Cinque Terre, check into a hotel in Riomaggiore or Vernazza; the latter is perhaps the most beautiful of these fishing ports that cling implausibly to the cliffs. From there, hike some of the impressive paths that connect the towns, including the Via dell' Amore between Manarola and Riomaggiore. Eat in whichever town you end up in at dinnertime, then take the train back to your hotel.

Logistics: The Via Aurelia (SS 1) first heads out of town past the Genoese neighborhoods of Quarto, Quinto, and then Nervi. If you're not in view of the water, you're probably on the wrong road. From there it's a slow but beautiful drive to the Cinque Terre. If you're running short on time, switch over to the parallel A10 autostrada.

Day 3: Parma

Your next stop will be the stately food capital of Parma. When you arrive, check out the city's harmonious piazzas and medieval architecture. Shop for Parmigiano-Reggiano cheese and prosciutto di Parma (Parma ham)—where better?—or simply acquaint yourself with the *dolce di far niente* (art of doing nothing), perhaps browsing the city's stately boutiques, with breaks for coffee, gelato, or an aperitivo. When night comes, seize the occasion to welcome yourself to Italy with an elaborate meal. There are many fine restaurants in this food town, but perhaps none finer than La Greppia.

Logistics: From the Cinque Terre, take the Via Aurelia to La Spezia, where you'll head north on the A15—it's no more than an hour up to Parma on this fast highway.

Day 4: Verona

After breakfast, depart from Parma for Verona, which might be the most quintessentially Italian city on this itinerary. Standing along the side of the fast-flowing Adige river, gazing at the rows of old palazzos along its banks and the rolling hills of cypress beyond, you'll find it hard not to fall in love with this city of Romeo and Juliet. Spend your morning wandering the city's medieval piazzas. Skip the touristy so-called "House of Juliet," but don't miss Verona's stunning Roman Arena, the Castelvecchio (old castle), and San Zeno Maggiore, possibly Italy's finest Romanesque church. Accompany your dinner with a bottle of the Amarone wine for which the region is known. If it's summer and you plan things right, you might even time your day in Verona to coincide with an opera performance in the Arena.

Logistics: Take the A1 autostrada and then turn onto the A22 after about 50 km, before you hit Modena. The A22 heads straight north past Mantua to Verona. Once there, park your car and go it on foot; Verona is definitely a walking city.

Day 5: Trento/Bolzano

Head north on the highway after breakfast, stopping for lunch and a walk around Trento's castle and Piazza del Duomo with its beautifully crenellated Palazzo Pretorio. After lunch, it's back on the road north. If you're not familiar with the region, you may be surprised, upon reaching beautiful Bolzano, to discover that everybody is speaking German. This is Alto Adige, also known as Südtirol, a semi-autonomous region of Italy in which Italian is only one of the two official languages. The feel of the town, with its dim beer halls and elegant Piazza Walther, is positively Germanic. Not to be missed in town is the archaeological museum and a face-to-5,300-year-old-face visit with its amazingly preserved Iceman. Have a casual dinner of grilled meats and microbrewed beer at the young and laid-back Hopfen & Co, or gorge yourself with rich Tirolean mountain food at the more formal Zür Kaiserkron.

Logistics: Trento is due north of Verona on the A22 autostrada. It shouldn't take more than an hour and a half to get there. Continue north on the A22 to reach Bolzano—it's only another 50 km.

Day 6: Padua/Venice

Leave bright and early and head back to the Veneto, where you'll be stopping in Padua, a wondrous university town full of bicycles and beautiful medieval architecture. The drive should take about two hours. Stop to see Giotto's unbelievable fresco cycle in the Cappella degli Scrovegni before continuing into the centro storico, parking wherever you can, and wandering through the streets of the Old Town (watch out for those bikes!). After lunch, drive straight to Venice (less than an hour), return your rental car, check into your hotel, and if all goes well, you'll still have time for some afternoon sightseeing. Get lost in the city's back canals for a couple of hours before finding your way to a seafood dinner. Afterward, consider having a nightcap around the Campo San Luca or Campo Santa Margherita.

Logistics: This day really requires an early start. Head south on the A22—back through Verona—and then east on the A4. Padua is on the way to Venice on the A4. When you arrive in Venice, return your car at Piazzale Roma, where most major companies have a garage. Then at the Piazzale Roma vaporetto stop, buy 72-hour vaporetto "travel cards," and take the vaporetto to your hotel. If you're not in the mood for such a hectic day, then skip Padua.

Day 7: Venice

Begin with a morning vaporetto cruise along the Grand Canal. Proceed with a visit to Piazza San Marco, the Byzantine spendor of the Basilica San Marco, and the imposing Palazzo Ducale. Stop for lunch, perhaps at a traditional Venetian *bacaro* (wine bar). Next, take the Accademia footbridge across the Grand Canal, and see the Gallerie dell'Accademia, Venice's most important art gallery. Wander through the Dorsoduro neighborhood, finishing up with a romantic sunset walk around the Zattere before proceeding to dinner.

Day 8: Venice/Departure

Have breakfast at your hotel and head by vaporetto to San Marco, where you'll transfer to the airport boat. Savor your last cup of the world's richest coffee at the airport's coffee bar before boarding.

Logistics: Alialunga operates the one-hour boat trip to the airport. Water taxis are much more expensive, but they pick you up at your hotel.

TIPS

❶ The itinerary can also be done by train. All these stops are well connected by Italy's rail network, and none of the trips will take more than a couple of hours. In most cases you'll want to take a taxi from the train station to your hotel. The only tricky parts will be on days 5 and 6, when you'll be stopping for lunch in Trento and Padua, respectively. You can check your luggage at the train station.

❷ Winter is not the time for this trip. Northern Italy can get very cold in December, January, and especially February.

GREAT ITINERARIES

CLASSICS OF CENTRAL ITALY

Day 1: Florence

If you're coming in on an international flight, you'll probably settle in Florence in time for an afternoon stroll or siesta (depending on your jet-lag strategy) before dinner.

Logistics: On your flight in, read through the restaurant listings in this guide and begin anticipating the first dinner of your trip. Look for a place near your hotel, and when you arrive, reserve a table (or have your concierge do it for you). Making a meal the focus of your first day is a great way to ease into Italian life.

Day 2: Florence

Begin your morning at the Uffizi Gallery (reserve your ticket in advance). The extensive collection will occupy much of your morning. Next, take in the neighboring Piazza della Signoria, Florence's most impressive square, then head a few blocks north to the Duomo. There, check out Ghiberti's famous bronze doors on the Battistero, and work up an appetite by climbing the 463 steps to the cupola of Brunelleschi's splendid cathedral dome, atop which you'll experience a memorable vista. Spend the afternoon relaxing, shopping, and wandering Florence's medieval streets; or, if you're up for a more involved journey, head out to Fiesole to experience the ancient amphitheater and beautiful views of the Tuscan countryside.

Day 3: Florence

Keep the energy level up for your second full day in Florence, sticking with art and architecture for the morning, trying to see most of the following: Michelangelo's *David* at the Galleria dell'Accademia, the Palazzo Pitti and Boboli Gardens, the Medici Chapels, and the churches of Santa Maria Novella and Santa Croce. If it's a clear day, spend the afternoon on a trip up to the Piazzale Michelangelo, high on a hill above Florence, for sweeping views of the idyllic Florentine countryside. Given all the walking you've been doing, tonight would be a good night to recharge by trying the famed *bistecca alla fiorentina* (a grilled T-bone steak with olive oil).

Logistics: You can get up to the Piazzale Michelangelo by taxi or by taking Bus #7 from Santa Maria Novella. Otherwise, do your best to get around on foot; Florence is a brilliant city for walking.

Day 4: San Gimignano

Now that you've been appropriately introduced to the bewildering splendor of Renaissance Italy, it's time for a change of pace—and time for a rental car, which will enable you to see the back roads of Tuscany and Umbria. After breakfast, pick up your car, stop back at your hotel for your luggage, and head on out. On a good day the lazy drive from Florence to San Gimignano, past vineyards and typical Tuscan landscapes, is truly spectacular. The first thing that will hit you when you arrive at the hill town of San Gimignano will be the towers everywhere. The medieval skyscrapers of Italy, they also once occupied the role now played by Ferraris or Hummers: they were public displays of wealth. After finding your way to a hotel in the Old Town, set out on foot and check out the city's turrets and alleyways, doing your best to get away from the trinket shops, and later enjoying a leisurely dinner with the light but delicious local white wine, Vernaccia di San Gimignano.

Logistics: Some hotels might be able to co-ordinate with some rental car agencies so that your car can be brought to your hotel for you. Once you navigate your way out of Florence (no easy task), San Gimignano is only 57 km (35 mi) to the southwest, so it's an easy drive; you could even take a detour on the SS 222 (Strada Chiantigiana), stop at one of the Chianti wine towns, and visit a winery along the way.

Day 5: Siena

In the morning, set out for nearby Siena, which is known worldwide for its Palio, a festival that culminates in an elaborate horse race competition between the 17 *contrade* (medieval neighborhoods) of the city. Because of the enormous influx of tourists, especially in summer, Siena isn't everyone's cup of tea, but it's still one of Tuscany's most impressive sights; however many tourists you have to bump elbows with, it's hard not to be blown away by the city's precious medieval streets and memorable fan-shaped Piazza del Campo. Not to be missed while in town are the spectacular Duomo, the Battistero, and the Spedale di Santa Maria della Scala, an old hospital and hostel that now contains and underground archaeological museum.

Logistics: It's a short and pretty drive from San Gimignano to Siena, but once there, parking can be a challenge. Look for the *stadio* (soccer stadium) where there's a lot that often has space.

Day 6: Arezzo/Cortona

Get an early start, because there's a lot to see today. From Siena you'll first head to Arezzo, home to the Basilica di San Francesco, which contains important frescoes by Piero della Francesca. Check out the Piazza Grande along with its beautiful Romanesque church of Santa Maria delle Pieve. Try to do all of this before lunch (La Torre di Gnicche is a good choice), after which you'll head straight to Cortona. If Arezzo didn't capture your imagination, Cortona, which dates back to the 5th century BC, will. Olive trees and vineyards give way to a medieval hilltown with views over ridiculously idyllic Tuscan countryside and Lake Trasimeno. Cortona is a town for walking and relaxing, not sightseeing, so enjoy yourself, wandering through the Piazza della Repubblica and Piazza Signorelli, perhaps doing a bit of shopping.

Logistics: Siena to Arezzo is 63 km (39 mi) on the E 78. From Arezzo to Cortona, it's just 30 km (18 mi)—take SS 71.

Day 7: Assisi

Today you'll cross over into Umbria, a region just as beautiful as Tuscany but still less trodden. Yet another impossibly beautiful hill town, Assisi, is the home of St. Francis and host to the many religious pilgrims that come to celebrate his legacy. Upon arriving and checking into your lodging, head straight for the Basilica di San Francesco, which displays the coffin of St. Francis and a bevy of unbelievable frescoes. From there take Via San Francesco to Piazza del Commune and see the Tempio di Minerva before a break for lunch; Osteria Piazzetta dell'Erba would be a fine and relaxed choice. After lunch, see San Rufino, the town cathedral, and then go back through the piazza to Corso Mazzini and see Santa Chiara. If you're a true Franciscan, you could instead devote the afternoon to heading out 16 km (10 mi) to Cannara, where St. Francis delivered his sermon to the birds.

Logistics: From Cortona take the SS 71 to the A1 autostrada toward Perugia. After about 40 km (24 mi), take the Assisi exit (E 45), and it's 14 km (8 mi) to Assisi.

Day 8: Spoleto

This morning will take you from a small hill town to a slightly bigger one: Spoleto, a walled city that's home to a world-renowned arts festival each summer. But Spoleto needs no festival to be celebrated. Its Duomo is wonderful. Its fortress is impressive. And the Ponte delle Torri, a 14th-century bridge that separates Spoleto from Monteluco, is a marvelous sight, traversing a gorge 260 feet below and built upon the foundations of a Roman aqueduct. See all these during the day, stopping for a light lunch of a panino or salad saving your appetite for a serious last dinner in Italy: Umbrian cuisine is excellent everywhere, but Spoleto is a memorable culinary destination. Do your best to sample black truffles, a proud product of the region; they're delicious on pasta or meat.

Logistics: One school of thought would be to time your visit to Spoleto's world-renowned arts festival that runs from mid-June through mid-July. Another would be to do anything you can to avoid it. It all depends on your taste for big festivals and big crowds. The trip from Assisi to Spoleto is a pretty 47-km (29-mi) drive (SS 75 to the SS 3) that should take you less than an hour.

Day 9: Spoleto/Departure

It's a fair distance from Spoleto to the Florence airport, your point of departure. Depending on your comfort level with Italian driving, allow at least two and a half hours to reach Florence's airport. If your flight out is at midday or before, this will mean getting an early start.

Logistics: An alternative possibility would be to try to get a flight out of Perugia's tiny airport, which is a lot closer to Spoleto than Florence. It offers connections to Milan and Rome (Ciampino)—but not many. Otherwise, just get an early start and drive to Florence along the A1 autostrada.

TIP

Because of spotty train service to Tuscan hill towns, this itinerary is extremely difficult to complete without a car. Driving is easy and relaxing in the region, whose roads can be windy but are generally wide, well kept, well marked, and not too crowded. If you absolutely don't want to drive, buses are the best way to go.

THE SULTRY SOUTH

Day 1: Naples

Fly into Naples's Aeroporto Capodichino, a scant 8 km (5 mi) from the city. Naples is rough around the edges and may be a bit jarring if you're a first-time visitor, but it's classic Italy, and most visitors end up falling in love with the city's alluring waterfront palazzos and spectacular pizza. First things first, though: recharge with a good caffè—Naples has some of Italy's best. Revive in time for an evening stroll down Naples's wonderful shopping street, Via Toledo—it's quintessential Italy—before dinner and bed.

Logistics: Under no circumstances should you rent a car for Naples. Take a taxi from the airport—it's not far, or overly expensive—and you should face few logistical obstacles on your first day in Italy.

Day 2: Naples

Start the day in Piazza Gesù, and head east along Spaccanapoli through the very heart of Old Naples, stopping at the churches of Gesù Nuovo and Santa Chiara. Farther up Spaccanapoli, try to check out Cappella Sansevero and the Duomo, before heading left on Via Foria to the Museo Archeologico Nazionale. From there take a taxi to Da Michele, and begin your afternoon with the best pizza in the world. Post pizza, check out the harbor and the Castel Nuovo; then head past the Teatro San Carlo to the enormous Palazzo Reale. Walk 15 minutes south to the Castello dell'Ovo in the Santa Lucia waterfront area, one of Naples' most charming neighborhoods. Then it's back up to Via Caracciolo and the Villa Comunale, before heading back to your hotel for a short

rest before dinner and perhaps a night out at one of Naples's lively bars or clubs.

Logistics: This entire day is easily done on foot, with the exception of the taxi for your midday pizza. Naples is one of the best walking cities in Italy.

Day 3: Pompeii/Sorrento

After breakfast, pick up your rental car, pack in your luggage, and drive from Naples to Pompeii, one of the true archaeological gems of Europe. If it's summer, be prepared for an onslaught of sweltering heat as you make your way through the incredibly preserved ruins of a city that was devastated by the whims of Mount Vesuvius nearly two thousand years ago. You'll see the houses of noblemen and merchants, brothels, political graffiti, and more. From Pompeii, get back in your car and it's on to Sorrento, your first taste of the wonderful peninsula that marks the beginning of the fabled Amalfi Coast. Sorrento is touristy, but it may well be the Italian city of your imagination: cliff-hanging, cobblestone-paved, and graced with an infinite variety of fishing-port and coastal views. There, have a relaxing dinner of fish and white wine before calling it a day.

Logistics: Naples to Pompeii is all about the A3: a short 24 km (15 mi) brings you to this archaeological gem. From Pompeii it's a short ride back on the A3 until the exit for Sorrento; from the exit, you'll take the S145 to reach Sorrento.

Day 4: Positano/Ravello

Your stay in Sorrento will be short, as there's much of the Amalfi Coast still to see: Positano, your next stop, is a must. It's one of the most visited towns in Italy for good reason: its blue-green seas, stairs "as steep as ladders," and white Moorish-style houses make for a truly memorable setting. Walk, gaze, and eat (lunch), before heading on to the less traveled, even higher-up town of Ravello, your Amalfi Coast dream come true, an aerie that is "closer to the sky than the sea." Don't miss the Duomo, Villa Rufolo, or Villa Cimbrone before settling in for a dinner in the sky.

Logistics: Sorrento to Positano is just a 34-km (21-mi) jaunt, but the winding roads will draw it out for the better part of an hour—a scenic hour. From Positano, Ravello is another slow 40 km (24 mi) to the east, perched high above the rest of the world. Be prepared to use low gears if you're driving a stick shift (as you almost surely will be).

Day 5: Matera
It will take a bit of a drive to get to Basilicata from the Amalfi Coast; leaving Campania and entering Basilicata is generally a lonely experience. Little-traveled roads, wild hills, and distant farms are the hallmarks of this province, which produces deep, dark Aglianico wines and has perfected the art of peasant food. You'll spend a while in your car to make it to Matera, a beautiful, ancient city full of Paleolithic *sassi* (cavelike dwellings hewn out of rock)—but it's worth it. Traversing the city is like taking a voyage through time. Spend the afternoon exploring the sassi, but take care not to miss the new part of the city too. Then enjoy a relaxing dinner at one of Matera's excellent restaurants—just decide whether you want flavorful local beef (Le Botteghe) or a flurry of Basilicatan tapas (Lucanerie). Basilicata, you'll soon discover, is full of unrivaled values at restaurants, and with such options you'll be guaranteed to sleep well in the sassi.

Logistics: It's a long haul from your starting point, Ravello, to Matera. Good thing Basilicata's landscape is so pretty. Once in Matera, if you're staying in the sassi, get extra-detailed driving and parking instructions from your hotel beforehand—navigating through thousand-year-old alleyways can be challenging.

Day 6: Lecce
This drive will take a good three hours, so get an early start. The baroque city of Lecce will mark your introduction to Puglia, the heel of Italy's boot. It's one of Italy's best-kept secrets, as you'll soon find out upon checking out the spectacular church of Santa Croce, the ornate Duomo, and the harmonious Piazza Sant'Oronzo. The shopping is great, the food is great, and the evening passeggiata is great. Don't miss the opportunity, if you wind up at a bar or café in the evening, to chat with Lecce's friendly residents—unfazed by tourism, the welcoming Leccesi represent southern Italians at their best.

Logistics: It's not far from Matera to Lecce as the crow flies, but the trip is more involved than you might think; patience is required. The best route is via Taranto—don't make the mistake of going up through Bari.

Day 7: Bari
The trip from Lecce to Bari is a short one. Check into the pleasant Hotel Palace and spend the morning and afternoon wandering through Bari's centro storico. The wide-open doors of the town's humble houses and apartments, with bickering families and grandmothers drying their pasta in the afternoon sun, will give you a taste of the true flavor of the mezzogiorno, Italy's deep south. Don't miss Bari's castle and the walk

around the ridge of the ancient city walls, with views of wide-open sea at every turn. Finish the day with a good fish dinner, and celebrate your last night in Italy by checking out one of the city's multitude of lively bars—Bari boasts one of southern Italy's most hopping bar scenes.

Logistics: This is one of your most straightforward, if not quickest, drives: just take the coastal SS 16 for 154 km (95 mi) until you hit Bari. They're two-lane highways, though, so don't be surprised if the trip takes two hours or more. If you get tired, beautiful Ostuni (the "Città Bianca," the white city) is a perfect hilltop pit stop halfway there.

Day 8: Bari/Departure

Bad news: this is your wake-up-and-leave day. Bari's Aeroporto Palese is small but quite serviceable. Exploit its absence of crowds and easy access and use it as your way out of Italy. Connections through Rome or Milan are more frequent than you might think. Plan on leaving southern Italy firmly established in your heart as the best way to see the Italy that once was—and be thankful that you were able to see it while it is still like this.

Logistics: Bari hotels offer easy airport transfers; take advantage of them. Return your

rental car at the Bari airport; you won't have to arrive at the airport more than an hour or so before your flight.

TIPS

❶ Alitalia usually doesn't mark up open-jaw trips. However, VolareWeb (www.volareweb.com) has inexpensive domestic air service, and is now operating Milan (Linate)-Naples and Bari-Milan (Linate) routes. Alpi Eagles (www.alpieagles.com) also has service along those routes. If you're able to find a deep-discount round-trip fare from your home to Milan plus those two flights on low-cost carriers, you might save some money. (The Malpensa-Linate connection can be done on regularly scheduled buses.)

❷ Also look at low-cost carriers that shuttle passengers between London and southern Italy; you can often save the most money of all by combining two such one-way fares with a round-trip discount fare to London; however, beware of inconvenient airport connections in London (Luton, for example).

ON THE CALENDAR

WINTER	The Italian calendar is filled with festivals and holidays. This list includes the biggest ones—those that could play a significant part in your trip planning.
January 30–February 8	A big do in the 18th century and revived in the latter part of the 20th century, **Carnevale** in Venice includes concerts, plays, masked balls, fireworks, and indoor and outdoor happenings of every sort. It is probably Italy's most famous festival, bringing in hundreds of thousands.
February 10–February 26 **SPRING**	For two weeks the sports world will focus its attention on Turin and the surrounding mountains as they host the **2006 Winter Olympics**.
April 16	Needless to say, the **Messa di Pasqua al Vaticana** (Easter Mass at the Vatican) in Rome is long, intense, and packed, with many people attending in elaborate holiday costumes.
Late April–Early July **SUMMER**	**Maggio Musicale Fiorentino** (Florence May Music Festival) is the oldest and most prestigious Italian festival of the performing arts.
Late June–Mid-July	The **Festival dei Due Mondi** (Festival of Two Worlds), in Spoleto, is perhaps Italy's most famous performing arts festival, bringing in a worldwide audience for concerts, operas, ballets, film screenings, and crafts fairs. Plan well in advance.
July 2 & August 16	The world-famous **Palio** in Siena is a bareback horse race with ancient Sienese factions showing their colors and participants competing for a prized *palio* (banner).
Early July–Late August	The **Arena di Verona Stagione Lirica** (Verona Arena Outdoor Opera Season) heralds spectacular productions in Verona's 22,000-seat Roman amphitheater.
July	The **Umbria Jazz Festival**, in Perugia, brings in many of the biggest names in jazz each summer.
July 15	Venice's **Festa del Redentore** (Feast of the Redeemer) is a procession of gondolas and other craft commemorating the end of the plague of 1575. The fireworks over the lagoon are spectacular.
Late August–Early September	The **Festival di Venezia** (Venice Film Festival), the oldest of the international film festivals, takes place mostly on the Lido.

SMART TRAVEL TIPS

Finding out about your destination before you leave home means you won't spend time organizing everyday minutiae once you've arrived. You'll be more streetwise when you hit the ground as well, better prepared to explore the aspects of Italy that drew you here in the first place. The organizations in this section can provide information to supplement this guide; contact them for up-to-the-minute details, and consult the A to Z sections that end each chapter for facts on the various topics as they relate to the country's many regions. Happy landings!

ADDRESSES

Addresses in Italy are fairly straightforward: the street is followed by the building number. However, you might see an address with a number plus "bis" or "A"; for instance, "Via Verdi 3/bis" or "Via Mazzini 8/A." This indicates that 3/bis and 8/A are the next doors down from Via Verdi 3 and Via Mazzini 8. In Rome, street numbers flow down one side of a street and back up the other. In central Florence, the letter "r" following an address (e.g., Via Santo Spirito 35/r) refers to "rosso" (red), the color of the number painted on the wall. Red addresses are commercial; blue or black numbers are residential. (Many hotels have blue or black street numbers.)

Venice addresses consist of the name of one of the city's six neighborhoods and a number. The hitch is that the numbers don't go in any sequential order, so San Marco 3672 and 3673 might well be several narrow winding streets away from each other. When helpful, the Venetian addresses in this book include the nearest *campo,* bridge, or *calle.*

In rural areas some addresses give only the route name or the distance in kilometers along a major road (e.g., Via Fabbri, Km 4.3), or sometimes only the name of the nearest small village.

AIR TRAVEL

The price of flying within Italy is often comparable to the cost of train travel, although be sure to factor in the expense of getting to and from the airport. When flying out of Italian airports, always check with the airport or tourist agency about upcoming strikes, which are frequent in Italy and often affect air travel.

BOOKING

When you book, look for nonstop flights and remember that "direct" flights stop at least once. Try to avoid connecting flights, which require a change of plane. Two airlines may operate a connecting flight jointly, so ask whether your airline operates every segment of the trip; you may find that the carrier you prefer flies you only part of the way. To find more booking tips and to check prices and make online flight reservations, log on to www.fodors.com.

CARRIERS

When flying internationally, you must usually choose between a domestic carrier, the national flag carrier of the country you are visiting (Alitalia for Italy), and a foreign carrier from a third country. National flag carriers have the greatest number of non stops. Domestic carriers may have better connections to your hometown and serve a greater number of gateway cities. Third-party carriers may have a price advantage.

On international flights, Alitalia serves Rome, Milan, and Venice. The major international hubs in Italy are Milan and Rome, served by Continental Airlines and Delta Air Lines. American Airlines flies into just Milan. US Airways serves only Rome.

Alitalia and British Airways have direct flights from London's Heathrow and Gatwick airports to Milan and Rome. From Manchester, British Airways has daily flights to Milan and Rome. Smaller, no-frills airlines also provide service between Great Britain and Italy. EasyJet connects Gatwick with Bologna. British Midland connects Heathrow and Milan. Ryanair, departing from London's Stansted Airport, has daily flights to Milan, Rome, Pisa, and Venice. Meridiana has two or three direct flights each week between Gatwick and Olbia on Sardinia in summer, and daily flights to Rome and Florence throughout the year. From its hub in Brussels, Virgin Express files to Milan, Catania, and Rome.

Alitalia connects Canada and Italy. Air Canada flies to Munich for connections to Rome, Florence, and Milan via Lufthansa. Qantas flies from various cities in Australia via Bangkok, arriving in Rome. Alitalia and New Zealand Air fly from Auckland to Rome with a stop in London. Another option if you're coming from Australia or New Zealand is Thai Airlines, landing in Rome via Bangkok.

Tickets for flights within Italy, on Alitalia and small carriers such as Meridiana and Air One, cost less when purchased from agents within Italy. Tickets are frequently sold at discounted prices, so check the cost of flights, even one-way, as an alternative to train travel.

🔖 International Carriers **Air Canada** ☎ 888/247-2262 in U.S. and Canada, 0870/524-7226 in U.K., 800/919091 in Italy ⊕ www.aircanada.com. **Air New Zealand** ☎ 800/262-1234 in U.S., 800/663-5494 in Canada, 0800/028-4149 in U.K., 13-24-76 in Australia, 0800/737-000 in New Zealand ⊕ www.airnz.com. **Alitalia** ☎ 800/223-5730 in U.S., 0870/544 in U.K., 61/292-44-2222 in Australia, 06/65641 in Rome, 848/865641 elsewhere in Italy ⊕ www.alitalia.it. **American Airlines** ☎ 800/433-7300 in U.S., 02/69682464 in Milan ⊕ www.aa.com. **British Airways** ☎ 800/403-0882 in U.S. and Canada, 0870/850-9850 in U.K., 1300/767-177 in Australia, 0800/274-847 in New Zealand, 06/52492800 in Italy ⊕ www.britishairways.com. **Continental** ☎ 800/231-0856 in U.S., 02/69633256 in Milan, 800/296230 elsewhere in Italy ⊕ www.flycontinental.com. **Delta** ☎ 800/241-4141 in U.S., 06/65954406 in Italy ⊕ www.deltaairlines.com. **EasyJet** ☎ 0870/6076543 in U.K., 848/887766 in Italy ⊕ www.go-fly.com. **Lufthansa** ☎ 800/399-5838 in U.S., 800/563-5954 in Canada, 0870/8377-747 in U.K., 1300-655-727 in Australia, 0800/945-220 in New Zealand ⊕ www.lufthansa.com. **Qantas,** ☎ 800/227-4500 in U.S., 13-11-31 in Australia, 06/52482725 in Rome ⊕ www.qantas.com. **Ryanair** ☎ 08701/569569 in U.K., 199/114114 in Italy ⊕ www.ryanair.com. **Thai Airlines** ☎ 800/426-5204 in U.S., 61-1300-651-960 in Australia, 64-9-377-3886 in New Zealand ⊕ www.thaiair.com. **US Airways** ☎ 800/428-4322 in U.S., 848/813177 in Italy ⊕ www.usairways.com. **Virgin Express** ☎ 32/70353637 in U.S., Canada, Australia, and New Zealand, 0207/744-0004 in U.K., 02/48296000 in Milan, 800/097097 elsewhere in Italy ⊕ www.virginexpress.com.

▸ National Carriers Air One ☎ 06/488800 in Rome, 800/900966 elsewhere in Italy ⊕ www. flyairone.it. **Meridiana** ☎ 199/111333 in Italy ⊕ www.meridiana.it.

CHECK-IN & BOARDING

Always **find out your carrier's check-in policy.** Plan to arrive at the airport about two hours before your scheduled departure time for domestic flights and 2½ to 3 hours before international flights. You may need to arrive earlier if you're flying from one of the busier airports or during peak air-traffic times. To avoid delays at airport-security checkpoints, try not to wear any metal. Jewelry, belt and other buckles, steel-toe shoes, barrettes, and underwire bras are among the items that can set off detectors.

Assuming that not everyone with a ticket will show up, airlines routinely overbook planes. When everyone does, airlines ask for volunteers to give up their seats. In return, these volunteers usually get a several-hundred-dollar flight voucher, which can be used toward the purchase of another ticket, and are rebooked on the next available flight out. If there are not enough volunteers, the airline must choose who will be denied boarding. The first to get bumped are passengers who checked in late and those flying on discounted tickets, so get to the gate and check in as early as possible, especially during peak periods.

Always **bring a government-issued photo ID** to the airport; even when it's not required, a passport is best.

CUTTING COSTS

The least expensive airfares to Italy are often priced for round-trip travel and must usually be purchased in advance. Airlines generally allow you to change your return date for a fee; most low-fare tickets, however, are nonrefundable. It's smart to call a number of airlines and check the Internet; when you are quoted a good price, book it on the spot—the same fare may not be available the next day, or even the next hour. Always check different routings and look into using alternate airports. Also, price off-peak flights and red-eye, which may be significantly less

expensive than others. Travel agents, especially low-fare specialists (⇨ Discounts & Deals), are helpful.

Consolidators are another good source. They buy tickets for scheduled flights at reduced rates from the airlines, then sell them at prices that beat the best fare available directly from the airlines. (Many also offer reduced car-rental and hotel rates.) Sometimes you can even get your money back if you need to return the ticket. Carefully read the fine print detailing penalties for changes and cancellations, purchase the ticket with a credit card, and confirm your consolidator reservation with the airline.

When you fly as a courier, you trade your checked-luggage space for a ticket deeply subsidized by a courier service. There are restrictions on when you can book and how long you can stay. Some courier companies list with membership organizations, such as the Air Courier Association and the International Association of Air Travel Couriers; these require you to become a member before you can book a flight.

Many airlines, singly or in collaboration, offer discount air passes that allow foreigners to travel economically in a particular country or region. These visitor passes usually must be reserved and purchased before you leave home. Information about passes often can be found on most airlines' international Web pages, which tend to be aimed at travelers from outside the carrier's home country. Also, try typing the name of the pass into a search engine, or search for "pass" within the carrier's Web site.

▸ Consolidators AirlineConsolidator.com ☎ 888/468-5385 ⊕ www.airlineconsolidator.com, for international tickets. **Best Fares** ☎ 800/880-1234 ⊕ www.bestfares.com; $59.90 annual membership. **Cheap Tickets** ☎ 800/377-1000 or 800/652-4327 ⊕ www.cheaptickets.com. **Expedia** ☎ 800/397-3342 or 404/728-8787 ⊕ www.expedia.com. **Hotwire** ☎ 866/468-9473 or 920/330-9418 ⊕ www.hotwire.com. **Now Voyager Travel** ✉ 1717 Avenue M, Brooklyn, NY 11230 ☎ 212/459-1616 🖶 718/504-4762 ⊕ www.nowvoyagertravel.com. **Onetravel.com** ⊕ www.onetravel.com. **Orbitz** ☎ 888/656-4546 ⊕ www.orbitz.com. **Priceline. com** ⊕ www.priceline.com. **Travelocity** ☎ 888/

709–5983, 877/282–2925 in Canada, 0870/111–7061 in U.K. ⊕ www.travelocity.com.

🖪 Courier Resources **Air Courier Association/ Cheaptrips.com** ☎ 800/211–5119 ⊕ www.aircourier. org or www.cheaptrips.com; $20 annual membership. **Courier Travel** ☎ 303/570–7586 🖷 313/625–6106 ⊕ www.couriertravel.org; $50 annual membership. **International Association of Air Travel Couriers** ☎ 308/632–3273 🖷 308/632–8267 ⊕ www.courier.org; $45 annual membership. **Now Voyager Travel** ✉ 1717 Avenue M, Brooklyn, NY 11230 ☎ 212/459–1616 🖷 718/504–4762 ⊕ www. nowvoyagertravel.com.

ENJOYING THE FLIGHT

State your seat preference when purchasing your ticket, and then repeat it when you confirm and when you check in. For more legroom, you can request one of the few emergency-aisle seats at check-in, if you're capable of moving obstacles comparable in weight to an airplane exit door (usually between 35 pounds and 60 pounds)—a Federal Aviation Administration requirement of passengers in these seats. Seats behind a bulkhead also offer more legroom, but they don't have under-seat storage. Don't sit in the row in front of the emergency aisle or in front of a bulkhead, where seats may not recline. SeatGuru.com has more information about specific seat configurations, which vary by aircraft.

Ask the airline whether a snack or meal is served on the flight. If you have dietary concerns, request special meals when booking. These can be vegetarian, low-cholesterol, or kosher, for example. It's a good idea to pack some healthful snacks and a small (plastic) bottle of water in your carry-on bag. On long flights, try to maintain a normal routine, to help fight jet lag. At night, get some sleep. By day, eat light meals, drink water (not alcohol), and **move around the cabin** to stretch your legs. For additional jet-lag tips consult *Fodor's FYI: Travel Fit & Healthy* (available at bookstores everywhere).

FLYING TIMES

Flying time to Milan or Rome is approximately 2½ hours from London, 8–8½ hours from New York, 10–11 hours from Chicago, 11½ hours from Los Angeles, and 23½ hours from Sydney.

HOW TO COMPLAIN

If your baggage goes astray or your flight goes awry, complain right away. Most carriers require that you **file a claim immediately.** The Aviation Consumer Protection Division of the Department of Transportation publishes *Fly-Rights,* which discusses airlines and consumer issues and is available online. You can also find articles and information on mytravelrights.com, the Web site of the nonprofit Consumer Travel Rights Center.

🖪 Airline Complaints **Aviation Consumer Protection Division** ✉ U.S. Department of Transportation, Office of Aviation Enforcement and Proceedings, C-75, Room 4107, 400 7th St. SW, Washington, DC 20590 ☎ 202/366–2220 ⊕ airconsumer.ost.dot.gov. **Federal Aviation Administration Consumer Hotline** ✉ For inquiries: FAA, 800 Independence Ave. SW, Washington, DC 20591 ☎ 800/322–7873 ⊕ www.faa.gov.

RECONFIRMING

Check the status of your flight before you leave for the airport. You can do this on your carrier's Web site, by linking to a flight-status checker (many Web-booking services offer these), or by calling your carrier or travel agent. Always confirm international flights at least 72 hours ahead of the scheduled departure time. Confirm flights within Italy the day before travel.

AIRPORTS

The major gateways to Italy are Rome's **Aeroporto Leonardo da Vinci,** better known as **Fiumicino** (FCO), and Milan's **Aeroporto Malpensa 2000** (MXP). There are direct connections from both airports to Florence and Venice. For information about regional airports, *see* the Essentials sections at the end of each chapter.

🖪 Airport Information **Aeroporto Leonardo da Vinci** ✉ 35 km [20 mi] southeast of Rome ☎ 06/5951 ⊕ www.adr.it. **Aeroporto Malpensa** ✉ 45 km [28 mi] north of Milan ☎ 02/7485–2200 ⊕ www. sea-aeroportimilano.it.

DUTY-FREE SHOPPING

Duty-free shopping in airports has been eliminated in Italy (and other European Union countries) when you are traveling within member nations; when flying out of or into Italy, however, duty-free shopping is still an option.

BEACHES

With 7,420 km (4,610 mi) of coastline facing three seas—the Adriatic to the northeast, the Ionian to the southeast, and the Tyrrhenian to the west—Italy offers every type of seaside scene. Italy has several world-famous beaches, like those along the Costa Smeralda in Sardinia, and great stretches of deserted and untouched coastline, many found in eastern Calabria, Sardinia, and the islands around Sicily. In Emilia-Romagna, Riccione and Rimini are famous for their nightlife and seaside fitness programs (Spinning to weight lifting, water gymnastics to dance). The Tremiti Islands (off the Adriatic Coast, between Molise and Puglia), the Gargano Peninsula (in Puglia), Tropea (in Calabria), Taormina (in Sicily), the islands of Capri and Ischia (in the Gulf of Naples), the Amalfi Coast (in Campania), Ponza (off the coast of Lazio), and the island of Elba (off the coast of Livorno in Tuscany) bring together a natural beauty with a low-key worldliness.

Public beaches are free, but offer no services. On the most popular ones it's sometimes possible to buy sandwiches and soft drinks, but don't depend on it. They often lack telephones, toilets, and showers. Private beaches charge admission and range from downright spartan (cold showers and portable toilets) to luxurious (with gardens, stylish bars, fish restaurants, and private guest huts). Admission policies and prices vary accordingly. Most establishments offer a chaise longue, chair, and umbrella for between €20 and €50 a day. Some of the most exclusive places cater only to patrons who pay by the week or month. Inquire at local tourist offices.

Don't underestimate the scorching power of the Italian sun. The "tanning season" begins in early May, and beach life starts in earnest in early June, with the opening of beach concessionaires, called *stabilimenti balneari* or *bagni*. During weekends and holidays and in August, most sea resorts and beaches tend to be very crowded, some posting "no vacancy" (*completo*) signs by 10 AM, so an early start is essential. In northern and central Italy, it's common to see sunbathing topless; in the south it could lead to undesired attention from local men. Nowhere in Italy, except at the rare nudist beach, is it common practice to walk around topless, and wearing beach attire (bare chests and thighs) in town is frowned upon. The summer season ends in early September.

BIKE TRAVEL

Biking is a terrific way to see Italy, particularly in places such as Tuscany, where two-lane roads wind through startlingly beautiful countryside. The best times to bike are in spring and fall; July and August are unbearably hot in most places. Rentals are easily obtained in most cities. Given the generally hilly terrain, it's essential to have a good map with elevations, distances, and the various types of roads clearly marked. An excellent map choice is the green regional series issued by the Italian Touring Club, available at major bookstores. Topographical maps by Kompass Wanderkarten, distributed by Omni Resources, show both hiking and biking routes and are available in large bookstores and map shops. The *Federazione Italiana Amici della Bicicletta* (Italian Federation of Friends of the Bicycle) has a useful Web site (in English as well as Italian) with information about bicycle routes, events, and services.

Road conditions are generally good throughout Italy, but, as you move along it's always a good idea to ask local tourist information offices about bike-friendly routes. Especially in smaller towns and villages cyclists do not go unnoticed, and if you speak a little Italian you'll be likely to meet sympathetic native cyclists eager to give valuable tips about the region. If you're not familiar with the countryside, joining an organized tour is a great idea. To be on the safe side, always lock your bike inside your hotel for the night.

🚲 Bike Maps Omni Resources ✉ 1004 S. Mebane St., Burlington, NC 27216-2096 ☎ 336/227–8300 🌐 www.omnimap.com.

🚲 Bike Organizations *Federazione Italiana Amici della Bicicletta* ✉ Viale Col Moschin 1, 30171 Mestre, Veneto ☎📠 041/921515 🌐 www.fiab-onlus.it.

Bike Tours Backroads ✉ 801 Cedar St., Berkeley, CA 94710 ☎ 510/527-1555 or 800/462-2848 ⊕ www.backroads.com. **Bike Riders** ⚲ Box 130254, Boston, MA 02113 ☎ 617/723-2354 or 800/473-7040 ⊕ www.bikeriderstours.com. **Butterfield & Robinson** ✉ 70 Bond St., Suite 300, Toronto, Ontario, Canada M5B 1X3 ☎ 416/864-1354 or 800/678-1147 ⊕ www.butterfield.com. **Ciclismo Classico** ✉ 30 Marathon St., Arlington, MA 02474 ☎ 781/646-3377 or 800/866-7314 ⊕ www.ciclismoclassico.com. **EEI Travel** ✉ 19021 120th Ave., Suite 102, Bothell, WA 98011 ☎ 425/487-6711 or 800/927-3876 ⊕ www.europeexpress.com. **Euro-Bike Tours** ⚲ Box 990, De Kalb, IL 60115 ☎ 800/321-6060 ⊕ www.eurobike.com. **Europeds** ✉ 761 Lighthouse Ave., Monterey, CA 93940 ☎ 831/646-4920 ⊕ www.europeds.com. **Naturequest** ✉ 30872 South Coast Hwy., Suite 185, Laguna Beach, CA 92651 ☎ 949/499-9561 or 800/369-3033 ⊕ www.naturequesttours.com.

Rentals Alinari ✉ Via Guelfa 85/r, Florence ☎ 005/271871. **Happy Rent** ✉ Via Farini 3, Rome ☎ 06/4818185. **I Bike Italy** ✉ Viale Galoppatoio 33, Rome ☎ 06/3225240 ⊕ www.ibikeitaly.com.

BIKES IN FLIGHT

Most airlines accommodate bikes as luggage, provided they are dismantled and boxed; check with individual airlines about packing requirements. Some airlines sell bike boxes, which are often free at bike shops, for about $20 (bike bags can be considerably more expensive). International travelers often can substitute a bike for a piece of checked luggage at no charge; otherwise, the cost is about $100. Most U.S. and Canadian airlines charge $40–$80 each way.

BOAT & FERRY TRAVEL

Ferries connect the mainland with all the major islands. To many destinations there is also *aliscafo* (hydrofoil) service, which is generally twice as fast (and twice as expensive). Service is considerably more frequent in summer. Car ferries go to Sicily and Sardinia and many islands, including Elba, Ponza, Capri, and Ischia. If you are traveling in July or August, try to make reservations at least a month ahead for Sicily or Sardinia. (Same-day ticket purchase is available for shorter trips.)

Tirrenia operates ferries from Naples to Liguria, Naples, Sicily, Sardinia, and

Tunisia. SNAV operates ferries between Naples and Palermo (high-speed ferries only from April to early October), and hydrofoils between Naples and Capri. Alilauro has hydrofoils and car ferries between Naples and Ischia and from Ischia and Capri to the Amalfi coast in summer. Caremar runs from Naples and Sorrento to Capri. Toremar serves Elba from Piombino. For the Lake District, contact Navigazione Laghi. Golfo Paradiso and Golfo dei Poeti serve the coast from Genova to Cinque Terre. Adriatica connects Italy with Greece.

FARES & SCHEDULES

Pick up schedules and buy tickets from any Italian travel agent, most of whom speak English. Credit cards are usually accepted, but cash is always preferred. Fares depend on whether you have a car and what type of accommodation you desire. Without a car, a ferry from Naples to Capri will cost about €7 per person. Between Naples and Palermo, fares range from €106 for a small car and no sleeping quarters to €231 for a large car and a sleeping cabin for two.

Adriatic Coast Ferries Adriatica ✉ Via San Nicola da Tolentino 27, Rome ☎ 06/4818341 ⊕ www.adriatica.it.

Mediterranean Ferries Alilauro ✉ Molo Beverello, Napoli ☎ 081/7611004 ⊕ www.alilauro.it. **Caremar** ✉ Molo Beverello, Napoli ☎ 081/5513882 ⊕ www.caremar.it. **Golfo Paradiso** ✉ Via Scalo 3, Camogli ☎ 0187/772091 ⊕ www.cinqueterre.it. **Golfo dei Poeti** ✉ Via Mazzini 21, La Spezia ☎ 0187/732987 ⊕ www.cinqueterre.it. **SNAV** ✉ Stazione Marittima Terminal Napoli, Naples ☎ 081/7612348 ⊕ www.snav.it. **Tirrenia** ✉ Rione Sirignano 2, Napoli ☎ 199/123199 within Italy, 081/3172999 from abroad ⊕ www.tirrenia.it. **Toremar** ✉ Piazzale Premuda 13/14, Piombino ☎ 0565/31100 ⊕ www.toremar.it.

Northern Lakes Ferries Navigazione Laghi ✉ Via Ludovico Ariosto 21, Milan ☎ 02/4676101, 800/551801 within Italy ⊕ www.navlaghi.it.

BUS TRAVEL

Italy's bus network is extensive, although buses are not as attractive an option as in other European countries, partly because of cheap, convenient train travel. In some areas buses are faster, so **compare bus and**

train schedules. To reach some smaller towns, a bus may be your only option.

If you're traveling by bus from the United Kingdom, **have some euros on hand** to spend along the way. Eurolines runs bus service to Rome once a week from London, three times a week June–September.

CUTTING COSTS

Bus service is provided by regional companies, some of which run day trips from their base of operations. Children under two usually ride for free, and children under eight travel at half price. If you need a car seat for your child, it's best to bring your own.

FARES & SCHEDULES

Unlike city buses, for which you must buy your ticket from a machine, newsstand, or tobacco shop and stamp it after you board, private bus lines usually have a ticket office in town or allow you to pay when you board.

🚌 Bus Information **Eurolines** ✉ 52 Grosvenor Gardens, London SW1W 0AU ☎ 020/7730-8235 or 020/7730-3499 ⊕ www.eurolines.com.

BUSINESS HOURS

Religious and civic holidays are frequent in Italy. Depending on the holiday's local importance, businesses may close for the day. Businesses do not close on a Friday or Monday when the holiday falls on the weekend.

BANKS & POST OFFICES

Banks are open weekdays 8:30 to 1:30 and for an hour in the afternoon, depending on the bank. Most post offices are open Monday–Saturday 9–12:30; central post offices are open 9–6:30 PM weekdays, 9–12:30 on Saturday. On the last day of the month all post offices close at midday.

MUSEUMS & SIGHTS

Most churches are open from early morning until noon or 12:30, when they close for three hours or more; they open again in the afternoon, closing at about 6 PM. A few major churches, such as St. Peter's in Rome and San Marco in Venice, remain open all day. Walking around during services is discouraged. Many museums are closed one day a week, often on Monday.

During low season, museums often close early; during high season, many stay open until late at night.

PHARMACIES

Pharmacies are generally open weekdays 8:30–1 and 4–8, and Saturday mornings 9–1. Local pharmacies cover the off-hours in shifts: on the door of every pharmacy is a list of which pharmacies in the vicinity will be open late.

SHOPS

Most shops are open Monday–Saturday 9–1 and 3:30 or 4–7:30. Clothing shops are generally closed on Monday mornings. Barbers and hairdressers, with some exceptions, are closed Sunday and Monday. Some bookstores and fashion and tourist-oriented shops in places such as Rome and Venice are open all day, as well as Sunday. Large chain supermarkets such as Standa, COOP, and Eselunga do not close for lunch and are usually open on Sunday; smaller *alimentari* (delicatessens) and other food shops are usually closed one evening during the week (it varies according to the town) and almost always on Sunday.

CAMERAS & PHOTOGRAPHY

Many museums restrict photography, so be on the lookout for signs indicating that picture-taking is not allowed. Many museums and churches forbid flash or tripods. Not everyone appreciates being photographed, particularly in smaller towns. Always ask for permission before taking someone's photograph. The *Kodak Guide to Shooting Great Travel Pictures* (available at bookstores everywhere) is loaded with tips.

📷 Photo Help **Kodak Information Center** ☎ 800/242-2424 ⊕ www.kodak.com.

EQUIPMENT PRECAUTIONS

Don't pack film or equipment in checked luggage, where it is much more susceptible to damage. X-ray machines used to view checked luggage are extremely powerful and therefore are likely to ruin your film. Try to ask for hand inspection of film, which becomes clouded after repeated exposure to airport X-ray machines, and keep videotapes and computer disks away from metal detectors. Always keep film, tape, and computer disks out of the sun. Carry an extra supply of batteries, and be prepared to turn on your camera, camcorder, or laptop to prove to airport security personnel that the device is real.

FILM & DEVELOPING

In Rome and most major cities you'll see scores of photo shops. In smaller towns look for any type of shop with a Kodak sign outside its door. All major brands (Kodak, Polaroid, Fuji) of film are available. Expect to pay between €4.20 and €6 for a roll of 36-exposure color print film. Because costs are higher in Italy, it's a good idea to **stock up on film** before you leave. One-hour developing is readily available in most cities; smaller towns usually have 24-hour service. Developing a roll of 36-exposure film costs €8 to €12.50.

VIDEOS

Italy, like other countries in Europe, doesn't use the same VHS tapes that are used in North America. This means tapes purchased in Italy won't work back home. This is also the case with European DVDs, which aren't compatible with American players.

Videotapes for camcorders are readily available throughout the country. A 90-minute tape costs €7.50–€9.50.

CAR RENTAL

Renting a car in Italy is essential for exploring the countryside, but not if you plan to stick to the cities. Signage on country roads is usually good, but be prepared for fast and impatient fellow drivers.

Hiring a car with a driver can come in handy, particularly if you plan to do some wine tasting or drive along the Amalfi Coast. Ask at your hotel for recommended drivers, or inquire at the local tourist office. Drivers are paid by the day, and are usually rewarded with a tip of about 15% upon completion of the journey.

Fiats and Fords in a variety of sizes are the most typical rental cars. Remember that most Italian cars have standard transmissions. **If you want to rent an automatic, be specific when you reserve the car.** Higher rates will apply.

🚘 **Major Agencies Alamo** ☎ 800/522-9696 ⊕ www.alamo.com. **Avis** ☎ 800/331-1084, 800/

879-2847 in Canada, 0870/606-0100 in U.K., 02/9353-9000 in Australia, 09/526-2847 in New Zealand ⊕ www.avis.com. **Budget** ☎ 800/527-0700 ⊕ www.budget.com. **Dollar** ☎ 800/800-6000, 0800/085-4578 in U.K. ⊕ www.dollar.com. **Hertz** ☎ 800/654-3001, 800/263-0600 in Canada, 0870/844-8844 in U.K., 02/9669-2444 in Australia, 09/256-8690 in New Zealand ⊕ www.hertz.com. **National Car Rental** ☎ 800/227-7368 ⊕ www.nationalcar.com.

CUTTING COSTS

Most American chains have affiliates in Italy, but the rates are usually lower if you book a car before you leave home. A company's rates are the same throughout the country: you will not save money, for example, if you pick up a vehicle in a city rather than at an airport. For a good deal, book through a travel agent who will shop around.

Do look into wholesalers, companies that do not own fleets but rent in bulk from those that do and often offer better rates than traditional car-rental operations. Prices are best during off-peak periods. Rentals booked through wholesalers often must be paid for before you leave home.
🚘 **Wholesalers Auto Europe** ☎ 207/842-2000 or 800/223-5555 🖷 207/842-2222 ⊕ www.autoeurope.com. **Destination Europe Resources** (DER) ✉ 9501 W. Devon Ave., Rosemont, IL 60018 ☎ 800/782-2424 🖷 800/282-7474. **Europe by Car** ☎ 212/581-3040 or 800/223-1516 🖷 212/246-1458 ⊕ www.europebycar.com. **Kemwel** ☎ 877/820-0668 or 800/678-0678 🖷 207/842-2124 or 866/726-6726 ⊕ www.kemwel.com.

INSURANCE

When driving a rented car you are generally responsible for any damage to or loss of the vehicle. Collision policies that car-rental companies sell for European rentals typically don't cover stolen vehicles. Indeed, all car-rental agencies operating in Italy require that you buy a theft-protection policy. Before you rent—and purchase collision coverage—see what coverage you already have under the terms of your personal auto-insurance policy and credit cards.

REQUIREMENTS & RESTRICTIONS

In Italy your driver's license is acceptable. However, a universally recognized International Driver's Permit may save you a problem with the local authorities. They are available from the American or Canadian Automobile Association and, in the United Kingdom, from the Automobile Association or Royal Automobile Club. In Italy you must be 21 to rent a car, and most companies require those under 23 to pay by credit card.

In Sicily there are some roads for which rental agencies deny coverage; ask in advance if you plan to travel in remote regions.

Children under three are required to ride in a car seat, which must be booked in advance. The cost ranges from €26 to €40 for the duration of the rental.

SURCHARGES

Before you pick up a car in one city and leave it in another, ask about drop-off charges or one-way service fees, which can be substantial. Also inquire about early-return policies; some rental agencies charge extra if you return the car before the time specified in your contract while others give you a refund for the days not used. Most agencies note the tank's fuel level on your contract; to avoid a hefty refueling fee, return the car with the same tank level. If the tank was full, refill it just before you turn in the car, but be aware that gas stations near the rental outlet may overcharge. It's almost never a deal to buy a tank of gas with the car when you rent it; the understanding is that you'll return it empty, but some fuel usually remains. The cost for an additional driver is about €5 per day.

CAR TRAVEL

Italy has an extensive network of *autostrade* (toll highways), complemented by equally well-maintained but free *superstrade* (expressways). Save the ticket you are issued at an autostrada entrance, as you need it to exit; on some shorter autostrade, you pay the toll when you enter. Viacards, on sale for €25 at many autostrada locations, allow you to pay for tolls in advance. At special lanes you simply slip the card into a designated slot.

An *uscita* is an "exit." A *raccordo* is a ring road surrounding a city. *Strade regionale*

and *strade provinciale* (regional and provincial highways, denoted by S, SS, SR, or SP numbers) may be single-lane roads, as are all secondary roads; directions and turnoffs aren't always clearly marked.

EMERGENCY SERVICES

Automobile Club Italiano offers 24-hour road service. English-speaking operators are available. Your rental-car company may also have an emergency tow service with a toll-free call. Be prepared to tell the operator which road you're on, the *verso* (direction) you're headed, and your *targa* (license plate number).

When you're on the road, always carry a good road map, a flashlight, and, if possible, a cellular phone for emergencies. On the autostrade and superstrade, emergency phones are available. To find the nearest one, look on the pavement for painted arrows and the term "SOS."

🚗 **Automobile Club Italiano** ☎ 803/116.

GASOLINE

Gas stations are located along the main highways. Those on autostrade are open 24 hours. Otherwise, gas stations generally are open Monday through Saturday 7–7, with a break at lunchtime. Self-service gas stations have pumps that accept only bills in denominations of 5, 10, 20, and 50 euros and do not give change. Those with attendants accept cash and credit cards. It's not customary to tip the attendant.

Gasoline (*benzina*) costs about €1.20 per liter and is available in unleaded (*verde*) and super unleaded (*super*). Many rental cars in Italy use diesel (*gasolio*), which costs about €1 per liter.

PARKING

Parking is at a premium in most towns, especially in the *centri storici* (historic centers). Fines for parking violations are high, and towing is common. Don't think about tearing up a ticket, as car rental companies may use your credit card to be reimbursed for any fines you incur. It's a good idea to park in a designated (and preferably attended) lot. And **don't leave valuables in your car,** as thieves often target rental cars.

In congested cities like Rome and Florence, indoor parking costs €23–€30 for 12–24 hours; outdoor parking costs about €10–€20. Parking in an area signposted ZONA DISCO (disk zone) is allowed for short periods (from 30 minutes to two hours or more—the time is posted); if you don't have a cardboard disk (get one at the tourist office or car rental company) to show what time you parked, you can use a piece of paper. The *parcometro,* a machine that prints a ticket that you leave on your dashboard, has been introduced in most metropolitan areas.

ROAD CONDITIONS
Autostrade are generally well maintained, well marked, and easy to navigate, as are most regional roads. The condition of smaller roads varies, but road maintenance is generally good in Italy.

ROAD MAPS
Street signs are often challenging—a good map and lots of patience are essential. Local maps are available at rental agencies. Most bookstores sell them, as do most gas stations. The best road maps are those produced by Michelin.

RULES OF THE ROAD
Driving is on the right. Regulations are largely the same as in Britain and the United States, except that the police have the power to levy on-the-spot fines. Using handheld mobile phones while driving is illegal; fines can exceed €100. In most Italian towns the use of the horn is forbidden in many areas; a large sign, ZONA DI SILENZIO, indicates a no-honking zone. Speed limits are 130 kph (80 mph) on autostrade and 110 kph (70 mph) on state and provincial roads, unless otherwise marked.

The blood-alcohol content limit for driving is 0.5 gr (stricter than U.S. limits) with fines up to €5,000 for surpassing the limit and the possibility of six months' imprisonment. Though enforcement of laws varies depending on region, fines for speeding are uniformly stiff: 10 kph over the speed limit can warrant a fine of up to €500; greater than 10 kph, and your license could be taken away from you.

Nonetheless, Italians drive fast and are impatient with those who don't. Tailgating is the norm here—the only way to avoid it is to get out of the way. Right turns on red lights are forbidden. Headlights are not compulsory in cities when it rains or snows, but it's a good idea to turn them on. However, you must **turn on your headlights** outside city limits at all hours. You must **wear seat belts** and **strap young children into car seats** at all times.

CHILDREN IN ITALY
Although Italians love children and are generally very tolerant and patient with them, they provide few amenities for them. Some discounts do exist. Always ask about a *sconto bambino* (child's discount) before purchasing tickets. Children under a certain height ride free on municipal buses and trams. Children under 18 who are EU citizens are admitted free to state-run museums and galleries, and there are similar privileges in many municipal or private museums. *Fodor's Around Rome with Kids* (available in bookstores everywhere) can help you plan your days together.

If you are renting a car, don't forget to arrange for a car seat when you reserve. For general advice about traveling with children, consult *Fodor's FYI: Travel with Your Baby* (available in bookstores everywhere).

FLYING
If your children are two or older, ask about children's airfares. As a general rule, infants under two not occupying a seat fly at greatly reduced fares or even for free. But if you want to guarantee a seat for an infant, you have to pay full fare. Consider flying during off-peak days and times; most airlines will grant an infant a seat without a ticket if there are available seats. When booking, confirm carry-on allowances if you're traveling with infants. In general, for babies charged 10% to 50% of the adult fare you are allowed one carry-on bag and a collapsible stroller; if the flight is full, the stroller may have to be checked or you may be limited to less.

Experts agree that it's a good idea to use safety seats aloft for children weighing less than 40 pounds. Airlines set their own policies: if you use a safety seat, U.S. carri-ers usually require that the child be tick-eted, even if he or she is young enough to ride free, because the seats must be strapped into regular seats. And even if you pay the full adult fare for the seat, it may be worth it, especially on longer trips. Do **check your airline's policy about using safety seats during takeoff and landing.** Safety seats are not allowed everywhere in the plane, so get your seat assignments as early as possible.

When reserving, request children's meals or a freestanding bassinet (not available at all airlines) if you need them. But note that bulkhead seats, where you must sit to use the bassinet, may lack an overhead bin or storage space on the floor.

FOOD
In restaurants you may find a high chair or a cushion for the child to sit on, but rarely is there a children's menu. You can **order a mezza porzione** (half portion) or **ask for a porzione da bambino** (child's portion) of any dish. Though spaghetti with meatballs is not found on menus, approximations to it, such as spaghetti *al pomodoro* (with tomato sauce) or *in bianco* (with butter) are suitable substitutions. Italian children are fond of spaghetti with Parmesan cheese; even if it's not on the menu most eateries will happily prepare it. Pizza is a familiar treat for children. Other foods likely to find favor include *pollo fritto* or *pollo arrosto* (fried chicken or roast chicken), *patate fritte* (french fries), and *gelato* (ice cream).

Italian families usually take their children to casual establishments such as trattorias. Only exceptionally well-behaved children should go to higher-end restaurants; indeed, it's rare to see Italian children in them.

LODGING
Most hotels will provide cots or cribs if you ask in advance; higher-end hotels normally have these on hand. The same holds true with babysitting; budget hotels will most likely be unable to provide the service. Some five-star hotels and *agritur-ismi* (farm stays) do not allow children, so inquire beforehand. Pools in city hotels are

a rarity, as are video games. If you're stay-ing at a hotel with satellite TV, you will have access to some English-language news programs, but little more. Even *The Simpsons* is dubbed into Italian.

Most hotels in Italy allow children under a certain age to stay in their parents' room at no extra charge, but others charge for them as extra adults; be sure to find out the cutoff age for children's discounts. Sheraton has 15 properties in Italy, all of which welcome families. Club Med has a "Mini Club" for kids ages 4–10 and a "Kids Club" at its ski village in Sestriere. There are also children's programs at sum-mer resort villages in Metaponto and on the islands of Sicily and Sardinia. Some of the Valtur vacation villages also have spe-cial facilities and activities for children. 🔳 **Best Choices Club Med** ☒ 7001 N. Scottsdale Rd., Suite 1010, Scottsdale, AZ 85253 ☎ 800/258-2633 or 888/WEBCLUB ⊕ www.clubmed.com. **Sher-aton** ☒ 1111 Westchester Ave., White Plains, NY 10604 ☎ 800/221-2340 ⊕ www.starwood.com. **Valtur** ☒ Piazza della Repubblica 59, Rome 00185 ☎ 06/471061 🖷 06/4706321 ⊕ www.valtur.it.

PRECAUTIONS
Italian tap water is safe to drink, but is heavily chlorinated. (That's why most Ital-ians drink bottled water.) Apple juice (*succo di mele*) is readily available in most bars and supermarkets, as are other fruit juices and soft drinks.

Mosquitoes can be pesky once the weather gets warm. Travel with your usual brand of children's insect repellent. There are several Italian brands—Autun, for in-stance—that also do the trick. They are available in pharmacies and supermarkets.

SIGHTS & ATTRACTIONS
Places that are especially appealing to chil-dren are indicated by a rubber-duckie icon (🐤) in the margin.

SUPPLIES & EQUIPMENT
Disposable diapers are available in phar-macies and supermarkets. American brands such as Pampers and Huggies cost slightly more than in the United States. Italian baby formula, available in pharma-cies, generally contains more vitamins than in America. Plasmon is a respected brand.

No-spill cups for toddlers are difficult to find; it's best to bring a few with you.

COMPUTERS ON THE ROAD

Getting online in Italian cities isn't difficult. Internet cafés, some open 24 hours a day, are common. Prices differ, so **shop for the best deal.** Some hotels have in-room modems, but using the hotel's line is usually expensive. Always check the rates before plugging in. You may need an adapter for your computer for the European-style plugs. As always, if you are traveling with a laptop, carry a spare battery and an adapter. Wireless Internet is available in high-end hotels, airports, train stations, and shopping centers.

CONSUMER PROTECTION

Most stores in Italy do not allow customers to return or exchange merchandise, even if there is a minor flaw in the product. Clothing stores are particularly inflexible.

Whether you're shopping for gifts or purchasing travel services, **pay with a major credit card** whenever possible, so you can cancel payment or get reimbursed if there's a problem (and you can provide documentation). If you're doing business with a particular company for the first time, contact your local Better Business Bureau and the attorney general's offices in your state and (for U.S. businesses) the company's home state as well. Have any complaints been filed? Finally, if you're buying a package or tour, always consider travel insurance that includes default coverage (⇨ Insurance).

🚩 **BBBs Council of Better Business Bureaus** ✉ 4200 Wilson Blvd., Suite 800, Arlington, VA 22203 ☎ 703/276-0100 🖷 703/525-8277 ⊕ www.bbb.org.

CRUISE TRAVEL

Several major companies give their customers a taste of Italy. Cunard calls at Genoa, Livorno, Rome, and Lipari. Festival Cruises sails from Venice to Malta, Tunisia, Sicily, and Croatia. Mediterranean Shipping Cruises take you to Sicily, Tunisia, the Balearic Islands, Spain, and France. Royal Olympic Cruises has multiple departures leaving from Venice with ports of call in Dubrovnik, Istanbul, Corfu, Mykonos, and Santorini.

To learn how to plan, choose, and book a cruise-ship voyage, consult *Fodor's FYI: Plan & Enjoy Your Cruise* (available in bookstores everywhere).

🚩 **Cruise Lines Cunard** ✉ 6100 Blue Lagoon Dr., Miami, FL 33126 ☎ 800/728-6273 in U.S. and Canada, 0800/0523840 in U.K., 612/92506666 in Australia and New Zealand ⊕ www.cunardline.com. **Festival Cruises** ✉ Via XX Settembre 28, 16121 Genoa ☎ 010/5490700. **Mediterranean Shipping Cruises** ✉ Via A. Depretis 31, 80133 Naples ☎ 081/7942400 or 081/794211 ⊕ www.msccruises.com. **Royal Olympia Cruises** ✉ 805 3rd Ave., New York, NY 10022-7513 ☎ 800/872-6400 in U.S. and Canada 🖷 888/662-6237 ⊕ www.royalolympiacruises.com.

CUSTOMS & DUTIES

When shopping abroad, keep receipts for all purchases. Upon reentering the country, **be ready to show customs officials what you've bought.** Pack purchases together in an easily accessible place. If you think a duty is incorrect, appeal the assessment. If you object to the way your clearance was handled, note the inspector's badge number. In either case, first ask to see a supervisor. If the problem isn't resolved, write to the appropriate authorities, beginning with the port director at your point of entry.

IN AUSTRALIA

Australian residents who are 18 or older may bring home A$900 worth of souvenirs and gifts (including jewelry), 250 cigarettes or 250 grams of cigars or other tobacco products, and 2.25 liters of alcohol (including wine, beer, and spirits). Residents under 18 may bring back A$450 worth of goods. If any of these individual allowances are exceeded, you must pay duty for the entire amount (of the group of products in which the allowance was exceeded). Members of the same family traveling together may pool their allowances. Prohibited items include meat products. Seeds, plants, and fruits need to be declared upon arrival.

🚩 **Australian Customs Service** 🗝 Locked Bag 3000, Sydney International Airport, Sydney, NSW 2020 ☎ 02/6275-6666 or 1300/363263, 02/

8334-7444 or 1800/020-504 quarantine-inquiry line 🖨 02/8339-6714 🌐 www.customs.gov.au.

IN CANADA

Canadian residents who have been out of Canada for at least seven days may bring in C$750 worth of goods duty-free. If you've been away fewer than seven days but more than 48 hours, the duty-free allowance drops to C$200. If your trip lasts 24 to 48 hours, the allowance is C$50 if the goods are worth more than C$50, you must pay full duty on all of the goods. You may not pool allowances with family members. Goods claimed under the C$750 exemption may follow you by mail; those claimed under the lesser exemptions must accompany you. Alcohol and tobacco products may be included in the seven-day and 48-hour exemptions but not in the 24-hour exemption. If you meet the age requirements of the province or territory through which you reenter Canada, you may bring in, duty-free, 1.5 liters of wine *or* 1.14 liters (40 imperial ounces) of liquor *or* 24 12-ounce cans or bottles of beer or ale. Also, if you meet the local age requirement for tobacco products, you may bring in, duty-free, 200 cigarettes, 50 cigars or cigarillos, and 200 grams of tobacco. You may have to pay a minimum duty on tobacco products, regardless of whether or not you exceed your personal exemption. Check ahead of time with the Canada Border Services Agency or the Department of Agriculture for policies regarding meat products, seeds, plants, and fruits.

You may send an unlimited number of gifts (only one gift per recipient, however) worth up to C$60 each duty-free to Canada. Label the package UNSOLICITED GIFT—VALUE UNDER $60. Alcohol and tobacco are excluded.

🇨🇦 **Canada Border Services Agency** ✉ Customs Information Services, 191 Laurier Ave. W, 15th fl., Ottawa, Ontario K1A 0L5 ☎ 800/461-9999 in Canada, 204/983-3500, 506/636-5064 🌐 www. cbsa.gc.ca.

IN ITALY

Of goods obtained anywhere outside the EU, the allowances are (1) 200 cigarettes or 100 cigarillos (under 3 grams) or 50 cigars or 250 grams of tobacco; (2) 2 liters of still table wine or 1 liter of spirits over 22% volume; and (3) 50 milliliters of perfume and 250 milliliters of toilet water.

Of goods obtained (duty and tax paid) within another EU country, the allowances are (1) 800 cigarettes or 400 cigarillos (under 3 grams) or 200 cigars or 1 kilogram of tobacco; (2) 90 liters of still table wine or 10 liters of spirits over 22% volume or 20 liters of spirits under 22% volume or 110 liters of beer.

There is no quarantine period in Italy, so if you want to travel with Fido or Fifi, it's possible. Contact your nearest Italian consulate to find out what paperwork is needed for entry into Italy with a pet; generally, it is a certificate noting that the animal is healthy and up-to-date on its vaccinations. Keep in mind, however, that the United States has some stringent laws about reentry: pets must be free of all disease, especially those communicable to humans, and they must be vaccinated against rabies at least 30 days before returning. This means that if you are in Italy for a short-term stay, you must find a veterinarian or have your pet vaccinated before departure. (This law does not apply to puppies younger than three months old.) Pets should arrive at the point of entry with a statement, in English, attesting to this fact.

🇮🇹 **Ministero delle Finanze, Direzione Centrale dei Servizi Doganali, Divisione I** ✉ Via Carucci 71, 00143 Rome ☎ 06/50242117. **Dogana Sezione Viaggiatori** ✉ Customs, Aeroporto Leonardo da Vinci, Fiumicino, 00054 Rome ☎ 06/65954343.

IN NEW ZEALAND

All homeward-bound residents may bring back NZ$700 worth of souvenirs and gifts; passengers may not pool their allowances, and children can claim only the concession on goods intended for their own use. For those 17 or older, the duty-free allowance also includes 4.5 liters of wine or beer; one 1,125-ml bottle of spirits; and either 200 cigarettes, 250 grams of tobacco, 50 cigars, *or* a combination of the three up to 250 grams. Meat products, seeds, plants, and fruits must be declared upon arrival to the Agricultural Services Department.

New Zealand Customs ⊠ Head office: The Customhouse, 17–21 Whitmore St., Box 2218, Wellington ☎ 09/300–5399 or 0800/428–786 ⊕ www.customs. govt.nz.

IN THE U.K.

If you are a U.K. resident and your journey was wholly within the European Union, you probably won't have to pass through customs when you return to the United Kingdom. If you plan to bring back large quantities of alcohol or tobacco, check EU limits beforehand. In most cases, if you bring back more than 200 cigars, 3,200 cigarettes, 400 cigarillos, 3 kilograms of tobacco, 10 liters of spirits, 110 liters of beer, 20 liters of fortified wine, and/or 90 liters of wine, you have to declare the goods upon return.

HM Customs and Excise ⊠ Portcullis House, 21 Cowbridge Rd. E, Cardiff CF11 9SS ☎ 0845/010– 9000 or 0208/929–0152 advice service, 0208/929– 6731 or 0208/910–3602 complaints ⊕ www.hmce. gov.uk.

IN THE U.S.

U.S. residents who have been out of the country for at least 48 hours may bring home, for personal use, $800 worth of foreign goods duty-free, as long as they haven't used the $800 allowance or any part of it in the past 30 days. This exemption may include 1 liter of alcohol (for travelers 21 and older), 200 cigarettes, and 100 non-Cuban cigars. Family members from the same household who are traveling together may pool their $800 personal exemptions. For fewer than 48 hours, the duty-free allowance drops to $200, which may include 50 cigarettes, 10 non-Cuban cigars, and 150 ml of alcohol (or 150 ml of perfume containing alcohol). The $200 allowance cannot be combined with other individuals' exemptions, and if you exceed it, the full value of all the goods will be taxed. Antiques, which U.S. Customs and Border Protection defines as objects more than 100 years old, enter duty-free, as do original works of art done entirely by hand, including paintings, drawings, and sculptures.

This doesn't apply to folk art or handicrafts, which are in general dutiable.

You may also send packages home duty-free, with a limit of one parcel per addressee per day (except alcohol or tobacco products or perfume worth more than $5). You can mail up to $200 worth of goods for personal use; label the package PERSONAL USE and attach a list of its contents and their retail value. If the package contains your used personal belongings, mark it AMERICAN GOODS RETURNED to avoid paying duties. You may send up to $100 worth of goods as a gift; mark the package UNSOLICITED GIFT. Mailed items do not affect your duty-free allowance on your return.

To avoid paying duty on foreign-made high-ticket items you already own and will take on your trip, register them with a local customs office before you leave the country. Consider filing a Certificate of Registration for laptops, cameras, watches, and other digital devices identified with serial numbers or other permanent markings; you can keep the certificate for other trips. Otherwise, bring a sales receipt or insurance form to show that you owned the item before you left the United States.

For more about duties, restricted items, and other information about international travel, check out U.S. Customs and Border Protection's online brochure, *Know Before You Go*. You can also file complaints on the U.S. Customs and Border Protection Web site, listed below.

U.S. Customs and Border Protection ⊠ For inquiries and complaints, 1300 Pennsylvania Ave. NW, Washington, DC 20229 ⊕ www.cbp.gov ☎ 877/227– 5551 or 202/354–1000.

DISABILITIES & ACCESSIBILITY

Italy has only recently begun to provide facilities such as ramps, telephones, and restrooms for people with disabilities; such things are still the exception, not the rule. Wheelchairs must be transported free of charge, according to Italian law, but the logistics of getting them on trains and buses can make this requirement irrelevant. Seats are reserved for people with disabilities on public transportation, but few buses have lifts for wheelchairs. High, narrow steps for boarding trains create additional problems. At many monuments and museums, and even in some hotels and restaurants, architectural barriers make access difficult. Wheelchair access to bathrooms in restaurants is nearly nonexistent. Capdarco or Roma per Tutti can provide information about events and services for disabled people.

Contact the nearest Italian consulate about bringing a guide dog into Italy. This requires an import license, a current certificate detailing the dog's inoculations, and a letter from your veterinarian certifying the dog's good health.

▣ Local Resources Capodarco ⌀ Via Enrico Giglioli 54/a, 00169 Rome ☏ 06/71290123 🖷 06/71290125. **Roma per Tutti** ✉ Via di Torricola 87, 00178 Rome ☏ 06/71623919 🖷 06/71290125 ⊕ www.romapertutti.it.

LODGING
Because Italian lodgings are often in buildings that are several hundred years old, many are not equipped with elevators. Many of them have steps at the entrance. When booking a hotel, inquire about entranceways, as ramps are still rare. In Rome, the Hotel de Russie has four rooms available for people who use wheelchairs. The Locarno, also near Piazza del Popolo, has one accessible room. A budget option is the Alimandi, near the Vatican.

The Hotel Excelsior in Florence is wheelchair accessible. In Venice the San Zulian and the luxurious Danieli both have two rooms that are wheelchair accessible. In Milan the Grand Hotel Duomo has a junior suite available for people who use wheelchairs. The equally luxurious and modern Westin Palace has two wheelchair-friendly rooms.

The Italian Government Travel Office (⇨ Visitor Information) can give you a list of hotels that provide access and addresses of Italian associations for travelers with disabilities.

RESERVATIONS
When discussing accessibility with an operator or reservations agent, ask hard questions. Are there any stairs, inside *or* out? Are there grab bars next to the toilet *and* in the shower/tub? How wide is the doorway to the room? To the bathroom? For the most extensive facilities meeting the latest legal specifications, opt for newer accommodations. If you reserve through a toll-free number, consider also calling the hotel's local number to confirm the information from the central reservations office. Get confirmation in writing when you can.

SIGHTS & ATTRACTIONS
Getting around in Italy with a wheelchair is difficult but not impossible. In Rome, for example, the Musei Vaticani and the Museo Nazionale di Castel Sant'Angelo are accessible (but the Colosseum and Forum are not). In Florence the Uffizi, Palazzo Pitti, Duomo, Baptistery, and Accademia are all accessible. Local tourist offices provide maps and lists, rated on degrees of ease and difficulty, of banks, supermarkets, sites, hotels, and restaurants.

TRANSPORTATION
The U.S. Department of Transportation Aviation Consumer Protection Division's online publication *New Horizons: Information for the Air Traveler with a Disability* offers advice for travelers with a disability, and outlines basic rights. Visit DisabilityInfo.gov for general information.

Most buses in Italy cannot accommodate wheelchairs; only a few have special ramps. A handful of subway stops in the Rome subway system are accessible to people who use wheelchairs. Local tourist offices are sometimes helpful with information about mass transit.

Getting around in Venice on the vaporetti is relatively easy; however, when *acqua alta* (high water) floods pedestrian areas, as it does sporadically between October and April, movement for people who use wheelchairs becomes virtually impossible.

More than 150 railroad stations throughout the country have a reception service to assist people who use wheelchairs; this service must be booked 24 hours in advance. To do so, consult a travel agency or go to www.trenitalia.com, select the Italian-language version, and click on "servizi per i disabili." The ferry line Tirrenia has two wheelchair-accessible cabins on their routes to Sardinia.

🔢 **Information & Complaints Aviation Consumer Protection Division** (⇨ Air Travel) for airline-related problems ⊕ airconsumer.ost.dot.gov/publications/horizons.htm for airline travel advice and rights. **Departmental Office of Civil Rights** ✉ For general inquiries, U.S. Department of Transportation, S-30, 400 7th St. SW, Room 10215, Washington, DC 20590 ☎ 202/366-4648, 202/366-8538 TTY ⊟ 202/366-9371 ⊕ www.dotcr.ost.dot.gov. **Disability Rights Section** ✉ NYAV, U.S. Department of Justice, Civil Rights Division, 950 Pennsylvania Ave. NW, Washington, DC 20530 ☎ ADA information line 202/514-0301, 800/514-0301, 202/514-0383 TTY, 800/514-0383 TTY ⊕ www.ada.gov. **U.S. Department of Transportation Hotline** ☎ For disability-related air-travel problems, 800/778-4838 or 800/455-9880 TTY.

TRAVEL AGENCIES

In the United States, the Americans with Disabilities Act requires that travel firms serve the needs of all travelers. Some agencies specialize in working with people with disabilities.

🔢 **Travelers with Developmental Disabilities Sprout** ✉ 893 Amsterdam Ave., New York, NY 10025 ☎ 212/222-9575 or 888/222-9575 ⊟ 212/222-9768 ⊕ www.gosprout.org.

🔢 **Travelers with Mobility Problems Access Adventures/B. Roberts Travel** ✉ 1876 East Ave., Rochester, NY 14610 ☎ 800/444-6540 ⊕ www.brobertstravel.com, run by a former physical-rehabilitation counselor. **CareVacations** ✉ No. 5, 5110-50 Ave., Leduc, Alberta, Canada, T9E 6V4 ☎ 780/986-6404 or 877/478-7827 ⊟ 780/986-8332 ⊕ www.carevacations.com, for group tours and cruise vacations. **Flying Wheels Travel** ✉ 143 W. Bridge St., Box 382, Owatonna, MN 55060 ☎ 507/451-5005 ⊟ 507/451-1685 ⊕ www.flyingwheelstravel.com.

DISCOUNTS & DEALS

Be a smart shopper and compare all your options before making decisions. A plane ticket bought with a promotional coupon from travel clubs, coupon books, and direct-mail offers or purchased on the Internet may not be cheaper than the least expensive fare from a discount ticket agency. And always keep in mind that what you get is just as important as what you save.

DISCOUNT RESERVATIONS

To save money, look into discount reservations services with Web sites and toll-free numbers, which use their buying power to get a better price on hotels, airline tickets (⇨ Air Travel), even car rentals.

🔢 **Hotel Rooms Accommodations Express** ☎ 800/444-7666 or 800/277-1064. **Hotels.com** ☎ 800/246-8357 ⊕ www.hotels.com. **International Marketing & Travel Concepts** ☎ 800/790-4682 ⊕ www.imtc-travel.com. **Steigenberger Reservation Service** ☎ 800/223-5652 ⊕ www.srs-worldhotels.com. **Turbotrip.com** ☎ 800/473-7829 ⊕ w3.turbotrip.com.

PACKAGE DEALS

Don't confuse packages and guided tours. When you buy a package, you travel on your own, just as though you had planned the trip yourself. Fly/drive packages, which combine airfare and car rental, are often a good deal. In cities, ask the local visitor's bureau about hotel and local transportation packages that include tickets to major museum exhibits or other special events. If you **buy a rail/drive pass,** you may save on train tickets and car rentals. All Eurailpass holders get a discount on Eurostar fares through the Channel Tunnel and often receive reduced rates for buses, hotels, ferries, sightseeing cruises, and car rentals.

EATING & DRINKING

The restaurants we list are the cream of the crop in each price category. Properties indicated by a ✕⊡ are lodging establishments whose restaurant warrants a special trip.

CATEGORY	COST
$$$$	over €22
$$$	€16-€22
$$	€11-€16
$	€7-€11
¢	under €7

Prices are for a second course (secondo piatto) and are given in euros.

A few pointers on Italian dining etiquette: menus are posted outside most restaurants (in English in tourist areas); if not, you might step inside and ask to take a look at the menu, but don't ask for a table unless you intend to stay. Italians take their food as it is listed on the menu, seldom making special requests such as "dressing on the side" or "hold the olive oil." If you have special dietary needs, though, make them known, and they can usually be accommodated. Although mineral water makes its way to almost every table, you can always order a carafe of tap water (*acqua di rubinetto* or *acqua semplice*). Doing this, however, will mark you as a tourist.

Spaghetti should be eaten with a fork rolled against the side of the dish, although a little help from a spoon will not horrify the locals the way cutting spaghetti into little pieces might. Wiping your bowl clean with a (small) piece of bread is fine in less formal eateries. Order your espresso (Italians almost never drink a cappuccino after breakfast) after dessert, not with it. You usually have to ask for *il conto* (the bill). Unless it's well past closing time, no waiter will put a bill on your table until you request him to do so. Don't ask for a doggy bag.

MEALS & SPECIALTIES

What's the difference between a ristorante and a trattoria? Can you order food at an enoteca? Can you go to a restaurant just for a snack, or order just a salad at a pizzeria? The following definitions should help.

Not too long ago, restaurants tended to be more elegant and expensive than trattorie and osterie, which served more traditional, home-style fare in an atmosphere to match. But the distinction has blurred considerably, and an osteria in the center of town might be far fancier (and pricier) than a ristorante across the street. In all these types of places you are generally expected to order at least a two-course meal, such as: a *primo* (first course) and a *secondo* (main course) or a *contorno* (vegetable side dish); an antipasto (starter) followed by either primo or secondo; or a secondo and a *dolce* (dessert).

In an *enoteca* (wine bar) or pizzeria it's common to order just one dish. An enoteca menu is often limited to a selection of cheese, cured meats, salads, and desserts, but if there's a kitchen you'll also find soups, pastas, and main courses. The typical pizzeria fare includes *affettati misti* (a selection of cured pork), simple salads, various kinds of bruschetta, crostini (similar to bruschetta, sometimes topped with cheese and broiled) and, in Rome, *fritti* (deep-fried finger food) such as *olive ascolane* (green olives with a meat stuffing) and *supplì* (rice balls stuffed with mozzarella). All pizzerias serve fresh fruit, ice cream, and simple desserts.

Throughout the country the handiest and least expensive places for a quick snack between sights are probably bars, cafés, and pizza *al taglio* (by the slice) spots. Bars in Italy are primarily places to get a coffee and a bite to eat rather than drinking establishments. Most have a selection of *panini* (sandwiches) warmed up on the griddle (*piastra*) and *tramezzini* (sandwiches made of untoasted white bread triangles). In larger cities, bars also serve vegetable and fruit salads, cold pasta dishes, and yogurt around lunchtime. Most bars offer beer and a variety of alcohol as well as wines by the glass (sometimes good but more often mediocre). A café (*caffè* in Italian) is like a bar but usually with more tables. Pizza at a café should be avoided—it's usually heated in a microwave. If you place your order at the counter, ask if you can sit down: some places charge for table service, others do not. In self-service bars and cafés it's good manners to clean your table before you leave. Note that in some places you have to pay a cashier, then place your order and show your *scontrino* (receipt) at the counter. Pizza al taglio shops sell pizza by weight: just point out which kind you want and how much. Very few pizza al taglio shops have seating.

Italian cuisine is still largely regional. Ask what the local specialties are: by all means, have spaghetti *alla carbonara* (with bacon and egg) in Rome, pizza in Rome or Naples, *bistecca alla fiorentina* (steak) in Florence, *chingale* (wild bore) in Tuscany, truffles in the Piedmont, and risotto *alla milanese* in Milan.

MEAL TIMES

Breakfast (*la colazione*) is usually served from 7 to 10:30, lunch (*il pranzo*) from 12:30 to 2:30, dinner (*la cena*) from 7:30 to 10. Peak times are usually 1:30 for lunch and 9 for dinner. Enoteche and bacari (wine bars) are open also in the morning and late afternoon for a snack at the counter. Most pizzerias open at 8 PM and close around midnight—later in summer and on weekends. Most bars and cafés are open from 7 AM until 8 or 9 PM; a few stay open until midnight. Unless otherwise noted, the restaurants listed in this guide are open daily for lunch and dinner.

PAYING

Most restaurants charge a "cover" charge per person, usually listed at the top of the check as *"coperto"* or *"pane e coperto."* It should be a modest charge (€1–€2.50 per person) except at the most expensive restaurants. Whenever in doubt, ask before you order to avoid unpleasant discussions later. It is customary to leave a small tip (around 10%) in appreciation of good service. If *servizio* is included at the bottom of the check, no tip is necessary. Tips are always given in cash.

The price of fish dishes is often given by weight (before cooking), so the price you see on the menu is for 100 grams of fish, not for the whole dish. An average fish portion is about 350 grams. In Tuscany, *bistecca alla fiorentina* (florentine steak) is also often priced by weight.

Major credit cards are widely accepted in Italy, though cash is usually preferred. More restaurants take Visa and Master-Card than American Express.

RESERVATIONS & DRESS

Reservations are always a good idea; we mention them only when they're essential or not accepted. Book as far ahead as you can, and reconfirm as soon as you arrive. (Large parties should always call ahead to check the reservations policy.) Pizzerias and enoteche usually accept reservations only for large groups.

We mention dress only when men are required to wear a jacket or a jacket and tie.

But unless they're dining outside are at an oceanfront resort, Italian men never wear shorts or running shoes in a restaurant. The same applies to women: no casual shorts, running shoes, and plastic sandals when going out to dinner. Shorts are acceptable in pizzerias and cafés.

WINE, BEER & SPIRITS

If you're in a restaurant or trattoria, ask your waiter about the house wine; sometimes it's very good indeed, sometimes it isn't. Wine in Italy is considerably less expensive than almost anywhere else. Beer, oddly, is more expensive than a glass of wine, and though Italy does produce beer it's not nearly as notable as its wine.

Beer, wine, and spirits can be purchased in any bar, grocery store, or enoteca, any day of the week. There's no minimum drinking age in Italy. Italian children begin drinking wine mixed with water at mealtimes when they are teenagers or even younger.

Many bars have their own *aperitivo della casa* (house aperitif). Italians are most imaginative with their mixed drinks—usually shaken, rarely blended.

ELECTRICITY

To use electric-powered equipment purchased in the United States or Canada, **bring a converter and adapter.** The electrical current in Italy is 220 volts, 50 cycles alternating current (AC); wall outlets take Continental-type plugs, with two or three round prongs.

If your appliances are dual-voltage, you'll need only an adapter. Don't use 110-volt outlets marked FOR SHAVERS ONLY for high-wattage appliances such as blow-dryers. Most laptops operate equally well on 110 and 220 volts and so require only an adapter.

EMBASSIES

🔽 Australia **Australian Embassy** ✉ Via Alessandria 215, 00198 Rome ☎ 06/852721 ⊕ www.australian-embassy.it.

🔽 Canada **Canadian Embassy** ✉ Via G. B. de Rossi 27, 00161 Rome ☎ 06/445981 ⊕ www.dfait-maeci.gc.ca/canadaeuropa/italy.

🔽 New Zealand **New Zealand Embassy** ✉ Via Zara 28, 00198 Rome ☎ 06/4417171.

🏛 United Kingdom **British Embassy** ⊠ Via XX Settembre 80A, 00187 Rome ☎ 06/42200001 ⊕ www.britain.it.
🏛 United States **U.S. Embassy** ⊠ Via Veneto 121 00187 Rome ☎ 06/46741 ⊕ www.usembassy.it.

EMERGENCIES

No matter where you are in Italy, you can **dial 113 in case of emergency.** Not all 113 operators speak English, so you may want to ask a local to place the call. Asking the operator for *"pronto soccorso"* (first aid) should get you an *ambulanza* (ambulance). If you just need a doctor, ask for *"un medico."*

Italy has the *carabinieri* (national police force) as well as the *polizia* (local police force). Both are armed and have the power to arrest and investigate crimes. Always **report the loss of your passport** to the police as well as to your embassy. When reporting a crime, you'll be asked to fill out a *una denuncia* (official report); keep a copy for your insurance company.

Local traffic officers, known as *vigili,* are responsible for, among other things, giving out parking tickets. They wear white (in summer) or black uniforms. Should you find yourself involved in a minor car accident, contact down the vigili.
🏛 Emergencies ☎ 113. **National police** ☎ 112.

ENGLISH-LANGUAGE MEDIA

BOOKS

Most major cities have bookstores that cater to an English speakers. The nationwide chain Feltrinelli International, for example, has a large English-language section (expensive, since they are all imported). Rome has several independent English-language bookstores, as do several other cities, including Florence.

NEWSPAPERS & MAGAZINES

The best source for news in English is the *International Herald Tribune,* sold at newsstands in major cities. *USA Today* and most of the London newspapers are also available. You can sometimes find a week-old Sunday *New York Times,* but be prepared to pay €12. Various national versions of *Vogue* are available, as are English-language versions of *Time, Newsweek, The Economist, The New Yorker, Vanity Fair, In Style,* and *People,* among others. But they don't come cheap: *Vanity Fair,* for example, costs more than €8.

RADIO & TELEVISION

Unless your hotel gets CNN or SkyNews, every television program you see will be in Italian. (MTV is sometimes broadcast in English with Italian subtitles—but that's the exception, not the rule.) Aside from Vatican Radio, which broadcasts world news in English three times a day, radio broadcasts are all in Italian.

ETIQUETTE & BEHAVIOR

Be sure to **dress appropriately** when visiting a church in Italy. Shorts, tank tops, and sleeveless garments are taboo in most churches throughout the country. In summer carry a sweater or other item of clothing to wrap around your bare shoulders before entering a church. You should **never bring food into a church,** and do not sip from your water bottle while inside. And **never enter a church when a service is in progress,** especially if it is a private affair such as a wedding or baptism.

Italians who are friends greet each other with a kiss, usually first on the right cheek, then on the left. When you meet a new person, shake hands.

GAY & LESBIAN TRAVEL

Same-sex couples traveling in major cities and popular resorts should meet with no raised eyebrows on the part of the locals. However, overt displays of affection in public are rare. Gay bars, mostly catering to men (and some of which ban women), can be found in all major cities. Some mainstream bars and nightclubs have a gay night during the week; inquire at the local tourist office. In Florence, the monthly events magazine *Firenze Spettacolo* has an informative section on gay bars, events, and services. The Web site *Azione Gay e Lesbica* has a list of gay bars in Florence.
🏛 Local Contacts & Community Centers **Azione Gay e Lesbica** ♂ c/o Andrea del Sarto, Via Manara 12, Florence ☎ 055/671298 ⊕ www.azionegayelesbica.it. **Circolo di Cultura Omosessuale Mario Mieli** ⊠ Via Corinto 5, Rome ☎ 06/59604622 ⊕ www.mariomieli.org.

⚑ Gay- & Lesbian-Friendly Travel Agencies Different Roads Travel ⊠ 1017 N. LaCienega Blvd., Suite 308, West Hollywood, CA 90069 ☎ 310/289-6000 or 800/429-8747 (Ext. 14 for both) 📠 310/855-0323 ✉ lgernert@tzell.com. **Kennedy Travel** ⊠ 130 W. 42nd St., Suite 401, New York, NY 10036 ☎ 800/237-7433 or 212/840-8659 📠 212/730-2269 ⊕ www.kennedytravel.com. **Now, Voyager** ⊠ 4406 18th St., San Francisco, CA 94114 ☎ 415/626-1169 or 800/255-6951 📠 415/626-8626 ⊕ www.nowvoyager.com. **Skylink Travel and Tour/Flying Dutchmen Travel** ⊠ 1455 N. Dutton Ave., Suite A, Santa Rosa, CA 95401 ☎ 707/546-9888 or 800/225-5759 📠 707/636-0951; serving lesbian travelers.

HEALTH

The Centers for Disease Control and Prevention (CDC) in Atlanta caution that most of Southern Europe is in the "intermediate" range for risk of contracting traveler's diarrhea. Part of this risk may be attributed to an increased consumption of olive oil and wine, which can have a laxative effect on stomachs used to a different diet. The CDC also advises all international travelers to swim only in chlorinated swimming pools unless they are certain the local beaches and freshwater lakes are not contaminated. Italy's private beaches are very clean, public ones less so.

OVER-THE-COUNTER REMEDIES

It's always best to **travel with your own tried and true medicines.** The regulations regarding what medicines require a prescription are not likely to be exactly the same in Italy and in your home country—all the more reason to bring what you need with you. Aspirin (*l'aspirina*) can be purchased at any pharmacy, but Tylenol and Advil are unavailable.

HIKING & WALKING

Italy has many good places to hike and an extensive network of long trails. The Sentiero Italia is a national trail running from Reggio Calabria on the toe of Italy's boot to the central section of the Apennine mountains. There are plans to lengthen it farther north and to the western Alps, and from there to the Dolomites and Udine in the Friuli region. For detailed information on the Sentiero Italia contact the Club

Alpino Italiano headquarters or one of the local offices. Local tourist information offices can also be helpful.

⚑ Hiking Organizations Club Alpino Italiano ⊠ Via Petrella 19, 20124 Milan ☎ 02/2057231 📠 02/205723201 ⊕ www.cai.it.

⚑ Hiking & Walking Tours Above the Clouds Trekking ✍ Box 388, Hinesburg, VT 05461 ☎ 802/482-4848 or 800/233-4499 📠 802/482-5011 www.aboveclouds.com. **Butterfield & Robinson** (⇨ Bike Travel). **Ciclismo Classico** (⇨ Bike Travel). **Country Walkers** ✍ Box 180, Waterbury, VT 05676-0180 ☎ 802/464-9255 or 800/464-9255 ⊕ www.countrywalkers.com. **EEI Travel** (⇨ Bike Travel). **Italian Connection, Walking & Culinary Tours** ⊠ 11 Fairway Dr., Suite 210, Edmonton, Alberta, Canada T6J 2W4 ☎ 800/462-7911 ⊕ www.italian-connection.com. **Mountain Travel-Sobek** ⊠ 6420 Fairmount Ave., El Cerrito, CA 94530 ☎ 510/527-8100 or 888/687-6235 📠 510/525-7710 ⊕ www.mtsobek.com. **Wilderness Travel** ⊠ 1102 9th St., Berkeley, CA 94710 ☎ 510/558-2488 or 800/368-2794 📠 510/558-2489 ⊕ www.wildernesstravel.com.

HOLIDAYS

If you can avoid it, don't travel through Italy in August, when much of the population is on vacation. Most cities are deserted and many restaurants and shops are closed.

National holidays in 2005 include January 1 (New Year's Day); January 6 (Epiphany); March 27 and March 28 (Easter Sun. and Mon.); April 25 (Liberation Day); May 1 (Labor Day or May Day); June 2 (Festival of the Republic); August 15 (Ferragosto); November 1 (All Saints' Day); December 8 (Immaculate Conception); December 25 and 26 (Christmas Day and the feast of St. Stephen).

Feast days of patron saints are observed locally. Many businesses and shops may be closed in Florence, Genoa, and Turin on June 24 (St. John the Baptist); in Rome on June 29 (Sts. Peter and Paul); in Palermo on July 15 (St. Rosalia); in Naples on September 19 (San Gennaro); in Bologna on October 4 (San Petronio); in Trieste on November 3 (San Giusto); and in Milan on December 7 (St. Ambrose). Venice's feast of St. Mark is April 25, the same as Liberation Day, so the Madonna della Salute on November 21 makes up for the lost holiday. (*Also see* Festivals and Seasonal Events *under* When to Go.)

INSURANCE

The most useful travel-insurance plan is a comprehensive policy that includes coverage for trip cancellation and interruption, default, trip delay, and medical expenses (with a waiver for preexisting conditions).

Without insurance you'll lose all or most of your money if you cancel your trip, regardless of the reason. Default insurance covers you if your tour operator, airline, or cruise line goes out of business—the chances of which have been increasing. Trip-delay covers expenses that arise because of bad weather or mechanical delays. Study the fine print when comparing policies.

If you're traveling internationally, a key component of travel insurance is coverage for medical bills incurred if you get sick on the road. Such expenses aren't generally covered by Medicare or private policies. U.K. residents can buy a travel-insurance policy valid for most vacations taken during the year in which it's purchased (but check preexisting-condition coverage). British and Australian citizens need extra medical coverage when traveling overseas.

Always **buy travel policies directly from the insurance company**; if you buy them from a cruise line, airline, or tour operator that goes out of business you probably won't be covered for the agency or operator's default, a major risk. Before making any purchase, review your existing health and homeowner's policies to find what they cover away from home.

Travel Insurers In the U.S.: **Access America** ⊠ 2805 N. Parham Rd., Richmond, VA 23294 ☎ 800/284-8300 🖷 804/673-1469 or 800/346-9265 ⊕ www.accessamerica.com. **Travel Guard International** ⊠ 1145 Clark St., Stevens Point, WI 54481 ☎ 800/826-1300 or 715/345-1041 🖷 800/955-8785 or 715/345-1990 ⊕ www.travelguard.com. **In the U.K.: Association of British Insurers** ⊠ 51 Gresham St., London EC2V 7HQ ☎ 020/7600-3333 🖷 020/7696-8999 ⊕ www.abi.org.uk.

In Canada: **RBC Insurance** ⊠ 6880 Financial Dr., Mississauga, Ontario L5N 7Y5 ☎ 800/387-4357 or 905/816-2559 🖷 888/298-6458 ⊕ www.rbcinsurance.com. In Australia: **Insurance Council of Australia** ⊠ Level 3, 56 Pitt St. Sydney, NSW 2000 ☎ 02/9253-5100 🖷 02/9253-5111 ⊕ www.ica.com.au. In New Zealand: **Insurance Council of New Zealand** ⊠ Level 7, 111-115 Customhouse Quay, Box 474, Wellington ☎ 04/472-5230 🖷 04/473-3011 ⊕ www.icnz.org.nz.

LANGUAGE

In larger cities such as Venice, Rome, and Florence, language is not a big problem. Most hotels have English speakers at their reception desks, and if not they can always find someone who speaks at least a little English. You may have trouble communicating in the countryside, but a phrase book and expressive gestures will go a long way. Try to **master a few phrases for daily use** and familiarize yourself with the words you'll need for deciphering signs and menus.

LANGUAGES FOR TRAVELERS

A phrase book and language-tape set can help get you started. *Fodor's Italian for Travelers* (available at bookstores everywhere) is excellent.

LODGING

The lodgings we list are the cream of the crop in each price category. We always list the facilities that are available, but we don't specify whether they cost extra; when pricing accommodations, always ask what's included and what costs extra. Properties are assigned price categories based on the range between their least and most expensive standard double room at high season (excluding holidays). Properties marked ✕⌐ are lodging establishments whose restaurants warrant a special trip. Hotels with the designation **BP** (for Breakfast Plan) at the end of their listing include breakfast in their rate; offerings can vary from coffee and a roll to an elaborate buffet. Those designated **EP** (European Plan) have no meals included; **MAP** (Modified American Plan) means you get breakfast and dinner; **FAP** (Full American Plan) includes all meals.

CATEGORY	MAIN CITIES	ELSEWHERE
$$$$	over €290	over €220
$$$	€210–€290	€160–€220
$$	€140–€210	€110–€160
$	€80–€140	€70–€110
¢	under €80	under €70

Prices are for two people in a standard double room in high season, including tax and service, and are given in euros. "Main cities" are Florence, Milan, Rome, and Venice.

APARTMENT & VILLA RENTALS

If you want a home base that's roomy enough for a family and comes with cooking facilities, consider a furnished rental. These can save you money, especially if you're traveling with a group. Home-exchange directories sometimes list rentals as well as exchanges.

In the capital, *Wanted in Rome* is a bimonthly magazine with extensive listings for short-term rentals all over the country. Another good source for rentals is *EYP*, available at English-language bookstores.

⌁ International Agents At Home Abroad ⌂ 163 3rd Ave., No. 319, New York, NY 10003 ☏ 212/421–9165 🖷 212/533-0095 ⊕ www.athomeabroadinc.com. **Drawbridge to Europe** ⊠ 98 Granite St., Ashland, OR 97520 ☏ 541/482–7778 or 888/268-1148 🖷 541/482-7779 ⊕ www.drawbridgetoeurope.com. **Hideaways International** ⊠ 767 Islington St., Portsmouth, NH 03801 ☏ 603/430–4433 or 800/843-4433 🖷 603/430-4444 ⊕ www.hideaways.com, annual membership $185. **Hometours International** ⊠ 1108 Scottie La., Knoxville, TN 37919 ☏ 865/690-8484 or 866/367-4668 ✆ hometours@aol.com ⊕ thor.he.net/~hometour/. **Interhome** ⊠ 1990 N.E. 163rd St., Suite 110, North Miami Beach, FL 33162 ☏ 305/940-2299 or 800/882-6864 🖷 305/940-2911 ⊕ www.interhome.us. **Solemar** ⊠ 1990 N.E. 163rd St., Suite 110, North Miami Beach, FL 33162 ☏ 305/940-2299 or 800/882-6864 🖷 305/940-2911 ⊕ www.solemar.us. **Vacation Home Rentals Worldwide** ⊠ 235 Kensington Ave., Norwood, NJ 07648 ☏ 201/767-9393 or 800/633-3284 🖷 201/767-5510 ⊕ www.vhrww.com. **Villanet** ⊠ 1251 N.W. 116th St., Seattle, WA 98177 ☏ 206/417-3444 or 800/964-1891 🖷 206/417-1832 ⊕ www.rentavilla.com. **Villas and Apartments Abroad** ⊠ 183 Madison Ave., Suite 201, New York, NY 10016 ☏ 212/213-6435 or 800/433-3020 🖷 212/213-8252 ⊕ www.vaanyc.com. **Villas International** ⊠ 4340 Redwood Hwy., Suite D309, San Rafael, CA 94903

☏ 415/499-9490 or 800/221-2260 🖷 415/499-9491 ⊕ www.villasintl.com.

⌁ Local Agents Homes International ⊠ Via Bissolati 20, 00187 Rome ☏ 06/4881800 🖷 06/4881808 ⊕ www.homeinternational.it. **Property International** ⊠ Viale Aventino 79, 00153 Rome ☏ 06/5743170 🖷 06/5743182 ⊕ www.propertyint.net.

⌁ Roman Publications *EYP* ⊕ www.intoitaly.it. *Wanted in Rome* ⊠ Via dei Delfini 17, 00186 Rome, Italy ☏ 06/6790190 🖷 06/6783798 ⊕ www.wantedinrome.com.

CAMPING

Camping is particularly common in the mountains and in beach towns. (Sleeping on the beach is illegal in Italy, which is not to say that people don't do it.) Campgrounds are generally crowded in summer. Amenities vary: some have restrooms, showers, pools, bars, and restaurants. Sicily and nearby islands have excellent summer camping facilities. The two best are El Bahira in San Vito Lo Capo, and Bazia in Furnari Marina, west of Milazzo.

Camping areas in the national parks are more rustic. You may be required to break camp every morning.

FARM HOLIDAYS & AGRITOURISM

Staying on working farms or vineyards, often in old stone farmhouses that accommodate a number of guests, has become more and more popular. Contact local tourist offices or consult *Agriturism* (www.agriturismo.com) for more than 1,600 farms in Italy. Although it's in Italian, the publication has photos and descriptions that make it a useful resource.

⌁ Agencies Italy Farm Holidays ⊠ 547 Martling Ave., Tarrytown, NY 10591 ☏ 914/631-7880 🖷 914/631-8831 ⊕ www.italyfarmholidays.com.

HOME EXCHANGES

If you would like to exchange your home for someone else's, join a home-exchange organization, which will send you its updated listings of available exchanges for a year and will include your own listing in at least one of them. It's up to you to make specific arrangements.

⌁ Exchange Clubs HomeLink USA ⊠ 2937 NW 9th Terrace, Wilton Manors, FL 33311 ☏ 954/566-2687 or 800/638-3841 🖷 954/566-2783 ⊕ www.homelink.org; $75 yearly for a listing and online access; $45 additional to receive directories. **Intervac U.S.** ✉ 30 Corte San Fernando, Tiburon, CA 94920 ☎ 800/756-4663 🖷 415/435-7440 ⊕ www.intervacus.com; $128 yearly for a listing, online access, and a catalog; $68 without catalog.

HOSTELS

No matter what your age, you can save on lodging costs by staying at hostels. Hostels in Italy are found both in remote towns and large cities. They range from the bare-bones dormitory-style rooms (no linens provided) to comfortable accommodations resembling bed-and-breakfasts. Many offer rooms for couples or families. When booking, inquire about the noise level—some hostels with a young clientele are lax in enforcing evening quiet hours.

In some 4,500 locations in more than 70 countries around the world, Hostelling International (HI), the umbrella group for a number of national youth-hostel associations, offers single-sex, dorm-style beds and, at many hostels, rooms for couples and family accommodations. Membership in any HI national hostel association, open to travelers of all ages, allows you to stay in HI-affiliated hostels at member rates; one-year membership is about $28 for adults (C$35 for a two-year minimum membership in Canada, £15 in U.K., A$52 in Australia, and NZ$40 in New Zealand); hostels charge about $10–$30 per night. Members have priority if the hostel is full; they're also eligible for discounts around the world, even on rail and bus travel in some countries.

🗂 **Organizations Hostelling International–USA** ✉ 8401 Colesville Rd., Suite 600, Silver Spring, MD 20910 ☎ 301/495-1240 🖷 301/495-6697 ⊕ www.hiusa.org. **Hostelling International–Canada** ✉ 205 Catherine St., Suite 400, Ottawa, Ontario K2P 1C3 ☎ 613/237-7884 or 800/663-5777 🖷 613/237-7868 ⊕ www.hihostels.ca. **YHA England and Wales** ✉ Trevelyan House, Dimple Rd., Matlock, Derbyshire DE4 3YH, U.K. ☎ 0870/870-8808, 0870/770-8868, or 0162/959-2600 🖷 0870/770-6127 ⊕ www.yha.org.uk. **YHA Australia** ✉ 422 Kent St., Sydney, NSW 2001 ☎ 02/9261-1111 🖷 02/9261-1969 ⊕ www.yha.com.au. **YHA New Zealand** ✉ Level 1, Moorhouse City, 166 Moorhouse Ave., Box 436, Christchurch ☎ 03/379-9970 or 0800/278-299 🖷 03/365-4476 ⊕ www.yha.org.nz.

HOTELS

All Italian hotels are graded on a star scale, from five stars for the most deluxe hotels to one star for the most modest. This system can be misleading, as it reflects a hotel's facilities, not how well it is maintained. Some four- or five-star accommodations are past their prime, and some two- and three-star places might be sparkling. Except in the most expensive hotels, rooms may be very small by U.S. standards.

The quality of rooms in older hotels may be very uneven; if you don't like the room you're given, request another. A front room may be larger or have a view, but it also may have a lot of street noise. If you're a light sleeper, **request a quiet room** when making a reservation. Rooms in lodgings listed in this guide have a shower and/or tub unless noted otherwise. (Hotels with three or more stars always have private bathrooms). Remember to **specify whether you prefer to have a bathtub or shower.**

In all hotels there will be a card inside the door of your room stating the basic rate (which often varies according to the location and size of the room). Any discrepancy between the posted rate and what you are charged is cause for complaint to the manager and to the police. By law, breakfast is supposed to be optional, but most hotels quote room rates including breakfast. When you book a room, **ask whether the rate includes breakfast.** You are under no obligation to take *colazione* (breakfast) at your hotel, and can have the charge removed from your bill if you decide to eat elsewhere.

You'll find some familiar chains, such as Best Western and Sheraton. Other chains include Atahotels, with mostly four- and five-star hotels; Agip, which has four-star motels along main highways; Jolly, which has four-star hotels; Space Hotels, which has 80 independently owned four- and three-star hotels; and Starhotels, which has mainly four-star lodgings.

RESERVING A ROOM

High season in Italy generally runs from Easter through the beginning of November, and then for two weeks at Christmas. During low season, many hotels reduce their prices. Always **inquire about special rates**. It's always a good idea to **confirm your reservation** by e-mail or fax. If you need to cancel your reservation, do so by e-mail or fax and keep a record of the transmission. If you don't have a reservation, most cities have reservation booths in train stations.

Useful terms to know when booking a room are *aria condizionata* (air-conditioning), *bagno in stanza* (private bath), *letto matrimoniale* (double bed), *letti singoli* (twin beds), and *letti singoli uniti* (twin beds pushed together). Italy does not really have queen- or king-size beds, but larger beds are sometimes available in four- and five-star accommodations.

Other useful phrases include: *una camera su un piano alto e con vista* (a room on a high floor with a view), *una camera a un piano basso* (a room on a low floor), and *una camera silenziosa* (a quiet room).

MAIL & SHIPPING

The Italian mail system is notoriously slow. Allow up to 15 days for mail to get to the United States, Canada, Australia, and New Zealand. It takes about a week to United Kingdom and within Italy. Posta Prioritaria (for Italy only) and Postacelere (for Italy and abroad) are special-delivery services from the post office that guarantee delivery within 24 hours in Italy and within three to five days abroad.

Most post offices are open Monday–Saturday 9–12:30; central post offices are open 9–6:30 weekdays, 9–12:30 on Saturday. On the last day of the month, post offices close at midday. You can buy stamps at tobacco shops as well as post offices.

OVERNIGHT SERVICES

Overnight mail is generally available during the week in all major cities and at popular resorts. Service is reliable; a Federal Express letter to the United States costs about €30, to the United Kingdom, €51, and to Australia and New Zealand, €33. Overnight delivery usually means 24–36 hours.

If your hotel can't assist you, try an Internet café, many of which also offer overnight mail services using major carriers at reasonable rates.

🔳 **Major Services DHL** ☎ 199-199-345 ⊕ www. dhl.it. **Federal Express** ☎ 800/123800 ⊕ www. fedex.com. **SDA** ☎ 800/016027 ⊕ www.sda.it.

POSTAL RATES

Airmail letters and postcards sent *ordinaria* to the United States and Canada cost €0.65 for up to 20 grams, €1 for 21 to 50 grams, and €1.30 for 51 to 100 grams. Always stick the blue airmail tag on your mail, or write AIRMAIL in big, clear letters beside the address. Mail sent *ordinaria* to Italy, the United Kingdom, and other EU countries costs €0.45 for the first 20 grams.

For faster service, use priority delivery *Posta Prioritaria* (for small letters and packages), which guarantees delivery within IItaly in three to five business days and abroad in five to six working days. The more expensive express delivery *Postacelere* (for larger letters and packages), which guarantees one-day delivery to most places in Italy and three- to five-day delivery abroad.

Mail sent as Posta Prioritaria to the United States and Canada costs €0.80 for up to 20 grams, €1.50 for 21 to 50 grams, and €1.80 for 51 to 100 grams; to Italy, the United Kingdom, and other EU countries it costs €0.62. Mail sent as Postacelere to the United States and Canada costs €35.05 for up to 500 grams. If you're shipping to the United Kingdom or elsewhere in Europe, the cost is €28.15.

Other package services to check are Quick Pack Europe, for delivery within Europe; and EMS ExpressMail Service, a global three- to five-day service for letters and packages that can be less expensive than Postacelere.

RECEIVING MAIL

Correspondence can be addressed to you in care of any Italian post office. Letters should be addressed to your name, "c/o Ufficio Postale Centrale," followed by "Fermo Posta" on the next line, and the name of the city (preceded by its postal code) on the next. You can **collect it at the central post office** by showing your passport or photo-bearing ID and paying a small fee. American Express also has a general-delivery service. There's no charge for cardholders, holders of American Express traveler's checks, or anyone who booked a vacation with American Express.

SHIPPING PARCELS

You can ship parcels via air or surface. Air takes about two weeks, and surface anywhere up to three months to most countries. If you have purchased antiques, ceramics, or other objects, **ask if the vendor will do the shipping** for you; in most cases, this is a possibility.

MONEY MATTERS

Prices vary from region to region and are substantially lower in the country than in the cities. Of Italy's major cities, Venice and Milan are by far the most expensive. Resorts such as the Costa Smeralda, Portofino, and Cortina d'Ampezzo cater to wealthy people and charge top prices. Good values can be had in the scenic Trentino–Alto Adige region and the Dolomites and in Umbria and the Marches. With a few exceptions, southern Italy, Sicily, and Sardinia also offer good values.

What do things cost? A cup of coffee is about €0.80. A soft drink (taken standing at a café) is about €2. An English-language newspaper costs €2. A short taxi ride in Rome costs €5.15. The cheapest seat at Rome's Teatro dell'Opera runs €16.55. Getting into a Milan nightclub will set you back about €20. An inexpensive dinner in Rome is €40, and a simple pasta dish runs about €10. A ½-liter carafe of house wine is €3.50, and a pint of beer is €3.70. An inexpensive hotel room for two, including breakfast, is about €100 in Rome or Florence.

Prices throughout this guide are given for adults. Substantially reduced fees are almost always available for children, students, and senior citizens from the EU; citizens of non-EU countries rarely get discounts. For information on taxes, *see* Taxes.

ATMs

An ATM (*bancomat* in Italian) is the easiest way to get euros in Italy. They are fairly common in large cities and small towns, as well as in airports and train stations. They are not common in grocery stores. Be sure to **memorize your PIN number,** as ATM keypads in Italy don't always display letters.

CREDIT CARDS

MasterCard and Visa are preferred by Italian merchants, but American Express is usually accepted in tourist spots. Credit cards aren't accepted everywhere; if you want to pay with a credit card in a small shop, hotel, or restaurant, it's a good idea to make your intentions known early on. Throughout this guide, the following abbreviations are used: **AE,** American Express; **DC,** Diners Club; **MC,** MasterCard; and **V,** Visa.

🛅 Reporting Lost Cards **American Express** ☎ 800/874 333 international collect. **Diners Club** ☎ 702/797–5532 collect. **MasterCard** ☎ 800/870866 toll-free within Italy. **Visa** ☎ 800/877232 toll-free within Italy.

CURRENCY

The euro is the main unit of currency in Italy, as well as in 11 other European countries. Under the euro system there are 100 *centesimi* (cents) to the euro. There are coins valued at 1, 2, 5, 10, 20, and 50 cents, as well as 1 and 2 euros. There are seven notes: 5, 10, 20, 50, 100, 200, and 500 euros.

CURRENCY EXCHANGE

At this writing, the exchange rate was about 0.83 euros to the U.S. dollar; 0.68 euros to the Canadian dollar; 1.46 euros to the pound sterling; 0.62 euros to the Australian dollar; and 0.56 euros to the New Zealand dollar.

For the most favorable rates, **change money through banks.** Although ATM transaction fees may be higher abroad than at home, ATM rates are excellent because they're based on wholesale rates offered only by major banks. You won't do as well at exchange booths in airports or rail and bus stations, in hotels, in restaurants, or in stores. To avoid lines at airport exchange booths, get a bit of local currency before you leave home.

🛅 Exchange Services **International Currency Express** ✉ 427 N. Camden Dr., Suite F, Beverly Hills,

CA 90210 ☎ 888/278-6628 orders ⊟ 310/278-6410 ⊕ www.foreignmoney.com. **Travel Ex Currency Services** ☎ 800/287-7362 orders and retail locations ⊕ www.travelex.com.

TRAVELER'S CHECKS

Do you need traveler's checks? It depends on where you're headed. If you're going to rural areas and small towns, go with cash; traveler's checks are best used in cities. Lost or stolen checks can usually be replaced within 24 hours. To ensure a speedy refund, buy your own traveler's checks—don't let someone else pay for them: irregularities like this can cause delays. The person who bought the checks should make the call to request a refund. Make sure to **get traveler's checks in euros,** not U.S. dollars.

PACKING

The weather is considerably milder, in the winter at least, in Italy than in the north and central United States or Great Britain. At the height of summer stick with very light clothing, as it can get steamy; even during summer months a sweater may be necessary for cool evenings, especially in the mountains and on the islands. Sunglasses, a hat, and sunblock are essential. Brief summer afternoon thunderstorms are common in Rome and inland cities, so an umbrella will come in handy. In winter bring a medium-weight coat and a raincoat for Rome and farther south. Northern Italy calls for heavier coats, gloves, hats, scarves, and boots. Bring sturdy shoes for winter and comfortable walking shoes in any season.

Living up to their reputation, Italians dress exceptionally well. Men aren't required to wear ties or jackets to dinner, except in some of the grander hotel dining rooms and top-level restaurants, but are expected to look reasonably sharp—and they do. Formal wear is the exception rather than the rule at the opera nowadays, though people in expensive seats usually do get dressed up.

For sightseeing **pack a pair of binoculars;** they will help you get a good look at painted ceilings and domes. If you stay in budget hotels **take your own soap and**

towel. Many such hotels either do not provide soap or give guests only one tiny bar per room, and towels often look like what you'd use to dry dishes.

In your carry-on luggage, pack an extra pair of eyeglasses or contact lenses and enough of any medication you take to last a few days longer than the entire trip. You may also ask your doctor to write a spare prescription using the drug's generic name, as brand names may vary from country to country. In luggage to be checked, **never pack prescription drugs, valuables, or undeveloped film.** And don't forget to carry with you the addresses of offices that handle refunds of lost traveler's checks. Check *Fodor's How to Pack* (available at online retailers and bookstores everywhere) for more tips.

To avoid customs and security delays, carry medications in their original packaging. Don't pack any sharp objects in your carry-on luggage, including knives of any size or material, scissors, nail clippers, and corkscrews, or anything else that might arouse suspicion.

To avoid having your checked luggage chosen for hand inspection, don't cram bags full. The U.S. Transportation Security Administration suggests packing shoes on top and placing personal items you don't want touched in clear plastic bags.

CHECKING LUGGAGE

You're allowed to carry aboard one bag and one personal article, such as a purse or a laptop computer. Make sure what you carry on fits under your seat or in the overhead bin. Get to the gate early, so you can board as soon as possible, before the overhead bins fill up.

Baggage allowances vary by carrier, destination, and ticket class. On international flights, you're usually allowed to check two bags weighing up to 70 pounds (32 kilograms) each, although a few airlines allow checked bags of up to 88 pounds (40 kilograms) in first class. Some international carriers don't allow more than 66 pounds (30 kilograms) per bag in business class and 44 pounds (20 kilograms) in economy. If you're flying to or through the

EXPLORE THE WONDERS OF ITALY IN STYLE...

EXPLORE THE WONDERS OF ITALY IN STYLE...

Milan

Venice

Florence

Sardinia

Rome

Naples
Capri
Sorrento
Amalfi Coast

Palermo

EXCLUSIVE LIMOUSINE SERVICE ITALY

A prestigious limousine company offers a countless range of memorable trips tailored to your personal requirements. Experience the beauty, in the most luxurious vehicles selected specifically for comfort and ease. Organised tours and excursions in and around the glories of Rome, Florence, Pompeii, Naples, Palermo and along the Amalfi Coast, (Amalfi, Positano and Ravello) will uncover spectacular sights that will turn an experience into something of a dream... Services are available for up to a maximum of 15 persons per vehicle, with a fully licensed guide, upon request. All drivers are multilingual and many years of experience enables them to provide a "personal touch". Other than tours and excursions, our services include; airport transfers, transfers to and from the port, wedding events and business conventions.

ROME CONTACT
DANIELE MELARAGNO
Telephone: +39 3384180978 - 333 7080868
Alternative number: +39 06 61522395
Fax: +39 06 61532259
Web: www.driverinrome.com
Email: info@driverinrome.com

AMALFI COAST/NAPLES CONTACT
GIOVANNI BENVENUTO
Telephone: +39 334-3078342
Alternative number: +39 089 874024
Fax: +39 089-8131091
Web: www.benvenutolimos.com
Email: info@benvenutolimos.com

United Kingdom, your luggage cannot exceed 70 pounds (32 kilograms) per bag. On domestic flights, the limit is usually 50 to 70 pounds (23 to 32 kilograms) per bag. In general, carry-on bags shouldn't exceed 40 pounds (18 kilograms). Most airlines won't accept bags that weigh more than 100 pounds (45 kilograms) on domestic or international flights. Expect to pay a fee for baggage that exceeds weight limits. Check baggage restrictions with your carrier before you pack.

Airline liability for baggage is limited to $2,500 per person on flights within the United States. On international flights it amounts to $9.07 per pound or $20 per kilogram for checked baggage (roughly $640 per 70-pound bag), with a maximum of $634.90 per piece, and $400 per passenger for unchecked baggage. You can buy additional coverage at check-in for about $10 per $1,000 of coverage, but it often excludes a rather extensive list of items, shown on your airline ticket.

Before departure, itemize your bags' contents and their worth, and label the bags with your name, address, and phone number. (If you use your home address, cover it so potential thieves can't see it readily.) Include a label inside each bag and **pack a copy of your itinerary.** At check-in, make sure each bag is correctly tagged with the destination airport's three-letter code. Because some checked bags will be opened for hand inspection, the U.S. Transportation Security Administration recommends that you leave luggage unlocked or use the plastic locks offered at check-in. TSA screeners place an inspection notice inside searched bags, which are resealed with a special lock.

If your bag has been searched and contents are missing or damaged, file a claim with the TSA Consumer Response Center as soon as possible. If your bags arrive damaged or fail to arrive at all, file a written report with the airline before leaving the airport.

Complaints U.S. Transportation Security Administration Contact Center ☎ 866/289-9673 ⊕ www.tsa.gov.

PASSPORTS & VISAS

When traveling internationally, carry your passport even if you don't need one (it's always the best form of ID) and **make two photocopies of the data page** (one for someone at home and another for you, carried separately from your passport). If you lose your passport, promptly call the nearest embassy or consulate and the local police.

U.S. passport applications for children under age 14 require consent from both parents or legal guardians; both parents must appear together to sign the application. If only one parent appears, he or she must submit a written statement from the other parent authorizing passport issuance for the child. A parent with sole authority must present evidence of it when applying; acceptable documentation includes the child's certified birth certificate listing only the applying parent, a court order specifically permitting this parent's travel with the child, or a death certificate for the nonapplying parent. Application forms and instructions are available on the Web site of the U.S. State Department's Bureau of Consular Affairs (⊕ travel.state.gov).

ENTERING ITALY

Citizens of Australia, Canada, New Zealand, and the United States need only a valid passport to enter Italy for stays of up to 90 days. Citizens of the United Kingdom need only a valid passport to enter Italy for an unlimited stay.

PASSPORT OFFICES

The best time to apply for a passport or to renew is in fall and winter. Before any trip, check your passport's expiration date, and, if necessary, renew it as soon as possible.

Australian Citizens Passports Australia Australian Department of Foreign Affairs and Trade ☎ 131-232 ⊕ www.passports.gov.au.

Canadian Citizens Passport Office ✉ To mail in applications: 70 Cremazie St., Gatineau, Québec J8Y 3P2 ☎ 819/994-3500 or 800/567-6868 ⊕ www.ppt.gc.ca.

New Zealand Citizens New Zealand Passports Office ☎ 0800/22-5050 or 04/474-8100 ⊕ www.passports.govt.nz.

U.K. Citizens U.K. Passport Service ☎ 0870/521-0410 ⊕ www.passport.gov.uk.

🔼 **U.S. Citizens National Passport Information Center** ☎ 877/487-2778, 888/874-7793 TDD/TTY ⊕ travel.state.gov.

RESTROOMS

Public restrooms are rather rare in Italy. Pay toilets are the exception, not the rule. In Rome, Florence, and Venice, a few public pay toilets costing €0.50 are strategically located in the city centers. Although private businesses can refuse to make their toilets available to the passing public, some bars will allow you to use the restroom if you ask politely. Alternatively, it is not uncommon to pay for a little something—a mineral water or coffee, for example—to get access to the facilities. Standards of cleanliness and comfort vary greatly. In cities, restaurants, hotel lobbies, and high-end department stores such as La Rinascente and Coin tend to have the cleanest restrooms. Pubs and bars rank among the worst. In general, it's in your interest to carry some toilet paper with you. There are bathrooms in museums and in airports and train stations (in major train stations you'll also find well-kept pay toilets for €0.50–€1). There are also bathrooms at highway rest stops and gas stations: a small tip (€.25–€.50) to the attendant is always appreciated. There are no bathrooms at churches, post offices, subway stations, or public beaches.

SAFETY

The best way to protect yourself against purse snatchers and pickpockets is to wear a concealed money belt or a pouch on a string around your neck. Be on your guard when in buses and subways, when making your way through crowded trains, and in busy piazzas and other tourist spots. Don't wear a waist pack, which pegs you as a tourist. Distribute your cash and any valuables (including your credit cards and passport) between a deep front pocket, an inside jacket or vest pocket, and a hidden money pouch. Do not reach for the money pouch once you're in public.

LOCAL SCAMS

In larger cities, some children have been trained to be adept pickpockets. One tactic is to proffer a piece of cardboard with writing on it. While you attempt to read the message *on* it, the children's hands are busy *under* it, trying to make off with purses or valuables. If you see such a group, avoid them—they are quick and know more tricks than you do. If traveling in a rental car, have someone remain near the car when you stop at rest areas. Thieves often target rental cars.

WOMEN IN ITALY

Purse-snatching is not uncommon, and thieves operate on foot as well as on *motorini* (mopeds). If you carry a purse, choose one with a zipper and a thick strap that you can drape across your body; adjust the length so that the purse sits in front of you at or above hip level. (Don't wear a money belt or a waist pack.) Store only enough money in the purse to cover casual spending. Distribute the rest of your cash and any valuables between deep front pockets, inside jacket or vest pockets, and a concealed money pouch.

The difficulties encountered by women traveling alone in Italy are often overstated. Younger women have to put up with much male attention, but it is rarely dangerous or hostile. Ignoring whistling and questions is the best response; a firm *no, vai via* ("no, go away") usually works, too.

SENIOR-CITIZEN TRAVEL

To qualify for age-related discounts, mention your senior-citizen status up front when booking hotel reservations (not when checking out) and before you're seated in restaurants (not when paying the bill). Be sure to have identification on hand. When renting a car, ask about promotional car-rental discounts, which can be cheaper than senior-citizen rates.

🔼 **Educational Programs Elderhostel** ✉ 11 Ave. de Lafayette, Boston, MA 02111 ☎ 877/426-8056, 978/323-4141 international callers, 877/426-2167 TTY 🖷 877/426-2166 ⊕ www.elderhostel.org. **Interhostel** ✉ University of New Hampshire, 6 Garrison Ave., Durham, NH 03824 ☎ 603/862-1147 or 800/733-9753 🖷 603/862-1113 ⊕ www.learn.unh.edu.

SHOPPING

Italy produces fine wines, beautiful clothes, and exquisite jewelry, among other things. The notice PREZZI FISSI (fixed prices) means just that—it's a waste of time to bargain unless you're buying a sizable quantity of goods or a particularly costly object. You can bargain, however, at outdoor markets and when buying from street vendors.

WATCH OUT

If you have purchased art, make sure it is less than 50 years old. Any painting, sculpture, or other work of art older than that must receive clearance from the Italian government to leave the country.

If you have purchased an antique, the dealer will provide you with a certificate attesting to the integrity of the piece and the price paid. Some dealers will ship the object for you; others leave it to you to arrange shipping.

SIGHTSEEING GUIDES

Every province in Italy has tour guides licensed by the government. Some are eminently qualified in relevant fields such as architecture and art history; others have simply managed to pass the test. Tourist offices can provide the names of knowledgeable guides and the rates for certain services. Before you hire a guide, ask about their background and qualifications and make sure you can understand each other. Tipping is appreciated but not obligatory.

SMOKING

In 2005 smoking was banned in many public places, including bars and restaurants. Although Italians are for the most part unrepentant smokers, they are begrudgingly obeying the law. Always check to see if there's a VIETATO FUMARE (no smoking) sign before lighting up. All Italian trains have no-smoking cars (ask for one when making reservations), and Eurostar trains are smoke-free.

STUDENTS IN ITALY

In the major art cities there are plenty of sources of information and lodging geared to students' needs. Students from member nations in the EU with valid ID cards may sometimes receive discounts at museums, galleries, exhibitions, and entertainment venues, and on some transportation. Stu-

dents who aren't EU citizens generally pay the usual entrance fees.

IDs & Services STA Travel ⊠ 10 Downing St., New York, NY 10014 ☎ 212/627-3111, 800/777-0112 24-hr service center 🖶 212/627-3387 ⊕ www.sta.com. **Travel Cuts** ⊠ 187 College St., Toronto, Ontario M5T 1P7, Canada ☎ 800/592-2887 in U.S., 416/979-2406 or 866/246-9762 in Canada 🖶 416/979-8167 ⊕ www.travelcuts.com.

LOCAL RESOURCES

The Centro Turistico Studentesco (CTS) is a student and youth travel agency with offices in major Italian cities. CTS helps its clients find low-cost accommodations and bargain fares for travel in Italy and elsewhere. CTS is also the Rome representative for EuroTrain International.

TAXES

HOTELS

A 9% V.A.T. (value-added tax) is included in the rate at all hotels except those at the upper end of the range. At luxury hotels a 12% tax is added to the bill.

RESTAURANTS

No tax is added to the bill in restaurants. A service charge of approximately 10%–15% is often added to your check; in some cases a service charge is included in the prices.

VALUE-ADDED TAX

The V.A.T. is 20% on clothing, wine, and luxury goods. On consumer goods it's already included in the amount shown on the price tag, whereas on services it may not be. If your purchases total more than €155 at a store displaying a EURO TAX FREE sign, present your passport and request a "Tax Free Shopping Check."

When making a purchase, **ask for a V.A.T. refund form** and find out whether the merchant gives refunds—not all stores do, nor are they required to. Have the form stamped like any customs form by customs officials when you leave the country or, if you're visiting several European Union countries, when you leave the EU. Be ready to show customs officials what you've bought (pack purchases together, in your carry-on luggage); budget extra time for this. After you're through passport control, take the form to a refund-service counter for an on-the-spot refund (which is usually the quickest and easiest option), or mail it to the address on the form (or the envelope with it) after you arrive home.

A service processes refunds for most shops. You receive the total refund stated on the form. Global Refund is a Europe-wide service with 210,000 affiliated stores and more than 700 refund counters—located at major airports and border crossings. Its refund form is called a Tax Free Check. The service issues refunds in the form of cash, check, or credit-card adjustment. If you don't have time to wait at the refund counter, you can mail in the form to an office in Europe or Canada instead.

🗹 V.A.T. Refunds **Global Refund Canada** ✆ Box 2020, Station Main, Brampton, Ontario L6T 3S3 ☎ 800/993-4313 📠 905/791-9078 ⊕ www.globalrefund.com.

TELEPHONES

Italy's telephone system is quite reliable. Remember that telephone numbers do not have a standard number of digits (they can range anywhere from four to seven) and that the entire area code must be included even when calling a number in the same city.

Cell phones are widely used by Italians, so there are fewer public pay phones. If you need to make a lot of calls, consider renting or even buying a cell phone. Renting one costs about €20 per week plus the cost of a calling card. There is no charge for the phone, but a €100 deposit is normal. Buying a basic phone runs between €80 and €125.

Public pay phones may take coins, but usually require a *carta telefonica* (phone card) purchased at newsstands and tobacco shops. There are national cards and international cards, so make sure to specify which you want.

AREA & COUNTRY CODES

The country code for Italy is 39. Here are the area codes for major cities: Bologna 051; Brindisi 0831; Florence 055; Genoa 010; Milan 02; Naples 081; Palermo 091;

Perugia 075; Pisa 050; Rome 06; Siena 0577; Turin 011; Venice 041; Verona 045. A call from the United States to Rome would be dialed as 011 + 39 + 06 + phone number.

The country code is 1 for the United States and Canada, 61 for Australia, 64 for New Zealand, and 44 for the United Kingdom.

DIRECTORY & OPERATOR ASSISTANCE

For general information in English, dial 4176. To place international calls through an operator, dial 170.

INTERNATIONAL CALLS

Since hotels charge exorbitant rates for long-distance and international calls, it's best to call from public phones using telephone cards. You can **make collect calls from any phone by dialing 170,** which will get you an English-speaking operator. Rates to the United States are lowest all day Sunday and 10 PM–8 AM the rest of the week.

LOCAL & LONG-DISTANCE CALLS

For all calls within Italy, whether local or long-distance, dial the area code followed by the number. Rates for long-distance calls vary according to the time of day; it's cheaper to call before 9 AM and after 7 or 8 PM.

LONG-DISTANCE SERVICES

AT&T, MCI, and Sprint access codes make calling long-distance relatively convenient, but you may find the local access number blocked in many hotel rooms. First ask the hotel operator to connect you. If the hotel operator balks, ask for an international operator, or dial the international operator yourself. One way to improve your odds of getting connected to your long-distance carrier is to travel with more than one company's calling card (a hotel may block Sprint, for example, but not MCI). If all else fails, call from a pay phone. If you are traveling for a longer period of time, consider renting a cell-phone from a local company.

🗹 Access Codes **AT&T Direct** ☎ 800/172-444. **MCI WorldPhone** ☎ 800/172-401/404. **Sprint International Access** ☎ 800/172-405.

PHONE CARDS

Prepaid *carte telefoniche* (phone cards) are available throughout Italy. Cards in different denominations are sold at post offices, newsstands, tobacco shops, and bars. For local or national cards, tear off the corner of the card and insert it in the slot. When you dial, its value appears in the window. After you hang up, the card is returned. International calling cards are different; you must call a toll-free number and dial a code number on the back of the card. The best card to use when calling North America or Europe is the €5 or €10 Europa card, which gives you a local number to dial and 180 minutes and 360 minutes of calling time.

PUBLIC PHONES

Public pay phones are scarce, although they can be found at train and subway stations, post offices, in hotel lobbies, and in some bars. In rural areas, town squares usually have a pay phone. Some accept coins, but most use only prepaid phone cards.

TIME

Italy is six hours ahead of Eastern Standard Time, one hour ahead of Great Britain, 10 hours behind Sydney, and 12 hours behind Auckland. Like the rest of Europe, Italy uses the 24-hour (or "military") clock, which means that after noon you continue counting forward: 13:00 is 1 PM, 23:30 is 11:30 PM.

TIPPING

In restaurants a service charge of 10% to 15% usually appears on your check. If so, it's not necessary to leave an additional tip. If service is not included, leave a tip of up to 10%. Tip checkroom attendants €1 per person and restroom attendants €0.50 (more in expensive hotels and restaurants). In major cities tip €0.05 for whatever you drink standing up at a coffee bar, €0.25 or more for table service in cafés. At a hotel bar tip €1 and up for a round or two of drinks.

Italians rarely tip taxi drivers, which is not to say that you shouldn't do it. A euro or two, depending on the length of the journey, is appreciated, particularly if the driver helps with luggage. Service-station attendants are tipped only for special services; give them €1 for checking your tires. Railway and airport porters charge a fixed rate per bag. Tip an additional €0.25 per person, more if the porter is helpful. Give a barber €1–€1.50 and a hairdresser's assistant €1.50–€4 for a shampoo or cut, depending on the type of establishment.

On sightseeing tours, tip guides about €1.50 per person for a half-day group tour, more if they are especially knowledgeable. In monasteries and other sights where admission is free, a contribution (€0.50–€1) is expected.

In hotels give the *portiere* (concierge) about 10% of his bill for services, or €2.50–€5 for help with dinner reservations and such. For two people in a double room leave the chambermaid about €0.75 per day, or about €4.50–€5 a week in a moderately priced hotel; tip a minimum of €1 for valet or room service. Double these amounts in an expensive hotel. In expensive hotels tip doormen €0.50 for calling a cab and €1.50 for carrying bags to the check-in desk, bellhops €1.50–€2.50 for carrying your bags to the room, and €2–€2.50 for room service.

TOURS & PACKAGES

Because everything is prearranged on a prepackaged tour or independent vacation, you spend less time planning—and often get it all at a good price.

BOOKING WITH AN AGENT

Travel agents are excellent resources. But it's a good idea to collect brochures from several agencies, as some agents' suggestions may be influenced by relationships with tour and package firms that reward them for volume sales. If you have a special interest, find an agent with expertise in that area. The American Society of Travel Agents (ASTA) has a database of specialists worldwide; you can log on to the group's Web site to find one near you.

Make sure your travel agent knows the accommodations and other services of the place being recommended. Ask about the hotel's location, room size, beds, and whether it has a pool, room service, or programs for children, if you care about these. Has your agent been there in person or sent others whom you can contact?

Do some homework on your own, too: local tourism boards can provide information about lesser-known and small-niche operators, some of which may sell only direct.

BUYER BEWARE

Each year consumers are stranded or lose their money when tour operators—even large ones with excellent reputations—go out of business. So check out the operator. Ask several travel agents about its reputation, and try to **book with a company that has a consumer-protection program.** (Look for information in the company's brochure.) In the United States, members of the United States Tour Operators Association are required to set aside funds (up to $1 million) to help eligible customers cover payments and travel arrangements in the event that the company defaults. It's also a good idea to choose a company that participates in the American Society of Travel Agents' Tour Operator Program; ASTA will act as mediator in any disputes between you and your tour operator.

Remember that the more your package or tour includes, the better you can predict the ultimate cost of your vacation. Make sure you know exactly what is covered, and beware of hidden costs. Are taxes, tips, and transfers included? Entertainment and excursions? These can add up.

🗂 Tour-Operator Recommendations **American Society of Travel Agents** (⇨ Travel Agencies). **CrossSphere—The Global Association for Packaged Travel** ✉ 546 E. Main St., Lexington, KY 40508 ☎ 859/226-4444 or 800/682-8886 🖷 859/226-4414 ⊕ www.CrossSphere.com. **United States Tour Operators Association** (USTOA) ✉ 275 Madison Ave., Suite 2014, New York, NY 10016 ☎ 212/599-6599 🖷 212/599-6744 ⊕ www.ustoa.com.

TRAIN TRAVEL

In Italy traveling by train is simple and efficient. Service between major cities is frequent, and trains usually arrive on schedule. You can either purchase your tickets in advance (all major credit cards

are accepted online at ⊕ www.raileurope.com) or after you arrive at any train station or travel agency. If you are considering using a Eurail Pass or any of its variations you must **buy the pass before leaving your home country,** as they are not sold in Italy.

You must **validate your ticket before boarding** the train by punching it at a yellow box located in the waiting area of smaller train stations or at the end of the track in larger stations. Always **purchase tickets before boarding the train,** as you can no longer purchase one from a conductor. Fines are steep for passengers without tickets.

The fastest trains on the *Trenitalia,* the Italian State Railways, are the Eurostar trains that run between major cities. You will be assigned a specific seat in a specific coach. To avoid having to squeeze through narrow aisles, board only at your designated coach (the number on your ticket matches the one on near the door of each coach). The next-fastest trains are the *Intercity* (IC) trains. Reservations, required for some IC trains, are always advisable. *Diretto* and *Interregionale* trains make more stops and are a little slower. *Regionale* and *locale* trains are the slowest; many serve commuters. There are refreshments on all long-distance trains, purchased from a mobile cart or a dining car.

Traveling by night is a good deal, as you do not pay extra for a bed. More comfortable trains run on the longer routes (Sicily–Rome, Sicily–Milan, Sicily–Venice, Rome–Turin, Lecce–Milan); ask for the good-value T3, Intercity Notte, and Carrozza Comfort. The Vagone Letto Excelsior has private bathrooms, coffee machines, microwave ovens, refrigerators, and a suite with a double bed and TV.

Some cities—Milan, Turin, Genoa, Naples, Florence, and Rome included—have more than one train station, so be sure you get off at the right place. Except for Pisa and Rome, none of the major cities have trains that go directly to the airports, but there are commuter bus lines connecting train stations and airports.

Train strikes of various kinds are also common, so it's a good idea to make sure your train is running.

Train Information Trentalia ☎ 892021 in Italy ⊕ www.trenitalia.com.

CLASSES

Most Italian trains have first and second classes. On local trains a first-class fare gets you little more than a clean doily on your headrest, but on long-distance trains you get wider seats, more legroom, and better ventilation and lighting. At peak travel times, a first-class fare is worth the price as the coaches are less crowded. In Italian, *prima classe* is first class; second is *seconda classe*.

CUTTING COSTS

To save money, **look into rail passes.** But be aware that if you don't plan to cover many miles, you may come out ahead by buying individual tickets. If Italy is your only destination, consider an Italian Flexi Rail Card Saver. Over the course of a month you can travel on four days ($239 first class, $191 second class) or eight days ($260 first class, $206 second class). These tickets are sold only outside Italy. They are cheaper if you travel in a group or are under 26.

Once in Italy, travelers over 60 can buy a *Carta d'Argento* (Silver Card). For €30 you get a 15% discount on first- and second-class tickets. Travelers under 26 can get the same deal with a *Cartaverde* (Green Card). Those under 26 can also get discount fares under the Billet International Jeune (BIJ) and Euro Domino Junior plans. *Comitive Ordinarie* (Ordinary Group Travel) entitle parties of at least six people to a 20% discount on most tickets.

Italy is one of 17 countries that accept Eurailpass, which allows unlimited first-class travel. If you plan to rack up the miles, get a standard pass. Passes are available for 15 days ($588), 21 days ($762), one month ($946), two months ($1,338), and three months ($1,654). You also get free or discounted fares on some ferry lines. The Eurail Selectpass allows for travel in three to five contiguous countries. Five days of

first-class travel in three countries is $370; four countries $414; five countries $446.

In addition to standard Eurailpasses, **ask about special plans.** Among these are the Eurail Youthpass (for those under 26), the Eurail Flexipass (which allows a certain number of travel days within a set period), the Eurail Saver Flexipass (which give a discount for two or more people traveling together), and the EurailDrive Pass (which combines travel by train and rental car). All Eurailpasses must be purchased before you leave home. Order them on the Rail Europe Web site.

Remember that you need to reserve seats even if you are using a rail pass.

Information & Passes CIT Rail ✉ 15 W. 44th St., New York, NY 10036 ☎ 800/248-7245. **DER Tours** ☎ 800/782-2424 🖷 800/282-7474. **Rail Europe** ✉ 44 S. Broadway, White Plains, NY 10601 ☎ 800/438-7245 or 877/257-2887 ⊕ www.raileurope.com.

PAYING

You can pay for your train tickets in cash or with a major credit card such as American Express, Diners Club, MasterCard, and Visa.

RESERVATIONS

Trains can be very crowded, so it's always a good idea to make a reservation. You can reserve seat up to two months in advance at the train station or at a travel agent. Simply holding a train ticket does not guarantee a seat. In summer it's fairly common to see people standing for part of the journey.

TRAVEL AGENCIES

A good travel agent puts your needs first. Look for an agency that has been in business at least five years, emphasizes customer service, and has someone on staff who specializes in your destination. In addition, **make sure the agency belongs to a professional trade organization.** The American Society of Travel Agents (ASTA) has more than 10,000 members in some 140 countries, enforces a strict code of ethics, and will step in to mediate agent-client disputes involving ASTA members. ASTA also maintains a directory of agents on its Web site; ASTA's TravelSense.org, a trip-planning and travel-advice site, can also help to locate a travel agent who caters to your needs. (If a travel agency is also acting as your tour operator, *see* Buyer Beware *in* Tours & Packages.)

⑦ Local Agent Referrals American Society of Travel Agents (ASTA) ⊠ 1101 King St., Suite 200, Alexandria, VA 22314 ☎ 703/739-2782 or 800/965-2782 24-hr hotline 🖶 703/684-8319 ⊕ www.astanet.com and www.travelsense.org. **Association of British Travel Agents** ⊠ 68-71 Newman St., London W1T 3AH ☎ 020/7637-2444 🖶 020/7637-0713 ⊕ www.abta.com. **Association of Canadian Travel Agencies** ⊠ 130 Albert St., Suite 1705, Ottawa, Ontario K1P 5G4 ☎ 613/237-3657 🖶 613/237-7052 ⊕ www.acta.ca. **Australian Federation of Travel Agents** ⊠ Level 3, 309 Pitt St., Sydney, NSW 2000 ☎ 02/9264-3299 or 1300/363-416 🖶 02/9264-1085 ⊕ www.afta.com.au. **Travel Agents' Association of New Zealand** ⊠ Level 5, Tourism and Travel House, 79 Boulcott St., Box 1888, Wellington 6001 ☎ 04/499-0104 🖶 04/499-0786 ⊕ www.taanz.org.nz.

VISITOR INFORMATION

Learn more about foreign destinations by checking government-issued travel advisories and country information. For a broader picture, consider information from more than one country.

⑦ Tourist Information Italian Government Tourist Board ⊠ 630 5th Ave., Suite 1565, New York, NY 10111 ☎ 212/245-4822 🖶 212/586-9249 ⊠ 500 N. Michigan Ave., Chicago, IL 60611 ☎ 312/644-0996 🖶 312/644-3019 ⊠ 12400 Wilshire Blvd., Suite 550, Los Angeles, CA 90025 ☎ 310/820-1898 🖶 310/820-6357 ⊠ 175 Bloor St. E, Suite 907, South Tower, Toronto, Ontario M4W 3R8 ☎ 416/925-4882 🖶 416/925-4799 ⊠ 1 Princes St., London W1B 2.8AY ☎ 020/7408-1254 🖶 020/73993567 ⊕ www.italiantourism.com.

⑦ Regional Offices Florence ⊠ Via Cavour 1/r, next to Palazzo Medici-Riccardi, 50129 ☎ 055/290832 ⊕ www.comune.firenze.it. **Milan** ⊠ Stazione Centrale, 20121 ☎ 02/72524370 ⊕ www.milaninfotourist.com. **Naples** ⊠ Piazza del Gesù, 80135 ☎ 081/5523328 ⊕ www.inaples.it. **Palermo** ⊠ Piazza Castelnuovo 35, 90141 ☎ 091/583847 ⊕ www.palermoturismo.com. **Rome** ⊠ Via Parigi 5, 00185 ☎ 06/36004399 ⊕ www.romaturismo.it. **Venice** ⊠ Stazione Ferroviaria Santa Lucia ☎ 041/5298727 ⊕ www.turismovenezia.it.

⑦ Government Advisories U.S. Department of State ⊠ Bureau of Consular Affairs, Overseas Citizens Services Office, 2201 C St. NW, Washington, DC 20520 ☎ 202/647-5225, 888/407-4747 or 317/472-2328 for interactive hotline ⊕ www.travel.state.gov. **Consular Affairs Bureau of Canada** ☎ 800/267-6788 or 613/944-6788 ⊕ www.voyage.gc.ca. **U.K. Foreign and Commonwealth Office** ⊠ Travel Advice Unit, Consular Directorate, Old Admiralty Bldg., London SW1A 2PA ☎ 0870/606-0290 or 020/7008-1500 ⊕ www.fco.gov.uk/travel. **Australian Department of Foreign Affairs and Trade** ☎ 300/139-281 travel advisories, 02/6261-1299 Consular Travel Advice ⊕ www.smartraveller.gov.au or www.dfat.gov.au. **New Zealand Ministry of Foreign Affairs and Trade** ☎ 04/439-8000 ⊕ www.mft.govt.nz.

WEB SITES

Do check out the World Wide Web when planning your trip. You'll find everything from weather forecasts to virtual tours of famous cities. Be sure to visit Fodors.com (⊕ www.fodors.com), a complete travel-planning site. You can research prices and book plane tickets, hotel rooms, rental cars, vacation packages, and more. In addition, you can post your pressing questions in the Travel Talk section. Other planning tools include a currency converter and weather reports, and there are loads of links to travel resources.

Venice

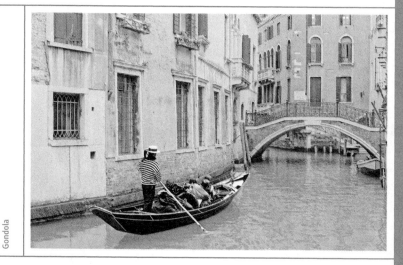

Gondola

WORD OF MOUTH

"There's no way to adequately describe the uniqueness, the beauty, and the charm that is Venice. It's like the Grand Canyon. It doesn't matter how many pictures you've seen, until you've come face to face with her, you can't begin to imagine her splendor."

—dcd

WELCOME TO VENICE

Gondola navigating a side canal

TOP 5
Reasons to Go

1. **Basilica di San Marco:** Whether its opulence seduces you or overwhelms you, it's a sight to be seen.

2. **Gallerie dell'Accademia:** It only makes sense that you find the world's best collection of Venetian painting here.

3. **Santa Maria Gloriosa dei Frari:** Of Venice's many gorgeous churches, this one competes with San Marco for top billing.

4. **Cruising the Grand Canal:** Whether seen by gondola or by water bus, Venice's Main Street is something from another world.

5. **Snacking at a bacaro:** The best way to sample genuine Venetian cuisine is to head for one of the city's classic wine bars.

Getting Oriented

Seen from the window of an airplane, central Venice looks like a fish laid out on a blue platter. The train station at the western end is the fish's eye, and the Castello *sestiere* (neighborhood) is the tail. In all, the "fish" consists of six sestieri—Cannaregio, Santa Croce, San Polo, Dorsoduro, San Marco, and Castello. More sedate outer islands swim around them—San Giorgio Maggiore and the Giudecca just to the south, beyond them the Lido, and to the east Murano, Borano, and Torcello.

The Grand Canal is Venice's major thoroughfare, lined with grand palazzos that once housed the city's richest families.

The neighboring sestieri of Santa Croce and San Polo are largely commercial districts, with many shops, several major sights, and the Rialto fish and produce markets.

Bridge to Mainland

Stazione Ferrovia Santa Luca

SANTA CROCE

Santa Maria ♦ Gloriosa dei Frari

Canal Della Guidecca

LA GUIDECCA

Santa Maria della Salute

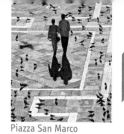
Piazza San Marco

Cannaregio is short on architectural splendor, but it provides some of the prettiest canal-side walks in town. **The Fondamenta della Misericordia** is a nightlife center, and the **Jewish Ghetto** has a fascinating history and tradition all its own.

CANNAREGIO

Fond. d. Misericordia

THE JEWISH GHETTO

CIMITERO SAN MICHELE

0   20 mi
0   20 km

Canal Grande

Ca' d'Oro

SAN POLO

Campo Santi Giovanni e Paolo

Castello, along with Cannaregio, is home to most of the locals. It's the sestiere that's least influenced by Venice's tourist culture—except when the Biennale art festival is on.

CASTELLO

Basilica di San Marco

Piazza San Marco

SAN MARCO

Palazzo Ducale

Canal Grande

Gallerie dell' Accademia

◆Peggy Guggenheim Collection

Santa Maria della Salute

DORSODURO

Zattere Promenade

SAN GIORGIO MAGGIORE

0   1/4 mile
0   400 meters

Piazza San Marco, called by Napoleon "the world's most beautiful drawing room," is the heart of Venice and the location of its two most distinctive sights, the **Basilica di San Marco** and the **Palazzo Ducale**.

Rio di Palazzo

Dorsoduro is an elegant residential area that's home to the **Gallerie dell'Accademia** and the **Peggy Guggenheim Collection**. The Zattere promenade is one of the best spots to stroll with a gelato or linger at an outdoor café.

The sestiere of **San Marco,** in the city's center, is one of Italy's most expensive neighborhoods. Its streets are lined with fashion boutiques, art galleries, and grand hotels.

VENICE PLANNER

Making the Most of Your Time

A great introduction to Venice is a ride on *vaporetto* (water bus) Line 1 from the train station all the way down the Grand Canal. If you've just arrived and have luggage in tow, you'll need to weigh the merits of taking this trip right away versus getting settled at your hotel first. (Crucial factors: your mood, the bulk of your bags, and your hotel's location.)

Seeing Piazza San Marco and the sights bordering it can fill a day, but if you're going to be around awhile, consider holding off on your visit there—the crowds can be overwhelming, especially when you're fresh off the boat. Instead, spend your first morning at Santa Maria Gloriosa dei Frari and the Scuola Grande di San Rocco, then wander through the Dorsoduro sestiere, choosing between visits to Ca' Rezzonico, the Gallerie dell'Accademia, the Peggy Guggenheim Collection, and Santa Maria della Salute—all A-list attractions. End the afternoon with a gelato-fueled stroll along the Zattere boardwalk. Then tackle San Marco on day two.

If you have more time, make these sights your priorities: the Rialto fish and produce markets; Ca' d'Oro and the Jewish Ghetto in Cannaregio; Santa Maria dei Miracoli and Santi Giovanni e Paolo in Castello; and, across the water from Piazza San Marco, San Giorgio Maggiore. (In Venice, there's a spectacular church for every day of the week, and then some.) A day on the outer islands of Murano, Burano, and Torcello is good for a change of pace.

Getting Around

It's true: there are no cars whatsoever in Venice. You get around primarily on foot, with occasional trips by boat on the famous canals that lace through the city. These are your basic boat-going options:

■ **Vaporetto.** Water buses run up and down the Grand Canal, around the city, and out to the surrounding islands. They're Venice's primary means of public transportation.

■ **Gondola.** Traveling by gondola is a romantic, pricey joy ride (rather than a way to get from one place to another). You pay by the hour. Be sure to agree on the fare before boarding, and ask to be taken down smaller side canals.

■ **Traghetto.** There are only three bridges across the Grand Canal. Traghetti are gondola-like ferries (rowed by gondoliers in training) that fill in the gaps, going from one bank to the other in eight spots. They can save a lot of walking, and they're a cheap (€.50), quick taste of the gondola experience.

■ **Water taxi.** A more accurate name might be "water limousine"—sky-high fares make taxis and indulgent way to get from place to place.

For details on getting around, see "Essentials" at the end of this chapter.

KNOWING WHERE YOU'RE GOING

Be sure to arrive in Venice with precise directions to your hotel (usually available on the hotel Web site). Getting lost in Venice can be a charming adventure, but the charm level drops to zero when you're hauling around luggage.

Venetian Vocabulary

Venetians use their own terms to describe their unique city. In fact, they have their own dialect; if you have an ear for Italian, you'll notice a distinct difference in the language. Here are some key words to know:

Sestiere: A neighborhood in central Venice. (There are six of them.)

Rio: A small canal.

Riva: A street running along a canal.

Fondamenta: Another name for a riva.

Calle: A street not running along a canal.

Campo: A square—what elsewhere in Italy would be called a piazza. (The only piazza in Venice is Piazza San Marco.)

Bacaro: A wine bar.

Ombra: A glass of wine served at a bacaro.

Cicchetto (pronounced "chick-ay-toh")*:* A snack served at a bacaro—roughly the Venetian equivalent of tapas.

How's the Weather?

One thing Venice has in common with much of Italy: spring and fall are the best times to visit. Summers are hot, sticky, and crowded. Winters are relatively mild and tourist-free, but there are frequent rainy spells, and at the beginning and end of the season there's the threat of *acqua alta*, when tides roll in and flood low-lying parts of the city, including Piazza San Marco.

Zattere

TOP PASSEGGIATA

With its streets given over to pedestrians, all of Venice is in a state of perpetual passeggiata, but Fondamenta delle Zattere, along the southern end of Dorsoduro, is a particularly prime spot.

Festivals to Build a Trip Around

■ Venice's most famous festival is **Carnevale**, drawing revelers from all over the world. For 10 days leading up to Ash Wednesday, it takes over the city—think Mardi Gras meets Casanova.

■ The prestigious **Biennale** is a century-old international art festival held in late summer and early fall of odd-numbered years. It's spawned several other festivals, including the **Biennale Danza, Biennale Musica,** and, most famously, **Biennale Cinema,** also known as the Venice Film Festival, held every year at the end of August.

■ The **Festa Redentore** (Feast of the Redeemer), on the third Sunday in July, is the biggest celebration of the year among locals, who float out in boats on Bacino San Marco and watch midnight fireworks displays.

■ There are three noteworthy annual contests of Venetian-style rowing: the **Regata delle Bafane**, on January 6; **Vogalonga** (long row), on a Sunday in May; and **Regata Storica**, on the first Sunday in September.

IT IS CALLED LA SERENISSIMA, or "the most serene," a reference to the monstrous power, majesty, and wisdom of this city that was for centuries the unrivaled mistress of trade between Europe and the Orient and the staunch bulwark of Christendom against the tides of Turkish expansion. "The most serene" also refers to the way in which those visiting have looked upon Venice, a miraculous city imperturbably floating on its calm blue lagoon.

Built entirely on water by men who dared defy the sea, Venice is unlike any other town. No matter how many times you have seen it in movies or TV commercials, the real thing is more dreamlike than you could ever imagine. Its landmarks, the Basilica di San Marco and the Palazzo Ducale, seem hardly Italian: delightfully idiosyncratic, they are exotic mixes of Byzantine, Gothic, and Renaissance styles. Shimmering sunlight and silvery mist soften every perspective here, and you understand how the city became renowned in the Renaissance for its artists' rendering of color. It's full of secrets, inexpressibly romantic, and at times given over entirely to pleasure.

You'll see Venetians going about their daily affairs in *vaporetti* (water buses), aboard the *traghetti* (traditional gondola ferries) that carry them across the Grand Canal, in the *campi* (squares), and along the *calli* (narrow streets). They are nothing if not skilled—and remarkably tolerant—in dealing with the veritable armies of tourists from all over the world who fill the city's streets almost year-round.

EXPLORING VENICE

Updated by
Pamela Santini

Many of Venice's major churches and museums are organized into two groups that coordinate hours and admissions. Fifteen art-laden churches are known as the **Chorus churches** (☎041/2750462 ⊕www.chorusvenezia. org): Santa Maria del Giglio, Santo Stefano, Santa Maria Formosa, Santa Maria dei Miracoli, Santa Maria Gloriosa dei Frari, San Polo, San Giacomo dell'Orio, San Stae, Sant'Alvise, Madonna dell'Orto, San Pietro di Castello, Santissimo Redentore, San Sebastiano, Gesuati, and San Giovanni Elemosinario. They're open to visitors all day except Sunday morning, and usually someone there can provide information and a free leaflet in English. Postcards and booklets about the sights are on sale. Single church entry costs €2.50, or you can visit them all with a €9 Chorus pass. The price of the pass includes audio guides except in the Frari, where they cost €1.60. The artwork in Chorus churches is labeled and the staff can show you where to switch on lighting for selected paintings.

Eleven museums currently make up Venice's **Musei Civici** (☎041/2715911 ⊕ www.museiciviciveneziani.it). A Museum Pass costing €15.50 and valid for three months lets you make one visit to each museum. A Museum Card, good only at the Piazza San Marco museums—Palazzo Ducale, Museo Correr, Museo Archeologico, and Biblioteca Nazionale Marciana—costs €11.

CRUISING THE GRAND CANAL

THE BEST INTRODUCTION TO VENICE IS A TRIP DOWN MAIN STREET

Venice's Grand Canal is one of the world's great thoroughfares. It winds its way in the shape of a backward "S" from Ferrovia (the train station) to Piazza San Marco, passing 200 palazzos born of a culture obsessed with opulence and fantasy. There's a theatrical quality to a boat ride on the canal: it's as if each pink- or gold-tinted façade is trying to steal your attention from its rival across the way.

The palaces were built from the 12th to 18th centuries by the city's richest families. A handful are still private residences, but many have been converted to other uses, including museums, hotels, government offices, university buildings, a post office, a casino, and even a television station.

It's romantic to see the canal from a gondola, but the next best thing, at a fraction of the cost, is to take the Line 1 *vaporetto* (water bus) from Ferrovia to San Marco. The ride costs €5 and takes about 35 minutes. Invest in a Travel Card (€10.50 buys 24 hours of unlimited passage) and you can spend the better part of a day hopping on and off at the vaporetto's 16 stops, visiting the sights along the banks. Either way, keep your eyes open for the highlights listed here; those with numbered bullets have fuller descriptions later in this chapter.

FROM FERROVIA TO RIALTO

Palazzo Labia

On September 3, 1951, during the Venice Film Festival, the Palazzo Labia hosted what's been dubbed "the party of the century." The Aga Khan, Winston Churchill, Orson Welles, and Salvador Dalí were among those who donned 18th-century costume and danced in the Tiepolo-frescoed ballroom.

Santa Maria di Nazareth

Ponte di Scalzi

R. Di BIASIO

FERROVIA

Stazione Ferrovia Santa Lucia

As you head out from Ferrovia, the baroque church immediately to your left is **Santa Maria di Nazareth**. Its shoeless friars earned it the nickname Chiesa degli Scalzi (Church of the Barefoot).

The first of only three bridges over the Grand Canal is the **Ponte di Scalzi**. The original version was built of iron in 1858; the existing stone bridge dates from 1934.

After passing beneath the Ponte di Scalzi, ahead to the left you'll spy **Palazzo Labia** ㉒, one of the most imposing buildings in Venice, looming over the bell tower of the church of San Geremia.

A hundred yards or so further along on the left bank, the uncompleted façade of the church of **San Marcuola** gives you an idea of what's behind the marble decorations of similar 18th-century churches in Venice. Across the canal, flanked by two *torricelle* (side wings in the shape of small towers) and a triangular

merlatura (crenellation), is the **Fondaco dei Turchi**, one of the oldest Byzantine palaces in Venice; it's now a natural history museum. Next comes the plain brick **Depositi del Megio**, a 15th-century granary—note the lion marking it as Serenissima property—and beyond it the obelisk-topped **Ca' Belloni-Battagia**. Both are upstaged by the **Palazzo Vendramin-Calergi** ㉔ on the opposite bank: this Renaissance gem was built in the 1480s, at a time when late-Gothic was still the prevailing style. A gilded banner identifies the palazzo as site of Venice's casino.

Palazzo Vendramin-Calergi

The German composer Richard Wagner died in Palazzo Vendramin-Calergi in 1883, soon after the success of his opera *Parsifal*. His room has been preserved—you can visit it on Saturday mornings by appointment.

Ca' d'Oro

Ca' d'Oro means "house of gold." but the gold is long gone—the gilding that once accentuated the marble carvings of the façade has worn away over time.

Church of San Marcuola

S. MARCUOLA ▲

Ca' Belloni-Battagia

S. STAE ▲

Ca' Pesaro

Fondaco dei Turchi

Depositi del Megio

San Stae Church

▲ CA' D'ORO

Ca' Corner della Regina

Pescheria

The pescheria has been in operation for over 1,000 years. Stop by in the morning to see the exotic fish for sale—one of which may wind up on your dinner plate. Produce stalls fill the adjacent *fondamenta*, and butchers and cheesemongers occupy the surrounding shops.

Fondaco dei Tedeschi

Ca' dei Camerlenghi

▲ RIALTO

The white, whimsically baroque church of **San Stae** ⑰ on the right bank is distinguished by a host of marble saints on its façade. Further along the bank is another baroque showpiece, **Ca' Pesaro** ⑯, followed by the tall, balconied **Ca' Corner della Regina**. Next up on the left is the flamboyant pink-and-white **Ca' d'Oro** ㉕, arguably the finest example of Venetian Gothic design.

Across from Ca' d'Oro is the loggia-like, neo-Gothic **pescheria,** Venice's fish market, where boats dock in the morning to deliver their catch.

The canal narrows as you approach the impressive Rialto Bridge. To the left, just before the bridge, is the **Fondaco dei Tedeschi**. This was once the busiest trading center of the republic—German, Austrian, and Hungarian merchants kept warehouses and offices here;

today it's the city's main post office. Across the canal stands the curiously angled **Ca' dei Camerlenghi**. Built in 1525 to accommodate the State Treasury, it had a jail for tax evaders on the ground floor.

FROM RIALTO TO THE PONTE DELL' ACCADEMIA

Ponte di Rialto

▲ **RIALTO**

Ca' Foscari
Positioned at one of the busiest junctures along the Grand Canal, Ca' Foscari has suffered severe foundation damage as a result of the relentless wake from passing boats.

Palazzo Barzizza

S. SILVESTRO ▲

Ca' Loredan

Ca' Farsetti

Ca' Grimani

Palazzo Pisani Moretta

▲ *S. ANGELO*

Ca' Corner-Spinelli
If Ca' Corner-Spinelli has a familiar look, that's because it became a prototype for later Grand Canal buildings—and because its architect, Mauro Codussi, himself copied the windows from Palazzo Vendramin-Calergi.

TOMA ▲

Ca' Garzoni

Palazzo Falier
Palazzo Falier is said to have been the home of Doge Martin Fallier, who was beheaded for treason in 1355.

Palazzo Grassi

Ca' Rezzonico

REZZONICO ▲

ACCADEMIA ▲

Gallerie dell'Accademia

Until the 19th century, the shop-lined **Ponte di Rialto** ⑭ was the only bridge across the Grand Canal.

Rialto is the only point along the Grand Canal where buildings don't have their primary entrances directly on the water, a consequence of the two spacious *rive* (waterside paths) once used for unloading two Venetian staples: coal and wine. On your left along Riva del Carbon stand **Ca' Loredan** and **Ca' Farsetti**, 13th-century Byzantine palaces that today make up Venice's city hall. Just past the San Silvestro vaporetto landing on Riva del Vin is the 12th- and 13th-century facade of **Palazzo Barzizza**, an elegant example of Veneto-Byzantine architecture that managed to survive a complete renovation the 17th century. Across the water, the sternly Renaissance

Ca' Grimani has an intimidating presence that seems appropriate for today's Court of Appeals. At the Sant'Angelo landing, the vaporetto passes close to another massive Renaissance palazzo, **Ca' Corner-Spinelli**.

Back on the right bank, in a salmon color that seems to vary with the time of day, is elegant **Palazzo Pisani Moretta**, with twin water entrances. To your left, four-storied **Ca' Garzoni**, part of the Universita di Venezia Ca' Foscari, stands beside the San Toma *traghetto* (gondola ferry), which has operated since 1354. The boat makes a sharp turn and, on the right, passes one of the city's tallest Gothic palaces, **Ca' Foscari**.

The vaporetto passes baroque **Ca' Rezzonico** ⑦ so closely that you get to look inside one of the most fabulous entrances along the canal. Opposite stands the

Grand Canal's youngest palace, **Palazzo Grassi**, commissioned in 1749. Just beyond Grassi and Campo San Samuele, the first house past the garden was once Titian's studio. It's followed by **Palazzo Falier**, identifiable by its twin loggias (windowed porches).

Approaching the canal's third and final bridge, the vaporetto stops at a former church and monastery complex that houses the world-renowned **Gallerie dell'Accademia** ⑪.

> The wooden pilings on which Venice was built (you can see them at the bases of the buildings along the Grand Canal) have gradually hardened into mineral form.

ARCHITECTURAL STYLES ALONG THE GRAND CANAL

BYZANTINE: 12th and 13th centuries.
Distinguishing characteristics: high, rounded arches, relief panels, multicolored marble.
Examples: Fondaco dei Turchi, Ca' Loredan, Ca' Farsetti, Palazzo Barzizza (and, off the canal, Basilica di San Marco).

GOTHIC: 14th and 15th centuries.
Distinguishing characteristics: Pointed arches, high ceilings, and many windows.
Examples: Ca' d'Oro, Ca' Foscari, Ca' Franchetti, Palazzo Falier (and, off the canal, Palazzo Ducale).

RENAISSANCE: 16th century.
Distinguishing characteristics: classically influenced emphasis on order, achieved through

symmetry and balanced proportions.
Examples: Palazzo Vendramin-Calergi, Ca' Grimani, Ca' Corner-Spinelli, Ca' dei Camerlenghi (and, off the canal, Libreria Sansoviniana on Piazza San Marco and the church of San Giorgio Maggiore).

BAROQUE: 17th century.
Distinguishing characteristics: Renaissance order wedded with a more dynamic style, achieved through curving lines and complex decoration.
Examples: churches of Santa Maria di Nazareth and San Stae, Ca' Pesaro, Ca' Rezzonico (and, off the canal, the church of Santa Maria della Salute).

FROM THE PONTE DELL'ACCADEMIA TO SAN ZACCARIA

Ca' Franchetti

Until the late 19th century, Ca' Franchetti was a *squero* (gondola workshop). A few active squeri remain, though none are on the Grand Canal. The most easily spotted is Squero di San Trovaso, in Dorsoduro on a small canal near the Zattere boat landing.

Ca' Barbaro

Monet, Henry James, and Cole Porter are among the guests who have stayed at Ca' Barbaro. Porter later lived aboard a boat in Giudecca Canal.

Ponte dell' Accademia

ACCADEMIA

Casetta Rossa

Ca' Pisani-Gritti

S. M. DEL GIGLIO

Ca' Barbarigo

SALUTE

Palazzo Salviati

Palazzo Venier dei Leoni

S. Maria della Salute

Ca' Dario

The wooden Ponte dell'Accademia, like the Eiffel Tower (with which it shares a certain structural grace), wasn't intended to be permanent. Erected in 1933 as a quick replacement for a rusting iron bridge built by the Austrian military in 1854, it was so well liked by Venetians that they kept it. (A perfect replica, with steel bracing, was installed 1986.)

You're only three stops from the end of the Grand Canal, but this last stretch is packed with sights. The lovely **Ca' Franchetti**, with a central balcony made in the style of Palazzo Ducale's loggia, dates from the late Gothic period, but its gardens are no older than the cedar tree standing at their center.

When she was in residence at Palazzo Venier dei Leoni, Peggy Guggenheim kept her private gondola parked at the door and left her dogs standing guard (in place of Venetian lions).

Ca' Barbaro, next door to Ca' Franchetti, was the residence of the illustrious family who rebuilt the church of Santa Maria del Giglio.

Farther along on the left bank, a garden, vibrant with flowers in summer, surrounds **Casetta Rossa** (small red house) as if it were the centerpiece of its bouquet. Across the canal, bright 19th-century mosaics on **Ca' Barbarigo** give you some idea how the frescoed facades of many Venetian palaces must have looked in their heyday. A

However tilted Dario might be, it has outlasted its many owners, who seem plagued by misfortune. They include the Italian industrialist Raul Gardini, whose 1992 suicide followed charges of corruption and an unsuccessful bid to win the America's Cup.

few doors down are the lush gardens within the walls of the unfinished **Palazzo Venier dei Leoni**, which holds the **Peggy Guggenheim Collection** ⓬ of contemporary art.

Lovely, leaning **Ca' Dario** on the right bank is notable for its colorful marble façade.

Past the landing of Santa Maria del Giglio stands the

Basilica di S. Marco

Palazzo Ducale

S. ZACCARIA

VALLARESSO

Punta della Dogana

THE GRAND CANAL is 2½ miles long, has an average depth of 9 feet, and is 76 yards wide at its broadest point and 40 yards at its narrowest.

15th-century **Ca' Pisani-Gritti**, now the Gritti Palace Hotel. On the other bank, narrow **Palazzo Salviati**, with its 20th-century mosaic facade, was among the last glass factories to operate within the Venice city center. At this point the cupola of **Santa Maria della Salute** ⑬ dominates the scene, but spare a glance for picturesque Rio di San Gregorio and what remains of its Gothic abbey. At

Punta della Dogana on the tip of Dorsoduro, note the former customhouse, topped by Palla della Fortuna—a golden ball and a weather vane depicting Fortune. At the Vallaresso vaporetto stop you've left the Grand Canal, but stay on board for a view of the **Palazzo Ducale** ❷, with **Basilica di San Marco** ❶ behind it, then disembark at San Zaccaria.

Piazza San Marco

One of the world's most evocative squares, Piazza San Marco (St. Mark's Square) is the heart of Venice, a vast open space bordered by an orderly procession of arcades marching toward the fairy-tale cupolas and marble lacework of the Basilica di San Marco. Perpetually packed by day with people and fluttering pigeons, it can be magical at night, especially in winter, when mists swirl around the lampposts and the Campanile.

If you face the basilica from in front of the Correr Museum, you'll notice that rather than being a strict rectangle, this square opens wider at the basilica end, creating the illusion that it's even larger than it is. On your left, the long, arcaded building is the Procuratie Vecchie, built in the early 16th century as offices and residences for the powerful procurators (magistrates) of San Marco. On your right is the Procuratie Nuove, built half a century later in a more grandiose classical style. It was originally planned by Venice's great Renaissance architect, Sansovino, to carry on the look of his Libreria Sansoviniana (Sansovinian Library), but he died before construction on the Nuove had begun. Vincenzo Scamozzi (circa 1552–1616), a neoclassicist pupil of Andrea Palladio (1508–80), completed the design and construction. Still later, the Procuratie Nuove was modified by architect Baldassare Longhena (1598–1682), one of Venice's baroque masters.

When Napoléon (1769–1821) entered Venice with his troops in 1797, he called Piazza San Marco "the world's most beautiful drawing room"— and promptly gave orders to redecorate it. His architects demolished a 16th-century church with a Sansovino facade in order to build the Ala Napoleonica (Napoleonic Wing), or Fabbrica Nuova (New Building), which linked the two 16th-century procuratie and effectively enclosed the piazza.

Piazzetta San Marco, the "little square" leading from Piazza San Marco to the waters of Bacino San Marco (St. Mark's Basin), is a *molo* (landing) that was once the grand entryway to the Republic. It's distinguished by two columns towering above the waterfront. One is topped by the winged lion, a traditional emblem of St. Mark that became the symbol of Venice itself; the other supports St. Theodore, the city's first patron, along with his dragon. Between these columns the Republic traditionally executed convicts.

It takes a full day to take in everything on the piazza thoroughly; so if time is limited you'll have to prioritize. Plan on 1½ hours for the Basilica and its Pala d'Oro, Galleria, and Museo Marciano. You'll want at least two hours to appreciate the Palazzo Ducale. Do take time to enjoy the piazza itself from a café table, or on a clear day, from atop the Campanile.

The Main Attractions

❶ Basilica di San Marco. An opulent synthesis of Byzantine and Romanesque styles, Venice's gem is laid out in a Greek-cross floor plan and topped with five plump domes. It didn't become the cathedral of Venice until

Fodor'sChoice
★

Piazza
San Marco

1807, but its role as the Chiesa Ducale (doge's private chapel) gave it immense power and wealth. The original church was built in 828 to house the body of St. Mark the Evangelist. His remains, filched from Alexandria by the doge's agents, were supposedly hidden in a barrel under layers of pickled pork to sneak them past Muslim guards. The escapade is depicted in the 13th-century mosaic above the door farthest left of the front entrance, one of the earliest mosaics on the heavily decorated facade; look closely to see the church as it appeared at that time.

A 976 fire destroyed most of the original church. It was rebuilt and reopened in 1094, and for centuries it would serve as a symbol of Venetian wealth and power, endowed with all the riches admirals and merchants could carry off from the Orient, to the point where it earned the nickname Chiesa d'Oro (Golden Church). The four bronze horses that prance and snort over the doorway are copies of sculptures that victorious Venetians took from Constantinople in 1204 after the fourth crusade (the originals are in the Museo di San Marco). The rich, colorful exterior decorations, including the numerous different marble columns, all came from the same source. Look for a medallion of red porphyry in the floor of the porch inside the main door. It marks the spot where, in 1177, Doge Sebastiano Ziani orchestrated the reconciliation between

Barbarossa—the Holy Roman Emperor—and Pope Alexander III. Dim lighting, galleries high above the naves—they served as the *matroneum* (women's gallery)—the *iconostasis* (altar screen) and the single massive Byzantine chandelier all seem to wed Christianity with the Orient, giving San Marco its exotic blend of majesty and mystery.

The basilica is famous for its 43,055 square feet of stunning mosaics, which run from floor to ceiling thanks to an innovative roof of brick vaulting. Many of the original windows were filled in to make room for even more artwork. At midday, when the interior is fully illuminated, the mosaics truly come alive, the shimmer of their tiny gold tiles becoming nothing short of magical. The earliest mosaics are from the 11th and 12th centuries, and the last were added in the early 1700s. One of the most recent is the *Last Judgment,* believed to have been designed by Tintoretto (1518–94), on the arch between the porch and the nave. Inside the main entrance, turn right on the porch to see the Book of Genesis depicted on the ceiling. Ahead through a glass door, 13th-century mosaics depict St. Mark's life in the **Cappella Zen** (Zen Chapel). The **Cappella della Madonna di Nicopeia,** in the left transept, holds the altar icon that many consider Venice's most powerful protector. In nearby **Cappella della Madonna dei Mascoli** the life of the Virgin Mary is depicted in fine 15th-century mosaics, believed to be based on drawings by Jacopo Bellini and Andrea Mantegna.

In the **Santuario** (Sanctuary), the main altar is built over the tomb of St. Mark, its green marble canopy lifted high on carved alabaster columns. Perhaps even more impressive is the **Pala d'Oro,** a dazzling gilt silver screen encrusted with 1,927 precious gems and 255 enameled panels. Originally commissioned in Constantinople by Doge Orseolo I (976–978), it was enlarged and embellished over four centuries by master craftsmen and wealthy merchants. The bronze door leading from the sanctuary into the sacristy is by Jacopo Sansovino (1486–1570). In the top left corner the artist included a self-portrait, and above that, he pictured friend and fellow artist Titian. The **Tesoro** (Treasury), entered from the right transept, contains many treasures carried home from conquests abroad.

Climb the steep stairway to the **Galleria** and the **Museo di San Marco** for the best overview of the basilica's interior. From here you can step outdoors for a sweeping panorama of Piazza San Marco and out over the lagoon to San Giorgio. The displays focus mainly on the types of mosaic and how they have been restored over the years. But the highlight is a close-up view of the original gilt bronze horses that were once on the outer gallery. The four were most probably cast in Rome and taken to Constantinople, where the Venetians pillaged them after sacking that city. When Napoléon (1769–1821) sacked Venice in 1797, he took them to Paris. They were returned after the fall of the French Empire, but came home "blind"—their big ruby eyes had been sold.

Be aware that guards at the basilica door turn away anyone with bare shoulders or knees; no shorts, short skirts, or tank tops are allowed. If you want a free guided tour in English during summer months (less cer-

CLOSE UP

Wading Through the Acqua Alta

1

You have to walk almost everywhere in Venice, and where you can't walk, you go by water. Occasionally you walk *in* water, when normally higher fall and spring tides are exacerbated by falling barometers and southeasterly winds. The result is *acqua alta*—flooding in the lowest parts of town, especially Piazza San Marco, which lasts a few hours, until the tide recedes.

Work has begun on the Moses Project, a plan that would close off the lagoon when high tides threaten, but it's a much-debated response to an emotionally charged problem. Protecting Venice and its lagoon from high tides—as well as high use and the damaging wave action caused by powerboats—is among the city's most contentious issues.

---

tain in winter, as the guides are volunteers), look for groups forming on the porch inside the main door. You may also arrange tours by appointment. ⊠ *Piazza San Marco* ☎ *041/5225205 Basilica, 041/5225697 tours* 🖾 *Basilica free, Tesoro € 2, Santuario and Pala d'Oro €1.50, Galleria and Museo di San Marco € 3* ⊙ *Mon.–Sat. 9:30–5, Sun. 2–4; last entry ½ hr before closing* Ⓥ *Vallaresso/San Zaccaria.*

★ ❷ **Palazzo Ducale** (Doge's Palace). Rising above the Piazzetta San Marco, this Gothic-Renaissance fantasia of pink-and-white marble is a majestic expression of the prosperity and power attained during Venice's most glorious period. Some architectural purists find the building top-heavy, its hulking upper floors resting upon a graceful ground-floor colonnade, but you can hardly imagine the palace with any other design. Always much more than a residence, it was White House, Senate, torture chamber, and prison rolled into one. Venice's participatory democracy began around 700 and had an elected doge who ruled for life. In practice he was little more than a figurehead; real power rested with the Great Council, which once had more than 2,000 members. Although originally an elected body, in the 13th century it became an aristocratic stronghold, members inheriting seats from noble ancestors. The Senate, a group of 200 elected from the Great Council, passed laws, but executive powers belonged to the College, a committee of 25. In the 14th century the Council of Ten was formed to protect state security and soon became the most powerful and most feared branch of government.

Though a fortress for the doge stood on this spot in the early 9th century, the building you see today was begun in the 12th century, and like the basilica next door was continually remodeled over the centuries. Near the basilica you'll see the ornately Gothic **Porta della Carta** (Gate of the Paper), where official decrees were traditionally posted, but visitors enter under the portico facing the water. You'll find yourself in an immense courtyard with the **Scala dei Giganti** (Stairway of the Giants) directly ahead, guarded by Sansovino's huge statues of Mars and Neptune. Though ordinary mortals must use the central interior staircase, its upper flight is the lavishly gilded **Scala d'Oro** (Golden Staircase), also by Sansovino. It may seem odd that you have to climb so many steps to reach the government's main council rooms and reception halls, but imagine how this extraordinary climb must have impressed, and perhaps intimidated, foreign emissaries.

The palace's sumptuous chambers are awe-inspiring in themselves, their walls and ceilings covered with works by Venice's greatest artists. Visit the **Anticollegio,** a waiting room outside the Collegio's chamber, where you'll see the *Rape of Europa* by Veronese (1528–88) and Tintoretto's *Bacchus and Ariadne Crowned by Venus.* Veronese also painted the ceiling of the adjacent **Sala del Collegio.** The ceiling of the **Sala del Senato** (Senate Chamber) features *The Triumph of Venice* by Tintoretto, magnificent surely, but dwarfed by his masterpiece *Paradise* in the **Sala del Maggiore Consiglio** (Great Council Hall). A vast work commissioned for a vast hall, this dark, dynamic piece is the world's largest oil painting (23 by 75 feet). The room's carved, gilt ceiling is breathtaking, especially with Veronese's majestic *Apotheosis of Venice* filling one of the center panels. Around the upper walls, study the portraits of the first 76 doges, and you'll notice one picture is missing near the left corner of the wall opposite *Paradise.* A black painted curtain, rather than a portrait, marks Doge Marin Falier's fall from grace; he was beheaded for treason in 1355, which the Latin inscription bluntly explains.

A narrow canal separates the Palace's east side from the cramped cell blocks of the **Prigioni Nuove** (New Prisons). High above the water arches the enclosed marble **Ponte dei Sospiri** (Bridge of Sighs), which earned its name from the sighs of those being led to their fate. Look out its windows to see the last earthly view these prisoners beheld.

The palazzo's "Secret Itinerary" tour takes you to the doge's private apartments, through hidden passageways to the interrogation (torture) chambers, and into the rooftop *piombi* (lead) prison, named for its lead roofing. Venetian-born writer and libertine Giacomo Casanova (1725–98), along with an accomplice, managed to escape from the piombi in 1756, the only men ever to do so. ⊠ *Piazzetta San Marco* ☎ *041/2715911* 🎫 *€11 Piazza San Marco museum card, €15.50 Musei Civici pass* ☉ *Apr.–Oct., daily 9–7; Nov.–Mar., daily 9–5; last tickets sold 1 hr before closing* 🎫 *€12.50 "Secret Itinerary" tour* ☎ *041/5209070* ☉ *English tours in morning; reservations advisable* Ⓥ *Vallaresso/San Zaccaria.*

need a break?

Caffè Florian (☎ 041/5205641), located in the Procuratie Nuove, has served coffee to the likes of Casanova, Charles Dickens, and Marcel Proust. It's Venice's oldest café, continuously in business since 1720 (though you'll find it closed on winter Wednesdays). Counter seating is less expensive than taking a table, especially when there's live music. In the Procuratie Vecchie, **Caffè Quadri** (☎ 041/5289299) exudes almost as much history as Florian across the way, and is similarly pricey. It was shunned by 19th-century Venetians when the occupying Austrians made it their gathering place. In winter it closes on Monday. If you'd like to aatend happy hour with the ghosts of Ernest Hemingway, Aristotle Onassis, and Orson Welles, head to **Harry's Bar** (☎ 041/5285777). Walk out Piazza San Marco near the Correr Museum and turn left at Calle Vallaresso; you'll find the legendary hangout right at the vaporetto landing. Harry's still boasts Venice's driest martinis and freshest Bellinis (white peach juice and sparkling Prosecco wine).

Also Worth Seeing

⑨ ❸ Campanile. Venice's famous brick bell tower (325 feet tall, plus the angel) had been standing nearly 1,000 years when in 1902, practically without warning, it collapsed, taking with it Jacopo Sansovino's 16th-century marble loggia at the base. The crushed loggia was promptly restored, and the new tower, rebuilt to the old plan, reopened in 1912. In the 15th century, clerics found guilty of immoral behavior were suspended in wooden cages from the tower. Some were forced to subsist on bread and water for as long as a year, and others were left to starve. The stunning view from the tower on a clear day includes the Lido, the lagoon, and the mainland as far as the Alps but, strangely enough, none of the myriad canals that snake through the city. ⊠ *Piazza San Marco* ☎ *041/ 5224064* 🔁 *€6* ☉ *Apr.–Sept., daily 9:30 AM–5:30; Oct.–Mar., daily 9:30–4:30; last entry ½ hr before closing* Ⓥ *Vallaresso/San Zaccaria.*

❹ Museo Correr. Exhibits in this museum of Venetian art and history range from the absurdly high-soled shoes worn by 16th-century Venetian ladies (who walked with the aid of a servant) to the huge *Grande Pianta Prospettica* by Jacopo de' Barbari (circa 1440–1515), which details in carved wood every nook and cranny of 16th-century Venice. The city's proud naval history is evoked in several rooms through highly descriptive paintings and numerous maritime objects, including ships' cannons and some surprisingly large iron mast-top navigation lights. The Correr has a room devoted entirely to antique games, and its second-floor **Quadreria** (Picture Gallery) has works by Venetian, Greek, and Flemish painters. The Correr exhibition rooms lead directly into the **Museo Archeologico** and the **Stanza del Sansovino,** the only part of the **Biblioteca Marciana** open to visitors. ⊠ *Piazza San Marco, Ala Napoleonica* ☎ *041/2405211* 🔁 *€11 Piazza San Marco museum card, €15.50 Musei Civici pass* ☉ *Apr.–Oct., daily 9–7; Nov.–Mar., daily 9–5; last tickets sold 1 hr before closing* Ⓥ *Vallaresso/San Zaccaria.*

❺ Torre dell'Orologio. Five hundred years ago, when this enameled clock was built, twin Moor figures would strike the hour, and three wise men with an angel would walk out and bow to the Virgin Mary on Epiphany (January 6) and during Ascension Week (40 days after Easter). An inscription on the tower reads HORAS NON NUMERO NISI SERENAS ("I only count happy hours"); if that's true, perhaps happy hours will return to Venice when they finally fix the clock. It's been under restoration for years and due to reopen sometime in 2006, but you can visit the three wise men in the Palazzo Ducale, where they are on display. ⊠ *North side of Piazza San Marco.*

Dorsoduro

The sestiere Dorsoduro (named for its "hard back" solid clay foundation) is across the Grand Canal to the south of San Marco. It is a place

VENICE THROUGH THE AGES

Venice was founded in the 5th century when the Veneti, inhabitants of the mainland region roughly corresponding to today's Veneto, fled their homes to escape invading Lombards. The unlikely city, built atop wooden posts driven into the marshes, would evolve into a great maritime republic. Its fortunes grew as a result of its active role in the Crusades, beginning in 1095 and culminating in the Venetian-led sacking of Constantinople in 1204. The defeat of rival Genoa in the Battle of Chioggia (1380) established Venice as the dominant sea power in Europe.

As early as the 7th century, Venice was governed by a participatory democracy, featuring a ruler, the doge, who was elected to a lifetime term. Beginning in the 12th century, the doge's power was increasingly subsumed by a growing number of councils, commissions, and magistrates. In 1268 a complicated procedure for the doge's election was established to prevent nepotism, but by this point power rested foremost with the Great Council, which at times numbered as many as 2,000 members. Laws were passed by the Senate, a group of 200 elected from the Great Council, and executive powers belonged to the College, a committee of 25 leaders. In 1310 the Council of Ten was formed to protect state security. When circumstances abroad or at home endangered the Republic's democracy, the doge could expedite decision-making by consulting only the Council of Ten. To avoid too great a concentration of power, these 10 served only one year and had to belong to different families.

Venice reached its height of power in the 15th and 16th centuries, during which time its domain extended inland to include all of the Veneto region and part of Lombardy. But beginning in the 16th century, the tide turned. The Ottoman Empire blocked Venice's Mediterranean trade routes, and newly emerging sea powers such as Britain and the Netherlands ended Venice's monopoly by opening oceanic trading routes. The republic underwent a long, slow decline. When Napoleon arrived in 1797, he took the city without a fight, eventually delivering it to the Austrians, who ruled until 1848. In that tumultuous year throughout Europe, the Venetians rebelled, an act that would ultimately lead to their joining the Italian republic in 1866.

In the 13th through 15th centuries the influence of Gothic architecture produced the characteristic type of palace in the Florid Gothic style, for which the town is famous. Renaissance sensibilities arrived in Venice comparatively late. Early Venetian Renaissance artists—Carpaccio, Giorgione, and the Bellini brothers, Giovanni and Gentile—were active in the late 15th and early 16th centuries. Along with the stars of the next generation—Veronese, Titian, and Tintoretto—they played a decisive role in the development of Western art, and their work still covers walls and ceilings all over the city.

Like its steadily dwindling fortunes, Venice's art and culture underwent a prolonged decline, leaving only the splendid monuments to recall a fabled past, with the 18th-century paintings of Canaletto and frescoes of Giambattista Tiepolo striking a glorious swan song.

of monumental churches, meandering canals, the city's finest art museums, and a boardwalk called the Zattere, where on sunny days you'll swear half the city is out for a *passeggiata,* or stroll. The eastern point of the peninsula, Punta della Dogana, has one of the best views in town. The Stazione Marittima, where in summer cruise ships line the dock, lies at the western end. Midway between these two points, just off the Zattere, is the Squero di San Trovaso, where gondolas have been built and repaired for centuries.

Dorsoduro is also home to the Gallerie dell'Accademia, which has an unparalleled collection of Venetian painting, and Ca' Rezzonico, the Museo del Settecento Veneziano. Another of its landmark sites, the Peggy Guggenheim Collection, has a fine selection of 20th-century art. The Gallerie dell'Accademia demands a few hours, but if time is short an audio guide can help you cover the highlights in about an hour. Give yourself at least 1½ hours for the Guggenheim Collection. Ca' Rezzonico deserves a couple of hours.

The Main Attractions

★ ❼ **Ca' Rezzonico.** Designed by Baldassare Longhena in the 17th century, this palace was completed nearly 100 years later by Giorgio Massari and became the last home of English poet Robert Browning (1812–89). Elizabeth Taylor and Richard Burton danced in the baroque ballroom in the 1960s. Today Ca' Rezzonico is the home of the **Museo del Settecento** (Museum of Venice in the 1700s). Its main floor is packed with period furniture and tapestries in gilded salons (note the four Tiepolo ceiling frescoes) and successfully retains the feel of an old Venetian palazzo. Upper floors contain hundreds of paintings, most from Venetian schools of artists. There's even a restored apothecary, complete with powders and potions. ⊠ *Fondamenta Rezzonico, Dorsoduro 3136* ☎ *041/2410100* 🎫 *€6.50, €15.50 Musei Civici pass* ☉ *Apr.–Oct., Wed.–Mon. 10–6; Nov.–Mar., Wed.–Mon. 10–5; last entry 1 hr before closing* Ⓥ *Ca' Rezzonico.*

★ ⓫ **Gallerie dell'Accademia.** Napoléon founded these galleries in 1807 on the site of a religious complex he'd suppressed, and what he initiated now amounts to the world's most extraordinary collection of Venetian art. Jacopo Bellini (1400–71) is considered the father of the Venetian Renaissance, and in Room 2 you can compare his *Madonna and Child with Saints* with such later works as *Madonna of the Orange Tree* by Cima da Conegliano (circa 1459–1517) and *Ten Thousand Martyrs of Mt. Ararat* by Vittore Carpaccio (1450–1526). Jacopo's son Giovanni (circa 1430–1516) draws your eye not with his subjects but with his rich color. Rooms 4 and 5 are full of his Madonnas; note the contrast between the young Madonna and child and the neighboring older Madonna after the crucifixion—you'll see the colors of dawn and dusk in Venice. Room 5 contains *Tempest* by Giorgione (1477–1510), a work that was revolutionary in its time and has continued to intrigue viewers and critics over the centuries. It depicts a storm approaching as a nude woman nurses her child and a soldier looks on. The overall atmosphere that Giorgione creates is as important as any of his figures.

Dorsoduro

KEY

▲ Vaporetto Stop

0 — 1/8 mile
0 — 1/8 km

In Room 10, *Feast in the House of Levi,* commissioned as a Last Supper, got Veronese dragged before the Inquisition over its depiction of dogs, jesters, and German (therefore Protestant) soldiers. The artist saved his neck by simply changing the title, so that the painting represented a different biblical feast. Titian's *Presentation of the Virgin* (Room 24) is the collection's only work originally created for the building in which it hangs. Don't miss Rooms 20 and 21, with views of 15th- and 16th-century Venice by Carpaccio and Gentile Bellini (1429–1507), Giovanni's brother—you'll see how little the city has changed.

Booking tickets in advance isn't essential but helps during busy seasons and costs only an additional €1. Booking is necessary to see the **Quadreria,** where additional works cover every inch of a wide hallway. A free map names art and artists, and the bookshop sells a more informative English-language booklet. In the main galleries a €4 audio guide saves reading but adds little to each room's excellent annotation; audio-video guides (€6) are more exhaustive and also ease navigating. ⌧ *Campo della Carità, Dorsoduro 1050* ☎ *041/5222247, 041/5200345 reservations* ⊕ *www.artive.arti.beniculturali.it* 🎟 *€6.50, €11 includes Ca' d'Oro and Museo Orientale* ☉ *Tues.–Sun. 8:15–7:15, Mon. 8:15–2* Ⓥ *Accademia.*

need a break?
There's no sunnier spot in Venice than **Fondamenta delle Zattere,** along the southern edge of Dorsoduro. It's the city's gigantic public terrace, with bustling bars and gelato shops; come here to stroll, read in the open air, and play hooky from sightseeing. The Zattere's most decadent treat is found at **Gelateria Nico** (⌧ Dorsoduro 922 ☎ 041/5225293)—order their famous *gianduiotto,* a nutty slab of chocolate ice cream floating on a cloud of whipped cream, and relax on the big, welcoming deck.

⟳ ⑫ **Peggy Guggenheim Collection.** A small but choice selection of 20th-century painting and sculpture is on display at this gallery in the heiress Guggenheim's former Grand Canal home. Through wealth and social connections, Guggenheim (1898–1979) became a serious art patron, and her collection here in Palazzo Venier dei Leoni includes works by Picasso, Kandinsky, Pollock, Motherwell, and Ernst (at one time her husband). The museum serves beverages, snacks,

> ### WORD OF MOUTH
>
> "Personally, I liked the garden and the villa itself at the Peggy Guggenheim museum better than the art."   –Dayle

and light meals in its refreshingly shady, artistically sophisticated garden. On Sunday at 3 PM the museum offers a free tour and art workshop for children 12 and under. ⌧ *Fondamenta Venier dei Leoni, Dorsoduro 701* ☎ *041/2405411* ⊕ *www.guggenheim-venice.it* 🎟 *€10* ☉ *Wed.–Mon. 10–6* Ⓥ *Accademia.*

⑬ **Santa Maria della Salute.** The view of La Salute (as this church is commonly called) from the Riva degli Schiavoni at sunset or from the Accademia Bridge by moonlight is unforgettable. Baldassare Longhena was

32 years old when he won a competition to design a shrine honoring the Virgin Mary for saving Venice from a plague that killed 47,000 residents. Outside, this simple white octagon is adorned with a colossal cupola lined with snail-like buttresses and a Palladian-style facade; inside are a polychrome marble floor and six chapels. The Byzantine icon above the main altar has been venerated as the Madonna della Salute (of health) since 1670, when Francesco Morosini brought it here from Crete. Above it is a sculpture showing Venice (left) on her knees while the plague (right) is driven from the city. The **Sacrestia Maggiore** contains a dozen works by Titian, including his *San Marco Enthroned with Saints* altarpiece. You'll also see Tintoretto's *The Wedding at Canaan*, and on special occasions the altar displays a 15th-century tapestry depicting the Pentecost. For the Festa della Salute, held November 21, Venetians make a pilgrimage here and light candles in thanksgiving for another year's health. ⊠ *Punta della Dogana, Dorsoduro* ☎ *041/ 5225558* ⊠ *Church free, sacristy €1.50* ⊗ *Apr.–Sept., daily 9–noon and 3–6:30; Oct.–Mar., daily 9–noon and 3–5:30* Ⓥ *Salute.*

need a break?

Filled with cafés and restaurants, **Campo Santa Margarita** also has produce vendors, pizza by the slice, and benches where you can sit and eat. For more than a portable munch, bask in the sunshine at popular **il Caffè** (☎ 041/5287998), commonly called Caffé Rossa for its bright red exterior. It's open past midnight, serving drinks and light refreshment every day except Sunday.

Also Worth Seeing

❻ Campo Santo Stefano. In Venice's most prestigious residential neighborhood, you'll find one of the city's busiest crossroads just over the Accademia bridge; it's hard to believe this square once hosted bullfights, with bulls (or oxen) tied to a stake and baited by dogs. For centuries the campo was grass except for a stone avenue called the *liston*. It was so popular for strolling that in Venetian dialect *"andare al liston"* still means "go for a walk." A sunny meeting spot popular with Venetians and visitors alike, the campo also hosts outdoor fairs during Christmas and Carnevale seasons. Check out the 14th-century **Chiesa di Santo Stefano** and its ship's-keel roof, created by shipbuilders. You'll see works by Tintoretto and the tipsiest bell tower in town—best appreciated from nearby Campo San Angelo. ⊠ *Campo Santo Stefano, San Marco* ☎ *041/2750462 Chorus* ⊠ *€2.50, €9 Chorus pass* ⊗ *Mon.–Sat. 10–5, Sun. 1–5* Ⓥ *Accademia.*

❿ Gesuati. When the Dominicans took over the church of Santa Maria della Visitazione from the suppressed order of Gesuati laymen in 1668, Giorgio Massari was commissioned to build this structure. It has a score of works by Giambattista Tiepolo (1696–1770), Giambiattista Piazzetta (1683–1754), and Sebastiano Ricci (1659–1734). ⊠ *Zattere, Dorsoduro* ☎ *041/2750462 Chorus* ⊠ *€2.50, €9 Chorus pass* ⊗ *Mon.–Sat. 10–5, Sun. 1–5* Ⓥ *Zattere.*

❾ San Sebastiano. Paolo Veronese (1528–88) established his reputation while still in his twenties with the frescoes at this, his parish church, and for decades he continued to embellish them with amazing trompe-l'oeil scenes. Don't miss his altarpiece *Madonna in Glory with Saints*. Veronese is buried beneath his bust near the organ. ✉ *Campo San Sebastiano, Dorsoduro* ☎ *041/2750462 Chorus* 💶 *€2.50, €9 Chorus pass* 🕐 *Mon.–Sat. 10–5, Sun. 1–5* Ⓥ *San Basilio.*

❽ **Scuola Grande dei Carmini.** When the order of Santa Maria del Carmelo commissioned Baldassare Longhena to build Scuola Grande dei Carmini in the late 1600s, their brotherhood of 75,000 members was the largest in Venice and one of the wealthiest. Little expense was spared in the decorating of stuccoed ceilings and carved ebony paneling, and the artwork was choice, even before 1739, when Tiepolo painted the **Sala Capitolare**. In what many consider his best work, Tiepolo's nine great canvases vividly transform some rather unpromising religious themes into flamboyant displays of color and movement. ✉ *Campo dei Carmini, Dorsoduro 2617* ☎ *041/5289420* 💶 *€5* 🕐 *Nov.–Mar., daily 9–4; Apr.–Oct., Mon.–Sat. 9–6, Sun. 9–4* Ⓥ *Ca' Rezzonico.*

San Polo & Santa Croce

The smallest of Venice's six sestieri, San Polo and Santa Croce were named after their main churches, though the Chiesa di Santa Croce was demolished in 1810. The city's most famous bridge, the Ponte di Rialto, which unites sestiere San Marco (east) with San Polo (west), takes its name from *Rivoaltus,* the high ground on which it was built. Shops abound here; on the San Marco side of the bridge they sell everything that's hip, on the San Polo side everything edible. Chiesa di San Giacometto, where you see the first fruit vendors as you come off the bridge on the San Polo side, was probably built in the 11th and 12th centuries, about the time the surrounding market came into being. Public announcements were traditionally read in the church's campo; its 24-hour clock, though lovely, has rarely worked. If you want to take part in the food shopping, come early to beat the crowds and bear in mind that a *metà kilo* is about a pound and an *etto* is a few ounces.

The sestiere has some other important sites, such as Santa Maria Gloriosa dei Frari and the Scuola Grande di San Rocco, as well as some worthwhile but lesser-known churches. There's a lot to see, so if you do any shopping, or even pop in at a few churches along the way, you'll need at least a half day. West of the main thoroughfare that takes you from the Ponte di Rialto to Santa Maria Gloriosa dei Frari is San Giacomo dell'Orio campo and church, a peaceful place for a drink, a rest, and a chance to glimpse daily life. Not far from

> **WORD OF MOUTH**
>
> "Scuola Grande di San Rocco is absolutely mind-boggling. It is near Santa Maria Gloriosa dei Frari—also well worth a visit. The bonus is that in the small street between these two places is Millevoglie, a sandwich/pizza shop with *the best* gelato." –Rosemary

the campo is the whimsically baroque church of San Stae and Ca' Pesaro, the site of both the Museum of Modern Art and the Oriental Museum. You'll want at least two hours to see both collections at Ca' Pesaro.

The Main Attractions

★ ⑭ **Ponte di Rialto** (Rialto Bridge). The competition to design a stone bridge across the Grand Canal (replacing earlier wooden versions) attracted the late 16th century's best architects, including Michelangelo, Palladio, and Sansovino, but the job went to the less famous but appropriately named Antonio da Ponte. His pragmatic design featured shop space and was high enough for galleys to pass beneath; it kept decoration and cost to a minimum at a time when the republic's coffers were low due to continual wars against the Turks and the opening of oceanic trade routes. Along the railing you'll enjoy one of the city's most famous views: the Grand Canal vibrant with boat traffic. Ⓥ *Rialto.*

⑳ **Santa Maria Gloriosa dei Frari.** This immense Gothic church of russet-color brick, completed in the 1400s after more than a century of work, is deliberately austere, befitting the Franciscan brothers' insistence on spirituality and poverty. However, *I Frari* (as it's known locally) contains some of the most brilliant paintings in any Venetian church. Visit the sacristy first, to see Giovanni Bellini's 1488 triptych *Madonna and Child with Saints* in all its mellow luminosity, painted for precisely this spot. The Corner Chapel on the other side of the chancel is graced by Bartolomeo Vivarini's 1474 altarpiece *St. Mark Enthroned and Saints John the Baptist, Jerome, Peter, and Nicholas,* of similar exquisite detail and color. There is also a fine sculpture of St. John the Baptist here by Jacopo Sansovino. You can see the rapid development of Venetian Renaissance painting by contrasting Bellini and Vivarini with the heroic energy of Titian's *Assumption,* over the main altar, painted only 30 years later. Unveiled in 1518, this work was not initially accepted by the church, precisely because of the innovative style and bright colors, especially Titian's trademark red, which would make it famous.

Fodor'sChoice
★

Titian's beautiful *Madonna di Ca' Pesaro,* in the left aisle, was modeled after his wife, who died in childbirth. The painting took almost 10 years to complete, and in it Titian totally disregarded the conventions of his time by moving the Virgin out of center frame and making the saints active participants. On the same side of the church look at the spooky, pyramid-shape monument to the sculptor Antonio Canova (1757–1822). Across the nave is a neoclassical 19th-century monument to Titian, executed by two of Canova's pupils. ✉ *Campo dei Frari, San Polo* ☎ *041/2728618, 041/2750462 Chorus* 🖾 *€2.50, €9 Chorus pass* 🕙 *Mon.–Sat. 9–6, Sun. 1–6* Ⓥ *San Tomà.*

> **need a break?**
>
> On a narrow passage between the Frari and San Rocco, **Gelateria Millevoglie** (a Thousand Desires ☎ 041/5244667) has pizza slices, calzones, and gelato so popular it backs up traffic. It's closed in December and January, but it's open seven days a week—10 AM to midnight in summer and until 9 PM October–March.

㉑ **Scuola Grande di San Rocco.** St. Rocco's popularity stemmed from his miraculous recovery from the plague and his care for fellow sufferers. Throughout the plague-filled Middle Ages, followers and donations abounded, and this elegant example of Venetian Renaissance architec-

San Polo
& Santa Croce

KEY

▲ *Vaporetto Stop*

ture was the result. Although it is bold and dramatic outside, its contents are even more stunning—a series of more than 60 paintings by Tintoretto. In 1564 Tintoretto edged out competition for a commission to decorate a ceiling by submitting not a sketch, but a finished work, which he moreover offered free of charge. *Moses Striking Water from the Rock, The Brazen Serpent,* and *The Fall of Manna* represent three afflictions—thirst, disease, and hunger—that San Rocco and later his brotherhood sought to relieve. ⊠ *Campo San Rocco, San Polo 3052* ☎ *041/5234864* ⊕ *www.scuolagrandesanrocco.it* ⊠ €*5.50; students up to 26* €*4; children up to 18 free if accompanied by parent* ⊙ *Mar. 28–Nov. 2, daily 9–5:30; Nov. 3–Mar. 27, daily 10–4; last entrance ½ hr before closing* Ⅴ *San Tomà.*

need a
break?

The bridge behind Scuola Grande di San Rocco leads to a bustling little student area of bars and restaurants. **Café Noir** (⊠ Calle Crosera, Dorsoduro 3805 ☎ 041/710925) has a good selection of sandwiches. It's open until 2 AM but is closed Sunday. **Pasticceria Tonolo** (⊠ Calle Crosera, Dorsoduro 3764 ☎ 041/5237209) has been fattening up Venetians since 1886. During Carnevale it's still the best place in town for *fritelle,* fried doughnuts (traditional raisin or cream-filled); during acqua alta, the staff dons rubber boots and

Venice's Scuola Days

An institution you'll inevitably encounter from Venice's glory days is the *scuola* (plural *scuole*). These weren't schools, as the word today translates, but an important network of institutions established by different social groups—enclaves of foreigners, tradesmen, followers of a particular saint, and parishioners.

For the most part secular despite their devotional activities, the scuole concentrated on charitable work, either helping their own membership or assisting the city's neediest citizens.

The tradesmen's and servants' scuole formed social security nets for elderly and disabled members. Wealthier scuole assisted orphans or provided dowries so poor girls could marry. By 1500, there were more than 200 major and minor scuole in Venice, some of which contributed substantially to arts and crafts guilds. The Republic encouraged their existence—the scuole kept strict records of the names and professions of contributors to the brotherhood, which helped when it came time to collect taxes.

keeps working. The place is closed on Monday, and there's no seating anytime.

Also Worth Seeing

⓳ **Campo San Polo.** Only Piazza San Marco is larger than this square, where not even the pigeons manage to look cozy, and the echo of children's voices bouncing off the surrounding palaces makes the space seem even more cavernous. Not long ago Campo San Polo hosted bull races, fairs, military parades, and packed markets, but now it only really comes alive on summer nights, when it hosts the city's outdoor cinema. The **Chiesa di San Polo** has been restored so many times that little remains of the original 9th-century church, and sadly, 19th-century alterations were so costly that the friars sold off many great paintings to pay bills. Though Giambattista Tiepolo is represented here, his work is outdone by 16 paintings of his son Giandomenico (1727–1804), including the *Stations of the Cross* in the oratory to the left of the entrance. The younger Tiepolo also created a series of expressive and theatrical renderings of the saints. Look for altarpieces by Tintoretto and Veronese that managed to escape auction. San Polo's bell tower remained unchanged through the centuries—don't miss the two lions guarding it, playing with a disembodied human head and a serpent. ⊠ *Campo San Polo* ☎ *041/2750462 Chorus* 🖼 *€2.50, €9 Chorus pass* ۞ *Mon.–Sat. 10–5, Sun. 1–5* Ⓥ *San Tomà.*

⓰ **Ca' Pesaro.** Baldassare Longhena's grand baroque palace is the beautifully restored home of two impressive collections. The **Galleria Internazionale d'Arte Moderna** has works by 19th- and 20th-century artists such as Klimt, Kandinsky, Matisse, and Miró. It also has a collection of representative works from Venice's Biennale art show that amounts to a panorama of 20th-century art. The **Museo Orientale** has a small but striking collection of oriental porcelains, musical instruments, arms,

and armor. ✉ *San Stae, Santa Croce 2076* ☎ *041/5240662 Galleria,*
041/5241173 Museo Orientale ⊙ *Apr.–Sept., Tues.–Sun. 10–6; Oct.–Mar.,*
Tues.–Sun. 10–5 🎟 *€5.50 includes both museums* Ⓥ *San Stae.*

⑱ San Giacomo dell'Orio. It was named after a laurel tree *(orio),* and today
trees give character to the square. Add benches and a fountain (with a
drinking bowl for dogs), and this pleasant, oddly shaped campo becomes
a welcoming place for friendly conversation, picnics, and neighborhood kids at play. Legend has it the **Chiesa di San Giacomo dell'Orio**
was founded in the 9th century on an island still populated by wolves.
The current church dates from 1225; its short unmatched Byzantine
columns survived renovation during the Renaissance, and the church
never lost the feel of an ancient temple sheltering beneath its 15th-cen-
tury ship's-keel roof. In the sanctuary, large marble crosses are surrounded
by a bevy of small medieval Madonnas. The altarpiece is *Madonna with*
Child and Saints (1546) by Lorenzo Lotto (1480–1556), and the sac-
risties contain works by Palma il Giovane (circa 1544–1628). ✉ *Campo*
San Giacomo dell'Orio, Santa Croce ☎ *041/2750462 Chorus* 🎟 *€2.50,*
€9 Chorus pass ⊙ *Mon.–Sat. 10–5, Sun. 1–5* Ⓥ *San Stae.*

⑮ San Giovanni Elemosinario. Storefronts make up the facade, and the altars were built by market guilds—poulterers, messengers, and fodder
merchants—at this church intimately bound to the Rialto Market. It's
as rich inside as it is simple outside. During San Giovanni Elemosinario's
restoration, workers stumbled upon a frescoed cupola by Pordenone
(1484–1539) that had been painted over centuries earlier. Don't miss
Titian's *St. John the Almsgiver* and Pordenone's *Sts. Catherine, Sebas-*
tian, and Roch, which in 2002 were returned after 30 years by the Gallerie dell'Accademia, a rare move for an Italian museum. ✉ *Rialto*
Ruga Vechia S. Giovanni ☎ *041/2750462 Chorus* 🎟 *€2.50, €9 Cho-*
rus pass ⊙ *Mon.–Sat. 10–5, Sun. 1–5* Ⓥ *San Silvestro or Rialto.*

⑰ San Stae. The most renowned Venetian painters and sculptors of the early
18th century—known as the Moderns—decorated this church with the
legacy left by Doge Alvise Mocenigo II, who's buried in the center aisle.
A broad sampling of these masters includes works by Tiepolo, Ricci,
Piazzetta, and Lazzarini. ✉ *Campo San Stae, Santa Croce* ☎ *041/*
2750462 Chorus 🎟 *€2.50, €9 Chorus pass* ⊙ *Mon.–Sat. 9–5, Sun.*
1–5 Ⓥ *San Stae.*

Castello & Cannaregio

Twice the size of tiny San Polo and Santa Croce, Castello and Cannaregio combined spread east to west from one end of Venice to the other.
From working-class shipbuilding neighborhoods to the world's first
ghetto, here you'll see a cross section of city life that's always existed beyond the palace walls. Churches that could make a Renaissance pope jeal-
ous await you, as does one of the Grand Canal's prettiest palaces, Ca'
d'Oro, but you'll also find detour options for leaving the crowds behind.

Visiting both sestieri involves a couple of hours of walking, even if you
never enter a building, and offers little chance to hop a boat and save
your legs. Some sights have restricted hours, making it virtually impos-

sible to see everything even in a full day. Your best bet is to choose a few sights as priorities, time your tour around their open hours, and then drop in at whatever others happen to be open as you're passing by. If you're touring on Friday, keep in mind that synagogues close at sunset.

The Main Attractions

Arsenale. The Venetian Republic never could have thrived without the Arsenale shipyard, which is said to have been founded in 1104 on twin islands. The immense facility that evolved was given the old Venetian dialect name *arzanà,* borrowed from the Arabic *darsina'a,* meaning "workshop." At times it employed as many as 16,000 *arsenalotti,* workers who were among the most respected shipbuilders in the world. (Dante immortalized these sweating men armed with pitch and boiling tar in his *Inferno.*) Their diligence was confirmed time and again—whether building 100 ships in 60 days to battle the Turks in Cyprus (1597) or completing one perfectly armed warship—start to finish—while King Henry III of France attended a banquet. The Arsenale's impressive Renaissance **gateway** (1460) is guarded by four lions, war booty of Francesco Morosini, who took the Peloponnese from the Turks in 1687. The 10-foot-tall lion on the left stood sentinel more than 2,000 years ago near Athens, and experts say its mysterious inscription is runic "graffiti" left by Viking mercenaries hired to suppress 11th-century revolts in Piraeus. If you look at the winged lion above the doorway, you'll notice that the Gospel at his paws is open but lacks the customary *Pax* inscription; praying for peace perhaps seemed inappropriate above a factory that manufactured weapons. The zone belongs to the Italian Navy and isn't regularly open to the public, but it opens for the Biennale and for Venice's festival of traditional boats, held every May. If you're here during those times, don't miss the chance for a look inside. ⊠ *Campo dell'Arsenale, Castello* Ⓥ *Arsenale.*

★ ㉕ **Ca' d'Oro.** This exquisite Venetian Gothic palace was once literally a "Golden House," when its marble traceries and ornaments were embellished with pure gold. Created in 1434 by the enamored patrician Marino Contarini for his wife, Ca' d'Oro became a love offering a second time when a 19th-century Russian prince gave it to Maria Taglioni, a celebrated classical dancer who collected palaces along the Grand Canal. The last proprietor, perhaps more taken with Venice than with any of his lovers, left Ca' d'Oro to the city, after having had it carefully restored and filled with antiquities, sculptures, and paintings that today make up the **Galleria Franchetti.** Besides Andrea Mantegna's celebrated *St. Sebastian* and other first-rate Venetian works, the Galleria Franchetti contains the type of fresco that once adorned the exteriors of Venetian buildings (commissioned by those who could not afford a marble facade). One such detached fresco displayed here was made by a young Titian for the (now grayish-white) facade of the Fondaco dei Tedeschi, now the main post office. ⊠ *Calle Ca' d'Oro, Cannaregio 3933* ☏ *041/5200345* 🎫 *€5, €11 includes Gallerie dell'Accademia and Museo Orientale* ⊙ *Tues.–Sun. 8:15–7:15, Mon. 8:15–2; last entry ½ hr before closing* Ⓥ *Ca' d'Oro.*

㉓ **Jewish Ghetto.** The neighborhood that gave the world the word *ghetto* is today a quiet warren of backstreets that is still home to Jewish institutions, a kosher restaurant, a rabbinical school, and five synagogues. Though Jews may have arrived earlier, the first synagogues weren't built and a cemetery wasn't founded until the Askenazim, or Eastern European Jews, came in the late 1300s. Dwindling coffers may have prompted the Republic to sell temporary visas to Jews, but over the centuries they were alternately tolerated and expelled. The Rialto commercial district, as vividly recounted in Shakespeare's *The Merchant of Venice,* depended on Jewish merchants and moneylenders for trade, and to help cover ever-increasing war expenses.

In 1516 relentless local opposition forced the Senate to confine Jews to an island in Cannaregio, named for its *geto* (foundry), which produced cannon. Gates at the entrance were locked at night, and boats patrolled the surrounding canals. The German accents of early residents changed "geto" into "ghetto." Jews were allowed only to lend money at low interest, operate pawnshops controlled by the government, trade in textiles, or practice medicine. Jewish doctors were highly respected and could leave the ghetto at any hour when on duty. Though ostracized, Jews were nonetheless safe in Venice, and in the 16th century the community grew considerably, with refugees from the Near East, southern and central Italy, Spain, and Portugal. The ghetto was allowed to expand twice, but it still had the city's densest population and consequently ended up with the city's tallest buildings (nine stories); notice the slanting apartment blocks on Campo del Ghetto Nuovo. Although the gates were pulled down after Napoléon's 1797 arrival, the Jews realized full freedom only in the late 19th century with the founding of the Italian state. On the eve of World War II there were about 1,500 Jews left in the ghetto: 247 were deported by the Nazis; eight returned.

The area has Europe's highest density of Renaissance-era synagogues, and visiting them is a unique cross-cultural experience. Though each is marked by the tastes of its individual builders, Venetian influence is evident throughout. Women's galleries resemble those of theaters from the same era, and some synagogues were decorated by artisans who were simultaneously active in local churches.

The small but well-arranged **Museo Ebraico** highlights centuries of Jewish culture with splendid silver Hanukkah lamps and torahs, and handwritten, beautifully decorated wedding contracts in Hebrew. Tours of the ghetto in Italian and English leave hourly from the museum. ⊠ *Campo del Ghetto Nuovo, Cannaregio 2902/b* ☎ *041/715359* ⊕ *www. museoebraico.it* 🎫 *Museum €3; museum and synagogues €8.50* ☉ *June–Sept., Sun.–Fri. 10–7; last tour 5:30; Oct.–May, Sun.–Fri. 10–5:30; last tour 4:30* Ⓥ *San Marcuola or Guglie.*

You might complete your circuit of Jewish Venice with a visit to the **Antico Cimitero Ebraico** (Ancient Jewish Cemetery) on the Lido, full of fascinating old tombstones half hidden by ivy and grass. The earliest grave dates from 1389; the cemetery remained in use until the late 18th century. ⊠ *Via Cipro, Lido* ☎ *041/715359* 🎫 *€8.50* ☉ *Tours Apr.–Oct., Sun. 2:30; call for arrangements* Ⓥ *Lido–S.M.E.*

★ ② **Santa Maria dei Miracoli.** Tiny yet perfectly proportioned, this early Renaissance gem is sheathed in marble and decorated inside with exquisite marble reliefs. Architect Pietro Lombardo (circa 1435–1515) miraculously compressed the building into its confined space, then created the illusion of greater size by varying the color of the exterior, adding extra pilasters on the building's canal side, and offsetting the arcade windows to make the arches appear deeper. The church was built in the 1480s to house *I Miracoli,* an image of the Virgin Mary that is said to perform miracles—look for it on the high altar. ⊠ *Campo Santa Maria Nova, Cannaregio* ☎ *041/2750462 Chorus* ⊠ *€2.50, €9 Chorus pass* ☉ *Mon.–Sat. 10–5, Sun. 1–5* Ⓥ *Rialto.*

★ ③ **Santi Giovanni e Paolo.** This massive Dominican church, commonly called San Zanipolo, contains a wealth of art. The 15th-century stained-glass window near the side entrance is breathtaking for its brilliant colors and beautiful figures, made from drawings by Bartolomeo Vivarini and Gerolamo Mocetto. The second official church of the Republic after San Marco, San Zanipolo is the Venetian equivalent of London's Westminster Abbey, with a great number of important people, including 25 doges, buried here. Artistic highlights include an outstanding polyptych by Giovanni Bellini (right aisle, second altar); Alvise Vivarini's *Christ*

Cannaregio

1

Carrying the Cross (sacrestia); and Lorenzo Lotto's *Charity of St. Antonino* (right transept). Don't miss the *Cappella del Rosario* (Rosary Chapel), off the left transept, built in the 16th century to commemorate the 1571 victory of Lepanto, in western Greece, when Venice led a combined European fleet to defeat the Turkish navy. The chapel was devastated by a fire in 1867 and restored in the early years of the 20th century with works from other churches, among them the sumptuous Veronese ceiling paintings. However quick your visit, don't miss the Pietro Mocenigo tomb to the right of the main entrance, a monument built by the ubiquitous Pietro Lombardo and his sons. ⊠ *Campo dei Santi Giovanni e Paolo, Castello* ☎ *041/5235913* 🖃 *€ 2.50* ◷ *7 AM–7 PM daily* Ⓥ *Fondamente Nuove or Rialto.*

need a break?

To satisfy your sweet tooth head for Campo Santa Marina and the family-owned and -operated **Didovich Pastry Shop** (☎ 041/5230017). It's a local favorite, especially for Carnevale-time *fritelle* (fried doughnuts). There is limited seating inside, but in the warmer months you can sit outside. **Bar ai Miracoli** (☎ 041/5231515) in Campo Santa Maria Nova is a good place to grab a quick bite and gaze across the canal at Maria dei Miracoli, Lombardo's miracle in marble.

Also Worth Seeing

26 **Gesuiti.** Extravagantly baroque, this 18th-century church completely abandons classical Renaissance straight lines in favor of flowing, twisting forms. Its interior walls resemble brocade drapery, and only touching will convince skeptics that rather than paint, the green-and-white walls are inlaid marble. Over the first altar on the left the *Martyrdom of St. Lawrence* is a dramatic example of Titian's feeling for light and movement. ⊠ *Campo dei Gesuiti, Cannaregio* ☎ *041/5286579* ⊘ *Daily 10–noon and 4–6* Ⓥ *Fondamente Nuove.*

35 **Museo Storico Navale** (Museum of Naval History). The boat collection here includes scale models such as the doges' ceremonial *Bucintoro,* and full-size boats such as Peggy Guggenheim's private gondola complete with romantic *felze* (cabin). There's a range of old galley and military pieces, and also a large collection of seashells. ⊠ *Campo San Biagio, Castello 2148* ☎ *041/5200276* ▨ *€1.55* ⊘ *Weekdays 8:45–1:30, Sat. 8:45–1* Ⓥ *Arsenale.*

31 **Ospedaletto.** This 16th-century "little hospital" was one of four church foundling homes that each had an orchestra and choir of orphans. Entering through **Santa Maria dei Derelitti** (St. Mary of the Destitute) you'll see a large gallery built for the young musicians. The orphanage is now a home for the elderly; its beautiful 18th-century **Sala della Musica** (Music Room) is the only one of its kind to survive. On the far wall the fresco by Jacopo Guarana (1720–1808) depicts Apollo, god of music, surrounded by the orphan musicians and their maestro, Pasquale Anfossi. ⊠ *Calle Barbaria delle Tole, Castello 6691* ☎ *041/2719012* ▨ *€2* ⊘ *Thurs.–Sat. 3:30–6:30* Ⓥ *Fondamente Nuove or Rialto.*

22 **Palazzo Labia.** Once the home of 18th-century Venice's showiest family, this palace is now the Venetian headquarters of the Italian media giant RAI—modern broadcasting goes baroque. In the **Tiepolo Room,** the Labia's gorgeous ballroom, the final flowering of Venetian painting is seen in Giambattista Tiepolo's playful frescoes of Antony and Cleopatra among dwarfs and Barbary pirates. You have to call ahead to arrange a visit here. ⊠ *Campo San Geremia, Cannaregio 275* ☎ *041/781277* ▨ *Free* ⊘ *Wed.–Fri. 3–4* Ⓥ *Ferrovia.*

24 **Palazzo Vendramin-Calergi.** This Renaissance classic with an imposing carved frieze is the work of Mauro Codussi (1440–1504). You can see some of its interior by dropping into the **Casinò di Venezia.** Fans of Richard Wagner (1813–83) might enjoy visiting the **Sala di Wagner,** the room (separate from the casino) in which the composer died. Though rather plain, it's loaded with music memorabilia. ⊠ *Cannaregio 2040* ☎ *041/5297111, 041/2760407 Fri. AM to reserve Wagner Room tours* ▨ *€10 casino, tour suggested €5 donation* ⊘ *Slots 2:45 PM–2:30 AM, tables 3:30 PM–2:30 AM Wagner Room Sat. AM by appointment* Ⓥ *San Marcuola.*

29 **Querini-Stampalia.** The art collection at this Renaissance palace includes Giovanni Bellini's *Presentation in the Temple* and Sebastiano Ricci's triptych *Dawn, Afternoon, and Evening.* Portraits of newlywed Francesco Querini and Paola Priuli were left unfinished on the death of Giacomo

Let's Get Lost

CLOSE UP

GETTING AROUND VENICE presents some unusual problems: the city's layout has few straight lines; house numbering seems nonsensical; and the sestieri (six districts) of San Marco, Cannaregio, Castello, Dorsoduro, Santa Croce, and San Polo all duplicate each other's street names. The numerous vaporetto lines can be bewildering, and often the only option for getting where you want to go is to walk. Yellow signs, posted on many busy corners, point toward the major landmarks—San Marco, Rialto, Accademia, etc.—but don't count on finding such markers once you're deep into residential neighborhoods. Even buying a good map at a newsstand—the kind showing all street names and vaporetto routes—

won't necessarily keep you from getting lost.

Fortunately, as long as you maintain your patience, getting lost in Venice can be a pleasure. For one thing, being lost is a sign that you've escaped the tourist throngs. And although you might not find the Titian masterpiece you'd set out to see, instead you could wind up coming across an ageless bacaro or a quirky shop that turns out to be the highlight of your afternoon. Opportunities for such serendipity abound. Keep in mind that the city is nothing if not self-contained: sooner or later, perhaps with the help of a patient native, you can rest assured you'll regain your bearings.

Palma il Vecchio (1480–1528); note the groom's hand and the bride's dress. Original 18th-century furniture and stuccowork are a fitting background for Pietro Longhi's portraits. Nearly 70 works by Gabriele Bella (1730–99) capture scenes of Venetian street life. Admission Friday and Saturday includes concerts with antique instruments at 5 and 8:30. ⊠ *Campo Santa Maria Formosa, Castello 5252* ☎ *041/2711411* ⊕ *www.querinistampalia.it* ⊠ €6 ☉ *Tues.–Thurs. and Sun. 10–6, Fri. and Sat. 10–10* Ⓥ *San Zaccaria.*

㉝ San Francesco della Vigna (St. Francis of the Vineyard). Legend says this is where an angel awakened St. Mark the Evangelist with the famous words, "Pax tibi Marce Evangelista meus" (Peace to you, Mark, my Evangelist), which became the motto of the Venetian Republic. The land was given in 1253 to the Franciscans, who kept the vineyard but replaced the ancient church. Bring some €.20 coins to light up the Antonio Vivarini (circa 1415–84) triptych of Sts. Girolamo, Bernardino da Siena, and Ludovico, which hangs to your right as you enter the main door, and Giovanni Bellini's *Madonna with Saints* inside the Cappella Santa. Antonio da Negroponte's glittering gold *Madonna Adoring the Child*, near the side door, is an inspiring work of the late 15th century. Here you'll see the transition from formal Gothic rigidity to naturalistic Renaissance composition and detailed decoration. Two cloisters open out from the left aisle, paved entirely with VIP tombstones. ⊠ *Campo San Francesco della Vigna, Castello* ☎ *041/5206102* ⊠ *Free* ☉ *Daily 8–12:30 and 3–7* Ⓥ *Celestia.*

36 San Pietro di Castello. This church's stark campanile, the first in Venice built from marblelike Istrian stone, stands out against the picturesque, workaday slips along the Canale di San Pietro and the Renaissance cloister, which for years was a squatters colony. The Veneti settled on the island where the church is located years

before Venice was officially founded, but today it's a sleepy, almost forgotten place, with little to suggest that for 1,000 years the church was Venice's cathedral—until the Basilica di San Marco superseded it in 1807. The interior has some minor 17th-century art and San Pietro's ancient *cattedra* (throne). ⊠ *Campo San Pietro, Castello* ☎ *041/2750462 Chorus* 🖃 *€2.50, €9 Chorus pass* ⊗ *Mon.–Sat. 10–5, Sun. 1–5* Ⓥ *San Pietro di Castello or Giardini.*

28 Santa Maria Formosa. Guided by his vision of a beautiful Madonna, 7th-century St. Magno is said to have followed a small white cloud and built a church where it settled. Gracefully white, the marble building you see today dates from 1492, built by Mauro Codussi on an older foundation. The interior is a blend of Renaissance decoration, a Byzantine cupola, barrel vaults, and narrow-columned screens. Of interest are two fine paintings: *Our Lady of Mercy* by Bartolomeo Vivarini (1415–84) and *Santa Barbara* by Palma il Vecchio. The surrounding square bustles with sidewalk cafés and a produce market on weekday mornings. ⊠ *Campo Santa Maria Formosa, Castello* ☎ *041/5234645, 041/2750462 Chorus* 🖃 *€2.50, €9 Chorus pass* ⊗ *Mon.–Sat. 10–5, Sun. 1–5* Ⓥ *Rialto.*

32 Scuola di San Giorgio degli Schiavoni. Founded in 1451 by the Dalmatian community, this small scuola was, and still is, a social and cultural center for migrants from what is now Croatia. It's dominated by one of Italy's most beautiful rooms, lavishly yet harmoniously decorated with the *teleri* (large canvases) of Vittore Carpaccio (circa 1465–1525). A lifelong Venice resident, Carpaccio painted legendary and religious figures against backgrounds of Venetian architecture. Here he focused on saints especially venerated in Dalmatia: St. George, St. Tryphone, and St. Jerome. He combined observation with fantasy, a sense of warm color with a sense of humor (don't miss the priests fleeing St. Jerome's lion, or the body parts in the dragon's lair). ⊠ *Calle dei Furlani, Castello 3259/a* ☎ *041/5228828* 🖃 *€3* ⊗ *Apr.–Oct., Tues.–Sat. 9:30–12:30 and 3:30–6, Sun. 9:30–12:30; Nov.–Mar., Tues.–Sat. 10–12:30 and 3–6, Sun. 10–12:30* Ⓥ *Arsenale/San Zaccaria.*

San Giorgio Maggiore & the Giudecca

Beckoning travelers across St. Mark's Basin, sparkling white through the mist, is the island of San Giorgio Maggiore, separated by a small channel from the Giudecca. A tall brick campanile on that distant bank perfectly complements the Campanile of San Marco. Beneath it looms the stately dome of one of Venice's greatest churches, San Giorgio Maggiore, the creation of Andrea Palladio.

You can reach San Giorgio Maggiore via vaporetto Line 82 from San Zaccaria. The next three stops on the line take you to the Giudecca. The island's past may be shrouded in mystery, but today it's about as down to earth as you can get and one of the city's few remaining neighborhoods that feels truly Venetian.

A half day should be plenty of time to visit the area. Allow about a half hour to see each of the churches, and an hour or two to look around the Giudecca.

The Main Attractions

Giudecca. The island's name is something of a mystery. It may come from a possible 14th-century Jewish settlement, or because 9th-century nobles condemned to *giudicato* (exile) were sent here. It became a pleasure garden for wealthy Venetians during the Republic's long and luxurious decline, but today, like Cannaregio, it's largely working class. The Giudecca provides spectacular views of Venice and is becoming increasingly gentrified. While here, visit the **Santissimo Redentore** church, designed by Palladio and built to commemorate a plague. The third weekend in July it's the site of Venetians' favorite festival, Redentore, featuring boats, fireworks, and outdoor feasting. Thanks to several bridges, you can walk the entire length of the Giudecca's promenade, relaxing at one of several restaurants or just taking in the lively atmosphere. Accommodations run the gamut from youth hostels to the city's most exclusive hotel, Cipriani. ⊠ *Fondamenta San Giacomo, Giudecca* ☎ *041/5231415, 041/2750462 Chorus* ✆ *€2.50, €9 Chorus pass* ☉ *Mon.–Sat. 10–5, Sun. 1–5* Ⓥ *Redentore.*

San Giorgio Maggiore. There's been a church on this island since the 8th century, with a Benedictine monastery added in the 10th century (closed to the public). Today's refreshingly airy and simply decorated church of brick and white marble was begun in 1566 by Palladio and displays his architectural hallmarks of mathematical harmony and classical influence. *The Last Supper* and the *Gathering of Manna,* two of Tintoretto's later works, line the chancel. To the right of the entrance hangs *The Adoration of the Shepherds* by Jacopo Bassano (1517–92); his affection for his foothills home, Bassano del Grappa, is evident in the bucolic subjects and terra-firma colors he chooses. The monks are happy to show Carpaccio's *St. George and the Dragon,* hanging in a private room, if they have time. The campanile is so tall that it was struck by lightning in 1993. Take the elevator to the top for some of the finest views in town. ⊠ *Isola di San Giorgio Maggiore* ☎ *041/5227827* ✆ *Church free, campanile €3* ☉ *Daily 7:30–12:30 and 2:30–6* Ⓥ *San Giorgio.*

Islands of the Lagoon

The perfect vacation from your Venetian vacation is an escape to Murano, Burano, and sleepy Torcello, the islands of the northern lagoon. Hitting all the sights on all the islands takes a full day. If you limit yourself to Murano and San Michele, a half day will suffice.

Torcello offers greenery, breathing space, and picnic opportunities (remember to pack lunch). Burano is a toy town of houses painted in a riot of colors—blue, yellow, pink, ochre, and dark red. Visitors still love to shop here for "Venetian" lace, even though the vast majority of it is machine-made in Taiwan. Murano is renowned for its glass, but also notorious for the high-pressure sales on its factory tours, even those organized by top hotels. Vaporetto connections to Murano aren't difficult, and for the price of a boat ticket you'll buy your freedom and more time to explore. The Murano "guides" herding new arrivals follow a rotation so that factories take turns giving tours, but you can avoid the hustle by just walking away.

In summer San Zaccaria is connected to Murano by express vaporetto Line 5; the trip takes 25 minutes. In winter the local Line 41 takes about 45 minutes. The boat leaves San Zaccaria (in front of the Savoia e Jolanda hotel) every 20 minutes, circling the east end of Venice and stopping at Fondamente Nuove before making the five-minute hop to the San Michele island cemetery and then heading on to Murano. To see glassblowing, get off at Colonna; the Museo stop will put you near the Museo Vetrario.

Line LN goes from Fondamente Nuove direct to Murano, Burano, and Torcello every 30 minutes, and the full trip takes 45 minutes each way. To get to Burano and Torcello from Murano, pick up Line LN at the Faro stop (Murano's lighthouse), which runs to Burano before continuing on to Torcello, only five minutes away.

The Main Attractions

★ ❸❾ **Burano.** Cheerfully painted houses line the canals of this quiet village where lace making rescued a faltering fishing-based economy centuries ago. As you walk the 100 yards from the dock to Piazza Galuppi, the main square, you pass stall after stall of lace vendors. These good-natured ladies won't press you with a hard sell, but don't expect precise product information or great bargains—real handmade Burano lace costs $1,000 to $2,000 for a 10-inch doily.

The **Museo del Merletto** (Lace Museum) lets you marvel at the intricacies of Burano's lace making. It's also a skills center—more sewing circle than school—where on weekdays you'll usually find women carrying on the tradition. They sometimes have authentic pieces for sale privately. ✉ *Piazza Galuppi 187* ☎ *041/730034* ✐ *€4, €6 with Museo Vetrario, €15.50 Musei Civici pass* ☉ *Apr.–Oct., Wed.–Mon. 10–5; Nov.–Mar., Wed.–Mon. 10–4* Ⓥ *Burano.*

☾ ❸❽ **Murano.** As in Venice, bridges here link a number of small islands, which are dotted with houses that once were workmen's cottages. In the 13th century the Republic, concerned about fire hazard, moved its glassworks

Venetian Lagoon

Mestre
Aeroporto Marco Polo
Malcontenta
Torcello **40**
39 Burano
38 Murano
PUNTA SABBIONI
Cavallino
Punta Sabbioni
37
San Michele
S.M.ELISABETTA
Venice
Lido
Malamocco
Alberoni
Golfo di Venezia
Laguna Veneta
Pellestrina
Chioggia

0 _____ 4 miles
0 _____ 6 km

to Murano, and today you can visit the factories and watch glass being made. Many of them line the Fondamenta dei Vetrai, the canal-side walkway leading from the Colonna vaporetto landing.

Before you reach Murano's Grand Canal (250 meters from the landing) you'll pass **Chiesa di San Pietro Martire.** Reconstructed in the 16th century, it houses Giovanni Bellini's *Madonna and Child* and Veronese's *St. Jerome.* ✉ *Fondamenta dei Vetrai* ☎ *041/739704* 🕙 *Mon.–Sat. 9–Noon and 3–6, Sun. 3–6* Ⓥ *Colonna.*

The collection at the **Museo Vetrario** (Glass Museum) ranges from priceless antiques to only slightly less expensive modern pieces. You'll see authentic Venetian styles and patterns, including the famous Barovier wedding cup (1470–80). ✉ *Fondamenta Giustinian 8* ☎ *041/739586* 🎫 *€4, €6 with Museo del Merletto, €15.50 Musei Civici pass* 🕙 *Apr.–Oct., Thurs.–Tues. 10–5; Nov.–Mar., Thurs.–Tues. 10–4; last tickets sold ½ hr before closing* Ⓥ *Museo.*

The **Basilica dei Santi Maria e Donato,** just past the glass museum, is among the first churches founded by the lagoon's original inhabitants. The elaborate mosaic pavement includes the date 1140; its ship's-keel roof and Veneto-Byzantine columns add to the semblance of an ancient temple. ✉ *Fondamenta Giustinian* ☎ *041/739056* 💳 *Free* 🕒 *Daily 8–noon and 4–7* Ⓥ *Museo.*

★ ㊵ **Torcello.** In their flight from barbarians 1,500 years ago, the first Venetians landed here, prospering even after many left to found the city of Venice. As malaria took its toll and the island's wool manufacturing was priced out of the market, Torcello became a ghost town. In the 16th century there were 10 churches and 20,000 inhabitants; today you'll be lucky to see one of the island's 16 permanent residents.

Santa Maria Assunta was built in the 11th century, and Torcello's wealth at the time is evident in the church's high-quality Byzantine mosaics. The massive *Last Judgment* shows sinners writhing in pain, while opposite, above the altar, the Madonna looks calmly down from her field of gold. Ask to see the inscription dated 639 and a sample of mosaic pavement from the original church. The adjacent **Santa Fosca** church, added when the body of the saint arrived in 1011, is still used for religious services. It's worth making the climb up the adjacent **Campanile** for an incomparable view of the lagoon wetlands. ✉ *Torcello* ☎ *041/730119* 💳 *Santa Maria Assunta €3, Campanile €3* 🕒 *Mar.–Oct., daily 10:30–6; Nov.–Feb., daily 10–5* Ⓥ *Torcello.*

need a break? | **Locanda Cipriani** (☎ *041/730150*), closed Tuesday and January, is famous for good food and its connection to Ernest Hemingway, who often came to Torcello seeking solitude. Today the restaurant (not to be confused with the Giudecca's Cipriani hotel) is busy, with well-heeled customers speeding in for lunch (dinner also on weekends). Dining is pricey, but you can relax in the garden with just a glass of Prosecco.

Also Worth Seeing

㊲ **San Michele.** This cypress-lined island is home to the pretty Renaissance church of **San Michele in Isola**—and to some of Venice's most illustrious deceased. The church was designed by Codussi; the graves include those of poet Ezra Pound (1885–1972), impresario and art critic Sergey Diaghilev (1872–1929), and composer Igor Stravinsky (1882–1971). Surrounded by the living sounds of Venice's lagoon, this would seem the perfect final resting place. However, these days newcomers are exhumed after 10 years and transferred to a less grandiose location. ☎ *041/7292811* 💳 *Free* 🕒 *Apr.–Sept., daily 7:30–6; Oct.–Mar., daily 7:30–4* Ⓥ *San Michele.*

WHERE TO EAT

Updated by
Jeff Booth

The general standard of Venetian restaurants suffers from the effects of mass tourism, but it is still possible to eat well in Venice at moderate prices. Most of the city's better restaurants change menus daily or frequently depending on the availability of seasonal ingredients.

It's always a good idea to reserve your table or have your hotel concierge do it for you. Dining hours are limited, starting at 12:30 or 1 for lunch and ending at 2:30 or 3, when restaurants close for the afternoon, opening up again to start serving about 7:30 and closing again at 11 or midnight on weekend nights and earlier (10–11) on weekdays and in the low season. Most close one day a week and are also likely to close without notice for vacation or renovation. Few have signs on the outside, so when the metal blinds are shut tight you can't tell a closed restaurant from a closed TV-repair shop.

Restaurants usually display a menu in the window so you can check out what's available before committing yourself. Also check the (very) fine print: most places add a cover charge of €1.50–€2 per person, often listed as a charge for bread. Some also add a service charge of 10%–15%. In such cases tipping is unwarranted. A sign of changing times is a law, in effect as of 2005, banning smoking in all public restaurants; most establishments comply but some do not.

	WHAT IT COSTS In euros				
	$$$$	**$$$**	**$$**	**$**	**¢**
AT DINNER	over €22	€16–€22	€11–€16	€7–€11	under €7

Prices are for a second course *(secondo piatto)*.

Cannaregio

$$$ ✕ **A la Vecia Cavana.** Since they took over in 2004, the owners have focused on presenting a highly refined menu. The young, talented kitchen staff creates winning Italian and Venetian dishes such as *filetti di pesce a cottura differenziata* (fish fillet, cooked on one side and quickly seared on the other), tender baby cuttlefish, and, among desserts, *gelato al basilico* (basil ice cream). The 18th-century *cavana* (boathouse) maintains its original low columns, arches, and brick walls, but has been decorated with contemporary flair. ⊠ *Rio Terà SS. Apostoli, Cannaregio 4624* ☎ *041/5287106* ⊟ *AE, DC, MC, V* ⊙ *Closed Mon., 2 wks in Jan., and Aug.* Ⓥ *Rialto/Ca' d'Oro.*

★ **$$–$$$** ✕ **Vini da Gigio.** A friendly, family-run trattoria on the quay side of a canal just off the Strada Nova, da Gigio is very popular with Venetians and other visiting Italians, who appreciate the affable service, the well-prepared homemade pasta, fish, and meat dishes, the imaginative and varied wine cellar, and the high-quality draft wine. It's good for a simple lunch at tables in the barroom. ⊠ *Fondamenta de la Chiesa, Cannaregio 3628/a* ☎ *041/5285140* ⊟ *DC, MC, V* ⊙ *Closed Mon., Tues., 2 wks Jan., and 3 wks Aug.* Ⓥ *Ca' d'Oro.*

$–$$ ✕ **Algiubagiò.** A waterfront table is relatively affordable here on Venice's largely forgotten northern Fondamente Nuove. Enjoy the summer shade and breeze off the water as you gaze toward San Michele and Murano; you can even see the Dolomites on a clear day. It's an excellent lunch choice, with big, creative salads—such as lettuce, arugula, tuna, prawns, capers, and onions—that are meals in themselves. There are also pasta dishes with freshly made seasonal sauces, pizzas, and main courses. The young, friendly staff serves ice cream, drinks, and snacks all day. A table here is worth the walk. ⊠ *Fondamente Nuove, Cannaregio 5039* ☎ *041/ 5236084* ⊟ *MC, V* Ⓜ *Fondamenta Nuove.*

$–$$ ✕ **Anice Stellato.** Hidden away on one of the most romantic fondamente of Cannaregio, this family-run bacaro-trattoria is the place to stop for fairly priced, great-tasting food in a part of town that doesn't teem with restaurants. The space has plenty of character: narrow columns rise from the colorful mosaiclike floor, dividing the room into cozy booths. Traditional Venetian fare is enriched with such offerings as *carpacci di pesce* (thin slices of raw tuna, swordfish, or salmon dressed with olive oil and fragrant herbs), tagliatelle with king prawns and zucchini flowers, and several tasty fish stews. Meat dishes are also served, including a tender beef fillet stewed in Barolo wine with potatoes. ⊠ *Fondamenta de la Sensa, Cannaregio 3272* ☎ *041/720744* ⊟ *AE, DC, MC, V* ◷ *Closed Mon. and Tues., and Aug.* Ⓥ *S. Alvise.*

★ $ ✕ **Alla Vedova.** This warm trattoria not far from the Ca' d'Oro (it's also known as Trattoria Ca' d'Oro) was opened as a bacaro by the owner's great-grandparents. A Venetian terrazzo floor, old marble counter, and rustic furnishings lend a pleasant authenticity that's matched by the food and service. Cicheti include tender *seppie roste* (grilled cuttlefish), *polpette* (meatballs), and baccalà mantecato. The house winter pasta is the *pastisso de radicio rosso* (lasagna with sausage, radicchio, and béchamel sauce). In spring the chef switches to pastisso *de asparagi* (with asparagus). ⊠ *Calle del Pistor, Cannaregio 3912* ☎ *041/5285324* ⊟ *No credit cards* ◷ *Closed Thurs. No lunch Sun.* Ⓥ *Ca' d'Oro.*

Castello

$$$$ ✕ **Do Leoni.** The Two Lions, in the Hotel Londra Palace, is a sumptuous candlelit setting in which to sample Venetian and other Italian cuisine. The kitchen turns out creative, nontraditional dishes like millet soup with bacon; the seven-course tasting menu utilizes such non-Italian ingredients as vanilla and ginger. The summer terrace occupies a good portion of the Riva. ⊠ *Riva degli Schiavoni, Castello 4171* ☎ *041/5200533* ▵ *Reservations essential* ⊟ *AE, DC, MC, V* Ⓥ *San Zaccaria.*

★ $$$–$$$$ ✕ **Alle Testiere.** A strong local following can make it tough to get one of the 22 seats at this tiny trattoria near Campo Santa Maria Formosa. With its decidedly unglamorous ceiling fans, the place feels as informal as a bistro (or a saloon); the food, however, is much more sophisticated. Chef Bruno Gavagnin's dishes stand out for lightness and balance: try the *gnocchetti con moscardini* (little gnocchi with tender baby octopus) or the linguine with *coda di rospo* (monkfish), or inquire about the carpaccio of the day. The well-assembled wine list is particularly strong on local whites. ⊠ *Calle del Mondo Novo, Castello 5801* ☎ *041/5227220* ▵ *Reservations essential* ⊟ *MC, V* ◷ *Closed Sun. and Mon., 3 wks Jan. and Feb., 4 wks July and Aug.* Ⓥ *Rialto/San Zaccaria.*

★ $–$$$ ✕ **Corte Sconta.** You're close to seafood heaven at this firm favorite on the Venetian dining scene. Simple wooden tables are arranged around an open courtyard with outdoor seating in summer. You could make a meal of the seafood antipasti alone, but you'd miss out on such delights as spaghetti *neri alle capesante e zucchine* (cuttlefish-ink pasta with scallops and zucchini) and *vongole veraci spadellate allo zenzero* (clams sauteed in ginger). The house dessert is a warm zabaglione with Venetian cookies, and the house pour is a smooth, still Prosecco, backed up by a good range of bottled wines. ⊠ *Calle del Pestrin, Castello 3886* ☎ *041/5227024* ⌕ *Reservations essential* ⊟ *MC, V* ۞ *Closed Sun. and Mon., 4 wks Jan. and Feb., 4 wks July and Aug.* Ⅴ *Arsenale.*

¢–$ ✕ **Da Remigio.** Locals almost always fill this place, especially on the weekend (you'll need to book ahead), and it's easy to see why: the food is good, the service prompt, and the atmosphere lively. The *canocchio bollite* (boiled, then chilled, shredded mantis shrimp) is a perfect starter, particularly when paired with an effervescent local white wine. Though the second course is strong on fish, Da Remigio also turns out respectable nonfish dishes such as the spaghetti *con porcini* (with mushrooms) and grilled meats. ⊠ *Salizzada dei Greci, Castello 3416* ☎ *041/5230089* ⌕ *Reservations essential* ⊟ *AE, DC, MC, V* ۞ *Closed Tues., 2 wks July and Aug., and 4 wks Dec. and Jan. No dinner Mon.* Ⅴ *Arsenale.*

Dorsoduro

$$$–$$$$ ✕ **Ai Gondolieri.** If you're tired of fish, this is the place to come, as meat and food of the mainland are menu mainstays. Despite the tourist-trap name, it's a favorite with Venetians. Feast on *filetto di maiale con castraure* (pork fillet with baby artichokes), duck breast with apple and sweet onion, or more traditional dishes from the Veneto hills such as horse meat and game, gnocchi, and polenta. The wine list is above average in quality and variety. ⊠ *Fondamenta dell'Ospedaletto, Dorsoduro 366* ☎ *041/5286396* ⊟ *AE, DC, MC, V* ۞ *Closed Tues. No lunch July and Aug.* Ⅴ *Accademia.*

★ $$–$$$ ✕ **Avogaria.** In terms of both food and architecture, ultrafashionable Avogaria lends modern flavor to the Venice restaurant scene. The clean, elegant design of the dining room and garden leaves no doubt that here, you're in the Venice of the present, not the past. The cuisine is Pugliese (from the region in the heel of Italy's boot); highlights among the primi include *orecchiette* (small, round pasta) with turnip tops, and zucchini *involtini* (roll-ups) made with fresh stracciatella cheese. Pugliese cooking, like Venetian, reveres fresh seafood, and you can taste this sensibility in the slow-cooked, sesame-encrusted tuna steak. ⊠ *Calle Avogaria, Dorsoduro 1629* ☎ *041/2960491* ⊟ *AE, DC, MC, V* ۞ *Closed Tues.*

★ $$ ✕ **La Bitta.** The decor is more discreet, the dining hours longer, and the service friendlier and more efficient here than in many small restaurants in Venice—and the creative nonfish menu is a temptation at every course. You can start with a light salad of Treviso radicchio and crispy bacon, followed by smoked-beef carpaccio or *gnocchetti ubriachi al Montasio* (small marinated gnocchi with Montasio cheese). Then choose from secondi such as lamb chops with thyme, *anatra in pevarada* (duck in a pepper sauce), or Irish Angus fillet steak. Secondi are served with vegetables, which helps bring down the price. The restaurant is open only for dinner, but serves much later than most, continuously from 6:30 to 11. ⊠ *Calle Lunga San Barnaba, Dorsoduro 2753/A* ☎ *041/5230531* ⊟ No *credit cards* ۞ *Closed Sun. No lunch.* Ⅴ *Ca' Rezzonico.*

$–$$ ✕ **Pizzeria al Profeta.** Though Pizzeria al Profeta offers more than 100 types of pizza, their real strength is massive portions of roast and grilled meats and, on occasion, fresh fish. Two or three people can split the baked pie filled with Angus beef, porcini mushrooms, and radichio. For a wonderfully medieval feeling, sit at a wooden table in the spacious, simple garden and use both hands to tear into a large leg of lamb. Sharing an ample dish can make this a great value. ✉ *Calle Lunga San Barnaba, Dorsoduro 2671* ☎ *041/5237466* 🖃 *MC, V.*

$ ✕ **Ai 4 Feri.** The paper tablecloths and cozy, laid-back ambience are all part of this small restaurant's charm. The menu varies according to what's fresh that day; imaginative combinations of ingredients in the primi— herring and sweet peppers, salmon and radicchio, giant shrimp and broccoli (with pumpkin gnocchi)—are the norm. A meal here followed by after-dinner drinks at Campo Santa Margherita, a five-minute walk away, makes for a lovely evening. The kitchen closes early on weekdays. ✉ *Calle Lunga San Barnaba, Dorsoduro 2754/a* ☎ *041/5206978* 🖃 *No credit cards* ☉ *Closed Sun. and June* Ⓥ *Ca' Rezzonico.*

San Marco

$$$$ ✕ **Al Graspo de Ua.** Opened in the 19th century as a small osteria, the "Bunch of Grapes" became the meeting place of artists and movie stars back in the 1960s. Today it serves a faithful clientele of wealthy Italians. The decor is a miscellany of plants, sculpture, candlelight, and paintings set against brick and white-stucco walls. The owner, Lucio Zanon, speaks fluent English and will introduce you to a wide-ranging menu of fresh pastas, seasonal risottos, and meat and seafood. A treat in late spring is the thick white asparagus from Bassano, which, with a couple of fried eggs, is eaten as a main course. Desserts are all homemade. ✉ *Calle dei Bombaseri, San Marco 5094* ☎ *041/5223647* 🖃 *AE, DC, MC, V* ☉ *Closed Mon. and 1 wk in Jan.* Ⓥ *Rialto.*

¢ ✕ **Enoteca al Volto.** Just steps away from the Rialto Bridge, this bar has been around since 1936; the fine cicheti and primi have a lot to do with its staying power. Two small, dark rooms with wooden tables and chairs are the backdrop for the enjoyment of simple fare. The place prides itself on its considerable wine list of both Italian and foreign vintages; if you stick to the *panini* (sandwiches) and a cicheto or two, you'll eat well for relatively little. If you opt for one of the primi of the day, the price category goes up a notch. ✉ *Calle Cavalli, San Marco 4081* ☎ *041/ 5228945* 🖃 *No credit cards* ☉ *Closed Sun.* Ⓥ *Rialto.*

San Polo

★ $$$$ ✕ **Osteria da Fiore.** Tucked away on a little calle off the top of Campo San Polo, Da Fiore is a favorite among high-end diners for its superbly prepared Venetian cuisine and refined yet relaxed atmosphere. A superlative seafood lunch or dinner here might include delicate hors d'oeuvres of moeche, scallops, and tiny octopus, followed by a succulent risotto or pasta *con scampi e radicchio* (with shrimp and radicchio), and a perfectly cooked main course of *rombo* (turbot) or *tagliata di tonno* (tuna steak). A jacket is not required, but is highly recommended. ✉ *Calle*

EATING WELL IN VENICE

Venetian cuisine is based on seafood—*granseola* (crab), *moeche* (soft-shell crab), and *seppie* or *seppioline* (cuttlefish) are all prominently featured, and trademark dishes include *sarde in saor* (fried sardines with olive oil, onions, pine nuts, and raisins) and *baccalà mantecato* (cod creamed with milk and olive oil). When served whole, fish is usually priced by the *etto* (100 grams, about ¼ pound) and can be quite expensive. Antipasti may take the form of a seafood salad, prosciutto, or pickled vegetables. As a first course, Venetians favor risotto, the creamy rice dish, prepared with vegetables or shellfish. Pasta, too, is paired with seafood sauces: *pasticcio di pesce* is pasta baked with fish, usually baccalà, and *bigoli* is a strictly local pasta shaped like short, thick spaghetti, usually served with *nero di seppia* (squid-ink sauce). A classic first course is *pasta e fagioli* (thick bean soup with pasta). Polenta (creamy cornmeal) is an-

other pillar of regional cooking; it's often served with *fegato alla veneziana* (calf's liver and onions).

Though it originated on the mainland, tiramisu is Venice's favorite dessert, a heavenly concoction of mascarpone (a rich, soft double-cream cheese), espresso, chocolate, and *savoiardi* (ladyfingers). Local wines are the dry white Tocai and Pinot Grigio from the Friuli region and bubbly white Prosecco, a naturally fermented sparkling wine that is a shade less dry. Popular red wines include merlot, cabernet, raboso, and refosco. You can sample all of these in Venice's *bacari* (little watering holes), a great Venetian tradition. For centuries, locals have gathered at these neighborhood spots to chat and have a glass of wine (known as an *ombra* in Venetian dialect) accompanied by *cicchetti* (snacks such as marinated fish, deep-fried vegetables, and meatballs), often substantial enough for a light meal.

del Scaleter, San Polo 2202 ☎ 041/721308 ⚴ *Reservations essential* ☲ *AE, DC, MC, V* ☺ *Closed Sun. and Mon., Aug., and Dec. 24–Jan. 15* Ⓥ *San Silvestro/San Stae.*

$ ✕ **Ostaria al Garanghelo.** Superior quality, competitive prices, and great ambience means this place is often packed with Venetians, especially for lunch and an after-work *ombra* (small glass of wine) and cicheti. Only a few steps from the Rialto market, chef Renato uses fresh ingredients to make his own pasta, fresh bread, and tomato sauces. He prefers cooking many dishes *al vapore* (steamed). The spicy *fagioli al uciletto* (literally beans, bird-style) has an unusual name and Tuscan origins, and is a perfect companion to plate of fresh pasta. Don't confuse this centrally located restaurant with one of the same name in Via Garibaldi. ☒ *Calle dei Boteri, San Polo 1570* ☎ 041/721721 ☲ *MC, V* ☺ *Closed Sun.*

Santa Croce

$$$ ✕ **Vecio Fritolin.** Until not so long ago, fish was fried and sold "to go" throughout Venice just as in London, except that it was paired with polenta rather than chips. A sign advertising fish to go still hangs out-

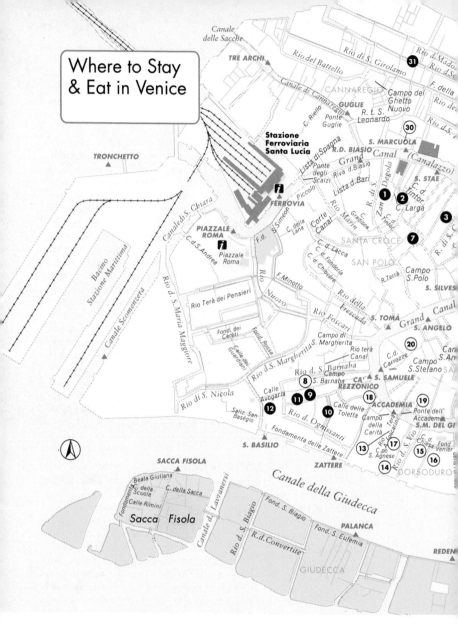

Where to Stay & Eat in Venice

Canale delle Sacche

TRE ARCHI

Canale di Cannaregio

CANNAREGIO

GUGLIE

C. Riello

Ponte
Guglie

R. T. S.
Leonardo

Rio del Battello

Rio di S. Girolamo

31

Rio d.Mado
Rio d.S

F. della
Rio de

Campo del
Ghetto
Nuovo

30

S. MARCUOLA

Rio d.S

TRONCHETTO

Canale di S. Chiara

Stazione
Ferroviaria
Santa Lucia

FERROVIA

Lista di Spagna

Ponte
degli
Scalzi

Piccolo
Canal

R.D. BIASIO

Grand

Riva d.Biasio

Lista d.Bari

Canal

(Canalazzo)

C. di
Tintor

S. STAE

1

2

C.po
C. Larga

3

C. d.
Tintor

PIAZZALE
ROMA

C. d.S. Andrea

Piazzale
Roma

F.d.

S. Simeon

C. della
Lana

Corte
Canal

Rio Marin

Gradisca

7

SANTA CROCE

C. d. Lacca

C. d. Fonderia
C. d. Chiovere

SAN POLO

R.Terra

Campo
S.Polo

S. SILVES

Rio d.S

Rio d. S. Maria Maggiore

Rio d. S. Nicola

Rio Terà dei Pensieri

Fond. dei
Cereti

Calle dei
Guardiani

Fond. Rossa

Rio d.S. Margherita

Rio

Nuovo

F.Minotto

Rio Foscari

Rio della
Frescada

S. TOMÀ

Grand Canal

S. ANGELO

Campo di
S. Margherita

Rio terà
Canal

C.d.
Carrozze

20

Campo
S.Stefano

Can
S.An

Bacino
Stazione Marittima

Canale Scomenzera

Calle
Avogaria

12

S. BASILIO

Saliz. San
Basegio

Rio d. S. Barnaba

Campo
S. Barnaba

8

11

9

Rio d. Ognissanti

10

Fondamenta delle Zattere

ZATTERE

CA'
REZZONICO

18

Calle della
Toletta

Campo
della
Carità

S. SAMUELE

ACCADEMIA

19

Ponte dell'
Accademia

S.M. DEL GI

13

14

C.po
S. Agnese

Rio Terà
Foscarini

17

C.d.
Chiesa

15

16

R.d.S. Vio

Fond
Venier

DORSODURO

Canale della Giudecca

SACCA FISOLA

Beata Giuliana

Fondamenta
C. della
Scuola

C. della Sacca

Calle Rimini

Sacca Fisola

Calle d. Lavraneresi

Rio d. S. Biagio

R.d.Convertite

Fond. S. Biagio

Fond. S. Eufemia

PALANCA

GIUDECCA

REDEN

Restaurants

Cannaregio

Algiubagiò	**32**
Anice Stellato	**31**
A la Vecia Cavana	**33**
Alla Vedova	**28**
Vini da Gigio	**29**

Castello

Alle Testiere	**34**
Corte Sconta	**42**
Da Remigio	**39**
Do Leoni	**43**

Dorsoduro

Ai 4 Fieri	**10**
Ai Gondolieri	**16**
Avogaria	**12**

La Bitta	**9**
Pizzeria al Profeta	**11**

San Marco

Al Graspo de Ua	**24**
Enoteca al Volto	**25**

San Polo

Ostaria al Garanghelo	**5**
Osteria da Fiore	**7**

Santa Croce

Al Prosecco	**1**
Bancogiro	**4**
La Zucca	**2**
Vecio Fritolin	**3**

Hotels

Cannaregio

Bernardi Semenzato	**27**

side the "Old Fry Shop," but nowadays you can only dine in. A second sign, announcing cicheti available to go, still holds true. At this tidy bacaro *con cucina* (with kitchen) you can have a traditional meal featuring such dishes as *bigoli in salsa* (thick spaghetti with anchovy sauce), baked fish with herbs, and non-Venetian lamb chops. ⊠ *Calle della Regina, Santa Croce 2262* ☎ *041/5222881* ⊟ *AE, DC, MC, V* ⊘ *Closed Mon.* Ⓥ *San Stae.*

$–$$ ✕ **Bancogiro.** Come to this casual spot in the heart of the Rialto market
Fodor'sChoice in a 15th-century loggia for a change from standard Venetian food. Yes,
★ fish is on the menu, but offerings such as mousse *di gamberoni con salsa di avocado* (shrimp mousse with an avocado sauce) and Sicilian-style *sarde incinte* (stuffed, or "pregnant," sardines) are far from typical fare—though portions can be small. The wine list and cheese plate are both divine. There are tables upstairs in a carefully restored room with a partial view of the Grand Canal; when it's warm you can sit outdoors and get the full canal view. ⊠ *Campo San Giacometto, Santa Croce 122 (under the porch)* ☎ *041/5232061* ⊟ *No credit cards* ⊘ *Closed Mon. No dinner Sun.* Ⓥ *Rialto.*

$–$$ ✕ **La Zucca.** The simple place settings, latticed-wood walls, a canal window, and mélange of languages make this place feel as much like a typical vegetarian restaurant as you could expect to find in Venice. Though the menu does have superb meat dishes such as the *piccata di pollo ai caperi e limone con riso* (sliced chicken with capers and lemon served with rice), more attention is paid to dishes from the garden: try the *radicchio di Treviso con funghi e scaglie di Montasio* (Treviso radicchio with mushrooms and shavings of Montasio cheese) or the *finocchi piccanti con olive* (fennel in a spicy tomato-olive sauce). ⊠ *Calle del Tintor, Santa Croce 1762* ☎ *041/5241570* ◁ *Reservations essential* ⊟ *AE, DC, MC, V* ⊘ *Closed Sun., 1 wk in Aug.* Ⓥ *San Stae.*

¢–$$ ✕ **Al Prosecco.** Locals stream into this place, down an order of "spritz bitter" (a combination of white wine, Campari, and seltzer water), and continue on their way. Or they linger over a glass of one of the numerous wines on offer, perhaps also tucking into a tasty panino, such as the *porchetta romane verdure* (roasted pig, Roman style, with greens). Proprietors Davide and Stefano preside over a young and friendly staff who reel off the day's specials with ease. There are a few tables in the enticing back room, and when the weather's warm you can eat outside on the beautiful campo. ⊠ *Campo S. Giacomo dal'Orio, Santa Croce 1503* ☎ *041/5240222* ⊟ *No credit cards* ⊘ *Closed Sun.* Ⓥ *San Stae.*

WHERE TO STAY

Updated by
Cristina
Gregorin

Most of Venice's hotels are in renovated palaces, but space is at a premium—and comes for a price—with all Venice lodging. The most exclusive hotels are indeed palatial, although even they may have some small, dowdy rooms. In lower price categories rooms may be cramped, and not all hotels have lounge areas. Because of preservation laws, some hotels are not allowed to have elevators. Air-conditioning can be essential if you suffer in summer heat; some hotels charge a supplement for it. Although the city has no cars, it does have boats plying the canals

VOICES OF ITALY

1

Lino and Sandra Gastaldi
bacaro owners, Dorsoduro

Husband and wife Lino and Sandra Gastaldi run the *bacaro* (wine bar) Cantinone Già Schiavi, on Fondamenta Nani, across from the *squero* (gondola workshop) in Dorsoduro. Following the bacaro tradition, they serve *cicchetti*—distinctly Venetian snacks—with their wine. Lino pours and handles distribution, while Sandra makes exquisite panini and crostini, for which she's received international acclaim. The couple works seven days a week, with assistance from three of their four sons.

All in the family. "We have been here since 1949," Lino explains. "My father took the business over from the Schiavi family—we kept the name. Soon I'll retire and my sons will take over. It's always been a family-run business, and I hope it stays that way. Over the years our business has continued to grow, and we have a wide range of customers—the regulars who come in every day at the same time, university students who stop in for a bite before class, as well as an increasing number of foreign visitors."

Ciccetti and ombre. "I love bacari and fight to keep the tradition alive," Sandra says. "There aren't many left in Venice that still follow the tradition of cicchetti and *ombre,* which has been around for over 500 years. *Il cicchetto* was the typical break taken by Venetians at about 10 o'clock in the morning. In past centuries, workers would stop and have a sandwich or piece of cheese with a small glass of wine in the shade of the bell tower in Piazza San Marco. The term *ombra,* which means shade or shadow in Italian, is the name for a glass of wine in Venetian dialect. Nowadays people come in throughout the day—it's busiest at lunchtime and early in the evening.

"Some typical Venetian cicchetti are *baccalà mantecato,* whipped codfish served on bread, chunks of *mortadella* or salted pork meat with peppers, hard-boiled eggs served with onion, *folpeti*—tiny octopus—and *polpette,* which are deep-fried meatballs. I've added my own recipes as well because I love creating new cicchetti—like my tuna and leek spread or crostini with cheese and figs."

The bacaro state of mind. Sandra surveys Cantinone and declares, "*This* is bacaro." Her husband and sons hustle at the counter; behind them, the wall is lined with wine bottles. Customers sip, snack, and chat, creating a pleasant buzz. "People come to socialize. That's the real bacaro—you come in, have a cicheto, and talk. It's like you're part of the family."

Despite the sociable atmosphere, bacari aren't meant for lingering—they're places to stop into for a quick bite, taken standing at the counter. "Many visitors don't understand this, and they come in and go all the way to our storage room at the back looking for a table, or sit outside on the steps of the San Trovaso bridge. This is a definite bacaro faux pas."

But as the population of native Venetians declines, such bacaro traditions are slowly eroding. Few places meet Sandra's high standards. "The only other traditional bacaro is Do Mori, near the Rialto market. It's run by the Schiavi family who used to own Cantinone. The bacaro there dates back to the 15th century."

and pedestrians chattering in the streets, even late at night, so ask for a quiet room if noise bothers you. In summer don't leave your room lights on at night *and* your window wide open: mosquitoes can descend en masse. If you find that these creatures are a problem, ask at your hotel's desk for a Vape, a plug-in antimosquito device.

It is *essential* to know how to get to your hotel when you arrive, as transport can range from arriving in a very expensive water taxi or gondola to wandering alleys and side streets—luggage in hand—with relapses of déjà vu. Many hotels accept reservations online; the handy Web site ⊕ www.veniceinfo.it offers free information (with photographs) about most hotels in town. It's advisable to book well in advance. If you don't have reservations, try **Venezia Si** (☎ 800/843006 toll-free in Italy Mon.–Sat. 9–7, 0039/0415222264 from abroad 🖷 0039/0415221242 from abroad), which offers a free reservation service over the phone. It's the public relations arm of **AVA** (Venetian Hoteliers Association) and has booths where you can make same-day reservations at **Piazzale Roma** (☎ 041/5231397 ☉ Daily 9 AM–10 PM), **Santa Lucia train station** (☎ 041/715288 or 041/715016 ☉ Daily 8 AM–9 PM), and **Marco Polo Airport** (☎ 041/5415133 ☉ Daily 9 AM–10 PM).

Prices

Venetian hotels cater to all tastes and come in all price ranges. Rates are about 20% higher than in Rome and Milan, but can be reduced by as much as half off-season (November–March, excluding Christmas and Carnevale, and also to some degree in August).

WHAT IT COSTS In euros					
	$$$$	**$$$**	**$$**	**$**	**¢**
FOR 2 PEOPLE	over €290	€210–€290	€140–€210	€80–€140	under €80

Prices are for two people in a standard double room in high season.

Cannaregio

★ **$$$–$$$$** ▦ **Hotel Antico Doge.** If you're looking for a small, intimate hotel in a quiet yet central location, look no farther. This delightful palazzo was once home to Doge Marino Falier. It has been completely modernized in elegant Venetian style, with a wealth of textiles and some fine original furnishings. Some rooms have *baldacchini* (canopied beds) and views; all have fabric walls and hardwood floors. On a small canal and only minutes away from San Marco and the Rialto Bridge, this is an oasis of tranquillity. An ample buffet breakfast is served in a room with a frescoed ceiling and a Murano chandelier. ⊠ *Campo SS. Apostoli, Cannaregio 5643, 30131* ☎ 041/2411570 🖷 041/2443660 ⊕ *www.anticodoge.com* ⬭ *20 rooms, 1 suite* ⚲ *In-room safes, minibars, cable TV, in-room data ports, bar* ⊟ *AE, DC, MC, V* ⦿❘ *BP* Ⓥ *Ca' D'oro.*

$ ▦ **Bernardi Semenzato.** This is a particularly inviting little place just off Strada Nova and near the gondola ferry to the Rialto market. Some rooms have exposed ceiling beams, and some have rooftop or garden views. Practical pluses include in-room coffee- and tea-making facilities. All rooms

1

are very basic, but those in the nearby *dipendenza* (annex) are larger with newer amenities. ✉ *Calle dell'Oca, Cannaregio 4366, 30121* ☎ *041/5211052* 🖷 *041/5222424* ⊕ *www.hotelbernardi.com* ⇆ *24 rooms, 20 with bath* ⚲ *In room safes, cable TV, Internet, some pets allowed, no-smoking rooms* ▭ *AE, DC, MC, V* ⊘ *Closed Jan.* ⍟ *BP* Ⓥ **Ca' d'Oro.**

$ 🖾 **Ca' San Marcuola.** Opened in 2002 in a busy area of shops, trattorias, and wine bars frequented by Venetians and tourists alike, this family-owned hotel stands out for its relaxed and familiar atmosphere. The comfortable rooms, all full of light and with spacious bathrooms, are furnished in a quiet Venetian mode with delicate pastel colors. An elevator that provides access to all floors and a very convenient location close to a waterbus stop on the Grand Canal make this a good choice for those with limited mobility. ✉ *Campo San Marcuola, Cannaregio 1763, 30121* ☎ *041/716048* 🖷 *041/2759217* ⊕ *www.casasanmarcuola. com* ⇆ *14 rooms* ⚲ *In-room safes, minibars, in-room data ports, cable TV, bar, Internet, concierge* ▭ *AE, DC, MC, V* ⊘ *Closed 4 wks Dec. and Jan.* ⍟ *BP* Ⓜ *San Marcuola.*

Castello

$$$$ 🖾 **Danieli.** You'll feel like a doge in Venice's largest luxury hotel, a complex of newer buildings and a 14th-century palazzo. Sumptuous Venetian decor prevails from the moment you set foot in the soaring atrium with its sweeping staircase. Long favored by world leaders and movie stars, Danieli is predictably expensive and very elegant. The rooftop terrace restaurant has a heavenly view but unexceptional food. May through October, you have access to the pool, tennis courts, and beach of the Hotel Excelsior on the Lido via a private (free) launch running on the hour. ✉ *Riva degli Schiavoni, Castello 4196, 30122* ☎ *041/ 5226480, 041/2961222 reservations in English* 🖷 *041/5200208* ⊕ *www. starwoodhotels.com/danieli* ⇆ *221 rooms, 12 suites* ⚲ *Restaurant, room service, in-room safes, minibars, cable TV, in-room data ports, bar, babysitting, dry cleaning, laundry service, concierge, Internet, business services, meeting rooms, some pets allowed, no-smoking rooms* ▭ *AE, DC, MC, V* ⍟ *EP* Ⓥ *San Zaccaria.*

$$$$ 🖾 **Hotel Londra Palace.** A wall of windows overlooking the lagoon and the island of San Giorgio makes this the hotel of choice for soaking up that extraordinary lagoon view—sweeping all the way from the Salute to the Lido. The downstairs restaurant is all glass, light, and water views, and 34 rooms offer the same spectacle. The view must have been pleasing to Tchaikovsky, who wrote his 4th Symphony here in 1877. Neoclassical public rooms, with splashes of blue-and-green glass suggesting the sea, play nicely off guest rooms, which have fine fabric, damask drapes, Biedermeier furniture, and Venetian glass. A change in management in 2003 has brought a breath of fresh air to the place; the staff is top-notch, as are the restaurant and bar. ✉ *Riva degli Schiavoni, Castello 4171, 30122* ☎ *041/5200533* 🖷 *041/5225032* ⊕ *www.hotellondra.it* ⇆ *36 rooms, 17 suites* ⚲ *Restaurant, room service, in-room fax, in-room safes, minibars, cable TV, in-room data ports, piano bar, wine bar, babysit-*

ting, dry cleaning, laundry service, concierge, Internet, business services, meeting room ⊟ *AE, DC, MC, V* ⫪⊙⫪ *BP* ⊻ *San Zaccaria.*

$$$$ ⌧ **Palazzo Contarini della Porta di Ferro.** Formerly the residence of the Contarinis, one of the most powerful families of Venice, this late-14th-century palace has been a hotel since 2001. The building's aristocratic past shows in the elegant inner courtyard with a majestic marble staircase. All differently furnished, the spacious, light-filled rooms have high wood-beam ceilings, while the apartments include a kitchen, dining room, and open mezzanine. The large Torcello Suite also has a wooden roof terrace from which you can take in a spectacular view of the city. On the *piano nobile* (main floor) is a large, well-appointed hall overlooking the garden; private dinners, meetings, and small conferences are sometimes held here. In sunny weather breakfast is served in the small garden. The hotel has an elevator and a private dock for boats. ⊠ *Salizada S. Giustina, Castello 2926, 30122* ☏ *041/2770991* 🖶 *041/2777021* ⊕ *www.palazzocontarini.com* ⇝ *6 rooms, 11 apartments* ⌂ *In-room safes, minibars, cable TV, in-room data ports, room service, babysitting, dry cleaning, Internet, concierge, some small pets allowed* ⊟ *AE, MC, V* ⫪⊙⫪ *BP.*

★ $$$–$$$$ ⌧ **Savoia e Jolanda.** Here you'll get the best deal from among the high-end hotels along the fabulous San Marco Basin waterfront. Fifteen of the guest rooms open directly onto the splendid lagoon panorama, and all are decorated with sumptuous tapestries, fine fabric curtains, and Murano glass chandeliers; they have high ceilings—some are coffered—and many get a great deal of light. There's a copious buffet breakfast, and the restaurant stays open all day. ⊠ *Riva degli Schiavoni, Castello 4187, 30122* ☏ *041/5206644* 🖶 *041/5207494* ⊕ *www.hotelsavoiajolanda.com* ⇝ *36 rooms, 15 suites* ⌂ *Restaurant, room service, in-room safes, some in-room hot tubs, minibars, cable TV, in-room data ports, bar, babysitting, dry cleaning, laundry service, concierge, Internet, some pets allowed, no-smoking rooms* ⊟ *AE, DC, MC, V* ⫪⊙⫪ *BP* ⊻ *San Zaccaria.*

$$–$$$ ⌧ **Ca' Formenta.** You're in residential rather than tourist Venice here, but the front rooms still have a wonderful lagoon view. Dating from the 15th century, the simple building underwent a complete makeover before opening in 2003 as a hotel with high-quality services, an elevator, and a canal-side entrance for guests arriving by water taxi. The 15-minute stroll along the waterfront between Piazzo San Marco and this friendly gem of a hotel is through a genuinely "local" part of the city, with plenty of cafés and restaurants. One of the rear rooms has direct access to a pleasant rooftop terrace with tables. ⊠ *Via Garibaldi, Castello 1650, 30122* ☏ *041/5285494* 🖶 *041/5204633* ⊕ *www.hotelcaformenta.it* ⇝ *14 rooms* ⌂ *In-room safes, minibars, cable TV, in-room data ports, laundry service* ⊟ *AE, DC, MC, V* ⫪⊙⫪ *BP* ⊻ *Arsenale/Giardini.*

$$ ⌧ **La Residenza.** The word *residenza* in Italian suggests a good deal of aristocratic elegance, and this hotel, with more the feeling of a private mansion than a hotel, does not disappoint. The grand hall on the *piano nobile* (main floor) of this 15th-century building looks almost disproportionately opulent. Well-preserved 18th-century stuccowork adorns the ceilings and walls, along with precious oil paintings. Oriental carpets partially hide the beautiful Venetian terrazzo floor. The rooms are

1

spacious—some with lordly views over the campo in front—and were all upgraded in late 2000, and stucco decorations and frescoes were carefully restored in 2003–04. ⊠ *Campo Bandiera e Moro, Castello 3608, 30122* ☎ *041/5285315* 🖷 *041/5238859* ⊕ *www.venicelaresidenza. com* 🛏 *14 rooms* ♿ *In-room safes, minibars, lounge; no smoking* 🚪 *MC, V* ¶⊙¶ *BP* Ⓥ *Arsenale.*

$ 🖼 **Santa Maria della Pietà.** There's more space—both public and private—in this *casa per ferie* (vacation house) than in many four-star hotels in Venice. It occupies two historic palaces and opened as a hotel in 1999. Completely restored with Venetian terrazzo floors throughout, it has big windows and a huge rooftop terrace with coffee shop, bar, and unobstructed lagoon views. On top of all this, it is excellently situated—100 yards from the main waterfront and about 10 minutes' walk from St. Mark's—meaning you'll have to book early to stay here. The spartan rooms have only beds and wardrobes, but the shared bathrooms are plentiful, spacious, and scrupulously clean. Some family rooms with up to six beds are available. ⊠ *Calle della Pietà, Castello 3701, 30122* ☎ *041/2443639* 🖷 *041/2411561* 🛏 *15 rooms* ♿ *Coffee shop, bar, lounge; no room phones, no room TVs* 🚪 *No credit cards* ¶⊙¶ *BP* Ⓥ *San Zaccaria/Arsenale.*

Dorsoduro

$$$$ 🖼 **Ca' Pisani.** Here's a breath of fresh air: a Venetian hotel with no brocades and chandeliers to be found. Instead there's a tasteful mix of modern design and well-chosen antique pieces. The entrance hall has marble floors and an interesting play of colors and lights; the rooms contain original art deco pieces from the 1930s and '40s (every bed is different). The no-smoking wine bar La Rivista serves light meals all day, and upstairs are a Turkish bath and a wooden rooftop terrace where you can take the sun. ⊠ *Rio Terà Antonio Foscarini, Dorsoduro 979/a, 30123* ☎ *041/2401411* 🖷 *041/2771061* ⊕ *www.capisanihotel.it* 🛏 *25 rooms, 4 suites* ♿ *Restaurant, room service, in-room safes, minibars, cable TV with movies, in-room data ports, Turkish bath, wine bar, dry cleaning, laundry service, concierge, Internet, some pets allowed, no-smoking floor* 🚪 *AE, DC, MC, V* ¶⊙¶ *BP* Ⓥ *Accademia.*

★ **$$$–$$$$**   🖼 **American–Dinesen.** This quiet, family-run hotel has a yellow stucco facade typical of Venetian houses. A hall decorated with reproduction antiques and Oriental rugs leads to a breakfast room reminiscent of a theater foyer, with red-velvet chairs and gilt wall lamps. Rooms are spacious and tastefully furnished in sage-green and delicate pink fabrics, with lacquered Venetian-style furniture throughout. Some front rooms have terraces with canal views. A 2002 overhaul has made the place sparkle, though the four-story building still has no elevator. ⊠ *San Vio, Dorsoduro 628, 30123* ☎ *041/5204733* 🖷 *041/5204048* ⊕ *www. hotelamerican.com* 🛏 *28 rooms, 2 suites* ♿ *In-room safes, minibars, cable TV, in-room data ports, babysitting, Internet, no-smoking rooms* 🚪 *AE, MC, V* ¶⊙¶ *BP* Ⓥ *Accademia/Salute.*

$$–$$$ 🖼 **Hotel Pausania.** From the moment you ascend the grand staircase rising above the fountain of this 14th-century palazzo, you sense the combination of good taste and modern comforts that characterizes Hotel Pausania. Light-color rooms are spacious, with comfortable furniture and carpets strewn with rugs. Some rooms face the small canal (which can become a bit noisy early in the morning) in front of the hotel, whereas others look out over the large garden courtyard. ☒ *Fondamenta Gherardini, Dorsoduro 2824, 30123* ☎ *041/5222083* 🖷 *041/5222989* ⊕ *www.hotelpausania.it* ⇆ *26 rooms* ♿ *Minibars, cable TV, Internet, bar, babysitting, dry cleaning, concierge, some pets allowed* ▭ *AE, MC, V* ⫯❶⫯ *BP* **V** *Ca' Rezzonico.*

$$–$$$ 🖼 **Pensione Accademia Villa Maravege.** A secret garden awaits just be-

Fodor'sChoice yond an iron gate, complete with a mini Palladian-style villa, flower beds,

★ stone cupids, and verdant trees—all rarities in Venice. Aptly nicknamed "Villa of the Wonders," this patrician retreat once served as the Russian embassy and was the residence of Katharine Hepburn in the movie *Summertime.* Conservative rooms are outfitted with Venetian-style antiques and fine tapestry. The location is on a promontory where two side canals converge with the Grand Canal, which can be seen from the garden. Book well in advance. ☒ *Fondamenta Bollani, Dorsoduro 1058, 30123* ☎ *041/5210188* 🖷 *041/5239152* ⊕ *www.pensioneaccademia. it* ⇆ *27 rooms* ♿ *In-room safes, minibars, cable TV, bar, babysitting, dry cleaning, laundry service* ▭ *AE, DC, MC, V* ⫯❶⫯ *BP* **V** *Accademia.*

$$ 🖼 **Agli Alboretti.** The Alboretti is one of the many hotels clustered at the foot of the Ponte dell'Accademia. Its unpretentious, rather small rooms are blessed with plenty of light. Their nautical decor, with original pieces taken from old ships' cabins, goes well with the cries of seagulls living along the nearby Giudecca Canal. In warm weather, breakfast is served in an inner courtyard under a rose bower and a small terrace with potted plants is open. The elevator is a welcome convenience for weary travelers. ☒ *Rio Terrà Foscarini, Dorsoduro 884, 30123* ☎ *041/5230058* 🖷 *041/5210158* ⊕ *www.aglialboretti.com* ⇆ *20 rooms* ♿ *Restaurant, cable TV, bar, dry cleaning, laundry service, concierge, some pets allowed, no-smoking rooms* ▭ *AE, MC, V* ⫯❶⫯ *BP* **V** *Accademia.*

★ **$–$$** 🖼 **La Calcina.** The Calcina sits in an enviable position along the sunny Zattere, with front rooms offering views across the wide Giudecca Canal. You can sunbathe on the *altana* (wooden roof terrace) or enjoy an afternoon tea in one of the reading corners of the lounge with flickering candlelight and barely perceptible classical music. A stone staircase (no elevator) leads to the rooms upstairs, which have parquet floors, original art deco furniture and lamps, and firm beds. Besides full meals at lunch and dinner, the Piscina bar and restaurant offers drinks and freshly made snacks all day in the elegant dining room or on the wooden waterside terrace out front. ☒ *Zattere, Dorsoduro 780, 30123* ☎ *041/5206466* 🖷 *041/5227045* ⊕ *www.lacalcina.com* ⇆ *27 rooms, 26 with bath, 5 suites* ♿ *Restaurant, in-room safes, cable TV* ▭ *AE, DC, MC, V* ⫯❶⫯ *BP* **V** *Zattere.*

Giudecca

$$$$ 🖼 **Cipriani.** It's impossible to feel stressed in this oasis of stunning rooms and suites, some with garden patios. The hotel launch whisks you to Giudecca from San Marco and back at any hour; those dining at the exceptional Ristorante Harry Cipriani can use it as well. For rooms the restored 17th-century-style Palazzo Vendramin is the premium choice, with views across to Piazza San Marco, but the main hotel and Palazzetto, a modern annex facing the Canale della Giudecca, also offer extraordinary luxury. Prices are high even by Venetian standards, but this is the only place in town with such extensive facilities and services, from an Olympic-size pool and tennis courts to cooking courses, fitness programs, and even a vineyard. ⊠ *Giudecca 10, 30133* ☎ *041/5207744* ☎ *041/5207745* ⊕ *www.hotelcipriani.it* ⇆ *54 rooms, 50 suites* ♨ *4 restaurants, room service, in-room safes, minibars, cable TV, Wi-Fi, Internet, tennis court, saltwater pool, health club, massage, sauna, spa, bar, babysitting, dry cleaning, laundry service, concierge, Internet room, meeting room* ▭ *AE, DC, MC, V* ☉ *Main hotel closed Nov.–Mar.; Palazzo Vendramin and Palazzetto closed 4 wks in Jan. and Feb.* ℟ *BP* Ⅴ *Zitelle.*

Lagoon

$$$$ ▨ **San Clemente Palace.** If you prefer wide-open spaces to the intimacy of Venice, this is your hotel. It occupies an entire island, about 15 minutes from Piazza San Marco by (free) shuttle launch, with acres of parkland, a swimming pool, tennis courts, wellness center, and three restaurants. The 19th-century buildings are on the site of a 12th-century monastery, of which only the chapel remains. They form a large quadrangle and contain spacious, modern rooms. The view back to Venice with the Dolomites behind on a clear day is stunning. This hotel, opened in 2003, offers all the five-star comforts: it even has three holes of golf. ⊠ *Isola di San Clemente 1, San Marco, 30124* ☎ *041/2445001* ☎ *041/2445800* ⊕ *www.sanclemente.thi.it* ⇆ *107 rooms, 96 suites* ♨ *3 restaurants, coffee shop, in-room safes, minibars, cable TV, in-room data ports, 3-hole golf course, 2 tennis courts, pool, exercise equipment, health club, hair salon, hot tub, massage, sauna, spa, bars, shop, laundry service, convention center, meeting rooms, some pets allowed, no-smoking rooms* ▭ *AE, DC, MC, V* ℟ *BP.*

Lido

$$–$$$$ ▨ **Quattro Fontane.** This fine hotel in a well-maintained mansion run by Danish sisters Bente and Pia Bevilacqua offers the serenity of the Lido in a location that's a 15-minute walk and 20-minute boat ride from Piazza San Marco. Well-decorated rooms with period furniture and tasteful tapestries overlook the lush surrounding garden of mature trees and shrubs, with clearings for dining tables in summer. Common areas contain an odd collection of masons' aprons, pipes, ex-votos, masks from Jakarta, Roman seals, and seashells. A huge fireplace adds warmth and character in the colder months. After a full day you can relax in the library, stocked with books in many languages. ⊠ *Via Quattro Fontane 16, Lido, 30126* ☎ *041/5260227* ☎ *041/5260726* ⊕ *www.quattrofontane.com* ⇆ *54 rooms, 4 apartments* ♨ *Restaurant, in-room safes, minibars, cable TV, Internet, tennis court, bar, library, babysitting, dry cleaning, laundry service, meeting room, some pets allowed* ▭ *AE, DC, MC, V* ☉ *Closed Nov.–Mar.* ℟ *BP* Ⅴ *Lido.*

San Marco

$$$$ 🏨 **Gritti Palace.** Queen Elizabeth, Greta Garbo, and Winston Churchill all made this their Venetian address. The feeling of being in an aristocratic private home pervades this legendary hotel replete with fresh flowers, fine antiques, sumptuous appointments, and old-style service. The dining terrace on the Grand Canal is best enjoyed in the evening, when the boat traffic dies down. May through October you have access to the pool, tennis courts, and beach of the Hotel Excelsior on the Lido via a private (free) launch. ⊠ *Campo Santa Maria del Giglio, San Marco 2467, 30124* ☎ *041/794611* 🖷 *041/5200942* ⊕ *www. starwoodhotels.com/grittipalace* 🛏 *84 rooms, 6 suites* ⚬ *Restaurant, room service, in-room safes, minibars, cable TV with movies, in-room data ports, bar, babysitting, dry cleaning, laundry service, concierge, Internet, Wi-Fi, business services, meeting rooms, some pets allowed, no-smoking rooms* ▤ *AE, DC, MC, V* ⏐⦿⏐ *BP* ⓥ *Giglio.*

$$$$ 🏨 **Il Palazzo at the Bauer.** Il Palazzo, under the same management as the larger Bauer Hotel, is the ultimate word in luxury. Bevilacqua and Rubelli fabrics cover the walls, and no two rooms are decorated the same. What they have in common, however, are high ceilings, Murano glass, marble bathrooms, and damask drapes. Many have sweeping views. Breakfast is served on Venice's highest terrace, appropriately named il Settimo Cielo (Seventh Heaven). The outdoor hot tub, also on the 7th floor, offers views of La Serenissima that won't quit. ⊠ *Campo San Moisè, San Marco 1413/d, 30124* ☎ *041/5207022* 🖷 *041/5207557* ⊕ *www. ilpalazzovenezia.com* 🛏 *36 rooms, 40 suites* ⚬ *Restaurant, room service, in-room fax, in-room safes, some in-room hot tubs, minibars, cable TV with movies, in-room data ports, golf privileges, health club, outdoor hot tub, massage, sauna, Turkish bath, dock, bar, babysitting, dry cleaning, laundry service, concierge, Internet, Wi-Fi, some pets allowed, no-smoking rooms* ▤ *AE, DC, MC, V* ⏐⦿⏐ *EP* ⓥ *Vallaresso.*

★ $$–$$$$ 🏨 **Monaco & Grand Canal.** Major upgrading and expansion of this landmark canal-side hotel have resulted in a blend of Venetian elegance and contemporary design. The centerpiece of the restored original section is the convivial waterfront restaurant; many guest rooms share the same panoramic lagoon views. A big, bright reception area, created by roofing an inner courtyard with glass, leads to the new rear section, which was once the Sala del Ridotto, a luxurious gambling house. It's almost worth staying here just to spend time in the sumptuous lounge with adjoining bar. Rooms in both sections are in modern Italian style, with spacious bathrooms in a warm, beige marble. ⊠ *Calle Vallaresso, San Marco 1332, 30124* ☎ *041/5200211* 🖷 *041/5200501* ⊕ *www.hotelmonaco.it* 🛏 *87 rooms, 12 suites* ⚬ *Restaurant, room service, in-room safes, minibars, cable TV, in-room data ports, dock, bar, piano bar, babysitting, dry cleaning, laundry service, concierge, meeting rooms, some pets allowed, no-smoking rooms* ▤ *AE, DC, MC, V* ⏐⦿⏐ *BP* ⓥ *Vallaresso.*

★ $$$ 🏨 **San Zulian.** A minimalist entrance hall leads to rooms that are a refined variation on the Venetian theme, with lacquered 18th-century-style furniture and parquet floors. Room 304 is on two levels and has its own delightful covered veranda. Two ground-floor rooms have bathrooms equipped for people with disabilities. The handy location near San Marco and the Rialto and the top-notch staff make a stay here eminently enjoyable. ⊠ *Campo della Guerra, San Marco 534/535, 30124* ☎ *041/5225872 or 041/5226598* 🖷 *041/5232265* ⊕ *www.hotelsanzulian. com* 🛏 *25 rooms* ⚓ *In-room safes, minibars, cable TV, some pets allowed* ⊟ *AE, DC, MC, V* ⧆ *BP* Ⓥ *Vallaresso/San Zaccaria.*

$$–$$$ 🖫 **Novecento.** In a quiet street just a 10-minute walk from St. Mark's Square is this small family-run hotel, opened in 2002. Inspired by the style of Mariano Fortuny, the early-1900s artist and fashion designer, the intimate rooms are a surprisingly elegant mélange of multiethnic and exotic furnishings. The Mediterranean, Indian, and Venetian fabrics, silverware, chandeliers, and furniture create a sensual turn-of-the-20th-century atmosphere. In fine weather breakfast is served in the inner courtyard. ⊠ *Calle del Dose (Campo San Maurizio), San Marco 2683/84, 30124* ☎ *041/2413765* 🖷 *041/5212145* ⊕ *www.novecento.biz* 🛏 *9 rooms* ⚓ *In-room safes, minibars, cable TV, in-room data ports, bar, dry cleaning, laundry service, Internet, Wi-Fi* ⊟ *AE, DC, MC, V* ⧆ *BP* Ⓜ *S. Maria del Giglio.*

$ 🖫 **Albergo San Samuele.** Near the Grand Canal and Palazzo Grassi, this friendly hotel has clean, sunny rooms in surprisingly good shape for the price. Five of the bathrooms are relatively new, with white-and-gray-blue tiles, and the walls are painted in crisp, pleasant shades of pale pink or blue. Curtains and bedspreads are made from antique-looking fabrics, and although the furniture is of the boxy modern kind, the owners are gradually adding more interesting-looking pieces. ⊠ *Salizzada San Samuele, San Marco 3358, 30124* ☎🖷 *041/5228045* 🛏 *10 rooms, 7 with bath* ⚓ *Fans, some pets allowed, no-smoking rooms; no a/c, no room TVs* ⊟ *No credit cards* ⧆ *EP* Ⓥ *San Samuele.*

San Polo

$$$ 🖫 **Sturion.** At the end of the 13th century this building housed foreign merchants selling their wares at the Rialto, and the painter Vittore Carpaccio depicted it in his 1494 *Miracle of the Cross* (on view at the Accademia). Now it's decorated in 18th-century Venetian style and run with great care by a Venetian family. Rooms (two with views of the Grand Canal) are done in red-and-gold brocade; there's also a small but inviting breakfast room. Two rooms comfortably sleep four and are perfect for families. All rooms have coffee- and tea-making facilities, an uncommon feature for Italy. Be warned that the stairs are steep here (the hotel is on the 4th and 5th floors), and there's no elevator. ⊠ *Calle del Sturion, San Polo 679, 30125* ☎ *041/5236243* 🖷 *041/5228378* ⊕ *www.locandasturion. com* 🛏 *11 rooms* ⚓ *In-room safes, minibars, Internet, some pets allowed, no-smoking rooms* ⊟ *MC, V* ⧆ *BP* Ⓥ *S. Silvestro/Rialto.*

NIGHTLIFE & THE ARTS

The Arts

A Guest in Venice, a monthly bilingual booklet free at most hotels, is your most accessible, up-to-date guide to Venice happenings. It also includes information about pharmacies, vaporetto and bus lines, and the main trains and flights. You can visit their Web site, ⊕ www. aguestinvenice.com, for a preview of musical, artistic, and sporting events. *Venezia News,* available at newsstands, has similar information but also includes in-depth articles about noteworthy events. The tourist office publishes *Leo* and *Bussola,* bimonthly brochures in Italian and English listing events and updated museum hours. *Venezia da Vivere* is a seasonal guide listing nightspots and live music. Several Venice Web sites allow you to scan the cultural horizon before you arrive; try ⊕ www.ombra.net, (which has a fantastic map function to find any address in Venice), ⊕ www.veniceonline.it, and ⊕ www.venicebanana.com. Last but not least, don't ignore the posters you see everywhere in the streets. They're often the most up-to-date information you can find.

Carnevale

The first historical evidence of Carnevale (Carnival) in Venice dates from 1097, and for centuries the city marked the days preceding *quaresima* (Lent, the 40 days of abstinence leading up to Palm Sunday) with abundant feasting and wild celebrations. The word *carnival* is derived from the words for meat (*carne*) and to remove (*levare*), as eating meat was prohibited during Lent. Venice earned its international reputation as the "city of Carnevale" in the 18th century, when partying would begin right after Epiphany (January 6) and the city seemed to be one continuous decadent masquerade. With the Republic's fall in 1797, the city lost a great deal of its vitality, and the tradition of Carnevale celebrations was abandoned.

Carnevale was revived in the 1970s when residents began taking to the calli and campi in their own impromptu celebrations. It didn't take long for the tourist industry to embrace the revival as a means to stimulate business during low season. The efforts were successful. Each year over the 10- to 12-day Carnevale period (ending on the Tuesday before Ash Wednesday) more than a half million people attend concerts, theater and street performances, masquerade balls, historical processions, fashion shows, and contests. **A Guest in Venice** (⊕ www.aguestinvenice.com) gives free advertising to public and private event festivities and is therefore one of the most complete Carnevale guides. For general Carnevale information, contact **Consorzio Comitato per il Carnevale di Venezia** (✉ Santa Croce 1714, 30135 ☎ 041/717065, 041/2510811 during Carnevale 🖷 041/5200410 ⊕ www.carnevale.venezia.it). The **Tourist Office** (☎ 041/5298711) has detailed information about daily events.

If you're not planning on joining in the revelry, you'd be wise to choose another time to visit Venice. Enormous crowds clog the streets (which become one-way, with police directing foot traffic), bridges are designated "no-stopping" zones to avoid gridlock, and prices absolutely skyrocket.

Festivals

The **Biennale** (⊕ www.labiennale.org) cultural institution organizes events year-round, including the Venice Film Festival, which begins the last week of August. The Biennale international exhibition of contemporary art is held in odd-numbered years, usually from mid-June to early November, at the Giardini della Biennale, and in the impressive Arsenale.

The third weekend of July, the **Festa del Redentore** (Feast of the Redeemer) commemorates the end of a 16th-century plague that killed about 47,000 city residents. Just as doges have done annually for centuries, you too can make a pilgrimage across the temporary bridge connecting Zattere to the Giudecca. Venetians take to the water to watch fireworks at midnight, but if you can't find a boat, the Giudecca is the best place to be. Young people traditionally greet sunrise on the Lido beach while their elders attend church.

Music

Although there are occasional jazz and Italian pop concerts in clubs around town, the vast majority of music you'll hear is classical, with Venice's famed composer, Vivaldi, frequently featured. A number of churches and palazzos regularly host concerts, as do the Ca' Rezzonico and Querini Stampalia museums. You'll find these events listed in publications such as *A Guest in Venice*; also try asking the tourist information office or your concierge. The **Vela Call Center** (☎ 041/2424 ☼ Daily 8–8) has information about musical events, and you can buy tickets at Vela sales offices in Piazzale Roma, Ferrovia, and Calle dei Fuseri (a 10-minute walk from San Marco). (When busy, the Vela Call Center number doesn't give a signal, but instead is silent.)

The travel agency **Kele & Teo** (✉ Ponte dei Bareteri, San Marco 4930 ☎ 041/5208722) has tickets for a number of venues and is conveniently located midway between Rialto and San Marco.

Opera

Teatro La Fenice (✉ Campo San Fantin, San Marco ☎ 041/786511 ⊕ www.teatrolafenice.it), one of Italy's oldest opera houses, has witnessed many memorable premieres, including the 1853 first-night flop of Verdi's *La Traviata*. It's also had its share of disasters, the most recent being a terrible fire, deliberately set in January 1996. It was completely and luxuriously restored, and reopened to great fanfare in 2004. Visit the Fenice Web site for a schedule of performances and to buy tickets.

Nightlife

Piazza San Marco is a popular meeting place in nice weather, when the cafés stay open late and all seem to be competing to offer the best live music. The younger crowd, Venetians and visitors alike, tends to gravitate toward the area around Rialto Bridge, with Campi San Bartolomeo and San Luca on one side and Campo Rialto Nuovo on the other. Especially popular with university students are the bars along Cannaregio's Fondamenta della Misericordia and around Campo Santa Margarita and San Pantalon. Pick up a booklet of *2Night* or visit their Web site ⊕ www.2night.it for nightlife listings and reviews.

Bars

L'Olandese Volante (✉ Campo San Lio, near Rialto ☎ 041/5289349) is a popular hangout for many young Venetians. Nothing special by day, **Bar Torino** (✉ Campo San Luca ☎ 041/5223914) is one of Venice's liveliest nightspots, open late and spilling out onto the campo in summer. **Bá-**

caro Jazz (✉ Across from Rialto Post Office ☎ 041/5285249) has music (not usually live) and meals until 2 AM, and its gregarious staff is unlikely to let you feel lonely. The **Martini Scala Club** (✉ Campo San Fantin, San Marco 1983 ☎ 041/5224121), the Antico Martini restaurant's elegant bar, has live music from 10 to 3:30. Full meals are served until 2.

One of the newest and hippest bars for the late night chill-out crowd, **Centrale** (✉ Piscina Frezzeria, San Marco 1659/B ☎ 041/2960664) is in a former movie theater—and the crowd does look more Hollywood than Venice. Excellent mojitos and other mixed drinks, black-leather couches, and dim lighting strike a loungey note, and the DJ keeps the beats cool.

Campo Santa Margarita is a student hangout all day and late into the night. Try **Orange** (✉ Campo Santa Margarita, Dorsoduro 3054/a ☎ 041/5234740) for piadine sandwiches, drinks, and soccer games on a massive screen. The bohemian **Il Caffè** (✉ Campo Santa Margarita, Dorsoduro 2963 ☎ 041/5287998), also known as Caffè Rosso for its red exterior, is especially popular in nice weather.

Casinos

The city-run gambling casino in the splendid **Palazzo Vendramin-Calergi** is a classic scene of well-dressed high-rollers playing French roulette, Caribbean poker, chemin de fer, 30–40, and slots. You must be 18 to enter, and men must wear jackets, no tennis shoes allowed. ✉ *Cannaregio 2040* ☎ *041/5297111* 💳 *€10 entry includes €10 in chips* ⊙ *Slots 2:45 PM–2:30 AM; tables 3:30 PM–2:30 AM* Ⓥ *San Marcuola.*

Mestre's **Ca' Noghera** casino, near the airport, has slots, blackjack, craps, poker, and roulette. Minimum age is 18. There's a free shuttle bus from Piazzale Roma from 4:05 PM until closing. ✉ *Via Triestina 222, Tessera, Mestre* ☎ *041/5297111* 💳 *€10 entry includes €10 in chips* ⊙ *Slots 11 AM–3:30 AM; tables 3:30 PM–3:30 AM.*

Nightclubs

Dancing and clubbing is a hard find on the Venetian islands, so your best bets are on the *terra firma*. **Magic Bus** (✉ Via delle Industrie, 118, Second Industrial Zone, Marcon ☎ 041/5952151) is an alternative rock club with pop art walls and zebra-stripe floors. It showcases new and established European acts every weekend.

Claiming to be Venice's only "real" disco club, **Casanova** (✉ Lista di Spagna, Cannaregio 158/a ☎ 041/2750199) undeniably has the largest dance floor. With no cover charge, Internet points, and student-night specials, it attracts mostly foreign students and some young Venetians.

SPORTS

Beaches

Those looking for a cooling break in summer should head for the **Lido** (Ⓥ S. M. Elizabetta). Large sections of the long, narrow beach are private, renting chairs and umbrellas and offering toilets, showers, and restaurants. If your hotel has no beach rights, you can pay for entry. The free beach areas, with no facilities, are generally crowded unless you head south by bus toward Malamocco and Alberoni.

Running

The most scenic running route (6–7 km [4–4½ mi] long) heads east from Piazza San Marco and skirts the lagoon along the Riva degli Schiavoni to the pine wood of Sant'Elena. You can return by way of the picturesque neighborhood of Castello and the island of San Pietro di Castello. This route can get packed with pedestrians from spring through fall, so if you don't want to run a slalom course, try Lido Beach or the area around Zattere.

SHOPPING

Updated by
Pamela Santini

Alluring shops abound in Venice. You'll find countless vendors of trademark Venetian wares such as glass and lace; the authenticity of some goods can be suspect, but they're often pleasing to the eye regardless of their place of origin. For more sophisticated tastes (and deeper pockets), there are jewelers, antiques dealers, and high-fashion boutiques on a par with those in Italy's larger cities but often maintaining a uniquely Venetian flair. There are also some interesting craft and art studios, where you can find high-quality, one-of-a-kind articles, from handmade shoes to decorative lamps and mirrors.

It's always a good idea to mark the location of a shop that interests you on your map; otherwise you may not be able to find it again in the maze of tiny streets. Regular store hours are usually 9–12:30 and 3:30 or 4–7:30; some stores are closed on Saturday afternoon or Monday morning. Food shops are open 8–1 and 5–7:30, and are closed Wednesday afternoon and all day Sunday. Many tourist-oriented shops are open all day, every day. Some shops close for both a summer and a winter vacation.

Food Markets

The morning open-air fruit and vegetable market at **Rialto** offers animated local color and commerce. On Tuesday through Saturday mornings the **fish market** (adjacent to the Rialto produce market) provides an impressive lesson in ichthyology, with species you've probably never seen before. In the Castello district you'll find a lively food market weekday mornings on **Via Garibaldi.**

Shopping Districts

The **San Marco** area is full of shops and couture boutiques such as Armani, Missoni, Valentino, Fendi, and Versace. **Le Mercerie,** along with the Frezzeria and Calle dei Fabbri, leading from Piazza San Marco, are some of Venice's busiest shopping streets. Other good shopping areas surround Calle del Teatro and Campi San Salvador, Manin, San Fantin, and San Bartolomeo. Less-expensive shops are between the Rialto Bridge and San Polo.

Specialty Stores

Glassware

Glass, most of it made in Murano, is Venice's number one product, and you'll be confronted by mind-boggling displays of traditional and contemporary glassware, much of it kitsch. Take your time and be selective. You will probably find that prices in Venice's shops and the showrooms of Murano's factories are pretty much the same. However, because of competition, shops in Venice with wares from various glassworks may charge slightly less.

Domus (✉ Fondamenta dei Vetrai, Murano 82 ☎ 041/739215) has a selection of smaller objects and jewelry from the best glassworks.

For chic, contemporary glassware, Carlo Moretti is a good choice; his designs are on display at **L'Isola** (✉ Campo San Moisè, San Marco 1468 ☎ 041/5231973 ⊕ www.carlomoretti.com). **Marina Barovier** (✉ Calle delle Botteghe, off Campo Santo Stefano, San Marco 3216 ☎ 041/5236748 ⊕ www.barovier.it) has an excellent selection of contemporary collectors' glass.

Go to Michel Paciello's **Paropàmiso** (✉ Frezzeria, San Marco 1701 ☎ 041/5227120) for stunning Venetian glass beads and traditional jewelry from all over the world. **Pauly** (✉ Piazza San Marco 73, 77, and 316; Ponte dei Consorzi ☎ 041/5209899 ⊕ www.paulyglassfactory.com) has four centrally located shops with an impressive selection of glassware at better prices than on Murano. **Venini** (✉ Piazzetta dei Leoncini 314, San Marco ☎ 041/5224045 ⊕ www.venini.com) has been an institution since the 1930s, attracting some of the foremost names in glass design.

Lace & Fabrics

Much of the lace and embroidered linen sold in Venice and on Burano is really made in China or Taiwan. However, at **Il Merletto** (✉ Sotoportego del Cavalletto, under the Procuratie Vecchie, Piazza San Marco 95 ☎ 041/5208406), you can ask for the authentic, handmade lace kept in the drawers behind the counter. This is the only place in Venice connected with the students of the Scuola del Merletto in Burano, who, officially, do not sell to the public. Hours of operation are 10–5. A top address for linen is **Jesurum** (✉ Cannaregio 3219, Fondamenta della Sensa ☎ 041/5242540 ⊕ www.jesurum.it).

Go to **Lorenzo Rubelli** (✉ Palazzo Corner Spinelli, San Marco 3877 ☎ 041/5236110 ⊕ www.rubelli.it) for the same brocades, damasks, and cut velvets used by the world's most prestigious decorators. **Venetia Studium** (✉ Calle Larga XXII Marzo, San Marco 2403 ☎ 041/5229281 ✉ Calle Larga XXII Marzo, San Marco 723 ☎ 041/5229859 ⊕ www.

Venetian Masks Revealed

IN THE TIME OF THE REPUBLIC, the mask trade was vibrant—Venetians wore masks all year to go about town incognito. Napoléon suppressed their use, a by-product of his effort to end Carnevale, and when Carnevale was revived in the late 1970s, mask making returned as well. Though many workshops use centuries-old techniques, none has been in business for more than 30 years.

A landmark date in the history of Venetian masks is 1436, when the *mascareri* (mask makers) founded their guild, but masks were popular well before then. Laws regulating their use appeared as early as 1268, intended to prevent wearers from carrying weapons and masked men disguised as women from entering convents to seduce nuns.

In the 18th century, masks started being used by actors playing the traditional roles of the commedia dell'arte. Inexpensive papier-mâché versions of these masks can be found everywhere. The character Arlecchino has the round face and surprised expression, Pantalone is the one with the curved nose and long mustache, and Pulcinella has the protruding nose.

The least expensive mask is the white Bauta, smooth and plain with a short, pointed nose intended to disguise the wearer's voice; in the 18th century it was commonly accompanied by a black three-cornered hat and a black cloak. The pretty Gnaga, which resembles a cat's face, was used by gay men to "meow" proposals to good-looking boys. The basic Moretta is a black oval with eyeholes. The Medico della Peste (the Plague Doctor) has a beaklike nose and glasses; during the plague of 1630 and 1631, doctors wore masks with herbs inside the nose intended to filter infected air and glasses to protect the eyes.

---

venetiastudium.com) sells silk scarves, bags, and cushion covers, as well as the famous Fortuny lamps.

Lamps
The studio **A Mano** (⊠ Rio Terà, San Polo 2616 ☏ 041/715742), near the Frari, is worth hunting down. Alessandro Savadori makes imaginative table, wall, and ceiling lamps that may well cross the boundary from craft into art.

Masks
Guerrino Lovato, proprietor of **Mondonovo** (⊠ Rio Terà Canal, Dorsoduro 3063 ☏ 041/5287344 ⊕ www.mondonovomaschere.it) is one of the most respected mask-makers in town. He was called on to oversee reconstruction of reliefs and sculptures in Teatro La Fenice after it burned to the ground in 1996.

Shoes
Fine shoes and boots are handmade to order at **Daniela Ghezzo, Segalin a Venezia** (⊠ Calle dei Fuseri, San Marco 4365 ☏ 041/5222115), op-

erated by one of the city's two female shoemakers. Ghezzo carries on the tradition established by the renowned Rolando Segalin.

Giovanna Zanella (✉ Calle Carminati, Castello 5641 ☎ 041 5235500) creates custom-made footwear with daring color combinations and unique styles. Her accessories make a statement as well.

VENICE ESSENTIALS

Transportation

BY AIR

Venice's Aeroporto Marco Polo is served by domestic and international flights, including connections from 21 European cities, plus direct flights from Moscow and New York's JFK. In addition, Treviso Airport, some 20 mi (32 km) north of Venice, receives daily arrivals from London's Stansted Airport.

A shuttle bus or 10-minute walk takes you from Marco Polo's terminal to a dock where public and private boats are available to deliver you direct to Venice's historic center. For €10 per person, including bags, Alilaguna operates regularly scheduled service from predawn until nearly midnight. It takes about an hour to reach the landing near Piazza San Marco, stopping at the Lido on the way. A *motoscafo* (water taxi) carries up to four people and four bags to the city center in a sleek, modern powerboat. The base cost is €80, and the trip takes about 25 minutes. Each additional person, bag, and stop costs extra, so it's essential to agree on a fare before boarding.

Blue ATVO buses take 20 minutes to make the nonstop trip from airport to Piazzale Roma; from here you can get a vaporetto to the landing nearest your hotel. The ATVO fare is €3, and tickets are available on the bus when the airport ticket booth (open 9–7:30) is closed. Orange ACTV local buses (Line 5) leave for Venice at 10 and 40 minutes past every hour (hourly service after 11:10 PM) and take 30 minutes; before boarding, you must buy a €2 ticket at the airport tobacconist-newsstand, open 6:30 AM–9 PM, or from the ATVO/ACTV booth in the arrivals hall on the ground floor. During rush hour, luggage can be a hassle on the local bus. A land taxi from the airport to Piazzale Roma costs about €40.

🛈 Airport Information **Aeroporto Marco Polo** ✉ Tessera, 10 km (6 mi) north of the city on the mainland ☎ 041/2609260 ⊕ www.veniceairport.it.

🛈 Taxis & Shuttles **Alilaguna** ☎ 041/5235775. **ATVO** ☎ 0421/383672. **Motoscafo** ☎ 041/5222303 airport transfers. **Radio Taxi** ☎ 041/5952080.

BY BOAT & FERRY

BY GONDOLA   It's hard to believe that Venice could get any more beautiful, but as your gondola glides away from the fondamenta, a magical transformation takes place—you've left the huddled masses behind to marvel at the city as visitors have for centuries before you. To some it feels like a Disney ride, and some complain about flotsam, jetsam, and less than pleasant odors, but if you insist that your gondolier take you winding through

1

the tiny side canals, you'll get out of the city's main salon and into her intimate chambers, where only private boats can go. San Marco is loaded with gondola stations, but to get off the circuit, and maybe even have a canal to yourself, try the San Tomà or Santa Sofia (near Ca' d'Oro) stations. The price of a 50-minute ride is supposed to be fixed at €73 for up to six passengers, rising to €91 between 8 PM and 8 AM, but these are minimums and you may have difficulty finding a gondolier who will work for that unless the city is empty. Bargaining can help, but in any case come to terms on cost and duration before you start, and make it clear that you want to see more than just the Grand Canal.

BY TRAGHETTO Many tourists are unaware of the two-man gondola ferries that cross the Grand Canal at numerous strategic points. At €.50, they're the cheapest and shortest gondola ride in Venice, and they can save a lot of walking. Look for TRAGHETTO signs and hand your fare to the gondolier when you board.

BY VAPORETTO ACTV water buses serve several routes daily and after 11 PM provide limited service through the night. Some routes cover the length of the Grand Canal, and others circle the city and connect Venice with the lagoon islands. Landing stages are clearly marked with name and line number, but check before boarding to make sure the boat is going in your direction.

Line 1 is the Grand Canal local, calling at every stop and continuing via San Marco to the Lido. The trip takes about 35 minutes from Ferrovia to Vallaresso, San Marco. Circular Line 41 (the odd number indicates it goes counterclockwise) will take you from San Zaccaria to Murano, and Line 42 (clockwise) makes the return trip. Likewise, take Line 42 from San Zaccaria to Giudecca's Redentore, but Line 41 to return. Line 51 (counterclockwise) runs from the station to San Zaccaria via Piazzale Roma, then continues to the Lido. From the Lido, Line 52 circles clockwise, stopping at San Zaccaria, Zattere, Piazzale Roma, the station, Fondamente Nuove (connect to northern lagoon islands), San Pietro di Castello, and back to the Lido. From San Zaccaria, Line 82 (same number both directions) loops past Giudecca and Zattere, then stops at Tronchetto (parking garage) on the way to Piazzale Roma and the station. From the station, Line 82 becomes the Grand Canal express to Rialto, with some boats continuing to Vallaresso (San Marco) and in summer going all the way to the Lido beaches. Line N runs from roughly midnight to 6 AM, stopping at the Lido, Vallaresso, Accademia, Rialto, the train station, Piazzale Roma, Giudecca, and San Zaccaria, then returning in the opposite direction.

BY WATER TAXI A motoscafo (water taxi) isn't cheap; you'll spend about €55 for a short trip in town, €60 to the Lido, and €80 per hour to visit the outer islands. The fare system is convoluted, with luggage handling, waiting time, early or late hours, and even ordering a taxi from your hotel adding expense. Always agree on the price first.

FARES & SCHEDULES An ACTV water bus ticket for all lines except the Grand Canal costs €3.50, or €6 round-trip (valid for 24 hours); a single ride on the Grand Canal line costs €5. (Children under four ride free.) Another option is

Travel Cards: €10.50 buys 24 hours and €22 buys 72 hours of unlimited travel on ACTV boats and buses. A shuttle ticket allows you to cross a canal, one stop only, for €1.80

Line information is posted at each landing, and complete timetables for all lines are available for €0.60 at ACTV/Vela ticket booths, located at most major stops. Buy tickets before getting on the boat and remember to validate them in the yellow time-stamp machines. Tickets are also sold on the boat; you must ask to buy one immediately upon boarding, which can be a hassle. When inspectors come aboard, ticketless riders are fined, as are those who haven't validated their tickets. Ignorance will not spare you; the fine is €40, and getting fined can be embarrassing. The law says you must also buy tickets for dogs, baby strollers left unfolded, and bags over 28 inches long (there's no charge for your bag if you have a Travel Card), but this is generally enforced only for very bulky bags. The telephone number for ferry information listed below has assistance in English.

Boat & Ferry Information ACTV ☎ 041/2424 ⊕ www.hellovenezia.it. **Water taxi** ☎ 041/5415084 or 041/5222303.

BY BUS
From Venice's Piazzale Roma terminal, buses connect with Mestre, the Brenta Riviera, Padua, Treviso, Cortina d'Ampezzo, and other regional destinations as well as many major European cities.

FARES & SCHEDULES   ACTV buses to Mestre (€1) are frequent, and there's night service; ACTV buses to Padua (€3.50) leave at 25 and 55 minutes past each hour and stop along the Brenta River. ATVO has daily buses to Cortina (€10.60) June–September and throughout the Christmas–New Year holidays. Buses leave Venice at 7:50 AM and depart from Cortina at 3:15 PM. Service is available only on weekends September–May.

Bus Information ACTV ☎ 041/2424. **ATVO** ☎ 0421/383671 ⊕ www.atvo.it. **Bus Terminal** ✉ Piazzale Roma, across the Grand Canal from the train station, Santa Croce.

BY CAR
Venice is on the east–west A4 autostrada, which connects with Padua, Verona, Brescia, Milan, and Turin. If you bring a car to Venice, you will have to pay for a garage or parking space.

You can take your car to the Lido; the car ferry (Line 17) makes the half-hour trip about every 50 minutes from a landing at Tronchetto, but in summer there can be long lines. It costs €10–€20, depending on the size of the car.

PARKING   Warning: don't be waylaid by illegal touts, often wearing fake uniforms, who may try to flag you down and offer to arrange parking and hotels; drive on to one of the parking garages. Parking at Autorimessa Comunale costs €19 for 24 hours. The private Garage San Marco costs €20 for up to 12 hours and €26 for 12–24 hours. You can reserve a space in advance at either of these garages; you'll come upon both immediately after crossing the bridge from the mainland. Another alternative is Tronchetto parking (€18 for 1–24 hours); watch for signs for it coming over the bridge—you'll have to turn right before you get to

Piazzale Roma. Many hotels have negotiated guest discounts with San Marco or Tronchetto garages; get a voucher when you check in at your hotel and present it when you pay the garage. Line 82 connects Tronchetto with Piazzale Roma and Piazza San Marco and also goes to the Lido in summer. When there's thick fog or extreme tides, a bus runs to Piazzale Roma instead. Avoid private boats—they're a rip-off. There's a luggage-check office, open daily 6 AM–9 PM, next to the Pullman Bar on the ground floor of the municipal garage at Piazzale Roma.

🚗 Garages **Autorimessa Comunale** ✉ Piazzale Roma, Santa Croce, end of S11 road ☎ 041/2727211 ⊕ www.asmvenezia.it. **Garage San Marco** ✉ Piazzale Roma 467/f, Santa Croce, turn right into bus park ☎ 041/5232213 ⊕ www.garagesanmarco.it. **Tronchetto** ☎ 041/5207555.

BY TRAIN

Venice has rail connections with every major city in Italy and Europe. Some Continental trains do not enter Venice but stop only at the mainland Mestre station. All trains traveling to and from Venice Santa Lucia stop at Mestre, and it's just a 10-minute hop on the next passing train. If you change from a regional train to an Intercity or Eurostar, you'll need to upgrade with a *supplemento* (extra charge) or be liable for a hefty fine. You'll also be fined if before boarding you forget to validate your train ticket in one of the yellow machines found on or near platforms.

🚆 Train Information **Stazione Ferroviaria Santa Lucia** ✉ Grand Canal, northwest corner of the city, Cannaregio ☎ 041/785670, 892021 Trenitalia train information ⊕ www.trenitalia.com. **Stazione Ferroviaria Venezia-Mestre** ✉ Mestre, 12 km [7 mi] northwest of Venice ☎ 041/784498, 892021 Trenitalia train information ⊕ www.trenitalia.com.

Contacts & Resources

DISABILITIES & ACCESSIBILITY

In Venice, bridges, historic buildings that cannot be modernized, and boat travel all complicate matters for people with mobility concerns. Don't rely on tourist maps that indicate lifts on certain bridges around town; these rarely if ever work. Vaporetto Lines 1, 82, and N have the most deck space, but boarding water taxis can sometimes be hazardous. Kiosks in the airport, train station, and parking areas that book hotels can dispense only information member hotels provide; there are no set criteria for designating a hotel as accessible. InformaHandicap's Web site has helpful information for chair users, and questions e-mailed in English are answered. Palazzo Ducale, Museo Correr, the Campanile di San Marco, Ca' Rezzonico, Palazzo Grassi, Ca' d'Oro, and the Scuola di San Rocco have either lifts or ramps. Most churches, including the Basilica di San Marco, have one or two low steps to overcome.

🚹 **InformaHandicap** ✉ San Marco 4136, Riva del Carbon, 30124 Venice ☎ 041/2748144 ⊕ www.comune.venezia.it/handicap.

EMERGENCIES

The U.K. Consulate can recommend doctors and dentists, as can your hotel or any pharmacy. The nearest pharmacy is never far, and they take turns staying open nights, Saturday afternoons, and Sunday; the list of after-hours pharmacies is posted on the front of every pharmacy and appears in daily newspapers.

🆘 Emergency Services **General Emergencies** ☎ 113. **Ambulance** ☎ 118. **Carabinieri** ☎ 112. **U.K. Consulate** ✉ Piazza Donatori di Sangue 2, Mestre ☎ 041/5055990.

ENGLISH-LANGUAGE MEDIA

BOOKS   Cafoscarina, close to Università Ca' Foscari, has a large selection of English literature, mainly classics. Mondadori and Studium stock books about Venice and Italian food, with a few fiction paperbacks. The Venice Pavilion, off Piazza San Marco near the Giardini Reali, has a good selection of books and novels featuring the city. For books about Venice's maritime culture, lagoon, and environment, try Maredicarta.

NEWSPAPERS &   You can find English-language newspapers at a stall beside the San
MAGAZINES   Marco post office (behind Museo Correr), at the train station, in Campo SS. Apostoli, between Rialto and Ca' d'Oro, and at the foot of the Accademia bridge.

🆘 **Cafoscarina** ✉ Campiello Squellini, Dorsoduro 3259 ☎ 041/5229602. **Maredicarta** ✉ Fondamenta dei Tolentini, Santa Croce 222, across from train station ☎ 041/716304. **Mondadori** ✉ Salizada San Moisè, San Marco 1345 ☎ 041/52222193. **Studium** ✉ Calle de la Canonica, San Marco 337/c, off Piazzetta dei Leoncini ☎ 041/5222382. **Venice Pavilion** ✉ San Marco 2 ☎ 041/5225150.

MAIL & SHIPPING

Venice's main post office (Monday–Saturday 8:30–6:30) is housed in the Fondaco dei Tedeschi, near the Rialto bridge. You'll find a Federal Express office just outside Piazza San Marco, opposite Hotel Luna.

TOURS

BOAT TOURS   Boat tours to the islands of Murano, Burano, and Torcello, organized by Serenissima Motoscafi and Consorzio San Marco, leave from various docks around Piazza San Marco daily. These 3½-hour trips cost €18 (Serenissima Motoscafi) or €40 (Consorzio San Marco) and can be annoyingly commercial, often emphasizing glass-factory showrooms and pressuring you to buy at prices even higher than normal. Trips depart at 9:30 and 2:30 April–October, at 2:30 November–March.

More than a dozen major travel agents in Venice have grouped together to provide frequent, good-quality tours of the city. Serenaded gondola trips, with or without dinner (€73, €35), can be purchased at any of their offices or at American Express. Nightly tours leave at 7:30 and 8:30 April–September, at 7:30 only in October, and at 3:30 November–March.

🆘 **American Express** ✉ Salizada San Moisè, San Marco 1471 ☎ 041/5200844 🖷 041/5229937. **Consorzio San Marco** ☎ 041/2406712. **Serenissima Motoscafi** ☎ 041/5224281.

PRIVATE GUIDES   Cooperativa Guide Turistiche Autorizzate has a list of more than 100 licensed guides. Tours lasting about two hours with an English-speaking guide start at €113 for up to 30 people. Agree on a total price before you begin, as there can be some hidden extras. Guides are of variable quality.

🆘 **Cooperativa Guide Turistiche Autorizzate** ✉ San Marco 750, near San Zulian ☎ 041/5209038 🖷 041/5210762.

TOURS OF THE
REGION

American Express and other agencies offer several excursions in the Veneto region of the Venetian Arc. A boat trip to Padua along the Brenta River makes stops at three Palladian villas, and you return to Venice by bus. The tours run three times a week (Tuesday, Thursday, and Saturday) from March to October and cost €62 per person (€86 with lunch); bookings need to be made a few days in advance.

Bassani offers excursions as well as personalized travel through the Veneto and other Italian cities.

🚩 Fees & Schedules **American Express** ⊠ Salizada San Moisè, San Marco 1471 ☎ 041/5200844 🖷 041/5229937. **Avventure Bellissime** ⊠ San Marco 2442/A ☎ 041/5208616 🖷 041/2960282 ⊕ www.tours-italy.com. **Bassani** ⊠ San Basilio, Santa Marta, Fab. 17 ☎ 041/5203644 🖷 041/5204009 ⊕ www.bassani.it

WALKING TOURS

More than a dozen major travel agents offer a two-hour walking tour of the San Marco area (€28), which ends with a glassblowing demonstration daily (no Sunday tour in winter). From April to October there's also an afternoon walking tour that ends with a gondola ride (€37). Venicescapes, an Italo-American cultural association, offers several themed itineraries focusing on history and culture as well as tourist sights. Their three- to seven-hour tours are private, and groups are small (generally six to eight people). Reservations are recommended during busy seasons, and prices start at €200 for two people. Walks inside Venice also does several themed tours for small groups starting at €65 per hour and lasting up to three hours.

🚩 Fees & Schedules **Alba Travel** ⊠ Calle del Magazin, San Marco 4538 ☎ 041/5210123 🖷 041/5200781 ⊕ www.albatravel.it. **Oltrex Viaggi** ⊠ Castello 4192 ☎ 041/5242840 🖷 041/5221986 ⊕ www.oltrex.it. **Venicescapes** ⊠ Campo San Provolo, Castello 4954 ☎🖷 041/5206361 ⊕ www.venicescapes.org. **Walks Inside Venice** ☎🖷 041/5202434 ⊕ www.walksinsidevenice.com.

TRAVEL AGENCIES

🚩 Local Agent Referrals **Gran Canal** ⊠ Ponte del Ovo, near Rialto Bridge, San Marco 4759 ☎ 041/2712111 🖷 041/5223380. **Kele & Teo** ⊠ Ponte dei Bareteri, San Marco 4930, between San Marco and Rialto ☎ 041/5208722 🖷 041/5208913.

VISITOR INFORMATION

The train-station branch of the Venice Tourist Office is open daily 8–6:30; other branches generally open at 9:30.

The Rolling Venice pass, costing €3 and valid throughout a calendar year, buys visitors ages 14–29 discounts on 72-hour vaporetto passes and admission to lots of museums, and at assorted hotels, restaurants, and shops. Just show your passport or ID at Vela ticket offices (major vaporetto stops), at the Assessorato alla Gioventù (weekdays 9:30–1, plus Tuesday and Thursday afternoons 3–5), or at the Associazione Italiana Alberghi per la Gioventù (Monday through Saturday 8–2). The Venice Card allows you to avoid lines at city museums and prepays for vaporetti and municipal toilets. Order online (www.venicecard.it) or by phone (☎ 041/2424) and pay cash when you pick up the card. Price depends on how many days you're staying; though convenient, it's not a significant discount.

🛈 **Assessorato alla Gioventù** ✉ Corte Contarina, San Marco 1529, behind Piazza San Marco post office ☎ 041/2747651. **Associazione Italiana Alberghi per la Gioventù** ✉ Calle Castelforte, San Polo 3101, near San Rocco ☎ 041/5204414. **Rolling Venice** ☎ 041/2714747 ⊕ www.comune.venezia.it/rol2/.

🛈 **Venice Tourist Offices** ☎ 041/5298711 ⊕ www.turismovenezia.it ✉ Marco Polo Airport ✉ Train Station, Cannaregio ✉ Procuratie Nuove, San Marco 71/f, near Museo Correr ✉ Venice Pavilion, San Marco, near Giardini Reali ✉ Garage Comunale, Piazzale Roma ✉ S. Maria Elisabetta 6/a, Lido ⊘ Summer only ☎ 041/5265711.

The Venetian Arc

Villa Cordellina Lombardi

WORD OF MOUTH

"Verona and Vicenza are both stunningly beautiful cities that we liked very much. Vicenza is smaller and seems to have more green space. It's also less touristy. Verona gives you the 'Romeo and Juliet' thing. Although I personally did not find any one attraction in Verona that impressive, the city as a whole stole my heart."

—Jocelyn P

WELCOME TO
THE VENETIAN ARC

Villa Barbaro, Maser

TOP 5
Reasons to Go

1 Giotto's frescoes in the Capella degli Scrovegni: At this chapel in Padua, Giotto's innovative painting techniques helped to launch the Renaissance.

2 Villa Barbaro in Maser: Master architect Palladio's most gracious Renaissance creation meets Veronese's opulent paintings in a one-time-only collaboration.

3 Opera in Verona's ancient arena: Even if the music doesn't move you, the spectacle will.

4 The café scene in Trieste: As you sip a cup of Trieste's superlative coffee, you'll feel like you have one foot in Venice, the other in Vienna.

5 The wine roads north of Treviso: A series of routes take you through beautiful hillsides to some of Italy's finest wines.

Shakespeare placed Romeo, Juliet, and a couple of gentlemen in Verona, one of the oldest, best-preserved, and most beautiful cities in Italy. Try to catch *Aida* at the gigantic Roman arena.

The elegant art city of Vicenza, nestled on the green plain reaching inland from Venice's lagoon, bears the signature of the great 16th-century architect Andrea Palladio. The **Corso Palladio**, a main road through the center of town, is lined with palaces he designed.

Bassano del Grappa

Cittadella

A22

Vicenza

Verona

A4

VENETO

A22

10

Legnago

434

Arena, Verona

Treviso

Juliet's House, Verona

Getting Oriented

The Venetian Arc is the sweep of land curving north and east from the Adige River to the Slovenian border. It's made up of two Italian regions—the Veneto and Friuli–Venezia Giulia—that were once controlled by Venice, and the culture is a mix of Venetian, Alpine, and central European sensibilities.

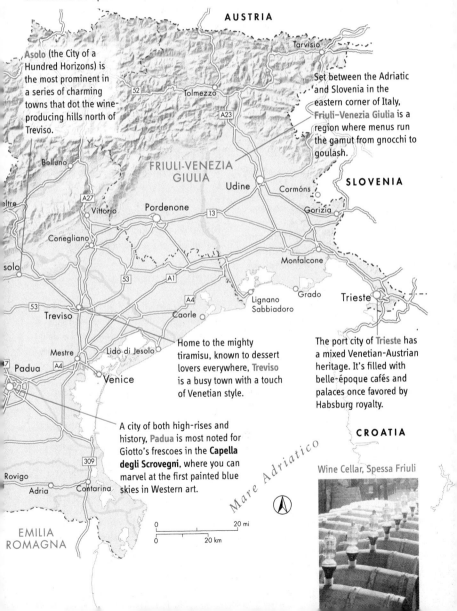

AUSTRIA

Tarvisio

Asolo (the City of a Hundred Horizons) is the most prominent in a series of charming towns that dot the wine-producing hills north of Treviso.

52
Tolmezzo
A23

Set between the Adriatic and Slovenia in the eastern corner of Italy, **Friuli–Venezia Giulia** is a region where menus run the gamut from gnocchi to goulash.

Belluno

FRIULI-VENEZIA GIULIA

Udine
Cormòns

SLOVENIA

A27
eltre
Vittorio

Pordenone
13
Gorizia

Coneglian o

Monfalcone

solo
53
A1

Grado
Lignano Sabbiadoro

Trieste

53
A4
Caorle

Treviso

Mestre
Lido di Jesolo

Home to the mighty tiramisu, known to dessert lovers everywhere, **Treviso** is a busy town with a touch of Venetian style.

The port city of **Trieste** has a mixed Venetian-Austrian heritage. It's filled with belle-époque cafés and palaces once favored by Habsburg royalty.

7
Padua
A4

Venice

A city of both high-rises and history, **Padua** is most noted for Giotto's frescoes in the **Capella degli Scrovegni**, where you can marvel at the first painted blue skies in Western art.

CROATIA

309
Rovigo

Adria
Contarina

Mare Adriatico

Wine Cellar, Spessa Friuli

EMILIA ROMAGNA

0   20 mi
0   20 km

THE VENETIAN ARC PLANNER

Making the Most of Your Time

The towns of the Veneto region should be on your itinerary if you're doing a tour of northern Italy, and they're good day-trip options if you're making an extended stay in Venice. Lined up in a row west of Venice are Padua, Vicenza, and Verona—three well-to-do towns, each with its own appealing character and worthwhile sights. Verona has the greatest charm, and it's probably the best choice for a base in the area (though this is no secret—Verona also draws the most tourists).

The hills north of Venice make for good drives. Treviso, the largest town, is worth a stop, but you're more likely to fall for the smaller towns of Asolo and Bassano del Grappa and the visitor-friendly wine country that surrounds them.

East of the Veneto, the region of Friuli-Venezia Giulia is off the main tourist circuit. You probably won't go here on a first trip to Italy, but by your second or third visit you may be drawn by its caves and castles, its battle-worn hills, and its mix of Italian and central European culture. The port city of Trieste, most famous for its elegant cafés, has quiet character that some people find dull and others find intriguing. (Famed travel writer Jan Morris's book in praise of the city is tellingly titled *Trieste and the Meaning of Nowhere*.) The vineyards of the Collio area on the Slovenian border have smaller yields than other Italian wine regions, but the quality of the final product is very high.

Getting Around

Padua, Vicenza, and Verona are neatly arranged on the highway and train line between Venice and Milan. Seeing them without a car isn't a problem, and having a car can complicate matters. The cities sometimes limit access, permitting only cars with plates ending in an even number on even days, odd on odd, or prohibiting cars altogether on weekends. There's no central source for information about these sporadic traffic restrictions; the best strategy is to check with your hotel before arrival for an update. On the other hand, you'll need a car to get the most out of the hill country that makes up much of the Venetian Arc. For details about getting around, see "Essentials" at the end of this chapter.

Prime Picnicking

One of the pleasures of this mellow region is buying provisions at an open-air market or *salumeria* (the Italian version of a deli) and relaxing over a picnic. In the countryside, good picnicking spots are countless. If you're limiting your trip to the cities, consider these two locations:

■ In Verona, the Ponte Scaligero footbridge across the Adige River, just behind the Castelvecchio, has a lookout area at the halfway point that's excellent for picnicking. You can find everything you need at the exceptional Salumeria Albertini.

■ Padua's Basilica di Sant'Antonio is one of the rare churches in Italy that welcomes picnickers—it even provides the tables. For supplies, head to the Palazzo della Ragione food market.

Planning Ahead

Three of the top sights in the region demand some advance planning:

■ Reservations are required to see the Giotto frescoes in Padua's Cappella degli Scrovegni—you can book by phone or online.

■ Outside Vicenza, Villa La Rotonda, one of star architect Palladio's masterpieces, is open to the public only on Wednesday from mid-March through October. (Hours for visiting the grounds are less restrictive.)

■ Another highly acclaimed Palladian villa, Villa Barbaro near Maser, is open from March through October on Tuesday, Saturday, and Sunday afternoons. For the rest of the year, it's only open on weekends.

For details about Cappela degli Scrovegni, look in this chapter under "The Main Attractions" in Padua. For the villas, see "Palladio Country."

In the Cards

If you're planning to see more than a sight or two in Padua, Verona, or Trieste, it pays to pick up one of the tourist cards each city offers. For one price, you get admission to most sights and unlimited use of public transportation. Specifics are listed at the beginning of the city write-ups in this chapter.

Finding a Place to Stay

There's a full range of accommodations throughout the region. It's a trend for hotels to renovate and subsequently hike their prices, but good low-cost options can still be found. Ask about weekend discounts, which are often available at hotels catering to business clients. Rates tend to be higher in towns near Venice, which absorb the overflow when Venice is most crowded (during Carnevale and from spring through autumn). Agriturismo (farm stay) information is available at local tourist information offices and sometimes on the offices' Web sites.

Dining & Lodging Price Categories

WHAT IT COSTS in Euros					
	$$$$	$$$	$$	$	¢
Restaurants	over €22	€16–€22	€11–€16	€7–€11	under €7
Hotels	over €220	€160–€220	€110–€160	€70–€110	under €70

Restaurant prices are for a second course (un secondo). Hotel prices are for two people in a standard double room in high season, including tax and service.

How's the Weather?

The ideal times to visit are late spring and early summer (May and June) and in September and October. If you're an opera buff, it's worth tolerating the summer heat in order to see a performance at the Arena di Verona (where the season runs from July through September). Winter is a good time to avoid travel to the region: foggy conditions and wet, bone-chilling cold are not unusual from November through March.

TOP PASSEGGIATA

An evening walk along Via Mazzini between Piazza dei Signori and Piazza Bra captures the essence of Verona's appeal. On nights when there's a performance, you can sit in one of Piazza Bra's cafés and make out strains of opera coming from the arena next door.

Piazza dei Signori

Updated by
Elaine Eliah

THE ARC AROUND VENICE—stretching from Verona to Trieste, encompassing the Veneto and Friuli–Venezia Giulia regions—falls under the historical and spiritual influence of its namesake city. Whether seaside or inland, the emblem of Venice, St. Mark's winged lion, is emblazoned on palazzos or poised on pedestals, and the art, architecture, and way of life all reflect the splendor of La Serenissima.

The area is mainly flat green farmland, spotted with low hills that swell and rise steeply inland in a succession of plateaus and high meadows to the snow-capped Alps. Much of the pleasure of exploring here comes from discovering the variations on the Venetian theme that confer a unique character to each of the towns you visit. Some, such as Verona, Treviso, and Udine, have a solid medieval look; Asolo, the town of a hundred horizons, has an idyllic setting; Bassano combines a bit of both of these qualities. Padua is ennobled by Giotto's frescoes, Vicenza by the villas of Palladio. Udine, often overlooked, is home to the first important frescoes by Giambattista Tiepolo (1696–1770). In Trieste, after a climb to the hill of San Giusto with its cathedral and castle, the aroma of freshly roasted coffee that fills the city center is hard to resist. And there are artistic jewels to find around the arc, from the great Venetian masters in Verona to Veronese's lighthearted frescoes in Villa Barbaro at Maser.

PADUA

Bustling Padua (Padova in Italian) has long been one of northern Italy's major cultural centers. It's home to the peninsula's second-oldest university, founded in 1222, which attracted the likes of Dante (1265–1321), Petrarch (1304–74), and Galileo Galilei (1564–1642). The artists Giotto (circa 1266–1337), Donatello (circa 1386–1466), and Mantegna (1431–1506) left great works here.

Exploring Padua

The Padova Card (€15) provides free access to city buses, entrance to some of the town's principal sights (including the Cappella degli Scrovegni, Museo Civico, Battistero del Duomo, and Orto Botanico) and discounts for many other attractions, including boat trips on the Brenta River. The cards are valid for 48 hours or an entire weekend (from Friday to Sunday evening), and are sold at the tourist information office and the railway station.

The Main Attractions

❼ **Basilica di Sant'Antonio.** Byzantine domes and slender, minaretlike towers give this huge basilica an Asian-inspired style reminiscent of San Marco in Venice. The interior is sumptuous with the highest artistic achievements all bearing Donatello's name: the 15th-century Florentine master did the remarkable series of bronze reliefs illustrating the life of St. Anthony—whose feast day, Festa di Sant'Antonio on June 13, draws pilgrims from all over Europe—as well as the bronze statues of the Madonna and saints on the high altar. Standing in front of the church is Donatello's powerful statue of the *condottiere* (mercenary general) Erasmo da Narni, known by the nickname Gattamelata. It was cast in

THE VENETIAN ARC, PAST & PRESENT

Long before Venetians had made their presence felt, Ezzelino III da Romano (1194–1259), a larger-than-life scourge who was excommunicated by Pope Innocent IV, laid claim to Verona, Padua, and the surrounding lands and towns. After he was ousted, powerful families such as Padua's Carrara and Verona's della Scala (Scaligeri) vied throughout the 14th century to annex these territories. With the rise of Venetian rule came a time of relative peace, when noble families from the lagoon and the mainland commissioned Palladio to design their palazzos and enlisted the three Ts—Titian, Tintoretto, and Tiepolo—to decorate their interiors. This opulent legacy, superimposed upon medieval castles and fortifications, is central to the identities of present-day Padua, Vicenza, and Verona.

Friuli–Venezia Giulia has a diverse cultural history that's reflected in its architecture, language, and cuisine. It's been marched through, fought over, hymned by patriots, and romanticized by James Joyce, Rainer Maria Rilke, and Jan Morris. It's seen Fascists and Communists, Romans, Habsburgs, and Huns. It survived by forging sheltering alliances—Udine beneath the wings of San Marco (1420), Trieste choosing Duke Leopold of Austria (1382) over Venetian domination.

Some of World War I's fiercest fighting took place in Friuli–Venezia Giulia, where memorials and cemeteries commemorate hundreds of thousands who died before the arrival of Italian troops in 1918 finally liberated Trieste from Austrian rule. During World War II one of Italy's two concentration camps, still visitable, was in Trieste. Thousands of ethnic Slav residents bore the brunt of Fascist persecution, and in Istria Italian residents suffered Yugoslavia's retaliation. When peace was declared in other parts of Europe, Trieste became a subject of Cold War conflict between Zone A and Zone B—the free-world Allies versus Tito's socialism. Only in 1976 was the "Trieste question" finally resolved with Treaty of Osimo: Italy retained the city but surrendered the entire Istrian Peninsula, now part of Croatia. With Slovenia's 1991 declaration of independence from Yugoslavia, confrontation again flared along the border, but the admission of Slovenia to the European Union (May 2004) may finally end the area's bloody legacy.

bronze, a monumental technical achievement in 1453, and had an enormous influence on the development of Italian Renaissance sculpture. In the church there are also marble reliefs by architect Jacopo Sansovino (1486–1570) and Tullio Lombardo (circa 1455–1532), who was the most talented in a family of marble carvers that decorated churches throughout the Veneto (including Santa Maria dei Miracoli in Venice). ⊠ *Piazza del Santo* ☎ *049/8242811* ⊕ *www.santantonio.org* ☉ *Weekdays 6:15 AM–6:45 PM, weekends 6:15 AM–7:45 PM.*

❶ Cappella degli Scrovegni. What's perhaps the most famous chapel in Italy after the Sistine was erected by wealthy Paduan Enrico Scrovegno to atone for the usury practiced by his deceased father, Reginaldo. Giotto and his assistants were commissioned to decorate the interior; they worked

Fodor'sChoice ★

from 1303 to 1305 on a magnificent fresco cycle illustrating the lives of Mary and Christ. In typical medieval comic-strip fashion, the 38 panels are arranged in tiers intended to be read from left to right. Opposite the altar is a powerful *Last Judgment,* where Enrico offers his chapel to the Virgin. The depth and perspective in these frescoes—which include the first blue skies in Western painting—were revolutionary. Mandatory reservations, available by Web or phone, are for a specific time and are nonrefundable. In order to preserve the artwork, doors are opened only every 15 minutes. A maximum of 25 visitors at a time must spend 15 minutes in an acclimatization room before making a 15-minute chapel visit. You can see fresco details as part of a virtual tour at Museo Civico Eremitani. ⊠ *Piazza Eremitani 8* ☎ *049/8204551 information, 049/2010020 reservations* ⊕ *www.cappelladegliscrovegni. it* 🖭*€12, includes Museo Civico Eremitani* ⊙ *Mar.–Jan. 6, daily 9 AM–10 PM; Jan. 7–Feb., daily 9–7.*

❺ **Piazza dei Signori.** Some fine examples of 15th- and 16th-century buildings line this square. On the west side, the **Palazzo del Capitanio** has an impressive **Torre dell'Orologio,** with an astronomical clock dating from 1344. The **Duomo,** just a few steps away, is not the most interesting church in town.

Villa Pisani. Extensive grounds with rare trees, ornamental fountains, and garden follies surround this extraordinary 18th-century palace in Stra, 13 km (8 mi) southeast of Padua. It was one of the last of many stately residences constructed along the Brenta River from the 16th to 18th century by wealthy Venetians for their *villeggiatura*—

> **WORD OF MOUTH**
>
> "To me, Padua, even more than Venice, is evocative of the 'old' Italy. In the old city *(città vecchia)*, the maze of tiny streets is just the thing for wandering around and getting lost."   –Wayne

vacation and escape from the midsummer humidity. Tiepolo's trompel'oeil frescoes on the ballroom ceiling alone are worth the visit. If you have youngsters in tow surfeited with old masters, explore the gorgeous **park** and **maze.** To get here from Venice, you can take the Brenta River bus that leaves from Piazzale Roma. ☒ *Via Doge Pisani 7, Stra* ☎ *049/ 502074* ☒ *Villa €5, maze and park €2.50* ☼ *Apr.–Sept., Tues.–Sun. 9–7; villa and park only Oct.–Mar., Tues.–Sun. 9–4; last entry 1 hr before closing.*

Also Worth Seeing

❻ **Battistero del Duomo** (Cathedral Baptistery). The often overlooked 12th-century baptistry contains mid-1370s frescoes depicting scenes from the Book of Genesis. They're the greatest work of Giusto de' Menabuoi, who further developed Giotto's style of depicting human figures naturally, using perspective and realistic lighting. The building is a refreshingly cool retreat from the city. ☒ *Piazza Duomo* ☎ *049/656914* ☒ *€2.50* ☼ *Daily 10–6.*

❷ **Museo Civico Eremitani** (Civic Museum). What was once a monastery now houses works of Venetian masters, as well as fine collections of archaeological pieces and ancient coins. ☒ *Piazza Eremitani 8* ☎ *049/8204551* ☒ *€10* ☼ *Tues.–Sun. 9–7.*

❽ **Orto Botanico** (Botanical Garden). The Venetian Republic ordered the creation of Padua's botanical garden in 1545 to supply the university with medicinal plants. You can stroll the arboretum and wander through hothouses and beds of plants that were first introduced to Italy in this Renaissance garden, which still maintains its original layout. A St. Peter's palm, planted in 1585, stands protected in its own private greenhouse. ☒ *Via Orto Botanico 15* ☎ *049/8272119* ☒ *€4* ☼ *Apr.–Oct., daily 9–1 and 3–6; Nov.–Mar., Mon.–Sat. 9–1.*

❸ **Palazzo del Bo'.** The University of Padua, founded in 1222, is housed in this 16th-century palazzo with an 18th-century facade. It's named after the Osteria del Bo' (*bo'* means "ox"), an inn that once stood on the site. It's worth a visit to see the exquisite and perfectly proportioned anatomy theater and a hall with a lectern used by Galileo. You can enter only as part of a guided tour. Most guides speak English, but it is worth checking ahead by phone. ☒ *Via VIII Febbraio* ☎ *049/8273047* ☒ *€3* ☼ *Mar.–Oct., Tues., Thurs., and Sat. at 9:15, 10:15, and 11:15, Mon., Wed., and Fri. at 3:15, 4:15, and 5:15; Nov.–Feb., Tues., Thurs., and Sat. at 10:15 and 11:15, Mon., Wed., and Fri. at 3:15 and 4:15.*

④ Palazzo della Ragione. In the Middle Ages this building was the seat of Padua's government. Today its street-level arcades shelter shops and cafés. Art shows are often held upstairs in the frescoed **Salone,** where there's an enormous 15th-century wooden replica of Gattamelata's bronze steed sculpted by Donatello. ⊠ *Piazza della Ragione* ☎ *049/8205006* ▣ *Salone €8* ☉ *Tues.–Sun. 9–7.*

Where to Stay & Eat

$$$ ✕ **La Vecchia Enoteca.** The ceiling is mirrored, the shelves are filled with books and wine, and the silverware once belonged to a cruise line. It's a luxurious setting in which to enjoy *branzino in crosta di patate* (sea bass with a potato crust) or beef with rosemary and balsamic vinegar, followed by a homemade dessert such as *crema catalana* (crème caramel). ⊠ *Via Santi Martino e Solferino 32* ☎ *049/8752856* ▤ *AE, MC, V* ☉ *Closed Sun., 3 wks July and Aug. No lunch Mon.*

$–$$ ✕ **Gigi Bar.** Simple and unpretentious: yellow walls and tablecloths brighten this inexpensive restaurant where high ceilings open up a second-floor seating area. The central kitchen is behind a counter low enough for the convivial owner-chef Ferrucio to see and supervise the equally friendly dining-room staff. The terrific and popular fish soup is one of the affordable seafood dishes that keep locals queuing up. There are also tasty steaks, salads, vegetable plates, and pizzas with a surprisingly light crust. ⊠ *Via Verdi 18/20* ☎ *049/8760028* ▤ *DC, MC, V* ☉ *Closed Tues., 2 wks in July.*

$ ✕ **Osteria L'Anfora.** At this loud and lively spot the framed rugby shirts hanging alongside vintage wine bottles seem to make sense. Padua's not-quite-students-anymore regularly come here for wine and jazz, especially at happy hour. The simple, reasonable menu of pastas, salads, and a couple of daily specials makes return clients of many. ⊠ *Via Dei Soncin 13* ☎ *049/656629* ▤ *AE, MC, V* ☉ *Closed Sun.*

¢ ✕ **Brek.** Workers in northern Italy flock to this modern chain of self-service restaurants for fast food Italian style. Browse the hot and cold buffet islands, make your choices, and watch your pasta or pizza be created—or your steak grilled—before your eyes. Brek won't take much time out of your touring schedule or much cash out of your wallet. ⊠ *Piazza Cavour 54* ☎ *049/8753788* ▤ *AE, DC, MC, V.*

$$$ ▦ **Methis.** The strikingly modern Methis takes its name from the Greek word for style and spirit. Four floors of minimalist guest rooms are designed to reflect the elements: gentle earth tones, firey red, watery cool blue, and airy whiteness (in the top-floor suites). Rooms have Japanese-style tubs, and four are equipped for guests with disabilities. The lobby bathroom is worth a visit just to wash your hands in the fountain. ⊠ *Riviera Paleocapa 70, 35141* ☎ *049/8725555* ▤ *049/8725135* ⊕ *www.methishotel.com* ▨ *52 rooms, 7 suites* ⌂ *In-room safes, mini-bars, cable TV with movies and video games, in-room data ports, gym, bar, Internet, meeting room, free parking, no-smoking floor* ▤ *AE, DC, MC, V* ▯◯▮ *BP.*

★ **$$$** ▦ **Villa Pisani.** The spacious high-ceiling rooms in this enormous 16th-century villa are furnished entirely with period pieces—some units even

EATING WELL IN THE VENETIAN ARC

With the decisive seasonal changes of the Venetian Arc, it's little wonder many restaurants shun printed menus. Some of the region's defining culinary elements are from the field and the forest, and are only available at certain times of year: in spring, highlights include white asparagus and wild herbs; in autumn, chestnuts, radicchio, and wild mushrooms. Any time of the year, you're sure to find Italian families and friends indulging in the Sunday tradition of lunching out; equally certain is the likelihood of finding nothing more than bar snacks open from 2:30 until 7 PM.

The catch of the day, whether from the Adriatic or Lake Garda, is always a good bet. Inland, meat prevails: pork and veal standards are supplemented with lamb and rabbit, and goose, duck, and guinea fowl are all common poultry options. North around Asolo, snails are popular. In Verona, a tradition of eating horse meat dates to a bloody 19th-century skirmish, when a starving populace created *pastisada*, a stew made with the animals killed in battle. In

Friuli–Venezia Giulia, menus show the influences of Austria, Hungary, Slovenia, and Croatia. You may find wild deer and hare on the menu, along with renowned San Daniele del Friuli prosciutto. And you can't get out of Treviso without eating the ubiquitous radicchio, found in soup, salad, pasta, and even dessert.

For starches, the Veneto dines on *bigoli* (thick, whole wheat pasta), and risotto is wine-saturated with Amarone in Verona and Prosecco in Conigliano. You'll encounter gnocchi made with pumpkin or plums in Udine, strudel filled with *bruscandoli* (wild greens) in Cormòns. Polenta is everywhere, varying from a stiff porridge topped with Gorgonzola or stews, to a patty grilled alongside meat or fish.

Austrian-style pastries will sweeten your stay in Trieste, and Verona scoops some of the best gelato. Treviso claims to have invented the area's signature dessert, tiramisu, but chefs in virtually every kitchen believe they hold the secret to making the best version.

have fully frescoed walls. All rooms look out over stunning formal gardens and beyond to a 15-acre park with rare trees, a chapel, a theater, and a concealed swimming pool. You have access to three big *sale* (lounges), where you can chat with the few other lucky guests and Signora Scalabrin, who shares her patrician living areas, music, and books. With breakfast served on silver platters, this is a bed-and-breakfast that outstrips almost all the hotel competition. ✉ *Via Roma 19, 35040 Vescovana, 30 km (19 mi) south of Padua, off Hwy A13* ☎ *0425/ 920016* ⊕ *www.villapisani.it* ➚ *7 rooms, 1 suite* ⚭ *Pool, horseback riding, Internet, convention center, free parking, some pets allowed; no a/c in some rooms, no room phones, no TV in some rooms, no smoking* ⊟ *AE, DC, MC, V* ⊙ *BP.*

$$ 🏨 **Majestic Toscanelli.** An elegant entrance, with potted evergreens flanking the steps, sets the tone in a hotel that has been family-operated since

1946. Plants figure strongly in the breakfast room as well, and the charming bedrooms are furnished in different styles—from 19th-century mahogany to French Empire. Your very welcoming hosts offer discounts to seniors, AAA members, and those carrying Fodor's guidebooks. ⊠ *Via dell'Arco 2, near Piazza della Frutta, 35122* ☎ *049/663244* 🖨 *049/8760025* ⊕ *www.toscanelli.com* ⤴ *31 rooms, 3 suites* ♻ *Café, some in-room safes, minibars, cable TV with movies, in-room data ports, bar, Internet, meeting room, parking (fee), some pets allowed (fee), no-smoking floor* ☰ *AE, DC, MC, V* ❑ *BP.*

$ ⊞ **Al Fagiano.** Some rooms in this peaceful hotel have views of the spires and cupolas at Basilica di Sant'Antonio. Facilities are modest, and rooms simply furnished, but an amiable staff and central location make this a pleasant and convenient place to stay. Breakfast is available for €6. ⊠ *Via Locatelli 45, 35100* ☎ *049/8750073* 🖨 *049/8753396* ⊕ *www.alfagiano.it* ⤴ *29 rooms* ♻ *Cable TV, in-room data ports, bar, parking (fee)* ☰ *AE, DC, MC, V* ❑ *EP.*

¢ ⊞ **Casa del Pellegrino.** Sharing the piazza with the Basilica di Sant'Antonio, this rather austere hotel has simple rooms arranged hospital-fashion along polished corridors. The newer annex, 100 yards behind the main building, has more modern amenities like air-conditioning. A cavernous restaurant downstairs serves cheap, simple fare. ⊠ *Via Cesarotti 21, 35123* ☎ *049/8239711* 🖨 *049/8239780* ⊕ *www.casadelpellegrino. com* ⤴ *157 rooms, 124 with bath* ♻ *Restaurant, cable TV, bar, parking (fee); no a/c in some rooms* ☰ *AE, MC, V* ☉ *Closed last wk Dec. and Jan.* ❑ *EP.*

Nightlife

Cafés

Since 1831 **Caffè Pedrocchi** (⊠ Piazzetta Pedrocchi ☎ 049/8781231) has been a place to sip and snack while musicians play jazz and intellectuals debate. An innovative bistro menu means you can now enjoy coffee-flavor pasta, or share zabaglione made from Pedrocchi's 150-year-old recipe. This neoclassical cross between a museum and stage set is open Sunday–Wednesday 9–9, and until midnight Thursday–Saturday.

Nightclubs & Bars

Kolar (⊠ Via dell'Arco 37 ☎ 049/8762385) is decoupaged floor to ceiling with recycled newspapers. This bar serves beverages, appetizers, and a lively mix of rock and jazz Tuesday through Sunday from 5 PM until 2 AM. **Victoria** (⊠ Via Savonarola 149 ☎ 049/8721530) is a *birreria* (bar serving primarily beer) that occasionally has live rock music; it's closed on Monday. **Limbo** (⊠ Via San Fermo 44 ☎049/656882), closed on Monday and Tuesday, is a restaurant-pizzeria that stays open late, with live music and a disco downstairs.

VICENZA

Vicenza bears the distinctive signature of the 16th-century architect Andrea Palladio, whose name has been given to the "Palladian" style of architecture. He gracefully incorporated elements of classical architecture—columns, porticoes, and domes—into a style that reflected the Renaissance celebration of order and harmony. His elegant villas and palaces were influential in propagating classical architecture in Europe, especially Britain, and later in America—most notably at Thomas Jefferson's Monticello.

In the mid-16th century Palladio was commissioned to rebuild much of Vicenza, which had been greatly damaged during wars waged against Venice by the League of Cambrai, an alliance of the papacy, France, the Holy Roman Empire, and several neighboring city-states. He made his name with the basilica, begun in 1549 in the heart of Vicenza, then embarked on a series of lordly buildings, all of which adhere to the same classicism.

Exploring Vicenza

Many of Palladio's works join the Venetian Gothic and baroque palaces that line Corso Palladio, an elegant shopping thoroughfare where Vicenza's status as one of Italy's wealthiest cities is evident.

The Main Attractions

⓭ Villa La Rotonda   See Page 85

★ ❾ **Teatro Olimpico.** Palladio's last, and perhaps most exciting, work was completed after his death by Vincenzo Scamozzi (1552–1616). Based closely on the model of an ancient Roman theater, it represents an important development in theater and stage design and is noteworthy for its acoustics and the cunning use of perspective in Scamozzi's permanent backdrop. The anterooms are frescoed with images of important figures in Venetian history. ⊠ *Piazza Matteotti* ☏ *0444/222800* ▢ *€8, includes admission to Palazzo Chiericati* ⊘ *Sept.–June, Tues.–Sun. 9–5; July and Aug., Tues.–Sun. 9–7.*

Also Worth Seeing

❿ **Palazzo Chiericati.** This exquisite and unmistakably Palladian palazzo houses Vicenza's **Museo Civico.** The museum's Venetian collection includes paintings by Tiepolo (1696–1770) and Tintoretto (1519–94). ⊠ *Piazza Matteotti* ☏ *0444/321348* ▢ *€8, includes admission to Teatro Olimpico* ⊘ *Sept.–June, Tues.–Sun. 9–5; July and Aug., Tues.–Sun. 9–7.*

⓫ **Palazzo Leoni Montanari.** In a city dominated by Palladio, this distinctly baroque building is often overlooked, as are its galleries. On display are more than 500 Orthodox icons dating back to the 13th century, making this one of the most significant such collections outside Russia. A second gallery of Veneto art includes paintings by Longhi (1702–85), Canaletto (1697–1768), and Francesco Guardi (1712–93). ⊠ *Contrà Santa Corona 25* ☏ *800/578875* ⊕ *www.palazzomontanari.com* ▢ *€3.50* ⊘ *Fri.–Sun. 10–6.*

⑫ **Piazza dei Signori.** At the heart of Vicenza sits this square, which contains the **Palazzo della Ragione,** commonly known as Palladio's basilica, though it wasn't a church at all but originally a courthouse and public meeting hall. Palladio made his name by successfully modernizing the medieval building, grafting a graceful two-story exterior loggia onto the existing Gothic structure. Take a look also at the **Loggia del Capitaniato,** opposite, which Palladio designed but never completed. Note that the palazzo and its loggia are open to the public only when there's an exhibition: ask at the tourist office.

⑭ **Villa Valmarana ai Nani.** Inside this 18th-century country house a series of frescoes by Tiepolo depict fantastic visions of a mythological world, including one of his most stunning works, the *Sacrifice of Iphigenia.* The neighboring *foresteria* (farm workers' dormitory) is also part of the museum; it contains more frescoes showing 18th-century Veneto life at its most charming by Tiepolo's son Giandomenico (1727–1804). You can reach the villa on foot by following the same path that leads to Palladio's Villa la Rotonda. ✉ *Via dei Nani 2/8* ☎ *0444/544546* 🎫 *€6* ⊙ *Mid-Mar.–Oct., Wed., Thurs., and weekends 10–noon and 3–6, Tues. and Fri. 10–noon.*

Continued on page 90

PALLADIO COUNTRY

They asked for a villa. Andrea Palladio gave them a lifestyle. Wealthy 16th-century Venetians by the score commissioned country houses from this architectural genius so they could pursue *la dolce vita*. Today, his Veneto villas are considered among the most beautiful structures ever conceived. When he managed to publish his designs in his *Four Books of Architecture* (1570), Palladio inspired a legion of wannabes that eventually spanned the globe. His influence was crucial in Thomas Jefferson's Monticello as well as, by unofficial count, half the state capitol structures in America. Jefferson wasn't lucky enough to visit the Veneto, but a tour of Palladio's finest buildings today will let you discover the seductions of *la dolce villa*.

TOWN & COUNTRY

Although the villa, or "country residence," was still a relatively new phenomenon in the 16th century, it quickly became all the rage once the great lords of Venice turned their eyes from the sea toward the fertile plains of the Veneto. They were forced to do this once their trade routes had faltered when Ottoman Turks conquered Constantinople in 1456 and Columbus opened a path to the riches of America in 1492. In no time, canals were built, farms were laid out, and the fashion for *villeggiatura*—the attraction of idyllic country retreats for the nobility—became a favored lifestyle. As a means of escaping an overheated

Rome, villas had been the original brainchild of the ancient emperors. But emperors, after all, required palatial, not rustic, lodgings—so it was no accident that Palladio zeroed in on this style of country residence. His process of evaluating the standards, and standbys, of ancient Roman life through the eye of the Italian Renaissance, combined with Palladio's innate sense of proportion and symmetry, became the lasting foundation of his art. In turn, Palladio threw out the jambalaya of styles prevalent in Venetian architecture—Oriental, Gothic, and Renaissance—for the pure, noble lines he had found in the buildings of the Caesars.

PALLADIO, STAR ARCHITECT

Andrea Palladio (1508–1580)

"Face dark, eyes fiery. Dress rich. His appearance that of a genius." So was Palladio described by his wealthy mentor, Count Trissino. In a brilliant bit of brand marketing, Trissino encouraged the young student to trade in his birth name, Andrea della Gondola, for the catchy Palladio, derived from Pallas, Greek deity of wisdom. He did, and it proved a wise move indeed. Born in Padua in 1508, Andrea moved to nearby Vicenza in 1524 and was quickly taken up

THE OLD BECOMES NEW

La Malcontenta

Studying ancient Rome with the eyes of an explorer, Palladio created a style that was surprisingly "modern." He linked old with new—but often did so in unexpected ways. Just take a look at Villa Foscari, nicknamed **"La Malcontenta"** (Mira, 041/5470012, € 5.15. Open May–Oct., Tues. and Sat. 9–noon; from Venice, take an ACTV bus from Piazzale Roma to Mira or opt for a boat ride up on the Burchiello). Shaded by weeping willows and mirrored by the Brenta Canal—the Beverly Hills of 16th-century Venice—"The Unhappy" was built for Nicolò and Alvise Foscari and is the quintessence of Palladian poetry. Its nickname was presumably coined for the recalcitrant wife of one of the original owners, as she had misbehaved so scandalously in Venice that she was kept locked up here. In revolutionary fashion, Palladio has applied the ancient Roman public motif of a temple facade to a private, domestic dwelling, topped off by a pediment, a construct previously used exclusively for religious structures. Stepping inside, he used the technique of vaulting seen in ancient Roman baths to enhance the spatial flow. With giant windows and immense white walls ready-made for the colorful frescoes painted by Zelotti, the resulting effect almost feels like a spacious New York City loft.

by the city's power elite. But he experienced a profound revelation on his first trip, in 1541, to Rome. Foregoing his earlier impulse to turn his adopted city, Vicenza, into a Gothic-mannered Venice, he decided instead to turn it into another Rome. This turnaround led to his spectacular conversion of the city's Palazzo della Ragione (1545) into a basilica modeled after the great meeting halls of antiquity. In years to come, after relocating to Venice, he created some memorable churches, such as S. Giorgio Maggiore (1564). Despite these varied projects, Palladio's unassailable position as one of the world's greatest architects is tied to the countryside villas, which he spread across the Veneto plains like a firmament of stars. Nothing else in the Veneto illuminates more clearly the idyllic beauty of the region than these elegant residences, their stonework now nicely mellowed and suntanned after five centuries.

VICENZA, CITY OF PALLADIO

Palazzo della Ragione

La Rotonda

To see Palladio's pageant of palaces, head for Vicenza, 53 km (33 mi) to the northwest of Mira's Malcontenta. His **Palazzo della Ragione**, or "Basilica," landmarks the city's heart, the Piazza dei Signori. This is where Palladio most brilliantly adopted the Serliana motif, an open arch framed by columns and circular windows. Across the way is his redbrick **Loggia dei Capitaniato**. One block past the Loggia is Vicenza's main street, appropriately named Corso Andrea Palladio. Just off this street is the Contrà Porti, where you'll find the **Palazzo Porto Barbaran** (1570) at No. 11, with its fabulously rich facade erupting with Ionic and Corinthian pillars. Today, this is the Centro Internazionale di Studi di Architettura Andrea Palladio (0444/323014, www.cisapalladio.org), a study center which mounts impressive temporary exhibitions. At No. 12 is Palladio's **Palazzo Thiene** (1558) while No. 21 is **Palazzo Porto Festa**, which he started. Contrà Reale leads to Corso A. Fogazzaro, where Palladio's **Palazzo Valmarana Braga** is found at No. 16, its grand facade ornamented with gigantic pilasters. A family cartouche once surmounted the roofline and was illuminated at night—à la Trump. Return to Corso Palladio and head left for five blocks to Piazza Mattotti and the **Palazzo Chiericati** (1550)—now the Museo Civico—Palladio's take on an imperial Roman loggia. Across the piazza the **Teatro Olimpico**, one of his final works (begun in 1579–80), reveals Palladio's knowledge of ancient Roman theaters. For a suitably grand finale, nothing will satisfy but a visit to one of the greatest buildings in all of Europe, **Villa La Rotonda** (Via della Rotonda 29, 0444/321793; villa €10, grounds €5. Villa open mid-Mar.–Oct., Wed. 10–noon and 3–6. Grounds mid-Mar.–Oct., Tues.–Sun. 10–noon and 3–6; Nov.–mid-Mar., Tues.–Sun. 10–noon and 2–5. Getting to the villa is a pleasant 20-minute walk from the city center, or take Bus 8 from Viale Roma. Created for papal prelate Paolo Almerico, La Rotonda seems less a villa than a Roman temple, which was precisely the architect's intention. Take sufficient time to admire it from all sides; you'll realize Palladio just repeated the temple portico on all four faces, to take advantage of the idyllic views. Inspired by the hillside site on Monte Berico and topped by a dome like Rome's Pantheon, La Rotonda is Palladio's only freestanding, centralized design, because it was intended to be a showplace, not a working farm. Still owned by the Counts Valmarana, La Rotonda's interior is rarely open. But it's no loss, as it's awash in florid frescoes Palladio would have detested.

THE "WINGED DEVICE"

Villa Barbaro

One of Palladio's most gracious Renaissance creations lies 48 km (30 mi) northeast of Vicenza: his **Villa Barbaro** (Via Cornuda 7, 0423/923004, €5. Open Mar.–Oct., Tues. and weekends 3–6; Nov.–Feb., weekends 2:30–5; closed Dec. 24–Jan. 6). Near Asolo and built just outside the town of Maser in 1549 for the two Barbaro brothers, this villa spectacularly illustrates Palladio's famous "winged device"—the utilization of a villa's outlying wings, often the *barchessa*, which housed granaries, to frame the main building and link them together with graceful loggias (the 16th-century answer to air-conditioning). With this one stroke, he brought everything together, making the parts subservient to the whole. His dramatic frontal designs have led historians to compare these facades to theater stages and to term his sense of space scenographic. Inside the cool halls of the villa, painted courtiers provocatively peek out behind frescoed doors. Legend has it that these famous paintings of Paolo Veronese were the cause of a rift, since Palladio felt these trompe l'oeil scenes distorted the purity of his architectural design. Today, the villa is still owned by Barbaro descendants, and its enduring beauty ensures that future generations of architects will continue to shape and enrich the Palladian style.

ALONG THE BRENTA CANAL

During the 16th century the Brenta was transformed into a landlocked version of Venice's Grand Canal with the building of nearly 50 waterside villas. Back then, boating parties viewed them in *"burchielli"*–beautiful boats. Today, the Burchiello excursion boat (Via Orlandini 3, Padua, 049/8206910, www.ilburchiello.it) makes an all-day villa tour along the Brenta, from March to November, departing from Padua on Wednesday, Friday, and Sunday and from Venice on Tuesday, Thursday, and Saturday; tickets are €62 and can also be bought at American Express at Salizzada San Moisè in Venice. You visit three houses, including the Villas Pisani and Foscari, with a lunchtime break in Oriago. Another canal excursion is run by the Battelli del Brenta (www.battellidelbrenta.it). Note that most houses are on the left side coming from Venice, or the right from Padua.

Where to Stay & Eat

$–$$ ✕ **Antico Ristorante agli Schioppi.** Veneto country-style decor matches simple yet imaginative cuisine in this family-run restaurant established in 1897. Begin with the Parma ham served with eggplant mousse and Parmesan. The *baccalà* (salt cod) is a delicacy, as are the *petto d'anitra all'uva moscata e indivia* (duck breast with muscat grapes and endive) and *coniglio alle olive nere*

(rabbit with black olives). Desserts include ever-so-light fruit mousse and a pear cake with red-wine sauce. ⊠ *Contrà del Castello 26* ☎ *0444/ 543701* ▤ *AE, DC, MC, V* ☺ *Closed Sun., last wk of July–mid-Aug., and Jan. 1–6. No dinner Sat.*

$–$$ ✕ **Dai Nodari.** Seven restaurant veterans—with a shared passion for good food and hard work—opened this exciting restaurant in January 2005. They must also share a flare for the dramatic: a silent film shows in the bar and Dante's Inferno plays in the men's room. Appetizers include interesting cheeses, such as *bastardo del drappa* (aged 60 days), and dishes like tuna marinated in orange. Move on to fish or steak, or try rabbit roasted with juniper berries. There are also several pasta and salad choices. ⊠ *Contrà do Rode 20* ☎ *0444/544085* ▤ *AE, DC, MC, V.*

★ $ ✕ **Ponte delle Bele.** With all the pine furniture and lacy lamps, you may feel like you've stumbled into an Alpine cabin, so it's no surprise when your homemade pasta resembles dumplings or spaetzle. At this friendly *Tyrolese* (Tirolean) restaurant, your prosciutto might be made from wild deer or boar, and venison in blueberry sauce is not usually found this far south of the mountains. Try guinea fowl roasted with white grapes, or the local cheese plate served with honey and preserves (but take care with the tough rye cracker-bread, which only a dentist could love). ⊠ *Contrà Ponte delle Bele 5* ☎ *0444/320647* ▤ *AE, DC, MC, V* ☺ *Closed Sun.*

¢–$ ✕ **Righetti.** After staking out seats, line up (with elbows ready) at the self-service food counters here. There's a daily pasta, a risotto, and a hearty soup such as *orzo e fagioli* (barley and bean) on the menu. Vegetables, salads, and baccalà are standards; at dinner meats are grilled to order. Once you have your meal on your tray, help yourself to bread, wine, and water. Sharing tables is the norm. After you've finished, tell the cashier what you had and he'll total your (very reasonable) bill. Low prices and simple, enjoyable food has generated a loyal following. ⊠ *Piazza Duomo 3* ☎ *0444/543135* ▤ *No credit cards* ☺ *Closed weekends and Aug.*

$$ 🛏 **Giardini.** The hotel Giardini is in good company near Palladio's Teatro Olimpico and Palazzo Chiericati, off the central Piazza Matteotti. Rooms have a modern Italian style, with sleek, mid-tone wood floors and multicolor bedspreads; two rooms are equipped for guests with dis-

2

abilities. ✉ *Viale Giurioli 10, 36100* ☎☎ *0444/326458* ⊕ *www. hotelgiardini.com* ⬎ *17 rooms* ♿ *In-room safes, minibars, cable TV, bar, meeting room, free parking* ☰ *AE, DC, MC, V* ♺ *Closed Dec. 23–Jan. 2* ♥⃝ *BP.*

$ 🛏 **Due Mori.** Antiques fill the rooms at the 1883 hotel Due Mori, one of the oldest in the city. Loyal regulars favor the place because it's light and airy (with tall ceilings and pale walls), yet at the same time cozy (with substantial wood beds). This comfortable, convenient bargain is off the Piazza dei Signori. ✉ *Contrà Do Rode 24, 36100* ☎ *0444/ 321886* 🖨 *0444/326127* ⊕ *www.hotelduemori.com* ⬎ *30 rooms* ♿ *Bar, some pets allowed, some free parking; no a/c, no room TVs* ☰ *MC, V* ♺ *Closed last 2 wks July* ♥⃝ *BP.*

Nightlife & the Arts

The **Teatro Olimpico** (✉ Piazza Matteotti ☎ 0444/222801 ⊕ www. comune.vicenza.it) hosts a jazz festival in May, classical concerts in June, and classical drama performances in September. Even if your Italian is dismal, it can be thrilling to see a performance in Palladio's magnificent theater.

VERONA

On the banks of the fast-flowing Adige River, 60 km (37 mi) west of Vicenza, enchanting Verona has timeless monuments, a picturesque town center, and a romantic reputation as the setting of Shakespeare's *Romeo and Juliet.* With its lively Venetian air and proximity to Lake Garda, it attracts hordes of tourists, especially during summer's renowned opera season and spring's Vinitaly, one of the world's most important wine expos, where for five days you can sample the wines of more than 3,000 wineries from dozens of countries.

Verona grew to power and prosperity within the Roman Empire as a result of its key commercial and military position in northern Italy. After the fall of the Empire, the city continued to flourish under the guidance of barbarian kings such as Theodoric, Alboin, Pepin, and Berenger I, reaching its cultural and artistic peak in the 13th and 14th centuries under the della Scala dynasty. (Look for the *scala*, or ladder, emblem all over town.) In 1404 Verona traded its independence for security and placed itself under the control of Venice. (The other recurring architectural motif is the lion of St. Mark, symbol of Venetian rule.) Verona remained under Venetian protection until 1797, when Napoléon invaded. In 1814 the entire Veneto region was won by the Austrians it wasn't reunited with Italy until 1866.

Exploring Verona

If you're going to visit more than a sight or two, it's worthwhile to purchase a Verona Card, available at museums, churches, and tobacconists for €8 (one day) or €12 (three days). You get a single admission to most of the city's significant museums and churches, and you can ride free on city buses. A €5 Chiese Vive Card is sold at Verona's major churches and gains you entry to the Duomo, San Fermo Maggiore, San Zeno Maggiore, and Sant'Anastasia. Do note that Verona's churches strictly enforce their dress code: no sleeveless shirts, shorts, or short skirts.

The Main Attractions

⑰ Arena di Verona. Only four arches remain of the arena's outer rings, but otherwise the structure is so complete that it's easy to imagine the days when the cruel deaths of countless gladiators, wild beasts, and Christians passed as entertainment here. Today the arena hosts Verona's summer opera (July–September), famous for spectacular productions staged before audiences of up to 16,000. ⊠ *Piazza Brà 5* ☎ *045/8003204* 🎫 *€4, €1 1st Sun. of month* ☉ *Mon. 1:45–7:15, Tues.–Sun. 8:30–7:15, on performance days 8:30–3; last entry 45 mins before closing.*

⑯ Castelvecchio (Old Castle). This crenellated, russet brick building with massive walls, towers, turrets, and a vast courtyard was built for Cangrande II della Scala in 1354. It presides over a street lined with attractive old buildings and palaces of the nobility. To really appreciate the massive castle complex, go inside the **Museo di Castelvecchio,** which gives you a good look at the vaulted halls and the collections of Venetian art and medieval weapons and jewelry. For the benefit of sightless visitors, some paintings have been rendered in plastic relief and have recorded explanations. Behind the castle is the Ponte Scaligero, a public walkway spanning the River Adige. ⊠ *Corso Castelvecchio 2* ☎ *045/ 8062611* 🎫 *€4, free 1st Sun. of month* ☉ *Mon. 1:30–7:30, Tues.–Sun. 8:30–7:30; last entry 6:45.*

㉕ Duomo. Verona's cathedral is an amalgamation of religious buildings, the earliest dating back to 380; it's ornately Romanesque but also shows Venetian and even Byzantine influences. Noteworthy inside are carvings of Oliver and Roland, two of Charlemagne's knights, guarding the main entrance, and Titian's *Assumption* gracing the first chapel on the left. ⊠ *Via Duomo* ☎ *045/592813* ⊕ *www.chieseverona.it* 🎫 *€2.50* ☉ *Nov.–Feb., Tues.–Sat. 10–1 and 1:30–4, Sun. 1:30–5; Mar.–Oct., Mon.–Sat. 10–5:30, Sun. 1:30–5:30.*

㉓ Loggia del Consiglio. This graceful structure, built in the 12th century as a site for city council meetings, still serves as seat of the provincial government. ⊠ *Piazza dei Signori* ☉ *Closed to the public.*

㉒ Palazzo degli Scaligeri. The iron-fisted della Scalas ruled Verona from this medieval stronghold. Though the palazzo is closed to the public, you can gaze into the adjacent **Arche Scaligere,** site of the suitably impressive marbled Gothic tombs of family members Cangrande I ("Big Dog"), Mastino II ("Mastiff"), and Cansignorio ("Top Dog"). ⊠ *Piazza dei Signori.*

⑳ Palazzo della Ragione. An elegant pink marble staircase leads up from the *mercato vecchio* (old market) courtyard to the magistrates' chambers in the 12th-century palace also known as the Palazzo del Comune. The building is undergoing renovation and will be turned into a con-

Verona

300 meters
300 yards

TO GIARDINI DI VILLA ARVEDI

Galleria d'Arte Moderna

STAZIONE F.S.

TO TOMBA DI GIULIETTA

Arena di Verona **17**
Casa di Giulietta **19**
Castelvecchio **16**
Duomo **25**
Giardino Giusti **27**
Loggia del Consiglio **23**

Museo Archeologico ... **26**
Palazzo degli
Scaligeri **22**
Palazzo della
Ragione **20**
Piazza dei Signori **21**

San Femo Maggiore ... **18**
San Zeno Maggiore ... **15**
Sant'Anastasia **24**

ference center. You can get the highest view in town from atop the attached 270-foot-tall **Torre dei Lamberti,** which is open during reconstruction. Would-be endurance athletes can save €1 by climbing the stairs; for everyone else there's an elevator. ⊠ *Piazza dei Signori* ☎ *045/ 8032726* 🖃 *€2, €3 with elevator* ⊗ *Mon. 1:30–7:30, Tues.–Sun. 8:30–7:30; last entry 6:45.*

㉑ Piazza dei Signori. Verona's most impressive piazza, the center of things for more than 1,000 years, is today lorded over by a pensive statue of Dante, often as not with a pigeon on his head. His back is toward the Loggia del Consiglio and his left hand points toward the Palazzo degli Scaligeri. He faces Palazzo del Capitanio (to his left) and Palazzo della Ragione (to his right). All these buildings are closed to the public except those on government business.

⑱ San Fermo Maggiore. From its humble Benedictine beginnings, San Fermo grew through the centuries, in part as a result of rebuilding after floods from the nearby River Adige. The tomblike lower church, dating from the 8th century, became usable again when the Adige was reengineered to stay within its banks. The mammoth upper church completed in the 14th century has the Veneto's oldest and perhaps finest ship's-keel ceiling, decorated with paintings of 400 saints. ⊠ *Stradone S. Fermo* ☎ *045/592813* ⊕ *www.chieseverona.it* 🖃 *€2.50* ⊗ *Nov.–Feb., Tues.–Sat. 10–1 and 1:30–4, Sun. 1–5; Mar.–Oct., Mon.–Sat. 10–6, Sun. 1–6.*

★ ⑮ San Zeno Maggiore. Possibly Italy's finest Romanesque church, San Zeno stands between two medieval bell towers. A 13th-century rose window depicts the wheel of fortune, and bronze doors from the 11th and 12th centuries are decorated with scenes from the Bible and from the life of Verona's patron saint, Zeno, who's buried in the crypt. Look for the statue *San Zeno Laughing* to the left of the main altar—the unknown artist, or perhaps the saint himself, must have had a sense of humor. A *Madonna and Saints* triptych by Andrea Mantegna (1431–1506) hangs over the main altar, and a peaceful cloister lies to the north (left) of the nave. ⊠ *Piazza San Zeno* ☎ *045/592813* ⊕ *www.chieseverona.it* 🖃 *€2.50* ⊗ *Nov.–Feb., Tues.–Sat. 10–1 and 1:30–4, Sun. 1–5; Mar.–Oct., Mon.–Sat. 8:30–6, Sun. 1–6.*

㉔ Sant'Anastasia. Verona's largest church, completed in 1481, is a fine example of Gothic brickwork and has a grand doorway with elaborately carved biblical scenes. The finest of its numerous frescoes is the pastel *St. George and the Princess* by Pisanello (1377–1455) above the Pellegrini Chapel right off the main altar, where the saint appears more gentleman than warrior. As you come in, look for the *gobbi* (hunchbacks) supporting holy-water stoups. ⊠ *Vicolo Sotto Riva 4* ☎ *045/592813* ⊕ *www.chieseverona.it* 🖃 *€2.50* ⊗ *Nov.–Feb., Tues.–Sat. 10–1 and 1:30–4, Sun. 1–5; Mar.–Oct., Mon.–Sat. 9–6, Sun. 1–6.*

Also Worth Seeing

⑲ Casa di Giulietta (Juliet's House). The small courtyard balcony evokes Shakespeare's play, even if it is part of a 20th-century remodel. Despite historians' belief that the famous lovers had no real-life counterparts, thousands of visitors refuse to let truth get in the way of a good story. ⊠ *Via Cappello 23* ☎ *045/8034303* ⊡ *€4* ⊙ *Mon. 1:30–7:30, Tues.–Sun. 8:30–7:30; last entry 6:45.*

㉗ Giardino Giusti. In 1570 Agostino Giusti designed these formal gardens on the hillside behind his villa. Though the toothy mask halfway up the hill no longer breathes flames, little has been changed of Giusti's maze, fountains, or stalactite grotto. And though Verona might no longer be recognizable to Johann Wolfgang von Goethe (1749–1832), you can still enjoy the terrace views that inspired this German poet and dramatist to record his impressions. ⊠ *Via Giardino Giusti 2* ☎ *045/8034029* ⊡ *€5* ⊙ *Apr.–Sept., daily 9–8; Oct.–Mar., daily 9–6.*

㉖ Museo Archeologico. The views of the city from this museum housed in an old monastery are even better than its archaeological exhibits. It sits high above the Teatro Romano, near the ⇨ **Arena di Verona,** which is used in summer for operatic productions. ⊠ *Rigaste del Redentore 2* ☎ *045/8000360* ⊡ *€3, free 1st Sun. of month* ⊙ *Mon. 1:30–7:30, Tues.–Sun. 8:30–7:30; last entry 6:45.*

off the beaten path

TOMBA DI GIULIETTA – If you want to believe the falsehood that Juliet is buried in this old chapel near the river, then put aside the fact that the structure is a former orphanage and Franciscan monastery. In the crypt there's an open sarcophagus labeled as Juliet's tomb; the city of Verona perpetuates the fantasy that Romeo and Juliet were married here by conducting civil weddings in the chapel. ⊠ *Via del Pontiere 35* ☎ *045/8000361* ⊡ *€3* ⊙ *Mon. 1:30–7:30, Tues.–Sun. 8:30–7:30; last entry 6:45.*

Where to Stay & Eat

$$$$ ✕ **Il Desco.** *Cucina dell' anima* (food of the soul) is how Chef Elia Rizzo describes his cuisine in which natural flavors are preserved through quick cooking and a limit of three ingredients per dish. He spares no expense in selecting those ingredients, and you pay accordingly. Suckling pig in black truffle sauce and guinea fowl in chocolate and balsamic vinegar sauce are two of the typically elegant options. For a real splurge, order the tasting menu (€110), which includes appetizers, two first courses, two second courses, and dessert. The fine food is complemented by the dining room's tapestries and paintings. ⊠ *Via Dietro S. Sebastiano 7* ☎ *045/595358* ⌕ *Reservations essential* ⊟ *DC, MC, V* ⊙ *Closed Sun., Dec. 25–Jan. 10, and 2–3 wks in June. No dinner Mon. Jan.–June, Sept., and Oct.*

$$–$$$ ✕ **Bottega Del Vino.** The prayer on the wall, *DIO MI GUARDI DO CHI NON BEVE VINO,* asks for protection from non–wine drinkers and a good-luck *gobbo* (hunchback) hovers above, holding a lantern and the key to a wine cellar of more than 100,000 bottles. Elbow your way through the crowd of locals to the bar for a sandwich and a glass of wine from the wall-size list. Or make it a full bottle and a full meal—try the Amarone wine risotto or *brasato Amarone,* a wine-marinated beef cutlet. ⊠ *Via Scudo di Francia 3* ☎ *045/8004535* ⊟ *AE, DC, MC, V* ⊙ *Closed Tues.*

¢–$ ✗ **Du de Cope.** Il Desco's star chef decided to branch into pizza making and the result is four-star, wood-fire pizza at one-star prices. Toppings like buffalo mozzarella and Parmiggiano Reggiano cheese cover the lightest crust that ever hovered on a plate. Notice how well modern drop lighting merges with old-fashioned, blue-and-white tile walls; placemats quilt the hardwood tables and burlap tapestries decorate the walls. ⊠ *Galleria Pellicciai 10* ☎ *045/595562* ▤ *AE, DC, MC, V* ☉ *Closed Tues. No lunch Sun.*

★ ¢ ✗ **Osteria al Duca.** Folks jam this place at lunchtime, sharing tables, wine, and conversation in a building that legend claims to have been Romeo's birthplace. Beneath low-slung ceilings, generous portions of local specialties are served for a very reasonable fixed-price along with a wine list that belies the simplicity of the surroundings. Try Gorgonzola served with polenta, vegetarian eggplant with mozzarella, or homemade *bigoli al torchio,* a thick spaghetti forced through a press. This may be some of the best food available for the price in town. ⊠ *Arche Scaligere 2* ☎ *045/594474* ▤ *MC, V* ☉ *Closed Sun. and mid-Dec.–mid-Jan.*

★ $$$$ ✗▥ **Villa del Quar.** Leopoldo and Evelina Montresor spared no expense when converting part of their 16th-century home into a sophisticated luxury hotel with antiques and marble bathrooms. The villa is surrounded by gardens and vineyards, 15 minutes by car from Verona's city center. Service is attentive but relaxed, whether at the poolside bar or in the acclaimed Arquade restaurant. Chef Bruno Barbieri's creative menu might include baked scallops with radicchio and *speck* (a thin, cured ham) or chocolate mousse served with crisp, caramelized eggplant. Sommelier Alberto Besco can help select wines for your meal or organize a visit to some of Valpolicella's best wineries. ⊠ *Via Quar 12, 37020 Pedemonte di San Pietro in Cariano, 10 km (6 mi) northwest of Verona* ☎ *045/6800681* 🖷 *045/6800604* ⊕ *www.hotelvilladelquar.it* ⃗ *18 rooms, 10 suites* ⟂ *Restaurant, in-room safes, minibars, cable TV, in-room data ports, pool, health club, massage, bar, Internet, meeting room, helipad, free parking, some pets allowed, no-smoking rooms* ▤ *AE, DC, MC, V* ☉ *Closed Jan.–mid-Mar. Restaurant closed Mon. Oct.–May. No lunch Tues.* ⎪⊙⎪ *BP.*

$$ ▥ **Hotel Europa.** The third generation of this innkeeping family, which has operated the Europa since 1956, welcomes you to a convenient downtown hotel. Expect hardwood floors and pastel *marmarino* (Venetian polished plaster) walls. Rooms are comfortable and up-to-date, and the breakfast room on the ground floor is exceptionally bright. ⊠ *Via Roma 8, 37121* ☎ *045/594744* 🖷 *045/8001852* ⊕ *www. veronahoteleuropa.com* ⃗ *46 rooms* ⟂ *In-room safes, minibars, cable TV, parking (fee), no-smoking rooms* ▤ *AE, DC, MC, V* ⎪⊙⎪ *BP.*

$ ▥ **Armando.** A few minutes' walk from the Arena, this contemporary hotel in a residential area offers respite from the busy city, as well as easier parking. Rooms are decorated with light, modern furniture, and some family rooms sleep up to five. In the airy breakfast room downstairs Signora Diana serves a breakfast of fresh-baked rolls, yogurt, juices, and coffee. ⊠ *Via Dietro Pallone 1, 37120* ☎ *045/8000206* 🖷🖷 *045/ 8036015* ⃗ *19 rooms* ⟂ *Free parking, no-smoking rooms* ▤ *MC, V* ☉ *Closed 2 wks late Dec.–early Jan.* ⎪⊙⎪ *BP*

2

$ ⊡ **Torcolo.** The warm owners Diana Castellani and Silvia Pomari run the hotel Torcolo, which has pleasant, unfussy rooms, and a central location close to Piazza Brà and the Arena. Breakfast, which costs an extra €7–€12, is served outside on the terrace in front of the hotel in summer. ✉ *Vicolo Listone 3, 37121* ☎ *045/8007512* 🖷 *045/8004058* ⊕ *www.hoteltorcolo.it* ↝ *19 rooms* ♿ *In-room safes, minibars, cable TV, parking (fee), some pets allowed* 🗏 *AE, DC, MC, V* ☺ *Closed mid-Jan.–mid-Feb.* ❙◯❙ *EP.*

Nightlife & the Arts

Opera

FodorśChoice   Of all the venues for enjoying opera in the region, pride of place must
★   go to the **Arena di Verona** (✉ Piazza Brà 28 ✉ Box office ✉ Via Dietro Anfiteatro 6/b ☎045/8005151 ⊕www.arena.it). During its summer opera season (July–September) audiences of as many as 16,000 sit on the original stone terraces or in the modern cushioned stalls. The best operas are the big, splashy ones, like *Aïda,* that demand huge choruses, lots of color and movement, and, if possible, camels, horses, or elephants. But the experience is memorable no matter what's playing. Order tickets by phone or online: if you book a place on the cheaper terraces, be sure to take or rent a cushion—four hours on a 2,000-year-old stone bench can be an ordeal. Sometimes you can even hear the opera from Piazza Brà cafés.

Nightclubs & Bars

Lounge, with your drink in-hand, on Kasbah cushions at **Cappa Café** (✉ Piazzetta Brà ☎ 045/8004516). You can also have a full meal while overlooking the River Adige and listening to jazz until 2 AM. **Alter Ego** (✉ Via Torricelle 9 ☎ 045/915130) packs in a hip, thirtyish crowd for disco and drinks Friday and Saturday from midnight to 5 or 6 AM. **Berfi's** (✉ Via Lussemburgo 1 ☎ 045/508024) is a popular and pricey restaurant-disco. It's open 9:30 PM to 4 AM Friday to Sunday. Take a taxi; Berfi's is in Verona's *zona industriale* (industrial area).

Shopping

Antiques

The area around the Gothic church of **Sant'Anastasia** is full of antiques shops, most catering to serious collectors.

Food & Wine

Salumeria Albertini (✉ Corso S. Anastasia 41 ☎045/8031074) is Verona's oldest delicatessen: look for the prosciutto and salami hanging outside. **De Rossi** (✉ Corso Porta Borsari 3 ☎ 045/8002489) sells baked bread and cakes, pastries, and biscotti that are lusciously caloric.

The famous international wine show, **Vinitaly** (✉ Fiera di Verona, Viale del Lavoro 8 ☎ 045/8298170 ⊕ www.vinitaly.com), takes place for five days in early April. It claims to make Verona the "world capital of quality wines" for the week, attracting more than 3,000 exhibitors from dozens of countries. The show costs €35 per day (€30 if purchased in advance) and runs daily 9–7.

Markets

Verona's two **markets,** on Piazza delle Erbe and Piazza Cittadella, have a selection of food, wine, clothing, antiques, and even pets. They're both open Monday–Saturday 8–1 and 3:30–dusk.

TREVISO & THE HILLSIDE TOWNS

In this area directly north of Venice, market towns cling to the steep foothills of the Alps and the Dolomites alongside streams raging down from the mountains. Villa Barbaro, one of Palladio's most graceful country villas, is here, as are the arcaded streets of Treviso and the graceful Venetian Gothic structures of smaller hill towns.

Marostica

28 *26 km (16 mi) northeast of Vicenza, 93 km (58 mi) northwest of Venice.*

From the 14th-century Castello Inferiore, where the town council still meets, an ancient stone wall snakes up the hill to enclose the Castello Superiore, with its commanding views. Marostica's most celebrated feature is the checker board–like square made with colored stone, Piazza Castello.

A game of human-scale chess known as **Partita a Scacchi** is acted out in Piazza Castello by players in medieval costume on the second weekend in September in even-number years. There's a game presented Friday–Sunday evenings and there's a Sunday afternoon show. Tickets go on sale in April; the tourist office can help with bookings.

Where to Stay

★ **$–$$** 🏨 **Due Mori.** Recessed lighting adds to the modern, minimalist design at this historic inn, which has been this medieval town's only refuge for travelers since the 18th century. Warm wooden floors and soft-beige marble bathrooms are all made of local materials. Some windows look out onto the city walls or olive tree–filled terraces, but rooms 7, 8, 11, and 12 have picture-perfect views of the upper castle. There's a comfortably chic restaurant ($$) downstairs. ⊠ *Corso Mazzini 73, 36063* 🕾 *0424/471777* 🖶 *0424/476920* 🌐 *www.duemori.com* 🛏 *12 rooms* ⌂ *Restaurant, minibars, cable TV, in-room data ports, free parking, some pets allowed, no-smoking rooms* 🚭 *AE, DC, MC, V* 🕔 *Closed 2 wks mid-Aug.* 🍽 *BP.*

Bassano del Grappa

29 *7 km (4½ mi) east of Marostica, 37 km (23 mi) north of Venice.*

Nestled at the base of the Mt. Grappa massif (5,880 feet), with the mountain-fresh Brenta River sluicing through, this town seems to be higher in the mountains than it actually is. Bassano has old streets lined with low-slung buildings adorned with wooden balconies and pretty flowerpots. Bright ceramic wares produced in the area are displayed in shops along byways that curve uphill toward a centuries-old square and, even higher, to a belvedere with a good view of Mt. Grappa and the beginning of the Val Sugana. Bassano is home to the famous Nardini distillery, where grappa has been made since 1779. Stop in for a sniff or a snifter of the liquor at any of the local cafés.

Bassano's most famous landmark is the **Ponte degli Alpini,** a covered bridge named for Italy's Alpine soldiers. There's been a bridge spanning the Brenta here since 1209, but floods and wars have required repeated rebuilding. The present version was constructed by Alpine soldiers following World War II. They used Andrea Palladio's 16th-century design, which astutely calls for easily replaceable wood as the building material.

The **Museo della Grappa** illustrates how the grape remnants from winemaking are turned into the liquor grappa. ⊠ *Ponte Vecchio* ☎ *0424/244366* 🖼 *Free* ☉ *Mon. 2:30–7:30, Tues.–Sat. 9–1 and 2:30–7:30.*

Nardini distillery has its own *bottega* (shop) in town: **Grapperia Nardini** is basically a bar that sells take-away bottles. From here you have an excellent view of the Ponte degli Alpini. ⊠ *Ponte Vecchio 2* ☎ *0424/524426.*

Where to Stay & Eat

$–$$ ✕ **Osteria Terraglio.** The creative modern menu here focuses on absolute freshness, from the wonderful array of savory snacks to the big, crisp *insalatone* (main-course salads with tuna or various cheeses), and the steak fillet, cut to order. Special tasting sessions of local delicacies such as asparagus, cold-pressed olive oil, and fine wines are a regular feature. October through May there's live jazz on Tuesday evening. ⊠ *Piazza Terraglio 28* ☎ *0424/521064* ▭ *AE, DC, MC, V* ☉ *Closed Mon.*

★ **$–$$** ✕ **Ristorante Al Sole.** With the personable Franco Chiurato in the dining room, and his 90-year-old mother Maria still in the kitchen after 40 years, you can't help but come out satisfied at the Ristorante Al Sole. Here Bassano home cooking flirts with the international: duck ends up in pomegranate, pheasant in Cognac, and cauliflower and cheese hand-stuffed into luscious pasta pillows. ⊠ *Via Vittorelli 41/43* ☎ *0424/23206* ▭ *AE, DC, MC, V* ☉ *Closed Mon. and 3 wks late July–mid-Aug.*

$$$ ✕🖼 **Ca' Sette.** Were it not for an engraving showing Napoléon's troops massed in the courtyard, you'd never guess the great age of this hotel, which has an ultramodern interior. Each room has a different tasteful design in local wood and marble. Light sleepers should request a room that doesn't face the rather busy road. **Ca' 7** restaurant ($$–$$$) is among the best in the area. From Chef Alex Lorenzon's menu you might choose a dish in which you dig into a deep-fried, bread crumb–covered egg yolk to find it bursts golden cream over your plate of polenta, fresh mushrooms, and Asiago cheese. ⊠ *Via Cunizza da Romano 4, 36061* ☎ *0424/383350* 🖼 *0424/393287* ⊕ *www.ca-sette.it* ⤴ *17 rooms, 2 suites* ♿ *Restaurant, in-room safes, minibars, in-room data ports, bicycles, some pets allowed, no-smoking rooms, free parking* ▭ *AE, DC, MC, V* ☉ *Restaurant closed Mon., 1st wk in Jan., and 2 wks mid-Aug. No dinner Sun.* �‖ *BP.*

$$ 🖼 **Hotel Belvedere.** This 15th-century hotel has richly decorated public rooms with period furnishings and Oriental rugs; the lounge has an open fireplace and a piano. Guest rooms are decorated in traditional Venet-

Treviso &
the Hillside Towns

ian or contemporary style. Two restaurants provide a choice between light, inexpensive dishes and full-course regional meals. ✉ *Piazzale G. Giardino 14, 36061* ☎ *0424/529845* 🖷 *0424/529849* ⊕ *www.bonotto. it* 🖙 *83 rooms, 4 suites* ⚐ *Restaurant, cable TV with movies, some in-room data ports, piano bar, Internet, meeting rooms, parking (fee), some pets allowed (fee), no-smoking rooms* 🝙 *AE, DC, MC, V* ☺ *Restaurant closed Sun.* 🍽 *BP.*

$ 🏨 **Al Castello.** In a restored town house at the foot of the medieval Torre Civica, the Cattapan family's Castello is a reasonably priced, attractive choice. The simply furnished rooms all differ in shape and size, some have wood beam ceilings. Request a room at the front for a small balcony with a view of the charming square below. ✉ *Piazza Terraglio 19, 36061* 🖷 *0424/228665* ⊕ *www.hotelalcastello.it* 🖙 *11 rooms* ⚐ *Bar, Internet* 🝙 *AE, MC, V* 🍽 *EP.*

Shopping

The Bassano del Grappa region is famous for ceramics. There are antiques, handmade reproductions of timeless designs, and kitschy souvenirs. Prices near the old bridge tend to run a bit higher than elsewhere in town.

Preserved foods are another Bassano specialty. **Il Melario** (✉ Via Angarano 13 ☎ 0424/502168) has one of the best selections in town, including dried wild mushrooms and myriad liqueurs, honeys, and jams. If the friendly proprietor neglects to offer, ask to taste his roasted fava beans, a wholesome snack.

Asolo

30 *11 km (7 mi) east of Bassano del Grappa, 33 km (20½ mi) northwest of Treviso.*

The romantic, charming hillside hamlet of Asolo was the consolation prize of an exiled queen. At the end of the 15th century, Venetian-born Caterina Cornaro was sent here by Venice's doge to keep her from interfering with Venetian administration of her former kingdom of Cyprus, which she had inherited from her husband. To soothe the pain of exile she established a lively and brilliant court in Asolo. Through the centuries, Venetian aristocrats continued to build gracious villas on the hillside, and in the 19th century Asolo once again became the idyllic haunt of musicians, poets, and painters. From the outside, you can explore villas once inhabited by Robert Browning and the actress Eleonora Duse. Be warned that the town's charm vaporizes on holiday weekends when the crowds pour in. At the center of town is the Piazza Maggiore, with Renaissance palaces and fin-de-siècle cafés. Asolo hosts a two-day antiques market on the second Sunday of every month except July and August.

Uphill from the Piazza Maggiore, past Caterina's ruined castle, are the remains of a medieval fortress, the **Rocca,** from which you can see Asolo's 100 horizons and amazing sunsets. Walk up for the view alone; the fortress is nothing more than a shell of crumbling walls with opening times that vary with season, weather, and whim.

Where to Stay & Eat

$$–$$$$ ✕ **Ca' Derton.** Just behind the main square you can choose between the formality of a restaurant's white-lace tablecloths or the rustic tables (and lower prices) of an *enoteca* (wine bar) at Ca' Derton. Either way, you order from the same menu, which includes such dishes as venison with pomegranate, pasta with partridge and radicchio, and vanilla ice cream with pure Modena balsamic vinegar. ⊠ *Piazza D'Annunzio 11* ☎ *0423/ 529648* ⊟ *AE, DC, MC, V* ☾ *Closed Mon. and 2 wks June–Aug. No dinner Sun.*

¢–$ ✕ **Al Bacaro.** Since 1892 this *osteria* (tavernlike restaurant) has been a second home to Asolani laborers and craftsmen. Whether you eat downstairs in the bar with hanging copper kettles or upstairs in the dining room lighted by lacy lamps, you get affordable wines and pastas and home-style food that includes goulash and dishes with escargot. ⊠ *Via R. Browning 165* ☎ *0423/55150* ⊟ *AE, DC, MC, V* ☾ *Closed Wed. and 2 wks in Aug.*

★ $$$ ✕▥ **Al Sole.** Perched over the town of Asolo, Al Sole's terrace is a relaxing and restorative respite. Overstuffed chairs fill the lobby, and all rooms are richly furnished in antiques. The hotel was once actress Eleonora Duse's preferred haunt, and her favorite room has been preserved and named after her. Two rooms are equipped for guests with disabilities. The restaurant ($$), closed Wednesday, serves quick salads and single-course lunches, or full-course meals accompanied by a choice wine selection. ⊠ *Via Collegio 33, 31011* ☎ *0423/951332* 🖷 *0423/951007* ⊕ *www.albergoalsole.com* ⟿ *22 rooms, 1 suite* ⟐ *Restaurant, in-room safes, minibars, cable TV with movies, in-room data ports, gym, massage, bar, Internet, meeting room, free parking, some pets allowed (fee), no-smoking rooms* ⊟ *AE, DC, MC, V* ⊙I *BP.*

$$$$ ⊞ **Villa Cipriani.** A romantic hillside garden surrounded by country homes is the setting for this 16th-century villa. Its 19th-century antiques are complemented by modern creature comforts, such as bathrobes, and discreet service. The restaurant ($$$$) has a terrace overlooking the garden and the Asolo Golf Club is close by. ⊠ *Via Canova 298, 31011* ☎ *0423/523411* 🖷 *0423/952095* ⊕ *www.sheraton.com/villacipriani* ⟿ *31 rooms* ⟐ *Restaurant, room service, in-room safes, minibars, cable TV with movies, gym, hot tub, bicycles, bar, concierge, babysitting, laundry service, shops, Internet, business services, meeting room, parking (fee), some pets allowed (fee), no-smoking floor* ⊟ *AE, DC, MC, V* ⊙I *BP.*

$$ ⊞ **Hotel Duse.** A spiral staircase winds it's way up this narrow building to rooms with a view of the town square. The scene gets lively on antique fair weekends, but if the sights don't make up for the sounds, ask for the larger and quieter attic room—skylights instead of windows mean your only view is the stars. Furnishings, such as small tables with pastel table cloths and slipcovered chairs, are simple and well tended. For Asolo, the price is a real deal. ⊠ *Via R. Browning 190, 31100* ☎ *0423/55241* 🖷 *0423/950404* ⊕ *www.hotelduse.com* ⟿ *14 rooms* ⟐ *Minibars, in-room data ports, parking (fee); no smoking* ⊟ *AE, MC, V* ⊙ *Closed 3 wks in Jan.* ⊙I *EP.*

Treviso

㉛ *35 km (22 mi) southeast of Maser, 30 km (19 mi) north of Venice.*

The heart of a busy manufacturing region, Treviso has fashionable shops and boutiques in Venetian style buildings along narrow walkways. The nickname "Little Venice" is a somewhat inflated claim, however, though there are several canals.

The **Piazza dei Signori** is the center of medieval Treviso and still the town's social hub, with outdoor cafés and some impressive public buildings. One of these, the Palazzo dei Trecento, has a small alley behind it that leads to the *pescheria* (fish market), on an island in one of the small canals that flow through town.

The most important church in Treviso is **San Nicolò,** an impressive Gothic structure with an ornate vaulted ceiling and frescoes of the saints by Tommaso da Modena (circa 1325–79); the depiction of *St. Agnes* on the north side is particularly charming. More remarkable are Tommaso's astoundingly realistic portraits of 40 Dominican friars in the seminary next door. They include one of the earliest-known paintings of a subject wearing glasses. ⊠ *Seminario Vescovile, Via San Nicolò* ☎ *0422/3247* ⊙ *Church Mon.–Sat. 8–noon and 4–6:30, Sun. 4–6:30.*

Seminary Sept.–June, daily 7 AM*–8* PM*; July and Aug., Mon.–Sat. 7* AM*–8* PM*, Sun. 7–1.*

Inside Treviso's seven-domed **Duomo,** the Malchiostro Chapel contains an *Annunciation* by Titian and frescoes by Pordenone (1484–1539), including an *Adoration of the Magi.* The crypt has 12th-century columns.

⊠ *Piazza del Duomo* ⊗ *Mon.–Sat. 7:30–noon and 3:30–7, Sun. 7:30–1 and 3:30–8.*

> **WORD OF MOUTH**
>
> "If you do stay in Treviso, make sure you have a cappuccino in Piazza dei Signori–the best place to people watch and enjoy the ambience!"   –Paulareg

off the beaten path

CONEGLIANO – The town of Conegliano, 23 km (14 mi) north of Treviso, is in wine-producing country. The town itself is attractive, with Venetian-style villas and frescoed houses, but the real draw is the wine, particularly the effervescent prosecco, sold in local wine bars and shops.

Where to Stay & Eat

$–$$ ✕ **Toni del Spin.** Wood-paneled with 1930s decor, this place oozes delightful, old-fashioned character. Locals love the friendly and bustling feel as well as the wholesome food. The menu is chalked on a hanging wooden board for immediate updating. Soups might include the filling zuppa d'orzo e fagioli. *Faraona* (guinea fowl) is a specialty, and autumn brings roast goose to the menu. Don't leave without quaffing a glass or two of *prosecco,* a dry sparkling white wine. ⊠ *Via Inferiore 7* ☎ *0422/543829* ▤ *AE, MC, V* ⊗ *Closed Sun. and Aug. No lunch Mon.*

¢–$ ✕ **Osteria Muscoli's.** The bar is busy with locals popping in for an *ombra* (colloquial for glass of wine), but there are rough-hewn tables in back where you can sit and enjoy traditional osteria fare. Open-face crostini sandwiches, sliced meats, and quichelike pies arrive on wood cutting boards. The daily menu might include soup with radicchio and chestnuts, polenta with cheese, or catch of the day from the fish market across the bridge. Muscoli's is open 7 AM–2 AM. ⊠ *Via Pescheria 23* ☎ *0422/583390* ▤ *No credit cards* ⊗ *Closed Sun. Apr.–Aug., Wed. Oct.–Mar., and 3 wks in Sept.*

$ ✕▥ **Locanda La Colonna.** Arranged around a vine-covered courtyard, this small, central 15th-century hotel is worth booking ahead (it's completely nonsmoking). Rich wood floors and decorative marble make the modestly furnished rooms seem lush. Flower-frescoed ceilings and old-fashioned washstands add to the charm. You can feel history seeping through the walls in Locanda's restaurant ($–$$), where you sit among pillars, frescoes, and arches. The chef favors fish, but the pork, delicately perfumed with rosemary, is good, too. The same menu is available in the adjacent wine bar, formerly the carriage house. ⊠ *Via Campana 27, 31100* ☎ *0422/544804* ▤ *0422/419177* ⤚ *7 rooms* ♿ *Restaurant, bar, some pets allowed; no smoking* ▤ *AE, DC, MC, V* ⊗ *Restaurant closed Mon. and 2 wks in mid-Aug.* ⍩ *EP.*

$$ ▥ **Carlton Hotel.** Pass the river flowing outside, walk through a lobby that's seen better days, and seek out the huge terrace right on top of the old city wall. Even the parking lot has a view from here. Five minutes from the train station, five minutes from the heart of Treviso, this hotel is very convenient for touring. That is if you're not too busy using the gym, enjoying free golf at Asolo, or tasting wines wines in the vineyards nearby. ⊠ *Largo di Porta Altinia 15, 31100* ☎ *0422/411661* 🖷 *0422/411620* ⊕ *www.hotelcarlton.it* ☎ *93 rooms* ♧ *Restaurant, in-room safes, minibars, cable TV, golf privileges, gym, bicycles, bar, meeting room, free parking, some pets allowed* ⊟ *AE, DC, MC, V* ⊘ *Restaurant closed Sun.* ⦿ *BP.*

FRIULI–VENEZIA GIULIA

The peripheral location of the Friuli–Venezia Giulia region in Italy's northeastern corner makes it easy to overlook, but with its ethnic mix of Italian, Slavic, and central European cultures, it's a fascinating area to explore. Venetian culture crept northward until it merged with northern European into the Veneto-Byzantine style evident in places like the medieval city of Udine. The Cividale del Friuli and the Collio wine regions around Cormòns are a short hop away from Udine and the old Austrian port of Trieste was once an important symbol of Italian nationalism.

Udine

③② *94 km (58 mi) northeast of Treviso, 127 km (79 mi) northeast of Venice.*

Udine commands a view from the Alpine foothills to the Adriatic Sea; it stands on a mound that, according to legend, was erected so Attila the Hun could watch the burning of Aquileia, an important Roman center to the south. In the Middle Ages Udine flourished, thanks to its favorable trade location and the right granted by the local patriarch to hold regular markets. There is a distinctly Venetian architectural feel to the medieval city, noticeable in the Piazza della Libertà under the stern gaze of the lion of St. Mark, symbol of Venetian power.

From the hilltop **Castello** panoramic views extend to Monte Nero (7,360 feet) in neighboring Slovenia. Here Udine's civic museums of art and archaeology are centralized under one roof. Particularly worth seeing is the national and regional art collection in the **Galleria d'Arte Antica,** which has canvases by Friulian Nicola Grassi (1682–1745), and Venetians Vittore Carpaccio (circa 1460–1525) and Giambattista Tiepolo. ⊠ *Castello di Udine* ☎ *0432/271591* ▱ *€3, €1 Sun.* ⊘ *Tues.–Sat. 9:30–12:30 and 3–6, Sun. 9:30–12:30.*

Where to Stay & Eat

$$–$$$ ✕ **Vitello d'Oro.** Udine's landmark restaurant is where locals go to celebrate special occasions. You can dine al fresco on the terrace, or beneath a stained-glass ceiling inside. Vitello d'Oro serves regional classics and newer creations. Try *carrè di cinghiale* (saddle of wild boar) or fish roasted with *ristretto al porto*, a port wine reduction. If you haven't left room for a rich sweet, at least try a taste of homemade chestnut ice cream.

Traveling the Wine Roads

YOU'D BE HARD-PRESSED to find a more stimulating and varied wine region than northeastern Italy. From the Valpolicella, Bardolino, and Soave produced near Verona to the superlative whites of the Collio region, wines from the Veneto and Friuli-Venezia Giulia earn more Denominazione di Origine Controllata (DOC) seals for uniqueness and quality than those of any other area of Italy.

You can travel on foot, by car, or by bicycle over hillsides covered with vineyards, each field nurturing subtly different grape varieties. On a casual trip through the countryside you're likely to come across wineries that will welcome you for a visit; for a more organized tour, check at local tourist information offices, which have maps of roads, wineries, and vendors. (If you find yourself in Bassano del Grappa, stop by Nardini distillery to pick up some grappa, the potent liquor made from grape husks.) Be advised that Italy has become more stringent about its driving regulations; seat belts and designated drivers can save fines, embarrassment, or worse.

One of the most hospitable areas in the Veneto for wine enthusiasts is the stretch of country north of Treviso, where you can follow designated wine roads—tours that blend a beautiful rural setting with the delights of the grape. Authorized wine shops where you can stop and sample are marked with a sign showing a triangular arrangement of red and yellow grapes. There are three routes to choose from, and they're managable enough that you can do them all comfortably over the course of a day or two.

Montello & Asolo Hills

This route provides a good balance of vineyards and non-wine-related sights. It winds its way from Nervesa della Battaglia, 18 km (10 mi) north of Treviso, past two prime destinations in the area, the lovely village of Asolo and the Villa Barbaro at Maser. Asolo produces good Prosecco, whereas Montello favors merlot and cabernet. Both areas also yield pinot and chardonnay.

Piave River

The circular route follows the river Piave and runs through orchards, woods, and hills. Among the area's gems are the DOC Torchiato di Fregona and Refrontolo Passito, both made according to traditional methods. Raboso del Piave, renowned since Roman times, ages well and complements local dishes such as beans and pasta or goose stuffed with chestnuts. The other reds are cabernet, merlot, and cabernet sauvignon. As an accompaniment to fish, choose a Verduzzo del Piave or, for an aperitif, the lovely warm-yellow Pinot Grigio del Piave.

Prosecco

This route runs for 47 km (29 mi) between Valdobbiadene and Conegliano, home of Italy's first wine institute, winding between knobby hills covered in grapevines. These hang in festoons on row after row of pergolas to create a thick mantle of green. Turn off the main route to explore the narrower country lanes, most of which eventually join up. They meander through tiny hamlets and past numerous family wineries where you can taste and purchase the wines. Spring is an excellent time to visit, with no fewer than 15 local wine festivals held between March and early June.

✉ *Via Valvason 4* ☎ *0432/508982* 🖃 *AE, DC, MC, V* ⊘ *Closed Sun. June–Aug., Wed. Sept.–May. No lunch Mon.*

★ ¢–$ ✕ **Al Cappello.** This whimsical wine tavern is painted orange, except for the blackboard wall that lists 100 wines available by the glass, and hats cover the ceiling. Grilled meats are served with a splash of vinegar and there are daily pasta specials. If you don't come for dinner, at least stop in for a glass of wine and a snack such as an appetizer-size sandwich or *frico* (a potato-and-cheese bake). You can sit at the counter, at one of the shared tables inside, or outside where you're served through the open window. ✉ *Via Paolo Sarpi 5* ☎ *0432/299327* 🖃 *No credit cards* ⊘ *Closed Mon., 3 wks in Jan. and 3 wks mid-summer. No dinner Sun.*

$$ 🏨 **Clocchiatti.** The 19th century meets the 21st at Clocchiatti: you can stay in the restored villa, where large double doors open onto canopy beds or Alpine-style wooden ceilings and paneling; or choose the ultra modern wing, "Next," which has rich colors, spare furnishings, and dramatic lighting. Daniela and Aldo are excellent hosts. The hotel is on a quiet street, not far from the train station. ✉ *Via Cividale 29, 33100* ☎🖷 *0432/505047* ⊕ *www.hotelclocchiatti.it* ➲ *27 rooms* ☐ *In-room data ports, in-room safes, minibars, cable TV with movies, pool, bicycles, bar, laundry service, free parking, some pets allowed, no-smoking rooms* ⭐◎⏐ *BP.*

Cividale del Friuli

㉝ *17 km (11 mi) east of Udine, 144 km (89 mi) northeast of Venice.*

Cividale was founded in AD 53 by Julius Caesar, then commander of Roman legions in the area. Locals say their Ponte del Diavolo, bridging the Natisone River, is supported by rocks the devil tossed down during a tantrum. Here you can find Celtic and Roman ruins alongside Venetian Gothic buildings, including the Palazzo Comunale. Cividale's Renaissance **Duomo** contains a magnificent 12th-century silver gilt altarpiece. ✉ *Piazza Duomo* ☎ *0432/731144* ⊘ *Apr.–Oct., Mon.–Sat. 9:30–noon and 3–7, Sun. 3–7; Nov.–Mar., Mon.–Sat. 9:30–noon and 3–6, Sun. 3–6.*

Trace the area's history at the **Museo Archeologico** and learn about the importance of Cividale and Udine in the period following the collapse of the Roman Empire. The collection includes weapons and jewelry from 6th-century Lombard warriors, who swept through much of what is now Italy. ✉ *Piazza Duomo 13* ☎ *0432/700700* 🎟 *€2* ⊘ *Mon. 9–2, Tues.–Sun. 8:30–7:30.*

The **Tempietto Longobardo,** perched above the meandering river, is a little gem of a Lombard church. It has an archway with a vine motif, guarded by an 8th-century procession of female figures. The fine carved wooden stalls date from the 14th century. ✉ *Via Monastero Maggiore* ☎ *0432/ 700867* 🎟 *€2* ⊘ *Apr.–Sept., Mon.–Sat. 9:30–12:30 and 3–6:30, Sun. 9:30–1 and 3–7:30; Oct.–Mar., Mon.–Sat. 9:30–12:30 and 3–5, Sun. 9:30–12:30 and 2:30–6.*

2

Where to Eat

$ ✕ **Ai Tre Re.** Here, legend says, three kings once divided up the country-side, and since the 1500s the Three Kings has refreshed travelers within its stone-wall garden or beside its 6-foot-square woodstove. Beneath the beamed ceiling everything is homemade, including the bread of wheat and *maize* (corn). Try pumpkin gnocchi with smoked ricotta, followed by sausage in cream sauce or cheese grilled with wild herbs. ✉ *Via Stretta San Valentino 31* ☎ *0432/700416* 🍽 *MC, V* ⊗ *Closed Tues., June, and Oct.*

Cormòns

34 *18 km (11 mi) south of Cividale del Friuli, 51 km (32 mi) northwest of Trieste.*

Southeast of Udine, in the rolling hills of Friuli–Venezia Giulia, Cormòns is the epicenter of the Collio region, a producer of exceptional white wine. Route 356, just west of the Slovenian border, winds through miles of vineyard-covered hills. Residents boast that Ribolla grapes have grown here for 1,000 years, the region's Tocai grape vines may be the original source for Hungary's famous Tokay wine. Local Picolit grapes

VOICES OF ITALY

Josko Gravner
wine maker, Collio region

Josko Gravner's Friuli home looks across a shallow valley into Slovenia. His vineyards, and the surrounding Collio hills, straddle the national divide, literally half-Italian and half-Slovene. It's an area that's been racked by political turmoil; it also produces exceptional white wines. "These hills here are drier," Josko explains. "The grapes are stressed, robbed. They suffer." Such conditions result in small yields but a rich final product.

Josko is one of the Italian wine world's leading innovators and iconoclasts—a reputation he cemented in the mid-1990s by becoming its most staunch traditionalist. He swapped his modern press for an antiquated model—"one that presses the grapes, instead of chewing them." He was labeled a madman when he replaced his refrigerated stainless steel tanks with terra-cotta amphorae from the Kakheti province of Georgia, where the first wine is thought to have been produced five millennia ago. These 3,000-liter vessels—pointed at the bottom, 7 feet tall, and 5½ feet across at their widest—are buried in the ground, and the wine is allowed to settle in them, making filtration unnecessary.

Josko describes his approach in straightforward terms. "It isn't a science, it's a philosophy. I have to make wine that I like." He forgoes chemical fertilizers, fortifiers, and clarifiers, and he bottles under a waning moon. "I don't have the goal to get rich but to make good wine, natural wine, as simple as possible. One is rich when one is content."

In this idyllic region along the banks of the Isonzo River, contentment has been hard to come by. In Friuli, 300,000 residents consider themselves ethnic Slovenes. "Mussolini's people closed my grandfather's trattoria because he would not join the Fascist party," Josko recalls. "After World War II, the border was drawn in London. It was possible to have the house in one country and the barn in another." The Slovene language was officially banned, but Josko, born in 1952—"after the war, but before the peace"—grew up speaking it nonetheless. So did his wife, Maria, the Yugoslavian girl next door.

Much has changed, to say the least, in recent years. May 2004 marked Slovenia's admission into the European Union, a telltale sign of the culture's growing acceptance among its neighbors. The change can be felt locally as well. Now, according to Miha, Josko's youngest son and winemaking partner, "When you interview for a job, you don't get it if you don't speak Slovene."

Meanwhile, the Gravners are earning accolades from those who once doubted Josko's sanity. According to Gambero Rosso, Italy's leading organization of wine critics, "Gravner's wines are exploring ways forward that are as exciting as their maker's personality. The amphorae are no mere exotic curiosities. They are serious cellar tools that produce stunningly rounded wines."

The Gravners welcome visitors when time allows. Try contacting Josko by e-mail at joskogravner@libero.it. Proprietors of La Subida in Cormòns can also help arrange a visit.

are said to have been the source of papal communion wine for centuries, and it is still made here by the Sovereign Military Order of Malta.

The region has changed hands in bloody battles since the days of imperial Rome. Following World War II, international arbitrators determined whose farms would be part of Italy and whose would end up within Tito's Yugoslavia. It's no surprise that many residents here speak Slovenian in their homes and have relatives or cultivate fields across the border. In May 2004 the border effectively dissolved when Slovenia was welcomed into the European Union.

Where to Stay & Eat

$$–$$$
Fodor'sChoice
★
✕ **La Cacciatore.** Set among the Collio's vineyards, La Cacciatore serves food that reflects the region's Slovenian-Austrian-Italian cultural blend: *zlikrofi* is a cross between ravioli and tortellini, and gnocchi are made with plum and with butter and cinnamon instead of savory ingredients. You may even find wild *sambuco* (elderflowers) and *dragoncello* (tarragon) in the desserts. The prix-fixe menu (€48–€55) provides a consistently delicious meal. The restaurant is the centerpiece of La Subida country lodging. ⊠ *La Subida, Loc. Monte 22* ☎ *0481/60531* ⚏ *Reservations essential* ☰ *MC, V* ⊗ *Closed Tues., Wed., and July 1–10. No lunch weekdays.*

$$–$$$
✕ **Trattoria Al Giardinetto.** The wrought-iron gate and wide front porch make it feel like you're entering a family home, and indeed this restaurant is run by three brothers. They call their cuisine Friulian and they've come up with creative cooking techniques such as *in conserva* (steaming food with wine inside canning jars); you open your jar at the table, unlocking delightful aromas. All Giardinetto's ingredients are fresh, seasonal, and local, except for the cocoa in their desserts, such as *fondente di Araguani 72%*, a fondue of designer chocolate so rich it could substitute for a main course. ⊠ *Via Matteotti 54/56* ☎ *0481/60257* ⚏ *Reservations essential* ☰ *AE, DC, MC, V* ⊗ *Closed Mon. and Tues.*

$$$
Fodor'sChoice
★
▦ **Castello Formentini.** Count Formentini's stunning castle has been ancestral property for five centuries. The restored complex today includes a winery, sports facilities, and superb accommodations that blend antique furnishings with modern conveniences. Not only is breakfast included, but there's complimentary wine, beer, and grappa, as well as a day-long buffet of antipasto and sweets. About once a month the hotel hosts a medieval banquet in the massive hall—complete with sword fights, fire-eaters, 15th-century recipes, and no forks. Though such events can feel contrived and tacky, here they pull it off with style; it's the closest thing there is to time travel. ⊠ *Via Oslavia 2, 34070 San Floriano del Collio, 20 km (12 mi) northeast of Cormòns* ☎ *0481/884051* 📠 *0481/884052* ⊕ *www.golfhotelformentini.com* ⌖ *14 rooms, 1 suite* ⚏ *Snack bar, minibars, cable TV, 9-hole golf course, tennis court, pool, bar, meeting room, some pets allowed, no-smoking rooms, free parking; no a/c in some rooms* ☰ *AE, DC, MC, V* ⊗ *Closed Dec. 20–Feb.* ❢○❢ *BP.*

$$
▦ **La Subida.** Josko and Loredana Sirk's painstakingly created country refuge has 13 rustic-yet-modern cottages. Wooden beams and white lace lend nostalgia to the lodgings. Wood is delivered to the rooms each day so you can enjoy the *fogolar*, a traditional Friulan fireplace. Be sure to

dine in the noteworthy restaurant, La Cacciatore; there is also the less formal (and less expensive) Osteria La Subida on-site. ⊠ *Loc. Monte 22, 34071* ☎ *0481/60531* 🖷 *0481/61616* ⊕ *www.lasubida.it* ⇥ *13 cottages* ⚭ *2 restaurants, kitchenettes, cable TV, tennis court, pool, bicycles, horseback riding, bar, some pets allowed; no a/c* ⊟ *MC, V* ⊗ *Closed 3 wks in Feb. Osteria closed Thurs. and Nov.* ⏐⊙⏐ *EP.*

Trieste

㉟ *51 km (32 mi) southeast of Cormòns, 163 km (101 mi) east of Venice.*

Surrounded by rugged countryside and beautiful Adriatic, Trieste is built on a mere fringe of coast and the rugged Karst plateau above. This town was once the chief port of the Austro-Hungarian Empire. Early Italian revolutionaries rallied their battle cry around Trieste, because of what they believed was foreign occupation of their rightful motherland. Like Vienna's coffeehouses, Trieste's belle-epoque cafés are social and cultural centers and much-beloved refuges from winter's bitter *bora* (wind from the north).

If you're visiting more than a sight or two pick up a T For You Card from the Tourist Information office. The €8 (24 hours) or €10 (48 hours) pass gets you free entrance to all civic museums, the Grotto Gigante, and some beach areas. You'll also be able to use all public transportation, including buses, the tram, and boat rides across the bay. Cardholders get discounts at some restaurants, shops, and hotels: ask when booking or ordering.

The sidewalk cafés on the vast seaside **Piazza dell'Unità d'Italia** are popular meeting places in the summer months. The square is similar to Piazzetta San Marco in Venice; both are focal points of architectural interest and command fine views of the water. On the inland side of the piazza is the majestic, Vienese **Palazzo Comunale** (Town Hall). Steps behind it lead uphill, tracing Trieste's upward expansion from its roots as a Roman fishing port.

A statue of Habsburg emperor Leopold I looks out over **Piazza della Borsa,** which contains Trieste's original stock exchange, the **Borsa Vecchia,** a neoclassical building now serving as the chamber of commerce.

The 1st century AD amphitheater **Teatro Romano** ruins, opposite the city's *questura* (police station), were discovered during 1938 demolition work. Its statues are now displayed at the Museo Civico and the space that once held 6,000 spectators is filled with grass and flowers. ⊠ *Via del Teatro Romano.*

The 14th-century **Cattedrale di San Giusto** contains remnants of two previous churches built on the same ground, the earliest dating from the 5th century. The exterior includes fragments of Roman tombs and temples, adding to the jumble of styles: the pillars of the main doorway are the most conspicuous Roman element. Inside, don't miss the 12th-century gold mosaic behind the main altar. ⊠ *Piazza della Cattedrale 2* ☎ *040/309666* ⊗ *Apr.–Sept., Mon.–Sat. 8–noon and 3:30–7:30, Sun. 8–1 and 3:30–8; Oct.–Mar., Mon.–Sat. 8–noon and 2:30–6:30, Sun. 8–1 and 3:30–8.*

2

The hilltop **Castello di San Giusto** was built on the ruins of the Roman town of Tergeste. Given the excellent view, it's no surprise that 15th-century Venetians turned the castle into a shipping observation point; the structure was further enlarged by Trieste's subsequent rulers, the Habsburgs. The castle is not open to the public; it has been judged structurally unsound. No one knows if or when it will reopen.

On the hill near the Castello is the **Museo Civico di Storia ed Arte,** an eclectic history and art museum with statues from the Roman theater and artifacts from Egypt, Greece, and Rome. There's also an assortment of glass and manuscripts. The **Orto Lapidario** (Lapidary Garden) has classical statuary, pottery, and a small Corinthian temple. ⊠ *Via Cattedrale 15* ☎ *040/310500* ✉ *€3* ☉ *Weekdays 9–12:30; and Mon. and Wed. 2–4.*

The **Civico Museo Revoltella e Galleria d'Arte Moderna** was founded in 1872, when the city inherited the palazzo, library, and art collection of shipping magnate Baron Pasquale Revoltella, vice president of the consortium that built the Suez Canal. The gallery holds one of the country's most important collections of 19th- and 20th-century art, with Italian artists particularly well represented. Hours vary for special exhibits, but don't miss a summer evening at the museum's rooftop café, where the view rivals the artwork. ⊠ *Via Armando Diaz 27* ☎ *040/6754350* ✉ *€5* ☉ *Mon. and Wed.–Sat. 9–1:30 and 4–7, Sun. 10–7; July 15–Aug., Thurs.–Sat. 9 AM–midnight.*

☼ At Trieste's **Museo del Mare** (Museum of the Sea) you can learn how Venetian galley rowers managed to sit three abreast and not smash one another with their oars. Displays include lots of boat models and a diorama with *casoni* (fishermen's grass huts) and submerged *seragi* (fishnet traps). Outside is a park area with giant anchors and shady benches. ⊠ *Via di Campo Marzio 5* ☎ *040/304987* ✉ *€3* ☉ *Tues.–Sun. 8:30–1:30.*

Where to Stay & Eat

$$–$$$ ✕ **Trattoria ai Fiori.** Fishermen still in their gum boots deliver their catch fresh off the boat to a restaurateur they've worked with for 20 years. Enjoy your fish simply grilled, or lying on a bed of wild mushrooms and truffles. Homemade pasta, bread, and gelato enliven any meal, and high ceilings brighten the dining room. ⊠ *Piazza Attilio Hortis 7* ☎☎ *040/ 300633* ⊟ *AE, DC, MC, V* ☉ *Closed Sun. and 2–3 wks in Aug.*

$–$$ ✕ **Suban.** Head for the hills—to the landmark trattoria operated by members of the hospitable Suban family since 1865. Sit by the dining room fire or relax on a huge terrace and watch the sunset. This is fish-free Italian food with a Slovene, Hungarian, and Austrian accent. Start with *jota carsolina* (a rich soup of cabbage, potatoes, and beans), and then you might order a steak grilled and sliced at your table. Lighter fare includes *insalatine tiepide* (warm salads with smoked pork or duck) and a locally smoked beef that is truly special. To get here you can take Bus 35 from Piazza Oberdan. ⊠ *Via Comici 2* ☎ *040/54368* ⊟ *AE, DC, MC, V* ☉ *Closed Tues., 3 wks in Aug., and 1 wk in early Jan. No lunch Mon.*

¢–$ ✕ **Antipastoteca di Mare.** Nautical kitsch provides homey charm to this
Fodor'sChoice little eatery that serves seafood exclusively, accompanied by salad, po-
★ tatoes, polenta, and house wine. Don't miss chef-owner Roberto Surian's

Trieste's Caffè Culture

TRIESTE IS JUSTLY FAMOUS for its coffee, and so it is perhaps no coincidence that its former mayor Riccardo Illy (now serving as governor of the Friuli–Venezia Giulia region) is an heir to the Illycaffè dynasty, supplier of top-quality caffeine fixes throughout Italy and the world. The elegant civility of Trieste plays out beautifully in a caffè culture rivaling that of Vienna. In Trieste, as elsewhere in Italy, ask for a *caffè* and you'll get a thimbleful of high-octane espresso. Your cappuccino here will also come in an espresso cup, with only half as much frothy milk as you'll find elsewhere and a dollop of whipped cream. Many cafés are part of a *torrefazione* (roasting shop), so you can sample a cup and then buy beans to take with you.

Few cafés in Italy–or in the world–can rival Antico Caffè San Marco (⊠ Via Battisti 18 ☎ 040/363538) for its art deco style and bohemian atmosphere. After being destroyed in World War I,

it was rebuilt in the 1920s and became a meeting place for local intellectuals. Cremcaffè (⊠ Piazza Carlo Goldoni 10 ☎ 040/636555) isn't the ideal place to sit and read the paper, but its downtown location and selection of 20 coffee blends make it one of the busiest cafés in town. Founded in 1830, classic Caffè Tommaseo (⊠ Piazza Tommaseo 4/c ☎ 040/362666) is a comfortable place to linger, especially on weekend evenings and Sunday morning when there's live music. For a great view of the great piazza, you couldn't do better than Caffè Degli Specchi (⊠ Piazza dell'Unità d'Italia 7 ☎ 040/365777), where the many mirrors heighten the opportunities for people-watching. The atmosphere is more modern than old-world at I Paesi del Caffè (⊠ Via Einaudi 1 ☎ 040/633897), which brews and sells beans of top international varieties, including Jamaica Blue Mountain.

slow-cooked fish soup—with tuna, mackerel, and sardines—served in a shell. Grilled or fried fish is generally available, but order the mixed antipasto and you get to taste just about everything on the menu except dessert. ⊠ *Via della Fornace 1* ☎ *040/309606* ▭ *No credit cards* ⊘ *Closed Mon. No dinner Sun.*

$$$$ 🏨 **Duchi d'Aosta.** Since 1327, hotels on this spot have hosted everyone from sailors and merchants to Austrian emperors. Continuously reincarnated like the city of Trieste itself, Duchi d'Aosta welcomes guests with valet parking, Oriental carpets, and rich brocade. Rooms are furnished in dark-wood antiques; some have balconies. The basement was excavated below sea level to engineer a pool and spa area that rivals the baths of ancient Rome. ⊠ *Piazza dell'Unità d'Italia 2, 34121* ☎ *040/7600011* 🖷 *040/366092* ⊕ *www.grandhotelduchidaosta.com* ⇝ *53 rooms, 2 suites* ⚲ *Restaurant, some in-room hot tubs, minibars, cable TV with movies, indoor pool, spa, bar, laundry service, meeting rooms, parking (fee), some pets allowed, no-smoking rooms* ▭ *AE, DC, MC, V* ⧖ *BP.*

★ **$$** 🏨 **Riviera & Maximilian's.** Leave the city behind, just 7 km (4 mi) to the north, and stay waterfront on the Gulf of Trieste. Rooms vary from modern design to vintage wood, and some have balconies and kitchenettes. The restaurant and the breakfast room also face the stunning panorama. From the hotel you take an elevator down to a private beach, pool, and children's area. ⊠ *Strada Costiera 22, 34010* ☎ *040/224551* 🖷 *040/224300* ⊕ *www.hotelrivieraemaximilian.com* ➪ *56 rooms, 2 suites, 9 apartments* ⚐ *Restaurant, fans, minibars, some kitchenettes, cable TV with movies, in-room data ports, pool, beach, bar, Internet, meeting rooms, some pets allowed, free parking no a/c in some rooms* ▤ *AE, DC, MC, V* ⦿ *BP.*

$ ▦ **Alabarda.** The staff of this family-operated hotel is happy to help you with local services, maps, and city bus tickets. Alabarda is in central Trieste, only a 10-minute walk from the train station. Bright, spacious rooms have wood laminate floors and peach color schemes. Some of the front rooms can be noisy; ask for one in the back. ⊠ *Via Valdirivo 22* ☎ *040/630269* 🖷 *040/639284* ⊕ *www.hotelalabarda.it* ➪ *18 rooms, 7 with bath* ⚐ *Cable TV, in-room data ports, bicycles, Internet, parking (fee), some pets allowed; no a/c in some rooms* ▤ *AE, DC, MC, V* ⦿ *BP.*

$ ▦ **Filoxenia.** The location on the city waterfront, and the reasonable prices, make this small hotel a choice accommodation. Members of Trieste's Greek community run the Filoxenia, and there's a good Greek restaurant on-site. The staff makes up in friendliness for what it might lack in professionalism. Rooms are simple and fresh, with white walls and two single beds covered in Mediterranean blue–stripe spreads; family rooms sleep four (€120). ⊠ *Via Mazzini 3, 34121* ☎ *040/3481644* 🖷 *040/661371* ⊕ *www.filoxenia. it* ➪ *20 rooms* ⚐ *Restaurant, in-room safes, bar, meeting rooms, no-smoking rooms; no a/c in some rooms* ▤ *DC, MC, V* ⦿ *BP.*

Nightlife & the Arts

The opera season at the **Teatro Verdi** (⊠ Piazza Verdi 1 ☎ 040/6722111 ⊕ www.teatroverdi-trieste.com) in Trieste runs from October through May, with a brief operetta festival in July and August.

Shopping

Trieste has some 60 local dealers in jewelry, antiques, and antique wannabes; the city's old center hosts a street market on the third Sunday of each month and a large antiques fair at the end of October. Trieste's busy shopping street, **Corso Italia**, is off the Piazza della Borsa.

Castello di Miramare

★ ☾ ㊱ *7 km (4½ mi) northwest of Trieste.*

Archduke Maximilian of Habsburg, brother of Emperor Franz Josef and retired commander of the Austrian navy, built this seafront extravaganza in the 19th century. It has ship's-keel wooden ceilings, marine-blue furnishings, and windows onto the Adriatic. His peaceful retirement was interrupted in 1864 when he reluctantly became Emperor of Mexico; he was killed three years later by a Mexican firing squad. The castle was later owned by the Duke of Aosta, who installed modern plumbing in his art deco bathroom. Within the 54-acre garden surrounding the castle is **Tropical Park** greenhouse, which is populated by butterflies and birds. Bus 36 from Piazza Oberdan in Trieste leaves for here every half hour. Guided tours in English are available by reservation. ✉ *Viale Miramare, off SS14, Miramare* ☎ *040/224143 castle, 040/224406 greenhouse* ⊕ *www.castello-miramare.it* ✉ *Castle €4, guided tour €3.50, park free, greenhouse €6.50* ⊙ *Castle daily 9–7, last entry 30 mins before closing. Park daily Apr.–Sept., 8–7; Nov.–Feb., 8–5; Mar. and Oct., 8–6. Greenhouse daily Apr.–Oct., 9–6; Nov.–Mar., 10–5.*

VENETIAN ARC ESSENTIALS

Transportation

BY AIR

The main airport serving the Venetian Arc is Aeroporto Marco Polo, 10 km (6 mi) north of Venice, which handles international and domestic flights to the region. A few European airlines schedule flights to Aeroporto Valerio Catullo, southwest of Verona; it's also served by a number of charter flights. A regular bus service connects the airport with Verona's Porta Nuova railway station.

Aeroporto di Treviso, 5 km (3 mi) southeast of Treviso, 32 km (19 mi) north of Venice, is also served by charter flights (check ⊕ www.ryanair. com for flights to and from London's Stansted airport). Flights to Treviso sometimes include transportation from the airport to Venice or other destinations; otherwise there is an ACTT local bus to Treviso every 30 minutes during the day (until 9 PM), or a taxi will come to the airport to pick you up from Treviso. There are domestic and some European flights (including a daily Ryanair London service) to Aeroporto Ronchi dei Legionari, 35 km (22 mi) northwest of Trieste, linked with the Trieste's Piazza della Libertà bus terminal (beside the railway station) by regular APT bus service, or you can take a convenient *servizio navetta* (shuttle).

🛫 Airport Information **Aeroporto Marco Polo** ✉ Tessera, 10 km (6 mi) north of Venice ☎ 041/2609260, 041/2609240 automated system ⊕ www.veniceairport.it. **Aeroporto Valerio Catullo di Verona Villafranca** ✉ 11 km (7 mi) southwest of Verona ☎ 045/8095666 ⊕ www.aeroportoverona.it. **Aeroporto Ronchi dei Legionari** ☎ 0481/773224 ⊕ www.aeroporto.fvg.it. **Aeroporto di Treviso** ☎ 0422/315111.

🛫 Taxis & Shuttles **APT** ☎ 0481/593511 ⊕ www.aptgorizia.it. **Taxi** ☞ For Trieste ☎ 0481/778000 or 335/6914776.

BY BUS

There are interurban and interregional connections throughout the Veneto and Friuli. Local tourist offices may be able to provide details of timetables and routes; otherwise contact the local bus station or, in some cases, the individual bus companies operating from the station, listed below.

🚌 Bus Information **ACTT buses** ✉ Piazzale Duca D'Aosta 25, Treviso ☎ 0422/3271. **ACTV buses** ✉ Piazzale Roma, Venice ☎ 041/24240 buses to Brenta Riviera ⊕ www. actv.it. **APTV buses** ✉ Autostazione di Verona Porta Nuova, Piazzale XXV Aprile, Verona ☎ 045/8057911 ⊕ www.aptv.it. **ATVO buses** ✉ Piazzale Roma, Venice ☎ 0421/383671 ⊕ www.atvo.it. **FTV buses** ✉ Piazzale della Stazione near Campo Marzio, Vicenza ☎ 0444/223115 ⊕ www.ftv.vi.it. **SITA buses** ✉ Piazzale Boschetti, Padua ☎ 049/

8206844 ⊕ www.sita-on-line.it. **TT buses** ✉ Piazza della Libertà, Trieste ☎ 800/016675 ⊕ www.triestetrasporti.it.

BY CAR

The two main access roads to the Venetian Arc from southern Italy are both linked to the A1 (Autostrada del Sole), which connects Bologna, Florence, and Rome. They are the A13, which culminates in Padua, and the A22, which passes through Verona running north–south. Linking the region from east to west is the A4, the primary route from Milan to Trieste, skirting Verona, Padua, and Venice along the way. The distance from Verona to Trieste via A4 is 263 km (163 mi), with one break in the autostrada near Venice/Mestre. Branches link the A4 with Treviso (A27), Pordenone (A28), and Udine (A23).

EMERGENCY ACI Emergency Service offers 24-hour roadside assistance.
SERVICES 🛈 **ACI dispatchers** ☎ 803/116.

BY TRAIN

Trains on the main routes from the south stop almost hourly in Verona, Padua, and Venice. From northern Italy and the rest of Europe, trains usually enter via Milan or through Porta Nuova station in Verona. Treviso and Udine both lie on the main line from Venice to Tarvisio, from which Eurocity trains continue to Vienna and Prague.

To the west of Venice, the main line running across the north of Italy stops at Padua (30 minutes from Venice), Vicenza (1 hour), and Verona (1½ hours); to the east is Trieste (2 hours). Local trains link Venice to Bassano del Grappa (1 hour), Padua to Bassano del Grappa (1 hour), Vicenza to Treviso (1 hour), and Udine to Trieste (1 hour).
🛈 Train Information **Trenitalia** ☎ 892021 ⊕ www.trenitalia.com.

Contacts & Resources

EMERGENCIES

For first aid, dial the general emergency number (118) and ask for *pronto soccorso* (first aid). Be prepared to give your address. (If you can find a concierge or some other Italian-speaker to call on your behalf, do so, as not all operators speak English.) All pharmacies post signs on the door with addresses of pharmacies that stay open at night, on Saturday afternoon, and on Sunday.
🛈 **Ambulance** ☎ 118, **Police** ☎ 113.

TOURS

Local tourist offices will be able to put you in contact with the Tourist Guides Association or provide you with a list of authorized guides, for whom there is an official tariff rate.
🛈 **Association of Trieste Authorized Guides** ☎ 040/365248. **Padua Authorized Guides** ☎ 049/8209711 ⊕ www.guidepadova.it

VISITOR INFORMATION

🛈 Tourist Information **Asolo** ✉ Piazza Garibaldi, 31011 ☎ 0423/529046 ⊕ www.asolo.it. **Bassano del Grappa** ✉ Largo Corona d'Italia 35, 36061 ☎ 0424/524351 ⊕ www.vicenzae.org. **Marostica** ✉ Piazza Castello 1, 36063 ☎ 0424/72127 ⊕ www.

marosticaonline.it. **Padua** ⊠ Padova Railway Station ☎ 049/8752077 ⊠ Vicolo Pedrocchi ☎ 049/8767927 ⊕ www.apt.padova.it. **Treviso** ⊠ Piazza Monte di Pietà 8, 31100 ☎ 0422/547632. **Trieste** ⊠ Piazza dell'Unità d'Italia 4/b, 34100 ☎ 040/3478312 ⊕ www.triestetourism.it. **Udine** ⊠ Piazza I Maggio 7, 33100 ☎ 0432/295972 ⊕ www.turismo.fvg.it. **Verona** ⊠ Piazza Brà, 37100 ☎ 045/8068680 ⊠ Porta Nuova Railway Station ☎ 045/8000861 ⊕ www.tourism.verona.it. **Vicenza** ⊠ Piazza Giacomo Matteotti 12, 36100 ☎ 0444/320854 ⊠ Piazza dei Signori 8 ☎ 0444/544122 ⊕ www.vicenza.org.

The Dolomites

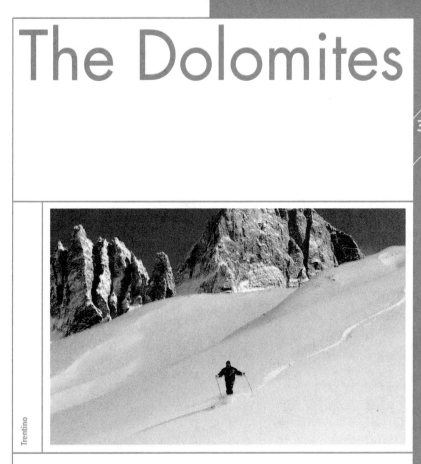

Trentino

WORD OF MOUTH

"There are so many beautiful valleys and mountains, it's hard to choose. My favorite drive is through the Val Gardena from north of Bolzano to Cortina. The area around Cortina, especially to the west, is full of great little villages."

—Wayne

WELCOME TO THE DOLOMITES

Merano

TOP 5
Reasons to Go

1. **Cortina d'Ampezzo:** The former hangout of the ultra hip has aged gracefully into the Grand Dame of Italian ski resorts.

2. **Museo Archeologico dell'Alto Adige, Bolzano:** The impossibly well-preserved body of the iceman Ötzi, the star attraction here, provokes countless questions about the meaning of life 5,000 years ago.

3. **Hiking:** No matter your fitness level, there's a memorable walk in store for you here.

4. **Trento:** A graceful fusion of Austrian and Italian styles, this breezy, frescoed town is famed for its imposing castle.

5. **Grande Strada delle Dolomiti (Great Dolomites Road):** Your rental Fiat will think it's a Ferrari as it wends its way along this gorgeous drive through the Heart of the Dolomites.

At the spa town of Merano you can soak in hot springs, take the "grape cure," and stroll along lovely walkways.

AUSTRIA

SWITZ.

40

Glorenza
Spondigna

Merano

38

Parco Nazionale dello Stelvio

Bormio

PIEMONTE

42

Madonna di Campiglio

Mezzolombardo

TRENTINO

Trento

237

Roveret?

12

Trentino

Butterfly-shaped Trentino province is Italy with a German accent. Its principal city, history-rich **Trento**, is situated at the center. To the northwest are **Madonna di Campiglio**, Italy's most fashionable ski resort, and **Bormio,** another notable skiing destination that doubles as a gateway to the **Parco Nazionale dello Stelvio**.

Getting Oriented

Shadowed by the Dolomite mountains—whose other-worldly pinnacles Leonardo depicted in the background of his *Mona Lisa*—the northeast Italian provinces of Trentino and Alto Adige are centered around the valleys of the Adige and Isarco rivers, which course from the Brenner Pass south to Bolzano.

Alto Adige

The **Alto Adige** region was a part of Austria until the end of World War I, and Austrian sensibilities still predominate over Italian.

AUSTRIA

Brenner Pass

12

49

Brunico

Bressanone

49

Dobbiaco

ALTO ADIGE

38 Bolzano

VAL GARDENA

Sella Mt. Range

48

Cortina d'Ampezzo

Grande Strada delle Dolomiti

Col Rodella

Canazei

12

VAL DI FASSA

Predazzo

48

Strigno

Lago di Caldonazzo

47

The spectacular Sella mountain range and the surrounding Val di Fassa and Val Gardena make up the area known as the **Heart of the Dolomites.** It's distinguished by great views and great mountain sports, both summer and winter. At the town of **Canazei,** the cable car 3,000 feet up to the Col Rodella lookout packages the vast panorama perfectly.

Bolzano, Alto Adige's capital, is the Dolomites' most lively city. Look for high-gabled houses, wrought-iron signs, and centuries-old wine cellars.

0   20 mi
0   20 km

Bolzano   Canazei

THE DOLOMITES PLANNER

Making the Most of Your Time

For a general pleasure tour (as opposed to a skiing- or hiking-intensive vacation), your best choice for a base is vibrant Bolzano, where you'll get a sense of the region's contrasts—Italian and German, medieval and ultramodern. The Archaeological Museum shouldn't be missed. After a day or two in town, venture out to history-laden Trento or the lovely spa town of Merano; both are viable day trips from Bolzano and good places to spend the night as well.

If you have more time in the region, you're going to want to get higher into the mountains. The trip on the Grande Strada delle Dolomiti (Great Dolomites Road) through the Heart of the Dolomites to Cortina d'Ampezzo is one of Italy's most spectacular mountain drives. You can either spend a full day on the road and return to Bolzano, splurge on a night in Cortina, or bed down in one of the homier towns along the way.

Getting Around

Driving is easily the most convenient way to travel in the Dolomites. It's also the most exhilarating, as you rise from broad valleys into mountains with narrow, winding roads straight out of a sports car ad. In summer there are several sight-seeing bus tours through the mountains. There's also regular bus service to most towns, but if you're aiming for anywhere beyond the major destinations, you'll need great patience or great luck catching the infrequent runs. Bressanone, Bolzano, Trento, Rovereto, and Morano are accessible by train. For more about car, bus, and train travel, see "Essentials" at the end of this chapter.

Speaking the Language

Alto Adige is the only region in Italy with two official languages: Italian and German. In Bolzano, Merano, and environs, street signs, menus, city names, and street chatter are completely bilingual. Trentino, Madonna di Campiglio, and Cortina d'Ampezzo are Italian-speaking, but there's a distinctive regional accent—notice the "r," which is guttural rather than rolled.

Hitting the Slopes

The Dolomites have some of the most spectacular downhill skiing in Europe, with the facilities to match. The most comprehensive centers are the upscale resorts of Cortina d'Ampezzo and Madonna di Campiglio, which draw an international clientele with impressive terrain, expansive lift systems, and lively après-ski. For traditional Tirolean *Gemütlichkeit* (congeniality), try one of the more rustic resorts: in the Val di Fassa or Val Gardena your liftmate is more likely to be a schoolteacher from a neighboring town than a businessman from Milan (or Tokyo). Both major resorts and out-of-the-way villages have well-marked trails for *sci di fondo* (cross-country skiing). With the exception of the main bargain period known as *settimane bianche* (white weeks) in January and February, the slopes are seldom overcrowded.

3

Hitting the Trails

Walking and hiking options are appealing, varied, and abundant. Whether on an hour's stroll in the foothills of Merano or a weeklong trek high above Ortisei and Canazei, you'll experience a pleasant climate and captivating vistas that have been attracting visitors to the Dolomites for centuries. The region is also a major draw for hardcore climbers—it's not surprising that Reinhold Messner, the first person to reach the summit of Everest without oxygen, is a lifelong resident.

Local tourist offices are the places to find maps and descriptions of hiking trails, as well as expert advice.

■ **The Club Alpino Italiano** (CAI), the world's oldest organization of its kind, is an excellent resource for more ambitious adventures. www.cai.

it. Bolzano: Piazza delle Erbe 46, 0471/ 981391; Merano: Corso della Libertà 188, 0473/448944; Trento: Via Manci 57, 0461/ 981871.

■ **The Scuole di Alpinismo** (Mountaineering Schools) in Madonna di Campiglio and

Cortina d'Ampezzo offer guided mountain trips for fit hikers of any experience level. Madonna di Campiglio: www. guidealpinecampiglio. it, 0465/442634. Cortina d'Ampezzo: www.guidecortina. com, 0436/868505.

Finding a Place to Stay

Classic Dolomite lodging options range from restored castles to chalets to stately 19th-century hotels. Small villages often have scores of places to stay, many of them inexpensive. Hotel information offices at train stations and tourist offices can help if you've arrived without reservations. The Bolzano train station has a 24-hour hotel service, and tourist offices will give you a list of all the hotels in the area, arranged by location and price.

Hotels at ski resorts cater primarily to longer stays at full or half board: you should book ski vacations as packages in advance. Nearly all rural accommodations close from early November to mid- or late December, as well as for a month or two after Easter.

Dining & Lodging Price Categories

WHAT IT COSTS in Euros					
	$$$$	**$$$**	**$$**	**$**	**¢**
Restaurants	over €22	€16–€22	€11–€16	€7–€11	under €7
Hotels	over €220	€160–€220	€110–€160	€70–€110	under €70

Restaurant prices are for a second course (un secondo). Hotel prices are for two people in a standard double room in high season, including tax and service.

How's the Weather?

The Dolomites are a two-season destination: winter and summer. Most ski resorts are open from mid-December through April, but snowfall in early winter is unreliable, and the best conditions often aren't seen until late February. Hiking trails can remain icy well into June, and mountain temperatures drop sharply in September. Spring and autumn are quiet—many of the mountain tourist facilities close down entirely. It can still be a pleasant time to visit; in the fall, cozy taverns serve up the new wine and roasted chestnuts.

TOP PASSEGGIATA

A stroll on Merano's Passeggiata Tappeiner is as relaxing as any of the town's spa treatments.

THE VAST, MOUNTAINOUS DOMAIN of northeastern Italy, unlike other famous Alpine regions, has remained relatively undeveloped. Strange, rocky pinnacles jutting straight up like chimneys (reminiscent more of Utah's Monument Valley than a European range) loom over scattered, pristine mountain lakes. Below, rivers meander through valleys dotted with peaceful villages and protected by picture-book castles. In the most secluded Dolomite vales, unique cultures have flourished: the Ladin language, an offshoot of Latin still spoken in the Val Gardena, owes its unlikely survival to centuries of isolation.

The more accessible parts of Trentino–Alto Adige, on the other hand, have a history of near-constant intermingling of cultures. The region's the Adige and Isarco valleys make up the main access route between Italy and central Europe, and as a result the language, cuisine, and architecture are a blend of north and south. Whereas the province of Trentino is largely Italian-speaking, Alto Adige is predominantly Germanic: until World War I, the area was Austria's South Tirol. As you move north toward the famed Brenner Pass—through the prosperous valley towns of Rovereto, Trento, and Bolzano—the Teutonic influence is increasingly dominant; by the time you reach Bressanone, it's hard to believe you're in Italy at all.

TRENTINO

Until the end World War I, Trentino was Italy's frontier with the Austro-Hungarian Empire, and the subtle Austro-German influence can still be felt in most aspects of life here—architecture, cuisine, culture, language. Numerous year-round mountain resorts, including fashionable Madonna di Campiglio, are nestled in the wings of this butterfly-shape province.The region also has sights to attract those with religious and war history interests: Trento was the headquarters of the Catholic Counter-Reformation; Rovereto the site of an emblematically bloody battle during World War I.

Trento

❶ *51 km (32 mi) south of Bolzano, 24 km (15 mi) north of Rovereto.*

Trento is a prosperous, cosmopolitan university town that retains an architectural charm befitting its historical importance. It was here, from 1545 to 1563, that the structure of the Catholic Church was redefined at the Council of Trent. This was the starting point of the Counter-Reformation, which brought half of Europe back to Catholicism. Look for the word *consiglio* (council), it appears everywhere in Trento—in hotel, restaurant, and street names, and even on wine labels.

Today the Piazza del Duomo remains splendid, and its enormous medieval palazzo dominates the city landscape in virtually its original form. The 24-hour Trento Card (€9) grants admission to all major town sights and can be purchased at the tourist office or any museum. A 48-hour option (€14) is also available, and includes entrance to the modern art museum in Rovereto. Both cards provide a number of other perks, including a free cable car ride to Belvedere di Sardagna.

Guided tours of Trento depart Saturday from the **tourist office.** You can meet at 10 AM for a visit to the Castello del Buonconsiglio (€6, including admission to the castle), or at 3 PM for a tour of the city center (€3). Reservations are not required. ✉ *Via Manci 2* ☎ *0461/983880* ⊕ *www. apt.trento.it.*

The massive Romanesque **Duomo,** also known as the Cathedral of San Virgilio, forms the southern edge of the Piazza del Duomo. Locals refer to this square as the city's *salotto* (sitting room), as in fine weather it's always filled with students and residents drinking coffee, enjoying an aperitif, or reading the newspaper. A baroque **Fontana del Nettuno** presides over it all. When skies are clear, pause here to savor the view of the mountaintops enveloping the city.

Within the Duomo, unusual arcaded stone stairways border the austere nave. Ahead is the *baldacchino* (altar canopy), a clear copy of Bernini's masterpiece in St. Peter's in Rome. In the small **Cappella del Crocifisso** (Chapel of the Crucifix) to the right is a mournful 15th-century crucifixion, with the Virgin Mary and John the Apostle. This crucifix, by German artist Sixtus Frei, was a focal point of the Council of Trent: each decree agreed on during the two decades of deliberations was solemnly read out in front of it. Outside, walk around to the back of the cathedral to see an exquisite display of 14th-century stonemason's art, from the small porch to the intriguing knotted columns on the graceful apse. ✉ *Piazza del Duomo* ☎ *0461/980132* ⊙ *Daily 7:30–noon and 2:30–7:30.*

★ The crenellated **Palazzo Pretorio,** situated so as to seem like a wing of the Duomo, was built in the 13th century as the fortified residence of the prince-bishops, who enjoyed considerable power and autonomy within the medieval hierarchy. The remarkable palazzo has lost none of its original splendor. The crenellations are not merely decorative: the square pattern represents ancient allegiance to the Guelphs (the triangular crenellations seen elsewhere in town represent Ghibelline loyalty). The Palazzo now houses the **Museo Diocesano Tridentino,** where you can see paintings showing the seating plan of the prelates during the Council of Trent; early-16th-century tapestries by Pieter van Aelst, the Belgian artist who carried out Raphael's 15th-century designs for the Vatican tapestries; carved wood altars and statues; and an 11th-century sacramentary, or book of services. These and other precious objects all come from the cathedral's treasury. Accessible through the museum, a subterranean **archaeological area** reveals ancient ruins of a 6th-century Christian basilica and a gate dating from the 9th century. ✉ *Piazza del Duomo 18* ☎ *0461/234419* ✉ *€3, includes archaeological area* ⊙ *Wed.–Mon. 9:30–12:30 and 2–5:30.*

need a break? **Scrigno del Duomo** (✉ Piazza del Duomo 30 ☎ 0461/220030) serves more than 30 wines by the glass, with an excellent selection of local cheeses to match, in a building with some of the oldest frescoes in town. Salads and regional specialties are also available; the *canederli* (seasoned bread balls in broth) are especially flavorful here. If you walk downstairs to the wine shop, you can see excavated

Roman-era walls—this was the level of the ancient square that became Piazza del Duomo.

Many sessions of the Council of Trent met at the Renaissance church **Santa Maria Maggiore.** Limited light enters through the simple rose window over the main door, so you have to strain to see the magnificent ceiling, an intricate combination of stucco and frescoes. The church is off the northwest side of the Piazza del Duomo, about 200 yards down Via Cavour. ⊠ *Via Cavour* ☉ *Daily 8:30–noon and 2:30–8.*

Locals refer to **Via Belenzani** as Trento's outdoor gallery because of the frescoed facades of the hallmark Renaissance palazzi. It's an easy 50-yard walk up the lane behind the church of Santa Maria Maggiore.

The **Torre Vanga** is a 13th-century tower near the Adige River and one of the bridges that crosses it, the Ponte San Lorenzo. You can take a cable car up to the **Belvedere di Sardagna,** a lookout point 1,200 feet above medieval Trento. The trip is free if you have a Trento card. *Cable car* ⊠ *Ponte San Lorenzo* ☎ *0461/983627* 🎫 *€2 round-trip* ☉ *Daily 7–5.*

★ The **Castello del Buonconsiglio** (Castle of Good Counsel) was once the stronghold of the prince-bishops; its position and size made it easier to defend than the Palazzo Pretorio. Look for the evolution of architectural styles: the medieval fortifications of the Castelvecchio section (on the far left) were built in the 13th century; the more decorative, Renaissance Magno Palazzo section (on the far right) wasn't completed until 300 years later. Part of the Castello now houses the **Museo Provinciale d'Arte,** where permanent and visiting exhibits of art and archaeology hang in frescoed medieval halls or under Renaissance coffered ceilings. The 13th-century **Torre dell'Aquila** (Eagle's Tower) is home to the highlight of the art works, a 15th-century *ciclo dei mesi* (cycle of the months). The four-wall fresco is full of charming and detailed scenes of medieval life in both court and countryside. To get to the tower, follow signs to the small office, and wait—you need a guide to accompany you up. ⊠ *Via Bernardo Clesio 5* ☎ *0461/233770* ⊕ *www.buonconsiglio.it* 🗎 *Museo €5, Torre dell'Aquila €1 extra* ⊗ *Apr.–Sept., Tues.–Sun. 10–6; Oct.–Mar., Tues.–Sun. 9–noon and 2–5.*

The **Museo Storico in Trento** (Trento Historical Museum), housed in the former joiner's shop inside the castle walls, has been undergoing restoration and is scheduled to reopen by late 2005. The focus is modern Trentino history, with dioramas and displays about the region from the unification of Italy in 1861 through World War II. ⊠ *Via Bernardo Clesio 3* ☎ *0461/230482* ⊕ *www.museostorico.tn.it.*

The **Torre Verde** (Green Tower) is part of Trento's 13th-century fortifications, standing alongside other fragments of the city walls. ⊠ *Piazza Raffaello Sanzio, near the castle.*

The **Museo d'Arte Moderna e Contemporanea di Trento** is installed in the Palazzo delle Albere, a Renaissance villa on the Adige River. Works in the permanent collection date from the 19th and 20th centuries, but the real focus here is the rotating exhibitions of contemporary artists. ⊠ *Palazzo delle Albere, Via Roberto da Sanseverino 45* ☎ *0461/234860* ⊕ *www.mart.tn.it* 🗎 *€5* ⊗ *Tues.–Sun. 10–6.*

About 20 km (12 mi) southeast of Trento in the Val Sugana, **Levico Terme** is a medieval spa town with thermal waters. This valley enclave was inhabited by the Celts and then conquered by the Romans; the Latin-derived Ladin dialect is still spoken today. Two weeks advance booking is recommended for the spa services at at **Palazzo delle Terme** ⊠ *Viale Vittorio Emanuele, 38056 Levico Terme* ☎ *0461/706481* 🖷 *0461/707722* ⊗ *May–Oct., Mon.–Sat. 7–12:30.*

Where to Stay & Eat

★ **$$$** ✕ **Le Due Spade.** This Tirolean tavern has been around the corner from the Duomo since the Council of Trent. Able servers bring superb local dishes to you amid the coziness created by the wood paneling and an antique stove. You can sample traditional *gnocchetti di ricotta* (miniature ricotta cheese dumplings) and such savory second courses as *tagliata di Angus alla griglia* (grilled slivers of beef) served with an aromatic herb sauce. Given the restaurant's deserved popularity with locals and the limited seating, reservations are a must. ⊠ *Via Rizzi 11* ☎ *0461/234343* 🖉 *Reservations essential* ⊟ *AE, DC, MC, V* ⊗ *Closed Sun. No lunch Mon.*

$$ ✕ **Chiesa.** Near the castle, a 15th-century building conceals a bright, modern restaurant that attracts romancing couples and power lunchers alike. Ubiquitous apple imagery and excellent risotto *alle mele* (with apples) celebrate the local produce—there's even a set meal featuring apples in every course. Otherwise, the food is traditional: specialties are *maccheroncini con salsiccia e verze* (short, narrow pasta tubes with sausage and cabbage) and *tonco de Pontesel* (a stew of mixed meat made according to a 15th-century recipe). ⌧ *Via San Marco 64* ☎ *0461/238766* 🗖 *AE, DC, MC, V* ⊗ *Closed Sun.*

¢–$ ✕ **Pizzeria Laste.** Owner Guido Rizzi is a deserving national pizza-making champion; he invented pizza Calabrese, a white pizza with garlic, mozzarella, and hot red-pepper flakes. Each of his 35 pies—including the *sedano* (mozzarella, celery root, aged Parmesan cheese, oregano)—is delectable. Save room for desserts like the pizza *dolce* (sweet), which is made with bananas, strawberries, kiwi, and caramel. In a pleasant hill-top villa above the city center, the pizzeria is a bit hard to reach, but worth it. ⌧ *Via alle Laste 39* ☎ *0461/231570* 🗖 *MC, V* ⊗ *Closed Tues.*

$–$$ ✕🏨 **Castel Pergine.** A 13th-century castle, appropriated by Trento's prince-bishops in the 16th century, is now skillfully managed by Theo Schneider, an Austrian architect, and his charming Swiss wife, Verena Neff (a former translator). Amid the labyrinth of stone and brick chambers, prisons, and chapels are sparse, rustic rooms with carved-wood trim, lace curtains, and heavy wooden beds, some canopied. The grounds host a different modern-art installation each year. The popular candlelit restaurant serves ages-old seasonal recipes from Trento in lighter guises: risotto with lemon and rosemary, for example. ⌧ *Via al Castello 10, 38057 Pergine Val Sugana, 12 km (7½ mi) east of Trento* ☎ *0461/531158* 🖷 *0461/531329* ⊕ *www.castelpergine.it* ⬎ *21 rooms, 14 with bath* ♨ *Restaurant, horseback riding, bar, library; no a/c, no room TVs* 🗖 *AE, DC, MC, V* ⊗ *Closed Nov.–Mar. No lunch Mon.* �î◎l *MAP.*

$$$–$$$$ 🏨 **Imperial Grand Hotel Terme.** For spa treatments and luxe comforts, choose the graciously restored, golden yellow palace in the nearby spa town of Levico Terme. It's not hard to imagine yourself as Austrian nobility (for whom this was once home) as you idle in the beautiful swiming pool amidst a restful garden, or dine at one of the elegant restaurants. Your room may even have a frescoed ceiling. In summer a poolside bar and grill is open. ⌧ *Via Silva Domini 1, 38056 Levico Terme, 20 km (12 mi) east of Trento* ☎ *0461/706104* 🖷 *0461/706350* ⊕ *www.imperialhotel.it* ⬎ *69 rooms, 12 suites* ♨ *4 restaurants, in-room safes, minibars, cable TV, 2 pools (1 indoor), gym, spa, billiards, 2 bars, babysitting, meeting rooms, some pets allowed (fee)* 🗖 *AE, DC, MC, V* ⊗ *Closed Nov.–mid-Mar.* �î◎l *BP.*

$$$ 🏨 **Boscolo Grand Hotel Trento.** Its contemporary rounded facade amid ancient palaces makes this hotel on Piazza Dante an anomaly. Inside the lush, modern appointments include marble and woodwork in the lobby and lounges to the Clesio restaurant's rich drapery. Rooms are ample, with thick carpets and clubby, wood-trim furniture. ⌧ *Via Alfieri 1, 38100* ☎ *0461/271000* 🖷 *0461/271001* ⊕ *www.grandtrento.boscolohotels.com* ⬎ *126 rooms, 10 suites* ♨ *Restaurant, in-room safes, minibars, cable TV, massage sauna, bar, laundry service, Internet, business services, meeting rooms* 🗖 *AE, DC, MC, V* �î◎l *EP.*

Eating Well in the Dolomites

Everything in Alto Adige (and, to a lesser extent, Trentino as well) has more than a tinge of the Teutonic—and the food is no exception. Germanic influence can be seen in the profusion of pastry shops, lively beer halls, and wood-panel Tirolean Stuben (pubs) serving hearty meat-and-dumpling fare. Although the early dining schedule you'll find in Germany or Austria is somewhat tempered here, your options for late-night meals are more limited than in southern Italy, where la dolce vita has a firmer grip. Thankfully, the coffee is every bit as good as in parts south.

Local dishes vary from one isolated mountain valley to the next; one universal is the thinly sliced *Speck tirolese* (smoked ham). Other specialties include *canederli* (also known as *Knoedel*), seasoned bread balls with many variations, served either in broth or with a sauce; *Würste* (sausages) and sauerkraut; ravioli made from rye flour, stuffed with spinach, and fried; and

apple or pear strudel. *Alimentari* (food shops) stock a bounty of regional cheeses, pickles, salami, and smoked meats—perfect for picnics—and bakeries turn out a wide selection of crusty dark rolls and caraway-studded rye breads. The best of the cheeses are the mild Asiago and *fontal* and the more pungent *puzzone di Moena* (literally, "stinkpot").

Not to be missed are the outdoor Wurst carts, even (or perhaps especially) in colder weather. After placing your order at these movable sausage stands you'll get a sheet of wax paper, followed by a dollop of mustard, a hard Kaiser roll, and your chosen Wurst. You can sometimes make your selection by pointing to whatever picture seems most appealing; if not, pass on the familiar-sounding *Frankfurter* and try the local *Meraner*. The carts can reliably be found in Bolzano (try Piazza delle Erbe, or in front of the archaeological museum) and Merano (Piazza del Grano, or along the river).

★ $$ ⌷ **Accademia.** This friendly hotel occupies an ancient, character-filled house in the historic center of Trento, close to Piazza del Duomo. Enter through a beautiful arched passage; the public rooms also retain the original vaulting. Bedrooms have comfortable beds and handsome lithographs of the town. In warm weather, you can enjoy a meal or a drink in the courtyard garden. ✉ *Vicolo Colico 4/6, 38100* ☎ *0461/233600* ⎙ *0461/230174* ⊕ *www. accademiahotel.it* ↪ *41 rooms, 2 suites* ⚒ *Restaurant, minibars, bar, meeting rooms* ⊟ *AE, DC, MC, V* ⊙ *Closed Dec. 24–Jan. 6* ⏐⌷⏐ *BP.*

$ ⌷ **Aquila d'Oro.** A prime location, steps from Piazza del Duomo, is a main selling point for the Aquila d'Oro. The friendly owner gives good suggestions about what to see, do, and eat while in town. Most rooms have nondescript contemporary veneer furniture. ✉ *Via Belenzani 76, 38100* ☎ *0461/986282* ⎙ *0461/986292* ⊕ *www.aquiladoro.it* ↪ *19 rooms* ⚒ *Cable TV, in-room data ports, minibars, bar* ⊟ *AE, DC, MC, V* ⊙ *Closed late Dec.–mid.-Feb.* ⏐⌷⏐ *BP.*

$ ⌷ **Buonconsiglio.** Near the train station, this efficient hotel has well-kept, sizable—and sound-resistant—rooms. Both singles and doubles are available. The prompt service also helps make Buonconsiglio ideal for the business traveler. Modern art decorates the public spaces. ⊠ *Via Romagnosi 18, 38100* ☎ *0461/272888* 🖷 *0461/272889* ⊕ *www. hotelbuonconsiglio.it* ⤶ *46 rooms, 1 suite* ⚿ *In-room safes, minibars, cable TV, bar, meeting rooms, parking (fee)* ⊟ *AE, DC, MC, V* ⊗ *Closed 2 wks mid-Aug.* ⦿ *BP.*

Nightlife & the Arts

The Sounds of the Dolomites, **I Suoni delle Dolomiti,** festival is held in July and August every year. This series of free concerts is held at refuges high in the hills of Trentino: experience of chamber music played in grassy meadows, echoing through the mountain air. Wine buffs can take part in the **Vinum Bonum** (☎ 0461/822820) with music and wine tastings for €8 at different cellars in Trentino July and August, each Tuesday, Thursday, and Friday from 4:30 to 7.

Townspeople don medieval clothing in honor of their patron saint **Festive Vigiliane,** a spectacular weeklong pageant in the Piazza del Duomo, culminating on June 26.

In late April or early May, Trento hosts the world's hosts a celebration of movies about mountains, the **Città di Trento Film Festival** (☎0461/986120 ⊕ www.mountainfilmfestival.trento.it).

Since 1936 the late-May wine festival, **Mostra dei Vini** (☎ 0461/497371), has attracted would-be Bacchuses of every stripe; farmers from surrounding hillside towns bend elbows with sommeliers from all over Italy. The weeklong festival includes tastings, tours, and prizes.

The **Festivale di Musica Sacra** (Sacred Music Festival ☎ 0462/983880) is a monthlong series of concerts in May and June held in Trentino's churches.

Shopping

A number of pleasant souvenir shops and glassware outlets line **Via Manci,** near the church of Santa Maria Maggiore. The small, morning **Mercato di Piazza Lodron** is held in Piazza Alessandro Vittoria. You can pick up meats, cheeses, produce, local truffles, and porcini mushrooms here. The **Enoteca di Corso** (⊠ Corso 3 Novembre 54 ☎ 0461/916424) is an extraordinary shop laden with local products, including cheese, salami, and wine.

Galleria Trentino Art (⊠ Via Belenzani 43/45 ☎ 0461/263721) sells the widest selection of traditional Trentino handicrafts. **Il Laboratorio** (⊠ Via Roma 12 ☎ No phone) specializes in terra-cotta pieces molded by local artists. You can buy excellent handcrafted wooden objects at **Il Pozzo** (⊠ Piazza Pasi 14 ☎ No phone).

Rovereto

❷ *24 km (15 mi) south of Trento, 75 km (47 mi) south of Bolzano.*

Some of the fiercest fighting of World War I took place in the wooded hills around the medieval town of Rovereto, with Italian and Austrian troops bogged down in prolonged and costly conflict. Every evening at nightfall you're reminded of the thousands who died by the ringing of the *Campana dei Caduti* (Bell of the Fallen). Today, Rovereto is Trentino's peaceful second city. Its 15th-century castle looks down on winding streets, long-shadowed piazzas, and crumbling pastel-color villas.

The **Museo Storico Italiano della Guerra** (Italian Historical War Museum) was founded after World War I to commemorate the conflict—and to warn against repeating its atrocities. An authoritative exhibition of military artifacts is displayed in the medieval castle perched above Rovereto; the views alone warrant a visit. May–November you can also see a collection of artillery from the Great War housed in a former air-raid shelter. ⊠ *Via Castelbarco 7* ☎ *0464/438100* ⊕ *www.museodellaguerra.it* 🖅 *€5.50* ☉ *July–Sept., Tues.–Sun. 10–6, weekends 9:30–6:30; Oct.–June, Tues.–Sun. 10–6.*

need a break? Weathered wine barrels serve as tables at **Bacchus** (⊠ Via Garibaldi 29 ☎ No phone), which has an excellent selection of local wines by the glass. Better yet, find a spot at the bar and ask for a bitter *negroni sbagliato* to be ladled out of the largest wine glass you've ever laid eyes upon (in addition to the usual Campari, gin, and vermouth, this "mistaken" negroni also employs vodka, oranges, and a few undisclosed ingredients).

The paintings of native son Fortunato Depero (1892–1960), a prominent futurist, can be found throughout town. There's a good selection of his work at the **Museo D'Arte Moderna e Contemporanea.** ⊠ *Corso Bettini 43* ☎ *0464/438887* ⊕ *www.mart.tn.it* 🖅 *€8* ☉ *Tues.–Thurs., weekends 10–6, Fri. 10–9.*

Where to Stay & Eat

$$$–$$$$ ✕ **Ristorante Al Borgo.** Renowned throughout Italy for its creative cuisine, Al Borgo has a modernist take on classics. Trentino specialties on the seasonal menu may include *strangola preti* (literally "priest-chokers," dumplings with a texture so heavy that they were considered unsuitable for the delicate throats of the clergy). You could try the simple *tagliolini ai frutti di mare* (long ribbons of pasta with shellfish), or in fall, you might choose *polentina* (soft, creamy polenta) with a fondue of Trentino cheeses and truffle. The restaurant's interior is elegant and calm, with attractive art adorning the walls. ⊠ *Via Garibaldi 13* ☎ *0464/ 436300* ⌕ *Reservations essential* ▭ *AE, DC, MC, V* ☉ *Closed Mon., 1 wk in late Jan., 3 wks in July, and Sun. in Aug. No dinner Sun.*

$$ ✕▤ **Hotel Rovereto.** Brothers Marco and Fausto Zani preside over welcoming public spaces and warm-color guest rooms at the modern, central Hotel Rovereto. Their mother, Wanda Zani, oversees the kitchen at the candlelit Ristorante Novecento ($$), one of the city's most appealing restaurants. Luscious dishes, paired with local wines, include *tortelli con fonduta di formaggi* (pasta squares stuffed with spinach and ricotta in a butter sauce) and *quaglia con finferli e polenta* (quail with wild mushrooms and polenta). ⊠ *Corso Rosmini 82/d, 38068* ☎ *0464/ 435222* 🖷 *0464/439644* ⊕ *www.hotelrovereto.it* ➪ *49 rooms* ↺ *Restaurant, in-room safes, minibars, cable TV, meeting rooms, parking (fee)* ▭ *AE, DC, MC, V* ☉ *Restaurant closed Sun. and Aug.* ⦿ *BP.*

Nightlife & the Arts

The **Rovereto Oriente Occidente Festival** (☎ 0464/431660 ⊕ www. orienteoccidente.it) in early September hosts exhibitions of contemporary dance, theater, and cuisine. Late September brings the **Festival Internazionale W. A. Mozart** (☎ 0464/439988), with classical performances. The exquisite 18th-century **Teatro Zandonai** (✉ Corso Bettini 82 ☎ 0464/452159) hosts many of the concerts in conjunction with the Mozart Festival.

en route   Traveling south from Rovereto to Madonna di Campiglio (about a two-hour drive), you zigzag through lovely mountain valleys and towns like Riva del Garda, and past small farming communities as in Tione. Outside the small mountain village of Pinzolo (on S239), stop at the church of **San Virgilio** to see the remarkable 16th-century fresco on the exterior south wall. Painted in 1539 by the artist Simone Baschenis, the painting describes the Dance of Death: a macabre parade of 40 sinners from all walks of life (in roughly descending order of worldly importance), each guided to his end by a ghoulish escort. Unfortunately, the church's interior is closed to the public.

Madonna di Campiglio

❸ *89 km (56 mi) northwest of Rovereto, 88 km (55 mi) southwest of Bolzano.*

The chichi winter resort of Madonna di Campiglio has surpassed Cortina d'Ampezzo as the most fashionable place for young Italians to ski and be seen in the Dolomites. Madonna's popularity is well deserved, with more than 130 km (80 mi) of well-groomed ski runs served by 39 lifts. The resort itself is a modest 5,000 feet above sea level, but the downhill runs, summer hiking paths, and mountain-biking trails venture high up into the surrounding peaks (including Pietra Grande at 9,700 feet). Madonna's cachet is evident in its increasingly well-organized lodging, skiing, and trekking facilities.

Ride the cable car up **Punta Spinale** (Spinale Peak, 6,900 feet) for magnificent views of the Brenta Dolomites. *Cable car ✉ Off Via Monte Spinale* ☎ *0465/447744* 🎫 *€8 round-trip* ☉ *Daily 8:30–5:30.*

The Madonna di Campiglio **tourist office** can supply maps of a dozen trails leading to waterfalls, lakes, and stupefying views. ✉ *Via Pradalago 4* ☎ *0465/447501* ⊕ *www.campiglio.to.*

The stunning pass at **Campo Carlo Magno** (5,500 feet) is 3 km (2 mi) north of Madonna di Campiglio. This is where Charlemagne is said to have stopped in AD 800 on his way to Rome to be crowned emperor. Stop here to glance over the whole of northern Italy. If you continue north, take the descent with caution—in the space of a mile or so, hairpin turns and switchbacks deliver you down more than 2,000 feet.

Where to Stay

$$$$ 🏨 **Golf Hotel.** You need to make your way north to the Campo Carlo Magno pass to reach this grand hotel, the former summer residence of Habsburg emperor Franz Josef. A modern wing has been added, but old-world charm

CLOSE UP

Enrosadira & the Dwarf King

THE DOLOMITES, the inimitable craggy peaks Le Corbusier called "the most beautiful work of architecture ever seen," are never so arresting as at dusk, when the last rays of sun create a pink hue that languishes into purple. In the Ladin language, spoken only in the isolated valleys below, this magnificent transformation has its own word—the *enrosadira*. You can certainly enjoy this phenomenon from a distance, but one of the things that makes the Dolomites such an appealing year-round destination is the multitude of options for getting onto the mountains themselves. Whether you come for a pleasant stroll or a technical ascent in summer, to plunge down sheer faces or glide across peaceful valleys in winter, or to brave narrow switchbacks in a rented Fiat, your perspective, like the peaks around you, can only become more rose-colored.

The enrosadira is so striking that it's prompted speculation about its origins. The French nobleman and geologist De'odat Guy Silvain Tancrède Gratet de Dolomieu (1750–1801) took the scientific

approach: he got his name applied to the range after demonstrating that the peaks have a particular composition of stratified calcium magnesium carbonate which generates the evening glow. For those unconvinced that such the phenomenon can be explained by geology alone, Ladin legend offers a compelling alternative.

Laurin, King of the Dwarfs, became infatuated with the daughter of a neighboring (human) king, and captured her with the aid of a magic hood that made him invisible. As he spirited her back to the mountains, the dwarf king was pursued by many knights, who were able to track the kidnapper after spotting his beloved rose garden. Laurin was captured and imprisoned, and when he finally managed to escape and return home, he cast a spell turning the betraying roses into rocks—so they could be seen neither by day nor by night. But Laurin forgot to include dusk in his spell, which is why the Dolomites take on a rosy glow just before nightfall. (This story is the subject of frescoes in the bar of Bolzano's Park Hotel Laurin.)

persists: rooms 114 and 214 retain the lavish imperial style, and the rest of the resort is replete with verandas, Persian rugs, and bay windows. In summer the golf course attracts a tony crowd. ⊠ *Via Cima Tosa 3, 38084* ☎ *0465/441003* 🖷 *0465/440294* ⊕ *www.golfhotelcampiglio.it* ⤴ *107 rooms, 8 suites* ⌂ *Restaurant, minibars, cable TV, 9-hole golf course, gym, spa, bar, convention center, free parking* ═ *AE, DC, MC, V* ⊙ *Closed mid-Apr.–May and Sept.–Nov.* ⫟◯⫠ *MAP.*

$$$$ 🏨 **Grifone.** A comfortable Alpine lodge sits catching the sun with a distinctive wood facade and flower-bedecked balconies. Contemporary singles, doubles, and triples have views of the forested slopes. The restaurant serves home cooking as well as international dishes. The hotel is south of the lake, a bit out of town, but the Spinale cable car is nearby. Half or full board is required. ⊠ *Via Vallesinella 7, 38084*

☎ *0465/442002* 🖶 *0465/440540* ⊕ *www.hotelgrifone.it* 🖂 *38 rooms, 2 suites* ⟁ *Restaurant, in-room safes, cable TV, spa, bar, free parking; no a/c* ▭ *AE, DC, MC, V* ⊗ *Closed May and June and Sept.–Nov.* ¶⊙¶ *MAP.*

★ **$$$$** 🖵 **Savoia Palace.** This central hotel is also Madonna's most traditional, full of carved-wood and mountain-style furnishings. Two fireplaces blaze away in the bar, where you can relax as you recall the day's exploits on the ski slopes. The elegant restaurant serves a mixture of local specialties and rich dishes combining Italian and Austrian influences. Full or half board is required. ⊠ *Viale Dolomiti di Brenta 18, 38084* ☎ *0465/441004* 🖶 *0465/440549* ⊕ *www.savoiapalace.com* 🖂 *55 rooms* ⟁ *Restaurant, in-room safes, minibars, cable TV, bar; no a/c* ▭ *AE, DC, MC, V* ⊗ *Closed Apr.–June and mid-Sept.–mid-Dec.* ¶⊙¶ *MAP.*

Sports & the Outdoors

GOLF   The 9-hole **Campo Carlo Magno** (⊠ Via Cima Tosa 15, near Golf Hotel ☎ 0465/440622) course is one of the highest in Europe, at 5,500 feet. It's open July–September.

HIKING &   Climbing and trekking adventures are organized by Madonna's **Scuola**
CLIMBING   **di Alpinismo** (Mountaineering School ⊠ Piazza Brenta Alta 16 ☎ 0465/ 442634 ⊕ www.guidealpinecampiglio.it).

SKIING   Kilometers of interconnecting ski runs—some of the best in the Dolomites—are linked by the cable cars and lifts of **Funivie Madonna di Campiglio** (Main cable car ⊠ Off Via Presanella, across from Piazza Righi ☎ 0465/447744 ⊕ www.campiglio.to). Advanced skiers will delight in the extremely difficult terrain found on certain mountain faces, but there are also many intermediate and beginner runs, all accessible from town. There are also plenty of off-piste opportunities. Ski passes (€34 per day) can be purchased at the main *funivia* (cable car) in town.

| en route | The route between Madonna di Campiglio and Bormio (2½ hours) takes you through a series of high mountain passes. After Campo Carlo Magno, turn left at Dimaro and continue 37 km (23 mi) west through another Passo del Tonale (6,200 feet). At Ponte di Legno, turn north on S300. You pass the *Lago Nero* (Black Lake) on your left just before the summit. Continue on to Bormio through the Passo di Gavia (8,600 feet). |

Bormio

❹ *97 km (60 mi) northwest of Madonna di Campiglio, 100 km (62 mi) southwest of Merano.*

At the foot of Stelvio Pass, Bormio is the most famous ski resort on the western side of the Dolomites, with 38 km (24 mi) of long pistes and a 5,000-plus-foot vertical drop. In summer its cool temperatures and clean air entice Italians away from cities in the humid Lombard plain. This dual-season popularity supports the plentiful shops, restaurants, and hotels in town. Bormio has been known for the therapeutic qualities of its waters since the Roman era, and there are numerous spas.

Bormio makes a good base for exploring the Alps' biggest national park, the **Parco Nazionale dello Stelvio,** spread over 1,350 square km (520 square mi) and four provinces. Opened in 1935 with the express intent to preserve flora and protect fauna, today it thrives, with more than 1,200 types of plants, 600 different mushrooms, and more than 160 species of animals, including the chamois, ibex, and roe deer. There are many entrances to the park, and nine visitor centers that are open at different times of the year. ⊠ *Off SS38 and SS42* ⊕ *www.parks.it/parco. nazionale.stelvio* ⓢ *Free.*

Where to Stay & Eat

$$–$$$ ✕ **Kuerc.** This central restaurant building was for centuries where justice was publicly served to accused witches, among others. These days, things are rather more refined: enjoy local specialties like *brasaola* (salted, air-dried beef) with lemon and olive oil, or *pizzoccheri* (buckwheat pasta) with garlic and winter vegetables. ⊠ *Piazza Cavour 7* ☎ *0342/904738* ⊟ *MC, V* ⊘ *Closed Tues.*

$$$ ▦ **Nazionale.** Bordering the Stelvio National Park, the Nazionale caters to both the winter and summer crowds. Behind the Alpine exterior, rooms are small but have solid wood furniture, minibars, and with balconies on all floors except the top one. The hotel operates a shuttle bus to the cable cars. ⊠ *Via al Forte 28, 23032* ☎ *0342/903361* ⊟ *0342/905294* ⊕ *www. hotelnazionale.info* ⤴ *48 rooms* ⟁ *2 restaurants, in-room safes, minibars, indoor pool, hot tub, sauna, bar, recreation room, shops; no a/c* ⊟ *AE, DC, MC, V* ⊘ *Closed mid-Sept.–Nov., Apr. and May* ⍟ *BP.*

$$$ ▦ **Posta.** Ostelli della Posta hotels, stagecoach inns of days gone by, are a time-honored tradition in northern Italy. The warm reception at this town-center hotel helps to temper the cold, as does the rustic decoration, with its warm wood detail in the low-vault areas. Rooms are cozy and comfortable, with heavy drapery and bed linens. Perks include a small health club with a pool, sauna, gym, and Turkish bath—and a shuttle bus to the slopes. ⊠ *Via Roma 66, 23032* ☎ *0342/904753* ⊟ *0342/ 904484* ⊕ *www.hotelposta.bormio.it* ⤴ *50 rooms* ⟁ *Restaurant, in-room safes, cable TV, indoor pool, health club, sauna, Turkish bath, pub; no a/c* ⊟ *AE, DC, MC, V* ⊘ *Closed May and June and Sept.–Nov.* ⍟ *BP.*

Sports

SKIING You can buy a ski pass (€32 per day) and pick up a trail map at the base **funivia** (cable car ☎ 0342/901451 ⊕ www.skipassaltavaltellina.it) in the center of town to connect to the Bormio 2000 station (6,600 feet) on Vallecetta, the main resort mountain. From there, you can ski down intermediate trails (which comprise the majority of Bormio's runs), use the extensive lift network to explore secondary ski areas, or get another funivia up to the Cima Bianca station (9,800 feet) for more challenging terrain. These cable cars are more for skiing than hiking.

Passo dello Stelvio

★ ❺ *20 km (12 mi) north of Bormio, 80 km (48 mi) west of Merano.*

At more than 9,000 feet, the Passo dello Stelvio is the second-highest pass in Europe, connecting the Valtellina in Lombardy with the Val Venosta in Alto Adige. The view from the top is well worth the drive; looking north you can see Switzerland. The pass is open from May or June to October, depending on weather conditions. Stelvio itself is a year-round skiing center, with many of its runs open in summer.

en route   Between the Stelvio Pass and the town of Spondigna, 30 km (19 mi) of road wind down 48 hair-raising hairpin turns. The views are spectacular, but this descent is not for the faint of heart. In Spondigna keep to the right for the road to Naturno.

BOLZANO (BOZEN)

32 km (19 mi) south of Merano, 50 km (31 mi) north of Trento.

Bolzano (Bozen), the capital of the autonomous province of Alto Adige, is tucked in among craggy peaks in a Dolomite valley just 77 km (48 mi) from the Brenner Pass and Austria. Tirolean culture dominates Bolzano's language, food, architecture, and people. It may be hard to remember that you're in Italy when walking the city's colorful cobblestone streets and visiting its lantern-lighted cafés, where you may enjoy sauerkraut and a beer among a lively crowd of blue-eyed German-speakers. However, fine Italian espresso, fashionable boutiques, and reasonable prices will help remind you where you are. With castles and steeples topping the landscape, this quiet city at the confluence of the Isarco (Eisack) and Talvera rivers has retained a provincial appeal. Proximity to fabulous skiing and mountain climbing—not to mention the world's oldest preserved mummy—make it a worthwhile, if undiscovered, tourist destination. And its streets are immaculate: with the highest per capita earnings of any city in Italy Bolzano's residents enjoy a standard of living that is second to none.

> **WORD OF MOUTH**
>
> "Bolzano is a fairly big town, a college town, lots of stores and places to eat. There are many gondolas to take, the tourist office has a great little book with about 10 walks/hikes. It's such a beautiful city, right in the middle of the mountains."   –Susanna

Exploring Bolzano

The Main Attractions

8 **Chiesa dei Domenicani.** The 13th-century Dominican Church is renowned as Bolzano's main repository for paintings, especially frescoes. In the adjoining **Cappella di San Giovanni** you can see works from the Giotto school, one of which is a *Triumph of Death* (circa 1340). Despite its macabre subject, this fresco shows the birth of a pre-Renaissance sense of depth and individuality. ⊠ *Piazza Domenicani* ☎ *0471/973133* ⊙ *Mon.–Sat. 9:30–5, Sun. noon–5.*

7 **Duomo.** A lacy spire looks down on the mosaiclike roof tiles of the city's Gothic cathedral, built between the 12th and 14th century. Inside are 14th- and 15th-century frescoes and an intricately carved stone pulpit dating from 1514. Outside, don't miss the **Porta del Vino** (Wine Gate) on the northeast side; decorative carvings of grapes and harvest workers attest to the long-standing importance of wine to this region. ⊠ *Piazza Walther* ☎ *0471/978676* ⊘ *Weekdays 10–noon and 2–5, Sat. 10–noon and 2–4, Sun. 1–5.*

⑪ Museo Archeologico dell'Alto Adige. This museum has gained international fame for Ötzi, its 5,300-year-old iceman, discovered in 1991 and the world's oldest naturally preserved body. In 1998 Italy acquired it from Austria after it was determined that the body lay 100 yards inside Italy. The iceman's leathery remains are displayed in a freezer, preserved along with his longbow, ax, and clothing. The rest of the museum relies on models and artifacts from nearby archaeological sites (an eloquent English audio guide is €2) to lead you not only through Ötzi's Copper Age, but also into the preceding Paleolithic and Neolithic eras, and the Bronze and Iron ages that followed. ⊠ *Via Museo 43* ☎ *0471/320100* ⊕ *www.iceman.it* 🎟 *€8* ⊘ *Tues., Wed., and Fri.–Sun. 10–6; Thurs. 10–8; last admission 1 hr before closing.*

⑨ Piazza delle Erbe. A bronze statue of Neptune, which dates back to 1745, presides over a bountiful fruit and vegetable market in this square. The stalls spill over with colorful displays of local produce; bakeries and grocery stores showcase hot breads, pastries, cheeses, and delicatessen meats—a complete picnic. Try the *speck tirolese* (a thinly sliced smoked ham) and the apple strudel.

⑥ Piazza Walther. This pedestrian-only square is Bolzano's heart; in warmer weather it serves as an open-air living room where locals and tourists alike can be found at all hours sipping a drink (such as a glass of chilled Riesling). In the center stands Heinrich Natter's white-marble, neo-Romanesque **Monument to Walther,** built in 1889. The piazza's namesake was the 12th-century German wandering minstrel Walther von der Vogelweide, whose songs lampooned the papacy and praised the Holy Roman Emperor.

Also Worth Seeing

Castel Mareccio (Schloss Maretsch). This castle, tucked below mountains and enveloped by vineyards, dates from the 13th century. It's been pressed into service as a modern conference center. You can only view the frescoes inside by calling ahead and joining a free guided tour on Tuesday (in German or Italian). ⊠ *Lungotalvera, Bolzano, head north along the river* ☎ *0471/976615* ⊠ *Free* ⊘ *Tues. by appointment.*

Castel Roncolo (Schloss Runkelstein). The green hills and farmhouses north of town surround the meticulously kept castle with a red roof. It was built in 1237, destroyed half a century later, and then rebuilt soon thereafter. There's a beautifully preserved cycle of medieval frescoes inside. A **tavern** in the courtyard serves excellent local food and wines from noon to 10. ⊠ *Via San Antonio, from Piazza delle Erbe, head north along Via Francescani and continue through Piazza Madonna, connecting to Via Castel Roncolo* ☎ *0471/329808 castle, 0471/324073 tavern* ⊕ *www.comune.bolzano.it/roncolo/ie* 🎟 *€8* ⊘ *Tues.–Sun. 10–6.*

Bolzano

● **Museo Civico.** Bolzano's municipal museum has a rich collection of traditional costumes, wood carvings, and archaeological exhibits. It's scheduled to reopen, following renovations, by late 2005. ⊠ *Via Cassa di Risparmio 14* ☎ *0471/974625* ⊡ *€5* ⊙ *Tues. 10–6, Wed. 10–8, Thurs.–Sun. 10–6.*

Passeggiata del Guncina. An 8-km (5-mi) botanical promenade dating from 1892 ends with a panoramic view of Bolzano. ⊠ *Entrance near Vecchia Parrocchiale, in Gries, across river and up Corso Libertà.*

Vecchia Parrocchiale (Old Parish Church). Visit this church, said to have been built in 1141, to see its two medieval treasures: an 11th-century Romanesque crucifix and an elaborately carved 15th-century wooden altar by Michael Pacher—a true masterpiece of the Gothic style. ⊠ *Via Martin Knoller, in Gries, across river and up Corso Libertà* ☎ *0471/ 283089* ⊙ *Apr.–Oct., weekdays 10:30–noon and 2:30–4.*

off the beaten path

RENON (RITTEN) PLATEAU – The earth pyramids of Renon Plateau are a bizarre geological formation where erosion has left a forest of tall, thin, needlelike spires of rock, each topped with a boulder. To get here, take the Soprabolzano funicular from Via Renon, about 300 yards left of the Bolzano train station. At the top, switch to the electric train that takes you to the plateau, which is in Collalbo, just above Bolzano. The two rides take about 12 minutes and cost €7 round-trip total. ⊠ *Via Renon, Collalbo* ☎ *0471/978479* 🖃 *€7 round-trip* ⊙ *Daily 7–7.*

Where to Stay & Eat

★ **$$$** ✕ **Zür Kaiserkron.** Traditional Tirolean opulence and attentive service set the stage for some of the best food in town. Appetizers might include potato blini with salmon caviar, and marinated artichokes with butter (not to be missed if available). Main dishes, such as veal with black truffle–and–spinach canederli make use of ingredients from the local valleys. This place is popular with dignified local businesspeople. ⊠ *Piazzetta Mostra* ☎ *0471/970770* 🖃 *AE, DC, MC, V* ⊙ *Closed Sun. No dinner Sat.*

$–$$ ✕ **Alexander.** Typical Tirolean dishes are served at this convivial city-center restaurant. The venison ham and the lamb cutlets *al timo con salsa all'aglio* (with thyme and garlic sauce) are particularly good, but make sure to leave room for the rich chocolate cake. ⊠ *Via Aosta 37* ☎ *0471/918608* 🖃 *MC, V* ⊙ *Closed Sat.*

★ **$–$$** ✕ **Batzenhausl.** Locals hold animated conversations over glasses of local wine in a modern take on the traditional Weinstube (wine tavern, often abbreviated to "stube"). Tasty South Tirolean specialties include speck tirolese and *mezzelune casarecce ripiene* (house-made stuffed half-moons of pasta). If you're seeking a quiet meal, ask for a table on the second floor, near the handsome stained-glass windows of this medieval building. ⊠ *Via Andreas Hofer 30* ☎ *0471/050950* 🖃 *MC, V.*

$ ✕ **Hopfen & Co. (Bozner Bier).** Fried white Würstel, sauerkraut, and grilled ribs complement the excellent home-brewed Austrian-style pilsner and wheat beer at this lively pub-restaurant. On some nights there's live music. ⊠ *Piazza delle Erbe 17* ☎ *0471/300788* 🖃 *MC, V.*

¢–$ ✕ **Cavallino Bianco.** Ask a local for a restaurant recommendation in Bolzano, and you're likely to be pointed toward this dependable favorite near Via dei Portici. A wide selection of Italian and German dishes is served in a spacious, comfortable dining room, where there are usually many extended families enjoying their meals together. ⊠ *Via Bottai 6* ☎ *0471/973267* 🖃 *No credit cards* ⊙ *Closed Sun. No dinner Sat.*

★ **$$$–$$$$** ✕🛏 **Park Hotel Laurin.** An exercise in art nouveau opulence, Park Hotel Laurin is considered the finest lodging in all of Alto Adige, with art-filled modern guest rooms and handsome public spaces (the frescoes in the bar tell the legend of the dwarf King Laurin). The hotel presides over a large park in the middle of town. Its history is speckled with visits from Europe's grand nobility, including Archduke Franz Ferdinand (whose murder in Sarajevo sparked World War I). Restaurant Laurin is superb, bringing an international sensibility to rustic regional dishes. ⊠ *Via Laurin 4, 39100* ☎ *0471/311000* 🖷 *0471/311148* ⊕ *www.laurin.it* ⇖ *88 rooms, 8 suites* ₺ *Restaurant, in-room safes, minibars, cable TV, pool, bar, convention center, parking (fee), no-smoking rooms* 🖃 *AE, DC, MC, V* 🍽 *BP.*

$$$–$$$$
Fodor'sChoice
★ 🛏 **Hotel Greif.** Even in a hospitable region, the Greif is a rare gem. This small central hotel has been a Bolzano landmark for centuries, and a beautiful renovation has set a standard for modernity in Alto Adige. In-

room computers with ISDN Internet and private whirlpool baths are just a few of the perks. Public spaces are airy and immaculate; each guest room was designed by a different local artist—contemporary installations are thoughtfully paired with 19th-century paintings and sketches. The clean-line modern furnishings contrast with views of the Gothic cathedral across the square. ⌧ *Piazza Walther 1, 39100* ☎ *0471/318000* 📠 *0471/318148* ⊕ *www.greif.it* 🛏 *33 rooms* ⟁ *In-room safes, minibars, cable TV, in-room hot tubs, Internet, parking (fee)* 🚭 *AE, DC, MC, V* ⍟*l BP.*

★ $$$–$$$$ 🏨 **Schloss Korb.** A romantic 13th-century castle hotel, with crenellations and a massive tower, perches in a park amid vine-covered hills. Much of the ancient character is preserved, and the public rooms are filled with antiques, elaborate wood carvings, paintings, and attractive plants. The guest rooms have solid, rustic, pine beds with pillowtop mattresses; some in the tower have striking Romanesque arched windows. It's well worth the 5-km (3-mi) drive west from Bolzano to get here. ⌧ *Via Castel d'Appiano 5, 39050 Missiano* ☎ *0471/636000* 📠 *0471/636033* ⊕ *www. schlosskorb.com* 🛏 *57 rooms, 5 suites* ⟁ *Restaurant, 2 tennis courts, 2 pools (1 indoor), sauna, bar, parking (fee); no a/c* 🚭 *No credit cards* ⊙ *Closed Dec.–Mar.* ⍟*l MAP.*

$$ 🏨 **Luna-Mondschein.** This central yet secluded hotel in a tranquil garden dates from 1798. The comfortable rooms have wood paneling throughout; those overlooking the garden have balconies, others have good views of the mountains. First-rate dining is available in both the cozy, convivial Tirolean stube and the art nouveau Ristorante Van Gogh, one of the city's best. ⌧ *Via Piave 15, 39100* ☎ *0471/975642* 📠 *0471/975577* ⊕ *www.hotel-luna.it* 🛏 *85 rooms* ⟁ *Restaurant, Weinstube, meeting rooms, parking (fee); no a/c* 🚭 *AE, DC, MC, V* ⍟*l BP.*

Nightlife & the Arts

Fairs

Spring is heralded each May with large **flower markets** in Piazza Walther as well as other events, including concerts and folklore and art exhibits. On August 24 the **Bartolomeo Horse Fair** takes place on Renon Mountain northeast of the town. Hundreds of farmers converge for a day of serious trading and merriment.

Nightlife

A centuries-old tradition of late-night merriment carries on at **Hopfen & Co.** (⌧ Piazza delle Erbe 17 ☎ 0471/300788), a beer hall and restaurant. If only a properly poured pint of Guinness will do, **Pogue Mahone's** (⌧ Vicolo Erbe 10 ☎ 0471/978339) is your place.

Batzenhausl (⌧ Via Andreas Hofer 30 ☎ 0471/050950) is a traditional, wine-bar favorite among locals. The bar at **Vögele** (⌧ Via Goethe 3 ☎ 0471/973938) stays open until 1 AM, serving an outstanding selection of wines by the glass in a relaxed setting.

The **Park Hotel Laurin Bar** (⌧ Via Laurin 4 ☎ 0471/311000) hosts jazz combos on Fridays and a jazz pianist all other nights.

Loden & Lederhosen

SHOPPING IS TRULY AN EVENT in the Alto Adige; in larger towns stores are clustered in a small clutch of arcaded streets, keeping shoppers dry on rainy and snowy days. The strong Tirolean influence makes for local products that are quite different from those elsewhere in Italy.

Traditional clothes—loden goods, lederhosen, dirndls, and linen suits with horn buttons—are a good buy, costing less than in neighboring Austria. Local crafts such as embroidered goods, wood carvings, and figures for nativity scenes also make excellent gifts. Of course there is no shortage of boutiques supplying the under-35 Italian dress code: jet-black and icy-gray designer clothes and accessories. Although store hours are not subject to the draconian store-closing laws that limit shopping across the northern border, neither are they immune from the midafternoon closure so fervently embraced to the south.

Concerts & Theater

There's a lively performance scene in town. A weekly schedule of what's on is available at the tourist office. Note that theater performances may be in German.

For opera information and schedules, call **Friends of Opera** (☎ 0471/913223). Orchestral concerts are held at **Haus der Kultur** (✉ Via Sciliar 1 ☎ 0471/977520).

A frequently used theater venue is the imposing **Nuovo Teatro Comunale** (✉ Piazza Verdi 40 ☎ 0471/304111 ⊕ www.ntbz.net). **Cortile Theater im Hof** (✉ Piazza delle Erbe 37 ☎ 0471/980756) specializes in children's theater.

Sports & the Outdoors

Biking

If you're in decent shape, a great way to see some of the surrounding castles, lakes, and forested valleys of the Dolomites is by bike. **Alp Bike** (☎ 0471/280795 ⊕ www.alpbike.it) leads different guided excursions almost every day, at all levels, but you must reserve a week or more ahead for the more ambitious trips.

Hiking

Club Alpino Italiano (✉ Piazza delle Erbe 46 ☎ 0471/981391 ⊕ www. cai.it) provides helpful information on area hiking and rock climbing.

Shopping

Local Crafts

The long, narrow arcades of **Via dei Portici** house shops that specialize in Tirolean crafts and clothing. The largest store for locally made hand-crafted goods is **Artigiani Atesini** (✉ Via Portici 39 ☎ 0471/978590).

Markets

From the end of November to Christmas Eve there's a traditional **Christkindlmarkt** (Christmas market) in Piazza Walther, with stalls selling all kinds of Christmas decorations and local handcrafted goods. An outdoor fruit and vegetable market takes over the central **Piazza delle Erbe** Monday through Saturday from 8 to 1. A weekly flea market takes place Saturday morning in **Piazza della Vittoria.**

Wine

Walk down a small alleyway near Piazza delle Erbe to discover **Il Baccaro** (⊠ Via Argentieri 17 ☎ 0471/971421), a tiny *enoteca* (wine bar) and wine shop. It's invariably filled with older men engrossed in conversation—you can't go wrong buying a bottle of whatever they're drinking. On Saturdays in October the **Bacchus Urbanus** program leads guided excursions to vineyards near Bolzano; contact the tourist office for details.

ALTO ADIGE & CORTINA

Prosperous valley towns (such as the famed spa center Merano) and mountain resorts (including the archetypical Cortina d'Ampezzo) entice those seeking both relaxation and adventure. Alto Adige (Südtirol) was for centuries part of the Austro-Hungarian Empire, only ceded to Italy at the end of World War I. Ethnic differences led to inevitable tensions in the 1960s and again in the '80s, though a large measure of provincial autonomy has, for the most part, kept the lid on nationalist ambitions. Today Germanic and Italian influences balance, and ancient castles often host contemporary art exhibitions.

Naturno (Naturns)

🄬 *44 km (27 mi) northwest of Bolzano, 61 km (38 mi) east of Passo dello Stelvio.*

Colorful houses covered with murals line the streets of Naturno (Naturns), a major horticultural center. Art lovers will appreciate the church of **San Procolo;** the frescoes inside are some of the oldest in the German-speaking world, dating from the 8th century. It's northeast of the town center, off S38. ⊠ *Via San Procolo* ☎ *0471/667312* ☉ *Easter–Nov., Tues.–Sun. 9:30–noon and 2:30–5:30.*

A five-minute drive west of Naturno, in the hills above the hamlet of Stava, is the 13th-century **Castel Juval,** since 1983 the home of the South Tirolese climber and polar adventurer Reinhold Messner—the first man to conquer Everest solo and the first to reach its summit without oxygen. Part of the castle has been turned into a museum, showing Messner's collection of Tibetan art, mountaineering illustrations, and masks from around the world. ⊠ *Viale Europa 2* ☎ *0473/221852* 🎫 *€7* ☉ *Palm Sun.–June, Sept., and Oct., Thurs.–Tues. 11–4.*

Where to Eat

$$ ✕ **Schlosswirt Juval.** Below Castel Juval, Reinhold Messner's restored farmhouse is home to an old-style restaurant serving Mediterranean stan-

dards and traditional local dishes. Not to be missed are the smoked hams and flavorful cheeses provisioned from the farm outside; they are well-paired with the estate's Castel Juval wine. Dinner is often accompanied by live jazz. ✉ *Via Municipio 1* ☎ *0473/668238* ▭ *No credit cards* ◷ *Closed Wed., July and Aug., and Nov.–Easter.*

<table>
<tr><td>en route</td><td>The source of the full-flavor beer served throughout the region is the striking Forst Brewery (✉ Via Venosta 8, Lagundo ☎ 0473/ 260111), on the road connecting Naturno and Merano. Tours are possible in summer (roughly June–August, daily 2–4), but you need to call ahead for reservations. You can turn up any time of year to sample the product line. In warm weather, cross a covered, flower-lined bridge to reach the delightful beer garden.</td></tr>
</table>

Merano (Meran)

★ ⑬ *16 km (10 mi) east of Naturno, 24 km (15 mi) north of Bolzano.*

The second-largest town in Alto Adige, Merano (Meran) was once the capital of the Austrian region of Tirol. When the town and surrounding area were ceded to Italy as part of the 1919 Treaty of Versailles, Innsbruck became the capital. Merano, however, continued to be known as a spa town, attracting European nobility for its therapeutic waters and its grape cure, which consists simply of eating the grapes grown on the surrounding hillsides. Sheltered by mountains, Merano has an unusually mild climate, with summer temperatures rarely exceeding 80°F and winters that usually stay above freezing, de-

spite the skiing that is within easy reach. Along the narrow streets of Merano's old town, houses have little towers and huge wooden doors, and the pointed arches of the Gothic cathedral sit next to neoclassical and art nouveau buildings. Merano serves as a good respite from mountain adventures, or from the bustle of nearby Trento and Bolzano.

The 14th-century Gothic **Duomo,** with a crenellated facade and an ornate campanile, sits in the heart of the old town. The Capella di Santa Barbara, just behind the cathedral, is an octagonal church containing a 15th-century pietà. ⊠ *Piazza del Duomo* ☉ *Easter–Sept., daily 8–noon and 2:30–8; Oct.–Easter, daily 8–noon and 2:30–7.*

Overlooking the town atop Mt. Tappeinerweg is a castle that was the home of poet Ezra Pound from 1958 to 1964. Still in the Pound family, the castle now houses the **Museo Agricolo di Brunnenburg** devoted to Tirolean country life. Among its exhibits are a blacksmith's shop and, not surprisingly, a room with Pound memorabilia. To get there, take Bus 3, which departs every hour on the hour, from Merano to Dorf Tirol (20 minutes). ⊠ *Via Castello 17, Brunnenburg* ☎ *0473/923533* ☑ *€3* ☉ *Apr.–Oct., Wed.–Mon. 10–5.*

The thermal baths at the **Terme di Merano** are scheduled to reopen by late 2005, after an extensive renovation and expansion of the spa complex (and the addition of a luxury hotel). ⊠ *Via Piave 6* ☎ *0473/ 237724* ⊕ *www.termemerano.it.*

FodorśChoice A stroll along one of Merano's well-marked, impossibly pleasant **Prom-**
★ **enades** may yield better relaxation than even a spa treatment. **Passeggiata Tappeiner** (Tappeiner's Promenade) is a 3-km (2-mi) path with panoramic views from the hills north of the Duomo, and the exceptionally mild climate gives way to diverse botanical pleasures along the walk. **Passeggiata d'Estate** (Summer Promenade) runs along the shaded south bank of the Passirio River, and the **Passeggiata d'Inverno** (Winter Promenade), on the exposed north bank, provides more warmth and the Wandelhalle—a suntrap decorated with idyllic paintings of surrounding villages. Sissi, the popular Austrian Empress Elisabeth, who put Merano on the map as a spa destination, was an inveterate ambler, and there is a trail named in her honor: **Sentiero di Sissi.** Sissi's Walk follows a path from **Castel Trauttmansdorff,** 2 km (1 mi) southeast of town, to the heart of Merano. The fortified Gothic castle was restored in the 19th century, and recently opened as a museum, celebrating 200 years of tourism in South Tyrol. Outside, a sprawling garden has an extensive display of exotic flora organized by country of origin. ⊠ *Via S. Valentino 51a* ☎ *0473/258819*

⊕ *www.trauttmansdorff.it* ⊠ €9.50 ⊙ *Mar. 15–May 15 and Sept. 15–Nov. 15, daily 9–6; May 15–Sept. 15, daily 9–9.*

need a break? **Cafe Saxifraga** (⊠ Passeggiata Tappeiner ☎ 0473/237249) occupies an enviable position overlooking Merano and the peaks enveloping the town; an extensive selection of teas and other beverages can be enjoyed on the patio, which has panoramic views. You can enjoy a rich hot chocolate or a cold beer above a gurgling waterfall at **Cafe Glif** (⊠ Passeggiata Glif 51 ☎ 0473/234701), at the northeast edge of the Passeggiata d'Inverno.

3

Where to Stay & Eat

★ **$$$–$$$$** ✕ **Sissi.** In this relaxed leafy restaurant just off Via dei Portici, rustic regional dishes are prepared with the precision of haute Italian cooking. Menu choices may include risotto *alle erbe* (with herbs) and *filetto di vitello con salsa di alloro* (veal fillet with bay-leaf sauce); a set menu (about €50) provides a complete five-course dinner. ⊠ *Via Galilei 44* ☎ *0473/231062* ⌑ *Reservations essential* ▤ *MC, V* ⊙ *Closed Mon. and Jan.–mid-Mar.*

$$ ✕ **Haisrainer.** Among the rustic wine taverns lining Via dei Portici, this one is most popular with locals and tourists alike; a menu in English is available for the latter. Warm wooden walls provide a comfortable setting for Tirolean and Italian standards: try the *zuppa al vino bianco* (stew with white wine) or the seasonal risottos (with asparagus in spring, or Barolo wine in chillier months). ⊠ *Via dei Portici 100* ☎ *0473/237944* ▤ *MC, V* ⊙ *Closed Sun.*

$$ ✕ **Seiben.** Young Meraners crowd the hip bar on the ground floor of this modern bistro, in the town's central arcade. Upstairs, a more mature crowd enjoys the contemporary cooking and attentive service in the jazz-themed dining room. Don't miss the Blues Brothers, poised over the staircase. ⊠ *Via dei Portici 232* ☎ *0473/210636* ▤ *MC, V* ⊙ *Closed Tues. No lunch Sun.*

¢–$ ✕ **Vinoteca-Pizzeria Relax.** You may have difficulty choosing from the long list of appetizing pizzas here. Ask the friendly English-speaking staff for help with the food and the wine. You're unlikely to find a better selection, or a more pleasant environment for browsing, if a glass of a locally produced vintage inspires you to bring a bottle or two home. ⊠ *Via Cavour 31, opposite Grand Hotel Palace* ☎ *0473/236735* ▤ *AE, MC, V* ⊙ *Closed Sun. and 2 wks in late Feb.*

★ **$$$$** ▥ **Grand Hotel Palace.** Merano's finest hotel is an old-world institution in an extensive garden. The art nouveau touches present in the public spaces—Tiffany glass, marble pillars, and high ceilings—spill over into the spacious guest rooms. The renowned spa has baths, massages, mud treatments, and other cures that attracts fatigued soccer stars and others in search of renewal. Rooftop suites have balconies with stunning views of Merano's steeples and the surrounding mountains. ⊠ *Via Cavour 2, 39012* ☎ *0473/271000* ⎙ *0473/271100* ⊕ *www.palace.it* ⇄ *125 rooms, 12 suites* ⌕ *2 restaurants, minibars, cable TV, pool, spa, bar, wine shop, meeting rooms, free parking* ▤ *AE, DC, MC, V* ⎟⊚⎟ *BP.*

$$$ ▥ **Castello Labers.** The red-tile gables, towers, and turrets give this castle its unmistakably Tirolean style, as it sits on a hilltop amid forested slopes. Ceiling beams, painted fresco decorations, and crossed halberds on the walls complete the look inside. The hospitable Stapf-Neubert family owns the hotel and takes an active part in its management. ⊠ *Via Labers 25, 39012, 3 km (2 mi) northeast of Merano's center* ☎ *0473/ 234484* 🖷 *0473/234146* 🌐 *www.castellolabers.it* 🛏 *32 rooms, 1 suite* ⚘ *Restaurant, in-room safes, tennis court, pool; no a/c* ▭ *AE, DC, MC, V* ⊙ *Closed Nov.–Mar.* ⦾| *BP.*

$ 🛌 **Conte di Merano.** If you don't feel like paying for one of Merano's resorts, this simple central hotel is a good alternative. Steps away from Via dei Portici and open year-round, it's an efficient base for exploring the town. Rooms have spartan furnishings, but are clean and comfortable. ⊠ *Via delle Corse 78, 39012* ☎ *0473/232181* 🖷 *0473/211874* 🛏 *23 rooms* ⚘ *Restaurant, in-room safes, cable TV, bar* ▭ *AE, DC, MC, V* ⦾| *BP.*

Nightlife & the Arts

Merano is a quiet town after dark, but there is no shortage of pleasant watering holes. Younger Meraners favor **Bar Piccolo** (⊠ Corso Libertà 5 ☎ 0473/236765). Mellow cafés such as **Cafe Darling** (⊠ Passegiata Inverno 5 ☎ 0473/237221) line the promenade along the river.

The **Grape Festival** on the third Sunday of October has parades and wine tastings in Piazza del Duomo. Farmers test indigenous Haflinger horses in the highly charged **horse race** on Easter Monday.

Shopping

Merano's main shopping street, the narrow arcaded **Via dei Portici** (Laubengasse), runs west from the cathedral. There are regional products—wood carvings, Tirolean-style clothing, embroidery, cheeses, salami, and fruit schnapps—for sale, along with more standard clothing-boutique shopping. You can taste a selection of locally grown varietals at the retail outlet of winemaker **Burggräfler** (⊠ Via dei Portici 218 ☎ 0473/237147). From the end of November until Christmas Eve, Merano holds a traditional **Christkindlmarkt** in the main square.

Chiusa (Klausen)

⑭ *30 km (19 mi) northeast of Bolzano.*

Beautiful narrow streets are lined with houses built in the 15th and 16th centuries in Chiusa (Klausen), the main town in the Val Isarco. Geraniums and begonias fill window boxes beneath the carved wooden shutters. From here you can catch a bus east to Val di Funes, where the church of Santa Maddalena is spectacularly hemmed in by the Geisler Peaks.

Above the town of Chiusa is the Benedictine monastery of **Saviona** (Saeben), built as a castle in the 10th century but occupying a site that was fortified in Roman times. The monastery buildings date from the late Middle Ages and are a mixture of Romanesque and Gothic architecture surrounded by walls and turrets. Guided visits to Saviona are organized by the **Tourist Association in Chiusa** (Tourist office ⊠ Piazza Tinne 6 ☎ 0472/847424).

Bressanone (Brixen)

⑮ *14 km (9 mi) north of Chiusa, 40 km (25 mi) northeast of Bolzano.*

Bressanone (Brixen) is an important artistic center and was the seat of prince-bishops for centuries. Like their counterparts in Trento, these medieval administrators had the delicate task of serving two masters—the pope (the ultimate spiritual authority) and the Holy Roman Emperor (the civil and military power), who were virtually at war throughout the Middle Ages. Bressanone's prince-bishops became experts at tact and diplomacy. The imposing **Duomo** was built in the 13th century but acquired a baroque facade 500 years later; its 14th-century cloister is decorated with medieval frescoes. Free guided tours are available Monday–Saturday at 10:30 and 3 (in German or Italian). ⊠ *Piazza Duomo* ⊙ *Daily 8–noon and 3–6.*

The Bishop's Palace houses the **Museo Diocesano** (Diocesan Museum) and its abundance of local medieval art, particularly Gothic wood carvings. The wooden statues and liturgical objects were all collected from the cathedral treasury. During the Christmas season, curators arrange the museum's large collection of antique nativity scenes; look for the shepherds wearing Tirolean hats. ⊠ *Palazzo Vescovile 2* ☎ *0472/830505* ⊕ *www.dioezesanmuseum.bz.it* ⊡ *€5, nativity scenes €3.50* ⊙ *Museum Mar. 15–Oct., Tues.–Sun. 10–5; nativity scenes only Dec. and Jan., daily 2–5.*

From the end of November until January 6, there is a traditional **Christkindlmarkt** in Piazza Duomo, with stalls selling Christmas decorations and local handcrafted goods.

They've been making wine at the Augustinian abbey, **Abbazia di Novacella** (founded 1142), for at least nine centuries. Sample varietals produced in the Isarco valley in the tasting room; Novacella is most famous for the delicate stone-fruit character of its dry white Sylvaner. You can also wander the delightful grounds; note the progression of Romanesque, Gothic, and baroque building styles. Guided tours of the abbey depart on the hour. ⊠ *Località Novacella 1, 39040 Varna, 3 km (2 mi) north of Bressanone* ☎☎ *0472/836189* ⊟ *AE, MC, V* ⊡ *Grounds and tasting room free, guided tours €4.50* ⊙ *Grounds Mon.–Sat. 10–7, tasting room Mon.–Sat. 9–noon and 2–6, guided tours 10–4.*

Where to Stay & Eat

$$–$$$ ✕ **Fink.** Try the *carré di maiale gratinato* (pork chops roasted with cheese and served with cabbage and potatoes) or the *castrato alla paesana,* a substantial lamb stew, here. In addition to hearty Tirolean specialties, there's an affordable daily set menu, as well as international dishes. The rustic wood-panel dining room is upstairs in this restaurant under the arcades of the pedestrian-only town center. ⊠ *Via Portici Minori 4* ☎ *0472/834883* ⊟ *MC, V* ⊙ *Closed Wed., July 1–14, and Feb. 1–14. No dinner Tues.*

★ $$$ ▥ **Elephant.** This cozy inn, one of the region's best, takes its name from the 1551 visit of King John III of Portugal, who stopped here while leading an elephant (a present for Austria's Emperor Ferdinand) over the Alps. Each room is unique, many with antiques and paintings. Housed on the park property is the separate Villa Marzari, with 14 rooms. A rustic three-room stube serves decent fare. ✉ *Via Rio Bianco 4, 39042* ☎ *0472/832750* 🖷 *0472/836579* ⊕ *www.hotelelephant.com* ⤳ *44 rooms* ♿ *Restaurant, minibars, cable TV, 2 tennis courts, pool, gym, sauna, bar, Internet* ▭ *DC, MC, V* ⊗ *Closed early Jan.–Mar. and Nov.* ▮⊘▮ *BP.*

$ ▦ **Croce d'Oro** (Goldenes Kreuz). A five-century-old tradition of hospitality is still practiced by the Reiserer family at this central, pink hotel. Interior styles range from a modern reception area to a tavern-style bar; guest rooms are spacious, with sturdy wood appointments. The hotel is open year-round. ✉ *Bastioni Minori 8, 39042* ☎ *0472/836155* 🖷 *0472/834255* ⊕ *www.goldeneskreuz.it* ⤳ *75 rooms* ♿ *Restaurant, in-room safes, cable TV, spa, bar; no a/c* ▭ *No credit cards* ▮⊘▮ *BP.*

Brunico (Bruneck)

★ ⓰ *33 km (20 mi) east of Bressanone, 65 km (40 mi) northwest of Cortina d'Ampezzo.*

With its medieval quarter nestling below the 13th-century bishop's castle, Brunico (Bruneck) is in the heart of the Val Pusteria. This quiet and quaint town is divided by the Rienza River, with the old quarter on one side and the modern town on the other.

The **Museo Etnografico dell'Alto Adige** (Alto Adige Ethnographic Museum) re-creates a Middle Ages farming village, built around a more modern 300-year-old mansion. The wood-carving displays are most interesting. The museum is in the district of Teodone, northeast of the center. ✉ *Via Duca Diet 24, Teodone* ☎ *0474/552087* ⊕ *www.provincia.bz.it/volkskundemuseen* 🎫 *€3.60* ⊗ *Mid-Apr.–Oct., Tues.–Sat. 9:30–5:30, Sun. 2–6.*

Where to Stay

$ ▦ **Post.** The Von Grebmer family maintains a traditional, homey hotel in an 1880s building, and provides efficient service. This is the most central, appealing lodging choice in town, especially if you've got a sweet tooth: the attached pastry shop is as popular with locals as with international guests. The hotel has its own parking, an unusual perk in the pedestrian-only center. ✉ *Via Bastioni 9, 39031* ☎ *0474/555127* 🖷 *0474/551603* ⊕ *www.hotelpost-bruneck.com* ⤳ *54 rooms, 45 with bath* ♿ *Restaurant, café, in-room safes, minibars, cable TV, spa, Weinstube, laundry service, shop, some pets allowed (fee); no a/c* ▭ *AE, MC, V* ⊗ *Closed 1st 2 wks Nov.* ▮⊘▮ *BP.*

Sports

The **Alta Badia ski area** (⊕ www.altabadia.org) can be reached by heading 30 km (19 mi) south on S244 from Brunico. It's less expensive—and more Austrian in character—than other, more famous ski destinations in this region.

Dobbiaco (Toblach)

⓱ *25 km (16 mi) east of Brunico, 34 km (21 mi) north of Cortina d'Ampezzo.*

In Dobbiaco (Toblach), Italian is spoken grudgingly, and the place seems more Germanic than Austria itself. Gustav Mahler (1860–1911), the great Austrian composer, came here often for inspiration. The same mountain vistas and pleasant climate that attracted Mahler continue to draw tourists to Dobbiaco, as does its proximity to low-key alternatives to the Dolomites' better known resorts.

Where to Stay

$$$ ⊞ **Cristallo.** Wood beams and paneling lend an Old Tirolean patina to this small hotel in a garden outside town. The architecture and furnishings reflect the local preference for combining traditional chalet design with functional, comfortable modern furniture. You can relax in the cozy and informal stube. ✉ *Viale S. Giovanni 37, 39034* ☎ *0474/972138* 🖷 *0474/972755* ⊕ *www.hotelcristallo.com* ➷ *30 rooms* ♨ *Restaurant, in-room safes, cable TV, indoor pool, sauna, bar; no a/c* ▭ *MC, V* ⊘ *Closed mid-Mar.–May and mid-Oct.–mid-Dec.* ¶⊙¶ *MAP.*

★ **$$** ⊞ **Alpenhotel Ratsberg.** To reach this traditional chalet you can drive up by car, or take the 10-minute cable-car ride from Santa Maria (5 km [3 mi] northwest of Dobbiaco) to Monte Rota (Ratsberg). Front rooms have balconies and stunning mountain views; those in the back look out over the dense mountain forest. The many windows, along with light-color furnishings, make the rooms feel open. You needn't take the cable car back down for sustenance: the hotel has a good restaurant, a bar, and a Tirolean-style stube. ✉ *Monte Rota 12, 39034 Monte Rota* ☎ *0474/ 972213* 🖷 *0474/972916* ⊕ *www.alpenhotel-ratsberg.com* ➷ *30 rooms* ♨ *Restaurant, cable TV, tennis court, indoor pool, sauna, bar; no a/c* ▭ *No credit cards* ⊘ *Closed Apr.–mid-May and Nov.–late Dec.* ¶⊙¶ *BP.*

Sports

SKIING   Groomed trails for **cross-country skiing** (usually loops marked off by the kilometer) accommodate differing degrees of ability. Inquire at the local tourist office. Downhill skiing can be found at the modest **Monte Elmo** (⊕ www.helmbahnen.com), 10 km (6 mi) southeast of Dobbiaco.

Cortina d'Ampezzo

18 *30 km (19 mi) south of Dobbiaco.*

Fodor'sChoice
   ★   Cortina d'Ampezzo has been the Dolomites' mountain resort of choice for more than 100 years; the Winter Olympics were held here in 1956. Although its glamorous appeal to younger Italians may have been eclipsed by steeper, sleeker Madonna di Campiglio, Cortina remains, for many, Italy's most idyllic incarnation of an Alpine ski town.

Surrounded by mountains and dense forests, the "The Pearl of the Dolomites" is in a lush meadow 4,000 feet above sea level. The town hugs the slopes beside a fast-moving stream, and a public park extends along one bank. Higher in the valley, luxury hotels and the villas of the rich are identifiable by their attempts to hide behind stands of firs and spruces. The bustling center of Cortina d'Ampezzo has little nostalgia, despite its Alpine appearance. The tone is set by smart shops and cafés as chic as their well-dressed patrons, whose corduroy knickerbockers may well have been tailored by Armani. Unlike neighboring resorts that have a strong Germanic flavor, Cortina d'Ampezzo is unapologetically Italian and distinctly fashionable.

On Via Cantore, a winding road heading up out of town to the northeast (becoming S48), you can stop and see the **Pista Olimpica di Bob** (Olympic Bobsled Course), a leftover from the 1956 Winter Games. The course is open to the public, but at unpredictable times.

Where to Stay & Eat

$$–$$$ ✕ **Tavernetta.** Near the Olympic ice-skating rink, this popular restaurant has Tirolean-style, wood-panel dining rooms and a local clientele. Here you can try Cortina specialties such as *zuppa di porcini* (porcini mushroom soup), ravioli *di cervo* (stuffed with venison), and game. ⊠ *Via Castello 53* ☎ *0436/868102* ⊟ *AE, DC, MC, V* ⊘ *Closed Nov.*

$$$$ ✕⊡ **De la Poste.** Loyal skiers return year after year to this lively hotel; its
Fodor'sChoice main terrace bar is one of Cortina's social centers. De la Poste has been
★ under the careful management of the Manaìgo family since 1936. Each unique room has antiques in characteristic Dolomite style; almost all have wooden balconies. A refined main dining room—with high ceilings and large chandeliers—serves nouvelle cuisine and superb soufflés; there's also a more informal grill room with wood paneling and the family's pewter collection. Sporadic off-season bed-and-breakfast rates can be a bargain. ⊠ *Piazza Roma 14, 32043* ☎ *0436/4271* ⊟ *0436/868435* ⊕ *www.delaposte.it* ⊡ *83 rooms* ⌂ *2 restaurants, minibars, cable TV, bar, free parking; no a/c* ⊟ *AE, DC, MC, V* ⊘ *Closed Apr.–mid-June and Oct.–mid-Dec.* ⟨Ⓞ⟩ *MAP.*

$$$$ ⊡ **Corona.** Noted ski instructor Luciano Rimoldi, who has coached such luminaries as Alberto Tomba, runs a cozy Alpine lodge. Modern art adorns small but comfortable pine-panel rooms; the convivial bar is a pleasant place to relax. The hotel is a five-minute walk—across the river—from the center of town, and a 10-minute ride from the lifts (a ski bus stops out front). ⊠ *Via Val di Sotto 12, 32040* ☎ *0436/3251* ⊟ *0436/867339* ⊕ *www.hotelcoronacortina.it* ⊡ *44 rooms* ⌂ *Restaurant, cable TV, bar, free parking; no a/c* ⊟ *AE, DC, MC, V* ⊘ *Closed Apr.–June and Sept.–Nov.* ⟨Ⓞ⟩ *MAP.*

$$$$ ⊡ **Miramonti Majestic.** This imposing and luxe hotel, more than a century old, has a magnificent mountain-valley position about 1 km (½ mi) south of town. A touch of formality comes through in the imperial Austrian design, and the interior reflects the period style throughout. There's always a roaring fire in the splendid bar, and the hotel's recreation rooms are lined with windows overlooking mountain vistas. The history of Cortina is intricately tied to the Miramonti, and you can feel a part of it all here. ⊠ *Località Peziè 103, 32043* ☎ *0436/4201* ⊟ *0436/ 867019* ⊕ *www.cortina.dolomiti.org/hmiramonti* ⊡ *105 rooms* ⌂ *Restaurant, minibars, cable TV, 9-hole golf course, 2 tennis courts, indoor pool, gym, sauna, bar, meeting rooms, free parking; no a/c* ⊟ *AE, DC, MC, V* ⊘ *Closed Apr.–June and Sept.–mid-Dec.* ⟨Ⓞ⟩ *MAP.*

Nightlife & the Arts

At the **Europa** (⊠ Corso Italia 207 ☎ 0436/3221) hotel you can mingle with the couture set at the VIP disco; nonguests are welcome, but don't expect to spend less than €30.

Sports

SKIING Cortina's long and picturesque ski runs will delight intermediates, but advanced skiers might lust for steeper terrain, which can be found only off-piste. Efficient ski bus service connects the town with the high-speed chairlifts and gondolas that ascend in all directions from the valley.

The **Dolomiti Superski pass** (✉ Via Marconi 15 ☎ 0471/795397 ⊕ www. dolomitisuperski.com) provides access to the surrounding Dolomites (€38 per day, excluding Bromio)—with 450 lifts and gondolas serving 1,200 km (750 mi) of trails. Buy one at the ticket office next to the bus station. The **Faloria gondola** (✉ Via Ria de Zeta 8 ☎ 0436/2517) runs from the center of town. From its top you can get up to most of the central mountains.

Some of the most impressive views (and steepest slopes) are on **Monte Cristallo,** based at Misurina, 15 km (9 mi) northeast of Cortina by car or bus. The topography of the **Passo Falzarego** ski area, 16 km (10 mi) east of town, is quite dramatic.

HIKING & CLIMBING Hiking information is available at the excellent local **tourist office** (✉ Piazzetta San Francesco 8 ☎ 0436/3231 ⊕ www.cortina.dolomiti.com).

Cortina's **Scuola di Alpinismo** (Mountaineering School) (✉ Corso Italia 69 ☎ 0436/868505 ⊕ www.guidecortina.com) organizes climbing trips and trekking adventures.

HEART OF THE DOLOMITES

The area between Bolzano and the mountain resort Cortina d'Ampezzo is dominated by two major valleys, Val di Fassa and Val Gardena. Both share the spectacular panorama of the Sella mountain range, known as the Heart of the Dolomites. The roads around the Sella mountains are among the most spectacular in Europe. Val di Fassa cradles the beginning of the Grande Strada delle Dolomiti (Great Dolomites Road—S48 and S241), which runs from Bolzano as far as Cortina d'Ampezzo. This route, opened in 1909, comprises 110 km (68 mi) of relatively easy grades and smooth driving between the two towns—a slower, more scenic alternative to traveling by way of Brunico and Dobbiaco along S49.

In both Val di Fassa and Val Gardena, recreational options are less expensive, though less comprehensive, than in better-known resorts like Cortina. The culture here is firmly Germanic. Val Gardena is freckled with well-equipped, photo-friendly towns with great views overlooked by the oblong *Sasso Lungo* (Long Rock), which is more than 10,000 feet above sea level. It's also home to the Ladins, descendants of soldiers sent by the Roman emperor Tiberius to conquer the Celtic population of the area in the 1st century AD. Forgotten in the narrow cul-de-sacs of isolated mountain valleys, the Ladins have developed their own folk traditions and speak an ancient dialect that is derived from Latin and similar to the Romansch spoken in some high valleys in Switzerland.

Canazei

🄳 *60 km (37 mi) west of Cortina d'Ampezzo, 52 km (32 mi) east of Bolzano.*

Of the year-round resort towns in the Val di Fassa, Canazei is the most popular. The mountains around this small town are threaded with hiking trails and ski slopes, surrounded by large clutches of conifers. Four kilometers (2½ mi) west of Canazei, an excursion from Campitello di Fassa to the vantage point at **Col Rodella** is a must. A cable car rises some 3,000 feet to a full-circle vista of the Heart of the Dolomites, including the Sasso Lungo and the rest of the Sella range.

Where to Stay

$$ 🏨 **Alla Rosa.** The view of the imposing Dolomites is the real attraction at this central hotel, so ask for a room with a balcony. The reception area is spacious and welcoming, and guest rooms pleasantly blend rustic and modern elements. There's a modest restaurant serving local and international cuisine, and a cozy bar. ☒ *Via del Faure 18, 38032* ☎ *0462/601107* ☐ *0462/601481* ⊕ *www.hotelallarosa.com* ➴ *49 rooms* ⚲ *Restaurant, minibars, cable TV, sauna, bar, recreation room, parking (fee); no a/c* ▭ *MC, V* |◯| *MAP.*

> **en route** | The **Passo di Sella** (Sella Pass) can be approached from the S48 and continues into Val Gardena through the most panoramic mountain scenery in Europe. The road descends to Ortisei, passing the smaller resorts of Selva Gardina and Santa Cristina.

Ortisei (St. Ulrich)

⓴ *28 km (17 mi) north of Canazei, 35 km (22 mi) northeast of Bolzano.*

Ortisei (St. Ulrich), the jewel in the crown of Val Gardena's resorts, is a hub of activity in both summer and winter; there are hundreds of miles of hiking trails and accessible ski slopes. Hotels and facilities are abundant—swimming pools, ice rinks, health spas, tennis courts, and bowling. Most impressive of all is the location, a valley surrounded by formidable views in all directions.

For centuries Ortisei has also been famous for the expertise of its woodcarvers, and there are still numerous workshops. Apart from making religious sculptures—particularly the wayside Calvaries you come upon everywhere in the Dolomites—Ortisei's carvers were long known for producing wooden dolls, horses, and other toys. As itinerant peddlers they traveled every spring on foot with their loaded packs as far as Paris, London, and St. Petersburg. Shops in town still sell woodcrafts. Fine historic and contemporary examples of local woodworking can be seen at the **Museo della Val Gardena.** ☒ *Via Rezia 83* ☎ *0471/797554* ⊕ *www. val-gardena.com* ☑ *€3* ☉ *Feb.–mid-Mar., Tues.–Fri. 2:30–5:30; June and Sept.–mid-Oct., Tues., Thurs., and Fri. 2–6, Wed. 10–noon and 2–6; July and Aug., Tues.–Sat. 10–noon and 2–6, Sun. 2–6.*

Where to Stay

★ $$$$ 🏨 **Adler.** This hotel, the best in the valley, has been under the same family management since 1810. The original building has been enlarged several times, yielding spacious guest rooms (with wireless Internet access) and an expansive spa complex but retaining much of the old turreted-castle appeal. Most guests stay for a full week, picking up the busy schedule of activities (such as guided ski tours and snowshoe walks) when they arrive on Saturday evening. The same activities, at a slower pace, are available for children. ⊠ *Via Rezia 7, 39046* ☎ *0471/775000* 🖷 *0471/775555* ⊕ *www.hotel-adler.com* 🛏 *123 rooms* ⚐ *Restaurant, in-room safes, minibars, cable TV, indoor pool, health club, hair salon, sauna, steam bath, spa, bar, Internet, children's programs (ages 4–12)* ▤ *MC, V* ⊗ *Closed Apr.–mid-May and Nov.* ⍟❘ *MAP.*

$$$$ ⌸ **Cavallino Bianco.** The pink Cavallino Bianco looks like a gigantic dollhouse, with delicate wooden balconies and an eye-catching wooden gable. Beyond this facade lies a sprawling, all-inclusive modern resort, but the cozy bar—with its large, handcrafted fireplace—retains some of the charm of the old postal hotel it was. Guest rooms have upholstered furniture with cheery, large-scale plaids and honey-tone wood accents. The hotel is only a five-minute walk from the main ski facilities; ski guides are available. ⊠ *Via Rezia 22, 39046* ☎ *0471/783333* 🖷 *0471/797517* ⊕ *www. cavallino-bianco.com* 🛏 *184 rooms* ⚐ *Restaurant, coffee shop, in-room safes, minibars, cable TV, indoor pool, sauna, spa, mountain bikes, bar, dance club, children's programs (ages 2–12), Internet; no a/c* ▤ *AE, DC, MC, V* ⊗ *Closed Apr.–mid-May and mid-Oct.–mid-Dec.* ⍟❘ *FAP.*

Sports

With almost 600 km (370 mi) of accessible downhill slopes and more than 90 km (56 mi) of cross-country skiing trails, Ortisei is one of the most popular ski resorts in the Dolomites. Prices are good, and facilities are among the most modern in the region. In warmer weather, the slopes surrounding Ortisei are a popular hiking destination, as well as a playground for vehicular mountain adventures: biking, rafting, even paragliding.

An immensely popular ski route, the **Sella Ronda** relies on well-placed chairlifts to connect 26 km (16 mi) of downhill skiing around the colossal Sella massif, passing through several towns along the way. You can ski the loop, which requires intermediate ability and a full day's effort, either clockwise or counterclockwise. Going with a guide is recommended. Chairlifts here, as elsewhere in the Dolomites, are covered by the €38-daily **Dolomiti Superski pass** (⊠ Sparkasse building, Via Rezia ☎ 0471/795397 ⊕ www.dolomitisuperski.com).

The **Val Gardena Tourist Office** (⊠ Str. Dursan 78, Santa Cristina ☎ 0471/ 792092 ⊕ www.valgardena.it) can provide detailed information about sport equipment rental outfits and guided tour operators.

Gardena Mountain Adventures (☎ 335/684903 ⊕ www.val-gardena.com/ gma) outfits a particularly large choice of year-round mountain sport activities.

Lago di Carezza

㉑ *22 km (14 mi) west of Canazei, 29 km (18 mi) east of Bolzano.*

Glacial Lake Carezza is some 5,000 feet above sea level. The azure blue of the waters can at times change to magical greens and purples, reflections of the dense surrounding forest and rosy peaks of the Dolomites. You can hike down to this most quintessential of mountain lakes from the nearby village of the same name; there's a fountain with two marmots in the center of town.

Hiking the Dolomites

FOR MANY OVERSEAS VISITORS, the Dolomites conjure images of downhill skiing at Cortina d'Ampezzo and Madonna di Campiglio. But summer, not winter, is high season here; Italians, German-speaking Europeans, and in-the-know travelers from farther afield come here for clear mountain air and world-class hiking. Nature has done most of the work—impressive terrain, inspiring vistas, an impossibly pleasant climate—but the man-made facilities for enjoying the mountains are also exceptional.

PICKING A TRAIL

The Dolomites boast a well-maintained network of trails for hiking and rock climbing. As long as you're in reasonably good shape, the number of appealing hiking options can be overwhelming. Trails are well marked and designated by grades of difficulty: T for tourist path, H for hiking path, EE for expert hikers, and EEA for equipped expert hikers. On any of these paths you're likely to see carpets of mountain flowers between clutches of dense evergreens, with chamois and roe deer mulling about. If you're just out for a day in the mountains, you can leave the particulars of your walk open until you're actually on the spot; local tourist offices (especially those in Cortina, Madonna, and the Heart of the Dolomites) can help you choose the right route based on trail conditions, weather, and desired exertion level.

TRAVELING THE VIE FERRATE

If you're looking for an adventure somewhere between hiking and climbing, consider a guided trip along the Vie Ferrate (Iron Paths). These routes offer fixed climbing aids (steps, ladders, bridges, safety cables) left by alpine divisions of the Italian and Austro-Hungarian armies and later converted for recreational use. Previous experience is generally not required, but vertigo-inducing heights do demand a strong stomach. Detailed information about Vie Ferrate in the eastern Dolomites can be found at ⊕ www.dolomiti.org. Capable tour organizers include Scuole di Alpinismo (Mountaineering Schools) in Madonna di Campiglio (☎ 0465/442634 ⊕ www.guidealpinecampiglio.it) and Cortina d'Ampezzo (☎ 0436/868505 ⊕ www.guidecortina.com).

BEDDING DOWN

One of the pleasures of an overnight adventure in the Dolomites is staying at a *rifugio*, one of the refuges that dot the mountainsides. There are hundreds of them, often in remote locations and ranging from spartan shelters to posh retreats. Most fall somewhere in between—they're cozy mountain lodges with dormitory-style accommodations. Pillows and blankets are provided (so there's no need to carry a sleeping bag), but you have to supply your own sheet. Bathrooms are usually shared, as is the experience of a cold shower in the morning.

The majority of rifugi are operated by the Club Alpino Italiano (CAI) (⊕ www.cai.it). Contact information for both CAI-run and private rifugi are available from local tourist offices; most useful are those in Madonna di Campiglio (⊕ www.campiglio.to), Cortina d'Ampezzo (⊕ www.dolomiti.org), Val di Fassa (⊕ www.fassa.com), and Val Gardena (⊕ www.valgardena.it). Reservations are a must, especially in August, although Italian law requires rifugi to accept travelers for the night if there is insufficient time to reach other accommodations before dark.

EATING WELL
Food, true to Italian priorities, is as much a draw at rifugi as location. While the dishes served are the sort of the rustic cuisine you might expect (salami, dumplings, hearty stews), the quality is uniformly excellent—an impressive feat, made all the more remarkable when you consider that supplies often have to arrive by helicopter. Your dinner may cost as much as your bed for the night—about €20 per person—and it's difficult to determine which is the better bargain.

Snacks and packed lunches are available for purchase, but many opt to sit down for the midday meal, to enjoy the camaraderie and diversity of their fellow explorers. Serving as both holiday hiking destination and base camp for difficult ascents, the rifugi welcome walkers and climbers of all stripes from intersecting trails and nearby faces. Multilingual stories are swapped, food and wine shared, and new adventures launched.

STUMBLING ON ÖTZI
It was at the Similaun rifugio in September 1991 that a German couple arrived talking of a dead body they'd discovered near a "curious pickaxe." This was to be the world's introduction to Ötzi, the oldest mummy ever found (now on display in Bolzano's Museo Archeologico dell'Alto Adige).

The couple, underestimating the age of the corpse by about 5,300 years, thought it was a matter for the police. World-famous mountaineers Reinhold Messner and Hans Kammerlander happened to be passing through the same rifugio during a climbing tour, and a few days later they were on scene, freeing the iceman from the ice. Ötzi's remarkable story was underway.

Caldaro (Kaltern)

❷ *45 km (28 mi) southwest of Lago di Carezza, 15 km (9 mi) south of Bolzano.*

A vineyard village with clear views of castles high up on the surrounding mountains represents the centuries of division that forged the unique character of the area. Caldaro architecture is famous for the way it blends Italian Renaissance elements of balance and harmony with the soaring windows and peaked arches of the Germanic Gothic tradition. The church of Santa Caterina, on the main square, is a good example.

Close to Caldaro's main square is the **Museo Provinciale del Vino,** with exhibits on how local wine has historically been made, stored, served, and worshipped. You can call ahead to reserve a wine tasting (€4.60) in the museum's cellar. ✉ *Via dell'Oro 1* ☎ *0471/963168* ⊕ *www. provinz.bz.it/volkskundemuseen* 🖃 *€2.10* ☉ *Apr.–mid.-Nov., Tues.–Sat. 9:30–noon and 2–6, Sun. 10–noon.*

DOLOMITES ESSENTIALS

Transportation

BY AIR

The nearest airport, but the least well connected, is Aeroporto Bolzano Dolomiti (BZO), with scheduled service to Rome (FCO) and Munich (MUC). A bit farther to the south, Verona (VRN) can be reached by plane from many European cities and is well connected by road and rail with the Dolomite area. Direct intercontinental flights are available into Milan Malpensa (MXP) to the southwest and Munich (MUC) to the north, both about a four-hour drive from Bolzano.

🛈 Airport Information **Aeroporto Bolzano Dolomiti** ☎0471/255255 ⊕www.abd-airport. it. **Aeroporto Milan Malpensa** ☎ 02/74852200 ⊕ www.sea-aeroportimilano.it. **Aeroporto Valerio Catullo di Verona Villafranca** ☎045/8095666 ⊕ www.aeroportoverona. it. **Munich International Airport** ☎ 049/8997500 ⊕ www.munich-airport.de.

BY BUS

Regular bus service connects larger cities to the south (Verona, Venice, and Milan) with valley towns in Trentino–Alto Adige (Rovereto, Trento, Bolzano, and Merano). You'll need to change to less-frequent local buses to reach resorts in the mountains beyond. For information, contact Trentino Trasporti or Alto Adige's SIT. A convenient bus service between Cortina d'Ampezzo and the Venice airport (€18 round-trip, complimentary at some hotels) is available on weekends from mid-December to March; bookings must be made through your hotel. DolomitiBus provides winter weekend service between Cortina and the Venice train station.

Local buses provide frequent service between the valley towns of Trento, Bolzano, and Merano. Although it's certainly possible to visit even the remotest villages without a car (if you're equipped with schedules and lots of time), most towns are designed for automobiles, and getting between your hotel, ski lifts, and après-ski locales without a vehicle can be very tricky. For detailed information on bus service within Trentino–Alto Adige, contact Trentino Trasporti or SIT. DolomitiBus serves the Eastern Dolomites, including Cortina d'Ampezzo.

⚡ Bus Information DolomitiBus ☎ 0437/217111 ⊕ www.dolomitibus.it. **SIT** (Servizio Integrato di Trasporto) ☎ 0471/415480 ⊕ www.sii.bz.it. **Trentino Trasporti** ☎ 0461/983627 ⊕ www.ttspa.it.

BY CAR

The most important route in the region is Autostrada A22, the main north–south highway linking Italy with central Europe by way of the Brenner Pass. It connects Innsbruck with Bressanone, Bolzano, Trento, and Rovereto, and near Verona joins Autostrada A4 (which runs east–west across northern Italy, from Trieste and Venice to Milan and Turin). By car, Trento is 3 hours from Milan and 2½ hours from Venice. Bolzano is another hour's drive to the north (with Munich 4 hours farther on).

Driving definitely has its advantages when exploring the Dolomites; it can be difficult to reach the ski areas (or any town outside of Rovereto, Trento, Bolzano, and Merano) without a car. Caution is essential, especially in winter, when roads are often covered in snow and buffeted by high winds. Sudden closures are common, especially on high mountain passes, and can occur as early as November and as late as May. Even under the best conditions, expect to negotiate mountain roads at speeds no greater than 50 kph (30 mph). Call Autostrada Weather Information Service in Bolzano for information on weather-related closures.

EMERGENCY ACI Emergency Service offers 24-hour roadside assistance.
SERVICES **⚡ ACI dispatchers** ☎ 803/116. **Autostrada Weather Information Service** ☎ 0471/413810.

BY TRAIN

The rail line following the course of the Isarco and Adige valleys—from Munich and Innsbruck, through the Brenner Pass, and southward past Bressanone, Bolzano, Trento, and Rovereto en route to Verona—is well trafficked, making trains a viable option for travel between these towns. Eurocity trains on the Dortmund–Venice and Munich–Innsbruck–Rome routes stop at these stations, and you can connect with other Italian lines at Verona. While branch lines from Trento and Bolzano do extend into some of the smaller valleys (including hourly service between Bolzano and Merano), most of the mountain attractions are beyond the reach of trains. Contact Trenitalia for more information. Contact Trenitalia for more information.

⚡ Train Information Trenitalia ☎ 892021 ⊕ www.trenitalia.com.

Contacts & Resources

EMERGENCIES

For first aid, ask for *pronto soccorso,* and be prepared to give your address. Pharmacies take turns staying open late and on Sunday; for the latest information, consult the current list posted on the front door of each pharmacy or ask at the local tourist office.

⚡ Ambulance ☎ 118. **Polizia** ☎ 113 local police.

TOURS

If you are without a car or don't care to drive mountain roads, guided tours from Bolzano or Trento can show you the Dolomites the easy way. However, tours are offered only in the snow-free summer months.

BUS TOURS   In Bolzano city sightseeing and local excursions are organized by the SAD bus company. In Trento city sightseeing can be arranged through the city tourist office.

🚌 Fees & Schedules **SAD** ✉ Via Conciapelli 60 ☎ 0471/450111 ⊕ www.sii.bz.it.

SINGLE-DAY TOURS   In July and August, the SAD bus company's full-day mountain tours include a "Great Dolomites Tour" from Bolzano to Cortina and a tour of the Val Venosta that climbs over the Stelvio Pass into Switzerland. A tour of the Val Gardena and the Siusi Alps is available from April to October.

From June through September the Calderari e Moggioli travel agency offers a full-day guided bus tour of the Brenta Dolomites and its own "Great Dolomites Tour," a full-day drive over the Pordoi and Falzarego passes to Cortina d'Ampezzo and Lake Misurina. The Trentino tourist office also organizes guided tours and excursions by train to castles in the region.

🚌 Fees & Schedules **Calderari e Moggioli** ✉ Via Manci 46 ☎ 0461/980275.

VISITOR INFORMATION

🛈 Tourist Information **Alto Adige Tourism** ☎ 0471/999999 🖷 0471/999800 ⊕ www.suedtirol.info. **Bolzano** ✉ Piazza Walther 8 ☎ 0471/307000 🖷 0471/980128 ⊕ www.bolzano-bozen.it. **Bormio** ✉ Via Roma 131/b ☎ 0342/903300 🖷 0342/904696 ⊕ www.valtellinaonline.com. **Bressanone** ✉ Via Stazione 9 ☎ 0472/836401 🖷 0472/836067. **Brunico** ✉ Piazza Municipio 7 ☎ 0474/555722 🖷 0474/555544. **Caldaro** ✉ Piazza Mercato 8 ☎ 0471/963169 🖷 0471/963469. **Canazei** ✉ Piazza Marconi 5 ☎ 0462/601113 🖷0462/602502. **Chiusa** ✉Piazza Tinne 6 ☎0472/847424 🖷0472/847244. **Cortina d'Ampezzo** ✉ Piazzetta San Francesco 8 ☎ 0436/3231 🖷 0436/3235 ⊕ www.cortina.dolomiti.com. **Dobbiaco** ✉ Via Dolomiti 3 ☎ 0474/972132 🖷 0474/972730. **Dolomites Tourism** ☎ 0437/941148 🖷 0437/944202 ⊕ www.dolomiti.org. **Fiè allo Sciliar** ✉ Via Bolzano 4 ☎ 0471/725047 🖷 0471/725488. **Madonna di Campiglio** ✉ Via Pradalago 4 ☎ 0465/447501 🖷0465/440404 ⊕www.campiglio.to. **Merano** ✉Corso Libertà 45 ☎0473/272000 🖷 0473/235524 ⊕ www.meraninfo.it. **Naturno** ✉ Piazza Municipio 1 ☎ 0473/666077 🖷 0473/666369. **Ortisei** ✉ Via Rezia 1 ☎ 0471/796328 🖷 0471/796749. **Rovereto** ✉ Corso Rosmini 6 ☎ 0464/430363 🖷 0464/435528. **Santa Cristina** ✉ Via Chemun 9 ☎0471/793046 🖷0471/793198. **Selva Gardena** ✉Via Mëisules 213 ☎0471/795122 🖷0471/794245. **Trentino Tourism** ☎ 0461/839000 🖷 0461/260245 ⊕ www.trentino.to. **Trento** ✉ Via Manci 2 ☎ 0461/983880 🖷 0461/232426 ⊕ www.apt.trento.it. **Val Gardena Tourism** ☎ 0471/792277 🖷 0471/792235 ⊕ www.valgardena.it.

Milan, Lombardy & the Lakes

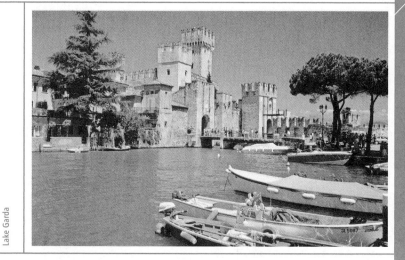

Lake Garda

WORD OF MOUTH

"Italy's Lake Maggiore is one of Europe's top vacation meccas for good reason. It's a long sliver of water ringed by Alpine scenery freckled with villas and resorts."

—PalQ

WELCOME TO MILAN, LOMBARDY & THE LAKES

Plaza and Duomo, Milan

TOP 5
Reasons to Go

1. **Lake Como:** Ferries crisscross the waters, taking you from stately villas to tiny towns.

2. **Leonardo Da Vinci's** *Last Supper*: Behold one of the world's most famous works of art.

3. **Bergamo Alta:** A funicular ride takes you up to the magnificent medieval city.

4. **Window shopping in Milan:** Italians' refined fashion sense is on full display in the famed *quadrilatero* shopping district.

5. **La Scala:** There's no better place to spend a night at the opera.

Getting Oriented

In Lombardy, jagged mountains and deep glacial lakes stretch from the Swiss border down to Milan's outskirts, where they meet the flat, fertile plain that extends from the banks of the River Po. Lake Como is north of Milan, while Lake Maggiore is to the northwest and Lake Garda is to the east. Scattered across the plains to the south are the Renaissance city-states of Pavia, Cremona, and Mantua.

La Scala, Milan

Lake Maggiore is smaller than Lake Garda and less famous than Lake Como, but with the Alps as a backdrop, it's impressively picturesque. One of the greatest pleasures here is exploring the lake's islands.

PIEDMONT

Stresa
Lago Maggiore Verbano
Varese
Orta San Giulio
Como
A26
A8
0   20 mi
0   20 km
Milan
Vigevano
Mortara
A7

Milan is Italy lived in the present tense. The country's leading city of commerce is also one of the world's fashion capitals, and there are cultural treasures here that rival those of Florence and Rome.

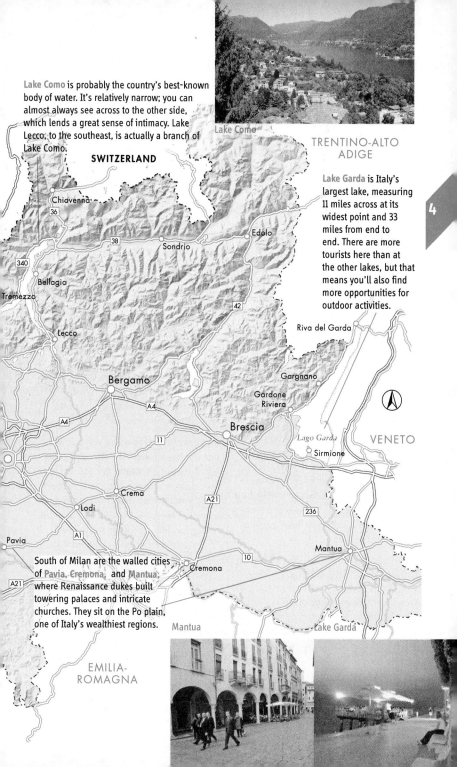

Lake Como is probably the country's best-known body of water. It's relatively narrow; you can almost always see across to the other side, which lends a great sense of intimacy. Lake Lecco, to the southeast, is actually a branch of Lake Como.

SWITZERLAND

Lake Como

TRENTINO-ALTO ADIGE

Lake Garda is Italy's largest lake, measuring 11 miles across at its widest point and 33 miles from end to end. There are more tourists here than at the other lakes, but that means you'll also find more opportunities for outdoor activities.

Chiavenna
36

Edolo

38
Sondrio

340

Bellagio

Tremezzo

42

Riva del Garda

Lecco

Bergamo

Gargnano

Gardone Riviera

A4

A4

Brescia

11

Lago Garda

VENETO

Sirmione

Crema

A21

236

Lodi

Pavia

A1

10

Mantua

South of Milan are the walled cities of Pavia, Cremona, and Mantua, where Renaissance dukes built towering palaces and intricate churches. They sit on the Po plain, one of Italy's wealthiest regions.

A21

Cremona

Mantua

Lake Garda

EMILIA-ROMAGNA

MILAN, LOMBARDY & THE LAKES PLANNER

Making the Most of Your Time

If you're visiting northern Italy, the odds are good you'll fly in and out of Milan's Malpensa airport, and for expediency you may end up spending your final night in Milan. Italy's capital of commerce isn't a top priority for most leisure travelers, but the city has a sophisticated urban appeal: its fashionable shops rival New York and Paris, its soccer teams are Italy's answer to the Yankees and the Mets, its opera performances set the standard for the world, and its art treasures are considerable. If that sounds appealing, think about giving Milan an additional day or two on your itinerary.

The biggest draw in the region, though, is the lake district. Lakes Como, Garda, Maggiore, and Orta all have long histories as travel destinations, and each has its own distinct character. If you're only spending a couple of days in the area, devote your time to the lake you think best suits your style, but if you have more time, make the rounds to two or three to get a sense of their contrasts.

Getting Around

Milan has an unmatched system of public transportation. Besides the trio of subway lines, there are dozens of bus and tram routes that connect all parts of the city. Buying an all-inclusive subway, bus, and tram pass good for 24 or 48 hours will save you the hassle of purchasing individual tickets. Taxis are expensive but reliable; they come in handy late at night.

Outside of Milan, driving is the best way to see the region. Getting almost anywhere is a snap, as several major highways intersect at Milan, all connected by the tangenziale, the road that rings the city. To get to the lakes you must exit onto well-maintained secondary roads, which have many places where you can stop and admire the view.

If you don't want to drive, you can still travel around Lombardy without a problem. Buses and trains both head out to the lakefront villages. Once you're there, you'll want to take one of the boats that crisscross the lakes themselves. For more about car, bus, and train travel, see "Essentials" at the end of this chapter.

A Night at the Opera

Attending a performance at the world's most venerated opera house, La Scala, is an unforgettable experience, regardless of whether you're an opera buff. Tickets go on sale two months in advance, and they sell out quickly. Your best bet is to order online at www.teatroallascala.org (phone orders aren't accepted). Once you're in Milan, you can check on ticket availability at the Scala box office, located in the Duomo metro station and open daily from noon to 6 PM. About 100 tickets for seats in the second gallery go on sale three hours before a performance—they're available at the ticket office of the theater itself.

Fashion Alerts

Milan becomes the world fashion capital par excellence four times a year, when the global fashion elite descend on the city for the ready-to-wear designer shows. The dates are late-February and late-September (for women) and late-June and mid-January (for men). The effect? Very little if you're outside the business, except that it's hard for mere mortals to get a taxi, a reservation in a top restaurant, or a hotel room.

Sales take place in mid-January and mid-July (dates set by law), with prices slashed by 30% to 50%. If you want the season's clothes as soon as they hit the shelves, plan your trip for mid-February or mid-August.

Supper Reservations

Reservations are required to see Leonardo da Vinci's *The Last Supper,* housed in the refectory of Milan's Santa Maria delle Grazie church. You should call as far in advance as possible to make them, particularly if you're planning to go on a weekend. For details, see the Santa Maria delle Grazie listing starting on p. 171.

Finding a Place to Stay

The hotels in Italy's wealthiest region generally cater to a clientele willing to pay for extra comfort. Many are converted from handsome old villas and have well-landscaped grounds—they can be worth visiting, even if you don't stay the night. Most of the famous lake resorts are expensive; more reasonably priced accommodations can be found in the smaller towns. Local tourism offices can be an excellent source of information about affordable accommodations. In Milan there's constant competition for rooms. Reservations are recommended year-round.

Dining & Lodging Price Categories

WHAT IT COSTS in Euros					
	$$$$	**$$$**	**$$**	**$**	**¢**
RESTAURANTS					
	over €22	€16–€22	€11–€16	€7–€11	under €7
HOTELS					
in Milan	over €290	€210–€290	€140–€210	€80–€140	under €80
Elsewhere	over €220	€160–€220	€110–€160	€70–€110	under €70

Restaurant prices are for a second course (un secondo). Hotel prices are for two people in a standard double room in high season, including tax and service.

How's the Weather?

Early summer and early fall are the best times to see the area—though October can be chilly for swimming. The throngs that descend on the lakes in July and August, particularly on weekends, make reservations absolutely necessary—especially at Lake Como, the quintessential Italian lake resort. Fewer people visit in spring and fall, and in winter the lakeside towns are deserted. Note that many of the ferry services stop running in October and recommence in May.

Lake Como

TOP PASSEGGIATA

The small-town charm of Cernobbio, at the southern end of Lake Como, is in full force when families take their evening stroll through the piazza.

IT'S TEMPTING TO DESCRIBE LOMBARDY as a region that offers something for everyone. Milan is the country's business capital and the center for everything that's up-to-the-minute. The great Renaissance cities of the Po plain—Pavia, Cremona, and Mantua—are stately and serene, embracing their past with nostalgia while at the same time keeping an eye on the present. Topping any list of the region's attractions are the lakes—glacial waters stretching out below the Alps have been praised as the closest thing to paradise by writers throughout the ages, from Virgil to Hemingway.

Millions of travelers have concurred: for sheer beauty, the lakes of northern Italy—Como, Maggiore, Garda, and Orta—have few equals. Along their shores are 18th- and 19th-century villas, exotic formal gardens, sleepy villages, and dozens of resorts that were once Europe's most fashionable, and still retain a powerful allure.

Milan can be disappointingly modern—a little too much like the place you've come to Italy to escape—but its historic buildings and art collections in many ways rival those of Florence and Rome. And if you love to shop, Milan is Mecca. It truly offers a fashion experience for every taste, from the broad Corso Buenos Aires, which has a higher ratio of stores per square foot than anywhere else in Europe, to elegant Via Montenapoleone, where a pair of cuff links can cost more than a four-course meal in a top-flight restaurant. Milan is home to global fashion giants such as Armani, Prada, and Trussardi; behind these famous names stands a host of smaller, less renowned designers who help fill all those fabulous shops.

MILAN

Updated by
Roberta
Kedzierski

Italy's business hub and crucible of chic is the country's most populous and prosperous city, serving as the capital of commerce, finance, fashion, and media. It's also Italy's transport hub, with the biggest international airport, most rail connections, and best subway system. Leonardo Da Vinci's *Last Supper* and other great works of art are here, as well as a spectacular Gothic Duomo, the finest of its kind. Milan even reigns supreme where it really counts (in the minds of many Italians), routinely trouncing the rest of the nation with its two premier soccer teams.

And yet, Milan hasn't won the battle for hearts and minds. Most tourists prefer Tuscany's hills and Venice's canals to Milan's hectic efficiency and wealthy indifference, and it's no surprise that in a country of medieval hilltop villages and skilled artisans, a city of grand boulevards and global corporations leaves visitors asking the real Italy to please stand up. They're right, of course. Milan is more European than Italian, a new buckle on an old boot, and although its old city can stand cobblestone for cobblestone against the best of them, seekers of Roman ruins and fairy-tale towns may pass. But Milan's new faces are hidden behind splendid beaux-arts facades and in luxurious 19th-century palazzos, and those lured by its world-class shopping and European sophistication enjoy the city's lively, cosmopolitan feel.

LOMBARDY THROUGH THE AGES

Lombardy has had a tumultuous history. Control by outsiders dates back more than 3,000 years, to when the Etruscans of central Italy first wandered north of the River Po. They dominated the region for centuries, to be followed by the Cenomani Gauls, then the Romans in the later days of the Republic. The region was known as Cisalpine Gaul ("Gaul this side of the Alps"), and under the rule of Augustus became a Roman province.

The decline of the Roman Empire was followed by invasion by Attila of the Huns and Theodoric of the Goths. These conquerors gave way to the Lombards, who then ceded to Charlemagne their iron crown, which became the emblem of his vast, unstable empire. Even before the bonds of the empire had begun to snap, the cities of Lombardy were erecting walls in defense against the Hungarians, and against each other.

These city-states formed the Lombard League, which in the 12th century finally defeated the German ruler Frederick Barbarossa. With the northern invaders gone, new and even bloodier strife began. In each city the Guelphs (bourgeois supporters of the popes) and the Ghibellines (noblemen loyal to the Holy Roman Empire) clashed. The city-states declined, falling under the yoke of a few powerful regional rulers. The Republic of Venice dominated Brescia and Bergamo. Mantua was ruled by the Gonzaga family, and the Visconti and Sforza families took over Como, Cremona, Milan, and Pavia.

The Battle of Pavia in 1525, in which the generals of Holy Roman Emperor Charles V defeated the French, brought on 200 years of occupation by the Spanish—who proved generally less cruel than the local tyrants. The War of the Spanish Succession in the early years of the 18th century brought in the Austrians. Napoléon and his generals defeated the Austrians at the turn of the 19th century. The Treaty of Campoformio resulted in the proclamation of the Cisalpine Republic, which soon became the Republic of Italy and then the Kingdom of Italy—which lasted only until Napoléon's defeat brought back the Austrians. In March of 1848, demonstrations in Milan took on surpising force: the Austrians were driven out of the city, and a provisional government of Milan soon became a provisional government of Lombardy. In June of the same year, Lombardy united with Sardinia—the first step toward Italian unification in 1870.

The spirit of 1848 was rekindled in 1943. Discontent with Fascism provoked workers to strike in Turin and Milan marking the beginning of the end of Fascist dominance. The Lombardy-based partisan insurrection against Mussolini and the German regime was better organized and more successful than in many other parts of the country. Indeed, Milan was liberated from the Germans by its own partisan organization before the Allied troops entered the city.

Dissatisfaction with the federal government is practically a given among Lombardy residents, and the prevailing attitude has been to ignore Rome and get on with business. It's an approach that's proven successful: Lombardy accounts for one-fifth of Italy's economy.

Virtually every invader in European history—Gaul, Roman, Goth, Longobard, and Frank—as well as a long series of rulers from France, Spain, and Austria, took a turn at ruling the city. After being completely sacked by the Goths in AD 539 and by the Holy Roman Empire under Frederick Barbarossa in 1157, Milan became one of the first independent city-states of the Renaissance. Its heyday of self-rule proved comparatively brief. From 1277 until 1500 it was ruled by the Visconti and subsequently the Sforza dynasties. These families were known, justly or not, for a peculiarly aristocratic mixture of refinement, classical learning, and cruelty, and much of the surviving grandeur of Gothic and Renaissance art and architecture is their doing. Be on the lookout in your wanderings for the Visconti family emblem—a viper, its jaws straining wide, devouring a child.

The city center is compact and walkable, while the efficient Metropolitana (subway), as well as buses and trams, provides access to locations farther afield. Driving the streets of Milan is difficult at best, and parking can be downright miserable, so leave the car behind. The **tourist office** (⊠ Via Marconi 1 ☎ 02/72524301 ⊕ www.milaninfotourist.com ☉ Mon.–Sat. 9–1 and 2–6, Sun. 9–1 and 2–5) in Piazza Duomo is an excellent place to begin your visit. Free maps on a variety of themes are available: one showing monuments, another shopping areas, another highlights of the design culture, and so on. Make sure to pick up a copy of the English-language *Hello Milano* (ask if it is not on display). As well as a comprehensive map of the city, this monthly magazine includes a day-to-day schedule of events of interest to visitors.

The Duomo & Points North

Milan's main streets radiate out from the massive Duomo, a late-Gothic cathedral that was started in 1386. Leading north is the handsome Galleria Vittorio Emanuele, an enclosed walkway that takes you to the world-famous opera house known as La Scala. Beyond are the winding streets of the Brera neighborhood, the traditional bohemian quarter. Here you'll find one of Italy's leading art galleries, as well as the academy of fine arts. Heading northeast from La Scala is Via Manzoni, which leads to the *quadrilatero della moda,* or fashion district. Its streets are lined with elegant window displays from the world's most celebrated designers—the Italians taking the lead, of course.

Leading northeast from the Duomo is Corso Vittorio Emanuele. Locals and visitors stroll along this pedestrian-only street, looking at the shop windows, buying ice cream, or stopping for a coffee at one of the sidewalk cafés. Northwest of the Duomo is Via Dante, at the top of which is the imposing outline of the Castello Sforzesco.

The Main Attractions

★ ❽ **Castello Sforzesco.** For the serious student of Renaissance military engineering, the Castello must be something of a travesty, so often has it been remodeled or rebuilt since it was begun in 1450 by the *condottiere* (hired mercenary) who founded the city's second dynastic family, Francesco Sforza, fourth duke of Milan. Though today the word "mercenary" has a pejorative ring, during the Renaissance all Italy's great

soldier-heroes were professionals hired by the cities and principalities that they served. Of them—and there were thousands—Francesco Sforza (1401–66) is considered one of the greatest, most honest, and most organized. It is said he could remember the names not only of all his men but of their horses as well. His rule signaled the enlightened age of the Renaissance, but preceded the next foreign rule by a scant 50 years.

Since the turn of the last century, the Castello has housed municipal museums devoted variously to Egyptian and other antiquities, musical instruments, paintings, and sculpture. Highlights include the **Sala delle Asse,** a frescoed room still sometimes attributed to Leonardo da Vinci (1452–1519). Michelangelo's unfinished *Rondanini Pietà* is believed to be his last work—an astounding achievement for a man nearly 90, and a moving coda to his life. Reopened in 2005, after a four-year restoration project, the *pinacoteca* (picture gallery) features paintings from medieval times to the 18th century. The 230 paintings on display include works by Antonello da Messina, Canaletto, Andrea Mantegna, and Bernardo Bellotto. ⊠ *Piazza Castello, Brera* ☎ *02/88463700* ⊕ *www. milanocastello.it* ☜ *€3, free Fri. 2–5* ☉ *Tues.–Sun. 9–5:30* Ⓜ *Cairoli.*

★ ❶ **Duomo.** This intricate Gothic structure has been fascinating and exasperating visitors and conquerors alike since it was begun by Galeazzo Visconti III (1351–1402), first duke of Milan, in 1386. Consecrated in the 15th or 16th century, it was not completed until just before the coronation of Napoléon as king of Italy in 1809. Whether or not you concur with travel writer H. V. Morton's 1964 assessment that the cathedral is "one of the mightiest Gothic buildings ever created," there is no denying that for sheer size and complexity it is unrivaled. It is the second-largest church in the world—the largest being Saint Peter's in Rome. The capacity is reckoned to be 40,000. Usually it is empty, a sanctuary from the frenetic pace of life outside and the perfect place for solitary contemplation.

The building is adorned with 135 marble spires and 2,245 marble statues. The oldest part is the **apse.** Its three colossal bays of curving and counter-curved tracery, especially the bay adorning the exterior of the stained-glass windows, should not be missed. At the end of the southern transept down the right aisle lies the **tomb of Gian Giacomo Medici.** The tomb owes some of its design to Michelangelo but was executed by Leone Leoni (1509–90) and is generally considered to be his masterpiece; it dates from the 1560s. Directly ahead is the Duomo's most famous sculpture, the gruesome but anatomically instructive figure of **San Bartolomeo** (St. Bartholomew), whose glorious martyrdom consisted of being flayed alive. It is usually said the saint stands "holding" his skin, but this is not quite accurate. It would appear more that he is luxuriating in it, much as a 1950s matron might have shown off a new fur stole.

As you enter the apse to admire those splendid windows, glance at the **sacristy doors** to the right and left of the altar. The lunette on the right dates from 1393 and was decorated by Hans von Fernach. The one on the left also dates from the 14th century and is ascribed jointly to Giacomo da Campione and Giovanni dei Grassi. Don't miss the view from the Duomo's **roof**; walk out the left (north) transept to the stairs and elevator. Sadly, air pollution drastically reduces the view on all but the rarest days. As you stand among the forest of marble pinnacles, remember that virtually every inch of this gargantuan edifice, including the roof itself, is decorated with precious white marble dragged from quarries near Lake Maggiore by Duke Visconti's team along road laid fresh for the purpose and through the newly dredged canals.

Inspection and possible repair of 12 of the northern spires means the facade facing the piazza may be shrouded in scaffolding through most of 2005, although as individual sections are restored, some scaffolding comes down. The rest of the Duomo's intricate masonry and statuary, including the gleaming, emblematic **Madonnina** perched on the highest spire, remain unencumbered. ☒ *Piazza del Duomo* ☎ *02/86463456* ⊕ *duomomilano.com* ☒ *Stairs to roof €3.50, elevator €5* ⊙ *Mid-Feb.–mid-Nov., daily 9–5:45; mid-Nov.–mid-Feb., daily 9–4:15. Closed Jan. 1, Easter Sun., Apr. 25, May 1, Dec. 25* Ⓜ *Duomo.*

Exhibits at the **Museo del Duomo** shed light on the cathedral's history and include some of the treasures removed from the exterior for preservation purposes. ☒ *Piazza del Duomo 14* ☎ *02/860358* ☒ *€6, €7 including ticket for elevator to Duomo roof* ⊙ *Daily 10–1:15 and 3–6.*

★ ❸ **Galleria Vittorio Emanuele.** This spectacular, late-19th-century glass-topped, barrel-vaulted tunnel is essentially one of the planet's earliest and most select shopping malls. Like its suburban American cousins, the Galleria Vittorio Emanuele fulfills numerous social functions. This is the city's heart, midway between the Duomo and La Scala. It teems with life, inviting people-watching from the tables that spill from the bars and restaurants, where you can enjoy an overpriced coffee. Books, records, clothing, food, pens, jewelry are all for sale, and you'll also find here Savini, one of Milan's classic restaurants.

Like the cathedral, the Galleria is cruciform in shape. Even in poor weather the great glass dome above the octagonal center is a splendid sight. And the floor mosaics are a vastly underrated source of pleasure, even if they are not to be taken too seriously. They represent Europe, Asia, Africa, and the United States; those at the entrance arch are devoted to science, industry, art, and agriculture. Be sure to follow tradition and spin your heels once or twice on the more "delicate" parts of the bull beneath your feet in the northern apse; the Milanese believe it brings good luck. ☒ *Piazza del Duomo* Ⓜ *Duomo.*

❺ **Museo Poldi-Pezzoli.** This exceptional museum opened in 1881 was once a private residence and collection, and contains not only pedigreed paintings but also porcelain, textiles, and a cabinet with scenes from Dante's life. The gem is undoubtedly the *Portrait of a Lady* by Antonio Pollaiolo (1431–98), one of the city's most prized treasures and the source of the museum's logo. The collection also includes masterpieces by Botticelli (1445–1510), Andrea Mantegna (1431–1506), Giovanni Bellini (1430–1516), and Fra Filippo Lippi (1406–69), whose uncomplicated, heartrending style won him the favor and patronage of Florence's Piero de' Medici (1416–69), son of Cosimo and father of Lorenzo il Magnifico (1449–92). ☒ *Via Manzoni 12, Brera* ☎ *02/ 794889* ⊕ *www.museopoldipezzoli.it* 🎫 €7 ⊙ *Tues.–Sun. 10–6. Closed Jan. 1, Easter Sun., Apr. 25, May 1, Aug. 15, Nov. 1, Dec. 8, Dec. 25–26* Ⓜ *Montenapoleone.*

★ ❼ **Pinacoteca di Brera** (Brera Gallery). The collection here is star-studded even by Italian standards. The entrance hall (Room I) displays 20th-century sculpture and painting, including Carlo Carrà's (1881–1966) confident, stylish response to the schools of cubism and surrealism. The museum has nearly 40 other rooms, arranged in chronological order—pace yourself.

The somber, moving *Cristo Morto* (*Dead Christ*) by Mantegna (1430–1506) dominates Room VI, with its sparse palette of umber and its foreshortened perspective. Mantegna's shocking, almost surgical precision—in the rendering of Christ's wounds, the face propped up on a pillow, the day's growth of beard—tells of an all-too-human agony. It is one of Renaissance painting's most quietly wondrous achievements, finding an unsuspected middle ground between the excesses of conventional gore and beauty in representing the Passion's saddest moment.

Room XXIV offers two additional highlights of the gallery. Raphael's (1483–1520) *Sposalizio della Vergine,* with its mathematical composition and precise, alternating colors, portrays the betrothal of Mary and Joseph (who, though older than the other men gathered, wins her hand when the rod he is holding miraculously blossoms). *La Vergine con il Bambino e Santi* (*Madonna with Child and Saints*), by Piero della Francesca (1420–92), is an altarpiece commissioned by Federico da Montefeltro (shown kneeling, in full armor, before the Virgin); it was intended for a church to house the Duke's tomb. The ostrich egg hanging from the apse, depending on whom you ask, either commemorates the miracle of his fertility—Federico's wife died months after giving birth to a long-awaited male heir—or alludes to his appeal for posthumous mercy, the egg symbolizing the saving power of grace. ☒ *Via Brera 28* ☎ *02/722631* ⊕ *www.brera.beniculturali.it* 🎫 €5 ⊙ *Tues.–Sun. 8:30–7:15; last admission 45 mins before closing. Closed Jan. 1, May 1, Dec. 25* Ⓜ *Montenapoleone.*

❹ **Teatro alla Scala.** You need know nothing of opera to sense that, like Carnegie Hall, La Scala is closer to a cathedral than an auditorium. Here Verdi established his reputation and Maria Callas sang her way into opera lore. It looms as a symbol—both for the performer who dreams of singing here and for the opera buff who knows every note of *Rigoletto* by heart. Audiences are notoriously demanding and are apt to jeer performers who do not measure up. The opera house was closed after destruction by Allied bombs in 1943, reopened at a performance led by Arturo Toscanini in 1946, and closed again in 2002 for long-overdue renovations. The massive modern reconstruction project, which left only the exterior shell standing, is now complete and the opera house officially reopened on December 7, 2004. This is the traditional first night of the opera season, which coincides with the feast day of Saint Ambrose, Milan's patron saint.

VOICES OF ITALY

Giampaolo Abbondio
gallery owner, Milan

Giampaolo Abbondio, 38, is a rising star in Milan's contemporary art scene. Although his gallery, **Galleria Pack** (✉ Foro Buonaparte 60 ☎02/86996395 ⊕www.galleriapack.com), has only been open for four years, he has attracted a number of important young artists to his stable. Giampaolo is a Milanese by birth, and unabashedly proud of what he calls "the least Italian city in Italy."

Q: Giampaolo, what exactly do you mean when you call Milan the least Italian city in Italy?

A: Well, it's not, of course. We're still Italians. But Milan has been a crossroads for many years, a meeting place from which Italy can access the rest of Europe, and from which the rest of Europe can be introduced to Italy. I think that has made Milan a little more European than other parts of the country. Some of that is good: we have excellent public transportation, stores that are open all day, things like that. And some of that is not so good: they say we work too much, we don't take the time to enjoy life like they do in the rest of Italy. But I'm sure that's clearer to Italians than from a foreigner's point of view. I mean, we still make an excellent risotto . . .

Q: Most people don't think of Milan when they're thinking of great Italian art; they think of places like Rome, Florence, and Venice. Are they making a mistake?

A: Of course! I mean, it's true that Milan isn't the most "artistic" place in Italy. It has a very strong private sector but a weak public sector, meaning there is not a lot of money for museums and other public cultural works. But it also means that there's a lot of private investment in art and culture here in Milan. Rome may have the museums, but Milan has the more fertile art scene.

Q: What are some of the features of Milan's contemporary art activities that a visitor to Milan should know about?

A: Well, the P.A.C., or **Padiglione di Arte Contemporanea** (✉ Via Palestro 14 ☎ 02/76009085 ⊕ www.comune.milano.it/pac). The P.A.C. is a public space that hosts a constantly changing series of temporary shows. It is a kind of city gallery that does four or five important shows a year. Another is the **Palazzo della Triennale** (✉ Via Alemagna 6 ☎ 02/724341 ⊕ www.triennale.it), which, like the Stazione Centrale, is interesting for its classic Fascist architecture no matter what's going on inside. And the Triennale is located in the middle of Parco Sempione, which has some important public artworks including a fountain by De Chirico and an amphitheater by Arman. And of course, at least as far as I'm concerned, no visit to Milan would be complete without a tour of the important contemporary art galleries! Besides my gallery, there are the **Emi Fontana** (✉ Viale Bligny 42 ☎ 02/58322237), **Salvatore & Carolina Ala** (✉ Via Monte di Pietà 1 ☎ 02/8900901), **Massimo De Carlo** (✉ Via Ventura 4 ☎ 02/70003987 ⊕ www.massimodecarlo.it), and **1,000 Eventi** (✉ Via Porro Lambertenghi 3 ☎02/45478297). This is the best way to avoid lines at the museums . . . you go see the art in a gallery before it gets too famous!

4

If you are lucky enough to be here during the opera season, which runs for approximately six months, do whatever is necessary to attend. Tickets go on sale two months before the first performance, and are usually sold out the same day. Hearing opera sung in the magical acoustic of La Scala is an unparalleled experience. ☒ *Piazza della Scala* ☎ *02/72003744* ⊕ *www.teatroallascala.org* Ⓜ *Duomo*.

At **Museo Teatrale alla Scala** you can admire librettos, posters, costumes, instruments, and design sketches for the theater, curtains, and viewing box decorations, along with an explanation of the reconstruction project and several interactive exhibits. A highlight is the collection of antique gramophones and phonographs. ☒ *Piazza della Scala* ☎ *02 43353521* ☒ *€5* ☉ *Daily 9–Noon, 1:30–5.*

Also Worth Seeing

❷ **Battistero Paleocristiano.** Beneath the Duomo's piazza lies this baptistery ruin dating from the 4th century. Although opinion remains divided, it is widely believed to be where Ambrose, Milan's first bishop and patron saint, baptized Augustine. Tickets are available at the kiosk inside the cathedral. ☒ *Piazza del Duomo, enter through Duomo* ☎ *02/86463456* ☒ *€1.50* ☉ *Daily 9:30–5:15* Ⓜ *Duomo.*

☾ ❻ **Museo Civico di Storia Naturale** (Municipal Natural History Museum). Exhibits here appeal to animal and nature lovers, and anyone else who can appreciate stilted arrangements of narwhals, elephant seals, and bug-besieged hippopotami. It's on the eastern edge of the **Giardini Pubblici** (Public Gardens), an outlet for active young children. ☒ *Corso Venezia 55, Porta Venezia* ☎ *02/88463337* ⊕ *www.assodidatticamuseale.it* ☒ *€3* ☉ *Tues.–Sun. 9–6, last admission 30 mins before closing* Ⓜ *Palestro.*

South & West of the Duomo

If the part of the city to the north of the Duomo is dominated by its shops, the section to the south is famous for its works of art. The most famous is *Il Cenacolo*—known in English as *The Last Supper*. If you have time for nothing else, make sure you see this masterwork, which has now been definitively restored, after many, many years of work. Reservations will be needed to see this fresco, housed in the refectory of Santa Maria delle Grazie. Make these before you depart for Italy, so you can plan the rest of your time in Milan.

There are other gems as well. Via Torino, the ancient road for Turin, leads to a half-hidden treasure: Bramante's Renaissance masterpiece, the church of San Satiro. At the intersection of Via San Vittore and Via Carducci is the medieval Basilica di Sant'Ambrogio, named for Milan's patron saint. Another lovely church southeast of Sant'Ambrogio along Via de Amicis is San Lorenzo Maggiore. It's also known as San Lorenzo alle Colonne because of the 16 columns running across the facade.

The Main Attractions

⓭ **Basilica di Sant'Ambrogio** (Basilica of St. Ambrose). Noted for its medieval architecture, the church was consecrated by St. Ambrose in AD 387 and is the model for all Lombard Romanesque churches. The church is often closed for weddings on Saturdays. ☒ *Piazza Sant'Ambrogio 15* ☎ *02/86450895* ☉ *Mon.–Sat. 7–noon and 2:30–7, Sun. 3–8* Ⓜ *Sant'Ambrogio.*

need a break? A bit overcrowded at night, the **Bar Magenta** (☒ Via Carducci 13, at Corso Magenta, Sant'Ambrogio ☎ 02/8053808) can be a good stop en route during the day. Beyond coffee at all hours, lunch, and beer, the real attraction is its casual but civilized, quintessentially Milanese ambience. It's open until 2 AM.

❿ Pinacoteca Ambrosiana. This museum, founded in the 17th century by Cardinal Federico Borromeo, is one of the city's treasures. Here you can contemplate works of art such as Caravaggio's *Basket of Fruit,* prescient in its realism, and Raphael's awesome preparatory drawing for *The School of Athens* that hangs in the Vatican, as well as paintings by Leonardo, Botticelli, Luini, Titian, and Brueghel. The adjoining library, the Biblioteca Ambrosiana, dates from 1609, and is thought to be the oldest public library in Italy. Admission these days is limited to scholars. ☒ *Piazza Pio XI 2, near Duomo* ☎ *02/806921* ⊕ *www.ambrosiana.it* ☞ *€7.50* ☉ *Tues.–Sun. 10–5:30. Closed Jan. 1, Easter Sun., May 1, Dec. 25.*

⓯ San Lorenzo Maggiore. Sixteen ancient Roman columns line the front of this sanctuary; 4th-century paleochristian mosaics survive in the Cappella di Sant'Aquilino (Chapel of St. Aquilinus). ☒ *Corso di Porta Ticinese 39, Porta Ticinese* ☎ *02/89404129* ☞ *Mosaics €2* ☉ *Daily 8:30–12:30 and 2:30–6:30.*

★ ❾ San Satiro. First built in 876, this architectural gem was later perfected by Bramante (1444–1514), demonstrating his command of proportion and perspective, keynotes of Renaissance architecture. Bramante tricks the eye with a famous optical illusion that makes a small interior seem extraordinarily spacious and airy, while accommodating a beloved 13th-century fresco. ☒ *Via Torino 9, near Duomo* ☉ *Weekdays 7:30–11:30 and 3:30–6:30, weekends 9–noon and 3:30–7.*

★ ⓬ Santa Maria delle Grazie. Leonardo da Vinci's *The Last Supper,* housed in the church and former Dominican monastery of Santa Maria delle Grazie, has had an almost unbelievable history of bad luck and neglect—its near destruction in an American bombing raid in August 1943 was only the latest chapter in a series of misadventures, including, if one 19th-century source is to be believed, being whitewashed over by monks. Well-meant but disastrous attempts at restoration have done little to rectify the problem of the work's placement: it was executed on a wall unusually vulnerable to climatic dampness. Yet Leonardo chose to work slowly and patiently in oil pigments—which demand dry plaster—instead of proceeding hastily on wet plaster according to the conventional fresco technique. Novelist Aldous Huxley (1894–1963) called it "the saddest work of art in the world." After years of restorers' patiently shifting from one square centimeter to another, Leonardo's masterpiece is free of the shroud of scaffolding—and centuries of retouching, grime, and dust. Astonishing clarity and luminosity have been regained. *Reservations are required* to view the work; call several days ahead for weekday visits and several weeks in advance for a weekend visit. The reservations office is open 9 AM–6 PM weekdays and 9 AM–2 PM on Saturday. Viewings are in 15-minute slots.

Despite Leonardo's carefully preserved preparatory sketches in which the apostles are clearly labeled by name, there still remains some small debate about a few identities in the final arrangement. But there can be no mistaking Judas, small and dark, his hand calmly reaching forward to the bread, isolated from the terrible confusion that has taken the hearts of the others. One critic, Frederick Hartt, offers an elegantly terse explanation for why the composition works: it combines "dramatic confusion" with "mathematical order." Certainly, the amazingly skillful and unobtrusive repetition of threes—in the windows, in the grouping of the figures, and in their placement—adds a mystical aspect to what at first seems simply the perfect observation of spontaneous human gesture.

> ### WORD OF MOUTH
>
> "What I loved about Milan was: attending a concert at La Scala and taking their backstage tour; walking amidst the marble spires on the roof of the Duomo on a sunny day, gazing at the Dolomites in the distance (a definite wow!); window shopping in the too-chic-for-words Via Montenapoleone area; and seeing the *Last Supper*."
> —Maribel

The painting was executed in what was the order's refectory, which is now referred to as the **Cenacolo Vinciano.** Take a moment to visit Santa Maria delle Grazie itself. It's a handsome church, with a fine dome, which Bramante added along with a cloister about the time that Leonardo was commissioned to paint *The Last Supper.* If you're wondering how two such giants came to be employed decorating and remodeling the refectory and church of a comparatively modest religious order, and not, say, the Duomo, the answer lies in the ambitious but largely unrealized plan to turn Santa Maria delle Grazie into a magnificent Sforza family mausoleum. Though Ludovico il Moro Sforza (1452–1508), seventh duke of Milan, was but one generation away from the founding of the Sforza dynasty, he was its last ruler. Two years after Leonardo finished *The Last Supper,* Ludovico was defeated by Louis XII and spent the remaining eight years of his life in a French dungeon. ⊠ *Piazza Santa Maria delle Grazie 2, off Corso Magenta, Sant'Ambrogio* ☎ *02/89421146, weekdays. 9–6, Sat. 9–2* ✉ *€6.50 plus €1.50 reservation fee* ◯ *Tues.–Sun. 8–7:30; last entry 6:45. Closed Jan. 1* Ⓜ *Cadorna.*

Also Worth Seeing

⓫ **Museo Civico Archeologico** (Municipal Archaeological Museum). Housed in a former monastery, this museum has some enlightening relics from Milan's Roman past—from everyday utensils and jewelry to several fine examples of mosaic pavement. ⊠ *Corso Magenta 15, Sant'Ambrogio* ☎ *02/86450011* ✉ *€2, free Fri. 2–5* ◯ *Tues.–Sun. 9–5:30. Closed Jan. 1, May 1, Dec. 25* Ⓜ *Cadorna.*

 ⓮ **Museo Nazionale della Scienza e Tecnica** (National Museum of Science and Technology). This museum houses an extensive, eccentric collection of engineering achievements, from metal-processing equipment to full-size locomotives. But the highlights are undoubtedly the exhibits based on the inventive technical drawings of Leonardo da Vinci. On the second floor a collection of models based on these sketches is artfully displayed, with Leonardo's paintings offering striking counterpoint overhead. Explanations are not offered in English, leaving you to ponder possible purposes for the contraptions. On the ground level—in the hallway between the courtyards—is a room featuring interactive, moving models of the famous *vite aerea* (aerial screw) and *ala battente* (beating wing), thought to be forerunners of the modern helicopter and airplane, respectively. ⊠ *Via San Vittore 21, Sant'Ambrogio* ☎ *02/48555200* ⊕ *www. museoscienza.org* 🖅 *€7* ☼ *Tues.–Fri. 9:30–4:50, weekends 9:30–6:20. Closed Jan. 1, Dec. 25* Ⓜ *Sant'Ambrogio.*

16 **Navigli district.** In medieval times, a network of *navigli*, or canals, crisscrossed the city. Almost all have been covered over, but two—Naviglio Grande and Naviglio Pavese—are still navigable. Once a down-at-heel neighborhood, the Navigli district has been gentrified over the last 20 years. Humble workshops have been replaced by trendy boutiques, art galleries, cafés, bars, and restaurants. Check out the antiques fair on the last Sunday of the month. ⊠ *South of Corso Porta Ticinese, Porta Genova* Ⓜ *Porta Genova.*

Where to Eat

★ **$$$$** ✕ **Cracco-Peck.** When a renowned local chef (Carlo Cracco) joined forces with the city's top gourmet food store (Peck), the results were not long in coming. Within three years, Cracco-Peck boasted two Michelin stars. The dining room is done in an elegant style that favors cool earth tones. Specialties include Milanese classics revisited—Cracco's take on saffron risotto and breaded veal cutlet should not be missed. Be sure to save room for the light, steam-cooked tiramisu. If you can't decide, opt for the gourmet menu (€88 for six courses, excluding wine). ⊠ *Via Victor Hugo 4, near Duomo* ☎ *02/876774* ⌂ *Reservations essential* ⊟ *AE, DC, MC, V* ☼ *No lunch Sat. Closed Sun., 10 days in Jan., and 2 wks in Aug. No dinner Sat. in July and Aug.* Ⓜ *Duomo.*

★ **$$$$** ✕ **Don Carlos.** This restaurant, in the Grand Hotel et de Milan, is nothing like its indecisive operatic namesake (whose betrothed was stolen by his father). Flavors are bold, their presentation precise and full of flair: broiled red mullet floats on a lacy layer of crispy leek. Walls are saturated with sketches of the theater, and the aria recordings are every bit as well chosen as the wine list, setting the perfect stage for discreet business negotiation or, better yet, refined romance. A gourmet menu costs €65 for five courses, excluding wine. ⊠ *Grand Hotel et de Milan, Via Manzoni 29, Duomo* ☎ *02/723141* ⌂ *Reservations essential* ⊟ *AE, DC, MC, V* ☼ *Closed Aug. No lunch* Ⓜ *Montenapoleone.*

★ **$$$$** ✕ **L'Antica Osteria del Ponte.** Rich, imaginative seasonal cuisine composed according to the inspired whims of chef Ezio Santin is reason enough to make your way 20 km (12 mi) southwest of Milan to one of Italy's finest restaurants. The setting is a traditional country inn, where a wood fire warms the rustic interior in winter. The menu changes regularly; in

EATING WELL IN LOMBARDY

Unlike most other Italian regions, Lombardy traditionally exhibits a northern European preference for butter rather than oil as its cooking medium, which imparts a rich and distinctive flavor to the cuisine. *Alla milanese*—Milanese-style cooking—usually means the food is dipped in egg and bread crumbs mixed with grated Parmesan, then sautéed in butter. One of the most popular specialties here, osso buco, is almost always paired with risotto, which the alla milanese preparation enriches with chicken broth and saffron.

The lakes are a good source of fish, particularly trout and pike. Gorgonzola, a strong, creamy, veined cheese, and panettone, a sweet yeast bread with raisins, citron, and anise, both hail from the Milan area and can be found throughout Lombardy. The most rewarding wines of the region, worth searching wine lists for, are the red Valtellina Superiore and Oltrepò Pavese, as well as the delicious light sparkling whites from the Franciacorta area.

fall, wild porcini mushrooms are among the favored ingredients. ⌧ *Cassinetta di Lugagnano, 3 km (2 mi) north of Abbiategrasso* ☎ *02/ 9420034* ⌕ *Reservations essential* ▭ *AE, DC, MC, V* ⊗ *Closed Sun., Mon., Dec. 25–Jan. 12, and Aug.*

$$$–$$$$ ✕ **Antica Trattoria della Pesa.** Fin-de-siècle furnishings, dark-wood paneling, and old-fashioned lamps still look much as they must have when this eatery opened 100 years ago. It's authentic Old Milan, and the menu is right in line, offering risotto, minestrone, and osso buco. Sample the *riso al salto con rognone trifolato,* which is fried rice with thinly sliced kidney. In winter, *polenta* is the best choice. ⌧ *Viale Pasubio 10, Porta Volta* ☎ *02/6555741* ▭ *AE, DC, MC, V* ⊗ *Closed Sun., Aug., and Dec. 24–Jan. 6* Ⓜ *Porta Garibaldi.*

$$$–$$$$ ✕ **Boeucc.** Milan's oldest restaurant, opened in 1696, is on the same square as novelist Alessandro Manzoni's house, not far from La Scala. With fluted columns, chandeliers, thick carpets, and a garden, it has come a long way from its basement origins (*boeucc,* pronounced "birch," is old Milanese for *buco,* or "hole"). You'll savor such dishes as penne *al branzino e zucchini* (with sea bass and zucchini). For desert, try the *gelato di castagne con zabaglione caldo* (chestnut ice cream with hot zabaglione). ⌧ *Piazza Belgioioso 2, Scala* ☎ *02/76020224* ⌕ *Reservations essential* ▭ *AE* ⊗ *Closed Sat., Easter Sun. and Mon., Aug., and Dec. 24–Jan. 4. No lunch Sun.* Ⓜ *Montenapoleone, Duomo.*

$$$–$$$$ ✕ **Joia.** At this haute-cuisine vegetarian restaurant near Piazza della Repubblica, delicious dishes are artistically prepared by chef Pietro Leemann. The ever-changing menu offers dishes such as ravioli with basil, potatoes, pine nuts, and crisp green beans. The dishes all have names, such as the onomatopoeic soup called "blub." In the depths of this thick mushroom and asparagus soup is an air bubble that makes a distinctive sound when it comes to the surface. Multicourse menus range from €50 to €95, excluding wine. ⌧ *Via Panfilo Castaldi 18, Porta Venezia*

☎ *02/29522124* ▤ *AE, DC, MC, V* ⊘ *Closed Sun., 3 wks in Aug., and Dec. 24–Jan. 7. No lunch Sat.* Ⓜ *Repubblica.*

$$$–$$$$ ✕ **Nobu.** From a minimalist corner of the Armani mini mall, Milan's Nobu serves the same delicious Japanese-Peruvian fusion as its siblings in the world's other culinary capitals. Cocktails, appetizers, and beautiful people can be found at the ground-floor bar, well worth a visit even if you're not dining upstairs. ✉ *Via Pisoni, 1, corner of Via Manzoni 31, Quadrilatero* ☎ *02/72318645* ⌕ *Reservations essential* ▤ *AE, DC, MC, V* ⊘ *No lunch Sun., Mon.* Ⓜ *Montenapoleone.*

$$$–$$$$ ✕ **Savini.** Classic, classy Savini, in the east wing of Galleria Vittorio Emanuele, is a Milanese institution, with red carpets and cut-glass chandeliers characteristic of its late-19th-century roots. Stick with the standards: the Milanese specialty risotto *al salto* (cooked as a pancake, grilled in the pan) is excellent here, as are the *cotoletta di vitello* (veal cutlet) and osso buco. Fish is also a specialty; try the thinly sliced carpaccio of sea bass. ✉ *Galleria Vittorio Emanuele, Duomo* ☎ *02/72003433* ▤ *AE, DC, MC, V* ⊘ *Closed Sun., Jan. 1–6, Easter Sun. and Mon., Aug. 6–31* Ⓜ *Duomo.*

$$–$$$$ ✕ **La Terrazza.** An office building at the edge of the fashion district is home to this stylish eatery where contemporary design dominates both food and decor. Well-dressed business executives don't seem to appreciate the inventive "Mediterranean sushi," which uses pearl barley instead of rice and incorporates pesto, blood oranges, or olive tapenade. A nine-piece sampler is about €21. In warmer weather, the scene shifts to the terrace, where you can see the treetops of the nearby Giardini Pubblici. Take-away is also available. ✉ *Via Palestro 2, Quadrilatero* ☎ *02/76002277* ▤ *AE, DC, MC, V* ⊘ *Closed weekends and last 3 wks in Aug.* Ⓜ *Turati, Palestro.*

$$–$$$$ ✕ **Trattoria Montina.** Twin brothers Maurizio and Roberto Montina have
Fodor'sChoice turned this restaurant into a local favorite. Don't be fooled by the "trat-
★ toria" name—Chef Roberto creates exquisite modern Italian dishes such as warmed bruschetta with brie and prosciutto, while Maurizio moves around the restaurant chatting and taking orders. Try the *frittura impazzita,* a wild-and-crazy mix of delicately fried seafood. The warm chocolate and pear pie also comes highly recommended. ✉ *Via Procaccini 54, Procaccini* ☎ *02/3490498* ▤ *AE, DC, MC, V* ⊘ *Closed Sun., Aug., and 2 wks in Jan. No lunch Mon.* Ⓜ *Trams 1, 19, 29, 33.*

$$–$$$ ✕ **La Libera.** Although this establishment in the heart of Brera calls itself a *birraria con cucina* (beer cellar with kitchen), locals come here for excellent evening meals in relaxed surroundings. A soft current of jazz and sylvan decor soothe the ripple of conversation. The creative cooking varies with the season, but could include *linguine al pescato* (pasta with a fish sauce), *fritto di gamberi, zucchine e totanetti* (fried shrimp, zucchini, and baby squid), or *rognone alla senape* (veal kidneys cooked in mustard). ✉ *Via Palermo 21, Brera* ☎ *02/8053603/02 86462773* ▤ *AE, DC, MC, V* ⊘ *Closed Dec. 25, Jan. 1, Aug. 15. No lunch* Ⓜ *Moscova.*

$–$$$ ✕ **Trattoria Milanese.** Between the Duomo and the Basilica di Sant'Ambrogio, this small, popular trattoria has been run by the same family in the same location since 1933. It's invariably crowded, especially at dinner, when the regulars love to linger. Food is classic regional in approach; good choices include risotto and cotoletta alla Milanese. ✉ *Via Santa Marta 11, near Duomo* ☎ *02/86451991* ▭ *AE, DC, MC, V* ☉ *Closed Tues., July 15–Sept. 1, and Dec. 24–Jan. 6* Ⓜ *Duomo, Cordusio, Missori.*

★ **$$** ✕ **Da Abele.** If you love risotto, then make a beeline for this neighborhood trattoria. The superb risotto dishes change with the season, and there may be just two or three on the menu at any time. It is tempting to try them all. The setting is relaxed, the service informal, the prices strikingly reasonable. Outside the touristy center of town but quite convenient by subway, this trattoria is invariably packed with locals. ✉ *Via Temperanza 5, Loreto* ☎ *02/2613855* ▭ *AE, DC, MC, V* ☉ *Closed Mon., late July–late Aug., and Dec. 15–Jan. 7. No lunch* Ⓜ *Pasteur.*

$–$$ ✕ **La Bruschetta.** This tiny, bustling first-class pizzeria near the Duomo serves specialties from Tuscany and other parts of Italy. The wood oven is in full view, so you can see your pizza cooking in front of you, although there are plenty of nonpizza dishes available, too, such as spaghetti *alle cozze e vongole* (with clam and mussel sauce) and grilled and skewered meats. ✉ *Piazza Beccaria 12, Duomo* ☎ *02/8692494* ▭ *AE, MC, V* ☉ *Closed Mon., 3 wks in Aug., and late Dec.–early Jan.* Ⓜ *Duomo.*

¢–$$ ✕ **Al Rifugio Pugliese.** Just outside the center of town, this is a fun place to sample specialties from the Puglia region of southern Italy. These include homemade *orecchiette* (a small, ear-shape pasta) with a variety of sauces. There is a choice of 60 first courses, as well as plenty of vegetable and fish dishes. At lunch, the buffet is a good deal. ✉ *Via Costanza 2, corner of Via Boni 16, Fiera* ☎ *02/48000917* ▭ *AE, DC, MC, V* ☉ *Closed Aug. 5–25 and late Dec.–early Jan.* Ⓜ *Wagner.*

¢–$ ✕ **Pizza Ok.** Pizza is almost the only item on the menu at this popular spot near Corso Buenos Aires, but it's very good and the dining experience will be easy on your pocketbook. Possibilities for toppings seem endless. ✉ *Via Lambro 15, Porta Venezia* ☎ *02/29401272* ▭ *No credit cards* ☉ *Closed Aug. and Dec. 24–Jan. 7. No lunch Sun.* Ⓜ *Porta Venezia.*

¢–$ ✕ **Taverna Morigi.** This dusky, wood-panel wine bar near the stock exchange is the perfect spot to enjoy a glass of wine with cheese and cold cuts. At lunch, pasta dishes and select entrées are available; pasta is the only hot dish served in the evening. Platters of cheese and coldcuts are always available; if you're coming for a meal, a reservation is a good idea. ✉ *Via Morigi 8, Sant'Ambrogio* ☎ *02/86450880* ▭ *AE, DC, MC, V* ☉ *Closed Sun. and Aug. No lunch Sat.* Ⓜ *Cairoli.*

Where to Stay

$$$$ ▦ **Carlton-Baglioni.** If you're in Milan to shop in the fashion district, this hotel is an ideal base. It's light and airy, with double-glazed windows, a parking garage, and lots of little touches such as complimentary chocolates and liqueurs to make up for the rather functional rooms. Some have terraces large enough for a table, a chair, and a shrub in a pot. ✉ *Via Senato 5, Quadrilatero, 20121* ☎ *02/77077* 🖷 *02/783300* ⊕ *www. baglionihotels.com* ⇱ *92 rooms* ᗧ *Restaurant, room service, minibars, cable TV, bar, laundry service, convention center, parking (fee), no-smoking rooms* ▭ *AE, DC, MC, V.*

$$$$ ☒ **Four Seasons.** The elegant restoration of a 15th-century monastery in the middle of Milan's most exclusive shopping district has produced a precious gem—for which you'll pay dearly. The hotel blends European sophistication with American comfort. In addition to opulent marble bathrooms, the rooms are individually decorated to maintain the complex's classic feel. Modern amenities are juxtaposed with antique furniture: you'll find Internet access alongside your four-poster bed. Most rooms face a quiet central courtyard. ⊠ *Via Gesù 6–8, Quadrilatero, 20121* ☎ *02/7708167* 🖷 *02/77085000* ⊕ *www.fourseasons.com* ⤳ *77 rooms, 41 suites* ⚙ *2 restaurants, room service, minibars, cable TV, fitness center, bar, laundry service, Internet, business services, meeting rooms, parking, no-smoking rooms* ⊟ *AE, DC, MC, V* ⦿| *EP* Ⓜ *Montenapoleone.*

$$$$ ☒ **Grand Hotel et de Milan.** This elegant hotel near La Scala opened its doors in 1863 and has served as a home away from home for everyone from old-world nobility to modern glitterati. (Giuseppe Verdi commandeered a suite here for 20 years.) The rooms are named for the famous people who have stayed in them, and decorated tastefully with corresponding period furniture. The hotel's bar and lounge offer late-19th-century charm, with marble, tapestries, and verdant palms. Make sure to dine at Don Carlos. ⊠ *Via Manzoni 29, Scala, 20121* ☎ *02/723141* 🖷 *02/86460861* ⊕ *www.grandhoteletdemilan.it* ⤳ *87 rooms, 8 suites* ⚙ *Restaurant, room service, minibars, cable TV, bar, laundry service, parking (fee), no-smoking rooms* ⊟ *AE, DC, MC, V* ⦿| *EP* Ⓜ *Montenapoleone.*

★ $$$$ ☒ **The Gray.** At this small luxury hotel you get the best of everything, from location to amenities—all for a price. The interiors are decorated by famed Italian designer Guido Ciompi (who handles Gucci boutiques the world over). The atmosphere is trendy chic, from bottom-lighted tables in the hotel restaurant to patterns of laser light that play across the walls of the lobby. Rooms come equipped with everything from plasma TVs to specially designed oversize toiletries. The entire facility is equipped for high-speed wireless Internet. ⊠ *Via San Raffaele 6, near Duomo, 20121* ☎ *02/7208951* 🖷 *02/866526* ⊕ *www.sinahotels.it* ⤳ *21 rooms* ⚙ *Restaurant, room service, minibars, cable TV, bar, laundry service, Wi-Fi, business services, no-smoking rooms* ⊟ *AE, DC, MC, V* ⦿| *EP* Ⓜ *Duomo.*

★ $$$$ ☒ **Park Hyatt Milano.** This hotel provides every luxury Hyatt prides itself in, all smack in the city's historic center. Rooms have high ceilings, spacious bathrooms, and pleasant light colors that brighten even the gloomiest Milan day. Although the original 19th-century building's facade is intact, the interiors have been completely renovated, including a skylit internal lounge, created from what was once the courtyard, that's a marvel. The staff is courteous to the point of clairvoyance, and the hotel restaurant serves excellent Italian as well as Continental fare. ⊠ *Via Tommaso Grossi 1, near Duomo, 20121* ☎ *02/88211234* 🖷 *02/88211235* ⊕ *www. milan.park.hyatt.com* ⤳ *117 rooms* ⚙ *Restaurant, room service, minibars, cable TV, health club, bar, laundry service, business services, meeting rooms, no-smoking rooms* ⊟ *AE, DC, MC, V* ⦿| *EP* Ⓜ *Duomo.*

★ $$$$ ☒ **Principe di Savoia.** Here you'll find all the trappings of an exquisite hotel: lavish mirrors, drapes, and carpets, and gracious bedrooms with eclectic fin-de-siècle furnishings. A newer wing, added when the Principe took over the neighboring Duca di Milan, has "English style" junior suites. The hotel's newly refurbished Galleria restaurant serves outstanding contemporary Italian cuisine under executive chef Paola Budel. The Caffè Doney serves lighter meals. The two are linked by a covered veranda. The presidential suite features its own marble pool. ⊠ *Piazza della Repubblica 17, Porta Nuova, 20124* ☎ *02/62301* 🖷 *02/653799* ⊕ *www.hotelprincipedisavoia.com* ⟿ *278 rooms, 126 suites ♿ 2 restaurants, room service, minibars, cable TV, health club, bar, laundry service, business services, convention center, meeting rooms, no-smoking rooms* ▭ *AE, DC, MC, V* ⦿I *EP* Ⓜ *Repubblica.*

$$$–$$$$ ▦ **Grand Hotel Duomo.** The location of this elegant, modern hotel is so central that if you look out of a front-facing window you'll find a Duomo gargoyle staring back at you. The comfortable, spacious rooms and suites are done in shades of gold, cream, and brown. ⊠ *Via San Raffaele 1, near Duomo, 20121* ☎ *02/88331* 🖷 *02/86462027* ⊕ *www.grandhotelduomo.com* ⟿ *162 rooms ♿ 3 restaurants, room service, minibars, cable TV, bar, laundry service, business services, meeting rooms, parking (fee), no-smoking rooms* ▭ *AE, DC, MC, V* ⦿I *EP* Ⓜ *Duomo.*

$$$–$$$$ ▦ **Pierre Milano.** No expense was spared to furnish each room of this intimate luxury hotel in a different style, with color-coordinated fabrics and both modern and antique furniture. Everything is electronic: you can open the curtains, turn off the lights, get personal messages on your TV screen—all at the touch of a button. It's on the inner beltway, near the medieval basilica of Sant'Ambrogio. ⊠ *Via de Amicis 32, Sant'Ambrogio, 20123* ☎ *02/72000581* 🖷 *02/8052157* ⊕ *www.hotelpierremilano.it* ⟿ *51 rooms ♿ Restaurant, room service, in-room safes, minibars, cable TV, bar, laundry service, parking (fee), no-smoking rooms* ▭ *AE, DC, MC, V* ⦿I *BP* Ⓜ *Sant'Ambrogio.*

$$$–$$$$ ▦ **Westin Palace.** Milan's premier business hotel offers comfort and connectivity, with high-speed Internet access in every room. Don't be fooled by the functional 1950s-era exterior: rooms are decorated with Empire-style antiques, and bathrooms are lined with Issoire green and Portugal pink marble in a mosaic effect. ⊠ *Piazza della Repubblica 20, Porta Nuova, 20124* ☎ *02/63361* 🖷 *02/63366337* ⊕ *www.westin.com/palacemilan* ⟿ *232 rooms ♿ 2 restaurants, room service, in-room safes, minibars, cable TV, in-room data ports, bar, laundry service, Internet, business services, meeting rooms, parking (fee), no-smoking rooms* ▭ *AE, DC, MC, V* ⦿I *EP* Ⓜ *Repubblica.*

$$$ ▦ **Hotel Spadari al Duomo.** This intimate boutique hotel near the Duomo and the Pinacoteca Ambrosiana has its own private art collection. Rooms are elegantly furnished; junior suites on the 7th floor have views of the cathedral. Simple fare is served in the bar. ⊠ *Via Spadari 11, near Duomo, 20123* ☎ *02/72002371* 🖷 *02/861184* ⊕ *www.spadarihotel.com* ⟿ *40 rooms, 3 suites ♿ Minibars, cable TV, bar, no-smoking rooms* ▭ *AE, DC, MC, V* ⦿I *BP* Ⓜ *Duomo.*

★ $$–$$$ ▦ **Antica Locanda dei Mercanti.** On a quiet side street off Via Dante, this 14-room hotel is minutes—and light-years—away from Milan's bustling downtown. There's no sign—look for the name on the bell. Four rooms have private terraces; book early if you want one of those. Breakfast, which costs extra, is served in your room. ⊠ *Via San Tomaso 6, Duomo, 20121* ☎ *02/8054080* 🖷 *02/8054090* ⊕ *www.lalocanda.it* ⟿ *14 rooms ♿ Cable TV, bar, Internet, Wi-Fi* ▭ *MC, V* ⦿I *EP* Ⓜ *Cordusio.*

$$–$$$ ⊞ **Ariston.** "Bio-architectural" principles prevail at this hotel near the Duomo, which was built using natural materials and has ionized air circulating throughout. As you might expect from such a progressive-minded place, the buffet breakfast includes organic foods. There's free Internet access in the lobby and in the rooms, and bicycles are available in summer. It's a longish walk from the nearest subway stop, the Duomo. ✉ *Largo Carrobbio 2, Duomo, 20123* ☎ *02/72000556* 🖷 *02/72000914* ⊕ *www.aristonhotel.com* ⇨ *52 rooms* ♨ *Minibars, cable TV, bicycles, bar, laundry service, Internet, parking (fee), no-smoking rooms* ⊟ *AE, DC, MC, V* ♨⃝ *BP* Ⓜ *Duomo.*

$$–$$$ ⊞ **Hotel Gran Duca di York.** Originally a seminary, this 1890s art nouveau building has a welcoming lobby and airy public spaces. Peaceful rooms done in muted hues open onto a small elevated courtyard. With an ideal location a few steps west of the Duomo, it offers good value by Milan standards. Call well ahead to reserve one of the four rooms with private terraces. ✉ *Via Moneta 1/a, Duomo, 20123* ☎ *02/874863* 🖷 *02/8690344* ⊕ *www.ducadiyork.com* ⇨ *33 rooms* ♨ *Minibars, cable TV, bar, laundry service, meeting rooms, parking (fee)* ⊟ *AE, MC, V* ⊘ *Closed Aug.* ♨⃝ *EP* Ⓜ *Cordusio.*

$–$$$ ⊞ **Hotel Vittoria.** This family-owned hotel sits on a quiet residential street 10 minutes by taxi from the Duomo. A complete renovation created more rooms and increased the size of the existing ones. The courteous staff is eager to ensure your comfort. In summer, breakfast is served in the small garden at the back. ✉ *Via Pietro Calvi 32, East Central Milan, 20129* ☎ *02/5456520* 🖷 *02/55190246* ⊕ *hotelvittoriamilano.it* ⇨ *40 rooms* ♨ *In-room safes, minibars, cable TV, no-smoking rooms* ⊟ *AE, DC, MC, V* ♨⃝ *EP.*

$$ ⊞ **Antica Locanda Leonardo.** Convenient to the church where you'll find *The Last Supper* and near the city center, this small hotel is in an inner courtyard, making it one step removed from the traffic outside. It's been run by the same family for more than 40 years, and the staff is welcoming and helpful. The rooms overlook the courtyard or the garden. ✉ *Corso Magenta 78, Sant'Ambrogio, 20123* ☎ *02/463317* 🖷 *02/48019012* ⊕ *www.anticalocandaleonardo.com* ⇨ *20 rooms* ♨ *Cable TV, bar, laundry service* ⊟ *AE, DC, MC, V* ⊘ *Closed Dec. 31–Jan. 7 and 3 wks in Aug.* ♨⃝ *BP* Ⓜ *Sant'Ambrogio.*

$ ⊞ **Gritti.** The Gritti is a bright, cheerful hotel with adequate rooms and good views (from the inside upper floor) of tiled roofs and the gold Madonnina statue on top of the Duomo, a few hundred yards away. ✉ *Piazza Santa Maria Beltrade 4, north end of Via Torino, Duomo, 20123* ☎ *02/801056* 🖷 *02/89010999* ⊕ *www.hotelgritti.com* ⇨ *48 rooms* ♨ *Minibars, cable TV, bar, laundry service, meeting room, parking (fee)* ⊟ *AE, DC, MC, V* ♨⃝ *BP* Ⓜ *Duomo.*

★ $ ⊞ **London.** On a quiet side street just round the corner from the castle, the London offers good value for money as well as convenient access to Milan's main sights. Well-appointed rooms are in a 1960s-era building. ✉ *Via Rovello 3, Castello, 20121* ☎ *02/72020166* 🖷 *02/8057037* ⊕ *www.hotellondonmilano.com* ⇨ *29 rooms* ♨ *Cable TV, bar, laundry service, Internet* ⊟ *MC, V* ⊘ *Dec. 23–Jan. 6* ♨⃝ *EP* Ⓜ *Cairoli.*

4

Nightlife & the Arts

The Arts

For events likely to be of interest to non-Italian speakers, see *Hello Milano* (www.hellomilano.it.), a monthly magazine available at the tourist office on Via Marconi. The tourist office publishes the monthly *Milano Mese,* which also includes some listings in English.

MUSIC The two halls belonging to the **Conservatorio** (⊠ Via del Conservatorio 12, Duomo ☎ 02/7621101 Ⓜ San Babila) host some of the leading names in classical music. The modern **Auditorium di Milano** (⊠ Corso San Gottardo, at Via Torricelli, Conchetta ☎ 02/83389201), known for its excellent acoustics, is home to the **Orchestra Verdi** under the baton of Milan-born conductor Richard Chailly. The season, which runs from September to June, includes many top international performers. The **Teatro Dal Verme** (⊠ Via San Giovanni sul Muro 2, Castello ☎ 02/87905201 Ⓜ Cairoli) recently reopened after many years of renovations. Frequent classical music concerts are heard throughout the season, which runs from October to May.

OPERA Milan's hallowed **Teatro alla Scala** (⊠ Piazza della Scala ☎ 02/86077 ⊕ www.teatroallascala.org) has undergone a complete renovation, with everything refreshed, refurbished, or replaced save the building's exterior walls. Special attention was paid to the acoustics, which have always been excellent. The season runs from early-December to mid-June. Plan well in advance, as tickets sell out quickly.

THEATER Milan's **Piccolo Teatro** (☎ 02/72333222 ⊕ www.piccoloteatro.org) is made up of three separate venues, each of which is noted for its excellent productions. The intimate **Teatro Paolo Grassi** (⊠ Via Rovello 2, Castello) is the traditional headquarters of the theater, and is named after its founder. The spacious, modern **Teatro Giorgio Strehler** (⊠ Largo Greppi 1, east of Piazzo Castello, Brera) takes its name from a famous Italian theater director. It hosts dance and musical performances as well as plays. The horseshoe-shaped **Teatro Studio** (⊠ Via Rivoli 6, Castello) is a popular venue for experimental theater and music concerts.

Nightlife

BARS Milan has a bar somewhere to suit any style; those in the better hotels are respectably chic. **El Brellin** (⊠ Vicolo Lavandai at Alzaia Naviglio Grande, Navigli ☎ 02/58101351) is one of the many bars in this arty district. It's only open on Sunday for brunch, which is fast becoming a Milanese tradition. For a quiet drink in a sophisticated setting, try **Fiori Oscuri** (⊠ Via Fiori Oscuri 3, Brera ☎ 02/45477057), in the heart of Brera. If you decide to stay for dinner, chefs Giovanni Valsecchi and Luca Marongiu will wow you with their creative Italian cuisine, savored with a fine wine from their cellar. Also in Brera, check out the **Giamaica** (⊠ Via Brera 32, Brera ☎ 02/876723), a traditional hangout for students from the nearby Brera art school. On summer nights this neighborhood pulses with life; street vendors and fortune-tellers jostle for space alongside the outdoor tables.

For a break from the traditional, check out ultra-trendy **SHU** (⊠ Via Molino delle Armi, Ticinese ☎ 02/58315720), whose gleaming interior looks like a cross between *Star Trek* and Cocteau's *Beauty and the Beast*. The **Trussardi Bar** (✉ Piazza della Scala 5 ☎ 02/80688295) has an enormous plasma screen that keeps hip barflies entertained with video art. Open throughout the day, it's a great place for coffee.

Blue Note (✉ Via Borsieri 37, Garibaldi ☎ 02/69016888 ⊕ www.bluenotemilano.com), the first European branch of the famous New York nightclub, features regular performances by some of the most famous names in jazz, as well as blues and rock concerts. There's a popular jazz brunch on Sunday. Monday evenings are reserved for Italian musicians. For an evening of live music—predominantly rock to jazz—head to perennial favorite **Le Scimmie** (✉ Via Ascanio Sforza 49, Navigli ☎ 02/89402874 ⊕ www.scimmie.it). It features international stars, some of whom jet in to play here, while others, including Ronnie Jones, are longtime residents in Milan.

NIGHTCLUBS **La Banque** (✉ Via Bassano Porrone 6, Scala ☎ 02/86996565 ⊕ www.labanque.it) is an exclusive and expensive bar, restaurant, and dance club, and is great for anything from an *aperitivo* to a night on the town. The dance floor starts hopping at 10:30 PM. The hip **Café l'Atlantique** (✉ Viale Umbria 42, Porta Romana ☎ 02/55193906 ⊕ www.cafeatlantique.com) is a popular place for dancing the night away and enjoying a generous buffet brunch on Sunday afternoon. **C-Side** (✉ Via Castelbarco 11, Porta Romana ☎ 02/58310682) is near Bocconi University. The music on the dance floor varies but includes Latin favorites.

Hollywood (✉ Corso Como 15/c, Centro Direzionale ☎ 02/6598996 ⊕ www.discotecahollywood.com) continues to be one of the most popular places for the sunglasses set. **Magazzini Generali** (✉ Via Pietrasanta 14, Porta Vigentina ☎ 02/55211313 ⊕ www.magazzinigenerali.it), in what was an abandoned warehouse, is a fun, futuristic venue for dancing and concerts.

Sports

Car Racing

Italy's Formula I fans are passionate about team Ferrari. Huge numbers of them converge on the second Sunday in September for the **Italian Grand Prix**, held 15 km (9 mi) northeast of Milan in Monza. The race track was built in 1922 within the Parco di Monza (⊕ www.monzanet.it).

Soccer

AC Milan and Inter Milan, two of the oldest and most successful teams in Europe, vie for the heart of soccer-mad Lombardy. For residents, the city is *Milano* but the teams are *Milan,* a vestige of their common founding as the Milan Cricket and Football Club in 1899. When an Italian-led faction broke off in 1908, the new club was dubbed Internazionale (or "Inter") to distinguish it from the bastion of English exclusivity that would become AC Milan (or simply "Milan"). Since then, the picture has become more clouded: although Milan prides itself as the true team of the city and of its working class, Inter can more persuasively claim pan-Italian support.

AC Milan and Inter Milan share the use of **San Siro Stadium (Stadio Meazza)** (✉ Via Piccolomini) during their August–May season. With more

Calcio Crazy

FOR THE VAST MAJORITY of Italians, *il calcio* (soccer) is much more than a national sport–it's a way of life. The general level of passion for the game exceeds that expressed by all but the most diehard sports fans in the U.S. In 2005 there were no fewer than seven primetime television shows and four major national newspapers dedicated to soccer–not to mention countless radio programs and local TV shows. In a country that's fine-tuned to nuance and inclined to see conspiracy around every corner, controversial referee calls can spark arguments that last weeks. In 2004, debate over questionable rulings in a match between Roma and Juventus (a perennial power from Turin) made it all the way to the floor of Parliament, where conflict between senators actually degenerated into a fistfight.

Nowhere is the passion more feverish than in big soccer cities, of which Milan is the prime example. It's home to two of the country's dominant teams: A.C. Milan and F.C. Internazionale. On game days, it is not unusual to see boisterous bands of fans wandering the city center, team colors draped across their shoulders and rousing team choruses issuing from their mouths. At the stadium, even the most innocuous games are events where chants, insults, and creative banners make crowd-watching an appealing sideshow–especially the banners, which Italians affectionately refer to as *sfotto* ("razzings"). In the 2004 matchup between the Milanese teams, A.C. Milan fans silenced their rivals by unrolling an enormous banner that made fun of Internazionale's decade-long streak as runners-up, stating simply: "We live your dreams." Adding injury to insult, A.C. Milan took the game, 3 goals to 1.

than 60,000 of the 85,000 seats appropriated by season-ticket holders and another couple of thousand allocated to visiting fans, tickets to the Sunday games can be difficult to come by, especially for high-profile matches. You can purchase advance AC Milan tickets at Cariplo bank branches, including one at Via Verdi 8, or at the club's **Web site** (⊕ www.acmilan. com). Inter tickets are available at Banca Popolare di Milano branches, including one at Piazza Meda 4, or at the club's **Web site** (⊕ www.inter. it). To reach San Siro, take subway Line 1 (red) toward Molino Dorino, exit at the Lotto station, and board a bus for the stadium. Alcohol is not sold inside, but beer poured into plastic cups by vendors outside is allowed past the gates.

If you're a soccer fan but can't get in to see a game, you might settle for a **stadium tour** (☎ 02/4042432 ⊕ www.sansirotour.com), which includes a visit to the Milan-Inter museum. Tours are available every half hour from Gate 21 from 10 AM to 5 PM, except on game Sundays; they cost €12.50. Call for reservations a few days before your visit.

Shopping

The heart of Milan's fashion scene is the **quadrilatero della moda** district north of the Duomo. Here the world's leading designers compete for shoppers' attention, showing off their ultrastylish clothes in stores that are works of high style themselves. You won't find any bargains, but regardless of whether you're making a purchase, the area is a great place for window shopping and people watching.

But fashion is not limited to one neighborhood. Wander around the **Brera** to find smaller shops with lesser-known names but with some interesting and exciting offerings. The densest concentration is along Via Brera, Via Solferino, and Corso Garibaldi.

Corso Buenos Aires, which runs northeast from the Giardini Pubblici, is a wide boulevard lined with boutiques. It has the highest concentration of clothing stores in Europe, so be prepared to give up half-way. Avoid Saturday after 3 PM, when it seems the entire city is here looking for bargains.

Department Stores

La Rinascente (⊠ Piazza del Duomo ☎ 02/88521) is Milan's most important department store, carrying everything from Armani cosmetics to Zegna men's suits over eight floors. An outstanding selection of household goods is found in the basement. Check out the restaurants on the top floor, where you can get everything from a quick sandwich to a gourmet meal, with prices to match.

Coin (⊠ Piazza Cinque Giornate, Porta Vittoria ☎ 02/55192083) has an impressive selection at moderate prices. Check out the handbags, accessories, and costume jewelry on the ground floor. The housewares in the basement are a good value. The eighth-floor bar called Globe is a fun place to have a drink.

Markets

Weekly open markets selling fruits and vegetables are still a common sight in Milan. Many also sell clothing and shoes. Bargains in designer apparel can be found at the huge **Mercato Papiniano** (⊠ Porta Genova) on Saturday and Tuesday from about 9–1. The stalls to look for are at the Piazza Sant'Agostino end of the market. It's very crowded—watch for pickpockets.

If you collect coins, stamps, or postcards, or if you just want to see Italian collectors in action, go on Sunday morning to the market at **Via Armorari** (⊠ Off Piazza Cordusio, near Duomo). Milan's most comprehensive antiques market is the **Mercatone dell'Antiquario,** held on the last Sunday of each month along the Naviglio Grande. The third Saturday of every month there's a major antiques and flea market on **Via Fiori Chiari,** near Via Brera.

THE FASHIONISTA'S MILAN

Opera buffs and lovers of Leonardo's *Last Supper,* skip ahead to the next paragraph. No one else should be dismayed to learn that clothing is Milan's greatest cultural achievement. The city is one of the fashion capitals of the world and home base for practically every top Italian designer. The same way art aficionados walk the streets of Florence in a state of bliss, the style-conscious come here to be enraptured.

It all happens in the *quadrilatero della moda,* Milan's toniest shopping district, located just north of the Duomo. Along the cobblestone streets, Armani, Prada, and their fellow *stilisti* sell the latest designs from flagship stores that are as much museums of chic as retail establishments. Any purchase here qualifies as a splurge, but you can have fun without spending a euro—just browse, window-shop, and

FLORENCE HAS THE *DAVID.*

ROME HAS THE PANTHEON.

MILAN HAS THE CLOTHES.

people-watch. Not into fashion? Think of the experience as art, design, and theater all rolled into one. If you wouldn't visit Florence without seeing the Uffizi, you shouldn't visit Milan without seeing the quadrilatero.

On these pages we give a selective, street-by-street list of stores in the area. Hours are from around 10 in the morning until 7 at night, Monday through Saturday.

VIA DELLA SPIGA
(east to west)

Prada (No. 1)
☎ 02/76014448
www.prada.com
lingerie: for down-to-the-skin Prada fans

Dolce & Gabbana (No. 2)
☎ 02/795747
www.dolcegabbana.it
women's accessories

Agnona (No. 3)
☎ 02/76316530
www.agnona.com

women's clothes:
Ermenegildo excellence
for women

Gio Moretti (No. 4)
☎ 02/76003186
women's and men's
clothes: many labels, as
well as books, CDs,
flowers, and an art
gallery

Sergio Rossi (No. 5)
☎ 02/76390927
www.sergiorossi.com
men's shoes

Bulgari Italia (No. 6)
☎ 02/777001
www.bulgari.com
jewelry, fragrances,
accessories

cross Via Sant'Andrea

Sergio Rossi (No. 15)
☎ 02/76002663
www.sergiorossi.com
women's shoes

Fay (No. 16)
☎ 02/76017597
www.fay.it
women's and men's
clothes, accessories: a
flagship store, designed
by Philip Johnson

Prada (No. 18)
☎ 02/76394336
www.prada.com
accessories

Giorgio Armani (No. 19)
☎ 02/783511
www.giorgioarmani.com
accessories

Tod's (No. 22)
☎ 02/76002423
www.tods.com
shoes and handbags:
the Tod's flagship store

Dolce & Gabbana (No. 26)
☎ 02 76001155
www.dolcegabbana.it
women's clothes, in a
baroque setting

✔ **Just Cavalli** (No. 30)
☎ 02/76390893
www.robertocavalli.net
**Women's and men's
clothes, plus a café
serving big salads and
carpaccio. It's the
offspring of the Just
Cavalli Café in Parco
Sempione, one of the
hottest places in town
for drinks (with or
without dinner).**

Moschino (No. 30)
☎ 02/76004320
www.moschino.it
women's, men's, and
children's clothes: Chic
and Cheap, so they say

Roberto Cavalli (No. 42)
☎ 02/76020900
www.robertocavalli.net
women's and men's
clothes, accessories:
3,200 square feet of
Roberto Cavalli

VIA MONTENAPOLEONE
(east to west)

Fratelli Rossetti (No. 1)
☎ 02/76021650
www.rossetti.it
shoes

Louis Vuitton (No. 2)
☎ 02/7771711
www.vuitton.com
leather goods, accessories, women's clothes

Armani Collezioni (No. 2)
☎ 02/76390068
www.giorgioarmani.com
women's and men's clothes: the "white label"

Tanino Crisci (No. 3)
☎ 02/76021264
www.taninocrisci.com
women's and men's shoes, leather goods

Etro (No. 5)
☎ 02/76005049
www.etro.it
women's and men's clothes, leather goods, accessories

Bottega Veneta (No. 5)
☎ 02/76024495
www.bottegaveneta.com
leather goods: signature woven-leather bags

Gucci (No. 5/7)
☎ 02/771271
www.gucci.com
women's and men's clothes

Prada (No. 6)
☎ 02/76020273
www.prada.com
men's clothes

Prada (No. 8)
☎ 02/7771771
www.prada.com
women's clothes

cross Via Sant'Andrea

Armani Junior (No. 10)
☎ 02/783196
www.giorgioarmani.com
children's clothes: for the under-14 fashionista

Versace (No. 11)
☎ 02/76008528
www.versace.com
everything Versace, except Versus and children's clothes

Corneliani (No. 12)
☎ 02/777361
www.corneliani.com
men's clothes: bespoke tailoring excellence

Versace in
Via Montenapoleone

Cartier
corner Via Gesù
☎ 02/3030421
www.cartier.com
jewelry: precious stones, fine gifts

FASHION SHOPPING, ACCESSORIZED

Milan's most ambitious shops don't just want to clothe you— they want to trim your hair, clean your pores, and put a cocktail in your hand. Some "stores with more" in and around the quadrilatero are indicated by a ✔.

Valentino
corner Via Santo Spirito
☎ 02/76020285
www.valentino.it
women's clothes: elegant designs for special occasions

Loro Piana (No. 27c)
☎ 02/7772901
www.loropiana.it
women's and men's clothes, accessories: cashmere everything

4

FASHIONISTA'S MILAN

REFUELING

If you want refreshments and aren't charmed by the quadrilatero's in-store cafés, try **Cova** (Via Montenapoleone 8, ☎ 02 76000578) or **Sant'Ambroeus** (Corso Matteotti 7, ☎ 02 76000540). Both serve coffee, tea, aperitifs, sandwiches, and snacks in an ambience of starched tablecloths and chandeliers.

Cova's courtyard café

When the hurly-burly's done, head for the **Bulgari Hotel** (Via Fratelli Gabba 7b, ☎ 02/8058051), west of Via Manzoni, for a quiet (if pricey) drink, In summer, the bar extends into a beautiful, mature garden over an acre in size.

VIA SAN PIETRO ALL'ORTO
(east to west)

Versus (No. 10)
☎ 02/76014722
www.versace.com
women's, men's, and children's clothes:
Versace Jeans and Sport

Jimmy Choo (No. 17)
☎ 02/45481770
www.jimmychoo.com
women's and men's shoes

CORSO VENEZIA
(south to north)

Miu Miu (No. 3)
☎ 02/76001799
www.prada.com
women's clothes:
Prada's playful line

D&G (No. 7)
☎ 02/76004091
www.dolcegabbana.it
swimwear, underwear, accessories: Dolce & Gabbana diffusion

✔ **Dolce & Gabbana** (No. 15)
☎ 02/76028485
www.dolcegabbana.it
Men's clothes, sold in a four-story, early 19th-century patrician home. Added features are a barbershop (☎ 02/76408881), a beauty parlor (☎ 02/76408888), and the

Martini Bar, which also serves light lunches.

Borsalino
corner Via Senato
☎ 02/76017072
www.borsalino.com
hats: for people who want to be streets ahead

VIA VERRI
(south to north)

Ermenegildo Zegna (No. 3)
☎ 02/76006437
www.zegna.com.
men's clothes, in the finest fabrics.

Borsalino
Via Verri/corner Via Bigli
☎ 02/76398539
www.borsalino.com
hats

cross Via Bigli

Etro Profumi
corner Via Bigli
☎ 02/76005450
www.etro.it
fragrances

D&G in Via della Spiga

VIA SANT'ANDREA
(south to north)

✔ **Trussardi** (No. 5)
☎ 02/76020380
www.trussardi.com
Women's and men's clothes. The nearby flagship store (Piazza della Scala 5) includes the Trussardi Marino alla Scala Café (☎ 02 80688201), a fashion-forward bar done in stone, steel, slate, and glass. For a more substantial lunch, and views of Teatro alla Scala, head upstairs to the Marino alla Scala Ristorante (☎ 02 80688201), which serves creative Mediterranean cuisine.

Banner (No. 8)
☎ 02/76004361
women's and men's clothes: a multibrand boutique

Giorgio Armani (No. 9)
☎ 02/76003234
www.giorgioarmani.com
women's and men's clothes: the "black label"

Moschino (No. 12)
☎ 02/76000832
www.moschino.it
women's clothes: world-renowned window displays

BARGAIN-HUNTING AT THE OUTLETS

Milan may be Italy's richest city, but that doesn't mean all its well-dressed residents can afford to shop at the boutiques of the quadrilatero. Many pick up their designer clothes at outlet stores, where prices can be reduced by 50 percent or more.

Salvagente (Via Bronzetti 16, ☎ 02/76110328, www.salvagentemilano.it) is the top outlet for designer apparel and accessories from both large are small houses. There's a small men's department. To get there, take the 60 bus, which runs from the Duomo to the Stazione Centrale, to the intersection of Bronzetti and Archimede. Look for the green iron gate with the bronze sign, between the hairdressers and an apartment building. No credit cards.

DMagazine Outlet (Via Montenapoleone 26, ☎ 02/76006027, www.dmagazine.it) has bargains in the

Marni (No. 14)
☎ 02 76317327
www.marni.com
women's clothes

✔ **Gianfranco Ferré**
(No. 15)
☎ 02/794864
www.gianfrancoferre. com
Everything Ferré, plus
a spa providing facials,
Jacuzzis, steam baths,
and mud treatments.
Reservations are
essential (☎
02/76017526), preferably
a week in advance.

Prada (No. 21)
☎ 02 76001426
www.prada.com
women's and men's
sportswear

VIA MANZONI
(south to north)

P-Box (No. 13)
☎ 02/89013000
www.aeffe.com
women's and men's
shoes, bags: Aeffe group

Armani in Via Manzoni

labels, including Alberta
Ferretti, Philosophy, and
Narciso Rodriquez

✔ **Armani Megastore**
(No. 31)
☎ 02/72318600
www.giorgioarmani.com
The quadrilatero's most
conspicuous shopping
complex. Along with
many Armani fashions,
you'll find a florist, a
bookstore, a chocolate
shop (offering Armani
pralines), the Armani
Caffè, and Nobu (of the
upscale Japanese
restaurant chain). The
Armani Casa furniture
collection is next door at
number 37.

CORSO COMO
✔ **10 Corso Como**
☎ 02/29000727
www.10corsocomo.com
Outside the quadrilatero,
but it's a must see for
fashion addicts. The
bazaar-like 13,000-
square-foot complex
includes women's and
men's boutiques, a bar
and restaurant, a
bookstore, a record shop,
and an art gallery
specializing in
photography. You can
even spend the night (if
you can manage to get a
reservation) at Milan's
most exclusive B&B,
Three Rooms (☎
02/626163). The
furnishings are a modern
design-lover's dream.

Prada store in the Galleria

**GALLERIA VITTORIO
EMANUELE**
(not technically part of
the quadrilatero, but
nearby)

✔ **Gucci**
☎ 02/8597991
www.gucci.com
Gucci accessories, plus
the world's first Gucci
café. Sit outside behind
the elegant boxwood
hedge and watch the
world go by.

Prada (No. 63-65)
☎ 02/876979
www.prada.com
the original store: look

for the murals
downstairs.

Louis Vuitton
☎ 02/72147011
www.vuitton.com
accessories, women's
and men's shoes,
watches

Tod's
☎ 02/877997
www.tods.com
women's and men's
shoes, leather goods,
accessories

Borsalino (No. 92
☎ 02/804337
www.borsalino.com
hats

Galleria Vittorio Emanuele

midst of the quadrilatero. Names on sale include Armani,
Cavalli, Gucci, and Prada.

DT-Intrend (Galleria San Carlo 6, ☎ 02/76000829)
sells last year's Max Mara, Max & Co, Sportmax, Marella,
Penny Black, and Marina Rinaldi. It's just 300 meters
from the Max Mara store located on Corso Vittorio
Emanuele at the corner of Galleria de Cristoforis.

At the **10 CorsoComo** outlet (Via Tazzoli 3, ☎ 02/29015130,
www.10corsocomo.com) you can find clothes, shoes,
bags, and accessories.

Fans of **Marni** who have a little time on their hands will
want to check out the outlet (Via Tajani 1, ☎ 02/70009735
or 02/71040332, www.marni.com). Take the 61 bus to the
terminus at Largo Murani, from which it's about 200 meters on foot.

Giorgio Armani has an outlet, but it's way out of town—
off the A3, most of the way to Como. The address is
Strada Provinciale per Bregnano 13, in the town of Verte-
mate (☎ 031 887373, www.giorgioarmani.com).

PAVIA, CREMONA & MANTUA

Once proud medieval fortress towns rivaling Milan in power, these centers of industry and commerce on the Po plain still play a key role in Italy's wealthiest, most populous region. Pavia is celebrated for its extraordinarily detailed Carthusian monastery, Cremona for its incomparable violin-making tradition. Mantua—the most picturesque of the three—was the home of the fantastically wealthy Gonzaga dynasty for almost 300 years.

Pavia

⑰ *41 km (25 mi) south of Milan.*

Pavia was once Milan's chief regional rival. The city dates from at least the Roman era and was the capital of the Lombard kings for two centuries (572–774). It was at one time known as "the city of a hundred towers," but only a handful have survived the passing of time. Its prestigious university was founded in 1361 on the site of a 10th-century law school, but has roots that can be traced to antiquity.

The 14th-century **Castello Visconteo** now houses the local **Museo Civico** (Municipal Museum), with an archaeological collection and a picture gallery featuring works by Correggio, Giovanni Bellini, Giambattista Tiepolo, and Vincenzo La Foppa, among others. ☒ *Viale 11 Febbraio, near Piazza Castello* ☏ *0382/33853* ☒ *€6* ☉ *Feb.–June and Sept.–Nov., Tues.–Sun. 10–5:45, (last entry 5:15), Dec. and Jan., July and Aug., Tues.–Sun. 9–1:30, (last entry 12:45).*

In the Romanesque church of **San Pietro in Ciel d'Oro** you can visit the tomb of Christianity's most celebrated convert, St. Augustine, housed in a Gothic marble ark on the high altar. ☒ *Via Matteotti* ☏ *0382/303040* ☉ *Mon.–Sun. 7–noon and 3–7; mass Mon.–Sat. 9 and 6:30, Sun. 9, 11, and 6:30.*

The main draw in Pavia is the **Certosa** (Carthusian monastery), 9 km (5½ mi) north of the city center. Its elaborate facade shows the same relish for ornamentation as the Duomo in Milan. The Certosa's extravagant grandeur was due in part to the plan to have it house the tombs of the family of the first duke of Milan, Galeazzo Visconti III (who died during a plague, at age 49, in 1402). The very best marble was used, taken undoubtedly by barge from the quarries of Carrara, roughly 240 km (150 mi) away. Though the floor plan may be Gothic—a cross shape divided into a series of squares—the gorgeous fabric that rises above it is triumphantly Renaissance. On the facade, in the lower frieze, are medallions of Roman emperors and Eastern monarchs; above them are low reliefs of scenes from the life of Christ and from the career of Galeazzo Visconti III.

The first duke was the only Visconti to be interred here, and then only some 75 years after his death, in a tomb designed by Gian Cristoforo Romano. Look for it in the right transept. In the left transept is a more appealing tomb—that of a rather stern middle-age man and a beautiful young woman. The man is Ludovico il Moro Sforza (1452–1508), seventh duke of Milan, who commissioned Leonardo to paint *The Last Supper.* The woman is Ludovico's wife, Beatrice d'Este (1475–97), one of the most celebrated women of her day, the embodiment of brains, culture, birth, and beauty. Married when he was 40 and she was 16, they had enjoyed six years together when she died while giving birth to a stillborn child. Ludovico commissioned the sculptor Cristoforo Solari to design a joint tomb for the high altar of Santa Maria delle Grazie in Milan. Originally much larger, the tomb for some years occupied the honored place as planned. Then for reasons that are still mysterious the Dominican monks, who seemed to care no more for their former patron than they did for their faded Leonardo fresco, sold the tomb to their Carthusian brothers to the south. Sadly, part of the tomb and its remains were lost. ⊠ *Certosa, 9 km (5½ mi) north of Pavia* ☎ *0382/925613* ⊕ *www.comune.pv.it/certosadipavia* ⊠ *Free* ☉ *Open Tues.–Sun. 9–11:30 and 2:30–5.*

Where to Eat

$$$$ ✕ **Locanda Vecchia Pavia al Mulino.** At this sophisticated art nouveau restaurant 150 yards from the Certosa you'll find creative versions of traditional regional cuisine, including *risotto alla certosina* (rice with sturgeon eggs, frogs' leg, and river shrimp). *Casoncelli* (stuffed pasta), *petto d'anatra* (duck breast), and veal cutlet alla milanese are done with style, as are the imaginative seafood dishes. For dessert, consider the hot chocolate soufflé with white-chocolate sauce. ⊠ *Via al Monumento 5, Certosa* ☎ *0382/925894* ♟ *Reservations essential* ⊟ *AE, DC, MC, V* ☉ *Closed Mon., 3 wks in Aug., and 3 wks in early-Jan. No lunch Wed.*

Cremona

🔞 *104 km (65 mi) east of Pavia, 106 km (66 mi) southeast of Milan.*

Cremona is where the world's best violins are made. Andrea Amati (1510–80) invented the modern instrument here in the 16th century. Though cognoscenti continue to revere the Amati name, it was an apprentice of Amati's nephew for whom the fates had reserved wide and lasting fame. In a career that spanned an incredible 68 years, Antonio Stradivari (1644–1737) made more than 1,200 instruments—including violas, cellos, harps, guitars, and mandolins, in addition to his fabled violins. Labeled simply with a small printed slip reading ANTONIUS STRADIVARIUS CREMONENSIS. FACIEBAT ANNO . . .—the date inserted in a neat italic hand—they remain the most coveted, most expensive stringed instruments in the world.

Strolling about this quiet, medium-size city, you cannot help noting that the violin making continues to flourish. There are, in fact, more than 50 *liutai,* many of them graduates of the Scuola Internazionale di Liuteria (International School of Violin Making). You are usually welcome to these ateliers, where traditional craftsmanship reigns supreme, especially if you are contemplating the acquisition of your own instrument; the tourist office can provide addresses.

The Po Plain
& Lake Garda

LOMBARDY

TRENTINO-ALTO ADIGE

VENETO

Riva del Garda **23**

Torbole

Limone sul Garda

Malcesine **22**

Tremosine

Tignale

Gargnano **24**

Toscolano-Maderno

Gardone Riviera **25**

Salò

Punta di San Vigilio **21**

Garda

Bardolino **20**

Lazise

Sirmione **26**

Peschiera

Desenzano

Castelnuovo del Garda

Verona

TO VENICE

Mantua **19**

Goito

Sabbioneta

Bozzolo

Castiglione d. Stiviere

Carpenedolo

Oglio

Brescia

Lago d'Iseo

Lovere

Cremona **18**

TO PARMA

Lago di Garda

San Pellegrino Terme

Lenna

Lecco

Chiesa della Madonna del Ghisallo

Bergamo

Capriate San Gervasio

Cassano d'Adda

Treviglio

Crema

Adda

Lodi

Po

Aeroporto Milano Linate

Milan

Aeroporto Malpensa

Abbiategrasso

Vigevano

Ticino

Certosa di Pavia

Pavia **17**

20 miles

30 km

ITALY

Varese

Cremona's other claim to fame is *torrone* (nougat), which is said to have been created here in honor of the marriage of Bianca Maria Visconti and Francesco Sforza, which took place in October 1441. The new confection, originally prepared by heating almonds, egg whites, and honey over low heat and shaped and named after the city's tower, was created in symbolic celebration. The annual Festa del Torrone is held in the main piazza on the third Sunday in October.

The **Piazza del Comune,** surrounded by the Duomo, tower, baptistery, and city hall, is distinctive and harmonious: the combination of old brick, rose- and cream-color marble, terra-cotta, and old copper roofs brings Romanesque, Gothic, and Renaissance together with unusual success. Dominating Piazza del Comune is the **Torrazzo** (Big Tower), the city's symbol and perhaps the tallest campanile in Italy, visible for a considerable distance across the Po plain. It's open to visitors, but in winter hours fluctuate depending on the weather. The tower's astronomical clock is the 1583 original. ⊠ *Piazza del Comune* 🎫 €6 ☉ *Daily 9–6.*

Cremona's Romanesque **Duomo** was consecrated in 1190. Here you'll find the beautiful *Story of the Virgin Mary and the Passion of Christ,* the central fresco of an extraordinary cycle commissioned in 1514 and featuring the work of local artists, including Boccacio Boccancino, Giovan Francesco Bembo, and Altobello Melone. ⊠ *Piazza del Comune* ☉ *Daily 7:30–noon and 3:30–7.*

Legendary violin maker Antonio Stradivari lived, worked, and died near the verdant square at No. 1 **Piazza Roma.** According to local lore, Stradivari kept each instrument in his bedroom for a month before varnishing, imparting part of his soul before sealing and sending it out into the world. In the center of the park is **Stradivari's grave,** marked by a simple tombstone.

The **Museo Stradivariano** (Stradivarius Museum) in Palazzo Affaitati houses the city's collection of stringed treasures: a viola and five violins, including the golden-orange "Il Cremonese 1715" Stradivarius. Informative exhibits display Stradivari's paper patterns, wooden models, and various tools. ⊠ *Via Ugolani Dati 4* 🕾 *0372/407770* 🎫 €7 ☉ *Tues.–Sat. 9–6, Sun. 10–6.*

Where to Stay & Eat

$$ ✕ **La Sosta.** This traditional Cremonese restaurant looks to the 16th century for culinary inspiration, following a time-tested recipe for a favored first course, gnocchi *Vecchia Cremona.* The homemade salami is also excellent. To finish off the evening, try the *semifreddo al torroncino* (chilled almond cake) and a dessert wine. ⊠ *Via Sicardo 9* 🕾*0372/456656* ▭*AE, DC, MC, V* ☉ *Closed Mon. and 3 wks in Aug. No dinner Sun.*

★ **$**   ✕ **Centrale.** Close to the cathedral, this old-style trattoria is a favorite among locals for traditional Cremonese fare, such as succulent *cotechino* (pork sausage) and *tortelli di zucca* (a small pasta with pumpkin filling), at moderate prices. ⊠ *Vicolo Pertusio 4* 🕾 *0372/28701* ▭ V ☉ *Closed Thurs. and July.*

$$–$$$ 🏨 **Delle Arti Design Hotel.** The name fits at this central hotel with elegant modern interiors and eclectic designer furniture. The contemporary feel provides a nice contrast to the surrounding historic center. ✉ *Via Bonomelli 8, 26100* ☎ *0372/23131* 🖷 *0372/21654* ⊕ *www.dellearti. com* ⇄ *33 rooms △ Minibars, cable TV, gym, sauna, bar, Internet, meeting rooms, parking (fee), no-smoking rooms* 🖃 *AE, DC, MC, V* ¶◎ *BP* ⊗ *Aug. 5–29, Dec. 25.*

$–$$ 🏨 **Hotel Continental.** This comfortable modern hotel is well equipped to satisfy its international business clientele. At the end of the road to the autostrade, on the periphery of the historic center, the Continental makes a convenient base for those wisely disinclined to navigate old Cremona by car. ✉ *Piazza Libertà 26, 26100* ☎ *0372/434141* 🖷 *0372/ 454873* ⊕ *www.hotelcontinentalcremona.it* ⇄ *62 rooms △ Restaurant, minibars, cable TV, bar, restaurant, Internet, meeting rooms, parking (fee)* 🖃 *AE, DC, MC, V* ¶◎ *BP.*

Nightlife & the Arts
At the end of May and the beginning of June, Cremona hosts an annual festival in honor of native composer Claudio Monteverdi, the great baroque pioneer of modern opera. For details, contact the **Teatro Ponchielli** (☎ 0372/22010 ⊕ www.teatroponchielli.it).

Shopping
For Cremona's specialty nougat, visit famed **Sperlari** (✉ Via Solferino 25 ☎ 0372/22346 ⊕ www.fieschi1867.com). In addition to nougat, Cremona's best *mostarda* (a condiment made from preserved fruit served with meat and cheese) has been sold from this handsome shop since 1836; Sperlari and parent company Fieschi have grown into a confectionery empire. Look for the historical product display in the back.

Mantua

🔞 *192 km (119 mi) southeast of Milan.*

Mantua stands tallest among the ancient walled cities of the Po plain. Its fortifications are circled on three sides by the passing Mincio River, which long provided Mantua with protection, fish, and a steady stream of river tolls as it meandered from Lake Garda to join the Po. It may not be flashy or dramatic, but Mantua's beauty is subtle and deep, hiding a rich trove of artistic, architectural, and cultural gems beneath its slightly somber facade.

Although Mantua first came to prominence in Roman times as the home of Virgil, its grand monuments date from the glory years of the Gonzaga dynasty. From 1328 until the Austrian Habsburgs sacked the city in 1708, the dukes and marquesses of the Gonzaga clan reigned over a wealthy independent *commune*, and the arts thrived in the relative peace of that period. Raphael's star pupil Andrea Mantegna (1431–1506), who served as court painter for 50 years, was the best known of a succession of artists and architects who served Mantua through the years, and some of his finest work, including his only surviving fresco cycle, can be seen here. Giulio Romano (circa 1499–1546), Mantegna's apprentice, built his masterpiece, Palazzo Te, on an island in the river. Leon Battista Alberti (1404–72), who designed two impressive churches in Mantua, was widely emulated later in the Renaissance.

★ The 500-room **Palazzo Ducale,** the palace that dominates the skyline, was built for the Gonzaga family. Unfortunately, as the Gonzaga dynasty waned in power and prestige, much of the art within the castle was sold or stolen. The highlight is the Camera Degli Sposi—literally, the "Chamber of the Wedded Couple"—where Duke Ludovico and his wife held court. Mantegna painted it over a nine-year period at the height of his power, finishing at age 44. He made a startling advance in painting by organizing the picture plane in a way that systematically mimics the experience of human vision. Even now, more than five centuries later, you can sense the excitement of a mature artist, fully aware of the great importance of his painting, expressing his vision with a masterly, joyous confidence. The circular tromp l'oeil around the vaulted ceiling is famous for the many details that attest to Mantegna's greatness: the three dimensional quality of the seven Caesars (the Gonzagas saw themselves as successors to the Roman Emperors and paid homage to classical culture throughout the palazzo); the self-portrait of Mantegna (in purple, on the right side of the western fresco), and the dwarf peering out from behind the dress of Ludovico's wife (on the northern fresco). Only 20 people are allowed at a time in the Camera Degli Sposi, and only for 10 minutes at a time. Read about the room before you enter so that you can spend your time looking up.

Walk-up visitors to Mantua's Palazzo Ducale may take a fast-paced guided tour conducted in Italian; signs in each room provide explanations in English. Alternatively, call the **tourist office** (✉ Piazza Mantegna 6 ☎ 0376/328253) to arrange for English-language tours. ✉ *Piazza Sordello* ☎ *0376/224832* 🎫 *€6.50* 🕐 *Tues.–Sun. 8:45–7:15, last entry 6:30.*

Serious Mantegna aficionados will want to visit the **Casa di Andrea Mantegna,** designed by the artist himself and built around an intriguing circular courtyard, which is usually open to view. The interior can be seen only by appointment or during occasional art exhibitions. ✉ *Via Acerbi 47* ☎ *0376/360506* 🎫 *€3* 🕐 *Tues.–Sun. 10–12:30; also 3–6 during exhibitions.*

Mantegna's tomb is in the first chapel to the left in the basilica of **Sant' Andrea,** most of which was built in 1472. The current structure, a masterwork by the architect Alberti, is the third built on this spot to house the relic of the Precious Blood. The crypt holds two reliquaries containing earth believed to be soaked in the blood of Christ, brought to Mantua by Longinus, the soldier who pierced his side. They are displayed only on Good Friday. ✉ *Piazza delle Erbe* 🕐 *Daily 8–12:30 and 3–6.*

★ **Palazzo Te** is one of the greatest of all Renaissance palaces, built between 1525 and 1535 by Federigo II Gonzaga. It is the mannerist masterpiece of artist-architect Giulio Romano, who created a pavilion where the strict rules of courtly behavior could be relaxed for libertine pastimes. Romano's purposeful

WORD OF MOUTH

"The Palazzo Te in Mantua was awesome—amazing, vivid, huge, almost grotesque frescoes throughout. Well worth the visit in itself, if you are interested much in art/architecture."   —Hadley breaks with classical tradition are lighthearted and unprecedented. For example, note the "slipping" triglyphs along the upper edge of the inside courtyard. Two highlights are the Camera di Amore e Psiche ("Room of Cupid and Psyche") that depicts a wedding set among lounging nymphs, frolicking satyrs, and even a camel and an elephant; and the gasp-producing Camera dei Giganti ("Room of the Giants") that shows Jupiter expelling the Titans from Mount Olympus. The scale of the work is overwhelming; the floor-to-ceiling work completely envelops the viewer. The room's rounded corners, and the river rock covering the original floor, were meant to give it a cavelike feeling. It is a "whisper chamber" in which words softly uttered in one corner can be heard in the opposite one. For fun, note the graffiti from as far back as the 17th century. ⊠ *Viale Te* ☎ *0376/323266* ⊕ *www.centropalazzote. it* ☎ *€8* ⊘ *Mon. 1–6, Tues.–Sun. 9–5:30.*

Where to Stay & Eat

★ **$$$$** ✕ **Al Bersagliere.** One of Lombardy's best restaurants is this rustic four-room tavern in the tiny riverside hamlet of Goito, 16 km (10 mi) north of Mantua on Route 236. It has been run by a single family for more than 150 years. The fish in particular is excellent, as is a Mantuan classic, frog soup. ⊠ *Via Goitese 260, Goito* ☎ *0376/60007* ⌕ *Reservations essential* ⊟ *AE, DC, MC, V* ⊘ *Closed Mon., Tues., and 3 wks in Aug.*

★ **$$$$** ✕ **Ambasciata.** Heralded by food critics the world over as one of Italy's finest restaurants, Ambasciata (Italian for "embassy") takes elegance and service to extremes rarely, if ever, achieved outside Europe. Chef Romano Tamani makes frequent appearances abroad (at New York's Le Cirque 2000, for one) but is at home in tiny Quistello, 20 km (12 mi) southeast of Mantua, where he offers to those willing to make the trek (and pay the bill) an ever-changing array of superlative creations such as *timballo di lasagne verdi con petto di piccione sauté alla crème de Cassis* (green lasagna with breast of pigeon and red currant). ⊠ *Via Martiri di Belfiore 33, Quistello* ☎ *0376/619169* ⌕ *Reservations essential* ⊟ *AE, DC, MC, V* ⊘ *Closed Mon., Jan. 1–20, and Aug. 5–25. No dinner Sun.*

$$$–$$$$ ✕ **L'Aquila Nigra.** Down a small side street opposite the Palazzo Ducale, this popular restaurant is set in a former medieval convent, where frescoes grace the walls. Diners choose from such local dishes as *medaglione di anguilla all'aceto balsamico* (medallion of eel with balsamic vinegar), *saltarelli e frittata di zucchine* (lightly fried freshwater shrimp and zucchini), and *petto di faraona in pane grattinata con rosmarino* (breaded guinea fowl with rosemary). Reservations are recommended. ⊠ *Vicolo Bonacolsi 4* ☎ *0376/327180* ⊟ *AE, DC, MC, V* ⊘ *Closed 3 wks in Aug., Sun. (except for Sun. lunch in Apr. and May, Sept. and Oct.), and Mon.*

$$–$$$ ✕ **Antica Osteria ai Ranari.** This mellow, inviting restaurant owned by the Giardi family serves such Mantuan specialties as *tortelli di zucca* (homemade pasta stuffed with sweetly spiced pumpkin in sage butter) and *ranne fritte* (fried frogs' legs). For dessert, try *sbrisolona*, which means "crumbs" in Mantuan dialect. This crumb cake with whole almonds and a deceptively large amount of butter is served warm and is meant to be eaten with the hands. ⊠ *Via Trieste 11* ☎ *0376/328431* ⊟ *AE, D, MC, V.*

$$–$$$ ✕ **Ristorante Pavesi.** Locals have been coming to this central restaurant for delicious food at reasonable prices since 1918. The menu changes every other month; homemade pasta is always a good bet. In warmer months you can dine on Mantua's handsome main square. ✉ *Piazza Erbe 13* ☎ *0376/323627* ▭ *AE, DC, MC, V* ⊗ *Closed Feb.*

$$$ ⊞ **San Lorenzo.** As if spacious, comfortable rooms, authentic early-19th-century furnishings, and a prime location weren't enough, many rooms here have wonderful views overlooking Piazza Concordia, and some have private terraces. In summer, breakfast is served on the roof. ✉ *Piazza Concordia 14, 46100* ☎ *0376/220500* 🖷 *0376/327194* ⊕ *www.hotelsanlorenzo.it* ⇝ *32 rooms* ⚬ *Minibars, cable TV, bar, Internet, meeting rooms, free parking* ▭ *AE, DC, MC, V* ¶⊙| *BP.*

$–$$ ⊞ **Hotel Broletto.** Here you'll get comfortable, clean digs in a perfect location. The furniture was new in the '60s and has stuck around long enough to come back in style. ✉ *Via Accademia 1, 46100* ☎ *0376/223678* 🖷 *0376/221297* ⊕ *space.tin.it/viaggi/fsmirnov* ⇝ *16 rooms* ⚬ *Minibars, cable TV* ▭ *AE, DC, MC, V* ⊗ *Closed for some time in July and late Dec.* ¶⊙| *BP.*

LAKE GARDA

Updated by
Maria
Sophocles

Lake Garda has had a perennial attraction for travelers and writers alike; even essayist Michel de Montaigne (1533–92), whose 15 months of travel journals contain not a single other reference to nature, paused to admire the view down the lake from Torbole, which he called "boundless."

Lake Garda is 50 km (31 mi) long, ranges roughly 1 km–16 km (½ mi–10 mi) wide, and is as much as 1,135 feet deep. The terrain is flat at the lake's southern base and mountainous at its northern tip. As a consequence, its character varies from stormy inland sea to crystalline Nordic-style fjord. It's the biggest lake in the region and by most accounts the cleanest. Drivers should take care on the hazardous hairpin turns on the lake road.

Bardolino

❷⓪ *24 km (15 mi) northeast of Sirmione, 157 km (97 mi) east of Milan.*

Famous for its red wine, Bardolino hosts the **Cura dell'Uva** (Grape Cure Festival) in late September–early October. It's a great excuse to indulge in the local vino, which is light, dry, and often slightly sparkling. (Bring aspirin, just in case the cure turns out to be worse than the disease.)

Bardolino is one of the most popular summer resorts on the lake. It stands on the eastern shore at the wider end of the lake. Here there are two handsome Romanesque churches: **San Severo,** from the 11th century, and **San Zeno,** from the 9th. Both are in the center of the small town.

Punta di San Vigilio

❷① *6 km (4 mi) north of Bardolino, 163 km (101 mi) east of Milan.*

Just about everyone agrees that this is the prettiest spot on Garda's eastern shore. Punta di San Vigilio is full of cypresses from the gardens of the 15th-century **Villa Guarienti di Brenzone** (✉ Frazione Punta San Vigilio 1); the villa itself is closed to the public.

Malcesine

㉒ *28 km (17 mi) north of Punta di San Vigilio, 190 km (118 mi) east of Milan.*

One of the loveliest areas along the upper eastern shore of Lake Garda, Malcesine is principally known as a summer resort with sailing and windsurfing schools. It tends to be crowded in season, but there are nice walks from the town toward the mountains. Six ski lifts and more than 11 km (7 mi) of runs of varying degrees of difficulty serve skiers. Dominating the town is the 12th-century **Castello Scaligero,** built by the Della Scalas.

The futuristic *funivia* (cable car) zipping visitors to the top of **Monte Baldo** (5,791 feet) is unique because it rotates. After a 10-minute ride you're high in the Veneto, where you can stroll while enjoying spectacular views of the lake. You can ride the cable car down or bring along a mountain bike (or hang glider) for the descent. ✉ *Via Navene Vecchia 12* ☎ *0457/7400206* ⊕ *www.montebaldo.com* 🎫 *€13 round-trip* ☉ *Daily 8–4.*

Riva del Garda

㉓ *18 km (11 mi) north of Malcesine, 180 km (112 mi) east of Milan.*

Set on the northern tip of Lake Garda against a dramatic backdrop of jagged cliffs and miles of beaches, Riva del Garda is the lake's quintessential resort town. The old city, set around a pretty harbor, was built up during the 15th century, when it was a strategic outpost of the Venetian Republic.

The heart of Riva del Garda, the lakeside **Piazza 3 Novembre** is surrounded by medieval palazzos. Standing in the piazza and looking out onto the lake you can understand why Riva del Garda has become a windsurfing mecca: air currents ensure good breezes on even the most sultry midsummer days.

The **Torre Apponale,** predating the Venetian period by three centuries, looms above the medieval residences of the main square; its crenellations recall its defensive purpose.

Where to Stay & Eat

$$$ ✕ **Castel Toblino.** A lovely stop for a lakeside drink or a romantic dinner, this castle is right on a lake in Sarche, about 20 km (12 mi) north of Riva toward Trento. The compound is said to have been a prehistoric, then Roman, village, and was later associated with the Church of Trento. Bernardo Clesio had it rebuilt in the 16th century in the Renaissance style. It's now a sanctuary of fine food, serving such local specialties as lake fish and guinea fowl. ✉ *Via Caffaro 1, Sarche* ☎ *0461/864036* ⊟ *MC, V* ☉ *Closed Tues., mid-Nov.–Feb. No dinner some Mon.*

$$$–$$$$ 🏨 **Hotel du Lac et du Parc.** Riva's most splendid hotel has elegance befitting its cosmopolitan name, with personalized service rarely found on Lake Garda since its aristocratic heyday. The airy public spaces include a dining room, bar, and beautifully manicured private garden leading to the public beach. The rooms are well appointed and comfortable; be sure to ask for air-conditioning. The outdoor pool has separate areas for adults and children. ⊠ *Viale Rovereto 44, 38066* ☎ *0464/566600* 📠 *0464/566566* ⊕ *www.hoteldulac-riva.it* 🛏 *164 rooms, 5 suites* 🍴 *2 restaurants, minibars, cable TV, 2 tennis courts, indoor pool, gym, hair salon, sauna, Turkish bath, beach, bar, free parking; no a/c in some rooms* 🖃 *AE, DC, MC, V* ☺ *Closed Jan.–Mar.* ✤ *BP.*

$$$ 🏨 **Hotel Sole.** Within a lakeside 15th-century palazzo in the center of town, this lovely, understated hotel offers comfortable, affordable rooms. The terraced front rooms open to breathtaking views of the lake, and a secluded rooftop terrace is a perfect retreat from crowded beaches in summer. ⊠ *Piazza 3 Novembre 35, 38066* ☎ *0464/552686* 📠 *0464/552811* ⊕ *www.hotelsole.net* 🛏 *52 rooms* 🍴 *Restaurant, room service, in-room safes, refrigerators, cable TV, sauna, bicycles, bar, parking (fee)* 🖃 *AE, DC, MC, V* ✤ *BP.*

$$–$$$ 🏨 **Luise.** This cozy, reasonably priced hotel has great amenities, including a big garden and a large swimming pool. The restaurant, La Limonaia, is recommended for its Trentino specialties. ⊠ *Viale Rovereto 9, 38066* ☎ *0464/550858* 📠 *0464/554250* ⊕ *www.feelinghotelluise.com* 🛏 *68 rooms* 🍴 *Restaurant, minibars, cable TV, tennis court, pool, laundry facilities, no-smoking rooms* 🖃 *AE, DC, MC, V* ✤ *BP.*

Sports

Contact **Circolo Surf Torbole** (⊠ Torbole sur Garda ☎ 0464/505385 ⊕ www.circolosurftorbole.com) for news on windsurfing in the area.

en route · After passing the town of Limone—where it is said the first lemon trees in Europe were planted—take the fork to the right about 5 km (3 mi) north of Gargnano and head to Tignale. The view from the Madonna di Monte Castello church, some 2,000 feet above the lake, is spectacular. Adventurous travelers will want to follow this pretty inland mountain road to Tremosine; be warned that the road winds its way up the mountain through hairpin turns and blind corners that can test even the most experienced drivers.

Gargnano

㉔ *30 km (19 mi) south of Riva del Garda, 144 km (89 mi) east of Milan.*

This small port town was an important Franciscan center in the 13th century, and now comes alive in the summer months when German tourists, many of whom have villas here, crowd the small pebble beach. An Austrian flotilla bombarded the town in 1866, and some of the houses still bear marks of cannon fire. Mussolini owned two houses in Gargnano: one is now a language school and the other, Villa Feltrinelli, has been restored and reopened as a luxury hotel.

Where to Stay & Eat

$$$$ ✕ **La Tortuga.** This rustic trattoria is more sophisticated than it first appears, with an extensive wine cellar and nouvelle-style twists on local dishes. Specialties include *agnello con rosmarino e timo* (lamb with rosemary and thyme), *persico con rosmarino* (perch with rosemary), and *carpaccio d'anatra all'aceto balsamico* (goose carpaccio with balsamic vinegar). ⊠ *Via XXIV Maggio at small harbor* ☎ *0365/71251* 🖷 *0365/ 71938* ▤ *AE, DC, MC, V* ⊘ *Closed Tues. No lunch Dec.–Mar.*

$$$$ 🏨 **Villa Feltrinelli.** This 1892 art nouveau villa hotel, named for the Italian publishing family that used to vacation here, is immersed in private gardens and faces the lake. Meticulously restored, it has frescoed ceilings, wood paneling, and original tile floors. The rooms are spacious and equipped with every luxury (as befits the final bill). If you can afford it, take the tower room. There's an extensive library open to guests. ⊠ *Via Rimembranza 38/40, 25084* ☎ *0365/798000* 🖷 *0365/798001* ⊕ *www.villafeltrinelli.com* ⇗ *21 rooms* ⚲ *Restaurant, room service, minibars, cable TV, pool, health club, bar, laundry service, business services, no-smoking rooms* ▤ *AE, DC, MC, V* ⊘ *Closed late Oct.–Easter* ⦿| *BP.*

¢ 🏨 **Hotel Bartabel.** This cozy hotel on the main street offers comfortable accommodations at a rock-bottom price. The restaurant has an elegant terrace overlooking the lake. ⊠ *Via Roma 39, 25084* ☎ *0365/713300* 🖷 *0365/790009* ⇗ *10 rooms* ⚲ *Restaurant; no a/c* ▤ *AE, DC, MC, V* ⊘ *Closed mid–late Nov. Restaurant closed Mon.* ⦿| *EP.*

Sports & the Outdoors

The **Upper Brescian Garda Park** stretches over nine municipalities on the western side of the lake, from Salò to Limone, covering 147 square mi. Call the **Limone Hotel Owners Association** (⊠ Via Quattro Novembre 2/C ☎ 0365/954720) for trail and bicycle-rental information. They're also the people to contact if you'd like to take part in one of the free treks led by the Gruppo Alpini Limone every Sunday from June to September.

Gardone Riviera

㉕ *12 km (7 mi) south of Gargnano, 139 km (86 mi) east of Milan.*

Gardone Riviera, a once-fashionable 19th-century resort now delightfully faded, is the former home of the flamboyant Gabriele d'Annunzio (1863–1938), one of Italy's greatest modern poets. D'Annunzio's estate, **Il Vittoriale,** perched on the hills above the town, is an elaborate memorial to himself, filled with the trappings of conquests in art, love, and war (of which the largest is a ship's prow in the garden), and complete with an imposing mausoleum. ⊠ *Gardone Riviera* ☎ *0365/296511* ⊕ *www. vittoriale.it* 🎟 *€11 for house or museum, €16 for both* ⊙ *Grounds Apr.–Sept., daily 8:30–8; Oct.–Mar., daily 9–5. House and museum Apr.–Sept., Tues.–Sun. 9:30–7; Oct.–Mar., Tues.–Sun. 9–1 and 2–5.*

More than 2,000 Alpine, subtropical, and Mediterranean species thrive at the **Giardino Botanico Hruska.** ⊠ *Via Roma* ☎ *0365/20347* 🎟 *€7* ⊙ *Mar. 15–Oct. 15, daily 9:30–6:30.*

> off the
> beaten
> path

SALÒ MARKET – Four kilometers (2½ mi) south of Gardone Riviera is the enchanting lakeside town of Salò, which history buffs may recognize as the capital of the ill-fated Social Republic set up in 1943 by the Germans after they liberated Mussolini from the Gran Sasso.

Every Saturday morning an enormous market is held in the Piazza dei Martiri della Libertà, with great bargains on everything from household goods to clothing to foodstuffs. In August or September a lone vendor often sells locally unearthed *tartufi neri* (black truffles) at affordable prices.

Where to Stay & Eat

★ **$$$–$$$$** ✕⊞ **Villa Fiordaliso.** The pink-and-white lakeside Villa Fiordaliso—once home to Claretta Petacci, given to her by Benito Mussolini—is a high-quality restaurant, but it also has seven tastefully furnished rooms, some overlooking the lake. The Claretta Suite is where Mussolini and Petacci were said to have carried on an affair. The art nouveau restaurant features seasonal ingredients such as zucchini flowers and porcini mushrooms, paramount in salads and soups. ⊠ *Corso Zanardelli 150* ☎ *0365/20158* 🖷 *0365/290011* ⊕ *www.villafiordaliso.it* ⇆ *6 rooms, 1 suite* ⎈ *Restaurant, cable TV, free parking* ▤ *AE, DC, MC, V* ☉ *Closed mid-Nov.–mid-Feb. Restaurant closed Mon. No lunch Tues.* ⫦ *BP.*

★ **$$$–$$$$** ⊞ **Villa del Sogno.** A narrow winding road takes you from town to this imposing villa, which surveys the valley and the lake below it. The large hotel terrace and the quiet surrounding grounds create a sense of escape. You may think twice about a busy sightseeing itinerary once you've settled into position in the sun, cool drink in hand. ⊠ *Corso Zanardelli 107* ☎ *0365/290181* 🖷 *0365/290230* ⊕ *www.villadelsogno.it* ⇆ *28 rooms, 5 suites* ⎈ *Restaurant, tennis court, pool* ▤ *AE, DC, MC, V* ☉ *Closed late Oct.–late Mar.* ⫦ *BP.*

$$–$$$$ ⊞ **Grand Hotel Fasano.** A former 19th-century hunting lodge between Gardone and Maderno, the Fasano has matured into a seasonal hotel of a high standard. To one side you face the deep waters of Lake Garda; on the others you're surrounded by a 12,000-square-mi private park where the original Austrian owners no doubt spent their days chasing game. Besides myriad activities on the water, there are two golf courses in the vicinity. All the rooms have a lakeview. There are older rooms filled with antiques, but these lack air-conditioning. ⊠ *Corso Zanardelli 190* ☎ *0365/290220* 🖷 *0365/290221* ⊕ *www.ght.it* ⇆ *68 rooms* ⎈ *Restaurant, minibars, cable TV, tennis court, indoor pool, beach, waterskiing, free parking* ▤ *No credit cards* ☉ *Closed mid-Oct.–mid-May* ⫦ *BP.*

★ **$$$** ⊞ **Gran Hotel Gardone.** Directly facing the lake, this majestic 1800s villa is surrounded by an attractive landscaped garden. Nearly all the rooms look out over the water. The ground-floor Winnie's Bar, named after Winston Churchill, a frequent guest, envelopes you in charming art nouveau furniture and decorations. ⊠ *Corso Zanardelli 84* ☎ *0365/20261* 🖷 *0365/22695* ⊕ *www.grangardone.it* ⇆ *180 rooms* ⎈ *Minibars, cable TV, pool, sauna, laundry service, meeting rooms, parking (fee)* ▤ *AE, DC, MC, V* ☉ *Closed mid-Oct.–Mar.* ⫦ *BP.*

¢ ⊞ **Villa Maria Elisabetta.** Many of the rooms in this charming hotel run by a group of hospitable nuns have views of Lago di Garda. You can sit in the hotel's garden or take one of the ground's trails down for a dip in the lake or a bask in the sun. ⊠ *Corso Zanardelli 180* ☎ *0365/20206* 🖷 *0365/2020818* ⇆ *42 rooms* ⎈ *Restaurant, bar; no a/c, no room TVs* ▤ *No credit cards* ☉ *Closed Oct. 18–Dec. 18* ⫦ *BP.*

Nightlife & the Arts

Gardone's tranquillity is its greatest attraction, but that doesn't inhibit conviviality. Visitors and locals alike relish a *passeggiata* (stroll) along the lakefront, stopping perhaps to enjoy an ice cream or aperitif. **La Terrazza** (⊠ Via Zanardelli 190 ☎ 0365/290220), in the Grand Hotel Fasano, is particularly elegant. Winston Churchill reputedly enjoyed more than a few brandies in the belle-epoque surroundings.

Sirmione

★ ❷ *138 km (86 mi) east of Milan.*

Dramatically rising out of Lake Garda is the enchanting town of Sirmione. *"Paene insularum, Sirmio, insularumque ocelle,"* sang Catullus in a homecoming poem: "it is the jewel of peninsulas and islands, both." The forbidding Castello Scaligera stands guard behind the small bridge connecting Sirmione to the mainland; beyond, cobbled streets wind their way through medieval arches past lush gardens, stunning lake views, and gawking crowds. Originally a Roman resort town, Sirmione served under the dukes of Verona and later Venice as Garda's main point of defense. It has now reclaimed its original function, bustling with visitors in summer. Cars aren't allowed into town; parking is available by the tourist office at the entrance.

Locals will almost certainly tell you that the so-called **Grotte di Catullo** (Grottoes of Catullus) were once the site of the villa of Catullus (87–54 BC), one of the greatest pleasure-seeking poets of all time. Present archaeological wisdom, however, does not concur, and there is some consensus that this was the site of two villas of slightly different periods, dating from about the 1st century AD. But never mind—the view through the cypresses and olive trees is lovely, and even if Catullus didn't have a villa here he is closely associated with the area and undoubtedly did have a villa nearby. The ruins are at the top of the isthmus and are poorly signposted: walk through the historic center and past the various villas to the top of the spit; the entrance is on the right. A small museum offers a brief overview of the ruins (on the far wall); for guided tours in English, call 02/20421469. ⊠ *Via Catullo Sirmione, Sirmione* ☎ *030/916157* 🎫 *€4* 🕑 *Mar.–mid-Oct., Tues.–Sun. 8:30–7; mid-Oct.–Feb., Tues.–Sun. 8:30–5.*

The **Castello Scaligero** was built, along with almost all the other castles on the lake, by the Della Scala family. As hereditary rulers of Verona for more than a century before control of the city was seized by the Visconti in 1402, they counted Garda among their possessions. You can go inside to take in the nice view of the lake from the tower, or you can swim at the nearby beach. ⊠ *Piazza Castello, Sirmione* ☎ *030/916468* 🎫 *€4* 🕑 *Tues.–Sun 8:30–7.*

off the
beaten
path

GARDALAND AMUSEMENT PARK – This park has more than 40 different rides and water slides, making it Italy's largest amusement park. It's 12 km (8 mi) east of Sirmione. ⊠ *Castelnuovo del Garda* ☎ *045/6449777* ⊕ *www.gardaland.it* 🎫 *€23* 🕑 *July and Aug.,*

daily 9 AM–midnight; Apr.–June and Sept., daily 9–6:30; Oct.,
weekends 9–6:30.

Where to Stay & Eat

$$$–$$$$ ✕ **La Rucola.** Next to Sirmione's castle, this elegant, intimate restaurant
has a creative menu, with seafood and meat dishes accompanied by a
good choice of wines. Three fixed-price menus are available. ✉ *Via*
Strentelle 3 ☎ *030/916326* 🖃 *AE, DC, MC, V* ☯ *Closed Thurs. and*
Jan.–mid-Feb. No lunch Fri.

$–$$ ✕ **Ristorante Al Pescatore.** Lake fish is the specialty at this simple, popular restaurant in Sirmione's historical center. Try grilled trout with a
bottle of local white wine and settle your meal with a walk in the nearby
public park. ✉ *Via Piana 20* ☎ *030/9199006* 🖃 *AE, DC, MC, V.*

★ $$$$ 🏨 **Villa Cortine.** This former private villa in a secluded park risks being
just plain ostentatious, but it's saved by the sheer luxury of its setting
and the extraordinary professionalism of its staff. The hotel dominates
a low hill, and the grounds—a colorful mixture of lawns, trees, statues,
and fountains—go down to the lake. The villa itself dates from the early
part of the 19th century, although a wing was added in 1952: the trade-
off is between the more charming decor in the older rooms and the better lake views from the newer ones. In summer a three-night minimum
stay and half board are required. ✉ *Via Grotte 6* ☎ *030/9905890*
🖶 *030/916390* ⊕ *www.palacehotelvillacortine.com* ⇗ *40 rooms*
♿ *Restaurant, minibars, cable TV, tennis court, pool, beach, bar, meet-*
ing rooms, free parking 🖃 *AE, DC, MC, V* ☯ *Closed late Oct.–mid-*
Apr. ⊓⊙⊏ *MAP.*

$$$–$$$$ 🏨 **Hotel Sirmione.** Just inside the city walls, near the Castello, this hotel
and spa sits amid lakeside gardens and terraces. Rooms are furnished with
comfortable Scandinavian slat beds, matching floral draperies and wall
coverings, and built-in white furniture. Many guests have been return-
ing for years, due largely to the homespun feel and the attentiveness of
the staff. ✉ *Piazza Castello 19* ☎ *030/916192* 🖶 *030/916558* ⊕ *www.*
termedisirmione.com ⇗ *101 rooms* ♿ *Restaurant, minibars, cable TV,*
pool, spa, 2 bars, Internet, parking (fee) 🖃 *AE, DC, MC, V* ⊓⊙⊏ *BP.*

LAKE COMO & BERGAMO

Updated by
Maria
Sophocles
For those whose idea of heaven is palatial villas, rose-laden belvederes,
hanging wisteria and bougainvillea, lanterns casting a glow over lakeshore
restaurants, and majestic Alpine vistas, heaven is Lake Como. In his *Char-*
terhouse of Parma, Stendhal described it as an "enchanting spot, un-
equaled on earth in its loveliness." Virgil called it simply "our greatest"
lake. Though summer crowds do their best to vanquish the lake's
dreamy mystery and slightly faded old-money gentility, they fail. Como
remains a consummate pairing of natural and man-made beauty. The
villa gardens, like so many in Italy, are a union of two landscape tradi-
tions: that of Renaissance Italy, which values order, and of Victorian
England, which strives to create the illusion of natural wildness. Such
gardens are often framed by vast areas of picturesque farmland—fruit
trees, olive groves, and vineyards.

Lake Como is some 47 km (30 mi) long north to south and is Europe's deepest lake (almost 1,350 feet). If not driving, you arrive at the lake by pulling into the railway station at Como, a leading textile center famous for its silks. Many travelers hasten to the vaporetti waiting to take them to Bellagio and the *centro di lago,* the center region of the lake's three branches, and its most beautiful section. The 2,000-year-old walled city of Como should not be missed, however. Car ferries traverse the lake, making it easy to get to the other main towns, Cernobbio, Tremezzo, and Varenna.

Bergamo

🅐 *55 km (34 mi) west of Brescia, 52 km (32 mi) east of Milan.*

From behind a set of battered Venetian walls high on an Alpine hilltop, medieval Bergamo majestically surveys the countryside. Behind are the snowcapped Bergamese Alps, and two funiculars connect the ancient **Bergamo Alta** (Upper Bergamo) to the modern **Bergamo Bassa** (Lower Bergamo). A worthwhile destination in its own right, Bergamo Bassa's long arteries and ornate piazzas speak to its centuries of prosperity, but it's nonetheless overshadowed by Bergamo Alta's magnificence. The massive **Torre Civica** offers a great view of the two cities. ✉ *Piazza Vecchia* ☎ *035/247116* ✉ *€3* ☉ *Apr.–Oct., Sun.–Tues. 9:30–7, Sat. 9:30–9:30; Nov.–Mar., Sat. 9:30–4:30, Tues.–Fri. by appointment only.*

> ### WORD OF MOUTH
>
> "Even the narrow crowded streets couldn't disguise the allure of Bergamo's Citta Alta. It seemed that around almost every corner there was a little square complete with fountain or statue."
>
> –JJBhoy

Bergamo's **Duomo** and **Battistero** are the most substantial buildings in Piazza Duomo. But the most impressive is the **Cappella Colleoni,** with stunning marble decoration. ✉ *Piazza Duomo* ✉ *Free* ☉ *Daily 10–12:30 and 2:30–5:30.*

In the **Accademia Carrara** you will find an art collection that is surprisingly rewarding given its size and remote location. Many of the Venetian masters are represented—Mantegna, Bellini, Carpaccio (circa 1460–1525/26), Tiepolo, Francesco Guardi (1712–93), Canaletto (1697–1768)—as well as Botticelli (1445–1510). ✉ *Bergamo Bassa, Piazza Carrara 82* ☎ *035/247149* ⊕ *www.accademiacarrara.bergamo.it* ✉ *€2.58, free Sun.* ☉ *Apr.–Sept., Tues.–Sun. 10–12:45 and 3–6:30; Oct.–Mar., Tues.–Sun. 9:30–12:30 and 2:30–5:30.*

Where to Stay & Eat

★ **$$–$$$$** ✕ **Taverna Colleoni dell'Angelo.** Angelo Cornaro is the name behind the Taverna del Colleoni, on the Piazza Vecchia right behind the Duomo. He serves imaginative fish and meat dishes, both regional and international, all expertly prepared. ✉ *Piazza Vecchia 7* ☎ *035/232596* ☲ *AE, DC, MC, V* ☉ *Closed Mon. and 1 wk in Aug.*

$$ ✕ **Da Ornella.** The vaulted ceilings of this popular trattoria on the main street in the upper town are marked with ancient graffiti, created by (patiently) holding candles to the stone overhead. Ornella herself is in the kitchen, turning out *casoncelli* (stuffed pasta) in butter and sage and platters of assorted roast meats. Three prix-fixe menus are available during the week, two on the weekend. Reservations are recommended. ⊠ *Via Gombito 15* ☎ *035/232736* ▭ *AE, DC, MC, V* ⊗ *Closed Thurs.*

$$ ✕ **La Trattoria del Teatro.** Traditional regional food tops the bill at this good-value restaurant in the upper town. The polenta is a silky delight, and game is recommended in season. Fettuccine *con funghi* (with mushrooms) is deceptively simple but a rich and memorable specialty. ⊠ *Piazza Mascheroni 3* ☎ *035/238862* ▭ *No credit cards* ⊗ *Closed Mon. and 2 wks mid-July.*

$–$$
FodorsChoice ✕ **Al Donizetti.** Find a table in the back of this central, cheerful *enoteca* ★ (wine bar) before choosing local hams and cheeses to accompany your wine (more than 800 bottles are available, many by the glass). Heartier meals are also available, such as eggplant stuffed with cheese and salami, but save room for the desserts, which are well paired with dessert wines. ⊠ *Via Gombito 17/a* ☎ *035/242661* ▭ *AE, MC, V* ⊗ *Closed Tues.*

$$ ✕▣ **Agnello d'Oro.** A 17th-century tavern on the main street in Upper Bergamo, with wooden booths and walls hung with copper utensils and ceramic plates, Agnello d'Oro is a good place to imbibe the atmosphere as well as the good local wine. Specialties are typical Bergamese risotto and varieties of polenta served with game and mushrooms. The same establishment has 20 modestly priced ($) rooms. ⊠ *Via Gombito 22* ☎ *035/249883* 🖷 *035/235612* 🛏 *20 rooms* ⸙ *Restaurant; no a/c* ▭ *AE, MC, V* ⊗ *Restaurant closed Mon. and Jan. 7–Feb. 5. No dinner Sun.* ⦿ *EP.*

$$–$$$$ ▣ **Excelsior San Marco.** The most comfortable hotel in Lower Bergamo, the Excelsior San Marco is only a short walk from the walls of the upper town. The rooms are surprisingly quiet considering the central location. You can breakfast on the rooftop terrace. ⊠ *Piazza della Repubblica 6, 24122* ☎ *035/366111* 🖷 *035/223201* ⊕ *www.hotelsanmarco.com* 🛏 *155 rooms* ⸙ *Restaurant, in-room safes, minibars, cable TV, bar, laundry service, Internet, parking (fee), no-smoking rooms* ▭ *AE, DC, MC, V* ⦿ *BP.*

Nightlife & the Arts

The annual summer **Festival Internazionale del Pianoforte** (International Piano Festival) is held in Bergamo's **Teatro Donizetti** (⊠ Piazza Cavour 15 ☎ 035/4160602 ⊕ www.teatrodonizetti.it). Call the theater for information about drama, opera, and ballet events throughout the year.

en route The Chiesa della Madonna del Ghisallo (Church of the Patroness of Bicyclists), open daily from March through November, is not far from the shores of Lake Como and affords a fine view. You will often see cyclists parked outside taking a breather after their uphill struggle, but many come simply in homage to this unique Madonna. It's located 48 km (30 mi) northwest of Bergamo, on the road to Bellagio.

Bellagio

28 *30 km (19 mi) northeast of Como, 56 km (35 mi) northwest of Bergamo.*

Fodor's Choice
★

Sometimes called the prettiest town in Europe, Bellagio always seems to be flag-bedecked, with geraniums ablaze in every window and bougainvillea veiling the staircases, or *montées,* that thread through the town. At dusk Bellagio's nightspots—including the wharf, where an orchestra serenades dancers under the stars—beckon you to come and make merry. It's an impossibly enchanting location, one that inspired French composer Gabriel Fauré to call Bellagio "a diamond contrasting brilliantly with the sapphires of the three lakes in which it is set."

Boats ply the lake to Tremezzo, where Napoléon's worst Italian enemy, Count Sommariva, resided at Villa Carlotta; and a bit farther south of Tremezzo, to Villa Balbianello. Check with the **Bellagio tourist office** (✉ Piazza Mazzini [Pontile Imbarcadero] ☎ 031/950204 ⊕ www.bellagiolakecomo.com) for the hours of the launch to Tremezzo.

★ **Villa Serbelloni,** a property of the Rockefeller Foundation, has celebrated gardens on the site of Pliny the Elder's villa overlooking Bellagio. There are only two guided visits per day, restricted to 30 people each, and in

May these tend to be commandeered by group bookings. ✉ *Near Palazza della Chiesa* ☎ *031/950204* ⌑ *€5* ☉ *Guided visits Apr.–Oct., Tues.–Sun. at 11 and 4; tours gather 15 mins before start.*

The famous gardens of the **Villa Melzi** were once a favorite picnic spot for Franz Lizst, who advised author Louis de Ronchaud in 1837: "When you write the story of two happy lovers, place them on the shores of Lake Como. I do not know of any land so conspicuously blessed by heaven." The gardens are open to the public, and though you can't get into the 19th-century villa, don't miss the lavish Empire-style family chapel. The Melzi were Napoléon's greatest allies in Italy (the family has passed down the name "Josephine" to the present day). ✉ *Via Lungolago Marconi* ☎ *031/951281* ⌑ *€5* ☉ *Apr.–Oct., daily 9–6.*

Where to Stay & Eat

$$ ✕◫ **La Pergola.** Try to reserve a table on the terrace at this popular lakeside restaurant about 1 km (½ mi) from Bellagio, on the other side of the peninsula. The best dining option is the freshly caught fish. You can also stay in one of the inn's 11 rooms, all of which have baths. ✉ *Pescallo, Piazza del Porte, 22021* ☎ *031/950263* 🖷 *031/950253* ⊕ *www.lapergolabellagio.it* ⇥ *11 rooms* ⟟ *Restaurant* 🖃 *AE, MC, V* ☉ *Restaurant closed Tues.* ⎮◯⎮ *BP.*

$ ✕◫ **Silvio.** At the edge of town, this family-owned trattoria with a lakeshore terrace specializes in fresh fish. Served cooked or marinated, with risotto or as a ravioli stuffing, the fish is caught by Silvio's family—it's local cooking at its best. Many of the modestly priced guest rooms have balconies and lake views. ✉ *Lòppia di Bellagio, Via Carcano 10, 22021* ☎ *031/950322* ⊕ *www.bellagiosilvio.com* ⇥ *21 rooms* ⟟ *Restaurant, cable TV* 🖃 *MC, V* ☉ *Closed Jan. and Feb.* ⎮◯⎮ *BP.*

★ **$$$$** ◫ **Grand Hotel Villa Serbelloni.** Designed to cradle nobility in high style, this hotel is a refined haven for the discreetly wealthy, set within a pretty park down the road from the Punta di Bellagio. The sense of 19th-century luxury has not so much faded as mellowed: the rooms are immaculate and plush; public areas are gilt and marble with thick, colorful carpets. The staff is unobtrusive and very knowledgeable about lake transportation. Churchill's and John Kennedy's former rooms face the Tremezzina, a group of towns across the lake. ✉ *Via Roma 1, 22021* ☎ *031/950216* 🖷 *031/951529* ⊕ *www.villaserbelloni.it* ⇥ *83 rooms* ⟟ *2 restaurants, room service, minibars, cable TV, tennis court, 2 pools, health club, hair salon, sauna, Turkish bath, laundry service, Internet, free parking, no-smoking rooms* 🖃 *AE, DC, MC, V* ☉ *Closed mid-Nov.–early Apr.* ⎮◯⎮ *BP.*

$$$ ◫ **Du Lac.** In the center of Bellagio, by the landing dock, this comfortable, medium-size hotel owned by an Anglo-Italian family has a relaxed and congenial feel. Most rooms have views of the lake and mountains, and there's a rooftop terrace garden for drinks or dozing. ✉ *Piazza Mazzini 32, 22021* ☎ *031/950320* 🖷 *031/951624* ⊕ *www.bellagiohoteldulac.com* ⇥ *48 rooms* ⟟ *Restaurant, minibars, cable TV, bar, free parking* 🖃 *MC, V* ☉ *Closed Nov.–Mar.* ⎮◯⎮ *BP.*

$$–$$$ ◫ **Hotel Florence.** This villa dating from the 1880s has an impressive lobby with vaulted ceiling and an imposing Florentine fireplace. Most of the rooms, furnished with interesting antiques, are large and comfortable and have splendid views of the lake. The restaurant and bar draw locals and visitors who appreciate the friendly and helpful staff. The hotel is across from the ferry stop. ⊠ *Piazza Mazzini 46, 22021* ☎ *031/950342* 🖶 *031/951722* ⊕ *www.hotelflorencebellagio.it* ⤻ *30 rooms* ♨ *Restaurant, cable TV, spa, bar; no a/c* ▭ *AE, MC, V* ℩◯℩ *MAP* ⊙ *Closed Nov.–Mar.*

$–$$$ 🏨 **Belvedere.** In Italian, Belvedere means "beautiful view," an apt description of this enchanting spot. The hotel has been in the Martinelli-Manoni family since 1880, and the unbroken tradition of service makes it one of the best places to stay in town. Antique chairs and eye-catching rugs complement the modern, understated rooms. The bathrooms are expertly designed for maximum comfort. Outstanding terraced gardens have replaced the vineyards that once surrounded the house. The restaurant is very good. ⊠ *Via Valassina 31, 22021* ☎ *031/950410* 🖶 *031/950102* ⊕ *www.belvederebellagio.com* ⤻ *68 rooms* ♨ *Restaurant, cable TV, pool, bar, meeting rooms, free parking, no-smoking rooms; no a/c* ▭ *AE, DC, MC, V* ⊙ *Closed Nov.–Mar.* ℩◯℩ *BP.*

> **WORD OF MOUTH**
>
> "We arrived in Varenna and almost immediately fell under the calming spell of Lake Como. It was so beautiful there words cannot describe it. Everything was slow, quiet and tranquil."   —daria

Varenna

㉙ *6 km (4 mi) northeast of Bellagio, 56 km (35 mi) northwest of Bergamo.*

You can reach Varenna by ferry from Bellagio. The principal sight here is the spellbinding garden of the **Villa Monastero**, which, as its name suggests, was originally a monastery. Now it's an international science and convention center. ⊠ *Varenna* ☎ *0341/295459* 🎫 *€2* ⊙ *Apr.–Oct., daily 9–7.*

Tremezzo

㉚ *34 km (21 mi) north of Cernobbio, 78 km (48 mi) north of Milan.*

If you're lucky enough to visit the small lakeside town of Tremezzo in late spring or early summer, you will find the magnificent **Villa Carlotta** a riot of color, with more than 14 acres of azaleas and dozens of varieties of rhododendrons in full bloom. The villa was built between 1690 and 1743 for the luxury-loving marquis Giorgio Clerici. The garden's collection is remarkable, particularly considering the difficulties of transporting delicate plants before the age of aircraft. Palms, banana trees, cacti, eucalyptus, a sequoia, orchids, and camellias are counted among the more than 500 species.

According to local lore, one reason for the Villa Carlotta's magnificence was a competition between the marquis's son-in-law, who inherited the estate, and the son-in-law's archrival, who built *his* summer palace directly across the lake (Villa Melzi, in Bellagio). Whenever either added to his villa and garden, it was tantamount to taunting the other in public. Eventually the son-in-law's insatiable taste for self-aggrandizement prevailed. The villa's last (and final) owners were Prussian royalty (including the "Carlotta" of the villa's name); the property was confiscated during World War I.

The villa's interior is worth a visit, particularly if you have a taste for the romantic sculptures of Antonio Canova (1757–1822). The best-known is his *Cupid and Psyche,* which depicts the lovers locked in an odd but graceful embrace, with the young god above and behind, his wings extended, while Psyche awaits a kiss that will never come. The villa can be reached by boats from Bellagio. ☎ *0344/40405* ⊕ *www.villacarlotta. it* ⊠ *€7* ⊗ *Apr.–Sept., daily 9–6; Mar. and Oct., daily 9–11:30 and 2–4:30.*

Villa Balbianello may be the most magical house in all of Italy. It sits on its own little promontory, Il Dosso d'Avedo—separating the bays of Venus and Diana—around the bend from the tiny fishing village of Ossuccio. Relentlessly picturesque, the villa is composed of loggias, terraces, and *palazzini* (tiny palaces), all spilling down verdant slopes to the lakeshore, where you'll find an old Franciscan church, a magnificent stone staircase, and a statue of San Carlo Borromeo blessing the waters. The villa is most frequently reached by launch from Como and Bellagio. Check with the **Como tourist office** (☎ 031/269712) for hours. Visits are usually restricted to the gardens, but if you plan in advance it's also possible to tour the villa itself. You pay €30 for a guide—regardless of how many are in your party—and an additional €5 entrance fee. ⊠ *Il Dosso di l'Avedo* ☎ *0344/56110* ⊠ *Gardens €5* ⊗ *Apr.–Oct., Tues., Thurs., and Fri. 10–1 and 2–6, weekends 10–6.*

Where to Stay

$$$$ 🏨 **Grand Hotel Tremezzo.** One hundred windows of this turn-of-the-20th-century building face the lake. The hotel, in the middle of a private park stretching over 12½ acres, has many creature comforts, from a heated swimming pool and private landing on the lake to a hillside for jogging. The 18-hole Menaggio & Cadenabbia golf course is about five minutes away by car. ⊠ *Via Regina 8, 22019* ☎ *0344/42491* 🖶 *0344/40201* ⊕ *www.grandhoteltremezzo.com* 🛏 *98 rooms, 2 suites* ⚐ *3 restaurants, room service, minibars, cable TV, tennis court, 2 pools, gym, hair salon, sauna, billiards, 3 bars, Internet, meeting room, helipad, free parking, no-smoking rooms* ⊟ *AE, DC, MC, V* ⊗ *Closed mid-Nov.–Feb.* ⊦⊙⊧ *BP.*

$ 🏨 **Rusall.** On the hillside above Tremezzo in the midst of a large garden, this small and reasonably priced hotel offers quiet and privacy. You can lie out on the terrace and enjoy a nice view. Rooms are simple and comfortable. ⊠ *Via S. Martino 2, 22019* ☎ *0344/40408* 🖶 *0344/ 40447* ⊕ *www.rusallhotel.com* 🛏 *19 rooms* ⚐ *Restaurant, tennis court, bar, Internet; no a/c* ⊟ *AE, DC, MC, V* ⊦⊙⊧ *EP.*

Cernobbio

31 *5 km (3 mi) north of Como, 53 km (34 mi) north of Milan.*

The legendary resort of Villa d'Este is reason enough to visit this jewel on the lake, but the town itself is worth a stroll. Despite the fact that

George Clooney lunches here regularly, the place still has a neighborhood feel to it, especially on summer evenings and weekends when the piazza is full of families and couples taking their passeggiata.

Built over the course of roughly 45 years for fisherman-turned-cardinal Tolomeo Gallio, the **Villa d'Este** has had a colorful and somewhat checkered history since its completion in 1615, swinging wildly between extremes of grandeur and dereliction. Its tenants have included the Jesuits, two generals, a ballerina, Caroline of Brunswick—the disgraced and estranged wife of the future king of England, George IV—a family of ordinary Italian nobles, and, finally, a czarina of Russia. Its life as a private summer residence ended in 1873, when it was turned into the fashionable hotel it has remained ever since.

Where to Stay & Eat

$$ ✕ **Il Gatto Nero.** This restaurant in the hills above Cernobbio has a splendid view of the lake. Specialties include *filetto con aceto balsamico* (filet mignon with balsamic vinegar), *pappardelle al ragù di selvaggini* (pasta with wild game sauce), and lake fish. Save room for the warm chocolate tort with its delicious liquid chocolate center. Reservations are encouraged as this is a regular haunt of Italian soccer stars as well as the jet set. ⊠ *Via Monte Santo 69, Rovenna* ☎ *031/512042* ⊟ *AE, DC, V* ☺ *Closed Mon. No lunch Tues.*

¢–$ ✕ **Pizzeria L'Ancora.** For the best pies in Como, and perhaps in the region, you won't want to miss this local haunt, run by a Neapolitan family that has been making pizza for three generations. Even Italians from out of town rave about the pizza here. Three sisters—Barbara, Grazie, and Linda—dish out hospitality as fine as the food. Their somewhat surly father (a dead-ringer for Santa Claus) looks like he has enjoyed a pizza or two in his time. ⊠ *Via Conciliazione 12, Tavernola* ☎ *031/340769* ⊟ *No credit cards* ☺ *Closed Wed.*

$$$$ ▥ **Villa d'Este.** One of the grandest hotels in Italy, the 17th-century Villa
Fodor'sChoice   d'Este has long welcomed Europe's rich and famous, from Napoléon
★   to the Duchess of Windsor. The chandeliers in the vast lobby illuminate marble staircases leading to guest rooms furnished in the Empire style: walnut paneling, sofas in striped silk, and gorgeous antiques. A broad veranda sweeps out to the lakefront, where a swimming pool extends above the water. The fanciful pavilions, temples, miniature forts, and mock ruins make for an afternoon's walk of quietly whimsical surprises. ⊠ *Via Regina 40, 22012* ☎ *031/3481* 🖷 *031/348844* ⊕ *www.villadeste. it* ⊯ *148 rooms, 13 suites* ⅙ *3 restaurants, room service, minibars, cable TV, 8 tennis courts, indoor pool, sauna, squash, bar, nightclub, laundry service, Internet, free parking, no-smoking rooms* ⊟ *AE, DC, MC, V* ☺ *Closed mid-Nov.–Feb.* �‖ *FAP.*

Como

㉜ *5 km (3 mi) south of Cernobbio, 30 km (19 mi) southwest of Bellagio, 49 km (30 mi) north of Milan.*

Como, on the south shore of the lake, is only part elegant resort, where cobbled pedestrian streets wind their way past parks and bustling cafés.

The other part is an industrial town renowned for its fine silks. If you're traveling by car, leave it at the edge of the town center in the clean, new, well-lighted underground parking facility right on the lake.

The splendid 15th-century Renaissance-Gothic **Duomo** was begun in 1396. The facade was added in 1455, and the transepts were completed in the mid-18th century. The dome was designed by Filippo Juvara (1678–1736), chief architect of many of the sumptuous palaces of the royal house of Savoy. The facade has statues of two of Como's most famous sons, Pliny the Elder and Pliny the Younger, whose writings are among the most important documents from antiquity. Inside, the works of art include Luini's *Holy Conversation,* a fresco cycle by Morazzone, and the *Marriage of the Virgin Mary* by Ferrari. ☒ *Piazza del Duomo* ☉ *Daily 7–noon and 3–7.*

At the heart of Como's medieval quarter, the city's first cathedral, **San Fedele,** is worth a peek, if only because it is one of the oldest churches in the region. ☒ *Piazza San Fedele* ☉ *Daily 7–noon and 3–7.*

If you brave Como's industrial quarter, you will find the beautiful church of **Sant'Abbondio,** a gem of Romanesque architecture begun by Benedictine monks in 1013 and consecrated by Pope Urban II in 1095. Inside, the five aisles of the church converge on a presbytery with a semicircular apse decorated with a cycle of 14th-century frescoes—now restored to their original magnificence—by Lombard artists heavily influenced by the Sienese school. In the nave the cubical capitals are the earliest example of this style in Italy. ☒ *Via Sant'Abbondio* ☉ *Daily 7–6.*

Exhibiting the path of production from silkworm litters to *moiré*-finishing machinery, the **Museo Didattico della Seta** (Silk Museum) is small but complete. The museum preserves the history of a manufacturing region that continues to supply almost three-fourths of Europe's silk. The friendly staffers will give you an overview of the museum; they are also happy to provide brochures and information about local retail shops. The museum's location isn't well marked: follow the textile school's driveway around to the low-rise concrete building on the left, and follow the shallow ramp down to the entrance. ☒ *Via Velleggio 3* ☏ *031/303180* ⊕ *www.museosetacomo.com* ▦ €8 ☉ *Tues.–Fri. 9–noon and 3–6. Tours in English available by reservation.*

Where to Stay & Eat

$$–$$$ ✕ **Raimondi.** This elegant restaurant in the Hotel Villa Flori (2 km [1 mi] toward Cernobbio) offers good value and a superb location, with a large terrace poised over the lake. The local freshwater fish is your best option, but a wide range of Italian dishes is capably prepared. The restaurant's season is longer than most, owing to its popularity with local residents. ☒ *Via Cernobbio 12* ☏ *031/338233* ▭ *AE, DC, MC, V* ☉ *Closed Mon. and Dec.–Feb. 14. No lunch Sat.*

★ **$$–$$$** ✕▦ **Terminus.** Commanding a panoramic view over Lake Como, this early-20th-century art nouveau building is the city's finest hotel. The marbled public spaces have an understated elegance, and the guest rooms are done in floral patterns and furnished with large walnut wardrobes and silk-covered sofas. In summer, the garden terrace is perfect for relaxing over a drink. Bar delle Terme ($$), the candelit restaurant, is worth a trip. The cranberry-hued space, filled with plush velvet sofas, resembles a large living room. The food and service as fine as the decor. Reservations are strongly advised, as there are only a few tables. It is closed Tuesday. ✉ *Lungolario Trieste 14, 22100* 🕾 *031/329111* 🖷 *031/302550* 🌐 *www.albergoterminus.com* 🛏 *40 rooms* ♨ *Restaurant, in-room safes, minibars, cable TV, in-room data ports, massage, sauna, meeting room, free parking, no-smoking rooms* ▤ *AE, DC, MC, V* ◎ *EP.*

$$–$$$ 🏨 **Barchetta Excelsior.** Though it has a rather unprepossessing exterior, this central, modern hotel is comfortable, with many rooms looking directly across Piazza Cavour to Lake Como. The rooms are airy and spacious, with those on the upper floors commanding the best views (though the noise of the piazza can be a distraction). The Barchetta is run by the group that owns Villa d'Este. ✉ *Piazza Cavour 1, 22100* 🕾 *031/3221* 🖷 *031/302622* 🌐 *www.hotelbarchetta.com* 🛏 *84 rooms* ♨ *2 restaurants, minibars, cable TV, bar, Internet, no-smoking rooms* ▤ *AE, DC, MC, V* ◎ *BP.*

$$–$$$ 🏨 **Villa Flori.** Italian patriot Garibaldi spent his wedding night here, in a suite that now bears his name. The hotel enjoys a panoramic view of Lake Como and attracts locals with its highly acclaimed restaurant, Raimondi. ✉ *Via Cernobbio 12, 22100* 🕾 *031/33820* 🖷 *031/570379* 🌐 *www.hotelvillaflori.com* 🛏 *45 rooms* ♨ *Restaurant, minibars, cable TV, meeting room* ▤ *AE, DC, MC, V* ◎ *EP.*

$ 🏨 **Tre Re.** This clean, spacious, welcoming hotel is a few steps west of the cathedral and convenient to the lake. Although the exterior gives away the age of this 16th-century former convent, the rooms are airy, comfortable, and modern. The moderately priced restaurant shares an ample terrace with the hotel. ✉ *Via Boldoni 20, 22100* 🕾 *031/265374* 🖷 *031/241349* 🌐 *www.hoteltrere.com* 🛏 *41 rooms* ♨ *Restaurant, cable TV, bar, Internet, free parking* ▤ *MC, V* ☯ *Closed mid-Dec.–mid-Jan.* ◎ *BP.*

Sports

The lake has many opportunities for sports enthusiasts, from windsurfing at the lake's northern end, to boating, sailing, and jet skiing at Como and Cernobbio. The lake is also quite swimmable in the summer months. For hikers there are lovely paths all around the lake. For an easy trek, take the funicular up to Brunate, and walk along the mountain to the lighthouse for a stunning view of the lake. For more information, contact the **Tourist Office** (✉ Piazza Cavour 17 🕾 031/269712).

Shopping

While in Como, seize the opportunity to shop for fine silk directly from its source. One of the biggest names is **Mantero** (✉ Via San Abbondio 8 🕾 031/321510), which supplies major design houses like Yves Saint Laurent, Nina Ricci, and Trussardi. Not far from the lake, good deals on ties, scarves, and shirts can be found at the factory store of **Binda** (✉ Viale Geno 6 🕾 031/3861629). **Frey** (✉ Via Garibaldi 10 🕾 031/267012) has a factory outlet on the western edge of the old town selling silk clothes and accessories. Another major name in silk production, **Ratti** (✉ Via Per Cernobbio 19 🕾 031/576000), has a factory store on the lake near Villa Flori.

On Saturday (except the first Saturday of every month), Piazza San Fedele holds a **local crafts market** from 9 to 7.

LAKE MAGGIORE & LAKE ORTA

Updated by
Maria
Sophocles

Magnificently scenic, Lake Maggiore has its mountainous western shore in Piedmont, its lower eastern shore in Lombardy, and its northern tip in Switzerland. The lake stretches nearly 50 km (30 mi) and is up to 5 km (3 mi) wide. The better-known resorts are on the western shore, particularly Stresa, a tourist town that provided one of the settings for Hemingway's *A Farewell to Arms*. A mountainous strip of land separates Lake Maggiore from Lake Orta, its smaller neighbor to the west, in Piedmont. Orta attracts fewer visitors than the three larger lakes, and can be a pleasant alternative in the summer.

Orta San Giulio

❸❸ *76 km (47 mi) northwest of Milan.*

At the end of a small peninsula jutting out into Lake Orta, this charming town is full of 18th-century buildings adorned with wrought-iron balustrades and balconies. The shady main square looks out across the lake to the small island of San Giulio. There is nothing more relaxing than sitting at one of the piazza cafés and watching sailboats catch the breezes that blow across the languid waters.

Rising up behind Orta, **Sacro Monte** (Sacred Mountain) is an interesting hike. Pass the Church of the Assumption at the edge of the old town, and just ahead is a gateway marked Sacro Monte. This leads to a comfortable climb that takes about 40 minutes round-trip. As you approach the top, you pass no fewer than 20 17th-century chapels, all devoted to St. Francis of Assisi. Within them, life-size terra-cotta statues (almost 400 in all) illustrate the saint's life. The campanile of the last chapel provides a view over the lake and the town, about 350 feet below.

The island of **San Giulio** is accessible by hired boat for about €6 round-trip per boatload of up to four people. The island takes its name from the 4th-century St. Julius, who—like St. Patrick in Ireland—is said to have banished snakes from the island. Julius is also said to have founded the **Basilica** in AD 390, although the present building shows more signs of its renovations in the 10th and 15th centuries. Inside, there's a black-marble pulpit (12th century) with elaborate carvings, and a crypt containing relics of the saint. In the sacristy of the church is a large bone said to be from one of the beasts destroyed by the saint, but it actually resembles a whalebone.

Much of the area is occupied by private villas; it takes only a few minutes to walk around the parts of the island open to the public. The view

> ### WORD OF MOUTH
>
> "If you are looking for a really cute village to stroll around in, nothing beats Orta San Giulio on Lago d'Orta. It's a nice place to stop for lunch and take in the views of the island basilica in the middle of the lake."   —BelTib

to Orta, with Sacro Monte behind it, is memorable, particularly in the late afternoon when the light picks up the glint of the wrought-iron traceries. Signs laud the virtues of silence and contemplation, and the island's quiet is broken only by the pealing of the basilica's bells.

Where to Stay & Eat

$$–$$$ ✕🖼 **Hotel San Rocco.** Half the rooms in this converted 17th-century lakeside convent on the edge of town have views of the water, garden, and surrounding mountains; many also have balconies. The restaurant ($$$) serves international cuisine and has beautiful views of the lake. ⊠ *Via Gippini 11, 28016* ☎ *0322/911977* 🖷 *0322/911964* ⊕ *www. hotelsanrocco.it* 🖵 *74 rooms* ⚖ *Restaurant, minibars, cable TV, pool, bar, parking (fee)* ▤ *AE, DC, MC, V* 🍴 *BP.*

---

en route — If you're going to Stresa from Orta San Giulio, you'll first pass through the town of Armeno, where in late summer and early fall you're likely to see whole families out in the woods, crouched down in their hunt for wild mushrooms, or—if they're lucky—truffles. Oaks blend into evergreens as you climb La Borromea, a 9-km (5½-mi) twisting, panoramic mountain road toward Mottarone (at 4,900 feet, the tallest peak between the lakes). The road continues through Gignese, which offers a last dramatic view of Maggiore before descending to Stresa on its western shore.

Stresa

🔟 *16 km (10 mi) east of Orta San Giulio, 80 km (50 mi) northwest of Milan.*

Stresa, which has capitalized on its central lakeside position, has to some extent become a victim of its own success. The luxurious elegance that distinguished its heyday has faded; the grand hotels are still grand, but traffic now encroaches upon their parks and gardens. Even the undeniable loveliness of the lakeshore drive has been threatened by the roar of diesel trucks and BMW traffic. One way to escape is to head for the Isole Borromee (Borromean Islands) in Lake Maggiore.

As you wander around the palms and semitropical shrubs of **Villa Pallavicino,** don't be surprised if you're followed by a peacock or even an ostrich: they're part of the zoological garden and are allowed to roam almost at will. From the top of the hill on which the villa stands you can see the gentle hills of the Lombardy shore of Lake Maggiore and, nearer and to the left, the jewel-like Borromean Islands. In addition to a bar and restaurant, the grounds also have picnic spots. ⊠ *Via Sempione 8* ☎ *0323/31533* ⊕ *www.parcozoopallavicino.it* 🎟 *€6.70* 🕙 *Early Mar.–Oct., daily 9–6.*

Boats to the **Isole Borromee** (⊕ www.borromeoturismo.it) depart every 15–30 minutes from the dock at Stresa's Piazza Marconi. Although you can hire a private boatman, it's cheaper and just as convenient to use the regular service. Make sure you buy a ticket allowing you to visit all the islands—Bella, Dei Pescatori, and Madre. The islands take their name from the Borromeo family, which has owned them since the 12th century.

Isola Bella (Beautiful Island) is the most famous of the three, and the first that you'll visit. It is named after Isabella, whose husband, Carlo III Borromeo (1538–84), built the palace and terraced gardens for her as a wedding present. Before Count Carlo began his project, the island was rocky and almost devoid of vegetation; the soil for the garden had to be transported from the mainland. Wander up the 10 terraces of the gardens, where peacocks roam among the scented shrubs, statues, and fountains, for a splendid view of the lake. Visit the palazzo to see the rooms where famous guests—including Napoléon and Mussolini—stayed in 18th-century splendor. ☎ *0323/30556* ✉ *Garden and palazzo €9* ☽ *Late Mar.–Sept., daily 9–5:30.*

Stop for a while at the tiny **Isola dei Pescatori** (Island of the Fishermen), less than 100 yards wide and only about ½ km (¼ mi) long. Of the three islands, this one has remained closest to the way it was before the Borromeos began building. The island's little lanes strung with fishing nets and dotted with shrines to the Madonna are the definition of picturesque; little wonder that in high season the village is crowded with postcard stands.

Isola Madre (Mother Island) is the largest of the three and, like Isola Bella, has a large botanical garden. Take time to see the profusion of exotic trees and shrubs running down to the shore in every direction. Two special times to visit are April (for the camellias) and May (for azaleas and rhododendrons). Also on the island is a 16th-century palazzo, where an antique puppet theater is on display, complete with string puppets, prompt books, and elaborate scenery designed by Alessandro Sanquirico, who was a scenographer at La Scala in Milan. ☎ *0323/31261* ✉ *€8.50* ☽ *Late Mar.–Sept., daily 9–5:30.*

For more information about the islands, contact the **Stresa tourist office** (✉ Piazza Marconi 16 ☎ 0323/30150) or ask at the docks (look for Navigazione Lago Maggiore signs).

Where to Stay

$$$$ 🏨 **Grand Hotel des Iles Borromées.** This palatial establishment has catered to a demanding European clientele since 1863. And though it still has the spacious salons and lavish furnishings of the turn of the 20th century, it has been discreetly modernized. The bathrooms are luxurious. ✉ *Corso Umberto I 67, 28838* ☎ *0323/938938* 🖷 *0323/32405* ⊕ *www. borromees.it* ⇆ *161 rooms, 11 suites* ♻ *Restaurant, room service, minibars, cable TV, in-room data ports, Wi-Fi, tennis court, indoor pool, spa, bar, laundry service, convention center, helipad, free parking* ⊟ *AE, DC, MC, V* ❤️ *BP.*

$ 🏨 **Primavera.** A few blocks up from the lake, Primavera has compact, simply furnished rooms in a 1950s building hung with flower boxes. Most rooms have balconies overlooking the streets of Stresa's old center. ✉ *Via Cavour 39, 28838* ☎ *0323/31286* 🖷 *0323/33458* ⇆ *31 rooms* ♻ *Cable TV, bar, Internet, meeting rooms, parking (fee); no a/c* ⊟ *AE, DC, V* ☽ *Closed mid-Nov.–mid-Mar.* ❤️ *BP.*

4

Verbania

③ *16 km (10 mi) north of Stresa, 95 km (59 mi) northwest of Milan.*

Verbania, across the Gulf of Pallanza from Stresa, is known for the **Villa Taranto,** which has magnificent botanical gardens. The villa was acquired in 1931 by Scottish captain Neil McEachern, who expanded the gardens considerably, adding terraces, waterfalls, more than 3,000 plant species from all over the world, and broad meadows sloping gently down to the lake. In 1938 McEachern donated the entire complex to the Italian people. ⊠ *Via Vittorio Veneto 111* ☎ *0323/404555* ⊕ *www. villataranto.it* ⊡ *€8* ☉ *Late Mar.–Oct., daily 8:30–7:30; last admission 1 hr before closing.*

Where to Stay & Eat

$–$$ ✕ **Da Cesare.** Off Piazza Cadorna and close to the embarcadero, this restaurant serves tasty risotto *con filetti di persico* (with perch fillets) and typical Piedmontese meat dishes, such as beef braised in Barolo wine. ⊠ *Via Mazzini 14* ☎ *0323/31386* ▭ *AE, DC, MC, V* ☉ *Closed Tues. and mid-Dec.–late Feb.*

$$$ ✕▥ **Il Sole di Ranco.** The same family has run this lakeside inn for more than 150 years. The present chefs, Davide Brovelli and his father, Carlo, do the family proud. Lake trout and perch find their way onto the menu, as do artichoke dishes in spring and eggplant in summer. Guest rooms ($$$–$$$$) are in two late-19th-century villas surrounded by a garden and overlooking the lake. Restaurant reservations essential. ⊠ *Piazza Venezia 5, Ranco, near Angera* ☎ *0331/976507* 🖷 *0331/ 976620* ⊕ *www.ilsolediranco.it* ➸ *14 rooms* ♪ *Restaurant, minibars* ▭ *AE, DC, MC, V* ☉ *Closed Dec. and Jan. Restaurant closed Tues. No lunch Mon.* ᠀⊙ǀ *BP.*

$ ▥ **Il Chiostro.** Originally a 17th-century convent, this hotel expanded into the adjoining 19th-century textile factory, adding some conference facilities. Rooms are clean and functional. ⊠ *Via Fratelli Cervi 14, 28900* ☎ *0323/404077* 🖷 *0323/401231* ⊕ *www.chiostrovb.it* ➸ *100 rooms* ♪ *Restaurant, cable TV, meeting rooms* ▭ *AE, DC, MC, V* ᠀⊙ǀ *BP.*

MILAN, LOMBARDY & THE LAKES ESSENTIALS

Transportation

BY AIR

Aeroporto Malpensa (MXP), 50 km (31 mi) northwest of Milan, is the major northern Italian hub for intercontinental flights and also sees substantial European and domestic traffic. The smaller Aeroporto Milano Linate (LIN), 10 km (6 mi) east of Milan, handles additional European and domestic flights.

The Malpensa Express Train connects Malpensa airport to Cadorna station near downtown Milan. The 40-minute train ride costs €9 (€12 round-trip), leaving Cadorna every half hour from 5:50 AM to 8:20 PM and Malpensa every half hour 6:45 AM to 9:45 PM. Malpensa Express Buses make the trip outside of these hours. In addition, Malpensa Shuttle Buses (€5) go to and from Milan's central train station (Stazione Centrale). There are departures every half hour from about 5 AM to 10 PM, and the trip takes about 75 minutes.

From Linate, the municipal Bus 73 runs every 10 minutes to Piazza San Babila in the heart of the city. The trip takes approximately 20 minutes. Tickets cost €1 and are sold at the Arrivals lounge newsstand (by the pharmacy). You can go from Linate to Stazione Centrale on the STARFLY bus, which runs every half hour; tickets are €2.50 and are sold on board.

If you need to get from one airport to the other, you can take the shuttle bus Airpullman (€8), which runs every 90 minutes. The trip takes approximately 90 minutes.

The drive from Malpensa to Milan is about an hour; take Route S336 east to the A8 autostrada southeast. From Linate it's about 10 minutes into the central city; head west following the signs.

Taxis wait directly outside the arrival building doors at Malpensa, and will take you downtown for about €80. The fare from Linate is about €25.

Malpensa is closer to lakes Como and Maggiore than to Milan itself. If that's where you're headed, it's perfectly feasible to skip the city altogether.
�⁷ Airport Flight Information **Aeroporto Malpensa & Aeroporto Milano Linate** ☎ 02/74852200 ⊕ www.sea-aeroportimilano.it.

BY BOAT & FERRY
Frequent daily ferry and hydrofoil services link the lakeside towns and villages. Residents take them to get to work and school, while visitors can use them for exploring the area. There are also special round-trip excursions, some with (optional) dining service on board. Schedules and ticket price are available on the Navigazione Laghi Web site and are posted at the landing docks.
🔷 Boat & Ferry Information **Navigazione Laghi** ✉ Via Ariosto 21, Milan ☎ 02/4676101 ⊕ www.navigazionelaghi.it. **Navigazione Lago di Como** ✉ Via per Cernobbio 18, Tavernola, near Como ☎ 031/579211. **Navigazione Lago di Garda** ✉ Piazza Matteotti 2, Desenzano ☎ 030/9149511. **Navigazione Lago Maggiore** ✉ Viale Baracca 1, Arona ☎ 800/551801.

BY BUS
Bus service isn't a good option for travel between cities here—it's neither faster, cheaper, nor more convenient than the train. For those determined to travel by bus, Autostradale goes to Turin, Bergamo, and Brescia from its hub at Autostazione Garibaldi, north of Milan's city center. Reservations are required.

There's regular bus service between the small towns on the lakes. It's less convenient than going by boat or by car, and it's used primarily by locals (particularly schoolchildren), but sightseers can use it as well. The bus service around Lake Garda serves mostly towns on the western shore. Call the bus operator SIA for information.
🔷 Bus Information **Autostradale** ☎ 02/637901. **SIA** ☎ 030/3774237.

BY CAR

Although trains are often more convenient for intercity travel, driving is the best way to get a sense of Lombardy's varied landscape. Several major autostrada routes intersect at Milan, all connected by the *tangenziale,* the road that rings the city. The A4 runs west to Turin and east to Venice; A1 leads south to Bologna, Florence, and Rome; A7 angles southwest down to Genoa. A8 goes northwest toward Lake Maggiore, and A9 north runs past Lake Como and over the St. Gotthard Pass into Switzerland.

To get around the lakes, you have to follow secondary roads—often of great beauty. S572 follows the southern and western shores of Lake Garda, S45b edges the northernmost section of the western shore, and S249 runs along the eastern shore. Around Lake Como, follow S340 along the western shore, S36 on the eastern shore, and S583 on the lower arms. S33 and S34 trace the western shore of Lake Maggiore.

Milan is well served by public transit, and taxis are readily available, so there's little motivation for taking on city driving yourself. Also, there's no free street parking—an added disincentive. For car service, contact Autonoleggio Pini. English-speaking drivers are available.

🚩 Car Service **Autonoleggio Pini** ☎ 02/29400555 🖷 02/2047843 ⊕ www.pini.it.

EMERGENCY SERVICES   Your car-rental company should be your first resource if you had a problem while driving in Italy, but it's also good to know that the ACI, the Italian auto club, offers 24-hour roadside assistance (free for members, for a fee for nonmembers). Regularly spaced roadside service phones are available on the autostrade.

🚩 **ACI dispatchers** ☎ 803/116.

BY MILAN PUBLIC TRANSIT

Milan has an excellent system of public transit, consisting of three subway lines and 120 tram and bus routes. Tickets are valid for one trip on the Metropolitana (subway) or 75 minutes on buses and trams, and must be purchased before you board and then stamped in machines at station entrances or on poles inside trolleys and buses. Standard tickets cost €1 and can be purchased from news vendors, tobacconists, and—at larger stops—machines (some of which require exact change). All-inclusive subway, bus, and tram tickets cost €3 for 24 hours or €5.50 for 48 hours; they're available at Duomo Metro and Stazione Centrale Metro stations. Trains run from 6 AM to 12:30 AM. For more information, check the ATM Web site (which has an English-language version) or visit the information office at the Duomo stop.

🚩 **ATM (Azienda Trasporti Milanesi)** ⊕ www.atm-mi.it.

BY TAXI

Taxi fares in Milan are high compared to those in American cities, but drivers are honest. A short downtown ride will come to about €15. Taxis wait at stands, or can be called at one of the numbers listed below. Dispatchers may speak some English; they'll ask for the phone number you're calling from, and they'll tell you the number of your taxi and how many minutes your wait will be. If you're in a restaurant or bar, ask the staff to call a cab for you. It's not customary to flag taxis down in the street, but drivers do sometimes stop if you hail them.

🗷 Taxi Companies **Autoradiotaxi** ☎ 02/8585. **Taxiblu** ☎ 02/4040. **Amicotaxi** ☎ 02/4000. **Radiotaxi** ☎ 02/6969.

BY TRAIN

Stazione Centrale, 3 km (2 mi) northwest of Milan's Duomo, is one of Italy's major passenger-train hubs, with service to destinations throughout Italy and the rest of Europe, as well as frequent direct service within the region to Como, Bergamo, Brescia, Sirmione, Pavia, Cremona, and Mantua. Milan has several other railway stations; the one you're most likely to encounter is Cardorna, the central-city destination for the shuttle train from Malpensa airport. If you're traveling at off hours, there's a chance you may have to venture to a suburban station—most notably Milano Lambrate for Bergamo.

For general information on trains and schedules, check with the FS–Trenitalia. The automated telephone line requires that you speak Italian, but the Web site has an English version.

🗷 Train Information **FS–Trenitalia** ☎ 892021 ⊕ www.trenitalia.com.

Contacts & Resources

EMERGENCIES

The nationwide ambulance number (118) connects you to the nearest emergency services provider. For first aid, ask for *pronto soccorso* and be prepared to give your address. Although the situation is gradually changing, do not expect emergency services workers to speak English, even at the highest levels. (A recent survey showed that only 10% of Italian doctors speak English.) It's wise to ask nonetheless, even if the answer is yes, the level of proficiency is likely to be low. If you need the emergency services, try to find someone (such as a member of your hotel staff) who speaks both languages to assist you.

There are two national police forces, the *carabinieri* and the *polizia di stato*. If you need to report a theft, or need the police for any other matter, first try contacting the carabinieri, who are both more likely to have jurisdiction and more likely to have an English-speaking officer in their number.

Pharmacies in Milan are open from about 8:30 AM to 12:30 PM and then from 4 PM to 7 PM. The most central after-hours pharmacy is Farmacia Carlo Erba on the north side of Piazza del Duomo between the Galleria Vittorio Emanuele and Piazza Mercanti. Another option is Ambreck, in Piazza Argentina near Corso Buenos Aires. The pharmacy on the upper level of Stazione Centrale is open 24 hours a day throughout the year, though the station itself closes in the early morning hours, at which time you need a police escort to get in. Throughout the region, pharmacies alternate late-night service. The address of the nearest open location is posted in every pharmacy window.

🗷 **Ambulance** ☎ 118. **Carabinieri** ☎ 112. **Police** ☎ 113.

📌 **24-Hour Pharmacies Ambreck** ✉ Piazza Argentina, Milan ☎ 02/29526966. **Farmacia Carlo Erba** ✉ Piazza del Duomo, Milan ☎ 02/86464832. **Stazione Centrale** ✉ Piazza Duca D'Aosta, Milan ☎ 02/6690735.

ENGLISH-LANGUAGE MEDIA

BOOKS **American Bookstore** (✉ Via Camperio at Via Dante, Castello, Milan ☎ 02/878920). **English Bookshop** (✉ Via Ariosto at Via Mascheroni, Porta Magenta, Milan ☎ 02/4694468 🌐 www.englishbookshop.it). **Feltrinelli Bookstore** (✉ Piazza del Duomo, Milan ☎ 02/86996897). **Feltrinelli International** (✉ Piazza Cavour 1, Duomo, Milan ☎ 02/6595644). **FNAC** (✉ Via Torino, at Via della Palla, Duomo, Milan ☎ 02/869541). **Hoepli** (✉ Via Hoepli 5, Duomo, Milan ☎ 02/864871).

TOURS

In Milan, a refurbished 1920s tram car operates a hop-on-hop-off tour of the city. Tickets (€20) are valid all day, and can be purchased on board. Departures are at 11 and 1 (also at 3, April–October) from Piazza Castello. The organization A Friend in Milan conducts walking tours of the city, including a visit to the *Last Supper*, day trips to the lakes, and shopping tours.

📌 **Resources A Friend in Milan** 🌐 friendinmilan.co.uk.

TRAVEL AGENCIES

📌 **Local Agent Referrals Compagnia Italiana Turismo** (CIT) ✉ Via Dante 6, Castello, Milan ☎ 02/863701. **American Express Travel Agency** ✉ Via Larga 4, Duomo, Milan ☎ 02/721041.

VISITOR INFORMATION

📌 **Tourist Information Bellagio** ✉ Piazza Mazzini (Pontile Imbarcadero) ☎🖷 031/950204 🌐 www.bellagiolakecomo.com. **Bergamo** ✉ Vicolo Aquila Nera at Piazza Vecchia, Upper Bergamo ☎ 035/242226 🖷 035/232730 ✉ Viale Vittorio Emanuele 20, Bergamo Bassa ☎ 035/210204 🖷 035/230184 🌐 www.provincia.bergamo.it/turismo. **Brescia** ✉ Corso Zanardelli 34 ☎ 030/43418 🖷 030/3756450 🌐 www.bresciaholiday.com. **Cernobbio** ✉ Via Regina ☎🖷 031/510198. **Como** ✉ Piazza Cavour 17 ☎ 031/269712 🖷 031/240111 🌐 www.lakecomo.org. **Cremona** ✉ Piazza del Comune 5 ☎ 0372/23233 🖷 0372/534080 🌐 www.aptcremona.it. **Malcesine** ✉ Via Capitanato 6/8 ☎ 045/7400044 🖷 045/7401633 🌐 www.aptgardaveneto.com. **Mantua** ✉ Piazza A. Mantegna 6 ☎ 0376/328253 🖷 0376/363292 🌐 www.turismo.mantova.it. **Milan** ✉ Via Marconi 1, Piazza Duomo ☎ 02/72524301 🖷 02/72524350 🌐 www.milanoinfotourist.com. **Pavia** ✉ Via Fabio Filzi 2 ☎ 0382/22156 🖷 0382/32221 🌐 www.apt.pavia.it. **Riva del Garda** ✉ Giardini di Porta Orientale 8 ☎ 0464/554444 🖷 0464/520308 🌐 www.gardatrentino.it. **Sabbioneta** ✉ Via Vespasiano Gonzaga 27 ☎🖷 0375/52039 ✉ Piazza D'Armi 1 ☎ 0375/221044 🖷 0375/222119 🌐 www.comune.sabbioneta.mn.it. **Sirmione** ✉ Viale Marconi 2 ☎ 030/916114 🖷 030/916222. **Stresa** ✉ Piazza Marconi 16 ☎ 0323/30150 🖷 0323/32561 🌐 www.distrettolaghi.it. **Tremezzo** ✉ Piazzale Trieste ☎ 0344/40493 🌐 www.tremezzina.com.

Piedmont &
Valle d'Aosta

Grape Harvest

WORD OF MOUTH

"Piedmont is way off the tourist track and as pretty as Tuscany. . . . Lots of wineries and wonderful undiscovered small towns."

—Barolo

"Valle d'Aosta is gorgeous. Old Roman ruins, neat towns, high peaks, rivers, and the day we were there, they had a festival for cows! . . . It's green and lush and just beautiful."

—Pat

WELCOME TO PIEDMONT & VALLE D'AOSTA

Landscape, Langhe

TOP 5
Reasons to Go

1 Sacra di San Michele: Explore one of the country's most spectacularly situated religious buildings.

2 Castello Fénis: This castle transports you back in time to the Middle Ages.

3 Monte Bianco: The cable car ride over the snowcapped mountain will take your breath away.

4 Turin's Museo Egizio: A surprising treasure—one of the word's richest collections of Egyptian art outside Cairo.

5 Regal wines: Some of Italy's most revered reds—led by Barolo, dubbed "the king wines"—come from the hills of southern Piedmont.

The mountains and valleys of Valle d'Aosta fairly cry out to be strolled, climbed, and skied. Here, the highest Alpine peaks—including **Monte Bianco** (aka Mont Blanc) and the **Matterhorn**—shelter resorts such as Breuil-Cervinia and Courmayeur and the great nature preserve known as the Gran Paradiso.

Gracing the Colline ("little hills") west of Turin are some opulent monuments of the 17th-century Piedmontese style, including the palace at **Stupinigi**, designed by Juvarra for the Savoy kings. Less worldly is the mesmerizingly medieval hilltop monastery of **Sacra di San Michele**.

Turin isn't just the car capital of Italy and home to the Holy Shroud. Neoclassical piazzas, shops filled with chocolates and chic fashions, and elegant baroque palazzos have all been prettied up for the 2006 Winter Olympics.

SWITZERLAND

Breuil-Cervinia

Courmayeur

Aosta

A5

VALLE D'AOSTA

Susa

A32

Sacra di San Michele

Turin

Stupinigi

23

Claviere

FRANCE

Pinerolo

Saluzzo

20 A6

589

Fossan

Cuneo

Mondovi

21

0   20 mi

0   20 km

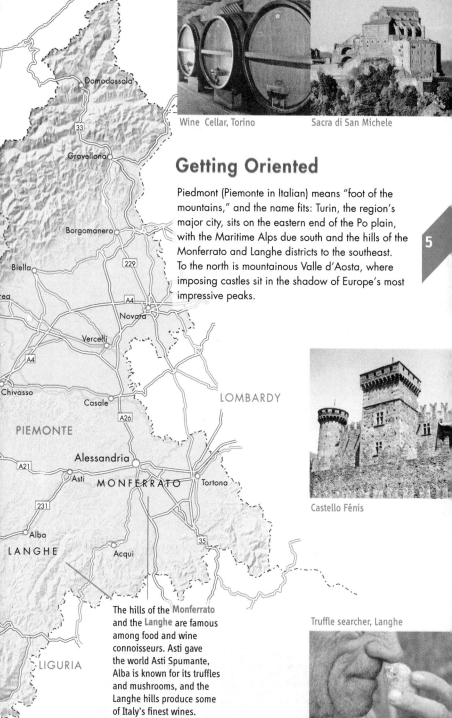

Wine Cellar, Torino

Sacra di San Michele

Getting Oriented

Piedmont (Piemonte in Italian) means "foot of the mountains," and the name fits: Turin, the region's major city, sits on the eastern end of the Po plain, with the Maritime Alps due south and the hills of the Monferrato and Langhe districts to the southeast. To the north is mountainous Valle d'Aosta, where imposing castles sit in the shadow of Europe's most impressive peaks.

Castello Fénis

The hills of the **Monferrato** and the **Langhe** are famous among food and wine connoisseurs. Asti gave the world Asti Spumante, Alba is known for its truffles and mushrooms, and the Langhe hills produce some of Italy's finest wines.

Truffle searcher, Langhe

PIEDMONT & VALLE D'AOSTA PLANNER

Making the Most of Your Time

The region is the site for the 2006 Winter Olympics, which is a good reason to pay a visit—and not just during the games. Lots of work, and many euros, have gone into development and renovation, the effects of which will linger well after the last medal has been handed out.

Turin is an underrated travel destination, and it's been polished to a shine for its role as Olympics host. If you like the idea of an Italian city with touches of Parisian sophistication, Turin is likely to strike your fancy.

Turin's residents will tell you how much it lifts their spirits when, on clear days, they have views of the surrounding mountains. In them you'll find exceptional hiking and climbing. Along the Piedmont–Valle d'Aosta border, the Gran Paradiso national park has beautiful, well-marked trails. Farther north is Monte Bianco, which should be a priority; you can ascend it by cable car, or, if you're an experienced climber, make a go of it with professional guides. If food and wine are your thing, also schedule a day or two on the less lofty slopes of the Langhe, south of Turin.

■ **The Truth about Turin's Shroud→→** When you hear the name Turin, the first thing that pops into your mind may be the Sacra Sindone (Holy Shroud), long held to be the burial shroud of Christ. Don't come to the city expecting to get a look at it—it's very rarely exhibited to the public, with the next appearance scheduled for 2025. Until then, you'll have to make do with a photocopy, on display in the Duomo.

Getting Around

Like any rugged, mountainous region, the Italian Alps can be tricky to navigate by car. Roads that look like superhighways on the map can be narrow and twisting, with steep slopes and cliff-side drops. Generally, roads are well maintained, but the sheer distance covered by all of those curves tends to take longer than you might expect, so it's best to figure in extra time for getting around. This is especially true in winter, when weather conditions can cause slow traffic and road closings. Check with local tourist offices, or in a pinch with the police, to make sure roads are passable and safe, and to find out whether you may need tire chains for snowy and icy roads.

Train service is extensive to the east of Turin along the Po plain. In the mountains, going by bus is the only public-transportation option; service is reliable, but slow. For more about car, bus, and train travel, see "Essentials" at the end of this chapter.

The French Connection

Napoleon's regime controlled Piedmont and Valle d'Aosta in the 19th century, and French influence remains evident in everything from traditional recipes redolent of mountain cheeses, truffles, and cream to Versailles-style gardens and wide, tree-lined boulevards. Well-dressed women in the cafés of Turin are addressed more often as *madama* than *signora*, and French is often spoken in the more remote mountain hamlets.

Hitting the Slopes

Skiing is the major sport in both Piedmont and Valle d'Aosta. Excellent facilities abound at resort towns such as Courmayeur and Breuil-Cervinia. The so-called Via Lattea (Milky Way)—five skiing areas near Sestriere with 400 km (almost 250 mi) of linked runs and 90 ski lifts—provides practically unlimited skiing. Lift tickets, running around €35 for a day's pass, are significantly less expensive than at major U.S. resorts.

To Italian skiers, a weeklong holiday on the slopes is known as a *settimana bianca* (white week). Ski resort hotels in the Piedmont and Valle d'Aosta encourage these getaways by offering six- and seven-day packages, and though they're designed with the domestic market in mind, you can get a bargain by taking advantage of the offers. The packages usually, though not always, include half- or full-board.

■ **Crossing Borders→→** You should have your passport with you if you plan to day-trip into France or Switzerland—though odds are you won't be asked to show it.

Finding a Place to Stay

High standards and opulence are characteristic of Turin's better hotels, and the same is true, translated into the Alpine idiom, at the top mountain resort hotels. The less-expensive hotels in cities and towns are generally geared to business travelers; make sure to ask if lower weekend rates are available.

Summer vacationers and winter skiers keep occupancy rates and prices high at the resorts during peak seasons. Many mountain hotels accept half- or full-board guests only and require that you stay for several nights; some have off-season rates that can reduce the cost by a full price category. If you're a skier, ask about package deals that can give you a break on the price of lift tickets.

Dining & Lodging Price Categories

WHAT IT COSTS in Euros					
	$$$$	**$$$**	**$$**	**$**	**¢**
Restaurants	over €22	€16–f22	€11–€16	€7–€11	under €7
Hotels	over €220	€160–€220	€110–€160	€70–€110	under €70

Restaurant prices are for a second course (un secondo). Hotel prices are for two people in a standard double room in high season, including tax and service.

How's the Weather?

Snow conditions for skiing vary drastically year to year—there is nothing approaching the consistency of, say, the Rockies—so keep apprised of weather conditions. Some years there's good snow beginning in November, while others don't see much more than a flake or two until February.

The mountains to the north tend to shield the lowlands from the harshest winter weather, resulting in something resembling a Mediterranean climate. Spring starts early, fall lingers, and winter is mercifully short. Locals only complain about the steamy summers.

5

TOP PASSEGGIATA

Turin's Piazza San Carlo is one of the city's highlights, with arcaded walkways and distinguished cafés.

Updated by
Peter Blackman

A PAIR OF CONTRASTING CHARACTERISTICS define the appeal of north-west Italy's Piedmont and Valle d'Aosta regions: mountain splendor and bourgeois refinement. Two of Europe's most famous peaks—Monte Bianco (aka Mont Blanc) and Monte Cervino (the Matterhorn)—straddle Valle d'Aosta's borders with France and Switzerland, and the entire region is a magnet for skiers and hikers. To the south, the mist-shrouded lowlands skirting the Po River are home to Turin, a city that may not have the artistic treasures of Rome or the cutting-edge style of Milan, but has developed a sense of urban sophistication that makes it a pleasure to visit. You also taste a mountain/city contrast in the cuisine: the hearty peasant cooking served in tiny stone villages and the French-accented delicacies found in the plain are both eminently satisfying. Meals are accompanied by Piedmontese wines commonly held to be Italy's finest.

TURIN

Turin—Torino, in Italian—is roughly in the center of Piedmont/Valle d'Aosta and 128 km (80 mi) west of Milan; it's on the Po River, on the edge of the Po plain, which stretches eastward all the way to the Adriatic. Turin's flatness and wide, angular, tree-lined boulevards are a far cry from Italian *metropoli* to the south; the region's decidedly northern European bent is quite evident in its nerve center. Apart from its role as northwest Italy's major industrial, cultural, intellectual, and administrative hub, Turin also has a reputation as Italy's capital of black magic and the supernatural. This distinction is enhanced by the presence of Turin's most famous, and controversial, relic, the Sacra Sindone (Holy Shroud), still believed by many Catholics to be the cloth in which Christ's body was wrapped when he was taken down from the cross.

Downtown Turin

Many of Turin's major sights are clustered around Piazza Castello, and others are on or just off the porticoed Via Roma, one of the city's main thoroughfares, which leads 1 km (½ mi) from Piazza Castello south to Piazza Carlo Felice, a landscaped park in front of the train station. First opened in 1615, Via Roma was largely rebuilt in the 1930s, during the Mussolini era.

The Main Attractions

1 Duomo di San Giovanni. The most impressive part of Turin's 15th-century cathedral is the shadowy, black marble–walled **Cappella della Sacra Sindone** (Chapel of the Holy Shroud), where the famous relic was housed before a fire in 1997. The chapel was designed by the priest and architect Guarino Guarini (1604–83), a genius of the baroque style who was official engineer and mathematician to the court of Duke Carlo Emanuele II of Savoy. The fire caused severe structural damage, and the chapel is closed indefinitely while restoration work proceeds.

The Sacra Sindone (Holy Shroud) is a 4-yard-long sheet of linen, thought by millions to be the burial shroud of Christ, bearing the light imprint of his crucified body. The shroud first made an appearance around the middle of the 15th century, when it was presented to Ludovico of Savoy

PIEDMONT & VALLE D'AOSTA, PAST & PRESENT

Ancient History. Piedmont and Valle d'Aosta were originally inhabited by Celtic tribes, who over time were absorbed by the conquering Romans. As allies of Rome, the Celts held off Hannibal when he came down through the Alpine passes with his elephants, but they were eventually defeated, and their capital—Taurasia, the present Turin—was destroyed. The Romans rebuilt the city, giving its streets the grid pattern that survives today. (Roman ruins can be found throughout both regions and are particularly conspicuous in the town of Aosta.)

The Middle Ages and the Savoy. With the fall of the Roman Empire, the region suffered the fate of the rest of Italy and was successively occupied and ravaged by barbarians from the east and the north. In the 11th century, the feudal French Savoy family ruled Turin briefly; toward the end of the 13th century it returned to the area, where it would remain, almost continuously, for 500 years. In 1798 the French republican armies invaded Italy, but when Napoléon's empire fell, the house of Savoy returned to power.

Risorgimento. Beginning in 1848, Piedmont was one of the principal centers of the Risorgimento, the movement for Italian unity. In 1861 the Chamber of Deputies of Turin declared Italy a united kingdom. Rome became the capital in 1870, effectively marking the end of Piedmont's prominence in national politics.

Industry and Affluence. Piedmont became one of the first industrialized regions in Italy, and the automotive giant FIAT—the Fabbrica Italiana Automobili Torino—was established here in 1899. Today the region is the center of Italy's automobile, metalworking, chemical, and candy industries, having attracted thousands of workers from Italy's south. The FIAT company, led by the Agnelli family—roughly Italy's equivalent of the Kennedys—has been arguably the most important factor in the region's rise to affluence.

5

in Chambéry. In 1578 it was brought to Turin by another member of the Savoy royal family, Duke Emanuele Filiberto. It was only in the 1990s that the Catholic Church began allowing rigorous scientific study of the shroud. Not surprisingly, results have bolstered both sides of the argument. On the one hand, three separate university teams—in Switzerland, Britain, and the United States—have concluded, as a result of carbon 14 dating, that the cloth is a forgery dating from between 1260 and 1390. On the other hand, they are unable to explain how medieval forgers could have created the shroud's image, which resembles a photographic negative, and how they could have had the knowledge or means to incorporate traces of Roman coins covering the eyelids and endemic Middle Eastern pollen woven into the cloth. Either way, the shroud continues to be revered as a holy relic, exhibited to the public on very rare occasions—the next official display is planned for 2025. In lieu of the real thing, a photocopy is on permanent display near the altar of the Duomo. ⊠ *Piazza San Giovanni, Centro* ☎ *011/4361540* ☉ *Mon.–Sat. 6:30–noon and 3–7, Sun. 8–noon and 3–7.*

8 **Galleria Sabauda.** Some of the most important paintings from the vast collections of the house of Savoy are displayed here. The collection is particularly rich in 16th- and 17th-century Dutch and Flemish paintings: note the *St. Francis with Stigmata* by Jan Van Eyck (1395–1441), in which the saint receives the marks of Christ's wounds while a companion cringes beside him. Other Dutch masterpieces include paintings by Anthony Van Dyck (1599–1641) and Rembrandt (1606–69). *Tobias and the Angel* by Piero del Pollaiuolo (circa 1443–96) is showcased, and other featured Italian artists include Fra Angelico (circa 1400–55), Andrea Mantegna (1431–1506), and Paolo Veronese (1528–88). Along with the Egyptian Museum, the gallery is housed in the **Palazzo dell'Accademia delle Scienze,** a baroque tour de force designed by priest-architect Guarino Guarini. ⊠ *Via Accademia delle Scienze 6, Centro* ☎*011/547440* ☜ *€4, €8 with admission to Museo Egizio* ☾ *Fri.–Tues. 8:30–2, Wed. and Thurs. 2–7:30.*

★ ☾ **⑪** **Mole Antonelliana.** You can't miss the unusual square dome and thin, elaborate spire of this Turin landmark above the city's rooftops. This odd structure, built between 1863 and 1889, was originally intended to be a synagogue, but costs escalated and eventually it was bought by the city of Turin. In its time it was the tallest brick building in the world. You can take the crystal elevator to reach the terrace at the top of the dome for an excellent view of the city, the plain, and the Alps beyond. Also worth a visit is the Mole Antonelliana's **Museo Nazionale del Cinema** (National Cinema Museum), which embraces more than 34,000 square feet and houses many items of film memorabilia as well as a film library with some 7,000 titles. ⊠ *Via Montebello 20, Centro* ☎ *011/8125658* ⊕ *www.museonazionaledelcinema.it* ☜ *Museum €5.20, elevator €3.62, combination ticket €6.80* ☾ *Museum Tues.–Fri. and Sun. 9–8, Sat. 9 AM–11 PM; ticket sales end 75 mins before closing; elevator Tues.–Fri. and Sun. 10–8, Sat. 10 AM–11 PM.*

9 **Museo Egizio.** The Egyptian Museum's superb collection includes statues
Fodor'sChoice of pharaohs and mummies and entire frescoes taken from royal tombs—
★ all in all, it's one of the world's finest and largest museums of its kind. Look for the magnificent 13th-century BC statue of Ramses II and the fascinating Tomb of Kha. The latter was found intact with furniture, supplies of food and clothing, writing instruments, and a complete set of personal cosmetics and toiletries. Unfortunately, the museum's objects are not always displayed according to modern standards. Along with carefully constructed exhibits with detailed information in English and Italian you will also find rooms that resemble warehouses filled with objects, with little or no information identifying what they are. ⊠ *Via Accademia delle Scienze 6, Centro* ☎ *011/5617776* ⊕ *www.museoegizio.it* ☜ *€6.50, €8 with admission to Galleria Sabauda* ☾ *Tues.–Sun. 8:30–7:30; ticket sales end 1 hr before closing.*

3 **Palazzo Madama.** In the center of Piazza Castello, this castle was named for the Savoy queen Maria Cristina, who made it her home in the 17th century. The building incorporates the remains of a Roman gate with later medieval and Renaissance additions. Filippo Juvarra (1678–1736) designed the castle's monumental baroque facade. Open to the public

Turin

are the atrium; the large central room known as Il Voltone, where a glass floor reveals the castle's Roman foundations; Juvarra's splendid baroque staircase; and the Salone del Senato, where you'll find temporary art exhibitions. At this writing the museum was closed for restoration, but was expected to open in December 2005. ⊠ *Piazza Castello, Centro* ☎ *011/4429912* ⊕ *www.comune.torino.it/palazzomadama* ⊠ *Free, exhibitions €3.50* ☉ *Tues.–Fri. and Sun. 10–8, Sat. 10 AM–11 PM.*

❼ **Piazza San Carlo.** Surrounded by shops, arcades, fashionable cafés, and elegant baroque palaces, this is one of the most beautiful squares in Turin. In the center stands a statue of Duke Emanuele Filiberto of Savoy, victor at the battle of San Quintino in 1557. The melee heralded the peaceful resurgence of Turin under the Savoy after years of bloody dynastic fighting. The fine bronze statue erected in the 19th century is one of Turin's symbols.

need a break?
A chocolate lover's pilgrimage to Turin inevitably leads to **Al Bicerin** (⊠ Piazza della Consolata 5, Centro ☎ 011/4369325 ⊕ www.bicerin.it ☉ Closed Wed.), which first opened its doors in 1763. Cavour, Nietzsche, Puccini, and Dumas have all sipped here, and if you order the house specialty, the *bicerin* (a hot drink with layers of chocolate, coffee, and cream), you'll understand why. Don't be surprised if the friendly and energetic owner, Marité Costa, also tries to tempt you with one of her flavored *zabajoni* (warm eggnogs). Chocolate goodies, including chocolate-flavored pasta, are on sale in the café store. The historic **Caffè San Carlo** (⊠ Piazza San Carlo 156, Centro ☎ 011/532586) is usually lively with locals gathered at the marble-top tables under the huge crystal chandelier. Breakfast and lunch, afternoon snack, and evening aperitifs are all served in this particularly elegant neoclassical setting.

❹ **San Lorenzo.** Architect Guarino Guarini was in his mid-60s when he began this church in 1668. The masterful use of geometric forms and the theatrical control of light and shadow show him working at his mature and confident best. Stand in the center of the church and look up into the cupola to enjoy the full effect. ⊠ *Piazza Castello, Centro* ☎ *011/4361527* ☉ *Daily 8:30–noon and 4–7.*

A GOOD WALK: BAROQUE TURIN

When the Savoy moved the seat of their Duchy from France to Turin in 1563, they instituted a process of urban renewal that was to employ some of the most important baroque architects of the day. During 200 years of almost continuous development, Turin was transformed into an elegant European capital more than twice its original size, with new churches, palaces, public squares, and streets.

The first section of town to be developed was the *contrada nuova* (new district), to the southwest of the old medieval fortifications. It was surrounded by extensive walls, which no longer exist. Only the name of the present-day train station serves as a reminder of the *porta nuova* (new gate) that was once the main entrance to this part of town.

This walk, encompassing some of Turin's most important baroque monuments, begins in what was de-

need a break?   **Baratti e Milano** (✉ Piazza Castello 27, Centro ☎ 011/5613060), in the glass-roof Galleria Subalpina near Via Po, is one of Turin's charming old cafés. It's famous for its exquisite chocolates—indulge your sweet tooth or buy some *gianduiotti* (hazelnut chocolates) or candied chestnuts to take home to friends. Light lunches are served at the tables to the rear of the café. The tiny café **Mulassano** (✉ Piazza Castello 15, Centro ☎ 011/547990), decorated with marble and finely carved wood panels, is famous for its *tramezzini* (small triangular sandwiches made with lightly toasted white bread), invented here in the 1920s. Popular with the pre- and post-theater crowd, the café also offers a unique roulette system for clients trying to decide on who pays the bill—ask the cashier for an explanation.

Also Worth Seeing

⓿ Palazzo Carignano. A baroque triumph by Guarino Guarini (the priest who designed several of Turin's most noteworthy structures), this red-brick palace was built between 1679 and 1685 and would play an important role in the 19th-century unification of Italy. Vittorio Emanuele II of Savoy (1820–78), united Italy's first king, was born within these walls, and Italy's first parliament met here from 1860 to 1865. The palace now houses the **Museo del Risorgimento,** a museum honoring the 19th-century movement for Italian unity. ✉ *Via Accademia delle Scienze 5, Centro* ☎ *011/5621147* ⊕ *www.regione.piemonte.it/cultura/risorgimento* 💶 *€5* ⊙ *Tues.–Sun. 9–7; ticket sales end 1 hr before closing.*

❷ Palazzo Reale. This 17th-century palace, the former Savoy royal residence, is an imposing work of brick, stone, and marble that stands on the site of one of Turin's ancient Roman city gates. In contrast to its sober exterior, the palace's interior is swathed in luxurious, mostly rococo trappings, including tapestries, gilt ceilings, and sumptuous 17th- to 19th-century furniture. Behind the palace you can relax in the royal gardens. ✉ *Piazza Castello, Centro* ☎ *011/4361455* 💶 *Gardens free, palace €6.50* ⊙ *Palace, Tues.–Sun. 8:30–6:15; guided visits depart every 40 mins; gardens, 9–1 hr before sunset.*

The **Armeria Reale** (Royal Armory), in a wing of the Royal Palace, holds one of Europe's most extensive collections of arms and armor. It's a must-

---

signed to be the focal point of the contrada nuova, **Piazza San Carlo** ⓻. Developed in the style of the French *place royales* (royal square), Piazza San Carlo was not only the most important public space of this new part of the city, but also a symbol of the authority of the Savoy family. At the southwestern end are the twin baroque churches of **San Carlo** ⓹ and **Santa Cristina** ⓺, while some of Turin's most famous cafés are to be found beneath the porticoes that line each side of the square.

Beyond the northeast end of Piazza San Carlo is the imposing **Palazzo dell'Accademia delle Scienze,** begun by priest/architect Guarino Guarini in 1679. If you're in the mood for museums, devote an hour or two to the collections housed inside, the **Galleria Sabauda** ⓼ and the **Museo Egizio** ⓽. To the east, across the street, is the graceful **Palazzo Carignano** ⓾, united Italy's first parliament building and another of Guarino Guarini's architectural masterpieces in Turin. (As a brief detour, you can follow Via Principe, to the right of the palazzo, to see the eastern facade of the palace on Piazza Carlo Alberto.)

see for connoisseurs. At time of writing the museum was closed for extensive renovations. ⊠ *Entrance at Piazza Castello 191, Centro* ☎ *011/543889* ◫ *€2.07* ⊙ *Tues.–Sun. 10:30–7:30.*

5 **San Carlo.** The ornate baroque facade of this 17th-century church was enhanced in the latter part of the 19th century to harmonize with the facade of neighboring Santa Cristina. ⊠ *Piazza San Carlo, south end of square, right corner, Centro* ☎ *011/5620922* ⊙ *Weekdays 8–noon and 4–6:30, Sat. 8–noon and 4–6, Sun. 9–12:45 and 4–6.*

6 **Santa Cristina.** Built in the mid-17th century, this church received a baroque-style face-lift by Juvarra in 1715. ⊠ *Piazza San Carlo, south end of square, left corner, Centro* ☎ *011/539281* ⊙ *Daily 7–noon and 3–7.*

> **off the beaten path**

GALLERIA CIVICA D'ARTE MODERNA E CONTEMPORANEA (GAM) – In 1863 Turin was the first Italian city to begin a public collection devoted to contemporary art. Housed in a modern building on the edge of downtown, a permanent display of more than 600 paintings, sculptures, and installation pieces provides an exceptional glimpse of how Italian contemporary art has evolved since the late 1800s. The Futurist, Pop, Neo Dada, and Arte Povera movements are particularly well represented, and the gallery has a fine video and art film collection. ⊠ *Via Magenta 31, Centro* ☎ *011/5629911* ⊕ *www.gamtorino.it* ◫ *€7.50* ⊙ *Tues.–Sun. 9–7.*

Along the Po

The Po River is narrow and unprepossessing here in Turin, only a hint of the broad waterway that it becomes as it flows eastward toward the Adriatic. It's flanked, however, by formidable edifices, a park, and a lovely pedestrian path.

The Main Attractions

15 **Borgo Medioevale.** Along the banks of the Po, this complex, built for a General Exhibition in 1884, is a faithful reproduction of a typical Piedmont village in the Middle Ages: craft shops, houses, a church, and stores cluster the narrow lanes, and in the center of the village the **Rocca**

Continue northeast on Via Accademia delle Scienze to reach **Piazza Castello.** The massive building occupying an entire block at the center of the square is **Palazzo Madama** , parts of which are open to the public. Don't miss the dramatic baroque staircase, in the entrance hall, that was begun by Juvarra in 1718. In the northwest corner of the same square is another example of Guarini's lively architectural vision, the church of **San Lorenzo** . Near San Lorenzo is the entrance to the imposing **Palazzo Reale** , where you can view sumptuous rococo interiors. The gate, flanked by statues of Castor and Pollux, is thought by some to be a focal point of otherworldly powers. It marks the apex of two international triangles alleged to have magical significance, one formed by Turin, London, and San Francisco, the other by Turin, Lyon, and Prague.

Wrap up your walk by taking the passage to the left of the Palazzo Reale to reach Piazza San Giovanni and the **Duomo di San Giovanni** . This hushed, shadowy repository of the city's famed relic, the Shroud of Turin, is yet another Guarini creation.

Medioevale, a medieval castle, provides the town's main attraction. ✉ *Southern end of Parco del Valentino, San Salvario* ☎ *011/4431701* ⊕ *www.borgomedioevaletorino.it* 🎫 *Village free, Rocca Medioevale €5* ⊙ *Village Apr.–Oct., daily 9–8; Nov.–Mar., daily 9–7; Rocca Medioevale Tues.–Sun. 9–7; groups of no more than 25 enter the castle every ½ hr; ticket counter closes at 6:15.*

★ ⑯ **Museo dell'Automobile.** No visit to car-manufacturing Turin would be complete without a pilgrimage to see perfectly conserved Bugattis, Ferraris, and Isotta Fraschinis. Here you'll get an idea of the importance of FIAT—and automobiles in general—to Turin's economy. There's a collection of antique cars from as early as 1896, and displays show how the city has changed over the years as a result of its premier industry. For the true automobile fan, there's even a section devoted to the history of car tires. (A yearlong closure for restoration is planned for 2006. At this writing the dates of were undetermined, so call ahead before visiting.) ✉ *Corso Unità d'Italia 40, Millefonti* ☎ *011/677666* ⊕ *www.museoauto.it* 🎫 *€5.50* ⊙ *Tues., Wed., Fri., and Sat. 10–6:30, Thurs. 10–10 PM, and Sun. 10–8:30.*

⑭ **Parco del Valentino.** This pleasant riverside park is a great place to stroll, bike, or jog. Originally the grounds of a relatively simple hunting lodge, the park owes its present arrangement to Madama Maria Cristina of France, who received the land and lodge as a wedding present after her marriage to Vittorio Amedeo I of Savoy. With memories of 16th-century French châteaux in mind, she began work in 1620 and converted the lodge into a magnificent palace, the **Castello del Valentino.** The building, now home to the University of Turin's Faculty of Architecture, is not open to the general public. Next to the palace are botanical gardens, established in 1729, where local and exotic flora can be seen in a hothouse, herbarium, and arboretum. ✉ *Parco del Valentino, San Salvario* ☎ *011/6707446 botanical gardens* 🎫 *Gardens €3* ⊙ *Gardens Apr.–Sept., weekends 9–1 and 3–7.*

⑰ **Pinacoteca Giovanni e Marella Agnelli.** This gallery was opened by Gianni Agnelli (1921–2003), the head of FIAT and patriarch of one of Italy's most powerful families, just four months before his death. The emphasis here is on quality rather than quantity: 25 works of art from the Agnelli private collection are on permanent display, along with temporary exhibitions. There are four magnificent scenes of Venice by Canaletto (1697–1768), two splendid views of Dresden by Canaletto's nephew, Bernardo Bellotto (1720–80), several works by Manet (1832–83), Renoir (1841–1919), Matisse (1869–1954), and Picasso (1881–1973), and fine examples of the work of Italian Futurist painters Balla (1871–1958) and Severini (1883–1966). The gallery is located on the top floor of the **Lingotto,** a former FIAT factory that was completely transformed between 1982 and 2002 by architect

WORD OF MOUTH

"The highlights of our stay in Turin were walking under the grand arcades that run alongside miles of the streets downtown, window-shopping, and stopping for coffee, pastries, or chocolate at one of the many elegant cafés."   –anne

Renzo Piano. The multilevel complex now contains two hotels, a shopping mall, several movie theaters, restaurants, and an auditorium. ✉ *Via Nizza 230, Lingotto* ☎ *011/0062008* ⊕ *www.pinacoteca-agnelli.it* 💷 *€4* ⊙ *Tues.–Sun. 9–7.*

> **off the beaten path**

SASSI–SUPERGA COG TRAIN – The 18-minute ride from Sassi up the Superga hill is an absolute treat on a clear day. The view of the Alps is magnificent at the hilltop **Parco Naturale Collina Torinese,** a tranquil retreat from the bustle of the city. If you feel like a little exercise, you can walk back down to Sassi (about two hours) on one of the well-marked, wooded trails that start from the upper station. Other circular trails lead through the park and back to Superga, where mountain bikes are also available for rent. ✉ *Piazza G. Modena, Sassi* ☎ *011/5764733 cog train, 011/8903667 bikes* ⊕ *www.gtt.to.it* 💷 *Weekdays €1.55 one-way; weekends €2.58 one-way* ⊙ *Hourly service Mon. and Wed.–Fri. 9–noon and 2–5; hourly service weekends 9–8; bus service replaces the train on Tues.*

BASILICA DI SUPERGA – Since 1731, the Basilica di Superga has been the burial place of kings. Visible from miles around, the thoroughly baroque church was designed by Juvarra in the early 18th century, and no less than 58 members of the Savoia family are memorialized in the crypt. ✉ *Strada della Basilica di Superga 73* ☎ *011/8980083 basilica, 011/8997456 crypt* 💷 *Free* ⊙ *Basilica: Apr.–Oct., daily 9–noon and 3–6; Nov.–Mar., daily 9–noon and 3–5. Crypt: Apr.–Oct., Mon.–Thurs. 9:30–1:30 and 2:30–6:30, weekends 9:30–7:30; Nov.–Mar., weekends 9:30–1:30 and 2:30–6:30.*

Also Worth Seeing

⓬ **Gran Madre di Dio.** On the east bank of the Po, this neoclassical church is modeled after the Pantheon in Rome. It was built between 1827 and 1831 to commemorate the return of the house of Savoy to Turin after the fall of Napoléon's empire. ✉ *Piazza Gran Madre di Dio, Borgo Po* ☎ *011/8193572* ⊙ *Mon.–Sat. 7:30–noon and 3:30–7, Sun. 7:30–1 and 3:30–7.*

⓭ **Santa Maria del Monte.** The church and convent standing on top of 150-foot Monte dei Cappuccini date from 1583. Don't be surprised if you find yourself in the middle of a wedding party, as couples often come here to be photographed. Next to the church is the tiny **Museo Nazionale della Montagna,** dedicated to mountains and to mountain climbing. ✉ *Monte dei Cappuccini, above Corso Moncalieri, Borgo Po* ☎ *011/6604414 church, 011/6604104 museum* ⊕ *www.museomontagna.org* 💷 *Church free, museum €5* ⊙ *Church, daily 9–noon, and 2:30–6; museum, daily 9–7.*

Where to Eat

★ **$$$–$$$$** ✕ **Al Garamond.** The ochre-color walls and the ancient brick vaulting set the stage in this small and brightly decorated restaurant. Traditional and innovative dishes of both meat and seafood are prepared with creative flair; you might try the tantalizing *rombo in crosta di patate al barbera* (turbot wrapped in sliced potatoes and baked with Barbera wine). For dessert, the mousse *di liquirizia e salsa di cioccolato bianco* (licorice mousse with white chocolate sauce) is a must, even if you don't usually like licorice. The level of service here is high, even by demanding Turin standards. ⊠ *Via G. Pomba 14, Centro* ☎ *011/8122781* ▭ *AE, MC, V* ⊗ *Closed Sun., Jan. 1–6, and 3 wks in Aug. No lunch Sat.*

$$$–$$$$ ✕ **Del Cambio.** Set in a palace dating from 1757, this is one of Europe's most beautiful and historic restaurants, with decorative moldings, mirrors, and hanging lamps that look just as they did when Italian national hero Cavour dined here more than a century ago. The cuisine draws heavily on Piedmontese tradition and is paired with fine wines of the region. Agnolotti with *sugo d'arrosto* (roast veal sauce) is a recommended first course. ⊠ *Piazza Carignano 2, Centro* ☎ *011/546690* 👔 *Jacket and tie* ⌂ *Reservations essential* ▭ *AE, DC, MC, V* ⊗ *Closed Sun., Jan. 1–6, and 3 wks in Aug.*

$$$–$$$$ ✕ **Vintage 1997.** The first floor of an elegant town house in the center of Turin makes a fitting location for this sophisticated restaurant. You might try such specialties as *vitello tonnato alla nostra maniera* (roast veal with a light tuna sauce) or *code di scampi con costolette di coniglio su crema di scalogno* (shrimp and rabbit in a scallion sauce). For the especially hungry gourmet there's the *menu del Vintage,* a 13-course feast that covers the full range of the restaurant's cuisine. There's an excellent wine list, with regional, national, and international vintages well represented. ⊠ *Piazza Solferino 16/h, Centro* ☎ *011/535948* ▭ *AE, DC, MC, V* ⊗ *Closed Sun. and 3 wks in Aug. No lunch Sat.*

$$–$$$ ✕ **L'Agrifoglio.** This intimate local favorite has just 10 tables. Specialties change with the seasons, but you might find such delicacies as risotto *al Barbaresco* (with Barbaresco wine) and *agnolotti dal plin al sugo d'arrosto* on the menu. L'Agrifoglio stays open late for the after-theater and after-cinema crowd. ⊠ *Via Accademia Albertina 38, Centro* ☎ *011/837064* ▭ *AE, DC, MC, V* ⊗ *Closed Sun. and Mon. No lunch.*

$$–$$$ ✕ **Hosteria La Vallée.** Small and romantic, with elegant tableware and linens, select pieces of antique furniture, and carefully designed lighting, this restaurant tucked away in a quiet section of central Turin has developed a devoted clientele. Recommended are *agnello scottato all'aglio e rosmarino* (lamb grilled with garlic and rosemary) followed by *sformato di cacao con cuore di fondente* (warm chocolate pudding). ⊠ *Via Provana 3b, Centro* ☎ *011/8121788* ▭ *AE, MC, V* ⊗ *Closed Sun., Jan. 1–7, and Aug. No lunch.*

$–$$ ✕ **Savoia.** The enthusiasm of chef and owner Mario Ferrero permeates three small rooms decorated with a few choice pictures and antique furniture. His kitchen turns out creative takes on Piedmontese specialties that change with the seasons. The bread and pasta are homemade, and the wine cellar is tended with equal care. ⊠ *Via Corta d'Appello 13, Centro* ☎ *011/4362288* ▭ *AE, DC, MC, V* ⊗ *Closed Sun. No lunch Sat.*

$ ✕ **Porto di Savona.** Look for this centuries-old tavern under the arcades of vast Piazza Vittorio Veneto, where it once served as a terminal for the Turin–Savona stagecoach line. The small street-level and upstairs din-

EATING WELL IN PIEDMONT & VALLE D'AOSTA

The Piedmontese take their food and their wine very seriously, and although you will find a similar range of eating establishments here as in other regions of Italy, the number of formal restaurants, with elaborate service and extraordinary wine lists, exceeds the national average. This holds true both in cities and in the country, where even simply named trattorias may offer a *menu di degustazione* (a multicourse tasting menu) accompanied by wines appropriate to each dish. In Turin the ritual of the *aperitivo* has been finely tuned, and most cafés from the early evening onward provide lavish buffets that are included in the price of a cocktail—a respectable substitute for dinner if you are traveling on a limited budget. As a result, restaurants in Turin tend to fill only after 9 PM.

In Piedmont and Valle d'Aosta you will find rustic specialties from farmhouse hearths, fine cuisine with a French accent—and everything in between. The area's best-known dish is probably polenta, creamy cornmeal served with *carbonada* (veal stew), melted cheese, or wild mushrooms. Also at the top of the favorites list are *agnolotti dal plin,* crescent-shaped stuffed pasta, served with the pan

juices of roast veal or with melted butter and shaved *tartufi bianchi* (white truffles) from Alba. Another regional specialty is *fonduta,* a local version of fondue, made with melted cheese, eggs, and sometimes grated truffles. Fontina and ham also often deck out the ubiquitous French-style *crepes alla valdostana,* served casserole style.

Throughout the region, though especially in Turin, you will find that most meals are accompanied by *grissini* (bread sticks). Invented in Turin in the 17th century to ease the digestive problems of little Prince Vittorio Amedeo II (1675–1730), these, when freshly made and hand-rolled, are a far cry from the thin and dry, plastic-wrapped versions available elsewhere. Napoléon called them *petits batons* and was, it seems, addicted to them.

Though desserts here are less sweet than in some other Italian regions, treats like *panna cotta* (a cooked milk custard), *torta di nocciole* (hazelnut torte), and *bonet* (a pudding made with hazelnuts, cocoa, milk, and macaroons) are delights. Turin is renowned for its delicate pastries and fine chocolates, especially for the hazelnut *gianduiotti.*

ing rooms have a decidedly old-fashioned air; the marble stairs are well worn, and the walls are decked with photos of Old Turin. Customers sit at long wooden tables to eat home-style Piedmontese cooking, including gnocchi with Gorgonzola and *bollito misto* (mixed boiled meats, appropriately served only in winter). The Barbera house wine is good. ⊠ *Piazza Vittorio Veneto 2, Centro* ☎ *011/8173500* ▤ *MC, V* ⊗ *Closed Mon., 1st 2 wks in Jan., and last 2 wks in Aug. No lunch Tues.*

¢–$ ✕ **Locanda da Betty.** At this small and homey trattoria, traditional Piedmont cuisine is served to a usually packed house. The inexpensive four-course menu di degustazione is an especially good deal. ⊠ *Via Bogino 17/e, Centro* ☎ *011/8170583* ▤ *No credit cards* ⊗ *Closed Sun.*

Where to Stay

The **Turin Tourist Board** (✉ Via Bogino 8, Centro ☎ 011/8185011 🖷 011/883426 ⊕ www.turismotorino.org) provides a booking service for hotels and bed-and-breakfast–style accommodations in the city. In order to use the service, you must book hotels 48 hours in advance and B&Bs seven days in advance. In anticipation of the Olympics, legislation governing alternative (usually inexpensive) types of lodging, such as B&Bs, has been relaxed. Whatever style of accommodations you choose, if you decide to attend the Olympics expect rates and availability to be at a premium—start your planning well in advance. The travel agency **Montagnedoc** (✉ Viale Giolitti 7/9, Pinerolo ☎ 0121/794003 🖷 0121/794932 ⊕ www.montagnedoc.it), which operates in conjunction with the tourist offices in the towns hosting the 2006 Winter Olympics, provides help locating and booking accommodations. It's also a good source for information about all-inclusive Olympics packages.

$$$$ 🏨 **Grand Hotel Sitea.** The finest of Turin's four-star hotels, the Sitea is ideally located in the city's historic center. Decorated in a warmly classical style, the public areas and guest rooms are elegant and comfortable. As might be expected from a first-rate hotel, top-notch service is a provided by a courteous and efficient staff. Weekend rates are available. ✉ *Via Carlo Alberto 35, Centro, 10123* ☎ *011/5170171* 🖷 *011/548090* ⊕ *www.thi.it* 🛏 *112 rooms, 2 suites* ♿ *Restaurant, minibars, cable TV with movies, in-room data ports, bar, meeting rooms, parking (fee), some pets allowed* 🍽 *AE, DC, MC, V* ⦿ *CP.*

$$$$ 🏨 **Le Meridien Art+Tech.** Designed by architect Renzo Piano, this luxury hotel is part of the former Lingotto FIAT factory. The approach throughout is typically minimalist, with ultramodern fixtures and designer furniture decorating the rooms. The track on the roof, once used by FIAT to test its cars, is available to clients for jogging. ✉ *Via Nizza 262, Lingotto, 10126* ☎ *011/6642000* 🖷 *011/6642001* ⊕ *www.lemeridien.com* 🛏 *141 rooms, 1 suite* ♿ *Restaurant, in-room safes, minibars, cable TV with movies, in-room data ports, bar, Internet, meeting rooms* 🍽 *AE, DC, MC, V* ⦿ *CP.*

★ $$$ 🏨 **Victoria.** Rare style, attention to detail, and comfort are the hallmarks of this boutique hotel furnished and managed to create the feeling of a refined town house. The newer wing has a grand marble staircase and individually decorated guest rooms. The same attention to detail is found in the refurbished rooms of the original wing, and the sitting room and breakfast room are particularly attractive. ✉ *Via Nino Costa 4, Centro, 10123* ☎ *011/5611909* 🖷 *011/5611806* ⊕ *www.hotelvictoria-torino.com* 🛏 *97 rooms, 9 suites* ♿ *Pool, bicycles, bar, parking (fee), no-smoking rooms; no a/c in some rooms* 🍽 *AE, DC, MC, V* ⦿ *CP.*

$$ 🏨 **Liberty.** The name of this small, conveniently located lodging comes from an Italian term for the art nouveau style, and the place is true to its name, with period-style furnishings and a stylish ambience. It's a favorite of academics, artists, and others who appreciate its solid, old-fashioned comfort and the Anfossi family's attentive courtesy. The hotel is on the upper floor of an otherwise poorly maintained building, so don't be put off by the shabby entrance and the rickety elevator. ⊠ *Via Pietro Micca 15, Centro, 10121* ☎ *011/5628801* 🖷 *011/5628163* ⊕ *www. hotelliberty-torino.it* ⌁ *35 rooms* ⌂ *Restaurant, bar* ▭ *AE, DC, MC, V* |◯| *CP.*

$$ 🏨 **La Maddalena.** It may be difficult to book a stay at this small B&B hotel (there are only three rooms), but it's worth a try. You'll be made to feel instantly at home by the proprietor, Maddalena Vitale, in this delightfully decorated and comfortably cluttered apartment not far from the main train station. One room has a double bed and en suite bathroom; the other two rooms have twin beds and private bathrooms across the hall. ⊠ *Via San Secondo 31, Centro, 10128* ☎🖷 *011/591267* ⊕ *www.iam-maddalena.com* ⌁ *3 rooms* ⌂ *In-room data ports; no a/c* ▭ *No credit cards* |◯| *CP.*

$–$$ 🏨 **Genio.** The Genio, like many hotels in Turin, has undergone a complete transformation in preparation for the Winter Olympics in 2006. Though steps away from the main train station, spacious and tastefully decorated rooms provide a quiet haven from the bustle of the city. Best of all is the service, which resembles that of a friendly family-run inn rather than a big-city business hotel. ⊠ *Corso Vittorio Emanuele II 47, Centro, 10125* ☎ *011/6505771* 🖷 *011/6508264* ⊕ *www.hotelgenio. it* ⌁ *120 rooms, 3 suites* ⌂ *Minibars, meeting rooms, parking (fee)* ▭ *AE, DC, MC, V* |◯| *CP.*

Nightlife & the Arts

The Arts

MUSIC Classical music concerts are held in the famous **Conservatorio Giuseppe Verdi** (⊠ Via Mazzini 11, Centro ☎ 011/8121268 ⊠ Piazza Bodoni, Centro ☎ 011/888470) throughout the year but primarily in winter. The **Settembre Musica Festival** (☎ 011/4424703), held for three weeks in September, highlights classical works. Traditional sacred music and some modern religious pieces are performed in the **Duomo** (⊠ Via Montebello 20, Centro ☎ 011/8154230) on Sunday evening; performances are usually advertised in the vestibule or in the local edition of Turin's nationally distributed newspaper, *La Stampa.* The Thursday edition comes with a supplement on music and other entertainment possibilities.

OPERA The **Teatro Regio** (⊠ Piazza Castello 215, Centro ☎ 011/8815557 ⊕ www.teatroregio.torino.it), one of Italy's leading opera houses, has its season from October to June. You can buy tickets for most performances (premieres sell well in advance) at the box office or on the Web site, where discounts are offered on the day of the show.

Nightlife

Two areas of Turin are enormously popular nightlife destinations: the Docks Dora, to the north of the city center, and the Murazzi embankment, near the Ponte Vittorio Emanuele I.

The **Docks Dora** (⊠ Via Valprato 68, Madonna di Campagna ☎ 011/280251 ◷ Mon.–Sat. 9 PM–4 AM) is a complex of old warehouses that have been converted into artists' studios, gallery spaces, bars, cafés, and theaters. Live music and performances keep the area hopping, and the disco **Café Blue**

The Olympics Come to Turin

TURIN PLAYS HOST to the 20th Winter Olympics in 2006, and the impact of the event will linger long after the international spotlight has moved on. With the Olympics as an impetus (and further spurred by recent crises in the auto industry), Turin is working to transcend its image as a city of industry to become identified as a dynamic cultural and recreational travel destination.

The Olympic events themselves take place between February 10 and 26 at several locations in the region. Turin is the site for ice hockey, figure skating, and speed skating. Curling is in nearby Pinerolo, and the remaining events take place in mountain resorts to the west: Bardonecchia (snowboarding), Cesana–San Sicario (biathlon, women's downhill trials, bobsled, luge, and skeleton), Pregelato (ski-jumping, Nordic combination, and cross-country skiing), Sestriere (downhill skiing), and Sauze d'Oulx (freestyle skiing). Three Olympic Villages—in Turin, Sestriere, and Bardonecchia—are equipped to house 5,000 athletes, coaches, and national officials, while the 10,000 members of the media have six media centers to call home. One and a half million spectators are expected to attend the Games. If you want to be one of them, contact the Organizing Committee (TOROC, ⇨ Sports) to find out about event tickets, and Montagnedoc (⇨ Where to Stay) for help with lodging and package deals.

The Olympics will have a significant long-term impact on Turin, bringing about nothing less than a fundamental reorientation of the city. The central train station, Porta Nuova, and the nearby historical center have long been the focal points of activity, but the Olympics have helped foster development both to the west and along the city's north–south axis. The Olympic Village and Olympic skating rink are near a former FIAT factory, the Lingotto, to the south of the city core. Once entirely an industrial zone, the area is being transformed into a residential and commercial center: new hotels and restaurants are sprouting up everywhere, and the Lingotto train station, little used after the closure of the FIAT factory, is being enlarged.

With the Olympics in mind, the city has developed its first subway system; construction wraps up on a section linking the Lingotto Olympic area with downtown Turin in late 2005. From the Porta Nuova station, the subway heads toward the now secondary Porta Susa station and then continues toward Turin's rapidly expanding western limits; the first stage of this plan is scheduled for completion in 2006. The intention is to transform Porta Susa into Turin's principal train station, making it a hub in Europe's high-speed train network. Eventually the Porta Nuova station will close; it may be turned into a museum, like the d'Orsay train station in Paris.

The impact of the Olympics will spread beyond the city limits. The most important developments in the mountain centers affect the range of skiing and hospitality services available: new runs and lifts are being added, new facilities are being built, and many of the existing hotels are receiving face-lifts.

serves up dance music all night long. Take the 51 bus from the Porta Susa train station or catch it heading north past the Duomo. On the Murazzi, near the Ponte Vittorio Emanuele I, is **Jammin's** (✉ Murazzi del Po 17, Centro ☎ 011/882869 ☼ May–Sept., Mon.–Sat. 9 PM–4 AM), a popular disco with a mixed crowd; there's live music on Friday.

The center of town is also popluar, especially earlier in the evening. With music, often live, that ranges from British pop and rock to punk, crossover, soul, and reggae, **Barrumba** (✉ Via San Massimo 1, Centro ☎ 011/883322 ⊕ www.barrumba.it ☼ Thurs.–Sat. 10:30 PM–4:30 AM) is usually packed with a mix of young Turinese, university students, and visitors. A trendy meeting place for an aperitif or a pre-disco drink in the piazza at the end of Via Po is the wine bar **Caffè Elena** (✉ Piazza Vittorio Veneto 5, Centro ☎ 011/8123341 ☼ Thurs.–Tues. 9 AM–2 AM). South of the main train station is **Rockcity** (✉ Via Bertini 2, San Salvario ☎ 011/3184737 ☼ Thurs.–Sat. 10:30 PM–4 AM), where you'll find a smart crowd in their mid-20s to mid-30s listening to rock, techno, and commercial music.

Sports

Soccer

Turin's two professional soccer clubs, Juventus and Torino, play their games in the **Stadio delle Alpi** (✉ 6 km [4 mi] northwest of city, Venaria). Juventus is one of Italy's most successful and most popular teams. There is fierce rivalry between its supporters and those of visiting clubs, especially Inter Milan and AC Milan. Home matches are usually played on Sunday afternoon during the season, which runs from late August to mid-May. It's possible to purchase tickets for Juventus and Torino games in any *tabaccheria* (tobacco shop) with a sign bearing a capital "T."

Winter Olympics

The **Organizing Committee for the Winter Olympics in Torino** (TOROC; ✉ Corso Novara 96, Centro ☎ 011/6310511 🖶 011/6310500 ⊕ www.torino2006.org) is responsible for managing the sports events for the 2006 Games, as well as the opening and closing ceremonies. They have detailed schedules of the events and information about how to obtain tickets. Their comprehensive Web site, which includes an online ticket service, is the first place to check for games-related information.

Shopping

Chocolate

The tradition of making chocolate began in Turin in the early 17th century. Chocolate at that time was an aristocratic drink, but in the 19th century a Piedmontese invention made it possible to further refine cocoa, which could then be used to create solid bars and candies. The most famous of all Turin chocolates is the gianduiotto (with cocoa, sugar, and hazelnuts), first concocted in 1867. The tradition of making these delicious treats has been continued at the small, family-run **Peyrano** (✉ Corso Moncalieri 47, Centro ☎ 011/6602202 ⊕ www.peyrano.it), where more than 80 types of chocolates are concocted. **Stratta** (✉ Piazza San

Carlo 191, Centro ☎ 011/547920), one of Turin's most famous chocolate shops, has been in business since 1836 and sells confections of all kinds—not just the chocolates in the lavish window displays but also fancy cookies, rum-laced fudges, and magnificent cakes.

Markets

Go to the famous **Balon Flea Market** (✉ Piazza Repubblica, Centro) on Saturday morning for excellent bargains on secondhand books and clothing and good browsing among stalls selling local specialties such as gianduiotti. (Be aware, however, that the market is also famous for its pickpockets.) The second Sunday of every month a special antiques market, appropriately called the **Gran Balon,** sets up shop in Piazza Repubblica.

Specialty Stores

Most people know that Turin produces more than 75% of Italy's cars, but they are often unaware that it's also a hub for clothing manufacturing. Top-quality boutiques stocking local, national, and international lines are clustered along Via Roma and Via Garibaldi. Piazza San Carlo, Via Po, and Via Maria Vittoria are lined with antiques shops, some—but not all—specializing in 18th-century furniture and domestic items.

Specialty food stores and delicatessens abound in central Turin. For a truly spectacular array of cheeses and other delicacies, try Turin's famous **Borgiattino** (✉ Via Accademia Albertina 38/a, Centro ☎ 011/8394686). For hand-rolled grissini—some as long as 4 feet—the bakery **Bersano** (✉ Via Barbaroux 5, Centro ☎ 011/5627579) is the best place in town. **Tabernalibraria** (✉ Via Bogino 5, Centro ☎ 011/836515) is a delightful combination of *enoteca* (wine bar), delicatessen, and bookstore.

THE COLLINE & SAVOY PALACES

As you head west from Turin into the Colline ("little hills"), castles and medieval fortifications begin to pepper the former dominion of the house of Savoy and the Alps come into better and better view. In the region lie the storybook medieval towns of Avigliana, Rivoli, and Saluzzo; 12th-century abbeys; and, farther west in the mountains, the ski resorts of Bardonecchia and Sestriere, two of the venues chosen for the 2006 Winter Olympics.

Stupinigi

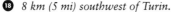 *8 km (5 mi) southwest of Turin.*

★ The **Palazzina di Caccia,** in the town of Stupinigi, was built by Juvarra in 1729 as a hunting lodge for the house of Savoy. More like a sumptuous royal villa, its many wings, landscaped gardens, and surrounding forests give a clear idea of the level of style to which the Savoy were accustomed. This regal aspect was not lost on Paolina Buonaparte, who briefly held court here during her brother Napoléon's reign over Italy. Today the Palazzina houses the **Museo d'Arte e Ammobiliamento** (Museum of Art and Decoration), a vast collection of paintings and furniture gathered from numerous Savoy palaces in the area. You can get there by taking Bus 41 from Turin's Porta Nuova train station. ⊠ *Via Principe Amedeo 7* ☎ *011/3581220* 🖾 *€6.20* ⏱ *Apr.–Oct., Tues.–Sun. 10–7:30, last entrance at 6:50; Nov.–Mar., Tues.–Sun. 9:30–4, last entrance at 3:20.*

Rivoli

🔞 *16 km (10 mi) northwest of Stupinigi, 13 km (8 mi) west of Turin.*

The Savoy court was based in Rivoli in the Middle Ages. The 14th- to 15th-century **Casa del Conte Verde** (House of the Green Count) sits right in the center of town, and the richness of its decorations hints at the wealth and importance of the owner (and of Rivoli) during the period. Inside, a small gallery hosts temporary exhibitions. ⊠ *Via Fratelli Piol 8* ☎ *011/9563020* ⊕ *www.casadelconteverde.it* 🖾 *Varies with exhibits* ⏱ *Varies with exhibits.*

★ The castle of Rivoli now houses the **Museo d'Arte Contemporaneo** (Museum of Contemporary Art). The building was begun in the 17th century and then redesigned but never finished by Juvarra in the 18th century; it was finally completed in the late 20th century by minimalist Turin architect Andrea Bruno. On display are changing international exhibitions and a permanent collection of 20th-century Italian art. To get to Rivoli from downtown Turin, take Tram 1 and then Bus 36. ⊠ *Piazzale Mafalda di Savoia* ☎ *011/9565222* ⊕ *www.castellodirivoli.org* 🖾 *€6.50* ⏱ *Tues.–Thurs. 10–5, Fri.–Sun. 10–7.*

Abbazia di Sant'Antonio di Ranverso

🔞 *6 km (3½ mi) west of Rivoli, 23 km (14 mi) west of Turin.*

This abbey was originally a hospital, founded in the 12th century by the Hospitallers of St. Anthony to care for victims of St. Anthony's Fire, a painful medical condition brought on by consuming contaminated rye. Pilgrims came here over the centuries for cures and to offer thanks for a miraculous recovery. The 15th-century frescoes with their lifelike depictions of pilgrims and saints retain their original colors. ⊠ *Buttigliera Alta west of Rivoli, off SS25* ☎ *011/9367450* 🖾 *€2.58* ⏱ *Nov.–Mar., Tues.–Sun. 9–12:30; Apr.–Oct., Tues.–Sun. 9–12:30 and 2–6; last entrance ½ hr before closing.*

Sacra di San Michele

★ 🔞 *20 km (13 mi) west of Abbazia di Sant'Antonio di Ranverso, 43 km (27 mi) west of Turin.*

Unless you plan a 14-km (9-mi) hike from the town of Avigliana, a car is essential for an excursion to the Abbey of St. Michael, perhaps best known as inspiration for the setting of Umberto Eco's novel *The Name of the Rose.* San Michele was built on Monte Pirchiriano in the 11th century so it would stand out: it occupies the most prominent location for miles around, hanging over a 3,280-foot bluff. When monks came to enlarge the abbey they had to build part of the structure on supports more than 90 feet high—an engineering feat that was famous in medieval

Europe and is still impressive today. By the 12th century this important abbey controlled 176 churches in Italy, France, and Spain; one of the abbeys under its influence was Mont-Saint-Michel in France. Because of its strategic position it came under frequent attacks over the next five centuries and was eventually abandoned in 1622. It was restored in the late 19th and early 20th centuries.

From **Porta dello Zodiaco,** a splendid Romanesque doorway decorated with the signs of the zodiac, you climb 150 steps, past 12th-century sculptures, to reach the church. On the left side of the interior are 16th-century frescoes representing New Testament themes; on the right are depictions of the founding of the church. Go down to the crypt to see the 9th- to 12th-century chapels. Some sections of the abbey are open only on weekends. ☎ *011/939130* ⊕ *www.sacradisanmichele.com* ✉ *Weekends €4; weekdays €3.50* ☉ *Mar. 16–Oct. 15, Tues.–Sat. 9:30–12:30 and 3–6, Sun. 9:30–noon and 2:40–6; Oct. 16–Mar. 15, Tues.–Sat. 9:30–12:30 and 3–5, Sun. 9:30–noon and 2:40–5; mandatory accompanied visits leave every 30 mins.*

Saluzzo

㉒ *58 km (36 mi) southwest of Turin.*

The russet-brick town of Saluzzo—a flourishing medieval center and later seat of a Renaissance ducal court—is a well-preserved gem with narrow, winding streets, frescoed houses, Gothic churches, and elegant Renaissance palaces. A map with instructions for a walking tour of the town's sights is available from the local **tourist information office** (✉ Via Griselda 6 ☎ 0175/46710 ⊕ www.comune.saluzzo.cn.it). The older and more interesting part of the town hugs a hilltop in the Po Valley and is crowned by **La Castiglia,** a 13th-century castle that has served as a prison since the 1820s.

The exterior of the **Castello di Manta,** 4 km (2½ mi) south of Saluzzo, is austere, but inside are frescoes and other decorations of the period. Knights and damsels from an allegorical poem written by Marquis Tommaso III of Saluzzo, humanist lord of the castle, parade in full costume in the 15th-century frescoes of the **Sala del Barone.** The castle sometimes hosts exhibits, at which time higher admission is charged. ✉ *Via al Castello 14, Manta* ☎ *0175/87822* ✉ *€4.50* ☉ *Mar.–mid-Dec., Tues.–Sun. 10–1 and 2–6.*

Sestriere

㉓ *32 km (20 mi) east of Briançon, 93 km (58 mi) west of Turin.*

In the early 1930s, before skiing became a sport for commoners, the patriarch of the FIAT automobile dynasty had this resort built, with two distinctive tower hotels and ski facilities that have been developed into some of the best in the Alps. The resort lacks the charm of older Alpine centers, overdevelopment has added some eyesores, and the mountains don't have the striking beauty of those in Valle d'Aosta. But skiers have an excellent choice of trails, some of them crossing the border into France.

VOICES OF ITALY

Ines Cavalcanti
Chambra d'Oc,
Western Piedmont

Ines Cavalcanti is a member of Piedmont's Chambra d'Oc. The organization promotes the little-known language and culture of the Occitan peoples, inhabitants of the mountain valleys of western Piedmont, as well as much of southern France (including, naturally, the Languedoc region) and parts of northern Spain. Ines provides some background:

"All the mountain valleys at one time were filled with people, and all the villages, though small, were active communities. When the major industrialization of Italy began in the 1960s, people left the valleys to look for work in major towns like Turin. The population fell by more than 80%. Everything, practically everything, was abandoned.

"I come from a small village, Elva, more than 5,000 feet above sea level. Until I was 10 years old, I'd lived in Elva, and then my family came down from the valley—we emigrated to the towns in the Piedmont plains. In some ways, treated like foreigners in our new homes, we were worse off than we had been before.

"Until the 1970s, all the people of my generation spoke Occitan, with most people speaking only the one language. We weren't aware that, just across the Alps, 13 million people spoke exactly the same language! It wasn't until between about 1965 and 1970 that linguistic studies proved the language spoken in the valleys of western Piedmont was Occitan. When this happened, it was as though a new window opened for us. The knowledge that we belonged to a larger cultural group gave us a new perspective.

"After the official recognition of Occitan as a language, there has been a boom in interest, and in the 1990s a commission was formed to standardize both the written and spoken language. We now have an Italian–Occitan dictionary and a newspaper, the *Occitano Vivo*. We've also started a project—because all the valleys involved in the 2006 Winter Olympics are Occitan valleys—to have the language recognized during the opening ceremonies of the Olympic Games. This would be an excellent way to bring us recognition."

For more information about the language of Occitania, contact **Chambra d'Oc** (⊠ Chamin Arnaud Daniel 18, 12020 Roccabruna ☎ 0171/918971). Though only in Italian and Occitan, the web site www.jari.it/html/ousitanio.html provides maps indicating the extent of Occitania.

Where to Stay

$$$ 🏨 **Principi di Piemonte.** Large and elegant, this luxurious hotel sits on the slopes above the town, near the lifts and the town's golf course. Its secluded location heightens the sense of exclusivity, and though showing signs of age the hotel still attracts a stylish clientele. The restaurant and a cozy bar invite après-ski relaxation. ⊠ *Via Sauze 3/B, 10058* ☎ *0122/7941* 🖷 *0122/755411* ⊕ *www.framon-hotels.com* ↻ *96 rooms, 4 suites* ⚐ *Restaurant, indoor pool, hot tub, sauna, Turkish bath,* bar, meeting rooms, some pets allowed ⊟ AE, DC, MC, V ⊘ Closed early Apr.–June and Sept.–Nov. ⦿ CP.

$$–$$$ ⌑ **Hotel Cristallo.** Half of the rooms at this hotel face the slopes of Sestriere, and the ski-lift station is just across the road. You'll find all the facilities you need for a stay in the mountains either in the hotel or just steps away from the lobby entrance. Rooms are elegantly and warmly furnished in the style of a modern ski lodge; ask for one with a terrace facing the view. ⊠ *Via Pinerolo 5, 10058* ☎ *0122/750707* 🖷 *0122/ 755152* ⊕ *www.newlinehotels.com* ⮡ *40 rooms* ⌂ *Restaurant, minibars, gym, sauna, Turkish bath, bar, Internet, parking (fee)* ⊟ AE, DC, MC, V ⦿ CP.

$ ⌑ **Miramonti.** Nearly every room has a terrace at this pleasant, central, modern chalet. The ample, comfortable rooms are done in traditional mountain style, with lots of exposed wood and coordinated floral-print fabrics. ⊠ *Via Cesana 3, 10058* ☎ *0122/755333* 🖷 *0122/755375* ⮡ *30 rooms* ⌂ *Restaurant, minibars, exercise equipment, bar, meeting rooms, some pets allowed* ⊟ AE, DC, MC, V ⦿ CP.

Sports & the Outdoors

SKIING At 6,670 feet, the ski resort of **Sestriere** (☎ 0122/799411 for conditions ⊕ www.vialattea.it) was built in the late 1920s under the auspices of Turin's Agnelli family. The slopes get good snow some years from November through May, other years from February through May. The **tourist office** (☎ 0175/46710 ⊕ www.comune.sestriere.to.it) in Sestriere provides complete information about lift tickets, ski runs, mountain guides, and equipment rentals, here and in neighboring towns such as Bardonecchia and Claviere. Its excellent Web site is also navigable in English. A quaint village with slate-roof houses, **Claviere** (⊠ 17 km [11 mi] west of Sestriere) is one of Italy's oldest ski resorts. Its slopes overlap with those of the French resort of Montgenèvre.

Bardonecchia

㉔ *36 km (22 mi) northwest of Sestriere, 89 km (55 mi) west of Turin.*

This sunny town is one of Italy's oldest winter ski resorts, attracting hardy sports enthusiasts from Turin since the 1920s. It's near the entrance to the Fréjus train and automobile tunnels.

Where to Stay

$$ ⌑ **Des Geneys-Splendid.** One of the best hotels in the area sits in a pine-filled private park near the town center. The 1930s style is evident in the arched windows on the ground floor, the stucco walls, and the wrought-iron balconies. The public rooms are spacious and comfortable, and there's a playroom for children. ⊠ *Via Einaudi 21, 10052* ☎ *0122/99001* 🖷 *0122/999295* ⊕ *www.desgeneys.it* ⮡ *53 rooms, 4 suites* ⌂ *Restaurant, gym, piano bar, meeting rooms* ⊟ AE, DC, MC, V ⊘ Closed mid-Apr.–mid-June and mid-Sept.–Nov. ⦿ CP.

$ ⌑ **Bucaneve.** Just a short walk from the ski lift, this small family-owned hotel is popular with the ski crowd. A cozy reading room and restaurant add to the allure of these affordable lodgings. ⊠ *Viale della Vecchia 2, 10052* ☎ *0122/999332* 🖷 *0122/999980* ⊕ *www.hotelbucanevebardonecchia.it*

↗ *20 rooms, 4 suites* ⌂ *Restaurant, bar, Internet, some pets allowed; no a/c* ▤ *AE, MC, V* ⊘ *Closed Oct. and Nov.* ⦿ *CP.*

★ ¢ ▥ **Asplenia.** Skiers love this small, modern version of a mountain chalet near the town center and the ski lifts. The ample rooms are comfortably furnished, with a small entryway and a balcony affording beautiful views. ⊠ *Viale della Vittoria 31, 10052* ☎ *0122/999870* 📠 *0122/901968* ⊕ *www.asplenia.it* ↗ *17 rooms, 4 suites* ⌂ *Restaurant, some pets allowed* ▤ *AE, DC, MC, V* ⦿ *CP.*

THE MONFERRATO & THE LANGHE

Southeast of Turin, in the hilly wooded area around Asti known as the Monferrato and farther south in a similar area around Alba known as the Langhe, the rolling landscape is a patchwork of vineyards and dark woods dotted with hill towns and castles. This is wine country, producing some of Italy's most famous reds and sparkling whites. And hidden away in the woods are the secret places where hunters and their dogs unearth the precious, aromatic truffles worth their weight in gold at Alba's truffle fair.

Casale Monferrato

㉕ *42 km (26 mi) northeast of Asti, 75 km (46 mi) southwest of Milan.*

Casale Monferrato, strategically situated on the southern bank of the Po, was held by the Gonzaga, rulers of Mantua, before falling into the hands of the Savoy. The 16th-century **Torre Civica,** marking the heart of town in Piazza Mazzini, commands extensive views up and down the Po. It's open the second Saturday and Sunday of every month for free guided visits. In the second half of March the **Festa di San Giuseppe** brings artisans, musicians, and vendors of traditional sweets to the central Piazza del Castello.

Casale's most enlightening sight is the **Museo Israelitico** (Jewish Museum) in the women's section of its synagogue. Inside is a collection of documents and sacred art of a community that was vital to the prosperity of this mercantile city. The synagogue dates from the late 16th century, and neighboring buildings on the same street formed the Jewish ghetto of that period. ⊠ *Vicolo Olper 44, south of Torre Civica* ☎ *0142/71807* ⊘ *Mar.–Dec., Sun. 10–noon and 3:30–5:30; other times by appointment.*

Asti

㉖ *60 km (37 mi) southeast of Turin.*

Asti is best known outside of Italy for its wines—excellent reds as well as the famous sparkling white Spumante—but its strategic position on trade routes between Turin, Milan, and Genoa has given it a broad economic base. In the 12th century Asti began to develop as a republic, at a time when other Italian cities were also flexing their economic and military muscles. It flourished in the following century, when the inhabitants began erecting lofty **towers** (⊠ West end of Corso Vittorio Alfieri) for its defense, giving rise to the medieval nickname "city of 100 towers." In the center of Asti some of these remain, among them the 13th-century **Torre Comentina** and the well-preserved **Torre Troyana**, a tall, slender tower attached to the **Palazzo Troya**. The 18th-century church of **Santa Caterina** has incorporated one of Asti's medieval towers, the **Torre Romana** (itself built on an ancient Roman base), as its bell tower. Corso Vittorio Alfieri is Asti's main thoroughfare, running west–east across the city. This road, known in medieval times as Contrada Maestra, was built by the Romans.

The **Duomo** is an object lesson in the evolution of the Gothic architecture. Built in the early 14th century, it's decorated so as to emphasize geometry and verticality: pointed arches and narrow vaults contrast with the earlier, Romanesque attention to balance and symmetry. The porch on the south side of the cathedral facing the square was built in 1470 and represents Gothic at its most florid and excessive. ⊠ *Piazza Cattedrale* ☎ *0141/592924* ☉ *Daily 8:30–noon and 3:30–5:30.*

The Gothic church of **San Secondo** is dedicated to Asti's patron saint, reputedly decapitated on the spot where the church now stands. Secondo is also the patron of the city's favorite folklore and sporting event, the annual Palio di Asti, the colorful medieval-style horse race (similar to Siena's) held each year on the third Sunday of September in the vast Campo del Palio to the south of the church. ⊠ *Piazza San Secondo, south of Corso Vittorio Alfieri* ☎ *0141/530066* ☉ *Mon.–Sat. 10:45–noon and 3:30–5:30, Sun. 3:30–5:30.*

Where to Stay & Eat

$$$ ✕ **Gener Neuv.** One of Italy's best restaurants, the family-run Gener Neuv
Fodor'sChoice is known for its rustic elegance. The setting on the bank of the Tanaro
★ River is splendid. The menu of regional specialties may include agnolotti *ai tre stufati* (with a filling of ground rabbit, veal, and pork), and to finish, *composta di prugne e uva* (prune and grape compote). Fixed-price menus are available with or without the wine included. As you might expect, the wine list is first-rate. ⊠ *Lungo Tanaro 4* ☎ *0141/557270* ⊕ *www.generneuv.it* ⊟ *AE, DC, MC, V* ☉ *Closed Aug. and Mon., no dinner Sun.; Jan.–July, closed Sun.*

$$ ✕ **L'Angolo del Beato.** Regional specialties such as bagna cauda and *tagliolini al ragu di anatra* (pasta with a duck sauce) are the main attraction at this central Asti restaurant, housed in a building that dates back to the 12th century. There's also a good wine list. ⊠ *Via Guttuari 12* ☎ *0141/531668* ⊟ *AE, DC, MC, V* ☉ *Closed Sun., last wk of Dec., 1st wk of Jan., and 3 wks in Aug.*

$$ ▥ **Reale.** This hotel in a 19th-century building is located on Asti's main square. The spacious rooms are somewhat eclectically decorated, with a mix of contemporary and period furniture. Though this is one of the oldest hotels in Asti, all the bathrooms have been modernized and are spotlessly maintained. ⊠ *Piazza Alfieri 6, 14100* ☎ *0141/530240* ⎙ *0141/34357* ⊕ *www.hotel-reale.com* ⇌ *25 rooms, 2 suites* ⚐ *Cable TV, parking (fee), some pets allowed; no a/c* ⊟ *AE, DC, MC, V* ❙◯❙ *CP.*

Continued on page 250

ON THE TRAIL OF BAROLO

Picture yourself in the background of a grand medieval mural, and you won't be far off from what you experience driving through the idyllic wooded landscape south of Turin, in Piedmont's Langhe district.

The crests of the graceful hills are dotted with villages, each lorded over by an ancient castle. The gentle slopes of the valleys below are lined with row upon row of Nebbiolo grapes, the choicest of which are used to make Barolo wine. Dubbed "the king of wines and wine of kings" in the 19th century after finding favor with King Carlo Alberto, Barolo still wears the crown, despite stiff competition from all corners of Italy.

The Langhe district is smaller and surprisingly less visited by food-and-wine enthusiasts than Chianti and the surrounding areas of Tuscany, but it yields similar rewards. The best way to tour the Barolo-producing region is on day trips from the delightful truffle town of Alba—getting around is easy, the country roads are gorgeous, and the wine is fit for a king.

Above, Alba's castle
Right, bottles of old vintage Barolo

ALL ABOUT BAROLO

The Nebbiolo grapes that go into this famous wine come not just from Barolo proper (the area surrounding the tiny town of Barolo), but also from a small zone that encompasses the hill towns of Novello, Monforte d'Alba, Serralunga d'Alba, Castiglione Falletto, La Morra, and Verduno. All are connected by small but easy-to-navigate roads.

When wine lovers talk about Barolo, they talk about tannins—the quality that makes red wine dry out your mouth. Tannins come from the grape skins; red wine—which gets its color from the skins—has them, white wine doesn't. Tannins can be balanced out by acidity (the quality that makes your mouth water), but they also soften over time. As a good red wine matures, flavors emerge more clearly, achieving a harmonious balance of taste and texture.

A bottle of Barolo is often born so overwhelmingly tannic that many aficionados won't touch the stuff until it has aged 10 or 15 years. But a good Barolo ages beautifully, eventually spawning complex, intermingled tastes of tobacco, roses, and earth. It's not uncommon to see bottles for sale from the 1960s, 1950s, or even the 1930s.

WHERE TO DRINK IT

The word *enoteca* in Italian can mean a wine store, or a wine bar, or both. The words "wine bar," on the other hand—which are becoming increasingly trendy—mean just that. Either way, these are great places to sample and buy the wines of the Langhe.

An excellent enoteca in Alba is Vincafé (Via V. Emanuele, 12, Alba, 0173/364603). It specializes in tastes of Langhe wines, accompanied by *salumi* (cured meats), cheeses, and other regional products. More than 350 wines, as well as grappas and liqueurs, grace Vincafé's distinguished list. It's open from noon to midnight, and there's food until 9 pm.

In the fortified hill town of Barolo, visit the Castello di Barolo (Piazza Falletti, 0173/56277, www.baroloworld.it) which has a little wine bar and a museum dedicated to Barolo.

HOW MUCH DOES IT COST?

The most reasonably priced, but still enjoyable Barolos will cost you €20 to €30. A very good, but not top-of-the-line bottle will cost €40 to €60. For a top-of-the-line bottle you may spend anywhere from €80 to €200.

LABELS TO LOOK FOR

Barolo is a strictly controlled denomination, but that doesn't mean all Barolos are equal. Legendary producers include Prunotto, Aldo Conterno, Giacomo Conterno, Bruno Giacosa, Famiglia Anselma, Mascarello, Pio Cesare, and Michele Chiarlo.

WINE ESTATES TO VISIT

Right in the town of Barolo, an easy, if touristy, option for a visit is Marchesi di Barolo (Via Alba 12, Barolo, 0173/564400, www.marchesibarolo.com). In the estate's user-friendly enoteca you can taste wine, buy thousands of different bottles from vintages going way back, and look at display bottles, including an 1859 Barolo. Marchesi di Barolo's *cantine* (wine cellars, Via Roma 1, Barolo) are open daily 10:30–5:30. The staff here is used to catering to visitors, so you won't have to worry too much about endearing yourself to them.

From there you might want to graduate to Famiglia Anselma (Loc. Castello della Volta, Barolo, 0173/787217, www.anselma.it). Winemaker Mauricio Anselma, in his mid-20s, is something of a prodigy in the Barolo world, and he's quite open to visitors. He is known for his steadfast commitment to produce only Barolo—nothing else—and for his policy of holding his wines for several years before release.

A good, accessible example of the new school of Barolo winemaking is Podere Rocche dei Manzoni (3, Loc. Manzini Soprano, Monforte d'Alba, 0173/78421, www.barolobig.com). The facade of the cantina is like a Roman temple of brick, complete with imposing columns. Rocche dei Manzoni's reds include four Barolos, one Dolcetto, one Langhe Rosso, two Langhe DOCs, and two Barbera d'Albas.

WINE TOUR TIPS

Keep in mind that visiting wineries in Italy is different from what you might have experienced in the Napa Valley or in France. Wherever you go, reservations are most definitely required, and you'll usually be the only person or group on the tour—so be sure to show up when you say you will, and keep in mind that it's impolite not to buy something in the end.

Wine buyers and wine professionals are the expected audience for tours. While this attitude is slowly changing and many winemakers are beginning to welcome interested outsiders, it's important to be humble and enthusiastic. You'll be treated best if you come in with an open mind, respect that the winemaker probably knows more about wine than you do, and make it clear that you aren't just looking to drink for free. It helps to speak Italian, but if you don't, the international language of effusive compliments can still go a long way.

BEYOND BAROLO

Neive, in the Barbaresco region

By no means do the fruits of the Langhe end with Barolo. The region boasts Italy's highest concentration of DOC (denominazione di origine controllata) and DOCG (denominazione di origine controllata e garantita) wines, the two most prestigious categories of appellation in Italy. The other DOCG in the Langhe is Barbaresco, which, like Barolo, is made from the Nebbiolo grape. Barbaresco is not quite as tannic as Barolo, however, and can be drunk younger.

$ 🏨 **Rainero.** An older hotel near the train station, the Rainero has been run by the same family for three generations. It's fitted with cheerful modern furnishings. Ask for one of the "green rooms," decked out in a green-and-white decor. ✉ *Via Cavour 85, 14100* ☎ *0141/353866* 📠 *0141/594985* ⊕ *www.hotelrainero.com* ⟳ *53 rooms, 2 suites* ⚴ *Bar, Internet, meeting rooms, parking (fee), some pets allowed* ⊟ *AE, V* ⊗ *Closed Jan. 1–15* |⊙| *CP.*

Festivals

September is a month of fairs and celebrations in Asti, and the **Palio di Asti,** a horse race run through the streets of town, highlights the festivities. First mentioned in 1275, this annual event has been going strong ever since. After an elaborate procession in period costumes, nine horses and jockeys representing different sections of town vie for the honor of claiming the *palio,* a symbolic flag of victory. For 10 days in early September Asti is host to the **Douja d'Or National Wine Festival**—an opportunity to see Asti and celebrate the product that made it famous. During the course of the festival a competition is held to award "Oscars" to the best wine producers, and stands for wine tastings allow visitors to judge the winners for themselves. Musical events and other activities accompany the festival. Contact the **tourist office** (☎0141/530357 ⊕www.atasti.it) for the schedule of events.

Shopping

The **Enoteca** on Piazza Alfieri, a square adjacent to Campo del Palio, is a wine center and shop, open Monday–Saturday 9–4:30, where you can try a range of Asti vintages, buy a bottle, and have a light snack. Be aware, though, that prices for Spumante in Asti are not necessarily lower than those elsewhere.

Alba

㉗ *30 km (18 mi) southwest of Asti.*

This small town has a gracious atmosphere and a compact core studded with medieval towers and Gothic buildings. In addition to being a wine center of the region, Alba is known as the "City of the White Truffle" for the dirty little tubers that command a higher price per ounce than diamonds. For picking out your truffle and having a few wisps shaved on top of your food, expect to shell out an extra €16—which is well worth it. Visit in October for the Fiera del Tartufo (National Truffle Fair), Cento Torri Joust (a medieval jousting festival), and the Palio degli Asini (donkey races), held the first Sunday of the month.

Where to Stay

$ 🏨 **La Meridiana.** If Alba strikes your fancy, consider a night at this reasonably priced belle-epoque–style B&B, on a hill overlooking the historic center and surrounded by Dolcetto and Nebbiolo grapevines. ✉ *Località Altavilla 9* ☎📠 *0173/ 440112* ✉ *cascinareine@libero.it*

WORD OF MOUTH
"I really like the Piedmont region in October. It is truffle season and there are many festivals going on! The Alba white truffles are heaven on earth." —SloJan

⏎ *7 rooms, 2 apartments* ⟁ *Pool, gym, cable TV; no a/c in some rooms, no room phones* ▭ *No credit cards* ⊙ *CP.*

VALLE D'AOSTA

The unspoiled beauty of the highest peaks in the Alps, the Matterhorn and Monte Bianco, competes with the magnificent scenery of Italy's oldest national park in Valle d'Aosta, a semiautonomous, bilingual region tucked away at the border with France and Switzerland. Luckily, you don't have to choose—the region is small, so you can fit skiing, après-ski, and wild ibex into one memorable trip. The main Aosta Valley, largely on an east–west axis, is hemmed in by high mountains where glaciers have gouged out 14 tributary valleys, six to the north and eight to the south. A car is very helpful here, but take care: though distances are relatively short as the crow flies, steep slopes and winding roads add to your mileage and travel time.

Coming up from Turin, beyond Ivrea the road takes you through countryside that becomes hillier and hillier, passing through steep ravines guarded by brooding, romantic castles. Pont St. Martin, about 18 km (11 mi) north of Ivrea, is the beginning of bilingual (Italian and French) territory.

Bard

28 *65 km (40 mi) north of Turin.*

A few minutes beyond the French-speaking village of Pont St. Martin you pass through the narrow Gorge de Bard and reach the **Forte di Bard** (closed to the public), a 19th-century reconstruction of a fort that stood for eight centuries, serving the Savoys for six of them. In 1800 Napoléon entered Italy through this valley and used the cover of darkness to get his artillery units past the castle unnoticed. Ten years later he remembered this inconvenience and had the fortress destroyed.

St. Vincent

29 *28 km (17 mi) north of Bard, 93 km (58 mi) north of Turin.*

The town of St. Vincent has been a popular spa resort since the late 18th century. Its main draw these days is the **Casinò de la Vallée,** one of Europe's largest gambling casinos. You must present identification and be at least 18 years old to enter. Dress is elegant, with jacket and tie requested at the French gaming tables. ⊠ *Via Italo Mus 1* ☎ *0166/5221* ⊕ *www. casinodelavallee.it* ⊡ *€5* ⊙ *Sun.–Fri. 3 PM–3:30 AM, Sat. 3 PM–4 AM.*

Where to Stay & Eat

★ **$$$–$$$$** ✕ **Nuovo Batezar—da Renato.** This tiny restaurant with only eight tables ranks among the best in all of Italy. The ambience is rustic yet elegant, with arches and beamed ceilings enhanced by local antiques and fine crystal. The menu, which changes with the seasons, is Valdostana and Piemontese, with creative variations. Mushrooms, fish, fresh game, and truffles often play prominent roles. As a starter, try the homemade pasta or the *pazzarella* (a small pizza with porcini mushrooms, mozzarella, and truffles). ✉ *Via Marconi 1, near the casino* ☎ *0166/513164* 🍴 *Reservations essential* 🍽 *AE, DC, MC, V* 🕓 *Closed Wed., 3 wks in June, and Nov. 15–30. No lunch weekdays.*

$$$$ 🏨 **Billia.** A luxury belle-epoque hotel with faux-Gothic touches, the Billia is in a park in the middle of town and connects directly to the casino by a passageway. Half the rooms are done in modern and half in period decor, but all have high ceilings, finely upholstered furniture, and well-stocked bathrooms. ✉ *Viale Piemonte 72, 11027* ☎ *0166/5231* 📠 *0166/523799* 🌐 *www.grandhotelbillia.com* 🛏 *233 rooms, 7 suites* 🍴 *Restaurant, cable TV, tennis court, pool, health club, sauna, bar, convention center, Internet* 🍽 *AE, DC, MC, V* 🍴 *CP.*

$ 🏨 **Elena.** A central location is the selling point of this hotel near the casino. The spacious rooms, some with balconies and king-size beds, are decorated in a comfortable modern style. ✉ *Via Biavaz 2 (Piazza Zerbion), 11027* ☎ *0166/512140* 📠 *0166/537459* ✉ *hotel.elena@libero.it* 🛏 *46 rooms, 2 suites* 🍴 *Restaurant, minibars, gym, sauna, Turkish bath, bar, meeting rooms, parking (fee), no-smoking rooms; no a/c in some rooms* 🍽 *AE, DC, MC, V* 🍴 *CP.*

Breuil-Cervinia/The Matterhorn

30 *30 km (18 mi) north of St. Vincent, 116 km (72 mi) north of Turin.*

Breuil-Cervinia is a village at the base of the **Matterhorn** (Monte Cervino in Italian; Mont Cervin in French). Like the village, the famous peak straddles the border between Italy and Switzerland, and all sightseeing and skiing facilities are operated jointly. Splendid views of the peak can be seen from **Plateau Rosa** and the **Cresta del Furggen,** both of which can be reached by cable car

> ## WORD OF MOUTH
>
> "I love nature, but I never thought a picture-perfect image of the Matterhorn would stay with me for as long as it has—it's been almost 10 years since that first time I saw it on a clear day in July."
>
> –Mitch

from the center of Breuil-Cervinia. Although many locals complain that the tourist facilities and condominiums in the village have changed the face of their beloved village, most would agree that the cable car has given them access to climbing and off-trail skiing in ridges that were once inaccessible.

Where to Stay & Eat

★ $$$ ✕🏨 **Les Neiges d'Antan.** In an evergreen forest at Perrères, just outside Cervinia, this family-run inn is quiet and cozy, with three big fireplaces and a nice view of the Matterhorn. An excellent restaurant ($$$–$$$$) serves French dishes and local specialties such as *zuppa Valpellinentze* (a hearty soup of bread, cabbage, and Fontina cheese) and an opulent antipasto (local salami, country pâté, *tomino* cheese, and much more). ✉ *Località Perrères, 3½ km (2 mi) outside Cervinia, 11021* ☎ *0166/948775* 📠 *0166/948852* 🌐 *www.lesneigesdantan.it* 🛏 *21 rooms, 3 suites* 🍴 *Restaurant, room TVs with movies, sauna, bar; no a/c* 🍽 *MC, V* 🕓 *Closed May and June, and mid-Sept.–Nov.* 🍴 *CP.*

$$ ×📷 **Cime Bianche.** This calm, quiet mountain-lodge restaurant is one of the few dining spots in town to offer regional Valdostana cuisine, serving fonduta, polenta, and wild game in a rustic setting. The wood beams and tables are typical of a ski resort, but meals are produced with greater care than your average après-ski affairs. The commanding view covers the Matterhorn and Grandes Murailles. Reservations are highly recommended. There are also 15 guest rooms, all with balconies. ⊠ *Località La Vieille 44, near the ski lift, 11021* ☎ *0166/949046* 🖷 *0166/948061* ⊕ *www.hotelcimebianche.com* ➷ *15 rooms* ♨ *Restaurant, bar; no a/c* ▭ *MC, V* ⊘ *Closed Mon., and May and June* ⊘⊙ *CP.*

★ **$$$$** 📷 **Hermitage.** The entryway's marble relief of St. Theodolus reminds you that this was the site of a hermitage, but asceticism has given way to comfort and elegance at what is now one of the most exclusive hotels in the region. It has the look of a relaxed but posh family chalet, with rustic antiques, petit-point upholstery, a fire always glowing in the enormous hearth, and a candlelit dining room. The bright bedrooms have balconies; suites have antique fireplaces and 18th-century furnishings. While here you can make use of Hermitage's extensive health and beauty facilities and play golf (for half price) at the Cervinia Golf Club. ⊠ *Via Piolet 1, Località Chapellette, 11021* ☎ *0166/948998* 🖷 *0166/*

949032 ⊕ *www.hotelhermitage.com* ⟳ *30 rooms, 6 suites* ⚘ *Restaurant, golf privileges, indoor pool, health club, massage, sauna, bar, Internet, meeting rooms* ⊟ *AE, DC, MC, V* ⊘ *Closed May, June, Sept., and Oct.* ¶⊙¶ *CP.*

$$$ ▥ **Bucaneve.** This small central hotel catering to longer stays is decorated in typical mountain style, with lots of wood paneling, cheery floral upholstery in spacious lounges, and terraces dripping with geraniums. Après-ski, there's a restaurant (half board is required) and a cozy bar with a big fireplace and pianist in the evening. ⊠ *Piazza Jumeaux 10, 11021* ☎ *0166/949119* ⊟ *0166/948308* ⊕ *www.hotel-bucaneve.it* ⟳ *20 rooms, 6 suites* ⚘ *Restaurant, gym, hot tub, sauna, piano bar, meeting rooms* ⊟ *AE, MC, V* ⊘ *Closed May–late June and Sept.–Nov., depending on weather* ¶⊙¶ *MAP.*

$$$ ▥ **Chalet Valdotain.** About 2 km (1 mi) outside of town on the road to Châtillon, this Alpine chalet has wooden balconies and snug rooms with terrific views of the Matterhorn. It's known for good food and a friendly atmosphere. ⊠ *Località Lago Bleu 2, 11021* ☎ *0166/949428* ⊟ *0166/948874* ⊕ *www.chaletvaldotain.it* ⟳ *35 rooms* ⚘ *Restaurant, pool, gym, sauna, Turkish bath, bar* ⊟ *AE, DC, MC, V* ⊘ *Closed May–mid-June and mid-Sept.–Oct.* ¶⊙¶ *CP.*

Sports & the Outdoors

CLIMBING Serious climbers can make the ascent of the Matterhorn from Breuil-Cervinia after registering with the local mountaineering officials at the **tourist office** (⊠ Via Carrel 29 ☎ 0166/949136). This climb is for experienced climbers only. Less demanding hikes follow the lower slopes of the valley of the River Marmore, to the south of town.

SKIING Because its slopes border the Cervino glacier, this resort at the foot of the Matterhorn offers year-round skiing. Sixty lifts and a few hundred miles of ski runs ranging from beginner to expert make the area one of the best and most popular in Italy. Contact the **tourist office** (⊠ Via Carrel 29 ☎ 0166/949136) for information.

Castello Fénis

③ 11 km (7 mi) west of St. Vincent, 104 km (65 mi) north of Turin.

Fodor'sChoice The best-preserved medieval fortress in Valle d'Aosta, the many-turreted
★ Castello Fénis was built in the mid-14th century by Aimone di Challant, a member of a prolific family related to the Savoys. The castle, which used a double ring of walls for its defense, is the sort imagined by schoolchildren, with pointed towers, portcullises, and spiral staircases. The 15th-century courtyard surrounded by wooden balconies is elegantly decorated with well-preserved frescoes. Inside you can see the kitchen, with an enormous fireplace that provided central heat in winter, the armory, and the spacious, well-lighted rooms used by the lord and lady of the manor. If you have time to visit only one castle in Valle d'Aosta, this should be it. ☎ *0165/764263* ⊠ *€5* ⊘ *Mar.–June, daily 9–6:30; July and Aug., daily 9–7:30; Sept., daily 9–6:30; Oct.–Feb., Wed.–Mon. 10–5; maximum of 25 people allowed to enter every ½ hr.*

en route | The highway continues climbing through Valle d'Aosta to the town of Aosta itself. The road at this point is heading almost due west, with rivulets from the wilderness reserve Parco Nazionale del Gran Paradiso streaming down from the left to join the Dora Baltea River, one of the major tributaries of the Po and an increasingly popular spot for rafting. Be careful driving here in late spring, when melting snow can turn some of these streams into torrents.

Aosta

㉜ *12 km (7 mi) west of Castello Fénis, 113 km (70 mi) north of Turin.*

Aosta stands at the junction of two of the important trade routes that connect France and Italy—the valleys of the Rhône and the Isère. Its significance as a trading post was recognized by the Romans, who built a garrison here in the 1st century BC. At the eastern entrance to town, in the Piazza Arco d'Augusto and commanding a fine view over Aosta and the mountains, is the **Arco di Augusto** (Arch of Augustus), built in 25 BC to mark Rome's victory over the Celtic Salassi tribe. (The sloping roof was added in 1716 in an attempt to keep rain from seeping between the stones.) The present-day layout of streets in this small city tucked away in the Alps more than 644 km (400 mi) from Rome is the clearest example of Roman urban planning in Italy. Well-preserved Roman walls form a perfect rectangle around the center of Aosta, and the regular pattern of streets reflects its role as a military stronghold. St. Anselm, born in Aosta, later became archbishop of Canterbury in England.

The **Collegiata di Sant'Orso** is the sort of church that has layers of history in its architecture. Originally there was a 6th-century chapel on this site founded by the Archdeacon Orso, a local saint. Most of this structure was destroyed or hidden when an 11th-century church was erected over it. This church, in turn, was encrusted with Gothic, and later baroque, features, resulting in a jigsaw puzzle of styles, but, surprisingly, not a chaotic jumble. The 11th-century features are almost untouched in the crypt, and if you go up the stairs on the left from the main church you can see the 11th-century frescoes (ask the sacristanto let you in). These restored frescoes depict the life of Christ and the Apostles: although only the tops are visible, you can see the expressions on the faces of the disciples. Take the outside doorway to the right of the main entrance to see thechurch's crowning glory, its 12th-century **cloister**. Next to the church, it's enclosed by some 40 stone columns with masterfully carved capitals depicting scenes from the Old and New Testaments and the life of St. Orso. The turrets and spires of Aosta peek out above. ⊠ *Via Sant'Orso* ☎ *0165/40614* ☉ *Apr.–Sept., daily 9–5; Oct.–Mar., daily 10–5.*

The huge **Roman Porta Pretoria**, regally guarding the city, is a remarkable relic from the Roman era. The area between the massive inner and outer gates was used as a small parade ground for the changing of the guard. ⊠ *West end of Via Sant'Anselmo.*

The 72-foot-high ruin of the facade of the **Teatro Romano** guards the remains of the 1st-century BC amphitheater, which once held 20,000 spec-

5

tators. Only a bit of the outside wall and seven of the amphitheater's original 60 arches remain, and these are built into the facade of the adjacent convent of the sisters of San Giuseppe. The nuns will usually allow you in to see these arches (ask at the entrance). ⊠ *Via Anfiteatro 4.*

Aosta's **Duomo** dates from the 10th century, but all that remains from that period are the bell towers. The decoration inside is primarily Gothic, but the main attraction of the cathedral predates that era by 1,000 years: a carved ivory diptych portraying the Roman Emperor Honorius and dating from AD 406 is among the many ornate objects housed in the treasury. ⊠ *Via Monsignor de Sales* ☎ *0165/40251* ☉ *Treasury Apr.–Sept., Tues.–Sun. 9–11:30 and 3–5:30; Oct.–Mar., Sun. 3–5:30.*

Where to Stay & Eat

$$–$$$ ✕ **Vecchio Ristoro.** Housed in a converted mill, this centrally located restaurant is furnished with antiques and a large ceramic stove. The chef-proprietor takes pride in creative versions of regional favorites, including *marbrè di bollito misto con bagnet verde* (terrine of mixed boiled meats with a parsley and anchovy sauce) and *carrè d'agnello gratinato alle erbe* (grilled loin of lamb in a pastry and herb crust). ⊠ *Via Tourneuve 4* ☎ *0165/33238* ⊟ *AE, DC, MC, V* ☉ *Closed Sun., June, and 1 wk in Nov. No lunch Mon.*

$–$$$ ✕ **Taverna Nando.** In a wine cellar with wooden floors and vaulted ceilings, this family-run tavern lets you sample regional specialties such as fonduta, carbonada, and *cervo* (venison) with mushrooms. In the center of Aosta, it also has a terrace for outdoor dining. ⊠ *Via de Tillier 41* ☎ *0165/44455* ⊟ *AE, DC, MC, V* ☉ *Closed Mon. and June 20–July 10.*

$–$$ ✕ **La Brasserie du Commerce.** In the heart of Aosta, this small and lively eatery is near the Piazza E. Chanoux. On a sunny summer day try to snag a table on the terrace. Typical valley dishes such as fonduta are on the menu, as well as many vegetable dishes and salads. ⊠ *Via de Tillier 10* ☎ *0165/35613* ⊛ *Reservations not accepted* ⊟ *AE, DC, MC, V* ☉ *Closed Sun.*

¢–$ ✕ **Praetoria.** Just outside the Porta Pretoria, this simple and unpretentious restaurant serves hearty local dishes such as *crespelle alla valdostana* (crepes with cheese and ham). The pasta is made on the premises, and all of the menu offerings are prepared from traditional recipes. ⊠ *Via S. Anselmo 9* ☎ *0165/44356* ⊟ *AE, DC, MC, V* ☉ *Closed Thurs.*

$$ ⊡ **Holiday Inn Aosta.** Attractive Provençal fabrics add some local color to this chain hotel's otherwise predictable amenities. The rooms, some equipped for people with disabilities, are modern and comfortable, and some have balconies overlooking the mountains. The central location is another plus. ⊠ *Corso Battaglione Aosta 30, 11100* ☎ *0165/236356* ⊟ *0165/236837* ⊕ *www.sixcontinentshotels.com* ⇆ *45 rooms, 5 suites* ⚘ *Restaurant, room TVs with movies, bar, business services, some pets allowed (fee), no-smoking rooms* ⊟ *AE, DC, MC, V* ⊺⊙⊺ *CP.*

★ **$–$$** ⊡ **Milleluci.** This small and inviting family-run hotel sits on a hillside overlooking Aosta, 1 km (½ mi) north of town. A huge brick hearth and rustic wooden beams highlight the lounge. Bedrooms, some with balconies, are bright and pleasantly decorated and have good views of the city and mountains. Ten rooms are reserved for nonsmokers and some rooms are equipped for people with disabilities. ✉ *Località Porossan Roppoz 15, 11100* ☎ *0165/235278* 🖷 *0165/235284* ⊕ *www.hotelmilleluci.com* ↩ *26 rooms, 5 suites* ⚬ *Tennis court, pool, sauna, bar, Internet, no-smoking rooms; no a/c* ➡ *AE, DC, MC, V* ⦿| *CP.*

$ 🏰 **Casa Ospitaliera del Gran San Bernardo.** Here's your chance to sleep in a 12th-century castle without emptying your wallet. In a monastery that Amedeo of Savoy gave to the Order of St. Bernard in 1137, this bargain-price lodging is still run by monks. Only 15 km (8 mi) north of Aosta, this simple pension is a good base for hikers and cross-country skiers. Hearty food is included in the full meal plan. ✉ *Rue de Flassin 3, 11010 Saint-Oyen* ☎ *0165/78247* 🖷 *0165/789512* ↩ *15 rooms* ⚬ *No a/c, no room phones, no room TVs* ➡ *No credit cards* ⊙ *Closed May* ⦿| *FAP.*

Nightlife & the Arts

Each summer a series of **concerts** is held in different venues around the city. Organ recitals in July and August attract performers of world renown. Call the **tourist board** (✉ Piazza E. Chanoux 8 ☎ 0165/236627) for information.

Shopping

Aosta and the surrounding countryside are famous for wood carvings and wrought iron. There's a permanent **crafts exhibition** in the arcades of Piazza E. Chanoux, in the heart of Aosta; it's a good place to pick up a bargain.

Courmayeur/Monte Bianco

★ ㉝ *35 km (21 mi) northwest of Aosta, 150 km (93 mi) northwest of Turin.*

The main attraction of Courmayeur is a knock-'em-dead view of Europe's tallest peak, **Monte Bianco** (Mont Blanc). Jet-set celebrities flock here, following a tradition that dates from the late 17th century, when Courmayeur's natural springs first began to draw visitors. The spectacle of the Alps gradually surpassed the springs as the biggest draw (the Alpine letters of the English poet Percy Bysshe Shelley were almost advertisements for the region), but the biggest change came in 1965 with the opening of the Mont Blanc tunnel. Since then, ever increasing numbers of travelers have passed through the area.

Luckily, planners have managed to keep some restrictions on wholesale development within the town, and its angled rooftops and immaculate cobblestone streets maintain a cozy (if prepackaged) feeling. There is no train directly into Courmayeur, so if you don't have a car you'll need to bus it from nearby Pré-Saint-Didier, which is accessible by train from Aosta.

From La Palud, a small town 4 km (3½ mi) north of Courmayeur, you can catch the cable car up to the top of Monte Bianco. In summer, if you get the inclination, you can then switch cable cars and descend into Chamonix, in France. In winter you can ski parts of the route off-piste. The Funivie La Palud whisks you up first to the Pavillon du Mont Fréty—a starting point for many beautiful hikes—and then to the Rifugio di Torino, before arriving at the viewing platform at **Punta Helbronner** (more than 11,000 feet), which is also the border post with France. Monte Bianco's attraction is not so much its shape (much less distinctive than that of the Matterhorn) as its expanse and the vistas from the top.

The next stage up—only in summer—is on the **Télépherique de L'Aiguille du Midi,** as you pass into French territory. The trip is particularly impressive: you dangle over a huge glacial snowfield (more than 2,000 feet below) and make your way slowly to the viewing station above Chamonix. It's one of the most dramatic rides in Europe. From this point you're looking down into France, and if you change cable cars at the Aiguille du Midi station you can make your way down to Chamonix itself. The return trip covers the same route. Schedules are unpredictable, depending on weather conditions and demand; contact the **Courmayeur tourist office** (☎ 0165/842060 ⊕ www.courmayeur.net) for more infromation. ⊠ *Fraz. La Palud 22* ☎ *0165/89925 Italian side, 00/33450536210 French side* ⊕ *www.montebianco.com* ✉ *€11 round-trip to Pavillon du Mont Fréty, €32 round-trip to Helbronner, €48 round-trip to Aiguille du Midi, €75 round-trip to Chamonix* ☉ *Call for hrs. Closed mid-Oct.–mid-Dec., depending on demand and weather.*

Where to Stay & Eat

★ **$$–$$$$** ✕**Cadran Solaire.** In what was the oldest tavern in Courmayeur, this warm and inviting restaurant been renovated by the Garin family to highlight its 17th-century stone vault, the old wooden floor, and the huge stone fireplace. The menu offers seasonal specialties and innovative interpretations of regional dishes. The cozy bar is a popular place for a before-dinner drink. ⊠ *Via Roma 122* ☎ *0165/844609* ⚑ *Reservations essential* ▭ *AE, MC, V* ☉ *Closed Tues., May, and Oct.*

★ **$$** ✕**Maison de Filippo.** Here you'll find country-style home cooking in a mountain house with lots of atmosphere, furnished with antiques, farm tools, and bric-a-brac of all kinds. There's a set menu only, which includes an abundance of antipasti and a tempting choice of local soups and pasta dishes. Cheese, dessert, and fresh fruit complete the meal. Reserve in advance, for it's one of the most popular restaurants in Valle d'Aosta. ⊠ *Entrèves* ☎ *0165/869797* ⚑ *Reservations essential* ▭ *MC, V* ☉ *Closed Tues., mid-May–June, and Oct. and Nov.*

$$$$ ✕▦ **Royal e Golf.** A longtime landmark in the center of Courmayeur, the Royal rises high above the surrounding town. With wide terraces and wood paneling, it is the most elegant spot in town. The cheery rooms have plenty of amenities. The main restaurant, Grill Royal e Golf, is renowned for such culinary creations as frogs' legs in a basil fish broth. Reservations are required, as are a jacket and tie for men. The hotel caters to longer stays with half- or full-board service. ⊠ *Via Roma 87, 11013* ☎ *0165/831611* ▦ *0165/842093* ⊕ *www.royalegolf.com* ⇨ *80 rooms, 6 suites* ⚏ *2 restaurants, minibars, pool, health club, sauna, Turkish bath, bar, piano bar, Internet, cable TV, meeting rooms, some pets allowed, no-smoking rooms; no a/c* ▭ *AE, DC, MC, V* ☉ *Closed wk after Easter–mid-June and mid-Sept.–Nov.* ▮◎▮ *MAP.*

$$$$ ▦ **Pavillon.** This modern take on an old-fashioned chalet comes complete with stylish furnishings and a clubby bar. Some stunning contemporary stained glass decorates the public areas and the well-equipped health center. Each room is individually decorated but all have the gold-hued wood paneling and solid furniture typical of mountain retreats. ⊠ *Strada Regionale 62, 11013* ☎ *0165/846120* 🖷 *0165/846122* ⊕ *www.pavillon.it* ➯ *40 rooms, 10 suites* ⚘ *Restaurant, indoor pool, health club, hot tub, massage, sauna, steam room, bar, meeting room, some pets allowed; no a/c* ☰ *AE, DC, MC, V* ⊗ *Closed end Apr.–June 15, Oct. and Nov.* ❦ *FAP.*

$$$–$$$$ 🏨 **Auberge de la Maison.** This modern hotel's stone-and-wood construction, typical of this region, gives it the feeling of a country inn. Most of the cozy rooms have views of Monte Bianco. Alpine prints on the walls, plush fabrics, and wood-burning stoves make the accommodations very comfortable. A massage here can be the perfect ending to a day of hiking or skiing. ⊠ *Via Passerin d'Entrèves, 11013* ☎ *0165/869811* 🖷 *0165/869759* ⊕ *www.aubergemaison.it* ➯ *30 rooms, 3 suites* ⚘ *Gym, hot tub, massage, sauna; no a/c* ☰ *AE, MC, V* ⊗ *Closed May* ❦ *CP.*

★ $$$ 🏨 **Palace Bron.** In a lovely stand of pines above the town, this tranquil hotel is an ideal spot to relax. Rooms are bright and pretty, furnished with antiques. The sitting room has picture windows with magnificent views of Monte Bianco, and for chilly nights the elegant restaurant offers a cozy fireplace. In winter there's a free shuttle between the hotel, the town center, and the ski lifts. ⊠ *Via Plan Gorret 41, 11013* ☎ *0165/846742* 🖷 *0165/844015* ⊕ *www.palacebron.it* ➯ *26 rooms, 1 suite* ⚘ *Restaurant, minibars, bar, piano bar, meeting room, some pets allowed (fee); no a/c* ☰*AE, DC, MC, V* ⊗*Closed Apr.–mid-June and mid-Sept.–Nov.* ❦CP.

$$$ 🏨 **Villa Novecento.** Run with the friendly charm and efficiency of Franco **Fodor'sChoice** Cavaliere and his son Stefano, the Novecento is a peaceful haven near Cour-**★** mayeur's busy center. In keeping with the style of a comfortable mountain lodge, the lounge is warmed by a fire in winter. The rooms are soothingly decorated with traditional fabrics, wooden furnishings, and early-19th-century prints. The restaurant, with only a few extra tables for nonguests, serves creative adaptations of traditional cuisine; it's a good choice for a relaxed evening meal. ⊠ *Viale Monte Bianco 64, 11013* ☎*0165/843000* 🖷*0165/844030* ⊕*www.villanovecento.it* ➯*24 rooms, 2 suites* ⚘ *Restaurant, gym, sauna, Turkish bath, bar, meeting rooms, some pets allowed; no a/c* ☰ *AE, DC, MC, V* ⊗ *Closed May and Oct.* ❦ *CP.*

$$ 🏨 **Croux.** This bright, comfortable hotel is near the town center on the road leading to Monte Bianco. Half the rooms have balconies, the other half have great views of the mountains. The friendly staff goes out of its way to make you feel welcome. ⊠ *Via Croux 8, 11013* ☎ *0165/846735* 🖷 *0165/845180* ⊕ *www.hotelcroux.it* ➯ *33 rooms* ⚘ *Sauna, Turkish bath, bar; no a/c* ☰ *AE, DC, MC, V* ⊗ *Closed mid-Apr.–mid-June and mid-Sept.–mid-Dec.* ❦ *CP.*

Sports & the Outdoors

SKIING Courmayeur pales in comparison to its French neighbor, Chamonix, in both the number (it has only 24) and the quality of its trails. But with good natural snow cover, the trails and vistas are spectacular. A huge gondola leads from the center of Courmayeur to Plan Checrouit, where gondolas and lifts lead to the slopes. The skiing around Monte Bianco is particularly good, and the off-piste options are among the best in Europe. The off-piste routes from Cresta d'Arp (the local peak) to Dolonne, and from the La Palud area into France, should be done with a guide. Contact the **Funivie Courmayeur/Mont Blanc** (☎ 0165/846658) for complete information about lift tickets, ski runs, and weather conditions. For Alpine guide services contact the **Società delle Guide Alpine** (✉ Strada Villair 2 ☎ 0165/842064 ⊕ www.guidecourmayeur.com).

Cogne & the Parco Nazionale del Gran Paradiso

③④ *52 km (32 mi) southeast of Courmayeur, 134 km (83 mi) northwest of Turin.*

Cogne is the gateway to the Parco Nazionale del Gran Paradiso. This huge park, once the domain of King Vittorio Emanuele II (1820–78) and bequeathed to the nation after World War I, is one of Europe's most rugged and unspoiled wilderness areas, with wildlife and many plant species protected by law. This is one of the few places in Europe where you can see the ibex (a mountain goat with horns up to 3 feet long) and the chamois (a small antelope). The park is open free of charge throughout the year and is managed by a park board, the **Ente Parco Nazionale Gran Paradiso** (✉ Via della Rocca 47, Turin, 10123 ☎ 011/8606211 ⊕ www.parks.it/parco.nazionale.gran.paradiso). Try to visit in May, when spring flowers are in bloom and most of the meadows are clear of snow.

Sports & the Outdoors

HIKING There's wonderful hiking to be done here, both on daylong excursions and longer journeys with overnight stops in the park's mountain refuges. The **Cogne tourist office** (✉ Piazza E. Chanoux 36 ☎ 0165/74040 ⊕ www.cogne.org) has a wealth of information and trail maps to help.

PIEDMONT & VALLE D'AOSTA ESSENTIALS

Transportation

BY AIR

The region's only international airport, Aeroporto Torino Caselle, is 18 km (11 mi) north of Turin. It's notoriously foggy in winter, and many flights are diverted to Genoa, on the coast, with bus connections provided for the two-hour drive to Turin. From Aeroporto Caselle, local buses to Turin arrive at the bus station on Corso Inghilterra in the city center.

🛈 Airport Information **Aeroporto Torino Caselle** ☎ 011/5676361.

BY BUS

The Turin-based SADEM and SAPAV lines service the autostrada network to Milan and other destinations in Italy. SITA buses, part of the nationwide system, also connect Turin with the rest of Italy.

Turin's main bus station is on the corner of Corso Inghilterra and Corso Vittorio Emanuele. Urban buses and trams are operated by the agency ATM. SADEM and SAPAV bus lines both have service throughout Piedmont and Valle d'Aosta. SAVDA specializes in mountain service, providing frequent links between Aosta, Turin, and Courmayeur as well as

Milan. There's also a major bus station at Aosta, across the street from the train station.

🚌 **Bus Information ATM** ✉ Corso Turati 19/6, 10128 Turin ☎ 800/019152 ⊕ www.atm. to.it. **SADEM** ✉ Via della Repubblica 14, Grugliasco, 10095 Turin ☎ 800801600. **SAPAV** ✉ Corso Torino 396, 10064 Turin ☎ 800/801901 ⊕ www.sapav.it. **SAVDA** ✉ Strada Ponte Suaz 6, 11100 Aosta ☎ 0165/361244. **SITA** ✉ Via Cadorna 105, 50123 Florence ☎ 055/47821 ⊕ www.sita-on-line.it.

BY CAR

Italy's autostrada network links the region with the rest of Italy and neighboring France. Aosta, Turin, and Alessandria all have autostrada connections, with the A4 heading east to Milan and the A6 heading south to the Ligurian coast and Genoa. Turin is the hub of all the transportation systems in Piedmont, with autostrada connections to the north, south, and east.

For travel across the French, Swiss, and Italian borders in Piedmont and Valle d'Aosta, only a few routes are practicable year-round: the 12-km (7-mi) Mont Blanc tunnel connecting Chamonix with Courmayeur, the Colle del Gran San Bernardo/Col du Grand St. Bernard (connecting Martigny with Aosta on Swiss highway E27 and Italian highway SS27, with 6 km [4 mi] of tunnel), and the Traforo del Fréjus (between Modane and Susa, with 13 km [8 mi] of tunnel). There are other passes, but they become increasingly unreliable between November and April.

EMERGENCY SERVICES If you have a breakdown on the road, you can walk to one of the roadside stations marked SOS and push the button. You'll be connected to the Automobile Club of Italy (ACI), which will come and assist you, for free if you have a membership card for the automobile club in your home country. (Otherwise, you must pay a fee.) For emergency road assistance, ACI can also be reached at the phone number below.
🚗 **ACI** ☎ 803/116.

BY TRAIN

Turin is on the main Paris–Rome TGV express line and is also connected with Milan, only 90 minutes away on the fast train. The fastest (Eurostar) trains cover the 667-km (400-mi) trip to Rome in about six hours, but most trains take about nine hours.

Services to the larger cities east of Turin are part of the extensive and reliable train network of the Lombard Plain. West of the region's capital, however, the train services soon peter out in the mountains. Continuing connections by bus serve these valleys; information about train-bus mountain services can be obtained from train stations and tourist information offices, or by contacting the Ferrovie dello Stato (FS), the Italian national train service.
🚆 **Train Information FS–Trenitalia** ☎ 892021 ⊕ www.trenitalia.com.

Contacts & Resources

EMERGENCIES

Pharmacies throughout the region take turns staying open late and on Sunday. Dial 192 for the latest information (in Italian) on which are open.

The Farmacia Boniscontro in Turin takes a lunch break between 12:30 and 3 but is open all night.

⌕ Ambulance service ☏ 118. **Emergencies** ☏ 113. **Farmacia Boniscontro** ✉ Corso Vittorio Emanuele II, 66, Turin ☏ 011/538271. **Police** ☏ 112.

TOURS

Turin's group and personally guided tours are organized by the city's tourist office. Here you can also get information about the Touristibus, a two-hour guided bus trip that leaves from Piazza Castello, at the corner of Via Po, every day but Tuesday at 2:30. Touristibus goes through the historic center of Turin, including Via Roma and Porta Nuova, and then out to view such locations as the Palazzina di Caccia in Stupinigi and the Parco Valentino.

PRIVATE GUIDES Alpine guides are not only recommended but essential if you're planning to traverse some of the dramatic ranges outside St. Vincent, Courmayeur, or Breuil-Cervinia. Before embarking on an excursion (however short) into the mountains in these areas, contact the representative of the CAI (Club Alpino Italiano) for information about hikes and the risks. Guides from the Alpine Guides Association can accompany you on treks and also lead skiing, canyoning, and ice-climbing excursions.

⌕ Alpine Guides Association ✉ Strada Villair 2, Courmayeur ☏ 0165/842064. **CAI** ✉ Piazza E. Chanoux 8, Aosta ☏ 0165/40194.

VISITOR INFORMATION

⌕ Tourist Information Alba ✉ Piazza Medford 3, 12051 ☏ 0173/35833 ⊕ www. langheroero.it. **Aosta** ✉ Piazza E. Chanoux 8, 11100 ☏ 0165/236627 ⊕ www.regione. vda.it/turismo. **Asti** ✉ Piazza Alfieri 29, 14100 ☏ 0141/530357 ⊕ www.atasti.it. **Bardonecchia** ✉ Viale Vittoria 44, 10052 ☏ 0122/99032 ⊕ www.comune.bardonecchia.to.it. **Breuil-Cervinia** ✉ Via Carrel 29, 11021 ☏ 0166/949136 ⊕ www.cervinia.it. **Cogne** ✉ Piazza E. Chanoux 36, 11012 ☏ 0165/74040 ⊕ www.cogne.org. **Courmayeur** ✉ Piazzale Monte Bianco 13, 11013 ☏ 0165/842060 ⊕ www.courmayeur.net. **Novara** ✉ Baluardo Quintino Sella 40, 28100 ☏ 0321/394059. **Saluzzo** ✉ Via Griselda 6, 12037 ☏ 0175/46710 ⊕ www.comune.saluzzo.cn.it. **Sestriere** ✉ Via Pinerolo 14, 10058 ☏ 0122/755444 ⊕ www.comune.sestriere.to.it. **Turin** ✉ Atrium Torino, Piazza Solferino ☏ 011/535181 ✉ Stazione Porta Nuova, 10121 ☏ 011/531327 ⊕ www.turismotorino.org. **Vercelli** ✉ Viale Garibaldi 90, 13100 ☏ 0161/58002 ⊕ www.turismovalsesiavercelli.it.

The Italian Riviera

Portovenere

WORD OF MOUTH

"Vernazza, in the Cinque Terre, is so wonderful because everyone there is just hanging out doing nothing. People sit in cafés and sip drinks and gaze at the sea. Or they stroll down the main street and gaze at each other. That's it. And it's wonderful."

—daria

WELCOME TO THE ITALIAN RIVIERA

Hiking trail, Cinque Terre

TOP 5
Reasons to Go

1 **Walking the Cinque Terre:** Hike the famous Cinque Terre trails past gravity-defying vineyards, rock-perched villages, and the deep blue sea.

2 **Genoa's "Street of Gold":** Renaissance or rococo, the palaces of Via Garibaldi bear witness to the gilded heyday of Genoese splendor.

3 **Giardini Botanici Hanbury, Ventimiglia:** A spectacular natural setting harbors one of Italy's largest, most exotic botanical gardens.

4 **Portofino:** See the world through rose-tinted sunglasses at this glamorous little harbor village.

5 **Pesto:** The basil-rich sauce was invented in Liguria, and it's never been equaled elsewhere.

Palazzo San Giorgio, Genoa

The **Riviera di Ponente** (Riviera of the Setting Sun), reaching from the French border to Genoa, has protected bays and sandy beaches. The seaside resorts of **Bordighera** and **San Remo** share some of the glitter of their French cousins to the west.

Getting Oriented

The Italians perfected *il dolce far niente*—the sweet art of idleness—right here in the coastal region of Liguria, also known as the Italian Riviera. It's a collection of villages dedicated to the sea and the sun, running along a broad curve between France to the west and Tuscany to the east. Smack in the middle is Genoa, one of Italy's great port cities.

Riomaggiore

The pastel-hued town of **Portofino**, at the tip of the Portofino Promontory, has charmed generations of the rich and famous.

TUSCANY

Golfo di Genova

Genoa, birthplace of Christopher Columbus, is the urban anomaly among Liguria's charming villages. At its heart is Italy's largest historic district.

East of Genoa, the **Riviera di Levante** (Riviera of the Rising Sun) has minuscule bays and inlets that accent dramatic cliffs.

The five isolated villages of the **Cinque Terre** seem removed from the modern world—despite the many hikers who populate the trails between them.

Manarola   Sant Andrea Cloister, Genoa   Portofino

ITALIAN RIVIERA PLANNER

Making the Most of Your Time

Genoa or no Genoa—that's your first question. The city has been working hard to shed its reputation as a seamy port town, and the efforts have largely been successful. Genoa's artistic and cultural treasures are significant—you won't find anything remotely comparable elsewhere in the region—and the historical center is a pleasure to explore. Unless your goal is to avoid urban life entirely, consider a night or more in the city.

Your second decision, particularly with limited time, is between the two Rivieras. The Riviera di Levante, east of Genoa, is quieter and has a more distinctive personality; high-end Portofino and the rustic Cinque Terre are arguably the coast's most appealing destinations. The Riviera di Ponente, west of Genoa, is more of a classic European resort experience, with better beaches and more nightlife—similar to, but not as glamorous as, the French Riviera across the border.

Getting Around

Though the pace of life in the region is leisurely, getting around the Riviera is an expedient affair. Public transportation is excellent: trains connect all sights along the coast, and buses snake inland.

With the freedom of a car, you could drive from one end of the Riviera to the other on the autostrada in less than three hours. The A10 and A12 on either side of Genoa—engineering wonders with literally hundreds of long tunnels and towering viaducts—skirt the coast, avoiding the local traffic on the beautiful Via Aurelia, which was laid out by the ancient Romans. The Via Aurelia, also known as highway S1, connects practically all the towns on the coast.

For more about car, bus, and train travel, see "Essentials" at the end of this chapter.

Liguria by Boat

With so much coastline—350 km (217 mi)—and so many pretty little harbors, Liguria is a great place to get around by boat. You can take a boat tour of Genoa harbor with Cooperativa Battellieri del Porto di Genova, and excursion cruises between coastal towns are operated by the main ferry lines. But you can have as much fun (or more) negotiating a price with a boat owner at one of the smaller ports. You're likely to deal with someone who has a rudimentary command of English at best, but that's all you need to discuss price, time, and destination. For details about excursions, see "Essentials" at the end of this chapter.

Liguria by Foot

Walking the Italian Riviera's hilly terrain, with its abundance of gorgeous views, is a major leisure activity. The mild climate and laid-back state of mind can lull you into underestimating just how strenuous these walks can be. Wear good shoes, slather on the sun screen, and carry water—you'll be glad you did. Trail maps are available from tourist information offices, or upon paying admission to the Cinque Terre national park, the region's top hiking destination. Other walks worth considering:

■ On Portofino promontory, the relatively easy walk from Portofino to the Abbazia di San Fruttuoso is a popular choice, and there's a more challenging hike from Ruta to the top of Monte Portofino.

■ From Genoa, you can take the Zecca-Righi funicular up to Righi and walk along the ring of fortresses that used to defend the city, or ride the Genova–Casella railroad to one of the many rugged trailheads near the station stops.

Finding a Place to Stay

One argument against staying in Genoa is a general shortage of first-rate lodging options. Most hotels are in modern buildings (rather than the grand old restored villas you might expect), and the city gets noisy—so look for a place with windows that are *doppi vetri* (double-glazed). Lodging throughout Liguria can be pricey, especially in summer. At other times of year, ask for a *sconto bassa stagione* (low-season discount). Reservations are a particularly good idea because the coast is popular convention territory: if there's one taking place in the town where you're planning to stay, rooms can be hard to come by.

Dining & Lodging Price Categories

WHAT IT COSTS in Euros					
	$$$$	**$$$**	**$$**	**$**	**¢**
Restaurants	over €22	€16–€22	€11–€16	€7–€11	under €7
Hotels	over €220	€160–€220	€110–€160	€70–€110	under €70

Restaurant prices are for a second course (un secondo). Hotel prices are for two people in a standard double room in high season, including tax and service.

How's the Weather?

Season is everything on the Italian Riviera. Shops, cafés, clubs, and restaurants stay open late in resorts during high season (at Easter and from June through August), but during the rest of the year they close early, if they're open at all. From October to February, the seaside towns go into hibernation, leaving little more than boarded-up cafés and waves crashing against the barren coast. April, May, and September may be the best times to visit: flowers are in bloom, the weather's mild, and the volume of tourist traffic is relatively low. October and November often bring torrential rains, and with them floods and landslides.

TOP PASSEGGIATA

In Nervi, just outside Genoa, the Passeggiata Anita Garibaldi runs along seaside cliffs, with deep blue water to one side, the lush gardens of the Parco Villa Grimaldi to the other, and great views of the city in the distance.

6

Updated by
Peter Blackman

LIKE THE FAMILY JEWELS that bedeck its habitual visitors, the Italian Riviera is glamorous, but in the old-fashioned way. The resort towns and coastal villages that stake intermittent claim on the rocky shores of the Ligurian Sea are the long-lost cousins of newer, overbuilt seaside paradises found elsewhere. Here the grandest palazzos share space with frescoed, angular, late-19th-century apartment buildings; high-rise glitz is far away. The rustic and elegant, the provincial and chic, the cosmopolitan and the small-town are blended together here in a sun-drenched pastiche that defines the Italian side of the Riviera.

Although the region bearing the name Liguria extends inland, its greatest charms are found on the coast, which has inspired poets and artists for centuries. Most famously, Percy Shelley praised the "soft blue Spezian bay," and his fellow Romantic poet, the daredevil Lord Byron, swam from Portovenere to Lerici. Today travelers escaping the stress of city living still head to the Italian Riviera. Mellowed by the balmy breezes blowing off the sea, they bask in the sun, explore the picturesque fishing villages, pamper themselves at the resorts that dot this ruggedly beautiful landscape.

RIVIERA DI LEVANTE

Of the two Ligurian Rivieras, the Riviera di Levante, east of Genoa, is overall the wilder and more rugged, yet here you can also find towns like Portofino and Rapallo, world famous for their classic, elegant style. Around every turn of this area's twisting roads the hills plummet sharply to the sea, forming deep, hidden bays and inlets. Beaches on this coast are rocky, backed by spectacular sheer cliffs. The Portofino promontory has one sandy beach, on the east side, at Paraggi. From Chiavari to Cavi di Lavagna, the coast becomes a bit gentler, with a few sandy areas. Sailing conditions along the rugged coast from Sestri Levante down to Portovenere are good. Waterskiing, tennis, and golf are also popular. You may want to choose a base and take short day trips or explore the area by boat from the larger towns. You can anchor your boat in the relatively calm waters of small *ciazze* (coves) found all along the coast.

Lerici

❶ *106 km (66 mi) southeast of Genoa, 65 km (40 mi) west of Lucca.*

Near Liguria's border with Tuscany, this town is set on a magnificent coastline of gray cliffs and pine forests. Shelley was one of Lerici's best-known visitors and spent some of the happiest months of his life in the lovely white village of San Terenzo, 2 km (1 mi) away. After his death in 1822 the bay was renamed the Golfo dei Poeti, in his and Byron's honor.

Lerici once belonged to Tuscan Pisa, and the 13th-century Pisan **Castello di Lerici** has stood above the splendid bay for centuries. The castle now houses a museum of paleontology. ⊠ *Piazza S. Giorgio 1* ☎ *0187/ 969042* ⊕ *www.museocastello.lerici.sp.it* 💰 *€4.60* ☉ *Mar. 16–June and Sept.–Oct. 19, Tues.–Sun. 10:30–1 and 2:30–6; July and Aug., daily*

10:30–12:30 and 6:30 PM–midnight; Oct. 20–Dec. 9 and Dec. 27–Mar. 15, Tues.–Fri. 10:30–12:30, weekends 10:30–12:30 and 2:30–5:30.

Where to Stay & Eat

$ ╳▦ **Miranda.** Perched amid the clustered old houses in seaside Tellaro, 4 km (2½ mi) southeast of Lerici, this small family-run inn has become a gourmet's destination ($$$$) because of chef Angelo Cabani's imaginative way with Ligurian cooking. His unusual seafood menu changes daily, but might include *insalata di gamberoni e aragosta con finocchio* (shrimp and lobster salad with fennel) and risotto *mantecato con asparagi e gamberi* (with butter, asparagus, and shrimp). If you stay in one of the seven comfortable rooms with bath you have the option of half board at €180 for two people. ⊠ *Via Fiascherino 92, 19030 Tellaro* ☎ *0187/968130* 🖷 *0187/ 964032* ⊕ *www.locandamiranda.com* 🛏 *5 rooms, 2 suites* ♿ *Restaurant; no a/c* ⊟ *AE, DC, MC, V* ⊗ *Closed Jan.; restaurant closed Mon.* ⫮⊙⫯ *BP.*

$$ ▦ **Florida.** This seafront, family-run establishment is not the most beautiful from the outside, but it has bright rooms with all the extras you would expect in a higher category, including soundproofing and a balcony with a sea view. For an even better view, loll in one of the deck chairs on the roof terrace. The Florida overlooks a small beach area and is close to tennis courts and a golf course; a solarium is also on the premises. ⊠ *Lungomare Biaggini 35, 19032* ☎ *0187/967332* 🖷 *0187/967344* ⊕ *www.hotelflorida.it* 🛏 *37 rooms* ♿ *In-room safes, minibars, beach, bar, Internet* ⊟ *AE, DC, MC, V* ⊗ *Closed Dec. 20–Mar. 1* ⫮⊙⫯ *BP.*

La Spezia

➋ *11 km (7 mi) northwest of Lerici, 103 km (64 mi) southeast of Genoa.*

La Spezia is a large, industrialized naval port on routes to the Cinque Terre and to Portovenere. It lacks the quiet charm of the smaller towns. However, its palm-lined promenade, fertile citrus parks, and lively, balcony-lined streets make parts of La Spezia surprisingly beautiful. The remains of the massive 13th-century **Castel San Giorgio** now house a small museum dedicated to local archaeology. ⊠ *Via XX Settembre* ☎ *0187/ 751142* 🎟 *€5* ⊗ *Wed.–Mon. 9:30–12:30 and 2–5.*

Portovenere

★ **➌** *12 km (7 mi) south of La Spezia, 114 km (70 mi) southeast of Genoa.*

Portovenere's small colorful houses, some dating from the 12th century, were once connected to the 12th- to 16th-century citadel, so that in times of attack the villagers could reach the safety of the battlements. The town commands a strategic position at the end of a peninsula that extends southeast from the Cinque Terre and forms the western border of the Gulf of La Spezia.

Lord Byron (1788–1824) is said to have written *Childe Harold's Pilgrimage* in Portovenere. Near the entrance to the huge, strange **Grotto Arpaia**, at the base of the sea-swept cliff, is a plaque recounting the poet's strength and courage as he swam across the gulf to the village of San Terenzo, near Lerici, to visit his friend Shelley (1792–1822); the feat is

0 ___ 10 miles
0 ___ 15 km

LIGURIA

Genoa
10 - **38**
see map
pages
290–291

ITALY

Nervi
39

Portofino Promontory

Camogli
9

Ruta

Santa Margherita Ligure
7

A12

Punta Chiappa

Monte Portofino

Pietre Strette

Olmi

Paraggi

Abbazia a di San Fruttuoso

Portofino
8

Rapallo
6 Zoagli

Chiavari
5 Lavagna

Cavi di Lavagna

Sestri Levante

Moneglia
4 SS1

Levanto

Golfo di Genova

RIVIERA DI LEVANTE

Monterosso al Mare

Vernazza

Corniglia

La Spezia

San Terenzo

Cinque Terre
see map
pages
272–273

Manarola

Riomaggiore
3

2

1

Portovenere

Lerici

Tellaro

KEY

Beach

Ferry

TO CORSICA

Riviera di Levante

TO ELBA, SARDINIA, SICILY, AND NAPLES

TO CORSICA

commemorated as well by the name of the stretch of water, Golfo dei Poeti (Poets' Gulf). **San Pietro**, a 13th-century Gothic church open daily 7–6, is built on the site of an ancient pagan shrine, on a formidable solid mass of rock above the Grotto Arpaia. With its black-and-white-stripe exterior, it is a landmark recognizable from far out at sea.

Where to Stay & Eat

$$–$$$$ ✕ **Da Iseo.** Try to get one of the tables outside at this waterfront restaurant with bistro accents and paintings of Portovenere. Seafood is the only choice, but it's fresh and plentiful. Pasta courses are inventive; try spaghetti *alla Giuseppe* (with shellfish and fresh tomato) or *alla Iseo* (with a seafood curry sauce). ⊠ *Waterfront* ☎ *0187/790610* ▭ *AE, DC, MC, V* ☉ *Closed Wed. and Jan. 2–Feb. 15.*

★ **$$$** ▦ **Royal Sporting.** Appearances are deceptive at this modern hotel on the beach about a 10-minute walk from the village. From the outside, the stone construction seems austere, but the courtyards and interior— with fresh flowers, potted plants, and cool, airy rooms—are colorful and vibrant. The sports facilities are among the best in the area. ⊠ *Via dell'Olivo 345, 19025* ☎ *0187/790326* ▤ *0187/777707* ⊕ *www. royalsporting.com* ↪ *56 rooms, 4 suites* ⚲ *Restaurant, minibars, tennis court, saltwater pool, beach, bar, Internet, meeting rooms, some pets allowed (fee)* ▭ *AE, DC, MC, V* ☉ *Closed Nov.–mid-Mar.* ❢◎❢ *BP.*

THE CINQUE TERRE

Five remote villages make one must-see destination

"Charming" and "breath-taking" are adjectives that get a workout when you're traveling in Italy, but it's rare that both apply to a single location. The Cinque Terre is such a place, and this combination of characteristics goes a long way toward explaining its tremendous appeal.

The area is made up of five tiny villages (Cinque Terre literally means "Five Lands") clinging to the cliffs along a gorgeous stretch of the Ligurian coast. The terrain is so steep that for centuries footpaths were the only way to get from place to place. It just so happens that these paths provide drop-dead views of the rocky coast tumbling into the sea, as well as access to secluded beaches and grottoes.

Backpackers "discovered" the Cinque Terre in the 1970s, and its popularity has been growing ever since. Despite summer crowds, much of the original appeal is intact. Each town has maintained its own distinct charm, and views from the trails in between are as breathtaking as ever.

Monterosso

Corniglia

Terracing around Corniglia

HIKING THE CINQUE TERRE

Mount Malpertuso

Mount Castello

Monterosso–Vernazza Trail
The most demanding portion of the trail. Often narrow, with significant climbs and descents, particularly near Vernazza. Your labors are rewarded with the Trail No. 2's best views.

Le Stalle

Trail No 8a

Mount Gaginara

Trail No 1

Drignana

Vernazza–Corniglia Trail
Ups and downs interspersed with olive groves and terraced vineyards.

Madonna di Soviore

Trail No 1 (Red Trail)

Santuario del Reggio

Santuario Bernardino

1hr 30min

370

Trail No 9

Trail No 3

1hr

S Bernardo

1hr

3 km (2 mi), 1 hr 30min

Trail No 7

3 km (2 mi), 2 hrs

Trail No 8

Trail No 2 (Blue Trail)

Vernazza

Palma Pt

Guvano Beach

Molinara Pt

del Frate Island

Monterosso al Mare

FERRY TO LÈVANTO

KEY
- - - - *Major footpaths*
- - - - *Sanctuary footpaths*
- - - - *Connecting footpaths*
1hr 30min *Hiking times*
⚓ *Sanctuaries*

Monterosso
The most resortlike of the villages, with the largest beach.

Vernazza
Pretty and visitor-friendly. The best spot for lingering in a café and watching waves crash against the shore.

THE CLASSIC HIKE

Hiking is the classic way to experience the Cinque Terre, and Trail No. 2, also known as the Sentiero Azzurro (Blue Trail), is the most popular path. It's perfect for a day trip: it's approximately 13 km (8 mi) in length, takes you to all five villages, and requires about five hours to complete. The best approach is to start at the east-ernmost town of Riomaggiore and warm up your legs on the easiest segment of the trail. As you work your way west, the hike gets progressively more demanding. For a less strenuous experience, you can choose to skip a leg or two and take the inland train running between the towns instead. You'll miss out on some of the views, but your feet may thank you.

Manarola

Along Trail No.2

Via dell'Amore

Corniglia–Manarola Trail
Runs through the hills near Manarola, descends to rocky beach near Corniglia.

Manarola–Riomaggiore Trail
Known as the Via dell'Amore (Lovers' Lane). A wide, paved, flat path with fine views.

0 — 1/2 mi

0 — 1/2 km

Mount Capri

Mount Cuna

Mount Galera

Mount Grosso

(Red Trail)

Trail No 6

Trail No 7a

Trail No 6d

Madonna della Salute

1hr 30min

1hr

Volastra

Trail No 02

Trail No 3

Madonna di Montenero

45min

370

TO LA SPEZIA

3 km (2 mi), 1 hr

Spiaggione di Corniglia

Corniglia

del Luogo Pt

Manarola

Buonfiglio Pt

Trail No 2 (Blue Trail)

30min

Via dell'Amore

Riomaggiore

Torre Guardiola

C di M Nero

Corniglia
Perched on a cliff high above the sea, reached by a switchback path (or by shuttle bus).

Manarola
The most photogenic of the villages, best seen from the cemetery a few minutes up the path toward Corniglia.

Riomaggiore
Cliff-clinging buildings are almost as striking as those in Manarola. Stairs to the left of the train station entrance cross over the tracks and lead to the trailhead.

6

THE CINQUE TERRE

BEYOND TRAIL NO.2

Trail No. 2 is just one of a network of trails crisscrossing the hills. If you're a dedicated hiker, spend a few nights and try some of the other routes. Trail No. 1, the Sentiero Rosso (Red Trail), climbs from Portovenere (east of Riomaggiore) and returns to the sea at Levanto (west of Monterosso al Mare). To hike its length takes from 9 to 12 hours; the ridge-top trail provides spectacular views from high above the villages, each of which can be reached via a steep path. Other shorter trails go from the villages up into the hills, some leading to religious sanctuaries. Trail No. 9, for example, starts from the old section of Monterosso and ends at the Madonna di Soviore Sanctuary.

VOICES OF ITALY

**Antonella Bongi &
Antonella Mariotti**
Cinque Terre

Antonella Bongi and Antonella Mariotti are the two energetic founders of La Spezia's Cooperativa Arte e Natura, which organizes guided walks, hikes, and visits to sites of interest in the Cinque Terre and La Spezia, as well as in the Province of Pisa, in Tuscany to the south.

Q: Most visitors to the Cinque Terre hike the standard route, the Trail No. 2, between Riomaggiore and Monterosso al Mare, and then leave to visit other places in Italy. What do you think they are missing?

Antonella B.: The entire *entroterra*, the hinterland that lies behind the coast. They miss coming into contact with the genuine part of the Cinque Terre that still exists, and they certainly miss contact with the real people who live here, the farmers and the wine-growers.

Antonella M.: You need a car or you can take the public bus, but a good way to start is to follow the SP 370, the Strada dei Santuari (the Road of the Sanctuaries), out of La Spezia. It climbs above the cliffs of the Cinque Terre and passes by each of the five sanctuaries that sit above each of the Cinque Terre towns. Did you know that each town has a sanctuary in the hills, that often predates the coastal town? There's the Madonna di Monte Nero above Riomaggiore, the Madonna della Salute above Manarola, San Bernardino above Corniglia, the Madonna di Reggio above Vernazza, and the Madonna di Soviore above Monterosso. There are walking trails that run up toward the sanctuaries as well—they're marked on the park's trail map.

Antonella B.: Yes, and there are some great viewpoints along the way. You can see the real nature of the landscape, with the #2 trail, the railway, the terraced vineyards, and the five villages far below. It's beautiful. The road goes through Groppo, where there's a wine cooperative . . .

Antonella M. (scandalized): But they give tastings in plastic cups!

Antonella B.: . . . and then continues through Volastra on the way to the other sanctuaries. (Antonella B. adds an aside:) How do you think they harvest the grapes on vines that are only 1 meter (3 feet) high on very narrow terraces? On their backs!

PRECAUTIONS

If you're hitting the trails, you'll want to carry water with you, wear sturdy shoes (hiking boots are best), and have a hat and sunscreen handy. ⚠ Check weather reports before you start out; especially in late fall and winter, thunderstorms can send townspeople running for cover and make the shelterless trails slippery and dangerous. Rain in October and November can cause landslides and close the trails. Note that the lesser-used trails aren't as well maintained as Trail No. 2. If you're undertaking the full Trail No. 1 hike, bring something to snack on as well as your water bottle.

ADMISSION

Entrance tickets for use of the trails, as well as tickets that combine use of the trails with unlimited use of the second-class trains or boats, are available at the Levanto, Monterosso, Vernazza, Corniglia, Manarola, Riomaggiore, and La Spezia train stations. For the price of your ticket you get trail maps, general information leaflets, and train and boat schedules. Prices: 1-day pass for footpaths €5, 1-day pass with train €6, 1-day pass with train and boat €15, 3-day pass with train €15, 7-day pass with train €20.

Working Cinque Terre's vertical vineyards

GETTING THERE & GETTING AROUND

The local train on the Genoa–La Spezia train line stops at each of the Cinque Terre. The train runs approximately every 30 minutes. A 24-hour Cinque Terre Tourist train ticket, which allows unlimited travel between the five towns, is available at the five train stations (€2.85).

Along the Cinque Terre coast two ferry lines operate. From June to September, Golfo Paradiso runs from Genoa and Camogli to Monterosso al Mare and Vernazza. The smaller, but more frequent, Golfo dei Poeti stops at each village from Portovenere (east of Riomaggiore) to Monterosso, with the exception of Corniglia, four times a day. A one-day ticket costs €11.50.

WHEN TO GO

The ideal times to see the Cinque Terre are September and May, when the weather is mild and the summer tourist season isn't in full swing.

SWIMMING & BEACHES

Each town has something that passes for a beach, but there are only two options where you'll find both sand and decent swimming. The more accessible is in Monterosso, opposite the train station; it's equipped with chairs, umbrellas, and snack bars. The other is the secluded, swimwear-optional Guvano Beach, between Corniglia and Vernazza. To reach it from the Corniglia train station, bypass the steps leading up to the village, instead following signs to an abandoned train tunnel. Ring a bell at the tunnel's entrance, and the gate will automatically open; after a dimly lit 10-minute walk, you'll emerge at the beach. Both beaches have a nominal admission fee.

Monterosso al Mare

THE TOWNS

Riomaggiore

At the eastern end of the Cinque Terre, Riomaggiore is the most accessible of the villages, reachable by car or train from La Spezia. It curves around a tiny harbor that's ringed with lively cafés and dotted with fishing boats, but doesn't have as much old-world charm as its sister villages—easy accessibility has brought traffic and more modern construction. According to legend, settlement along the narrow valley of the River Maior dates back to the 8th century, when Greek religious refugees came here to escape persecution by the Byzantine emperor.

Manarola

The enchanting pastel houses of Manarola spill down a steep hill overlooking a spectacular turquoise swimming cove and a bustling harbor. The whole town is built on black rock. Above the town, ancient terraces still protect abundant vineyards and olive trees. This village is the center of the wine and olive oil production of the region, and its streets are lined with shops selling local products.

Corniglia

The buildings, narrow lanes, and stairways of Corniglia are strung together amid vineyards high on the cliffs; on a clear day views of the entire coastal strip are excellent. The high perch and lack of harbor make this farming community the most remote of the Cinque Terre. On a pretty pastel square sits the 14th-century church of **San Pietro.** The rose window of marble imported from Carrara is impressive, particularly considering the work required to get it here. ⊠ *Main Sq.* ☎ *0187/ 3235582* ⊘ *Wed. 4–6, Sun. 10–noon.*

Vernazza

With its narrow streets and small squares, Vernazza is arguably the most charming of the five towns. Because it has the best access to the sea, it became wealthier than its neighbors—as evidenced by the elaborate arcades, loggias, and marblework. The village's pink, slate-roof houses and colorful squares contrast with the remains of the medieval fort and castle, including two towers, in the old town. The Romans first inhabited this rocky spit of land in the 1st century.

Today Vernazza has a fairly lively social scene. It's is a great place to refuel with a hearty seafood lunch or linger in a café between links of the hike on Trail No. 2.

Monterosso al Mare

Beautiful beaches, rugged cliffs, crystal-clear turquoise waters, and plentiful small hotels and restaurants make Monterosso al Mare, the largest of the Cinque Terre villages (population 1,730), busiest in mid-summer. The village center bustles high on a hillside. Below, connected by stone steps, are the port and seaside promenade, where there are boats for hire. The medieval tower, Aurora, on the hills of the Cappuccini, separates the ancient part of the village from the more modern part. The village is encircled by hills covered with vineyards and olive groves, and by a forest of scrubby bushes and small trees.

Monterosso has the most festivals of the five villages, starting with the Lemon Feast on the Saturday preceding Ascension Sunday, followed by the Flower Festival of Corpus Christi, celebrated yearly on the second Sunday after Pentecost. During the afternoon, the streets and alleyways of the *centro storico* (historic center) are decorated with thousands of colorful flower petals set in beautiful designs that the evening procession passes over. Finally, the Salted Anchovy and Olive Oil Festival takes place each year during the second weekend of September.

Thursday, the **market** attracts mingled crowds of tourists and villagers from along the coast to shop for everything from pots and pans and underwear to fruits, vegetables, and fish. Often a few stands sell local art and crafts as well as olive oil and wine. ⊠ *Old town center* ☉ *Thurs. 8–2.*

The **Chiesa di San Francesco,** was built in the 12th century in the Ligurian Gothic style. Its distinctive black stripes and marble rose window make it one of the most photographed sites in the Cinque Terre. ⊠ *Piazza Garibaldi* ☎ *No phone* ▣ *Free* ☉ *Daily 9–1 and 4–7.*

6

THE CINQUE TERRE

Main Square, Vernazza

WHERE TO STAY & EAT

Reservations are essential if you plan to stay in a hotel here in July or August. The area's numerous *affittacamere* (rooms for rent in private homes) are often indicated only by a simple handwritten sign on a front door. Tourist offices in Riomaggiore and Monterosso—a booking service is provided by the latter—have a list of officially licensed affittacamere. These rooms vary considerably in comfort, amenities, and cost.

Riomaggiore

$–$$ ✕ **Ripa del Sole.** Try some of the great local wine with one of the house specialties: *calamari con gran farro* (steamed squid with lemon sauce and barley), *tagliatelle fresche con scampi e tartufo bianco* (fresh pasta with scampi and white truffles), or *filetto di branzino al piatto rovente* (sea bass cooked on the griddle with herbs and garlic). In summer you can have your meal on the terrace. ⊠ *Via de' Gaspari 282* ☎ *0187/920143* ➦ No credit cards ☺ Closed mid-Jan.–mid-Feb. and Mon. Nov.–Mar.

$ ▦ **Due Gemelli.** Set above the sea, this small hotel has fabulous views of the turquoise water. The rooms have simple, mismatched furnishings, but they all have balconies, making them bright and airy. ⊠ *Via Litoranea 1, 19017* ☎ *0187/ 920111* ⊟ *0187/920678* ⊕ *www.*

duegemelli.it ➦ *14 rooms* �&ldots; *Restaurant, bar; no a/c* ➦ *AE, DC, MC, V* ¶⃝ *BP.*

Manarola

$ ▦ **Ca' d'Andrean.** If you want to stay in one of the less crowded of the Cinque Terre, this tiny, simple hotel is one of your best options. White-tile floors cool off the rooms, some of which have balconies. In summer, breakfast, an optional extra at €6 per person, is served in a flower garden. ⊠ *Via Discovolo 101, 19010* ☎ *0187/920040* ⊟ *0187/920452* ⊕ *www.cadandrean.it* ➦ *10 rooms* �&ldots; *Bar; no a/c* ⊟ *No credit cards* ☺ *Closed mid-Nov.–mid-Dec.*

Corniglia

$–$$ ✕▦ **Cecio.** On the outskirts of Corniglia, many of the spotless rooms at the family-run Cecio have spectacular views of the town clinging to the cliffs above the bay. The same memorable vista can be enjoyed from the hotel's restaurant, which serves inexpensive and well-prepared local seafood dishes. Try the delicious lasagna with pesto sauce as a first course. ⊠ *Via Serra 58, 19010, toward Vernazza* ☎ *0187/812043* ⊟ *0187/ 812138* ➦ *12 rooms* �&ldots; *Restaurant; no a/c, no room phones, no TV in some rooms* ⊟ *DC, MC, V* M ¶⃝ *BP.*

Vernazza

$–$$$ ✕ **Gambero Rosso.** Relax on Vernazza's main square at this fine trattoria looking out at a church. Enjoy such delectable dishes as shrimp salad, vegetable torte, and squid-ink risotto. The creamy pesto, served atop spaghetti, is some of the best in the area. End your meal with Cinque Terre's own *sciacchetrà*, a dessert wine served with semisweet biscotti. Don't drink it out of the glass—dip the biscotti in the wine instead. ⊠ *Piazza Marconi 7* ☎ *0187/812265* ▤ *AE, DC, MC, V* ⊗ *Closed Mon. Jan. and Feb.*

¢ ✕ 🍴 **Trattoria Gianni Franzi.** Order your pesto with *fagiolini* (green beans), a Ligurian specialty that somehow tastes better when you're eating it outside in a beautiful *piazzetta* (small square) with a view of the port, as you can here. Above the restaurant, a number of simply furnished, economical rooms are available. Your choice here is between the smaller, older rooms without private bathrooms, but with tiny balconies and great views of the port, or those in the newer section, with bathrooms but no view. ⊠ *Via G. Marconi 1, 19018* ☎ *0187/821003* 🖨 *0187/812228* ⊕ *www.giannifranzi.it* 🔁 *20 rooms, 12 with bath* 🍴 *Restaurant, bar* ▤ *AE, DC, MC, V* ⊗ *Closed Jan. 8–Mar. 8; restaurant closed Wed. early Mar.–mid-July and mid-Sept.–early Jan.* ⊙! *BP.*

Monterosso al Mare

$$$ ✕ **Il Gigante.** A good introduction to Ligurian seafood is the *zuppa di pesce* (fish soup) served at this traditional trattoria. It's usually served as a first course but is filling enough to be an entrée. Daily specials might include risotto *ai frutti di mare* (with a seafood sauce) and spaghetti with an octopus sauce. ⊠ *Via IV Novembre 9* ☎ *0187/817401* 🍴 *Reservations essential* ▤ *AE, DC, MC, V* ⊗ *Closed Mon.*

★ **$$$** ✕ **Miki.** Specialties here are anything involving seafood. The *insalata di mare* (seafood salad), with squid and fish, is more than tasty; so are the grilled fish and any pasta with seafood. If you're in the mood for a pizza, you can order that here as well. Miki has a beautiful little garden in the back, perfect for lunch on a sunny day. ⊠ *Via Fegina 104* ☎ *0187/817608* ▤ *AE, DC, MC, V* ⊗ *Closed Nov. and Dec., and Tues. Sept.–July.*

★ **$$–$$$** ✕ **Il Pirata.** Bright and rustic, this trattoria near the port should be the first stop for lunch, especially if you make it in time to grab a seat at one of the long tables on the front porch. Specialties are those of the region, with a few surprising gourmet touches like the French wines lining the shelves and Maine lobster on the menu. Reservations are essential on weekends and in summer. ⊠ *Via Molinelli 6/8* ☎ *0187/817536* ▤ *MC, V* ⊗ *Closed Wed. and mid-Jan.–mid.-Feb.*

¢ ✕ **Il Frantoio.** Some of the best focaccia on the coast is available here. It's a good place for a light lunch or a snack before heading out on the walk to Vernazza. ⊠ *Via Gioberti 1* ☎ *0187/818333* ▤ *No credit cards.*

$$$–$$$$ 🏨 **Porto Roca.** In a panoramic position above the sea, Porto Roca is set slightly apart, blessedly removed from the crowds. It has the look of a well-kept villa; its interiors have authentic antiques, and there are ample terraces. The rooms with views of the sea are bright and airy; avoid the back rooms, which are dark, dank, and without a view. ⊠ *Via Corone 1, 19016* ☎ *0187/817502* 🖨 *0187/817692* ⊕ *www.portoroca.it* 🔁 *43 rooms* 🍴 *Restaurant, bar, some pets allowed* ▤ *AE, MC, V* ⊗ *Closed Nov. 4–Mar. 27* ⊙! *BP.*

6

THE CINQUE TERRE

Moneglia

❹ 34 km (21 mi) northwest of Monterosso al Mare, 56 km (35 mi) southeast of Genoa.

The town of Moneglia, sheltered by the wooded hills of a nature preserve, faces a little bay guarded by ruined castles. An out-of-the-way alternative to fussier resorts, it's a quiet base for walks and excursions by boat, car, or tran to Portofino and the Cinque Terre towns. A classical guitar festival is held here in September.

Where to Stay

$–$$ 🏨 **Villa Edera.** Ingeniously merging an older building on a verdant hillside with a smart stone-and-glass wing, Villa Edera has a contemporary style. Terraces, a garden, luminous bedrooms, and lounges with stylish wicker armchairs are among the comforts. This hotel is owned by a family committed to personal attention; Mamma Ida's cooking is special, too. ⊠ *Via Venino 12, 16030* ☏ *0185/49291* 🖷 *0185/49470* ⊕ *www.villaedera.com* ⇆ *27 rooms* ⚘ *Restaurant, cable TV, pool, gym, sauna, bar, Internet, no-smoking rooms* ▱ *AE, MC, V* ⊗ *Closed Nov. 8–Feb.* ⎢◯⎢ *BP.*

Chiavari

❺ 19 km (12 mi) northwest of Moneglia, 38 km (23 mi) southeast of Genoa.

Chiavari is a fishing town (rather than village) of considerable character, with narrow, twisting streets and a good harbor. Chiavari's citizens were intrepid explorers, and many emigrated to South America in the 19th century. The town boomed, thanks to the wealth of the returning voyagers, but Chiavari retains many medieval traces in its buildings.

In the town center, the **Museo Archeologico** displays objects from an 8th-century BC necropolis, or ancient cemetery, excavated nearby. The museum closes the first and third Sunday of the month. ⊠ *Palazzo Costaguta, Via Costaguta 4, Piazza Matteotti* ☏ *0185/320829* ⛋ *Free* ⊗ *Tues.–Thurs. 9–1, Fri.–Sun. 2–7.*

Shopping

The traditional, light—they weigh only 3 pounds—*campanine*, wood chairs made of olive or walnut, are still produced by a few Chiavari craftsmen. Macramé lace can also be found here.

Rapallo

❻ 9 km (5½ mi) northwest of Chiavari, 28 km (17 mi) east of Genoa.

Rapallo was once one of Europe's most fashionable resorts, but it passed its heyday before World War II and has suffered from the building boom brought on by tourism. Ezra Pound and D. H. Lawrence lived here, and many other writers, poets, and artists have been drawn to it. Today, the town's harbor is filled with yachts. A single-span bridge on the eastern side of the bay is named after Hannibal, who is said to have passed through the area after crossing the Alps.

The highlight of the town center, the cathedral of **Santi Gervasio e Protasio,** at the western end of Via Mazzini, was founded in the 6th century. ⊠ *Via Mazzini* ☎ *0185/52375* 🖃 *Free* ☉ *Daily 6:30–noon and 3–6:30.*

The **Museo del Pizzo a Tombolo,** in a 19th-century mansion, has a collection of antique lace, a dying art for which Rapallo was once renowned. ⊠ *Villa Tigullio* ☎ *0185/63305* 🖃 *Free* ☉ *Oct.–Aug., Tues., Wed., Fri., and Sat. 3–6, Thurs. 10–11:30* AM.

Where to Stay & Eat

$$–$$$
Fodor'sChoice
★

✕ **U' Giancu.** Owner Fausto Oneto is a man of many hats—don't be surprised if he wears six different ones during the course of a meal. Though original cartoons cover the walls and a children's playground is the main feature of the outdoor seating area, Fausto is completely serious about his cooking. Lamb dishes are particularly delicious, and the vegetables from his own garden provide the freshest of ingredients. Those who want to learn the secrets of Ligurian cuisine can attend lively morning cooking lessons. ⊠ *Via San Massimo 28, Località San Massimo, 3 km (2 mi) northwest of Rapallo* ☎ *0185/261212* 🖃 *DC, MC, V* ☉ *Closed Wed. and mid.-Dec.–early Jan. No lunch.*

$–$$
✕ **Da Mario.** Simply decorated and brightly lighted, this small and usually crowded trattoria serves some of the best seafood in Rapallo. Don't miss the spaghetti with seafood and tomatoes. A small terrace provides outdoor seating in summer. ⊠ *Piazza Garibaldi 23* ☎ *0185/51736* 🍴 *Reservations essential* 🖃 *AE, DC, MC, V* ☉ *Closed Wed., and Oct. and Nov.*

$$$$
🏨 **Grand Hotel Bristol.** This Victorian showcase outside Rapallo is set in lush gardens with a huge seawater pool. Spacious rooms, many with balcony overlooking the sea, are decorated in soft blues and greens in a smart, contemporary style and have extra-large beds. You can choose between a Rapallo view and a Portofino view. In summer, dinner is served on the roof terrace. ⊠ *Via Aurelia Orientale 369, 16035* ☎ *0185/ 273313* 🖷 *0185/55800* ⊕ *www.tigullio.net/bristol* ⇄ *85 rooms, 6 suites* ⚖ *2 restaurants, minibars, cable TV, saltwater pool, hot tub, sauna, billiards, horseback riding, bar, meeting rooms, some pets allowed* 🖃 *AE, MC, V* ☉ *Closed Dec.–Feb.* 🍴 *BP.*

Shopping

Guido Porati's aromatic shop, **Bottega dei Sestieri** (⊠ Via Mazzini 44 ☎ 0185/230530), sells Ligurian cheeses, wines, and other delicacies. For something truly regional, try the *trarcantu,* a cow's-milk cheese aged in grape skins. The store is on a narrow lane that runs parallel to Rapallo's waterfront.

The attractive coastal village of **Zoagli** (⊠ On S1, 4 km [2½ mi] east of Rapallo) has been famous for silk, velvet, and damask since the Middle Ages.

Santa Margherita Ligure

➐ *3 km (2 mi) south of Rapallo, 31 km (19 mi) southeast of Genoa.*

A beautiful old resort town favored by well-to-do Italians, Santa Margherita Ligure has everything a Riviera playground should have—plenty of palm trees and attractive hotels, cafés, and a marina packed with yachts. Some of the older buildings here are still decorated on the outside with the trompe-l'oeil frescoes typical of this part of the Riviera. This is a pleasant, convenient base, which for many represents a perfect balance on the Italian Riviera: bigger and less Americanized than the Cinque Terre; less glitzy than San Remo; more relaxing than Genoa and environs; and ideally situated for day trips, such as an excursion to Portofino.

Where to Stay & Eat

$$$–$$$$ ✕ **La Paranza.** From the piles of tiny *bianchetti* (young sardines) in oil and lemon that are part of the antipasto *di mare* (of the sea) to the simple, perfectly grilled whole sole, fresh seafood in every shape and form is the specialty here. Mussels, clams, octopus, salmon, or whatever else is fresh that day is what's on the menu. Locals say this is the town's best restaurant, but if you're looking for a stylish evening out, look elsewhere—La Paranza is about food, not fashion. It's just off Santa Margherita's port. ✉ *Via Jacopo Ruffini 46* ☎ *0185/283686* ♟ *Reservations essential* ☰ *AE, DC, MC, V* ⊗ *Closed Mon. and Nov.*

$$$–$$$$ ✕ **La Stalla.** The breathtaking, hilltop views of Santa Margherita from this villa-turned-restaurant are worth the harrowing 3-km (2-mi) drive northwest to get here from Santa Margherita's port. Cesare Frati, your congenial host, is likely to tempt you with his homemade fettuccine ai frutti di mare followed by the *pescato del giorno alla moda ligure* (catch of the day baked Ligurian style, with potatoes, olives, and pine nuts) and a delightfully fresh lemon sorbet to complete the feast. ✉ *Via G. Pino 27, Nozarego* ☎ *0185/289447* ☰ *AE, DC, MC, V* ⊗ *Closed Mon. and Nov.*

★ $$$–$$$$ ✕ **Oca Bianca.** Angelo, son of Cesare Frati at Santa Margherita's La Stalla, has broken away from the norm at this excellent small restaurant—there is no seafood on the menu. Meat dishes are the specialty, and choices may include mouthwatering preparations of lamb from France or New Zealand, steak from Ireland or Brazil, South African ostrich, and Italian pork. Delicious antipasti, an extensive wine list, and the attentive service add to the experience. The Oca Bianca serves dinner until 1 AM. ✉ *Via XXV Aprile 21* ☎ *0185/288411* ♟ *Reservations essential* ☰ *AE, DC, MC, V* ⊗ *Closed Mon. and Jan.–mid-Feb. No lunch Tues.–Thurs. Sept.–Dec.*

$$–$$$ ✕ **Trattoria Cesarina.** This typical trattoria serves classic local fare—and that means seafood. The white interior is refreshingly free of bric-a-brac, allowing you to focus on your meal. Don't expect a menu; instead, allow the friendly staff to tell you what to eat. Among other treats, you may encounter a delectable antipasto of local frutti di mare, a seafood-theme pasta dish, and the catch of the day delicately grilled or baked in that

EATING WELL IN THE ITALIAN RIVIERA

Liguria's cooking might surprise you; it does employ all sorts of seafood—especially anchovies, sea bass, squid, and octopus—but it makes even wider use of vegetables and the aromatic herbs that grow wild on the hillsides, together with liberal amounts of olive oil and garlic. Basil- and garlic-rich pesto is Liguria's classic pasta sauce. You may also find *pansoti* (round pockets of pasta filled with a cheese mixture) and *trofie* (doughy, short pasta twists sometimes made with chestnut flour) with *salsa di noci*, an intense sauce of garlic, walnuts, and cream that, as with pesto, is ideally pounded with a mortar and pestle. Spaghetti *allo scoglio* is mixed with a tomato-based sauce containing an assortment of local *frutti di mare* (seafood). Fish is the best bet for a second course: the classic preparation is a whole grilled or baked whitefish—*branzino* (sea bass) and *orato* (dorado) are good choices—served with olives, potatoes, Ligurian spices, and a drizzle of olive oil. A popular meat dish is

cima alla Genovese, breasts of veal stuffed with a mixture of eggs and vegetables and rolled, served as a cold cut. You should also try the succulent *agnello* (lamb), *coniglio* (rabbit), and fresh wild mushrooms foraged from the hills.

When you're hankering for a snack, turn to bakeries and small eateries serving focaccia, the flatbread that's the region's answer to the pizza. It comes simply salted and dribbled with olive oil; flavored with rosemary and olives; covered with cheese or anchovies; and even *ripiena* (filled), usually with cheese and/or vegetables and herbs. Local vineyards produce mostly light and refreshing whites such as Pigato, Vermentino, and Cinque Terre. Rossese di Dolceacqua, from near the French border, is the best red wine the region has to offer, but for a more robust accompaniment to meats opt for the more full-bodied reds of the neighboring Piedmont region.

laissez-faire Ligurian style. ⊠ *Via Mameli 2/C* ☎ *0185/286059* ▤ *MC, V* ⊗ *Closed Tues., and Dec. and Jan.*

★ **$$$$** ▥ **Grand Hotel Miramare.** Classic Riviera elegance prevails at this palatial hotel overlooking the bay south of the town center. Stroll through the lush garden, then take a dip in the curvaceous heated swimming pool or at the private swimming area on the sea. Antique furniture, such as crystal chandeliers and Louis XV chairs, fills the high-ceiling rooms, and there are marble bathrooms. ⊠ *Via Milite Ignoto 30, 16038* ☎ *0185/287013* ▤ *0185/284651* ⊕ *www.grandhotelmiramare.it* ⊅ *75 rooms, 9 suites* ⚄ *2 restaurants, in-room safes, minibars, pool, beach, water-skiing, 2 bars, Internet, meeting rooms, some pets allowed* ▤ *AE, DC, MC, V* ⫿⦿⫿ *BP.*

$$$$ ▥ **Imperiale Palace.** As Via Pagana climbs north out of Santa Margherita Ligure on its way toward Rapallo it passes this traditional luxury hotel. Set in an extensive park, the main building is a former villa built in 1889. Reception rooms with tall windows, plush chairs, and potted plants create a warm welcome. The rooms are furnished with antiques; many over-look the shore drive to the sea. ⊠ *Via Pagana 19, 16038* ☎ *0185/288991* 🖷 *0185/284223* ⊕ *www.hotelimperiale.com* ⇆ *71 rooms, 18 suites* ⌂ *Restaurant, in-room safes, minibars, pool, beach, gym, 2 bars, babysitting, meeting rooms* ▤ *AE, DC, MC, V* ⊙ *Closed Nov.–Mar.* ⦀◎⦀ *BP.*

$$$ 🔲 **Continental.** Built in the early 1900s, this stately seaside mansion with a columned portico stands in a lush garden shaded by tall palms and pine trees. The style is a blend of classic furnishings, mostly inspired by the 19th century, with some more functional pieces. There's also a modern wing. The hotel's own cabanas and swimming area are at the bottom of the garden. ⊠ *Via Pagana 8, 16038* ☎ *0185/286512* 🖷 *0185/ 284463* ⊕ *www.hotel-continental.it* ⇆ *68 rooms, 4 suites* ⌂ *Restaurant, in-room safes, minibars, bar, meeting rooms, some pets allowed* ▤ *AE, DC, MC, V* ⊙ *Closed Jan. 8–Mar. 5* ⦀◎⦀ *BP.*

Portofino

❽ *5 km (3 mi) south of Santa Margherita Ligure, 36 km (22 mi) east of Genoa.*

One of the most photographed villages along the coast, with a decid-edly romantic and affluent aura, Portofino has long been a popular des-tination for foreigners. Once an ancient Roman colony and taken by the Republic of Genoa in 1229, it has also been ruled by the French, English, Spanish, and Austrians, as well as marauding bands of 16th-century pirates. Elite British tourists first flocked to the lush harbor in the mid-1800s. Some of Europe's wealthiest lay anchor in Portofino in summer, but they stay out of sight by day, appearing in the evening after buses and boats have carried off the day-trippers.

There's not actually much to *do* in Portofino other than stroll around the wee harbor, see the castle, walk to Punta del Capo, browse at the pricey boutiques, and sip a coffee while people-watching. However, weaving through picture-perfect cliff-side gardens and gazing at yachts framed by the turquoise Ligurian Sea and the cliffs of Santa Margherita can make for quite a relaxing afternoon. There are also several tame, photo-friendly hikes into the hills to nearby villages. Note the meticulous up-keep of streets and public flora in what is surely Italy's cleanest town.

Unless you're traveling on a deluxe budget, you may want to stay in Ra-pallo or Santa Margherita Ligure rather than at one of Portofino's few very expensive hotels. Restaurants and cafés are good but also pricey (don't expect to have a beer here for much under €8). Trying to reach Portofino by bus or car on the single narrow road can be a nightmare in summer and on holiday weekends. No trains go directly to Portofino: you must stop at Santa Margherita and take the public bus from there (€1). An alternative is to take a boat from Santa Margherita, though even this can be a harrowing experience, as cruise ships also anchor here to disgorge their passengers for outings.

From the harbor, follow the signs for the climb to the **Castello di San Giorgio,** the most worthwhile sight in Portofino, with its medieval relics, impeccable gardens, and sweeping views. The castle was founded in the Middle Ages but restored in the 16th through 18th century. In true Portofino form, it was owned by Genoa's English consul from 1870 until its opening to the public in 1961. ⊠ *Above harbor* ☎ *0185/269046* 💶 €3 🕙 *Apr.–Sept., Wed.–Mon. 10–6; Oct.–Mar., Wed.–Mon. 10–5.*

The small church **San Giorgio**, sitting on a ridge, was rebuilt four times during World War II. It is said to contain the relics of its namesake, brought back from the Holy Land by the Crusaders. Portofino enthusiastically celebrates St. George's Day every April 23. ⊠ *Above harbor* ☎ *0185/ 269337* 🕙 *Daily 7–6.*

Pristine views can be had from the deteriorating *faro* (lighthouse) at **Punta Portofino,** a 15-minute walk along the point that begins at the southern end of the port. Along the seaside path you can see numerous impressive, sprawling private residences behind high iron gates.

The only sand beach near Portofino is at **Paraggi,** a cove on the road between Santa Margherita and Portofino. The bus will stop there on request.

off the beaten path

ABBAZIA A DI SAN FRUTTUOSO – On the sea at the foot of Monte Portofino, the medieval Abbey of San Fruttuoso—built by the Benedictines of Monte Cassino—protects a minuscule fishing village that can be reached only on foot or by water (a 20-minute boat ride from Portofino and also reachable from Camogli, Santa Margherita Ligure, and Rapallo). The restored abbey is now the property of a national conservation fund (FAI) and occasionally hosts temporary exhibitions. The church contains the tombs of some illustrious members of the Doria family. The old abbey and its grounds are a delightful place to spend a few hours, perhaps lunching at one of the modest beachfront trattorias nearby (open only in summer). Boatloads of visitors can make it very crowded very fast; you might appreciate it most off-season. Last entrance is 30 minutes before closing time. ⊠ *15-min boat ride or a 2-hr walk northwest of Portofino* ☎ *0185/772703* 💶 *€4, €6 during exhibitions* 🕙 *Mar.–May and Oct., Tues.–Sun. 10–4; June–Sept., daily 10–6; Dec.–Feb., weekends 10–4.*

Where to Stay & Eat

$$$–$$$$ ✕ **Il Pitosforo.** A chic clientele, many from the luxury yachts in the harbor, gives this waterfront restaurant a high glamour quotient, which is augmented by outlandish prices. Spaghetti ai frutti di mare is recommended; adventurous diners might try *lo stocco accomodou* (dried cod in a sauce of tomatoes, raisins, and pine nuts). ⊠ *Molo Umberto I 9* ☎ *0185/269020 or 0335/5615833* 🔸 *Reservations essential* 🖃 *AE, DC, MC, V* 🕙 *Closed Mon. and Tues., and Jan.–mid-Feb. No lunch.*

$$–$$$ ✕ **Ristorante Puny.** A table at this tiny restaurant is difficult to come by in summer, as the manager caters mostly to friends and regulars. If you are lucky enough to get in, however, the food will not disappoint you, nor will the cozy but elegant yellow interior. The unforgettable *pappardelle* (large, flat noodles) *al portofino* delicately blends two of Liguria's tastes,

tomato and pesto. Ligurian seafood specialties include baked fish with bay leaves, potatoes, and olives as well as the inventive *moscardini al forno* (baked octopus with lemon and rosemary in tomato sauce). ☒ *P. Martiri dell'Olivetta 4–5, on the harbor* ☎ *0185/269037* ⌳ *Reservations essential* ▭ *AE, DC, MC, V* ☉ *Closed Thurs., and Jan. and Feb.*

¢ ✕ **Canale.** If the staggering prices of virtually all of Portofino's restaurants put you off, the long line outside this family-run bakery indicates that you're not alone and that something special is in store. Here all the focaccia is baked on the spot and served fresh from the oven, along with all kinds of sandwiches, pastries, and other refreshments. The only problem is there's nowhere to sit—time for a picnic! ☒ *Via Roma 30* ☎ *0185/269248* ▭ *No credit cards* ☉ *Closed Nov. and Dec. No lunch Oct. and Jan.–Apr.*

$$$$ ▥ **San Giorgio.** If you decide to stay in Portofino, this is perhaps your best choice. Tucked away on a quiet backstreet with no views of the harbor, the San Giorgio offers rooms that are immaculate, comfortable, and soothingly designed with canopy beds, pastel walls, and ultramodern bathrooms. Two small 19th-century town houses were joined to form the hotel, making the hallways seem like a labyrinth, but the level of service is high and the peaceful location—there's a secluded garden at the back—is a definite plus. ☒ *Via Del Fondaco 11, 16034* ☎ *0185/26991* ⎙ *0185/267139* ⊕ *www.portofinohsg.it* ➥ *17 rooms, 1 suite* ⌂ *Bar, Internet, some pets allowed* ▭ *AE, DC, MC, V* ☉ *Closed Dec.* ⦿ *BP.*

$$$$ ▥ **Splendido.** Arriving at this 1920s luxury hotel is so much like entering a Jazz Age film set that you'd almost expect to see a Bugatti or Daimler roll up the winding drive from the seaside below. There's a particular attention to color, from the coordinated floral linens in corals and gold to the fresh flowers in the reception rooms and on the large terrace. Even grander than the hotel are its prices (more than €500), and the large numbers of American guests smoking Cuban cigars. ☒ *Salita Baratta 16, 16034* ☎ *0185/267801* ⎙ *0185/267806* ⊕ *www.splendido.orient-express.com* ➥ *34 rooms, 32 suites* ⌂ *Restaurant, tennis court, pool, gym, sauna, 2 bars, meeting rooms, some pets allowed* ▭ *AE, DC, MC, V* ☉ *Closed mid-Nov.–late Mar.* ⦿ *BP.*

Sports & the Outdoors

HIKING If you have the stamina, you can hike to the Abbazia di San Fruttuoso from Portofino. It's a steep climb at first, and the walk takes about 2½ hours one-way. If you're extremely ambitious and want to make a day of it, you can hike another 2½ hours all the way to Camogli. Much more modest hikes from Portofino include a one-hour uphill walk to Cappella delle Gave, a bit inland in the hills, from where you can continue downhill to Santa Margherita Ligure (another 1½ hours) and a gently undulating paved trail leading to the beach at Paraggi (½ hour). Finally, there's a 2½-hour hike from Portofino that heads farther inland to Ruta, through Olmi and Pietre Strette. The trails are well marked and maps are available at the tourist information offices in Rapallo, Santa Margherita, Portofino, and Camogli.

Camogli

★ ❾ *15 km (9 mi) northwest of Portofino, 20 km (12 mi) east of Genoa.*

Camogli, at the edge of the large promontory and nature reserve known as the Portofino Peninsula, has always been a town of sailors. By the 19th century it was leasing its ships throughout the continent. Today, multicolor houses, remarkably deceptive trompe-l'oeil frescoes, and a massive 17th-century seawall mark this appealing harbor community, perhaps as beautiful as Portofino but without the glamour. When exploring on foot, don't miss the boat-filled second harbor, which is reached by ducking under a narrow archway at the northern end of the first one.

The Castello Dragone, built onto the sheer rock face near the harbor, is home to the **Acquario** (Aquarium), which has tanks filled with local marine life built into the ramparts. ⊠ *Via Isola* ☎ *0185/773375* 🎫 *€3* ☉ *May–Sept., daily 10–noon and 3–7; Oct.–Apr., Fri.–Sun. 10–noon and 2:30–6, Tues.–Thurs. 10–noon.*

6

off the beaten path

SAN ROCCO, SAN NICCOLÒ & PUNTA CHIAPPA – You can reach these hamlets along the western coast of the peninsula on foot or by boat from Camogli. They are more natural and less fashionable than those facing south on the eastern coast. In the small Romanesque church at San Niccolò, sailors who survived dangerous voyages came to offer thanks.

RUTA – The footpaths that leave from Ruta, 4 km (2½ mi) east of Camogli thread through rugged terrain and contain a multitude of plant species. Weary hikers are sustained by stunning views of the Riviera di Levante from the various vantage points along the way.

Where to Stay & Eat

$$–$$$ ✕ **Vento Ariel.** This small, friendly restaurant serves some of the best seafood in town. Dine on the shaded terrace in summer months and watch the bustling activity in the nearby port. Only the freshest of seafood is served; try the spaghetti *alle vongole* (with clams) or the mixed grilled fish. ⊠ *Calata Porto* ☎ *0185/771080* 🍽 *AE, DC, MC, V* ☉ *Closed Wed. and Jan. 2–15.*

¢–$ ✕ **Pizzeria Il Lido.** As the name suggests, this popular spot is right across from Camogli's narrow beach, and the outside tables have great views of the sea. If you don't fancy one of the many varieties of pizza, you can choose one of the pasta dishes. ⊠ *Via Garibaldi 133* ☎ *0185/ 770141* 🍽 *MC, V* ☉ *Closed Tues.*

★ $$$$ 🛏 **Cenobio dei Dogi.** Perched majestically a step above Camogli, overlooking harbor, peninsula, and sea, Cenobio dei Dogi is indisputably the best address in town. Genoa's

> **WORD OF MOUTH**
>
> "Camogli was really charming–great seafood, ferries to various other towns along the coast, and a wonderful Fellini cast of characters along the passeggiata."
> —marktynenyc

doges once summered here. Ask for one of the rooms with expansive balconies; though unimaginative in design, they have commanding vistas of Camogli's cozy port. You can relax in the well-kept park or enjoy a game of tennis. Cenobio dei Dogi can be crowded with business travelers and conventions. ⊠ *Via Cuneo 34, 16032* ☎ *0185/7241* 🖷 *0185/772796* ⊕ *www.cenobio.it* 🛏 *102 rooms, 4 suites* ⚐ *Restaurant, tennis court, pool, gym, beach, bar, Internet, business services, meeting rooms* 🖃 *AE, DC, MC, V* ◎ *BP.*

$$ 🏨 **Hotel Augusta.** This friendly, family-run hotel is an economic choice in the center of Camogli. Though you won't have a view of the sea, it's just a short walk away. Quiet guest rooms, all with parquet floors, are bright and modern. A satisfying buffet awaits you in the breakfast room each morning. ⊠ *Via Schiaffino 100, 16032* ☎ *0185/770592* 🖷 *0185/770593* ⊕ *www.htlaugusta.com* 🛏 *15 rooms* ⚐ *Restaurant, bar, in-room safes* 🖃 *AE, DC, MC, V* ◎ *BP.*

Nightlife & the Arts

The highlight of the festival of San Fortunato, held on the second Sunday of May each year, is the **Sagra del Pesce,** a crowded, festive, and free-to-the-public feast of freshly caught fish, cooked outside at the port in a frying pan 12 feet wide.

GENOA

Genoa was the birthplace of Christopher Columbus, but the city's proud history predates that explorer by several hundred years. Genoa was already an important trading station by the 3rd century BC, when the Romans conquered Liguria. The Middle Ages and the Renaissance saw its rise into a jumping-off place for the Crusaders, a commercial center of tremendous wealth and prestige, and a strategic bone of international contention. A network of fortresses defending the city connected by a wall second only in length to the Great Wall of China was constructed in the hills above, and Genoa's bankers, merchants, and princes adorned the city with palaces, churches, and impressive art collections.

Known as *La Superba* (The Proud), Genoa was a great maritime power in the 13th century, rivaling Venice and Pisa in power and splendor. But its luster eventually diminished, and the city was outshined by these and other formidable cities. By the 17th century it was no longer a great sea power. It has, however, continued to be a profitable port. Modern container ships now unload at docks that centuries ago served galleons and vessels bound for the spice routes. Genoa (Genova, in Italian) is now a busy, sprawling, and cosmopolitan city, apt to break the spell of the coastal towns in a hurry. Crammed into a thin crescent of land between sea and mountains, Genoa expanded up rather than out, taking on the form of a multilayer wedding cake, with churches, streets, and entire residential neighborhoods built on others' rooftops. Public elevators and funiculars are as common as buses and trains.

But with more than two millennia of history under its belt, magnificent palaces and museums, the largest medieval city center in Europe, and an elaborate network of ancient hilltop fortresses, Genoa may be just the dose of culture you are looking for. Europe's biggest boat show, the annual Salone Nautico Internazionale, is held here. Fine restaurants are abundant, and classical dance and music are richly represented; the Teatro Carlo Felice is the local opera venue, and where the internationally renowned annual Niccolò Paganini Violin Contest takes place.

With the occasional assistance of public transportation, the only way to visit Genoa is on foot. Many of the more interesting districts are either entirely closed to traffic, have roads so narrow that no car could fit, or are, even at the best of times, blocked by gridlock. Although it might seem a daunting task, exploring the city is made simple by its geography. The historical center of Genoa occupies a relatively narrow strip of land running between the mountains and the sea. You can easily visit the most important monuments in one or two days.

The Medieval Core & Points Above

The medieval center of Genoa, threaded with tiny streets flanked by 11th-century portals, is roughly the area between the port and Piazza de Ferrari. This mazelike pedestrian zone is officially called the Caruggi District, but the Genovese, in their matter-of-fact way, simply refer to the area as the place of the *vicoli* (narrow alleys). In this warren of narrow, cobbled streets extending north from Piazza Caricamento, the city's oldest churches sit among tiny shops selling antique furniture, coffee, cheese, rifles, wine, gilt picture frames, camping gear, and even live fish. The 500-year-old apartment buildings lean so precariously that penthouse balconies nearly touch those across the street, blocking what little sunlight would have shone down onto the cobblestones. Wealthy Genovese built their homes in this quarter in the 16th century, and prosperous guilds, such as the goldsmiths for whom Vico degli Indoratori and Via degli Orefici were named, set up shop here.

The Main Attractions

★ ❷ **Cimitero Monumentale di Staglieno.** One of the most famous of Genovese landmarks is this bizarrely beautiful cemetery; its fanciful marble and bronze sculptures sprawl haphazardly across a hillside on the outskirts of town. A **Pantheon** holds indoor tombs and some remarkable works like an 1878 *Eve* by Villa. Don't miss Rovelli's 1896 **Tomba Raggio,** which shoots Gothic spires out of the hillside forest. The cemetery began operation in 1851 and has been lauded by such visitors as Mark Twain and Evelyn Waugh. It covers a good deal of ground; allow at least half a day to explore. It's difficult to locate; the number 12 and 14 buses from the Stazione Genova Brignole, or a taxi, take you there. ⊠ *Piazzale Resasco, Piazza Manin* ☎ *010/870184* ⊕ *www.cimiterodistaglieno. it* ⊠ *Free* ☉ *Daily 7:30–5.*

❶ **Galleria Nazionale.** This gallery, housed in the richly adorned **Palazzo Spinola** north of Piazza Soziglia, contains masterpieces by Luca Giordano and Guido Reni. The *Ecce Homo,* by Antonello da Messina, is a hauntingly beautiful painting, of historical interest because it was the Sicilian da Messina who first brought Flemish oil paints and techniques to Italy from his sojourns in the Low Countries. ⊠ *Piazza Pellicceria*

1, *Maddalena* 🕾 *010/2705300* ⊕ *www.museigenova.it* 🎫 *€4, €6 including Palazzo Reale* ☉ *Tues.–Sat. 8:30–7:30, Sun. 1–8.*

⑲ Palazzo Bianco. It's difficult to miss the splendid white facade of this town palace as you walk down Via Garibaldi, once one of Genoa's most important streets. The building, completely restored in 2003–04, houses a fine collection of 17th-century art, with the Spanish and Flemish schools well represented. ⊠ *Via Garibaldi 11, Maddalena* 🕾 *010/5572013* ⊕ *www.stradanuova.it* 🎫 *€7, includes Palazzo Rosso and Sala Paganini in Palazzo Doria Tursi* ☉ *Tues.–Fri. 9–7, weekends 10–7.*

⑪ Palazzo Reale. Lavish rococo rooms provide sumptuous display space for paintings, sculptures, tapestries, and Asian ceramics. The 17th-century palace—also known as Palazzo Balbi Durazzo—was built by the Balbi family, enormously wealthy Genovese merchants. Its regal pretensions were not lost on the Savoy, who bought the palace and turned it into a royal residence in the early 19th century. The gallery of mirrors and the ballroom on the upper floor are particularly decadent. Look for works by Sir Anthony Van Dyck, who lived in Genoa for six years, beginning in 1621, and painted many portraits of the Genovese nobility. The formal gardens, which you can visit for €1, provide a welcome respite from the bustle of the city beyond the palace walls, as well as great views of the harbor. ⊠ *Via Balbi 10, Pré* 🕾 *010/27101* ⊕ *www. palazzorealegenova.it* 🎫 *€4, €6 including Galleria Nazionale* ☉ *Tues. and Wed. 9–1:30, Thurs.–Sun. 9–7.*

FodorsChoice
★

⑱ Palazzo Rosso. This 17th-century baroque palace was named for the red stone used in its construction. It now contains, apart from a number of lavishly frescoed suites, works by Titian, Veronese, Reni, and Van Dyck. ⊠ *Via Garibaldi 18, Maddalena* 🕾 *010/2476351* ⊕ *www.stradanuova. it* 🎫 *€7, includes Palazzo Bianco and Sala Paganini in Palazzo Doria Tursi* ☉ *Tues.–Fri. 9–7, weekends 10–7.*

⑭ Zecca-Righi funicular. This is a seven-stop commuter funicular beginning at Piazza della Nunziata and ending at a high lookout on the fortified gates in the 17th-century city walls. Ringed around the circumference of the city are a number of huge fortresses; this gate was part of the city's

---

A GOOD WALK: GENOA'S STREET OF GOLD

This walk starts from Piazza delle Fontane Marose and heads west along **Via Garibaldi,** one of Genoa's most famous streets. Between 1551 and 1558, three auctions sold off the lots of land along what was then known as the Via Aurea (Golden Street) to wealthy Genovese families, who proceeded to build the extravagant palaces you see there now. Several have become museums housing world-class collections. Many of the rest have courtyards open to the public.

Palazzo Cambiaso, at Via Garibaldi 1, is the first palace on the right, and like several of the other palaces along the street, it's now a bank. Built between 1558 and 1560 for Agostino Pallavicino, it is also one of the street's more traditionally designed buildings. The **Palazzo Gambaro,** at No. 2, is the first palace on your left. Perhaps fittingly, given that this building too is now a bank, the marble statues flanking the entrance represent Vigilance and Prudence. Number 3 is the **Palazzo Lercari Parodi,** built between 1571 and 1578. It's said that the broken noses system of defenses. From Righi you can undertake scenic all-day hikes from one fortress to the next. ✉ *Piazza della Nunziata, Pré* ☎ *010/ 5582414* ⊕ *www.amt.genova.it* 🎫 *€1, free with bus ticket* ⊙ *Daily 6 AM–11:45 PM.*

Also Worth Seeing

㉑ **Castelletto.** One of Genoa's handy municipal elevators whisks you skyward from Piazza Portello, at the end of Galleria Garibaldi, for a good view of the old city. ✉ *Piazza Portello, Castelletto* 🎫 *€1* ⊙ *6:40 AM–midnight.*

㉔ **Ferrovia Genova–Casella.** In continuous operation since 1929, the Genova–Casella Railroad runs from Piazza Manin in Genoa (follow Via Montaldo from the center of town, or take Bus 33 or 34 to Piazza Manin) through the beautiful countryside above the city, finally arriving in the rural hill town of Casella. On the way, the tiny train traverses a series of precarious switchbacks that afford sweeping views of the forested Ligurian hills. In Casella Paese (the last stop) you can hike, eat lunch, or just check out the view and ride back. There are two restaurants and two pizzerias near the Casella station; try local cuisine at Trattoria Teresin in Località Avosso. **Canova** (two stops from the end of the line) is the start of two possible hikes through the hills: one a two-hour, one-way trek to a small sanctuary, **Santuario della Vittoria,** and the other a more grueling four-hour hike to the hill town of **Creto.** Another worthwhile stop along the rail line is **Sant'Olcese Tullo,** where you can take a half-hour (one-way) walk along a river and through the **Sentiero Botanico di Ciaé,** a botanical garden and forest refuge with labeled specimens of Ligurian flora and a tiny medieval castle. For Canova and Sant'Olcese, inform your conductor that you want him to stop. The Casella railroad is a good way to get a sense of the rugged landscape around Genoa, and you may have it to yourself. The train runs about every hour. ✉ *Piazza Manin* ☎ *010/837321* ⊕ *www.ferroviagenovacasella.it* 🎫 *€4 round-trip Mon.–Sat., €6 Sun.* ⊙ *Mon.–Sat. 7:30–7:30, Sun. 9–9.*

⊙ ⑩ **Granarolo funicular.** Take a cog railway up the steeply rising terrain to another part of the city's fortified walls. It takes 15 minutes to hoist you

6

---

of the figures on either side of the door are representative of Mengollo Lercari's penchant for cutting off the noses of prisoners. Note that the courtyard, rather than being centrally located, sits in front of the main portion of the building. At No. 4, the **Palazzo Carrega Cataldi,** built between 1558 and 1561 by Tobia Pallavicino, the "King of Alum" (a fixative used for dyeing cloth), is now home to Genoa's Chamber of Commerce. It was built on a relatively small lot, hence the claim that the architect, Giovanni Battista Castello (1509–69), *fece grande in poco spazio* (basically, did a lot with a little). In fact, there's a fair bit of theatricality to the design. For example, if the main entrance is open, you can see the grand double staircase that leads to the first floor. Only one side actually goes somewhere—the other is there simply for show.

Farther down the street, at No. 5, is the **Palazzo Spinola,** one of many palaces built in Genoa by the fabulously wealthy Spinola family. It was built in 1558 for Angelo Giovanni Spinola, Genovese ambassador to the court of Spain and banker to Philip II. Rather austere on the outside, it's sumptuously stuccoed and frescoed within.

from Stazione Principe, on Piazza Acquaverde, to **Porta Granarolo,** 1,000 feet above, where the sweeping view gives you a sense of Genoa's size. The funicular departs about every half hour. ⊠ *Piazza del Principe, San Teodoro* ☎ *010/5582414* ⊕ *www.amt.genova.it* 🎫 *€1, free with bus ticket* ⊙ *Daily 6 AM–10 PM, at 10:40 PM and 11:20 PM.*

⑰ Loggia dei Mercanti. This merchants' row dating from the 16th century is lined with shops selling local foods and gifts as well as raincoats, rubber boots, and fishing line. ⊠ *Piazza Banchi, Maddalena.*

㉒ Museo d'Arte Orientale Chiossone. In the Villetta di Negro park on the hillside above Piazza Portello, the Chiossone Oriental Art Museum has one of Europe's most noteworthy collections of Japanese, Chinese, and Thai objects. There's a fine view of the city from the museum's terrace. ⊠ *Piazzale Mazzini 1, Maddalena* ☎ *010/542285* ⊕ *www. museochiossonegenova.it* 🎫 *€4, free Sun.* ⊙ *Tues.–Fri. 9–1, weekends 10–7.*

⑫ Palazzo dell'Università. Built in the 1630s as a Jesuit college, this has been Genoa's university since 1803. The exterior is unassuming, but climb the stairway flanked by lions to visit the handsome courtyard, with its portico of double Doric columns. ⊠ *Via Balbi 5, Pré.*

⑳ Palazzo Doria Tursi. In the 16th century, wealthy resident Nicolò Grimaldi had a palace built of pink stone quarried in the region. It's been reincarnated as Genoa's Palazzo Municipale (Municipal Building), and so most of the goings-on inside are the stuff of local politics and quickie weddings. You can visit the richly decorated **Sala Paganini,** where the famous Guarnerius violin that belonged to Niccolò Paganini (1782–1840) is displayed, along with the gardens that connect the palace with the neighboring Palazzo Bianco. ⊠ *Via Garibaldi 9, Maddalena* ☎ *010/ 557111* ⊕ *www.stradanuova.it* 🎫 *€7, includes Palazzo Bianco and Palazzo Rosso* ⊙ *Tues.–Fri. 9–7, weekends 10–7.*

⑮ San Siro. Genoa's oldest church was the city's cathedral from the 4th to the 9th century. Rebuilt in the 16th and 17th centuries, it now feels a bit like a haunted house—imposing frescoes line dank hallways, and chandeliers hold crooked candles flickering in the darkness. ⊠ *Via San Luca, Maddalena* ☎ *010/22461468* ⊙ *Daily 7:30–noon and 4–7.*

The brothers Giovanni Battista and Andrea Spinola built the palace at No. 6, now the **Palazzo Doria.** In the atrium hangs a wrought-iron chandelier with the eagles symbolizing the Doria family, who bought the place in 1723. Moving along to No. 7, you reach the **Palazzo Podestà** (1559–66), named after one of Genoa's longest-sitting mayors, Andrea Podestà. In office almost continuously between 1866 and 1895, Podestà didn't have much of a commute to work—the town hall is right next door, at No. 9.

The **Palazzo Cattaneo Adorno,** at Nos. 8 and 10, was the last palace built on the land auctioned between 1551 and 1558. Shortly after the auction, the lot was resold, at an inflated price, to Lazzaro and Giacomo Spinola. Despite the homogeneous appearance of the facade, the building contains two separate palaces. Number 8 was purchased by a member of the Cattaneo family in 1875, while No. 10 passed to Giovanni Battista Adorno, Giacomo Spinola's son-in-law. It still belongs to the Adorno family. At No. 12 is the **Palazzo Campanella,** unfortunately considerably damaged during a World War II bombardment. The facade has been restored, but the

🔞 **Santissima Annunziata.** Exuberantly frescoed vaults decorate the 16th- to 17th-century church, which is an excellent example of Genovese baroque architecture. ⊠ *Piazza della Nunziata, Pré* ☎ *010/297662* ⊙ *Daily 9–noon and 3–7.*

Southern Districts & the Aquarium

Inhabited since the 6th century BC, the oldest section of Genoa lies on a hill to the southwest of the Caruggi District. Today, apart from a section of 9th-century wall near Porta Soprana, there is little to show that an imposing castle once stood here. Though the neighborhood is considerably run-down, some of Genoa's oldest churches make it a worthwhile excursion. No visit to Genoa is complete, however, without at least a stroll along the harborfront. Once a squalid and unsafe neighborhood, the port was given a complete overhaul during Genoa's preparations for the Columbus quincentennial celebrations of 1992, and additional restorations in 2003 and 2004 have done much to revitalize the waterfront. You can easily reach the port on foot by following Via San Lorenzo downhill from Genoa's cathedral, Via delle Fontane from Piazza della Nunziata, or any of the narrow *viccoli* (alleyways) that lead down from Via Balba and Via Pré.

The Main Attractions

🐚 🔞 **Acquario di Genova.** Europe's biggest aquarium, second in the world only to Osaka's in Japan, is the third most-visited museum in Italy and a must for children. Fifty tanks of marine species, including sea turtles, dolphins, seals, eels, penguins, and sharks, share space with educational displays and re-creations of marine ecosystems, including a tank of coral from the Red Sea. If arriving by car, take the Genova Ovest exit from the autostrada. Entrance is permitted every half hour and the ticket office closes 1½ hours before the aquarium. ⊠ *Ponte Spinola, Porto Vecchio* ☎ *0101/ 23451* ⊕ *www.acquario.ge.it* ☑ *€13* ⊙ *July and Aug., daily 9 AM–11 PM; Sept.–June, Mon.–Wed. and Fri. 9:30–7:30, Thurs. 9:30 AM–10 PM, and weekends 9:30–8:30.*

🔞 **Harbor.** A boat tour gives you a good perspective on the layout of the harbor, which dates back to Roman times. The Genoa inlet, the largest along the Italian Riviera, was also used by the Phoenicians and Greeks

palace's claim to fame, the Salon of the Sun—a French-style room filled with mirrors sculpture—is lost forever. The largest of Via Garibaldi's palaces is at No. 9. This is the **Palazzo Doria Tursi** 🔞, built between 1565 and 1579 by the enormously wealthy banker Niccolò Grimaldi, nicknamed "the monarch." Later purchased by Giovanni Andrea Doria, the palace then passed on to his son Carlo, the Duke of Tursi, and now serves as Genoa's town hall. Directly opposite, at Nos. 14 and 16, and set slightly back from the street, is the **Palazzo delle Torrette** (1562–66). Built by the Doria Tursi as a

pendant to their main palace, the building also served as a passage to the workshops and other properties the family owned in the Caruggi District, just to the south.

Next to the Palazzo Doria Tursi, and the last palace to the right on Via Garibaldi, is the **Palazzo Bianco** 🔞, which was transformed in 1714 by Maria Durazzo Brignole Sale. It has a classical facade covered with white plaster (from which it gets its name). Maria Brignole Sale gave the palace to the city of Genoa in 1884 on condition that it become an art gallery. The Brignole as a harbor and a staging area from which they could penetrate inland to form settlements and to trade. The port is guarded by the Diga Foranea, a striking wall 5 km (3 mi) long built into the ocean. The **Lanterna,** a lighthouse more than 360 feet high, was built in 1544 at the height of Andrea Doria's career; it's one of Italy's oldest lighthouses and a traditional emblem of Genoa. Boat tours of the harbor, provided by the Cooperativa Battellieri, launch from the aquarium pier (€7.50, 1 hour). ⊠ *Stazione Marittima, Ponte dei Mille* ☎ *010/265712* ⊕ *www. battellierigenova.it.*

㊲ **Museo del Mare.** Devoted entirely to the city's seafaring history, this museum is probably the best way, at least on dry land, to get an idea of the changing shape of Genoa's busy port. Highlighting the displays is a full-size replica of a 17th-century Genovese galleon. ⊠ *Calata De Mari 1, Ponte dei Mille* ☎ *010/2345655* ⊕ *www.galatamuseodelmare.it* ✎ *€8* ⊙ *Mar.–Oct., daily 10–7:30; Nov.–Feb., Tues.–Fri. 10–6, and weekends 10–7:30; last entrance 1½ hours before closing.*

㉙ **Palazzo Ducale.** This palace was built in the 16th century over a medieval hall, and its facade was rebuilt in the late 18th century and later restored. It now houses temporary exhibitions and a restaurant-bar serving fusion cuisine. Reservations are necessary to visit the dungeons and tower. Guided tours of the palace and its exhibitions are sometimes available. ⊠ *Piazza Matteotti 9, Portoria* ☎ *010/5574004* ⊕ *www.palazzoducale. genova.it* ✎ *Free* ⊙ *Tues.–Sun. 9–9.*

㉛ **San Lorenzo.** Contrasting black slate and white marble, so common in Liguria, embellished the cathedral at the heart of medieval Genoa—inside and out. Consecrated in 1118, the church honors St. Lawrence, who passed through the city on his way to Rome in the 3rd century. For hundreds of years the building was used for state and religious purposes such as civic elections. Note the 13th-century Gothic portal, fascinating twisted barbershop columns, and the 15th- to 17th-century frescoes inside. The last campanile dates from the early 16th century. The **Museo del Tesoro di San Lorenzo** (San Lorenzo Treasury Museum) housed inside has some stunning pieces from medieval goldsmiths and silversmiths, for which medieval Genoa was renowned. ⊠ *Piazza San Lorenzo, Molo*

Sale also owned the last palace on the left-hand side of Via Garibaldi, the **Palazzo Rosso** ⑱, built between 1671 and 1677 with a red-stone facade. It was also given by Maria Brignole Sale to the city, in 1874.

One block past the Palazzo Rosso, turn left onto Via 4 Canti di San Francesco and follow it down to Via della Madonna, where you turn right, and shortly thereafter left onto Via Pellicceria. Here stands perhaps the grandest of the Spinola family's palaces, the **Palazzo Spinola.** Built for Grimaldi in 1593, it passed to the Spinola in the early 17th century. It was partially rebuilt and

then turned over to the Italian State, which made it the **Galleria Nazionale** ⑯. In passing, don't miss the 15th-century sculpted doorway, with a relief of Saint George, across the street.

After this substantial dose of Genoa at its most luxurious, you can see another side of Genoa by dipping into the **Caruggi District,** the warren of medieval alleys positioned directly below, and only a few steps away from, Via Garibaldi's opulence.

010/2471831 *Cathedral free, museum €5* ⊘ *Cathedral daily 8–11:45 and 3–6:45, museum Mon.–Sat. 9–11:30 and 3–5:30.*

㉝ Sant'Agostino. This 13th-century Gothic church was damaged during World War II, but it still has a fine campanile and two well-preserved cloisters that house an excellent museum displaying pieces of medieval architecture and fresco paintings. Highlighting the collection are the enigmatic fragments of a tomb sculpture by Giovanni Pisano (circa 1250–circa 1315). ✉ *Piazza Sarzano 35/r, Molo* ☎ *010/2511263* ✆ *€4, free Sun.* ⊘ *Tues.–Fri. 9–7, weekends 10–7.*

㉞ Santa Maria di Castello. One of Genoa's most significant religious buildings, an early-Christian church, was rebuilt in the 12th century and finally completed in 1513. You can visit the adjacent cloisters and see the fine artwork contained in the museum. Museum hours vary during religious services. ✉ *Salita di Santa Maria di Castello 15, Molo* ☎ *010/ 2549511* ✆ *Free* ⊘ *Daily 9–noon and 3:30–6.*

Also Worth Seeing

㉘ Accademia delle Belle Arti. Founded in 1751, the Academy of Fine Arts, as well as being a school, houses a collection of paintings from the 16th to the 19th century. Genovese artists of the baroque period are particularly well represented. ✉ *Largo Pertini 4, Portoria* ☎ *010/581957* ⊕ *www.accademialigustica.it* ✆ *Free* ⊘ *Mon.–Sat. 9–1.*

㉖ Childhood home of Christopher Columbus. The ivy-covered remains of this fabled medieval house stand in the gardens below the Porta Soprana. A small and rather disappointing display of objects and reproductions relating to the life and travels of Columbus are on display inside. ✉ *Piazza Dante, Molo* ☎ *No phone* ✆ *€4* ⊘ *Tues.–Sun. 9–5.*

㉟ Il Bigo. The bizarre white structure erected in 1992 to celebrate the Columbus quincentennial looks like either a radioactive spider or an overgrown potato spore, depending on your point of view. Its most redeeming feature is the **Ascensore Panoramico Bigo** (Bigo Panoramic Elevator), from which you can take in the harbor, city, and sea. Next to the elevator, in an area covered by sail-like awnings, there's an ice-skating rink in winter. ✉ *Ponte Spinola, Porto Vecchio* ☎ *010/23451, 010/2461319 ice skating* ✆ *Elevator €4, skating rink €7.50* ⊘ *Elevator Feb. and Nov., weekends 10–5; June–Aug., Tues., Wed., and Sun. 10–8, Thurs.–Sat. 10 AM–11 PM; Mar.–May and Sept., Tues.–Sun. 10–6; Oct., Tues.–Sun. 10–5; Dec. 26–Jan. 6, daily 10–5; skating rink Nov. or Dec.–Mar., weekdays 8 AM–9:30 PM, Sat. 10 AM–2 AM, Sun. 10 AM–midnight.*

㉕ Porta Soprana. A striking 12th-century twin-tower structure, this medieval gateway stands on the spot where a road from ancient Rome entered the city. It is just steps uphill from Columbus's boyhood home, and legend has it that the explorer's father was employed here as a gatekeeper. It's also known as Porta di Sant'Andrea (note the flags, with a red cross on a white background, flying atop the towers). ✉ *Piazza Dante, Molo.*

㉜ San Donato. Although somewhat marred by 19th- and 20th-century restorations, the 12th-century San Donato—with its original portal and octagonal campanile—is a fine example of Genovese Romanesque ar-

6

chitecture. Inside, an altarpiece by the Flemish artist Joos Van Cleve (circa 1485–1540) depicts the Adoration of the Magi. ⊠ *Piazza San Donato, Portoria* ☎ *010/2468869* ⊙ *Mon.–Sat. 8–noon and 3–7, Sun. 9–12:30 and 3–7.*

㉚ San Matteo. This typically Genovese black-and-white-stripe church dates from the 12th century; its crypt contains the tomb of Andrea Doria (1466–1560), the Genovese admiral who maintained the independence of his native city. The well-preserved Piazza San Matteo was, for 500 years, the seat of the Doria family, which ruled Genoa and much of Liguria from the 16th to the 18th century. The square is bounded by 13th- to 15th-century houses decorated with portals and loggias. ⊠ *Piazza San Matteo, Maddalena* ☎ *010/2474361* ⊙ *Mon.–Sat. 8–noon and 4–7, Sun. 9:30–10:30 and 4–5.*

㉗ Teatro Carlo Felice. The World War II–ravaged opera house in Genoa's modern center, Piazza de Ferrari, was rebuilt and reopened in 1991 to host the fine Genovese opera company; its massive tower has been the subject of much criticism. ⊠ *Passo Eugenio Montale 4, Piazza De Ferrari, Portoria* ☎ *010/53811* ⊕ *www.carlofelice.it.*

Where to Stay & Eat

$$$–$$$$ ✕ **Antica Osteria del Bai.** Look out from a large dark-wood–paneled room over the Ligurian Sea from this romantic upscale restaurant perched high on a cliff. A seaside theme pervades the art and menu, which might include black gnocchi with lobster sauce or ravioli ai frutti di mare. The restaurant's traditional elegance is reflected in its white tablecloths, its dress code, and its prices. ⊠ *Via Quarto 16, Quarto* ☎ *010/387478* ⌂ *Jacket and tie* ⊟ *AE, DC, MC, V* ⊙ *Closed Mon., Jan. 10–20, and Aug. 1–20.*

$$$–$$$$ ✕ **Gran Gotto.** Innovative regional dishes are served in this posh, spacious restaurant brightened by contemporary paintings. Try *cappellacci di borragine con vellutata di pinoli* (pasta with a pine-nut sauce) followed by *calamaretti brasati con porri e zucchine* (braised baby squid with leeks and zucchini), one of the many excellent second courses. Service is quick and helpful. ⊠ *Viale Brigata Bisagno 69/r, Piazza della Vittoria, Foce* ☎ *010/564344* ⌂ *Reservations essential* ⊟ *AE, DC, MC, V* ⊙ *Closed Sun. and Aug. 12–31. No lunch Sat.*

$$$–$$$$ ✕ **Zeffirino.** The five Belloni brothers share chef duties at a well-known restaurant full of odd combinations, including decor that has both rustic wood and modern metallic pieces. Try the *passutelli* (ravioli stuffed with ricotta cheese, herbs, and fruit) or any of the homemade pasta dishes. With a Zeffirino restaurant in Las Vegas and another in Hong Kong, the enterprising Bellonis have gone international. ⊠ *Via XX Settembre 20, Portoria* ☎ *010/591990* ⌂ *Reservations essential* ⌂ *Jacket required* ⊟ *AE, DC, MC, V.*

$$–$$$ ✕ **Enoteca Sola.** Menus are chosen specifically to complement wines at Pino Sola's airy, casually elegant *enoteca* (wine bar) in the heart of the modern town. The short menu emphasizes seafood and varies daily but might include stuffed artichokes or baked stockfish. The real draw, though, is the wine list, which includes some of the winners of the *Tre*

Bicchieri (Three Glasses) award denoting only the very best. ⊠ *Via C. Barabino 120/r, Foce* ☎ *010/594513* ⊟ *AE, DC, MC, V* ☾ *Closed Sun. and Aug.*

$–$$ ✕ **Bakari.** Hip styling and ambient lighting hint at this eatery's creative, even daring, takes on Ligurian classics. Sure bets are the spinach-and-cheese gnocchi, any of several carpaccios, and the delicate beef dishes. Reserve ahead, requesting a table on the more imaginative ground floor. ⊠ *Vico del Fieno 16/r, northwest of Piazza San Matteo, Maddalena* ☎ *010/291936* ⊟ *AE, MC, V* ☾ *Closed Sun. No dinner Wed. or Fri.*

$–$$ ✕ **Da Domenico.** Don't be dismayed by the labyrinth of rooms and wood passages that lead to your table at this restaurant in a quiet square near Piazza Dante—you've found one of those hidden corners that only the Genovese know. Traditional seafood and meat dishes make up most of the menu. ⊠ *Piazza Leonardo 3, Molo* ☎ *010/540289* ✍ *Reservations essential* ⊟ *AE, DC, MC, V* ☾ *Closed Mon.*

$$$$ 🏨 **Best Western City.** The location of this hotel can't be beat—it's in the heart of the city near Via Roma, the grand shopping street, and one block from Piazza de Ferrari, which divides new Genoa from old Genoa. A bland apartment-building exterior gives way to a polished lobby and light, modern rooms that are a bit small but very comfortable. Most have only mediocre views; try for a street-side room on a high floor. ⊠ *Via San Sebastiano 6, Portoria, 16123* ☎ *010/5545* 🖷 *010/586301* ⊕ *www. bwcityhotel-ge.it* ⇱ *63 rooms, 3 suites* ☊ *Restaurant, in-room safes, in-room data ports, bar, parking (fee)* ⊟ *AE, DC, MC, V* ⫶◯⫶ *BP.*

★ $$$ 🏨 **Bristol Palace.** The 19th-century grand hotel in the heart of the shopping district carefully guards its reputation for courtesy and service. Spacious guest rooms all have high ceilings and elegant wood wardrobes or headboards. Public spaces, all connected to the hotel's central oval staircase, are comfortable, small, and pleasantly discreet with paneled walls and soft lighting. ⊠ *Via XX Settembre 35, Portoria, 16121* ☎ *010/592541* 🖷 *010/561756* ⊕ *www.hotelbristolpalace.com* ⇱ *128 rooms, 5 suites* ☊ *Restaurant, room TVs with movies, gym, bar, Internet, meeting rooms, parking (fee), some pets allowed* ⊟ *AE, DC, MC, V* ⫶◯⫶ *BP.*

$ 🏨 **Agnello d'Oro.** The friendly owner at Agnello d'Oro does double duty as a travel agent: he's happy to help you with plane reservations and travel plans. Only a few of the simple, modern rooms have balconies, but a surprisingly varied continental breakfast awaits you in the morning. The hotel is about 100 yards from Stazione Principe, near the Palazzo Reale. ⊠ *Vico delle Monachette 6, Pré, 16126* ☎ *010/2462084* 🖷 *010/2462327* ⊕ *www.hotelagnellodoro.it* ⇱ *25 rooms* ☊ *Restaurant, bar, parking (fee), some pets allowed, no-smoking rooms; no a/c in some rooms* ⊟ *AE, DC, MC, V* ⫶◯⫶ *BP.*

$ 🏨 **Cairoli.** This family-run hotel has an enviable location on a pedestrian street not far from the Acquario di Genova. The accommodations are plain, but three rooms open onto the pleasant rooftop terrace. A simple continental breakfast is served in a room off the lobby. ⊠ *Via Cairoli 14/4, Maddalena, 16124* ☎ *010/2461454* 🖷 *010/2467512* ⊕ *www. hotelcairoligenova.com* ⇱ *12 rooms* ☊ *Bar* ⊟ *AE, DC, MC, V* ⫶◯⫶ *BP.*

6

The Art of the Pesto Pestle

YOU MAY HAVE KNOWN GENOA primarily for its salami or its brash explorer, but the city's most direct effect on your life away from Italy may be through its cultivation of one of the world's best pasta sauces. The sublime blend of basil, extra-virgin olive oil, garlic, pine nuts, and grated pecorino and Parmigiano Reggiano cheeses that forms *pesto alla Genovese* is one of Italy's crowning culinary achievements, a concoction that Italian food guru Marcella Hazan has called "the most seductive of all sauces for pasta." Unlike in the United States, where various versions of pesto bedeck everything from pizza to grilled-chicken sandwiches, Ligurian pesto is served only over spaghetti, gnocchi, lasagne, or—most authentically—*trenette* (a flat, spaghettilike pasta) or *trofie* (short, doughy pasta twists), and then typically mixed with boiled potatoes and green beans. Pesto is also occasionally used to flavor minestrone. The small-leaf basil

grown in the region's sunny seaside hills is considered by many to be the best in the world, and your visit to Liguria affords you the chance to savor pesto in its original form. Pesto sauce was invented primarily as a showcase for that singular flavor, and the best pesto brings out the fresh basil's alluring aroma and taste rather than masking it with the complementary ingredients. The simplicity and rawness of pesto is one of its virtues, as cooking (or even heating) basil ruins its delicate flavor. In fact, pesto aficionados refuse even to subject the basil leaves to an electric blender; Genovese (and other) foodies insist that true pesto can be made only with mortar and pestle. Although satisfactory versions can surely be prepared less laboriously, the pesto purists' culinary conservatism is supported by etymology: the word *pesto* is derived from the Italian verb *pestare* (to pound or grind).

Nightlife & the Arts

Especially in summer, the place for nightlife is on the waterfront near the *levante* (southeast) side of the city. From the center, take Corso Italia in the direction of Quarto, Quinto, and nearby Nervi to reach the outdoor nighttime hub. Several beachfront *bagni* (literally, baths) and their accompanying restaurants and bars in the area serve as nighttime summer hangouts.

Nightclubs

Makò. Big, well-known discotheques such as the famous Makò perch on a cliff about halfway to Nervi, attracting attention from Genovese twenty- and thirtysomethings. ⊠ *Corso Italia 28/r, Quarto* ☎ *010/367652.*

Opera

Teatro Carlo Felice. Genoa's well-respected opera company, Fondazione Teatro Carlo Felice, stages lavish productions of old favorites and occasionally world premieres from October to May. ⊠ *Passo Eugenio Montale 4, Piazza De Ferrari, Portoria* ☎ *010/53811* ⊕ *www.carlofelice.it.*

Shopping

Liguria is famous for its fine laces, silver and gold filigree work, and ceramics. Look also for bargains in velvet, macramé, olive wood, and marble. Genoa is the best spot to find all these specialties. In the heart of the medieval quarter, Via Sozigilia is lined with shops selling handicrafts and tempting foods. Via XX Settembre is famous for its exclusive shops. High-end shops line Via Luccoli. The best shopping area for trendy-but-inexpensive Italian clothing is near San Siro, on Via San Luca.

Clothing & Leather Goods

Bruno Magli. The Bologna-based designer makes an impeccable line of leather shoes, boots, handbags, and jackets. ⊠ *Via XX Settembre 135, Foce* ☎ *010/561890.*

Pescetto. Look for designer clothes, perfumes, and gifts at this fancy shop. ⊠ *Via Scurreria 8, Molo* ☎ *010/2473433.*

Jewelry

Codevilla. The well-established Codevilla is one of the best jewelers on a street full of goldsmiths. ⊠ *Via Orefici 53, Maddalena* ☎ *010/2472567.*

Wines

Vinoteca Sola. At this shop you can purchase the best Ligurian wines and have them shipped home. You can even buy futures for advance purchase. ⊠ *Piazza Colombo 13–15/r, near Stazione Brignole, Foce* ☎ *010/594513* ⊕ *www.vinotecasola.it.*

Side Trip from Genoa

Nervi

🟆 *11 km (7 mi) east of Genoa, 19 km (12 mi) west of Rapallo.*

★ The identity of this stately late-19th-century resort, famous for its seaside promenade, the **Passeggiata Anita Garibaldi** (1½ km [1 mi] long), its palm-lined roads, and its 300 acres of parks rich in orange trees, is given away only by the sign on the sleepy train station. Although Nervi is technically part of the city, its peace and quiet are as different from Genoa's hustle and bustle as its clear blue water is from Genoa's crowded port. From the centrally located train station, walk east along the seaside promenade to reach the beaches, a cliff-hanging restaurant, and the 2,000 varieties of roses in the public **Parco Villa Grimaldi,** all the while enjoying one of the most breathtaking views on the Riviera. Nervi—and the road along the way—is known for its nightlife in the summer. Take one of the frequent trains for the 15-minute ride from Stazione Principe or Brignole (buy a ticket for Genova–Nervi), or take Bus 15 or 17 from Brignole or Piazza de Ferrari. Alternatively, a taxi from town center runs about €20 one-way.

WHERE TO ✗ **Marinella.** The impressive wrought-iron chandelier inside takes sec-
STAY & EAT ond billing to the great sea views from the dining room and the terrace.
$–$$ Try the *zuppa di pesce* (fish soup); main dishes change according to the

day's catch. The restaurant, which perches on seaside shoals, has an inexpensive hotel, too. ✉ *Passeggiata Anita Garibaldi 18/r* ☎ *010/ 3728343* ☰ *MC, V* ☾ *Closed Mon. and Nov.*

★ $$$ ▦ **Romantik Hotel Villa Pagoda.** In a 19th-century merchant's mansion modeled after a Chinese temple, this luxury hotel has a private park, access to the famed cliff-top walk, and magnificent ocean views. Request a tower room for the best vantage point. Villa Pagoda is the best of both worlds, as you can enjoy peace and quiet or be in bustling Genoa in 15 minutes. ✉ *Via Capolungo 15, 16167* ☎ *010/3726161* 🖶 *010/321218* ⊕*www.villapagoda.it* ⤴*13 rooms, 4 suites* ☖ *Restaurant, in-room safes, minibars, tennis court, pool, piano bar, meeting room, some pets allowed* ☰ *AE, DC, MC, V* ◉ *BP.*

NIGHTLIFE & An **International Ballet Festival** (Tourist office ✉ Stazione Principe, San
THE ARTS Teodoro ☎ 010/2462633) is held every July in the Villa Gropallo park, drawing performers and audiences from all over the world.

Extraordinarily popular with locals, **Senhor do Bonfim** (✉ Passeggiata Anita Garibaldi ☎ 010/3726312), a nightclub along the water on Nervi's beautiful seaside promenade, has dancing every night and live music until late on weekends.

RIVIERA DI PONENTE

The Riviera di Ponente (Riviera of the Setting Sun) stretches from Genoa to Ventimiglia on the French border. For the most part it's an unbroken chain of beach resorts sheltered from the north by the Ligurian and Maritime Alps, mountain walls that guarantee mild winters and a long growing season—resulting in its other nickname, the Riviera dei Fiori (Riviera of Flowers). Actually, the name is more evocative than the sight of once-verdant hillsides now swathed in massive plastic greenhouses. Many towns on the western Riviera have suffered from an epidemic of overdevelopment, but most have preserved their old cores, usually their most interesting features. In major resorts, large, modern marinas cater to the pleasure-craft crowd. The Riviera di Ponente has both sandy and pebbly beaches with some quiet bays.

Pegli

🔟 *13 km (8 mi) west of Genoa.*

Once a popular summer home for many patrician Genovese families, Pegli has museums, parks, and some regal old homes with well-tended gardens. Two lovely villas—Villa Doria and Villa Durazzo Pallavicini— make Pegli worth an excursion. This suburb manages to maintain its dignity despite industrial development and the proximity of airport and port facilities. Pegli can be reached by convenient commuter train from Stazione Porta Principe in Genoa.

Villa Doria, near the Pegli train station, has a large park. The villa itself, built in the 16th century by the Doria family, has been converted into a **naval museum.** ✉*Piazza Bonavino 7* ☎*010/6969885* ⊕*www.museonavale. it* 🎫 *€4* ☾ *Villa Tues.–Fri. 9–1, Sat. 10–1, park daily 9–noon and 2–6.*

Villa **Durazzo Pallavicini,** set in 19th-century gardens with temples and artificial lakes, contains an **archaeological museum.** ⊠ *Via Pallavicini 11* ☏ *010/6981048* 🎟 *€3.10* ♥ *Tues.–Fri. 9–7, weekends 10–7.*

Varazze

41 *23 km (14 mi) southwest of Pegli, 35 km (22 mi) west of Genoa.*

Well-preserved medieval ramparts surround the town, with the remains of a Romanesque church built directly into one of the walls. Varazze is nicknamed *la città delle donne* (the city of women) after an annual festival. The name has remained but the celebration, last given in 1999, has passed, at least for the moment, from fashion.

Albisola Marina

42 *11 km (7 mi) southwest of Varazze, 43 km (26 mi) west of Genoa.*

Albisola Marina has a centuries-old tradition of ceramic-making. Numerous shops here sell the distinctive wares, and a whole sidewalk, **Lungomare degli Artisti,** has been transformed by the colorful ceramic works of well-known artists. It runs along the beachfront. The 18th-century **Villa Farag-**

giana, near the parish church, has exhibits on the history of pottery. ⊠ *Via dell'Oratorio* ☎ *019/480622* 🗺 *Free* ☉ *Apr.–Sept., Wed.–Mon. 3–7.*

Shopping

Ceramiche San Giorgio (⊠ Corso Matteotti 5 ☎ 019/482747) has been producing ceramics since the 17th century, and is known for both classic and modern designs. **Ernan** (⊠ Corso Mazzini 77, Albisola Superiore ☎ 019/489916) sells blue-and-white patterns typical of the 18th century. **Mazzotti** (⊠ Corso Matteotti 25 ☎ 019/481626) has an exclusive ceramics selection and a small museum.

Savona

43 *5 km (3 mi) southwest of Albisola Marina, 46 km (29 mi) southwest of Genoa.*

Savona is the fifth-largest seaport in Italy and handles vast oil and coal cargoes, as well as car and truck ferries. As it was considerably damaged during World War II, much of the town is modern and not very interesting, although a small austere older quarter near the harbor contains some fine homes of the town's merchant class. The large **Palazzo della Rovere** (⊠ Via Pia 28) was designed for Pope Julius II by the Florentine Giuliano da Sangallo in 1495. It is closed to the public. The 12th-century **Torre del Brandale** (⊠ Piazza del Brandale 2 ☎ 019/821915), with its 14th-century annex, the **Palazzo degli Anziani,** and two other remaining medieval towers, is open by appointment.

Shopping

Watch for shops selling crystallized fruit, a local specialty. In Millesimo, a town 4 km (2½ mi) west and 36 km (18 mi) inland from Savona, little rum chocolates known as *millesimi* are produced. Look for bargains, too, in wrought iron, copper, and and carvings from local sandstone.

Finale Ligure

44 *24 km (15 mi) southwest of Savona, 72 km (44 mi) southwest of Genoa.*

Finale Ligure is actually made up of three small villages: Finalmarina, Finalpia, and Finalborgo. The former two have fine sandy beaches and modern resort amenities. The most attractive of the villages is Finalborgo, less than 1 km (½ mi) inland, a hauntingly preserved medieval settlement, planned to a rigid blueprint, with 15th-century walls. The surrounding countryside is pierced by deep, narrow valleys and caves; the limestone outcroppings provide the warm pinkish stone found in many buildings in Genoa. Here lurk rare reptiles and exotic flora.

Finalborgo is crowned by the impressive ruins of the huge **Castel Gavone.** ⊠ *Via Beretta.*

The baroque church of **San Biagio** houses many works of art. ⊠ *Piazza San Biagio, Finalborgo* ☎ *019/695617* ☉ *Daily 8–11:30 and 2:30–5.*

Enjoy the shade of the courtyard in the 14th- to 15th-century Dominican convent **Santa Caterina,** or step in to see the museum of local paleontology and natural history. ⊠ *Museo Civico, Finalborgo* ☎ *019/*

690020 🖂 €2.60 ⊙ *July–Oct., Tues.–Sat. 9–noon and 3–6, Sun.*
9–noon; Nov.–June, Tues.–Sat. 9–noon and 2:30–4:30, Sun. 9–noon.

Where to Stay & Eat

$$$–$$$$ ✕ **Ai Torchi.** You could easily become a homemade-pesto snob at this
Finalborgo eatery. The high prices are justified by excellent inventive
seafood and meat dishes and by the setting—a restored 5th-century olive-
oil refinery. 🖂 *Via dell'Annunziata 12* ☎ *019/690531* 🖃 *AE, DC,*
MC, V ⊙ *Closed Jan. 7–Feb. 10, and Tues. Sept.–July.*

¢–$ 🏨 **Hotel Riviera.** Your agreeable host, Marzio Alberto, welcomes you to
this smartly run hotel in Finalmarina, close to the waterfront. Rooms
are cheerfully furnished and brightly lighted, and some have views of
the sea. There's an additional charge for breakfast if you stay for less
than three nights during August. 🖂 *Via Ruffini 11, 17024* ☎ *019/*
692814 🖷 *019/680013* ⊕ *www.hotelrivierafinale.it* 🛏 *20 rooms*
🖒 *Bar; no a/c in some rooms* 🖃 *AE, DC, MC, V* ⊙ *Closed mid-*
Oct–mid-Dec. ⦿| *BP.*

off the
beaten
path

NOLI – Just 9 km (5½ mi) northeast of Finale Ligure, the ruins of a
castle loom benevolently over the tiny medieval gem of Noli. It's hard
to imagine that this charming village was—like Genoa, Venice, Pisa,
and Amalfi—a prosperous maritime republic in the Middle Ages. If
you don't have a car, get a bus for Noli at Spotorno, where local
trains stop.

6

Albenga

45 *20 km (12 mi) southwest of Finale Ligure, 90 km (55 mi) southwest of*
Genoa.

Albenga has a medieval core, with
narrow streets laid out by the an-
cient Romans. A network of alleys
is punctuated by centuries-old tow-
ers surrounding the 18th-century
Romanesque cathedral, with a late-
14th-century campanile and a bap-
tistery dating back to the 5th
century.

> ### WORD OF MOUTH
>
> "The pesto is incredible in
> Liguria. . . . We often would go to
> an *alimentari* and get pesto,
> bread, cheese, tomatoes (the best
> I've ever had), prosciutto, melon,
> etc. And relax."   –Skatterfly

off the
beaten
path

BARDINETO – For a look at some of the Riviera's mountain scenery,
make an excursion by car to this attractive village in the middle of an
area rich in mushrooms, chestnuts, and raspberries, as well as local
cheeses. A ruined castle stands above the village. From Borghetto
Santo Spirito (between Albenga and Finale Ligure), drive inland 25
km (15 mi).

Where to Stay

$$$$ 🏨 **La Meridiana.** An oasis of hospitality and refinement occupies a hand-
some farmhouse compound surrounded by a garden. The interiors are
those of a comfortable home, with brightly colored prints, freshly cut

flowers, and a mix of traditional and period-style furniture in the common and guest rooms. Il Rosmarino restaurant serves fine wines and seafood dishes. You can enjoy privileges at the golf, tennis, and equestrian clubs nearby. ⊠ *Via ai Castelli, off A10, 17033 Garlenda, 8 km (5 mi) north of Albenga* ☎ *0182/580271* 📠 *0182/580150* ⊕ *www.relaischateaux.com/meridiana* ➬ *13 rooms, 15 suites* ♿ *Restaurant, golf privileges, pool, sauna, bicycles, Ping-Pong, bar, Internet, some pets allowed (fee)* ⊟ *AE, DC, MC, V* ⊗ *Closed Nov.–Mar.* ◯ *BP.*

Cervo

46 *23 km (14 mi) southwest of Albenga, 106 km (65 mi) southwest of Genoa.*

Cervo is the quintessential sleepy Ligurian coastal village, nicely polished for the tourists who come to explore its narrow byways and street staircases. It's a remarkably well-preserved medieval town, crowned with a big baroque church. In July and August the square in front of the church is the site of chamber music concerts.

Imperia

47 *12 km (7 mi) west of Cervo, 116 km (71 mi) southwest of Genoa.*

Imperia actually consists of two towns: Porto Maurizio, a medieval town built on a promontory, and Oneglia, now an industrial center for oil refining and pharmaceuticals. Porto Maurizio has a virtually intact medieval center, an intricate spiral of narrow streets and stone portals, and some imposing 17th- and 18th-century palaces. There's little of interest in modern Oneglia, but the 1½-km (1-mi) trip northeast along the seafront from Porto Maurizio to Oneglia is worth taking for a visit to the olive-oil museum.

Imperia is king when it comes to olive oil, and the story of the olive is the theme of the small **Museo dell'Olivo.** Displays of the history of the olive tree, farm implements, presses, and utensils show how olive oil has been made in many countries throughout history. ⊠ *Via Garessio 11, Oneglia* ☎ *0183/720000* ⊕ *www.museodellolivo.com* 🎟 *Free* ⊗ *Wed.–Mon. 9–noon and 3–6:30.*

Where to Eat

★ ¢–$ ✕ **Candidollo.** In this rustic country inn, with checkered tablecloths and worn terra-cotta floors, host Bruno Ardissone uses fresh, local ingredients to make traditional, seasonal recipes. The menu usually includes *coniglio al timo* (rabbit with thyme and other herbs) and *lumache all'agliata* (grilled snails in piquant sauce). It's well worth the detour to get to the village of Diano Borello, a mile or so north of Diano Marina. ⊠ *Corso Europa 23, Diano Borello, 6 km (4 mi) east of Imperia* ☎ *0183/43025* ⊟ *No credit cards* ⊗ *Closed Tues. and Nov.–Mar. No lunch Mon.*

Taggia

48 *20 km (12 mi) west of Imperia, 135 km (84 mi) southwest of Genoa.*

The town of Taggia has a medieval core and one of the most imposing medieval bridges in the area. The church of **San Domenico,** with a small museum, was once part of a monastery founded in the 15th century that remained a beacon of faith and learning in Liguria for 300 years. An antiques market is held here, just south of Taggia, on the fourth weekend of the month. ⊠ *Piazzale San Domenico, Arma di Taggia* ☎ *No phone* ☞ *Free* ⊘ *Fri.–Wed. 9–5.*

San Remo

㊾ *10 km (6 mi) west of Taggia, 146 km (90 mi) southwest of Genoa.*

The self-styled capital of the Riviera di Ponente, San Remo is also the area's largest resort, lined with polished hotels, exotic gardens, and seaside promenades. Renowned for its royal visitors, glittering casino, and romantic setting, San Remo still maintains some of the glamour of its heyday from the late 19th century to World War II. Waterside palm fronds conceal a sizable old center that, unlike in other Ponente towns, is lively even in the off-season. Restaurants, wine bars, and boutiques are second in Liguria only to Genoa's, and San Remo's cafés bustle with afternoon activity.

The newer parts of San Remo suffer from the same epidemic of overbuilding that changed so many towns on the western Riviera for the worse. The Mercato dei Fiori, Italy's most important wholesale flower market, is held here in a market hall between Piazza Colombo and Corso Garibaldi and open to dealers only. More than 20,000 tons of carnations, roses, mimosa flowers, and innumerable other cut flowers are dispatched from here each year. As the center of northern Italy's flower-growing industry, the town is surrounded by hills where verdant terraces are now blanketed with plastic to form immense greenhouses. Consult the San Remo **tourist office** for information on the flowers and about events in town. ⊠ *Palazzo Riviera, Largo Nuvoloni 1* ☎ *0184/571571* ⊕ *www.sanremonet.com.*

Explore the warren of alleyways in the old part of San Remo, **La Pigna** ("the pinecone"), which climbs upward to Piazza Castello and a splendid view of the town.

The onion-domed Russian Orthodox church of **San Basilio** is a legacy of Russian empress Maria Alexandrovna, wife of Czar Alexander II, who built a summerhouse here. ⊠ *Corso dell'Imperatrice* ☎ *0184/531807* ⊘ *Daily 9:30–12 and 3–6.*

In addition to gaming, the Art Nouveau **San Remo Casinò** has a restaurant, a nightclub, and a theater that hosts concerts and the annual San Remo Music Festival. If you want to try our luck at the gaming tables, there's a €7.50 cover charge on weekends. ⊠ *Corso Inglese* ☎ *0184/5951* ⊘ *Slot machines Sun.–Fri. 10 AM–2:30 AM, Sat. 10 AM–3:30 AM, tables Sun.–Fri. 2:30 PM–2:30 AM, Sat. 2:30 PM–3:30 AM.*

off the beaten path

BUSSANA VECCHIA – In the hills where flowers are cultivated for export sits Bussana Vecchia, a self-consciously picturesque former ghost town largely destroyed by an earthquake in 1877. The inhabitants packed up and left en masse after the quake, and for almost a century the houses, church, and crumbling bell tower were empty shells, overgrown by weeds and wildflowers. Since the 1960s an artists colony has evolved among the ruins. Painters, sculptors, artisans, and bric-a-brac dealers have restored dwellings. ⊠ *8 km (5 mi) east of San Remo.*

Where to Stay & Eat

★ ¢–$ ✗ **Nuovo Piccolo Mondo.** Old wooden chairs dating from the 1920s, when the place opened, evoke the homey charm of this small, family-run trattoria. The place has a faithful clientele, so get there early to grab a table and order Ligurian specialties such as *sciancui* (a roughly cut flat pasta with a mixture of beans, tomatoes, zucchini, and pesto) and *polpo e patate* (stewed octopus with potatoes). ⊠ *Via Piave 7* ☎ *0184/509012* ⊟ *No credit cards* ✆ *Closed Sun. and Mon., and July.*

$$$$ 🏨 **Royal.** It's a toss-up whether this hotel or the Splendido in Portofino is the most luxurious in Liguria. Rooms here have a mixture of modern amenities and antique furnishings. The heated seawater swimming pool, open April–September, is in a tropical garden. On the terrace, candlelight dining and music are of-

> ### WORD OF MOUTH
>
> "San Remo is certainly a more 'happening' place than quiet, tranquil Portofino. It's full of shops and restaurants."   –Huitres

fered each night in warm weather. Keep your eyes open for spectacular off-season discounts. The Royal is only a few paces from the casino and the train station. ⊠ *Corso Imperatrice 80, 18038* ☎ *0184/5391* 🖷 *0184/ 661445* ⊕ *www.royalhotelsanremo.com* 🛏 *121 rooms, 17 suites* ⚏ *2 restaurants, room service, in-room safes, cable TV, in-room data ports, golf privileges, miniature golf, tennis court, saltwater pool, gym, hair salon, 2 bars, babysitting, playground, dry cleaning, laundry service, convention center* ⊟ *AE, DC, MC, V* ✆ *Closed Oct. 8–Dec. 20* ⦿ *MAP.*

$$ 🏨 **Paradiso.** A quiet palm-fringed garden gives the Paradiso an air of seclusion in this sometimes hectic resort city. Rooms are modern and bright; many have little terraces. The hotel restaurant has a good fixed-price menu. This small central hotel is adjacent to a lush public park. ⊠ *Via Roccasterone 12, 18038* ☎ *0184/571211* 🖷 *0184/578176* ⊕ *www.paradisohotel.it* 🛏 *41 rooms* ⚏ *Restaurant, pool, bar, Internet, no-smoking rooms* ⊟ *AE, DC, MC, V* ⦿ *BP.*

Bordighera

🔟 *12 km (7 mi) west of San Remo, 155 km (96 mi) southwest of Genoa.*

This garden spot was the first town in Europe to grow date palms, and its citizens still have the exclusive right to provide the Vatican with palm fronds for Easter celebrations. Bordighera, on a large, lush promontory, wears its genteel past as a famous winter resort with unstudied ease. A large English colony, attracted by the mild climate, settled here in the second half of the 19th century and is still very much in evidence today; you regularly find people taking afternoon tea in the cafés, and streets named after Queen Victoria and Shakespeare. Thanks partly to its many year-round English residents, Bordighera does not close down entirely in the off-season like some Riviera resorts but rather serves as a quiet winter haven for an older clientele. With plenty of hotels and restaurants, Bordighera makes a good base for exploring the region and is quieter and less commercial than San Remo.

Running parallel to the ocean, **Lungomare Argentina** is a pleasant promenade, 1½ km (1 mi) long, which begins at the western end of the town and provides good views westward to the French Côte d'Azur.

Where to Stay & Eat

$$$$ ✕ **Le Chaudron.** A charming rustic interior, with ancient Roman arches, has the look of restaurants across the French border in Provence. Ligurian specialties are highlights on the predominantly seafood menu: try the cheese *pansoti con salsa di noci* (ravioli with walnut sauce) and the branzino with artichokes or mushrooms. ⊠ *Via Vittorio Emanuele 9* ☎ *0184/263592* ⌛ *Reservations essential* ▤ *DC, MC, V* ☉ *Closed Mon., 1st 2 wks in Feb., and 1st 2 wks in July.*

$$–$$$ ✕ **La Reserve.** This informal trattoria has access to the beach and excellent views from the dining room; there are even changing rooms for anyone who wants to take an after-lunch dip. Concentrate on the seafood here: specialties are seafood ravioli *al finocchio selvatico* (with wild fennel) and assorted grilled fish. La Reserve is part of the Hotel Parigi, 1½ km (1 mi) east of the center on the road to San Remo. ⊠ *Via Arziglia 20* ☎ *0184/261322* ▤ *AE, DC, MC, V* ☉ *Closed Mon. and mid-Nov.–mid-Dec. No dinner Wed.*

$–$$ ✕ **Il Tempo Ritrovato.** A small wine bar and restaurant combine forces here on Bordighera's main street. Simple pasta dishes and a spectacular wine list make this a great choice. ⊠ *Via Vittorio Emanuele 144* ☎ *0184/261207* ▤ *AE, DC, MC, V* ☉ *Closed Sun. and Mon.*

$–$$ ✕ **Piemontese.** Both the Ligurian seafood and the hearty cuisine of the neighboring Piedmont region served here are popular with locals. Risotto *al Barolo* is cooked with Barolo wine, sausage, and porcini mushrooms, and the winter specialty is *bagna cauda* (raw vegetables with a garlic, oil, and anchovy sauce). ⊠ *Via Roseto 8, off Via Vittorio Emanuele* ☎ *0184/261651* ▤ *AE, MC, V* ☉ *Closed Tues. and mid-Nov.–mid-Dec.*

$ 🏠 **Pensione Villa Miki.** Tucked away on a quiet residential street, this family-run pension has simple rooms, half of which have balconies and private bathrooms. Full- and half-pension plans are available, which, because the food is good and the price is right, are worth considering. ⊠ *Via Lagazzi 14, 18012* ☎ *0184/261844* 🖷 *0184/265808* ⇥ *8 rooms, 4 with bath* ⌂ *Restaurant, bar; no a/c* ▤ *No credit cards* ❏ *BP.*

Ventimiglia

❺❶ *5 km (3 mi) west of Bordighera, 159 km (98 mi) southwest of Genoa.*

From its past life as a pre-Roman settlement known as Albintimilium, Ventimiglia retains some important archaeological remains, including a 2nd-century AD amphitheater. A vital trade center for hundreds of years, it declined in prestige as Genoa grew and is now little more than a frontier town that lives on tourism and the cultivation of flowers. (The Friday flower market, open to the trade only, creates traffic gridlock; it's best to avoid the town on that day.)

Ventimiglia is divided in two by the Roia River. The Città Vecchia is a well-preserved medieval old town on the western bank. Walk up Via del Capo to reach the ancient walls, which have fine views of the coast. The 11th-century **Duomo** has a Gothic portal dating from 1222. ✉ *Piazza Cattedrale* ☎ *0184/229507* ✆ *Thurs.–Tues. 8:30–Noon and 3–5:30, Wed. 3–5:30.*

Where to Stay

$$ ▦ **La Riserva.** More than 1,100 feet above sea level is the village of Cas-
Fodor'sChoice tel d'Appio, where you'll find this innlike establishment. Rooms are bright,
★ airy, and simply decorated with contemporary furnishings and rich fabrics. The staff is very helpful, providing, for example, regular lifts into town if you have no car. In addition to its excellent restaurant, La Riserva has numerous activities and a lovely panoramic terrace for sunbathing, afternoon drinks, or candlelight dinners. Full-board rates are a good deal. ✉ *Via Peidago 79, 18039 Castel d'Appio, 5 km (3 mi) west of Ventimiglia* ☎ *0184/229533* 📠 *0184/229712* ⊕ *www.lariserva.it* 🔽 *16 rooms, 3 suites* 🖒 *Restaurant, pool, bicycles, billiards, Ping-Pong, bar, Internet* ▭ *AE, DC, MC, V* ✆ *Closed mid-Oct.–Mar.* ⅋ *BP.*

| en route | From Ventimiglia, a provincial road swings 10 km (6 mi) up the Nervi River valley to a lovely-sounding medieval town, Dolceacqua (its name translates as Sweetwater), with a ruined castle. Liguria's best-known red wine is the local Rossese di Dolceacqua. A farther 6 km (4 mi) along the road lies Pigna, a fascinating medieval village built in concentric circles on its hilltop. |

Giardini Botanici Hanbury

★ ㊵ *6 km (4 mi) west of Ventimiglia, 165 km (102 mi) southwest of Genoa.*

Mortola Inferiore, only 2 km (1 mi) from the French border, is the site of the world-famous Giardini Botanici Hanbury (Hanbury Botanical Gardens), one of the largest in Italy. Planned and planted in 1867 by a wealthy English merchant, Sir Thomas Hanbury, and his botanist brother Daniel, the terraced gardens contain species from five continents, including many palms and succulents. There are panoramic views of the sea from the gardens. The ticket office closes one hour before the garden. ✉ *Località Mortola* ☎ *0184/229507* 💶 *€7.50* ✆ *Mar.–June 15, daily 9:30–6; June 16–Sept. 15, daily 9:30–7; Sept. 16–last Sat. in Oct., daily 9:30–6; last Sun. in Oct.–Feb., Tues.–Sun. 10–5.*

| off the beaten path | **BALZI ROSSI –** Prehistoric humans left traces of their lives and magic rites in the Balzi Rossi (Red Rocks), caves carved in the sheer rock. You can visit the caves and a small museum displaying some of the objects found there. ✉ *Via Balzi Rosso 9, 2 km (1 mi) west of Giardini Botanici Hanbury* ☎ *0184/38113* 💶 *€2* ✆ *Tues.–Sun. 8:30–5:30.* |

ITALIAN RIVIERA ESSENTIALS

Transportation

BY AIR

There is daily air service between Genoa and Zürich (on Swiss International Air Lines), London (on British Airways), Paris (on Air France), Munich (on Air Dolomiti), and Milan and Rome (on Alitalia).

Aeroporto Internazionale Cristoforo Colombo is only 6 km (4 mi) from the center of Genoa. The nearest airports for direct U.S. flights are Nice, in France, about 2½ hours west of Genoa (an easy bus connection), and Milan's Linate and Malpensa, about two hours northeast.

Volabus services from Cristoforo Colombo Airport connect with Genoa's Stazione Brignole, stopping also at Piazza Acquaverde (Stazione Principe). Tickets cost €2.10 and may be purchased on the bus.

🚩 Airport Information Aeroporto Internazionale Cristoforo Colombo ⊠ Sestri Ponente, Genoa ☎ 010/60151.

🚩 Carriers Air Dolomiti ☎ 800/013366 ⊕ www.airdolomiti.it. **Air France** ☎ 848/884466 ⊕ www.airfrance.com. **Alitalia** ☎ 848/865641 ⊕ www.alitalia.com. **British Airways** ☎ 848/812266 ⊕ www.britishairways.com. **Swiss International Air Lines** ☎ 848/852000 ⊕ www.swiss.com.

🚩 Transfers Volabus ☎ 010/5582414.

BY BOAT & FERRY

Genoa, Italy's largest port, can be reached by sea from the United States as well as from other Italian and European ports, including Sardinia and Sicily. Ships berth in the heart of Genoa; ferries to various ports around the Mediterranean are operated by Tirrenia Navigazione, whose most popular destination is Sardinia (a 13-hour trip). Grimaldi Lines sends overnight ferries to Barcelona (an 18-hour trip) and Palermo, Sicily (a 20-hour trip). Corsica Ferries runs car ferries from Savona to Bastia and Ile-Rousse in Corsica.

Within Liguria, boat or ferry travel can be the most pleasant—and sometimes only—way to get from place to place. A busy network of local ferry lines, such as Servizio Marittimo del Tigullio and Alimar, connects many of the resorts. Golfo Paradiso lines run between Camogli, San Fruttuoso (on the Portofino promontory), and Recco, and in summer from the port of Genoa and Nervi to Portofino, Cinque Terre, and Portovenere, stopping in Recco and Camogli. Navigazione Golfo dei Poeti runs regular ferry services between Lerici, Portovenere, the Cinque Terre, Santa Margherita, and Genoa.

🚩 Boat & Ferry Resources, Interregional Corsica Ferries ⊠ Calata Nord, Porto Vado, Savona ☎ 019/2155300 ⊕ www.corsicaferries.com. **Grimaldi Lines** ⊠ Stazione Marittima, Ponte dei Mille, Genoa ☎ 010/589331. **Tirrenia Navigazione** ⊠ Stazione Marittima, Ponte dei Mille, Genoa ☎ 010/2758041 ⊕ www.tirrenia.it.

🚩 Boat & Ferry Resources Within Liguria Alimar ⊠ Calata Zingari, Molo, Genoa ☎ 010/256775. **Golfo Paradiso** ⊠ Via Scalo 3, Camogli ☎ 0185/772091 ⊕ www.golfoparadiso.it. **Navigazione Golfo dei Poeti** ⊠ Viale Mazzini 21, La Spezia ☎ 0187/732987 ⊕ www.

navigazionegolfodeipoeti.it. **Servizio Marittimo del Tigullio** ✉ Via Palestro 8/1b, Santa Margherita Ligure ☎ 0185/284670 ⊕ www.traghettiportofino.it.

BY BUS & FUNICULAR

Generallly speaking, buses are a difficult way to come and go in Liguria. Diana Tours provides service from the airport in Nice, but there's no bus service between Genoa and other major Italian cities such as Turin, Milan, Bologna, and Florence. Traveling from town to town by bus within Liguria is challenging due to the myriad of bus companies servicing small segments of the region. There's no regular service connecting Genoa with the towns along the Riviera di Ponente. Things are somewhat easier along the Riviera di Levante where Tigullio Trasporti runs regular service.

The main bus station in Genoa is at Piazza Principe. Local buses, operated by the municipal transport company AMT, serve the steep valleys that run to some of the towns along the western coast. Tickets may be bought at local bus stations or at newsstands. (You must have a ticket before you board.) AMT also operates the funicular railways and the elevators that service the steeper sections of the city.

🚌 **Bus Information AMT** ✉ Piazza Acquaverde, Genoa ☎ 010/5582414 ⊕ www.amt. genova.it. **Diana Tours** ✉ Via G. Ardoino 151, Diano Marina ☎ 800/651931. **Tigullio Trasporti** ✉ Piazza Nostro Signore dell'Orto, Chiavari ☎ 0185/373233 ✉ Piazza Vittorio Veneto 1, Santa Margherita Ligure ☎ 0185/288834.

BY CAR

Autostrada A12 southeast from Genoa links up with the autostrada network for all northern and southern destinations; Rome is a six-hour drive from Genoa. The 150-km (93-mi) trip north to Milan on A7 takes two hours. Nice is 2½ hours of tunnels west on A10.

Two good roads run parallel to each other along the coast of Liguria. Closer to shore and passing through all the towns and villages is S1, the Via Aurelia, which has excellent views at almost every turn but gets crowded in July and August. More direct and higher up than S1 is the autostrada, A10 west of Genoa and A12 to the south. These routes save time on weekends, in summer, and on days when festivals slow traffic in some resorts to a standstill.

Be forewarned: driving in Genoa is harrowing and is best avoided whenever possible—if you want to see the city on a day trip, go by train; if you're staying in the city, park in a garage or by valet and go by foot and by taxi throughout your stay.

CAR EMERGENCIES
If you break down on the highway, walk along the side of the road until you come to an emergency telephone. Call and the emergency highway road service comes to tow you to the nearest service station—for a hefty fee. On a smaller road, unless you have a cell phone you'd be better off walking to the nearest town or gas station (usually not too far) and calling ACI Emergency Service (a free call) from any pay phone. In order to describe where you are, be prepared to seek out the help of locals. (*Dove siamo?*—Where are we?)

🚗 **Emergencies ACI** ☎ 803/116.

BY TRAIN

Frequent and fast train service by the Ferrovie dello Stato (Italian State Railways), also known as Trenitalia, connects Liguria with the rest of Italy. Genoa is 1½ hours from Milan and 5½–6 hours from Rome (4½ with the Eurostar). Many services from France (in particular, the French Riviera) pass along the Ligurian Coast on the way to all parts of Italy.

Within Liguria, it takes two hours for an express train to cover the entire coast; local trains make innumerable stops and take upward of five hours. Regular service operates from Genoa's two stations: departures from Stazione Principe travel to points west and Stazione Brignole to points east and south. All the coastal resorts are on this line.

7 Train Information **Ferrovie dello Stato** ☎ 892021 ⊕ www.trenitalia.com.
7 Train Stations **Stazione Brignole** ✉ Piazza Giuseppe Verdi, Foce, Genoa ☎ 892021.
Stazione Principe ✉ Piazza del Principe, San Teodoro, Genoa.

EMERGENCIES

Europa and Ghersi are two late-night pharmacies in Genoa.

7 Ambulance ☎ 118. **Europa** ✉ Corso Europa 676, Genoa ☎ 010/380239. **Police** ☎ 112.
Ghersi ✉ Corso Buenos Aires 18/r, Genoa ☎ 010/541661. **Ospedale Generale Regionale San Martino** ✉ Largo Rosanna Benzi 10, Genoa ☎ 010/5551. **General emergencies** ☎ 113.

TOURS

You can also take a boat tour of Genoa harbor with Cooperativa Battellieri del Porto di Genova. The tour, which starts from the aquarium pier, costs €6, lasts about an hour, and includes a visit to the breakwater outside the harbor, the Bacino delle Grazie, and the Molo Vecchio (Old Port).

A bus tour of Genoa with an English-speaking guide is a good way to see the city and its panoramic upper reaches. A coach leaves every afternoon at 3 from Piazza Caricamento, by the port, and does the Giro Giro Tour, a two-hour narrated loop of the city (€15). It's operated by Genoa's municipal transport company in conjunction with the agency Macrame Viaggi.

Individual or group walking and hiking tours can introduce you to the lesser known aspects of the region. For the Cinque Terre and the rest of the Province of La Spezia, the Cooperativa Arte e Natura is a good source for well-trained, English-speaking, licenced guides. A half-day costs approximately €150. **7** Boat Tours **Cooperativa Battellieri** ✉ Stazione Marittima, Ponte dei Mille, Genoa ☎ 010/265712 ⊕ www.battellierigenova.it.
7 Bus Tours **Macrame Viaggi** ✉ Piazza Colombo 3, Maddalena, Genoa ☎ 010/5959779.
7 Walking Tours **Coopertiva Arte e Natura** ✉ Via Firenze 27, La Spezia ☎ 0187/712038 🖷 0187/767892.

VISITOR INFORMATION

Most towns have a local tourist office, called Agenzia di Promozione Turistica (APT), that can provide general information, and for a small fee can help you book accommodations Monday–Saturday 9–5. Note that the Terminale Crociere branch in Genoa is open only May–September, for the arrival of major ferries and cruise ships.

🚩 Tourist Information **Genoa** ✉ Stazione Principe, San Teodoro ☎ 010/2462633 ⊕ www.apt.genova.it ✉ Aeroporto Internazionale Cristoforo Colombo, Sestri Ponente ☎ 010/6015247 ✉ Via Roma 11 ☎ 010/576791 ✉ Terminale Crociere, Ponte dei Mille ☎ 010/6015247. **Alassio** ✉ Viale Mazzini 62, 17021 ☎ 0182/647027 ⊕ www.inforiviera.it. **Albenga** ✉ Viale Martiri della Libertà 1, 17031 ☎ 0182/558444 ⊕ www.inforiviera.it. **Bordighera** ✉ Via Roberto 1, 18012 ☎ 0184/262322 ⊕ www.rivieradeifiori.org. **Camogli** ✉ Via XX Settembre 33, 16032 ☎ 0185/771066. **Imperia** ✉ Viale Matteotti 37, 18100 ☎ 0183/660140 ⊕ www.rivieradeifiori.org. **La Spezia** ✉ Via Mazzini 45, 19100 ☎ 0187/770900 ⊕ www.aptcinqueterre.sp.it. **Lerici** ✉ Via Biaggini 6, 19032 ☎ 0187/967346 ⊕ www.aptcinqueterre.sp.it. **Levanto** ✉ Piazza Cavour 12, 19015 ☎ 0187/808125 ⊕ www.aptcinqueterre.sp.it. **Monterosso** ✉ Via Fegina 38, 19016 ☎ 0187/817506 ⊕ www.aptcinqueterre.sp.it. **Portofino** ✉ Via Roma 35, 16034 ☎ 0185/269024 ⊕ www.apttigullio.liguria.it. **Rapallo** ✉ Lungomare V. Veneto 7, 16035 ☎ 0185/230346 ⊕ www.apttigullio.liguria.it. **Riomaggiore** ✉ Stazione Ferroviaria, 19017 ☎ 0187/920633 ⊕ www.aptcinqueterre.sp.it. **San Remo** ✉ Palazzo Riviera, Largo Nuvoloni 1, 18038 ☎ 0184/571571 ⊕ www.rivieradeifiori.org. **Santa Margherita Ligure** ✉ Via XXV Aprile 28, 16038 ☎ 0185/2929 ⊕ www.apttigullio.liguria.it. **Varazze** ✉ Viale Nazioni Unite, 17019 ☎ 019/935043 ⊕ www.inforiviera.it. **Ventimiglia** ✉ Via Cavour 61, 18039 ☎ 0184/351183 ⊕ www.rivieradeifiori.org.

Emilia-Romagna

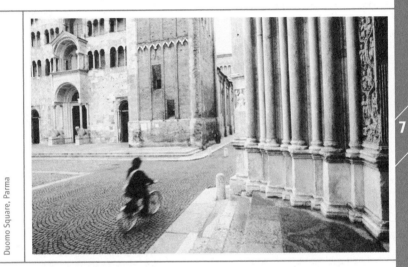

Duomo Square, Parma

WORD OF MOUTH

"Ah, Bologna . . . one of Italy's truly underrated gems. Sitting in an outdoor café in Piazza Maggiore is a true Italian experience."

—HowardR

"The cities in Emilia-Romagna are: (1) gastronomic heavens, (2) off the beaten tourist path, and (3) gastronomic heavens. Did I say that they were gastronomic heavens?"

—tdyls

WELCOME TO EMILIA-ROMAGNA

Tortellacci

TOP 5
Reasons to Go

1. **The signature food of Emilia:** This region's food—the prosciutto crudo, the Parmigiano-Reggiano, the balsamic vinegar, and perhaps above all, the pasta—alone makes the trip to Italy worthwhile.

2. **Mosaics that take your breath away:** The intricate tile creations in Ravenna's Mausuleo di Galla Placidia, in brilliantly well-preserved primary colors, depict pastoral scenes that transport you to another age.

3. **Europe's oldest wine bar:** You won't be the first to have a glass of wine at Osteria al Brindisi, in the heart of medieval Ferrara, beneath an apartment once inhabited by Copernicus—this venerable establishment has been continuously pouring since 1435.

4. **The nightlife of Bologna:** The red-roofed, left-leaning city of Bologna has the oldest student culture in Europe, and still one of the liveliest, from hopping Irish pubs to cutting-edge lounges.

5. **The medieval castles of San Marino:** The three castles are dramatically perched on a rock more than 3,000 feet above the flat landscape of Romagna.

LOMBARDY

Busseto

Piacenza

Fidenza

A1

Parma

Fornovo

Reggio Emilia

A15

63

Castelnovo

LIGURIA

TUSCANY

45

A landscape of medieval castles and crumbling farmhouses begins just east of Milan, in Emilia, where you'll first find the delicious delights of **Parma,** with its buttery prosciutto, famous cheese, and crenellated palaces. Next along the road, continuing east, comes **Modena,** the city of bicycles and balsamic vinegar.

Piazza Grande, Modena
Cattedrale e Torre della Ghirlandina

Getting Oriented

Emilia-Romagna owes its beginnings to the Romans, who built the Via Emilia in 187 BC. Today the road bisects the flat, foggy region, paralleling the Autostrada del Sole (A1), making it easy to drive straight through. Bologna is in the middle of everything, with Piacenza, Parma, and Modena to the west, and Rimini to the east. Ferrara and Ravenna are the only detours—they're to the north of Via Emilia.

Ravenna

Ferrara is a wonderfully characteristic medieval city to the north of Bologna, toward Padua and Venice; the Ferraresi consider themselves part of **Emilia**.

The highlight of Romagna, to the north of the autostrada, is the well-preserved city of **Ravenna**, with its memorable mosaics—glittering treasures left from Byzantine rule.

Emilia's principal cultural and intellectual center is **Bologna**, where rows of street arcades wind around ancient university buildings and grandiose towers, and conceal some of the best food in Italy.

Romagna begins east of Bologna, where spa towns span to the north and south of the Via Emilia and the autostrada, and extends east to the Adriatic, where **Rimini's** murky beaches fill with partying tourists in August.

San Marino, south of Rimini, is an anomaly in every way—it's its own tiny republic, perched incongruously on a cliff above the Romagna plain.

*Map labels:*
A22 · VENETO · Ferrara · Po di Volano · Comacchio · Modena · A13 · 16 · Mare Adriatico · A1 · Bologna · 12 · EMILIA · Ravenna · Pavullo · A1 · Imola · Faenza · A14 · 64 · Vado · Forlì · 9 · Cesenatico · 67 · ROMAGNA · Cesena · Rimini · 71 · 72 · SAN MARINO · THE MARCHES

0   20 mi
0   20 km

Bologna

7

EMILIA-ROMAGNA PLANNER

Making the Most of Your Time

Plan on spending at least two days or nights in Bologna, the region's cultural and historical capital. The next two priorities should be the elegant food center of Parma and the wonderfully characteristic medieval city of Ferrara, followed—in this order—by Ravenna and its memorable Byzantine mosaics, and Modena with its bicycles, harmonious architecture, and famous balsamic vinegar.

If you only have a few days in the region, it's virtually impossible to do all five of those cities justice. If you're a dedicated gourmand, move from Bologna west along the Via Emilia (SS9), to Modena and Parma. If you're more interested in architecture, art, and history, choose the eastern route, heading north on A13 to Ferrara and then southeast on S16 to Ravenna.

If you have more time, you won't have to make such tough choices. You can start in Milan, go east, and finish on the Adriatic—or vice versa. Don't bother with the Adriatic beach resort of Rimini unless it's the peak of summer and you absolutely can't imagine not being on the beach.

Getting Around

Driving is the best way to get around Emilia-Romagna. Roads are wide, flat, and well-marked; distances are short, and beautiful farmhouses and small villages make for easily accessible detours. A car is particularly useful for visiting the spa towns of Romagna, which aren't well connected by train. With the exception of Bologna, the cities themselves are more or less navigable by car as well, although they're also easily walkable, so you may just want to park your car and get around by foot once you hit your hotel. Public transportation, too, is easy, aside from the Romagnan hilltowns. Trains are better than buses. They're fairly efficient and quite frequent, and most stations aren't too far from the center of town. For more about car, bus, and train travel in the region, see "Essentials" at the end of this chapter.

Seeing Through the Fog

Emilia-Romagna is famous for the low-lying fog that comes in from the Adriatic and blankets much of the region in fall and winter. In the cities, the mist can be ghostly and beautiful, but it can also be a driving hazard, with little visibility beyond about 10 yards. You should avoid driving at night in winter, but the problem can arise in the day, too—if it gets too bad, pull off at an Autogrill or café and wait for the fog to lift, and if you're on the road, keep your headlights on and don't exceed 60 km/h. Road signs throughout the region indicate speed limits in fog (nebbia).

Tips for Foodies

Emilia-Romagna is famous for its food tradition. It's the region where tortellini, fettucine, and Parmesan cheese were invented, and it's justly famous worldwide for its balsamic vinegar and hams.

Along with these perfect primary ingredients, the region is dotted with spectacular, out-of-the-way restaurants with haute cuisine to rival any in Europe. These are places that might break your budget but are also likely to blow your mind. If you're moving east into Romagna, take time out to stop for a memorable meal at one of the region's top tables, either in Imola near Dozza, or a Romagnan spa town such as Castrocaro Terme near Forlì or Bagno di Romagna, where you might want to spend a relaxing night after dinner—you won't want to drive after such a meal.

Finding a Place to Stay

Emilia-Romagna has a reputation for an efficiency uncommon in most of the rest of Italy. Even the smallest hotels are well run, with high standards of quality and service. Bologna is very much a businessperson's city, and many hotels there cater to the business traveler, but there are smaller, more intimate hotels as well.

Though prices are high, you can expect an experience delightfully free of the condescending attitude and manipulative pricing schemes that sometimes mar Italy's tourist meccas. The one exception to the rule is Rimini, where the main business is tourism. Its numerous hotels, unlike those in the rest of Emilia-Romagna, have tourist-oriented full- and half-board packages. They overflow during July and August and close down for much of the off-season.

How's the Weather?

You would never visit Emilia-Romagna for the weather—so the season matters less here than it might in other regions. As elsewhere in Italy, fall and spring are best, especially in the Romagna countryside. Cold, gray winters can bring temperatures well below freezing, although the dense fog can be beautiful. It usually snows in the region a few times a year. Summers tend to be hot and humid.

Dining & Lodging Price Categories

WHAT IT COSTS in Euros					
	$$$$	**$$$**	**$$**	**$**	**¢**
Restaurants	over €22	€16–€22	€11–€16	€7–€11	under €7
Hotels	over €220	€160–€220	€110–€160	€70–€110	under €70

Restaurant prices are for a second course (un secondo). Hotel prices are for two people in a standard double room in high season, including tax and service.

TOP PASSEGGIATA

A walk down the Via delle Volte and around the cobble-stoned medieval district of Ferrara is a trip back through time.

Updated by
Robin S.
Goldstein

GOURMETS THE WORLD OVER claim that Emilia-Romagna's greatest contribution to humankind has been gastronomic. Birthplace of fettuccine, tortellini, lasagna, prosciutto, and Parmesan cheese, the region has a spectacular culinary tradition. But there are many reasons to come here aside from the desire to be well fed: Parma's Correggio paintings, Giuseppe Verdi's villa at Sant'Agata, the medieval splendor of Bologna's palazzos and Ferrara's alleyways, and, perhaps foremost, the Byzantine beauty of mosaic-rich Ravenna—glittering as brightly today as it did 1,500 years ago.

As you travel through the region, you encounter sprawling plants of the industrial food giants of Italy, such as Barilla and Fini, standing side by side with the fading villas and farmhouses that have long punctuated the flat, fertile land of the Po plain. Each fall the region's trademark low-lying fog rolls in off the Adriatic and hangs over the Romagnan flatlands for the winter, coloring cities and countryside alike with a spooky, gray glow.

Bologna, the principal city in the region, is a busy cultural capital, less visited but in many ways just as engaging as Italy's more famous tourist destinations—particularly given its acknowledged position as the leading city of Italian cuisine. The rest of the region follows suit: eating is a seminal part of any Emilia-Romagnan experience. The area's history is replete with culinary legends, such as how the original *tortellino* (singular of tortellini) was modeled on the shape of Venus's navel and the original *tagliolini* (long, thin egg pasta) were served at the wedding banquet of Annibale Bentivoglio and Lucrezia d'Este—a marriage uniting two of the noblest families in the region. It's almost impossible to eat badly in Emilia-Romagna, and everything is worth trying—Parma's famed prosciutto and Parmigiano Reggiano cheese, Modena's balsamic vinegar, and the best pasta in the world.

EMILIA

The Via Emilia runs through Emilia's heart in a straight shot from medieval Piacenza, only 67 km (42 mi) southeast of Milan, to thoroughly modern Modena. On the way from the past to the present you encounter many of Italy's cultural riches—from the culinary and artistic treasures of Parma to the birthplace and home of Giuseppe Verdi and the mist-shrouded tangle of streets that make up Ferrara's old Jewish ghetto. It may be tempting to imitate Modena's Ferraris and zoom along the portion of the A1 highway spanning the region, but take time to detour into the countryside, with its decaying farmhouses and 800-year-old abbeys, and to stop for a taste of prosciutto.

Piacenza

 66 km (41 mi) southeast of Milan, 150 km (94 mi) northwest of Bologna.

The city of Piacenza has always been associated with industry and commerce. Its position on the Po River has made it an important inland port since the earliest times; the Etruscans, and then the Romans, had thriv-

EMILIA-ROMAGNA THROUGH THE AGES

Ancient History. Emilia-Romagna owes its beginnings to a road. In 187 BC the Romans laid out the Via Aemilia, a long highway running straight northwest from the Adriatic port of Rimini to the central garrison town of Piacenza, and it was along this central spine that the primary towns of the region developed.

Despite the unifying factor of the Via Emilia, the region has had a fragmented history. Its eastern portion, roughly the area from Faenza to the coast, known as Romagna, has looked first to the Byzantine east and then to Rome for art, political power, and, some say, national character. The western portion, Emilia, from Bologna to Piacenza, had a more northern, rather dour sense of self-government and dissent.

The principal city of Bologna was founded by the Etruscans and eventually came under the influence of the Roman Empire. The Romans established a garrison there, renaming the old Etruscan settlement Bononia. It was after the fall of Rome that the region began its fragmentation. Romagna, centered in Ravenna, was ruled from Constantinople. Ravenna eventually became the capital of the empire in the west in the 5th century, passing to papal control in the 8th century. Even today, the city is still filled with reminders of two centuries of Byzantine rule.

Family Ties. The other cities of the region, from the Middle Ages on, became the fiefs of important noble families—the Este in Ferrara and Modena, the Pallavicini in Piacenza, the Bentivoglio in Bologna, and the Malatesta in Rimini. Today all these cities bear the marks of their noble patrons.

When in the 16th century the papacy managed to exert its power over the entire region, some of these cities were divided among the papal families—hence the stamp of the Farnese family on Parma, Piacenza, and Ferrara.

A Leftward Tilt. Bologna and Emilia-Romagna have established a robust tradition of rebellion and dissent. The Italian socialist movement was born in the region, as was Benito Mussolini—in keeping with the political climate of his home state, he was a firebrand socialist during the early part of his career. Despite having Mussolini as a native son, Emilia-Romagna did not take to fascism: it was here that the antifascist resistance was born, and during World War II the region suffered terribly at the hands of the Fascists and the Nazis.

Despite a long history of bloodletting, turmoil, and rebellion, the arts have always flourished. The great families financed painters, sculptors, and writers. (Dante found a haven in Ravenna after being expelled from his native Florence.) In modern times Emilia-Romagna has given to the arts such famous figures as painter Giorgio Morandi, filmmakers Michelangelo Antonioni and Federico Fellini, and tenor Luciano Pavarotti.

ing settlements on this site. As you approach the city today you could be forgiven for thinking that it holds little of interest. Piacenza is surrounded by ugly industrial suburbs (with particularly unlovely concrete factories and a power station), but forge ahead to discover that they surround a delightfully preserved medieval downtown and an unusually clean city. The prosperity is evidenced by the great shopping along Corso Vittorio Emanuele II.

The heart of the city is the **Piazza dei Cavalli** (Square of the Horses). The flamboyant equestrian statues from which the piazza takes its name are depictions of Ranuccio Farnese (1569–1622) and, on the left, his father, Alessandro (1545–92). Alessandro was a beloved ruler, enlightened and fair; Ranuccio, his successor, was less admired. Both statues are the work of Francesco Mochi, a master sculptor of the baroque period. Dominating the square is the massive 13th-century **Palazzo del Comune**, also known as the Palazzo Gotico. This two-tone, marble-and-brick, turreted and crenellated building was the seat of town government before Piacenza fell under the iron fists of the ruling Pallavicini and Farnese families.

Attached like a sinister balcony to the bell tower of Piacenza's 12th-century **Duomo** is a *gabbia* (iron cage), where miscreants were incarcerated naked and subjected to the scorn (and projectiles) of the crowd in the marketplace below. Inside the cathedral a less-evocative but equally impressive medieval stonework decorates the pillars and the crypt, and there are extravagant frescoes by Il Guercino (aka Giovanni Barbieri, 1591–1666) in the dome of the cupola. The Duomo can be reached by following Via XX Settembre from Piazza dei Cavalli. ⊠ *Piazza Duomo* ☎ *0523/335154* ⊙ *Daily 7:30–12:30 and 4–7:30.*

The **Museo Civico,** the city-owned museum of Piacenzan art and antiquities, is housed in the vast **Palazzo Farnese.** The ruling family had commissioned a monumental palace, but construction, begun in 1558, was never completed as planned. The highlight of the museum's rather eclectic exhibit is the 2nd-century BC Etruscan *Fegato di Piacenza,* a bronze tablet in the shape of a *fegato* (liver), with the symbols of the gods of good and ill fortune marked on it. By comparing this master "liver" with one taken from the body of a freshly slaughtered sacrifice, priests could predict the future. The collection also contains Botticelli's *Madonna with St. John the Baptist.* Reserve ahead for free one-hour guided tours. ⊠ *Piazza Cittadella 29* ☎ *0523/326981* ⊕ *www.musei.piacenza.it* ▣ *€5.25* ⊙ *Tues.–Thurs. 9–1, Fri. and Sat. 9–1 and 3–6, Sun. 9:30–1 and 3–6. Tours Tues.–Thurs. 10, Fri. 10 and 3:30, weekends 9:30, 11, 3, and 4:30.*

The **Galleria d'Arte Moderna Ricci Oddi** has been getting increasing attention for its unusually good collection of paintings from the 1800s and 1900s by luminaries from all over northern and central Italy—with a focus on Tuscany and Emilia. ⊠ *Via San Siro 13* ☎ *0523/320742* ⊕ *www.musei.piacenza.it* ▣ *€4* ⊙ *Tues.–Sun. 10–noon and 3–6.*

Where to Eat

★ $$$$ ✕ **Antica Osteria del Teatro.** On a lovely little square in the center of town, this restaurant is one of the best in all Emilia-Romagna. The 15th-century building, with coffered ceilings and sober furniture, effuses elegance.

The pricey, French-influence menu might be best described as haute Italian; some of the more nouveau flights of fancy might include, for example, a terrine of duck liver with marzipan-stuffed dates. The two tasting menus are an excellent way to sample the kitchen at its best. Service is excellent and the wine list impeccable. ⊠ *Via Verdi 16* ☎ *0523/323777* ⌂ *Reservations essential* ▭ *AE, DC, MC, V* ☉ *Closed Sun. and Mon., Aug. 1–25, and Jan. 1–10.*

$ × **Agnello da Renato.** Simple, small, and cheap: Agnello is an excellent place to plop down for lunch. Try the *tortelli* (small pasta pillows) served *alla Piacentina*, stuffed with ricotta and spinach and bathed in butter and Parmesan, or the *coniglio alla cacciatore* (rabbit in a tomato and white-wine sauce). The restaurant is very central, just steps from the Palazzo Gotico. ⊠ *Via Calzolai 9* ☎ *0523/320874* ▭ *No credit cards* ☉ *Closed Mon.*

Busseto

❷ *30 km (19 mi) southeast of Piacenza, 25 km (15 mi) southeast of Cremona in Lombardy.*

Busseto's main claim to fame is its native son, master composer Giuseppe Verdi (1813–1901). The 15th-century **Villa Pallavicino** is where Verdi

EATING WELL IN EMILIA-ROMAGNA

Emilia-Romagna's reputation as Italy's gourmet haven is well deserved; a visit wouldn't be complete without sampling what the region does best. The specialties are nothing new in name, they're just better here, where they were born—for example, Parma's world-famous prosciuttos and crumbly Parmigiano Reggiano cheese. Bologna's pasta (especially tagliatelle) *al ragù* is in a heavenly, slow-cooked sauce of onions, carrots, minced pork and beef, milk, and (sometimes) fresh tomatoes. The rich, soft, garlicky *mortadella* has been reincarnated elsewhere to its detriment as "baloney."

Pasta Pillows. Among the many Emilian variations on stuffed pasta, *tortelli* and *cappellacci* are larger pasta pillows, about the size of a Brussels sprout, but with the same basic form as tortellini; they're often stuffed with pumpkinlike squash or spinach and cheese. Tortelloni are, in theory, even bigger, although their size varies. Stuffed pastas are generally served simply, with melted butter, sage, and (what else) Parmigiano Reggiano cheese, or *in brodo* (in beef or chicken broth), which brings out the subtle richness of the fillings.

Going Local. Look for the local specialties: although most are served throughout the region, traditionalists have *zampone* (a sausage made from pig's trotter) and *aceto balsamico* (balsamic vinegar) in Modena; their risotto *in padella* (with fresh herbs and tomatoes) in Piacenza; their *brodetto* (tangy seafood stew) in Rimini; their ancient Roman *piadine* (chewy, flat griddle breads)

in Romagna; their *cappellacci di zucca* (pasta filled with pumpkinlike squash) and *salama da sugo* (salty, oily sausage aged and then cooked) in Ferrara; and everything else in Bologna.

Also along the Adriatic coast, don't miss the simply grilled seafood: the *scampi* from the Adriatic, for instance, are a thin, shrimplike crustacean whose tender meat is so sweet that you may swear there's something added. (It's also great in tomato-based pasta sauce.) Razor clams, mussels, and little *noci* (tiny clamlike mussels) are among the sweet, warm-water shellfish available.

Parma is synonymous with prosciutto, but it's not alone in making the meat a specialty. Parma ham's even more prized, and pricey, cousin is the sweet and flavorful *culatello di Zibello*, which is produced along the banks of the Po River, and is cured and aged for more than 11 months.

Wines. Emilia-Romagna's wines accompany the region's fine food rather than vying with it for accolades. The best known is Lambrusco, a sparkling red produced on the Po plain that has some admirers and many detractors. It's praised for its tartness and condemned for the same quality. The region's best wines include Sangiovese di Romagna, which can be similar to Chianti, from the Romagnolan hills, and Barbera, from the Colli Piacentini and Apennine foothills. Castelluccio, Bonzara, Zerbina, Leone Conti, and Tre Monti are among the region's top producers—keep your eyes out for their bottles.

worked and lived with his mistress (and later wife) Giuseppina Strepponi. On display are the maestro's piano, scores, composition books, and walking sticks. At this writing the villa was closed for renovation with the reopening date uncertain. ⌧ *Via Provesi 36* ☎ *0524/92239.*

In the center of Busseto is the lovely **Teatro Verdi,** dedicated, as one might expect, to the works of the hamlet's famous son. Once inside the well-preserved, ornate 19th century–style theater, use your imagination to get a feel for where he worked. Check with the Busseto tourist office for the performance schedule. Nonperformance visits are by appointment only. ⌧ *Piazza G. Verdi 10* ☎ *0524/931732 reservations* ⌧ *€4* ☉ *By appointment Mar.–Oct., Tues.–Sun. 9:30–1 and 3:30–6:30; Nov.–Feb., Tues.–Sun. 9:30–1 and 2:30–5.*

off the
beaten
path

VILLA SANT'AGATA – For Verdi lovers, Sant'Agata (also known as Villa Verdi) is a veritable shrine. It's the grand country home Verdi built for himself in 1849, the place where some of his greatest works were composed. Tours are required, and you have to reserve a few days in advance by phone or on the Web. ⌧ *Via Verdi 22, Sant'Agata Villanova sull'Arda, 4 km (2½ mi) north of Busseto on S588, toward Cremona* ☎ *0523/830000* ⊕ *www.villaverdi.org* ⌧ *€6* ☉ *Apr.–Sept., Tues.–Sun. 9–11:45 and 3–6:45; Jan. 16–Mar. and Oct.–Dec. 15, Tues.–Sun. 9–11:45 and 2:30–5:30; Dec. 16–Jan. 15, Tues.–Sun. by appointment.*

Parma

❸ *40 km (25 mi) southeast of Busseto, 97 km (61 mi) northwest of Bologna.*

Dignified, delightful Parma stands on the banks of a tributary of the Po River. Much of the stately old center has been untouched by modern times, despite damage during World War II. Almost every major European power has had a hand in ruling Parma at one time or another. The Romans founded the city—then little more than a garrison on the Via Emilia—after which a succession of feudal lords held sway. In the 16th century came the ever-avaricious Farnese family (who are still the dukes of Parma) and then, in fast succession, the Spanish, French, and Austrians (after the fall of Napoléon). The French influence is strong. The novelist Stendhal (1783–1842) lived in the city for several years and set his classic *The Charterhouse of Parma* here.

Bursting with gustatory delights, Parma now draws crowds for its sublime cured ham, prosciutto *crudo di Parma* (known locally simply as prosciutto *crudo*). The pale yellow Parmigiano Reggiano cheese produced here and in nearby Reggio Emilia is the original—and best—of a class known around the world as Parmesan. The city's prosperity has long been tied to the Parmalat dairy empire, but at the end of 2003 the once-proud company was brought down by a huge corporate scandal. As the public learned of fictional $4 billion bank accounts and shell holding companies offshore, Parmalat went bankrupt (and even sold off the star players of Parma, the company-owned soccer team that wore trademark blue-and-yellow stripe shirts).

★ **Piazza Garibaldi** is at the heart of Parma. This square is where pedestrians and bicycles come together in a bustle of activity, where all ages sit together at big old cafés, and where the evening *passeggiata* begins. Strada Cavour, leading off the piazza, is Parma's prime shopping street. This square and its buildings, together with the nearby Piazza del Duomo, make up one of the most harmonious, tranquil city centers in Italy.

The delightful, 16th-century domed church **Santa Maria della Steccata** has a wonderful fresco cycle by Parmigianino. The painter took so long to complete it that his patrons imprisoned him briefly for breach of contract. ✉ *Piazza Steccata 9, off Via Dante near Piazza Garibaldi* ☎ *0521/ 234937* ⊕ *www.santuari.it/steccata* ☉ *Daily 9–noon and 3–6.*

The **Teatro Regio** opera house is a local landmark and the site of regular performances. ✉ *Via Garibaldi 16* ☎ *0521/039393* ⊕ *www. teatroregioparma.org* 🎟 *€2* ☉ *Tours by reservation Mon.–Sat. 10:30–noon.*

The **Piazza del Duomo** contains the cathedral, the Battistero, the church of San Giovanni, and the palaces of the bishop and other notables. The magnificent 12th-century **Duomo** has two vigilant stone lions standing guard beside the main door. The arch of the entrance is decorated with a delicate frieze of figures representing the months of the year, a motif repeated inside the baptistery on the right-hand side of the piazza. Some of the church's original artwork still survives, notably the simple yet evocative *Descent from the Cross*, a carving in the right transept by Benedetto Antelami (1150–1230), a sculptor and architect whose masterwork is this cathedral's baptistery.

It is odd to turn from this austere work of the 12th century to the exuberant fresco in the dome, the *Assumption of the Virgin* by Antonio Correggio (1494–1534). The fresco was not well received when it was unveiled in 1530. "A mess of frogs' legs," the bishop of Parma is said to have called it. Today Correggio is acclaimed as one of the leading masters of Mannerist painting. Note that the front facade of the Duomo is undergoing a major renovation and will likely remain hidden by scaffolding through 2006. ✉ *Piazza del Duomo* ☎ *0521/235886* ☉ *Daily 9–12:30 and 3–7.*

The impressive **Battistero** (Bapitstry) has a simple pink-stone Romanesque exterior and an uplifting Gothic interior. The doors are richly decorated with figures, animals, and flowers, and the interior is adorned with figures carved by Antelami showing the months and seasons. ✉ *Piazza del Duomo* ☎ *0521/235886* 🎟 *€3* ☉ *Daily 9–12:30 and 3–6:30.*

Once beyond the elaborate baroque facade of **San Giovanni Evangelista**, the Renaissance interior reveals several works by Correggio; his *St. John the Evangelist* (left transept) is considered the finest. Also in this church (in the second and fourth chapels on the left) are works by Girolamo Parmigianino (1503–40)—a contemporary of Correggio's and the spearhead of the Mannerist art movement. Once seen, Parmigianino's swan-necked Madonnas are never forgotten: they pose with all the precious élan of today's fashion models. The church is next to the Battistero. ⊠ *Piazzale San Giovanni 1, off the Piazza del Duomo* ☎ *0521/235311* ⏱ *Daily 8–noon and 3–7:45.*

In the monastery adjoining the church of San Giovanni Evangelista is the **Spezieria di San Giovanni**—once a pharmacy where Benedictine monks mixed medicines and herbals. Although production stopped in 1881, the 16th-century decorations survive. ⊠ *Borgo Pipa 1, off Piazzale San Giovanni* ☎ *0521/233309* 🎟 *€2* ⏱ *Tues.–Sun. 8:30–1:45.*

Works by Parma's own Correggio and Parmigianino as well as Leonardo da Vinci (1452–1519), El Greco (1541–1614), and Bronzino (1503–72) hang at the **Galleria Nazionale.** The museum is on the ground floor of the rather grim-looking **Palazzo della Pilotta,** which was constructed on the riverbank in about 1600. It's so big that from the air the building is Parma's most recognizable sight—hence the destruction it suffered from Allied bombs in 1944. Much of the building has been restored. The palazzo takes its name from the game *pilotta,* a sort of handball played within the palace precincts in the 17th century.

To enter the Galleria Nazionale, of the palace, you pass through the magnificent baroque **Teatro Farnese,** built in 1628 and based on Palladio's theater in Vicenza. Built entirely of wood, it was burned badly during Allied bombing but has been flawlessly restored. ⊠ *Piazza Pilotta* ☎ *0521/233309* ⊕ *www.artipr.arti.beniculturali.it* 🎟 *€6, theater only €2* ⏱ *Tues.–Sun. 8:30–1:45.*

The **Camera di San Paolo** is the former dining room of the abbess of the Convent of St. Paul. It was extensively frescoed by Correggio, and despite the building's religious character the decorations aren't Christian but rather ravishingly beautiful depictions of mythological scenes—the *Triumphs of the Goddess Diana,* the *Three Graces,* and the *Three Fates.* ⊠ *Via Melloni, off Strada Garibaldi, near Piazza Pilotta* ☎ *0521/233309* 🎟 *€2* ⏱ *Tues.–Sun. 8:30–1:45.*

Where to Stay & Eat

$$–$$$$ ✕ **La Greppia.** The most elegant, most talked-about restaurant in the city is also one of the best. Taste well-known chef Paola Cavazzini's innovative treats like the *anelli con cavolo nero e mostarda della Paola* (small ring-shape pasta with black cauliflower and caramelized fruits) and the *faraona al tartufo nero di Fragno* (guinea hen with black truffle and chestnut puree). Service is personal and friendly, thanks to the place's tiny size, and the unpretentious surroundings keep the focus on the food. There's often a bargain set-price lunch for less than €30. ⊠ *Via Garibaldi 39/a* ☎ *0521/233686* ♤ *Reservations essential* ☐ *AE, DC, MC, V* ⏱ *Closed Mon. and Tues., July, and 1 wk in Dec.–Jan.*

$–$$$$ ✕ **Parma Rotta.** In an old inn 2 km (1 mi) south of the center is an informal neighborhood trattoria with impressive culinary ambitions.
Fodor'sChoice ★ Parma Rotta serves absolutely spectacular grilled steaks, spit-roast lamb, and other meats cooked on a wood-fire grill. The homemade pasta, which

might include ravioli or tortelli, is no less impressive. Dine outdoors under a pleasant trellis in warm weather. ⊠ *Via Langhirano 158* ☎*0521/966738* 🖃*AE, DC, MC, V* ☺ *Closed Mon., Dec. 24–Jan. 10, and Sun. June–Aug.*

$$–$$$ ✕ **Parizzi.** Named for its exciting young chef, Marco Parizzi, this restaurant rivals La Greppia for the title of Parma's finest. A stylish art nouveau interior with Persian rugs complements traditional Parma classics like stuffed tortelli and sublime risotto with Parmigiano Reggiano and shaved white truffles (in season). Try antipasti such as *culatello di Zibello* (the most highly touted of Parma prosciuttos, aged more than 11 months). The wine list is top-notch. ⊠ *Strada Repubblica 71* ☎ *0521/285952* 🍴 *Reservations essential* 🖃 *AE, DC, MC, V* ☺ *Closed Mon., Aug., and 3 wks in Dec. and Jan.*

$–$$$ ✕ **Croce di Malta.** The appealing, old-fashioned restaurant occupies what was once a convent and then an inn. Traditional local fare includes delicate homemade pasta—try the tortelli (with squash filling) or tagliatelle in any fashion. Second courses include well-prepared, hearty versions of classic veal and cheese dishes. The place is also quite serious about wine. ⊠ *Borgo Palmia 8* ☎ *0521/200272* 🍴 *Reservations essential* 🖃 *AE, DC, MC, V* ☺ *Closed Sun.*

$$ ✕ **Osteria dei Mascalzoni.** Carefully placed mood lighting and expensive table settings exude romance: Osteria dei Mascalzoni is thoroughly refined in both conception and execution, yet the place remains somehow young and approachable. Meat dishes, such as the fillet of beef with a delicate cream of leek sauce, are good. The wine list is carefully chosen, with a particularly good selection from Sicily. Leave satisfied and charmed, if a bit poorer for your wine tab. The restaurant is usually open until 1 AM. ⊠ *Vicolo delle Cinque Piaghe 1* ☎ *0521/281809* 🖃 *AE, DC, MC, V* 🍴 *Reservations essential* ☺ *Closed Sun. and 3 wks in Aug.*

★ ¢ ✕ **Enoteca Antica Osteria Fontana.** Gregarious locals flock to the bright yellow, old-school *enoteca* (wine bar) that has a star-studded selection of wines at shockingly good prices. You have to queue up in anarchic fashion for a table—or eat at the bar—and service is brusque. But that's all part of the experience. The grilled *panini* (sandwiches), filled with Emilia's best *salumi* (cured meats), are delicious. Try the *coppa* (an interesting, full-flavor pork sausage) with artichokes, for example. The panini come quartered, so you can share. The place is the best take-out wine store in town, but it closes early (9 PM or before). ⊠ *Strada Farini 24/a, near the Piazza del Duomo* ☎ *0521/286037* 🖃 *MC, V* 🍴 *Reservations not accepted* ☺ *Closed Sun.*

$$$$ 🏨 **Palace Hotel Maria Luigia.** Top-quality and convenient to Old Parma and the train station, the Maria Luigia is popular with business travelers. Some of the traditional rooms, with heavy draperies and wood furniture, have lovely vistas of Parma. It's part of the Italian Sina Hotel chain. ⊠ *Viale Mentana 140, 43100* ☎ *0521/281032* 🖷 *0521/231126* 🌐 *www.sinahotels.com* 🛏 *93 rooms, 12 suites* 🍴 *Restaurant, minibars, bar, meeting room* 🖃 *AE, DC, MC, V* 🍴 *BP.*

$$$ 🏨 **Hotel Stendhal.** The Stendhal is one of Parma's finest hotels. Rooms are smallish, but thickly carpeted and some have chandeliers and antique furniture. A few rooms have views of the Palazzo della Pilotta on the edge of the old center of town. The hotel is newly affiliated with the

Jolly chain, but it's best to reserve through the property directly. ⊠ *Via Bodoni 3, 43100* ☎*0521/208057* 🖷*0521/285655* ⊕*www.hotelstendhal. it* ➟ *62 rooms* ⚫ *Restaurant, minibars, cable TV, bar, Internet, meeting room, some pets allowed* ⊟ *AE, DC, MC, V* ¶◎¶ *BP.*

$–$$ 🖼 **Hotel Torino.** A warm reception and pleasant, relaxed surroundings welcome you to this former convent tucked away in a quiet pedestrian zone in the heart of town. Correggio reproductions hang on the walls of modern, compact rooms. If traveling by car, look online or fax ahead for a detailed map or directions—it's difficult to find. ⊠ *Via Mazza 7, 43100* ☎ *0521/281046* 🖷 *0521/230725* ⊕ *www.hotel-torino.it* ➟ *33 rooms* ⚫ *Cable TV, bar, Internet, some pets allowed* ⊟ *AE, DC, MC, V* ¶◎¶ *BP.*

Nightlife & the Arts

Opera in Parma is taken just as seriously as in Milan, although tickets are a little easier to come by. Performances are staged at the landmark **Teatro Regio** (⊠ Via Garibaldi 16 ☎0521/218678 ⊕ www.teatroregioparma. org). The main opera season is January–March, and the Verdi festival is May–mid-June.

Modena

❹ *56 km (35 mi) southeast of Parma, 38 km (23 mi) northwest of Bologna.*

The area around Modena has gained recognition for three very contemporary names: the opera star Luciano Pavarotti comes from here, and so do the high-performance cars Maserati and Ferrari (sorry no public tours available).With apologies to the Tenor and the Testarossa, however, it's Modena's syrupy balsamic vinegar, aged for up to 40 years, that may still be its greatest achievement. The town has become another Emilian food mecca, with delicious home cooking at every turn. Extensive modern industrial sprawl encircles the center; although the old quarter is small, it is filled with narrow medieval streets, pleasant piazzas, and typical Emilian architecture.

The 12th-century **Duomo,** also known as the Basilica Metropolitana, is a fine example of Romanesque architecture. The exterior is decorated with medieval sculptures depicting scenes from the life of San Geminiano, the city's patron saint, and fantastic beasts, as well as a realistic-looking scene of the sacking of a city by barbarian hordes—a reminder to the faithful to be ever vigilant in defense of the church. The bell tower is made of white marble and is known as **La Ghirlandina** (The Little Garland) because of its distinctive weather vane. The somber church interior is divided by an elaborate gallery carved with scenes of the Passion of Christ. The carvings took 50 years to complete and are by an anonymous Modenese master of the 12th century. The tomb of San Geminiano is in the crypt. ⊠ *Piazza Grande* ☎ *059/216078* ⊕ *www. duomodimodena.it* ◔ *Daily 7–12:30 and 3:30–7.*

Modena's principal museum is housed in the **Palazzo dei Musei,** a short walk from the Duomo. The collection was assembled in the mid-17th century by Francesco d'Este (1610–58), Duke of Modena, and the **Gal-**

leria Estense is named in his honor. The gallery also houses the duke's **Biblioteca Estense,** a huge collection of illuminated books, of which the best known is the beautifully illustrated 15th-century *Bible of Borso d'Este.* A map dated 1501 was one of the first in the world to show Columbus's discovery of America. To get here, follow Via Emilia, the old Roman road that runs through the heart of the town, to Via di Sant'Agostino. ⊠ *Piazza Sant'Agostino 337* ☎ *059/4395711* ⊕ *www.galleriaestense.it* 🖼 *€4* ⊗ *Tues.–Sun. 8:30–7:30, last entrance at 7.*

At the **Consorzio Produttori Aceto Balsamico Tradizionale di Modena** you can do a tasting, have a tour of the small facility with the friendly staff, and, of course, buy their famous balsamic vinegar. ⊠ *Strada Vaciglio Sud 1085/1* ☎ *059/395633* ⊕ *www.balsamico.it* 🖼 *Free* ⊗ *By appointment.*

Where to Stay & Eat

$$$–$$$$ ✕ **Hosteria Giusti.** The ancient stone walls here are shared with what is reputedly the world's oldest deli, the Salumeria Giusti, founded in 1605. There are only four tables and a host of antique furnishings in the tiny room, where the kitchen turns out dishes like your Italian grandmother might have cooked—handmade tagliolini, *gnocco fritto* (fried dough) with salumi from next door, and items using Modena's famous balsamic vinegar. Reserve well ahead; it's an unforgettable Modena experience. ⊠ *Vicolo Squallore 46* ☎ *059/222533* ⚐ *Reservations essential* ▭ *AE, DC, MC, V* ⊗ *Closed Sun. and Mon., Dec., and Aug. No dinner.*

$–$$$ ✕ **Da Enzo.** This big, cheerful, well-patronized trattoria is in the old town's pedestrian zone, a few steps from Piazza Mazzini. All the classic Modenese specialties are represented, including *zampone* (bladder) and *cotechino* (creamy pork sausage). For starters, try the *tortelloni di ricotta e spinaci* (large tortellini stuffed with ricotta and spinach). Reserve ahead for Friday and Saturday night dining. ⊠ *Via Coltellini 17* ☎ *059/225177* ▭ *AE, DC, MC, V* ⊗ *Closed Mon. and Aug. No dinner Sun.*

$$$ 🏨 **Canalgrande.** Once a ducal palace, the Canalgrande today has large, airy rooms appointed with ornate dark-wood and upholstered pieces. The garden has a fountain in back and breakfast is served on a pretty terrace there in summer. The hotel's restaurant, La Secchia Rapita (closed August), gets rave reviews. ⊠ *Corso Canalgrande 6, 41100* ☎ *059/217160* 🖷 *059/221674* ⊕ *www.canalgrandehotel.it* 🛏 *75 rooms, 3 suites* ⚐ *Restaurant, in-room safes, minibars, bar* ▭ *AE, DC, MC, V* ⦿ *BP.*

$–$$ 🏨 **Hotel Centrale.** The name says it all: this old-school hotel couldn't be more central, right around the corner from Piazza Grande. Rooms are basic and functional, with the classic feel of an Italian building whose layers of renovation don't quite cover up its aging design. The beige lobby is spiced up with cheery checkered floors. ⊠ *Via Rismondo 55, 41100* ☎ *059/218808* 🖷 *059/238201* ⊕ *www.hotelcentrale.com* 🛏 *40 rooms, 36 with bath* ⚐ *In-room safes, cable TV, bar, laundry service* ▭ *AE, DC, MC, V* ⊗ *Closed 3 wks in Aug.*

EMILIA:
ONE TASTE AT A TIME

4 towns, dozens of foods, and a mouthful of flavors you'll never forget

Imagine biting into the silkiest prosciutto in the world or the most delectable homemade tortellini you've ever tasted. In Emilia, Italy's most acclaimed food region, you'll discover simple tastes that exceed all expectations. Beginning in Parma and moving eastward to Bologna, you'll find the epicenters of such world-renowned culinary treats as *prosciutto crudo*, Parmigiano-Reggiano, *aceto balsamico*, and tortellini. The secret to this region is not the discovery of new and exotic delicacies, but rather the rediscovery of foods you thought you already knew—in much better versions than you've ever tasted before.

TASTE 1 | PROSCIUTTO CRUDO

From Piacenza to the Adriatic, ham is the king of meats in Emilia-Romagna, but nowhere is this truer than in **Parma.**

Parma is the world's capital of *prosciutto crudo*, raw cured ham (*crudo* for short). Ask for *crudo di Parma* to signal its local provenance; many other regions also make their own crudo.

Quality testing

CRUDO LANGUAGE
It's easy to get confused with the terminology. Crudo is the product that Americans simply call "prosciutto" or the Brits might call "Parma ham." *Prosciutto* in Italian, however, is a more general term that means any kind of ham, including *prosciutto cotto*, or simply *cotto*, which means "cooked ham." Cotto is an excellent product and frequent pizza topping that's closer to (but much better than) what Americans would put in a deli sandwich.

Greasing the ham

Crudo is traditionally eaten in one of three ways: in a dry sandwich (*panino*); by itself as an appetizer, often with shaved butter on top; or as part of an appetizer or snack platter of assorted *salumi* (cured meats).

WHAT TO LOOK FOR
For the best crudo di Parma, look for slices, always cut to order, that are razor thin and have a light, rosy red color (not dark red). Don't be shy about going into a simple *salumeria* (a purveyor of cured meats) and ordering crudo by the pound. You can enjoy it straight out of the package on a park bench—and why not?

Fire branding

BEST SPOT FOR A SAMPLE
You can't go wrong with any of Parma's famed salumerie, but **Salumeria Garibaldi** (Via Farini 9) is one of the town's oldest and most reliable. You'll find not only spectacular prosciutto crudo, but also delectable cheeses, wines, porcini mushrooms, and more.

Quality trademark

LEARN MORE
For more information on crudo di Parma, contact the **Consorzio del Prosciutto di Parma** (Via Marco dell'Arpa 8/b, 0521/243987, www.prosciuttodiparma.com/eng).

Prosciutto di Parma

TASTE 2 | PARMIGIANO-REGGIANO

From Parma, it's only a half-hour trip east to **Reggio Emilia,** the birthplace of the crumbly and renowned Parmigiano-Reggiano cheese. Reggio (not to be confused with Reggio di Calabria in the south) is a cute and characteristic little Emilian town that has been the center of production for this legendary cheese for more than 70 years.

Warming milk in copper cauldrons

SAY CHEESE
Grana is the generic Italian term for hard, aged, full-flavored cheese that can be grated. Certain varieties of Pecorino Romano, for example, or Grana Padano, also fall under this term, but Parmigiano-Reggiano is the foremost example.

NOT JUST FOR GRATING
In Italy, Parmigiano-Reggiano is not only grated onto pasta, but also often served by itself in chunks, either as an appetizer—perhaps accompanied by local salumi—or even for dessert, when it might be drizzled with honey or Modena's balsamic vinegar.

Breaking up the curds

MEET THE MAKERS
If you're a cheese enthusiast, you shouldn't miss the chance to take a free two-hour guided tour of a Parmigiano-Reggiano–producing farm. You'll witness the entire process and get to meet the cheesemakers. Tours can be arranged by contacting the **Consorzio del Formaggio Parmigiano-Reggiano** in Reggio Emilia (0522/506160, sezionere@parmigiano-reggiano.it, www.parmigiano-reggiano.it) at least 20 days in advance. (Ask specifically for an English-language tour if that's what you want.)

Placing cheese in molds

7

BEST SPOT FOR A SAMPLE
The production of Parmigiano-Reggiano is heavily controlled by the Consorzio del Formaggio, so you can buy the cheese at any store or supermarket in the region and be virtually guaranteed equal quality and price. For a more distinctive shopping experience, however, try buying Parmigiano-Reggiano at the street market on Reggio's central square. The market takes place on Tuesday and Friday from 8 AM to 1 PM year-round.

Aging cheese wheels

Parmigiano-Reggiano

TASTE 3 | ACETO BALSAMICO DI MODENA

Tasting tradizionale vinegar

Modena is home to *Aceto Balsamico Tradizionale di Modena*, a species of balsamic vinegar unparalleled anywhere else on Earth. The balsamic vinegar you've probably tried—even the pricier versions sold at specialty stores—may be good on salads, but it bears only a fleeting resemblance to the real thing.

HOW IS IT MADE?

The *tradizionale* vinegar that passes strict government standards is made with Trebbiano grape must (unfermented grape juice), which is cooked over an open fire, reduced, and fermented from 12 to 25 or more years in a series of specially made wooden casks. As the vinegar becomes more concentrated, so much liquid evaporates that it takes more than 6 gallons of must to produce one quart of vinegar 12 years later. The result is an intense and syrupy concoction best enjoyed sparingly on grilled meats, strawberries, or Parmigiano Reggiano cheese. The vinegar has such a complexity of flavor that some even drink it as an after-dinner liqueur.

Wooden casks for fermenting

BEST SPOT FOR A SAMPLE

The **Consorzio Produttori Aceto Balsamico Tradizionale di Modena** (Corso Cavour 60, 059/236981, www.balsamico.it) offers tours and tastings by reservation only. The main objective of the consortium is to monitor the quality of the authentic balsamic vinegar, made by only a few licensed restaurants and small producers.

The consortium also limits production, keeping prices sky high. Expect to pay €50 for a 100-ml (3.4 oz) bottle of tradizionale, which is generally aged 12 to 15 years, or €80 and up for the older tradizionale extra vecchio variety, which is aged 25 years.

OTHER TASTES OF EMILIA

❏ **Cotechino**: a sausage made from pork and lard, a specialty of Modena

❏ **Culatello de Zibello**: raw cured ham produced along the banks of the Po River, and cured and aged for more than 11 months

❏ **Mortadella**: soft, smoked sausage made with beef, pork, cubes of pork fat, and seasonings

❏ **Ragù**: a sauce made from minced pork and beef, simmered in milk, onions, carrots, and tomatoes

❏ **Salama da sugo**: salty, oily sausage aged and then cooked, a specialty of Ferrara

❏ **Tortelli and cappellacci**: pasta pillows with the same basic form as tortellini, but stuffed with cheese and vegetables

WHERE TO EAT

In Modena, it's hard to find a bad meal. Local trattorie do great versions of tortellini and other stuffed pasta. If you can find *zampone* (a sausage made from stuffed pig's trotter), don't miss it—it's an adventurous Modena specialty. **Hosteria Giusti** (Vicolo Squallore 46, 059/222533, www.giusti1605.com) is a particularly good place to try local specialties; the adjacent **Salumeria Giusti** is reputedly the world's oldest deli, founded in 1605.

TASTE 4 | TORTELLINI

The venerable city of **Bologna** is called "Bologna the Fat" for a reason: this is the birthplace of tortellini, not to mention other specialties such as mortadella and ragù. Despite the city's new reputation for chic nightclubs and flashy boutiques, much of the food remains as it ever was.

You'll find the many Emilian variations on stuffed pasta all over the region, but they're perhaps at their best in Bologna, especially the native tortellini.

INSPIRED BY THE GODS
According to one legend, tortellini was inspired by the bellybutton of Venus, goddess of love. As the story goes, Venus and some other gods stopped at a local inn for the night. A nosy chef went to their room to catch a glimpse of Venus. Peering through the keyhole, he saw her lying only partially covered on the bed. He was so inspired after seeing her perfect navel that he created a stuffed pasta, tortellini, in its image.

ON THE MENU
Tortellini is usually filled with beef (sometimes cheese), and is served two ways: *tortellini asciutta* is "dry," meaning it is served with a sauce such as ragù, or perhaps just with butter and Parmigiano. *Tortellini in brodo* is immersed in a lovely, savory beef broth.

BEST SPOT FOR A SAMPLE
Don't miss **Tamburini** (Via Drapperie 1, 051/234726), Bologna's best specialty food shop, where smells of Emilia-Romagna's famous spoils waft out through the room and into the streets.

Making the dough

Stretching the dough

Adding the filling

Shaping each piece

WHERE TO EAT

The classic art deco restaurant **Rosteria Luciano** (Via Nazario Sauro 19, 051/231249, www.rosterialuciano.it) is a great place to try tortellini in brodo, one of the best choices on their fixed menu. A changing list of daily specials augments the menu. For a meat course it's usually best to order whatever special the kitchen has that day. The selection of local cheeses is also good. Please note that the restaurant is closed on Wednesday, the whole month of August, and Sunday from June through September.

Tortellini di Bologna

BOLOGNA

The centuries of wars, sackings, rebellions, and bombings that left such dramatic evidence in other cities of Emilia-Romagna have not taken their toll on Bologna's old city center. Narrow, cobblestone streets remain intact, as do the ancient churches, massive palaces, and medieval towers. Arcades line many of the main thoroughfares, shading the walkways to such an extent that you can stroll around town in a rainstorm for hours without feeling a drop.

Through its long history, first as an Etruscan city then a Roman one, then as an independent city-state in the Middle Ages, Bologna has always played a significant role in the north of Italy. Over the centuries the city has acquired a number of nicknames: Bologna the Learned, in honor of its venerable university, the oldest in the world; Bologna the Red, for its rosy rooftops and communist leanings; Bologna the Turreted, recalling the forest of medieval towers that once rose from the city center (two remarkable examples survive); and Bologna the Fat, a tribute to its preeminent position in the world of cuisine, the birthplace of mortadella, tortellini, and ragù.

Today one might also be tempted to dub it Bologna the Hip, for its position at the cutting edge of Italian culture. Recent years have brought an explosion of trendy *newyorkese* bars and lounges with postmodern music and Germanic track lighting, American brunches and California construction cuisine, and pricey boutiques in primary colors. The result is a jarring juxtaposition of leaning medieval towers and towering modernist fashion billboards. Unfortunately, the influx of people and industry that has accompanied these changes has also brought air and noise pollution, a further distraction from the city's architectural and culinary gems.

Although foreign tourists have lately begun to discover Bologna's special charm and arrive (along with Italians) in increasing numbers, the city's urban vitality still comes in large part from its student population. The university was founded in about the year 1088, and by the 13th century already had more than 10,000 students. It was a center for the teaching of law and theology, and it was ahead of its time in that many of the professors were women. Guglielmo Marconi, the inventor of the wireless telegraph, first formulated his groundbreaking theories in the physics labs of the university. Today the university has prominent business and medical faculties.

Exploring Bologna

Piazza Maggiore and the adjacent Piazza del Nettuno make up the core of the city. Arranged around these two squares are the imposing Basilica di San Petronio, the massive Palazzo Comunale, the Palazzo del Podestà, the Palazzo di Re Enzo, and the Fontana del Nettuno—one of the most visually harmonious groupings of public buildings in the entire country. From here, sights that aren't on one of the piazzas are but a short walk away, along delightful narrow cobbled streets or under the ubiquitous arcades that double as municipal umbrellas. Take at least a full day to explore Bologna; it's compact and lends itself to easy exploration, but there is plenty to see.

The Main Attractions

⑤ **Basilica di San Petronio.** Construction on this cathedral began in the 14th century, and work was still in progress on this vast building some 300 years later. It's not finished yet, as you can see: the wings of the transept are missing and the facade is only partially decorated, lacking most of the marble face the architects had intended. The main doorway was carved by the great Sienese master of the Renaissance, Jacopo della Quercia. Above the center of the door is a Madonna and Child flanked by Saints Ambrose and Petronius, the city's patrons.

The interior of the basilica is huge: the Bolognans had planned an even bigger church—you can still see the columns erected to support the larger church outside the east end—but had to tone down construction when the university seat was established next door in 1561. The **Museo di San Petronio** contains models showing how the church was originally intended to look. The most important artworks in the church are in the left aisle, frescoes by Giovanni di Modena dating from the first years of the 1400s. ✉ *Piazza Maggiore* ☎ *051/225442* ✆ *Free* ☼ *Church*

Apr.–Sept., daily 7:30–1:15 and 2:30–6; Oct.–Mar., daily 7:30–1 and 2:30–6. Museum Mon.–Sat. 9:30–12:30 and 2:30–5:30, Sun. 2:30–5:30.

Fontana del Nettuno. Sculptor Giambologna's elaborate 1566 baroque monument to Neptune occupying Piazza Nettuno has been aptly nick-named *Il Gigante* (The Giant). Its exuberantly sensual mermaids and undraped God of the Sea drew fire when it was constructed, but not enough, apparently, to dissuade the populace from using the fountain as a public washing stall for centuries. It's also known for another reason: walk behind Neptune and to his right for an infamously lewd angle on the statue. ✉ *Piazza Nettuno, next to the Palazzo Re Enzo, Piazza Maggiore area.*

★ ❾ **Le Due Torri.** Two landmark towers, mentioned by Dante in *The Inferno,* stand side by side in the compact Piazza di Porta Ravegnana. Every family of importance had a tower as a symbol of prestige and power, and as a potential fortress; only 60 remain out of more than 200 that once presided over the city. **Torre Garisenda** (from the late 11th century), tilting 10 feet, was shortened to 165 feet for safety in the 1300s and is now closed to visitors. **Torre degli Asinelli** (circa 1109) is 320-feet tall. It leans an alarming 7½ feet off perpendicular. If you're up to a serious physical challenge—and you're not claustrophobic—you may want to climb the 500 narrow, wooden steps to get to the view over Bologna. ✉ *Piazza di Porta Ravegnana, east of Piazza Maggiore* 🎫 €3 ⊙ *Apr.–Sept., daily 9–6; Oct.–Mar., daily 9–5.*

❿ **Santo Stefano.** This splendid and unusual basilica actually contains between four and seven connected churches (authorities differ). Originally
on this site there was a 4th-century pagan temple to Iside, but the oldest remaining component is **Santi Vitale e Agricola,** which dates from
the 8th century. It contains a 14th-century nativity scene much loved
by Bologna's children, who come at Christmastime to pay their respects
to the baby Jesus. Within the church of **San Sepolcro** (12th century) is
the **Cortile di Pilato** (Courtyard of Pilate), named for the basin in its center said to be where Pontius Pilate washed his hands after condemning
Christ. Also in the building is a **museum** displaying various medieval
religious works and with a shop where you can buy sundry items such
as honey, shampoo, and jam made by the monks. ✉ *Via Santo Stefano
24, Piazza Santo Stefano, University area* ⊕ *www.settechiese.it* 🕾 *051/
223256* 🎫 *Free* ⊙ *Mon.–Sat. 9–noon and 3:30–6, Sun. 9–12:45 and
3:30–7.*

FodorsChoice
★

⓭ **Università di Bologna.** Take a stroll through the streets of the university area, a jumble of buildings, some dating as far back as the 15th century and most to the 17th and 18th. The neighborhood, as befits a college town, is full of bookshops, coffee bars, and cheap restaurants. None of them are particularly distinguished, but they're all characteristic of student life in the city. Try eating at the *mensa universitaria* (cafeteria) if you want to strike up a conversation with local students (most speak English). Political slogans and sentiments are scrawled on walls all around the university and tend to be ferociously leftist. The **university museums,** in Palazzo Poggi, display scientific instruments and paleontological, botanical, and university-related artifacts. ⊠ *Via Zamboni 33, University area* ☎ *051/2099602* ⊕ *www.unibo.it/musei-universitari* 🎟 *Free* ⊙ *Mon.–Sat. 9–4, Sun. 10:30–3:30.*

off the beaten path

BASILICA DI SAN LUCA – It's a spectacular one-hour walk (or 10-minute drive) uphill from Porta Saragozza to the Basilica di San Luca at the edge of Bologna's center (follow Via Saragozza). It's an impressive hilltop church that has perched dramatically atop Monte della Guardia since 1160. The entire road is remarkably arcaded the entire way; you walk beneath 666 arches before arriving at the round basilica, which has a famous Madonna icon. But it's the sweeping views of the Emilian countryside and city from the 990-foot altitude that make the trip worthwhile—most of all in autumn, when the leaves of the hills on one side play off the blazing red rooftops of Bologna on the other. If you go by car (or, better yet, scooter), it's possible to ask for directions at the church and take an unmarked route back through the hills, winding past wonderful, rustic Emilian restaurants before reentering the city center through Porta San Mammolo. ⊠ *Via Saragozza, 3½ km (2 mi) southwest of Bologna* ☎ *051/6142339* ⊙ *Oct.–Feb., Mon.–Sat. 7–12:30 and 2:30–5, Sun. 7–5; Mar., Mon.–Sat. 7–12:30 and 2:30–6, Sun. 7–6; Apr.–Sept., 7–12:30 and 2:30–7, Sun. 7–7.*

Also Worth Seeing

❻ Palazzo Comunale. A mélange of building styles and constant modifications characterize this huge palace dating from the 13th to 15th centuries. When Bologna was an independent city-state, this was the seat of government, a function it still serves today. Over the door is a statue of Bologna-born Pope Gregory XIII, most famous for reorganizing the calendar. There are good views from the upper stories of the palace. The first-floor Red Room (City Council Hall) is open on advance request and during some exhibitions.

Within the palazzo there are also two museums. The **Collezioni Comunali d'Arte** exhibits paintings from the Middle Ages as well as some Renaissance works by Luca Signorelli (circa 1445–1523) and Tintoretto. The **Museo Morandi** is dedicated to the 20th-century still-life artist Giorgio Morandi; in addition to his paintings, there's a re-creation of his studio and living space. Underground caves and the foundations of the old cathedral can be visited by appointment made through the tourist office. ⊠ *Piazza Maggiore 6* ☎ *051/203111 Palazzo, 051/203526 Collezioni, 051/203332 Museo* ⊕ *www.museomorandi.it* 🎟 *Palace free, each museum €4, combined ticket €6* ⊙ *Collectoni Tues.–Sat. 9–6:30, Sun. 10–6:30, Museo Tues.–Sun. 10–6.*

The **Biblioteca Sala Borsa,** connected to the Palazzo Comunale, has an impressive interior courtyard surrounded by the library. ⊠ *Entrance from Piazza Nettuno, Piazza Maggiore area* ☎ *051/204400* ⊕ *www.bibliotecasalaborsa.it* 🎟 *Free* ⊙ *Mon. 2:30–9, Tues.–Fri. 9 AM–9:30 PM, Sat. 9–7.*

❼ Palazzo del Podestà. This classic Renaissance palace facing the Basilica di San Petronio was erected in 1484, and attached to it is the soaring **Torre dell'Arengo.** The bells in the tower have rung whenever the city has celebrated, mourned, or called its citizens to arms since 1453. ✉ *Piazza Nettuno, Piazza Maggiore area* ☎ *051/224500* ◷ *During exhibitions only.*

❽ Palazzo Re Enzo. King Enzo of Sardinia was imprisoned in this 13th-century medieval palace for 23 years, until his death in 1272. He had waged war on Bologna and was captured after the fierce battle of Fossalta in 1249. The palace has other macabre associations: common criminals received the last rites of the Church in the tiny courtyard chapel before being executed in Piazza Maggiore. The courtyard is worth peeking into, but the palace merely houses government offices. ✉ *Piazza Re Enzo, Piazza Maggiore area* ☎ *051/224500* ◷ *During exhibitions only.*

⓬ Pinacoteca Nazionale. Bologna's principal art gallery contains many works by the immortals of Italian painting, including the famous *Ecstasy of St. Cecilia* by Raphael. There's also a beautiful multipanel painting by Giotto, as well as *Madonna and Saints* by Parmigianino. ✉ *Via delle Belle Arti 56, University area* ☎ *051/4209411* ⊕ *www.pinacotecabologna.it* ✐ *€4* ◷ *Tues.–Sun. 9–7.*

⓫ San Domenico. The tomb of St. Dominic, who died here in 1221, is called the **Arca di San Domenico** and is found in this church in the sixth chapel on the right. Many artists participated in its decoration, notably Niccolò di Bari, who was so proud of his contribution that he changed his name to Niccolò dell'Arca to recall this famous work. The young Michelangelo carved the angel on the right. In the right transept of the church is a tablet marking the last resting place of the hapless King Enzo, the Sardinian ruler imprisoned in the Palazzo Re Enzo. The attached **museum** displays religious relics and art. ✉ *Piazza San Domenico 13, off Via Garibaldi, south of Piazza Maggiore* ☎ *051/6400411* ◷ *Church daily 7:30–1 and 3:30–7:30; museum weekdays 10–noon and 3:30–6, Sat. 9:30–noon and 3:30–5:30, Sun. 3:30–5:30.*

Bologna walking tours. English-language walking tours (€13) run by the tourist office in Piazza Maggiore depart at 10:30 AM Wednesday, Sat-

WORKING UP AN APPETITE IN BOLOGNA

This tour through the heart of Bologna should take two or three hours. It's the perfect way to work up your appetite for an indulgent lunch—or to walk lunch off in the afternoon—while seeing some of the cities top sights.

Start at the southern end of sprawling Piazza Maggiore at the 14th-century **Basilica di San Petronio ❺**. Its interior is stark and expansive, and the half-finished facade is interesting in its own right. On the west side of Piazza Maggiore is the **Palazzo Comunale ❻**, and at the north end, in the adjoining Piazza Nettuno, is the **Palazzo del Podestà ❼** and its Torre dell'Arengo. In Piazza Nettuno you'll also find the Fontana del Nettuno, aka Il Gigante, the city's informal nerve center and meeting place. To the left (west) is **Palazzo Re Enzo ❽**, a palace with dark medieval associations.

urday, and Sunday. Tours by affiliated organizations also depart the office Monday and Friday at 11 AM and Tuesday, Thursday, and Saturday at 3 PM; bike tours leave Wednesday at 10 AM. ☒ *Tourist office, Piazza Maggiore 1* ☎ *051/246541* ⊕ *www.guidebologna.com.*

Where to Stay & Eat

$$$ ✕ **Al Pappagallo.** The well-known restaurant steps from Le Due Torre has hosted just about everyone, including Alfred Hitchcock. Its long and storied past is documented in the many black-and-white photos that line the tall, white walls. Al Pappagallo is formal and expensive, but this is a classic Bologna experience. Menu options might include the region's famed culatello di Zibello wonderfully paired with a Parmesan mousse and tomato chutney, a filled pasta in an impossibly rich sauce of foie gras and cheese, or an interesting plate of deep-fried meats and fruits. ☒ *Piazza della Mercanzia 3/C, Piazza Maggiore area* ☎ *051/232807* ⚜ *Reservations essential* ⊟ *AE, DC, MC, V* ⊗ *Closed Sun. and Aug.*

★ **$$–$$$** ✕ **Godot Wine Bar.** The buzzing, modern, bi-level Godot (open until 2 AM) is equally popular with students as with wine aficionados. This is the new face of Bologna. The extraordinary wine list is so diverse that you might be able to have, say, a scarce Pugliese bottle that is impossible to find in Puglia. Although the food may be the side attraction here, the basics are solid: they make a mean tagliatelle *al ragù* (with a slow-cooked, tomato-base meat sauce), for instance. ☒ *Via Cartoleria 12, University area* ☎ *051/226315* ⊟ *AE, MC, V* ⊗ *Closed Sun. and 3 wks in Aug.*

★ **$$** ✕ **Da Cesari.** It's the creative menu options—such as delicate squash gnocchi, or a slowly braised veal cheek—that make Da Cesari truly memorable. Area standards such as veal cutlet Bolognese (with ham and melted cheese) are also reasonably priced and well executed. Accompany your meal with wine made by the owner's brother: Cesari's Liano is excellent. The gentle romantic buzz in the dining room is warm and welcoming; the restaurant is in the very heart of the *centro storico* (historic center). ☒ *Via de' Carbonesi 8, south of Piazza Maggiore* ☎ *051/237710* ⚜ *Reservations essential* ⊟ *AE, DC, MC, V* ⊗ *Closed Sun., Aug., and Jan. 1–7.*

Toward the busy, chic Via Rizzoli, which runs east from Piazza Nettuno, is the gleaming glass tourist office complex, which has drawn mixed reviews from locals.

From this central piazza, follow Via Rizzoli directly into the medieval section of the city. At Piazza di Porta Ravegnana, if you're feeling courageous, you can climb the slightly off-kilter Torre degli Asinelli, the taller of **Le Due Torri** ⑨, Bologna's two landmark towers. From Piazza di Porta Ravegnana, take Via Santo Ste-

fano southeast and walk five minutes to the remarkable **Santo Stefano** ⑩, made up of seven connected churches. It's free, and it's one of Bologna's most impressive sights. Wander through the ancient chapels, mausoleums, and courtyards, and you'll eventually come upon the fountain where Pontius Pilate is said to have washed his hands after condemning Christ. From there, head west on Via Farini. Take a left on Via Garibaldi and another left two blocks down to reach the piazza and church of **San Domenico** ⑪. By now,

¢–$$ ✕ **Cantina Bentivoglio.** This two-floor wine-jazz extravaganza is a classic place to relax by night. The ground floor is a dim, bottle-clad wine cellar; the cavernlike basement downstairs has live jazz. The extraordinarily reasonable wine list includes labels from many of Italy's lesser-known regions, and the menu lists pastas, meats, and interesting salads and lighter plates, such as *crostini* (toasted bread) with mozzarella, eggplant, tomato, and roasted peppers. Vegetarian options are plentiful. Doors stay open until 2 AM, and wine is also available to go. ✉ *Via Mascarella 4, University area* ☎ *051/265416* ⊙ *Closed Sun. Oct.–May. No lunch Sat.* ▤ *AE, DC, MC, V.*

¢–$$ ✕ **Victoria.** It's not unusual for this unpretentious and charming trattoria-pizzeria off Via dell'Indipendenza to have lines, so reserve ahead. Locals come for the cheap pizzas, which are indisputably the highlight (*mozzarella di bufala,* buffalo mozzarella, is an excellent topping choice). Pastas and salads are less impressive. The back room has a lovely 17th-century painted wooden ceiling. ✉ *Via Augusto Righi 9/c, north of Piazza Maggiore* ☎ *051/233548* ▤ *AE, DC, MC, V* ⊙ *Closed Thurs.*

$ ✕ **Da Bertino.** Happy diners don't seem to mind the close quarters in the large, bustling space here. Maybe it's because of the incredibly low prices, or maybe it's because popularity hasn't spoiled this traditional neighborhood trattoria and its simple home-style dishes. Highlights are the homemade *paglia e fieno* (yellow and green, plain and spinach, pasta) with sausage and the choices on the steaming tray of *bollito misto* (boiled meats). Ask to be seated in the back, rather than the less attractive room up front. ✉ *Via delle Lame 55, Porta San Felice* ☎ *051/522230* ▤ *AE, DC, MC, V* ⊙ *Closed Sun. and Aug. 4–31. No dinner Sat. June and July. No dinner Mon. Aug.–May.*

¢–$ ✕ **La Scuderia.** A bit of New York chic comes to Bologna via the cutting-edge café–wine bar–performance space in a stunning vaulted ballroom of an old palazzo. Next door to the university, La Scuderia serves as an informal meeting place for hip students and intellectuals. Salads, desserts, lunches, wines by the glass, and American-style Sunday brunch are options. You can just as easily drink coffee over a newspaper at breakfast as flirt over a piña colada in the evening. Many nights there's live jazz. ✉ *Piazza G. Verdi 2, off Via Zamboni, University area* ☎ *051/6569619* ▤ *AE, DC, MC, V* ⊙ *Closed Mon.*

you're probably ready to make lunch your next stop. After your meal, consider spending some time in the university district. Return to the Piazza di Porta Ravegnana (home of the two towers), and head northeast along Via Zamboni. Continue along that street until you reach the **Università di Bologna** ⑬. Wander around the university and take in the student culture—lively cafés, outdoor book stalls, and so on. The university spirit isn't limited to Via Zamboni—also check out Via delle Belle Arti, Via Mascarella, and Via delle Moline. Only the true devotees of Italian painting will want to spend time at the **Pinacoteca Nazionale** ⑫, at the intersection of Belle Arti and Zamboni; it's a comprehensive collection, but nothing is likely to leave you in awe. Linger long enough in the district, and you may be ready for a snack at one of the cafés.

★ ¢–$ ✕ **Tamburini.** Smells of all that is good about Bolognese food waft through the room and out into the streets. Breads, numerous cheeses, salumi such as Parma and Bologna hams and prosciuttos, roasted peppers, inventive salads, balsamic vinegars, local olive oils, smoked salmon, and fresh pasta are among the delights. This upscale deli–cum–self-service buffet is *the* lunch spot. Tamburini also vacuum-packs foods for shipping or air travel. ☒ *Via Drapperie 1, Piazza Maggiore area* ☎ *051/ 234726* ▤ *AE, MC, V* ☽ *No dinner.*

★ $$$$ ⌂ **Corona d'Oro 1890.** A medieval printing house in a former life, this hotel is delightful—lyrically art nouveau in its reception and atrium, with enough flowers for a wedding. Guest rooms make opulent use of original 15th- and 16th-century decorations such as painted wood ceilings and Gothic-vault windows. The morning English breakfast buffet is worth getting up for. ☒ *Via Oberdan 12, north of Piazza Maggiore, 40126* ☎ *051/236456* ⎙ *051/262679* ⊕ *http://corona.hotel-bologna.net* ↩ *35 rooms* ♿ *In-room safes, minibars, cable TV, bicycles, bar, Internet, meeting room, parking (fee), some pets allowed, no-smoking rooms* ▤ *AE, DC, MC, V* ☽ *Closed 1st 3 wks in Aug.* ⦿ *BP.*

★ $$$$ ⌂ **Grand Hotel Baglioni.** Sixteenth-century paintings and frescoes by the Bolognese Carracci brothers are rarely seen outside a museum or church, but in this 15th-century palazzo they provide the stunning backdrop for the public rooms and restaurant of one of Italy's most glamorous hotels. Lady Di slept here, and you may feel no less royal in a handsome room with antique furniture and brocaded walls. The highly regarded I Carracci restaurant serves top-notch food in regal, formal surroundings. ☒ *Via dell'Indipendenza 8, north of Piazza Maggiore, 40121* ☎ *051/225445* ⎙ *051/ 234840* ⊕ *www.baglionihotels.com* ↩ *113 rooms, 11 suites* ♿ *Restaurant, in-room data port, some in-room fax, in-room safes, minibars, cable TV, bar, babysitting, meeting room, laundry service, Internet, business services, parking (fee), no-smoking rooms* ▤ *AE, DC, MC, V* ⦿ *BP.*

$$$–$$$$ ⌂ **Art Hotel Commercianti.** Rooms here were designed to retain the structural integrity of the 11th-century palace and tower the hotel occupies, and are therefore cozy and unique, with original wood beams built into the walls. Tower rooms and suites have balconies with magnificent views of San Domenico church; all are stylishly furnished with, among other things, Carrara marble desks custom-built following a 15th-century design. ☒ *Via De' Pignattari 11, south of Piazza Maggiore, 40124* ☎ *051/7457511* ⎙ *051/7457522* ⊕ *http://commercianti.hotel-bologna. net* ↩ *32 rooms, 2 suites* ♿ *Dining room, in-room safes, minibars, bicycles, bar, parking (fee)* ▤ *AE, DC, MC, V* ⦿ *BP.*

★ $$$–$$$$ ⌂ **Art Hotel Novecento.** A design-oriented hotel inspired by 1930s Europe, Novecento is at its core modern, modern, modern. Clean lines and elegant restraint are the hallmarks of the rooms, the lobby, and even the elevators. Breakfast is great and happy hour comes with free wine and snacks. The hotel's in the middle of everything in downtown Bologna: call ahead if you need a parking space, and be advised that the garage closes for the night. ☒ *Piazza Gallilei, Piazza Maggiore area, 40126* ☎ *051/7457311* ⎙ *051/7457322* ⊕ *http://novecento.hotel-bologna. net* ↩ *25 rooms* ♿ *Dining room, in-room safes, minibars, bar, parking (fee), no-smoking rooms* ▤ *AE, DC, MC, V* ⦿ *BP.*

$$$-$$$$ ▦ **Art Hotel Orologio.** Although occupying an old palazzo, which was originally a public building, the Orologio achieves a contemporary effect. A mid-level lounge and Internet room is a pleasant place to relax, and top-floor rooms have good views of Bologna's skyline. Under the same ownership as the other Art Hotels and the Corona d'Oro, this hotel is in a quiet pedestrian zone off Piazza Grande—an ideal sightseeing location. Fax ahead or check the Web site for driving directions. ⊠ *Via IV Novembre 10, Piazza Maggiore area, 40123* ☎ *051/7457411* 📠 *051/ 7457422* ⊕ *http://orologio.hotel-bologna.net* ⤳ *29 rooms* ♨ *Dining room, in-room safes, minibars, cable TV, bicycles, Internet, parking (fee), some pets allowed* ▭ *AE, DC, MC, V* ⊚⊚ *BP.*

$$ ▦ **Accademia.** Looking for a midrange, comfortable base for exploring the area? This small hotel is right in the center of the university quarter. The rooms are adequate, the staff friendly. Look for discounted prices on the Web site. A few more inexpensive rooms have a shared bath. ⊠ *Via delle Belle Arti 6, at Via delle Moline, University area, 40126* ☎ *051/ 232318* 📠 *051/263590* ⊕ *www.hotelaccademia.com* ⤳ *28 rooms, 24 with bath* ♨ *Bar, minibars, cable TV, parking (fee), pets allowed* ▭ *MC, V* ⊚⊚ *BP.*

$ ▦ **San Vitale.** Modern furnishings and a garden distinguish this modest hostelry, about 1 km (½ mi) east of the center of town. The service is courteous, and rooms are clean and bright. There are private bathrooms, but facilities are very basic. ⊠ *Via San Vitale 94, University area, 40125* ☎ *051/225966* 📠 *051/239396* ⤳ *17 rooms* ♨ *Internet, parking (fee)* ▭ *No credit cards.*

Nightlife & the Arts

The Arts
Bologna's arts scene is one of the liveliest in Italy, reaching out not just to the traditional older crowds of operagoers and ballet fans, but also to younger generations and food lovers with regional festivals.

BALLET You can see ballet performances at the **Arena del Sole** (⊠ Via Indipendenza 44, north of Piazza Maggiore ☎ 051/2910910 ⊕ www. arenadelsole.it); the theater opened in 1810.

FESTIVALS The first weekend in October crowds celebrate the **Festa di San Petronio** with bands, fireworks, and free mortadella sandwiches in Piazza Maggiore. Named after city's two-letter license-plate abbreviation, **Made in BO** (☎051/533880 ⊕www.madeinbo.it) is a popular local series of nightly outdoor concerts that runs for a month and a half June–August in the Parco Nord, near the Fiera. Free movies are shown at the **Open-air Cinema** in Piazza Unità June–August. The tourist office has the schedule.

MUSIC & OPERA The 18th-century **Teatro Comunale** (⊠ Largo Respighi 1, University area ☎ 199/107070 ⊕ www.comunalebologna.it) presents concerts by Italian and international orchestras throughout the year, but is dominated by the highly acclaimed opera performances November–May. Reserve seats well in advance. The ticket office is open Tuesday–Saturday 11–6:30.

Accademia Filarmonica, the city's principal music school, calls the **Sala Mozart** (⊠ Via Guerazzi 13, University area ☎ 051/222997) home.

Come to **Sala Bossi** (⊠ Piazza Rossini 2, University area ☎ 051/233975) for all types of classical music—and opera.

Nightlife

As a university town, Bologna has long been known for its hopping nightlife. As early as 1300 it was said to have had 150 taverns. Most of the city's current 200-plus pubs and lounges are frequented by Italian students, young adults, and the international study-abroad crowd, with the university district forming the epicenter. In addition to the university area, the pedestrian-only zone on Via del Pratello, lined with a host of pubs, is also a hopping night scene, as is Via delle Moline, with cutting-edge cafés and bars. A more upmarket, low-key evening experience can be had at one of Bologna's many new wine bars that are also restaurants, such as Cantina Bentivoglio and Godot Wine Bar. And then there are the hypertrendy bar-lounges that represent the newest, and most *newyorkese*, of Bologna's many faces; some of these joints make even Milan look old-school.

With live jazz staged every night (€4 cover), **Cantina Bentivoglio** (⊠ Via Mascarella 4/b, University area ☎ 051/265416) is one of Bologna's most appealing nightspots. You can light meals and nibbles as well. At **Le Stanze del Tenente** (⊠ Via del Borgo di S. Pietro 1, University area ☎ 051/228767) you can sip an *aperitivo* (aperitif) or a late-night drink at a modern bar under 17th-century frescoes in what was the private chapel of the 1576 Palazzo Bentivoglio. The adjoining avant-garde restaurant serves modern Italian fusion cooking.

The casually hip **Divinis** (⊠ Via Battibecco 4/c, University area ☎ 051/2961502) wine bar has a remarkable, if pricey, selection by the glass (as well as high-end food) served in chichi surroundings until 1:30 AM. A wine bar with romantic ambient lighting and a good draft beer selection, **Cantavalli** (⊠ Via Belle Arti 2, University area ☎ 051/268395) is relaxing choice.

To find a young, tipsy, boisterous international crowd, head for **The Cluricaune** (⊠ Via Zamboni 18/b, University area ☎ 051/263419) Irish pub. If your taste runs toward the English pub, try **Lord Lister** (⊠ Via Zamboni 56, University area ☎ 051/240886), which draws loads of students, study-abroaders, and expats.

The elegant and trendy **Bar Calice** (⊠ Via Clavature 13/a, at Via Marchesana, Piazza Maggiore area ☎ 051/264508) runs an indoor-outdoor operation year-round (with heat lamps); it's a cocktail and wine bar that's extremely popular with the see-and-be-seen thirtysomethings. The loud, modern, haywire **Nu Bar Lounge** (⊠ Off Buco San Petronio, Via de' Musei 6, Piazza Maggiore area ☎ 051/222532) hosts a self-confident crowd. Join the crowd sipping *prosecco,* a dry, sparkling white wine, or cocktails here and sometimes munching on light food. **Room** (⊠ Via Fossalta 3, Piazza Maggiore area ☎ 051/2961274) is a postmodern fantasy lounge with exposed pipes, industrial furnishings, and low-to-the-ground pillow-seats. The staff is composed entirely of beautiful people.

7

Shopping

Books

Next to the Due Torri is the best bookstore in the region, **Feltrinelli** (✉ Piazza Ravegnana 1, east of Piazza Maggiore ☎ 051/266891 ⊕ www.lafeltrinelli.it), which capitalizes on the university town setting. Look at **Feltrinelli International** (✉ Via Zamboni 7/b, east of Piazza Maggiore ☎ 051/268070), one of Italy's best selectiona of English and other foreign-language books, and innumerable travel guides and maps.

Clothing

A host of small clothing and jewelry shops lines Via d'Azeglio in the center of town. For cheaper goods, Via dell'Indipendenza between the station and downtown is often lined with street vendors hawking bargain-basement clothing.

One of the most upscale malls in Italy, the **Galleria Cavour** (✉ Piazza Cavour, south of Piazza Maggiore) houses many of the fashion giants, including Gucci, Versace, and the jeweler and watchmaker Bulgari.

Wine & Food

Bologna is a good place to buy wine. Several shops have a bewilderingly large selection—to go straight to the top, ask the managers which wines were awarded the prestigious *Tre Bicchieri* (Three Glasses) award from Gambero Rosso's wine bible, *Vini d'Italia*.

Repeatedly recognized as one of the best wine stores in Italy, **Enoteca Italiana** (✉ Via Marsala 2/b, north of Piazza Maggiore ☎ 051/227132) lives up to its reputation with shelves lined with excellent selections from all over Italy at reasonable prices. Their delicious sandwiches with wine by the glass also make a great stand-up light lunch. Friendly owners run the midsize, down-to-earth **Scaramagli** (✉ Strada Maggiore 31/d, University area ☎ 051/227132) wine store.

For fresh produce, meats, and other foods sold in traditional Italian markets, head to **Via Oberdan,** the street just off Via dell'Indipendenza downtown (✉ Piazza Maggiore). The gargantuan **City Market** (✉ Piazza VIII Agosto, off Via dell'Indipendenza north toward the train station) has vendors of every imaginable sort hawking wares of variable quality, including food, clothing, shoes, books, and every imaginable household necessity. It's open Monday–Saturday during daylight hours.

FERRARA

⓮ *47 km (29 mi) northeast of Bologna, 74 km (46 mi) northwest of Ravenna.*

Today you are likely to be charmed by Ferrara's prosperous air and meticulous cleanliness, its excellent local restaurants and fin-de-siècle coffeehouses, and its hospitable, youthful spirit: a boisterous mass of winedrinkers gathers outside the Duomo on even the foggiest of weekend evenings. Though Ferrara is a UNESCO world heritage site, the city still draws amazingly few tourists—which only adds to its appeal. The legendary Ferrarese filmmaker Michelangelo Antonioni called his beloved hometown "a city that you can see only partly, while the rest disappears to be imagined," and perhaps he was referring to the low-lying mist that rolls in off the Adriatic each winter and shrouds Ferrara's winding knot of medieval alleyways, turreted pleasure palaces, and ancient wine bars—once inhabited by the likes of Copernicus—in a ghostly fog. But perhaps Antonioni was also suggesting that Ferrara's striking beauty often conceals a dark and tortured past.

Although the site was first settled before the time of Christ and was once ruled by Ravenna, Ferrara's history really begins with an ominous event—the arrival of the Este in 1259. For more than three centuries the infamous dynasty ruled with an iron fist; brother killed brother, son fought father, husband murdered wife. The majestic castle with moat, which now guards the heart of Ferrara's old town in innocuous splendor, was originally built as a fortress to protect the ruthless Este dukes from their own citizens; deep within the castle's bowels the Este kept generations of political dissidents in dank cells barely larger than a human body. The greatest of the dukes, Ercole I (1433–1505), attempted to poison a nephew who challenged his power, and when that didn't work he beheaded him. Yet it is to this pitiless man that Ferrara owes its great beauty. In one of his more empathetic moments, Ercole invited Sephardic Jews exiled from Spain to settle in Ferrara, spawning half a millennium of Jewish history that came to a spectacular end as Italy succumbed to Axis ideology. The maze of twisting cobblestone streets that forms the old ghetto witnessed the persecution of its Jews once fascist Italy came under the spell of Nazi Germany, a tragedy documented in Giorgio Bassani's book and Vittorio De Sica's canonical neorealist film, *The Garden of the Finzi-Continis.*

If you plan to explore the city fully, consider buying a museum card (€12.40) at the Palazzo dei Diamanti or at one of the art museums around town; it grants admission to every museum, palace, and castle in Ferrara. A combined ticket for the Palazzo Schifanoia and its museum, the Palazzina Marfisa d'Este, and the Museo della Cattedrale costs €6.70. The first Monday of the month is free at many museums.

★ Naturally enough, the building that was the seat of Este power dominates the town: the massive **Castello Estense** is a perfectly preserved castle in the center of the city in Piazza Castello. The building was a suitable symbol for the ruling family: cold and menacing on the outside, lavishly decorated within. The public rooms are grand, but deep in the bowels of the fortress are chilling dungeons where enemies of the state were held in wretched conditions—a function these quarters served as recently as 1943, when antifascist prisoners were detained there. In particular, the **Prisons of Don Giulio, Ugo, and Parisina** have some fascinating features, like 15th-century smoke graffiti protesting the imprisonment of the young lovers Ugo and Parisina, who were beheaded in 1425.

The castle was established as a fortress in 1385, but work on its luxurious ducal quarters continued into the 16th century. Representative of Este grandeur are the **Sala dei Giochi,** extravagantly painted with pagan athletic scenes, and the **Sala dell'Aurora**, decorated to show the times of the day. The tower, the terraces of the castle, and the hanging garden—once reserved for the private use of the duchesses—have fine views of the town and the surrounding countryside. You can cross the castle's moat, traverse its drawbridge, and wander through many of its arcaded passages at any time; in the still of a misty night, the experience is haunting. ⊠ *Piazza Castello* ☎ *0532/299233* ⌨ *Castle €6, tower €1 extra* ⊙ *Castle Tues.–Sun. 9:30–5:30, ticket office closes at 4:45; tower Tues.–Sun. 10–4:45.*

★ The magnificent Gothic **Duomo,** a few steps away from the Castello Estense, has a three-tier facade of bony arches and beautiful carvings over the central door. It was begun in 1135 and took more than 100 years to complete. The interior was completely remodeled in the 17th century. ⊠ *Piazza Cattedrale* ☎ *0532/207449* ⊙ *Mon.–Sat. 7:30–noon and 3–6:30, Sun. 7:30–12:30 and 3:30–7:30.*

Some of the original decorations of the town's main church, the Ex-chiesa e chiostro di San Romano, reside in the **Museo del Duomo** across the street from today's Duomo. ⊠ *Via San Romano* ☎ *0532/209988* ⊕ *www. comune.fe.it/musei-aa/schifanoia/catte.html* ⌨ *€5* ⊙ *Tues.–Sun. 9–2.*

The oldest and most characteristic area of Ferrara is to the south of the Duomo, stretching between the Corso Giovecca and the city's ramparts. Here various members of the Este family built pleasure palaces, the most famous of which is the **Palazzo Schifanoia** (*schifanoia* means "carefree" or, literally, "fleeing boredom"). Begun in the 14th century, the palace was remodeled in 1466 and was the city's first Renaissance palazzo. The interior is lavishly decorated, particularly the **Salone dei Mesi,** with an extravagant series of frescoes showing the months of the year and their mythological attributes. The adjacent **Museo Civico Lapidario** has a collection of coins, statuary, and paintings. ⊠ *Via Scandiana 23* ☎ *0532/ 209988* ⊕ *www.comune.fe.it/musei-aa/schifanoia/skifa.html* ⌨ *€ 5* ⊙ *Tues.–Sun. 9–6.*

The grand but unfinished courtyard is the most interesting part of the luxurious **Palazzo di Ludovico il Moro,** a magnificent 15th-century dwelling built for Ludovico Sforza, husband of Beatrice d'Este. The palazzo contains the region's **Museo Archeologico,** a repository of relics of early man, Etruscans, and Romans found in the country surrounding the city. ⊠ *Via XX Settembre 124, near Palazzo Schifanoia* ☎ *0532/66299* ⌨ *€4* ⊙ *Tues.–Sun. 9–2.*

The courtyard of the peaceful **Palazzo del Paradiso** contains the tomb of the great writer Ariosto (1474–1533), author of the most popular work of literature of the Renaissance, the poem *Orlando Furioso*. The building now houses the city library, the **Biblioteca Ariostea.** ⊠ *Via delle Scienze 17* ☎ *0532/418200* ⌨ *Free* ⊙ *Weekdays 9–7:30, Sat. 9–5:30.*

One of the best-preserved of the Renaissance palaces along Ferrara's old streets is the charming **Casa Romei.** Downstairs are rooms with 15th-century frescoes and several sculptures collected from destroyed churches. The house stands not far from the Palazzo del Paradiso, in the area behind Ferrara's castle. The schedule varies with exhibits. ⊠ *Via Savonarola 30* ☎ *0532/240341* 🎫 *€2* ☉ *Tues.–Sun. 8:30–7:30.*

On the busy Corso Giovecca is the **Palazzina di Marfisa d'Este,** a grandiose 16th-century home that belonged to a great patron of the arts. The house has painted ceilings, fine 16th-century furniture, and a garden containing a grotto and an outdoor theater. ⊠ *Corso Giovecca 170* ☎ *0532/209988* ⊕ *www.comune.fe.it/musei-aa/schifanoia/marfi.html* 🎫 *€3* ☉ *Tues.–Sun. 9–1 and 3–6.*

The collection of ornate religious objects in the **Museo Ebraico** (Jewish Museum) bears witness to the long history of the city's Jewish community. This history had its high points—1492, for example, when Ercole I invited the Jews to come over from Spain—and its lows, notably 1624, when the papal government closed the **ghetto,** which was reopened only with the advent of a united Italy in 1859. The triangular warren of narrow, cobbled streets that made up the ghetto originally extended as far as Corso Giovecca (originally Corso Giudecca, or Ghetto Street); when it was enclosed, the neighborhood was restricted to the area between Via Scienze, Via Contrari, and Via di San Romano. The museum, in the center of the ghetto, was once Ferrara's synagogue. A guided tour is required to visit. ⊠ *Via Mazzini 95* ☎ *0532/210228* 🎫 *€4* ☉ *Guided tours Sun.–Thurs. at 10, 11, and noon.*

One of the streets most characteristic of Ferrara's past, the 2-km-long (1-mi-long) **Via delle Volte,** is also one of the oldest preserved medieval streets in Europe. The series of ancient *volte* (arches) along the narrow cobblestone alley once joined the merchants' houses on the south side of the street to their warehouses on the north side. The street ran parallel to the banks of the river Po, which was home to the busy port of ancient Ferrara.

The **Palazzo dei Diamanti** (Palace of Diamonds) is so called because of the 12,600 small, pink-and-white marble pyramids ("diamonds") that stud the facade. The building was designed to be viewed in perspective—both faces at once—from diagonally across the street. Originally built in the 15th and 16th centuries, today the palazzo contains the Pinacoteca Nazionale, which has an extensive art gallery and rotating exhibits. ⊠ *Corso Ercole I d'Este 19–21* ☎ *0532/205844* 🎫 *€4* ☉ *Tues., Wed., Fri., and Sat. 9–2, Thurs. 9–7, Sun. 9–1.*

WORD OF MOUTH

"Check out what special exhibits are at Ferrara's Palace of Diamonds at the time of your visit. We were lucky enough to hit a John Singer Sargent exhibit, exclusively his work in Italy."   –Ralstonlan

Where to Eat

★ **$$$–$$$$** ✕ **Max.** A modern, minimalist restaurant steps from the Castello Estense is quietly turning the Ferrara dining scene on its head. Exciting *alta cucina* (haute cuisine) dishes at Max include an absolutely spectacular plate of raw shellfish from the nearby Adriatic. In the deconstructed eggplant parmigiana, pieces of eggplant are molded into an impossibly soft *sformatino* (soufflelike dish) with a bechamel sauce and sweet *scampi* (a Mediterranean shellfish); a whole crisped tomato sits off to the side. In spite of the restaurant's relative formality, the service is friendly. ⊠ *Piazza Reppublica 16* ☎ *0532/209309* ⌔ *Reservations essential* ▤ *AE, DC, MC, V* ☉ *Closed Mon.*

$$–$$$ ✕ **Quel Fantastico Giovedì.** Naming the restaurant after a Steinbeck novel, *Sweet Thursday,* is not where the artistic ambitions here end. The restaurant's "art director" chooses the outlandishly modern work that lines the walls of the warm, cozy space. Food preparations are no less creative: the excellent plate of sashimi is sliced more like carpaccio, and might include Sicilian red tuna and Mediterranean bass. Even the steamed shrimp and the gnocchi carbonara are impressive. You can enjoy all this, accompanied by a selection from the extraordinary wine list until about midnight. ⊠ *Via Castelnuovo 9* ☎ *0532/760570* ⌔ *Reservations essential* ▤ *AE, DC, MC, V* ☉ *Closed Wed.*

$$–$$$ ✕ **Trattoria La Romantica.** The former stables of a 17th-century merchant's house have been transformed into this casually elegant, welcoming restaurant, which is a great favorite among well-fed locals. Although the decor (warm light and wood-beam ceilings, incongruous prints, and a piano) seems to be in perpetual transition, the haute-rustic food is fully realized. Ferrarese specialties like *cappellacci di zucca* (large, squash-filled pasta pillows in a cream sauce with tomato, walnuts, and Parmesan) are served side by side with French oysters. ⊠ *Via Ripagrande 36* ☎ *0532/765975* ▤ *AE, DC, MC, V* ☉ *Closed Wed., Jan. 7–17, and July 1–17.*

$$ ✕ **Hostaria Savonarola.** Into the wee hours an avant-garde buzz emanates from the bright, bustling bar that is an informal restaurant at lunch. Despite the hip clientele, the menu—scrawled on a chalkboard—is simple and traditional, focusing on a few daily preparations of good local ingredients. Risotto *in crema di zucca* makes creamy use of Ferrara's trademark small, pumpkinlike squash, and *papardelle al sugo d'anatra* pairs wide, flat noodles with a duck sauce. Service is warm, and outdoor tables couldn't be better for castle views. You can also buy good local salumi to go. ⊠ *Piazza Savonarola 12/16* ☎ *0532/200214* ▤ *AE, DC, MC, V* ☉ *Closed Mon. No dinner.*

$$ ✕ **Osteria del Ghetto.** Though the casually elegant *osteria* (tavernlike restaurant) is buried deep in the old Jewish ghetto, its seasonal menu is anything but old-fashioned. Dishes here represent the cutting edge of Ferrarese cooking: basmati rice torte with Colonnata lard and boletus mushrooms; eggplant flan with cold *grana* (aged, granulated cheese) cream; a lukewarm pheasant salad with balsamic vinegar. The dining room is modern and relaxing, with wood-beamed ceilings, a no-smoking section, and tables on the street in summer. ⊠ *Via Vittorio 26/28* ☎ *0532/764936* ▤ *AE, DC, MC, V* ☉ *Closed Tues.*

$–$$ ✕ **Antica Trattoria Volano.** Local businessmen often fill this white-wall, traditional-to-the-core neighborhood trattoria. The decor is rustic and the food includes such local treats as cappellacci di zucca and a good version of *salama da sugo,* a salty and oily boiled sausage served over mashed potatoes. *Tris* is a first course sampler of three pastas that change nightly. ⊠ *Via Volano 20* ☎ *0532/761421* ▤ *AE, DC, MC, V* ☉ *Closed Fri.*

Talking Politics

Emilia-Romagna might seem staid: city after city has immaculate streets filled with smartly dressed businessmen in impeccable shoes, covertly murmuring to each other through the winter fog over cups of coffee. But after dark, from Parma to Bologna, Piacenza to Ferrara, the middle managers are replaced on the streets by young, energetic would-be intellectuals, and the murmurs turn into impassioned political discussion—usually with a leftist slant—over jugs of table wine. If you enjoy this type of conversation, take time to stop for a drink after dinner in a student cafeteria, cozy café, or back-alley bar. Don't be afraid to join in—all ages are welcome, and divergent opinions, thoughtfully argued, are treated with respect. (Locals are usually happy to practice their English, which can often be quite good.) You'll experience another side of the region—a side that's important to understanding the culture and history.

$–$$ ✕ **Guido Ristorante.** Locals in the know frequent this restaurant on a cobbled street in the Jewish ghetto. The menu here has Ferrarese specialties plus a few inventive combinations you won't find elsewhere, such as gnocchi in curry sauce with black olives and zucchini. The fish is fresh, and pastas are delicate and perfectly cooked. Exposed brick and old wooden beams make the dining space intimate. ⊠ *Via Vignatagliata 61* ☎ *0532/761052* ▤ *AE, DC, MC, V* ⊙ *Closed Thurs. and July.*

★ ¢–$ ✕ **Osteria Al Brindisi.** Ferrara is a city of wine bars, beginning with this, Europe's oldest, which began pouring in 1435. This might just be the most perfect place to drink wine in Italy—Copernicus, who once lived upstairs, seemed to think so. Prices are low, the ambient lighting soft, and even the music (usually good jazz) somehow feels just right. There's a great selection by the glass, or you can choose from among the thousands of national and international bottles that line the ancient walls. A memorable spread of salumi and local cheeses is available, as well as tasty hot meals such as tortellini in brodo. ⊠ *Via degli Adelardi 11* ☎ *0532/209142* ▤ *AE, DC, MC, V* ⊙ *Closed Mon.*

The **Prenotel hotel reservation hot line** (☎ 0532/462046), run by the city, allows you to make reservations at any of the accommodations listed below, among many others.

$$–$$$ 🛏 **Hotel Ripagrande.** The courtyards, vaulted brick lobby, and breakfast room of this 15th-century noble's palazzo retain much of their lordly Renaissance flair. Rooms are decidedly more down-to-earth, but standard doubles and some of the enormous bi- and tri-level suites have faux-Persian rugs, tapestries, and cozy antique furniture; top-floor rooms and suites resemble a Colorado ski lodge, with terraces, and are roomy—especially good for families. Everything here, including the room service is impeccable. You can't beat the prime but quiet location. ⊠ *Via Ripagrande 21, 44100* ☎ *0532/765250* ▤ *0532/764377* ⊕ *www.ripagrandehotel.it* ⇗ *20 rooms, 20 suites* ⚱ *Restaurant, room service,*

Fodor's Choice
★

in-room safes, minibars, cable TV, bar, meeting room, free parking ⊟ *AE, DC, MC, V* ⦿⦿ *BP.*

$ 🏨 **Hotel San Paolo.** On the edge of the old city, San Paolo is the best inexpensive choice in town. The 10-minute walk from the heart of Ferrara's medieval quarter is pleasant, and there are good restaurants in the vicinity. Singles are a particularly good value (about €65); triples are available. ⊠ *Via Baluardi 9, 44100* ☎ *0532/762040* 🖷 *0532/ 762040* ⊕ *www.hotelsanpaolo.it* ⤴ *29 rooms* ⚭ *Cable TV, bicycles, some pets allowed; no a/c in some rooms* ⊟ *AE, DC, MC, V* ⦿⦿ *EP.*

$ 🏨 **Locanda Borgonuovo.** This lovely bed-and-breakfast is in a 17th-century monastery on a quiet but central pedestrians-only street. It books up months in advance, partly because musicians and actors from the local theater make this their home away from home. Rooms are furnished with antiques, and one has its own kitchen for longer stays. Summer breakfasts are served in the leafy courtyard. ⊠ *Via Cairoli 29, 44100* ☎ *0532/211100* 🖷 *0532/246328* ⊕ *www.borgonuovo.com* ⤴ *4 rooms* ⚭ *Dining room, in-room safes, some kitchens, minibars, bicycles, library, free parking* ⊟ *AE, MC, V* ⦿⦿ *BP.*

Nightlife

The dim, stylish **Enobar Estense** (⊠ Piazza Cattedrale 7 ☎ 339/4831510), right next to the cathedral, accompanies wines from all over Italy with endless plates of delightful free Italian tapas and soothing jazz. **Enoteca I Contrari** (⊠ Via Contrari 52, at Via Mazzini ☎ 0532/242422) has huge wooden beams, high ceilings, good music, and good feelings. They serve panini, plates of local salumi and cheeses, specialty rums and Scotches, and great wines by the glass.

For live jazz, check out the **Jazz Club Ferrara** (⊠ Torrione San Giovanni ☎ 0532/211573 ⊕ www.jazzclubferrara.com), which has a star-studded lineup.

Orsatti 1860 (⊠ Via Cortevecchia 33 ☎ 0532/207572) is one of the oldest and best places in town for local pastries and great espresso (standing at the bar, of course). The low-key **Leon d'Oro** (⊠ Piazza Cattedrale 2–10 ☎ 0532/209318) is a grand old café serving expensive drinks, coffee, and signature Ferrarese fruitcakes (as well as a few basic pasta dishes at lunchtime) in a truly regal environment. It's closed Wednesday.

Sports & the Outdoors

Bicycles
Cycling is extremely popular in Ferrara. **Pirana e Bagni** (⊠ Piazzale Stazione 2 ☎ 0532/772190) rents bicycles. Call **Cicloclub Estense** (☎ 0532/ 900931) to arrange a guided bike trip.

ROMAGNA

Anywhere in Emilia-Romagna, the story goes, a weary, lost traveler will be invited into a family's home and offered a drink. But the Romagnesi claim that he'll be served water in Emilia and wine in Romagna. The hilly, mostly rural, and largely undiscovered Romagna region has crumbling farmhouses dotting rolling hills, smoking chimneys, ancient Christian temples, and rowdy local bars dishing out rounds and rounds of *piadine* (flat griddle breads). Ravenna, the site of shimmering Byzantine mosaics, dominates the region, and Rimini is an overpopulated seaside resort.

Heading southeast out of Bologna, Via Emilia (SS9) and the parallel A14 Autostrada lead to the towns of Dozza and Faenza. From there, cut north to the Adriatic coast on the S71 to reach Ravenna, or continue on southeast on the A14 to reach Rimini. Alternatively, the slower S16 cuts a northwest–southeast swath through Romagna, directly connecting Ravenna and Rimini.

Dozza

⑮ *85 km (53 mi) southeast of Ferrara, 31 km (19 mi) southeast of Bologna.*

Dozza is a beautiful little village just off the Via Emilia (SS9) where artists from all over flock in September of odd years to take part in a mural competition. As a result, virtually every square foot of the town is covered with colorful scenes, executed with varying degrees of skill.

Dozza is crowned with a splendidly restored medieval castle museum, the **Rocca Sforzesca di Dozza.** ☎ *0542/678240* 🎟 *€4* 🕙 *Apr.–Sept., Tues.–Sat. 10–1 and 3–7, Sun. 10–1 and 3–7:30; Oct.–Mar., Tues.–Sat. 10–12:30 and 3–5, Sun. 10–1 and 2:30–6.*

The **Enoteca Regionale,** in Dozza's castle, is *the* wine shop for the region. While browsing in this cozy stone building, you can sample different vintages from the surrounding countryside. Try Dozza's own Albana, a white wine that comes dry or sweet. For further consumption, the on-site wine bar is open Sunday afternoon 2:30–5:30. ⊠ *Rocca di Dozza* ☎ *0542/678089* 🕙 *Tues.–Fri. 9:30–1 and 2:30–6, weekends 10–1 and 2:30–6.*

Where to Eat

$$$$ ✕ **San Domenico.** Some superstar
Fodor'sChoice restaurants come and go, but San
★ Domenico has defended its position as one of Italy's most refined dining destinations year after year. The majestic appointments complement celebrity chef Valentino Marcattilii's wondrous creations like the memorable *uovo in raviolo San Domenico,* in which one egg is stuffed into a large ravioli, the yolk spills out and mixes with sweet Paremsan cheese, *burro di malga* (butter from an Alpine dairy farm), and sensational white truffles. Service is like a silent, perfectly cho-

> **WORD OF MOUTH**
>
> "Dozza was such a surprising, improbable combination of a traditional-looking medieval town and a unique offbeat art site. I was just amazed by it. Every two years artists paint murals on the houses and streets and other walls of the town. The works vary tremendously in style, but somehow the overall effect, though startling, is interesting rather than tacky."
>
> –cmt

reographed ballet, and the staggering wine list has more than 3,000 choices. Reserve well in advance. ⊠ *Via G. Sacchi 1, Imola, 15 km (9 mi) east of Dozza* ☎ *0542/29000* ⌁ *Reservations essential* ⊟ *AE, DC, MC, V* ⊘ *Closed Mon., Sun. June–Aug., 1 wk in Jan., and 1 wk in Aug. No dinner Sun. Sept.–May. No lunch Sat. June–Aug.*

Faenza

⓰ *23 km (14 mi) southeast of Dozza, 49 km (30 mi) southeast of Bologna.*

The renowned style of pottery called faience has been produced in Faenza, on the Via Emilia, since the 12th century. In the central **Piazza del Popolo** are dozens of shops selling the native wares. Faenza, not surprisingly, is home to the **Museo delle Ceramiche,** one of the largest ceramics museums in the world. During a renovation of indeterminate length, the 17th- to 19th-century pottery is not accessible. ⊠ *Viale Baccarini 19* ☎ *0546/697311* ⊕ *www.racine.ra.it/micfaenza* ☑ *€6, €4.50 during renovation* ⊘ *Apr.–Oct., Tues.–Sat. 9–7, Sun. 9:30–1 and 3–7; Nov.–Mar., Tues.–Fri. 9–1:30, weekends 9:30–5:30.*

Forlì

⓱ *16 km (10 mi) southeast of Faenza, 74 km (46 mi) southeast of Bologna.*

The biggest city on the Via Emilia between Bologna and Rimini is Forlì. It's a pretty, prosperous, provincial Romagnan city with a huge but harmonious piazza and duomo. Some of the true riches of Romagna lie along the smaller roads branching off to the north and south of Forlì.

★ **$$$$** ✕ **La Frasca.** Chef Gianfranco Bolognesi is an artist with fresh Adriatic seafood, delectable fowl, and Romagnan produce. Expect far-fetched, haute-cuisine delights such as a pastry-crust quail stuffed with foie gras and black truffle. A set-price lunch menu is a relative bargain at €45 per person. In the warm weather you can dine in the garden. This elegant country restaurant is in the secluded spa town of Castrocaro Terme, a beautiful drive southeast of Forlì. ⊠ *Viale Mateotti 34, Castrocaro Terme, 11 km (7 mi) southeast of Forlì* ☎ *0543/767471* ⌁ *Reservations essential* ⊟ *AE, DC, MC, V* ⊘ *Closed Tues., Jan. 1–21, and Aug. 15–Sept. 1.*

Bagno di Romagna

⓲ *66 km (41 mi) southeast of Forlì, 81 km (51 mi) south of Ravenna.*

Bagno di Romagna is one of the spa hill towns that dot the bucolic Romagnan countryside. There's not a lot to see, but the hot springs in the center can be enjoyed year-round. You access the town's thermal waters through hotel spas, including the **Euroterme.** ⊠ *Via Lungosavio 2* ☎ *0543/911414* ⊕ *www.euroterme.com* ☑ *€7* ⊘ *Daily 10–7.*

Where to Stay & Eat

★ **$$$$** ✕ **Paolo Teverini.** The chef-owner—and restaurant's namesake—is one of the star culinary personalities of the region. His relentlessly modern preparations are punctuated by essences, foams, gelatins, and reductions that display an almost conniving flair for drama, matched only by the out-

Romagna

landishly pink and posh decor. Most impressive of all is the voluminous wine list, a showcase of older vintages from Italy's best producers at lower-than-wine-store prices. ⊠ *Piazza Dante 2* ☎ *0543/911260* ✍ *Reservations essential* ⊟ *AE, DC, MC, V* ⊘ *Closed Mon. and Tues. Sept.–June.*

$–$$$ 🏨 **Tosco Romagnolo.** Right near Bagno di Romagna's thermal baths, the Tosco Romagnolo is in the same spa complex (and under the same ownership) as the inimitable Paolo Teverini restaurant. Rooms are reasonably priced (rates drop dramatically in winter) and suites, though more expensive, are top-notch and sparkling. The hot tub and pool (heated) on the hotel's roof command calming views of the surrounding Romagnan hills. The attached spa, Gaia Teverini, has all manner of health treatments, massage, and so on. ⊠ *Piazza Dante 2, 47021* ☎ *0543/911260* 🖷 *0543/911014* ⊕ *www.paoloteverini.it* ⇄ *45 rooms, 4 suites* ⌂ *2 restaurants, some in-room safes, minibars, pool, health club, outdoor hot tub, spa, bicycles, bar, meeting rooms, car rental* ⊟ *AE, DC, MC, V* ⓧ*BP.*

en route

Beyond the turnoff for Bagno di Romagna taking the Via Emilia toward Rimini, you pass Savignano and a small stream outside of town, the **Rubicone.** Cross it and you, too, have crossed the Rubicon, made famous by Julius Caesar when in 49 BC he defied the Roman

Senate by bringing his army across the river and plunging the country into civil war.

Rimini

⑲ *52 km (32 mi) southeast of Ravenna, 121 km (76 mi) southeast of Bologna.*

Rimini is the principal summer resort on the Adriatic Coast and one of the most popular holiday destinations in Italy, flooded with Italians and other Europeans. That said, the water is murky, the beaches are ugly and overcrowded, and the nightlife is largely a teenage pick-up scene. Though there are hundreds of hotels—some very fine—with private beach turf, they all seem to be full in August. In the off-season (October–March) Rimini is a cold, windy ghost town with few places open.

The town stands at the junction of two great Roman consular roads, the Via Emilia and the Via Flaminia. In addition, in Roman times it was an important port, making it a strategic and commercial center. From the 13th century onward, Rimini was controlled by the Malatesta family, an unpredictable group capable of grand gestures and savage deeds. The famous lovers immortalized in Dante's *Inferno,* Paolo (died 1304) and Francesca (died 1283 or 1284), were Malatestas.

Sigismondo Malatesta (1417–68), lord of the city in the middle of the 15th century, banished his first wife, strangled his second, and poisoned his third. He lived with his beautiful mistress Isotta until her death, upon which he was so grief-stricken that he had the **Tempio Malatestiano** built in her honor. The masterful Renaissance facade is by Leon Battista Alberti (1404–72); the interior is light and spacious and contains the tombs of both the lovers. The dollar-sign-like intertwined *I,* for Isotta, and *S,* for Sigismondo, are everywhere. Inside the gift shop there's a wonderful fresco by Piero della Francesca (1420–92); when the shop is closed, one of the cathedral's staff can unlock the room. ⊠ *Via IV Novembre 35* ☎ *0541/51130* ⊕ *www.diocesi.rimini.it/diocesi/tempio.htm* 🔳 *Free* ⊗ *Mon.–Sat. 8–12:30 and 3:30–6:30, Sun. 9–1 and 3:30–7.*

Rimini's oldest monument is the **Arco d'Augusto,** now stranded in the middle of a square just inside the city ramparts. It was erected in 27 BC, making it the oldest surviving Roman arch. ⊠ *Largo Giulio Cesare.*

Where to Stay & Eat

★ **$$** ✕ **La Locanda di San Martino.** Patrons have been known to drive all the way from the Ligurian coast just for the seafood delights here. Dishes such as the *spaghettoni ai frutti di mare* (thick spaghetti with seafood sauce) and a grilled mixed seafood platter are uniformly fresh and superbly prepared; the mixed antipasto served with lunch is exquisite. An outdoor patio in the back is more romantic than the large main dining rooms. To get here take the road out of Rimini heading toward Bologna. ⊠ *Via Emilia 226* ☎ *0541/680127* 🔳 *AE, MC, V* ⊗ *Closed Mon.*

¢ ✕ **Piada e Cassoni da Jonny.** Come here for the *piada* (grilled flatbread), one of the traditional specialties of Romagnan cooking. A brisk staff member fills the flatbread, or a *cassoni* (a bigger pocket of bread, more like a calzone, but also grilled), with cheese, tomato, and meat or vegetables, to order while you wait. Don't expect to sit down at this bustling take-out place (open until about 9:15 PM daily), but Jonny also delivers. ⊠ *Via Giovanni XXIII 101* ☎ *0541/29675* 🖃 *No credit cards.*

★ $$$$ 🏨 **Grand Hotel.** This fin-de-siècle extravaganza, made famous by Fellini in his *Amarcord,* is grander than ever. The hyperluxe stage is set by enormous crystal chandeliers in the lobby, bright pink hallways, and inlaid wood in the rooms that seems playful rather than formal. A spotless private beach completes the scene. Entourages and steamer trunks would not be out of place here; neither would it be a surprise to see a greyhound loping through the restaurant on her way to the pool with her owner. ⊠ *Via Ramusio 1, Parco Federico Fellini, 47900* ☎ *0541/56000* 🖷 *0541/56866* ⊕ *www.grandhotelrimini.com* ⤳ *98 rooms, 19 suites* ♨ *2 restaurants, minibars, tennis court, 2 outdoor pools, health club, hair salon, massage, sauna, beach, 2 bars, nightclub, meeting room* 🖃 *AE, DC, MC, V* ❑ *BP.*

en route | There are two routes between Ravenna and Rimini. The coastal road, S16, hugs the shoreline much of the way, passing through Cervia. Although its length of 52 km (32 mi) is not great, this scenic route is naturally slower (beware of fog in winter). The coast north of Rimini is lined with dozens of small resort towns, only one having any charm—the seaport of Cesenatico; the others are mini-Riminis, and in summer the narrow road is hopelessly clogged with traffic. A faster route is to take the S71 and the A14; the distance is 64 km (39 mi).

RAVENNA

A small, quiet city, Ravenna has brick palaces, cobbled streets, magnificent monuments, and spectacular Byzantine mosaics to remind you of its storied past. The high point in Ravenna's history was 1,500 long years ago, when it became the capital of the Roman Empire. The honor was short-lived—the city was taken by the barbarian Ostrogoths in the 5th century; in the 6th century it was conquered by the Byzantines, who ruled it from Constantinople.

Because Ravenna spent much of its past looking to the East, its greatest art treasures show that influence. Churches and tombs with the most unassuming exteriors contain within them walls covered with tiny, glittering tiles. The beautifully preserved Byzantine mosaics put an emphasis on nature—green pastures, sheep, and starry skies, for instance—not found in Italy's other ancient artistic treasures. Outside Ravenna, the town of Classe hides even more mosaic gems.

Exploring Ravenna

A requisite combination ticket (available at ticket offices of all included sights) admits you to six of Ravenna's most important monuments: the Mausoleo di Galla Placidia, the Basilica di San Vitale, the Battistero Neoniano, Sant'Apollinare Nuovo, the church of Spirito Santo, and the Museo Arcivescovile e Cappella Sant'Andrea. Start out early in the morning to

San Marino, a Country on a Cliff

THE WORLD'S SMALLEST and oldest republic, as San Marino dubs itself, is landlocked entirely by Italy. It consists of three ancient castles perched high on cliffs of sheer rock rising implausibly out of the flatlands of Romagna, and a tangled knot of cobblestoned streets below, lined with tourist boutiques, cheesy hotels and restaurants, and gun shops. The 45-minute drive from Rimini is easily justified, however, by the castle-top view of the countryside far below. The 1,000-meter-plus precipices will make jaws drop and acrophobes quiver.

San Marino was founded in the 4th century AD by a stonecutter named Marino who settled with a small community of Christians, escaping persecution by pagan emperor Diocletian. Over the millennia, largely because of the logistical nightmares associated with attacking a fortified rock, San Marino was more or less left alone by Italy's various conquerors, and continues to this day to be an independent country (population 26,000), supported almost entirely by its 3-million-visitor-per-year tourist industry.

San Marino's headline attractions are its tre castelli (three castles)—medieval architectural wonders that appear on every coat of arms in the city. Starting in the center of town, you can walk quickly past the trinket shops along a paved cliff-top ridge from the 10th-century Rocca della Guaita to the 13th-century Rocca della Cesta (which contains a museum of ancient weapons that's worthwhile mostly for the views from its terraces and turrets), and finally to the 14th-century Rocca Montale (closed to the public), the most remote of the castles. Every

step of the way affords spectacular views of Romagna and the Adriatic; it is said that on a clear day you can see Croatia. The walks make for a good day's exercise but are by no means arduous. Even if you arrive after visiting hours, they're supremely worthwhile. ✉ *Rocca della Guaita and Rocca della Cesta:* €*3* ⊙ *Oct.–Mar., daily 8:50–5; Apr.–Sept., daily 8–8.*

A must-see is the Piazza della Libertà, whose Palazzo Pubblico is guarded by soldiers in green uniforms. As you'll notice by peering into the shops along the old town's winding streets, the republic is famous for crossbows—and more: shopping for fireworks, firearms, and other items illegal for sale elsewhere is another popular tourist activity.

Visiting San Marino in winter—off-season—increases the appeal of the experience, as tourist establishments shut down and you more or less have the castles to yourself. In August, every inch of walkway on the rock is mobbed with sightseers. To get to San Marino by car, take highway SS72 west from Rimini. From Borgo Maggiore, at the base of the rock, a cable car will whisk you up to the castles and town. Alternatively, you can drive all the way up the winding road; public parking is available in the town itself. Don't worry about changing money, showing passports, and the like (although the tourist office will stamp your passport for €1); San Marino is, for all practical purposes, Italy—except, that is, for its majestic perch, its gun laws, and its reported 99% national voter turnout rate.

avoid lines (reservations are necessary for the Mausoleo and Basilica in May and June). A half day should suffice to walk the town alone; allow an hour each for the Mausoleo, the Basilica, and the Museo Nazionale. Ticket offices often close 15–30 minutes before the sight themselves.

The Main Attractions

㉑ Basilica di San Vitale. The octagonal church of San Vitale was built in AD 547, after the Byzantines conquered the city, and its interior shows a strong Byzantine influence. In the area behind the altar are the most famous works in the church, accurate portraits of the Emperor of the East, Justinian, attended by his court and the bishop of Ravenna, Maximian. Notice how the mosaics seamlessly wrap around the columns and curved arches on the upper sides of the altar area. Reservations are recommended from March through mid-June. ⊠ *Via San Vitale, off Via Salara* ☎ *0544/219518* 🎫 *Combination ticket €9.50 Mar.–June, €7.50 July–Feb.* ☉ *Daily 10–5.*

㉓ Battistero Neoniano. The baptistry, next door to Ravenna's 18th-century cathedral, is one of the town's most important mosaic sights. In keeping with the building's role, the great mosaic in the dome shows the baptism of Christ, and beneath that scene are the Apostles. The lowest band of mosaics contains Christian symbols, the Throne of God, and the Cross. Note the naked figure kneeling next to Christ—he is the personification of the River Jordan. The Battistero building is said to have been a Roman bath dating from the 5th century AD. ⊠ *Via Battistero* ☎ *0544/ 215201* 🎫 *Combination ticket €9.50 Mar.–June, €7.50 July–Feb.* ☉ *Daily 10–5.*

㉒ Mausoleo di Galla Placidia. The little tomb and the great church stand side by side, but the tomb predates the Basilica di San Vitale by at least a hundred years. These two adjacent sights are decorated with the best-known, and most elaborate, mosaics in Ravenna. Galla Placidia was the sister of Rome's emperor, Honorius, the man who moved the imperial capital to Ravenna in AD 402. She is said to have been beautiful and strong-willed, and to have taken an active part in the governing of the crumbling empire. This tomb, constructed in the mid-5th century, is her memorial.

Fodor's Choice
★

Outside, the tomb is a small, unassuming redbrick building; the exterior's seeming poverty of charm only serves to enhance by contrast the richness of the interior mosaics, in deep midnight blue and glittering gold. The tiny, low central dome is decorated with symbols of Christ and the evangelists and striking gold stars. Over the door is a depiction of the Good Shepherd. Eight of the Apostles are represented in groups of two on the four inner walls of the dome; the other four appear singly on the walls of the two transepts. Notice the small doves at their feet, drinking from the water of faith. Also in the tiny transepts are some delightful pairs of deer (representing souls), drinking from the fountain of resurrection. There are three sarcophagi in the tomb, none of which are believed to contain the remains of Galla Placidia. She died in Rome in AD 450, and there is no record of her body having been transported back to the place where she wished to lie. Reservations are required for the Mausoleo from March through mid-June. ⊠ *Via San Vitale, off Via Salara* ☎ *0544/541688 reservations, 800/303999 toll-free information* ☒ *Combination ticket €9.50 Mar.–June, €7.50 July–Feb.* ☉ *Daily 9:30–5.*

❷❺ **Sant'Apollinare Nuovo.** The mosaics displayed in this church date from the early 6th century, making them slightly older than the works in San Vitale. Since the left side of the church was reserved for women, it's only fitting that the mosaic decoration there is a scene of 22 virgins offering crowns to the Virgin Mary. On the right wall are 26 men carrying the crowns of martyrdom. They are approaching Christ, surrounded by angels. ⊠ *Via Roma and Via Guaccimanni* ☎ *0544/219518* ☒ *Combination ticket €9.50 Mar.–June, €7.50 July–Feb.* ☉ *Daily 10–5.*

**off the
beaten
path**

SANT'APOLLINARE IN CLASSE – This church, about 5 km (3 mi) southeast of Ravenna, is landlocked now, but when it was built it stood in the center of the busy shipping port of Classis. The arch above and the area around the high altar are rich with mosaics. Those on the arch, older than the ones behind it, are considered superior.

They show Christ in Judgment and the 12 lambs of Christianity leaving the cities of Jerusalem and Bethlehem. In the apse is the figure of Sant'Apollinare himself, a bishop of Ravenna, and above him is a magnificent Transfiguration against blazing green grass, animals in skewed perspective, and flowers. ⊠ *Via Romea Sud, Classe* ☎ *0544/ 473569* 🔲 *€2* ⊙ *Mon.–Sat. 8:30–7:30, Sun. 1–7:30.*

Also Worth Seeing

Domus dei Tappeti di Pietra (Ancient Home of the Stone Carpets). This underground archaeological site was uncovered during the course of routine maintenance work by the city in 1993 and opened to the public in 2002. Below ground level (10 feet down) lie the remains of a 6th-century AD Byzantine palace, in which a beautiful and well-preserved network of floor mosaics display themes that are fascinatingly un-Christian. ⊠ *Via Barbiani, enter through Sant'Eufemia* ☎ *0544/32512* 🔲 *€3* ⊕ *www.ravennantica.it* ⊙ *Mar.–Oct., Tues.–Sun. 10–6:30; Nov.–Feb., Tues.–Sat. 10–4:30.*

㉒ **Museo Nazionale.** The National Museum of Ravenna, next to the Church of San Vitale, contains artifacts from ancient Rome, Byzantine fabrics and carvings, and pieces of early Christian art. The collection is housed in a former monastery, but is well displayed and artfully lighted. ⊠ *Via Fiandrini* ☎ *0544/34424* 🔲 *€4* ⊙ *Tues.–Sun. 8:30–7:30.*

㉔ **Tomba di Dante.** The tomb of Dante is in a small neoclassical building next door to the large church of St. Francis. Exiled from his native Florence, the author of *The Divine Comedy* died here in 1321. The Florentines have been trying to reclaim their famous son for hundreds of years, but the Ravennans refuse to give him up, arguing that since Florence did not welcome Dante in life it does not deserve him in death. The small **Museo Dantesco** has displays on the writer's life and the history of the tomb. ⊠ *Via Dante Alighieri 4 and 9* ☎ *0544/30252* 🔲 *Free* ⊙ *Tomb daily 9–noon and 2–5, museum Tues.–Sun. 9–noon.*

Where to Stay & Eat

$–$$ ✕ **Bella Venezia.** Graceful low archways lead into this attractive restaurant's two small dining rooms. Lighting is bright and styling is pink and white. Try the beans with olive oil and *bottarga* (cured roe) or the owner's special risotto with butter, Parmesan, cured ham, mushrooms, and peas to start. For the second course, the *fegato alla Veneziana* (grilled liver with onions) is a good choice. The outdoor garden is quite pleasant in season. ⊠ *Via IV Novembre 16* ☎ *0544/212746* ▤ *AE, DC, MC, V* ⊙ *Closed Sun. and 3 wks in Jan.*

★ **$–$$** ✕ **Ca' de Ven.** A vaulted wine cellar in the heart of the old city, the Ca' de Ven is great for a hearty meal. You sit at long tables with other diners and feast on platters of delicious cold cuts, flat breads, and cold, heady white wine. The tortelli *di radicchio e pecorino* (stuffed with radicchio and goat cheese) makes the best first course. ⊠ *Via C. Ricci 24* ☎ *0544/ 30163* ▤ *AE, DC, MC, V* ⊙ *Closed Mon., 3 wks in Jan. and Feb., and 1st wk of June.*

$–$$ ✕ **La Gardèla.** The kitchen seems to operate with an otherworldly efficiency, making this bright, bustling downtown restaurant extremely popular with the local business crowd—especially at lunch (always a good sign). The place is best for classics like tagliatelle al ragù and Adriatic fish, such as *sardoncini* (sardines, breaded and fried). ⊠ *Via Ponte Marino 3* ☎ *0544/217147* ⊟ *AE, DC, MC, V* ⊘ *Closed Thurs., 10 days in Aug., and 10 days in Jan.*

$$–$$$ ⊡ **Hotel Bisanzio.** Steps from San Vitale and the Tomb of Galla Placidia, this Best Western hotel is the most convenient lodging for mosaic enthusiasts. The exterior is drab, but rooms are comfortable and modern; the lobby's Florentine lamps add a touch of style. Ask to be on the top floor and you may get a view of the basilica. ⊠ *Via Salara 30, 48100* ☎ *0544/217111* 🖷 *0544/32539* ⊕ *www.bisanziohotel.com* ↩ *38 rooms* ⚲ *Dining room, in-room safes, minibars, 2 bars, meeting room, Internet, parking (fee)* ⊟ *AE, DC, MC, V* ⦿ *BP.*

$ ⊡ **Hotel Centrale Byron.** Tranquillity is assured here in the center of Ravenna's old town, because it's in a pedestrian zone. The old-fashioned, well-managed hotel has spotless if uninspired rooms. You can drop off your luggage at the door, but you have to park your car in one of the nearby garages or lots. ⊠ *Via IV Novembre 14, 48100* ☎ *0544/33479* 🖷 *0544/34114* ⊕ *www.hotelbyron.com* ↩ *54 rooms* ⚲ *In-room safes, minibars, cable TV, bar, parking (fee)* ⊟ *AE, DC, MC, V* ⦿ *BP.*

$ ⊡ **Hotel Ravenna.** A functional stopover near the train station, the Ravenna is still only a few minutes' walk from the center. This modern hotel has smallish rooms; two rooms are equipped for people with disabilities. ⊠ *Via Maroncelli 12, 48100* ☎ *0544/212204* 🖷 *0544/212077* ⊕ *www.hotelravenna.ra.it* ↩ *26 rooms* ⚲ *Bar, parking (fee); no a/c* ⊟ *MC, V* ⦿ *BP.*

Nightlife & the Arts

Friday evenings in July and August bring **Mosaics by Night,** when the Byzantine mosaic masterpieces in town are illuminated. Guided tours are available from the tourist office.

The **Ravenna Festival** is a musical extravaganza, held every year June and July. Orchestras from all over the world come to perform in Ravenna's mosaic-clad churches and theaters.

EMILIA-ROMAGNA ESSENTIALS

Transportation

BY AIR

Bologna is an important business and convention center, well served by European airlines linking it with Italian cities and European capitals, including Rome and Milan (on Alitalia), Paris (on Air France), London (on British Airways and easyJet), Barcelona (on Iberia), Amsterdam (on KLM), and Frankfurt (on Lufthansa)—among others. There are no direct flights from the United States, however. Those wishing to fly direct often choose instead to fly into and rent a car at Milan Malpensa airport, a 45-minute drive on the A1 Autostrada from Piacenza and an easy two hours from Bologna. Alternatively, if your itinerary runs east-to-west, you might choose to fly into the Venice airport and rent a car there; it's about an hour's drive from Ferrara.

Parma, Rimini, and Forlì are the smaller hubs in the region. Air Alps connects Rimini with Rome. Alitalia and Air Alps operate Rome–Parma service. The low-cost operator Ryanair connects Forlì with London (Stansted) and Frankfurt (Hahn).

The main airport of the region, Guglielmo Marconi, is 10 km (6 mi) northwest of Bologna. Aerobus service (Bus 54, €4.15) connects Guglielmo Marconi with Bologna's central train station as well as a downtown stop. It runs every half hour from 6 AM to 11:30 PM. Parma's small airport is Aeroporto G. Verdi, and Rimini's is called Aeradria; both are connected by bus to their respective cities during arrival and departure times. The airport at Forlì, 6 km (4 mi) from the A14 autostrada, is convenient to Ravenna, Rimini, and Bologna; a Bologna-bound bus waits for all Ryanair arrivals.

🛦 Airport Information **Aeradria Rimini Airport** ✉ Rimini ☎ 0541/715711 ⊕ www.riminiairport.com. **Aeroporto di Forlì** ✉ Forlì ☎ 0543/474990 ⊕ www.forli-airport.it. **Aeroporto G. Verdi** ✉ Parma ☎ 0521/982626 ⊕ www.aeroportoparma.it. **Aeroporto Guglielmo Marconi** ✉ Via Triumvirato 84, Bologna ☎ 051/6479615 ⊕ www.bologna-airport.it.

🛦 Carriers **Air Alps** ☎ 899/500004 ⊕ www.airalps.at. **Air France** ☎ 848/884466 ⊕ www.airfrance.com. **Alitalia** ☎ 848/865641 ⊕ www.alitalia.com. **British Airways** ☎ 848/81266 ⊕ www.british-airways.com. **easyJet** ☎ 848/887766 ⊕ www.easyjet.com. **Iberia** ☎ 848/870000 ⊕ www.iberia.com. **KLM** ☎ 02/218981 ⊕ www.northwest.com. **Lufthansa** ☎ 0516477730 ⊕ www.lufthansa.com. **Ryanair** ☎ 199/114114 ⊕ www.ryanair.com.

BY BUS

There's little reason to travel by bus in Emilia-Romagna. Trains are fast, efficient, and relatively inexpensive; they run frequently and connect most towns in the region. A bus might be helpful for travel in rural Romagna and to the smallest of towns. ATR buses travel between places such as Bagno di Romagna and the train stations of larger towns. Still, given the inconvenience and limited schedules, it's questionable whether such a trip is worthwhile. You're likely to find yourself wishing you had a car.

🛦 Bus Information **ATR** ☎ 199/115577 ⊕ www.atr-online.it.

BY CAR

Entering Emilia-Romagna by car is as easy as it gets. Coming in from the west on the Autostrada del Sole (A1), Piacenza will be the first city you'll hit. It's a mere 45 minutes from Milan, which is why some visitors to the region choose to fly into Milan's well-connected Malpensa airport and rent a car there. If you're starting on the other side of the region, the Venice airport, with good car-rental options and international plane connections, is only about an hour from Ferrara by car on the A13.

Bologna is on the autostrada network, so driving between cities is a breeze. The Via Emilia (SS9), one of the oldest roads in the world, runs through the heart of the region. It's a straight, low-lying modern road, the length of which can be traveled in a few hours. Although less scenic, the A1 toll highway, which runs parallel to the Via Emilia from Bologna, to west Modena, Parma, and Piacenza, can get you where you're going about twice as fast. From Bologna, the A13 runs north to Ferrara, and the A14 takes you east to Ravenna and Rimini. Note that much of the historic center of Bologna is closed off to cars daily 7 AM–8 PM.

BY TRAIN
Bologna is an important rail hub for the entire northern part of Italy and has frequent, fast service to Milan, Florence, Rome, and Venice. Piacenza is less than an hour from Milan by train, Parma an hour and a half, and Bologna about two hours. The routes from Bologna to the south tend to go through Florence, which is only an hour away. The Eurostar takes 2½ hours to and from Rome; the same trip takes four hours on the Intercity train. On the northeastern edge of the region, Venice is an hour and a half east of Ferrara by train, and Trieste and Slovenia are not much farther.

Within the region, the railway line follows the Via Emilia (SS9). In Emilia, it's generally a half hour to 45 minutes from one major city to the next. To reach Ferrara or Ravenna, you'll usually have to change to a local train at the Bologna station. Trains run frequently, and connections are easy. Ferrara is a half hour north of Bologna on the train, and Ravenna is just over an hour.

🚺 Train Information **Ferrovie dello Stato (FS)** ☎ 892021 ⊕ www.trenitalia.com.

Contacts & Resources

EMERGENCIES
For first aid, call the police and ask for *pronto soccorso*. Be prepared to give your address. Pharmacies take turns staying open late and on Sunday; for the latest information, consult the current list posted on the front door of each pharmacy or ask at the local tourist office. ACI emergency service provides 24-hour roadside assistance.

🚺 **ACI** ☎ 803/116. **Carabinieri** ☎ 112. **Police, ambulance** ☎ 113. **Doctors and dentists** ☎ 113.

VISITOR INFORMATION
🚺 Tourist Information **Bologna** ⊠ Guglielmo Marconi airport ☎ 051/246541 ⊠ Stazione Centrale, 40121 ☎ 051/246541 ⊠ Piazza Maggiore 1, 40124 ☎ 051/246541 ⊕ www.comune.bologna.it/bolognaturismo. **Busseto** ⊠ Comune, Piazza G. Verdi 10, 43011 ☎ 0524/92487 ⊕ www.bussetolive.com. **Dozza** ⊠ Via XX Settembre, 40050 ☎ 0542/678052. **Faenza** ⊠ Piazza del Popolo 1, 48018 ☎ 0546/691602. **Ferrara** ⊠ Castello Estense, 44100 ☎ 0532/209370 ⊕ www.ferrarainfo.com ⊠ Piazza Municipale 11, 44100 ☎ 0532/419474. **Modena** ⊠ Via Scudari 12, 41100 ☎ 059/206660 ⊠ Palazzo dei Musei, Via Vittorio Veneto 5 ☎ 059/200125. **Parma** ⊠ Via Melloni 1/a, 43100 ☎ 0521/218889 ⊕ turismo.comune.parma.it. **Piacenza** ⊠ Piazza Cavalli 7, 29100 ☎ 0523/329324 ⊕ www.provincia.pc.it. **Ravenna** ⊠ Via Salara 8, 48100 ☎ 0544/35404 ⊕ www.turismo.ravenna.it. **Rimini** ⊠ Piazzale Cesare Battisti, 47037 ☎ 0541/51331 ⊠ Piazzale Fellini 3, Marina Centro, 47037 ☎ 0541/56902 ⊕ www.riminiturismo.it. **San Marino** ⊠ Contra Omagnano 20, 47890 ☎ 0549/882400.

Florence

Piazza della Signoria

WORD OF MOUTH

"Michelangelo, Dante, Galileo. Gelato, red wine, amazing food. Some of the most wonderful art and architecture. Firenze is a magical city (and where my fiancé and I got engaged). It is an absolute gem."

—Kristin

WELCOME TO FLORENCE

David, Piazza della Signoria

TOP 5
Reasons to Go

 Galleria degli Uffizi: Italian Renaissance art doesn't get much better than this vast collection bequeathed to the city by the last Medici.

② **The dome of the Duomo:** Brunelleschi's work of engineering genius is the city's undisputed centerpiece.

③ **Michelangelo's *David*:** One look and you'll know why this is the western world's most famous sculpture.

④ **The view from Piazzale Michelangelo:** From this perch the city is laid out before you. Being there at sunset heightens the experience.

⑤ **Piazza Santa Croce:** After you've had your fill of Renaissance masterpieces, hang out here and watch the world go by.

Getting Oriented

The historic center of Florence is flat and compact—you could walk from one end to the other in half an hour. In the middle of everything is the Duomo, with its huge dome towering over the city's terracotta rooftops. Radiating out from the Duomo are Renaissance-era neighborhoods identified by their central churches and piazzas. Though the majority of sights are north of the Arno River, the area to the south, known as the Oltrarno, has its charms as well.

The quarter from Santa Maria Novella to the Arno includes the train station, 15th-century palaces, and the city's most chic shopping street, **Via Tornabuoni**.

The Oltrarno contrasts the massive Palazzo Pitti and the narrow streets of the **Santo Spirito** district, which is filled with artisans' workshops and antique stores. A climb up to the **Piazzale Michelangelo** gives you a spectacular view of the city.

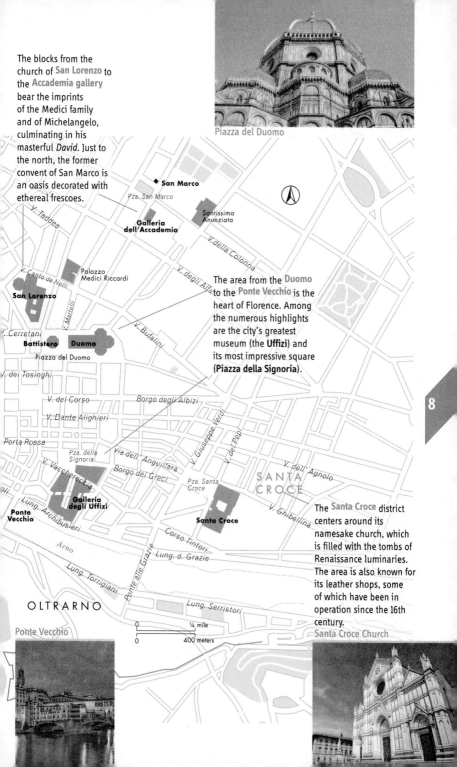

The blocks from the church of **San Lorenzo** to the **Accademia gallery** bear the imprints of the Medici family and of Michelangelo, culminating in his masterful *David*. Just to the north, the former convent of San Marco is an oasis decorated with ethereal frescoes.

Piazza del Duomo

The area from the **Duomo** to the **Ponte Vecchio** is the heart of Florence. Among the numerous highlights are the city's greatest museum (the **Uffizi**) and its most impressive square (**Piazza della Signoria**).

The **Santa Croce** district centers around its namesake church, which is filled with the tombs of Renaissance luminaries. The area is also known for its leather shops, some of which have been in operation since the 16th century.

Santa Croce Church

Ponte Vecchio

OLTRARNO

SANTA CROCE

San Marco
Pza. San Marco
Galleria dell'Accademia
Santissima Anunziata
V. Taddea
V. della Colonna
V. Canto de Nelli
Palazzo Medici Riccardi
V. degli Alfa
San Lorenzo
V. Martelli
V. Bufalini
V. Cerretani
Battistero Duomo
Piazza del Duomo
V. dei Tosinghi
V. del Corso
Borgo degli Albizi
V. Dante Alighieri
Porta Rossa
Pza. della Signoria
Via dell' Anguillara
V. Giuseppe Verdi
V. dei Pepi
V. dell' Agnolo
V. Vaccherecia
Borgo dei Greci
Pza. Santa Croce
V. Ghibellina
Lung. Archibusieri
Galleria degli Uffizi
Ponte Vecchio
Santa Croce
Arno
Corso Tintori
Lung. d. Grazie
Lung. Torrigiani
Ponte alle Grazie
Lung. Serristori

0   ¼ mile
0   400 meters

8

FLORENCE PLANNER

Making the Most of Your Time

With some planning, you can see Florence's most famous sights in a couple of days. Start off at the city's most awe-inspiring work of architecture, the Duomo, climbing to the top of the dome if you have the stamina. On the same piazza, check out Ghiberti's bronze doors at the Battistero. (They're actually high-quality copies; the Museo dell'Opera del Duomo has the originals.) Set aside the afternoon for the Galleria degli Uffizi, making sure to reserve tickets in advance.

On day two, visit Michelangelo's *David* in the Galleria dell'Accademia—reserve tickets here too. Linger in the Piazza della Signoria, Florence's central square, where a copy of *David* stands in the spot the original occupied for centuries, then head east a couple of blocks to Santa Croce, the city's most artistically rich church. Double back and walk across Florence's landmark bridge, the Ponte Vecchio.

Do all that, and you'll have seen some great art, but you've just scratched the surface. If you have more time, put the Bargello, the Museo di San Marco, and the Cappelle Medicee at the top of your list. When you're ready for an art break, stroll through the Boboli Gardens or explore Florence's lively shopping scene, from the food stalls of the Mercato Centrale to the chic boutiques of the Via Tornabuoni.

Getting Around

Florence's flat, compact city center is made for walking, but when your feet get weary, you can use the efficient bus system, which includes small electric buses making the rounds in the center. Buses also climb to Piazzale Michelangelo and San Miniato south of the Arno.

An automobile in Florence is a liability. If your itinerary includes parts of Italy where you'll want a car (such as Tuscany), pick the vehicle up on your way out of town. For more information on getting into, out of, and around Florence, see "Essentials" at the end of this chapter.

Titian's *Venus of Urbino*

Avoiding an Art Hangover

Trying to take in Florence's amazing art can be a headache—there's just too much to see. Especially if you're not a dedicated art enthusiast, remember to pace yourself. Allow time to wander and follow your whims, and ignore any pangs of guilt if you'd rather relax in a café and watch the world go by than trudge on sore feet through another breathtaking palace or church.

Florence isn't a city that can be "done." It's a place you can return to again and again, confident there will always be more treasures to discover.

Florence Hours

Florence's sights keep tricky hours. Some are closed on Wednesday, some on Monday, some on *every other* Monday. Quite a few shut their doors each day (or on most days) by 2 in the afternoon. Things get even more confusing on weekends. Make it a general rule to check the hours closely for any place you're planning to visit; if it's somewhere you have your heart set on seeing, call to confirm.

Here's a selection of major sights that might not be open when you'd expect—consult the sight listings within this chapter for the full details. And be aware that, as always, hours can and do change.

■ The Uffizi and the Accademia are both closed Monday. All but a few of the galleries at Palazzo Pitti are closed Monday as well.

■ The Duomo closes at 3:30 on Thursday (as opposed to 5 on other weekdays, 4:45 on weekends). The dome of the Duomo is closed on Sunday.

■ The Battistero is open from noon until 7, Monday through Saturday, and on Sunday from 8:30 to 2.

■ The Bargello closes at 1:50 in the afternoon, and is closed entirely on alternating Sundays and Mondays.

■ The Cappelle Medicee are closed on alternating Sundays and Mondays.

■ Museo di San Marco closes at 1:50 on weekdays but stays open till 7 on weekends—except for alternating Sundays and Mondays, when it's closed entirely.

■ Palazzo Medici-Riccardi is closed Wednesday.

Making Reservations

At most times of day you'll see a line of people snaking around the Uffizi. They're waiting to buy tickets, and you don't want to be one of them. Instead, call ahead for a reservation (055/294883; reservationists speak English). You'll be given a reservation number and a time of admission—the further in advance you call, the more time slots you'll have to choose from. Go to the museum's reservation door at the appointed hour, give the clerk your number, pick up your ticket, and go inside. You'll pay €3 for this privilege, but it's money well spent.

Use the same reservation service to book tickets for the Galleria dell'Accademia, where lines rival those of the Uffizi. (Reservations can also be made for the Palazzo Pitti, the Bargello, and several other sights, but they aren't needed.) An alternative strategy is to check with your hotel—many will handle reservations.

How's the Weather?

The best times to visit Florence are in the spring and the fall. Days are warm, nights are cool, and the city is crowded, but not overly so. Avoid July and August if at all possible: the heat is unbearable, air-conditioning something of a rarity, mosquitoes are rampant, and so are tour groups. Those who want to find the city at its emptiest should consider visiting in November or January. It rains quite a bit and can get cold, but you'll spare yourself waits at museums and have reduced competition at restaurant tables.

8

Piazza Signoria

TOP PASSEGGIATA

Via dei Calzaiuoli, between Piazza del Duomo and Piazza della Signoria, is where Florence comes out for its evening stroll.

Updated by
Patricia Rucidlo

FLORENCE, THE CITY OF THE LILY, gave birth to the Renaissance and changed the way we see the world. For centuries it has captured the imagination of travelers, who come here to walk in the footsteps of Dante, Donatello, Botticelli, and Michelangelo. You'll find sublime art at almost every turn, but Florence (Firenze in Italian) isn't simply one large museum. Even if *David* and the Duomo didn't exist, you could still fall in love with the city for its winding streets, its earthy yet sophisticated food and wine, or the way the natives manage to lead thoroughly modern lives in a place that hasn't changed all that much since the 16th century.

Florence was "discovered" in the 1700s by upper-class northerners making the grand tour. It became a mecca for travelers, particularly the Romantics, who were inspired by the elegance of its palazzos and its artistic wealth. Today millions of modern visitors follow in their footsteps. When the sun sets over the Arno and, as Mark Twain described it, "overwhelms Florence with tides of color that make all the sharp lines dim and faint and turn the solid city to a city of dreams," it's hard not to fall under the city's spell.

EXPLORING FLORENCE

Most sights in Florence are concentrated in the relatively small historic center, and walking through its streets and alleyways is a discovery in itself. Today a handful of the more than 200 towers built in the 12th and 13th centuries survive; look for them them as you explore. The town has managed to preserve its predominantly medieval street plan and mostly Renaissance infrastructure while successfully adapting to the insistent demands of 21st-century life.

Centro Storico: The Duomo to the Ponte Vecchio

Florence's *centro storico* (historic center), stretching from the Piazza del Duomo south to the Arno, is as dense with artistic treasures as anyplace in the world. The churches, medieval towers, Renaissance palaces, and world-class museums and galleries contain some of the most outstanding aesthetic achievements of Western history.

Much of the centro storico is closed to automobile traffic, but you still must dodge mopeds, cyclists, and masses of fellow tourists as you walk the narrow streets, especially in the area bounded by the Duomo, Piazza della Signoria, Galleria degli Uffizi, and Ponte Vecchio.

The Main Attractions

★ ❼ **Bargello.** During the Renaissance, this building was headquarters for the *podestà*, or chief magistrate. It was also used as a prison, and the exterior served as a "most wanted" billboard: effigies of notorious criminals and Medici enemies were painted on its walls. Today it houses the **Museo Nazionale**, containing what is probably the finest collection of Renaissance sculpture in Italy. The concentration of masterworks by Michelangelo (1475–1564), Don-

> **WORD OF MOUTH**
>
> "I think the Bargello might be the most underrated museum in Florence, if not Italy." —Jess

FLORENCE THROUGH THE AGES

Guelph vs. Ghibelline. Though Florence can lay claim to a modest importance in the ancient world, it didn't come into its own until the Middle Ages. In the early 1200s, the city, like most of the rest of Italy, was rent by civic unrest. Two factions, the Guelphs and the Ghibellines, competed for power. The Guelphs supported the papacy, and the Ghibellines supported the Holy Roman Empire. Bloody battles—most notably one at Montaperti in 1260—tore Florence and other Italian cities apart. By the end of the 13th century the Guelphs ruled securely and Ghibellines had been vanquished. This didn't end civic strife, however: the Guelphs split into the Whites and the Blacks for reasons still debated by historians. Dante, author of the *Divine Comedy*, was banished from Florence in 1301 because he was a White.

The Guilded Age. Local merchants had organized themselves into guilds by 1250. In that year they proclaimed themselves the *"primo popolo"* (literally, "first people"), making a landmark attempt at elective, republican rule. Though the episode lasted only 10 years, it constituted a breakthrough in Western history. Such a daring stance by the merchant class was a by-product of Florence's emergence as an economic powerhouse. Florentines were papal bankers; they instituted the system of international letters of credit; and the gold florin became the international standard of currency. With this economic strength came a building boom. Palaces and basilicas were erected, enlarged, or restructured. Sculptors such as Donatello and Ghiberti decorated them; painters such as Giotto and Botticelli frescoed their walls.

Mighty Medici. Though ostensibly a republic, Florence was blessed (or cursed) with one very powerful family, the Medici, who came to prominence in the 1430s and were the de facto rulers of Florence for several hundred years. It was under patriarch Cosimo il Vecchio (1389–1464) that the Medici's position in Florence was securely established. Florence's golden age occurred during the reign of his grandson Lorenzo de' Medici (1449–92). Lorenzo was not only an astute politician but also a highly educated man and a great patron of the arts. Called "Il Magnifico" (the Magnificent), he gathered around him poets, artists, philosophers, architects, and musicians.

Lorenzo's son, Piero (1471–1503), proved inept at handling the city's affairs. He was run out of town in 1494, and Florence briefly enjoyed its status as a republic while dominated by the Dominican friar Girolamo Savonarola (1452–98). After a decade of internal unrest, the republic fell and the Medici were recalled to power, but Florence never regained its former prestige. By the 1530s most of the major artistic talent had left the city—Michelangelo, for one, had settled in Rome. The now-ineffectual Medici, eventually attaining the title of grand dukes, remained nominally in power until the line died out in 1737, after which time Florence passed from the Austrians to the French and back again until the unification of Italy (1865–70), when it briefly became the capital under King Vittorio Emanuele II.

8

atello (circa 1386–1466), and Benvenuto Cellini (1500–71) is remarkable; they're distributed among an eclectic array of arms, ceramics, and enamels. For Renaissance art lovers, the Bargello is to sculpture what the Uffizi is to painting.

In 1401 Filippo Brunelleschi (1377–1446) and Lorenzo Ghiberti (circa 1378–1455) vied for the most prestigious commission of the day: the decoration of the north doors of the baptistery in Piazza del Duomo. For the competition, each designed a bronze bas-relief panel depicting the Sacrifice of Isaac; both panels are displayed, together, in the room devoted to the sculpture of Donatello on the upper floor. The judges chose Ghiberti for the commission; see if you agree with their choice. ⊠ *Via del Proconsolo 4, Bargello* ☎ *055/2388606* ⊕ *www.arca.net/db/musei/bargello.htm* ☜ *€4* ⊙ *Daily 8:15–1:50. Closed 2nd and 4th Mon. of month and 1st, 3rd, and 5th Sun. of month.*

★ ❷ **Battistero** (Baptistery). The octagonal Baptistery is one of the supreme monuments of the Italian Romanesque style and one of Florence's oldest structures. Local legend has it that it was once a Roman temple of Mars; modern excavations, however, suggest that its foundations date from the 4th to 5th and the 8th to 9th century AD, well after the collapse of the Roman Empire. The round-arched Romanesque decoration on the exterior probably dates from the 11th century. The interior dome mosaics from the early 14th century are justly renowned, but—glittering beauties though they are—they could never outshine the building's famed bronze Renaissance doors decorated with panels crafted by Lorenzo Ghiberti. The doors—or at least copies of them—on which Ghiberti spent most of his adult life (1403–52) are on the north and east sides of the Baptistery, and the Gothic panels on the south door were designed by Andrea Pisano (active circa 1290–1348) in 1330. The original Ghiberti doors were removed to protect them from the effects of pollution and have been beautifully restored; some of the panels are now on display in the Museo dell'Opera del Duomo.

Ghiberti's north doors depict scenes from the life of Christ; his later east doors (dating 1425–52), facing the Duomo facade, render scenes from the Old Testament. Very different in style, they illustrate the artistic changes that marked the beginning of the Renaissance. Look at the far right panel of the middle row on the earlier (1403–24) north doors (*Jesus Calming the Waters*). Ghiberti captured the chaos of a storm at sea with great skill and economy, but the artistic conventions he used are basically pre-Renaissance: Jesus is the most important figure, so he is the largest; the disciples are next in size, being next in importance; the ship on which they founder looks like a mere toy.

The exquisitely rendered panels on the east doors are larger, more expansive, more sweeping—and more convincing. Look at the middle panel on the left-hand door. It tells the story of Jacob and Esau, and the various episodes—the selling of the birthright, Isaac ordering Esau to go hunting, the blessing of Jacob, and so forth—have been merged into a single beautifully realized street scene. Ghiberti's use of perspective suggests depth: the background architecture looks far more credible than on the north door panels, the figures in the foreground are grouped realistically, and the naturalism and grace of the poses (look at Esau's left leg and the dog next to him) have nothing to do with the sacred message being conveyed. Although the religious content remains, the figures and their place in the natural world are given new prominence and are portrayed with a realism not seen in art since the fall of the Roman Empire more than a thousand years before.

As a footnote to Ghiberti's panels, one small detail of the east doors is worth a special look. To the lower left of the Jacob and Esau panel, Ghiberti placed a tiny self-portrait bust. From either side, the portrait is extremely appealing—Ghiberti looks like everyone's favorite uncle—but the bust is carefully placed so that there is a single spot from which you can make direct eye contact with the tiny head. When that contact is made, the impression of intelligent life is astonishing. It is no wonder that these doors received one of the most famous compliments in the history of art from an artist known to be notoriously stingy with praise: Michelangelo himself declared them so beautiful that they could serve as the Gates of Paradise. ⌂ *Piazza del Duomo* ☎ *055/2302885* ⊕ *www.operaduomo.firenze.it* 🎫 *€3* ⊗ *Mon.–Sat. noon–7, Sun. 8:30–2.*

❸ **Campanile.** The Gothic bell tower designed by Giotto (1266–1337) is a soaring structure of multicolored marble originally decorated with reliefs that are now in the Museo dell'Opera del Duomo. A climb of 414 steps rewards you with a close-up of Brunelleschi's cupola on the Duomo next door and a sweeping view of the city. ⌂ *Piazza del Duomo* ☎ *055/2302885* ⊕ *www.operaduomo.firenze.it* 🎫 *€6* ⊗ *Daily 8:30–7:30.*

★ ❶ **Duomo** (Cattedrale di Santa Maria del Fiore). In 1296 Arnolfo di Cambio (circa 1245–circa 1310) was commissioned to build "the loftiest, most sumptuous edifice human invention could devise" in the Romanesque style on the site of the old church of Santa Reparata. The immense Duomo was not completed until 1436, the year when it was consecrated. The imposing facade dates only from the 19th century; it was added in the neo-Gothic style to complement Giotto's genuine Gothic

> **WORD OF MOUTH**
>
> "The Duomo was a truly amazing cathedral. We visited it twice, once to attend mass (in English, which we appreciated), and once to look at its architecture and art and to climb up to the top. Although the climb is definitely a bit tiring, it was well worth it—the view from the top was incredible."
> —Gina

14th-century campanile. The real glory of the Duomo, however, is Filippo Brunelleschi's dome, presiding over the cathedral with a dignity and grace that few domes to this day can match.

Brunelleschi's **cupola** was an ingenious engineering feat. The space to be enclosed by the dome was so large and so high above the ground that traditional methods of dome construction—wooden centering and scaffolding—were of no use whatsoever. So Brunelleschi developed entirely new building methods, which he implemented with equipment of his own design (including a novel scaffolding method). Beginning work in 1420,

he built not one dome but two, one inside the other, and connected them with common ribbing that stretched across the intervening empty space, thereby considerably lessening the crushing weight of the structure. He also employed a new method of bricklaying, based on an ancient Roman herringbone pattern, interlocking each new course of bricks with the course below in a way that made the growing structure self-supporting. The result was one of the great engineering breakthroughs of all time: most of Europe's later domes, including that of St. Peter's in Rome, were built employing Brunelleschi's methods, and today the Duomo has come to symbolize Florence in the same way that the Eiffel Tower symbolizes Paris. The Florentines are justly proud, and to this day the Florentine phrase for "homesick" is *nostalgia del cupolone* (homesick for the dome).

The interior is a fine example of Florentine Gothic. Much of the cathedral's best-known art has been moved to the nearby Museo dell'Opera del Duomo. Notable among the works that remain, however, are two towering equestrian frescoes honoring famous soldiers: *Niccolò da Tolentino*, painted in 1456 by Andrea del Castagno (circa 1419–57), and *Sir John Hawkwood*, painted 20 years earlier by Paolo Uccello (1397–1475); both are on the left-hand wall of the nave. A 10-year restoration, completed in 1995, repaired the dome and cleaned the vast and crowded fresco of the *Last Judgment*, executed by Vasari and Zuccaro, on its interior. Originally Brunelleschi wanted mosaics to cover the interior of the great ribbed cupola, but by the time the Florentines got around to commissioning the decoration, 150 years later, tastes had changed. Too bad: it's a fairly dreadful *Last Judgment* and hardly worth the effort of craning your neck to see it.

You can explore the upper and lower reaches of the cathedral. The remains of a Roman wall and an 11th-century cemetery have been excavated beneath the nave; the way down is near the first pier on the right. The climb to the top of the dome (463 steps) is not for the faint of heart, but the view is superb. ⊠ *Piazza del Duomo* ☎ *055/2302885* ⊕ *www.operaduomo. firenze.it* 🕾 *Church free, crypt €3, cupola €6* ⊘ *Church Mon.–Wed. and Fri. 10–5, Thurs. 10–3:30, Sat. 10–4:45, Sun. 1:30–4:45, 1st Sat. of month 10–3:30. Crypt weekdays 10–5, Sat. 10–5:45, 1st Sat. of month 10–3:30. Cupola weekdays 8:30–7, Sat. 8:30–5:40, 1st Sat. of month 8:30–4.*

⓫ **Galleria degli Uffizi.** The venerable Uffizi Gallery occupies the top floor

FodorśChoice
★

of the U-shape **Palazzo degli Uffizi** fronting on the Arno, designed by Giorgio Vasari (1511–74) in 1560 to hold the *uffizi* (administrative offices) of the Medici grand duke Cosimo I (1519–74). Later, the Medici installed their art collections here, creating what was Europe's first modern museum, open to the public (at first only by request) since 1591. Hard-core museum aficiona-

> **WORD OF MOUTH**
>
> "I strongly recommend making reservations for both the Accademia and the Uffizi. We saved ourselves a ton of time. We walked right into the Accademia and right past the line of unreserved people."   –Ivy

dos can pick up a complete guide to the collections at bookshops and newsstands.

Among the highlights are Paolo Uccello's *Battle of San Romano,* its brutal chaos of lances one of the finest visual metaphors for warfare ever captured in paint; the *Madonna and Child with Two Angels,* by Fra Filippo Lippi (1406–69), in which the impudent eye contact established by the angel would have been unthinkable prior to the Renaissance; the *Birth of Venus* and *Primavera* by Sandro Botticelli (1445–1510), the goddess of the former seeming to float on air and the fairy-tale charm of the latter exhibiting the painter's idiosyncratic genius at its zenith; the portraits of the Renaissance duke Federico da Montefeltro and his wife, Battista Sforza, by Piero della Francesca (circa 1420–92); the *Madonna of the Goldfinch* by Raphael (1483–1520), which, though darkened by time, captures an aching tenderness between mother and child; Michelangelo's *Doni Tondo* (the only panel painting that can be securely attributed to him); a *Self-Portrait as an Old Man* by Rembrandt (1606–69); the *Venus of Urbino* by Titian (circa 1488/90–1576); and the splendid *Bacchus* by Caravaggio (circa 1571/72–1610). In the last two works, the approaches to myth and sexuality are diametrically opposed, to put it mildly. Six additional exhibition rooms opened in 2004, convoluting the way you exit the museum. Many of the more than 400 works now displayed would have been better left in storage.

> **WORD OF MOUTH**
>
> "The Uffizi has gorgeous high Renaissance art, but in my experience it is a user-unfriendly museum: lots of stairs, no captions or signs to speak of, no a/c. I was glad I went but I was also glad to leave. I'll go again, but with a headache tablet in hand."
>
> –elaine

Late in the afternoon is the least crowded time to visit. For a fee, advance tickets can be reserved by phone or, once in Florence, at the Uffizi reservation booth at least one day in advance of your visit. If you book by phone, remember to keep the confirmation number and take it with you to the door at the museum marked "Reservations." Usually you're be ushered in almost immediately. Come with cash, because credit cards are not accepted. When there's a special exhibit on, which is often, the base ticket price goes up to €9.50. ⊠ *Piazzale degli Uffizi 6, near Piazza della Signoria* ☎ *055/23885* ✉ *Advance tickets* ⊠ *Consorzio ITA, Piazza Pitti 1, 50121* ☎ *055/294883* ⊕ *www.uffizi.firenze. it* ✉ *€7.50, reservation fee €3* ☉ *Tues.–Sun. 8:15–6:50.*

need a break? **GustaVino** (⊠ Via della Condotta 37/r, near Piazza della Signoria ☎ 055/2399806) calls itself an *enoteca con cucina* (wine bar with a kitchen). Its handy location makes it a perfect spot to recover after a trip to the Uffizi. Next door, La Canova di Gustavino specializes in sandwiches.

★ ❾ **Piazza della Signoria.** This is by far the most striking square in Florence. It was here, in 1497, that the famous "bonfire of the vanities" took place, when the fanatical friar Savonarola induced his followers to hurl their worldly goods into the flames; it was also here, a year later, that he was hanged as a heretic and, ironically, burned. A bronze plaque in the pavement marks the exact spot of his execution.

The statues in the square and in the 14th-century **Loggia dei Lanzi** on the south side vary in quality. Cellini's famous bronze *Perseus* holding the severed head of Medusa is certainly the most important sculpture in the loggia. Other works include *The Rape of the Sabines* and *Hercules and the Centaur,* both late-16th-century works by Giambologna (1529–1608), and, in the back, a row of sober matrons dating from Roman times.

In the square, the Neptune Fountain, dating from between 1550 and 1575, wins the booby prize. It was created by Bartolomeo Ammannati (1511–1592), who considered it a failure himself. The Florentines call it *Il Biancone,* which may be translated as "the big white one" or "the big white thing." Giambologna's equestrian statue to the left of the fountain pays tribute to Grand Duke Cosimo I. Occupying the steps of the Palazzo Vecchio are a copy of Donatello's heraldic lion of Florence, known as the *Marzocco* (the original is in the Bargello); a copy of Donatello's *Judith and Holofernes* (the original is inside the Palazzo Vecchio); a copy of Michelangelo's *David* (the original is now in the Galleria dell'Accademia); and Baccio Bandinelli's insipid *Hercules* (1534).

㉛ Ponte Santa Trinita. Take a moment to study the bridge down river from the Ponte Vecchio: it was designed by Bartolomeo Ammannati in 1567 (possibly from sketches by Michelangelo), blown up by the retreating Germans during World War II, and painstakingly reconstructed after the war. The view from Ponte Santa Trinita is beautiful, which might explain why so many young lovers hang out there. ⊠ *Near Ponte Vecchio.*

⓮ Ponte Vecchio (Old Bridge). This charming bridge was built in 1345 to replace an earlier bridge that was swept away by flood, and its shops housed first butchers, then grocers, blacksmiths, and other merchants. But in 1593 the Medici grand duke Ferdinand I (1549–1609), whose private corridor linking the Medici palace (Palazzo Pitti) with the Medici offices (the Uffizi) crossed the bridge atop the shops, decided that all this plebeian commerce under his feet was unseemly. So he threw out the butchers and blacksmiths and installed 41 goldsmiths and eight jewelers. The bridge has been devoted solely to these two trades ever since.

Also Worth Seeing

❽ Badia Fiorentina. This ancient church was rebuilt in 1285; its graceful bell tower, best seen from the interior courtyard, is beautiful for its unusual construction—a hexagonal tower built on a quadrangular base. The interior of the church was halfheartedly remodeled in the baroque style during the 17th century; its best-known work of art is the delicate *Vision of St. Bernard* by Filippino Lippi (circa 1457–1504), on the left as you enter. The painting—one of Lippi's finest—is in superb condition; note the Virgin Mary's beautifully rendered hands. ⊠ *Via Dante Alighieri 1, near Bargello* ☎ *055/264402* ⊇ *Free* ☉ *Mon. 3–6.*

⓭ Istituto e Museo di Storia della Scienza (Institute and Museum of the History of Science). Though it tends to be obscured by the glamour of the

Uffizi, this science museum has much to recommend it: Galileo's own instruments, antique armillary spheres—some of them real works of art—and other reminders that the Renaissance made not only artistic but also scientific history. ☒ *Piazza dei Giudici 1, near Piazza della Signoria* ☎ *055/ 265311* ⊕ *www.imss.fi.it* 🖰 €5 ☉ *Mon. and Wed.–Sat. 9:30–5, Tues. 9:30–1. May–Oct., also open 2nd Sun. of month 10–1.*

☾ ⑫ **Mercato Nuovo** (New Market). This open-air loggia was new in 1551. Beyond its slew of souvenir stands, its main attraction is a copy of Pietro Tacca's bronze *Porcellino* (which translates as "little pig," despite the fact that the animal is, in fact, a wild boar) on the south side, dating from around 1612 and copied from an earlier Roman work now in the Uffizi. The Porcellino is Florence's equivalent of the Trevi Fountain: put a coin in his mouth, and if it falls through the grate below (according to one interpretation), it means that one day you'll return to Florence. ☒ *Corner of Via Por Santa Maria and Via Porta Rossa, near Piazza della Repubblica* ☉ *Tues.–Sat. 8–7, Mon. 1–7.*

❹ **Museo dell'Opera del Duomo** (Cathedral Museum). Ghiberti's original Baptistery door panels and the *cantorie* (choir loft) reliefs by Donatello and Luca della Robbia (1400–82) keep company with Donatello's *Mary Magdalen* and Michelangelo's *Pietà* (not to be confused with his more famous *Pietà* in St. Peter's in Rome). Renaissance sculpture is in part defined by its revolutionary realism, but in its palpable suffering Donatello's *Magdalen* goes beyond realism. Michelangelo's heart-wrenching *Pietà* was unfinished at his death; the female figure on the left was added by one Tiberio Calcagni (1532–65), and never has the difference between competence and genius been manifested so clearly. ☒ *Piazza del Duomo 9* ☎ *055/2302885* ⊕ *www.operaduomo.firenze.it* 🖰 €6 ☉ *Mon.–Sat. 9–7:30, Sun. 9–1:40.*

❻ **Orsanmichele.** This multipurpose structure, closed indefinitely for restoration, began as an 8th-century oratory, then in 1290 was turned into an open-air loggia for selling grain. Destroyed by fire in 1304, it was rebuilt as a loggia-market. Between 1367 and 1380 the arcades were closed and two stories added above; finally, at century's end it was turned into a church. Inside is a beautifully detailed 14th-century Gothic tabernacle by Andrea Orcagna (1320–68). The exterior niches contain copies of sculptures dating from the early 1400s to the early 1600s by Donatello and Verrocchio (1435–88), among others, that were paid for by the guilds. Though it is a copy, Verrocchio's *Doubting Thomas* (circa 1470) is particularly deserving of attention. Here you see Christ, like the building's other figures, entirely framed within the niche, and St. Thomas standing on its bottom ledge, with his right foot outside the niche frame. This one detail, the positioning of a single foot, brings the whole composition to life. ☒ *Via dei Calzaiuoli, near Piazza della Repubblica* ☎ *055/284944* ☉ *Closed indefinitely.*

❿ **Palazzo Vecchio** (Old Palace). Florence's forbidding, fortresslike city hall, presumed to have been designed by Arnolfo di Cambio, was begun in 1299, and its massive bulk and towering campanile dominate the Piazza della Signoria. It was built as a meeting place for the elected guilds-men who governed the city at the time; over the centuries it has served lesser purposes, but today it is once again City Hall. The interior court-yard is a good deal less severe, having been remodeled by Michelozzo (1396–1472) in 1453; the copy of Verrocchio's bronze *puttino* (little child), topping the central fountain, softens the space.

Two adjoining rooms on the second floor supply one of the starkest con-trasts in Florence. The vast **Sala dei Cinquecento** (Room of the Five Hun-dred) is named for the 500-member Great Council, the people's assembly established by Savonarola, which met here. The Sala was later decorated by Giorgio Vasari, around 1563–65, with huge—almost grotesquely huge—frescoes celebrating Florentine history; depictions of battles with nearby cities predominate. Continuing the martial theme, the Sala also contains Michelangelo's *Victory* group, intended for the never-com-pleted tomb of Pope Julius II (1443–1513), plus other lesser sculptures.

The little **Studiolo** is to the right of the Sala's entrance. The study of Cosimo I's son, the melancholy Francesco I (1541–87), was designed by Vasari and decorated by Vasari and Bronzino (1503–72). It's intimate, civilized, and filled with allegorical art. ⊠ *Piazza della Signoria* ☎ *055/2768465* 🎫 *€6* ⊙ *By reservation Mon.–Wed., Fri.–Sun. 9–7, Thurs. 9–2.*

❺ Piazza della Repubblica. This was the site of the ancient forum at the core of the original Roman settlement. The street plan in the area around the piazza still reflects the carefully plotted grid of the Roman military encampment. The Mercato Vecchio (Old Market), dating from the Mid-dle Ages, was demolished and the current piazza was constructed be-tween 1885 and 1895 as a neoclassical showpiece. The piazza is lined with outdoor cafés affording excellent spots to people-watch.

In Michelangelo's Footsteps: San Lorenzo to the Accademia

A sculptor, painter, architect, and even a poet, Florentine native son Michelangelo was a consummate genius, and some of his finest creations remain in his hometown. The Biblioteca Medicea Laurenziana is per-haps his most fanciful work of architecture. A key to understanding Michelangelo's genius can be found in the magnificent Cappelle Medicee, where both his sculptural and architectural prowess can be clearly seen. Planned frescoes were never completed, sadly, for they would have shown in one space the artistic triple threat that he certainly was. The towering yet graceful *David*, his most famous work, resides in the Gal-leria dell'Accademia.

After visiting San Lorenzo, resist the temptation to explore the market that surrounds the church. You can always come back later, after the churches and museums have closed; the market is open until 7 PM. Note that the Museo di San Marco closes at 1:50 on weekdays.

The Main Attractions

★ **⓱ Cappelle Medicee** (Medici Chapels). This magnificent complex includes the **Cappella dei Principi,** the Medici chapel and mausoleum that was begun

Continued on page 387

WHO'S WHO OF RENAISSANCE ART

Michelangelo. Leonardo da Vinci. Raphael. The heady triumvirate of the Italian Renaissance is synonymous with artistic genius. Yet they are only three of the remarkable cast of characters whose work inspired the Renaissance, that extraordinary flourishing of art and culture in Italy, especially in Florence, as the Middle Ages drew to a close. The artists were visionaries, who redefined painting, sculpture, architecture, and even what it means to be an artist.

THE PIONEER. In the mid-14th century, a few artists began to move away the flat, two-dimensional painting of the Middle Ages. **Giotto**, who painted seemingly three-dimensional figures who show emotion, had a major impact on the artists of the next century.

THE GROUNDBREAKERS. The generation of **Brunelleschi** and **Botticelli** took center stage in the 15th century. **Ghiberti, Donatello, Uccello, Fra Angelico, Masaccio,** and **Filippo Lippi** were other major players. Part of the Renaissance (or "rebirth") was a renewed interest in classical sources—the texts, monuments, and sculpture of Ancient Greece and Rome. Perspective and the illusion of three-dimensional space in painting was another theme of this era, known as the Early Renaissance. Suddenly the art appearing on the walls looked real, or more realistic than it used to.

Roman ruins were not the only thing to inspire these artists. There was an incredible exchange of ideas going on. In Santa Maria del Carmine, Filippo Lippi was inspired by the work of Masaccio, who in turn was a friend of Brunelleschi. Young artists also learned from the masters via the apprentice system. Ghiberti's workshop (*bottega* in Italian) included, at one time or another, Donatello, Masaccio, and Uccello. Botticelli was apprenticed to Filippo Lippi.

THE BIG THREE. The mathematical rationality and precision of 15th-century art gave way to what is known as the High Renaissance. **Leonardo, Michelangelo,** and **Raphael** were much more concerned with portraying the body in all its glory and with achieving harmony and grandeur in their work. Oil paint, used sparingly and unknowingly up until this time, became more widely employed: as a result, Leonardo's colors are deeper, more sensual, more alive. For one brief time, all three were in Florence at the same time. Michelangelo and Leonardo surely knew one another, as they were simultaneously working on frescoes (never completed) inside Palazzo Vecchio.

When Michelangelo left Florence for Rome in 1508, he began the slow drain of artistic exodus from Florence, which never really recovered her previous glory.

A RENAISSANCE TIMELINE

IN THE WORLD

Black Death in Europe kills one third of the population, 1347-50.

Joan of Arc burned at the stake, 1431.

IN FLORENCE

Founding of the Medici bank, 1397.

Medici family made official papal bankers.

1434, Cosimo il Vecchio becomes de facto ruler of Florence. The Medici family will dominate the city until 1494.

Dante, a native of Florence, writes *The Divine Comedy*, 1302-21.

1300

1400

IN ART

EARLY RENAISSANCE

Giotto frescoes in Santa Croce, 1320-25.

Masaccio and Masolino fresco Santa Maria del Carmine, 1424-28.

GIOTTO (ca. 1267-1337)

BRUNELLESCHI (1377-1446)

LORENZO GHIBERTI (ca. 1381-1455)

DONATELLO (ca. 1386-1466)

PAOLO UCCELLO (1397-1475)

FRA ANGELICO (ca. 1400-1455)

MASACCIO (1401-1428)

FILIPPO LIPPI (ca. 1406-1469)

Donatello sculpts his bronze *David*, ca. 1440.

Fra Angelico frescoes monks' cells in San Marco, ca. 1438-45.

Uccello's *Sir John Hawkwood*, ca. 1436.

1334, 67-year-old Giotto is appointed chief architect of Santa Maria del Fiore, Florence's Duomo (above). He begins to work on the Campanile, which will be completed in 1359, after his death.

Ghiberti wins the competition for the Baptistery doors (above) in Florence, 1401.

Brunelleschi wins the competition for the Duomo's cupola (below), 1418.

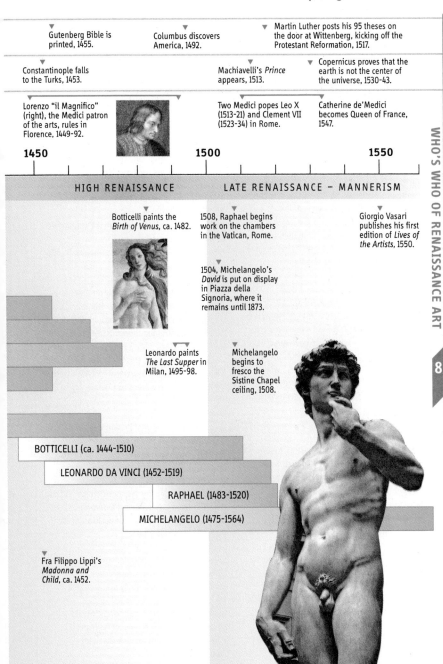

▼ Gutenberg Bible is printed, 1455.

▼ Columbus discovers America, 1492.

▼ Martin Luther posts his 95 theses on the door at Wittenberg, kicking off the Protestant Reformation, 1517.

▼ Constantinople falls to the Turks, 1453.

▼ Machiavelli's *Prince* appears, 1513.

▼ Copernicus proves that the earth is not the center of the universe, 1530-43.

▼ Lorenzo "il Magnifico" (right), the Medici patron of the arts, rules in Florence, 1449-92.

Two Medici popes Leo X (1513-21) and Clement VII (1523-34) in Rome.

Catherine de'Medici becomes Queen of France, 1547.

1450   **1500**   **1550**

HIGH RENAISSANCE   LATE RENAISSANCE – MANNERISM

▼ Botticelli paints the *Birth of Venus*, ca. 1482.

▼ 1508, Raphael begins work on the chambers in the Vatican, Rome.

▼ Giorgio Vasari publishes his first edition of *Lives of the Artists*, 1550.

▼ 1504, Michelangelo's *David* is put on display in Piazza della Signoria, where it remains until 1873.

▼ Leonardo paints *The Last Supper* in Milan, 1495-98.

▼ Michelangelo begins to fresco the Sistine Chapel ceiling, 1508.

BOTTICELLI (ca. 1444-1510)

LEONARDO DA VINCI (1452-1519)

RAPHAEL (1483-1520)

MICHELANGELO (1475-1564)

▼ Fra Filippo Lippi's *Madonna and Child*, ca. 1452.

Giotto's *Death and Ascension of St. Francis*   Donatello's *St. John the Baptist*   Ghiberti's *Gates of Paradise*

GIOTTO (CA. 1267-1337)
Painter/architect from a small town north of Florence.
He unequivocally set Italian painting on the course that led to the triumphs of the Renaissance masters. Unlike the rather flat, two-dimensional forms found in then prevailing Byzantine art, Giotto's figures have a fresh, life-like quality. The people in his paintings have bulk, and they show emotion, which you can see on their faces and in their gestures. This was something new in the late Middle Ages. Without Giotto, there wouldn't have been a Raphael.
In Florence: **Santa Croce; Uffizi; Campanile; Santa Maria Novella**
Elsewhere in Italy: **Scrovegni Chapel, Padua; Vatican Museums, Rome**

FILIPPO BRUNELLESCHI (1377-1446)
Architect/engineer from Florence.
If Brunelleschi had beaten Ghiberti in the Baptistery doors competition in Florence, the city's Duomo most likely would not have the striking appearance and authority that it has today. After his loss, he sulked off to Rome, where he studied the ancient Roman structures first-hand. Brunelleschi figured out how to vault the Duomo's dome, a structure unprecedented in its colossal size and great height. His Ospedale degli Innocenti employs classical elements in the creation of a stunning, new architectural statement; it is the first truly Renaissance structure.
In Florence: **Duomo; Ospedale degli Innocenti; San Lorenzo; Santo Spirito; Baptistery Doors Competition Entry, Bargello; Santa Croce**

LORENZO GHIBERTI (CA. 1381-1455)
Sculptor from Florence.
Ghiberti won a competition—besting his chief rival, Brunelleschi—to cast the gilded bronze North Doors of the Baptistery in Florence. These doors, and the East Doors that he subsequently executed, took up the next 50 years of his life. He created intricately worked figures that are more true-to-life than any since antiquity, and he was one of the first Renaissance sculptors to work in bronze. Ghiberti taught the next generation of artists; Donatello, Uccello, and Masaccio all passed through his studio.
In Florence: **Door Copies, Baptistery; Original Doors, Museo dell'Opera del Duomo; Baptistry Door Competition Entry, Bargello; Orsanmichele**

DONATELLO (CA. 1386-1466)
Sculptor from Florence.
Donatello was an innovator who, like his good friend Brunelleschi, spent most of his long life in Florence. Consumed with the science of optics, he used light and shadow to create the effects of nearness and distance. He made an essentially flat slab look like a three-dimensional scene. His bronze *David* is probably the first free-standing male nude since antiquity. Not only technically brilliant, his work is also emotionally resonant; few sculptors are as expressive.
In Florence: ***David*, Bargello; *St. Mark*, Orsanmichele; Palazzo Vecchio; Museo dell'Opera del Duomo; San Lorenzo; Santa Croce**
Elsewhere in Italy: **Padua; Prato**

Fra Angelico's *The Deploration*   Masaccio's *Holy Trinity*   Filippo Lippi's *Madonna and Child*

PAOLO UCCELLO (1397-1475)
Painter from Florence.
Renaissance chronicler Vasari once observed that had Uccello not been so obsessed with the mathematical problems posed by perspective, he would have been a very good painter. The struggle to master single-point perspective and to render motion in two dimensions is nowhere more apparent than in his battle scenes. His first major commission in Florence was the gargantuan fresco of the English mercenary Sir John Hawkwood (the Italians called him Giovanni Acuto) in Florence's Duomo.
In Florence: ***Sir John Hawkwood***, Duomo; ***Battle of San Romano***, Uffizi; **Santa Maria Novella**
Elsewhere in Italy: **Urbino**

FRA ANGELICO (CA. 1400-1455)
Painter from a small town north of Florence.
A Dominican friar, who eventually made his way to the convent of San Marco, Fra Angelico and his assistants painted frescoes for aid in prayer and meditation. He was known for his piety; Vasari wrote that Fra Angelico could never paint a crucifix without a tear running down his face. Perhaps no other painter so successfully translated the mysteries of faith and the sacred into painting. And yet his figures emote, his command of perspective is superb, and his use of color startles even today.
In Florence: **Museo di San Marco; Uffizi**
Elsewhere in Italy: **Vatican Museums, Rome**

MASACCIO (1401-1428)
Painter from San Giovanni Valdarno, southeast of Florence.
Masaccio and Masolino da Panicale, a frequent collaborator, worked most famously together at Santa Maria del Carmine. Their frescoes of the life of St. Peter use light to mold figures in the painting by imitating the way light falls on figures in real life. Masaccio also pioneered the use of single-point perspective, masterfully rendered in his *Trinity*. His friend Brunelleschi probably introduced him to the technique, yet another step forward in rendering things the way the eye sees them. Masaccio died young and under mysterious circumstances.
In Florence: **Santa Maria del Carmine;** ***Trinity*, Santa Maria Novella**

FILIPPO LIPPI (CA. 1406-1469)
Painter from Prato.
At a young age, Filippo Lippi entered the friary of Santa Maria del Carmine, where he was highly influenced by Masaccio and Masolino's frescoes. His religious vows appear to have made less of an impact; his affair with a young nun produced a son, Filippino (Little Philip, who later apprenticed with Botticelli), and a daughter. His religious paintings often have a playful, humorous note; some of his angels are downright impish and look directly out at the viewer. Lippi links the earlier painters of the 15th century with those who follow; Botticelli apprenticed with him.
In Florence: **Uffizi; Palazzo Medici Riccardi; San Lorenzo; Palazzo Pitti**
Elsewhere in Italy: **Prato**

Botticelli's *Primavera*   Leonardo's *Portrait of a Young Woman*

Raphael's *Madonna on the Meadow*

BOTTICELLI (CA. 1444-1510)

Painter from Florence.

Botticelli's work is characterized by stunning, elongated blondes, cherubic angels (something he undoubtedly learned from his time with Filippo Lippi), and tender Christs. Though he did many religious paintings, he also painted monumental, nonreligious panels—his *Birth of Venus* and *Primavera* being the two most famous of these. A brief sojourn took him to Rome, where he and a number of other artists frescoed the Sistine Chapel walls.

In Florence: **Birth of Venus, Primavera, Uffizi; Palazzo Pitti**

Elsewhere in Italy: **Vatican Museums, Rome**

LEONARDO DA VINCI (1452-1519)

Painter/sculptor/engineer from Anchiano, a small town outside Vinci.

Leonardo never lingered long in any place; his restless nature and his international reputation led to commissions throughout Italy, and took him to Milan, Vigevano, Pavia, Rome, and, ultimately, France. Though he is most famous for his mysterious *Mona Lisa* (at the Louvre in Paris), he painted other penetrating, psychological portraits in addition to his scientific experiments: his design for a flying machine (never built) predates Kitty Hawk by nearly 500 years. The greatest collection of Leonardo's work in the world can be seen on one wall in the Uffizi.

In Florence: **Adoration of the Magi, Uffizi**

Elsewhere in Italy: **Last Supper, Santa Maria delle Grazie, Milan**

RAPHAEL (1483-1520)

Painter/architect from Urbino.

Raphael spent only four highly productive years of his short life in Florence, where he turned out made-to-order panel paintings of the Madonna and Child for a hungry public; he also executed a number of portraits of Florentine aristocrats. Perhaps no other artist had such a fine command of line and color, and could render it, seemingly effortlessly, in paint. His painting acquired new authority after he came up against Michelangelo toiling away on the Sistine ceiling. Raphael worked nearly next door in the Vatican, where his figures take on an epic, Michelangelesque scale.

In Florence: **Uffizi; Palazzo Pitti**

Elsewhere in Italy: **Vatican Museums, Rome**

MICHELANGELO (1475-1564)

Painter/sculptor/architect from Caprese.

Although Florentine and proud of it (he famously signed his St. Peter's *Pietà* to avoid confusion about where he was from), he spent most of his 90 years outside his native city. He painted and sculpted the male body on an epic scale and glorified it while doing so. Though he complained throughout the proceedings that he was really a sculptor, Michelangelo's Sistine Chapel ceiling is arguably the greatest fresco cycle ever painted (and the massive figures owe no small debt to Giotto).

In Florence: **David, Galleria dell'Accademia; Uffizi; Casa Buonarroti**

Elsewhere in Italy: **St. Peter's Basilica, Vatican Museums, and Piazza del Campidoglio in Rome** in 1605 and kept marble workers busy for several hundred years, and the **Sagrestia Nuova** (New Sacristy), designed by Michelangelo and so called to distinguish it from Brunelleschi's *Sagrestia Vecchia* (Old Sacristy).

Michelangelo received the commission for the New Sacristy in 1520 from Cardinal Giulio de' Medici (1478–1534), who later became Pope Clement VII and who wanted a new burial chapel for his cousins Giuliano (1478–1534) and Lorenzo (1492–1519). The result was a tour de force of architecture and sculpture. Architecturally, Michelangelo was as original and inventive here as ever, but it is, quite properly, the powerful sculpture that dominates the room. The scheme is allegorical: on the tomb to the right are figures representing Day and Night, and on the tomb to the left are figures representing Dawn and Dusk; above them are idealized sculptures of the two men, usually interpreted to represent the active life and the contemplative life. But the allegorical meanings are secondary; what is most important is the intense presence of the sculptural figures. Michelangelo's contemporaries were so awed by this force (in his sculpture here and elsewhere) that they invented an entirely new word to describe the phenomenon: *terribilità* (dreadfulness). To this day it's used only when describing his work, and it's in evidence here at the peak of its power. During his stormy relations with the Medici, Michelangelo once hid out in a tiny room that is accessed from the left of the altar. Charcoal sketches on the wall were once thought to be Michelangelo's; art historians now think otherwise, but they're a nice example of centuries-old graffiti. Admission to the room is on the hour (at 9, 10, 11, and noon) and is limited to 12 people; tell the ticket seller that you want to go in. Your chances are better for one of the earlier hours. ⊠ *Piazza di Madonna degli Aldobrandini, near San Lorenzo* ☎ *055/294883 reservations* 🖼 *€6* ⊙ *Daily 8:15–5. Closed 1st, 3rd, and 5th Mon. and 2nd and 4th Sun. of month.*

★ ⓴ **Galleria dell'Accademia** (Accademia Gallery). The collection of Florentine paintings here, dating from the 13th to the 18th century, is largely unremarkable, but the sculptures by Michelangelo are worth the price of admission. The unfinished *Slaves,*

> **WORD OF MOUTH**
>
> "Seeing *David* is a must. It is one of those magical moments in life."
> –Janda0

fighting their way out of their marble prisons, were meant for the tomb of Michelangelo's overly demanding patron, Pope Julius II (1443–1513). But the focal point is the original *David,* moved here from Piazza della Signoria in 1873. The *David* was commissioned in 1501 by the Opera del Duomo (Cathedral Works Committee), which gave the 26-year-old sculptor a leftover block of marble that had been ruined by another artist. Michelangelo's success with the block was so dramatic that the city showered him with honors, and the Opera del Duomo voted to build him a house and a studio in which to live and work.

Today *David* is beset not by Goliath but by tourists, and seeing the statue at all—much less really studying it—can be a trial, as it is surrounded by a Plexiglas barrier. Anxious Florentine art custodians determined not

Florence's Trial by Fire

ONE OF THE MOST STRIKING figures of Renaissance Florence was Girolamo Savonarola, a Dominican friar who, for a moment, captured the conscience of the city. In 1491 he became prior of the convent of San Marco, where he adopted a life of austerity and delivered sermons condemning Florence's excesses and the immorality of his fellow clergy. Following the death of Lorenzo de' Medici, Savonarola was instrumental in the formation of the republic of Florence, ruled by a representative council with Christ enthroned as monarch. In one of his most memorable acts, he urged Florentines to toss worldly possessions—from frilly dresses to Botticelli paintings—onto a "bonfire of the vanities" in Piazza della Signoria. Savonarola's antagonism toward church hierarchy led to his undoing: he was excommunicated in 1497, and the following year was hanged and burned on charges of heresy. Today, at the Museo di San Marco, you can visit Savonarola's cell and see his arresting portrait.

to limit the number of tourists (whose entrance fees help preservation), have suggested installing an "air blaster" behind *David* that would remove the dust and humidity that each tourist brings in. A two-year study is underway, and a decision will probably be reached sometime in 2007. The statue is not quite what it seems. It is so poised and graceful and alert—so miraculously alive—that it is often considered the definitive embodiment of the ideals of the High Renaissance in sculpture. But its true place in the history of art is a bit more complicated.

As Michelangelo well knew, the Renaissance painting and sculpture that preceded his work were deeply concerned with ideal form. Perfection of proportion was the ever-sought Holy Grail; during the Renaissance, ideal proportion was equated with ideal beauty, and ideal beauty was equated with spiritual perfection. But *David,* despite its supremely calm and dignified pose, departs from these ideals. Michelangelo did not give the statue perfect proportions. The head is slightly too large for the body, the arms are too large for the torso, and the hands are dramatically large for the arms. The work was originally commissioned to adorn the facade of the Duomo and was intended to be seen from below at a distance. Michelangelo knew exactly what he was doing, calculating that the perspective of the viewer would be such that, in order for the statue to appear properly proportioned, the upper body, head, and arms would have to be bigger, as they are farther away from the viewer's line of vision. But he also did it to express and embody, as powerfully as possible in a single figure, an entire biblical story. David's hands *are* big, but so was Goliath, and these are the hands that slew him. Save yourself a long and tiresome wait at the museum entrance by reserving your tickets in advance. ✉ *Via Ricasoli 60, near San Marco* ☎ *055/294883 reservations, 055/2388609 gallery* ⊕ *www.polomuseale.firenze.it* 💶 *€6.50, reservation fee €3* ☺ *Tues.–Sun. 8:15–6:50.*

★ ⓲ **Museo di San Marco.** A former Dominican convent adjacent to the church of San Marco now houses this museum, which contains many stunning works by Fra Angelico (circa 1400–55), the Dominican friar famous for his piety as well as for his painting. When the friars' cells were restructured between 1439 and 1444, he decorated many of them with frescoes meant to spur religious contemplation. His paintings are simple and direct and furnish a compelling contrast to those in the Palazzo Medici-Riccardi chapel. Whereas Gozzoli's frescoes celebrate the splendors of the Medici, Fra Angelico's exalt the simple beauties of the contemplative life and quiet reflection. Fra Angelico's works are everywhere in this complex, from the friars' cells to the superb panel paintings on view in the museum. Don't miss the famous *Annunciation* on the upper floor and the works in the gallery off the cloister as you enter. Here you can see his beautiful *Last Judgment*; as usual, the tortures of the damned are far more inventive and interesting than the pleasures of the redeemed. ✉ *Piazza San Marco 1* ☎ *055/2388608* 🎫 *€4* ☉ *Weekdays 8:30–1:50, weekends 8:30–7. Closed 1st, 3rd, and 5th Sun., and 2nd and 4th Mon. of month.*

⓯ **San Lorenzo.** The interior of this church, like that of Santo Spirito on the other side of the Arno, was designed by Filippo Brunelleschi in the early 15th century. Both proclaim with ringing clarity the beginning of the Renaissance in architecture (neither was completed by Brunelleschi, and which he worked on first is unknown). San Lorenzo's most dramatic element is its floor grid of dark, inlaid marble lines. The grid makes the rigorous geometry of the interior immediately visible and is an illuminating lesson on the laws of perspective. If you stand in the middle of the nave at the church entrance, on the line that stretches to the high altar, every element in the church—the grid, the nave columns, the side aisles, the coffered nave ceiling—seems to march inexorably toward a hypothetical vanishing point beyond the high altar, exactly as in a single-point-perspective painting. Brunelleschi's **Sagrestia Vecchia** (Old Sacristy) has stucco decorations by Donatello; it's at the end of the left transept. The facade of the church was never finished. ✉ *Piazza San Lorenzo* ☎ *055/290184* 🎫 *€2.50* ☉ *Mon.–Sat. 10–5.*

Also Worth Seeing

⓰ **Biblioteca Medicea Laurenziana** (Laurentian Library). Michelangelo the architect was every bit as original as Michelangelo the sculptor. Unlike Brunelleschi (the architect of San Lorenzo), however, he was not obsessed with proportion and perfect geometry. He was interested in experimentation, invention, and expressing a personal vision at times highly idiosyncratic.

It was never more idiosyncratic than in the Laurentian Library, begun in 1524 and finished in 1568, and its famous **vestibolo.** This strangely shaped anteroom has had scholars scratching their heads for centuries. In a space more than two stories high, why did Michelangelo limit his use of columns and pilasters to the upper two-thirds of the wall? Why didn't he rest them on strong pedestals instead of on huge, decorative curlicue scrolls, which rob them of all visual support? Why did he re-cess them into the wall, which makes them look weaker still? The architectural elements here do not stand firm and strong and tall, like those inside the church next door; instead, they seem to be pressed into the wall as if into putty, giving the room a soft, rubbery look that is one of the strangest effects ever achieved by aping classical architecture. It is almost as if Michelangelo purposely set out to defy his predecessors, intentionally flouting the conventions of the High Renaissance to see what kind of bizarre, mannered effect might result. His innovations were tremendously influential and produced a period of architectural experimentation. As his contemporary Giorgio Vasari put it, "Artisans have been infinitely and perpetually indebted to him because he broke the bonds and chains of a way of working that had become habitual by common usage."

Nobody has ever complained about the anteroom's staircase (best viewed head-on), which emerges from the library with the visual force of an unstoppable lava flow. In its highly sculptural conception and execution, it's quite simply one of the most original and fluid staircases in the world. A restoration project may mean the opening hours are limited; call ahead. ⊠ *Piazza San Lorenzo 9, entrance to the left of San Lorenzo* ☎ *055/210760* ⊕ *www.bml.firenze.sbn.it* ▭ *Library free, special exhibitions €5* ☉ *Daily 8:30–1:30.*

㉓ Museo Archeologico. Of the Etruscan, Egyptian, and Greco-Roman antiquities in this museum, the Etruscan collection is particularly notable—one of the largest in Italy. The famous bronze *Chimera* was discovered (without the tail, a reconstruction) in the 16th century. ⊠ *Via della Colonna 38, near Santissima Annunziata* ☎ *055/23575* ⊕ *www.comune. firenze.it/soggetti/sat/didattica/museo.html* ▭ *€4* ☉ *Mon. 2–7, Tues. and Thurs. 8:30–7, Wed. and Fri.–Sun. 8:30–2.*

㉑ Museo dell'Opificio delle Pietre Dure. Ferdinand I established a workshop in 1588 to train craftsmen in the art of working with precious and semiprecious stones and marble. Four hundred–plus years later, the workshop is renowned as a center for the restoration of mosaics and inlays in semiprecious stones. The little museum is highly informative and includes some magnificent antique examples of this highly specialized and beautiful craft. ⊠ *Via degli Alfani 78, near San Marco* ☎ *055/26511* ▭ *€2* ☉ *Mon.–Sat. 8:15–1:50.*

⑱ Palazzo Medici-Riccardi. The upper floor **Cappella dei Magi** is the main attraction of this palace begun in 1444 by Michelozzo for Cosimo il Vecchio. Benozzo Gozzoli's famous *Procession of the Magi* (finished in 1460) adorns the walls, it celebrates both the birth of Christ and the splendor of the Medici family. Gozzoli's gift was for entrancing the eye, not challenging the mind, and on those terms his success here is beyond question. The paintings are full of activity yet somehow frozen in time in a way that fails utterly as realism but succeeds triumphantly when the demand for realism is set aside. Entering the chapel is like walking into the middle of a magnificently illustrated children's storybook, and this beauty makes it one of the most enjoyable rooms in the entire city. ⊠ *Via Cavour 1, near San Lorenzo* ☎ *055/2760340* ▭ *€4* ☉ *Thurs.–Tues. 9–7.*

25 **Santa Maria Maddalena dei Pazzi.** One of Florence's hidden treasures, Perugino's (circa 1445/50–1523) cool and composed *Crucifixion* is in the chapter house of the monastery below this church. Here you can see the Virgin Mary and St. John the Evangelist with Mary Magdalen and Sts. Benedict and Bernard of Clairvaux posed against a simple but haunting landscape. The figure of Christ crucified occupies the center of this brilliantly hued fresco. Perugino's colors radiate—note the juxtaposition of the yellow-green cuff against the orange tones of the Magdalen's robe. ⊠ *Borgo Pinti 58, near Santissima Annunziata* ☎ *055/2478420* 🖂 *Donation requested* ⊗ *Mon.–Sat. 9–noon, 5–5:20, and 6–7; Sun. 9–noon and 5–6:20.*

22 **Santissima Annunziata.** Dating from the mid-13th century, this church was restructured in 1447 by Michelozzo, who gave it an uncommon (and lovely) entrance cloister with frescoes by Andrea del Sarto (1486–1530), Pontormo (1494–1556), and Rosso Fiorentino (1494–1540). The interior is a rarity for Florence: an over-the-top baroque design. But it's not really a fair example, since it is merely 17th-century baroque decoration applied willy-nilly to an earlier structure—exactly the sort of violent remodeling exercise that has given the baroque a bad name. The **Cappella dell'Annunziata,** immediately inside the entrance to the left, illustrates the point. The lower half, with its stately Corinthian columns and carved frieze bearing the Medici arms, was commissioned by Piero de' Medici in 1447; the upper half, with its erupting curves and impish sculpted cherubs, was added 200 years later. Each is effective in its own way, but together they serve only to prove that dignity is rarely comfortable wearing a party hat. ⊠ *Piazza di Santissima Annunziata* ☎ *055/266186* ⊗ *Thurs.–Tues. 9–noon and 4–5.*

> **WORD OF MOUTH**
>
> "You can walk *anywhere* in Florence easily–it's one of my favorite cities because it is so compact. Every time I go I am surprised by how close all the major sights are."   –Travelday

24 **Spedale degli Innocenti.** Brunelleschi constructed this hospital in 1419; it takes the prize for the very first Renaissance construction employing the two shapes he considered mathematically (and therefore philosophically and aesthetically) perfect—the square and the circle. Below the level of the arches the portico encloses a row of perfect cubes; above the arch level the portico encloses a row of intersecting hemispheres. The whole geometric scheme is articulated with Corinthian columns, capitals, and arches borrowed directly from antiquity. At the same time Brunelleschi was also designing the interior of San Lorenzo, using the same basic ideas, but the portico here was finished before the church. As exterior decoration, there are 10 ceramic medallions that depict swaddled infants, done in about 1487 by Andrea della Robbia (1435–1525/28). Inside there's a small museum devoted to lesser-known Renaissance works. ⊠ *Piazza di Santissima Annunziata 12* ☎ *055/20371* 🖂 *€3* ⊗ *Thurs.–Tues. 8:30–2.*

8

Santa Maria Novella to the Arno

Piazza Santa Maria Novella is near the train station and is marked by a degree of squalor, especially at night. Nevertheless, the streets in and around the piazza have their share of architectural treasures, including some of Florence's most tasteful palaces. Between Santa Maria Novella and the Arno is Via Tornabuoni, Florence's finest shopping street.

The Main Attractions

㉗ Palazzo Strozzi. The Strozzi family built this imposing palazzo in an attempt to outshine the nearby Palazzo Medici. The design is based on a circa 1489 model by Giuliano da Sangallo (circa 1452–1516). Construction took place between 1489 and 1504 under Il Cronaca (1457–1508) and Benedetto da Maiaino (1442–97). The exterior is simple, severe, and massive: it's a testament to the wealth of a patrician, 15th-century Florentine family. The interior courtyard is another matter altogether. It is here that the classical vocabulary—columns, capitals, pilasters, arches, and cornices—is given uninhibited and powerful expression. Blockbuster art shows frequently take place here. ⊠ *Via Tornabuoni, near Piazza della Repubblica* ☎ *055/2776461* ⊕ *www.firenzemostre.com* 🎟 *Free except during exhibitions* ☉ *Daily 10–7.*

㉖ Santa Maria Novella. The facade of Santa Maria Novella looks distinctly clumsy by later Renaissance standards, and with good reason: it is an architectural hybrid. The lower half was completed mostly in the 14th century; its pointed-arch niches and decorative marble patterns reflect the Gothic style of the day. About a hundred years later (around 1456), architect Leon Battista Alberti was called in to complete the job. The marble decoration of his upper story clearly defers to the already existing work below, but the architectural motifs he added evince an entirely different style. The problem was to soften the abrupt transition between a wide ground floor and the narrow upper story. Alberti designed S-curve scrolls surmounting the decorative circles on either side of the upper story: this had no precedent in antiquity but set one in his time. Once you start to look for them, you see scrolls such as these (or sculptural variations of them) on churches all over Italy, and every one of them derives from Alberti's example here.

The architecture of the interior is, like the Duomo, a dignified but somber example of Florentine Gothic. Exploration is essential, however, because the church's store of art treasures is remarkable. Of special interest for its great historical importance and beauty is Masaccio's *Trinity,* on the left-hand wall, almost halfway down the nave. Painted around 1426–27 (at the same time he was working on his frescoes in Santa Maria del Carmine), it unequivocally announced the arrival of the Renaissance in painting. The realism of the figure of Christ was revolutionary in itself, but what was probably even more startling to contemporary Florentines was the barrel vault in the background. The mathematical rules for employing perspective in painting had just been discovered (probably by Brunelleschi), and this was one of the first works of art to employ them with utterly convincing success.

Other highlights include the 14th-century stained-glass rose window depicting the *Coronation of the Virgin* (above the central entrance); the Cappella Filippo Strozzi (to the right of the altar), containing late-15th-century frescoes and stained glass by Filippino Lippi; the Cappella Maggiore (the area around the high altar), displaying frescoes by Domenico Ghirlandaio (1449–94); and the Cappella Gondi (to the left of the altar), containing Filippo Brunelleschi's famous wood crucifix, carved around 1410 and said to have so stunned the great Donatello when he first saw it that he dropped a basket of eggs. Early, well-preserved frescoes painted between 1348 and 1355 by Andrea da Firenze are in the chapter house, or the **Cappellone degli Spagnoli** (Spanish Chapel). ✉ *Piazza Santa Maria Novella* ☎ *055/210113* ✆ *Church €2.70, chapel €2.50* ⊙ *Mon.–Thurs. and Sat. 9–5, Sun. 1–5.*

In the cloisters of the **Museo di Santa Maria Novella,** to the left of Santa Maria Novella, is a faded fresco cycle by Paolo Uccello depicting tales from Genesis, with a dramatic vision of the Flood. ✉ *Piazza Santa Maria Novella 19* ☎ *055/282187* ✆ *€2.70* ⊙ *Mon.–Thurs. and Sat. 9–5, Sun. 9–2.*

㉚ **Santa Trinita.** Started in the 11th century by Vallombrosian monks in Romanesque style, this church underwent a Gothic remodeling during the 14th century. (Remains of the Romanesque construction are visible on the interior front wall.) Its major work is the cycle of frescoes and the altarpiece in the Cappella Sassetti, the second to the high altar's right, painted by Domenico Ghirlandaio between 1480 and 1485. Ghirlandaio was a wildly popular but conservative painter for his day, and generally his paintings show little interest in the laws of perspective that other Florentine painters had been experimenting with for more than 50 years. But his work here has such graceful decorative appeal it hardly seems to matter. The frescoes illustrate the life of St. Francis, and the altarpiece, depicting the Adoration of the Shepherds, veritably glows. At this writing, some of the work is hidden behind renovation scaffolding. ✉ *Piazza Santa Trinita, near Santa Maria Novella* ☎ *055/216912* ⊙ *Mon.–Sat. 9–noon and 3:30–6.*

Also Worth Seeing

㉘ **Museo Marino Marini.** One of the few 20th-century art museums in Florence is dedicated to Marino Marini's (1901–80) paintings, sculptures, drawings, and engravings. A 21-foot-tall Etruscanesque bronze of a horse and rider dominates the main gallery. The museum itself is an eruption of contemporary space in a deconsecrated 9th-century church, designed with a series of open stairways, walkways, and balconies that allow you to peer at Marini's work from all angles. ✉ *Piazza San Pancrazio, near Santa Maria Novella* ☎ *055/219432* ✆ *€4* ⊙ *Oct.–Apr., Mon. and Wed.–Sat. 10–5; May–Sept., Mon. and Wed.–Fri. 10–5.*

㉙ **Palazzo Rucellai.** Architect Leon Battista Alberti (1404–72) designed what is perhaps the very first private residence (built between 1455 and 1470) that was inspired by antiquity. A comparison between the Palazzo Rucellai's facade and that of the severe Palazzo Strozzi is illuminating. An ordered arrangement of elements is seen on both, but Alberti devoted a larger proportion of his wall space to windows, which lightens the appearance. He filled in the space with rigorously ordered classical details. Though still severe, the result is less fortresslike (Alberti is on record as saying that only tyrants need fortresses). Ironically, the Palazzo Rucellai was built some 30 years *before* the Palazzo Strozzi. Alberti's civilizing ideas had little influence on the Florentine palaces that followed. To Renaissance Florentines, power—in architecture, as in life—was as impressive as beauty. ⊠ *Via della Vigna Nuova, near Santa Maria Novella.*

The Oltrarno

A walk through the Oltrarno (literally "the other side of the Arno") takes in two very different aspects of Florence: the splendor of the Medici, manifest in the riches of the mammoth Palazzo Pitti and the gracious Giardino di Boboli; and the charm of the Oltrarno, a slightly gentrified but still fiercely proud working-class neighborhood with artisans' and antiques shops.

Farther east across the Arno, a series of ramps and stairs climbs to Piazzale Michelangelo, where the city lies before you in all its glory (skip this trip if it's a hazy day). More stairs (behind La Loggia restaurant) lead to the church of San Miniato al Monte. You can avoid the long walk by taking Bus 12 or 13 at the west end of Ponte alle Grazie and getting off at Piazzale Michelangelo; you still have to climb the monumental stairs to and from San Miniato, but you can then take the bus from Piazzale Michelangelo back to the center of town. If you decide to take a bus; remember to buy your ticket before you board.

The Main Attractions

 ③③ Giardino di Boboli (Boboli Garden). The Italian gift for landscaping— less formal than the French but still full of sweeping drama—is displayed here at its best. The garden began to take shape in 1549, when the Pitti family sold the palazzo to Eleanora da Toledo, wife of the Medici grand duke Cosimo I. The initial horticul-

> **WORD OF MOUTH**
>
> "A good idea for Oltrarno: get lost between Borgo San Jacopo and Santo Spirito for wonderful antiques and restoration workshops. Extremely charming." –lcquinn2

tural plans were laid out by Niccolò Tribolo (1500–50). After his death, Vasari, Ammannati, Giambologna, Bernardo Buontalenti (circa 1536–1608), Giulio (1571–1635), and Alfonso Parigi (1606–56), among others, continued the work. The result was the most spectacular backyard in Florence. A copy of the famous *Morgante* statue, Cosimo I's favorite dwarf astride a particularly unhappy tortoise, is near the exit. Sculpted by Valerio Cioli (circa 1529–99), the work shows a perfectly executed potbelly. ⊠ *Enter through Palazzo Pitti* ☎ *055/294883* 🎟 *€4 combined ticket with Museo delle Porcellane and Museo degli Argenti* 🕐 *Apr.–May and Sept., daily 8:15–6:30; June–Aug., daily 8:15–7:30; Mar. and Oct., daily 8:15–5:30. Closed 1st and last Mon. of month.*

③② Palazzo Pitti. This palace is one of Florence's largest—if not one of its best—architectural set pieces. The original palazzo, built for the Pitti family around 1460, comprised only the main entrance and the three windows on either side. In 1549 the property was sold to the Medici, and Bartolomeo Ammannati was called in to make substantial additions. Although he apparently operated on the principle that more is better, he succeeded only in proving that more is just that: more. Today the palace houses several museums. The **Galleria Palatina** contains a collection of paintings from the 15th to the 17th century. High points include a number of portraits by Titian and an unparalleled group of paintings by Raphael, notably the double portraits of Angelo Doni and his wife, the sullen Maddalena Strozzi. The rooms here remain much as the Medici left them. The floor-to-ceiling paintings are considered by some to be Italy's most egregious exercise in conspicuous consumption, aesthetic overkill, and trumpery. Admission to the Galleria Palatina also allows you to explore the former **Appartamenti Reali,** containing furnishings from a remodel done in the 19th century. The **Museo degli Argenti** displays a vast collection of Medici household treasures; the **Galleria del Costume** showcases fashions from the past 300 years. In the **Galleria d'Arte Moderna** there's a collection of 19th- and 20th-century paintings, mostly Tuscan. ⊠ *Piazza Pitti* ☎ *055/210323* 🖅 *Galleria Palatina €6.50, Museo degli Argenti €4 combined with Giardino di Boboli, Galleria del Costume and Galleria d'Arte Moderna € 5 combined* ☉ *Tues.–Sun. 8:15–6:50. All but Galleria Palatina closed 2nd and 4th Sun. and 1st, 3rd, and 5th Mon. of month.*

㊳ Piazzale Michelangelo. From this lookout you have a marvelous view of Florence and the hills around it, rivaling the vista from the Forte di Belvedere. It has a copy of Michelangelo's *David* and outdoor cafés packed with tourists during the day and with Florentines in the evening. The **Giardino dell'Iris** (Iris Garden) off the piazza is in full flower in May. The **Giardino delle Rose** (Rose Garden) on the terraces below the piazza is in full bloom in May and June, and open only then. ⊠ *Lungarno South.*

㊱ Santa Maria del Carmine. Within the **Cappella Brancacci,** at the end of the right transept of this church, is a fresco cycle that changed the course of Western art forever. This masterpiece of Renaissance painting is the creation of three artists: Masaccio and Masolino (1383–circa 1440/47), who began it around 1424, and Filippino Lippi, who finished it some 50 years later, after a long interruption during which the sponsoring Brancacci family was exiled.

It was Masaccio's work that opened a new frontier for painting, as he was among the first to employ single-point perspective. He painted the *Tribute Money* on the upper-left wall; *St. Peter Baptizing* on the upper altar wall; the *Distribution of Goods* on the lower altar wall; and, most famous, the *Expulsion of Adam and Eve* on the chapel's upper-left entrance pier. If you look closely at the last painting and compare it with some of the chapel's other works, you see a pronounced difference. The figures of Adam and Eve have a startling presence, primarily due to the dramatic way in which their bodies seem to reflect light. Masaccio here shaded his figures consistently, so as to suggest a single, strong source of light within the world of the painting but outside its frame. In so doing, he succeeded in imitating with paint the real-world effect of light on mass, and he thereby imparted to his figures a sculptural reality unprecedented in his day. But his skill went beyond mere technical innovation. In the faces of Adam and Eve you see more than finely modeled figures. You see terrible shame and suffering depicted with a humanity rarely achieved in art. Tragically, Masaccio did not live to experience the revolution his innovations caused—he died in 1428 at the age of 27. Fire nearly destroyed the church in the 18th century; miraculously, the Cappella Brancacci survived almost intact.

Reservations to visit the church are mandatory, but can be booked on the same day. Your time inside is limited to 15 minutes—a frustration that's only partly mitigated by the 40-minute DVD about the history of the chapel you can watch either before or after your visit. ⊠ *Piazza del Carmine, near Santo Spirito* ☎ *055/276558, 055/2768224 reservations* ☞ *€4* ⊙ *Mon. and Wed.–Sat. 10–5, Sun. 1–5.*

㊲ San Miniato al Monte. A fine example of Romanesque architecture, San Miniato al Monte dates from the 11th century. The lively green-and-white marble facade has a 12th-century mosaic topped by a gilt bronze eagle, emblem of San Miniato's sponsors, the Calimala (cloth merchants' guild). Inside are a 13th-century marble floor and apse mosaic. Spinello Aretino (1350–1410) covered the walls of the **Sagrestia** with frescoes on the life of St. Benedict. The adjacent **Cappella del Cardinale del Portogallo** is one of the richest Renaissance works in Florence. Built to hold the tomb of a Portuguese cardinal, Prince James of Lusitania, who died young in Florence in 1459, it has a glorious ceiling by Luca della Robbia, a sculptured tomb by Antonio Rossellino (1427–79), and inlaid pavement in multicolor marble. ⊠ *Viale Galileo Galilei, Piazzale Michelangelo, Lungarno South* ☎ *055/2342731* ⊙ *Apr.–Oct., daily 8:30–7; Nov.–Mar., daily 8–noon and 2:30–7.*

Also Worth Seeing

㉞ Santa Felicita. This late baroque church (its facade was remodeled 1736–39) contains the Mannerist Jacopo Pontormo's (1494–1556) tour de force, the *Deposition* (executed 1525–28), which is a masterpiece of 16th-century Florentine art and the centerpiece of the **Cappella Capponi.** The remote figures, which transcend the realm of Renaissance classical form, are portrayed in tangled shapes and intense pastel colors (well pre-

A GOOD WALK: FLORENTINE PIAZZAS

You may come to Florence for the art, but once here you're likely to be won over by the vibrant, pedestrian-friendly street life played out on its numerous and wonderfully varied piazzas—which are often works of art themselves. This walk, designed for a beautiful day, takes you through many of them (but bypasses some of the most prominent ones you'll inevitably encounter while sightseeing). Stopping along the way for gelato, a caffè, or an aperitivo isn't mandatory, but when the urge strikes you, don't resist.

Start off in **Piazza Santa Maria Novella,** by the train station; note the glorious facade by Leon Battista Alberti decorating the square's church. Take Via delle Belle Donne, a narrow street running southeast from the piazza, and go left heading toward Via del Trebbio. Here you'll see a cross marking the site of a 13th-century street scuffle between Dominican friars and Patarene heretics. (The Dominicans won.) A right on Via Tornabuoni takes you to tiny **Piazza Antinori**; the 15th-century Antinori palace has been in the hands of its wine-producing namesake family for generations.

served because of the low lights in the chapel), in a space and depth that defy reality. Note, too, the exquisitely frescoed *Annunciation,* also by Pontormo, at a right angle to the *Deposition.* The granite column in the piazza was erected in 1381 and marks a Christian cemetery. ⊠ *Piazza Santa Felicita, Via Guicciardini, near Palazzo Pitti* ⊙ *Mon.–Sat. 9–noon and 3–6, Sun. 9–1.*

㉟ Santo Spirito. The plain, unfinished facade gives nothing away, but the interior is one of a pair designed in Florence by Filippo Brunelleschi in the early 15th century (the other is San Lorenzo). It was here that Brunelleschi supplied definitive solutions to the two main problems of interior Renaissance church design: how to build a cross shape using architectural elements borrowed from antiquity, and how to reflect the order and regularity that Renaissance scientists (including himself) were discovering in the natural world around them at the time. Brunelleschi's solution to the first problem was brilliantly simple: turn a Greek temple inside out. To see this clearly, look at one of the stately arch-topped arcades that separate the side aisles from the central nave. Whereas ancient Greek temples were walled buildings surrounded by classical colonnades, Brunelleschi's churches were classical arcades within walled buildings. This brilliant architectural idea overthrew the previous era's religious taboo against pagan architecture once and for all, triumphantly reclaiming that architecture for Christian use.

Brunelleschi's solution to the second problem—making the entire interior orderly and regular—was mathematically precise: he designed the church so that all its parts were proportionally related. The transepts and nave have exactly the same width; the side aisles are precisely half as wide as the nave; the little chapels off the side aisles are exactly half as deep as the side aisles; the chancel and transepts are exactly one-eighth the depth of the nave; and so on, with dizzying exactitude. For Brunelleschi, such a design technique would have been a matter of passionate conviction. Like most theoreticians of his day, he believed that mathematical regularity and aesthetic beauty were flip sides of the same coin, that one was not possible without the other. In the **refectory of Santo Spirito,** adjacent to the church, you can see the remains of Andrea Orcagna's fresco of the *Crucifixion.* ⊠ *Piazza Santo Spirito* ☎ *055/210030 church,*

8

Continue south on Tornabuoni, stopping in **Piazza Strozzi** to admire (or recoil at) the gargantuan Palazzo Strozzi, a 15th-century family palace designed specifically to dwarf the Palazzo Medici. Step into the courtyard, which is as graceful and delicate as the facade is not. Next stop on Tornabuoni is the lovely little **Piazza Trinita.** Take a quick look into the church of Santa Trinita; in its Sassetti Chapel in the right transept, Ghirlandaio's 15th-century frescoes neatly depict the square in which you were just standing.
Continue south to the Arno and cross it on the Ponte

Trinita, which affords an excellent view of the Ponte Vecchio upriver. Go south on Via Maggio, then make a right on Via Michelozzi, which leads to **Piazza Santo Spirito,** one of the loveliest—and liveliest—squares in Florence. Walking away from the piazza's church (heading south), make a left on Via Sant'Agostino, which quickly turns into Via Mazzetta. Stop briefly in **Piazza San Felice** and note No. 8, home of the English poets Elizabeth Barrett Browning and Robert Browning from 1849 to 1861.
From here Via Guicciardini takes you to the massive

055/287043 refectory ✉ *Church free, refectory* €2.20 ☉ *Church Thurs.–Tues. 10–noon and 4–6, Wed. 10–noon. Refectory Dec.–Mar., Tues.–Sat. 10:30–1:30; Apr.–Nov., Tues.–Sun. 9–2.*

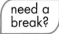

Cabiria (✉ Piazza Santo Spirito 4/r ☎ 055/215732), across the piazza from the church of Santo Spirito, draws a funky crowd in search of a cappuccino or a drink. When it's warm, sit outside on the terrace. Snacks and light lunches are also available.

Santa Croce

The Santa Croce quarter, on the southeast fringe of the historic center, was built up in the Middle Ages outside the second set of medieval city walls. The centerpiece of the neighborhood was the basilica of Santa Croce, which could hold great numbers of worshippers; the vast piazza could accommodate any overflow and also served as a fairground and playing field for traditional, no-holds-barred soccer games. A center of leather working since the Middle Ages, the neighborhood is still packed with leather craftsmen and leather shops.

The Main Attractions

③⑨ Santa Croce. Like the Duomo, this church is Gothic, but, also like the
Fodor's Choice Duomo, its facade dates from the 19th century. As a burial place, the
★ church probably contains more skeletons of Renaissance celebrities than any other in Italy. The tomb of Michelangelo is immediately to the right as you enter; he is said to have chosen this spot so that the first thing he would see on Judgment Day, when the graves of the dead fly open, would be Brunelleschi's dome through Santa Croce's open doors. The tomb of Galileo Galilei (1564–1642) is on the left wall; he was not granted a Christian burial until 100 years after his death because he produced evidence that Earth is not the center of the universe. The tomb of Niccolò Machiavelli (1469–1527), the political theoretician whose brutally pragmatic philosophy so influenced the Medici, is halfway down the nave on the right. The grave of Lorenzo Ghiberti, creator of the Baptistery doors, is halfway down the nave on the left. Composer Gioacchino Rossini (1792–1868) is entombed at the end of the nave on the right. The monument to Dante Alighieri (1265–1321), the greatest

---

Piazza dei Pitti. Palazzo Pitti was intended to outstrip Palazzo Strozzi in size and ostentatiousness, and it certainly succeeds. Behind the palazzo is the Giardino di Boboli. Walking the straight axis to its top, you'll pass man-made lakes, waterfalls, and grottoes. Head for the 18th-century Giardino dei Cavalieri; when you get there, pause and admire the view. It's hard to believe the pastoral scene in front of you, complete with olive groves, is in the city center.

If you have a climb left in you, head back toward the Arno along Via Guicciardini. Just before the Ponte Vec-

chio, turn right onto Via de' Bardi. Stop for a moment in **Piazza Maria Sopr'Arno** and check out the eerie 20th-century sculpture of John the Baptist, patron saint of Florence. Continue along Via de' Bardi until it becomes Via San Niccolò. Make a right on Via San Miniato, passing through the city walls at Porta San Niccolò. Head up, steeply, on Via Monte alle Croci and veer left, taking the steps of Via di San Salvatore al Monte. At the top is **Piazzale Michelangelo**, where your effort is rewarded with a breathtaking view of Florence below. Don't forget your camera.

Italian poet, is a memorial rather than a tomb (he is buried in Ravenna); it's on the right wall near the tomb of Michelangelo.

The collection of art within the church complex is by far the most important of any church in Florence. Historically, the most significant works are probably the Giotto frescoes in the two chapels immediately to the right of the high altar. They illustrate scenes from the lives of St. John the Evangelist and St. John the Baptist (in the right-hand chapel) and scenes from the life of St. Francis (in the left-hand chapel). Time has not been kind to these frescoes; through the centuries, wall tombs were placed in the middle of them, they were whitewashed and plastered over, and in the 19th century they suffered a clumsy restoration. But the reality that Giotto introduced into painting can still be seen. He did not paint beautifully stylized religious icons, as the Byzantine style that preceded him prescribed; he instead painted drama—St. Francis surrounded by grieving friars at the very moment of his death. This was a radical shift in emphasis: before Giotto, painting's role was to symbolize the attributes of God; after him, it was to imitate life. His work is indeed primitive compared with later painting, but in the early 14th century it caused a sensation that was not equaled for another 100 years. He was, for his time, the equal of both Masaccio and Michelangelo.

Among the church's other highlights are Donatello's *Annunciation,* a moving expression of surprise (on the right wall two-thirds of the way down the nave); 14th-century frescoes by Taddeo Gaddi (circa 1300–66) illustrating scenes from the life of the Virgin Mary, clearly showing the influence of Giotto (in the chapel at the end of the right transept); and Donatello's *Crucifix,* criticized by Brunelleschi for making Christ look like a peasant (in the chapel at the end of the left transept). Outside the church proper, in the **Museo dell'Opera di Santa Croce** off the cloister, is the 13th-century *Triumphal Cross* by Cimabue (circa 1240–1302), badly damaged by the flood of 1966. A model of architectural geometry, the Cappella Pazzi, at the end of the cloister, is the work of Brunelleschi. ⊠ *Piazza Santa Croce 16* ☎ *055/2466105* ☞ *€4* ⊘ *Daily 9:30–5.*

④ **Sinagoga.** Jews were already well settled in Florence by 1396, when the first money-lending operations were officially sanctioned. Medici patronage helped Jewish banking houses to flourish at first. Then in 1570, by decree of Pope Pius V (1504–72), Jews were required to live within the large ghetto, near today's Piazza della Repubblica. Construction of the modern Moorish-style synagogue, with its lovely garden, began in 1874 as a bequest of David Levi, who wished to endow a synagogue "worthy of the city." Falcini, Micheli, and Treves designed the building on a domed Greek-cross plan with galleries in the transept and a roofline bearing three distinctive copper cupolas. The exterior has alternating bands of tan travertine and pink granite, reflecting an Islamic style repeated in Giovanni Panti's ornate interior. Of particular interest are the cast-iron gates by Pasquale Franci, the eternal light by Francesco Morini, and the Murano glass mosaics by Giacomo dal Medico. The gilded doors of the Moorish ark, which fronts the pulpit and is flanked by extravagant candelabra, are decorated with symbols of the ancient Temple of Jerusalem and bear bayonet marks from vandals. The synagogue was used as a garage by the Nazis, who failed to inflict much damage in spite of one attempt to blow up the place with dynamite. Only the columns on the left side were destroyed, and, even then the women's balcony above did not collapse. Note the Star of David in black and yellow marble inlaid in the floor. The original capitals can be seen in the garden.

Some of the oldest and most beautiful Jewish ritual artifacts in all of Europe are displayed in the small **Museo Ebraico,** accessible by stairs or elevator. Exhibits document the Florentine Jewish community and the building of the synagogue. The donated objects all belonged to local families and date from as early as the late 16th century. Take special note of the exquisite needlework and silver objects. A small but well-stocked gift shop is downstairs. ⊠ *Via Farini 4, near Santa Croce* ☎ *055/2346654* ✆ *€3* ⊙ *Apr., May, Sept., and Oct., Sun.–Thurs. 10–5, Fri. 10–2; June–Aug., Sun.–Thurs. 10–6, Fri. 10–2; Nov.–Mar., Sun.–Thurs. 10–3, Fri. 10–2. English-guided tours 10:10, 11, noon, 1, 2 (no tour at 2 on Fri.).*

Also Worth Seeing

40 Casa Buonarroti. Michelangelo Buonarroti the Younger, the grandnephew of the famed Michelangelo, turned his family house into a shrine honoring the life of his great-uncle. It's full of works executed by Michelangelo, including a marble bas-relief, the *Madonna of the Steps,* carved when Michelangelo was a teenager, and his wooden model for the facade of San Lorenzo. ⊠ *Via Ghibellina 70, near Santa Croce* ☎ *055/241752* ⊕ *www.casabuonarroti.it* ✆ *€6.50* ⊙ *Fri.–Wed. 9:30–2.*

WHERE TO EAT

Dining hours start at around 1 for the midday meal and at 8 for dinner. Many of Florence's restaurants are small, so reservations are a must. You can sample such specialties as creamy *fegatini* (a chicken-liver spread) and *ribollita* (minestrone thickened with bread and beans and swirled with extra-virgin olive oil) in a bustling, convivial trattoria, where you share long wooden tables set with paper place mats, or in an upscale *ristorante* with linen tablecloths and napkins. Follow the Florentines' lead and take a break at an *enoteca* (wine bar) during the day and discover some excellent Chiantis and Super Tuscans from small producers who rarely export.

WHAT IT COSTS In euros				
$$$$	**$$$**	**$$**	**$**	**¢**
AT DINNER over €22	€16–€22	€11–€16	€7–€11	under €7

Prices are for a second course (*secondo piatto,* or *secondi*).

The Duomo to the Ponte Vecchio

$–$$ ╳ **Frescobaldi Wine Bar.** Enjoy a wide selection of wines by the glass at this small wine bar and romantic restaurant. The plates of pasta are terrific. ⊠ *Via de'Magazzini 2–4/r, near Piazza della Signoria* ☎ *055/ 284724* ▤ *MC, V* ⊙ *Closed Sun. No lunch Mon.*

¢–$ ✕ **Coquinarius.** After seeing the Duomo, you can rest and replenish at the tranquil enoteca Coquinarius one block away. They serve tasty salads and sandwiches here, as well as clever pastas such as the *raviolini ripieni di formaggio e pere* (small ravioli stuffed with cheese and pear). ✉ *Via delle Oche 15/r, near Duomo* ☎ *055/2302153* ▤ *MC, V* ⊘ *Closed Sun.*

San Lorenzo & Beyond

★ $$$$ ✕ **Taverna del Bronzino.** Want to have a sophisticated meal in a 16th-century Renaissance artist's studio? The former workshop of Santi di Tito, a student of Bronzino's, is now a restaurant with simple formality and white tablecloths. Lots of classic, superb Tuscan food graces the artful menu, and the presentation is often dramatic. Try the *i cappellacci al cedro* (round pasta pillows stuffed with ricotta and served in a citrus sauce). The wine list has solid, affordable choices. Book far ahead if you want to dine at the wine cellar's only table; the service is outstanding. ✉ *Via delle Ruote 25/r, near San Marco* ☎ *055/495220* ⌕ *Reservations essential* ▤ *AE, DC, MC, V* ⊘ *Closed Sun. and 3 wks in Aug.*

$–$$ ✕ **Le Fonticine.** Owner Silvano Bruci is from Tuscany, his wife, Gianna, from Emilia-Romagna; their ristorante near the train station combines the best of two Italian cuisines. Start with the mixed-vegetable antipasto plate and then move on to any of their house-made pastas. The feathery light *tortelloni nostro modo* is large stuffed tortellini with fresh ricotta, served with a tomato and cream sauce. The dining room, filled with the Brucis' painting collection, provides an upbeat space for this soul-satisfying food. Note that a 12% service charge may be automatically added to the bill. ✉ *Via Nazionale 79/r, near San Lorenzo* ☎ *055/282106* ▤ *AE, DC, MC, V* ⊘ *Closed Sun. and Mon., Nov. 24–Jan. 5, and July 25–Aug. 25.*

¢ ✕ **Casa del Vino.** Come here for the creative *panini* (sandwiches), such as *sgrombri e carciofini sott'olio* (mackerel and marinated baby artichokes), and the ever-changing list of significant wines by the glass. There's also a well-stocked collection of bottles to-go, at more than fair prices. ✉ *Via dell'Ariento 16/r, near San Lorenzo* ☎ *055/215609* ▤ *MC, V* ⊘ *Closed Sun.*

★ ¢ ✕ **Mario.** Florentines flock to this narrow family-run trattoria to feast on Tuscan favorites served at simple tables under a wooden ceiling dating from 1536. Genuine Florentine hospitality prevails: you're seated wherever there's room, which often means with strangers. Yes, there's a bit of extra oil in most dishes, which imparts calories as well as taste, but aren't you on vacation in Italy? Worth the splurge is *riso al ragù* (rice with ground beef and tomatoes). ✉ *Via Rosina 2/r, at Piazza del Mercato Centrale, near San Lorenzo* ☎ *055/218550* ⌕ *Reservations not accepted* ▤ *No credit cards* ⊘ *Closed Sun. and Aug. No dinner.*

¢ ✕ **Pugi.** This counter-service eatery sells pizza *a taglio* (by the slice) that is much favored by locals; their focaccia and other breads are equally good. The pizzeria is in a handy spot, directly across from the church of San Marco. ✉ *Piazza San Marco 9/b* ☎ *055/280981* ▤ *No credit cards* ⊘ *Closed Sun.*

8

EATING WELL IN FLORENCE

A typical Florentine meal starts with an antipasto of *crostini* (grilled bread spread with various savory toppings) or cured meats such as prosciutto *crudo* (ham thinly sliced) and *finocchiona* (salami seasoned with fennel). *Primi piatti* (first courses) can consist of local versions of pasta dishes available throughout Italy. More distinctly Florentine are the vegetable-and-bread soups such as *pappa al pomodoro* (bread and tomato soup) and *ribollita* (minestrone with bread and beans), and, in summer, a salad called *panzanella* (tomatoes, onions, vinegar, oil, basil, and bread). Before they are eaten, these dishes are often christened with un *"C" d'olio*, a generous C-shape drizzle of the sumptuous local olive oil.

Unparalleled among the *secondi piatti* (second courses) is *bistecca alla fiorentina*—a thick slab of local Chianina beef, often grilled over charcoal, seasoned with olive oil, salt, and pepper, and served rare. Arista (roast loin of pork seasoned with rosemary) is also a local specialty, as are many other roasted meats that pair especially well with Chianti. A *secondo* is usually served with a *contorno* (side dish) of white beans, sautéed greens, or artichokes in season, all of which can be drizzled with more of that fruity olive oil.

Desserts in Florence are more or less an afterthought. The meal often ends with a glass of *vin santo* (literally, "holy wine"), an ochre-color dessert wine that pairs beautifully with *biscotti* ("twice-cooked" cookies).

Santa Maria Novella to the Arno

$$–$$$ ✕ **Cantinetta Antinori.** After a rough morning of shopping on Via Tornabuoni, stop in this 15th-century palazzo and dine in the company of Florentine ladies (and men) who lunch. The kitchen reliably turns out Tuscan standards and a few unusual dishes like the *insalata di gamberoni con carciofi freschi* (shrimp salad with shaved raw artichokes). Most selections on the stellar wine list can be had by the glass, so that sampling Tignanello, the Super Tuscan that kicked off the entire Italian wine revolution, becomes affordable. ⊠ *Piazza Antinori 3, near Santa Maria Novella* 🕾 *055/292234* ▤ *AE, DC, MC, V* ⊘ *Closed weekends, 20 days in Aug., and Dec. 25–Jan. 6.*

☾ **$$** ✕ **Il Latini.** Although Il Latini may well be the noisiest, most crowded trattoria in Florence, it's also one of the most fun, precisely because of the liveliness. A genial Torello ("little bull") Latini presides over his four big, homey dining rooms. Ample portions of ribollita prepare the palatte for the hearty meat dishes that follow. Both Florentines and tourists alike praise the *agnello fritto* (fried lamb). Though reservations are advised, there's always a wait anyway. ⊠ *Via dei Palchetti 6/r, near Santa Maria Novella* 🕾 *055/210916* ⌂ *Reservations essential* ▤ *AE, DC, MC, V* ⊘ *Closed Mon. and 15 days at Christmas.*

$–$$ ✕ **Osteria delle Belle Donne.** Ropes of garlic and other dried vegetables adorn the walls, and checkered cloth napkins add cheer to this *osteria* (tavernlike restaurant) down the road from Santa Maria Novella. The kitchen reliably serves Tuscan standards, but shakes up the menu with alternatives such as *sedani con bacon, verza, e uova* (thick noodles sauced with bacon, cabbage, and egg). An ever-changing menu and prompt, friendly service make for a relaxed dining experience. If you want to eat alfresco, request a table outside when booking. ⊠ *Via delle Belle Donne 16/r, near Santa Maria Novella* ☎ *055/2382609* ◈ *Reservations essential* ▤ *AE, DC, MC, V.*

Oltrarno

$–$$ ✕ **Borgo Antico.** Near San Spirito, Borgo Antico serves pizza and other traditional trattoria pastas and such seven days a week. ⊠ *Piazza Santo Spirito 6/r* ☎ *055/210437* ▤ *AE, MC, V.*

$–$$ ✕ **Quattro Leoni.** The eclectic staff at this trattoria is an appropriate match for the diverse menu. Classics such as *taglierini con porcini* (long, thin, flat pasta with porcini mushrooms) are on the list, but so, too, are less typical dishes such as the earthy cabbage salad with avocado, pine nuts, and drops of *olio di tartufo* (truffle oil). In cold weather, dine in one of two rooms with high ceilings, and in summer you can sit outside. ⊠ *Piazza della Passera, Via dei Vellutini 1/r, near Palazzo Pitti* ☎ *055/ 218562* ◈ *Reservations essential* ▤ *AE, DC, MC, V* ☉ *No lunch Wed.*

¢–$ ✕ **La Casalinga.** The nostalgic charm of a 1950s kitchen pervades "The Housewife" restaurant, and it has the Tuscan comfort food to match. If you eat ribollita anywhere in Florence, do so here—the soup couldn't be more authentic. The menu is long, portions are plentiful, and service is prompt and friendly. Save room for dessert: the *sorbetto al limoncello* (lemon sorbet) perfectly caps off the meal. Mediocre paintings clutter the semi-paneled walls and tables are set close together in a place that is usually jammed. ⊠ *Via Michelozzi 9/r, near Santo Spirito* ☎ *055/ 218624* ▤ *AE, DC, MC, V* ☉ *Closed Sun., 1 wk at Christmas, and 3 wks in Aug.*

★ ¢–$ ✕ **Fuori Porta.** One of the oldest and best wine bars in Florence serves cured meats and cheeses, as well as daily specials such as the sublime spaghetti *al curry.* ⊠ *Via Monte alle Croci 10/r, near San Niccolò* ☎ *055/2342483* ▤ *AE, MC, V.*

¢ ✕ **Osteria Antica Mescita San Niccolò.** Always crowded, always good, and always cheap: this is simple Tuscan at its best. If you sit in the lower dining area, you're in what was once a chapel dating from the 11th century (the osteria is next to the church of San Niccolò). Such subtle but dramatic background plays off nicely with the food, such as *pollo con limone,* tasty pieces of chicken in a lemon-scented broth. In winter try the *spezzatino di cinghiale con aromi* (wild boar stew with herbs). ⊠ *Via San Niccolò 60/r, near San Niccolò* ☎ *055/2342836* ◈ *Reservations essential* ▤ *AE, MC, V* ☉ *Closed Sun. and Aug.*

¢ ✕ **Le Volpi e l'Uva.** Just off Piazza Santa Trinita is a oenophile's dream: here the well-informed barmen pour significant wines by the glass and serve equally impressive cheeses and other savory delights. ⊠ *Piazza de'Rossi 1, near Palazzo Pitti* ☎ *055/2398132* ▤ *AE, MC, V* ☉ *Closed Sun.*

Santa Croce

$$$$
Fodor'sChoice
★
✕ **Cibrèo.** From the crostini with a savory chicken-liver spread to the melt-in-your-mouth desserts, the food at this upscale trattoria is fantastic and creative. If you thought you'd never try tripe—let alone like it—this is the place to lay any doubts to rest: the *trippa in insalata* (cold tripe salad)

8

Where to Stay & Eat in Florence

Stazione Centrale

V. Fiume
V. Valfonda
V. Nazionale
V. Panicale
V. Taddea

1

2

Piazza Mercato Centrale

V. Canto de Nelli

V. S.
V. dell'Ariento
V. Antonino
V. Faenza
Borgo la Noce
V. della Stufa
V. de' Ginori

Piazza dell'Unità Italiana

V. del Melarancio
del Giglio
V. dei Conti
V. dell'Amore
V. dell'Oriuolo

Cappelle Medicee

Piazza S. Lorenz

27

V. Martelli

Santa Maria Novella

Piazza S. Maria Novella

V. dei Panzani

35

V. Cerretani

Battistero

Piazza di S. Giovanni

V. d. Belle Donne
V. del Trebbio
V. dei Banchi
V. dei Rondinelli

36

37

V. dei Pecori
V. Vecchietti
V. dei Tosinghi

Piazza Ognissanti
Lung. Amerigo Vespucci

V. della Scala
V. dell' Alberto
V. del Canacci
V. dei Benedetta
V. Maso Finiguerra
V. Palazzuolo
Borgo Ognissanti
V. d. Porcellana

V. de' Fossi
V. del Moro
V. del Sole
V. Spada
V. dei Federighi
V. dei Palchetti
V. d. Vigna Nuova

38

33

34

V. dei Pescioni
Pza. Strozzi
V. Strozzi
V. de' Sassetti
V. Anselmi

Piazza della Repubblica

28

V. degli Spe.
V. del Calzaiuoli
V. dei Calimala
V. dei Lamberti

V. Arno

Piazza Goldoni
V. dei Purgatorio
V. del Parione

32

31

Lung. Corsini

V. Tornabuoni

Piazza Santa Trinita
V. Porta Rossa
V. delle Terme
Borgo SS. Apostoli

Piazza Sign

V. Vacchere

Piazza di Cestello

San Frediano in Cestello

Lung. Soderini
Ponte alla Carraia

29

30

C. de' Medici
Via Por S. Maria

Piazza

Borgo S. Frediano

Piazza N. Sauro

40

Lung. Guicciardini
Via Santo Spirito

Ponte S. Trinita
Lung. Acciaioli

Ponte Vecchio

Galleria degli Uffizi

Lung. Archib

Arno

Piazza del Carmine

V. S. Monaca
V. dell'Ardiglione
V. dei Serragli
V. Sant'Agostino
V. Maffia

Borgo Sant'Jacopo

44

43

V. delle Sdrucciolo

V. del Ramaglianti

46

Piazza S. Maria Sopr'Arno

Costa dei Magnoli

Piazza S. Spirito

41

42

V. Michelozzi
V. Squazza
Borgo Tegolaio
V. Maggio
Sdrucciolo dei Pitti
V. Guicciardini

45

V. della Chiesa
V. delle Caldaie

Giardino Torrigiani
V. del Campuccio

Piazza S. Felice

Piazza dei Pitti

Palazzo Pitti

V. Romana

Boboli Gardens

Forte di Belvedere

KEY

- **3** Hotels
- **1** Restaurants
- 🛈 Tourist information

with parsley and garlic is an epiphany. If chef Fabio Picchi provides un-solicited advice, take it as a sign of his enthusiasm for cooking. Around the corner is Cibreino, Cibrèo's budget sibling, with a shorter menu and a no-reservations policy. ⊠ *Via A. del Verrocchio 8/r, near Santa Croce* ☎ *055/2341100* ⌨ *Reservations essential* ▭ *AE, DC, MC, V* ☾ *Closed Sun. and Mon., July 25–Sept. 5, and Dec. 31–Jan. 7.*

$$$$ ✕ **Enoteca Pinchiorri.** A sumptuous Renaissance palace—with high, fres-coed ceilings and floral bouquets in silver vases—provides the backdrop for one of the most expensive restaurants in Italy. Some consider it one of the best, and others consider it a non-Italian rip-off; the kitchen is presided over by a Frenchwoman with sophisticated, yet internation-al-ist, leanings. Interesting pasta combinations such as the *ignudi* (ricotta-and-spinach dumplings with a lobster-and-coxcomb fricassee) are always on the menu. Though portions are small, the holdings of the wine cel-lar are vast and service is top-notch. ⊠ *Via Ghibellina 87, near Santa Croce* ☎ *055/242777* ⌨ *Reservations essential* ▭ *AE, MC, V* ☾ *Closed Sun. and Mon., and Aug. No lunch Tues. or Wed.*

★ **$$–$$$** ✕ **La Giostra.** The clubby La Giostra, which means "carousel" in Ital-ian, is owned and run by Prince Dimitri Kunz d'Asburgo Lorena, and his way with mushrooms is as remarkable as his charm. The unusually good pastas may require explanation from Soldano, one of the prince's good-looking twin sons. In perfect English he'll describe a favorite dish, *taglierini con tartufo bianco,* a decadently rich, ribbonlike pasta with white truffles. All of this pairs with the well-culled wine list. Do leave room for sweets, as this is the only show in town serving a sublime tiramisu *and* a wonderfully gooey Sacher torte. ⊠ *Borgo Pinti 12/r, near Santa Croce* ☎ *055/241341* ▭ *AE, DC, MC, V.*

¢–$$$ ✕ **Baldovino.** Here the standard pizzas delight the kids, and to satisfy the parents, there are pizzas with more sophisticated toppings, such as the *lombardo,* with potatoes, *Taleggio* (soft, whole-milk cheese), and truffles. Pasta dishes are also served. ⊠ *Via San Giuseppe 22/r, near Santa Croce* ☎ *055/241773* ▭ *MC, V* ☾ *Closed Mon.*

$–$$ ✕ **Acquacotta.** Closely spaced tables with red-checker tablecloths: it doesn't get much more "Italian" than this; you'd almost expect some-one to come out of the kitchen with an accordion. Not to worry, the chef has better things to do than break into song. The highlight of the menu, with the usual list of grilled meats and pasta starters, is the *ac-quacotta,* literally "cooked water"—a favorite from southern Tuscany that rarely appears on Florentine menus. It's a vegetable-based soup with mushrooms and onions that's topped with a poached egg. Service can be offhand (if not dismissive). ⊠ *Via dei Pilastri 51/r, near Santa Croce* ☎ *055/242907* ▭ *MC, V* ☾ *Closed Mon. and Aug.*

★ **$–$$** ✕ **Antico Noe.** If Florentines voted for a favorite dive, this would be it. The 30-seat restaurant is on one of the more unsavory half blocks in town, but it serves Tuscan meals with flare. The chef relies heavily on fresh ingredients (the menu particularly comes alive during truffle and artichoke season). Locals rave about the tagliatelle *ai porcini* (with mushrooms). The mixed meat plate is noteworthy, and the *lardo di colonnata* (Colonnata lard—don't ask, just eat it) is sublime. The wine list is short but has some great bargains. ⊠ *Volta di San Piero*

6/r, Santa Croce ☎ *055/2340838* ▭ *AE, DC, MC, V* ⊗ *Closed Sun. and 2 wks in Aug.*

★ **$-$$** ✕ **Osteria de'Benci.** A few minutes from Santa Croce, this charming osteria serves grilled meats that are justifiably famous; the *carbonata* is a succulent piece of grilled beefsteak served rare. You might also try the *eliche del profeta* (a short pasta served with fresh ricotta, oregano, olive oil, tomatoes, and grated pecorino Romano cheese). When it's warm, you can dine outside with a view of the 13th-century tower belonging to the prestigious Alberti family. Next door the Osteria de'Benci Caffè (¢) serves coffee, aperitifs, and sandwiches 8 AM–midnight. ⊠ *Via de'Benci 11–13/r, near Santa Croce* ☎ *055/2344923* ▭ *AE, DC, MC, V* ⊗ *Closed Sun.*

$-$$ ✕ **Pallottino.** With its tiled floor, photograph-filled walls, and wooden tables, Pallottino is the quintessential Tuscan trattoria. Hearty, heartwarming classics include *peposa alla toscana* (a beef stew laced with black pepper). The menu changes frequently to reflect what's seasonal; the staff is friendly, as are the diners, who often share a table and, eventually, conversation. ⊠ *Via Isola delle Stinche 1/r, near Santa Croce* ☎ *055/ 289573* ▭ *AE, DC, MC, V* ⊗ *Closed Mon. and 2–3 wks in Aug.*

$ ✕ **Pizzeria Caffè Italiano.** Locals swear by the pizzeria associated with the Osteria del Caffè Italiano, two doors down. Come early to grab one of the few tables, and ignore the fact that service here is intentionally rushed. ⊠ *Via Isole delle Stinche, near Santa Croce* ☎ *055/289368* ▭ *No credit cards* ⊗ *Closed Mon.*

¢-$ ✕ **Le Campane.** The *pizziauoli* (pizza-makers) here successfully create both the Roman (thin) crust and the Neapolitan (thick) crust varieties, as well as some entrées. ⊠ *Borgo La Croce 85–87/r, near Santa Croce* ☎ *055/ 2341101* ▭ *AE, DC, MC, V* ⊗ *Closed Mon.*

¢ ✕ **da Rocco.** At one of Florence's biggest markets you can grab lunch to go, or you could cram yourself into one of the booths and pour from the straw-cloaked flask (wine here is *da consumo,* which means they charge you for how much you drink). Food is abundant, Tuscan, and fast; locals pack in. The menu changes daily, and the prices are so right. ⊠ *In Mercato Sant'Ambrogio, Piazza Ghiberti, near Santa Croce* ☎ *No phone* ⌂ *Reservations not accepted* ▭ *No credit cards* ⊗ *Closed Sun. No dinner.*

Beyond the City Center

$$-$$$ ✕ **Targa.** It looks and feels like California on the Arno at this sleek, airy restaurant a short ride from the city center. Owner-chef Gabriele Tarchiani has spent time in the United States, which shows in the plant-decorated interior. Creative touches on the frequently changing menu include combinations such as fusilli *al ragù di anatra e finferli* (with a minced duck and wild mushroom sauce). The desserts are culinary masterpieces. ⊠ *Lungarno Colombo 7, east of center* ☎ *0055/677377* ⌂ *Reservations essential* ▭ *AE, DC, MC, V* ⊗ *Closed Sun.*

Cafés

Cafés in Italy serve not only coffee concoctions and pastries but also drinks and some light lunches as well. They open early in the morning and usually close around 8 PM.

What Tripe!

WHILE IN FLORENCE, those with a sense of culinary adventure should seek out a tripe sandwich, which is just about as revered by local gourmands as the bistecca alla fiorentina. In this case, however, the treasure comes on the cheap—sandwiches are sold from small stands found in the city center, topped with a fragrant green sauce or a piquant red hot sauce, or both. *Bagnato* means that the hard, crusty roll is first dipped in the tripe's cooking liquid; it's advisable to say *"sì"* when asked if that's how you like it. Sandwiches are usually taken with a glass of red wine poured from the tripe seller's *fiasco* (flask). If you find the tripe to your liking, you might also enjoy *lampredotto*, another, some say better, cut of stomach. For an exalted, high-end tripe treat, try Fabio Picchi's

cold tripe salad, served gratis as an *amuse-bouche* at the restaurant Cibrèo. It could make a convert of even the staunchest "I'd never try *that*" kind of eater.

Tripe carts are lunchtime favorite of Florentine working men—it's uncommon, but not unheard of, to see a woman at a tripe stand. Afficionados will argue which sandwich purveyor is best; here are three that frequently get mentioned: **La Trippaia** (⊠ Via dell'Ariento, near Santa Maria Novella ☎ No phone ⊙ Closed Sun.). **Il Trippaio** (⊠ Via de'Macci, at Borgo La Croce, near Santa Croce ☎ No phone ⊙ Closed Sun.). **Nerbone** (⊠ Inside the Mercato Centrale, near Santa Maria Novella ☎ No phone ⊙ Closed Sun.)

The always-crowded **Caffè Giacosa/Roberto Cavalli** (⊠ Via della Spada 10, near Santa Maria Novella ☎ 055/2776328), joined at the hip with a Florentine fashion designer's shop, is open for breakfast, lunch, tea, and cocktails. Classy **Procacci** (⊠ Via Tornabuoni 64/r, near Santa Maria Novella ☎ 055/211656) is a Florentine institution dating back to 1885; try one of the panini *tartufati* (a small roll with truffled butter) and swish it down with a glass of *prosecco* (a dry, sparkling white wine). It's closed Sunday and Monday.

Gran Caffè (⊠ Piazza San Marco 11/r ☎ 055/215833) is down the street from the Accademia, so it's a perfect stop for a marvelous *panino* (sandwich) or sweet while raving about the majesty of Michelangelo's *David*. Perhaps the best café for people-watching is **Rivoire** (⊠ Piazza della Signoria, Via Vacchereccia 4/r, ☎ 055/214412). Stellar service, light snacks, and terrific *aperitivi* (aperitifs) are the norm. Think twice, however, before ordering the more substantial fare, which is not as good.

Gelaterie & Pasticcerie
The convenient **Caffè delle Carrozze** (⊠ Piazza del Pesce 3–5/r, near Piazza Signoria ☎ 055/2396810) is around the corner from the Uffizi; their gelati, according to some, are the best in the historic center. **Gelaterie Carabe** (⊠ Via Ricasoli 60/r, San Marco ☎ 055/289476) specializes in desserts Sicilian (including cannoli). Its *granità* (granular-flavor ices), made only in the summer, are tart and flavorful—perfect thirst-quenchers.

Dolci e Dolcezze (⊠ Piazza C. Beccaria 8/r, near Santa Croce ☎ 055/2345458), a *pasticceria* (bakery) in Borgo La Croce, probably has the prettiest and tastiest cakes, sweets, and tarts in town. It's closed Monday. Most visitors consider **Vivoli** (⊠ Via Isola delle Stinche 7/r, near Santa Croce ☎ 055/292334) the best gelateria in town; Florentines find it highly overrated. **Vestri** (⊠ Borgo Albizi 11/r, near Santa Croce ☎ 055/2340374) is devoted to chocolate in all its guises. The small but sublime selection of chocolate-base gelati includes one with hot peppers.

Salumerie

Delicatessens and gourmet food shops specializing in fresh and cured meats and cheeses, *salumerie,* can be a great places to assemble a picnic or purchase dinner. Most are closed Sunday.

Looking for some cheddar cheese to pile in your panino? **Pegna** (⊠ Via dello Studio 8, near Duomo ☎ 055/282701) has been selling both Italian and non-Italian food since 1860. The cheese collection at **Baroni** (⊠ Mercato Central, enter at Via Signa, near San Lorenzo ☎ 055/289576) may be the most comprehensive in Florence. **Perini** (⊠ Mercato Centrale, enter at Via dell'Aretino, near San Lorenzo ☎ 055/2398306) sells everything from prosciutto and mixed meats to sauces for pasta and a wide assortment of antipasti. They're generous with free samples. Hungry for lunch or a snack in the Oltrarno? Drop into **Azzarri Delicatesse** (⊠ Borgo S. Jacopo 27b/cr, near Santo Spirito ☎ 055/2381714) for a sandwich, meat for the grill, wine, or French cheeses.

WHERE TO STAY

8

Whether you are in a five-star hotel or a more modest establishment, one of the greatest pleasures of all is—a room with a view. E. M. Forster may have been referring specifically to a view of the Duomo, but Florence has so many famous landmarks that it's not hard to find lodgings with a panoramic vista. And the equivalent of the genteel pensions of yesteryear still exists, with the benefit of modern plumbing.

Florence's importance not only as a tourist city but as a convention center and site of the Pitti fashion collections throughout the year means a high demand for rooms. Except in winter, reservations are a must. If you find yourself in Florence with no reservations, go in person to **Consorzio ITA** (⊠ Stazione Centrale, near Santa Maria Novella ☎ 055/282893) to make a booking.

WHAT IT COSTS In euros					
	$$$$	**$$$**	**$$**	**$**	**¢**
FOR 2 PEOPLE	over €290	€210–€290	€140–€210	€80–€140	under €80

Prices are for a standard double room in high season.

Centro Storico

★ **$$$$** ▣ **Hotel Helvetia & Bristol.** Painstaking care has gone into making this hotel one of the prettiest and most intimate in town. From the cozy-yet-sophisticated lobby with its *pietra serena* (gray sandstone) columns to the guest rooms decorated with ornate art, you might feel as if you're a guest in a sophisticated manor house. The restaurant serves sumptuous fare among the romance of dark walls, red velvet chairs, and cascading chandeliers. Staying here you're at the center of the centro storico. ⊠ *Via dei Pescioni 2, Piazza della Repubblica, 50123* ☎ *055/26651* 🖷 *055/288353* ⊕ *www.royaldemeure.com* ⇨ *44 rooms, 23 suites* ⌕ *Restaurant, room service, in-room safes, some in-room hot tubs, minibars, cable TV, in-room VCRs, bar, babysitting, dry cleaning, laundry service, concierge, Internet, meeting room, parking (fee), some pets allowed, no-smoking rooms* ▭ *AE, DC, MC, V* ¶◎¶ *EP.*

$$$$ 🏨 **Hotel Savoy.** From the outside, the Hotel Savoy looks very much like the turn-of-the-19th-century building that it is. Inside, sleek minimalism and up-to-the-minute amenities prevail. Sitting rooms have a funky edge, their cream-color walls dotted with contemporary prints. Streamlined furniture sits in guest rooms outfitted in muted colors. Many rooms look out at the Duomo's cupola or the Piazza della Repubblica. The deep marble tubs might be reason enough to stay here—but you may also appreciate the efficient and courteous staff. ⊠ *Piazza della Repubblica 7, 50123* ☎ *055/27351* 🖷 *055/2735888* ⊕ *www.roccofortehotels.com* ⇨ *92 rooms, 11 suites* ⌕ *Restaurant, room service, in-room fax, in-room safes, minibars, cable TV with movies and video games, in-room VCRs, in-room data ports, exercise equipment, bar, children's programs (ages infant–12), dry cleaning, laundry service, concierge, Internet, business services, meeting rooms, parking (fee), no-smoking rooms* ▭ *AE, DC, MC, V* ¶◎¶ *EP.*

☾ $ 🏨 **Albergo Firenze.** A block from the Duomo, Albergo Firenze is on one of the oldest piazzas in Florence, and for the location, the place is a great bargain. Though the reception area and hallways have all the charm of a dormitory, the similarity ends when you enter the spotlessly clean rooms with tile floors and wood veneer. A good number of singles, triples, and quads make this an attractive alternative for families and budget travelers. ⊠ *Piazza Donati 4, near Duomo, 50122* ☎ *055/214203* 🖷 *055/212370* ⊕ *www.hotelfirenze-fi.it* ⇨ *58 rooms* ⌕ *Parking (fee)* ▭ *MC, V* ¶◎¶ *BP.*

San Lorenzo & Beyond

$$ 🏨 **Loggiato dei Serviti.** Though the hotel was not designed by Brunelleschi, it might as well have been; it's a mirror image of the architect's famous Spedale degli Innocenti across the way. Occupying a 16th-century former convent building, this was once an inn for traveling priests. Vaulted ceilings, tester canopy beds, and rich fabrics help make this spare Renaissance building with modern comforts a find. The Loggiato is on one of the city's loveliest squares. ⊠ *Piazza Santissima Annunziata 3, 50122* ☎ *055/289592* 🖷 *055/289595* ⊕ *www.loggiatodeiservitihotel.it* ⇨ *38 rooms* ⌕ *In-room safes, minibars, cable TV, in-room data ports, bar, babysitting, dry cleaning, laundry service, parking (fee), some pets allowed* ▭ *AE, DC, MC, V* ¶◎¶ *BP.*

$$ 🏨 **Morandi alla Crocetta.** Near Piazza Santissima Annunziata is a charming and distinguished residence in which you're made to feel like privileged friends of the family. The former convent is close to the sights but

FodorsChoice
★

very quiet, and is furnished comfortably in the classic style of a gracious Florentine home. One room retains original 17th-century fresco fragments, and two others have small private terraces. The Morandi is not only an exceptional hotel but also a good value. It's very small, so try to book well in advance. ☒ *Via Laura 50, near Santissima Annunziata, 50121* ☎ *055/2344747* 🖷 *055/2480954* ⊕ *www.hotelmorandi.it* ↘ *10 rooms* ⚹ *In-room safes, minibars, cable TV, in-room data ports, dry cleaning, laundry service, concierge, Internet, parking (fee), some pets allowed* ➾ *AE, DC, MC, V* ¶◉ *EP.*

$–$$ 🏨 **Antica Dimora Firenze.** Each room in the intimate *residenza* (a residence property, this one opened in May 2004) is painted a different pastel color—peach, rose, powder blue. Furnishings are simple and homey (that could be your grandmother's handmade quilt on the bed) and double-glaze windows ensure a peaceful night's sleep. You might ask for one of the rooms that has a small private terrace. Coffee and tea, available all day in the sitting room, are on the house. Note that the staff goes home at 7 PM. ☒ *Via San Gallo 72, near San Marco, 50129* ☎ *055/4627296* 🖷 *055/4634450* ⊕ *www.anticadimorafirenze.it* ↘ *6 rooms* ⚹ *In room data ports, in-room safes, minibars, refrigerators, cable TV, in-room VCRs, no smoking rooms* ➾ *No credit cards* ¶◉ *BP.*

$ 🏨 **Residenza Johanna I.** Savvy travelers and those on a budget know the Johanna I has a tremendous price-to-location ratio. Here you're very much in the centro storico. Rooms have high ceilings, traditional furniture (iron beds, wooden desks), and bedspreads done in pastel floral prints. Morning tea and coffee (but no breakfast) are taken in one's room. You're given a large set of keys to let yourself in, as the staff goes home at 7 PM. ☒ *Via Bonifacio Lupi 14, near San Marco, 50129* ☎ *055/481896* 🖷 *055/482721* ⊕ *www.johanna.it* ↘ *11 rooms* ⚹ *Fans, parking (fee); no a/c, no room phones, no room TVs* ➾ *No credit cards* ¶◉ *EP.*

Fodor'sChoice
★

Santa Maria Novella to the Arno

$$$ 🏨 **Antica Torre di Via Tornabuoni.** If you're looking for the proverbial view, stop here, where just about every room has a window that frames the awe-inspiring Duomo or the Arno (some even have small terraces). When it's warm, you can sit on the rooftop terrace with a glass of wine and enjoy a 360-degree panorama. The tastefully furnished rooms, with their high ceilings and sweeping draperies, create a fine backdrop for historic Florence. This is the perfect place if you desire luxe privacy; since it's a residenza, the staff goes home at 7 PM. Charming host Jacopo d'Albasio strives to ensure that all his guests are not only happy, but yearn to come back. ☒ *Via Tornabuoni 1, near Santa Maria Novella, 50122* ☎ *055/2658161* 🖷 *055/218841* ⊕ *www.tornabuoni1.com* ↘ *11 rooms, 1 suite* ⚹ *In-room data ports, in-room safes, minibars, cable TV, bar, Internet, meeting rooms, parking (fee), some pets allowed, no-smoking rooms* ➾ *AE, DC, MC, V* ¶◉ *EP.*

★ $$–$$$ 🏨 **Beacci Tornabuoni.** Florentine pensioni do not come any more classic than this one in a 14th-century palazzo. There's an old-fashioned grace, and enough modern comforts. Wallpaper or tapestrylike wall hangings make rooms inviting. The sitting room has a large fireplace, and the terrace has a tremendous view of some major Florentine monuments, such as the church of Santa Trinita. On Monday, Wednesday, and Friday nights

8

May–October, the dining room opens to serve Tuscan specialties. ✉ *Via Tornabuoni 3, near Santa Maria Novella, 50123* ☎ *055/212645* 🖷 *055/ 283594* ⊕ *www.bthotel.it* 🖘 *28 rooms* ᓬ *Restaurant, minibars, cable TV, bar, babysitting, dry cleaning, laundry service, Internet, parking (fee), some pets allowed* ☰ *AE, DC, MC, V* �|◉| *BP.*

$$ 🔲 **Alessandra.** The building, known as the Palazzo Roselli del Turco, was designed in 1507 by Baccio d'Agnolo, a contemporary of Michelangelo's. Though little remains of the original design save for the high wood ceilings, there's still an aura of grandeur in the ample rooms. Several have views of the Arno; the sole suite is spacious. Friendly hosts Anna and Andrea Gennarini speak fluent English. The location, a block from the Ponte Vecchio, helps make this a good choice. ✉ *Borgo Santi Apostoli 17, near Santa Maria Novella, 50123* ☎ *055/283438* 🖷 *055/ 210619* ⊕ *www.hotelalessandra.com* 🖘 *26 rooms, 19 with bath, 1 suite, 1 apartment* ᓬ *In-room safes, some minibars, cable TV, dry cleaning, laundry service, Internet, parking (fee), no-smoking rooms* ☰ *AE, MC, V* ⊘ *Closed Dec. 10–26* �|◉| *BP.*

$$ 🔲 **Torre Guelfa.** Enter this hidden hotel through an immense wooden door on a narrow street, continue through the iron gate and up a few steps to an elevator that takes you to the third floor. A few more steps and you're in a 13th-century Florentine *torre* (tower) that once protected the fabulously wealthy Acciaiuoli family. Now it's one of the best-located small hotels in Florence. Each guest room is different—some with canopied beds, some with balconies. Those on a budget might want to consider one of the six less-expensive rooms on the second floor that have no TVs. ✉ *Borgo Santi Apostoli 8, near Santa Maria Novella, 50123* ☎ *055/2396338* 🖷 *055/2398577* ⊕ *www.hoteltorrequelfa.com* 🖘 *24 rooms, 2 suites* ᓬ *Some in-room safes, babysitting, dry cleaning, laundry service, Internet, parking (fee), some pets allowed, no-smoking rooms; no TV in some rooms* ☰ *AE, MC, V* ⁘◉| *BP.*

$ 🔲 **Bellettini.** You're in good hands at this small, three-floor pensione run by sisters Marzia and Gina Naldini and their husbands. Public rooms are simple but comfortable; the good-size guest rooms have Venetian or Tuscan provincial decor; bathrooms are bright and modern. The top floor has two rooms with a view, and a handful of triples and quadruples make this the perfect place for families or friends traveling together. There's an ample buffet breakfast, including tasty homemade cakes. ✉ *Via dei Conti 7, near Santa Maria Novella, 50123* ☎ *055/213561* 🖷 *055/283551* ⊕ *www.hotelbellettini.com* 🖘 *28 rooms* ᓬ *In-room safes, minibars, cable TV, bar, Internet, parking (fee), some pets allowed* ☰ *AE, DC, MC, V* ⁘◉| *BP.*

$ 🔲 **Pensione Ferretti.** Minutes away from Piazza Santa Maria Novella, this pensione has views onto the tiny piazza containing the Croce al Trebbio, as well as easy access to the historic center. English-speaking owner Luciano Michel and his South African–born wife, Sue, do just about anything to make you feel at home (including providing 24-hour, free Internet access). Ceiling fans make warmer months more bearable. Though it's housed in a 16th-century palazzo, accommodations are no-frills. ✉ *Via delle Belle Donne 17, near Santa Maria Novella, 50123* ☎ *055/2381328* 🖷 *055/219288* ⊕ *www.emmeti.it/Hferretti* 🖘 *16 rooms, 6 with bath;*

1 apartment ♿ *Fans, Internet, parking (fee), some pets allowed; no a/c, no room TVs* 🖃 *AE, DC, MC, V* ❢⊙❢ *BP.*

The Oltrarno

$$$$ ✕⊞ **Villa La Vedetta.** A former family villa, turned luxury hotel, sits in the hills on the south bank of the Arno. Everything is elegantly under-stated: sleek black, gray, and red tones and contemporary Baccarat chandeliers adorn public spaces. Nineteenth-century consoles outfit rich, color-coordinated guest rooms: a sea of azure velvet bed coverings offsets pale blue canopies, for example. Phenomenal views of Florence, along with a stellar staff, set this place apart. Andrea Accordi is at the helm of Onice Restaurant. His inventive Italian dishes, such as a veal chop served with curried salsa, allude to the five years he spent in Thailand. ⊠ *Viale Michelangelo 78, Lungarno South, 50125* ☎ *055/681631* 🖷 *055/6582544* ⊕ *www.villalavedettahotel.com* ⤵ *10 rooms, 8 suites* ♿ *Restaurant, room service, in-room data ports, in-room safes, mini-bars, cable TV, some in-room DVDs, pool, sauna, 2 bars, babysitting, dry cleaning, laundry service, Internet, meeting rooms, free parking, some pets allowed, no-smoking rooms* 🖃 *AE, DC, MC, V* ❢⊙❢ *BP.*

$$$$ ⊞ **Lungarno.** Many rooms and suites here have private terraces that jut out over the Arno, affording sumptuous views of the palaces that line the river. Four suites in the 13th-century tower retain details like exposed stone walls and old archways; they face onto a little square with a me-dieval tower covered in jasmine. The very chic decor approximates a breezily wealthy home, with lots of crisp white fabrics with blue trim. A wall of windows and a sea of white couches make the lobby bar one of the nicest places in the city to stop for a drink. The Lungarno Suites, across the river, are apartmentlike lodgings that have kitchens. ⊠ *Borgo San Jacopo 14, Lungarno South, 50125* ☎ *055/27261* 🖷 *055/268437* ⊕ *www.lungarnohotels.com* ⤵ *60 rooms, 13 suites* ♿ *Restaurant, in-room fax, cable TV with movies, in-room data ports, bar, babysitting, dry cleaning, laundry service, concierge, Internet, meeting rooms, park-ing (fee), no-smoking rooms* 🖃 *AE, DC, MC, V* ❢⊙❢ *BP.*

$$$$ ⊞ **Palazzo Magnani Feroni.** Play the part of a Florentine aristocrat in a 16th-century palazzo with a massive halls and sweeping staircase. Suites include large sitting rooms and bedrooms, all decorated with luxurious fabrics, chandeliers, and Renaissance-inspired furniture. The rooftop ter-race, complete with bar, has citywide views that startle. Though it's only a five-minute walk from the Ponte Vecchio, the street is surprisingly quiet. ⊠ *Borgo San Frediano 5, near Santo Spirito, 50124* ☎ *055/2399544* 🖷 *055/2608908* ⊕ *www.florencepalace.com* ⤵ *11 suites* ♿ *Room service, in-room safes, minibars, cable TV, in-room data ports, exercise equipment, billiards, bar, dry cleaning, laundry service, parking (fee), no-smoking rooms* 🖃 *AE, DC, MC, V* ❢⊙❢ *BP.*

$ ⊞ **Albergo La Scaletta.** For a tremendous view of the Boboli Garden, near the Ponte Vecchio and Palazzo Pitti, come to this exquisite pensione run by a mother-and-son team. It has simply furnished yet rather large rooms and a sunny breakfast room. In warm weather two flower-be-decked terraces are open, one with a stunning 360-degree view of Flo-rence. ⊠ *Via Guicciardini 13, near Palazzo Pitti, 50125* ☎ *055/283028*

8

🖩 *055/289562* ⊕ *www.hotellascaletta.com* ➽ *11 rooms, 10 with bath* ⛨ *Parking (fee), some pets allowed; no TV in some rooms* ▭ *MC, V* 𝌆 *BP.*

Santa Croce

$$$–$$$$ ▦ **J&J.** Cavernous suites in the 16th-century convent are ideal for honeymooners, families, and small groups of friends. Some are bi-level, and many are imaginatively arranged around the central courtyard. The smaller rooms are more intimate, some opening onto a little shared courtyard. Some bathrooms have been refitted with pale travertine tiles. The gracious owners enjoy chatting in the light and airy lounge; breakfast is served in a glassed-in Renaissance loggia or in the central courtyard. ✉ *Via di Mezzo 20, near Santa Croce, 50121* ☎ *055/26312* 🖩 *055/240282* ⊕ *www.jandjhotel.com* ➽ *19 rooms, 7 suites* ⛨ *Cable TV, in-room data ports, bar, babysitting, dry cleaning, laundry service, parking (fee), no-smoking rooms* ▭ *AE, DC, MC, V* 𝌆 *BP.*

★ **$$$–$$$$** ▦ **Monna Lisa.** Housed in a 15th-century palazzo, with parts of the building dating from the 13th century, this hotel retains some of its original wood-coffered ceilings from the 1500s, as well as its original marble staircase. Though some rooms are small, they are tastefully decorated, each with different floral wallpaper. The public rooms retain a 19th-century aura, and the intimate bar, with its red velveteen wallpaper, is a good place to unwind. ✉ *Borgo Pinti 27, near Santa Croce, 50121* ☎ *055/ 2479751* 🖩 *055/2479755* ⊕ *www.monnalisa.it* ➽ *45 rooms* ⛨ *In-room safes, minibars, cable TV, bar, babysitting, dry cleaning, laundry service, concierge, parking (fee), some pets allowed, no-smoking rooms* ▭ *AE, DC, MC, V* 𝌆 *BP.*

¢ ▦ **Albergo Losanna.** Most major sights are within walking distance of this tiny pensione just within the Viale, the edge of the city center. Though dated and a little worn around the edges, the property is impeccably clean and the rooms have high ceilings; the mother and son who run the place are enthusiastic and cordial. Try to get a room facing away from the street; you won't have a view but you can get a quiet night's sleep. ✉ *Via V. Alfieri 9, near Santa Croce, 50121* ☎☎ *055/245840* ⊕ *www.albergolosanna.com* ➽ *8 rooms, 3 with bath* ⛨ *Parking (fee); no a/c in some rooms, no room TVs* ▭ *MC, V* 𝌆 *BP.*

¢ ▦ **Istituto Oblate dell'Assunzione.** Twelve nuns run this perfectly situated convent just minutes from the Duomo. Rooms are spotless and simple; some of them have views of the cupola, and others look out onto a carefully tended garden where guests are encouraged to relax. Several rooms have three and four beds. Curfew is at 11:30 PM, and those of you who want to attend Mass can do so every morning at 7:30. The nuns will provide half or full pension for groups of 10 or more. ✉ *Borgo Pinti 15, near Santa Croce, 501201* ☎ *055/2480582* 🖩 *055/2346291* ➽ *28 rooms, 22 with bath* ⛨ *Parking (fee), no-smoking rooms; no a/c in some rooms, no room phones, no room TVs* ▭ *No credit cards* 𝌆 *BP.*

Outside the City

🌙 **$$** ▦ **Relais Villa l'Olmo.** If you're looking for a country experience but crave easy access to the city, this place just outside the small town of Impruneta does the trick. Alberto and Claudia Giannotti have turned a 16th-century country villa into an elegantly comfortable agriturismo 20 minutes south of the center of Florence. Many of the cheerful one- and two-bedroom apartments—plaid couches, terra-cotta tile floors—look out at a gently terraced field of olive trees; some adjoin. Unlike at many agriturismi, there's no minimum stay during high season here. The estate produces top-notch olive oil, as well as some respectable wine. ⊠ *Via Impruneta 19, 50023 Impruneta* ☎ *055/2311311* 🖷 *055/2311313* ⊕ *www.relaisfarmholiday.com* ↪ *8 apartments, 1 farmhouse, 2 cottages* ⌂ *Picnic area, BBQs, fans, in-room safes, kitchens, refrigerators, cable TV with movies, golf privileges, 3 pools, massage, mountain bikes, babysitting, dry cleaning, laundry facilities, laundry service, Internet, free parking, some pets allowed, no-smoking rooms* ⊟ *AE, MC, V* ⦿l *EP.*

★ **$$** 🏨 **Villa Poggio San Felice.** Livia Puccinelli Sannini, the descendant of a famed 19th-century Florentine hotelier, and her husband, Lorenzo Magnelli, have turned the family's former country villa (documented to the 15th century) into a lovely hotel 5 km (3 mi) southwest of the city limits. With only five rooms available, the villa still feels like a single-family dwelling. Some of the high-ceiling rooms have divine views of Brunelleschi's cupola below, others have working fireplaces. The landscaped gardens help make a stay here serene. Though there is daily shuttle service to the center of town, a car is vital. ⊠ *Via San Matteo in Arcetri 24, Lugarno South, 50125* ☎ *055/220016* 🖷 *055/2335388* ⊕ *www. villapoggiosanfelice.com* ↪ *4 rooms, 1 suite* ⌂ *Golf privileges, pool, wading pool, babysitting, laundry service, Internet, free parking, some pets allowed, no-smoking rooms* ⊟ *AE, MC, V* ⦿l *BP* ⊗ *Closed Jan. 10–Feb. 28.*

NIGHTLIFE & THE ARTS

The Arts

Florence is justifiably famous for its musical offerings. The annual Maggio Musicale attracts the best international talent. Theaters also host visiting American rock stars and cabaret performers. Opera, ballet, and concerts occur regularly throughout the year at different venues in town. Major traveling art exhibitions are mounted at Palazzo Strozzi throughout the year. There's a little publication available at bars and hotels called *Informacittà* (⊕ www.informacittafirenze.it): even though it's in Italian, it's pretty easy to read for event times and addresses.

Film

You can find movie listings in *La Nazione,* the daily Florentine newspaper. Note that most American films are dubbed into Italian rather than subtitled. The **Odeon** (⊠ Piazza Strozzi, near Piazza della Repubblica ☎ 055/214068 ⊕ www.cinehall.it) shows first-run English-language films on Monday, Tuesday, and Thursday at its magnificent art deco theater.

Concerts & Operas

The **Teatro Comunale** (⊠ Corso Italia 16, Lungarno North ☎ 055/213535) hosts the opera season September—December, as well as concerts, festivals, and dance performances throughout the year.

Teatro della Pergola (✉ Via della Pergola 18/32, box office Via Ala-manni 39, near Santissima Annunziata ☏ 055/210804 ⊕ www.pergola. firenze.it) is home to classical concerts, Maggio Musicale events, and other dramatic performances.

The **Maggio Musicale Fiorentina** (☏ 055/213535 ⊕ www.maggiofiorentino. com) is a series of internationally acclaimed concerts and dance and opera performances that runs May–June in venues across the city. Tickets can be purchased online and at the Teatro Comunale box office.

November to June is the concert season for the **Orchestra della Toscana** (✉ Via Ghibellina 101, near Santa Croce ☏ 055/210804 ⊕ www. orchestradellatoscana.it), with performances staged at the Teatro Verdi. **Amici della Musica** (☏ 055/210804 ⊕ www.amicimusica.fi.it) organizes classical concerts at the Teatro della Pergola.

Nightlife

Florentines are rather proud of their nightlife options. Most bars have some sort of happy hour, which usually lasts for many hours, often accompanied by substantial snacks. Dance clubs typically don't open until very late in the evening and don't get crowded until 1 or 2 in the morning. Cover charges are steep, but it's fairly easy to find free passes in trendier bars around town. Most clubs are closed either Sunday or Monday.

Bars

Zona 15 (✉ Piazza Brunelleschi, Via del Castellaccia 53–55/r, near Duomo ☏ 055/211678) is coolly chic with its pale interior, blond wood-work, and metallic surfaces. Lunch, dinner, cocktails, and live music are on offer for Florentine cognoscenti and others. The oh-so-cool—bor-dering on pretentious—vibe at **La Dolce Vita** (✉ Piazza del Carmine 6/r, near Santo Spirito ☏ 055/284595) attracts Florentines and the occa-sional visiting American movie star.

Negroni (✉ Via dei Renai 17/r, near San Niccolò ☏ 055/243647) teems with well-dressed young Florentines at happy hour. **Zoe** (✉ Via dei Renai 13/r, near San Niccolò ☏ 055/243111) calls itself a café, and al-though coffee may indeed be served, twentysomething Florentines flock here for the fine (and expensive) cocktails.

Moyo (✉ Via de'Benci 23/r, near Santa Croce ☏ 055/247 9738) opened in December 2004; high ceilings, dramatic lighting, and superb aperi-tivi (with equally superb snacks) draw trendy Florentines. **Rex** (✉ Via Fiesolana 23–25/r, near Santa Croce ☏ 055/2480331) attracts a trendy, artsy clientele. **Sant'Ambrogio Caffè** (✉ Piazza Sant'Ambrogio 7–8/r, near Santa Croce ☏ 055/241035) has outdoor summer seating with a view of an 11th-century church (Sant'Ambrogio) directly across the street. When last call's come and gone and you're not finished with your evening, go where the bartenders unwind after their shift: **Loch Ness** (✉ Via de' Benci 19/r, near Santa Croce) pours drinks there until 5 AM. For a swanky experience lubricated with trademark Bellinis and fine marti-nis, head to **Harry's Bar** (✉ Lungarno Vespucci 22/r, Lungarno North ☏ 055/2396700).

Nightclubs

Yab (✉ Via Sassetti 5/r, near Piazza della Repubblica ☎ 055/215160) is one of the largest clubs; it attracts a young clientele. **Maracaná** (✉ Via Faenza 4, near Santa Maria Novella ☎ 055/210298) is a restaurant and pizzeria featuring Brazilian specialties; at 11 PM it transforms itself into a cabaret floor show and then it opens the floor to dancing. Book a table if you want to eat. If you had a transvestite grandmother, her home would look like **Montecarla** (✉ Via de' Bardi 2, near San Niccolò ☎ 055/2340259). On its two crowded floors people sip cocktails against a backdrop of exotic flowers, leopard-print chairs and chintz, and red walls and floors.

Jazz Club (✉ Via Nuova de' Caccini 3, at Borgo Pinti, near Santa Croce ☎ 055/2479700) puts on live music in a smoky basement.

SHOPPING

Since the days of the medieval guilds, Florence has been synonymous with fine craftsmanship and good business. Such time-honored Florentine specialties as antiques (and reproductions), bookbinding, jewelry, lace, paper products, leather goods, and silks attest to this. The various shopping areas are mostly a throwback to the Middle Ages, when each district supplied a different product. The Ponte Vecchio houses reputable but very expensive jewelry shops, as it has since the 16th century. The area around Santa Croce is the heart of the leather merchants' district. The fanciest clothing designers are mainly on Via Tornabuoni and Via della Vigna Nuova. There's a large concentration of antiques shops on Borgo Ognissanti and near Santo Spirito. Across the river in the Oltrarno, there's also a variety of artisans—goldsmiths, leatherworkers, and antique furniture restorers—plying their trade.

Shops are generally open 9–1 and 3:30–7:30 and are closed Sunday and Monday morning most of the year. Summer (June–September) hours are usually 9–1 and 4–8, and some shops close Saturday afternoon instead of Monday morning. When looking for addresses of shops, notice the two-color numbering system: the red numbers are commercial addresses; the blue or black numbers are residential.

Markets

Roam through the stalls under the loggia of the **Mercato Nuovo** (✉ Via Por Santa Maria and Via Porta Rossa, near Piazza della Repubblica) for cheery, inexpensive trinkets. In the huge, two-story **Mercato Centrale** (✉ Off Via Nazionale, near San Lorenzo ☉ Mon.–Sat. 7–2), food is everywhere, some of it remarkably exotic. The ground floor contains meat and cheese stalls, as well as some very good bars selling panini, and the second floor teems with vegetable stands. If you're looking for dill or mangoes in Florence, this is most likely where you'll find them. In the streets next to the church of San Lorenzo, shop for bargains at stalls full of clothing and leather-goods that are part of the **Mercato di San Lorenzo.**

The flea market on **Piazza dei Ciompi** (✉ Sant'Ambrogio, near Santa Croce) takes place on the last Sunday of the month. An open-air produce and flea market is held in **Le Cascine park** (⊠ Off Viale Fratelli Rosselli, near Santa Maria Novella), just before the Ponte della Vittoria, every Tuesday morning.

Specialty Stores

Antiques
Giovanni Pratesi (⊠ Via Maggio 13, near Santo Spirito ☎ 055/2396568) specializes in furniture, with some fine paintings, sculpture, and decorative objects turning up from time to time. Vying with Luigi Bellini as one of Florence's oldest antiques dealers, **Guido Bartolozzi** (⊠ Via Maggio 18/r, near Santo Spirito ☎ 055/215602) sells predominately period Florentine pieces. **Galleria Luigi Bellini** (⊠ Lungarno Soderini 5, Lungarno South ☎ 055/214031) claims to be Italy's oldest antiques dealer, which may be true, since father Mario Bellini was responsible for instituting Florence's international antiques biennial.

Books & Paper
Libreria d'Arte Galleria degli Uffizi (⊠ Piazzale degli Uffizi 6, near Piazza della Signoria ☎☎ 055/284508) carries monographs on famous artists, some of whose work can be found in the Uffizi; it also carries scholarly works from both the Italian and Anglophone worlds. Long one of Florence's best art-book shops, **Libreria Salimbeni** (⊠Via Matteo Palmieri 14–16/r, near Santa Croce ☎ 055/2340905) has an outstanding selection.

Alberto Cozzi (⊠ Via del Parione 35/r, near Santa Maria Novella ☎ 055/294968) keeps an extensive line of Florentine papers and paper products, and the artisans in the shop rebind and restore books and works on paper. One of Florence's oldest paper-goods stores, **Giulio Giannini e Figlio** (⊠ Piazza Pitti 37/r ☎ 055/212621) is *the* place to buy the marbleized stock, which comes in many shapes and sizes, from flat sheets to boxes and even pencils. Photograph albums, frames, diaries, and other objects dressed in handmade paper can be purchased at **Il Torchio** (⊠ Via dei Bardi 17, San Niccolò ☎ 055/2342862). The stuff is high-quality, and the prices lower than usual. **La Tartaruga** (⊠ Borgo Albizi 60/r, Santa Croce ☎ 055/2340845) sells brightly colored, recycled paper in lots of guises (such as calendars and stationery), as well as toys for children.

Ceramics
The mother-daughter team of Antonella Chini and Lorenza Adami, sell their Florentine-inspired ceramic designs, based on Antonella's extensive ceramics training in Faenza, at **Sbigoli Terrecotte** (⊠ Via Sant'Egidio 4/r, near Santa Croce ☎ 055/2479713). They carry traditional Tuscan terra-cotta and ceramic vases, pots, and cups and saucers. **Rampini Ceramiche** (⊠ Borgo Ognissanti 32/34, Lungarno North ☎ 055/219720) sells exquisitely crafted ceramics in various patterns, shapes, and sizes.

Clothing
The usual fashion gurus—such as Prada and Armani—all have shops in Florence; more and more Via Tornabuoni resembles a giant *passarella* (catwalk). If you want to buy Florentine haute fashion while in Florence, stick to Pucci, Gucci, Ferragamo, and Roberto Cavalli, all of which call Florence home.

Florentine **Patrizia Pepe** (✉ Piazza San Giovanni 12/r, near Duomo ☎ 055/2645056) has body-conscious clothes perfect for all ages, especially for women with a tiny streak of rebelliousness. For cutting-edge fashion, the fun and funky window displays at **Spazio A** (✉ Via Porta Rossa 109–115/r, Piazza della Repubblica ☎ 055/212995 ⊕ www. aeffe.com) merit a stop. The shop carries such well-known designers as Alberta Ferretti and Narciso Rodriguez, as well as lesser-known Italian, English, and French designers. **Bernardo** (✉ Via Porta Rossa 87/r, near Piazza della Repubblica ☎ 055/283333) specializes in men's trousers, cashmere sweaters, and shirts with details like mother-of-pearl buttons. At **L'essentiel** (✉ Via del Corso 10/r, near Piazza della Signoria ☎ 055/ 294713) Lara Caldieron has spun her club-going years into fashion that also works well on the street and in the office. Though it may seem American, **Diesel** (✉ Via dei Lamberti 13/r, near Piazza della Signoria ☎ 055/ 2399963) started in Vicenza; its gear is on the "must-have" list of many self-respecting Italian teens.

The aristocratic Marchese di Barsento, **Emilio Pucci** (✉ Via Tornabuoni 20–22/r, near Santa Maria Novella ☎ 055/2658082), became an international name in the late 1950s when the stretch ski clothes he designed for himself caught on with the dolce vita crowd—his pseudopsychedelic prints and "palazzo pajamas" became all the rage. You can take home a custom-made suit or dress from **Giorgio Vannini** (✉ Via Borgo Santi Apostoli 43/r, near Santa Maria Novella ☎ 055/ 293037), who also has a showroom for his prêt-à-porter designs. **Prada** (✉ Via Tornabuoni 51–53/r, near Santa Maria Novella ☎ 055/267471 ✉ Outlet ✉ Levanella Spacceo, Estrada Statale 69, Montevarchi ☎ 055/91911) appeals to an exclusive clientele. Cognoscenti will drive or taxi about 45 minutes out of town to the Prada Outlet. Native son **Roberto Cavalli** (✉ Via Tornabuoni 83/r, near Santa Maria Novella ☎ 055/2396226), whose outlandish designs appeal to Hollywood celebrities and those who want to look like more expensive versions of Britney Spears, has a corner shop with a trendy café attached.

Geraldine Tayar (✉ Sdrucciolo de Pitti 6/r, Palazzo Pitti ☎ 055/290405) makes clothing and accessories of her own design in eclectic fabric combinations. **Il Guardaroba/Stock House** (✉ Borgo Albizi 78/r, Santa Croce ☎ 055/2340271) is where savvy Florentines shop for designer clothes at affordable prices. **Piccolo Slam** (✉ Via de'Neri 9/11r, near Santa Croce ☎ 055/214504) has classic styles for members of the junior set.

Embroidery & Linens

Sumptuous silks, beaded fabrics, lace, wool, and tweeds can be purchased at **Valli** (✉ Via Strozzi 4/r, near Piazza della Repubblica ☎ 055/282485). It carries fabrics created by Armani, Valentino, and other high-end designers. **Valmar** (✉ Via Porta Rossa 53/r, near Piazza della Repubblica ☎ 055/284493) is filled with tangled spools of cords, ribbons, and fringes, plus buttons, tassels, sachets, and hand-embroidered cushions. You can also bring in your own fabric, choose the adornments, and they will custom-make your cushion or table runner.

Loretta Caponi (✉ Piazza Antinori 4/r, near Santa Maria Novella ☎ 055/ 213668) is synonymous with Florentine embroidery, and her luxury lace,

8

VOICES OF ITALY

Valentino Adami
*ceramics shop owner,
Santa Croce area*

Since 1970, Valentino Adami, a native of southern Tuscany who has lived all over the world, and his wife, Antonella Chini, a Florentine, have been owners of the ceramics shop Sbigoli Terrecotte. The operation is a family affair: Antonella studied in Faenza, the ceramics center in Emilia-Romagna, and daughter Lorenza holds two certificates in ceramics. Most days, they can be found in the back of the shop, painting vases. Valentino and daughter Chiara run the front of the store, two plain rooms bursting with colorful objects—vases, espresso cups, plates, and patio tables.

Valentino explains what makes Italian ceramics distinctive: "First of all, it's the type of clay we use. The clay we find here is softer. We fire it at a lower temperature [950 degrees

Centigrade]. You get better color if you fire it at a lower temperature."

The use of color is crucial. "The color of the sun, of the sea—it gives us confidence with color. Our colors are similar to what the Renaissance masters used, only we don't use lead. Like those Renaissance masters, we used to fire with wood. It would take three or four days. Now we use an electric kiln."

According to Valentino, works from major ceramics-making areas within Italy can be distinguished both by color and type of design. "The further you go south, you'll find that the colors are stronger. Deruta [in Umbria] makes one kind of ceramics, and Montelupo [near Florence] another. The main difference in ceramics from Faenza is that they use faces and produce lots of hunting scenes. In Florence, it's more geometric. Our portraits are rougher compared to Faenza."

linens, and lingerie have earned her worldwide renown. **Sant' Jacopo Show** (✉ Borgo Sant'Jacopo 66/r, near Santo Spirito ☎ 055/2396912) is an offbeat shop specializing in mannequins, decorations, and shop fittings.

Food
Conti (✉ Mercato Centrale, enter at Via Signa, near San Lorenzo ☎ 055/2398501) sells top-quality wines, olive oils, and dried fruits; they'll shrink-wrap the highest-quality dried porcini for traveling. **La Bottega dell'Olio** (✉ Piazza del Limbo 2/r, near Santa Maria Novella ☎ 055/2670468) sells a great collection of fine olive oil, as well as bath products made from olive oil. **Antico Salumificio Anzuini-Massi** (✉ Via de'Neri 84/r, near Santa Croce ☎ 055/294901) shrink-wraps their own pork products, making it a snap to take home some *salame di cinghiale* (wild boar salami).

Fragrances
Antica Officina del Farmacista Dr. Vranjes (✉ Borgo La Croce 44/r, near Santa Croce ☎ 055/241748 ✉ Via San Gallo 63/r, near San Marco ☎ 055/494537) makes aromatic oils

WORD OF MOUTH

"Officina Profumo Farmeceutica Santa Maria Novella is the grandest perfume salon in the world."
–ThinGorjus

and perfumes for people and for spaces. The essence of a Florentine holiday is captured in the sachets of the **Officina Profumo Farmaceutica di Santa Maria Novella** (✉ Via della Scala 16, near Santa Maria Novella ☎ 055/216276), a turn-of-the-19th-century emporium of herbal cosmetics and soaps that are made following centuries-old recipes created by friars.

Jewelry

Carlo Piccini (✉ Ponte Vecchio 31/r, near Piazza della Signoria ☎ 055/292030) has sold antique jewelry as well as made pieces to order for several generations; you can also get old jewelry reset. **Cassetti** (✉ Ponte Vecchio 54/r, near Piazza della Signoria ☎ 055/2396028) combines precious and semiprecious stones and metals in contemporary settings.

Gherardi (✉ Ponte Vecchio 5/r, near Piazza della Signoria ☎ 055/211809), Florence's king of coral, has the city's largest selection of finely crafted pieces, as well as cultured pearls, jade, and turquoise. One of Florence's oldest jewelers, **Tiffany** (✉ Via Tornabuoni 25/r, near Santa Maria Novella ☎ 055/215506), has supplied Italian (and other) royalty with finely crafted gems for centuries. Its selection of antique-looking classics has been updated with a choice of contemporary silver. **Gatto Bianco** (✉ Borgo Santi Apostoli 12/r, near Santa Maria Novella ☎ 055/282989) has breathtakingly beautiful jewelry worked in semiprecious and precious stones; the look is completely contemporary.

Affordable necklaces and rings, mostly in silver, can be purchased at **La Gazza Ladra** (✉ Piazza Salvemini 6, near Santa Croce ☎ 055/2466008).

Shoes & Leather Accessories

Furla (✉ Via Calzaiuoli 47/r, near Piazza della Repubblica ☎ 055/2382883) makes beautiful leather bags and wallets in up-to-the-minute designs. **Pollini** (✉ Via Calimala 12/r, near Piazza della Repubblica ☎ 055/214738) has beautifully crafted shoes and leather accessories for those willing to pay that little bit extra. For sheer creativity in both color and design, check out the shoes at **Sergio Rossi** (✉ Via Roma 15/r, near Duomo ☎ 055/294873) and fantasize about having a life to go with them.

Cellerini (✉ Via del Sole 37/r, near Santa Maria Novella ☎ 055/282533) is a Florentine institution in a city where it seems that nearly everybody is wearing an expensive leather jacket. Born near Naples, the late Salvatore **Ferragamo** (✉ Via Tornabuoni 2/r, near Santa Maria Novella ☎ 055/292123) earned his fortune custom-making shoes for famous feet, especially Hollywood stars'. The elegant store, in a 13th-century Renaissance palazzo, also displays designer clothing and accessories in addition to shoes. Though the Florentine family is no longer involved with the store that bears its name, **Gucci** (✉ Via Tornabuoni 73/r, near Santa Maria Novella ☎ 055/264011) still manages to draw a crowd. **Il Bisonte** (✉ Via del Parione 31/r, off Via della Vigna Nuova, near Santa Maria Novella ☎ 055/215722) is known for its natural-looking leather goods, all stamped with the store's bison symbol.

Madova (✉ Via Guicciardini 1/r, near Palazzo Pitti ☎ 055/2396526) has a rainbow of high-quality leather gloves. **Paolo Carandini** (✉ Via de' Macci

8

73/r, near Santa Croce ☎ 055/245397) works exclusively in leather, producing exquisite objects such as picture frames, jewelry boxes, and desk accessories. The **Scuola del Cuoio** (✉ Piazza Santa Croce 16 ☎ 055/355644 ⊕ www.leatherschool.com), in the former dormitory of Santa Croce, is a consortium for leatherworkers who ply their trade and sell their wares on the premises. **Giotti** (✉ Piazza Ognissanti 3–4/r, Lungarno North ☎ 055/ 294265) has a full line of leather goods and leather clothing.

SIDE TRIPS FROM FLORENCE

Gracious Gardens Around Florence

Like any well-heeled Florentine, you too can get away from Florence's hustle and bustle by heading for the hills. Take a break from city sightseeing to enjoy the gardens and villas set like jewels in the hills around the city. Villa di Castello and Villa La Petraia, both 6 km (4 mi) northwest of the center of town in Castello, can be explored in one trip. The garden at Villa Gamberaia is a quick 8-km (5-mi) jaunt east of the center near Settignano. Plan for a full-day excursion, picnic lunch included, if visiting all three. Spring and summer are the ideal time to visit, when flowers are in glorious bloom. For a taste of Medici living, venture farther afield to the family's Villa Medicea in Poggio a Caiano, south of Prato.

Villa di Castello

A fortified residence in the Middle Ages, Villa di Castello was rebuilt by the Medici in the 15th century. The Accademia della Crusca, the 400-year-old institution that is the official arbiter of the Italian language, now occupies the palace, which is not open to the public. The gardens are the main attraction. From the villa entrance, walk uphill through the 19th-century park set above part of the formal garden. From the terrace, which affords a good view of the geometric layout of the Italian garden below, stairs on either side descend to the parterre.

Though the original garden design has been altered somewhat over the centuries, the allegorical theme of animals devised by Tribolo to the delight of the Medici in 1537 is still evident. The artificial cave, **Grotta degli Animali** (Animal Grotto), displays an imaginative menagerie of sculpted animals by Giambologna and his assistants. An Ammannati sculpture, a figure of an old man *Gennaio* (January), is at the center of a pond on the terrace overlooking the garden. Two bronze sculptures by Ammannati, centerpieces of fountains studding the Italian garden, can now be seen indoors in Villa La Petraia. Allow about 45 minutes to visit the garden; you can easily visit Villa La Petraia from here, making for a four-hour trip in total.

To get to Villa di Castello by car, head northwest from Florence on Via Reginaldo Giuliani (also known as Via Sestese) to Castello, about 6 km (4 mi) northwest of the city center in the direction of Sesto Fiorentino; follow signs to Villa di Castello. Or take Bus 28 from the city center and tell the driver you want to get off at Villa di Castello; from the stop, walk north about ½ km (¼ mi) up the tree-lined allée from the main road. ✉ *Via di Castello 47, Castello* ☎ *055/454791* 🎫 *€2, includes* *entrance to Villa La Petraia* ☉ *Garden Nov.–Feb., daily 8:15–4:30; Mar.–Oct., daily 9–7. Closed 2nd and 3rd Mon. of month* ☞ *Palace closed to public.*

Villa La Petraia

The splendidly planted gardens of Villa La Petraia lie high above the Arno plain with a sweeping view of Florence. The villa was built around a medieval tower and reconstructed after it was purchased by the Medici sometime after 1530. Virtually the only trace of the Medici having lived here is the 17th-century courtyard frescoes depicting glorious episodes from the clan's history. In the 1800s the villa served as a hunting lodge for King Vittorio Emanuele II (1820–78), who kept his mistress here while Florence was the temporary capital of the newly united country of Italy.

The garden—also altered in the 1800s—and the vast park behind the palace suggest a splendid contrast between formal and natural landscapes. Allow 60 to 90 minutes to explore the park and gardens, plus 30 minutes for the guided tour of the villa interior. This property is best visited after the Villa di Castello.

To reach Villa La Petraia by car, travel as though you're going to Villa di Castello (head northwest from Florence on Via Reginaldo Giuliani), but take the right off Via Reginaldo Giuliani, following the sign for Villa La Petraia. You can walk from Villa di Castello to Villa La Petraia in about 15 minutes; turn left beyond the gate of Villa di Castello and continue straight along Via di Castello and the imposing Villa Corsini; take Via della Petraia uphill to the entrance. ⊠ *Via della Petraia 40, Località Castello* ☎ *055/451208* ✉ *€2, includes entrance to Villa di Castello* ☉ *Garden Oct.–Mar., daily 8:15–4:30; Apr., May, and Sept., daily 9–5; June–Aug., daily 9–7. Villa tours Oct.–Mar., daily at 9:15, 10, 10:45, 11:30, 12:10, 1:30, 2:20, 3, and 3:40; Apr., May, and Sept., daily at 9:15, 10, 10:45, 11:30, 12:10, 1:30, 2:20, 3, 3:40, and 4:45; June–Aug., daily at 9:15, 10, 10:45, 11:30, 12:10, 1:30, 2:20, 3, 3:40, 4:45, 5:35, and 6:35. Closed 2nd and 3rd Mon. of month.*

Villa Gamberaia

Villa Gamberaia, near the village of Settignano on the eastern outskirts of Florence, was the rather modest 15th-century country home of Matteo di Domenico Gamberelli, the father of noted Renaissance sculptors Bernardo, Antonio, and Matteo Rossellino. In the early 1600s the villa passed into the hands of the wealthy Capponi family. They spared no expense in rebuilding it and, more important, creating its garden, one of the finest near Florence. Studded with statues and fountains, the garden suffered damage during World War II but has been restored according to the original 17th-century design. This excursion takes about 1½ hours, allowing 45 minutes to visit the garden.

To get here by car, go to Piazza Beccaria and turn onto Via Gioberti. This eventually becomes Via Aretina; follow the sign to the turnoff to the north to Villa Gamberaia, about 8 km (5 mi) from the center. To arrive by bus, take Bus 10 to Settignano. From Settignano's main Piazza Tommaseo, walk east on Via di San Romano; the second lane on the right is Via del Rossellino, which leads southeast to the entrance of Villa

Gamberaia. The walk from the piazza takes about 10 minutes. ✉ *Via del Rossellino 72, near Settignano* ☎ *055/697205* 🎫 *€10* ⊙ *Nov.–Mar., weekends 9–5; Apr.–Oct., daily 9–6.*

Fiesole

A half-day excursion to Fiesole, in the hills 8 km (5 mi) northeast of Florence, gives you a pleasant respite from museums and a wonderful view of the city. Fiesole began life as an ancient Etruscan and later Roman village that held some power until it succumbed to barbarian invasions. Eventually it gave up its independence in exchange for Florence's protection. The medieval cathedral, ancient Roman amphitheater, and lovely old villas behind garden walls are clustered on a series of hilltops. The trip from Florence by car or bus takes 20–30 minutes. Take Bus 7 from the Stazione Centrale di Santa Maria Novella, Piazza San Marco, or the Duomo. (You can also get on and off the bus at San Domenico.) There are several possible routes for the two-hour walk from central Florence to Fiesole. One route begins in residential Salviatino (Via Barbacane, near Piazza Edison, on the Bus 7 route), and after a short time you can peeks over garden walls of beautiful villas, as well as a panorama of Florence in the valley. A walk around Fiesole can take a couple of hours, depending on how far you stroll from the main piazza.

The **Duomo** reveals a stark medieval interior. In the raised presbytery, the **Cappella Salutati** was frescoed by 15th-century artist Cosimo Rosselli, but it was his contemporary the sculptor Mino da Fiesole (1430–84) who put the town on the artistic map. The Madonna on the altarpiece and the tomb of Bishop Salutati are fine examples of his work. ✉ *Piazza Mino da Fiesole* ☎ *055/59400* ⊙ *Nov.–Mar., daily 7:30–noon and 2–5; Apr.–Oct., daily 7:30–noon and 3–6.*

Fiesole's beautifully preserved 2,000-seat **Anfiteatro Romano** (Roman Amphitheater) dates from the 1st century BC and is used for the summer concerts of the **Estate Fiesolana** (✉ Teatro Romano ☎ 055/5978403), a festival of theater, music, dance, and film that also utilizes the churches of Fiesole. To the right of the amphitheater are the remains of the **Terme Romane** (Roman Baths), where you can see the gymnasium, hot and cold baths, and rectangular chamber where the water was heated. A beautifully designed **Museo Archeologico,** an intricate series of levels connected by elevators, is built amid the ruins and contains objects dating from as early as 2000 BC. The nearby **Museo Bandini** is a small collection with a lot of interesting paintings. It's filled with the private collection of Canon Angelo Maria Bandini (1726–1803); he fancied 13th- to 15th-century Florentine paintings, terra-cotta pieces, and wood sculpture, which he later bequeathed to the Diocese of Fiesole. ✉ *Via Portigiani 1* ☎ *055/59477* 🎫 *€6.50, includes access to the archaeological park and museums* ⊙ *Apr.–Sept., daily 9:30–7; Oct.–Mar., Wed.–Mon. 9:30–5.*

Via Vecchia Fiesolana is a narrow lane in use since Etruscan times; walk 4 km (2½ mi) back toward Florence on it to get to the church of **San Domenico.** Sheltered in the church is the *Madonna and Child with Saints* by Fra Angelico, who was a Dominican friar here. ⊠ *Piazza San Domenico, off Via Giuseppe Mantellini* ☎ *055/59230* ☉ *Daily 9–noon.*

Where to Stay

$$$$ 🏨 **Villa San Michele.** The cypress-lined driveway provides an elegant pre-amble to this incredibly gorgeous (and incredibly expensive) hotel nes-tled in the hills of Fiesole. The 16th-century building was originally a Franciscan convent designed by Santi di Tito. Not a single false note is struck in the reception area (formerly the chapel) or in the dining rooms (a covered cloister and former refectory). Tasteful antiques and art that decorate the rooms. Even seasoned travelers sometimes find the space cramped; do keep in mind that this was once a convent. The open-air loggia, where lunch and dinner are served, provides one of the most stun-ning views of Florence, which might compensate for the exorbitant prices. ⊠ *Via Doccia 4, 50014* ☎ *055/59451* 🖷 *055/5678250* ⊕ *www.villasanmichele.com* ➷ *19 rooms, 26 suites* ☖ *Restaurant, room ser-vice, in-room fax, in-room safes, minibars, cable TV with movies, in-room VCRs, in-room data ports, pool, gym, mountain bikes (fee), piano bar, babysitting, dry cleaning, laundry service, concierge, Internet, free parking, some pets allowed, no-smoking rooms* ⊟ *AE, DC, MC, V* ☉ *Closed Dec.–Easter* ⊠ *BP.*

$ 🏨 **Fattoria di Maiano.** In the foothills of Fiesole you have all the pleas-ures of the country with Florence 5 km (3 mi) to the south. Here there are splendid views of olive tree groves (olive oil is produced by the Fat-toria owners). The lovely apartments—wood floors, simple and sturdy furniture, and very modern kitchens—sleep 4–11 people and are rented by the week. ⊠ *Via Benedetto da Maiano 11, 50016* ☎ *055/599600* 🖷 *055/599640* ⊕ *www.fattoriadimaiano.com* ➷ *13 apartments* ☖ *Kitch-enettes, some pets allowed; no a/c* ⊟ *DC, MC, V* ⊠ *EP.*

FLORENCE ESSENTIALS

Transportation

BY AIR

Florence's Aeroporto A. Vespucci, commonly called Peretola, receives flights from Milan, Rome, London, and Paris. To get into the city cen-ter from the airport by car, take the A11. Tickets for the local bus ser-vice into Florence are sold at the airport's second-floor bar. Take Bus 62, which goes directly to the train station at Santa Maria Novella; the airport's bus shelter is beyond the parking lot.

Pisa's Aeroporto Galileo Galilei is the closest landing point with signif-icant international service. It's relatively easy to get to Florence, as the SS67 leads directly there. For flight information, call the airport or Florence Air Terminal (which is an office at Santa Maria Novella, Flor-ence's main train station). A train service connects Pisa's airport station with Santa Maria Novella, roughly a 1½-hour trip. Trains start running about 7 AM from the airport, 6 AM from Florence, and continue service every hour until about 7 PM from the airport, 4 PM from Florence. You can check in for departing flights at the Florence Air Terminal, which is around the corner from train tracks 1 and 2.

🛈 **Airport Information Aeroporto Galileo Galilei** ✉ 12 km [7 mi] south of Pisa and 80 km [50 mi] west of Florence ☎ 050/500707 ⊕ www.pisa-airport.com. **Florence Air Terminal** ✉ Stazione Centrale di Santa Maria Novella ☎ 055/216073. **Peretola** ✉ 10 km [6 mi] northwest of Florence ☎ 055/373498 ⊕ www.airport.florence.it.

BY BIKE & MOPED

Brave souls (cycling in Florence is difficult at best) may rent bicycles at easy-to-spot locations at Fortezza da Basso, the Stazione Centrale di Santa Maria Novella, and Piazza Pitti. Otherwise try Alinari. You'll be up against hordes of tourists and those pesky *motorini* (mopeds). Le Cascine, a former Medici hunting ground turned into a large public park with paved pathways, admits no cars. The historic center can be circumnavigated via bike paths lining the *viali,* the ring road surrounding the historic center. If you want to go native and rent a noisy Vespa (Italian for "wasp") or other make of motorcycle or motorino, you may do so at Maxirent. Massimo also rents mopeds. However unfashionable, helmets must be rented at either place, and by law are mandatory, much to the chagrin of many Italians.

🛈 **Rentals Alinari** ✉ Via Guelfa 85/r, San Marco ☎ 055/280500 ⊕ www.alinarirental. com. **Massimo** ✉ Via Campo d'Arrigo 16/r ☎ 055/573689. **Maxirent** ✉ Borgo Ognissanti 155/r, Santa Maria Novella ☎ 055/265420.

BY BUS

Long-distance buses provide inexpensive if somewhat claustrophobic service between Florence and other cities in Italy and Europe. Lazzi Eurolines and SITA are the major lines; they have neatly divided up their routes, so there's little overlap.

Maps and timetables for local bus service are available for a small fee at the ATAF (Trasporti Area Fiorentina) booth, or for free at visitor information offices. Tickets must be bought in advance at tobacco shops, newsstands, from automatic ticket machines near main stops, or at ATAF booths. The ticket must be canceled in the small validation machine immediately upon boarding.

You have several ticket options, all valid for one or more rides on all lines. A €1 ticket is valid for one hour from the time it is first canceled. A multiple ticket—four tickets, each valid for 60 minutes—costs €3.90. A 24-hour tourist ticket costs €4.50. Two-, three-, and seven-day passes are also available.

🛈 **Bus Information ATAF** ✉ Next to train station; Piazza del Duomo 57/r, Santa Maria Novella ☎ 800/019794 toll free. **Lazzi Eurolines** ✉ Via Mercadante 2, Santa Maria Novella ☎ 055/363041 ⊕ www.lazzi.it. **SITA** ✉ Via Santa Caterina da Siena 17/r, Santa Maria Novella ☎ 055/214721 ⊕ www.sita-on-line.it.

BY CAR

Florence is connected to the north and south of Italy by the Autostrada del Sole (A1). It takes about one hour of driving on scenic roads to get to Bologna (although heavy truck traffic over the Apennines often makes for slower going), about 3 hours to Rome, and 3 to 3½ hours to

Milan. The Tyrrhenian Coast is an hour west on the A11. For help with car trouble, call the ACI (Automobile Club Firenze).

🔢 ACI ✉ Viale Amendola 36, outside town ☎ 055/2486246.

BY TAXI

Taxis usually wait at stands throughout the city (in front of the train station and in Piazza della Repubblica, for example), or you can call for one. The meter starts at €2.30, with a €3.60 minimum and extra charges at night, on Sunday, and for radio dispatch.

🔢 Taxi Companies **Taxis** ☎ 055/4390 or 055/4798.

BY TRAIN

Florence is on the principal Italian train route between most European capitals and Rome, and within Italy it is served frequently from Milan, Venice, and Rome by Intercity (IC) and nonstop Eurostar trains. Stazione Centrale di Santa Maria Novella is the main station and is in the center of town. Be sure to avoid trains that stop only at the Campo di Marte or Rifredi stations, which are not convenient to the center.

🔢 Train Information **Stazione Centrale di Santa Maria Novella** ☎ 892021 ⊕ www. trenitalia.com.

Contacts & Resources

EMERGENCIES

You can get a list of English-speaking doctors and dentists at the U.S. Consulate, or contact the Tourist Medical Service. If you need hospital treatment and an interpreter, you can call AVO, a group of volunteer interpreters; it's open Monday, Wednesday, and Friday 4–6 PM and Tuesday and Thursday 10–noon. Comunale No. 13, a local pharmacy, is open 24 hours a day, seven days a week. For a complete listing of other pharmacies that have late-night hours on a rotating basis, dial 192.

🔢 **AVO** ☎ 055/2344567. **Tourist Medical Service** ✉ Via Lorenzo il Magnifico, 59 ☎ 055/475411. **U.S. Consulate** ✉ Lungarno Vespucci 38, Lungarno North ☎ 055/ 266951 ⊕ www.usembassy.it.

🔢 Emergency Services **Ambulance** ☎ 118. **Emergencies** ☎ 113. **Misericordia** (Red Cross) ✉ Piazza del Duomo 20 ☎ 055/212222. **Police** ✉ Via Zara 2, near Piazza della Libertà ☎ 055/49771.

🔢 24-Hour Pharmacies **Comunale No. 13** ✉ Stazione Centrale di Santa Maria Novella ☎ 055/289435.

TOURS

BIKE TOURS   Florence by Bike has a variety of guided bike tours setting off from Florence and returning the same day; there's a half-day trip to Fiesole, and then several different full-day options into Chianti. I Bike Italy has one-day tours around Fiesole and Chianti.

🔢 Companies **Florence by Bike** ✉ Via San Zanobi 120-122/r, San Lorenzo ☎ 055/488992 ⊕ www.florencebybike.it. **I Bike Italy** ☎🖰 055/2342371 ⊕ www.ibikeitaly.com.

WALKING TOURS   🔢 Companies **Custom Travel and Special Events** ✉ Via dell'Ardiglione 19, near Santo Spirito, 50124 ☎ 055/2645526 ⊕ www.customitaly.com. **Abercrombie & Kent** ✉ Via de' Fossi 13, near Santa Maria Novella ☎ 055/2648029. **Context Florence** ✉ Via Baccina 40 00186 Rome ☎ 06/4820911 ⊕ www.contextflorence.com.

8

VISITOR INFORMATION

The main Florence tourist office, APT, has locations next to the Palazzo Medici-Riccardi, in the main train station, and around the corner from the Basilica di Santa Croce. Its Web site is in Italian only. Fiesole's office is on the main piazza.

🄵 Tourist Information **Fiesole** ✉ Via Portigiani 3, 50014 ☎ 055/598720 ⊕ www.comune. fiesole.fi.it. **Florence** Agenzia Promozione Turistica (APT) ✉ Via Cavour 1/r, next to Palazzo Medici-Riccardi, near San Lorenzo, 50100 ☎ 055/290832 ✉ Stazione Centrale di Santa Maria Novella, 50100 ☎ 055/212245 ✉ Borgo Santa Croce 29/r ☎ 055/2340444 ⊕ www.comune.firenze.it.

Tuscany

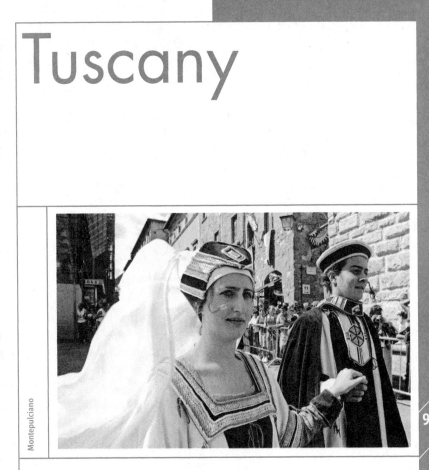

Montepulciano

WORD OF MOUTH

"The food in Tuscany, while simple and even rustic, can be some of the most satisfying in all of Italy. Wild boar ragu over papardelle pasta, tagliatelle with sauteed porcini mushrooms, and savory grilled sausages are just some of the dishes we lust after stateside."

—MLT

WELCOME TO TUSCANY

TOP 5
Reasons to Go

1 **Piazza del Campo, Siena:** Sip a cappuccino, lick some gelato, and take in this spectacular shell-shaped piazza.

2 **Piero della Francesca's *True Cross* frescoes, Arezzo:** If your holy grail is great Renaissance art, seek out these 12 silently enigmatic scenes.

3 **San Gimignano:** Grab a spot at sunset on the steps of the Collegiata church as flocks of swallows swoop in and out of the famous medieval towers.

4 **Wine-tasting in Chianti:** Sample the fruits of the region's gorgeous vineyards, at either the wineries themselves or the wine bars found in the towns.

5 **Leaning Tower of Pisa:** It may be touristy, but now that you can once again climb to the top, it's touristy fun.

Relaxed yet elegant Lucca is a little world of its own, surrounded by tree-bedecked 16th-century ramparts now used as delightful promenades.

Thanks to an engineering mistake, the name Pisa is instantly recognized the world over. The Leaning Tower, the cathedral, and the baptistery (above) are grouped together on the Piazza del Duomo.

Pontremoli

LIGURIA

Carrara

La Spezia

12

Viareggio   Lucca

A12   E74

Pisa

Livorno   A12

Cecina

Mare Tirreno

Piombino   Golfo Di Follónica

Elba   Portoferraio

Pianosa

0 ——————— 20 mi

0 ——————— 20 km

Lucca

San Gimignano

Getting Oriented

Hillsides blanketed with vineyards, silver-green olive groves, and enchanting towns are the essence of Tuscany, one of Italy's most beautiful landscapes. Little seems changed since the Renaissance: to the west of Florence, Pisa's tower still leans; to the south, Chianti's roads wind through cypress groves, taking you to Siena, with its captivating piazza.

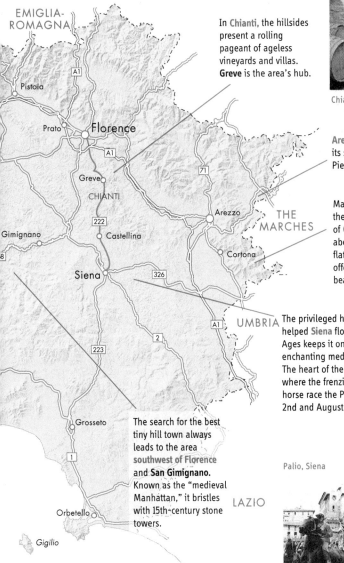

In **Chianti,** the hillsides present a rolling pageant of ageless vineyards and villas. **Greve** is the area's hub.

Chianti

Arezzo is best known for its sublime frescoes by Piero della Francesca.

Magnificently situated, the ancient stone town of **Cortona** sits high above the perfectly flat Valdichiana valley, offering great views of beautiful countryside.

The privileged hilltop site that helped **Siena** flourish in the Middle Ages keeps it one of Italy's most enchanting medieval towns today. The heart of the town is Il Campo, where the frenzied 700-year-old horse race the Palio is held every July 2nd and August 16th.

The search for the best tiny hill town always leads to the area **southwest of Florence** and **San Gimignano.** Known as the "medieval Manhattan," it bristles with 15th-century stone towers.

Palio, Siena

TUSCANY PLANNER

Making the Most of Your Time

Tuscany isn't the place for a jam-packed itinerary. One of the greatest pleasures here is indulging in rustic hedonism, marked by long lunches and show-stopping sunsets. Whether by car, bike, or foot, you'll want to get out into the glorious landscape, but it's smart to keep your plans modest. Set a church or a hill town or an out-of-the-way restaurant as your destination, knowing that half the pleasure is in getting there—admiring as you go the stately palazzos, the tidy geometry of row upon row of grape vines, the fields vibrant with red poppies and yellow scotch broom.

You'll need to devise a Siena strategy. The place shouldn't be missed; it's compact enough that you can see the major sights on a day trip, and that's exactly what most people do. Spend the night, and you'll get to see the town breathe a sigh and relax upon the day-trippers' departure. The flip side is, your favorite Tuscan hotel isn't likely to be in Siena. (See the comments under "Finding a Place to Stay.")

You face similar issues with Pisa and Lucca in the northwest. Pisa's famous tower is worth seeing, but ultimately Lucca has greater charms, making it a better choice for an overnight.

Getting Around

It's a tremendous advantage to have a car in Tuscany; driving is the only way (other than hiking or biking) to get to many of the small towns and vineyards. Roads are well maintained, but they're largely of the winding, two-lane variety—you need to be alert behind the wheel, and designated drivers are a must when wine tasting. The Strada Chiantigiana, also known as SS222, is the classic Tuscan drive.

If a car isn't an option, you can go by bus. Lines crisscross the region, connecting smaller towns and cities on the autostradas and superhighways. But making arrangements for bus travel, particularly for a non-Italian speaker, can be a test of patience. There's regular train service to the larger towns—most notably Pisa, Lucca, and Arezzo—but traveling by train makes it difficult to get a feel for the Tuscan countryside. For more about car, bus, and train travel, see "Essentials" at the end of this chapter.

Hidden Pleasures

These classic Tuscan experiences will take you away (sometimes far away) from the standard tourist path. And none of them will cost you a euro.

■ Hang out in Greve on market day.

■ Walk through the tiny town of Volpaia.

■ Listen to Gregorian chants at Abbazia di Sant'Antimo, outside Montalcino.

■ Visit the ruins of Abbazia di San Galgano.

■ Take a dip in the Mediterranean at Biodola beach in Elba.

■ Soak in the thermal waters of Saturnia.

Biking & Hiking

In spring, summer, and fall, bicyclists pedaling up and down Tuscany's hills are as much a part of the landscape as the cypress trees. Many are on weeklong organized tours, but it's also possible to rent bikes for jaunts in the countryside or to join afternoon or daylong rides.

Hiking is a simpler matter: all you need is a pair of road-worthy shoes. The tourist information offices in most towns can direct you on walks ranging from an hour to a full day in duration. You can also sign on for more elaborate guided tours.

■ **Italy by Design** (Via degli Artigiani 20, Panzano in Chianti 055/852418 or 055/852418 www.italybydesign.com) provides you with bikes and hand-tailored itineraries, and will pick you up and drop you off at your hotel. The Massachusetts-based ■ **Ciclismo Classico** (30 Marathon St, Arlington, MA 02474, 800/866-7314 www.ciclismoclassico.com) offers guided bike tours throughout Italy. ■ **Country Walkers** (Box 180, Waterbury, VT 05676 802/244-5661 or 888/742-0770) conducts weeklong (and longer) trips throughout Tuscany in spring and fall. ■ **Italian Connection**, Walking & Culinary Tours (11 Fairway Dr. Suite 210, Edmonton, Alberta, Canada, 800/462-7911) offers walking and food itineraries to Tuscan hill towns.

Finding a Place to Stay

A visit to Tuscany is a trip into the country. There are plenty of good hotels in the larger towns, but the classic experience is to stay in one of the rural accommodations—often converted private homes, sometimes working farms or vineyards (known as *agriturismi*). Though it's tempting to think of this as an area where you can wander the hills and then stumble upon a little out-of-the-way hotel at the end of the day, you're better off not testing your luck. Reservations are the way.

Dining & Lodging Price Categories

WHAT IT COSTS in Euros				
	$$$$	**$$$**	**$$**	**$**	**¢**
Restaurants over €22	€16–€22	€11–€16	€7–€11	under €7
Hotels over €220	€160–€220	€110–€160	€70–€110	under €70

Restaurant prices are for a second course (un secondo). Hotel prices are for two people in a standard double room in high season, including tax and service.

How's the Weather?

Spring and fall are the best times to visit Tuscany, when the weather is mild and the volume of tourists comparatively low. In summer try to start your days early and hit major sights first—that way you'll beat the crowds and the often-oppressive midday heat. Rising early isn't hard, as Tuscany is not about late nights; most restaurants and bars close well before midnight. Come winter, you'll meet with rain and chill. It's not a bad time to visit the cities—museums and monuments are uncrowded, and locals fill the restaurants. In the countryside, though, many restaurants and hotels close in November and reopen in the spring.

9

TOP PASSEGGIATA

Lucca's Passeggiata delle Mura is a pleasing walkway atop the thick walls that surround the old city.

Updated by
Patricia Rucidlo

MIDWAY DOWN THE ITALIAN PENINSULA, Tuscany (Toscana in Italian) is distinguished by rolling hills, snowcapped mountains, dramatic cypress trees, and miles of coastline on the Tyrrhenian Sea—all of which adds up to gorgeous views at practically every turn. The beauty of the landscape proves a perfect foil for the region's abundance of superlative art and architecture. It also produces some of Italy's finest wines and olive oils. The combination of unforgettable art, sumptuous views, and eminently drinkable wines that pair beautifully with its simple food makes a trip to Tuscany something beyond special.

Many of Tuscany's cities and towns have retained the same fundamental character over the past 500 years. Civic rivalries that led to bloody battles centuries ago have given way to soccer rivalries. Renaissance pomp lives on in the celebration of local feast days and centuries-old traditions such as the Palio in Siena and the Giostra del Saraceno (Joust of the Saracen) in Arezzo. Often present-day Tuscans look as though they might have served as models for paintings produced hundreds of years ago. In many ways, the Renaissance still survives in Tuscany.

NORTHWESTERN TUSCANY

In the shadows of the rugged coastal Alpi Apuane, where Michelangelo quarried his marble, this area isn't as lush as southern Tuscany—the hills flatten out, and there are hints of industry. It's well worth the effort to visit these spots, however—there's wonderful art, and there are some very fine restaurants with prices slightly lower than those in Florence.

Prato

❶ *17 km (11 mi) northwest of Florence.*

The wool industry in this city, one of the world's largest manufacturers of cloth, was known throughout Europe as early as the 13th century. It was further stimulated in the 14th century by a local cloth merchant, Francesco di Marco Datini, who built his business, according to one of his ledgers, "in the name of God and of profit." A cumulative €5 ticket provides admission to the Museo dell'Opera del Duomo, Museo di Pittura Murale, and the Castello.

Prato's Romanesque **Duomo** is famous for its **Pergamo del Sacro Cingolo** (Chapel of the Holy Girdle), to the left of the entrance, which enshrines the girdle of the Virgin Mary. It is said that the Virgin presented it to the apostle Thomas in a miraculous appearance after her Assumption. The Duomo also contains 15th-century frescoes by Prato's most famous son, Fra Filippo Lippi (1406–69), who executed scenes from the life of St. Stephen on the left wall and scenes from the life of John the Baptist on the right in the **Cappella Maggiore** (Main Chapel). As of this writing, the frescoes were undergoing restoration: call about possible guided visits on the scaffolding. ⊠ *Piazza del Duomo* ☎ *0574/26234 general information, 0574/24112 scaffolding visits* 🖃 *€8* ☉ *Mon.–Sat. 7–12 and 3–7, Sun. 7–12:30 and 3–8.*

Sculptures by Donatello (circa 1386–1466) that originally adorned the Duomo's exterior pulpit are now on display in the **Museo dell'Opera del Duomo** (Cathedral Museum). ☒ *Piazza del Duomo 49* ☎ *0574/29339* 🖃 *€3* ⊙ *Mon. and Wed.–Sat. 9:30–12:30 and 3–6, Sun. 9:30–12:30.*

Treasures of the City, a special exhibit running through 2006 at the **Museo di Pittura Murale** (Museum of Mural Painting), contains works by Fra Filippo Lippi and other artisanss from the 13th to 15th century. The permanent collection contains frescoes removed from sites in Prato and environs. ☒ *Piazza San Domenico 8* ☎ *0574/440501* 🖃 *€3* ⊙ *Sun., Mon, Wed., and Thurs. 9–1; weekends 9–1 and 3–6.*

The church of **Santa Maria delle Carceri** was built by Giuliano Sangallo in the 1490s and is a landmark of Renaissance architecture. ☒ *Piazza Santa Maria delle Carceri, off Via Cairoli and southeast of the cathedral* ☎ *0574/27933* ⊙ *Daily 7–noon and 4–7.*

Though in ruins, the formidable **Castello** (Castle) built for Frederick II Hohenstaufen, adjacent to Santa Maria delle Carceri, is an impressive sight, the only castle of its type outside southern Italy. ☒ *Piazza Santa Maria delle Carceri* ☎ *0574/38207* 🖃 *€2* ⊙ *Nov.–Mar., Wed.–Mon. 9–1; Apr.–Oct., Wed.–Mon. 9–1 and 4–7.*

off the
beaten
path

VILLA MEDICEA – For a look at gracious country living Renaissance style, detour south of Prato to the Villa Medicea in Poggio a Caiano. Lorenzo "il Magnifico" (1449–92) commissioned Giuliano da Sangallo (circa 1445–1516) to redo the villa, which was lavished with frescoes by important Renaissance painters such as Andrea del Sarto (1486–1530) and Pontormo (1494–1557). You can also take a walk around the austerely ornamented grounds. Tours start every hour on the half hour beginning at 8:30; the last tour begins at 3:30. ☒ *7 km (4½ mi) south of Prato, Poggio a Caiano* ☎ *055/877012* 🖃 *€2* ⊙ *Sept. and Oct., daily 8:15–5:30; Nov.–Feb., daily 8:15–3:30; Mar., daily 8:15–4:30; Apr.–May, daily 8:15–5:30; June–Aug., daily 8:15–6:30.*

9

Where to Eat

★ $$–$$$ ✕ **Da Delfina.** Delfina Cioni began cooking many years ago for hungry hunters, and now her son Carlo is proprietor. Dishes celebrate Tuscan food, with an emphasis on fresh local ingredients. *Secondi* (second courses) such as *coniglio con olive e pignoli* (rabbit sautéed with olives and pine nuts) are a real treat. The seasonal menu is complemented by a fine wine list, and service is gracious. From the restaurant's four comfortably rustic rooms you have a glorious view of the Tuscan countryside, including of a Medici villa (Ferdinando I de'Medici also enjoyed hunting in the area). ☒ *Via della Chiesa 1, Artimino, 16 km (10 mi) southwest of Prat, 24 km (38 mi) north of Florence* ☎ *055/8718074* 🖃 *Reservations essential* ⊟ *No credit cards* ⊙ *Closed Mon. and 2 wks in Aug. No lunch Tues. No dinner Sun. Oct.–May.*

¢–$ ✕ **La Vecchia Cucina di Soldano.** You could be sitting in your Italian grandmother's kitchen: the place is completely unpretentious, tablecloths are red-and-white checked, and the servers are like old friends. Local Pratesi specialties include the odd but tasty *sedani ripieni* (stuffed cel-

Northwestern
Tuscany

ery), in which celery's pressed and stuffed with a minced veal and mortadella filling, then coated in flour and egg before being fried in olive
oil and served with a meat sauce. Or you might enjoy the superb *tagliolini sui fagioli* (thin noodles with beans). The restaurant teems with
locals. Clearly they, too, like the rock-bottom prices. ⊠ *Via Pomeria
23* ☎ *0574/34665* ▭ *No credit cards* ⊙ *Closed Sun.*

Shopping
Prato's biscotti, twice-cooked cookies, have an extra-dense texture,
lending themselves to submersion in caffè or *vin santo* (a sweet dessert
wine). The best in town are at **Antonio Mattei** (⊠ Via Ricasoli 20/22
☎ 0574/25756).

The centuries-old tradition of selling fine textiles crafted into fine clothing continues in Prato. **Enrico Pecci di A. Pecci & C** (⊠ Via del Pantano
16/e ☎ 055/89890) sells fabric by the meter.

Pistoia

❷ *18 km (11 mi) northwest of Prato, 36 km (22 mi) northwest of Florence.*

Pistoia can claim a Roman past, as well as a bloody history during the
Middle Ages, when the town was rent by civil strife. Its historic center

is a jewel and little visited, which makes coming here all the more worthwhile. The **Cattedrale di San Zeno** in the main piazza houses the Dossale di San Jacopo, a magnificent silver altar. The two half figures on the left were executed by Filippo Brunelleschi (1377–1446). ⊠ *Piazza del Duomo* ☎ *0573/25095* 🎫 *Illumination of altarpiece €2* ⊙ *Church daily 8:30–12:30 and 3:30–7; altar daily 10–noon and 4–5:45.*

The **Palazzo del Comune,** begun around 1295, houses the **Museo Civico,** with works by local artists from the 14th to 20th century. ⊠ *Piazza del Duomo 1* ☎ *0573/371296* 🎫 *€3.50, Sat. 3–7 free* ⊙ *Apr.–Oct., Tues.–Sat. 10–6, Sun. 9–12:30; Nov.–Mar., Tues.–Sat. 10–5, Sun. 9–12:30.*

Founded in the 13th century and still a working hospital today, the **Spedale del Ceppo** (literally, Hospital of the Tree Stump) has a glorious early-16th-century exterior terra-cotta frieze begun by Giovanni della Robbia (1469–1529) and completed by the workshop of Santi and Benedetto Buglioni in 1526–28. ⊠ *Piazza Ospedale, a short way down Via Pacini from Piazza del Duomo.*

An architectural gem in green-and-white marble, the medieval church of **San Giovanni Fuorcivitas** contains the *Visitation* by Luca della Robbia (1400–82), a painting attributed to Taddeo Gaddi, and a holy-water font that may have been executed by Fra Guglielmo around 1270. ⊠ *Via Cavour* ☎ *0573/24784* ⊙ *Daily 8–noon and 4–6:30.*

Although it's not as grand as the silver altar in Pistoia's cathedral, Giovanni Pisano's powerfully sculpted pulpit (created 1298–1301) in the church of **Sant'Andrea** is considered by many the town's greatest art treasure. ⊠ *Via Sant'Andrea* ☎ *0573/21912* ⊙ *Nov.–Mar., daily 8–12:30 and 3:30–6; Apr.–Oct., daily 8–12:30 and 3:30–7.*

ⓒ The **Giardino Zoologico,** a small zoo, is a 20-minute drive out of town. Take Bus 29 from the train station. ⊠ *Via Pieve a Celle 160/a* ☎ *0573/ 911219* 🎫 *€9.50* ⊙ *Apr.–Sept., daily 9–7; Oct.–Mar., daily 9–5.*

Where to Eat

¢–$ ✕ **La BotteGaia.** Jazz plays softly in the background as patrons sip wine at rustic tables in rooms with exposed brick-and-stone walls. In warm weather you can also dine alfresco with a splendid view of the Piazza del Duomo. Typical wine-bar fare, such as plates of cured ham and cheese, shares the menu with a surprisingly sophisticated list of daily specials. For example, you might try *insalatina con foie gras condita con vinaigrette* (foie gras with dressed greens). ⊠ *Via del Lastrone 17* ☎ *0573/ 365602* ✍ *Reservations essential* ▤ *AE, DC, MC, V* ⊙ *Closed Mon. and 15 days in Aug. No lunch Sun.*

San Miniato

❸ *42 km (26 mi) southeast of Pisa, 43 km (27 mi) southwest of Florence.*

Dating from Etruscan and Roman times, San Miniato was so named when the Lombards erected a church here in the 8th century and consecrated

TUSCANY THROUGH THE AGES

Tuscany was populated, at least by the 7th century BC, by the Etruscans, a mysterious lot who chose to live on hills—the better to see the approaching enemy—in such places as present-day Arezzo, Chiusi, Cortona, Fiesole, and Volterra. Some 500 years later, the Romans came, saw, and conquered; by 241 BC they had built the Aurelia, a road from Rome to Pisa that is still in use today. The crumbling of the Roman Empire and subsequent invasions by marauding Lombards, Byzantines, and Holy Roman Emperors meant centuries of turmoil. By the 12th century city-states were being formed throughout Tuscany in part, perhaps, because it was unclear exactly who was in charge.

The two groups vying for power were the Guelphs and the Ghibellines, champions of the pope and the Holy Roman Emperor, respectively. They jostled for control of individual cities and of the region as a whole. Florence was more or less Guelph, and Siena more often than not Ghibelline. This led to bloody battles, most notably the 1260 battle of Montaperti, in which the Ghibellines roundly defeated the Guelphs.

Eventually—by the 14th century—the Guelphs became the dominant force. But this did not mean that the warring Tuscan cities settled down to a period of relative peace and tranquility. The age in which Dante wrote his *Divine Comedy* and Giotto and Piero della Francesca created their incomparable frescoes was one of internecine strife. Florence was the power to be reckoned with; it coveted Siena, which it conquered, lost, and reconquered during the 15th and 16th centuries. Finally, in 1555, following in the footsteps of Volterra, Pisa, Prato, and Arezzo, Siena fell for good. They were all united under Florence to form the grand duchy of Tuscany. The only city to escape Florence's dominion was Lucca, which remained fiercely independent until the arrival of Napoléon. Eventually, however, even Florence's influence waned, and the 17th and 18th centuries saw the decline of the entire region as various armies swept across it.

it to the saint. The Holy Roman Empire had very strong ties to San Miniato. Today the pristine, tiny hill town's narrow, cobbled streets are lined with austere facades dating from the 13th to 17th century. Its artistic treasures are on a par with those of other similar-size towns in the area, but the real reason for a trip is simply that the place is so pretty. St. Francis founded the 1211 **Convento e Chiesa di San Francesco** (Convent and Church of St. Francis), containing two cloisters and an ornate wooden choir. For a dose of monastic living, you can stay overnight. ⊠ *Piazza San Francesco* ☎ *0571/43051* ⊙ *Daily 9–noon and 3–7; or ring bell.*

Although the **Museo Diocesano** is small, the collection has a number of subtle and pleasant works of art. Note the rather odd Fra Filippo Lippi *Crucifixion, Il Redentore* by Verrocchio (1435–88), and the small but sublime *Education of the Virgin,* by Tiepolo (1696–1770). ⊠ *Piazza del Castello* ☎ *0571/418071* 🎟 *€2.60* ⊙ *Nov.–Mar., Tues.–Sun. 10–12:30 and 3–6; Apr.–Oct., Tues.–Sun. 9–noon and 3–6.*

Where to Stay & Eat

$-$$ ✕ **Il Convio.** A short drive down a steeply serpentine road from San Miniato brings you to a rustic country ristorante with sponged walls, stenciled decoration, and checkered table cloths. The main courses are mostly Tuscan classics, such as *bistecca fiorentina* (steak Florentine, a generous cut of grilled meat). The primi, however, are a bit more daring—tortelli stuffed with pecorino cheese and chestnut puree is a rarity on any menu. Local wines are well represented on the reasonable wine list, and service is courteous. ⊠ *Via San Maiano 2* ☎ *0571/408114* ▤ *AE, DC, MC, V* ⊘ *Closed Wed.*

¢ ▥ **Convento di San Francesco.** For a complete change of pace, stay at a 13th-century convent in the company of nine Franciscan friars. Rooms are simple, bordering on spartan, but are clean and quiet. You can participate in religious devotions or skip them altogether. All rooms have baths, and there are five rooms that groups can rent. It's a 10-minute walk from the town center. Plan to arrive before 8 PM and they'll give you a set of keys—thus sparing the usually obligatory convent curfew. ⊠ *Piazza San Francesco, 56020* ☎ *0571/43051* 🖷 *0571/43398* ◪ *30 rooms* ⚲ *No a/c, no room phones, no room TVs, no kids under 12* ▤ No *credit cards* ¶⊙ *EP.*

LUCCA

In this fortress town, Caesar, Pompey, and Crassus agreed to rule Rome as a triumvirate in 56 BC; it was one of the first Tuscan towns to establish a Christian community, which it had by 343–344 AD. Lucca still has a mind of its own, and when most of Tuscany was voting Communist as a matter of course, its citizens rarely followed suit. Within the city's ramparts, built between 1544 and 1645, the composer Giacomo Puccini (1858–1924) was born. He is celebrated, along with his peers, during the summer Opera Theater of Lucca Festival.

9

Exploring Lucca

The historic center of Lucca, 51 km (31 mi) west of Florence, is walled and motorized traffic is restricted. Walking or biking is the most efficient and most enjoyable way to get around. You can rent bicycles, and the center is quite flat, so biking is easy without the threat of traffic. A combination ticket that includes the Museo Nazionale di Villa Guinigi and the Museo Nazionale di Palazzo Mansi is €6.50

The Main Attractions

★ ❻ **Duomo.** The round-arched facade of the cathedral is an example of the rigorously ordered Pisan Romanesque style, in this case happily enlivened by a varied collection of small carved columns. Take a closer look at the decoration of the facade and of the portico below, which make for one of the most entertaining church exteriors in Tuscany. The Gothic interior contains a moving wood crucifix (called the *Volto Santo,* or Holy Face) brought here, as legend has it, in the 8th century (though it probably dates from between the 11th and early 13th century). The marble **tomb of Ilaria del Carretto** (1408) is the masterpiece of the Sienese sculp-

Lucca

0   200 yards

0   200 meters

tor Jacopo della Quercia (circa 1371–1438). ⊠ *Piazza del Duomo* ☎ *0583/490530* 🖾 *Duomo free, tomb of Ilaria del Carretto €2* ⊗ *Duomo: weekdays 7–5:30, Sat. 9:30–6:45, Sun. 11:30–11:50 and 1–5:30. Tomb: Nov.–Mar., weekdays 9:30–4:45, Sat. 9:30–6:45, Sun. 11:30–11:50 and 1–5; Apr.–Oct., weekdays 9:30–5:45, Sat. 9–6:45, Sun. 9–10 and 1–5:45.*

★ ⏱ **Passeggiata delle Mura** (walk on the walls). Any time of day when the weather is agreeable, you can find the citizens of Lucca cycling, jogging, strolling, or playing ball in this large, unusual park atop the ring of ramparts that surrounds the *centro storico* (historic center). Sunlight streams through two rows of tall plane trees to dapple the walkway, a loop almost 5 km (3 mi) in total length. Ten bulwarks are topped with lawns, many containing picnic tables, some with play equipment for children. One caution: there are no railings along the ramparts' edge and the drop to the ground is a precipitous 40 feet.

need a break?

Gelateria Veneta (⊠ Via V. Veneto ☎ 0583/47037 ⊠ Via Beccheria ☎ 0583/496856) makes outstanding ice creams, sorbets, and ices (some sugar-free). The pièces de résistance are frozen fruits stuffed with their own creamy filling: don't miss the apricot sorbet-filled apricot.

❾ Piazza del Anfiteatro Romano. A Roman amphitheater once stood on this spot; the medieval buildings constructed over the amphitheater retain its original oval shape and brick arches. It's a popular gathering place, with numerous cafés and some eclectic shops. ⊠ *Off Via Fillungo.*

⏱ **❽ San Frediano.** The church contains a gorgeous sculpted polyptych by Jacopo della Quercia. The bizarrely lace-clad mummy of the patron saint of domestic servants, St. Zita, really seems to make kids shriek—in a good way, that is—when they see her. ⊠ *Piazza San Frediano, Anfiteatro* ⊗ *Mon.–Sat. 8:30–noon and 3–5, Sun. 10:30–5.*

❺ San Michele in Foro. The facade of this church, slightly west of the centro storico, is even more fanciful than the Duomo's. Check out the superb panel painting of Sts. Girolamo, Sebastian, Rocco, and Helen by Filippino Lippi (1457/58–1504) in the right transept. ⊠ *Piazza San Michele, San Michele* ⊗ *Daily 7:40–noon and 3–6.*

⏱ **❼ Torre Guinigi.** The tower of the medieval palace contains one of the city's most curious sights: six ilex trees have established themselves at the top, and their roots have grown into the room below. From the tower there's a magnificent view of the city and the surrounding countryside. ⊠ *Palazzo Guinigi, Via Sant'Andrea 42, Amfiteatro* ☎ *0583/583150* 🖾 *€3.50* ⊗ *Mar.–Apr., daily 9–7:30; May–Sept., daily 9–midnight; Oct.–Feb., daily 9–5.*

Also Worth Seeing

❿ Museo Nazionale di Villa Guinigi. On the east end of the historic center, the museum houses an extensive collection of local Romanesque and Renaissance art. ⊠ *Villa Guinigi, Via della Quarquonia, Lucca East* ☎ *0583/496033* 🖾 *€4* ⊗ *Tues.–Sat. 8:30–7, Sun. 8:30–1.*

❹ **Pinacoteca Nazionale di Palazzo Mansi.** Highlights here are the brightly colored *Portrait of a Youth* by Pontormo and portraits of the Medici painted by Bronzino (1503–72) and others. ✉ *Palazzo Mansi, Via Galli Tassi 43, San Donato* ☎ *0583/55570* 🖰 *€4* 🕓 *Tues.–Sat. 8:30–7, Sun. 8:30–1.*

off the
beaten
path

VILLA REALE – Napoléon's sister, Princess Elisa, once called Villa Reale home. Restored by the Counts Pecci-Blunt, the estate is celebrated for its spectacular gardens, it was originally laid out in the 16th century and redone in the middle of the 17th century. Gardening buffs adore the legendary **teatro di verdura,** a theater carved out of hedges and topiaries. The Lucca tourist office has information about the occassional concerts held here. ✉ *Villa Reale, Marlia, 8 km (5 mi) north of Lucca* ☎ *0583/30108* 🖰 *€6* 🕓 *Mar.–Nov., guided visits Tues.–Sun. at 10, 11, noon, 3, 4, 5, and 6; Dec.–Feb., by appointment.*

Where to Stay & Eat

$$$–$$$$ ✕ **La Mora.** A former stagecoach station now serves classic Lucchese food. Start with the *minestra di farro* (soup made with emmer, a grain that resembles barley) with beans, or the exquisite homemade *tacconi* (a thin, short, wide pasta) with rabbit sauce. Though Lucca is not near the sea, La Mora's rendition of *cacciucco* (a Livornese fish stew) is succulent and not to be missed. The wine list has some great wines from the area, as well as from just about everywhere else in Italy. ✉ *Via Sesto di Ponte a Moriano 1748, 9 km (5½ mi) north of Lucca* ☎ *0583/406402* ▤ *AE, DC, MC, V* 🕓 *Closed Wed., Jan. 1–15, and June 15–30.*

$$ ✕ **Bucadisantantonio.** The staying power of Bucadisantantonio—it's been
FodorsChoice around since 1782—is the result of superlative Tuscan food brought to
★ the table by waitstaff that doesn't miss a beat. The menu includes the simple-but-blissful, like *tortelli lucchesi al sugo* (meat-stuffed pasta with a tomato-and-meat-sauce), and such daring dishes as roast *capretto* (kid) with herbs. A white-wall interior hung with copper pots and brass musical instruments creates a classy, enjoyable dining space. ✉ *Via della Cervia 3, San Michele* ☎ *0583/55881* 🕭 *Reservations essential* ▤ *AE, DC, MC, V* 🕓 *Closed Mon., 2 wks in Jan., and 2 wks in July. No dinner Sun.*

$$ ✕ **Il Giglio.** High ceilings, a large chandelier, and a big fireplace evoke the 19th century inside, and there is a terrace for dining outside in summer. Waiters in black double-breasted suits provide wise counsel on the wine choices, which complement the mostly Lucchesi dishes on the menu. Among the regional favorites are *farro garfagnino* (a thick soup made with emmer, a grain that resembles barley, and beans) and *coniglio con olive* (rabbit stew with olives). Save room for one of the desserts, including *la frutta carmellata in forno con gelato di castagne* (carmelized fruit with chestnut ice cream)—wow! ✉ *Piazza del Giglio 2, off Piazza Napoleone, Duomo* ☎ *0583/494058* ▤ *AE, DC, MC, V* 🕓 *Closed Wed. and 15 days in Feb. No dinner Tues.*

$–$$ ✕ **Osteria del Neni.** All the pasta here is made in house, and the menu, filled with tasty treats, changes regularly. If you're lucky enough to find ravioli *spinaci ed anatra in salsa di noci* (stuffed with duck and spinach,

EATING WELL IN TUSCANY

Just as the ancient Etruscans introduced cypress trees to the Tuscan landscape, their influence on regional food—in the use of fresh herbs—still lingers after more than three millennia. Simple and earthy, Tuscan food celebrates the seasons with a host of fresh vegetable dishes, wonderful bread-based soups, and savory meats and game perfumed with sage, rosemary, and thyme. Saltless Tuscan bread is grilled and drizzled with olive oil *(crostino)*, spread with chicken liver *(crostino di fegatini)*, or rubbed with garlic and topped with tomatoes *(bruschetta* or *fettunta)*. For their love of beans—particularly cannellini simmered in olive oil and herbs until creamy—Tuscans have been disparagingly nicknamed *mangiafagioli* (bean eaters) by Italians from other regions. Pecorino, a cheese made from sheep's milk, is particularly good in these parts—try it when it's young and in a soft, practically spreadable state, as well as when it's *stagionato* (aged). At its best, it's the equal of the finest Parmesan. Relatively new to Tuscan cuisine is the reintroduction of dishes featuring *cinta senese*, a once nearly extinct pig.

Grape cultivation here also dates from Etruscan times, and particularly in Chianti vineyards are abundant. The resulting medium-bodied red wine is a staple on most tables; however, the discerning can select from a multitude of other varieties, including such reds as Brunello di Montalcino and Vino Nobile di Montepulciano and such whites as Vermentino and Vernaccia. Super Tuscans, a fanciful name given to a group of wines by American journalists, now command attention as some of the best produced in Italy; they have great depth and complexity. The dessert wine *vin santo* is made throughout the region and is often sipped with biscotti (twice-baked cookies), perfect for dunking.

in a creamy but light walnut sauce) as an option, by all means order it. The walls of the warm, welcoming dining room are sponge-painted in two different shades of orange and wooden tables with paper placemats furnish the small space. In warm weather you can dine alfresco. Osteria del Neni is tucked away on a side street a block from San Michele. ⊠ *Via Pescheria 3, San Michele* ☎ *0583/492681* ✍ *Reservations essential* ☰ *AE, MC, V* ☉ *Closed Sun. and Jan.*

$$$$ ✕⌂ **Locanda l'Elisa.** A stay here could evoke home for you—that is if home is a neoclassical villa with a lush garden and a caring staff that caters to your needs. Most rooms are suites, outfitted with fresh flowers, antiques, and fine fabrics. The restaurant il Gazebo is in a former Victorian conservatory. The Tuscan food-with-flair is deftly served by English-speaking waiters. Locanda l'Elisa is a short ride from the city. ⊠ *Via Nuova per Pisa 1952, 5 km (3 mi) southwest of town center, 55050* ☎ *0583/379737* 🖷 *0583/379019* ⊕ *www.locandalelisa.com* ↙ *3 rooms, 7 suites* ⌂ *Restaurant, in-room safes, minibars, cable TV, in-room data ports, pool, massage, bar, babysitting, dry cleaning, laundry service, concierge, Internet, free parking* ☰ *AE, DC, MC, V* ☉ *Closed Jan. 7–Feb. 11* ⑩ *EP.*

$$$$ ⬚ **Hotel Ilaria.** The former stables of the Villa Bottini have been transformed into a modern hotel within the historic center. A second-floor terrace, overlooking the villa, makes a comfortable place to relax. Rooms are done in a warm wood veneer. The availability of free bicycles is a great bonus in this bike-friendly city. ⊠ *Via del Fosso 26, Lucca East, 55100* ☎ *0583/47615* 🖷 *0583/991961* ⊕ *www.hotelilaria. com* ⬩ *40 rooms* ⟷ *In-room safes, minibars, cable TV, bicycles, bar, babysitting, dry cleaning, laundry service, concierge, meeting room, free parking, some pets allowed (fee), no-smoking rooms* ⊟ *AE, DC, MC, V* ⦿| *BP.*

★ **$$$** ⬚ **Palazzo Alexander.** Relax in a style that Lucchesi nobility would have been comfortable with. The building housing this small boutique hotel dates from the 12th century and has timber ceilings and warm yellow walls. Brocade chairs adorn the public rooms, and the elegance is carried into the guest rooms, all of which have that same glorious damask upholstery and high ceilings. Top-floor suites have sweeping views of the town. Palazzo Alexander is on a quiet side street, a stone's throw from San Michele in Foro. ⊠ *Via S. Giustina 48, San Michele, 55100* ☎ *0583/583571* 🖷 *0583/583610* ⊕ *www.palazzo-alexander.com* ⬩ *9 rooms, 3 suites, 1 apartment* ⟷ *In-room safes, minibars, cable TV, in-room data ports, bicycles, wine bar, dry cleaning, laundry service, concierge, Internet, parking (fee), no-smoking rooms* ⊟ *AE, DC, MC, V* ⦿| *BP.*

$ ⬚ **Piccolo Hotel Puccini.** Steps away from the busy square and church of San Michele, this little hotel is quiet and calm—and a great deal. Wallpaper, hardwood floors, and throw rugs are among the handsome decorations. Paolo, the genial manager, speaks fluent English and dispenses great touring advice. ⊠ *Via di Poggio 9, San Michele, 55100* ☎ *0583/ 55421* 🖷 *0583/53487* ⊕ *www.hotelpuccini.com* ⬩ *14 rooms* ⟷ *Fans, in-room safes, cable TV, bar, babysitting, dry cleaning, laundry service, Internet, parking (fee), some pets allowed, no-smoking floors; no a/c* ⊟ *AE, DC, MC, V* ⦿| *EP.*

Nightlife & the Arts

The **Lucca Tourist Office** (⊠ Piazzale Verdi, Lucca East ☎ 0583/583150) has schedule and ticket information for many of the local festivals. The **Opera Theater of Lucca Festival,** sponsored by the Opera Theater of Lucca and the school of music of the University of Cincinnati, runs from mid-June to mid-July; performances are staged in open-air venues. Throughout the summer you can enjoy concerts in conjunction with the **Estate Musicale Lucchese** music festival.

From September through May you can see operas, plays, and concerts staged at the **Teatro del Giglio** (⊠ Piazza del Giglio, Duomo ☎ 0583/46531 ⊕ www.teatrodelgiglio.it).

Sports & the Outdoors

The centro storico is flat and easily navigated because automobile traffic is severely limited. A splendid bike ride (rental €10.50 per day) may be had by circling the entire historic center along the top of the bastions—

affording something of a bird's-eye view. **Barbetti Cicli** (✉ Via dei Gaspari 83/r, Anfiteatro ☎ 0583/517073) rents bikes near the Piazza di Anfiteatro. **Poli Antonio Biciclette** (✉ Piazza Santa Maria 42, Lucca East ☎ 0583/493787) is an option for bicycle rental on the east side.

Shopping

Lucca's justly famed olive oil, available throughout the city, is exported around the world. Look for those made by Fattoria di Fubbiano and Fattoria Fabbri—two of the best. On the second Sunday of the month there's a **flea market** in Piazza San Martino.

★ Chocoholics can get their fix at **Caniparoli** (✉ Via S. Paolino 96, San Donato ☎ 0583/53456). They are so serious about their sweets here that they do not make them from June through August because of the heat. Bargain-hunters won't want to miss **Benetton Stock Outlet** (✉ Via Mordini 17/19, Anfiteatro ☎ 0583/464533), with its brightly colored garments at reduced prices.

PISA

Pisa may have been inhabited as early as the Bronze Age. It was certainly populated by the Etruscans and, in turn, became part of the Roman Empire. In the early Middle Ages it flourished as an economic powerhouse—along with Amalfi, Genoa, and Venice, it was one of the maritime republics. The city's economic and political power ebbed in the early 15th century as it fell under the domination of Florence, though it enjoyed a brief resurgence under Cosimo I in the mid-16th century. Pisa endured heavy Allied bombing—miraculously, the Duomo and Leaning Tower, along with some other grand Romanesque structures, were spared though the Camposanto sustained heavy damage. Beyond the kitsch that the Leaning Tower has spawned, Pisa has much to see. Its treasures are more subtle than Florence's, to which it is inevitably compared, but the cathedral-baptistery-campanile complex on Piazza del Duomo is among the most dramatic ensembles in Italy.

9

Exploring Pisa

Pisa is 84 km (52 mi) west of Florence. Like many other Italian cities, the town is best seen on foot. The views along the Arno are particularly grand and shouldn't be missed—there's a sense of spaciousness here that the Arno in Florence lacks. You should weigh the different options for combination tickets to sights on the Piazza del Duomo when you begin your visit. Combination tickets are sold at each sight (one monument costs €5, two monuments €6, up to €8.50) for all the main sights).

The Main Attractions

❸ **Battistero.** The Gothic Baptistery, which stands across from the Duomo's facade, is best known for the pulpit carved by Nicola Pisano in 1260. Ask one of the ticket takers if he'll sing for you inside the baptistery: the acoustics are remarkable (a tip of €3 is appropriate). ✉ *Piazza del Duomo, Campo dei Miracoli* ☎ *050/561820* ⊕ *www.duomo.pisa.it*

✉ €5 ⏱ *June 22–Sept. 21, daily 8–7:40; Mar. 22–June 21 and Sept. 22–Dec. 21, daily 9–5:40; Dec. 22–Mar. 21, daily 9–4:40.*

⑫ **Duomo.** Pisa's cathedral was the first building to use the horizontal marble stripe motif (borrowed from Moorish architecture in the 11th century) common to Tuscan cathedrals. It's famous for the Romanesque panels depicting the life of Christ on the transept door facing the tower and for its expertly carved 14th-century pulpit by Giovanni Pisano. ✉ *Piazza del Duomo, Campo dei Miracoli* ☎ *050/3872210* ⊕ *www.duomo.pisa.it* ✉ *€2, Oct.–Mar. free* ⏱ *Nov.–Mar., daily 10–1 and 3–5; Apr.–Oct., daily 8–8.*

★ ⏳ ⑪ **Leaning Tower.** The final addition to the complex comprised of the Duomo, Baptistery, and the Camposanto was what is today known as the Torre Pendente (Leaning Tower). Construction started in 1174, and the lopsided settling was evident by the time work began on the third story. The tower's architects attempted to compensate by making the remaining floors slightly taller on the tilting side, but the extra weight only made the problem worse. The settling continued, to a point that by the end of the 20th century many feared it would simply topple over, despite all efforts to prop the structure up. In early 2000 the final step of restoring the tower to its original tilt of 300 years ago was executed, and it appears to have been successful. It has been firmly anchored to the earth and after years of being closed is once again open to the public for climbing. Legend holds that Galileo conducted an experiment on the nature of gravity by dropping metal balls from the top of the 187-foot-high tower; historians say this legend has no basis in fact (which is not quite to say that it is false). If you're visiting in low season (November–March), it's pretty easy to climb the tower without a reservation; if you come in high season, by all means book in advance. Tickets are available online 16–45 days in advance. ✉ *Campo dei Miracoli* ☎ *050/560547* ⊕ *www.opapisa.it* ✉ *€15* ⏱ *Nov.–Mar., daily 9–5:50; Apr.–Oct., daily 8–8.*

Also Worth Seeing

⑭ **Camposanto.** According to legend, this cemetery, a walled structure on the western side of the Campo dei Miracoli, is filled with earth from the Holy Land brought back by returning Crusaders. Contained within are numerous frescoes, notably the *Drunkenness of Noah* by Renaissance artist Benozzo Gozzoli and the disturbing *Triumph of Death* (14th century), whose authorship is disputed but whose subject matter shows what was on people's minds in a century that saw the ravages of the Black Death. ✉ *Camposanto, Campo dei Miracoli* ☎ *050/561820* ⊕ *www. duomo.pisa.it* ✉ *€5* ⏱ *June 22–Sept. 21, daily 8–7:40; Mar. 22–June 21 and Sept. 22–Dec. 21, daily 9–5:40; Dec. 22–Mar. 21, daily 9–4:40.*

⑮ **Museo dell'Opera del Duomo.** At the southeast corner of the sprawling Campo dei Miracoli, a marginally interesting museum holds numerous medieval sculptures and the ancient Roman sarcophagi that inspired the figures of Nicola Pisano (circa 1220–84). ✉ *Via Arcivescovado, Campo dei Miracoli* ☎ *050/560547* ⊕ *www.duomo.pisa.it* ✉ *€5* ⏱ *Nov.–Mar., daily 10–5; Apr.–Oct., daily 8–8.*

⑯ **Museo Nazionale di San Matteo.** On the north bank of the Arno, this museum contains wonderful early Renaissance sculpture and a stunning reli-

quary by Donatello (circa 1386–1466). ✉ *Lungarno Mediceo, Lungarni*
☎ *050/541865* 🎫 *€4* ⊙ *Tues.–Sat. 8:30–7:30, Sun. 8:30–1.*

Where to Stay & Eat

★ **$$$** ✗ **La Mescita.** Tall, vaulted ceilings, and stenciled walls lined with wine
bottles provide the simple background at this trattoria. There's nothing
basic, however, about the inventive,
Tuscan dishes that chef-owner Stefano
Saviozzi and his wife, Elisabetta Bauti,
turn out. They draw inspiration—
and fresh produce—from the market
outside the door. *Tagliolini al sugo e
piccolo ragù di salsiccia toscano,* thin
noodles with sausage and a red wine
sauce, is one option you might find
on the constantly changing menu.
Desserts are not to be missed, espe-
cially the *ricotta montata col ciocco-
lato fuso* (fresh sheep's milk cheese
topped with chocolate sauce). ✉ *Via*

> **WORD OF MOUTH**
>
> "At Pisa we discovered a peaceful
> haven with relatively few tourists
> compared with Florence, and a
> magnificent lawn you could actu-
> ally walk and sit on. I lay down in
> the lovely grass and slept in the
> sun until I was awakened by the
> cool shadow of the Leaning Tower.
> It was magic and peaceful and
> beautiful."   –Jo

Cavalca 2, Santa Maria ☎*050/544294* ☰*AE, DC, MC, V* ☼*Closed Mon., 3 wks in Jan., and last 3 wks in Aug. No lunch Tues.*

$$ ✕ **Osteria dei Cavalieri.** This charming white-wall *osteria* (a down-to-earth, tavernlike restaurant) has a versatile menu pleasing to carnivores and vegetarians alike. There are three reasonable, set price menus—from the sea, garden, and earth—or you can order à la carte. *Piatti veloci* (fast plates) are available at lunch only. The kitchen reliably turns out grilled fish, and the *tagliata* (thin slivers of rare beef) is a treat. A lemon sorbet bathed in *prosecco* (a dry sparkling wine), or chilled vodka, makes a perfect finish to your meal—even if service can be a bit rushed. ✉ *Via San Frediano 16, off Piazza dei Cavalieri, Santa Maria* ☎ *050/580858* ☰ *AE, DC, MC, V* ☼ *Closed Sun., July 25–Aug. 25, Dec. 29–Jan. 7. No lunch Sat.*

¢ ✕ **Vineria alla Piazza.** Translated, the name means, "wine store on the square," and the food here is just as straightforward: a simple blackboard lists two or three *primi* (first courses) and secondi. When the kitchen runs out of something, a choice is erased and a new one chalked in—a sure sign the food is made-that-moment fresh. The polenta *gratinata al gorgonzola* (mixed with Gorgonzola and run briefly under the broiler) is light as a feather. ✉ *Piazza delle Vettovaglie 13, Santa Maria* ☎ *No phone* ⌕ *Reservations not accepted* ☰ *No credit cards* ☼ *Closed Sun.*

$$$$ 🏨 **Hotel Relais dell'Orologio.** What used to be a private family palace opened as an intimate hotel in the spring of 2003. Eighteenth-century antiques fill the rooms and public spaces; some rooms have stenciled walls and wood-beam ceilings. On the third floor, sloped ceilings add romance. A large shared sitting room, complete with fireplace, provides a relaxing spot to read or sip a glass of wine. ✉ *Via della Faggiola 12/14, off Campo dei Miracoli, Santa Maria, 56126* ☎ *050/830361* 🖷 *050/551869* ⊕ *www.hotelrelaisorologio.com* ➾ *16 rooms, 5 suites* ⌕ *Dining room, room service, in-room safes, minibars, refrigerators, cable TV, in-room data ports, bar, babysitting, dry cleaning, laundry service, concierge, business services, meeting rooms, parking (fee), some pets allowed, no-smoking rooms* ☰ *AE, DC, MC, V* ⦿ *EP.*

$$ 🏨 **Royal Victoria.** The Piega family has owned and operated the Royal Victoria since 1837—such dedication probably explains why Charles Dickens and Charles Lindbergh, among others luminaries, have stayed here in the past. The hotel faces the Arno and though rooms are simply furnished and a bit dated, many have splendid river views. A fourth-floor terrace is a perfect spot for an *apertivo* (aperitif) or postcard writing. The hotel's rental-car service helps provide easy access to beaches and points of interest outside town. From here it's a 10-minute walk to the Campo dei Miracoli. ✉ *Lungarno Pacinotti 12, Lungarni, 56126* ☎ *050/940111* 🖷 *050/940180* ⊕ *www.royalvictoria.it* ➾ *48 rooms, 40 with bath* ⌕ *Room service, some fans, cable TV, in-room data ports, bicycles, bar, babysitting, dry cleaning, laundry service, concierge, parking (fee), some pets allowed; no a/c in some rooms* ☰ *AE, DC, MC, V* ⦿ *BP.*

Nightlife & the Arts

The **Luminaria** feast day on June 16 honors San Ranieri, the city's patron saint. Palaces along the Arno are lighted with white lights, and there are plenty of fireworks; this is the city at its most beautiful.

Pisa has a lively arts scene, most of which happens at the 19th-century Teatro Verdi. Music and dance performances are presented from September through May. Contact **Fondazione Teatro di Pisa** (✉ Via Palestro 40, Lungarni ☎ 050/941111 ⊕ www.teatrodipisa.pi.it) for schedules and information.

CHIANTI

Directly south of Florence is the Chianti district, one of Italy's most famous wine-producing areas; its hill towns, olive groves, and vineyards are quintessential Tuscany. Many British and northern Europeans have relocated here, drawn by the unhurried life, balmy climate, and charming villages; there are so many Britons, in fact, that the area has been nicknamed Chiantishire. Still, it remains strongly Tuscan in character: the views framing vine-quilted hills and elegantly elongated cypress trees.

The sinuous SS222, known as the Strada Chiantigiana, runs from Florence through the heart of Chianti. Its most scenic section connects Strada in Chianti, 16 km (10 mi) south of Florence, and Greve in Chianti, whose triangular central piazza is surrounded by restaurants and vintners offering *degustazioni* (wine tastings), 11 km (7 mi) farther south.

Greve in Chianti

⑰ *40 km (25 mi) northeast of Colle Val d'Elsa, 27 km (17 mi) south of Florence.*

If there is a capital of Chianti, it is Greve, a friendly market town with no shortage of cafés, *enoteche* (wine bars), and craft shops lining its main square. The sloping, asymmetrical **Piazza Matteotti** is attractively arcaded and has a statue of Giovanni da Verrazano (circa 1480–1528), the explorer who discovered New York harbor, in the center. At one end of the piazza is the **Chiesa di Santa Croce.** The church contains works from the school of Fra Angelico (circa 1400–55). ✉ *Piazza Matteotti* ☉ *Daily 9–1 and 3–7.*

Where to Stay & Eat

★ **$$$** ✕ **Osteria di Passignano.** Sophisticated country dining may not get better than at the deceptively simple restaurant next to the Vallombrosan abbey. A tiny sampling (maybe *sformatino di pecorino di fosso,* a flan made with aged pecorino) whets the appetite for what's to come. The kitchen team, a group of chefs all under 30, can do traditional as well as whimsical Tuscan—and then divine things such as the *maccheroni del Martelli al ragù bianco di agnelli e carciofi morellini* (tubular pasta with a lamb and artichoke sauce), which really isn't Tuscan at all. The wine list is unbeatable, as is the service. ✉ *Via Passignano 33, Località Badia a Passignano, 15 km (9 mi) east of Greve in Chianti* ☎ *055/801–1278* ▭ *AE, DC, MC, V* ☉ *Closed Sun., Jan. 7–Feb. 1, and 15 days in Aug.*

★ **$$** ✕ **Ristoro di Lamole.** Although off the beaten path (in this case, the SS222), this place is worth the effort to find down a narrow, winding road lined with olive trees and vineyards. The view from the outdoor

Siena
24 · **32**
see map
page 462

terrace is divine, as is the simple, exquisitely prepared Tuscan cuisine. Start with the bruschetta drizzled with olive oil or the sublime *verdure sott'olio* (vegetables marinated in oil) before moving on to any of the fine secondi. The kitchen has a way with *coniglio* (rabbit); don't pass it up if it's on the menu. ⊠ *Off SS222, Lamole in Chianti* ☎ *055/8547050* ▭ *AE, DC, MC, V* ⊙ *Closed Jan. 6–Feb. 28.*

★ ¢–$ ✕ **Enoteca Fuoripiazza.** Detour off Greve's flower-strewn main square for food that relies heavily on local ingredients (especially those produced by nearby cheese- and salami-makers). The lengthy wine list provides a bewildering array of choices to pair with *affettati misti* (a plate of cured meats) or one of their primi—the *pici* (a thick, short noodle) is deftly prepared here. All the dishes are made with great care. ⊠ *Via I Maggio 2, Piazza Trenta* ☎ *055/8546313* ▭ *AE, DC, MC, V* ⊙ *Closed Mon.*

$$$ ▥ **Fonte de' Medici.** The Antinori family has been making wine since 1180,
Fodor'sChoice and in 2001 they extended their efforts into an agriturismo—appropri-
★ ately, each of the individually decorated rooms and apartments bears the name of a grape. All are decorated with sponged walls, some with canopy beds, most with fireplaces and deep bathtubs, and nearly all with views of the tranquil countryside. Rooms are scattered between three structures, the busiest being Santa Maria a Macerata, and the most remote Podere Vivaio. If you're after bliss in the middle of Chianti, look

no farther. ✉ *Via Santa Maria a Macerata 31, 50020 Montefiridolfi* ☎ *055/8244700* 🖷 *055/8244701* ⊕ *www.fontedemedici.com* ⤳ *26 apartments, 2 cottages* ⚐ *Restaurant, picnic area, BBQs, some fans, in-room safes, some kitchens, some microwaves, refrigerators, cable TV, tennis court, pool, wading pool, exercise equipment, massage, sauna, steam room, mountain bikes, soccer, wine bar, wineshop, babysitting, laundry facilities, laundry service, Internet, meeting rooms, free parking, some pets allowed (fee); no a/c in some rooms* ▭ *AE, DC, MC, V* ⊙ *Restaurant closed Nov.–Feb.*

$$ 🏨 **Villa Vignamaggio.** The villa, surrounded by manicured classical Italian gardens, dates from the 14th century but was restored in the 16th. It's reputedly the birthplace of Mona Lisa, the woman later made famous by Leonardo da Vinci. There are guest rooms, suites, and apartments in the villa and other buildings, and a cottage on the grounds. The place also hosts tastings of its very fine wine: inquire at reception to organize one. Dinner can also be arranged sometimes. ✉ *Via Petriolo 5, 50022* ☎ *055/854661* 🖷 *055/854-4468* ⊕ *www.vignamaggio. com* ⤳ *3 rooms, 4 suites, 13 apartments, 1 cottage* ⚐ *Dining room, minibars, cable TV, tennis court, 2 pools, mountain bikes, bar, babysitting, playground, laundry service, some pets allowed, no-smoking rooms* ▭ *AE, DC, MC, V* ⊙ *Closed mid-Nov.–mid-Mar.* ❙◯❙ *BP.*

Panzano

⑱ *7 km (4½ mi) south of Greve, 29 km (18 mi) south of Florence.*

The little town of Panzano, between Greve in Chianti and Castellina in Chianti, has enoteche pouring samples of the local wine (in this case, Chianti), inviting shops, and a couple of breathtaking views as you're leaving town—if you walk up the steep incline to the hilltop church.

The town centerpiece is the church of **Santa Maria Assunta,** where you can see an *Annunciation* attributed to Michele di Ridolfo del Ghirlandaio (1503–77). ✉ *Panzano Alto* ⊙ *Daily 7–noon and 4–6.*

Where to Stay & Eat

$$–$$$ ✗**Oltre il Giardino.** An ancient stone farmhouse has been converted into a cozy dining area with a large terrace and spectacular views of the valley. Terra-cotta–color, stenciled walls and simple wood tables provide the background for very tasty Tuscan food. The *peposo* (a beef stew laced with black pepper) is particularly piquant, the tagliatelle *sul piccione* (with a delicate squab sauce) delightfully fragrant. The wine list is particularly strong on the local variety, which in this case is Chianti Classico. ✉ *Piazza G. Bucciarelli 42* ☎ *055/852828* ▭ *AE, DC, MC, V* ⊙ *Closed Mon. and mid-Nov.–mid-Dec.*

$–$$ 🏨 **Villa La Barone.** Formerly the home of the Viviani della Robbia family, this 16th-century villa retains many aspects of a private home. The honor bar allows you to enjoy an aperitivo in the tile barroom or on the terrace while admiring the view. And there are views here in abundance, from the pool to the rose garden to the back of the villa. Guest rooms have tile floors, white walls, and timber ceilings. The once-mandatory meal plan has been abolished, making this place a delight

VOICES OF ITALY

Dario Cecchini, Butcher Panzano

Dario Cecchini loves meat. At the half-century mark and standing over six feet tall, he could be a poster boy for the American beef lobby. He breathes health, vitality, vigor.

By trade, Dario is a butcher, but his Antica Macelleria Cecchini is not your typical butcher shop. From its intimate confines at Via XX Luglio 11 in Panzano, he holds forth behind a counter teeming with luscious meats. Opera plays in the background; sometimes customers sing along. Dario quotes Dante as he offers up samples of his wares. In March 2001, when beef cuts near the spine were banned by the European Union due to fears of mad cow disease, he held a funeral for such cuts, and most of the town turned out to watch. A beef auction was part of the solemnities, with Sir Elton John the high bidder; proceeds went to a nearby children's hospital.

Dario calls himself *un artigiano* (an artisan)—an indication of the pride he takes in his work. His shop has been in the family since the late 1700s, and his father trained Dario in the craft. "At 13," he says, "my grandmother made me a butcher's jacket. My mother began to cry. I guess she hoped I'd choose something else." The same grandmother is responsible for Dario's habit of offering wine to his customers. "She said a glass of wine brings people together, and I like to bring people together."

Dario is perhaps the world's greatest devotee of *bistecca fiorentina*, the definitive Tuscan steak. To get one of his *bistecche*, you must request it

seven days in advance. Ask him to halve its width, and you will incur this genial man's scorn. About its preparation, Dario brooks no compromises. "It must be very thick, seared on both sides, and very, very rare in the middle." If you prefer your steak well done? "You shouldn't order it." This is not to say that Dario is an unwavering traditionalist. One of his prized creations is sushi del Chianti, which took him five years to develop. After a taste of the coarsely ground raw beef, it can be difficult to stop eating.

What wine does Dario pair with his bistecca? "A young, simple, unstructured Chianti." If—heaven forbid—such a Chianti is not on the wine list? "Any young, honest red will do—no dallying in oak casks. Anything disliked by the *Wine Spectator*."

Where does Dario like to eat out these days? "Il Cipresso in Loro Ciuffena (some 20 minutes from Arezzo). Top-notch cooking with good seasonal ingredients." As a lifelong resident of Chianti, Dario has a firm view on views. After a good meal, where should you go to contemplate the finest vista in Tuscany? "If I had only a short time, I'd say the hills around Volpaia (just outside Radda in Chianti). If I had more time, the Crete Senesi. It's *un luogo dell'anima*—a place to feed your soul."

And supposing he couldn't live in Chianti, where would he go? "I wouldn't go to another place in the country, because I'd have too many memories. I tell you . . . when I was in Berkeley . . . not knowing the history. It was strange. I felt good. I was told that Berkeley was *una repubblica dei pazzi* (a republic of crazies). I'd like to go to a place that respects craziness."

for budgeteers. ✉ *Via San Leolino 19, 50020* ☎ *055/852621* 📠 *055/ 852277* 🛏 *30 rooms* ♿ *Dining room, tennis court, pool, babysitting, laundry service, concierge, Internet; no a/c in some rooms, no room TVs* 💳 *AE, MC, V* ⊗ *Closed Nov.–Easter* 🍽 *BP.*

Radda in Chianti

★ **⑲** *26 km (15 mi) south of Panzano, 52 km (32 mi) south of Florence.*

Radda in Chianti sits on a hill separating two valleys, Val di Pesa and Val d'Arbia. It's one of many tiny Chianti villages that invite you to stroll their steep streets; follow the signs pointing you toward the *camminamento,* a covered medieval passageway circling part of the city inside the walls. In Piazza Ferrucci, is the **Palazzo del Podestà** (or Palazzo Comunale), the city hall that has served the people of Radda for more than four centuries. It has 51 coats of arms embedded in its facade.

off the beaten path

VOLPAIA – Perched atop a hill 10 km (6 mi) north of Radda is Volpaia, a fairy-tale hamlet that was a military outpost from the 10th to the 16th century and once a shelter for religious pilgrims. Every August, for the Festa di San Lorenzo, people come to Volpaia to watch for falling stars and a traditional fireworks display put on by the family that owns the adjacent wine estate and agriturismo lodging, **Castello di Volpaia** (✉ Piazza della Cisterna 1, 53017 ☎ 0577/738066).

Where to Stay & Eat

¢ ✕ **Osteria Le Panzanelle.** Nada Michelassi and Silvia Bonechi combined their accumulated wisdom in the hospitality industry to create this welcoming restaurant a few minutes outside Radda. The small but carefully crafted menu has typical tastes of Tuscany, such as the exquisite *trippa alla fiorentina* (tripe Florentine, with tomatoes, onions, and bay leaves), and unexpected treats like *crostone con salsiccia fresca* (toasted bread with fresh sausage). The wine list, equally well thought out, is particularly strong on the local Chianti Classicos and Super Tuscans. Two small, simple rooms and tables outdoors provide the setting for your meal. ✉ *Località Lucarellia 29* ☎ *0577/733511* 💳 *MC, V* ⊗ *Closed Mon.*

★ **$$$–$$$$** ✕🏨 **Relais Fattoria Vignale.** On the outside it's an unadorned manor house with an annex across the street. Inside it's refined country-house comfortable, with terra-cotta floors, sitting rooms, and nice stone- and woodwork. White rooms with exposed brick and wood beams contain simple wooden bed frames and furniture, charming rugs and prints, and modern white-tile bathrooms. The grounds, flanked by vineyards and olive trees, are equally inviting, with lawns, terraces, and a pool. The sophisticated Ristorante Vignale ($$$–$$$$) serves excellent wines and Tuscan specialties, such as Chianina beef; the in-house *enoteca* (wine bar), less expensive fare. ✉ *Via Panigiani 9, 53017* ☎ *0577/738300 hotel, 0577/738701 restaurant, 0577/738012 enoteca* 📠 *0577/738592* 🌐 *www. vignale.it* 🛏 *35 rooms, 5 suites* ♿ *2 restaurants, in-room safes, minibars, cable TV, pool, bar, wineshop, library, laundry service, concierge,*

9

Internet, free parking, no-smoking rooms ☰ *AE, DC, MC, V* ⊘ *Closed Jan.–Mar. 15. Restaurant closed Thurs. Enoteca closed Wed.* �‖ *BP.*

$$$ 🏨 **Palazzo Leopoldo.** A contemporary interpretation of neoclassicism predominates at Palazzo Leopoldo. The former 15th-century palazzo on Radda's main street is now an invitingly intimate small hotel. Rooms have high ceilings and chandeliers—in the suites and in public rooms some are handcrafted 19th-century reproductions of Venetian Renaissance originals. The staff speaks English, and there's an inviting terrace. You might want to book a beauty treatment at the on-site spa. The tasty breads served at breakfast are made locally, and the restaurant has mostly Tuscan food; full and half board are options. ⊠ *Via Roma 33, 53017* 🕾 *0577/735605* 🖷 *0577/738031* ⊕ *www.palazzoleopoldo.it* ⟳ *8 rooms, 9 suites* ⚒ *Restaurant, room service, in-room safes, some kitchenettes, minibars, refrigerators, cable TV, indoor pool, hot tub, massage, sauna, spa, bar, babysitting, dry cleaning, laundry service, concierge, Internet, meeting room, free parking, some pets allowed, no-smoking rooms* ☰ *AE, DC, MC, V* ⊘ *Closed Jan. and Feb.* �‖ *BP.*

¢ 🏨 **La Bottega di Giovannino.** The name is actually that of the wine bar run by Giovannino Bernardoni; rentals are run by his children Monica and David in the house next door. This is a fantastic place for the budget-conscious traveler, as rooms are immaculate and beds comfortable. Most rooms have a stunning view of the surrounding hills. All have their own baths, though most of them necessitate taking a short trip outside one's room. ⊠ *Via Roma 6–8, 53017* 🕾🕾 *0577/738056* ⟳ *10 rooms* ⚒ *Bar; no a/c, no room phones* ☰ *MC, V* �‖ *EP.*

Castellina in Chianti

⓴ *14 km (8 mi) west of Radda, 42 km (26 mi) south of Florence.*

Castellina in Chianti, or simply Castellina, is on a ridge above the Val di Pesa, Val d'Arbia, and Val d'Elsa, and the panorama is bucolic in almost every direction you look. The imposing 15th-century tower hints at the history of this village, which was an outpost during the continuing wars between Florence and Siena.

Where to Stay & Eat

$$$–$$$$ ✕ **Alberghaccio.** The simple interior, with white-wash walls and cypress-beam ceilings, stands in high contrast to the sophisticated subtleties that come from the kitchen at Alberghaccio. The chef pays attention to the seasons, and the menu reflects what the market produces. The *sformato di cavolo nero* (creamy polenta with Tuscan kale) is a highlight in fall and winter; the outstanding *arista* (roast pork with rosemary and sage) should not be missed. A comprehensive wine list has selections from all over the world. This upscale trattoria is a short walk from Castellina's tiny center. ⊠ *Via Fiorentina 63* 🕾 *0577/741042* ⚒ *Reservations essential* ☰ *MC, V* ⊘ *Closed Sun.*

$$ 🏨 **Palazzo Squarcialupi.** This refurbished 15th-century palace on the main street in town is a pleasant, restful place to stay. Rooms have high ceilings, white walls, and tile floors; bathrooms are tiled in local stone. Many of the rooms have a view of the valley below. Common areas are elegant but comfortable, and the breakfast buffet is ample. The multilingual staff goes out of its way to be helpful. Though there's no restaurant, the hotel will arrange for a light lunch in the warmer months. ⊠ *Via Ferruccio 22, 53011* ☎ *0577/741186* 🖷 *0577/740386* ⊕ *www. chiantiandrelax.com* 🛏 *9 rooms, 8 suites* ⚒ *Minibars, cable TV, bar, babysitting, dry cleaning, laundry service, Internet, free parking, some pets allowed* ☰ *AE, DC, MC, V* ⊗ *Closed Nov.–Mar.* ⼚ *BP.*

$–$$ ⌂ **Collelungo.** One of the loveliest agriturismi in the area, Collelungo consists of a series of once-abandoned farmhouses that have been carefully remodeled. Set amid a notable vineyard (it produces internationally recognized Chianti Classico), the apartments—all with cooking facilities and dining areas—have exposed stone walls and that typical Tuscan tile floor. The *salone* (lounge), which possibly dates from the 14th century, has satellite TV; adjacent to it is an honor bar. In high season a minimum one-week stay is required. ⊠ *Podere Collungo, 53011* ☎ *0577/740489* 🖷 *0577/741330* ⊕ *www.collelungo.it* 🛏 *12 apartments* ⚒ *BBQs, pool, bar, laundry service, free parking; no a/c, no room phones, no room TVs, no kids under 8* ☰ *MC, V* ⊗ *Closed Nov.–Mar.* ⼚ *EP.*

HILL TOWNS SOUTHWEST OF FLORENCE

Submit to the draw of Tuscany's enchanting fortified cities that crown the hills west of Siena, many dating to the Etruscan period. San Gimignano, known as the "medieval Manhattan" because of its forest of stout medieval towers built by rival families, is perhaps the most heavily visited. This one-time Roman outpost, with its tilted cobble streets and ancient buildings, can make the days of Guelph-Ghibelline conflicts palpable. Rising from a series of bleak gullied hills and valleys, Volterra has always been popular for its minerals and stones, particularly alabaster, which was used by the Etruscans for many implements. Examples are now displayed in the exceptional and unwieldy Museo Etrusco Guarnacci.

9

Volterra

㉑   *48 km (30 mi) south of San Miniato, 75 km (47 mi) southwest of Florence.*

Unlike other Tuscan hill towns rising above sprawling vineyards and rolling fields of green, Volterra is surrounded by desolate terrain marred with industry and mining equipment. D. H. Lawrence described it as "somber and chilly alone on her rock" in his *Etruscan Places*. The fortress, walls, and gates still stand mightily over Le Balze, a stunning series of gullied hills and valleys to the west that were formed by irregular erosion. The town has long been known for its alabaster, which has been mined since Etruscan times; today the Volterrans use it to make ornaments and souvenirs sold all over town. A €7 combined ticket is your only option for visiting the Museo Etrusco Guarnacci and the Pinacoteca e Museo Civico.

Volterra has some of Italy's best small museums. The extraordinarily large and unique collection of the **Museo Etrusco Guarnacci** is a treasure in the region. Many of the other area Etruscan artifacts have landed in state museums and at the Vatican. If only a curator had thought to cull the best of the 700 funerary urns rather than to display every last one of them. ⊠ *Via Don Minzoni 15* ☎ *0588/86347* ⊕ *www.comune. volterra.pi.it* ☒ *Combined ticket €7* ⊙ *Mar. 16–Nov. 3, daily 9–7; Nov. 4–Mar. 15, daily 9–2.*

The **Pinacoteca e Museo Civico** houses a highly acclaimed collection of religious art, including a *Madonna and Child with Saints* by Luca Signorelli (1445/50–1523) and a *Deposition* by Rosso Fiorentino (1494–1541) that is reason enough to visit Volterra. ⊠ *Via dei Sarti 1* ☎ *0588/87580* ⊕ *www.comune.volterra.pi.it* ☒ *Combined ticket €7* ⊙ *Mar. 16–Nov. 3, daily 9–7; Nov. 4–Mar. 15, daily 9–2.*

Next to the altar in the town's unfinished **Duomo** is a magnificent 13th-century carved-wood *Deposition*. Note the fresco by Benozzo Gozzoli (1420–97) in the Cappella della Addolorata. Along the left wall of the nave you can see the arrival of the Magi. ⊠ *Piazza San Giovanni* ☎ *0588/86192* ⊙ *Daily 9–1 and 3–6.*

Among Volterra's best-preserved ancient remains is the Etruscan **Porta all'Arco,** an arch dating from the 4th century BC now incorporated into the city walls. The ruins of the 1st-century BC **Teatro Romano,** a beautifully preserved Roman theater, are worth a visit. Adjacent to the theater are the remains of the **terme** (baths). The complex is outside the town walls past Porta Fiorentina. ⊠ *Viale Francesco Ferrucci* ☎ *0586/ 260837* ☒ *€2* ⊙ *Mar.–May and Sept.–Nov., daily 10–1 and 2–4; June–Aug., daily 10–6:45; Dec.–Feb., weekends 10–1 and 2–4.*

Where to Stay & Eat

$ ✕ **Il Sacco Fiorentino.** Start with the *antipasti del Sacco Fiorentino*—a medley of sautéed chicken liver, porcini mushrooms, and polenta drizzled with balsamic vinegar. The meal just gets better when you move on to a dish like tagliatelle *del Sacco Fiorentino,* a riot of curried pasta with chicken and roasted red peppers. The wine list is a marvel, as it's long and affordably priced. Unremarkable white walls, tile floors, and red tablecloths are easily forgiven once the food starts arriving. ⊠ *Piazza XX Settembre 18* ☎ *0588/88537* ⊟ *AE, DC, MC, V* ⊙ *Closed Wed.*

$ ⊞ **Il Giardino di Venzano.** Terraced gardens bloom with native and exotic specimens: this agriturismo is run by two transplanted Australians with serious green thumbs. The grounds and buildings are what remains of an Augustinian monastery complete with Romanesque chapel. Three apartments, each sleeping two to four people, have high ceilings with light-color timbers, white walls and linens, and terra-cotta tile floors. Windows provide sweeping views of the surrounding countryside. A minimum one-week stay is required. ⊠ *Localita' Venzano, 56048 Mazzolla, 10 km (6 mi) south of Volterra* ☎☎ *0588/39095* ⊕ *www.venzanogardens. com* ⇨ *3 apartments* ⚒ *BBQs, kitchens, fans; no a/c, no room phones, no room TVs* ⊟ *No credit cards* ⊙ *Closed Nov. 1–Apr. 14* ⦿ *EP.*

$ ⊞ **San Lino.** Within the town's medieval walls a convent-turned-hotel pairs wood-beam ceilings, archways, and terra-cotta floors in public spaces with modern-day comforts in your private domain. Hair dryers and some carpeting in the guest rooms accompany contemporary wood laminate furnishings and straight-line ironwork pieces. Sip a drink on the small terrace with tables, umbrellas, and potted geraniums; the pool area is framed on one side by a church with a stained-glass window of the Last Supper. The restaurant serves Tuscan classics and local specialties such as *zuppa alla volterrana*, a thick vegetable soup. Half board is an option. ⊠ *Via San Lino 26, 56048* ☎ *0588/85250* 🖷 *0588/80620* ⊕ *www. hotelsanlino.com* ⇆ *43 rooms* ⌂ *Restaurant, in-room data ports, minibars, cable TV, pool, bar, dry cleaning, laundry service, concierge, Internet, parking (fee), some pets allowed, no-smoking rooms* ▭ *AE, DC, MC, V* ⊘ *Closed Nov.–Jan.* ⦿ *BP.*

Shopping

A number of shops in Volterra sell boxes, jewelry, and other objects made of alabaster. The **Cooperativa Artieri Alabastro** (⊠ Piazza dei Priori 5 ☎ 0588/87590) has two large showrooms of alabaster pieces. In what was once a medieval monastery, the **Galleria Agostiniane** (⊠ Piazza XX Settembre 3 ☎ 0588/86868) crafts alabaster objects of all kinds. You can also see a free video on how the mineral is quarried and carved. At **Camillo Rossi** (⊠ Via Lungo le Mura del Mandorlo 7 ☎ 0588/86133) you can actually see craftspeople at work, creating alabaster objects for all tastes and budgets.

Anna Maria Molesini weaves scarves, shawls, jackets, throws, and jackets—mostly in mohair—on her loom in her small shop. ⊠ *Via Gramsci 45* ☎ *0588/88411.*

San Gimignano

㉒ *27 km (17 mi) east of Volterra, 57 km (35 mi) southwest of Florence.*

When you're high on a hill surrounded by centuries-old towers silhouetted against the blue sky, it's difficult not to fall under the medieval spell of San Gimignano. Today 15 towers remain, but at the height of the Guelph-Ghibelline conflict there was a forest of more than 70, and it was possible to cross the town by rooftop rather than street. The towers were built partly to defend the town—they provided a safe refuge and were useful for pouring boiling oil on attacking enemies—and partly to bolster the egos of their owners, who competed with deadly seriousness to build the highest tower in town. When the Black Death devastated the population in 1348, power and independence faded fast and civic autonomy was ultimately surrendered to Florence.

Today San Gimignano isn't much more than a gentrified walled city, amply prepared for its booming tourist trade but still very much worth exploring. Despite the remarkable profusion of chintzy souvenir shops lining its main drag, there's some serious Renaissance art to be seen here and an equally important local wine (Vernaccia, a light white) to be savored. Escape at midday to the uninhabited areas outside the city walls for a hike and a picnic, and return to explore the town in the afternoon and evening, when things quiet down and the long shadows cast by the imposing towers take on fascinating shapes. A €7.50 combination ticket covers sights except for the private Museo di Criminologia Medievale.

San Gimignano's most noteworthy medieval buildings are clustered around the central **Piazza del Duomo**. The imposing **Torre Grossa** is the biggest tower in town (177 feet), with views that are well worth the climb. ⊠ *Piazza del Duomo 1* ☎ *0577/940008* 🎟 *€5* 🕐 *Mar.–Oct., daily 9:30–7:30; Nov.–Feb., daily 10–5:30.*

The **Palazzo del Popolo** houses the **Museo Civico**, featuring Taddeo di Bartolo's celebratory scenes from the life of San Gimignano. The town's namesake was a bishop of Modena who achieved sainthood by driving hordes of barbarians out of the city in the 10th century. Dante visited San Gimignano as an ambassador from Florence for only a single day in 1300, but it was long enough to get a room named after him, which now holds a *Maestà* by 14th-century artist Lippo Memmi. A small room (probably the private domain of the commune's chief magistrate) contains frescoes by Memmo di Filippuccio (active 1288–1324) depicting a young couple's courtship. ⊠ *Piazza del Duomo* ☎ *0577/940008* 🎟 *€5* 🕐 *Mar.–Oct., daily 9:30–7:30; Nov.–Feb., daily 10–5:30.*

★ The Romanesque **Collegiata** is a treasure trove of frescoes, including Bartolo di Fredi's cycle of scenes from the Old Testament on the left nave wall dating from 1367. Taddeo di Bartolo's otherworldly *Last Judgment*, on the arch inside the facade, depicts distorted and suffering nudes—avant-garde stuff for the 1390s. The New Testament scenes on the right wall, which may have been executed by Barna da Siena in the 1330s, suggest a more reserved, balanced Renaissance manner. The **Cappella di Santa Fina** contains glorious frescoes by Domenico Ghirlandaio (1449–94) depicting the story of this local saint. ⊠ *Piazza del Duomo* ☎ *0577/940316* 🎟 *€3.50* 🕐 *Mar.–Oct., weekdays 9:30–7:30, Sat. 9:30–5, Sun. 1–3; Nov.–Jan. 20, Mon.–Sat. 9:30–5, Sun. 1–5.*

The **Museo di Criminologia Medievale** (Museum of Medieval Criminology) has exhibits on medieval torture technology, along with operating instructions and a clear description of the intended effect. Though some scholars dispute the historical accuracy of many of the instruments, the final, very contemporary object—an electric chair imported from the United States—does give pause. ⊠ *Via del Castello 1–3* ☎ *0577/942243* 🎟 *€8* 🕐 *Mar. 16–July 18, daily 10–7; July 19–Sept. 17, daily 10–midnight; Sept. 18–Nov. 1, weekdays 10–7, weekends 10–8; Nov. 2–Mar. 15, Mon.–Sat. 10–6, Sun. 10–7.*

Before leaving San Gimignano, be sure to see its most revered work of art: Benozzo Gozzoli's utterly stunning 15th-century fresco cycle depicts scenes from the life of St. Augustine in the church of **Sant'Agostino**. ⊠ *Piazza Sant'Agostino, north end of town* ☎ *0577/907012* 🕐 *Nov.–Mar., daily 7–noon and 3–6; Apr.–Oct., daily 7–noon and 3–7.*

Where to Stay & Eat

$$ ✕ **La Mangiatoia.** Bright-color gingham tablecloths provide an interesting contrast from 13th-century, rib-vault ceilings. The lighthearted feminine touch might be explained by chef Susi Cuomo, who has been presiding over her kitchen for more than 20 years. The menu is seasonal—in the autumn, don't miss her *sacottino di pecorino al tartufo* (little packages of pasta stuffed with sheep's cheese and truffles), and in summer enjoy lighter fare on the intimate, flower-bedecked terrace in the back. ⊠ *Via Mainardi 5, off Via San Matteo* ☎ *0577/941528* ▭ *MC, V* ⊘ *Closed Tues., 3 wks in Nov., and 1 wk in Jan.*

★ ¢ ✗**Enoteca Gustavo.** The ebullient Maristella Becucci reigns supreme in this tiny wine bar (three small tables in the back, two in the bar, two bar stools) serving divine, and ample, crostini. The *crostino con carciofini e pecorino* (toasted bread with artichokes topped with semi-aged pecorino) packs a punch. The changing list of wines by the glass has about 16 reds and whites, mostly local, all good. The cheese plate is a bit more expensive than the crostini, but it's worth it. ⊠ *Via San Matteo 29* ☎ *0577/940057* ♨ *Reservations not accepted* ▭ *AE, DC, MC, V* ⊘ *Closed Tues.*

$$$$ 🏠 **La Collegiata.** After serving as a Franciscan convent and then residence of the noble Strozzi family, the Collegiata has been transformed into a fine hotel. Antiques and precious tapestries furnish the rooms, and bathrooms have whirlpool tubs. A park surrounds the building: ask for a room with a private balcony to enjoy the view more closely. The restaurant occupies the deconsecrated church. ⊠ *Località Strada 27, 53037, 1 km (½ mi) north of town center* ☎ *0577/943201* 🖷 *0577/940566* ⊕ *www.lacollegiata.it* ⇦ *19 rooms, 1 suite* ♨ *Restaurant, room service, some in-room hot tubs, in-room safes, cable TV, pool, bar, wine bar, Internet, meeting room, free parking, some pets allowed* ▭ *AE, DC, MC, V* ⊘ *Closed Nov.–mid-Mar.* ⦿| *EP.*

$–$$ ✗🏠 **Bel Soggiorno.** Beyond the wall of glass in the spacious dining room is a sweeping view of a Tuscan hillside. The *petto di faraona con mele condite, salsa al miele e pecorino di fossa* (breast of guinea fowl with apples, honey, and aged pecorino) is a real treat. Both the restaurant ($$$) and the hotel attached have been in the same family since 1886. Simple, airy rooms have contemporary beds in white. If you're looking for a place right within the town center, look no farther. ⊠ *Via San Giovanni 91, 53037* ☎ *0577/940375* 🖷 *0577/940375* ⊕ *www.hotelbelsoggiorno.it* ⇦ *17 rooms, 4 suites* ♨ *Restaurant, minibars, cable TV, babysitting, dry cleaning, parking (fee)* ▭ *AE, DC, MC, V* ⊘ *Closed Jan. 6–Feb. Restaurant closed Wed.* ⦿| *BP.*

$$ 🏠 **Pescille.** A rambling farmhouse 4 km (2½ mi) outside San Gimignano has been transformed into a handsome hotel with understated contemporary furniture in the bedrooms. Country-classic motifs, such as farm implements hanging on the walls, dominate in the bar. From this charming spot you get a splendid view of San Gimignano and its towers. ⊠ *Località Pescille, Strada Castel San Gimignano, 53037* ☎ *0577/940186* 🖷 *0577/943165* ⊕ *www.pescille.it* ⇦ *38 rooms, 12 suites* ♨ *Cable TV, tennis court, pool, gym, bar, Internet, free parking; no a/c in some rooms* ▭ *AE, DC, MC, V* ⊘ *Closed Nov.–Mar.* ⦿| *BP.*

Colle Val d'Elsa

㉓ *15 km (9 mi) southeast of San Gimignano, 50 km (31 mi) southwest of Florence.*

On the road from Florence to Siena, Colle Val d'Elsa rises dramatically along a winding road, its narrow streets lined with palazzos dating from the 15th and 16th centuries. For art enthusiasts, it's perhaps best known as the birthplace of Arnolfo di Cambio (circa 1245–1310), architect of Florence's Duomo. Once a formidable producer of wool, the town now produces glass and crystal sold in local shops. Colle has two distinct parts: the relatively modern and less interesting lower town, Colle Bassa, and the older, upper town, Colle Alta.

Where to Stay & Eat

★ $$$$ ✕ **Ristorante Arnolfo.** Food lovers with money should not miss Arnolfo, one of Tuscany's most highly regarded restaurants. Chef Gaetano Trovato sets high standards of creativity; his dishes daringly ride the line between innovation and tradition, almost always with spectacular results. The menu changes frequently and has two fixed-price options, but there are always plenty of fresh vegetables and herbs. You're in for a treat if *medaglioni di sogliola e gamberi rossi con finocchi allo zafferano* (sole and shrimp with fennel flavored with saffron) is on the list. The restaurant is in a tranquil spot at the center of town. ⊠ *Piazza XX Settembre 52* ☎ *0577/920549* ▤ *AE, DC, MC, V* ⊗ *Closed Tues. and Wed., mid-Jan.–mid-Feb., and 2 wks in Aug.*

★ $$$$ ▦ **La Suvera.** Pope Julius II once owned this luxurious estate in the valley of the River Elsa. The papal villa and adjacent building have magnificently furnished guest rooms and suites appointed with antiques and modern comforts. La Suvera's first-rate facilities, including drawing rooms, a library, an Italian garden, a park, and the Oliviera restaurant (serving organic estate wines), make it hard to tear yourself away. ⊠ *Pievescola (Casola d'Elsa), off SS541, 15 km (9 mi) south of Colle di Val d'Elsa, 53030* ☎ *0577/960300* ▤ *0577/960220* ⊕ *www.lasuvera. it* ▱ *16 rooms, 16 suites* ⊝ *Restaurant, room service, in-room safes, minibars, cable TV, tennis court, pool, exercise equipment, massage, Turkish bath, mountain bikes, bar, library, dry cleaning, laundry service, concierge, Internet, meeting room; no kids under 12* ▤ *AE, DC, MC, V* ⊗ *Closed Nov.–Easter* ◯| *BP.*

⟳ $ ▦ **Villa Belvedere.** The Conti-Iannone family has been running this place since 1984, and they provide the intimacy that you might find in a family home. Some of the 17th-century villa's rooms have three beds (with an option for adding a fourth), making this a good choice for families. A classic garden provides a place to read or have a drink, and an on-site restaurant serves Tuscan specialties. On a good day you can glimpse San Gimignano from here, but there's a fair amount of traffic that goes by on the road in front of the hotel. Half board is available. ⊠ *Località Belvedere, 53034, 1½ km (1 mi) south on SS2* ☎ *0577/920966* ▤ *0577/92412* ⊕ *www.villabelvedere.com* ▱ *15 rooms* ⊝ *Restaurant, cable TV, tennis court, pool, bar, Internet, free parking, some pets allowed; no a/c* ▤ *AE, DC, MC, V* ◯| *EP.*

SIENA

One of Italy's most enchanting medieval cities, Siena is the one place in Tuscany you should visit if you see no other. Florence's great historical rival was in all likelihood founded by the Etruscans. During the late Middle Ages it was both wealthy and powerful, for it saw the birth of the world's oldest bank, the Monte dei Paschi, still very much in business. It was bitterly envied by Florence, which in 1254 sent forces that besieged the city for more than a year, reducing its population by half and laying waste to the countryside. The city was finally absorbed by the grand duchy of Tuscany, ruled by Florence, in 1559.

Sienese identity is still defined by its 17 medieval *contrade* (neighborhoods), each with its own church, museum, and emblem. Look for streetlights painted in the contrada's colors, plaques displaying its symbol, and statues embodying the spirit of the neighborhood. The various contrade uphold ancient rivalries during the centuries-old Palio, a twice-yearly horse race (held in July and August) around the main piazza.

Exploring Siena

Practically unchanged since medieval times, Siena stretches over the slopes of three steep hills, but the most interesting sights are in a fairly compact area. Be sure to leave some time to wander off the main streets. Most sights are concentrated in the pedestrian-only centro storico, so you end up walking up and down a lot of steep streets. If you have only one day in Siena, see the Piazza del Campo, the Duomo, the Cripta, and the Palazzo Pubblico. If you are seeing more sights, it's usually worthwhile to buy a cumulative ticket (valid for three days, €7.50), good for entrance to the Duomo's Biblioteca Piccolomini, the Battistero, and the Museo dell'Opera Metropolitana. If you can overnight here, by all means do so: the city is filled with day-trippers and tour buses, and in the late afternoon and evening it empties out.The *passeggiata* (evening stroll) along the main shopping streets should not be missed: Siena's medieval charm and narrow streets are thrown into high relief, and Piazza del Campo positively glows. Keep in mind that most shops are closed on Sunday and museums have variable hours.

Siena is 69 km (43 mi) south of Florence; there are two basic routes. The speedy modern SS2 is good if you're making a day trip from Florence, as it's a four-lane divided highway. For a jaunt through Chianti, take the narrower and more meandering SS222, known as the Strada Chiantigiana. It's a gorgeous ride on only two lanes—patience is a necessity.

The Main Attractions

★ ㉖ **Duomo.** A few minutes' walk west of Piazza del Campo, Siena's Duomo is beyond question one of the finest Gothic cathedrals in Italy. The facade, with its multicolor marbles and painted decoration, is typical of the Italian approach to Gothic architecture, lighter and much less austere than the French. The cathedral as it now stands was completed in the 14th century, but at the time the Sienese had even bigger plans. They had decided to enlarge the building by using the existing church as a transept for a new one, with a new nave running toward the southeast. But in 1348 the Black Death decimated Siena's population, the city fell into decline, funds dried up, and the plans were never carried out. The beginnings of the new nave can be seen from the steps outside the Duomo's right transept.

The Duomo's interior, with its coffered and gilded dome, is striking. The magnificent inlaid marble floors took almost 200 years to complete (beginning around 1370); more than 40 artists contributed to the work, made up of 56 separate compositions depicting biblical scenes, allegories, religious symbols, and civic emblems. They are covered for most of the year for conservation purposes

WORD OF MOUTH

"Wandering Siena's streets and alleys was a mystical experience, one our seven-year-old loved. It got his imagination going, thinking about centuries past. Bring a comfortable pair of shoes and lots of water!"   –Jeff

but are usually unveiled every September for the entire month. The Duomo's pulpit, also much appreciated, was carved by Nicola Pisano between 1266 and 1268; the life of Christ is depicted on the rostrum frieze. In the **Biblioteca Piccolomini,** a room painted by Pinturicchio (circa 1454–1513) between 1502 and 1509, frescoes show scenes from the life of native son Aeneas Sylvius Piccolomini (1405–64), who became Pope Pius II in 1458. They are in excellent condition and reveal a freshness rarely seen in Renaissance frescoes. ⊠ *Piazza del Duomo, Città* ☎ *0577/ 283048* 🖃 *Church free, Biblioteca Piccolomini €3* ⊙ *Nov.–Feb.,*

Mon.–Sat. 10:30–6:30, Sun. 1:30–5:30; Mar.–Oct., Mon.–Sat. 10:30–7:30, Sun. 1:30–6:30.

㉗ **Duomo Cripta.** Rediscovered during routine excavation work, the crypt—
Fodor'sChoice under the grand *pavimento* (floor) of the Duomo upstairs—was opened
★ to the public in the fall of 2003. An unknown master executed the breath-takingly beautiful frescoes here sometime between 1270 and 1280; they retain their original colors and pack an emotional punch even with sporadic paint loss. The *Deposition/Lamentation* gives strong evidence that the Sienese school could paint emotion just as well as the Florentine school, some 20 years before Giotto. Guided tours in English take place more or less every half hour and are limited to no more than 35 persons. ⊠ *Piazza del Duomo, Città* ☎ *0577/283048* 🎫 *€6* ⏱ *Nov.–Mar. 14, daily 9–1:30; Mar. 15–Sept., daily 9–7:30; Oct., daily 9–6.*

need a break? Not far from the Duomo and the Pinacoteca, Siena's **Orto Botanico** (Botanical Garden; ⊠ Via Pier Andrea Mattioli 4, Città ☎ 0577/ 232874) is a great place to relax and enjoy views of the countryside. It's open weekdays 8–12:30 and 2:30–5:30, Sat. 8–noon, with an entrance fee of €8. Guided tours in English are available with a reservation.

Also Worth Seeing

㉘ **Battistero.** The Duomo's 14th-century Gothic Baptistery was built to prop up one side of the Duomo. There are frescoes throughout, but the highlight is a large bronze 15th-century baptismal font designed by Jacopo della Quercia and adorned with bas-reliefs by various artists, including two by Renaissance masters: the *Baptism of Christ* by Lorenzo Ghiberti (1378–1455) and the *Feast of Herod* by Donatello. ⊠ *Piazza San Giovanni, Duomo* 🎫 *€3* ⏱ *Nov.–Mar. 14, daily 10:30–1 and 2–5; Mar. 15–Sept., daily 9–7:30; Oct., daily 9–6.*

㉙ **Museo dell'Opera Metropolitana.** Built into part of the unfinished new cathedral's nave, the museum contains a small but important collection of Sienese art and the cathedral treasury. Its masterpiece is unquestionably the *Maestà* by Duccio (circa 1255–1318), painted around 1310 and magnificently displayed in a room devoted entirely to the artist's work. The tower inside the museum has a splendid view. ⊠ *Piazza del Duomo, next to the Duomo, Città* ☎ *0577/283048* 🎫 *€6* ⏱ *Nov.–mid-Mar., daily 9–1:30; mid-Mar.–Sept., daily 9–7:30; Oct., daily 9–6.*

㉛ **Pinacoteca Nazionale.** The national picture gallery contains an excellent collection of Sienese art, including works by native sons Ambrogio Lorenzetti (active 1319–48), Duccio, and Domenico Beccafumi (1486–1551). ⊠ *Via San Pietro 29, Città* ☎ *0577/281161* 🎫 *€4* ⏱ *Sun. and Mon. 8:30–1:15, Tues.–Sat. 8:30–7:15.*

㉜ **San Domenico.** In the church of San Domenico is the **Cappella di Santa Caterina,** with frescoes by Sodoma portraying scenes from the life of St. Catherine of Siena. Catherine was a much-respected diplomat, noted for ending the Great Schism by persuading the pope to return to Rome from Avignon. The saint's preserved head and finger are on display in

Continued on page 468

Climbing the 500 narrow steps of the **Torre del Mangia** rewards you with unparalleled views of Siena's rooftops and the countryside beyond.

The **Palazzo Pubblico**, Siena's town hall since the 14th century.

Something about the fan-shaped, sloping design of **Il Campo** encourages people to sit and relax (except during the Palio, when they stand and scream). The communal atmosphere here is unlike that of any other Italian piazza.

PIAZZA DEL CAMPO

24 The fan-shaped **Piazza del Campo,** known simply as Il Campo (The Field),

FodorsChoice ★ is one of the finest squares in Italy. Constructed toward the end of the 12th century on a market area unclaimed by any contrada, it's still the heart of town. The bricks of the Campo are patterned in nine different sections—representing each member of the medieval Government of Nine. At the top of the Campo is a copy of the **Fonte Gaia,** decorated in the early 15th century by Siena's greatest sculptor, Jacopo della Quercia, with 13 sculpted reliefs of biblical events and virtues. Those lining the rectangular fountain are 19th-century copies; the originals are in the Spedale di Santa Maria della Scala. On Palio horse race days (July 2 and August 16), the Campo and all its surrounding buildings are packed with cheering, frenzied locals and tourists craning their necks to take it all in.

25 The Gothic **Palazzo Pubblico,** the focal point of the Piazza del Campo, has served as Siena's town hall since the 1300s. It now also contains the **Museo Civico,** with walls covered in early Renaissance frescoes. The nine governors of Siena once met in the Sala della Pace, famous for Ambrogio Lorenzetti's frescoes called *Allegories of Good and Bad Government,* painted in the late 1330s to demonstrate the dangers of tyranny. The good government side depicts utopia, showing first the virtuous ruling council surrounded by angels and then scenes of a perfectly running city and countryside. Conversely, the bad government fresco tells a tale straight out of Dante. The evil ruler and his advisers have horns and fondle strange animals, and the town scene depicts the seven mortal sins in action. Interestingly, the bad government fresco is severely damaged, and the good government fresco is in terrific condition. The **Torre del Mangia,** the palazzo's famous bell tower, is named after one of its first bell ringers, Giovanni di Duccio (called Mangiaguadagni, or earnings eater). The climb up to the top is long and steep, but the view makes it worth every step. ⊠ *Piazza del Campo 1, Città* ☎ *0577/292226* ⊡ *Museo €7, Torre €6, combined ticket €10* ☉ *Museo Nov.–Mar. 15, daily 10–6:30; Mar. 16–Oct., daily 10–7. Torre Nov.–Mar. 15, daily 10–4; Mar. 16–Oct., daily 10–7.*

THE PALIO

The three laps around a makeshift racetrack in Piazza del Campo are over in less than two minutes, but the spirit of Siena's Palio—a horse race held every July 2 and August 16—lives all year long.

The Palio is contested between Siena's contrade, the 17 neighborhoods that have divided the city since the Middle Ages. Loyalties are fiercely felt. At any time of year you'll see on the streets contrada symbols—Tartuca (turtle), Oca (goose), Istrice (porcupine), Torre (tower)—emblazoned on banners and engraved on building walls. At Palio time, simmering rivalries come to a boil.

It's been that way since at least August 16, 1310, the date of the first recorded running of the Palio. At that time, and for centuries to follow, the race went through the streets of the city. The additional July 2 running was instituted in 1649; soon thereafter the location was moved to the Campo and the current system for selecting the race entrants established. Ten of the contrade are chosen at random to run in the July Palio. The August race is then contested between the 7 contrade left out in July, plus 3 of the 10 July participants, again chosen at random. Although the races are in theory of equal importance, Sienese will tell you that it's better to win the second and have bragging rights for the rest of the year.

The race itself has a raw and arbitrary character—it's no Kentucky Derby. There's barely room for the 10 horses on the makeshift Campo course, so falls and collisions are inevitable. Horses are chosen at random three days before the race, and jockeys (who ride bareback) are mercenaries hired from surrounding towns. Almost no tactic is considered too underhanded. Bribery, secret plots, and betrayal are commonplace—so much so that the word for "jockey," *fantino,* has come to mean "untrustworthy" in Siena. There have been incidents of drugging (the horses) and kidnapping (the jockeys); only sabotaging a horse's reins remains taboo.

Above: The tension of the starting line. Top left: The frenzy of the race. Bottom left: A solemn flag bearer follows in the footsteps of his ancestors.

| AQUILA | BRUCO | CHIOCCIOLA |

17 MEDIEVAL CONTRADE

Festivities kick off three days prior to the Palio, with the selection and blessing of the horses, trial runs, ceremonial banquets, betting, and late-night celebrations. Residents don their contrada's colors and march through the streets in medieval costumes. The Campo is transformed into a racetrack lined with a thick layer of yellow sand. On race day, each horse is brought to the church of the contrada for which it will run, where it's blessed and told, "Go little horse and return a winner." The Campo fills through the afternoon, with spectators crowding into every available space until bells ring and the piazza is sealed off. Processions of flag wavers in traditional dress march to the beat of tambourines and drums and the roar of the crowds. The *palio* itself—a banner for which the race is named, dedicated to the Virgin Mary—makes an appearance, followed by the horses and their jockeys.

The race begins when one horse, chosen to ride up from behind the rest of the field, crosses the starting line. There are always false starts, adding to the frenzied mood. Once underway, the race is over in a matter of minutes. The victorious rider is carried off through the streets of the winning contrada (where in the past tradition dictated he was entitled to the local girl of his choice), while winning and losing sides use television replay to analyze the race from every possible angle. The winning contrada will celebrate into the night, at long tables piled high with food and drink. The champion horse is guest of honor.

Reserved seating in the stands is sold out months in advance of the races; contact the Siena Tourist Office (⊠ Piazza del Campo 56 ☎ 0577/280551) to find out about availability, and ask your hotel if it can procure you a seat. The entire area in the center is free and unreserved, but you need to show up early in order to get a prime spot against the barriers.

CIVETTA	DRAGO
GIRAFFA	ISTRICE
LEOCORNO	LUPA
NICCHIO	OCA
ONDA	PANTERA
SELVA	TARTUCA
TORRE	VALDIMONTONE

PIAZZA DEL CAMPO

9

the chapel. ✉ *Costa di Sant'Antonio, Camollìa* ☎ *0577/280893* ⊗ *Nov.–mid-Mar., daily 9–1 and 3–6; mid-Mar.–Oct., daily 7–1 and 2:30–6:30.*

③⓪ Spedale di Santa Maria della Scala. A former *ospedale* (hospital) and hostel for weary pilgrims, built beginning in the late 9th century, continues to evolve into a grand exhibition space, hosting major contemporary art shows and housing, among other gems, some of the Fonte Gaia sculpted reliefs by Jacopo della Quercia (1371/74–1438). Even if you are not particularly taken with Etruscan objects, the subterranean archaeological museum contained within is not to be missed. Its interior design is sheer brilliance—it's beautifully lighted, eerily quiet, and an oasis of cool on hot summer days. ✉ *Piazza del Duomo, opposite front of Duomo, Città* ☎ *0577/224811* ☜ *€5.20* ⊗ *Mar. 17–Oct., daily 10–6; Nov.–Dec. 23, daily 10:30–4:30; Dec. 24–Jan. 6, daily 10–6; Jan. 7–Mar. 16, daily 10:30–4:30.*

Where to Stay & Eat

$$$–$$$$ ✕ **Antica Trattoria Botteganova.** Chef Michele Sorrentino's cooking is all about clean flavors, balanced combinations, and inviting presentation. Look for inspiring dishes such as spaghetti *alla chitarra in salsa di astice piccante* (with a spicy lobster sauce). The dining room's interior, with high vaulting, is relaxed yet classy, and there's a small room for nonsmokers. Service is first rate. ✉ *Strada per Montevarchi (SS408) 29, 2 km (1 mi) north of Siena along road to Chianti* ☎ *0577/284230* ☰ *AE, DC, MC, V* ⊗ *Closed Sun.*

$$–$$$ ✕ **Le Logge.** Bright flowers add a dash of color in this classic Tuscan dining room with stenciled ceilings. The wooden cupboards (now filled with wine bottles) recall the turn-of-the-19th-century food store it once was. A small menu, with four or five primi and secondi, changes regularly, but almost always includes *malfatti all'osteria*, ricotta and spinach dumplings in a cream sauce. Try inventive desserts such as *coni con mousse al cioccolato e gelato allo zafferano*, which is two diminutive ice-cream cones with chocolate mousse and saffron ice cream. ✉ *Via del Porrione 33, San Martino* ☎ *0577/48013* ☰ *AE, DC, MC, V* ⊗ *Closed Sun. and 3 wks in Jan.*

★ ☻ $$ ✕ **Osteria del Coro.** Chef-owner Stefano Azzi promotes local fare, uses age-old Sienese recipes, and backs up all his creations with a stellar wine list. His *pici con le briciole alla mio modo* (thick spaghetti with breadcrumbs), liberally dressed with fried *cinta senese* (a local bacon), dazzles. Pizza at lunch and dinner ensures the happiness of the junior set. In fact, the place was once a pizzeria, and it retains its unadorned, unpretentious nature—you certainly wouldn't come because of the decor. ✉ *Via Pantaneto 85–87, San Martino* ☎ *0577/222482* ⚇ *Reservations essential* ☰ *No credit cards.*

$$ ✕ **La Taverna del Capitano.** Not far from the Duomo you can step into a comfortable little taverna that is simplicity itself. The *pici al pomodoro fresco*, thick noodles topped with a lively fresh tomato sauce and a bit of cheese dusted on top, proves that less can indeed be more. Tuscan specialties and flavorful primi are strong suits here. Waiters dash between the closely spaced tables and can speak knowledgeably about the fine wine list. ⊠ *Via del Capitano 8, Città* ☎ *0577/288094* 🖃 *AE, DC, MC, V* ☺ *Closed Tues.*

¢ ✕ **da Trombicche.** Wiped out from too much sightseeing? Consider an invigorating snack at this one-room eatery. Here they do tasty things with eggs (the frittata is exceptional), plates of cured meats, and made-to-order *panini* (sandwiches). The list of daily specials reflects the season, and the collection of *verdure sott'olio* (marinated vegetables) is refreshing. Anything you choose can be washed down with the inexpensive, eminently drinkable, house red. ⊠ *Via delle Terme 66, Camollìa* ☎ *0577/288089* 🖃 *No credit cards* ☺ *Closed Sun.*

$$$$ 🏨 **Certosa di Maggiano.** A former 14th-century monastery has been converted into an exquisite country hotel. The officious staff is a drawback, but rooms have the style and comfort of an aristocratic villa—with classic prints and bold colors such as a happy, daffodil yellow. Common spaces are luxurious, with fine woods and leather. In warm weather, breakfast is served on the patio next to the garden ablaze with flowers. Half board is required in high season. ⊠ *Via Certosa 82, take the Siena Sud exit off superstrada, 53100* ☎ *0577/288180* 🖷 *0577/288189* ⊕ *www.certosadimaggiano.it* 🛏 *6 rooms, 11 suites* ⚖ *Restaurant, minibars, cable TV, tennis court, pool, exercise equipment, dry cleaning, laundry service, concierge, helipad, no-smoking rooms; no kids under 12* 🖃 *AE, MC, V* ⑩ *MAP.*

$$$$ 🏨 **Park.** What began life in the 16th century as a home for the prosperous Gori family is now an elegant hotel a short ride from the centro storico. Many of the rooms, with plush carpeting, large bathrooms, and flowered drapery, face a courtyard complete with well and stunning view of olive trees and Siena beyond. Public rooms have sweeping ceilings, highly polished terra-cotta floors, and comfortable couches. The Olivo restaurant serves regional cuisine, and the breakfast buffet includes splendid scrambled eggs. The staff is extraordinarily helpful and polite. ⊠ *Via Marciano 18, 53100* ☎ *0577/290290* 🖷 *0577/49020* ⊕ *www.royaldemeure.com* 🛏 *65 rooms, 1 suite* ⚖ *Restaurant, room service, minibars, cable TV, 6-hole golf course, tennis court, pool, bar, babysitting, dry cleaning, laundry service, concierge, Internet, business services, meeting rooms, some pets allowed, no-smoking rooms* 🖃 *AE, DC, MC, V* ☺ *Closed Nov.–Mar.* ⑩ *BP.*

★ $$$ 🏨 **Palazzo Ravizza.** There might not be a more romantic place in the center of Siena than this quietly charming pension, a 10-minute walk to the Duomo. Rooms exude a faded gentility, with high ceilings, antique furniture, big windows, and bathrooms done in hand-painted tiles. The restaurant serves Tuscans favorites, which, when it's warm, can be enjoyed outside in a lovely, tranquil garden complete with trickling fountain. ⊠ *Pian dei Mantellini 34, near Porto San Marco, Città, 53100* ☎ *0577/280462* 🖷 *0577/221597* ⊕ *www.palazzoravizza.it* 🛏 *40 rooms, 4 suites* ⚖ *Restaurant, some in-room safes, some minibars, cable TV, bar, laundry service, concierge, free parking, some pets allowed* 🖃 *AE, DC, MC, V* ⑩ *BP.*

$$ 🏨 **Antica Torre.** An old stone staircase, wooden beams, and original brick vaults here and there are reminders that the building is a 16th-century

tower. The lodging is the work of a cordial couple who have carefully evoked a private home, with only eight simply but tasteful guest rooms. Antica Torre is a 10-minute walk from Piazza del Campo. ⊠ *Via Fieravecchia 7, San Martino, 53100* 🏠 *0577/222255* ⊕ *www. anticatorresiena.it* ↩ *8 rooms* ⌂ *Cable TV, parking (fee)* ⊟ *AE, DC, MC, V* ⦿| *BP.*

¢ 🔳 **Alma Domus.** If you're after a contemplative, utilitarian experience, seek refuge at the former convent run by the committed parishioners of the Santurario Santa Caterina (Sanctuary of St. Catherine); it's around the corner from the church of San Domenico. Rooms are spartan and very clean. Many have a view of the Duomo and the rest of Siena, which might make the 11:30 curfew liveable. ⊠ *Via Camporeggio 37, Camollìa, 53100* 🕾 *0577/44177* 🕾 *0577/47601* ↩ *31 rooms* ⌂ *No-smoking floors; no room phones, no room TVs* ⊟ *No credit cards* ⦿| *EP.*

Nightlife & the Arts

Music

In the last week of July, Siena hosts the **Settimane Musicali Senesi,** a series of concerts held in churches and courtyards with performances of local and other music. The **Estate Musicale Chigiana** (⊠ Accademia Musicale Chigiana, Via di Città 89, Città 🕾 0577/22091 ⊕ www.chigiana.it) sponsors music master classes and workshops during July and August, and concerts from June through August. Age-old venues such as Santa Maria della Scala and the church of Sant'Agostino provide the setting.

Shopping

Siena is known for its cakes and cookies, their recipes of medieval origin—look for *cavallucci* (sweet spice biscuits), *panforte* (a densely packed concoction of honey, hazelnuts, almonds, and spices), and *ricciarelli* (almond-paste cookies). The best place in town to find Sienese baked goods, as well as to grab a cappuccino, is **Nannini** (⊠ Banchi di Sopra 24, Camollìa 🕾 0577/236009).

Siena has excellent specialty food and wine shops. **La Bottega dei Sapori Antichi** (⊠ Via delle Terme 41, Camollìa 🕾 0577/285501) is a good option for local products. Italy's only state-sponsored enoteca, **Enoteca Italiana** (⊠ Fortezza Medicea, Camollìa 🕾 0577/288497), sells wines from all across Italy.

Siena Ricama (⊠ Via di Città 61, Duomo 🕾 0577/288339) has embroidered linens and other housewares for sale. Chiara Perinetti Casoni at **Bottega dell'Arte** (⊠ Via Stalloreggi 47, Città 🕾 0577/40755) creates high-quality copies of 14th- and 15th-century Sienese paintings using tempera and gold leaf on panels.

AREZZO & CORTONA

The hill towns of Arezzo and Cortona carry on age-old local traditions—in June and September, for example, Arezzo's Romanesque and Gothic churches are enlivened by the Giostra del Saracino, a costumed medieval joust. Arezzo has been home to important artists since ancient times, when Etruscan potters produced their fiery-red vessels here. Fine examples of the work of Luca Signorelli are preserved in Cortona, his hometown.

Arezzo

33 *63 km (39 mi) northeast of Siena, 81 km (50 mi) southeast of Florence.*

Arezzo was the birthplace of both the poet Petrarch and the Renaissance artist and art historian Giorgio Vasari. Guido d'Arezzo, who was important in the development of musical notation, was also born here. Today Arezzo is best known for the magnificent frescoes by Piero della Francesca (circa 1420–92) in the **Basilica di San Francesco.** Painted between 1452 and 1466, they depict scenes from the *Legend of the True Cross* on three walls of the *cappella maggiore,* or high altar choir. What Sir Kenneth Clark called "the most perfect morning light in all Renaissance painting" may be seen in the lowest section of the right wall, where the troops of the emperor Maxentius flee before the sign of the cross. A 15-year project restored the works to their original brilliance. Reservations are required to see the choir area with the frescoes. ⊠ *Piazza San Francesco 6* ☎ *0575/900404* ⊕ *www.pierodellafrancesca.it* ✎ *Church free, choir €6* ⊙ *Weekdays 9–6, Sat. 9–5:30, Sun. 1–5:30.*

Some historians maintain that Arezzo's oddly shaped, sloping **Piazza Grande** was once the site of an ancient Roman forum. Now it plays host to a first-Sunday-of-the-month antiques fair as well as the **Giostra del Saracino** (Joust of the Saracen), featuring medieval costumes and competition, held here in the middle of June and on the first Sunday of September. Check out the 16th-century loggia designed by native son Giorgio Vasari on the northeast side of the piazza.

The curving, tiered apse on Piazza Grande belongs to **Santa Maria della Pieve,** one of Tuscany's finest Romanesque churches, built in the 12th century. Don't miss the Portale Maggiore (great door) with its polychromed figures representing the months; restored in 2002, they are remarkably vibrant. ⊠ *Corso Italia* ☎ *0575/377678* ⊙ *Daily 8–noon and 3–6.*

Arezzo's medieval **Duomo** (at the top of the hill) contains a fresco of a somber *Magdalen* by Piero della Francesca; look for it next to the large marble tomb near the organ. ⊠ *Piazza del Duomo 1* ☎ *0575/23991* ⊙ *Daily 7–12:30 and 3–6:30.*

The region's leading art historian and architect designed and decorated his private home, **Casa di Giorgio Vasari** in about the year 1540. ⊠ *Via XX Settembre 55* ☎ *0575/409040* ✎ *€2* ⊙ *Mon. and Wed.–Sat. 8:30–6:30, Sun. 8:30–1:30.*

Where to Stay & Eat

$$ ✕ **Le Logge Vasari.** Indulge yourself in terrific Tuscan food prone to flights of delicious fantasy. Try the *capelletti tiepidi al cacao amaro ripieno di pecorino* (thin pasta made with chocolate, stuffed with pecorino, and sauced with walnuts, mint, and tomato)—surprisingly it works. Grilled meats here are superb, as is the wine list. In warmer months,

9

enjoy outdoor seating under an airy loggia with views of Piazza Grande; in cooler months, tuck into the intimate dining room. ⊠ *Piazza Grande* ☎ *0575/295894* 🖃 *AE, DC, MC, V* ⊘ *Closed Tues.*

¢ ✕ **La Torre di Gnicche.** Looking for Italian home cooking? Eating *ribollita* (a hearty, traditional Tuscan soup) here is heightened experience when accompanied by an affordable glass of red. The short menu includes assorted crostini, sensational vegetables marinated in oil, cheese plates, and an earthy *polpettone* (meat loaf). This one-room restaurant, seating about 30, is part of a Renaissance palazzo. ⊠ *Piaggia San Martino 8* ☎ *0575/352035* 🖃 *MC, V* ⊘ *Closed Wed.*

$–$$ ✕🖾 **Castello di Gargonza.** Enchantment reigns at this tiny 13th-century hamlet in the countryside near Monte San Savino, part of the fiefdom of the aristocratic Florentine Guicciardini and restored by the modern Count Roberto Guicciardini as a way to rescue a dying village. A castle, church, and cobbled streets set the stage. A minimum two-night stay in any of the rooms is appreciated; apartments (sleeping 2–10 people) rent Saturday to Saturday. La Torre restaurant serves local fare, such as *zuppa di porcini* (a thick puree of porcini mushrooms). Follow with any of the superb grilled meats. Regional wines are well represented. ⊠ *52048 Monte San Savino* ☎ *0575/847021* 🖳 *0575/847054* ⊕ *www.gargonza. it* 🖘 *18 rooms, 11 apartments, 1 suite* ⚭ *Restaurant, minibars, pool, meeting room; no a/c, no room TVs* 🖃 *AE, DC, MC, V* ⊘ *Closed 3 wks in Jan. and 3 wks in Nov. Restaurant closed Tues.* ⦿ *BP.*

★ $ 🖾 **Calcione Country and Castle.** The elegant Marchesa Olivella Lotteringhi della Stufa has turned her six-centuries-old family homestead into invitingly comfortably rental apartments. Think sophisticated rustic: many of the apartments have open fireplaces. The houses have a private pool (the rest share the estate pool), and there are two nearby lakes for fishing and swimming. A stay here is restorative, since it's blissfully quiet. Calcione is convenient to Arezzo, Siena, San Gimignano, and the delights of Umbria. A one-week minimum stay is mandatory. ⊠ *Lucignano, 52046* ☎ *0575/837100* 🖳 *0575/837153* ⊕ *www.calcione.com* 🖘 *2 houses, 1 cottage, 6 apartments* ⚭ *BBQ, 3 pools, lake, babysitting, some pets allowed; no a/c, no phones, no room TVs* 🖃 *No credit cards* ⊘ *Closed Nov.–Mar.* ⦿ *EP.*

Shopping

On the first Sunday of each month a colorful flea market with antiques and other less precious objects for sale takes place in the **Piazza Grande.**

GOLD   Gold production here is on an industrial scale. Uno-A-Erre is the largest of several factories supplying local shops. **Prosperi** (⊠ Corso Italia 76 ☎ 0575/20746) works wonders in gold, silver, and platinum.

OUTLET MALLS   Savvy shoppers head to **I Pelletieri d'Italia** (⊠Località Levanella, SS69, Montevarchi, 29 km (18 mi) west of Arezzo ☎055/91901) for discounted Prada products. Go during the week, or if a weekend is your only option remember that patience is a virtue. If you're on an outlet roll, continue north to **The Mall** (⊠ Via Europa 8, Leccio Reggello, 52 km (33 mi) northwest of Arezzo ☎ 055/8657775), where discounted lines such as Gucci, Yves Saint Laurent, Armani, Sergio Rossi—to name but a few—abound.

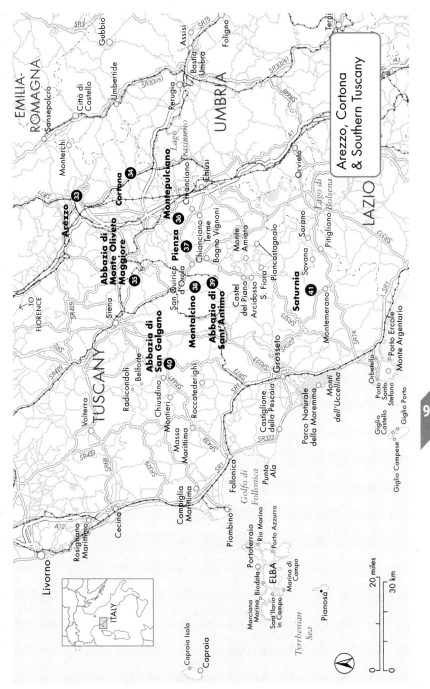

Arezzo, Cortona & Southern Tuscany

9

TEXTILES   At **Busatti** (⊠ Corso Italia 48 ☎ 0575/355295 ⊕ www.busatti.com), the Busatti-Sassolini family has been making sumptuous handwoven linen, wool, hemp, and cotton since 1842. Look for hand-stitched hems, embroideries, and lace.

Cortona

㉞ *29 km (18 mi) south of Arezzo, 79 km (44 mi) east of Siena, 117 km (73 mi) southeast of Florence.*

With olive trees and vineyards creeping up to its walls, pretty Cortona—popularized by Francis Mayes' *Under the Tuscan Sun*—commands sweeping views over Lake Trasimeno and the plain of the Valdichiana. Its two galleries and churches are rarely visited; its delightful medieval streets are a pleasure to wander for their own sake. The heart of town is formed by Piazza della Repubblica and the adjacent Piazza Signorelli, which both contain pleasant shops to browse through.

Cortona is considered one of Italy's oldest towns—popularly known as the "Mother of Troy and Grandmother of Rome." Tradition claims that it was founded by Dardanus, also the founder of Troy (after whom the Dardanelles were named). He was fighting a local tribe, so the story goes, when he lost his helmet (*corythos* in Greek) on Cortona's hill. In time a town grew up that took its name (Corito) from the missing headgear. By the 5th century BC the Etruscans had built the first set of town walls, whose cyclopean traces can still be seen in the 3-km (2-mi) sweep of the present fortifications.

The **Museo Diocesano** (Diocesan Museum) houses an impressive number of large and splendid paintings by native son Luca Signorelli, as well as a stunning *Annunciation* by Fra Angelico, a delightful surprise in this small town. ⊠ *Piazza del Duomo 1* ☎ *0575/62830* ☑ *€5* ⊘ *Nov.–Mar., Tues.–Sun. 10–5; Apr.–Oct., Tues.–Sun. 10–7.*

Where to Stay & Eat

$–$$ ✕ **Osteria del Teatro.** Walls filled with photographs of theater stars provide the backdrop for a two-room restaurant much frequented by locals. They come for good reason: the food here is tasty and abundant. If you're lucky enough to be around during truffle season (fall and early winter), start with the *fonduta al tartufo* (truffle fondue), in this case made with melted pecorino served with little toast squares. The *fagottini di pollo con carciofi* (chicken-stuffed pasta) proves that it's possible to have divine, dairy-free filled pasta. ⊠ *Via Maffei 2, off Piazza del Teatro* ☎ *0575/630556* ▤ *AE, DC, MC, V* ⊘ *Closed Wed. and 2 wks in Nov.*

$$$$ ✕▥ **Il Falconiere.** The husband-and-wife team of Riccardo and Silvia
Fodor'sChoice   Baracchi run a hotel with rooms in an 18th-century villa, just minutes
★   outside Cortona. Suites are in the *chiesetta* (little church) that once belonging to an obscure 19th-century Italian poet and hunter. You can also stay in the very private Le Vigne del Falco building at the end of the property, where suites have individual entrances and grand views of the plain. The restaurant's inventive menu is complemented by a wine list that's the product of Silvia's sommelier training. By all means sample

their estate-produced olive oil. Week long cooking classes are available. ⊠ *Località San Martino 370, 52044* ☎ *0575/612679* 🖷 *0575/612927* ⊕ *www.ilfalconiere.com* ↝ *13 rooms, 6 suites* ♧ *Restaurant, room service, in-room safes, minibars, cable TV, 2 pools, bar, babysitting, dry cleaning, laundry service, concierge, Internet, free parking, some pets allowed (fee), no-smoking rooms* ⊟ *AE, MC, V* ⊘ *Closed 3 wks in Jan. Restaurant closed Mon. Nov.–Mar.* ⦿ *BP.*

SOUTHERN TUSCANY

Along the roads leading south from Siena, soft green olive groves give way to a blanket of oak, cypress, and reddish-brown earth. Towns are the size of the roads—small—and as old as the hills. The scruffy mountain landscapes of Monte Amiata make up some of the wildest parts of Tuscany, and once you're across the mountains the landscape is still full of cliffs, like the one Pitigliano perches on. Southern Tuscany has good wine (try Brunello di Montalcino or the exceptional, lesser-known Morellino di Scansano for a true treat), thermal baths at Saturnia, Etruscan ruins, and the strands and fishing villages of Elba.

Abbazia di Monte Oliveto Maggiore

㉟ *52 km (32 mi) southeast of Cortona, 37 km (23 mi) southeast of Siena.*

This Benedictine abbey, Tuscany's most visited religious house, is an oasis of olive and cypress trees amid the harsh landscape of a zone known as the Crete, where erosion has sculpted the hills starkly, laying open barren rock in lush farmland. Surrounded by thick woodlands in the deep-cut hills south of Siena, it is accessible by car but not easily by bus.

Olivetans, or "White Benedictines," founded the abbey in 1313; this breakaway group sought to return to the simple ideals of the early Benedictine order. The monastery's mellow brick buildings in one of Tuscany's most striking landscapes protect a treasure or two. Only portions of the **park** and the **main cloister** are open to the public. In the main cloister, frescoes by Luca Signorelli and Sodoma depict scenes from the life of St. Benedict with earthy realism, a quality that came easily to Sodoma, described by Vasari as "a merry and licentious man of scant chastity." The wooden choir, with its intarsia designs, is an understated work of art that dates from 1503 to 1505. The monks make herbal liqueurs on-site. ⊠ *SS451, south of Asciano* ☎ *0577/707611* ⊘ *Daily 9:15–noon and 3:15–5:45.*

Montepulciano

㊱ *36 km (22 mi) southeast of Monte Oliveto Maggiore, 64 km (40 mi) southeast of Siena.*

Perched high on a hilltop, Montepulciano is made up of a pyramid of clustered Renaissance buildings set within a circle of cypress trees. At an altitude of almost 2,000 feet, it's cool in summer and chilled in winter by biting winds that sweep its spiraling streets. In the 21st century, vino nobile di Montepulciano, a robust red wine, is justifiably the town's greatest claim to fame. You can sample it in various wine shops and bars lining the twisting roads, as well as in most restaurants. The town is 13 km (8 mi) west of the A1 highway.

Montepulciano has an unusually harmonious look, the result of the work of three architects, Michelozzo (1396–1472), Antonio da Sangallo il Vecchio (circa 1455–1534), and Giacomo da Vignola (1507–73), who graced it with palaces and churches in an attempt to impose Renaissance architectural ideals on an ancient Tuscan hill town. The pièce de résis-
★ tance is the **Piazza Grande,** a wide expanse of urban space lined with 15th-century family palazzos and the equally grand, but facadeless, Duomo. On the hillside below the town walls is the church of **San Biagio,** designed by Sangallo, a paragon of Renaissance architectural perfection considered to be his masterpiece. ⊠ *Via di San Biagio* ☎ *0578/7577761* ☉ *Daily 9–12:30 and 3:30–7:30.*

Where to Stay & Eat

★ $$$ ✕ **La Grotta.** You might be tempted to walk by the innocuous entrance across the street from the Tempio di San Biagio (Church of San Biagio). Don't, for the food is fantastic. The *tagliolini con carciofi e rigatino* (thin noodles with artichokes and bacon) is superb, as is the tagliatelle *di grano saraceno con asparagi e zucchine* (with asparagus and zucchini). Follow with any of the wonderful secondi, and wash it down with the local wine, which just happens to be one of Italy's finest—vino nobile di Montepulciano. ⊠ *Località San Biagio* ☎ *0578/757479* ⊟ *AE, MC, V* ☉ *Closed Wed. and Jan. 8–Feb. 28.*

★ $$$$ ✕▦ **Locanda dell'Amorosa.** A self-sufficient hamlet with its own chapel in the 14th century is now a romantically refined place to rest your head. A majestic cypress-lined drive leads to the main gate of this country inn outside Sinalunga. Owners Carlo and Alessandra Citterio live on-site and tend to every detail. Some rooms have stunning views, others a private garden or terrace; all have sumptuous fabrics. Many of the bathrooms are large bathrooms. Color dominates the lusciously landscaped grounds in spring and summer. The restaurant, which once stabled horses, has candlelit tables, stone walls, and a menu grounded in Tuscan classics. ⊠ *Località Amorosa, west of Valdichiana exit off A1, 53048 Sinalunga, 17 km (11 mi) north of Montepulciano* ☎ *0577/677211* ⬚ *0577/632001* ⊕ *www.amorosa.it* ⇆ *17 rooms, 8 suites* ⬙ *Restaurant, room service, in-room safes, minibars, cable TV, in-room data ports, pool, mountain bikes, wine bar, wineshop, babysitting, dry cleaning, laundry service, concierge, Internet, meeting rooms, no-smoking rooms* ⊟ *AE, DC, MC, V* ☉ *Closed Jan. and Feb.* ⑩ *EP.*

$$$ ▦ **Villa Poggiano.** Two kilometers (1 mi) west of Montepulciano's historic center, a delightful, intimate 18th-century villa has been lovingly restored by the Savini family and turned into a bed-and-breakfast. Though the villa is definitely in the country (a winding, narrow unpaved road takes you there), there's nothing rustic about the decor. This is sweet luxury all the way—tumbled marble tiles, rich upholstered headboards, hand-painted details, fluffy bathrobes. Most rooms are suites; enjoy the blissful silence while ensconced on your divan. An on-staff beautician gives manicures and massages by appointment. ⊠ *Va di Poggiano 7,*

Bacchus in Tuscany

Tuscany produces some of Italy's finest wines. Here's a primer to help you navigate both the Tuscan wine list and the region's wine roads.

Varieties

The name Chianti evokes Tuscany as readily as gondolas evoke Venice, but if you think Chianti is about straw-covered jugs and deadly headaches, think again. This firm, full-bodied wine pressed from mostly Sangiovese grapes is the region's most popular, and it's easy to taste why. More difficult to understand is the difference between the many kinds of Chianti: there are seven subregions, including Chianti Classico, the oldest, whose wines have a *gallo nero* (black rooster) on the label. Each subregion has its own particularities, but the most noticeable—and costly—difference is between regular Chianti and the *riserva* (reserve) stock, aged at least four years.

Beginning in the 1970s, some winemakers, chafing at the strict regulations for making Chianti, chose to buck tradition and blend their wines in innovative ways. Thus was born the Super Tuscan (a name coined by American journalists). These pricey, French oak-aged wines continue to be the toast of Tuscany.

Montepulciano, south of Chianti, has a wine-making tradition dating back to the Etruscans. Vino Nobile di Montepulciano, the "Noble Wine," gained its title by virtue of royal patronage: in 1669, England's William III sent a delegation to procure the prized wine. Less noble but no less popular is Rosso di Montepulciano, a light, fruity DOC red.

With its velvety black berries and structured tannins, Brunello di Montalcino is just as sophisticated as Vino Nobile. The strain of Sangiovese grape used to make it was developed in 1870 by a winemaker in need of vines that could cope with windy weather. The resulting wine was a hit. Brunello has a younger sibling, Rosso di Montalcino.

Not all of Tuscany's great wines are reds; in fact, top honors often go to a white, Vernaccia di San Gimignano. This golden wine is made from grapes native to Liguria. Its name is thought to be a corruption of Vernazza, one of the Cinque Terre villages.

Winery Visits

The SS222 (aka the Strada Chiantigiana) running through the heart of Chianti and other Strade del Vino (Wine Roads) throughout the region will lead you to an abundance of producers. You can do preliminary research at www.terreditoscana. regione.toscana.it (click on "Strade del Vino"). When you're on the ground, visit any tourist information center in wine country (Greve, Montalcino, and Montepulciano are the best places to start) for maps and guidance. Then hit the road. Many wineries—especially smaller producers—offer free tastings without an appointment. Larger producers usually charge a small fee for a three-glass tasting, and sometimes require a reservation for a tour. Remember: always have a designated driver. Vineyards are usually off narrow, curving roads. Sobriety is a must.

9

53045 ☎ *0578/758292* 🖶 *0578/715635* ⊕ *www.villapoggiano.com*
⇨ *3 rooms, 6 suites* ♿ *In-room safes, minibars, cable TV, in-room data ports, pool, dry cleaning, laundry service, free parking, no smoking rooms; no kids under 12* ⊟ *AE, DC, MC, V* ⊘ *Closed Nov.–Mar.* ⦿ *BP.*

$$–$$$ ▥ **Montorio.** A cluster of five apartments perched 1,980 feet above sea level, with a commanding view of San Biagio below, provides the perfect mix of country and city life. Each apartment, sleeping from two to four, is self-catering and has its own separate entrance. A housekeeper comes every day except Sunday to clean the kitchen and make the beds; a home-baked breakfast cake awaits you upon arrival. Stays are usually run Saturday–Saturday, but four-day stays may be arranged. ⊠ *Strada per Pienza 2, 53045* ☎ *0578/717442* 🖶 *0578/715456* ⊕ *www.montorio. com* ⇨ *5 apartments* ♿ *Picnic area, some fans, kitchens, refrigerators, cable TV, massage, laundry facilities, free parking; no a/c* ⊟ *AE, DC, MC, V* ⊘ *Closed Dec. 15–Jan. 31* ⦿ *EP.*

Nightlife & the Arts

The **Cantiere Internazionale d'Arte** (⊠ Piazza Grande 7 ☎ 0578/757341 for tourist information office), held in July and August, is a festival of art, music, and theater ending with a major theatrical production in Piazza Grande. The tourist office has information on scheduling and events.

Pienza

㊲ *15 km (9 mi) east of Montepulciano, 52 km (32 mi) southeast of Siena.*

Pienza owes its urban design to Pope Pius II, who had grand plans to transform his home village of Corsignano—the town's former name—into a model Renaissance town. The man entrusted with the project was Bernardo Rossellino (1409–64), a protégé of the great Renaissance architectural theorist Leon Battista Alberti (1404–74). His mandate was to create a cathedral, a papal palace, and a town hall (plus miscellaneous other buildings) that adhered to the humanist pope's principles. The result was a project that expressed Renaissance ideals of art, architecture, and civilized good living in a single scheme: it stands as a fine example of the architectural canons that Alberti formulated in the early Renaissance and that were utilized by later architects, including Michelangelo (1475–1564), in designing many of Italy's finest buildings and piazzas. Today the cool nobility of Pienza's center seems almost surreal in this otherwise unpretentious village, known locally for its pecorino. Although the sheep's cheese is made all over Italy, here it is a superior gastronomic experience.

The **Palazzo Piccolomini,** the seat of Pius II's papal court, was designed by Rossellino in 1459, using Florence's Palazzo Rucellai by Alberti as a model. You can visit the papal apartments, including a library, as well as the **Sala delle Armi,** with an impressive weapons collection. Look for the extravagant wooden ceiling in the music room. ⊠ *Piazza Pio II* ☎ *0578/748503* 🎫 *€3.50* ⊘ *Guided tours Tues.–Sun. 10–noon and 3–5:30. Closed 2nd half of Feb., 1st wk in Mar., Nov. 16–Dec. 7.*

The interior of the **Duomo** is simple but richly decorated with paintings from the Sienese school. Begun in 1459 and finished in a record three years' time, the facade is divided into three parts. Renaissance pilasters on the facade draw attention to the pope's coat of arms encircled by a wreath of fruit, the papal tiara, and keys above it. ✉ *Piazza Pio II* ⊙ *Daily 8:30–1 and 2:30–7.*

Where to Stay & Eat

¢–$$ ✕ **La Porta.** Montichiello is a hamlet minutes away from Pienza, where this wine bar is basically the only show in town. But what a show it is— from start to finish, the food is delicious. The menu changes regularly, but you can always count on top-quality cheeses (pecorino di Pienza, among others) and lively pasta dishes such as *tagliolini alla chianina* (thin noodles with a hearty minced beef sauce). Second courses are just as strong; if rabbit's on the menu, don't miss it. Reservations are a good idea, especially in summer. ✉ *Off SP88, Montichiello* ☎ *0578/755163* ⌲ *Reservations essential* ▤ *MC, V* ⊙ *Closed Thurs. and mid-Jan.–mid-Feb.*

¢–$ ✕ **La Chiocciola.** Enjoy typical Pienza fare, including homemade pici with hare or wild boar sauce, at a no-frills trattoria a few minutes' walk from the historic center. La Chiocciola's take on *formaggio in forno* (baked cheese), with assorted accompaniments such as fresh porcini mushrooms, is reason enough to come. ✉ *Via Mencattelli 4* ☎ *0578/748683* ▤ *MC, V* ⊙ *Closed Wed. and 10 days in Jan.*

★ $ ▨ **La Foce.** The former estate of noted Anglo-American historian Iris Origo and her husband, Antonio, has become an agriturismo with various farmhouses and apartments scattered about the property. Furnishings have a simple, rustic style—wood farm tables, sponged walls—and there are extraordinary views of rolling hills. Kitchens come fully equipped, and some of the rooms have working fireplaces. If you're searching for peace and quiet, look no farther. From May through October, a minimum one-week stay is obligatory. ✉ *Strada della Vittoria 61, Chianciano Terme, 53042* ☎ *0578/69101* ⊕ *www.lafoce.com* ⇗ *9 apartments, 6 farmhouses* ⌂ *Fans, kitchens, refrigerators, some cable TV, tennis court, 8 pools, playground, laundry facilities, laundry service, free parking; no a/c* ▤ *MC, V* ⦿ *EP.*

Montalcino

38 *24 km (15 mi) west of Pienza, 41 km (25 mi) south of Siena.*

Another medieval hill town with a special claim to fame, Montalcino is the source for Brunello di Montalcino, one of Italy's most esteemed red wines. You can sample it in wine cellars in town or visit a nearby winery for a free guided tour and tasting; you must call ahead for reservations.

In the very heart of the centro storico is **Alle Logge,** a sophisticated wine bar where selections by the glass always include a significant Brunello. ✉ *Piazza del Popolo* ☎ *0577/846186.*

The 14th-century **La Fortezza** has a tower you can climb and an enoteca for tasting wines. ✉ *Via Panfilo dell'Oca* ☎ *0577/849211* ▨ *€3.50* ⊙ *Nov.–Mar., Tues.–Sun. 9–6; Apr.–Oct., daily 9–8.*

9

CLOSE UP

Sorry, Vasari

To many, Tuscan art is synonymous with the art of Florence. While Florence is indeed littered with masterpieces, its exalted status is due in no small part to the biases of Giorgio Vasari (1511–74), whose seminal book *Lives of the Artists* glorified the works of the Florentines above all others. In fact, even if Florence didn't exist, Tuscany would still be a place of phenomenal artistic achievement with a crucial role in the Renaissance. A few cases in point: Nicola Pisano (circa 1215/20–1278/84) carved a groundbreaking pulpit in Pisa, then worked with his son Giovanni on another in Siena. Giovanni carried the tradition to Pistoia. Ambrogio Lorenzetti (documented 1319–48) produced wonderful frescoes representing good and bad government in the Palazzo Pubblico in Siena. The frescoes of the *Legend of the True Cross* by Piero della Francesca (circa 1420–92) in Arezzo are among the 15th century's most stunning achievements. And Siena-born Aeneas Silvius Piccolomini (1405–64), later Pope Pius II, carried out his vision of Renaissance ideals on a citywide scale in Pienza.

One Montalcino winery worth visiting is **Fattoria dei Barbi e del Casato.** The cellars date back to the 17th century. ⊠ *Località Podernuovi* ☎ *0577/841200* ⊕ *www.fattoriadeibarbi.it* 🔲 *Free* ☉ *Weekdays 10–1 and 2:30–6.*

Where to Stay & Eat

$$$$ ✕ **Poggio Antico.** One of Italy's renowned chefs, Roberto Minnetti, abandoned his highly successful restaurant in Rome and moved to the country outside Montalcino. Now he and his wife, Patrizia, serve Tuscan cuisine masterfully interpreted by Roberto in a relaxed but regal dining room with arches and beam ceilings. The seasonal menu includes *pappardelle al ragù di agnello* (flat, wide noodles in a lamb sauce) and venison in a sweet-and-sour sauce. ⊠ *Località I Poggi, 4 km (2½ mi) southwest of Montalcino on road to Grosseto* ☎ *0577/849200* ▤ *MC, V* ☉ *Closed Mon. Nov.–Mar. and 20 days in Jan. No dinner Sun. Nov.–Mar.*

$ ✕▥ **Fattoria dei Barbi e del Casato.** Excellent Brunello as well as its younger cousin, Rosso di Montalcino, is produced by this family-owned wine estate and agriturismo. The rustic taverna ($$, reservations essential) has a large stone fireplace and is right among vineyards. The estate farm produces many of the ingredients used in such traditional specialties as *stracotto nel brunello* (braised beef cooked with beans in Brunello wine). Two comfortable, traditionally furnished apartments are next to the taverna; a two-night minimum stay is required throughout the year. ⊠ *Località Podernuovi, 53024* ☎ *0577/841111* ⊕ *www.fattoriadeibarbi. it* 🖷 *0577/841112* ⇱ *2 apartments* ♿ *Fans, kitchenettes, cable TV, some pets allowed; no a/c* ▤ *AE, DC, MC, V* ☉ *Taverna closed Wed. and mid-Jan.–mid Feb. No dinner Tues. Nov.–Mar.* ❑ *EP.*

Abbazia di Sant'Antimo

★ ㊴ *10 km (6 mi) south of Montalcino, 51 km (32 mi) south of Siena.*

The pale stone of the 12th-century abbey sits amid the silvery green of an olive grove, making this Romanesque gem well worth a visit. The exterior and interior sculpture is outstanding, particularly the nave capitals, a combination of French, Lombard, and Spanish influences. According to legend, the **sacristy** (rarely open) formed part of the primitive Carolingian church (founded in AD 781), its entrance flanked by 9th-century pilasters. The small **vaulted crypt** dates from the same period. An unusual element is the ambulatory, with three radiating chapels (rare in Italian churches) that were probably copied from the French model. Throughout the day the monks fill this magnificent space with Gregorian chant. ⊠ *Castelnuovo dell'Abate* ☎ *0577/835659* ⊕ *www.antimo. it* ⊙ *Daily 10–12:30 and 6–8.*

Abbazia di San Galgano

★ ㊵ *80 km (49 mi) northwest of the Abbazia di Sant'Antimo, 33 km (20 mi) southwest of Siena.*

This Gothic cathedral missing its roof is a hauntingly beautiful sight. The church was built in the late 12th century by Cistercian monks, who modeled it after churches built by their order in France. Starting in the 15th century it fell into ruin, declin-

> **WORD OF MOUTH**
>
> "San Galgano is beautiful and worth the trip. A very romantic setting." –Nutella

ing gradually over the centuries. Grass has grown through the floor, and the roof and glass windows are gone. What's left of its facade and walls makes a grandiose and desolate picture. Behind it, a short climb up a hill brings you to the charming little church of San Galgano, with frescoes by Ambrogio Lorenzetti (active 1319–48), as well as a famous sword of local legend. As the story goes, Galgano, a medieval knight, had an epiphany on this spot and gave up fighting. He thrust his sword into a stone, where it remains to this day.

Saturnia

㊶ *130 km (81 mi) southeast of Pimbino, 129 km (77 mi) south of Siena.*

Etruscan and pre-Etruscan tombs cut into the local rock can be seen in this town, a lively center in pre-Etruscan times. Today it is known for its hot sulfur thermal waters. You can soak for free at the tiered natural thermal pools of **Cascate del Gorello,** which get very crowded in August. ⊠ *2 km (1 mi) east on road to Montemerano* ☎ *No phone.*

There are four hot-spring pools at the **Terme di Saturnia;** it's attached to a hotel of the same name. ⊠ *Strada Saturnia–Pitigliano, 3 km (2 mi) east toward Montemerano* ☎ *0564/601061* ⊕ *www.saturnia-terme.it* ☞ *Full day €16, half day €12* ⊙ *May–Sept., daily 9:30–7:30; Oct.–Apr., daily 9:30–5:30.*

Where to Stay & Eat

$$$$ ✕**Da Caino.** Specialties include tomatoes and peppers on crisp phyllo dough, lasagna with pumpkin, and hearty dishes like *cinghiale lardolato con olive* (wild boar larded with olives) at an excellent restaurant in the town of Montemerano. Prices are among the highest in the region; locals consider it a serious splurge. ⊠ *Via della Chiesa 4, Montemerano, 7 km (4½ mi) south of Saturnia* ☎ *0564/602817* ⚜ *Reservations essential* ▭ *AE, DC, MC, V* ⊘ *Closed Wed., and Jan. and Feb. No dinner Thurs.*

$–$$$ ✕**I Due Cippi–Da Michele.** Owner Michele Aniello has a terrific restaurant with a lengthy and creative menu. Emphasis is placed on Maremman regional cuisine such as wild boar and duck—though there are other options as well; try the *tortelli di castagne al seme di finocchio* (chestnut-stuffed tortelli with butter sauce and fennel seeds). In good weather you can enjoy your meal on a terrace overlooking the town's main square. ⊠ *Piazza Veneto 26/a* ☎ *0564/601074* ⚜ *Reservations essential* ▭ *AE, DC, MC, V* ⊘ *Closed Tues. Oct.–June, Dec. 20–26, and Jan. 10–25.*

$$$$ 🏨 **Terme di Saturnia.** Roam elegant public rooms in your bathrobe (provided in every room) between beauty treatments or on your way to take a dip into the 37.5°C (99.5°F) sulfurous thermal pools. Guest rooms have cherry-stain wood furnishings. Half and full board are options and should be considered, as the on-site restaurant is good. The multilingual staff can be helpful. ⊠ *Strada Saturnia–Pitigliano, 3 km (2 mi) east toward Montemerano, 58050 Sinalunga* ☎ *0564/601061* 🖷 *0564/601266* ⊕ *www.termedisaturnia.it* ⟿ *140 rooms, 10 suites* ⚐ *Restaurant, snack bar, room service, in-room safes, minibars, cable TV with movies, some in-room VCRs, driving range, tennis court, 2 pools, 2 wading pools, health club, hair salon, sauna, spa, steam room, bar, piano bar, shops, dry cleaning, laundry facilities, concierge, Internet, helipad, some pets allowed* ▭ *AE, DC, MC, V* ⊠ *BP.*

$ 🏨 **Villa Garden.** Each of the 10 rooms, named for a flower, is charmingly furnished with comfortable beds, floral curtains and bedspreads, and tiled bathrooms. A few minutes from the center of town, it's a perfect place to stay if you want to take the waters without breaking the bank. The buffet breakfast is good and filling, the staff courteous and efficient. ⊠ *Via Sterpeti 56, 58014* 🖷 *0564/601182* ⊕ *www.laltramaremma.it/villa_garden* ⟿ *10 rooms* ⚐ *Minibars, cable TV, bar, Internet, free parking, some pets allowed; no a/c in some rooms* ▭ *AE, DC, MC, V* ⊠ *BP.*

TUSCANY ESSENTIALS

Transportation

BY AIR

The largest airports in the region are Pisa's Aeroporto Galileo Galilei and Florence's Aeroporto Amerigo Vespucci, known as Peretola, which connects to Amsterdam, Brussels, Frankfurt, London, Munich, and Paris.

🛈 Airport Information **Aeroporto Galileo Galilei** ☎ 050/849300 ⊕ www. pisa-airport.com. **Peretola** ⊠ 10 km [6 mi] northwest of Florence ☎ 055/315874 ⊕ www.airport.florence.it.

BY BUS

SENA connects Rome with Siena on several scheduled daily trips. When traveling to Tuscany from elsewhere in Italy, the train is almost always a better option than the bus; buses are subject to the vagaries of road traffic, and the seats are narrow and cramped.

Within Tuscany, bus service between towns is conducted primarily by two private companies, Tra-In and Lazzi.

🛈 **Bus Information CPT** (Compagnia Pisana Trasporti) ✉ Piazza Sant'Antonio 1, Pisa 🕾🖷 050/505511 ⊕ www.cpt.pisa.it. **Lazzi Eurolines** ✉ Via Mercante 2, Florence 🕾 055/363041 ⊕ www.lazzi.it. **Tra-In** ✉ Statale 73, Levante 23, Due Ponti, Siena 🕾 0577/204111. **SENA** ✉ Piazza Gramsci, Siena 🕾 0577/283203 🖷 0577/40731.

BY CAR

The Autostrada del Sole (A1), northern and central Italy's major north–south highway, connects Florence with Bologna, 105 km (65 mi) to the north, and beyond that with Milan. Rome is 277 km (172 mi) south of Florence via the A1.

Within Tuscany, the cities west of Florence are easily reached by the A11, which leads to Lucca and then to the sea. The A1 takes you south from Florence to Arezzo and Chiusi (where you turn off for Montepulciano). Florence and Siena are connected by a *superstrada* and also the panoramic SS222, which threads through Chianti wine country. The hill towns north and west of Siena lie along superstrade and winding local roads—all are well marked, but you should still arm yourself with a good map.

Drivers should be prepared to navigate through suburban sprawl around Pisa and Arezzo, and to a lesser degree Lucca and Cortona; to reach the historic centers where most sights are, look for the CENTRO STORICO signs. In many small towns you must park outside the city walls.

EMERGENCY SERVICES   If you have a breakdown on the autostrada, or any toll road, you will find along the side of the road "SOS" boxes placed every couple of kilometers. You push a button on the box, a green light pops on, and help is sent—you don't actually talk to a person. If you are on other roads, call ACI, the Italian Auto Club.

🛈 **ACI** 🕾 803/116.

BY TRAIN

Italy's main rail line, which runs from Milan in the north to Calabria in the toe of the boot, links Florence to Rome, Bologna, and numerous other Italian cities. Within Tuscany, trains on this line stop in Prato, Arezzo, and Chiusi as well as Florence. Another major line connects Florence with Pisa, and the coastal line between Rome and Genoa passes through Pisa and the Tuscan beach resorts (which, though popular with locals, aren't counted among the region's allures). There's also regular, nearly hourly service from Florence to Lucca via Prato, Pistoia, and Montecatini. If you want to visit other areas of Tuscany—Chianti, Montalcino, and Montepulciano, for example—you are better off going by bus or by car. Train stations in these towns, when they exist, are far from the historic centers, run infrequently, and are slow. Visit the Web site of FS, the Italian State Railway, for schedules and booking.

🛈 **Train Information FS** 🕾 892021 ⊕ www.trenitalia.com.

Contacts & Resources

EMERGENCIES

Pharmacies stay open at off hours on a rotating basis. To find out who's open, check the schedule posted in all pharmacy windows.

🔢 **Ambulance, medical emergency** ☎ 118. **Police, fire** ☎ 113.

TOURS

From Florence, American Express operates one-day excursions to Siena and San Gimignano and can arrange for cars, drivers, and guides for special-interest tours in Tuscany. Another option is the Florence-based, American-owned and -operated Custom Travel and Special Events, which runs day trips into Chianti wine country and other selected spots in Tuscany.

🔢 Fees & Schedules **American Express** ⊠ Via Dante Alighieri 22/r, Florence ☎ 055/50981. **Custom Travel and Special Events** ⊠ Via dell'Ardiglione 19, Florence ☎ 055/264-5526 ⊕ www.customitaly.com.

TRAVEL AGENCIES

🔢 Local Agent Referrals **American Express** ⊠ Via Dante Alighieri 22, Florence ☎ 055/50981. **Artemisia** ⊠ Via Soccorso Saloni 7, Montalcino ☎ 0577/846021 🖨 0577/846020 ⊕ www.artemisiaviaggi.it. **CIT Italia** ⊠ Piazza Stazione 51/r, Florence ☎ 055/284145. **Solimano Viaggi** ⊠ Via Don Minzoni 29, Volterra ☎ 0588/81364 🖨 0588/81356.

VISITOR INFORMATION

🔢 Agritourist Information **Terranostra** ⊠ Villa Demidoff 64/d, 50122 Florence ☎ 055/3245011 ⊕ www.terranostra.it.

🔢 Tourist Information **Arezzo** ⊠ Piazza della Repubblica 28 ☎ 0575/377678 ⊕ www.apt.arezzo.it. **Colle Val d'Elsa** ⊠ Via F. Campana 43 ☎ 0577/922791. **Cortona** ⊠ Via Nazionale 42 ☎ 0575/630352 ⊕ www.cortonaweb.net. **Greve in Chianti** ⊠ Piazza Ferrante Mori 1, by the post office ☎ 055/8546299 ⊕ www.chiantislowtravel.it. **Lucca** ⊠ Piazzale Verdi ☎ 0583/583150 ⊕ www.luccatourist.it. **Montalcino** ⊠ Costa del Municipio 1 ☎ 0577/849331 ⊕ www.prolocomontalcino.it. **Montepulciano** ⊠ Piazza Don Minzoni 1 ☎ 0578/757341 ⊕ www.prolocomontepulciano.it. **Pienza** ⊠ Corso Rossellino 51 ☎ 0578/8749071 ⊕ www.infinito.it/utenti/ufficio.turistico. **Pisa** ⊠ Piazza del Duomo ☎ 050/560464 ⊕ www.pisa.turismo.toscana.it. **Pistoia** ⊠ Palazzo dei Vescovi, Via Roma 1 ☎ 0573/21622 ⊕ www.pistoia.turismo.toscana.it. **Prato** ⊠ Piazza delle Carceri 15 ☎ 0574/24112 ⊕ www.prato.turismo.toscana.it. **Radda in Chianti** ⊠ Piazza Castello 1 ☎ 0577/738494. **San Gimignano** ⊠ Piazza del Duomo 1 ☎ 0577/940008 ⊕ www.sangimignano.com. **San Miniato** ⊠ Piazza del Popolo 1 ☎ 0571/42745 ⊕ www.cittadisanminiato.it. **Siena** ⊠ Piazza del Campo 56 ☎ 0577/280551 ⊕ www.terresiena.it; www.comune.siena.it. **Volterra** ⊠ Piazza dei Priori 20 ☎ 0588/87257 ⊕ www.volterratour.it.

WELCOME TO UMBRIA & THE MARCHES

Todi

TOP 5
Reasons to Go

❶ **Palazzo Ducale, Urbino:** A visit here reveals more about the ideals of the Renaissance than a shelfful of history books.

❷ **Assisi, shrine to St. Francis:** Recharge your soul in this rose-color hill town with a visit to the gentle saint's majestic Basilica, adorned with great frescoes.

❸ **Spoleto, Umbria's musical Mecca:** Crowds may descend and prices ascend here during summer's Festival dei Due Mondi, but Spoleto's hushed charm enchants year-round.

❹ **Tantalizing truffles:** Are Umbria's celebrated "black diamonds" coveted for their pungent flavor, their rarity, or their power in the realm of romance?

❺ **Orvieto's Duomo:** Arresting visions of heaven and hell on the facade and brilliant frescoes within make this Gothic cathedral a dazzler.

Many Umbrian towns are set atop hills, providing magnificent views—none more so than from **Assisi**—sanctified by St. Francis—and from the Piazza della Signoria in medieval **Gubbio**, the "City of Silence."

Umbria's largest town, **Perugia,** is easily reachable from Rome, Siena, or Florence. Home to some of Perugino's great frescoes and a hilltop *centro storico*, it is also beloved by chocoholics: "Kisses"—the hazelnut Baci candies—were born here.

In southern Umbria, the town of **Orvieto** is famed for its cathedral, its dry white wines, and its spectacular hilltop location. To the east is the village of **Todi,** another historic jewel.

Duomo , Orvieto   Perugia

TUSCANY

Sansepolcro

Città Di Castello

E45

Lago Di Trasimeno

Perugia

71

UMBRIA

448

Todi

A1

Orvieto

LAZIO

Umbria &
the Marches

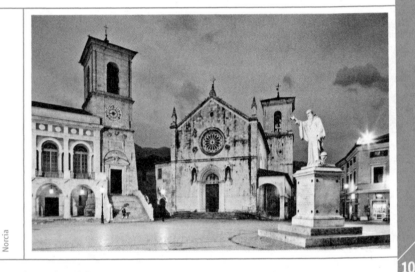

Norcia

WORD OF MOUTH

"I would suggest the Marches as a great, off-the-beaten-path region to visit. It has a very beautiful landscape and is just as central as Tuscany and Umbria (although, unlike Umbria, it has a coastline, and a nice one at that)."

—Jackie in Italy

Getting Oriented

Central Italy doesn't begin and end with Tuscany; the pastoral, hilly provinces of Umbria and the Marches pick up where the more famous neighbor leaves off. Divided by the Apennine range, both regions are studded with Renaissance-era villages and fortresses—a landscape hallowed by St. Francis and immortalized in the works of native son Raphael.

The steep, twisting roads of the **Marches** lead to well-preserved medieval towns before settling down to the sandy beaches of the Adriatic. Here you'll find **Urbino,** the best surviving example of the ideal Renaissance city.

Spoleto offers much more than Puccini on its Piazza del Duomo every summer: there are Filippo Lippi frescoes in the cathedral, a massive castle towering over the town, and a bridge across the neighboring valley that's an engineering marvel.

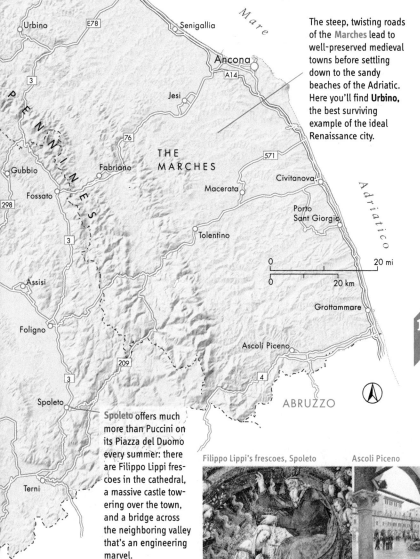

Filippo Lippi's frescoes, Spoleto

Ascoli Piceno

UMBRIA &
THE MARCHES
PLANNER

Making the Most of Your Time

Umbria is a nicely compact collection of character-rich hill towns; you can settle in one, then explore the others, as well as the countryside and forest in between, on day trips.

Perugia, Umbria's largest and most lively city, is a logical choice for your base, particularly if you're arriving from the north. If you want something a little quieter, virtually any other town in the region will suit your purposes; even Assisi, which overflows with bus tours during the day, is delightfully quiet in the evening and early morning. Spoleto and Orvieto are the most developed town to the south, but they're still of modest proportions.

If you have the time to venture farther afield, consider trips to Gubbio, northeast of Perugia, and Urbino, in the Marches. Both are worth the time it takes to reach them, and both make for pleasant overnight stays. In southern Umbria, Valernia and the Piano Grande are out-of-the-way spots with the region's best hiking.

Getting Around

Umbria and the Marches are mountainous regions divided by the Apennines, Italy's backbone. The main geographic difference is that Umbria's valleys run north to south, while those in the Marches run east to west. As a result, travel through Umbria is much easier in a north–south direction; in the Marches, the only easy going north to south is along the coast. Crossing from valley to valley in either region involves slow, winding, sometimes treacherous roads that can occasionally be closed by snow in December and January.

Buses run throughout the region, but some routes in rural areas, especially in the Marches, are designed to serve as many destinations as possible, making for a slow trip. There's frequent train service to Orvieto (which is on the main Florence-Rome line), Perugia, and Assisi, and many towns are accessible on regional lines—though Gubbio and Urbino are not. For more about car, bus, and train travel, see "Essentials" at the end of this chapter.

What to Bring Home: Umbrian Ceramics

The most celebrated Umbrian export (and souvenir) is pottery, and Deruta, south of Torgiano on S3bis, is Umbria's pottery-making capital. Flamboyant designs fill the town's multitude of shops, and there's a fine museum displaying examples of ceramics dating back to the Renaissance. Gubbio also has a pottery tradition—its red glazes have been renowned since medieval times. The secret of the original glaze died with its inventor some 500 years ago, but the town's present-day potters produce a fair facsimile.

Festivals to Plan a Trip Around

Each summer Umbria hosts two of Italy's biggest music festivals. Spoleto's **Festival dei Due Mondi** (www. spoletofestival.it), from mid-June through mid-July, features classical music and also ventures into theater and the visual arts. Perugia is hopping for 10 days in July, when famous names in contemporary music perform at the **Umbria Jazz Festival** (www. umbriajazz.com).

If you want to attend either event, you should make arrangements in advance … and if you don't want to attend, you should plan to avoid the cities during festival time, when hotel rooms and restaurant tables are at a premium. A similar caveat applies for Assisi during religious festivals at Christmas, Easter, the feast of St. Francis (October 4), and Calendimaggio (May 1), when pilgrims arrive en masse.

If you've got a sweet tooth and you're visiting during the fall, head to Perugia for the **Eurochocolate Festival** (www. eurochocolate. perugia.it) in the third week of October.

How's the Weather?

The forested hills of Umbria and the Marches are marked by rich fall colors and an explosion of greenery in spring, making those two seasons prime visiting time. Fall and winter are longer and colder here than in nearby Rome; you'll want to have warm clothes with you as early as October and as late as April. The consolation is that winter is the best season for the region's cuisine: January to April is truffle season in Norcia and Spoleto, and October to December brings a bounty of fresh local mushrooms. Summer, when the top of Monte Subasio and the Piano Grande are blanketed with wildflowers, is an excellent time for a hiking trip.

Finding a Place to Stay

Virtually every older town in Umbria and the Marches, no matter how small, has some kind of hotel. A trend in Umbria, particularly around Gubbio, Orvieto, and Todi, is to convert old villas, farms, and monasteries into first-class hotels. The natural splendor of the countryside more than compensates for the distance from town—provided you have a car. Hotels in town tend to be simpler than their country cousins, with a few notable exceptions in Spoleto, Gubbio, and Perugia.

10

Dining & Lodging Price Categories

WHAT IT COSTS in Euros					
	$$$$	**$$$**	**$$**	**$**	**¢**
Restaurants	over €22	€16–€22	€11–€16	€7–€11	under €7
Hotels	over €220	€160–€220	€110–€160	€70–€110	under €70

Restaurant prices are for a second course (un secondo). Hotel prices are for two people in a standard double room in high season, including tax and service.

TOP PASSEGGIATA

Perugia's stately, palace-lined Corso Vannucci is where residents of Umbria's capital stretch their legs in style before dinner.

BIRTHPLACE OF SAINTS and home to some of the country's greatest artistic treasures, central Italy is a collection of misty green valleys and picture-perfect hill towns laden with centuries of history. Umbria and the Marches are the Italian countryside as you've imagined it: verdant farmland, steep hillsides topped with fairy-tale fortresses, winding country roads traveled by horses and Fiat 500s carrying crates of fresh olives. No single town here has the extravagant wealth of art and architecture of Florence, Rome, or Venice, but this works in your favor: small jewels of towns feel knowable, not overwhelming. And the cultural cupboard is far from bare. Orvieto's cathedral and Assisi's basilica are two of the most important sights in Italy, while Perugia, Todi, Gubbio, and Spoleto are rich in art and architecture.

East of Umbria, the Marches (Le Marche to Italians) stretch between the Apennines and the Adriatic Sea. It's a region of great turreted castles on high peaks defending passes and roads—a testament to the centuries of battle that have taken place here. Rising majestically in Urbino is a splendid palace, built by Federico da Montefeltro, where the humanistic ideals of the Renaissance came to their fullest flower, while the town of Ascoli Piceno can lay claim to one of the most beautiful squares in Italy. Virtually every small town in the region has a castle, church, or museum worth a visit—but even without them, you'd still be compelled to stop for the interesting streets, panoramic views, and natural beauty.

PERUGIA

The painter Perugino (the Perugian) filled his work with images of his home: soft hills with sparse trees, wide plains dotted with lakes. Despite the development of undistinguished modern suburbs, this peaceful landscape still survives, and venerable Perugia's medieval hilltop city remains almost completely intact. Perugia is the best-preserved hill town of its size; there are few better examples of the self-contained city-state that so shaped the course of Italian history. Little remains of Perugia's earliest ancestors, although the Arco di Augusto (Arch of Augustus) in Piazza Fortebraccio, the northern entrance to the city, is of Etruscan origin.

Exploring Perugia

The best approach to the city is by train—the station is in the unlovely suburbs, but there are frequent buses running directly to Piazza d'Italia, the heart of the old town. If you are driving, leave your car in one of the parking lots near the station and then take the bus or the escalator, which passes through subterranean excavations of the city's Roman foundations, from Piazza Partigiani to the Rocca Paolina. A half day is sufficient to visit the major sights in the center of town.

The Main Attractions

 Collegio del Cambio. The series of elaborate rooms at Bankers' Guild Hall housed the meeting hall and chapel of the guild of bankers and money changers. The walls were frescoed from 1496 to 1500 by the most important Perugian painter of the Renaissance, Pietro Vannucci, better known as Perugino (circa 1450–1523). The iconography prevalent in the works includes common religious themes, like the Nativity and the Transfiguration (on the end walls), but also figures intended to inspire the businessmen who congregated here. On the left wall are female figures representing the Virtues, beneath them the heroes and sages of antiquity. On the right wall are the prophets and sibyls. Perugino's most famous pupil, Raffaello Sanzio, or Raphael (1483–1520), is said to have painted here, his hand, experts say, most apparent in the figure of Fortitude. On one of the pilasters is a remarkably honest self-portrait of Perugino, surmounted by a Latin inscription. The Collegio is on the ground floor of the Palazzo dei Priori, and is entered from Corso Vannucci. ⊠ *Corso Vannucci 25* ☏ *075/5728599* 💶 *€2.60* ⊙ *Daily 9–1 and 2:30–5:30.*

Corso Vannucci. The heart of the city is the broad stately pedestrian street that runs from Piazza d'Italia to Piazza IV Novembre. As evening falls, Corso Vannucci is filled with Perugians out for their evening *passeggiata,* a pleasant predinner stroll that may include a pause for an *aperitivo* (aperitif) at one of the many cafés that line the street.

❸ **Galleria Nazionale dell'Umbria.** On the fourth floor of the ⇨ **Palazzo dei Priori** is the region's most comprehensive art gallery. Well-placed infor-

UMBRIA THROUGH THE AGES

The earliest inhabitants of Umbria, the Umbri, were thought by the Romans to be the most ancient inhabitants of Italy. Little is known about them; with the coming of Etruscan culture the tribe fled into the mountains in the eastern portion of the region. The Etruscans, who founded some of the great cities of Umbria, were in turn supplanted by the Romans. Unlike Tuscany and other regions of central Italy, Umbria had few powerful medieval families to exert control over the cities in the Middle Ages—its proximity to Rome ensured that it would always be more or less under papal domination.

In the center of the country, Umbria has for much of its history been a battlefield where armies from north and south clashed. Hannibal destroyed a Roman army on the shores of Lake Trasimeno, and the bloody course of the interminable Guelph-Ghibelline conflict of the Middle Ages was played out here. Dante considered Umbria the most violent place in Italy. Trophies of war still decorate the Palazzo dei Priori in Perugia, and the little town of Gubbio continues a warlike rivalry begun in the Middle Ages—every year it challenges the Tuscan town of Sansepolcro to a crossbow tournament. Today the bowmen shoot at targets, but neither side has forgotten that 500 years ago its ancestors shot at each other. In spite of—or perhaps because of—this bloodshed, Umbria has produced more than its share of Christian saints. The most famous is St. Francis, the decidedly pacifist saint whose life shaped the Church of his time. His great shrine at Assisi is visited by hundreds of thousands of pilgrims each year. St. Clare, his devoted follower, was Umbria-born, as were St. Benedict, St. Rita of Cascia, and the patron saint of lovers, St. Valentine.

mation panels (in Italian and English) describe work by native artists—most notably Pinturicchio (1454–1513) and Perugino—along with others of the Umbrian and Tuscan schools. The gallery also exhibits frescoes, sculptures, and several superb painted crucifixes from the 13th and 14th centuries; other rooms are dedicated to Perugia itself, illustrating the evolution of the medieval city. The last entry is a half hour before closing, and the gallery is closed the first Monday of the month. ⊠ *Corso Vannucci 19, Piazza IV Novembre* ☎ *075/5721009* ⊕ *www. gallerianazionaledellumbria.it* ✎ *€6.50* ☉ *Daily 8:30–7:30.*

★ ❷ **Palazzo dei Priori.** The imposing palace, begun in the 13th century, has an unusual staircase that fans out into Piazza IV Novembre. The facade is decorated with symbols of Perugia's former power: the griffin is the city's symbol; the lion denotes Perugia's allegiance to the medieval Guelph (or papal) cause. Both figures support the heavy chains of the gates of Siena, which fell to Perugian forces in 1358. Most of the building now houses the town's municipal offices, which are not open to tourists, with access permitted only to the fourth floor ⇨ **Galleria Nazionale dell'Umbria.** ⊠ *Corso Vannucci 19* ☎ *075/5771.*

Also Worth Seeing

❶ Duomo. This church's prize relic is the Virgin Mary's wedding ring, stolen in 1488 from the nearby town of Chiusi. The ring, kept in a chapel on the left aisle, is the size of a large bangle and is kept under lock—15 locks actually—and key year-round except July 30 and the second-to-last Sunday in January. The first date commemorates the day the ring was brought to Perugia, the second Mary's wedding anniversary. The cathedral itself is large and rather plain, dating from the Middle Ages but with many additions from the 15th and 16th centuries. There are some elaborately carved choir stalls, executed by Giovanni Battista Bastone in 1520. Precious objects associated with the cathedral are on display at the associated **Museo Capitolare,** including vestments, vessels, manuscripts, and gold work. An early masterpiece by Luca Signorelli (circa 1450–1523) is the altarpiece showing the Madonna with St. John the Baptist, St. Onophrio, and St. Lawrence (1484). Note that sections of the church may be closed to visitors during religious services and the last admission is a half hour before closing. ☒ *Piazza IV Novembre* ☎ *075/5723832* 🎫 *Duomo free, museum €3* ☉ *Duomo Mon.–Sat. 7–12:30 and 4–6:45, Sun. 8–12:30 and 4–6:45; museum daily 10–1 and 4–6.*

La Città della Domenica. Umbria's only attraction aimed directly at the younger set is this theme park–like complex. Five hundred acres contain buildings based on fairy tales—Snow White's House, the Witches' Wood—as well as a reptile house, aquarium, medieval museum, exhibit of shells from all over the world, game rooms, and a choice of restaurants. Entrance is free for children under four years of age. West from Perugia, take the secondary road that leads to Corciano. ☒ *Via Col di Tenda 140, Località Montepulito, 8 km (5 mi) west of Perugia* ☎ *075/5054941* 🎫 *€10* ☉ *Easter–mid-Sept., daily 10–7; mid-Sept.–Oct., weekends 10–7; Nov.–Easter, aquarium and reptile house only, Sat. 2–7, Sun. 10–7.*

❺ Museo Archeologico Nazionale. Perugia was a flourishing Etruscan site long before it fell under Roman domination in 310 BC. This museum next to the imposing church of San Domenico contains an excellent collection of Etruscan artifacts from throughout the region. ☒ *Piazza G. Bruno 10* ☎ *075/5727141* ⊕ *www.archeopg.arti.beniculturali.it* 🎫 *€4* ☉ *Mon. 2:30–7:30, Tues.–Sun. 8:30–7:30.*

Where to Stay & Eat

$$ ✕ **La Taverna.** Medieval steps lead to a rustic two-story restaurant where wine bottles and artful clutter decorate the walls. Good choices from the regional menu include *caramelle al gorgonzola* (pasta rolls filled with red cabbage and mozzarella with a Gorgonzola sauce) and grilled meat dishes, such as the *medaglioni di vitello al tartuffo* (grilled veal with truffles). ☒ *Via delle Streghe 8, off Corso Vannucci* ☎ *075/5724128* 🖃 *AE, DC, MC, V* ☉ *Closed Mon.*

$–$$ ✕ **Il Falchetto.** Exceptional food at reasonable prices makes this Perugia's best bargain. Service is smart but relaxed in the two medieval dining rooms that put the kitchen and chef on view. The house specialty is

10

EATING WELL IN UMBRIA & THE MARCHES

Central Italy is mountainous, and its food is hearty and straightforward, with a stick-to-the-ribs quality that sees hardworking farmers and artisans through a long day's work and helps them make the steep climb home at night. The region has made several important contributions to Italian cuisine. Particularly prized are winter's *tartufi neri* (black truffles) from the area around Spoleto and from the hills around the tiny town of Norcia. The delicacy shows up on menus stuffed in ravioli, layered in lasagna, and mixed with risotto. Local pasta specialties, such as thick, handmade *ciriole* (roughly shaped, fat spaghetti) or *strangozzi* (long, thin pasta)—also spelled *stringozzi* or *strengozzi*—are even better prepared *al tartufo*, enriched with excellent local olive oil and truffles. Norcia's pork products—especially sausages, salami, and *arista* (roast loin perfumed with rosemary)—are so famous that pork butchers throughout Italy are called *norcini*, and pork butcher shops are called *norcinerie*. Bakeries and storefronts sell *torta al testo* in Umbria, and *crescie* in the Marches. Both are traditional forms of flat, pitalike bread that can be filled to order with various combinations of meat, cheese, and vegetables, and make for delicious light meals.

falchetti (homemade gnocchi with spinach and ricotta cheese). ⊠ *Via Bartolo 20* ☎ *075/5731775* 🖃 *AE, DC, MC, V* ☺ *Closed Mon. and last 2 wks in Jan.*

★ ¢ ✗ **Dal Mi' Cocco.** A great favorite with Perugia's university students, this is a fun, crowded, and truly inexpensive place to enjoy a multicourse fixed-price meal (€13). You may find yourself seated at a long table with other diners, but some language help from your neighbors could come in handy—the menu is in pure Perugian dialect. Meals change with the seasons, and each day of the week brings some new creation *dal cocco* (from the "coconut," or head) of the chef. ⊠ *Corso Garibaldi 12* ☎ *075/5732511* 🖎 *Reservations essential* 🖃 *No credit cards* ☺ *Closed Mon. and July 25–Aug. 15.*

$$$$ 🏨 **Brufani Palace.** A 19th-century palazzo has been turned into an elegant lodging choice. The Brufani's public rooms and first-floor guest rooms have high ceilings and are done in grand belle epoque style. Second-floor rooms are more modern; many on both floors have a marvelous view of the Umbrian countryside or the city. ⊠ *Piazza d'Italia 12, 06121* ☎ *075/5732541* 🖎 *075/5720210* ⊕ *www.brufanipalace. com* 🛏 *63 rooms, 31 suites* ♿ *Restaurant, pool, gym, bar, meeting rooms* 🖃 *AE, DC, MC, V* 🍽 *BP.*

$$$ 🏨 **Locanda della Posta.** Reside at the center of Perugia's old district in an 18th-century palazzo. Renovation has left the reception and other public areas rather bland, but the rooms, all of which are carpeted, are tastefully and soothingly decorated in muted colors. Though soundproof, rooms at the front of the hotel face the busy Corso Vannucci and should be avoided in favor of those on the upper floors at the back

of the building, which also have great views. ⊠ *Corso Vannucci 97, 06121* ☎ *075/5728925* 🖷 *075/5732562* 📞 *38 rooms, 1 suite* ♨ *Minibars, bar, parking (fee)* 🚍 *AE, DC, MC, V* 🍽 *BP.*

$ 🏨 **Hotel Fortuna.** The elegant furnishings in this friendly hotel complement the 18th-century frescoes that decorate several of the guest rooms. Some rooms have balconies. The building itself, just out of sight of Corso Vannucci, dates back to the 1300s. ⊠ *Via Bonazzi 19, 06123* ☎ *075/ 5722845* 🖷 *075/5735040* ⊕ *www.umbriahotels.com* 📞 *51 rooms* ♨ *Some in-room hot tubs, minibars, cable TV, bar, meeting rooms, parking (fee)* 🚍 *AE, DC, MC, V* 🍽 *BP.*

¢ 🏨 **Rosalba.** Here's a bright and friendly choice with scrupulously clean, basic rooms; the ones at the back enjoy a view. On the top floor, Room 9 has a private terrace and sleeps up to five people, making it perfect for a family or group of friends. Although somewhat out of the way, the hotel is only a matter of minutes from Corso Vannucci by virtue of a nearby public escalator stop. ⊠ *Via del Circo 7, 06100* ☎ *075/ 5728285* 🖷 *075/5720626* 📞 *11 rooms* ♨ *Free parking; no room TVs* 🚍 *No credit cards* 🍽 *EP.*

Nightlife & the Arts

The monthly *Viva Perugia* (sold at newsstands), with a section in English, is a good source of information about what's going on in town. Summer sees several music festivals in Perugia. The **Festival delle Nazioni di Musica da Camera** (International Chamber Music Festival ⊠ On S3bis, 80 km (50 mi) north of Perugia, Città di Castello ☎ 075/8521142 🖷 075/8552461) is a two-week event held in late August and early September. **Sagra Musicale Umbra** (☎ 075/5732800 ⊕ www.umbria.org/eng/ eventi) celebrates the traditional music of the region at performances during 10 days in September. The **Umbria Jazz Festival** (☎ 075/5732432 🖷 075/572256 ⊕ www.umbriajazz.com) a world-famous concert series lasts for 10 days in July.

Shopping

Judging by the expensive shops around the Corso Vannucci, the Perugians are not afraid to part with their euros. Clothing shops selling Italian designers such as Gucci, Ferragamo, Armani, and Fendi line the streets. The town is also known for its famous Perugina chocolate, although the brand (a Nestlé company since the early 1990s) is easily found throughout Italy. *Cioccolato al latte* (milk chocolate) and *fondente* (dark chocolate) are sold in tiny jewel-like containers, and in giant boxes the size of serving trays, all over town. Round hazelnut-filled chocolate candies, *baci* (literally, "kisses"), come wrapped in silver foil and, like fortune cookies, contain romantic sayings in several languages, English included.

The third week in October is especially sweet, when Perugia hosts the **Eurochocolate Festival** (☎ 075/5732670 ⊕ www.eurochocolate.perugia. it) and the streets are filled with stands, sculptures, and—best of all—tastings.

ASSISI

Assisi, 47 km (30 mi) north of Spoleto and 25 km (16 mi) east of Perugia, began as an Umbri settlement in the 7th century BC and was conquered by the Romans 400 years later, following the pattern of most towns in the region. It was Christianized by St. Rufino, its patron saint, in AD 238, but it is the spirit of St. Francis, patron saint of Italy, that is felt throughout the narrow medieval streets. The famous 13th-century basilica built in his honor was decorated by the greatest artists of the period. Assisi is pristinely medieval in architecture and appearance, due in large part to relative neglect from the 16th century until 1926, when the celebration of the 700th anniversary of St. Francis's death brought more than 2 million visitors. Since then, Assisi has become one of the most important pilgrimage destinations in the Christian world.

Exploring Assisi

The train station is 4 km (2½ mi) from town, with bus service about every half hour. The walled town is closed to outside traffic, so cars must be left in the parking lots at Porta San Pietro, near Porta Nuova, or beneath Piazza Matteotti. Frequent minibuses run between the parking lots and the center of town. You can see the major sights in Assisi in half a day, but set aside more time if you want to fully explore the town.

What to See

Eremo delle Carceri. In the caves on the slope of Monte Subasio, Francis and his followers established their first home, to which he returned often. The church and monastery—in dense woodlands—retain a tranquil, contemplative air. True to their Franciscan heritage, the friars here are entirely dependent on alms from visitors. ☒ *Via Santuario delle Carceri, 4 km (2½ mi) east of Assisi* ☎ *075/812301* ✉ *Donations accepted* ☼ *Nov.–Mar., daily 6:30–5; Apr.–Oct., daily 6:30* AM*–7* PM.

❼ San Rufino. St. Francis and St. Clare were among those baptized in Assisi's Duomo, the principal church in town until the 12th century. The baptismal font has since been redecorated, but it is possible to see the **crypt** of San Rufino, the martyred 3rd-century bishop who brought Christianity to Assisi. Admission to the crypt includes a look at the small **Museo Capitolare** and its detached frescoes and artifacts. ☒ *Piazza San Rufino* ☎ *075/812283* ✉ *Duomo free, crypt and museum €2.07* ☼ *Duomo daily 7–noon and 2–sunset; crypt and museum Mar. 16–Oct. 15, daily 10–1 and 2–5; Oct. 16–Mar. 15, daily 10:30–1 and 3–6.*

❽ Santa Chiara. This striking red-striped 13th-century church is dedicated to St. Clare, one of the earliest and most fervent of St. Francis's followers and the founder of the Order of Poor Clares, in imitation of the Franciscans. The church contains the body of the saint, and in the **Cappella del Crocifisso** is the crucifix that spoke to St. Francis and led him to a life of piety. A heavily veiled member of St. Clare's order is stationed before the cross in perpetual adoration of the image. ☒ *Piazza Santa Chiara* ☎ *075/812282* ☼ *Daily 7–noon and 2–sunset.*

Assisi

Basilica di San Francesco

Rocca Maggiore

Anfiteatro Romano

TO EREMO DELLE CARCERI

Porto Nuova

TO SAN DAMIANO

San Pietro

TO STAZIONE CENTRALE

TO SANTA MARIA DEGLI ANGELI

KEY

Steps

0   200 yards
0   200 meters

San Rufino **7**
Santa Chiara **8**
Tempio di Minerva **6**

Santa Maria degli Angeli. The shrine here is much venerated because it was in the **Cappella del Transito,** then a humble cell, that St. Francis died in 1226. This baroque church is built over the **Porziuncola,** a chapel restored by St. Francis. It's on the outskirts of town, near the train station. ⊠ *Località Santa Maria degli Angeli* ⊙ *Daily 7 AM–sunset.*

❻ Tempio di Minerva. Pieces of a Roman temple dating from the time of Augustus (63 BC–AD 14) make up this sanctuary dedicated to the goddess of wisdom. The expectations raised by the perfect classical facade are not met by the interior, subjected to a thorough baroque assault in the 17th century, but both are worth a look. ⊠ *Piazza del Comune* ⊙ *Daily 7–noon and 2:30–sunset.*

off the
beaten
path

CANNARA – A pleasant excursion 16 km (10 mi) southwest of Assisi leads to this tiny town; a half-hour's walk then brings you to the fields of Pian d'Arca, the legendary site of St. Francis's sermon to the birds. The first week of September the town's *Sagra della Cipolla* (Onion Festival) is in full swing, with everything from soup to ice-cream flavored with the town's favorite vegetable. *Pro Loco tourist office* ⊠ *Piazza Umberto I* ☎ *0742/72177.*

Where to Stay & Eat

Advance room reservations are absolutely essential if you are visiting Assisi between Easter and October or during Christmastime; latecomers are often left to choose from lodging in modern Santa Maria degli Angeli, 8 km (5 mi) out of town. Ask at the Assisi **tourist office** for a list of pilgrim hostels, an interesting and economical alternative to conventional lodgings. Private convents, churches, or other Catholic organizations run these *ostelli* (hostels) or *conventi* (convents). Rooms are on the spartan side, but you are virtually assured of a peaceful night's stay (€20–€32). ⊠ *Piazza del Comune 12, 06081* ☎ *075/812534* ⊕ *www.comune.assisi.pg.it.*

$–$$ ✕ **Buca di San Francesco.** In summer dine in a cool green garden; in winter under the low brick arches of the restaurant's cozy cellars: no wonder this central restaurant is Assisi's busiest. The food is first-rate, too. Try spaghetti *alla buca,* homemade pasta served with a roasted mushroom sauce. ⊠ *Via Brizi 1* ☎ *075/812204* ⊟ *AE, DC, MC, V* ⊙ *Closed Mon. and July.*

$ ✕ **La Fortezza.** Romans built parts of the walls that make up this family-run restaurant. The service is personable and the kitchen reliable. A particular standout is *anatra al finocchio selvatico* (duck with wild fennel). La Fortezza also has seven simple but clean guest rooms available. ⊠ *Vicolo della Fortezza 2/b* ☎ *075/812418* ⌂ *Reservations essential* ⊟ *AE, DC, MC, V* ⊙ *Closed Thurs. and Feb.*

★ ¢–$ ✕ **Osteria Piazzetta dell'Erba.** Avoid stodgy tourist eateries and come here for an informal meal or a light snack. There are two different *primi piatti* (first courses) every day, along with various salads and a good se-

Continued on page 503

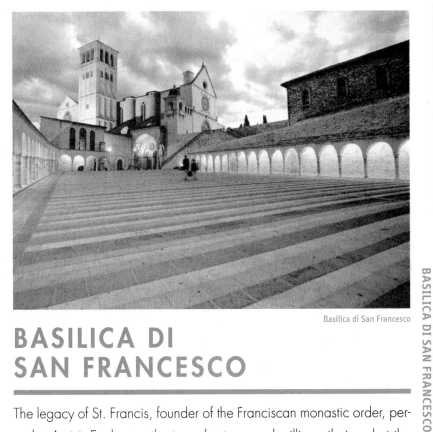

Basilica di San Francesco

BASILICA DI SAN FRANCESCO

The legacy of St. Francis, founder of the Franciscan monastic order, pervades Assisi. Each year the town hosts several million pilgrims, but the steady flow of visitors does nothing to diminish the singular beauty of one of Italy's most important religious centers. The pilgrims' ultimate destination is the massive Basilica di San Francesco, which sits halfway up Assisi's hill, supported by graceful arches.

The basilica is not one church but two. The Romanesque **Lower Church** came first; construction began in 1228, just two years after St. Francis's death, and was completed within a few years. The low ceilings and candlelit interior make an appropriately solemn setting for St. Francis's tomb, found in the crypt below the main altar. The Gothic **Upper Church**, built only half a century later, sits on top of the lower one, and is strikingly different, with soaring arches and tall stained-glass windows (the first in Italy). Inside, both churches are covered floor to ceiling with some of Europe's finest frescoes: the Lower Church is dim and full of candlelit shadows, and the Upper Church is bright and airy.

VISITING THE BASILICA

THE LOWER CHURCH

The most evocative way to experience the basilica is to begin with the dark Lower Church. As you enter, give your eyes a moment to adjust. Keep in mind that the artists at work here were conscious of the shadowy environment—they knew this was how their frescoes would be seen.

In the first chapel to the left, a superb fresco cycle by Simone Martini depicts scenes from the life of St. Martin. As you approach the main altar, the vaulting above you is decorated with the *Three Virtues of St. Francis* (poverty, chastity, and obedience) and *St. Francis's Triumph*, frescoes attributed to Giotto's followers. In the transept to your left, Pietro Lorenzetti's *Madonna and Child with St. Francis and St. John* sparkles when the sun hits it. Notice Mary's thumb; legend has it Jesus is asking which saint to bless, and Mary is pointing to Francis. Across the way in the right transept, Cimabue's *Madonna Enthroned Among Angels and St. Francis* is a famous portrait of the saint. Surrounding the portrait are painted scenes from the childhood of Christ, done by the assis-

tants of Giotto. Nearby is a painting of the crucifixion attributed to Giotto himself.

You reach the crypt via stairs midway along the nave—on the crypt's altar, a stone coffin holds the saint's body. Steps up from the church's transepts lead to the cloister, where there's a gift shop, and the treasury, which contains a collection of holy objects.

THE UPPER CHURCH

The St. Francis fresco cycle is the highlight of the Upper Church. (See facing page.) Also worth special note is the 16th-century choir, with its remarkably delicate inlaid wood. When a 1997 earthquake rocked the basilica, the St. Francis cycle sustained little damage, but portions of the ceiling above the entrance and altar collapsed, reducing their frescoes (attributed to Cimabue and Giotto) to rubble. The painstaking restoration is ongoing. ⚠ The dress code is strictly enforced—no bare shoulders or bare knees. Piazza di San Francesco, 075/819001, Lower Church Easter–Oct., daily 6 AM–6:50 PM; Nov.–Easter, daily 6–5:50. Upper Church Easter–Oct., daily 8:30–6:50; Nov.–Easter, daily 8:30–5:50.

FRANCIS, ITALY'S PATRON SAINT

PREGANDO ASPETTERO' CHE TORNI

St. Francis was born in Assisi in 1181, the son of a noblewoman and a well-to-do merchant. His troubled youth included a year in prison. He planned a military career, but after a long illness Francis heard the voice of God, renounced his father's wealth, and began a life of austerity. His mystical embrace of poverty, asceticism, and the beauty of man and nature struck a responsive chord in the medieval mind; he quickly attracted a vast number of followers. Francis was the first saint to receive the stigmata (wounds in his hands, feet, and side corresponding to those of Christ on the cross). He died on October 4, 1226, in the Porziuncola, the secluded chapel in the woods where he had first preached the virtue of poverty to his disciples. St. Francis was declared patron saint of Italy in 1939, and today the Franciscans make up the largest of the Catholic orders.

THE UPPER CHURCH'S ST. FRANCIS FRESCO CYCLE

The 28 frescoes in the Upper Church depicting the life of St. Francis are the most admired works in the entire basilica. They're also the subject of one of art history's biggest controversies. For centuries they were thought to be by Giotto (1267-1337), the great early-Renaissance innovator, but inconsistencies in style, both within this series and in comparison to later Giotto works, have thrown their origin into question. Some scholars now say Giotto was the brains behind the cycle, but that assistants helped with the execution; others claim he couldn't have been involved at all.

Two things are certain. First, the style is revolutionary, which argues for Giotto's involvement. The tangible weight of the figures, the emotion they show, and the use of perspective all look familiar to modern eyes, but in the art of the time there was nothing like it. Second, these images have played a major part in shaping how the world sees St. Francis. In that respect, who painted them hardly matters.

Starting in the transept, the frescoes circle the church, showing events in the saint's life (and afterlife). Some of the best are grouped near the church's entrance—look for the nativity at Greccio, the miracle of the spring, the death of the knight at Celano, and, most famously, the sermon to the birds.

BASILICA DI SAN FRANCESCO

10

Basilica di San Francesco

VOICES OF ITALY

Sister Marcellina, Order of St. Bridget

Sister Marcellina of the Order of St. Bridget talks about her life in Assisi, where she and 11 other sisters live in a convent and guesthouse on the outskirts of the town:

"Before coming to Assisi, I lived in various countries. I've lived in India, and in England, and been to Holland, to Sweden, and to Finland, as well as lived in Rome. But Assisi is the place that I would never want to change for any other. I don't know, I think there is something very special about this place. I've been here 13 years now, and each year I pray that I won't be sent somewhere else. I'm very happy here.

"I like the atmosphere of Assisi, it's very friendly, and of course with St. Francis and St. Claire, but especially St. Francis, there is a simplicity to life that I like very much. Even though I'm in the Order of St. Bridget, living here I feel very much a part of Franciscan spirituality. There is also a very strong ecumenical feeling to Assisi and this is very nice. There are over 60 different religious

communities, with people from all over the world. And even though they come from different religious backgrounds they still feel a part of Assisi. Living here, you don't see the people of Assisi, you see people who have come from all over the world.

"There is something you feel when you come to Assisi, something you feel in your heart that makes you want to come back. And people do return! They feel the peacefulness and tranquility. Not that there aren't other aspects, like the commercialism—but these things happen. People return for the simplicity of this place. People feel attracted to Assisi. There's always something that people feel when they come here—even the hard-hearted ones!"

Asked if she thinks Assisi is changing, Sister Marcellina answers, with laughter in her voice, "When they wanted to make all the changes in the year 2000, the Jubilee Year, our Lord said, 'I must stop everything.' They had lots of projects to build new accommodations to house the people coming for the Jubilee Year, but the Lord said, 'No!' "

lection of fillings to go in the ever-present *torta al testo* (flat, pitalike bread that can be filled to order with various combinations of meat, cheese, and vegetables). The goat cheese is from Sardinia and is a delicious surprise. ⊠ *Via San Gabriele dell'Addolorata 15b* ☎ *075/815352* ⊟ *AE, DC, MC, V* ⊘ *Closed Mon. and 3 wks in Jan.*

¢ ✕ **La Stalla.** A simple and rustic restaurant occupies a onetime stable. The kitchen turns out hearty country fare; for something light, try the torta al testo with your choice of local cheeses, salami, grilled meats, and vegetables. In summer enjoy your meal outside under a trellis shaded with vines and flowers. This is a good place to stop on your way to or from the Eremo delle Carceri. ⊠ *Via Santuario delle Carceri 8, 1 km (½ mi) east of center* ☎ *075/812317* ⊟ *No credit cards* ⊘ *Closed Mon. Oct.–June.*

¢ ✕🏠 **La Pallotta.** One of the best hotels in its category—and a great family-run restaurant—are found here under one roof. Upstairs, the beds are firm, and some of the upper-floor rooms look out across the rooftops of town. Downstairs, with a separate entrance on the alley around the corner, Vicolo della Volta Pinta ($) is a cozy trattoria with a fireplace and stone walls. The *menu di degustazione* (tasting menu) is a good way to sample the tasty local dishes, such as *strangozzi* (a long, thin pasta also spelled *stringozzi* and *strengozzi*) with *salsa di funghi* (mushroom sauce). ⊠ *Via San Ruffino 6, 06081* ☎ *075/812649* 🖷 *075/812307* ⊕ *www.pallottaassisi.it* 🛏 *8 rooms* ⚐ *Restaurant, bar; no a/c* ⊟ *AE, DC, MC, V* ⫯⊙⫯ *BP.*

FodorsChoice ★

$$$ 🏠 **Castello di Petrata.** Built as a fortress in the 14th century, the Petrata rightfully dominates its position—with Monte Subasio, Assisi, and the distant hills and valleys of Perugia all in view. Every room is different from the last: wood beams and sections of exposed medieval stonework make up the background and comfortable couches and upholstered chairs turn each room into a delightful retreat. The bathrooms with tubs are considerably more spacious than those with showers. ⊠ *Località Petrata 22, Pieve San Nicolò, 06081, 6 km (4 mi) east of Assisi* ☎ *075/815451* 🖷 *075/8043026* ⊕ *www.castellopetrata.com* 🛏 *21 rooms, 2 suites* ⚐ *Restaurant, minibars, pool, bar, Internet, meeting rooms, some pets allowed; no a/c* ⊟ *AE, DC, MC, V* ⊘ *Closed Jan. and Feb.* ⫯⊙⫯ *BP.*

FodorsChoice ★

$$$ 🏠 **Hotel Subasio.** The Subasio, housed in a converted monastery, has counted Marlene Dietrich and Charlie Chaplin among its guests. Some of the rooms remain a little monastic, but the splendid views, comfortable old-fashioned sitting rooms, flower-decked terraces, and lovely garden more than balance out a certain austerity in the furnishings. Ask for a room overlooking the valley. The hotel is close to the Basilica di San Francesco. ⊠ *Via Frate Elia 2, 06082* ☎ *075/812206* 🖷 *075/816691* ⊕ *www.hotelsubasio.com* 🛏 *54 rooms, 8 suites* ⚐ *Restaurant, bar, parking (fee)* ⊟ *AE, DC, MC, V* ⫯⊙⫯ *BP.*

$$ 🏠 **San Francesco.** You can't beat the location—the roof terrace and some of the rooms look out onto the Basilica di San Francesco, which is opposite the hotel. Rooms and facilities range from simple to homely, but you may be reminded that looks aren't everything by the nice touches like slippers, a good-night piece of chocolate, and soundproofing. Fruit, homemade tarts, and fresh ricotta make for a first-rate break-

10

fast. ⊠ *Via San Francesco 4, 06082* ☎ *075/812281* 🖷 *075/816237* ⊕ *www.hotelsanfrancescoassisi.it* ⤹ *44 rooms* ♿ *Restaurant, minibars, bar, Internet, some pets allowed* ▤ *AE, DC, MC, V* ⦿I *BP.*

$ 🏨 **Hotel Umbra.** A 16th-century town house is the setting for this charming hotel in a tranquil part of the city, an area closed to traffic and near Piazza del Comune. The rooms are arranged as small suites, each with tiny living room and balcony. Ask for an upper room with a view over the Assisi rooftops to the valley below. The restaurant, closed for lunch on Tuesday and Wednesday, has a charming vine-covered terrace leading to a secluded garden. ⊠ *Via degli Archi 6, 06081* ☎ *075/812240* 🖷 *075/813653* ⊕ *www.hotelumbra.it* ⤹ *25 suites* ♿ *Restaurant, minibars, bar* ▤ *AE, DC, MC, V* ⊗ *Closed mid-Jan.–mid-Mar.* ⦿I *BP.*

NORTHERN UMBRIA

To the north of Perugia, placid, walled Gubbio watches over green countryside, true to its nickname, City of Silence—except for its fast and furious festivals in May, as lively today as when they began more than 800 years ago. To the south, along the Tiber River valley, are the towns of Deruta and Torgiano, best known for their hand-painted ceramics and wine—as locals say, go to Deruta to buy a pitcher and to Torgiano to fill it.

Gubbio

❾ *48 km (30 mi) north of Assisi, 40 km (25 mi) northeast of Perugia.*

There is something otherworldly about this small jewel of a medieval town tucked away in a rugged, mountainous corner of Umbria. Even at the height of summer the cool serenity of the City of Silence's streets remains intact. Since medieval times Gubbio has been known for its red pottery. The town teeters on the slopes of Monte Ingino, and the streets are dramatically steep. Parking in the central Piazza dei Quaranta Martiri (40 Martyrs Square), named for 40 hostages murdered by the Nazis in 1944, is easy and secure, and it is wise to leave your car there and explore the narrow lanes on foot.

★ The striking Piazza Grande is dominated by the **Palazzo dei Consoli,** the 14th-century meeting place of Gubbio's parliament. The palace is the home of a small museum, famous chiefly for the *Tavole Eugubine* (Gubbio Tablets), seven bronze tablets written in the ancient Umbrian language, employing Etruscan and Latin characters and providing the best key to understanding this obscure tongue. Also in the museum are a captivating miscellany of coins, medieval arms, paintings, and majolica and earthenware pots, not to mention the exhilarating views over Gubbio's roofscape and beyond from the lofty loggia. For a few days at the beginning of May the palace also displays the famous *ceri* (ceremonial pillars) that are the focus of Gubbio's annual festivities. ⊠ *Piazza Grande* ☎ *075/9274298* ⊕ *www.comune.gubbio.pg.it* 🎟 *€5* ⊗ *Apr.–Oct., daily 10–1 and 3–6; Nov.–Mar., daily 10–1 and 2–5.*

The **Duomo,** on a narrow street on the highest tier of the town, dates from the 12th century, with some Baroque additions—in particular, a

Northern Umbria

ITALY

Urbino
Marotta
Senigallia
Adriatic Sea

Fossombrone
Metauro

Pergola

Città di Castello

THE MARCHES

Gubbio ❾

Umbertide
Fabriano
Macerata

Perugia
❶ - ❺
see map
page 491

UMBRIA

Passignano
sul Trasimeno

Assisi
❻ - ❽
see map
page 497

Lago di
Trasimeno
Corciano

Castiglione
del Lago

Nocera Umbra
Camerino

Fontignano

Torgiano ❿
Sta. Maria
d. Angeli
Spello

Panicale
❶❶
Cannara
❶❷

Città della
Pieve
Deruta
Foligno
Amandola

Montefalco
Trevi
0   30 miles

Todi
Fonti del
Clitunno
0   45 km

Orvieto
Norcia
PIANO GRANDE

lavishly decorated bishop's chapel. ✉ *Via Ducale* ☉ *Daily 8–12:45 and 3–7:30.*

The **Palazzo Ducale** is a scaled-down copy of the Palazzo Ducale in Urbino (Gubbio was once the possession of that city's ruling family, the Montefeltro). Gubbio's version contains a museum with a small collection of period furniture and paintings; the courtyard closely resembles that of the ducal palace in Urbino. ✉ *Via Ducale* ☎ *075/927–5872* 💶 *€2* ☉ *Tues.–Sun. 8:30–7:30.*

☺ Outside Gubbio's walls at the eastern end of town, a **gondola** (actually a metal basket made for two) provides a bracing panoramic ride to the top of Monte Ingino. ✉ *Via S. Girolamo, follow Corso Garibaldi or Via XX Settembre to end* ☎ *075/927–3881* 💶 *€ 5 round-trip* ☉ *Nov.–Feb., Thurs.–Tues. 10–1:15 and 2:30–5; Mar., Mon.–Sat. 10–1:15 and 2:30–5:30; Apr. and May, Mon.–Sat. 10–1:15 and 2:30–6:30, Sun. 9:30–1:15 and 2:30–7; June, Mon.–Sat. 9:30–1:15 and 2:30–7, Sun. 9–7:30; July and Aug., Mon.–Sat. 8:30–7:30, Sun. 8:30–8; Sept., Mon.–Sat. 9:30–1:15 and 2:30–7, Sun. 9–1:15 and 2:30–7:30; Oct., daily 10–1:15 and 2:30–6.*

Monte Ingino, along with its spectacular views, has the basilica of **Sant'Ubaldo,** repository of Gubbio's famous ceri. Statues of Sts. Ubaldo,

10

George, and Anthony crown the three 16-foot pillars, which are transported to the Palazzo dei Consoli on the first Sunday of May in preparation for the race that takes place during the Festival of the Ceri. You can reach the church by car from the SP298, by hiking, or by taking a gondola. ⊠ *Top of Monte Ingino* ⊗ *Daily 9–noon and 4–7.*

Where to Stay & Eat

$$–$$$ ✕ **Taverna del Lupo.** One of the city's most famous taverns, this popular restaurant seats 150 people and gets hectic on weekends and during the high season. Lasagna made in the Gubbian fashion—with ham and truffles—is an unusual indulgence, and the *coniglio di "Buon Ricordo,"* rabbit stew with herbs and spices, is a specialty. Peruse the extensive wine list and save room for the excellent desserts. ⊠ *Via Ansidei 21* ☎ *075/927–4368* ▭ *AE, DC, MC, V* ⊗ *Closed Mon. Oct.–Apr.*

$–$$$ ✕ **Bosone Garden.** Succulent treats here include a two-mushroom salad with truffles, risotto *alla porcina* (with porcini mushrooms, sausage, and truffles), and leg of pork. This was once the stables of the palace that now houses the Hotel Bosone. A pleasant garden provides outdoor seating in summer. ⊠ *Via Mastro Giorgio 2* ☎ *075/922–1246* ▭ *AE, DC, MC, V* ⊗ *Closed Wed. Oct.–May, and 2 wks in Jan.*

¢ ✕🏨 **Grotta dell'Angelo.** Angel's Grotto is a simple, rustic hotel and trattoria in the lower part of the old town, near the main square and tourist information office. Rooms are basic, with spare wood desks and chairs. Breakfast is optional at €3 per person. The restaurant ($), with a few tables under a pergola in the hotel's garden, serves simple local specialties, including salami, stringozzi, and lasagna *tartufata* (with truffles). ⊠ *Via Gioia 47, 06024* ☎🖷 *075/927–3438* ⊕ *www.grottadellangelo.it* ⤴ *18 rooms* ⚐ *No a/c* ▭ *AE, DC, MC, V* ⊗ *Closed 3 wks in Jan.* ⏉ *EP.*

$$ 🏨 **Relais Ducale.** Three 15th-century town palaces unite to form this hotel with small, antiques-filled guest rooms. Ask for one on the upper floors to enjoy views of the town and valley. Especially impressive is the panorama from the hotel's hanging garden, where tables are set for breakfast during the summer months. The hotel is off Gubbio's Piazza Grande. ⊠ *Via Galeotti 19, 06024* ☎ *075/922–0157* 🖷 *075/9220159* ⊕ *www.mencarelligroup.com* ⤴ *20 rooms, 5 suites* ⚐ *Bar, meeting rooms* ▭ *AE, DC, MC, V* ⏉ *BP.*

$ 🏨 **Hotel Bosone Palace.** Palazzo Raffaelli, a former palace, is home to the Hotel Bosone. Elaborate frescoes grace the ceilings of the two enormous suites, furnished with painted antiques, and top the hotel's small and delightful breakfast room. Standard rooms are comfortably though soberly decorated with heavy wooden furniture. Ask for a room facing the valley and away from the sometimes noisy street. ⊠ *Via XX Settembre 22, 06024* ☎ *075/922–0688* 🖷 *075/9220552* ⊕ *www.mencarelligroup.com* ⤴ *28 rooms, 2 suites* ⚐ *Dining room, minibars, bar; no a/c* ▭ *AE, DC, MC, V* ⊗ *Closed 3 wks in Jan.* ⏉ *BP.*

Nightlife & the Arts

☾ Gubbio explodes with exuberance every May 15 during the **Corsa dei Ceri** (Race of the Ceremonial Pillars), held annually since 1151 in honor of St. Ubaldo, the town's patron saint. Three 16-foot poles, elaborately decorated and crowned with statues of Sts. Ubaldo, George, and Anthony (representing three medieval guilds), are carried by teams who race up Mount Ingino. Don't place any bets, though; Ubaldo always wins.

At Christmastime, kitsch is king in Gubbio. From December 7 to January 10, colored lights are strung down the mountainside in a tree pattern as the town stakes its claim as the home of the **world's largest Christmas tree.**

Sports & the Outdoors

A costumed medieval pageant with its roots in Gubbio's warring past, the Crossbow Tournament, **Palio della Balestra** (Gubbio tourist office ✉ Piazza Oderisi 6, 06024 ☎ 075/922–0693), takes place on the last Sunday in May.

Torgiano

🔟 *48 km (30 mi) southeast of Gubbio, 15 km (9 mi) southeast of Perugia.*

On the right bank of the Tiber River, Torgiano sits on a low-lying hill surrounded by the vineyards that have made the town famous since the Middle Ages. Even the town's coat of arms, a tower wrapped in a parchment covered with bunches of grapes, indicates the age-old importance of wine to the area.

Torgiano's **Cantine Lungarotti** winery is best known for Rubesco Lungarotti, San Giorgio, and chardonnay. ✉ *Via Mario Angeloni 12* ☎ *075/988–0348* 🎫 *Free* ⊙ *Tours weekdays 8–1 and 3–6 by appointment.*

The **Museo del Vino** has a large collection of ancient wine vessels, presses, documents, and tools that tell the story of viticulture in Umbria and beyond. ✉ *Corso Vittorio Emanuele 31* ☎ *075/988–0200* 🎫 *€4* ⊙ *Apr.–Oct., daily 9–1 and 3–7; Nov.–Mar., daily 9–1 and 3–6.*

The **Osteria del Museo,** next door to the Museo del Vino, is a tavern devoted exclusively to the Lungarotti winery. You can buy the highly regarded wines there and, for €4–€10, take part in a tasting. ✉ *Corso Vittorio Emanuele 33* ☎ *075/988–0069.*

Deruta

1️⃣1️⃣ *7 km (4 mi) south of Torgiano, 20 km (12 mi) southeast of Perugia.*

Deruta has been known for its ceramics since the 16th century. Notable in this medieval hill town are the 14th-century church of San Francesco and the Palazzo Comunale, but Deruta's main attraction is the magnificent ceramics collection in the **Museo Regionale della Ceramica.** ✉ *Largo San Francesco* ☎ *075/971–1000* 🎫 *€3* ⊙ *Apr.–June, daily 10:30–1 and 3–6; July–Sept., daily 10–1 and 3:30–7; Oct.–Mar., Wed.–Mon. 10:30–1 and 2:30–5.*

Shopping

Deruta has more than 70 ceramics workshops and boutiques. Start your browsing in the central Piazza dei Consoli.

> **WORD OF MOUTH**
>
> "Best purchase *and* encounter with local people was going to a ceramic studio in Deruta. There are lots of places to buy ceramics, and a couple of places where there are true artists."   —marcy

10

Maioliche Cynthia (⊠ Via Umberto I 1 ☎ 075/971–1255) specializes in reproductions of antique ceramic designs. **Ceramiche El Frate** (⊠ Piazza dei Consoli 29 ☎ 075/971–1435) sells unusual ceramic tiles and jugs. The workshop at **Fabbrica Maioliche Tradizionali** (⊠ Via Tiberina Nord 37 ☎ 075/971–1220) is open for visits weekdays 8:30–1 and 2:30–4:30 and also operates one of the largest shops in the area. **Maioliche Monotti** (⊠ Via Tiberina Sud 276 ☎ 075/972002) focuses on the colors used in traditional designs.

Spello

⑫ *12 km (7 mi) southeast of Assisi, 32 km (24 mi) east of Deruta.*

Only a few minutes south of Assisi by car or train, the hill town of Spello, at the edge of Monte Subasio, makes an excellent base from which to explore the surrounding towns. Although it's half the size of Assisi, and has more than twice as many inhabitants, chances are you'll find the town relatively tourist-free. Spello's charms include a maze of quiet and picturesque backstreets, first-rate frescoes by Pinturicchio (1454–1513), and fine Roman ruins. The Romans called the town Hispellum, and traces remain of their walls, gates, amphitheater, and theater. Built, like Assisi, with pale pink stone from Monte Subasio, Spello is particularly attractive in the glowing light of an autumn sunset. The town is 1 km (½ mi) east of the train station, and buses run every 30 minutes for Porta Consolare; the dilapidated Roman gate at the south end of town and the best place to enter on foot. If you have a car, park in the lots outside the city walls and walk in.

Halfway up the main street that runs through town is the basilica of **Santa Maria Maggiore,** with vivid frescoes by Pinturicchio in the **Cappella Baglioni** (1501). The *Nativity,* the *Dispute at the Temple,* and *Annunciation* (with a self-portrait on the far right)—with rich colors, finely dressed figures, and complex symbolism—are among his finest works. Pinturicchio painted here after he had already won great acclaim for his work on the Palazzi Vaticani in Rome. Two pillars on either side of the apse are decorated with frescoes by Perugino (circa 1450–1523), the other great Umbrian artist of the 16th century. ⊠ *Piazza Matteotti 18* ☎ *0742/301792* ☉ *May–Sept., daily 8–12:30 and 2:30–7; Oct.–Apr., daily 8–12:30 and 2:30–6.*

The festival on the **Feast of Corpus Christi** (the ninth Sunday after Easter) is the region's most famous and most colorful. The streets of Spello are literally covered with *fiore* (flowers), arranged in vast canvases depicting religious subjects. Contact the tourist office form more information.

Where to Stay & Eat

$ ╳▦ **La Bastiglia.** A renovated grain mill serves as home to a tidy hotel
Fodor's Choice where soft, light colors and a mix of antique and modern furnishings
★ make the sitting rooms and bedrooms cozy. Ask for a top-floor room for a view. The terrace looks out onto the green and tranquil valley behind Spello and is used by the hotel's outstanding restaurant ($$$–$$$$). The refined and unusual menu changes with the season, but you might

try the *costoletto di agnello in crosta di pistacchi* (pistachio encrusted lamb chops) followed by *rocciata di ananas con sorbetto di peperoncino* (pineapple strudel with a hot-pepper sorbet). ⊠ *Piazza Valle Gloria 17, 06038* ☎ *0742/651277* 🖷 *0742/301159* ⊕ *www.labastiglia.com* ➟ *31 rooms, 2 suites* ♨ *Restaurant, some in-room hot tubs, pool, bar, Internet* ☰ *AE, DC, MC, V* ☉ *Closed Jan. 9–31* ⎟◎⎟ *BP.*

$$ 🏨 **Palazzo Bocci.** Hints of this old town house's past are retained in the first floor reading room, where vaulted ceilings and walls are decorated with bright trompe l'oeil frescoes. The solid colors and wooden furniture of the guest rooms are more modern. The staff here should win awards for their attentiveness and an ample buffet breakfast, with eggs in addition to cheese and cold cuts, is a welcome change from standard Continental fair. ⊠ *Via Cavour 17, 06038* ☎ *0742/301021* 🖷 *0742/301464* ⊕ *www.palazzobocci.com* ➟ *17 rooms, 6 suites* ♨ *Restaurant, bar, meeting rooms* ☰ *AE, DC, MC, V* ⎟◎⎟ *BP.*

SPOLETO

For most of the year Spoleto is one in a pleasant succession of sleepy hill towns. But for three weeks every summer it shifts into high gear for its turn in the spotlight: the Festival dei Due Mondi, a world-class extravaganza of theater, opera, music, painting, and sculpture, where the world's top artists vie for honors and throngs of art aficionados vie for hotel rooms.

But there is good reason to visit Spoleto any time of the year. Roman and medieval attractions and superb natural surroundings make it one of Umbria's most inviting towns. From the churches set among silvery olive groves on the outskirts of town to the soaring Ponte delle Torri behind it, Spoleto has sublime views in every direction.

Exploring Spoleto

Spoleto is small, and its sights are clustered in the upper part of town, so it's best explored on foot. Several walkways cut down the hill, crossing the Corso Mazzini, which turns up the hill. Parking in Spoleto is always difficult; park outside the walls in Piazza della Vittoria. One day in Spoleto allows you to see the highlights and still have time for a leisurely lunch and a walk across the Ponte delle Torri.

10

The Main Attractions

⑬ **Duomo.** A Renaissance loggia, eight rose windows, and an early-13th-century gold mosaic of the Benedictory Christ lightens the church's rather dour 12th-century Romanesque facade. The contrast makes this one of the finest church exteriors in the region. Inside, the Duomo holds the most notable art in town, including the immaculately restored frescoes in the apse by Fra Filippo Lippi (1406–69), showing the *Annunciation,* the *Nativity,* and the *Dormition of Mary,* with a marvelous *Coronation of the Virgin* adorning the dome. Be ready with a €.50 coin to illuminate the masterpiece. The Florentine artist died shortly after completing the work, and his tomb—designed by his son, Filippino Lippi

(1457–1504)—lies in the right transept. Another fresco cycle, including work by Pinturicchio, is in the **Cappella Eroli** off the right aisle. ✉ *Piazza Duomo* ☎ *0743/44307* ◷ *Mar.–Oct., daily 8–1 and 3–6:30; Nov.–Feb., daily 8–1 and 3–5:30.*

★ **⑯ Ponte delle Torri.** Spanning massively and gracefully across the gorge that separates Spoleto from Monteluco, this 14th-century bridge is one of Umbria's most-photographed sights, and justifiably so. Built by Gattapone over the foundations of a Roman-era aqueduct, it's 750 feet long and soars up to 262 feet above the forested gorge. Postcard valley views make a walk across the bridge a must, particularly on a starry night. Beyond are the slopes of Monteluco, where well-marked trails invite further exploration on foot. ✉ *Via del Ponte.*

Also Worth Seeing

⑱ Arco di Druso. This arch was built in the 1st century AD by the Senate of Spoleto to honor the Roman general Drusus (circa 13 BC–AD 23), son of the emperor Tiberius. It once marked the entrance to the Foro Romano (Roman Forum). ✉ *Piazza del Mercato.*

⑰ Casa Romana. The house excavated at the end of the 19th century is thought to have belonged to Vespasia Polla, the mother of the Roman

Emperor Vespasian. The design is typical for houses of the 1st century AD, and some of the original decoration is still intact, including geometrically patterned marble mosaics and plaster moldings. ⊠ *Palazzo del Municipio, Via Visiale 9* ☎ *0743/224656* ✉ *€2.50* ⊘ *Oct. 16–Mar., daily 10–6; Apr.–Oct. 15, daily 10–8.*

ⓖ La Rocca. The fortress built in 1359–63 by the Gubbio-born architect Gattapon dominates Spoleto. The structure served as a prison between 1860 and 1982 and now houses a small museum dedicated to medieval Spoleto. Plans for future development include an open-air theater and an international school for book restoration. You can admire the formidable exterior from the road that circles the extensive park beneath the castle. Tickets include a shuttle up to the entrance. Guided visits start on the hour; the last tour starts an hour before closing. ⊠ *Via del Ponte* ☎ *0743/223055* ✉ *€4.65* ⊘ *Mid-Mar.–June 10 and Sept. 16–Oct., weekdays 10–noon and 3–7, weekends 10–7; June 11–Sept. 15, weekdays 10–7, weekends 10–9; Nov.–mid-Mar., weekdays 10–noon and 3–5, weekends 10–5.*

ⓐ Sant'Eufemia. Ancient and austere, this 11th-century church sits in the courtyard of the archbishop's palace. Its most interesting feature is the gallery, unique in Umbira, where female worshippers were required to sit. Enter through the attached **Museo Diocesano,** which contains paintings including a Madonna by Fra Filippo Lippi. ⊠ *Via Saffi, between Piazza del Duomo and Piazza del Mercato* ☎ *0743/23101* ✉ *€3* ⊘ *Oct.–Mar., Wed.–Sat. and Mon. 10–12:30 and 3–6, Sun. 11–5; Apr.–Sept., Wed.–Sat. and Mon. 10–1 and 4–7, Sun. 10:30–1 and 3–6.*

ⓣ Teatro Romano. The small but well-preserved Roman theater was the site of a gruesome episode in Spoleto's history. During the medieval struggle between Guelph (papal) and Ghibelline (imperial) factions for control of central and northern Italy, Spoleto took the side of the Holy Roman Emperor. And woe to those who disagreed: 400 Guelph supporters were massacred in the theater, their bodies burned in an enormous pyre. In the end, however, the Guelphs were triumphant, and Spoleto was incorporated into the states of the Church in 1354. Through a door in the west portico, the **Museo Archeologico** displays assorted artifacts and the *Lex Spoletina* (Spoleto Law) tablets dating from 315 BC. This ancient legal document prohibited the destruction of the *Bosco Sacro* (Sacred Forest), south of town on Monteluco, a pagan prayer site later frequented by St. Francis. The theater is used in summer for Spoleto's arts festival. ⊠ *Piazza della Libertà* ☎ *0743/223277* ✉ *€2* ⊘ *Daily 8:30–7:30.*

10

off the
beaten
path

SAN SALVATORE – The church and cemetery of San Salvatore seem very much forgotten, ensconced in solitude and cypress trees on a peaceful hillside, with the motorway rumbling below. One of the oldest churches in the world, it was built by eastern monks in the 4th century, largely of Roman-era materials. The highlight is the facade, with three exquisite marble doorways and windows, one of the earliest and best preserved in Umbria. It dates from a restoration in the 9th century and has hardly been touched since. ✉ *Via della Basilica di San Salvatore, 1 km (½ mi) northeast of town, off Via Flaminia* ☉ *Nov.–Feb., daily 7–5; Mar., Apr., Sept., and Oct., daily 7–6; May–Aug., daily 7–7.*

Where to Stay & Eat

$$-$$$ ✕ **Ristorante Panciolle.** In the heart of Spoleto's medieval quarter, this restaurant has one of the most appealing settings you could wish for: a small piazza filled with lemon trees. Dishes change throughout the year, and may include pastas served with asparagus or mushrooms, as well as grilled meats. When in season, more expensive dishes prepared with fresh truffles are also available. ✉ *Vicolo degli Eroli 1* ☎ *0743/45598* ⌂ *Reservations essential* ▤ *AE, DC, MC, V* ☉ *Closed Wed. and last 2 wks in Nov.*

$$-$$$ ✕ **Il Tartufo.** As the name, the Truffle, indicates, dishes prepared with truffles are the specialty here—don't miss the risotto al tartufo—but there are also choices not perfumed with this expensive delicacy. Traditional fare is spiced up to appeal to the cosmopolitan crowd attending (or performing in) the summertime Festival dei Due Mondi. Incorporating the ruins of a Roman villa, the restaurant's decor is rustic on the ground floor; furnishings are more modern upstairs, and there's outdoor seating in warm weather. ✉ *Piazza Garibaldi 24* ☎ *0743/40236* ⌂ *Reservations essential* ▤ *AE, DC, MC, V* ☉ *Closed Mon. and last 2 wks in July. No dinner Sun.*

$-$$$ ✕ **Apollinare.** Low wooden ceilings and candlelight make Apollinare the romantic "in" spot in town. The kitchen serves good-size portions of sophisticated, innovative variations on local cooking: cherry tomatoes, mint, and a touch of red pepper top the usual long, thin pasta, or strangozzi. The *caramella* (light puff pastry roll filled with local cheese), served with a creamy Parmesan sauce, is a must-have. In late spring and summer you can dine under a pergola on the piazza. ✉ *Via Sant'Agata 14* ☎ *0743/223256* ▤ *AE, D, MC, V* ☉ *Closed Tues. Nov.–Mar.*

$-$$ ✕ **Il Pentagramma.** A former stable-turned-restaurant serves fresh local dishes such as *tortelli ai carciofi e noci* (artichoke-filled pasta with a hazelnut sauce) and lamb in a truffle sauce. It's quite central, off the Piazza della Libertà. ✉ *Via Martani 4* ☎ *0743/223141* ▤ *DC, MC, V* ☉ *Closed Mon. No dinner Sun.*

★ $$$ ▥ **Cavaliere Palace Hotel.** Turn into an arched passage off one of Spoleto's busy shopping streets and enter an elegant world through a quiet courtyard. Built in the 17th century for an influential cardinal, the rooms, particularly on the second floor, retain their sumptuously frescoed ceilings; care has been taken to retain a sense of old-world comfort throughout. In warm weather enjoy breakfast on a terrace and in a peaceful garden at the back of the hotel. ✉ *Corso Garibaldi 49, 06049* ☎ *0743/220350* 🖷 *0743/224505* ⊕ *www.cavalierehotels.com* ⇥ *29 rooms, 2 suites* ⌂ *Restaurant, in-room safes, minibars, cable TV, bar, meeting rooms* ▤ *AE, DC, MC, V* ⦿ *BP.*

$$ ▥ **Hotel San Luca.** The elegant San Luca is Spoleto's finest hotel, thanks
FodorśChoice   to its commendable attention to detail: hand-painted friezes decorate
★   guest-room walls, linen sheets cover firm beds, and some of the spacious

CLOSE UP

Truffle Trouble

Umbria is rich with truffles—more are found here than anywhere else in Italy—and those not consumed fresh are processed into pastes or flavored oils. The primary truffle areas are around the tiny town of Norcia, which holds a truffle festival every February, and near Spoleto, where signs warn against unlicensed truffle hunting at the base of the Ponte delle Torri. Although grown locally, the rare delicacy can cost a small fortune, up to $200 for a quarter pound— fortunately, a little goes a long way. At such a price there's great competition among the nearly 10,000 registered truffle hunters in the province, who use specially trained dogs to sniff them out among the roots of several types of trees, including oak and ilex. Despite one or two incidences of poisoning truffle-hunting dogs and importing inferior tubers from China, you can be reasonably assured that the truffle shaved onto your pasta has been unearthed locally.

rooms are wheelchair accessible. Enjoy an ample breakfast buffet, including homemade cakes, which is served in a pleasant room facing the central courtyard. You can sip afternoon tea in oversize armchairs by the fireplace, and the hotel's rose garden provides a sweet-smelling backdrop for a walk or a nap. Service is cordial and prices are surprisingly modest. ⊠ *Via Interna delle Mura 21, 06049* ☎ *0743/223399* 🖷 *0743/223800* ⊕ *www.hotelsanluca.com* 🛏 *33 rooms, 2 suites* ⚴ *Some in-room hot tubs, in-room safes, bar, laundry service, Internet, parking (fee)* ▱ *AE, DC, MC, V* ❙◯❙ *BP.*

$$ 🏠 **Palazzo Dragoni.** Housed in the 15th-century palazzo of a Spoletan noble and decorated with antiques and frescoes, all the rooms of this hotel differ in size and aspect. Room 8 with a canopied bed and Room 10 with elegant picture windows are particularly beautiful. The plain tile bathrooms, although simple and functional, lack the charm of the rest of the building. Look out at the cathedral and the sloping rooftops of the town from the guest rooms that face the valley and from the loggia, where the buffet breakfast is served. ⊠ *Via del Duomo 13, 06049* ☎ *0743/222220* 🖷 *0743/222225* ⊕ *www.palazzodragoni.it* 🛏 *15 rooms* ⚴ *Bar, meeting rooms, parking (fee), some pets allowed; no a/c* ▱ *MC, V* ❙◯❙ *BP.*

$ 🏠 **Hotel Clitunno.** A renovated 18th-century building houses this pleasant hotel in the center of town. Cozy bedrooms and intimate public rooms, some with timbered ceilings, have the sense of a traditional Umbrian home—albeit one with a good restaurant. The hotel staff is glad to light the fireplace in Room 212 in advance of winter arrivals. Upper-floor rooms look over Spoleto's rooftops. ⊠ *Piazza Sordini 6, 06049* ☎ *0743/223340* 🖷 *0743/222663* ⊕ *www.hotelclitunno.com* 🛏 *47 rooms* ⚴ *Restaurant, minibars, bar, library, babysitting, laundry service, meeting rooms; no a/c in some rooms* ▱ *AE, DC, MC, V* ❙◯❙ *BP.*

10

Nightlife & the Arts

Thousands of spectators flock to the **Festival dei Due Mondi** (Festival of Two Worlds ✉ Box office, Piazza Duomo 8 ☎ 800/565600 ⊕ www. spoletofestival.it), held mid-June–mid-July, to watch music, opera, and theater artists perform. Order tickets as far in advance as possible; full program information is available starting in February.

SOUTHERN UMBRIA

Orvieto, built on a tufa mount, produces one of Italy's favorite white wines and has one of the country's greatest cathedrals and most compelling fresco cycles. Nearby Narni and Todi are pleasant medieval hill towns. The former stands over a steep gorge, its Roman pedigree evident in dark alleyways and winding streets; the latter is a fairy-tale village with incomparable views and one of Italy's most perfect piazzas.

Todi

❷⓿ *41 km (27 mi) northwest of Spoleto, 47 km (29 mi) south of perugia.*

As you stand on **Piazza del Popolo,** it's easy to see why Todi is often described as Umbria's prettiest hill town. The square is a model of spatial harmony, with stunning views over the surrounding countryside. Narrow cobblestone streets go winding around the hill, every so often finishing in a tiny quiet piazza. Todi's 12th-century Romanesque-Gothic **Duomo** is famed for its choir stalls by Antonio Bencivenni da Mercatello and his son Sebastiano, dating from 1530. Its simple square facade is echoed by the solid Palazzo dei Priori across the way. ✉ *Piazza del Popolo* ☎ *075/894–3041* ⊗ *Apr.–Oct., Mon.–Sat. 8:30–12:30 and 2:30–6:30, Sun. 8:30–12:30 and 2:30–5:30; Nov.–Mar. 20, Mon.–Sat. 8:30–4:30, Sun. 8:30–12:30 and 2:30–5:30.*

The Renaissance church of **Santa Maria della Consolazione,** with an elegant pale-green dome, is a pleasant surprise on the outskirts of town. ✉ *Via Menecali* ☎ *075/894–8482* ⊗ *Apr.–Oct., Wed.–Mon. 9–1 and 2:30–6; Nov.–Mar., Wed.–Mon. 10–12:30 and 2:30–6.*

Where to Stay & Eat

$–$$ ✕ **Ristorante Umbria.** Todi's most popular restaurant for more than four decades, the Umbria is reliable for sturdy country food, plus a wonderful view from the terrace. There's always a hearty soup simmering, as well as homemade pastas with truffles, game, and the specialty of the house, *palombaccio alla ghiotta* (roasted squab). ✉ *Via San Bonaventura 13* ☎ *075/894–2737 or 075/894–2390* ▭ *AE, DC, MC, V* ⊗ *Closed Tues. and July.*

★ $$$ 🏠 **Tenuta di Canonica.** The affable hosts here, Daniele and Maria Fano, have retained the architectural integrity of this brick farmhouse and medieval tower in the Tiber Valley. You're bound to marvel at the exposed stone walls, high-beam ceilings, brick floors, and terra-cotta tiles—all in soothing earthy colors. Guest rooms are filled with family furniture and antique pieces. You can hike or ride on horseback through olive

Southern Umbria

groves, orchards, and the forest on the grounds. ✉ *Località La Canonica 75–76, 06059, 5 km (3 mi) northwest of center* ☎ *075/8947545* 🖶 *075/8947581* ⊕ *www.tenutadicanonica.com* ⇆ *10 rooms, 3 apartments* ⚒ *Dining room, pool, bar, library; no a/c, no room TVs* ⊟ *MC, V* ⅏ *BP.*

$ 🏨 **San Lorenzo Tre.** Surrounded by antique furniture, paintings, and period knickknacks, you get the sense of a place more in tune with the 19th than the 21st century. The hotel doesn't pamper you with modern comforts; only three of the six rooms have private bathrooms, but all share a magnificent view over the valleys and hills to the north of town. A narrow alley off Todi's main square and a long flight of stairs lead up to this tiny guesthouse. ✉ *Via San Lorenzo 3, 06059* ☎☎ *075/894–4555* ⊕ *www.todi.net/lorenzo* ⇆ *6 rooms, 3 with bath* ⚒ *No a/c, no room phones, no room TVs* ⊟ *No credit cards* ⊙ *Closed Jan. and Feb.* ⅏ *BP.*

Orvieto

㉑ *30 km (19 mi) west of Todi, 81 km (51 mi) west of Spoleto.*

Carved out of an enormous plateau of volcanic rock high above a green valley, Orvieto has natural defenses that made the high walls seen in many

Umbrian towns unnecessary. The Etruscans were the first to settle here, digging a honeycombed network of more than 1,200 wells and storage caves out of the soft stone. The Romans attacked, sacked, and destroyed the city in 283 BC; since then, it has grown up out of the rock into an enchanting maze of alleys and squares. Orvieto was solidly Guelph in the Middle Ages, and for several hundred years popes sought refuge in the city, at times needing protection from their enemies, at times from the summer heat of Rome.

When painting his frescoes inside the Duomo, Luca Signorelli asked that part of his contract be paid in Orvietan wine, and he was neither the first nor the last to appreciate the region's popular white. In past times the caves carved underneath the town were used to ferment the Trebbiano grapes used in making Orvieto Classico; now local wine production has moved out to more traditional vineyards, but you can still while away the afternoon in tastings at any number of shops in town.

★ Orvieto's **Duomo** is a dazzling triumph of Romanesque-Gothic architecture. It was built to commemorate a local miracle: a priest in the nearby town of Bolsena suddenly found himself assailed by doubts about the transubstantiation—he could not bring himself to believe that the body of Christ was contained in the consecrated communion host. His doubts were put to rest, however, when a wafer he had just blessed suddenly started to drip blood onto the linen covering the altar. The pope certified the miracle and declared a new religious holiday—the Feast of Corpus Christi.

> ### WORD OF MOUTH
>
> "When you go to Orvieto, stop first at the tourist information office across the piazza from the Duomo. Get tickets there to see the Signorelli frescoes inside the cathedral—they are stunning. Bring binoculars so you can get good closeup views, as many of them are high up." —nonnafelice

The stunning carved-stone church facade is the work of some of Italy's finest artists and took 300 years to complete. The bas-reliefs on the lower parts of the pillars by Lorenzo Maitani (circa 1275–1330), one of the Duomo's architects, show scenes from the Old Testament and some scary renderings of the *Last Judgment and Hell,* as well as a more tranquil *Paradise.*

Inside the cathedral a vast expanse of space leads to the major works, at the far end of the church in the transepts. To the left is the **Cappella del Corporale,** where the famous stained altar cloth is kept in a golden reliquary modeled after the cathedral and inlaid with enamel images of the miracle. The cloth is removed for public viewing on Easter and on Corpus Christi (the ninth Sunday after Easter). A trio of local artists executed frescoes depicting the miracle on the chapel walls. Signorelli's *Stories of the Antichrist,* the artistic jewel of the Duomo, decks the walls of the **Cappella Nuova** (or Cappella di San Brizio), in the right transept (buy tickets in the tourist office across the square). In these delightfully gruesome works, the damned fall to hell, and lascivious demons bite off ears, step on heads, and spirit away young girls. Dante would surely have approved; his portrait accompanies *Scenes from Purgatorio*. Signorelli and Fra Angelico, who also worked on the chapel, witness the gory scene. ✉ *Piazza del Duomo* ☎ *0763/342477* 🔖 *Church free, Cappella Nuova €3* ⊙ *Nov.–Feb., daily 7:30–12:45 and 2:30–5:15; Mar. and Oct., daily 7:30–12:45 and 2:30–6:15; Apr.–Sept., daily 7:30–12:45 and 2:30–7:15.*

The **Museo Claudio Faina,** across the piazza from the Duomo, holds Etruscan and Roman artifacts. Its Roman coins, bronze pieces, and sarcophagi are accessible and interesting. ✉ *Piazza del Duomo 29* ☎ *0763/341511* ⊕ *www.museofaina.it* 🔖 *€4.50* ⊙ *Apr.–Sept., daily 9:30–6; Oct. and Mar., daily 10–5; Nov.–Feb., Tues.–Sun. 10–5.*

There is no better way to get a sense of Orvieto's multilayered history than to take a tour of the maze of tunnels and chambers that make up **Orvieto Underground.** Members of an Umbrian speleological club lead small groups down below street level to explain the origins of the tufa plateau on which Orvieto sits and to reveal the fascinating purposes to which these hidden caverns where put. Tickets and information are available from the Orvieto Tourist Office, which also serves as the meeting place for tour groups. ✉ *Piazza Duomo 24* ☎ *0763/344891* ⊕ *www. orvietounderground.it* 🔖 *€5.50* ⊙ *Visits daily at 11, 12:30, 4, and 5:15.*

On Piazza Cahen, the **Fortezza,** built in the mid-14th century, encloses a public park with benches, shade, and an incredible view. The **Pozzo di San Patrizio** (Well of St. Patrick) was commissioned by Pope Clement VII (1478–1534) in 1527 to ensure a plentiful water supply in case of siege. Descend into the well on a pair of winding mule paths designed to avoid traffic jams. ✉ *Viale Sangallo, off Piazza Cahen* ☎ *0763/343768* 🔖 *€3.50* ⊙ *Oct.–Mar., daily 10–5:45; Apr.–Sept., daily 9:30–6:45.*

Where to Stay & Eat

\$\$\$ ✕ **Osteria dell'Angelo.** Come here for a decidedly nouvelle alternative to heavy Umbrian cuisine; tempting ingredients are delicately spiced and thoughtfully prepared. From the changing menu you might try the *sformato di sogliola e scampi in fondente di verza e fonduta* (sole and prawn flan with a cabbage and cheese sauce) as a starter, and continue with the *carrè d'agnello in crosta di nocciole tostate* (rack of lamb baked in a crust of toasted hazelnuts). Desserts are spectacular, and the wine list is a book with an intoxicating array of wines and vintages. ✉ *Piazza XXIX Marzo 8/a* ☎ *0763/341805* ♿ *Reservations essential* ▭ *MC, V* ⊙ *Closed Tues. and July 28–Aug. 16.*

\$–\$\$ ✕ **Le Grotte del Funaro.** This restaurant has an extraordinary location, deep in a series of caves within the volcanic rock beneath Orvieto. Once you have negotiated the steep steps, typical Umbrian specialties like tagliatelle *al vino rosso* (with red wine sauce) and grilled beef with truffles await. Sample the fine Orvieto wines, either the whites or the lesser-known reds. ✉ *Via Ripa Serancia 41* ☎ *0763/343276* ♿ *Reservations essential* ▭ *AE, DC, MC, V* ⊙ *Closed Mon. and 1 wk in July.*

¢–\$ ✕ **Cantina Foresi.** For a light lunch of cheese, salami, bread, and salad accompanied by a glass of cool white wine, this small *enoteca* (wine bar) is hard to beat. The umbrella-shade tables have one of the best views

10

of the cathedral facade in town. ✉ *Piazza del Duomo 2* ☎ *0763/ 341611* 🖃 *AE, DC, MC, V* ⊘ *Closed Tues. Nov.–Mar.*

$ ✕🖼 **Villa Bellago.** Three farmhouses overlooking Lake Corbara have been completely renovated, resulting in a lodging with bright, spacious guest rooms and ample facilities. The hotel's fine restaurant specializes in imaginatively prepared Umbrian and Tuscan dishes, such as *umbrichelli alla norcina* (local hand-made spaghetti with a cream and sausage sauce), and fresh fish is always on the menu. ✉ *On S448, 05023 Baschi, 7 km (4½ mi) south of Orvieto* ☎ *0744/950521* 🖨 *0744/950524* ⊕ *www. argoweb.it/hotel_villabellago* ⤢ *12 rooms, 2 suites* ♨ *Restaurant, minibars, tennis court, pool, gym, sauna, bar; no a/c* 🖃 *AE, DC, MC, V* ⊘ *Closed 4 wks in Jan.–Feb. Restaurant closed Tues.* ⦿ *BP.*

★ $$$$ 🖼 **Hotel La Badia.** One of the best-known country hotels in Umbria occupies a 12th-century building—a former monastery. Vaulted ceilings and exposed stone walls establish the rustic elegance in the guest rooms, which have hand-knotted rugs and upholstered furniture. The rolling park around the hotel provides wonderful views of the valley and the town of Orvieto in the distance. ✉ *Località La Badia, 05018 Orvieto Scalo, 4 km (2½ mi) south of Orvieto* ☎ *0763/301959* 🖨 *0763/305396* ⊕ *www. labadiahotel.it* ⤢ *21 rooms, 7 suites* ♨ *Restaurant, 2 tennis courts, pool, bar, meeting room* 🖃 *AE, MC, V* ⊘ *Closed Jan. and Feb.* ⦿ *BP.*

$$ 🖼 **Palazzo Piccolomini.** Once a 16th-century palace, this is perhaps your best bet in central Orvieto for a pleasant stay. Though the entrance hall and bar are austere, the guest rooms, which vary in size, are modern and comfortable. Try for one of the larger rooms on an upper floor. Service is friendly and efficient. ✉ *Piazza Ranieri 36, 05018* ☎ *0763/ 341743* 🖨 *0763/391046* ⤢ *34 rooms* ♨ *Bar, Internet* 🖃 *AE, DC, MC, V* ⊘ *Closed Jan. 15–31* ⦿ *BP.*

Shopping

Excellent Orvieto wines are justly prized throughout Italy and the world. The whites pressed from the region's Trebbiano grapes are fruity, with a tart finish. Orvieto also produces its own version of the Tuscan dessert wine *vin santo*. It's darker than its Tuscan cousin and is aged five years before bottling. You can stop for a glass of vino at the **Wine Bar Nazzaretto** (✉ Corso Cavour 40 ☎ 0763/340868), where there's also a good selection of sandwiches and snacks, and vin santo is for sale.

With a few small tables, a cheese counter that is second to none, a short menu, and a carefully chosen wine list, the specialty store **Carraro** (✉ Corso Cavour 101 ☎ 0763/342870) is an excellent place for either a *degustazione* (tasting) of Orvietan cheese or a light lunch.

Orvieto artisans do particularly fine inlay and veneer woodwork. The Corso Cavour has a number of shops, the best known being the **Michelangeli family studio** (✉ Via Michelangeli 3, at Corso Cavour ☎ 0763/ 342377), chock-full of imaginatively designed creations ranging in size from a giant *armadio* (wardrobe) to a simple wooden spoon.

Embroidery and lace making are not lost arts; **Duranti** (✉ Corso Cavour 105 ☎ 0763/342222) is a good shop in which to find handmade *merletto* (lace).

Hiking the Umbrian Hills

Magnificent scenery makes the heart of Italy excellent walking, hiking, and mountaineering country. In Umbria, the area around Spoleto is particularly good; several pleasant, easy, and well-signed trails begin at the far end of the Ponte alle Torri bridge over Monteluco. From Cannara an easy half-hour walk leads to the fields of Pian d'Arca, the site of St. Francis's sermon to the birds. For slightly more arduous walks, you can follow the saint's path, uphill from Assisi to the Eremo delle Carceri, and then continue along the trails that criss-cross Monte Subasio. At 4,250 feet, the Subasio's treeless summit affords views of Assisi, Perugia, far-off Gubbio, and the distant mountain ranges of Abruzzo.

For even more challenging hiking, the northern reaches of the Valnerina are exceptional; the mountains around Norcia should not to be missed. Throughout Umbria and the Marches, you'll find that most recognized walking and hiking trails are marked with the distinctive red and white blazes of the Club Alpino Italiano (CAI). Tourist offices are a good source for walking and climbing itineraries to suit all ages and levels of ability, while bookstores, *tabacchi* (tobacconists), and *edicole* (newsstands) often have maps and hiking guides that detail the best routes in their area. Depending on the length and location of your walk, it can be important that you have comfortable walking shoes or boots, appropriate attire, and plenty of water to drink.

Narni

22 *66 km (41 mi) southeast of Orvieto, 45 km (28 mi) southwest of Spoleto.*

At the edge of a steep gorge, Narni—like so many other towns in Umbria—is a medieval city of Roman origins. Below its finely paved streets and pretty Romanesque churches, excavations provide glimpses of an intriguing past. The **Lacus,** under **Piazza Garibaldi,** is an ancient Roman cistern with remnants of a Roman floor that was in use until the late Middle Ages. Two cisterns and assorted Roman fragments are visible in the crypt of the 8th-century church of **Santa Maria Impensole.** ⊠ *Via Mazzini* ☎ *0744/242226* ✆ *Daily 9:30–noon and 4:30–6:30.*

A macabre note is struck by the symbols and dates on the walls of the rooms under the former church of **San Domenico,** inscribed by prisoners held there during the Inquisition. Tours are given in English. ⊠ *Via Mazzini* ☎ *0744/722292* ✆ *€4* ✆ *Apr.–Oct., Sun. 10–1 and 3–6; Nov.–Mar., Sun. 11–1 and 3–5.*

You can take a unique tour of Narni's underground **Roman aqueduct**— the only one open to the public in all of Italy, but it's not for the claustrophobic. Contact the Associazione Culturale Subterranea at least one week ahead to book a visit. ⊠ *Associazione Culturale Subterranea, Via*

San Bernardino 12 ☎ *0744/722292* ⊕ *www.narnisotterranea.it* ☉ *Sun. 10–1 and 3–6, and by appointment.*

Where to Eat

$–$$ ✕ **Il Cavallino.** Run by the third generation of the Bussetti family, Il Cavallino is a first-rate trattoria outside Narni. There are always several pastas to choose from, but it's the meat that makes this a worthy detour. Rabbit roasted with rosemary and sage and juicy grilled T-bone steaks are house favorites. The wine list has the best of what's local. ⊠ *Via Flaminia Romana 220, 3 km (2 mi) south of center* ☎ *0744/761020* ▭ *AE, DC, MC, V* ☉ *Closed Tues., July 13–30, and Dec. 20–26.*

Valnerina

❷ *Terni is 13 km (8 mi) northeast of Narni, 27 km (17 mi) southwest of Spoleto.*

The Valnerina (the valley of the River Nera, to the east of Spoleto) is the most beautiful of Central Italy's many well-kept secrets. The twisting roads that serve the rugged landscape are poor, but the drive is well worth the effort for its forgotten medieval villages and dramatic mountain scenery. You can head into the area from Terni on the S209, or on the SP395bis north of Spoleto, which links the Via Flaminia (S3) with the middle reaches of the Nera valley through a tunnel.

The **Cascata delle Marmore** are waterfalls engineered by the Romans in the 3rd century BC. To find them, drive east from Terni on the road to Lake Piediluco and Rieti. The waters are diverted on weekdays to provide hydroelectric power. On summer evenings, when the falls are

> ## WORD OF MOUTH
>
> "I highly recommend a drive up the Valnerina. The highlight is the miraculous Paino Grande, which is an enormous and strange flat plain surrounded by mountains."
> –pfeldman

in full spate, the cascading water is floodlighted. *Falls information office* ⊠ *SP79, 3 km (2 mi) east of Terni* ☎ *0744/62982* 🎫 *Free* ☉ *Light displays May, weekends 8 PM–10 PM; June–Aug., daily 8 PM–10 PM; mid-Mar.–Apr. and Sept., weekends 8 PM–9 PM.*

The Terni **tourist office** can provide information on the operating schedule of the Cascata delle Marmore, and on the region in general. ⊠ *Viale Cesare Battisti 7/a, 05100* ☎ *0744/423047.*

Close to the town of Ferentillo is the outstanding 8th-century abbey of **San Pietro in Valle,** with fine frescoes in the church nave and a peaceful cloister. One of the abbey outbuildings houses an excellent restaurant with moderate prices. ⊠ *S209, 22 km (14 mi) northeast of Terni* ☎ *0743/54395.*

Norcia, the birthplace of St. Benedict, is better known for its Umbrian pork and truffles. Norcia exports truffles to France and hosts a truffle festival, the Mostra Internazionale del Tartufo Nero di Norcia, every November. The surrounding mountains provide spectacular hiking. ⊠ *67 km (42 mi) northeast of Terni.*

Piano Grande, a mountain plain 25 km (15 mi) to the northeast of the valley, is a hang-glider's paradise and a wonderful place for a picnic or to fly a kite.

THE MARCHES

Less touristed than Tuscany or Umbria, the Marches (Le Marche in Italian) have comparably diverse and attractive landscapes. Like those of its neighbors, the region's patchwork of hills is stitched with grapevines and olive trees producing delicious wine and oil. You're off the beaten path here and services tend to be less luxurious than in the regions to the west, but with a little luck you may have the place to yourself.

A car is recommended; train travel is slow and stops are limited, although you can reach Ascoli Piceno by rail. There is efficient bus service between the coastal town of Pésaro and Urbino, the principal tourist destinations of the region. Beyond the narrow coastal plain and away from major towns the roads are steep and twisting, but the only way to get around.

Urbino

② *101 km (63 mi) northeast of Perugia, 107 km (66 mi) northeast of Arezzo.*

Majestic Urbino, atop a steep hill with a skyline of towers and domes, is something of a surprise—it's oddly remote—and it's humbling to reflect that it was once a center of learning and culture almost without rival in western Europe. The city takes great pride in its intellectual and humanistic heritage: it's home to the small but distinguished Università di Urbino, one of the oldest in the world. Very much a college town—with the usual bookshops, record stores, bars, and coffeehouses—during school term Urbino's streets are filled with Italian students. In summer they are replaced by foreigners who come to study Italian language and arts at several prestigious academies.

Urbino's fame rests on the reputations of three of its native sons: Duke Federico da Montefeltro (1422–82), the enlightened warrior-patron who built the Palazzo Ducale; Raffaello Sanzio (1483–1520), or Raphael, one of the most influential painters in history and an embodiment of the spirit of the Renaissance; and the architect Donato Bramante (1444–1514), who translated the philosophy of the Renaissance into buildings of grace and beauty. Unfortunately, there's little work by either Bramante or Raphael in the city, but the duke's influence can still be felt strongly, even now, some 500 years after his death. The town looks much as it did in the glory days of the 15th century, a cluster of warm brick and pale stone buildings, all topped with russet-color tiled roofs.

10

Fodor'sChoice The immense and beautiful **Palazzo Ducale** holds the place of honor in
★ the city. In no other palace of its era are the tenets of the Renaissance better illustrated—in ideal form, it's a celebration of the nobility of man and his works, of the light and purity of the soul.

Today the palace houses the **Galleria Nazionale delle Marche,** with a superb collection of paintings, sculpture, and objets d'art, well arranged and properly lighted. Masterworks in the collection include Paolo Uccello's *Profanation of the Host,* Titian's *Resurrection* and *Last Supper,* and Piero della Francesca's *Madonna of Senigallia.* But the gallery's highlight is Piero's enigmatic masterpiece, long known as *The Flagellation of Christ.* Much has been written about this painting, and few experts agree on its meaning. It's one of the few works Piero signed (on the lowest step supporting the throne). The last tickets are sold 90 minutes before closing. ⊠ *Piazza Duca Federico* ☎ *0722/2760* ⊕ *www.comune. urbino.ps.it* ▱ *€4* ☉ *Apr.–Oct., Mon. 8:30–2, Tues.–Sun. 8:30* AM*–10* PM*; Nov.–Mar., Mon. 8:30–2, Tues.–Sun. 8:30–7:15.*

The **Casa Natale di Raffaello** is where the painter Raphael was born and, under the direction of his artist father, took his first steps in painting. There is debate about the fresco of the Madonna here; some say it is by Raphael, whereas others attribute it to the father—with Raphael's mother and the young painter himself standing in as models for the Madonna and Child. ⊠ *Via Raffaello 57* ☎ *0722/320105* ▱ *€3* ☉ *Mon.–Sat. 9–2, Sun. 10–1.*

Where to Stay & Eat

$–$$ ✕ **La Vecchia Fornarina.** Locals often fill the small, two-room trattoria near the Piazza della Repubblica to capacity. The specialty is meaty country fare, such as *coniglio* (rabbit) and *vitello alle noci* (veal cooked with walnuts) or *ai porcini* (with mushrooms). There's also a good selection of pasta dishes. ⊠ *Via Mazzini 14* ☎ *0722/320007* ⌲ *Reservations essential* ▤ *AE, DC, MC, V.*

¢ ⊞ **Hotel San Giovanni.** This hotel in the old town is housed in a renovated medieval building. The rooms are basic, clean, and comfortable— with a wonderful view from Rooms 24 to 30. There's a handy restaurant-pizzeria below. ⊠ *Via Barocci 13, 61029* ☎ *0722/2827* 🖷 *0722/329055* ⇋ *31 rooms, 17 with bath* ⚖ *Restaurant; no a/c* ▤ *No credit cards* ☉ *Closed July and Christmas wk* ⦿ *BP.*

Shopping

Historically, Urbino has been a center for the production of fine majolica ceramic designs, and you can find pretty reproductions as well as contemporary designs at shops around town. A unique, though hard-to-carry, gift would be the Stella Ducale (Ducal Star), a complex three-dimensional decorative wooden star designed out of pyramid shapes by Renaissance mathematician Luca Pacioli.

Ancona

㉕ *87 km (54 mi) southeast of Urbino, 139 km (87 mi) northeast of Perugia.*

Set on an elbow-shaped bluff (hence its name; *ankon* is Greek for "elbow") jutting out into the Adriatic, Ancona is one of Italy's most important ports. It's well served by trains, which makes it a good base for an excursion to Loreto or to Ascoli Piceno, farther south along the Adriatic coast. The city was the target of serious aerial bombing during World War II, and much was reduced to rubble, only to be rebuilt in a nondescript sprawl of boxy concrete. A few blocks from the main ferry terminal, what's left of the city's old center proves that Ancona was, and still is in parts, a lovely city. Narrow, cobbled streets wind steeply up from the waterfront, opening onto wide piazzas edged with handsome 19th-century brick-and-stucco buildings painted deep orange, pink, and ochre. The alleys leading downhill from central Piazza del Plebiscito are lined with chic shops selling everything from handmade linens to herbal cosmetics, and there are cafés and *pasticcerie* (pastry shops) aplenty to stave off hunger before your ferry leaves. There are enough sights to fill the longest layover, too.

The **Duomo di San Ciriaco,** built over a Greek temple, was redesigned in the 13th century to make it more visible to ships coming in to Ancona's port. ⊠ *Via Giovanni XXIII* ☎ *No phone* ☉ *Apr.–Sept., daily 8–noon and 3–7; Oct.–Mar., daily 8–noon and 3–6.*

Beginning in the 15th century the **Loggia dei Mercanti,** on the street of the same name, was Ancona's bazaar, where merchants and traders dealt in all manner of goods from the Far East. The Venetian Gothic building was restored in 2003 and is now used as a conference hall.

The 12th-century Romanesque church of **Santa Maria della Piazza** is built over a church from the 5th century; parts of the foundation and original hand-cut mosaic pavement are visible through handy glass cutouts in the floor. You can visit by appointment during the very irregular hours; call ahead. ✉ *Via della Loggia* ☎ *071/200391.*

The 2nd-century **Arco di Traiano** (Trajan's Arch), out on the point at the end of Via Vanvitelli, is worth a look.

Where to Stay & Eat

$–$$ ✕ **La Moretta.** This family-run trattoria is on the central Piazza del Plebiscito, and in summer there's dining outside in the square. Among the specialties here are *stoccafisso all'Anconetana* (cod baked with capers, anchovies, potatoes, and tomatoes) and the famous *brodetto* (fish stew). ✉ *Piazza del Plebiscito 52* ☎ *071/202317* ☰ *AE, DC, MC, V* ⊘ *Closed Sun., Jan. 1–10, and Aug. 13–18.*

$–$$ ✕ **Osteria del Pozzo.** The *antipasto di mare* (seafood appetizer), delicately flavored with a few drops of light olive oil and mixed with tiny pieces of seasonal fruit, is one reason the predominantly seafood restaurant is popular with locals. Pastas and main courses are equally delicious, and you should definitely finish with the restaurant's *sorbetto di limone* (lemon sorbet), served in a glass as a cool refreshing drink. This small, plain place is on a narrow cobblestone street between the port and Piazza del Plebiscito. ✉ *Via Bonda 2* ☎ *071/207–3996* ☰ *AE, DC, MC, V* ⊘ *Closed Sun., Jan. 6–15, and Aug. 7–31.*

$$$ 🏨 **Grand Hotel Palace.** Widely held to be the best hotel in town, it's the extras here—slippers, bath salts, and shaving kits—that earn the ranking. Rooms are on the small side but beautifully furnished with French beds dressed in yellow damask, and half have a view directly over the port. Public rooms are grand and elegant, and the breakfast room is on the top floor with a panoramic view. ✉ *Lungomare Vanvitelli 24, 60100* ☎ *071/201813* 🖷 *071/2074832* ⊕ *www.alberghiancona.it* ↩ *39 rooms, 1 suite* ⚐ *Dining room, gym, bar, Internet, meeting rooms* ☰ *AE, DC, MC, V* ⊘ *Closed Dec. 23–Jan. 1* ⊙ *BP.*

Loreto

➋➏ *31 km (19 mi) south of Ancona, 118 km (73 mi) southeast of Urbino.*

★ Thousands of pilgrims come to Loreto every year to visit one of the world's best-loved shrines, the **Santuario della Santa Casa** (House of the Virgin Mary), within the basilica. According to legend, angels moved the house from Nazareth to this hilltop in 1295, when Nazareth fell into the hands of Muslim invaders. Excavations made at the behest of the Church have shown that the house did once stand elsewhere and was brought to the hilltop—either by crusaders or a family named Angeli (tranlated, "angels")—around that time.

Easter week and the Feast of the Holy House on December 10 are marked by processions, prayers, and a deluge of pilgrims; the rest of the year the shrine is relatively quiet. The house itself consists of three rough stone walls contained within an elaborate marble tabernacle;

built around this centerpiece is the giant basilica of the Holy House, which dominates the town. The basilica was begun in Gothic style in 1468 and continued in Renaissance style through the late Renaissance with the help of some of the period's greatest architects: Bramante, Antonio da Sangallo (the Younger, 1483–1546), Giuliano da Sangallo (circa 1445–1516), and Sansovino (1467–1529).

The Holy Virgin of Loreto is the patroness of air travelers; you can pick up Pope John Paul II's prayer for a safe flight in the church, where it's available in a dozen languages. ⊠ *Piazza della Madonna* ☎ *071/970104* ⊕ *www.santuarioloreto.it* ⊗ *June–Sept., daily 6:45–12:30 and 2:30–8; Oct.–May, daily 6:45–12:30 and 2:30–7.*

Ascoli Piceno

㉗ *74 km (38 mi) south of Loreto, 175 km (109 mi) southeast of Perugia.*

Ascoli Piceno is not a hill town; rather, it sits in a valley ringed by steep hills and cut by the fast-racing Tronto River. You can drive *around* the quaint old town, but much of the center of town is closed to traffic. This makes Ascoli Piceno one of the most pleasant large towns in the country for exploring on foot.

★ The heart of Ascoli Piceno is the majestic **Piazza del Popolo,** dominated by the Gothic church of **San Francesco** and the **Palazzo dei Capitani del Popolo,** a 13th-century town hall that contains a graceful Renaissance courtyard. The square functions as the city's living room: at dusk each evening the piazza fills with people strolling and exchanging news and gossip.

☾ Ascoli Piceno's **Giostra della Quintana** (Joust of the Quintana) is held on the first Sunday in August. Children love this medieval-style joust and the processions of richly caparisoned horses that wind through the streets of the old town. *Ascoli tourist office* ⊠ *Piazza del Popolo 1* ☎ *0736/253045.*

Where to Stay & Eat

10

★ **$–$$** ✕ **Ristorante Tornasacco.** At one of Ascoli Piceno's oldest restaurants you won't find nouvelle cuisine: the owners pride themselves on meaty local specialties such as olives *ascolane* (stuffed with minced meat, breaded and deep-fried), *maccheroncini alla contadina* (homemade short pasta in a lamb, pork, and veal sauce), and *bistecca di toro* (bull steak). ⊠ *Piazza del Popolo 36* ☎ *0736/254151* ▭ *AE, DC, MC, V* ⊗ *Closed Fri., July 15–31, and Dec. 23–28.*

$ ▦ **Il Pennile.** Look for this modern, family-run hotel in a quiet residential area outside the old city center, amid a grove of olive trees. Rooms are functional singles, doubles, and triples some have views of the city. ⊠ *Via G. Spalvieri, 63100* ☎ *0736/41645* ▤ *0736/342755* ⊕ *www.hotelpennile.com* ⊶ *33 rooms* ⚑ *Minibars, gym, bar, Internet* ▭ *DC, MC, V* ⎰ *BP.*

UMBRIA & THE MARCHES ESSENTIALS

Transportation

BY AIR

Central Italy's closest major airports are in Florence, Rome, and Pisa— 2-, 2½-, and 3-hour drives, respectively. Perugia's tiny Aeroporto Sant'Egidio has flights to and from Milan, Rome Ciampino, and Palermo.
🗐 **Aeroporto Sant'Egidio** 🕾 075/592141 ⊕ www.airport.umbria.it. **Alitalia** 🕾 848/ 865642 ⊕ www.alitalia.it.

BY BUS

Perugia is served by the Sulga Line, with daily departures from Rome's Stazione Tiburtina and from Piazza Adua in Florence. Connections between Rome, Spoleto, and Urbino are provided by the associated bus companies Bucci and Soget, while Ascoli Piceno can be reached from Rome using the La Start company.

These same companies operate local bus service between all the major and minor towns within Umbria and the Marches. In addition, service between Loreto and Ancona is provided by the company Reni. Bus information is available from local tourist information offices or directly from area bus companies.
🗐 **Bus Information Bucci–Soget** ⊠ Strada delle Marche 56, Pesaro 🕾 0721/32401 ⊕ www.autolineebucci.com. **Reni** ⊠ Via Albertini 18, Ancona 🕾 071/804-6504 ⊕ www. anconarenibus.it. **La Start** ⊠ Viale Kennedy 22 🕾 0763/263053 ⊕ www.startspa.it. **Sulga Line** ⊠ Stazione Tiburtina, Rome 🕾 075/500-9641 ⊕ www.sulga.it.

BY CAR

On the western edge of the region is the Umbrian section of the Autostrada del Sole (A1), Italy's principal north–south highway. It links Florence and Rome with Orvieto and passes near Todi and Terni. The S3 intersects with A1 and leads on to Assisi and Urbino. The Adriatica superhighway (A14) runs north–south along the coast, linking the Marches to Bologna and Venice.

The steep hills and deep valleys that make Umbria and the Marches so idyllic also make for challenging driving. Fortunately, the area has an excellent, modern road network, but be prepared for tortuous mountain roads if your explorations take you off the beaten track. Central Umbria is served by a major highway, the S75bis, which passes along the shore of Lake Trasimeno and ends in Perugia. Assisi is served by the modern highway S75; S75 connects to S3 and S3bis, which cover the heart of the region. Major inland routes connect coastal A14 to large towns in the Marches, including Urbino, Jesi, Macerata, and Ascoli Piceno, but inland secondary roads in mountain areas can be winding and narrow. Always carry a good road map, a flashlight, and, if possible, a cell phone in case of a breakdown.
🗐 Car Rental Agencies **Avis** ⊠ Sant'Egidio airport, Perugia 🕾 075/692-9796 ⊠ Stazione Ferroviaria Fontivegge, Perugia 🕾 075/500-0395 ⊠ Località S. Chiodo 164, Spoleto 🕾 0743/46272 ⊠ Via XX Settembre 80/d, Terni 🕾 0744/287170. **Europ-**

car ✉ Via Ruggero d'Andreotto 7, Perugia ☎ 075/573-1704 ✉ Via degli Artigiani 10, Terni ☎ 0744/817337 ✉ Raffaello Sanzio airport, Ancona ☎ 071/916-2240. **Hertz** ✉ Via 7 Martiri 32/f, Orvieto ☎ 0763/301303 ✉ Piazza Vittorio Veneto 4, Perugia ☎ 075/ 500-2439 ✉ Sant'Egidio airport, Perugia ☎ 075/500-2439 ✉ Via Cerquiglia 144, Spoleto ☎ 0743/46703.

BY TRAIN

Frequent intercity trains link Florence and Rome with Perugia and Assisi, and local service to the same area is available from Terontola (on the Rome–Florence line) and from Foligno (on the Rome–Ancona line). Intercity trains between Rome and Florence make stops in Orvieto, and the main Rome–Ancona line passes through Narni, Terni, Spoleto, and Foligno. Branch lines link Ancona with the inland towns of Fabriano and Ascoli Piceno. In Umbria, a small, privately owned railway operated by Ferrovia Centrale Umbra (FCU) runs from Città di Castello in the north to Terni in the south via Perugia. Note, train service is available neither to Gubbio nor to Urbino.

🚆 Train Information **Ferrovia Centrale Umbra** (FCU) ☎ 075/572-9121 ⊕ www.fcu.it. **Ferrovie dello Stato** ☎ 892021 ⊕ www.trenitalia.com.

Contacts & Resources

EMERGENCIES

Emergency numbers are accessible from every phone, including cellular phones, all over Italy. If you have ongoing medical concerns, it's a good idea to make sure someone is on duty all night where you're staying—not a given in Umbria, less so in the Marches. As elsewhere in Italy, every pharmacy in Umbria and the Marches bears a sign at the door listing area pharmacies open in off-hours. Perugia, Spoleto, Assisi, Gubbio, and Urbino all have at least one so-called "night" pharmacy, but out in the countryside you may need a car to get to one. Try to bring extras with you of all medications you take regularly.

In car emergencies, call ACI for towing and repairs—you can ask to be transferred to an English-speaking operator; be prepared to tell the operator which road you're on, the direction you're going (e.g., "*verso* [in the direction of] Perugia") and the *targa* (license plate number) of your car. The great majority of Italians carry cellular phones, so if you don't have one, flag down someone who does for help.

🚗 **ACI** ☎ 803/116. **Ambulance** ☎ 118. **Carabinieri** (Military Police) ☎ 112. **Emergencies** ☎ 113. **Fire** ☎ 115.

VISITOR INFORMATION

Turismo Verde, as well as local tourist offices, can provide you with information about *agriturismi* (farm stays) in the countryside. Though officially working farms, these range in style from rustic, with little more than a bed-and-breakfast, to luxury resorts with swimming pools and restaurants.

🚩 Tourist Information **Ancona** ✉ Via Thaon de Revel 4, 60100 ☎ 071/358991 ⊕ www. comune.ancona.it. **Ascoli Piceno** ✉ Piazza del Popolo 1, 63100 ☎ 0736/253045 ⊕ www.comune.ascolipiceno.it. **Assisi** ✉ Piazza del Comune 12, 06081 ☎ 075/812534

⊕ www.comune.assisi.pg.it. **Gubbio** ⊠ Via Ansidei 32, 06024 ☎ 075/9220790 ⊕ www. comune.gubbio.pg.it. **Loreto** ⊠ Via Solari 3, 60025 ☎ 071/970276 ⊕ www.turismo. marche.it. **Narni** ⊠ Piazza dei Priori 3, 05035 ☎ 0744/715362 ⊕ www.comune.narni. tr.it. **Orvieto** ⊠ Piazza Duomo 24, 05018 ☎ 0763/341772 ⊕ www.comune.orvieto.tr.it. **Perugia** ⊠ Piazza IV Novembre 3, 06123 ☎ 075/572-3327 ⊕ www.umbria2000.it. **Spoleto** ⊠ Piazza della Libertà 7, 06049 ☎ 0743/49890 ⊕ www.comune.spoleto.pg. it. **Terni** ⊠ Viale Cesare Battisti 7/a, 05100 ☎ 0744/423047. **Todi** ⊠ Piazza Umberto I 6, 06059 ☎ 075/8943395 ⊕ www.comune.todi.pg.it. **Turismo Verde** ⊠ Via Maria Angeloni 1, 06124 Perugia ☎ 075/5002953 🖷 075/5002956 ⊕ www.turismoverde.it. **Urbino** ⊠ Piazza Duca Federico 35, 61029 ☎ 0722/2613 ⊕ www.turismo.marche.it.

Rome

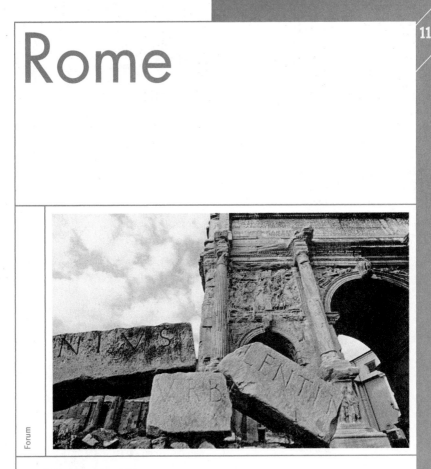

Forum

WORD OF MOUTH

"There's something very powerful to being surrounded by all that history (and I'm not a history buff). It's not a place where you walk up, snap a picture, and say, 'All right I've seen it.' It's an imposing experience (in a good way). The effect is very strong. There are other beautiful scenic places in the world, but there's only one Rome."

—flatfeet

WELCOME TO ROME

St. Peter's Basilica

TOP 5
Reasons to Go

1 The Pantheon: Of ancient Rome's remains, this is the best preserved and most impressive.

2 St. Peter's Square and Basilica: The primary church of the Catholic faith is truly awe-inspiring.

3 Galleria Borghese: With a setting as exquisite as its collection, this small, elegant museum showcases some of the finest baroque and Renaissance art in Italy.

4 A morning walk through Campo de' Fiori: The city comes alive in this wonderful square.

5 Roman pizza: Maybe it's the ovens, maybe the crust, maybe the cheese, but they just don't make it like this back home.

Getting Oriented

Rome is a sprawling city, but you'll likely spend all your time in and around the historic center. The area is split by the River Tiber (Tevere in Italian). To its west are the Vatican and the Trastevere neighborhood. To its east is everything else you've come to see: the Colosseum, the Pantheon, and scores of other exceptional sights, not to mention piazzas, fountains, shops, and restaurants. This is one of the most culturally rich plots of land in the world.

At the Vatican, headquarters of the Roman Catholic Church, everything is done in bold measures, from **St. Peter's Basilica** to the ceiling of the **Sistine Chapel.**

CITTÀ DEL VATICAN

Sistine Chapel

Borgo Pio

Castle St. Angelo

St. Peter's   V. d. Conciliazione

V. del Coronari

Corso Vittorio Emanuele I.

Pza Navc

Tiber

V. della Lungara

Parco Gianicolense

Campo de' Fiori

S. Maria in Trastevere

TRASTEVERE

From Via del Corso to the Tiber, the cobblestone streets of Baroque Rome lead from one landmark to another, including the **Pantheon, Piazza Navona,** and **Campo de' Fiori.**

Trastevere residents pride themselves on being the most authentic Romans, and though the neighborhood has become trendy, it retains a tight-knit feel.

Villa Borghese

Villa Borghese is Rome's answer to Central Park. Within it is the exceptional Galleria Borghese art museum.

The Spanish Steps, rising up from the Piazza di Spagna, have been a popular gathering place for centuries. Radiating out from them is Rome's toniest shopping district.

The Quirinale area is filled with palaces, including the home of the Italian president, as well as several works by the baroque master Bernini.

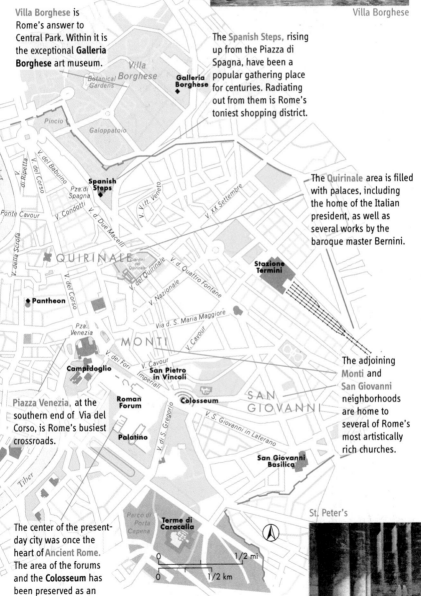

Piazza Venezia, at the southern end of Via del Corso, is Rome's busiest crossroads.

The adjoining Monti and San Giovanni neighborhoods are home to several of Rome's most artistically rich churches.

The center of the present-day city was once the heart of Ancient Rome. The area of the forums and the Colosseum has been preserved as an archaeological treasure.

St. Peter's

**Map labels:**
Villa Borghese
Botanical Gardens
Galleria Borghese
Pincio
Galoppatoio
Tiber
V. di Ripetta
V. del Babuino
V. del Corso
Spanish Steps
Pza. di Spagna
V. Condotti
Ponte Cavour
V. d. Due Macelli
V. Vitt. Veneto
V. XX Settembre
QUIRINALE
Giardini del Quirinale
V. del Quirinale
V. d. Quattro Fontane
Stazione Termini
V. della Scrofa
Pantheon
V. del Corso
V. Nazionale
Pza. Venezia
Via d. S. Maria Maggiore
MONTI
V. Cavour
Campidoglio
V. dei Fori Imperiali
V. Cavour
San Pietro in Vincoli
Roman Forum
Colosseum
SAN GIOVANNI
V. S. Giovanni in Laterano
Palatino
V. di S. Gregorio
San Giovanni Basilica
Tiber
Parco di Porta Capena
Terme di Caracalla
0   1/2 mi
0   1/2 km

ROME PLANNER

Making the Most of Your Time

"Roma, non basta una vita" (Rome, a lifetime is not enough): this famous saying should be stamped on the passport of every first-time visitor to the Eternal City. On the one hand, it's a warning: Rome is so packed with sights that it's impossible take them all in; it's easy to run yourself ragged trying to check off the items on your "must see" list. At the same time, the saying is a celebration of the city's abundance. There's so much here, you're bound to make discoveries you hadn't anticipated.

To conquer Rome, strike a balance between visits to major sights and leisurely neighborhood strolls. In the first category, the Vatican and the remains of ancient Rome loom the largest. Both require at least half a day; a good strategy is to devote your first morning to one and your second to the other. Leave the afternoons for exploring the neighborhood we label "Baroque Rome" and the shopping district around the Spanish Steps and Via del Corso.

If you have more days at your disposal, continue with the same approach. Among the sights, Galleria Borghese and the multilayered church of San Clemente are particularly worthwhile, and the neighborhoods of Trastevere and the Jewish Ghetto make for great wandering.

Getting Around

Most of Rome's sights are concentrated in the city center, but the area is too large to cover exclusively on foot. Transportation options are the metro (subway), bus, tram, and taxi—the pros and cons of each are detailed in the "Essentials" section at the end of the chapter. No matter what method you use to get around, try to avoid rush hours (8–9, 1–2:30, 7–8). Driving is always a mistake.

Expect to do lots of walking. Cobblestone streets call for comfortable shoes (though some natives seem willing to endure any pain in the name of fashion). Try to avoid the congestion and noise of major thoroughfares; plan routes along parallel side streets instead. Most hotels will give you a functional city map, and you can also pick maps up for free at tourist information booths. If you crave greater detail, purchase better maps at newsstands.

Safety Tips

Chances are your visit will be incident-free, but it's smart to be alert to the following:

■ The young pickpockets described under "Safety" in the Smart Travel Tips section at the front of this book are a common presence around Rome's major sights.

■ Pickpockets like to work public transit, particularly bus lines 64 and 40 Express between Termini station and St. Peter's. Gropers are also a presence on buses and subways. If you encounter one, react like the locals: forcefully and loudly.

■ Termini station is the site of numerous scams. Keep an eye on your belongings at all times.

■ They may not qualify as criminals, but the men who linger around the Colosseum in gladiator costume are con artists. They'll happily pose for a photograph with you, then demand a ridiculous fee.

Roman Hours

As you make your plans, keep in mind the following timing issues:

■ Most churches open at 8 or 9 in the morning, close from noon to 3 or 4, then reopen until 6:30 or 7. The notable exception is St. Peter's, which has continuous hours from 7 AM to 7 PM (6 in the fall and winter).

■ Many museums are closed on Monday, including the Galleria Borghese, the Etruscan Museum at Villa Giulia, and the museums of the Campidoglio.

■ The Vatican Museums are open

on Monday but closed on Sunday, except for the last Sunday of the month (when admission is free and crowds are large). From November through mid-March, the museums close for the day at 1:45.

Not surprisingly, spring and fall are the best times to visit, with mild temperatures and many sunny days; the famous Roman sunsets are also at their best. Summers are often sweltering. In July and August, come if you like, but learn to do as the Romans do—get up and out early, seek refuge from the afternoon heat (nap if you can), resume activities in early evening, and stay up late to enjoy the nighttime breeze. Come August, many shops and restaurants close as natives head for the beach or the countryside. Roman winters are relatively mild, with persistent rainy spells.

Piazza Navona

Sistine Chapel

Reservations

You should reserve tickets for the following sights. See the listings within the chapter for contact information:

■ Galleria Borghese requires reservations. Visitors are admitted in two-hour shifts, and prime time slots can sell out days in advance, so it pays to plan ahead. You can reserve by phone or through the gallery's Web site.

■ In the ancient Rome archaeological area,

reservations for the Colosseum save you from standing in a ticket line that sometimes takes upward of an hour; at the Domus Aurea, a reservation guarantees you one of the limited of admission spots. You can reserve for both at the same time, by phone or on the Web.

■ At the Vatican, you need to reserve several days in advance to see the necropolis and the gardens. For information about attending a papal audience, see the CloseUp box "A Morning with the Pope" several pages into this chapter.

ROME IS A HEADY BLEND of artistic and architectural masterpieces, classical ruins, and extravagant baroque churches and piazzas. The city's 2,700 years of history are on display everywhere you look. The ancient rubs shoulders with the medieval, the modern runs into the Renaissance, and the result is like nothing so much as an open-air museum. Julius Caesar and Nero, the Vandals and the Borgias, Raphael and Caravaggio, Napoléon and Mussolini—they and countless other political, cultural, and spiritual luminaries have left their mark on the city. More than Florence, more than Venice, Rome is Italy's treasure trove, packed with masterpieces from more than two millennia of artistic achievement. This is where a metropolis once bustled around the carved marble monuments of the Roman Forum, where centuries later Michelangelo Buonarotti painted Christian history in the Sistine Chapel, where Gian Lorenzo Bernini's nymphs and naiads dance in their fountains, and where an empire of gold was worked into the crowns of centuries of rulers.

Today Rome's formidable legacy is upheld by its people, their history knit into the fabric of their everyday lives. Students walk dogs in the park that was once the mausoleum of the family of the emperor Augustus; Raphaelesque madonnas line up for buses on busy corners; priests in flowing robes walk through medieval piazzas talking on cell phones. Modern Rome has one foot in the past, one in the present—a delightful stance that allows you to have an espresso in a square designed by Bernini, then take the metro back to your hotel room in a renovated Renaissance palace. "When you first come here you assume that you must burrow about in ruins and prowl in museums to get back to the days of Numa Pompilius or Mark Antony," Maud Howe observes in her book *Roma Beata*. "It is not necessary; you only have to live, and the common happenings of daily life—yes, even the trolley car and your bicycle—carry you back in turn to the Dark Ages, to the early Christians, even to prehistoric Rome."

EXPLORING ROME

Updated by
Valerie
Hamilton

Though spread out, Rome invites walking, and taxis are rarely far off. Plan your day taking into account the varying opening hours of the sights you want to visit, which usually means mixing the ancient, classical, and baroque, museums and parks, the center and the environs. Keep in mind that an uncharted ramble through the heart of the old city can be just as satisfying as the quiet contemplation of a chapel or a trek through marbled museum corridors. The Rome Archeologia Card, a combination ticket for the Colosseum, Palatine, and the various branches of the Museo Nazionale Romano (Palazzo Altemps, Crypta Balbi, Terme di Diocleziano, Terme di Caracalla, Villa dei Quintili, the Mausoleo di Cecilia Metella, and Palazzo Massimo alle Terme), valid for seven consecutive days, is available at each participant's ticket office for €20—a good deal for ancient-history buffs.

The Vatican: Rome of the Popes

This tiny walled city-state, capital of the Catholic Church, draws millions every year to its wealth of treasures and spiritual monuments. You might visit the Vatican for its exceptional art holdings—Michelangelo's frescoes, rare archaeological marbles, and Bernini's statues—or you may want to appreciate the singular and grandiose architecture of St. Peter's Square. Many come here on pilgrimage, spiritual or otherwise, to see the seat of world Catholicism and the most overwhelming architectural achievement of the Renaissance, St. Peter's Basilica. At the Vatican Museums there are magnificent rooms decorated by Raphael, sculptures such as the *Apollo Belvedere* and the *Laocoön,* frescoes by Fra Angelico, paintings by Giotto and Leonardo, and the celebrated ceiling of the Sistine Chapel. The Church power that emerged as the Rome of the emperors declined gave impetus to a profusion of artistic expression and shaped the destiny of the city for a thousand years.

Allow yourself an hour to see the Basilica, 30 minutes for the Museo Storico, 15 minutes for the Vatican Grottoes, an hour for Castel Sant'Angelo, and an hour to climb to the top of the dome. Ushers at the entrance of St. Peter's Basilica and the Vatican Museums bar entry to people with "inappropriate" clothing—which means no bare knees or shoulders.

The Main Attractions

★ ❸ **Basilica di San Pietro.** The physical proportions of the sublime St. Peter's Basilica are staggering: it covers about 18,100 square yards, extends 212 yards in length, and carries a dome that rises 435 feet and measures 138 feet across its base. The church's history dates back to the year AD 319, when the emperor Constantine built a basilica over the site of the tomb of St. Peter (died AD 64). This early church stood for more than 1,000 years, undergoing a number of restorations, until it was on the verge of collapse.

In 1506 Pope Julius II (1443–1513) commissioned the architect Bramante to build a new and greater basilica, but construction would take more than 170 years. In 1546 Michelangelo was persuaded to take over the job, but the magnificent cupola was finally completed by Giacomo della Porta (circa 1537–1602) and Domenico Fontana (1543–1607). The new church wasn't dedicated until 1626; by that time Renaissance had given way to baroque, and many of the plan's original elements had gone the way of their designers. At the entrance, the 15th-century bronze doors by Filarete (circa 1400–69) fill the central portal. Off the entry portico, architect and sculptor Gianlorenzo Bernini's famous *Scala Regia,* the ceremonial entry to the Vatican Palace, is one of the most magnificent staircases in the world and is graced with Bernini's dramatic statue of Constantine the Great.

Entering the sanctuary, take a moment to adjust to the enormity of the space stretching in front of you. The cherubs over the holy-water fonts have feet as long as the distance from your fingertips to your elbow. It is because the proportions are in such perfect harmony that the vastness may escape you at first. The megascale was inspired by the size of the ancient Roman ruins.

The Vatican

KEY

🛈 *Tourist information*

Basilica di San Pietro ...**3**

Castel Sant'Angelo **1**

Giardini Vaticani **6**

Musei Vaticani **5**

Piazza San Pietro **2**

Vatican Necropolis **4**

Over an altar in a side chapel near the entrance is Michelangelo's *Pietà*, a sculpture of Mary holding her son Jesus's body after crucifixion—the star attraction here other than the basilica itself. Legend has it that the artist, only 22 at the time the work was completed, overheard passersby expressing skepticism that such a young man could have executed such a sophisticated and moving piece. It's said that his offense at the implication was why he crept back that night and signed the piece—in big letters, on a ribbon falling from the Virgin's left shoulder across her breast.

Inlaid in the gorgeous marble pavement of the nave's central aisles are the names of the world's great cathedrals organized by church size—the message is clear, St. Peter's has them all beaten. At the crossing of the aisles four massive piers support the dome, and the mighty Bernini **baldacchino** (canopy) rises high above the papal altar, where the pope celebrates mass. "What the barbarians didn't do, the Barberini did," 17th-century wags quipped when Barberini Pope Urban VIII had the bronze stripped from the Pantheon's portico and melted down to make the baldacchino (using what was left over for cannonballs). The bronze throne behind the main altar in the apse, the *Cathedra Petri* (Chair of St. Peter), is Bernini's work (1656), and it covers a wooden-and-ivory chair that St. Peter himself is said to have used. However, scholars contend that this throne probably dates only from the Middle Ages. See how the adoration of a million lips has completely worn down the bronze on the right foot of the statue of St. Peter in front of the near right pillar in the transept. Free one-hour English-language tours of the basilica depart Monday–Saturday at 10 and 3, Sunday at 2:30 (sign up at the little desk under the portico). St. Peter's is closed during ceremonies in the piazza. ⊠ *Piazza San Pietro* ⊕ *www.vatican.va* ⊗ *Apr.–Sept., daily 7–7; Oct.–Mar., daily 7–6.*

The **Grotte Vaticane** (Vatican Grottoes) in the basilica contain the tombs of many popes including John Paul II, and the Tomb of St. Peter. The entrance is opposite the baldacchino, near a pillar where the dome begins. The only exit leads outside the church, so don't go down until you're finished elsewhere. ⊡ *Free* ⊗ *Apr.–Sept., daily 7–6; Oct.–Mar., daily 7–5.*

A small but rich collection of Vatican treasures is housed in the **Museo Storico** in St. Peter's Sacristy, among them precious antique chalices and the massive 15th-century sculptured bronze tomb of Pope Sixtus V (1520–90) by Antonio del Pollaiuolo (1431–98). ⊡ €9 ⊗ *Daily 8–5.*

The **roof** of St. Peter's basilica, reached by elevator or stairs, provides a view among a landscape of domes and towers. A short interior staircase leads to the base of the dome for a dove's-eye look at the interior of St. Peter's. Then, only if you are stout of heart and sound of lung should you attempt the taxing and claustrophobic climb up the hundreds of narrow stairs to the balcony of the lantern, where the view embraces the Vatican Gardens and all of Rome. The up and down staircases are one-way; once you commit to climbing, there's no turning back. ☎ *06/69883462* ⊡ *Elevator €5, stairs €4* ⊗ *Daily 8–5.*

🐾 ❶ **Castel Sant'Angelo.** For hundreds of years this fortress guarded the Vatican, to which it is linked by the **Passetto**, an arcaded passageway. According to legend, Castel Sant'Angelo got its name during the plague of 590, when Pope Gregory the Great (circa 540–604), passing by in a religious

A Morning with the Pope

THE POPE HOLDS AUDIENCES in a large, modern hall (or in St. Peter's Square in summer) on Wednesday morning at 10. To attend, you must get tickets; apply in writing at least 10 days in advance to the Papal Prefecture (Prefettura della Casa Pontificia; ☐ 00120 Vatican City ☎ 06/69883273 🖷 06/69885863), indicating the date you prefer, your language, and your hotel. Or go to the prefecture, through the Porta di Bronzo, the bronze door at the end of the colonnade on the right side of the piazza; the office is open Monday–Saturday 9–1, and last-minute tickets may be available. You can also arrange to pick up free tickets on Tuesday from 5 to 6:45 at the Santa Susanna American Church (⊠ Via XX Settembre 15, near Termini ☎ 06/42014554); call first. For a fee, travel agencies make arrangements that include transportation. Arrive early, as security is tight and the best places fill up fast.

procession, had a vision of an angel sheathing its sword atop the stone ramparts. Though it may look like a stronghold, Castel Sant'Angelo was in fact built as a tomb for the emperor Hadrian (76–138) in AD 135. By the 6th century it had been transformed into a fortress, and it remained a refuge for the popes for almost 1,000 years. It has dungeons, battlements, cannon and cannonballs, and a collection of antique weaponry and armor. The lower levels formed the base of Hadrian's mausoleum; ancient ramps and narrow staircases climb through the castle's core to courtyards and frescoed halls, where temporary exhibits are held. Off the loggia is a café.

The upper terrace, with the massive angel statue commemorating Gregory's vision, evokes memories of Tosca, Puccini's poignant heroine in the opera of the same name, who threw herself off these ramparts with the cry, *"Scarpia, avanti a Dio!"* ("Scarpia, we meet before God"). On summer evenings a book fair with musical events and food stalls surrounds the castle. One of Rome's most beautiful pedestrian bridges, **Ponte Sant'Angelo** spans the Tiber in front of the fortress and is studded with graceful angels designed by Bernini. ⊠ *Lungotevere Castello 50, San Pietro* ☎ *06/39967700* ⊕ *www.pierreci.it* 🎫 *€5* ⊙ *Tues.–Sun. 9–8.*

❺   **Musei Vaticani** (The Vatican Museums). The Vatican Palace has been the
 papal residence since 1377; it's a collection of buildings covering more
★   than 13 acres, with an estimated 1,400 rooms, chapels, and galleries. Other than the pope and his court, the occupant is the Musei Vaticani (Vatican Museums), containing some of art's greatest masterpieces. The Sistine Chapel is the headliner here, but in your haste to get there, don't overlook the Museo Egizio, with its fine Egyptian collection; the famed classical sculptures of the Chiaramonti and the Museo Pio Clementino; and the Stanze di Raffaelo (Raphael Rooms), a suite of halls covered floor-to-ceiling in some of the master's greatest works.

On a first visit to the Vatican Museums, you may just want to see the highlights—even that will take several hours and a good, long walk. The collection is divided among different galleries, halls, and wings connected end to end. Pick up a leaflet at the main entrance to the museums to see the overall layout. The Sistine Chapel is a must, of course, and that's why you may have to wait in line to see it; after all, every tourist in Rome has the same idea. The Sistine Chapel is at the far end of the complex, and the leaflet charts two abbreviated itineraries through other collections to reach it. An audio guide (€5.50, about 90 minutes) for the Sistine Chapel, the Stanze di Raffaello, and 350 other works and locations are worth it. Phone at least a day in advance to book a guided tour (€16.50) through the Guided Visit to Vatican Museums.

The main entrance to the museums, on Viale Vaticano, is a long walk from Piazza San Pietro. Some city buses stop near the main entrance: Bus 49 from Piazza Cavour stops right in front; Buses 81 and 492 and Tram 19 stop at Piazza Risorgimento, halfway between St. Peter's and the museums. The Ottaviano–S. Pietro and the Cipro–Musei Vaticani stops on Metro A also are in the vicinity. Entry is free the first Sunday of the month, and the museum is closed on Catholic holidays. Last admission is an hour before closing. ⊠ *Main museum entrance, Viale Vaticano; guided visit office, Piazza San Pietro* ☎ *06/69883332, 06/69884676 guided visit reservations* 🖷 *06/69885100 guided visit reservations* ⊕ *www.vatican.va* 🖼 *€12* ☉ *Mid-Mar.–Oct., weekdays 8:45–4:45, Sat. and last Sun. of month 8:45–1:45; Nov.–mid-Mar., Mon.–Sat. and last Sun. of month 8:45–1:45.*

Besides the galleries we list here, there are many other wings along your way—full of maps, tapestries, classical sculpture, Egyptian mummies, Etruscan statues, and even Aztec treasures. From the main entrance of the Vatican Museums take the escalator up to the **Pinacoteca** (Picture Gallery) on your right. This is a self-contained section, and it's worth visiting first for works by such artists as Leonardo, Giotto (circa 1266–1337), Fra Angelico, and Filippo Lippi (circa 1406–69), and Raphael's exceptional *Transfiguration, Coronation* and *Foligno Madonna.*

The **Cortile Ottagano** (Octagonal Courtyard) of the Vatican Museum displays some of sculpture's most famous works, including the 4th century BC *Apollo Belvedere* (and Canova's 1801 *Perseus,* heavily influenced by it) and the 2nd century *Laocoön.*

The **Stanze di Raffaello** (Raphael Rooms) are second only to the Sistine Chapel in artistic interest—and draw crowds comparable. In 1508 Pope Julius II (1503–1513) employed Raphael, on the recommendation of Bramante, to decorate the rooms with biblical scenes. The result was a Renaissance tour de force. Of the four rooms, the second and third were decorated mainly by Raphael. The others were decorated by Giulio Romano (circa 1499–1546) and other assistants of Raphael; the first room is known as the Stanza dell'Incendio, with frescoes by Romano of the *incendio* (fire) in the Borgo neighborhood.

The frescoed **Stanza della Segnatura** (Room of the Signature), where papal bulls were signed, is one of Raphael's finest works; indeed, they are thought by many to be some of the finest paintings in the history of Western art. This was Julius's private library, and the room's use is reflected in the frescoes' themes, philosophy and enlightenment. A paradigm of High Renaissance painting, the works demonstrate the revolutionary ideals of naturalism (Raphael's figures lack the awkwardness of those painted only a few years earlier); humanism (the idea that human beings are the noblest and most admirable of God's creations); and a profound interest in the ancient world, the result of the 15th-century rediscovery of classical antiquity. The *School of Athens* glorifies some of philosophy's greats, including Plato (pointing to Heaven) and Aristotle (pointing to Earth) at the fresco's center. The pensive figure on the stairs is thought to be modeled after Michelangelo, who was painting the Sistine ceiling at the same time Raphael was working here. Michelangelo does not appear in preparatory drawings, so Raphael may have added his fellow artist's portrait after admiring his work.

The tiny **Cappella di Nicholas V** (Chapel of Nicholas V) is aglow with frescoes by Fra Angelico (1387–1455), the Florentine monk whose sensitive paintings were guiding lights for the Renaissance. The **Appartamento Borgia** (Borgia Apartment) is worth seeing for the elaborately painted ceilings, designed and partially executed by Pinturicchio. Among the frescoes, look for the Borgia's family emblem, the bull, and for the blond Lucrezia, the Borgia pope's daughter, posing piously as St. Catherine.

In 1508, just before Raphael started work on his rooms, the redoubtable Pope Julius II commissioned Michelangelo to paint single-handedly the more than 10,000-square-foot ceiling of the **Cappella Sistina** (Sistine Chapel). The task cost the artist four years of mental and physical anguish. It's said that for years afterward Michelangelo couldn't read anything without holding it up over his head. The result, however, was the masterpiece that you now see, its colors cool and brilliant after restoration. Bring a pair of binoculars to get a better look at this incredible work (unfortunately, you're not allowed to lie down on the floor to study the frescoes above, the viewing position of choice in decades past). Tourists in the 19th century used pocket mirrors so as not to strain their necks.

WORD OF MOUTH

"At the Vatican Museums, we did the audio tour, and took our time looking at the Map Room, the tapestries, trompe l'oeil ceilings, the stunning Borgia Papal Apartments, and the Raphael Rooms. Finally, we got to the Sistine Chapel. Wow! We just sat on the benches along the wall for 30 minutes, looking at the Old and New Testament friezes." –Bardo

The exhibition halls of the **Biblioteca Vaticana** (Vatican Library) are bright with frescoes and contain a sampling of the library's rich collections of precious manuscripts. The **Room of the Aldobrandini Marriage** (Room X) holds a beautiful Roman fresco of a nuptial rite, which deserves a look after you've seen the rest of the museum.

need a break? You don't have to snack at the touristy joints outside the Vatican Museums; a short walk away are neighborhood restaurants catering to locals. Among them is the **Hostaria Dino e Toni** (⊠ Via Leone IV 60, near San Pietro), where you can dine on typical Roman fare at

moderate, even inexpensive prices. **La Caravella** (⊠ Via degli
Scipioni 32, at Via Vespasiano, off Piazza Risorgimento, near San
Pietro) serves pizza at lunch every day but Thursday, when it's closed.

❷ Piazza San Pietro. As you enter St. Peter's Square you are officially entering Vatican territory. The piazza is one of Bernini's most spectacular masterpieces. Completed in 1667 after 11 years' work—a relatively short time
in those days, considering the vastness of the task—the piazza can hold
400,000 people. It's surrounded by a curving pair of quadruple colonnades, which are topped by a balustrade and statues of 140 saints. Look
for the two disks set into the pavement on either side of the obelisk at
the center of the piazza. When you stand on either disk, a trick of perspective makes the colonnades seem to consist of a single row of columns.
Bernini had an even grander visual effect in mind when he designed the
square. By opening up this immense, bright, airy space in a neighborhood of narrow, shadowy streets, he created a contrast that would surprise and impress anyone who emerged from the darkness into the light,
in a characteristically baroque metaphor. But in the 1930s Mussolini spoiled
the effect. To celebrate the "conciliation" between the Vatican and the
Italian government under the Lateran Pact of 1929, he conceived of the
Via della Conciliazione, the broad, rather soulless avenue that now forms
the main approach to St. Peter's and gives the eye time to adjust to the
enormous dimensions of the square and church. Remember to take a look
at the Swiss Guards in their colorful 16th century–style uniforms; they
stand at the Vatican City entrances to the right and left of St. Peter's.

Also Worth Seeing

❻ Giardini Vaticani (Vatican Gardens). Generations of popes and cardinals
have mulled over affairs of church and state in these beautifully manicured gardens, originally laid out in the 16th century. A two-hour guided
tour, half by bus and half on foot, with a guide, takes you through a
haven of shady walkways, elaborate fountains, and exotic plants. Make
reservations two or three days in advance and pick up your tickets in
the Guided Visit to Vatican Museums Office at the museum entrance.
If you have a reservation, you can skip the line (go in through the
"Exit" door); the office window is inside the atrium. ⊠ *Viale Vaticano*
☎ *06/69884466 reservations* ⊕ *www.vatican.va* 💰 *€9* 🕐 *Garden
tours Mon.–Sat. 10 AM, office Mon.–Sat. 8:30–7.*

❹ Vatican Necropolis. Visit the pre-Constantine necropolis under St. Peter's
for a fascinating glimpse of the underpinnings of the great basilica,
which was built over the cemetery where archaeologists believe they have
found St. Peter's tomb. Apply in advance by sending a fax or e-mail with
the name of each visitor, language spoken, proposed days for the visit,
and a local phone number. Reservations will be confirmed a few days
in advance. No children under 15 are admitted. Tickets are sometimes
available for same-day tours; apply in person at the Ufficio Scavi (Excavations Office), on the right beyond the Arco delle Campane (Arch
of the Bells) entrance to the Vatican, which is to the left of the basilica.
Tell the Swiss Guard you want the Ufficio Scavi, and he will let you by.
⊠ *Piazza San Pietro* ☎ *06/69885318* 🖷 *06/69873017* 💰 *€10* 🕐 *Ufficio Scavi Mon.–Sat. 9–5.*

Piazza Venezia

Piazza M. di Loreto

Piazza S. Marco

Colonna di Traiano

V. d. Plebiscito

V.S. Marco

Piazza S. Marco

Pza. Campitelli

V.S. Marco

V. d. Grillo

V. Panisperna

V.S. Agata d. Goti

V. d. Serpenti

V. d. Boschetto

F.I.S.H.

FORO DI TRAIANO

V. di Marcello

MONUMENTO A VITTORIO EMANUELE II

FORO DI CESARE

S. MARIA IN ARACOELI

PAL. NUOVO

V. Alessandrina

V. Baccina

V. Madonna d. Mont

Cavour 313

V. d. Cardello

Fori Imperiali

Pza. del Campidoglio

V. dei Fori

V. Cavour

V. Frangipane

Musei Capitolini

CAMPIDOGLIO

PAL. SENATORIO

S. LUCA

CURIA

Via Salara Vecchia

BAS. EMILIA

Entrance

V. d. Colosseo

V. d. Carine

V. d. AnniBald

V. del Teatro

PAL. DEI CONSERVATORI

TEMPIO DI VESPASIANO

ARCO DI S. SEVERO

BAS. DI MASSENZIO

Imperiali

Musei Capitolini Café

V. d. Consolazione

BASILICA GIULIA

FORO ROMANO

Colosseo M

V. d. Foraggi

V. di S. Teodoro

TEMPIO DI VESTA

Foro Romano

TEMP. D. V. ROMA

ARCO DI TITO

Entrance

Arco di Constantino

ORTI FARNESIANI

COLLE PALATINO

V. di S. Gregorio

V. Celio

HOUSE OF LIVIA

PAL. DEI FLAVI

Tevere

DOMUS AUGUSTO

Entrance

V. dei Cerchi

Circo Massimo

Terme di Caracalla

Admission	
Rome Archeologia Card**	€ 20
Arco di Constantino	Free
Circo Massimo	Free
Colonna di Traiano	€ 6.20
Colosseo & Colle Palatino*	€ 10
Domus Aurea*	€ 5
Foro Romano	Free
Musei Capitolini	€ 6.20
Piazza del Campidoglio	Free
Santa Maria d'Aracoeli	Free
Terme di Caracalla	€ 5

*Reservation fee €1.50

**This is a combination ticket for the Colosseo, Colle Palatino, and the various branches of the Museo Nazionale Romano (Palazzo Altemps, Crypta Balbi, Terme di Diocleziano, Terme di Caracalla, Villa dei Quintili, the Mausoleo di Cecilia Metella, and Palazzo Massimo alle Terme), good for seven consecutive days.

CAPITOLINE HILL: The original capitol hill. The seat of government in Rome since its founding now also holds the Capitoline Museums, chock-full of the treasures of antiquity.

ROMAN FORUM: Downtown Ancient Rome. People from all corners of the empire crowded into the Forum to do business, to hear the latest news, and to worship.

PALATINE HILL: Home of the empire's rich and famous. Luxurious homes lined Palatine Hill; emperors held court on its heights and vied with their predecessors for lasting renown.

CAMPIDOGLIO

FORO ROMANO

COLLE PALATINO

ANCIENT ROME
GLORIES OF
THE CAESARS

Time has reduced ancient Rome to fields of silent ruins, but the powerful impact of what happened here, of the genius and power that made Rome the center of the Western world, echoes across the millennia.

In this one compact area of the city, you can step back into the Rome of Cicero, Julius Caesar, and Virgil. Walk along the streets they knew, cool off in the shade of the Colosseum that towered over their city, see the sculptures that watched over their piazzas. At the end of a day of exploring, climb one of the famous seven hills and watch the sun set over what was once the heart of the civilized world.

Today, this part of Rome, more than any other, is a perfect example of that layering of historic eras, the overlapping of ages, of religions, of a past that is very much a part of the present. Christian churches rise from the foundations of ancient pagan temples. An immense marble monument to a 19th-century king shares a square with a medieval palace built by a pope. Still, the history and memory of ancient Rome dominate the area. It's fitting that in the aftermath of centuries of such pageantry Percy Bysshe Shelley and Edward Gibbon reflected here on the meaning of *sic transit gloria mundi* (so passes away the glory of the world).

COLOSSEUM: Gladiators fought for the chance to live another day on the floor of the Colosseum, iconic symbol of ancient Rome.

COLOSSEO

CAMPIDOGLIO

⌄ **TIMING TIPS**

The Capitoline Museums are closed on Monday; admission is free on the last Sunday of the month. Late evening is an option for this area. Though the church is closed, the museums are open until 9 PM, and the views of the city lights and the illuminated Victor Emmanuel II monument and the Foro Romano are striking.

CLIMB MICHELANGELO'S DRAMATIC RAMP TO THE SUMMIT OF ONE OF Rome's seven hills, the Campidoglio (also known as Capitoline Hill), for views across the rooftops of modern Rome in one direction and across the ruins of ancient Rome in the other. Check out the stellar Musei Capitolini, crammed with a collection of masterpieces rivaled only by the Vatican museums.

★ **Piazza del Campidoglio.** In Michelangelo's piazza at the top of the Campidoglio stands a bronze equestrian statue of Marcus Aurelius (AD 121–180). A legend foretells that some day the statue's original gold surface will return, heralding the end of the world. Pending the arrival of that day, the original 2nd century statue was moved inside the Musei Capitolini; a copy sits on the piazza. Stand with your back to it to survey central Rome.

The Campidoglio, the site of the Roman Empire's first and holiest temples, had fallen into ruin by the Middle Ages and was called *Monte Caprino* (Goat Hill). In 1536 Pope Paul III (1468–1549) decided to restore its grandeur for the triumphal entry into the city of Charles V (1500–1558), the Holy Roman Emperor. He called upon Michelangelo to create the staircase ramp, the buildings and facades

on the square, the pavement decoration, and the pedestal for the bronze statue.

The two buildings that make up the **Musei Capitolini** are on the piazza, flanking the **Palazzo Senatorio**. The Campidoglio has always been the seat of Rome's government; its Latin name is the root for the word capitol. Today, Rome's city hall occupies the Palazzo Senatorio. Head to the vantage points in the belvederes on the sides of the palazzo for great views of the ruins of ancient Rome.

★ **Musei Capitolini** (Capitoline Museums). This immense collection, housed in the twin Palazzi del Museo Capitolino and Palazzo dei Conservatori buildings, is a greatest hits collection of Roman art through the ages, from the ancients to the baroque.

The **Palazzi del Museo Capitolino** contains hundreds of Roman busts of philoso-

AN EMPEROR CHEAT SHEET

OCTAVIAN/AUGUSTUS (27 BC–AD 14)
After the death of Julius Caesar, Octavian gained control of Rome after a series of battles that culminated with the defeat of Antony and Cleopatra at Actium. Later known as Caesar Augustus, he was Rome's first emperor. His rule began a 200-year period of peace known as the Pax Romana.
Colle Palatino

CALIGULA (AD 37–41)
Caligula was tremendously popular when he came to power at the age of 25, but he very soon became infamous for his excessive cruelty, immorality, and erratic behavior. His contemporaries universally considered him to be insane. He was murdered by his own guard within four years.

phers and emperors—a fascinating Who's Who of the ancient world. Forty-eight Roman emperors are represented. Unlike the Greeks, whose portraits are idealized, the Romans preferred the warts-and-all school of representation. Other notable sculptures include the poignant *Dying Gaul* and the regal *Capitoline Venus*. In the Capitolino courtyard is a gigantic, reclining sculpture of Oceanus, found in the Roman Forum and later dubbed *Marforio*. This was one of Rome's talking statues to which citizens from the 1500s to the 1900s affixed anonymous satirical verses and notes of political protest. (Another talking statue still in use today sits at Piazza Pasquino, near Piazza Navona.)

Lining the courtyard of the **Palazzo dei Conservatori** are the colossal fragments of a head, leg, foot, and hand—all that remains of the famous statue of the emperor Constantine the Great, who believed that Rome's future lay with Christianity. These immense effigies were much in vogue in the later days of the Roman Empire. The renowned symbol of Rome, the *Capitoline Wolf*, a 6th-century

BC Etruscan bronze, holds a place of honor in the museum; the suckling twins were added during the Renaissance to adapt the statue to the legend of Romulus and Remus. The Palazzo also contains some of baroque painting's great masterpieces, including Caravaggio's *La Buona Ventura* (1595) and *San Giovanni Battista* (1602), Peter Paul Rubens's *Romulus and Remus* (1614), and Pietro da Cortona's sumptuous portrait of Pope Urban VIII (1627). When museum fatigue sets in, enjoy the view and refreshments on a large open terrace in the Palazzo dei Conservatoria. ☎ *06/39967800 or 06/67102475* ⊕ *www.pierreci.it* ⊘ *Tues.–Sun. 9–8.*

Santa Maria d'Aracoeli. Seemingly endless, steep stairs climb from Piazza Venezia to the Santa Maria. There are 15th-century frescoes by Pinturicchio (1454–1513) in the first chapel on the right. ⊘ *Oct.–May, daily 7–noon and 4–6; June–Sept., daily 7–noon and 4–6:30.*

NERO (AD 54–68)

Nero is infamous as a violent persecutor of Christians. He also murdered his wife, his mother, and countless others. Although it's not certain whether he actually fiddled as Rome burned in AD 64, he was well known as a singer and a composer of music.

Domus Aurea

DOMITIAN (AD 81–96)

The first emperor to declare himself "Dominus et Deus" (Lord and God), he stripped away power from the Senate. After his death, the Senate retaliated by declaring him "Damnatio Memoriae" (his name and image were erased from all public records).

Colle Palatino

FORO ROMANO

⊗ **TIMING TIPS**

It takes about an hour to explore the Roman Forum. There are entrances on the Via dei Fori Imperiali and near the Colosseum. Another hour's walk will cover the Imperial Fora. With exception of the overpriced stands along the avenue and cafés on Largo Corrado Ricci, there are few places nearby for food and drink, so bring a snack and water.

EXPERIENCE THE ENDURING ROMANCE OF THE FORUM. WANDER AMONG its lonely columns and great, broken fragments of sculpted marble and stone— once temples, palaces, and shops crowded with people from all corners of the known world. This was the heart of ancient Rome and a symbol of the values that inspired Rome's conquest of an empire.

★ **Foro Romano** (Roman Forum). Built in a marshy valley between the Capitoline and Palatine hills, the Forum was the civic core of Republican Rome, the austere era that preceded the hedonism of the emperors. The Forum was the political, commercial, and religious center of Roman life. Hundreds of years of plunder and the tendency of later Romans to carry off what was left of the better building materials reduced it to the series of ruins you see today. Archaeological digs continue to uncover more about the sight; bear in mind that what you see are the ruins not of one period but of almost 900 years, from about 500 BC to AD 400.

The **Basilica Giulia**, which owes its name to Julius Caesar who had it built, was where the Centumviri, the hundred-or-so judges forming the civil court, met to hear cases. The open space before it was the core of the forum proper and prototype of Italy's famous piazzas. Let your imagination dwell on Mark Antony (circa 81 BC–30 BC), who delivered the funeral address in Julius Caesar's honor from the rostrum left of the **Arco di Settimio Severo**. This arch, one of the grandest of all antiquity, was built hundreds of years later in AD 203 to celebrate the victory of the emperor Severus (AD 146–211) over the Parthians, and was topped by a bronze equestrian statuary group with six horses. You can explore the reconstruction of the large brick senate hall, the **Curia**; three Corinthian columns (a favorite of 19th-century poets) are all that remains of the **Tempio di Vespasiano**. In the **Tempio di Vesta**, six highly privileged vestal virgins kept the sacred fire, a tradition that dated back to the very earliest days of Rome, when guarding the community's precious fire was essential to its well-being. The cleaned and restored

AN EMPEROR CHEAT SHEET

TRAJAN (AD 98–117)

Trajan, from Southern Spain, was the first Roman emperor not born in Italy. He enlarged the empire's boundaries to include modern-day Romania, Armenia, and Upper Mesopotamia.

Colonna di Traiano

HADRIAN (AD 117–138)

He expanded the empire in Asia and the Middle East. He's best known for designing and rebuilding the Pantheon, constructing a majestic villa at Tivoli, and initiating myriad other constructions across the empire, including the famed wall across Britain.

Pantheon, in Baroque Rome

Arco di Tito, which stands in a slightly elevated position on a spur of the Palatine Hill, was erected in AD 81 to celebrate the sack of Jerusalem 10 years earlier, after the great Jewish revolt. A famous relief shows the captured contents of Herod's Temple—including its huge seven-branched menorah—being carried in triumph down Rome's Via Sacra. Making sense of the ruins isn't always easy; consider renting an audio guide (€4) or buying a booklet that superimposes an image of the Forum in its heyday over a picture of it today. Guided tours in English usually begin at 10:30 AM. In summer the Forum is sometimes open for midnight (guided) tours—look for signs at the entrance or ask at your hotel. ☎ *06/39967700* ⊕ *www.pierreci.it* ⊗ *Daily 9–1 hr before sunset.*

THE OTHER FORA
Fori Imperiali (Imperial Fora). These five grandly conceived squares flanked with columnades and temples were built by the emperors Caesar, Augustus, Vespasian, Nerva, and Trajan. The original Roman Forum, built up over 500 years of Republican Rome, had grown crowded, and Julius Caesar was the first to attempt to rival it.

He built the **Foro di Cesare** (Forum of Caesar), including a temple dedicated to himself and the goddess Minerva. Four later emperors followed his lead, creating their own fora. The grandest was the **Foro di Traiano** (Forum of Trajan) a veritable city unto itself built by Trajan (AD 53–117). The adjoining Mercati Traianei (Trajan's Markets), a huge multilevel brick complex of shops, walkways, and terraces, was one of the marvels of the ancient world. In the 20th century, Benito Mussolini built the Via dei Fori Imperiali directly through the Imperial Fora area. Marble and bronze maps on the wall along the avenue portray the extent of the Roman Empire and Republic, and many of the remains of the Imperial Fora lay buried beneath its surface.

Colonna di Traiano (Trajan's Column). The ashes of Trajan were buried inside the base of this column (the ashes have since been removed). Remarkable reliefs spiral up its sides, celebrating his military campaigns in Dacia (Romania). The column has stood in what was once the Forum of Trajan since AD 113. ☎ *06/69780532* ⊗ *Tues.–Sun. 9–4:30.*

MARCUS AURELIUS (AD 161–180)
Remembered as a humanitarian emperor, Marcus Aurelius was a Stoic philosopher and his *Meditations* are still read today. Nonetheless, he was an aggressive leader devoted to expanding the empire.
Piazza del Campidoglia

CONSTANTINE I (AD 306–337)
Constantine changed the course of history by legalizing Christianity. He legitimized the once-banned religion and paved the way for the papacy in Rome. Constantine also founded Constantinople, an Imperial capital in the East.
Arco di Constantino

COLLE PALATINO

⌚ **TIMING TIPS**

A stroll on the Palatino, with a visit to the Museo Palatino, takes about two hours. You can reserve tickets online or by phone—operators speak English. If you are buying tickets in person, remember that there are often shorter lines here than at the Colosseum and the ticket is good for both sights. The entrances are in the Roman Forum and on Via S. Gregorio.

IT ALL BEGAN HERE. IT IS BELIEVED THAT ROMULUS, THE FOUNDER OF ROME, lived on the Colle Palatino (Palatine Hill). It was an exclusive address in ancient Rome, and emperors built palaces upon its slopes. Tour the Palatine's hidden corners and shady lanes, take a welcome break from the heat in its peaceful gardens, and enjoy a view of the Circo Massimo fit for an emperor.

★ **Colle Palatino** (Palatine Hill). A lane known as the Clivus Palatinus, paved with worn stones that were once trod by emperors and their slaves, climbs from the Forum area to a site that historians identify with Rome's earliest settlement. The legend goes that the infant twins Romulus and Remus were nursed by a she-wolf on the banks of the Tiber and adopted by a shepherd. Encouraged by the gods to build a city, the twins chose this site in 735 BC, fortifying it with a wall that archaeologist Rudolfo Lanciani identified in the late 19th century when digging on Palatine Hill.

During the Republican era the hill was an important religious center, housing the Temple of Cybele and the Temple of Victory, as well as an exclusive residential area. Cicero, Catiline, Crassus, and Agrippa all had homes here. Augustus was born on the hill, and as he rose in power, he built libraries, halls, and temples here; the **House of Livia,** reserved for his wife, is best preserved. Emperor Tiberius was the first to build a palace here; others followed. The structures most visible today date back to the late 1st century AD, when the Palatine experienced an extensive remodeling under Emperor Domitian. His architects put up two separate palaces, the **Domus Augustana** and the **Domus Livia.** During the Renaissance, the powerful Farnese family built gardens atop the ruins overlooking the Forum. Known as the **Orti Farnesiani,** they were Europe's first botanical gardens. The **Museo Palatino** charts the history of the hill. Splendid sculptures, frescoes, and mosaic intarsia from various imperial buildings are on display. ☎ *06/39967700* ⊕ *www.pierreci.it* ⌚ *Tues.–Sun. 9–1 hr before sunset.*

THE RISE AND FALL OF ANCIENT ROME

218 BC

ca. 800 BC	Rise of Etruscan city-states.
510	Foundation of the Roman republic; expulsion of Etruscans from Roman territory.
343	Roman conquest of Greek colonies in Campania.
264–241	First Punic War (with Carthage): increased naval power helps Rome gain control of southern Italy and then Sicily.
218–200	Second Punic War: Hannibal's attempted conquest of Italy, using elephants, is eventually crushed.

NEAR THE COLLE PALATINO

Circo Massimo (Circus Maximus). Ancient Rome's oldest and largest racetrack lies in the natural hollow between Palatine and Aventine hills. From the imperial box in the palace on Palatine Hill, emperors could look out over the oval course. Stretching about 650 yards from end to end, the Circus Maximus could hold more than 300,000 spectators. On certain occasions there were as many as 24 chariot races a day, and competitions could last for 15 days. The central ridge was the sight of two Egyptian obelisks (now in the Piazza del Popolo and Piazza San Giovanni in Laterano). Check out the panoramic views of the Circus Maximus from the Palatine Hill's Belvedere. You can also see the green slopes of the Aventine and Celian hills, as well as the bell tower of Santa Maria in Cosmedin.

Terme di Caracalla (Baths of Caracalla). For the Romans, public baths were much more than places to wash. The baths also had recital halls, art galleries, libraries, massage rooms, sports grounds, and gardens. Even the smallest public baths had at least some of these amenities, and in the capital of the Roman Empire, they were provided on a lavish scale. Ancient Rome's most beautiful and luxurious public baths were opened by the emperor Caracalla in AD 217 and were used until the 6th century.

Taking a bath was a long and complex process, and a social activity first and foremost. Remember, too, that for all their sophistication, the Romans didn't have soap. You began by sweating in the *sudatoria*, small rooms resembling saunas. From these you moved on to the *calidarium* for the actual business of washing, using a *strigil*, or scraper, to get the dirt off. Next was the *tepidarium*, where you gradually cooled down. Finally, you splashed around in the *frigidarium*, the only actual "bath" in the place, in essence a cold water swimming pool. There was a nominal admission fee, often waived by officials and emperors wishing to curry favor with the plebians. The baths' functioning depended on the slaves who cared for the clients and stoked the fires that heated the water. ☎ *06/39967700* ⊕ *www.pierreci.it* ☉ *Tues.–Sun. 9 AM–1 hr hour before sunset, Mon. 9–2.*

44 BC

150 BC	Roman Forum begins to take shape as the principal civic center in Italy.
146	Third Punic War: Rome razes city of Carthage and emerges as the dominant Mediterranean force.
133	Rome rules entire Mediterranean Basin except Egypt.
49	Julius Caesar conquers Gaul.
44	Julius Caesar is assassinated.
27	Rome's Imperial Age begins; Octavian (now named Augustus) becomes the first emperor and is later deified. The Augustan Age is celebrated in the works of Virgil (70 BC–AD 19), Ovid (43 BC–AD 17), Livy (59 BC–AD 17), and Horace (65–8 BC).

COLOSSEO

You can give the Colosseum a cursory look in about 30 minutes, but it deserves at least an hour. Make reservations by phone (there are English-speaking operators) or online at least a day in advance to avoid long lines at both the Colosseum and the Domus Aurea. Or buy your ticket for the Colosseum at Palatine Hill, where the lines are usually shorter.

LEGEND HAS IT THAT AS LONG AS THE COLOSSEUM STANDS, ROME WILL stand; and when Rome falls, so will the world. No visit to Rome is complete without a trip to the crumbling oval that has been the iconic symbol of the city for centuries.

★ **Colosseo.** A program of games and shows lasting 100 days celebrated the opening of the massive and majestic Colosseum in AD 80. On the opening day alone, 5,000 wild beasts perished. More than 70,000 spectators could sit within the arena's 573-yard circumference, which had marble facing, hundreds of statues for decoration, and a *velarium*—an ingenious system of sail-like awnings rigged on ropes manned by imperial sailors—to protect the audience from the sun and rain. Before the imperial box, gladiators would salute the emperor and cry, "*Ave, imperator, morituri te salutant*" ("Hail, emperor, men soon to die salute you"); it is said that when one day they heard the emperor Claudius respond, "Or maybe not," they were so offended that they called a strike.

Originally known as the Flavian Amphitheater, it took the name Colosseum after a truly colossal gilt bronze statue of Nero that stood nearby. Gladiator combat and staged animal hunts ended by the 6th century. The arena later served as a quarry from which materials were looted to build Renaissance churches and palaces. Finally, it was declared sacred by the Vatican in memory of the many Christians believed martyred here. (Scholars now maintain that Christians met their death elsewhere.) During the 19th century, romantic poets lauded the glories of the ruins when viewed by moonlight. Now its arches glow at night with mellow golden spotlights—less romantic, perhaps, but still impressive.

Expect long lines at the entrance and actors dressed as gladiators who charge a hefty fee to pose for pictures while you wait. Once inside you can walk around much of the outer ring of the structure and look down into the exposed passages under what was once the arena floor, now represented by a thin gangway and a small stage at one end. Climb the steep stairs for panoramic views in the Colosseum and out to the Forum and Arch of Constantine. A

THE RISE AND FALL OF ANCIENT ROME

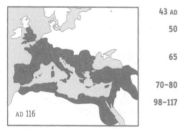

AD 116

43 AD	Rome invades Britain.
50	Rome is the largest city in the world, with a population of a million.
65	Emperor Nero begins the persecution of Christians in the Empire; Saints Peter and Paul are executed.
70–80	Vespasian builds the Colosseum.
98–117	Trajan's military successes are celebrated with his Baths (98), Forum (110), and Column (113); the Roman Empire reaches its apogee.

museum space on the upper floor holds temporary archaeological exhibits. ☎ *06/ 7005469, 06/39967700 reservations* ⊕ *www.pierreci.it* ⊘ *Daily. 8:30–1 hr before sunset.*

Arco di Costantino. The largest (69 feet high, 85 feet long, 23 feet wide) and the best preserved of Rome's triumphal arches was erected in AD 315 to celebrate the victory of the emperor Constantine (280–337) over Maxentius (died 312). It was just before this battle that Constantine, the emperor who converted Rome to Christianity, had a vision of a cross in the heavens and heard the words "In this sign, thou shalt conquer."

NEAR THE COLOSSEO

Domus Aurea. Nero's "Golden House" gives a good sense of the excesses of Imperial Rome. After fire destroyed much of the city in AD 64, Nero took advantage of the resulting open space to construct a lavish palace so large that it spread over four of Rome's seven hills. It had a facade of pure gold, seawater piped into the baths, decorations of mother-of-pearl, and vast gardens. Not much has survived of all this; a good portion of the building and grounds was buried under the public works with which subsequent emperors sought to make reparation to the Roman people for Nero's phenomenal greed. As a result, the site of the Domus Aurea itself remained unknown for many centuries. A few of Nero's original halls were discovered underground at the end of the 15th century. Raphael (1483–1520) was one of the artists who had themselves lowered into the rubble-filled rooms, which resembled grottoes. The artists copied the original painted Roman decorations, barely visible by torchlight, and scratched their names on the ceilings. Raphael later used these models—known as *grotesques* because they were found in the so-called grottoes—in his decorative motifs for the Vatican Loggia.

The palace remains impressive in scale; a bit of imagination is required to envision the original (a mediocre audio guide is €2). One wing caved in early 2000 and remains closed at least through 2005. The underground site is cold even in summer, so take something warm to wear. ☎ *06/ 39967700 reservations* ⊕ *www.pierreci.it* ⊘ *Wed.–Mon. 9–7:45.*

AD 450

238 AD	The first wave of Germanic invasions penetrates Italy.
293	Diocletian reorganizes the Empire into West and East.
330	Constantine founds a new Imperial capital (Constantinople) in the East.
410	Rome is sacked by Visigoths.
476	The last Roman emperor, Romulus Augustus, is deposed. The Roman Empire falls.

Baroque Rome: Gold & Grandeur

The area between the Corso and the Tiber bend is one of Rome's most beautiful districts, filled with narrow streets bearing curious names, airy piazzas, and half-hidden courtyards. Some of Rome's most coveted residential addresses are here. It includes such world-famous sights as the ancient Pantheon and the medieval square of Campo de' Fiori, but it is mainly a trip back in time to the baroque world of the 16th and 17th centuries.

The Main Attractions

★ ⑱ **Campo de' Fiori.** This bustling square is home to a famed morning market, a must-see dose of local culture. Each morning, vendors fill temporary stalls with all manner of local produce, nuts, cheese, spices, flowers, and seafood; by early afternoon it's all gone, to resurface in the city's homes and restaurants at dinnertime. Many pleasant cafés border the market. The view has certainly improved since the Middle Ages, when the square was the scene of public executions, including that of philosopher-monk Giordano Bruno (1548–1600). His statue still broods in the center of the square.

> **need a break?** Some of Rome's best pizza comes out of the ovens of **Il Forno di Campo de' Fiori** (☎ 06/68806662 ⊠ Campo de' Fiori). Choose pizza *bianca*, topped with olive oil, or *rossa*, with tomato sauce. Move to the annex next door to have your warm pizza filled with prosciutto and figs, or other mouthwatering combinations.

⑨ **Largo di Torre Argentina.** In the middle of this busy piazza lies Rome's largest fully excavated Republican-era ruins. The **area sacra** (sacred area) has columns, altars, and foundations from four temples dating as far back as the 1st century BC. On the west side of the square lies the **Curia Pompeia,** the site where Caesar was slain in 44 BC. The frescoes on the taller brickwork are from the 12th-century church of San Nicola de' Cesarini, which was built into one of the temples. The ruins serve as a cat sanctuary for hundreds of the city's strays: take the staircase down to visit the cats and the cat ladies who look after them. Volunteer cat tenders are welcome, even for a few hours. ⊠ *Near Piazza Venezia.*

⑭ **Museo Nazionale Romano.** The ancient Roman and Egyptian sculptures in the **Palazzo Altemps,** part of the Museo Nazionale Romano, make up a terrific antiquities collection. Look for two works in the famed Ludovisi collection: the large, intricately carved Ludovisi Sarcophagus and *Galata,* a poignant work portraying a barbarian warrior who chooses death for himself and his wife rather than humiliation by the enemy. The 16th-century palazzo, with gorgeously frescoed ceilings and loggia, is an impressive home for the sculptures. This is a must-see for serious art buffs. ⊠ *Piazza Sant'Apollinare 46, near Piazza Navona* ☎ *06/39967700* ☞ *€5* ☼ *Tues.–Sun. 9–7:45.*

⑪ **Pantheon.** One of Rome's most impressive and best-preserved ancient monuments, the Pantheon is particularly close to the hearts of Romans. The emperor Hadrian designed it around AD 120 and had it built on the site
Fodor'sChoice
★

Baroque Rome

1/8 mile

200 meters

of an earlier temple that had been damaged by fire. The most striking thing about the Pantheon is not its size, immense though it is (until 1960 the dome was the largest ever built); rather, it is the remarkable harmony of the building. Notice that the height of the dome is equal to the diameter of the circular interior. The oculus, or opening in the dome, is meant to symbolize the all-seeing eye of heaven; in practice, it illuminates the building and lightens the

heavy stone ceiling. The original bronze doors have survived more than 1,800 years, centuries longer than the interior's rich gold ornamentation, which was plundered by popes and emperors. Art lovers can pay homage to the tomb of Raphael, who is buried in an ancient sarcophagus under the altar of Madonna del Sasso. ⊠ *Piazza della Rotonda, Pantheon* ☎ *06/68300230* ⊑ *Free* ☉ *Mon.–Sat. 9–7:30, Sun. 9–5:30.*

★ ☾ ⑮ **Piazza Navona.** This famed piazza has the carefree air of the days when it was the scene of Roman circus games, medieval jousts, and 17th-century carnivals. Today it often attracts fashion photographers on shoots and Romans out for their evening *passeggiata* (evening stroll). Bernini's splashing **Fontana dei Quattro Fiumi** (Fountain of the Four Rivers), with an enormous rock squared off by statues representing the four corners of the world, makes a fitting centerpiece. Behind the fountain is the church of **Sant'Agnese in Agone,** an outstanding example of baroque architecture built by the Pamphili Pope Innocent X and still owned by his descendants, the Doria Pamphili. The facade—a wonderfully rich mélange of bell towers, concave spaces, and dovetailed stone and marble—is by Borromini, a contemporary and sometime rival of Bernini, and by Carlo Rainaldi (1611–91). One story has it that the Bernini statue nearest the church, which represents the River Plate, has its hand up before its eye because it can't bear the sight of the Borromini facade. Though often repeated, the story is a fiction: the facade was built after the fountain.

From early December through January 6 a Christmas market fills the square with games, nativity scenes (some well crafted, many not so), and multiple versions of the Befana, the ugly but good witch who brings candy and toys to Italian children on Epiphany. (Her name is a corruption of the Italian word for "epiphany," *Epifania.*)

⑫ **San Luigi dei Francesi.** The clergy of San Luigi considered Caravaggio's roistering and unruly lifestyle scandalous enough, but his realistic treatment of sacred subjects—seen in three paintings depicting the life of St. Matthew in the last chapel—was too much for them. They rejected outright his first version of the altarpiece, and they weren't especially happy with the other two works. Thanks to the intercession of Caravaggio's patron, the influential Cardinal Francesco del Monte, they were persuaded to keep them—a lucky thing, since they are now thought to be among the artist's finest paintings. Have a few one-euro coins handy for the

Roman Baroque

11

FLAGRANTLY EMOTIONAL, heavily expressive, and sensuously visual, the 17th-century artistic movement known as the baroque was born in Rome. It was the creation of three geniuses: the sculptor and architect Gianlorenzo Bernini (1598–1680), the painter and architect Pietro da Cortona (1596–1669), and the architect and sculptor Francesco Borromini (1599–1667). From the drama found in the artists' paintings to the jewel-laden, gold-on-gold detail of 17th-century Roman palaces, baroque style was intended both to shock and delight by upsetting the placid, "correct" rules of proportion and scale in the Renaissance. If a building looks theatrical—like a stage or a theater, especially with curtains being drawn back—it is usually baroque. Look for over-the-top, curvaceous marblework, tromp l'oeil, allusions to other art, and high drama to identify the style. Baroque's appeal to the emotions made it a powerful weapon in the hands of the Counter-Reformation.

light machine. ⊠ *Piazza San Luigi dei Francesi, near Piazza Navona* ☎ 06/688271 ⊗ *Fri.–Wed. 8–12:30 and 3:30–7:30.*

⑬ Sant'Agostino in Campo Marzio. Caravaggio's celebrated *Madonna of the Pilgrims*—which scandalized all Rome because it pictured pilgrims with dirt on the soles of their feet—can be found in this small church over the first altar on the left. Also of interest are Raphael's *Prophet,* on the first pilaster on the left, and the dozens of heart-shape ex-votos to *Madonna del Parto* (Mary of Childbirth) at the entrance. ⊠ *Piazza di Sant'Agostino, near Piazza Navona* ☎ 06/68801962 ⊗ *Mon.–Sat. 7–1 and 4:30–7:30, Sun. 7–1 and 3:30–7:30.*

Also Worth Seeing

❽ Crypta Balbi (Crypt of Balbus). After 20 years of excavation and restoration, these fascinating remains of a porticoed courtyard and theater built in 13 BC, curated by the Museo Nazionale Romano, afford a unique look at Roman history. Rather than focus on one era, the museum peels back the layers of the site, following the latest techniques in conservation. The well-explained exhibits (with text in English and Italian) give you a tangible sense of the sweeping changes that this spot—and Rome—underwent from antiquity to the 20th century. A partially restored wall provides an example of what marble and tufa constructions looked like before weather took its toll and medieval builders stripped the marble off for reuse. Copies of documents and reconstructed coins and other everyday objects found in drains, rubbish dumps, and tombs are a window into the world of the people who lived and worked here over the ages. ⊠ *Via Delle Botteghe Oscure 31, near Piazza Venezia* ☎ 06/39967700 ▣ €4 ⊗ *Tues.–Sun. 9–7:45.*

❼ Il Gesù. Grandmother of all baroque churches, this huge structure was designed by the architect Vignola (1507–73) to be the tangible symbol of Jesuits, a major force in the Counter-Reformation in Europe. It remained unadorned for about 100 years, but when it finally was decorated, no expense was spared: the interior drips with gold and lapis lazuli, precious marbles, gold and more gold. A fantastically painted ceiling by Baciccia (1639–1709) seems to merge with the painted stucco figures at its base. St. Ignatius's apartments, reached from the side entrance of the church, are also worth a visit (afternoons only) for the trompe-l'oeil frescoes and relics of the saint. ⊠ *Piazza del Gesù, near Piazza Venezia* ☎ *06/3613717* ⊘ *Daily 6:30–12:30 and 4–7.*

㉔ Palazzo Farnese. The Farnese family rose to great power during the Renaissance, in part due to the favor Pope Alexander VI showed to the beautiful Giullia Farnese. The large palace was begun when, with Alexander's aid, Giullia's brother became cardinal; it was further enlarged on his election as Pope Paul III in 1534. The uppermost frieze decorations and main window overlooking the piazza are the work of Michelangelo, who also designed part of the courtyard (viewable through windows on Via Giulia), as well as the graceful arch over Via Giullia at the back. The facade on Piazza Farnese has been recently cleaned, further revealing geometrical brick configurations that have long been thought to hold occult meaning. When looking at the palace from outside you can catch a glimpse of the splendid frescoed ceilings, including the **Galleria Carracci** vault painted by Annibale Carracci between 1597 and 1604—the second-greatest ceiling in Rome. For permission to view it from the inside, write to the French Embassy, which now occupies the palace. Specify the number in your party, when you wish to visit, and a local phone number for confirmation a few days before the visit. ⊠ *French Embassy, Servizio Culturale, Piazza Farnese 67, 00186 Rome* ☎ *06/686011* ⊠ *Free* ⊘ *By appointment only.*

㉑ Palazzo Spada. A dazzling stuccoed facade on Piazza Capo di Ferro, west of Piazza Farnese, fronts an equally magnificent inner courtyard. On the southeast side of the inner courtyard, the gallery designed by Borromini creates an elaborate optical illusion, appearing to be much longer than it really is. On the first floor there are paintings and sculptures that belonged to Cardinale Bernardino Spada, an art connoisseur who collected works by Italian and Flemish masters. ⊠ *Piazza Capo di Ferro*

A GOOD WALK: CARAVAGGIO'S ROME

Michelangelo Merisi—better known by the name of his birthplace, Caravaggio—may have been Rome's greatest painter. He certainly was one of its most notorious—he cultivated a reputation as a rebel, keeping low company and frequently fighting (and landing in jail). That spirit found its way into his painting: his dramatic, vibrant work was a major innovation in Western art. This walk introduces you to Caravaggio's art and his world. It covers approximately 1½ km (1 mi), including the final stretch to Piazza del Popolo.

Start at the **Palazzo Doria Pamphilj** ㉓, home to some of Caravaggio's most famous early works, including *Rest on the Flight to Egypt* and *Penitent Magdalene*, both from 1595. The latter created a scandal: Caravaggio used a real model for the sacred figure of Mary Magdalene, something prohibited by the church at the Council of Trent 30 years earlier. To compound the sin, the model was his lover, the prostitute Maddalena Antonietti. It wouldn't be the last time Caravaggio employed profane models for sacred subjects—later, his patrons drew the line at the *Death*

13, Campo de' Fiori ☎ *06/6832409* ⊕ *www.galleriaborghese.it* ✉ *€5* ⊘ *Tues.–Sun. 8:30–7:30.*

⑩ Santa Maria sopra Minerva. Michelangelo's *Risen Christ* and the tomb of the gentle 15th-century artist Fra Angelico are in practically the only Gothic-style church in Rome. Have some coins handy to light up the **Cappella Carafa** in the right transept, where exquisite 15th-century frescoes by Filippino Lippi (circa 1457–1504) are well worth the small investment. (Lippi's most famous student was Botticelli.) In front of the church, Bernini's charming elephant bearing an Egyptian obelisk has an inscription on the base stating that it takes a strong mind to sustain solid wisdom. ⊠ *Piazza della Minerva, Pantheon* ☎ *06/6793926* ⊘ *Daily 7–noon and 4–7.*

⑰ Sant'Andrea della Valle. This huge 17th-century church looms mightily over a busy intersection. Puccini set the first act of his opera *Tosca* here; fans have been known to hire a horse-drawn carriage at night to trace the course of the opera from Sant'Andrea up Via Giulia to Palazzo Far-nese—Scarpia's headquarters—to the locale of the opera's climax, Castel Sant'Angelo. Inside, above the apse are striking frescoes depicting scenes from St. Andrew's life by the Bolognese painter Domenichino (1581–1641). ⊠ *Corso Vittorio Emanuele II, near Campo de' Fiori* ☎ *06/6861339* ⊘ *Daily 7–noon and 4:30–7:30.*

⑯ Sant'Ivo alla Sapienza. Borromini's eccentric church has what must surely be Rome's most unusual dome—topped by a golden spiral said to have been inspired by a bee's stinger. ⊠ *Corso Rinascimento 40, near Piazza Navona* ⊘ *Sun. 10–noon.*

㉑ Via Giulia. Named after Pope Julius II and serving for more than four centuries as the "salon of Rome," this street is still the address of choice for Roman aristocrats. Built with funds garnered by taxing prostitutes, the street is lined with elegant palaces, including the Palazzo Falconieri, and old churches (one, San Eligio, reputedly designed by Raphael himself). The area around Via Giulia is a wonderful place to wander in to get the feeling of daily life as carried on in a centuries-old setting—an experience enhanced by the dozens of antiques shops in the neighborhood.

---

of Mary, the model for which was said to be the drowned body of a prostitute taken from the Tiber. Exit the gallery and walk left along Piazza Collegio Romano, continuing on Via Piè di Marmo. The street bends right through Piazza Minerva, with its elephant obelisk, and continues alongside of the Pantheon. In front of the Pantheon, walk around the fountain and take the street extending left from the far left corner of the piazza, Via Giustiniani. Follow it until it ends at the church **San Luigi dei Francesi** ⑫. Inside, in the far left corner, is the painting cycle of the Life of St.

Matthew (1600), which shocked the public with its contemporary depiction of sacred subjects and thrilled the art world with its realism and use of light.

Leave the church, turn left along the piazza, then take the third right, Vicolo Vaccarella. Follow it until it ends, then turn left onto Vicolo Coppelle. This alley soon opens into Piazza Campo Marzio, with the entrance to the church of **Sant'Agostino** ⑬ on the right. Inside is the *Madonna of the Pilgrims* (1605), which caused another sensation for its depiction of filthy, ragged pilgrims, and for its model, once again the for-

Piazza Venezia to the Spanish Steps: Vistas & Views

Though it has a bustling commercial air, this part of the city also holds great visual allure, from the gaudy marble confection that is the monument to Vittorio Emanuele II to the theatrical Piazza di Sant'Ignazio. Among the things to look for are stately palaces, baroque ballrooms, and the greatest example of portraiture in Rome, Velázquez's incomparable *Innocent X* at the Galleria Doria Pamphilj. Highlights are the Trevi Fountain and the Spanish Steps, 18th-century Rome's most famous example of city planning.

The Main Attractions

★ ❷ **Fontana di Trevi** (Trevi Fountain). The huge fountain designed by Nicola Salvi (1697–1751) is a spectacular fantasy of mythical sea creatures amid cascades of splashing water. The fountain is the world's most spectacular wishing well: legend has it that you can ensure your return to Rome by tossing a coin into the fountain. It was featured in the 1954 film *Three Coins in the Fountain* and was the scene of Anita Ekberg's aquatic frolic in Fellini's *La Dolce Vita*. By day this is one of the busiest sites in town, and at night the spotlighted piazza takes on the festive air of a crowded outdoor party. ⊠ *Off Via del Tritone, Piazza di Trevi.*

❷ **Monumento a Vittorio Emanuele II.** Known as the Vittoriano, this vast marble monument was erected in the late 19th century to honor Italy's first king, Vittorio Emanuele II (1820–78), and the unification of Italy. Aesthetically minded Romans have derided the oversize structure that can be seen from many parts of the city, calling it "the typewriter" or "the wedding cake." Whatever you think of its design, the views from the top are unforgettable. Here also is the **Tomb of the Unknown Soldier** with its eternal flame. A side entrance in the monument leads to the **Museo del Risorgimento,** which charts Italy's struggle for nationhood. The red shirt and boots of revolutionary hero Giuseppe Garibaldi (1807–82) are among the mementos. Opposite the Vittoriano, note the name "Bonaparte" still visible on the enclosed wooden veranda fronting the palace on the corner of Via del Plebiscito and Via Corso. Napoléon's mother had a fine view from here of the local goings-on for the many years that she lived in Rome. ⊠ *Entrance at Piazza Ara Coeli, near Piazza Venezia*

midable Maddalena, dressed as the Mother of God. Exit the church and continue up Via Metastasio to Vicolo Divino Amore. At its corner with Vicolo San Biagio is the apartment where Caravaggio lived. It was here, on a mission from the irate landlady, that a debt collector discovered Caravaggio's secret method—he arranged glass and mirrors in order to create intense, focused light and shadow on subjects, which he then would view with a mirror as he painted. Continue on Vicolo Divino Amore one block to Via Fontanella Borghese and turn left, then left again on

to Via Pallacorda, the site of a duel that changed Caravaggio's life. On May 29, 1606, the artist fought with and killed Ranuccio Tomassoni, a gangster said to have been a contender for the favors of Lena. Condemned to death for the deed, Caravaggio fled Rome, never to return. He first went to Naples, then to Malta, where he died in 1610. From here, you can continue north up Via Ripetta about 1 km (½ mi) to Piazza del Popolo and the church of **Santa Maria del Popolo** ❹, at the far end of the piazza. The Cappella Cerasi there holds two more masterpieces.

☎ *06/6991718* ⊕ *www.ambienterm.arti.beniculturali.it/vittoriano/ index.html* ✉ *Monument free, museum €5* ☉ *Daily 9:30–5:30.*

㉔ Palazzo Colonna. Inside the fabulous, private Palazzo Colonna, the 17th-century **Sala Grande**—more than 300 feet long, with bedazzling chandeliers, colored marble, and enormous paintings—is best known as the site where Audrey Hepburn met the press in *Roman Holiday.* The entrance to the picture gallery, the **Galleria Colonna,** hides behind a plain, inconspicuous door. The private palace is open to the public Saturday only; reserve ahead to get a free guided tour in English. ✉ *Via della Pilotta 17, near Piazza di Trevi* ☎ *06/6784350* ⊕ *www.galleriacolonna. it* ✉ *€7* ☉ *Sept.–July, Sat. 9–1.*

㉖ Sant'Ignazio. The interior dome in this sumptuous 17th-century church is a trompe-l'oeil oddity: the cupola is painted as, well, a cupola—but open at the top, and full of flying angels, saints, and heavenly dignitaries who float about in what appears to be a rosy sky above. To get the full effect of the illusionistic ceiling painted by Andrea del Pozzo (1642–1709), stand on the small disk set into the floor of the nave. The church also contains some of Rome's most splendorous, jewel-encrusted altars. If you're lucky, you might be able to catch an evening concert performed here (check with the tourist office). Step outside the church to look at it from Filippo Raguzzini's 18th-century piazza, where the buildings, as in much baroque art, are arranged almost as in a stage set. ✉ *Piazza Sant'Ignazio, near Pantheon* ☎ *06/6794406* ☉ *Daily 7:30–12:30 and 4–7:30.*

★ **㉚ Spanish Steps.** Both the steps and the Piazza di Spagna get their names from the Spanish Embassy to the Vatican on the piazza, though the staircase was actually built with French funds in 1723. In an allusion to the church of *Trinità dei Monti* (Trinity of the Mount), at the top of the hill, the staircase is divided by three landings (beautifully banked with azaleas from mid-April to mid-May). This area has always welcomed tourists: 18th-century dukes and duchesses on their Grand Tour, 19th-century artists and writers in search of inspiration—among them Stendhal, Balzac, Thackeray, and Byron—and today's enthusiastic hordes. The **Fontana della Barcaccia** (Fountain of the Old Boat) at the base of the steps is by Pietro Bernini, father of the famous Gian Lorenzo. ✉ *Piazza di Spagna.*

Also Worth Seeing

㉗ Colonna di Marco Aurelio. This ancient column, like the Colonna di Traiano, is an extraordinary stone history book. Its detailed reliefs spiraling up to the top illustrate the victorious campaigns of emperor Marcus Aurelius against the barbarians. It stands in front of a different kind of monument to power: the offices of the prime minister. ✉ *Piazza Colonna, near Piazza di Spagna.*

㉙ Keats-Shelley Memorial House. English Romantic poet John Keats (1795–1821) once lived in what is now a museum dedicated to him and his great contemporary and friend Percy Bysshe Shelley (1792–1822). You can visit his tiny rooms, preserved as they were when he died here. ✉ *Piazza di Spagna 26, next to the Spanish Steps* ☎ *06/6784235*

Piazza Venezia
to the
Spanish Steps

⊕ *www.keats-shelley-house.org* ✉ €3 ⊙ *Weekdays 9–1 and 3–6, Sat. 11–2 and 3–6.*

㉕ Palazzo Doria Pamphilj. The 18th-century facade of this palazzo on Via del Corso is only a small part of a bona fide patrician palace, still home to a princely family that rents out many of its 1,000 rooms. You can visit the remarkably well preserved **Galleria Doria Pamphilj** (pronounced pom-*fee*-lee), a picture gallery that gives you a sense of the sumptuous living quarters. Notice the way art was once put on display: numbered paintings (the bookshop's museum catalog comes in handy) are packed onto every available inch of wall space. Pride of place is given to the famous (and pitiless) portrait of the 17th-century Pamphilj pope Innocent X by Diego Velázquez (1599–1660), but don't overlook Caravaggio's affecting *Rest on the Flight into Egypt.* The audio guide (included in admission) is narrated by the current Doria Pamphilj prince himself and gives a fascinating personal history of the palace. ✉ *Piazza del Collegio Romano 2, near Piazza Venezia* ☏ *06/6797323* ⊕ *www. doriapamphilj.it* ✉ *€7.30* ⊙ *Fri.–Wed. 10–5.*

㉓ Palazzo Venezia. A Roman landmark on the city's busiest square, this palace is best-known for the balcony over the main portal, from which Mussolini gave public addresses to crowds in Piazza Venezia during the dark days of Fascism. Today it's home to a haphazard collection of mostly early-Renaissance weapons, ivories, and paintings in its grand salons, some of which Il Duce used as his offices. The palace also hosts major touring art exhibits, so check to see what's currently showing. ✉ *Piazza San Marco 49, near Piazza Venezia* ☏ *06/69994318* ⊕ *www. ticketeria.it/palazzovenezia-eng.asp* ✉ *€4* ⊙ *Tues.–Sun. 9–7.*

Monti & San Giovanni: Centuries of Worship

Through the centuries, the development of Christian worship has shaped Rome's history; the monuments to Christianity, still used today, are a living record of the faith and the city. Rome is home to hundreds of old churches, and their art, their histories, and their continuing existence bear witness to the centuries they have withstood; they have something for every visitor, regardless of faith. Monti and San Giovanni, adjoining neighborhoods east of Rome's historic center, are awash with some of Rome's greatest art and architecture, all executed for the glory of the Church.

The Main Attractions

★ **㉜ San Clemente.** A 12th-century church built on top of a 4th-century church, which in turn was built over a 2nd-century pagan temple to the god Mithras: San Clemente is an extraordinary archaeological site. Little of the temple remains, but the 4th-century church is largely intact, perhaps because it wasn't unearthed until the 19th century. (It was discovered by Irish Dominican monks; members of the order still live in the adjacent monastery.) The upper church, which you enter from street level, holds a beautiful early-12th-century mosaic showing a cross on a gold background, surrounded by swirling green acanthus leaves teeming with little scenes of everyday life. The marble choir screens, salvaged from the 4th-century church, are decorated with early Christian symbols: doves, vines, and fish. The **Cappella Castiglioni,** off the left aisle, holds frescos painted around 1400 by the Florentine artist Masolino da Panicale (1383–1440), a key figure in the introduction of realism and one-point perspective into Renaissance painting. Note the large Crucifixion and scenes from the lives of Sts. Catherine, Ambrose, and Christopher, plus an Annunciation (over the entrance). Before you leave the upper church, take a look at the pretty cloister—evening concerts are held here in summer.

From the right aisle, stairs lead down to the remains of the **4th-century church,** which was active until 1084, when it was damaged beyond repair during a siege of the neighborhood by the Norman prince Robert Guiscard. The vestibule is decorated with marble fragments found during the excavations (which are still under way), and in the nave are colorful 11th-century frescoes depicting stories from the life of St. Clement. Another level down is the **Mythraeum,** a shrine dedicated to the god Mithras, whose cult spread from Persia and gained a hold in Rome during the 2nd and 3rd centuries. ⊠ *Via San Giovanni in Laterano 108, San Giovanni* ☎ *06/70451018* 🖃 *€3* ⊗ *Mon.–Sat. 9–noon and 3–6, Sun. 10–12:30 and 3–6.*

㉛ **Santa Maria Maggiore.** One of Rome's four great pilgrimage churches was built on the spot where a 3rd-century pope witnessed a miraculous midsummer snowfall (reenacted every August 15). The gleaming mosaics on the arch in front of the main altar date from the 5th century, and the opulently carved wood ceiling is believed to have been gilded with the first gold brought from the New World. To view the elaborate 14th-century facade mosaics, inquire at the souvenir shop. ⊠ *Piazza Santa Maria Maggiore, off Via Cavour* ☎ *06/4465836* ⊗ *Daily 7 AM–8 PM.*

㉝ **Santi Quattro Coronati.** The 12th-century church of the Four Crowned Martyrs, part of a fortified abbey that provided refuge to early popes and emperors, is in an unusual corner of Rome, a quiet island that has resisted the tide of time and traffic flowing beneath its ramparts. Few places are so reminiscent of the Middle Ages. Don't miss the cloister with its well-tended gardens and 12th-century fountain. The entrance is the door in the left aisle; ring the bell if it's not open. You can also ring at the adjacent convent for the key to the **Oratorio di San Silvestro** (Oratory of St. Sylvester), with 13th-century frescoes. ⊠ *Largo Santi Quattro Coronati, San Giovanni* ☎ *06/70475427* ⊗ *Easter–Christmas, daily 9:30–12:30 and 3:30–6; Christmas–Easter, daily 9:30–12:30.*

Also Worth Seeing

㉞ **San Giovanni in Laterano.** You may be surprised to discover that the cathedral of Rome is not St. Peter's but this church. (St. Peter's is in Vatican City, technically not a part of Rome.) Dominating the piazza whose name it shares, this immense building is where the pope officiates in his capacity as bishop of Rome. The towering facade and Borromini's cool baroque interior emphasize the majesty of its proportions. The **cloister** is one of the city's finest, with beautifully carved columns surrounding a peaceful garden.

The adjoining **Palazzo Laterano** was the official papal residence until the 13th century, and is still technically part of the Vatican. It houses the offices of the Rome Diocese and the rather bland **Museo Storico Laterano** (Lateran Historical Museum). Behind the palace are the 4th-century octagonal **Battistero di San Giovanni** (St. John's Baptistery), forerunner of many similar buildings throughout Italy, and Rome's oldest and tallest obelisk, brought from Thebes and dating from the 15th century BC. ⊠ *Piazza San Giovanni in Laterano* ☎ *06/69886464* 💷 *Church free, cloister €2.50, museum €4* ☉ *Church Apr.–Sept., daily 7–7; Oct.–Mar., daily 7–6. Cloister 9–½ hr before church closing. Museum Sat. guided tours at 9:15, 10:30, and noon. 1st Sun. of each month 8:45–1. Baptistery daily 9–1 PM and 5 PM–1 hr before sunset.*

35 **Scala Santa** (Sacred Stairs). A small building opposite the Palazzo Laterano houses what is claimed to be the staircase from Pilate's palace in Jerusalem. The faithful climb it on their knees. ⊠ *Piazza San Giovanni in Laterano* ☉ *Daily 6:15–noon and 3:30–6:30.*

Il Quirinale to Piazza della Repubblica: Palaces & Fountains

Near the Piazza della Repubblica you can see ancient Roman sculptures, early Christian churches, and highlights from the 16th and 17th centuries, when Rome was conquered by the baroque—and by Bernini. Il Quirinale is the highest of Rome's seven hills, and was once home to the popes, housed in the massive Palazzo Quiriale, now Italy's presidential palace.

The Main Attractions

40 Fontana del Tritone (Triton Fountain). The centerpiece of busy Piazza Barberini is Bernini's graceful fountain designed in 1637 for the sculptor's patron, Pope Urban VIII. The pope's Barberini family coat of arms, featuring bees, is at the base of the large shell. Close by is the **Fontana delle Api** (Fountain of the Bees), the last fountain designed by Bernini. ⊠ *Piazza Barberini, near Via Veneto.*

36 Il Quirinale. The highest of ancient Rome's seven hills, this is where ancient Romans, and later popes, built their residences in order to escape the deadly miasmas and malaria of the low-lying area around the Forum. The fountain in the square has ancient statues of Castor and Pollux reining in their unruly steeds and a basin salvaged from the Roman Forum. The **Palazzo del Quirinale** passed from the popes to Italy's kings in the 19th century; it's now the official residence of the nation's president. Every day at 4 PM the ceremony of the changing of the guard at the portal includes a miniparade complete with band. ⊠ *Piazza del Quirinale, near Piazza di Trevi* ☎ *06/39967500 or 06/696271* ☒ *€5* ☉ *Sept.–July, Sun. 8:30–noon.*

Directly opposite the main entrance of the Palazzo del Quirinale sits **Le Scuderie Papale al Quirinale** (the Quirinal Stables), which once housed more than 120 horses for the exclusive use of the pope and his guests. The low-lying building was designed by Alessandro Specchi (1668–1729) in 1722 and was among the major achievements of baroque Rome. The stables were remodeled in the late 1990s by eminent architect Gae Aulenti and now serve as a venue for touring art exhibits. ⊠ *Piazza del Quirinale, near Piazza di Trevi* ☎ *06/39967500 or 06/696271* ⊕ *www. scuderiequirinale.it* ☒ *€9* ☉ *Sun.–Thurs. 10–7, Fri. and Sat. 10–9:30.*

44 Palazzo Massimo alle Terme. This 19th-century palace in neobaroque style holds part of the collections of antiquities belonging to the Museo Nazionale Romano (also exhibited in the Palazzo Altemps). Here you can see extraordinary examples of the fine mosaics and masterful paintings that decorated ancient Rome's palaces and villas. Don't miss the fresco—depicting a lush garden in bloom—that came from the villa that Livia, wife of Emperor Augustus, owned outside Rome. ⊠ *Largo Villa Peretti 1, near Termini* ☎ *06/480201* ☒ *€6* ☉ *Tues.–Sun. 9–7:15.*

☾ **41 Santa Maria della Concezione.** In the crypt under the main Capuchin church, the bones of some 4,000 dead Capuchin monks are arranged in odd decorative designs around the shriveled and decayed skeletons of their kinsmen, a macabre reminder of the impermanence of earthly life. Signs declare WHAT YOU ARE, WE ONCE WERE. WHAT WE ARE, YOU SOMEDAY WILL

Il Quirinale to Piazza della Repubblica

11

BE. Although not for the easily spooked, the crypt is touching and oddly beautiful. ⊠ *Via Veneto 27, Piazza di Spagna* ☎ *06/4871185* ✉ *Donation expected* ⊕ *Fri.–Wed. 9–noon and 3–6.*

42 Santa Maria della Vittoria. The most famous feature here is Bernini's baroque decoration of the **Cappella Cornaro,** an exceptional fusion of architecture, painting, and sculpture in which the *Ecstasy of St. Teresa* is the focal point. Bernini's audacious conceit was to model the chapel after a theater: members of the Cornaro family—sculpted in white marble—watch from theater boxes as, center stage, St. Teresa, in the throes of mystical rapture, is pierced by a gilded arrow held by an angel. To quote one 18th-century observer, President de Brosses: "If this is divine love, I know it well." ⊠ *Via XX Settembre 17, Termini* ☎ *06/42740571* ⊕ *Daily 8:30–noon and 4:30–6.*

Also Worth Seeing

39 Palazzo Barberini. Along with architect Carlo Maderno (1556–1629), Borromini helped make the splendid 17th-century Palazzo Barberini a residence worthy of Rome's leading art patron, Pope Urban VIII, who began the palace for his family in 1625. Inside, the **Galleria Nazionale d'Arte Antica** has some fine works by Caravaggio and Raphael, including the latter's portrait of his lover, *La Fornarina.* Rome's biggest ballroom is here; its ceiling, painted by Pietro da Cortona, depicts Immortality bestowing a crown upon Divine Providence escorted by a "bomber squadron"—to quote Sir Michael Levey—of mutant bees. (Bees featured prominently in the heraldic device of the Barberini.) ⊠ *Via Barberini 18, near Via Veneto* ☎ *06/328101* ⊕ *www.galleriaborghese.it* ☑ €6 ⊙ *Tues.–Sun. 9–7.*

㊸ Piazza della Repubblica. Smog-blackened porticoes, a subway station, and a McDonald's make this grand piazza feel a bit derelict. The racy **Fontana delle Naiadi** (Fountain of the Naiads), an 1870 addition to the square, depicts voluptuous bronze ladies wrestling happily with marine monsters. In ancient times, the Piazza della Repubblica was but the entrance to the immense **Terme di Diocleziano** (Baths of Diocletian), an archaeological site today. Built in the 4th century AD, these were the largest and most impressive of the baths of ancient Rome, with vast halls, pools, and gardens that could accommodate 3,000 people at a time. The *aula ottagonale* (octagonal hall) now holds a sampling of the ancient sculptures unearthed here, including two beautiful bronzes. ⊠ *Via Romita 8, near Termini* ☎ *06/4870690* ☑ *Free* ⊙ *Tues.–Sat. 9–2, Sun. 9–1.*

The curving ancient Roman brick facade on one side of the Piazza della Repubblica marks the church of **Santa Maria degli Angeli,** adapted by Michelangelo from the vast central chamber of the colossal baths. Look for the sundial carved on the floor. ⊠ *Via Cernaia 9* ☎ *06488/0812* ⊕ *www.santamariadegliangeliroma.it* ⊙ *Mon.–Sat. 7–6:30, Sun. 7 AM–7:30 PM.*

㊳ San Carlino alle Quattro Fontane. In a church no larger than the base of one of the piers of St. Peter's, Borromini attained geometric architectural perfection. Characteristically, he chose a subdued white stucco for the interior decoration, so as not to distract from the form. Don't miss the cloister, which you reach through the door to the right of the altar. The exterior of the church is Borromini

> **WORD OF MOUTH**
>
> "The Borghese Gallery is one of the most precious places I have ever had the good fortune to visit—twice. The Bernini Statues bring tears to my eyes. The building is gorgeous. Just a little jewel box of a museum."   –bugswife1

at his bizarre best, all curves and rippling movement. Outside the *quattro fontane* (four fountains) frame views in four directions. ⊠ *Via del Quirinale 23, near Piazza di Trevi* ☎ *06/4883261* ⊙ *Daily 9–1 and 4–6.*

㊲ Sant'Andrea al Quirinale. This small but imposing baroque church was designed and decorated by Bernini, who considered it one of his finest works. ⊠ *Via del Quirinale, Piazza di Trevi* ☎ *06/48903187* ⊙ *Mon. and Wed.–Sat. 8–noon and 4–6, Sun. 4–7.*

Villa Borghese to the Ara Pacis: Amid Sylvan Glades

Touring Rome's artistic masterpieces while staying clear of its hustle and bustle can be, quite literally, a walk in the park. Some of the city's finest sights are tucked away in or next to green lawns and pedestrian piazzas, offering a breath of fresh air for weary sightseers. Villa Borghese,

11

Villa Borghese
to the Ara Pacis

one of Rome's largest parks, can alleviate gallery gout by offering an oasis in which to cool off under the ilex trees. If you feel like a picnic, have an *alimentare* (food shop) make you some *panini* (sandwiches) before you go; food carts within the park are overpriced.

The Main Attractions

51 **Ara Pacis Augustae** (Altar of Augustan Peace). The altar was erected in 13 BC to celebrate the era of peace ushered in by Augustus's military victories. There is no access to the Ara Pacis while a museum to house it is under construction. Adjacent, the imposing bulk of the marble-clad **Mausoleo di Augusto** (Mausoleum of Augustus) was built by the emperor for himself and his family. ⊠ *Piazza Augusto Imperatore, Via Ripetta, near Piazza di Spagna* ☎ *06/68806848.*

45 **Galleria Borghese.** The palace that was completed in 1613 for Cardinal
Fodor'sChoice Scipione Borghese (1576–1633) is a monument to 18th-century Roman
★ interior decoration at its most luxurious, dripping with porphyry and alabaster. Today it contains the art collection of the cardinal. The grand salons have ancient Roman mosaic pavements and statues of various deities, including one officially known as *Venus Victrix*. There has never been any doubt, however, as to the statue's real subject: Pauline Bonaparte, Napoléon's sister, who married Prince Camillo Borghese in one

of the storied matches of the 19th century. Sculpted by Canova (1757–1822), the princess reclines on a chaise, bare-bosomed, her hips swathed in classical drapery, the very model of haughty detachment and sly come-hither. Pauline is known to have been shocked that her husband took pleasure in showing off the work to his guests. This coyness seems curious given the reply she is supposed to have made to a lady who asked her how she could have posed for the work: "Oh, but the studio was heated." Other rooms hold important sculptures by Bernini, including *David* and *Apollo and Daphne.* The renowned picture collection has splendid works by Titian, Caravaggio, and Raphael, among others. Reservations are required; be sure to book at least a day ahead of time. ⊠ *Piazza Scipione Borghese 5, off Via Pinciana, Villa Borghese* ☎ *06/8513979 information, 06/32810 reservations* ⊕ *www.galleriaborghese.it* 🖅 *€10.50, audio guide or English guided tour €5* ⊘ *Tues.–Sun. 9–7.*

㊿ Piazza del Popolo. Designed by neoclassical architect Giuseppe Valadier (1762–1839) in the early 1800s, this piazza is one of the largest in Rome, and it has a 3,000-year-old obelisk in the middle. Always a favorite spot for café-sitting and people-watching, the piazza is closed to motorized traffic. The bookend baroque churches **Santa Maria dei Miracoli** and **Santa Maria in Montesanto** are not, first appearances to the contrary, twins. On the plaza's eastern side, stairs lead uphill to the ⇨ **Pincio.** To the north, at the end of the square, is the 400-year-old **Porta del Popolo,** Rome's northern city gate, and next to it the church of Santa Maria del Popolo. The city gate was designed by Bernini to welcome the Catholic convert Queen Christina of Sweden to Rome in 1605. ⊠ *Near Villa Borghese.*

㊾ Santa Maria del Popolo. This church next to the Porta del Popolo goes almost unnoticed, but it has one of the richest art collections of any church in Rome. Here is Raphael's High Renaissance masterpiece the **Cappella Chigi,** as well as two stunning Caravaggios in the **Cappella Cerasi.** Each December an exhibit of Christmas nativity scenes is held in the adjacent building. ⊠ *Piazza del Popolo, near Villa Borghese* ☎ *06/3610836* ⊘ *Mon.–Sat. 7–noon and 4–7, Sun. 7:30–1:30 and 4:30–7:30.*

Also Worth Seeing

🄲 ㊼ Explora: Il Museo dei Bambini di Roma. Explore: the Museum for the Children of Rome is one of the very few sights in the city geared specifically to kids. There are two floors of open space filled with hands-on activities and games for toddlers to 12 year olds, and a child-friendly restaurant. Steps from the car-free Piazza del Popolo and a short hike downhill from the playground in Villa Borghese park, the museum is well suited to a child-oriented day in the neighborhood. Reservations are essential on weekends. You're let in for two-hour shifts. ⊠ *Via Flaminia 82, near Villa Borghese* ☎ *06/3613776* ⊕ *www.mdbr.it* 🖅 *€7 for children 3 and up, €6 for adults* ⊘ *Tues.–Fri. admission at 9:30, 11:30, 3, and 5; weekend admission at 10, noon, 3, and 5.*

㊻ Museo Nazionale Etrusco di Villa Giulia (National Etruscan Museum at Villa Giulia). Known for their sophisticated art and design, the Etruscans left a legacy of sarcophagi, bronze sculptures, terra-cotta vases, and stunning jewelry. (Unlike the Greeks, Etruscan women sat at the banquet tables with men and enjoyed displaying their wealth on their bodies.) Acclaimed pieces of statuary in the gallery include the *Goddess with Infant* and the *Sarcophagus of the Married Couple.* In the villa's courtyard visit the atmospheric underground **Ninfeo,** the remains of the Virgin's Aqueduct from the Augustan period. ✉ *Piazzale Villa Giulia 9, near Villa Borghese* ☎ *06/3226571* 💶 *€4* ☉ *Tues.–Sun. 8:30–7:30.*

need a break?   **Caffè delle Arti** (✉ Viale delle Belle Arti 131, near Villa Borghese ☎ 06/32651236), an exquisite, light-filled space with towering ceilings and bronze statues, is inside the not-so-noteworthy Galleria Nazionale d'Arte Moderna, across the street from Villa Giulia. The menu includes tea with a variety of homemade pastries as well as Roman and Neapolitan dishes. In warm weather sit out on the huge terrace and take in the splendor of the surrounding Villa Borghese.

🖐 **48** **Pincio.** At the southwestern corner of Villa Borghese, the Pincio belvedere and gardens were laid out by architect Giuseppe Valadier as part of his overall plan for Piazza del Popolo. Nineteenth-century counts and countesses liked to take their evening passeggiata here in the hope of meeting Pius IX (1792–1878), the last pope to go about Rome on foot. Nowadays you're more likely to see runners and in-line skaters, as well as throngs of Romans out for a stroll. It's a good place to take in the summer concerts and New Year's fireworks staged in Piazza del Popolo below. ✉ *Piazza del Popolo.*

Crossing the Tiber: The Ghetto, Tiberina Island & Trastevere

Despite rampant gentrification, Trastevere remains about the most tightly knit community in the city, its natives proudly proclaiming their descent from the ancient Romans. The old Jewish Ghetto is a warren of twisting, narrow streets, where Rome's Jewish community was once confined, then deported, and now, barely, persists. Ancient bridges, the Ponte Fabricio and Ponte Cestio, link the Ghetto and Trastevere to Tiberina Island; this area is Rome's medieval heart.

The Main Attractions

56 **Fontana delle Tartarughe.** The 16th-century Fountain of the Turtles in Piazza Mattei is one of Rome's loveliest. Designed by Giacomo della Porta (1539–1602) in 1581 and sculpted by Taddeo Landini (1550–96), the piece revolves around four bronze boys, each clutching a dolphin that jets water into marble shells. Several bronze tortoises, thought to have been added by Bernini, are held in each of the boys' hands and drink from the fountain's upper basin. The piazza is lined by a few interesting cafés and shops. It was named for the Mattei family, who built the **Palazzo Mattei** on Via Caetani. (The palace is not open to the public, but it's worth a peek at the sculpture-rich courtyard and staircase if the door is open.) ✉ *Piazza Mattei, Ghetto.*

59 **Isola Tiberina** (Tiberina Island) is where a city hospital stands on a site that has been dedicated to healing ever since a temple to Aesculapius was erected here in 291 BC. If you have time, and if the river's not too high, walk down the stairs for a different perspective on the island and the Tiber River. Every July, the city's Estate Romana hosts an open-air cinema on the island's paved shores. ⊠ *Ponte Fabricio and Ponte Cestio, near Ghetto.*

Jewish Ghetto. Rome has had a Jewish community since the 1st century BC, and from that time until the present its living conditions have varied widely according to its relations with the city's rulers. In 1555 Pope Paul II established Rome's Jewish ghetto in the neighborhood marked off by the Portico d'Ottavia, the Tiber, and Via Arenula. The area quickly became Rome's most squalid and densely populated. At one point, Jews—who had engaged in many businesses and professions in Trastevere—were limited to the sale of used iron and clothing as a trade. The laws were rescinded around the time of the Italian unifications in the 1870s. German troops occupied Rome during World War II, and on October 16, 1943, many of Rome's Jews were rounded up and deported to Nazi concentration camps. In 1982 the synagogue here was attacked with grenades and machine guns by Palestinian terrorists, and in 1986, as a gesture of reconciliation, Pope John Paul II paid a visit to Rabbi Elio Toaff, becoming the first pope ever to pray in a Jewish synagogue. Today some of Rome's 15,000 Jewish residents still live in the area; there are a few Judaica shops

VOICES OF ITALY

Dana Prescott
Artist/Arts Director,
American Academy in Rome

For nearly two decades, Rome has been American artist Dana Prescott's home—and her muse. Between her painting and her work as Andrew Heiskell Arts Director of the venerable American Academy in Rome, she's immersed in the Eternal City's creative life. Dana shares some thoughts on the pleasures of her adopted hometown:

On Rome as inspiration: "I love Rome's ability to continue to surprise me. I bicycle around and keep falling in love with the shapes of things, the proportions, the sheer unfussy beauty of a city living and working amidst its monuments.

"As a painter, I tend to respond to things visually but somewhat randomly, so Rome is a perfect companion. From braided loaves of bread on a bakery shelf to the clutter of Porta Portese, from the polish on a Bernini sculpture to Italian moms wheeling kids around in baby carriages, from peeling facades to *ragazzi* on *motorini*, how ice cream is stacked in a gelateria, the twists on the end of a *bocconcino* of mozzarella, it's all a constant bombardment of visual stimulation."

On connecting with the ancient city: "Above all, take time in the Pantheon—not taking pictures there, just sitting. Feel the vast proportions, the amazing light, the swell of the floor. Move around; reconsider your position in time and space."

On her neighborhood, the Jewish Ghetto: "Its mesh of history, of humanity, of great food, its charming Turtle Fountain, *spoglie* tucked into facades, and its stories and legends all make the city instantly accessible."

On her favorite places: "I have so many. Sant'Ignazio, with its amazing anamorphic frescoes by Pozzo, how they change while you walk through the room. I love the botanical gardens (off Via della Lungara in Trastevere), especially the unmanicured edges of the park with bamboo and wild flowers sprawled all over the lawn. By far my favorite church is Santa Maria sopra Minerva, for its Filippino Lippi frescoes, the tomb of Saint Catherine, the Madonna of the Dowery by Antoniaccio Romano, the tomb of Fra Angelico—the patron saint for artists—and two—two!—Berninis and one Michelangelo. The list goes on and on: the Pantheon, Raphael's Galatea in the Villa Farnesina in Trastevere, Cavallino's scenes from the life of St. Mary at Santa Maria in Trastevere . . ."

On Rome's artistic spirit: "Every street corner reveals another trace of history or of a hand at work, a carving, a construction, a beautiful view. I don't need to go to a museum to see art and to feel its presence on a daily basis. Every fountain, church, roadway, facade, *san pietrino*—everything reveals the skill and labor of an artist or artisan. Rome humbles me. "

and kosher groceries, bakeries, and restaurants—as well as linen and shoe stores run by Jewish families—especially on Via di Portico d'Ottavia. **Tours of the Ghetto** (€8, about two hours) that explore Rome's Jewish history can be booked through the SIDIC historical society. ⊠ *SIDIC Office, Via Garibaldi 28, Ghetto* ☎ *06/58333615* ⊕ *www.sidic.org.*

★ ② **Piazza di Santa Maria in Trastevere.** This piazza is a popular spot for afternoon coffee and evening cocktails at its outdoor cafés. But the showpiece of the Piazza di Santa Maria is the 12th-century church of **Santa Maria in Trastevere.** The 13th-century mosaics on the church's facade—which add light and color to the piazza, especially at night when they are in spotlight—are believed to represent the Wise and Foolish Virgins. Inside, the enormous golden mosaic in the apse is the city's finest, a shining burst of Byzantine color and light set off by giant columns filched from an ancient Roman building. Make sure to look down at the splendid Cosmati work, a mosaic style from the 12th and 13th centuries in which tiny squares and triangles were laid with larger stones to form geometric patterns, in the church floors. In August, processions honoring the Virgin Mary gather at the church as part of Trastevere's traditional feast, called *Festa de Noantri* (Our Own Feast). ⊠ *Piazza di Santa Maria, Trastevere* ☎ *06/5814802* ⊗ *Daily 7:30–1 and 4–7.*

⑤ **Sinagoga.** The imposing, square-dome synagogue on the Tiber is a Roman landmark. The **Museo Ebraico** documents the history of the Jewish community in Rome. Most of the decorative crowns, prayer books, holy chairs, and tapestries dating from the 17th century were donated by prominent Jewish families whose ancestors once lived in the Ghetto. The collection is a change of pace from the predominantly Christian art found elsewhere in Rome. ⊠ *Lungotevere Cenci 15, Ghetto* ☎ *06/ 68400661* ⊠ €6 ⊗ *Mon.–Thurs. 9–7:30, Fri. 9–2, Sun. 9–12:30.*

⑤ **Teatro di Marcello.** The Teatro, hardly recognizable as a theater today, was originally designed to hold 20,000 spectators. It was begun by Julius Caesar; today, the 16th-century apartment building that sprouted out of its remains has become one of Rome's most prestigious residential addresses. The area south of the theater makes a grand stage for chamber music concerts in summer. ⊠ *Via del Teatro di Marcello, Ghetto* ☎ *06/87131590 concert information* ⊕ *www.tempietto.it* ⊗ *Open during concerts only.*

Trastevere. This area consists of a maze of narrow streets that is still, despite evident gentrification, one of the city's most authentically Roman neighborhoods. Literally translated, its name means "across the Tiber," and indeed Trastevere and the Trasteverini—the neighborhood's natives—are a breed apart. The area is hardly undiscovered, but among its self-consciously picturesque trattorias and trendy tearooms you can also find old shops and dusty artisans' workshops in alleys festooned with laundry hung out to dry. Stroll along Via dell'Arco dei Tolomei and Via dei Salumi, shadowy streets showing the patina of the ages. One of the least affected parts of Trastevere centers on Piazza in Piscinula, north of Via dei Salumi and south of the Ponte Cestio Fabricio, where the smallest medieval church in the city, San Benedetto, stands opposite the restored medieval Casa dei Mattei.

⑤ **Via del Portico d'Ottavia.** Along this street in the heart of the Jewish Ghetto are buildings where medieval inscriptions, ancient friezes, and half-buried classical monuments attest to the venerable history of the neighborhood. The old **Chiesa di Sant'Angelo in Pescheria** was built right into the ruins of the Portico d'Ottavia, which was a monumental area enclosing a temple, library, and other buildings within colonnaded porticoes. ⊠ *Ghetto.*

★ **64** **Villa Farnesina.** Money was no object to extravagant patron Agostino Chigi, a Sienese banker who financed many a papal project. His munificence is evident in his elegant villa, built about 1511. When Raphael could steal some precious time from his work on the Vatican Stanze and from his wooing of the Fornarina, he executed some of the frescoes, notably a luminous *Galatea.* Chigi delighted in impressing guests by having his servants cast precious dinnerware into the Tiber when it was time to clear the table. The guests didn't know of the nets he had stretched under the waterline to catch everything. ⊠ *Via della Lungara 230, Trastevere* ☎ *06/68027268* ⊕ *www.lincei.it* ☒ *€5* ☉ *Mon.–Sat. and 1st Sun. of month 9–1.*

Also Worth Seeing

65 **Palazzo Corsini.** This elegant palace holds the 16th- and 17th-century painting collection of the **Galleria Nazionale d'Arte Antica**; even if you're not interested in the paintings, stop in to climb the extraordinary 17th-century stone staircase, itself a drama of architectural shadows and sculptural voids. The adjacent Corsini gardens, now Rome's **Giardino Botanico,** offer a welcome break with native and exotic plants and a stunning view at the top. ⊠ *Via della Lungara 10, Trastevere* ☎ *06/ 68802323* ⊕ *www.galleriaborghese.it* ☒ *€4* ☉ *Tues.–Sun. 8:30–1:30.*

52 **Piazza Bocca della Verità.** On the site of the Forum Boarium, ancient Rome's cattle market, this square was later used for public executions. Its name is derived from the marble **Bocca della Verità** (Mouth of Truth), a huge medieval drain cover in the form of an open-mouth face that is now set into the entry portico of the 12th-century church of **Santa Maria in Cosmedin.** In the Middle Ages,

> ### WORD OF MOUTH
>
> "At Santa Cecilia in Trastevere, the splendid *Last Judgment,* a huge fresco by Pietro Cavallini, can be admired by entering the choir of the nuns. The fresco is the greatest masterpiece of Roman medieval painting." –hansikday

legend had it that any person who told a lie with his hand in the mouth would have it chomped off. Today tour groups line up in this noisy, traffic-jammed piazza to give this ancient lie detector a try. ⊠ *Ghetto.*

61 **San Francesco a Ripa.** Ask the sacristan to show you the cell where St. Francis slept when he came to seek the pope's approval for his new order. Also in this church is one of Bernini's most dramatic sculptures, the figure of the *Blessed Ludovica Albertoni,* ecstatic at the prospect of entering heaven. ⊠ *Piazza San Francesco d'Assisi, Trastevere* ☎ *06/5819020* ☉ *Daily 7–noon and 4–7.*

63 **San Pietro in Montorio.** One of Rome's key Renaissance buildings, the **Tempietto,** stands in the cloister of this church built by order of Ferdinand and Isabella of Spain in 1481. Bramante built the Tempietto over the spot where St. Peter was thought to have been crucified. It's an architectural gem and was one of his earliest and most successful attempts to design a building in an entirely classical style. ☒ *Via Garibaldi, Gianicolo, Trastevere* ☏ *06/5813940* ⊘ *Church daily 9–noon and 4–6. Tempietto, Oct.–Mar., daily 9:30–12:30 and 2–4; Apr.–Sept., daily 4–6.*

⟲ ⑥⓪ Santa Cecilia in Trastevere. Mothers and children love to dally in the delightful little garden in front of this church. Duck inside for a look at the 9th-century mosaics and the languid statue of St. Cecilia under the altar. Fragments of a *Last Judgment* fresco cycle by Cavallini, dating from the late 13th century, remain one of his most important works. Though the Byzantine-influenced fragments are obscured by the structure, what's left reveals a rich luminosity in the seated apostles' drapery and a remarkable depth in their expressions. A pretty cloister and remains of Roman houses are visible under the church. Ask to see them at the booth to the left of the main nave. ☒ *Piazza Santa Cecilia, Trastevere* ☏ *06/5899289* ☒ *Church free, frescoes €2* ⊘ *Daily 10–noon and 4–6; frescoes Tues. and Thurs. 10–11:30, Sun. 11:30–noon.*

⑤④ Tempio della Fortuna Virilis. This rectangular temple devoted to "manly fortune" dates from the 2nd century BC and is built in the Greek style, as was the norm in the early years of Rome. For its age, its remains are remarkably well preserved, in part due to its subsequent consecration as a Christian church. ☒ *Piazza Bocca della Verità, near Piazza Venezia.*

⑤③ Tempio di Vesta. All but one of the 20 original Corinthian columns in Rome's most evocative small ruin remain intact. It was built in the 2nd century BC. Researchers now believe the temple was devoted to Hercules by a successful olive merchant. ☒ *Piazza Bocca dell Verità, near Piazza Venezia.*

---

off the
beaten
path

COLLE AVENTINO (Aventine Hill) – One of the seven hills of ancient Rome, Aventino is now a quiet residential neighborhood that most tourists don't see. It's home to some of the city's oldest and least-visited churches and some unusual views. The city panorama from the walled park next to the church of **Santa Sabina,** off Via Santa Sabina, is wide. Peek through the keyhole in the gate to the **Garden of the Knights of Malta** for a surprise perspective of the dome of St. Peter's. ☒ *Piazza Cavalieri di Malta, Colle Aventino.*

The Catacombs & Via Appia Antica

The Early Christian sites on the ancient Appian Way are some of the religion's oldest. Catacombs, where early Christians (whose religion prohibited cremation) buried their dead and gathered to worship in secret, lie below the very road where tradition says Christ appeared to St. Peter. The Via Appia Antica, built 400 years before, is a quiet, green place to walk and ponder the ancient world. The Rome APT office provides an informative free pamphlet for this itinerary.

Resist any temptation to undertake the 1½-km (1-mi) walk between Porta San Sebastiano and the catacombs; it's a dull and tiring hike on a heavily trafficked cobblestone road, with stone walls the only scenery. Instead, hop on Bus 660 from the Colli Albani metro stop on Line A to the end of the line, at Via Appia Antica. (Bus 218 from San Giovanni in

The Catacombs
& Via Appia Antica

Laterano also passes near the catacombs, but you have to walk about ½ km [¼ mi] east from Via Ardeatina to Via Appia Antica.) A slightly more expensive but hassle-free option is to take Bus 110 from Piazza Venezia; it's air-conditioned and allows you to hop on and off as you please.

The Main Attractions

67 **San Callisto.** A friar will guide you through its crypts and galleries of the well-preserved San Callisto catacombs. ⊠ *Via Appia Antica 110* ☎ *06/ 4465610* ⊠ *€5* ☉ *Mar.–Jan., Thurs.–Tues. 8:30–12:30 and 2:30–5.*

68 **San Sebastiano.** The 4th-century catacomb, named for the saint who was buried here, burrows underground on four levels. The only one of the catacombs to remain accessible during the Middle Ages, it's the origin of the term "catacomb," for it was in a spot where the road dips into a hollow, a place the Romans called *catacumbas* ("near the hollow"). Eventually the Christian cemetery that had existed here since the 2nd century came to be known by the same name, which was applied to all underground cemeteries discovered in Rome in later centuries. ⊠ *Via Appia Antica 136* ☎ *06/7850350* ⊠ *€5* ☉ *Mid-Nov.–mid-Oct., Mon.–Sat. 8:30–noon and 2:30–5:30.*

70 **Tomba di Cecilia Metella.** The circular mausoleum of a Roman noblewoman, who lived at the time of Julius Caesar, was transformed into a fortress in the 14th century. The tomb houses a small museum with sculptures from the Via Appia Antica and an interesting reconstruction of the area's geological and historical past. ⊠ *Via Appia Antica 161* 🕾 *06/78021465 or 06/39967700* ⊕ *www.pierreci.it* 🎫 *€2* 🕐 *Mon.–Sat. 9 AM–1 hr before sunset.*

★ ⑥⑥ **Via Appia Antica.** This Queen of Roads, "Regina Viarium," was the most important of the extensive network of roads that traversed the Roman Empire, a masterful feat of engineering that made possible Roman control of a vast area by allowing for the efficient transport of armies and commercial goods. Completed in 312 BC by Appius Claudius, the road was ancient Europe's first highway, connecting Rome with Brindisi, 584 km (365 mi) away on the Adriatic coast. Part of the route exists as Via Appia (SS7), but it is a paved, modern highway. The stretch indicated here is closed to traffic; the ancient roadway passes through grassy fields and shady groves and by the villas of movie stars (Marcello Mastroianni and Gina Lollobrigida had homes here) and other VIPs. This part is still paved with the ancient *basoli* (basalt stones) over which the Romans drove their carriages—look for the wheel ruts. Taverns, houses, temples, and tombs flanked the ancient road, and the occasional lone statue, crumbling wall, or column is still visible, draped in ivy or alone in a patch of wildflowers. Pick a sunny day for your visit, wear comfortable shoes, and bring a bottle of water. You can take Bus 660 from the Colli Albani metro station (Line A) for Via Cecilia Metella at Via Appia Antica. ✛ *Exit Via Cristoforo Colombo at Circonvallazione Ardeatina, follow signs to Appia Antica parking lot.*

Also Worth Seeing

⑥⑨ **Circo di Massenzio.** On the east side of Via Appia Antica are the ruins where the obelisk now in Piazza Navona once stood. ⊠ *Via Appia Antica 153* 🕾 *06/7801324* 🎫 *€3* 🕐 *Oct.–Mar., Tues.–Sun. 9–5; Apr.–Sept., Tues.–Sun. 9–7.*

WHERE TO EAT

Updated by
Dana Klitzberg

Rome has been known since ancient times for its great feasts and banquets, and though the days of the triclinium and the Saturnalia are long past, dining out is still the Romans' favorite pastime. The city is distinguished more by its good attitude toward eating out than by a multitude of world-class restaurants; simple, traditional cuisine reigns, although things are slowly changing as talented young chefs explore new culinary frontiers. Many of the city's restaurants cater to a clientele of regulars, and atmosphere and attitude are usually friendly and informal. The flip side is that in Rome the customer is not always right—the chef and waiters are in charge, and no one will beg forgiveness if you wanted *skim* milk in that cappuccino. Be flexible and you're sure to *mangiar bene* (eat well). Lunch is served from 12:30 to 2:30 and dinner from 8 until about 11, though some restaurants stay open later, especially in summer, when patrons linger at sidewalk tables to enjoy the parade of people and the *ponentino* (evening breeze).

WHAT IT COSTS In euros					
	$$$$	$$$	$$	$	¢
AT DINNER	over €22	€16–€22	€11–€16	€7–€11	under €7

Prices are for a second course (*secondi*).

Campo de' Fiori

★ **$$$–$$$$** ✕ **Osteria del Pesce.** The entrance to this restaurant looks like an up-scale *pescheria* (fish market). Awaiting you inside is seafood from the coast south of Rome that's beautiful enough to display like aquatic jewels: from starters such as tuna or sea bass carpaccio to seafood pasta dishes, to *secondi* (second course) of grilled or sautéed fish and crustaceans, all is simply prepared and of the highest quality. The space—hardwood floors, subtle lighting, and walls in royal blue and chili-pepper red—brims with energy. The extensive wine list has mostly whites; there are numerous after-dinner liqueurs available. ⊠ *Via di Monserrato 32, near Campo de' Fiori* ☎ *06/6865617* ▤ *AE, DC, MC, V* ⊘ *Closed Sun. and 2 wks in Aug. No lunch.*

$$–$$$ ✕ **Roscioli.** Marco Roscioli opened this restaurant (with an upscale deli counter and wine shop) around the corner from his famous *forno* (bakery). The menu has a mix of tasty and often uncommon Italian meats and cheeses, as well as pasta, meat, and fish dishes, all of which are meant to be paired with one of the 800 wines. Try the homemade pasta with duck prosciutto, the potato gnocchi with sea-urchin sauce, or splurge on the foie gras. If you book ahead you can get a table in the cozy, appealing wine cellar. ⊠ *Via dei Giubbonari 21/22, near Campo de' Fiori* ☎ *06/6875287* ▤ *AE, DC, MC, V* ⊘ *Closed Sun.*

$–$$ ✕**Acchiapafantasmi.** The name translates as "ghostbusters," after the restaurant's award-winning pizza shaped like a ghost with mozzarella, cherry tomatoes, and oregano. But the menu extends beyond pizza to spicy treats of the Commisso brothers' native Calabria, such as the spreadable *'nduja* sausage (half pork, half hot peppers) and an innovative version of eggplant parmigiana. The gelato, brought up from the southern town of Pizzo Calabria, is considered by some the best in Italy. ⊠ *Via dei Cappellari 66, near Campo de' Fiori* ☎ *06/6873462* ⌦ *Reservations not accepted* ▤ *AE, DC, MC, V* ⊘ *Closed Tues. and 1 wk in Aug.*

$–$$ ✕ **Grappolo d'Oro Zampanò.** This Campo area favorite has both a pizzeria and a restaurant, which serves eclectic regional Italian cuisine such as an eggplant flan with Gorgonzola sauce. Second courses include beef stewed in Sangiovese wine and a delicate grouper fillet oven-baked in foil with potatoes, tomatoes, and oregano. There's a well-selected (though not bargain-price) wine list. ⊠ *Piazza della Cancelleria 80, near Campo de' Fiori* ☎ *06/6897080* ▤ *AE, MC, V* ⊘ *Closed Mon. and Aug.*

¢ ✕ **Il Forno di Campo de' Fiori.** Crowds fill this counter-service pizzeria throughout the day. Try the *farcita* (stuffed) pizza, filled with meats, cheeses, vegetables—even prosciutto and warm figs in season—at their adjacent sandwich bar. ⊠ *Piazza Campo de' Fiori 22* ☎ *06/66806662* ⌦ *Reservations not accepted* ▤ *No credit cards* ⊘ *Closed Sun.*

Where to Eat in Rome

¢ ✕ **Le Piramidi.** Come here for great falafel, *schewerma* (spit-roast meat, in this case, veal), and other to-go Middle Eastern specialties. Sundry desserts are sure to include phyllo pastry, honey, and nuts. ⊠ *Vicolo del Gallo 11, Campo de' Fiori* ☎ *06/6879061* ▭ *No credit cards* ⊘ *Closed Mon.*

Piazza di Spagna

$$–$$$ ✕ **Dal Bolognese.** The classic Dal Bolognese is both a convenient shopping-spree lunch spot, and an in-crowd dinner destination. The tables on the expansive pedestrian piazza are prime people-watching real estate, and tables inside are perfectly spaced for table-hopping and lots of two-cheek kisses. As the name promises, the cooking here adheres to the hearty tradition of Bologna, with delicious homemade tortellini *in brodo* (in broth), fresh pastas in creamy sauces, and steaming trays of boiled meats. Among the desserts, try the *dolce della mamma* (a concoction of gelato, zabaglione, and chocolate sauce) and the fruit-shape gelato. ⊠ *Piazza del Popolo 1, near Piazza di Spagna* ☎ *06/3611426* ▭ *AE, DC, MC, V* ⊘ *Closed Mon. and Aug.*

$–$$ ✕ **GINA.** "Homey minimalism" isn't a contradiction at this whitewashed café with a modern edge (block seats, single flowers in mason jars, white chandeliers, and mirrors). With a reasonable menu of salads, sandwiches, and pastas to American-style desserts, this is the perfect spot for a late lunch or a light dinner that won't break the bank despite the high-end neighborhood. Upscale picnic baskets are stocked and ready to pick up on the way to nearby Villa Borghese park. For a relaxed Saturday evening, join the friendly owners for live jazz from 9:30 to midnight. ⊠ *Via San Sebastianello 7A, near Piazza di Spagna* ☎ *06/6780251* ▭ *AE, MC, V* ⊘ *Closed Sun. and Aug.*

★ ¢–$$ ✕ **Osteria della Frezza.** You can get regular tavern fare and service at this member of the 'Gusto restaurant empire (which dominates the surrounding block), or you can sample *ciccheti* (Venetian dialect for bar snacks). These are miniature portions of what's on the regular menu: cured meats and a head-spinning selection of cheeses; cooked meats like lamb chops and meatballs in tomato sauce; and pastas, including thick spaghetti with octopus, tomato, and pecorino cheese. Homemade desserts are also available in tiny portions. The wine list is full of interesting choices; trust the knowledgable staff to point you in the right direction. ⊠ *Via della Frezza 16, near Piazza di Spagna* ☎ *06/3226273* ▭ *AE, DC, MC, V.*

Piazza Navona & the Pantheon

$$$$ ✕ **Il Convivio.** The Troiani brothers came to Rome in the late 1980s; since
Fodor'sChoice   then they've been the leaders of a small circle of top Italian food elite.
★   Their inventive fare can be characterized as Italian cuisine revisited—classic dishes made from the best ingredients, given a unique, elegant tweak. The raw "lacquered" tuna and the foie gras are luscious starters, and Roman broccoli soup has disappeared from other menus. For secondi, the pigeon is exquisitely cooked, and the fish are all first-rate. Desserts are delicious, if a bit restrained, service is excellent, and the wine selection, although pricey, would impress any connoisseur. ⊠ *Vicolo dei Soldati 31, near Piazza Navona* ☎ *06/6869432* ⚐ *Reservations essential*

EATING WELL IN ROME

Roman cooking is simple, rustic cuisine, perfected over centuries. Dishes rarely have more than a few ingredients, and meat and fish are most often roasted, baked, or grilled. The best meat is often *abbacchio* (milk-fed lamb)—legs are usually roasted with rosemary and potatoes, and chops served *alla scottadito* (literally "burn your finger"—hot off the grill). Most Mediterranean fish are light, yet flavorful, among them *spigola* (the Roman name for sea bass, more commonly called *branzino* elsewhere), *orata* (gilthead bream), and *rombo* (turbot). Romans swoon for batter-fried *baccalà* (cod).

The quintessential Roman pasta dishes are made with *guanciale* (cured pork cheek) and pecorino Romano cheese. *All'amatriciana* adds onion and tomato to the mix and is classically served with *bucatini* (a thick, hollow spaghetti); *alla carbonara* tosses the pork and cheese with egg yolk and black pepper; and *alla gricia* is amatriciana without tomatoes. Potato gnocchi with a tomato sauce and Parmesan or pecorino is a favorite for Thursday dinner.

Seasonal vegetables may not appear on the menu but are usually available. Romans love their greens—*cicoria* and *spinaci ripassati* (sautéed chicory and spinach) are perennial favorites—and many restaurants specialize in vegetable *fritto misto* (literally "mixed fried"). Rome is famous for *carciofi* (artichokes)—available from November to April—prepared *alla romana* (stuffed with garlic and mint and braised) or *alla giudia* (fried whole, making each petal crisp). A springtime treat is *vignarola*, a mixture of tender peas, fava beans, artichokes, and guanciale.

Typical wines of Rome are from the Castelli Romani, the towns in the hills to the southeast: Frascati, Colli Albani, Marino, and Velletri. Though tap water in Rome is drinkable, restaurants usually offer bottled water, either *gassata* (sparkling) or *liscia* (still).

It was not so long ago that wine in Rome (and other towns) was strictly local; you didn't have to walk far to find an *osteria*, a tavernlike establishment where you could buy wine straight from the barrel or sit down to drink and nibble a bit, chat, or play cards. The tradition continues today, as many Roman wineshops are also open as *enoteche* (wine bars). Most have done away with the folding chairs and rickety tables in favor of designer interiors and chic ambience. Shelves are lined with hundreds of bottles from all over the country, representing the best in Italian wine making, and many selections are available by the glass. Behind the bar you'll usually find a serious wine enthusiast, maybe even a sommelier.

⊟ *AE, DC, MC, V* ☯ *Closed Sun., 1 wk in Jan., and 2 wks in Aug. No lunch.*

$$$–$$$$ ✕ **L'Altro Mastai.** Executive chef Fabio Baldassare (former sous-chef to La Pergola's renowned Heinz Beck) turns out beautiful Mediterranean dishes. Pastas are homemade and flavored with a delicate hand (think Roman broccoli ravioli in a truffle-scented sauce), and secondi such as

sea bass with tomatoes and olives taste of the sea and sun. Portions are small, especially for the prices, so partake heartily in the breads and *assaggini* (nibbles) throughout the meal. Desserts are luscious and beautifully executed, and the wine list ample. The restaurant has a casual wine-bar sibling across the street. ⊠ *Via G. Giraud 53, Via dei Banchi Nuovi, near Piazza Navona* ☎ *06/68301296* ☐ *AE, DC, MC, V* ☉ *Closed Sun. and Mon., and Aug.*

★ **$$$–$$$$** ✕ **Myosotis.** Don't overlook the traditional Myosotis in favor of trendier choices in the area. Secondi include a hearty veal chop *alla Milanese*, breaded and pan-fried, as well as a delicate catch of the day in a garlic, olive oil, and tomato broth. A soup of whitefish, fava beans, and chicory is a study in bittersweet. The chocolate mousse in chocolate raspberry sauce is elegant in its simplicity. Bright and fresh, the space has parquet floors, creamy table linens, and walls sponge-painted the color of fresh fettucine. Even though service is sometimes slow, owners and staff obviously care about the food. ⊠ *Vicolo della Vaccarella 3/5, near Piazza Navona* ☎ *06/6865554* ☐ *AE, DC, MC, V* ☉ *Closed 2 wks in Aug.*

$$$–$$$$ ✕ **Sangallo.** A quiet and intimate restaurant snuggled between Piazza Navona and the Pantheon serves high-quality seafood. The owner hails from Anzio, a coastal town south of Rome. The menu has some sophisticated touches, such as oysters tartare, snapper with foie gras, and pasta dishes made with toothsome *Gragnano* pasta (made in Gragnano of 100% Italian wheat, and dried to strict specifications). There are precious few tables in the tiny dining room, so make sure to book ahead. ⊠ *Vicolo della Vaccarella 11/a, near Piazza Navona* ☎ *06/6865549* ☝ *Reservations essential* ☐ *AE, DC, MC, V* ☉ *Closed Sun., 1 wk in Jan., and 2 wks in Aug. No lunch Mon.*

$$–$$$ ✕ **Osteria dell'Ingegno.** This casual but trendy spot is great for a glass of wine or a meal in the city center. The simple but innovative menu focuses on regional and seasonal produce and changes weekly. The walls are hung with colorful paintings by local artists, and service is friendly. ⊠ *Piazza di Pietra 45, near Piazza Navona* ☎ *06/6780662* ☐ *AE, DC, MC, V* ☉ *Closed Sun. and 2 wks in Aug.*

★ **$–$$** ✕ **Cul de Sac.** This is a classic Roman *enoteca* (wine bar), frequented by everyone from local soccer fans to the Fendi sisters. Quarters are cramped, both inside and out on the small piazza, but once you begin sipping the wine and sampling the food, you realize it's worth any discomfort. The selection of Italian regional cheeses and cured meats is vast, and the soups, pastas, and salads have homemade appeal. Especially refreshing are the international dishes: hummus, Greek salad, and pâtés that can be difficult to find in these parts. The wine list is tremendous and constantly changing. ⊠ *Piazza Pasquino 73, near Piazza Navona* ☎ *06/68801094* ☐ *AE, MC, V* ☉ *Closed 2 wks in Aug.*

$–$$ ✕ **Ōbikā.** The owners of this concept restaurant are trying something original: a "mozzarella bar." Varieties of the cheese—from the familiar cow's milk variety to the delectable buffalo milk mozzerella from the Campagnia region—are showcased. Try the sinfully rich *burrata* (fresh cow's milk mozzerella that encases a creamy center of unspun curds), which comes from Puglia. Accompanying cured meats, vegetables, sauces, and breads are available. Fresh salads and pasta dishes, including interesting lasagnas, are also on the menu. The wines tend to come from the southern Italian regions like the cheeses. ✉ *Piazza di Firenze and Via dei Prefetti, near Pantheon* ☎ *06/6832630* ▤ *AE, DC, MC, V.*

San Pietro

$$$$
Fodor'sChoice
★
✕ **La Pergola.** High atop Monte Mario, the Cavalieri Hilton's rooftop restaurant has a commanding view of the city below. Trompe-l'oeil ceilings and handsome wood paneling combine with low lighting to enhance the intimate dining experience. Celebrated wunder-chef Heinz Beck brings Rome its most polished example of Mediterranean *alta cucina* (haute cuisine): dishes are balanced and light (a perfectly cooked lobster) and presentation is striking (a plate of spiralling sea scallops and black truffles, each one the exact same size). For a window table reserve a month in advance; for others, two weeks. ✉ *Cavalieri Hilton, Via Cadlolo 101, Monte Mario* ☎ *06/3509221* ⚐ *Reservations essential* 🏛 *Jacket and tie* ▤ *AE, DC, MC, V* ⊘ *Closed Sun. and Mon., and 2 wks in Dec. No lunch.*

$$–$$$$
✕ **Il Simposio di Costantini.** The most sophisticated wine bar in town is done in wood paneling and velvet, and has sculptured iron vines as decoration. Here you can choose from about 30 wines by the glass. Food is appropriately fancy: marinated and smoked fish, composed salads, top-quality salami and other cured meats, terrines and pâtés, vegetable dishes, and several inventive secondi, mostly meat-game selections. Finish off with a plate from an assortment of 80 cheeses grouped according to origin or type, and a well-balanced dessert menu. ✉ *Piazza Cavour 16, near San Pietro* ☎ *06/3211502* ▤ *AE, DC, MC, V* ⊘ *Closed Sun. and last 2 wks of Aug. No lunch Sat.*

★ $–$$$
✕ **Siciliainbocca.** Looking for a straight-up, no-nonsense Sicilian restaurant? The owners, both Sicily natives, decided to open up Siciliainbocca after years of frustration at not finding a decent pasta *alla norma,* with eggplant, tomato sauce, and aged ricotta cheese. Try the risotto *ai profumi di Sicilia,* with lemon, orange, mozzarella, and zucchini. You might also opt for the delicious grilled swordfish, shrimp, or squid. Even in the dead of winter, Siciliainbocca's yellow walls and brightly colored ceramic plates are warming. There's outdoor seating in summer. ✉ *Via E. Faà di Bruno 26, near San Pietro* ☎ *06/37358400* ▤ *AE, DC, MC, V* ⊘ *Closed Sun.*

$$
✕ **Taverna Angelica.** The area surrounding St. Peter's Basilica isn't known for culinary excellence, but Taverna Angelica is an exception to the rule. The chef concentrates on each individual dish, and the results are impressive: lentil soup with pigeon breast, breast of duck in balsamic vinegar, and warm octopus salad on a bed of mashed potatoes with a basil-parsley pesto drizzle are all exquisitely executed. The narrow, candlelit dining room has plenty of space between tables; excellent service is icing on the cake. ✉ *Piazza A. Capponi 6, near San Pietro* ☎ *06/ 6874514* ⚐ *Reservations essential* ▤ *AE, V.*

$
✕ **Alfredo e Ada.** Squeeze into a table at this lovable hole-in-the-wall and make yourself at home. There's no menu, just plate after plate of whatever Ada thinks you should try, from hearty, classic pastas to *involtini di vitello* (savory veal rolls with tomato) and homemade sausage. Sit back, relax, and enjoy—it's all good. By the time you leave you may have made

some new friends, too. The cost depends on how many courses you eat and how much wine you consume, but an average meal might run around €25. Alfredo e Ada is across the river from Castel Sant'Angelo. ⊠ *Via dei Banchi Nuovi 14, near San Pietro* ☎ *06/6878842* ▭ *No credit cards* ⊘ *Closed weekends.*

Near Termini & San Lorenzo

★ **$$$–$$$$** ✕ **Agata e Romeo.** The husband-and-wife team of Agata Parisella and Romeo Caraccio runs one of Rome's top restaurants. Agata puts an inspired twist on Roman cuisine with dishes such as crepes with chestnut flour and ewe's-milk ricotta, and breaded lamp chops. Romeo acts as maître d' and expert sommelier. The tasting menu, complete with wine, changes monthly to reflect seasonal dishes and allows you to try a range of specialties. Desserts are scrumptious and the wine list is excellent. ⊠ *Via Carlo Alberto 45, near Termini* ☎ *06/4466115* ▭ *AE, DC, MC, V* ⊘ *Closed weekends, 2 wks in July, and 2 wks in Aug.*

$$–$$$$ ✕ **F.I.S.H.** The name stands for Fine International Seafood House, which sums up the kitchen's approach. This is fresh, fresh fish in capable and creative hands—from Italian fish-base pastas to a Thai mollusk soup with lemongrass and coconut milk that is a party for the senses. The menu is divided into three sections: sushi, Asian, and Mediterranean. Seating is limited, so book ahead, especially on weekends. ⊠ *Via dei Serpenti 16, Monti* ☎ *06/47824962* ⊰ *Reservations essential* ▭ *AE, D, MC, V* ⊘ *Closed Mon. and 2 wks in Aug.*

$$–$$$ ✕ **Trattoria Monti.** The cuisine of Le March is under-represented in the capital, especially considering that more Marchegiani live in Rome than in their native region—thank goodness for Trattoria Monti. The hearty regional food here includes soups, and roasted meats and game. A selection of soufflés and *timbales* (a molded, custardlike dish), generally vegetarian, changes seasonally. For dessert there are cheeses with dried fruits, nuts, and honey. The brothers who run the place are always welcoming. ⊠ *Via San Vito 13/a, Esquilino* ☎ *06/4466573* ▭ *AE, DC, MC, V* ⊘ *Closed Aug., 2 wks at Easter, 10 days at Christmas.*

$–$$$ ✕ **Bistro.** High, pale-yellow arched ceilings, immense guilt mirrors, rich oak paneling, and the original wrought-iron bar counter are all true to the art nouveau style. Chef Emanuele Vizzini serves fusion dishes such as fettuccine *al cabernet con scampi* (with red wine, shrimp, and vegetables) and *Nasdaq taglionini* (dollar-green pasta made with curaçao liqueur) topped with lobster. The sommelier has selected 300 labels (12 available by the glass) of high-quality, but lesser-known. ⊠ *Via Palestro 40, Termini* ☎ *06/44702868* ▭ *AE, DC, MC, V* ⊘ *No lunch Sun.*

$$ ✕ **Uno e Bino.** Giampaolo Gravina's restaurant in an artsy corner of the **Fodor'sChoice** San Lorenzo neighborhood is popular with Romans from all over town. ★ He works the dining room, offering suggestions from an impressive wine list, and his sister Gloria is in the kitchen turning out inventive cuisine inspired by the family's Umbrian and Sicilian roots. Octopus salad with asparagus and carrots is a specialty, and perfectly prepared pigeon can satisfy the most critical foodies on an autumn night. ⊠ *Via degli Equi 58, San Lorenzo* ☎ *06/4460702* ▭ *AE, D, MC, V* ⊘ *Closed Mon. and Aug. No lunch.*

CLOSE UP

Pizza, Roman Style

PIZZA MAY HAVE BEEN invented somewhere else, but in Rome it's hard to walk a block without encountering it in one form or another. You'll see it in bakeries, usually made without cheese—either pizza *bianca* (just olive oil and salt) or pizza *rossa* (with tomato sauce). Many small shops specialize in pizza *al taglio* (by the slice), priced by the *etto* (100 grams, about 1/4 pound), according to the kind of topping. These places are great for a snack on the go any time of day.

But don't leave Rome without sitting down to a classic, wafer-thin, crispy

Roman pizza in a lively, no-frills pizzeria. Most are open only for dinner, usually from 8 PM to midnight. Look for a place with a *forno a legna* (wood-burning oven), a must for a good thin crust on your plate-size Roman pizza. Standard models are the *margherita* (tomato, mozzarella, and basil) and the *capricciosa* (a little bit of everything, depending upon the "caprices" of the pizza chef: tomato, mozzarella, sausage, olives, artichoke hearts, prosciutto, even egg), and most pizzerias have a long list of additional options, including tasty mozzarella *di bufala* (made from buffalo milk).

$ ✕ **Arancia Blu.** Owner-chef Fabio Passan has a mission—to prove that "vegetarian cuisine" isn't an oxymoron. He succeeds, with flavorful, creative dishes that have won him a devoted, omnivorous clientele. Start with a leek-and-almond quiche or lemon-ricotta ravioli with squash and sage, and move on to *polpettine vegetali* (meatless meatballs) with a tomato-and-coriander seed sauce. For dessert you might tickle your palate with a chocolate tasting, 14 chocolate wafers of different flavors and origins. Vegan and wheat-free dishes are available on request. ⊠ *Via dei Latini 65, San Lorenzo* ☎ *06/4454105* ▭ *No credit cards* ☺ *No lunch.*

$ ✕ **La Soffitta.** This is Rome's hottest spot for classic Neapolitan pizza (thick, though crunchy on the bottom, rather than paper-thin and crispy like the Roman kind), and one of the few pizzerias in town certified by the True Neapolitan Pizza Association. Desserts are brought in daily from Naples. You pay more here, but hey, it's imported. ⊠ *Via dei Villini 1/ e, Termini* ☎ *06/4404642* ◈ *Reservations not accepted* ▭ *AE, DC, MC, V* ☺ *Closed Aug. 10–31. No lunch.*

★ ¢–$ ✕ **Cavour 313.** Wine bars are popping up all over the city, but Cavour 313 has been around much longer than most. It serves an excellent choice of cured meats, cheeses, and salads. Choose from about 25 wines by the glass or uncork a bottle (there are more than 1,200) and stay a while. ⊠ *Via Cavour 313, Colosseo* ☎ *06/6785496* ▭ *AE, DC, MC, V* ☺ *Closed Aug. No lunch weekends. No dinner Sun. June 15–Sept.*

¢–$ ✕ **Pommidoro.** Mamma's in the kitchen and the rest of the family greets, serves, and keeps you happy and well fed at this trattoria popular with artists, filmmakers, and actors. It's near Rome's main university in the counterculture San Lorenzo neighborhood, a short cab ride east of the Termini train station. The menu has especially good grilled meats and game birds as well as classic home-style cucina. You can dine outside in warm weather. ⊠ *Piazza dei Sanniti 44, San Lorenzo* ☎ *06/4452692* ▭ *AE, DC, MC, V* ☽ *Closed Sun. and Aug.*

Trastevere, Testaccio & the Ghetto

$$$ ✕ **Antico Arco.** Founded by three friends with a passion for wine and fine food, Antico Arco has won the hearts of foodies from Rome and beyond with its culinary inventiveness and high style. The menu changes with the season, but you may find such delights as *flan di taleggio con salsa di funghi* (cheese flan with mushrooms), or a *carré d'agnello* (rack of lamb) with foie-gras sauce and pears in port wine. Don't miss the chocolate soufflé with melted chocolate center: it's justly famous among chocoholics all over the city. ⊠ *Piazzale Aurelio 7, Trastevere* ☎ *06/5815274* ⌕ *Reservations essential* ▭ *AE, DC, MC, V* ☽ *Closed Sun. and 2 wks in Aug. No lunch.*

$$–$$$ ✕ **Ferrara.** What used to be a well-stocked *enoteca* (wine bar) with a few nibbles has expanded to become a full-fledge restaurant, wine bar, and gastronomic boutique—known as the "Ferrara block." It's a modernist destination with a frequently changing menu and tasty antipasti and *primi* (first courses). Keep in mind that consistency is neither the kitchen's nor the servers' strong point: you can have a wonderful experience one visit and a drawn-out, disappointing meal the next. The wine list never lets you down though, and the sinful desserts end things on a positive note. ⊠ *Via del Moro 1A, Trastevere* ☎ *06/58333920* ▭ *DC, MC, V* ☽ *Closed Tues. and 2 wks in Aug.*

$$–$$$ ✕ **Spirito di Vino.** At this restaurant on the less-traveled side of Viale Trastevere, the food ranges from inventive (mini meatballs seasoned with coriander) to traditional (spaghetti with *cacio,* an aged sheep's milk cheese) to ancient (braised pork shoulder with apple and leeks is from a recipe that dates back to the time of Apicius, Rome's first cookbook author). The dining room is welcoming and refined, with walls in tomato-red and dark wood. The proud owner is happy to explain every dish on the menu and give you the history of his wine cellar, where several ancient sculptures, now in the Vatican and Capitoline museums, were unearthed. ⊠ *Via dei Genovesi 31 A/B, Trastevere* ☎ *06/5896689* ▭ *AE, MC, V* ☽ *Closed Sun. and 2 wks in Aug.*

★ $–$$ ✕ **Alle Fratte.** Here staple Roman trattoria fare shares the menu with dishes that have a Neapolitan slant: spaghetti carbonara, as well as penne *alla Sorrentina,* with tomato, basil, and fresh mozzarella, for example. Try the pressed octopus carpaccio with arugula to start, followed by a mixed seafood pasta or a grilled sea bass with oven-roast potatoes. Boisterous owner Francesco, his American wife, and their trusted waiter Peppe make you feel at home. ⊠ *Via delle Fratte di Trastevere 49/50* ☎ *06/5835775* ▭ *AE, DC, MC, V* ☽ *Closed Wed. and 2 wks in Aug.*

$–$$ ✕ **Perilli.** A bastion of authentic Roman cooking since 1911 (the decor has changed very little), this trattoria is the place to go to try rigatoni *con pajata* (with calves' intestines)—if you're into that sort of thing. The pasta carbonara is also a classic. House wine is a hearty white from the Castelli Romani estate. ⊠ *Via Marmorata 39, Testaccio* ☎ *06/5742415* ▭ *AE, DC, MC, V* ☽ *Closed Wed.*

★ ¢–$ ✕ **Dar Poeta.** It's always crowded and lively at the innovative Dar Poeta. Pizza is served in traditional Roman style (paper-thin) or as the thicker

Neapolitan version, *alta* (tall or high). Topping choice goes beyond the usual: try the house specialty with sautéed zucchini, sausage, and hot pepper). There are several types of *bruschette* (grilled, topped breads) and salads. A must-try: the dessert calzone, filled with ricotta cheese and chocolate-hazelnut Nutella. ⊠ *Vicolo del Bologna, Trastevere* ☎ *06/5880516* 🚍 *AE, MC, V.*

¢–$ ✗ **Remo.** Expect a wait at this perennial favorite in Testaccio frequented by students and neighborhood locals. You won't find tablecloths or other nonessentials, just classic Roman pizza and boisterous conversation. ⊠ *Piazza Santa Maria Liberatrice 44, Testaccio* ☎ *06/5746270* ⌦ *Reservations not accepted* 🚍 *No credit cards* ☉ *Closed Sun., Aug., and Christmas wk. No lunch.*

¢ ✗ **Zí Fenizia.** This kosher pizzeria is something of an institution in the Jewish quarter. Thin crusts overflow with everything from eggplant and zucchini to beef sausage and arugula. Since the mingling of dairy and meat is prohibited, you can expect to find one or the other on your pizza, but not both. The falafel sandwiches here are also great. ⊠ *Via Santa Maria del Pianto 64, Ghetto* ⌦ *Reservations not accepted* 🚍 *No credit cards* ☉ *Closed Sat. No dinner Fri.*

Via Veneto

$$$$ ✗ **La Terrazza dell'Eden.** The Hotel Eden's La Terrazza restaurant has an unparalleled view of Rome's seven hills and food as spectacular as the view. The culinary expertise of the well-traveled young chef is reflected in his refined touch with Mediterranean dishes and his pairing the finest primary ingredients with accents like candied celery and pearl barley. If you're a wine enthusiast, ask the maître d' to let you view the restaurant's showcase cellar. ⊠ *Hotel Eden, Via Ludovisi 49, near Via Veneto* ☎ *06/47812752* ⌦ *Reservations essential* 🏛 *Jacket and tie* 🚍 *AE, DC, MC, V.*

★ $$$–$$$$ ✗ **Papá Baccus.** Italo Cipriani takes his meat as seriously as any Tuscan, in fact he brings in many ingredients from his hometown on the border of Emilia-Romagna and Tuscany. Real Chianina beef is the prized breed used for the house-specialty *bistecca alla fiorentina*, a thick grilled steak left rare in the middle. Try the sweet and delicate prosciutto from Pratomagno or the *ribollita* (a traditional bread-base, minestronelike soup). The welcome is warm, the service excellent. ⊠ *Via Toscana 36, near Via Veneto* ☎ *06/42742808* 🚍 *AE, DC, MC, V* ☉ *Closed Sun. and 2 wks in Aug. No lunch Sat.*

$$–$$$$ ✗ **Tullio.** For years members of the international business and the entertainment industries have frequented this upscale trattoria. The decor is basic—wood paneling and white linens—with the requisite older, often grumpy, waiters. But fresh seafood is available in abundance, as are greens like *brocoletti* (broccoli florets), sautéed to perfection with garlic and olive oil. The menu is heavy on Tuscan classics such as ribollita and grilled steak Florentine; the wild hare sauce, served over flat noodles, is delectable. The wine list favors robust Tuscan reds and those who have thick wallets. ⊠ *Via San Nicola da Tolentino 26, off Piazza Barberini, near Via Veneto* ☎ *06/4745560* 🚍 *AE, DC, MC, V* ☉ *Closed Aug.*

Cafés

Café-sitting is the most popular leisure-time activity in Rome, practiced by all and involving nothing more strenuous than gesturing to catch the waiter's eye. Cafés are meant for relaxing, chatting with a companion, and watching the passing parade, possibly within view of one of the city's spectacular fountains or churches. Part of the pleasure is resting your tired feet; you won't be rushed, even when the cafés are most crowded, just before lunch and dinner. (Be aware, though, that you pay for your seat—prices are higher at tables than at the counter.) Nearly every corner in Rome holds a faster paced coffee bar, where locals stop for a quick caffeine hit at the counter. You can get coffee drinks, fruit juices, pastries, sandwiches, liquor, and beer there, too.

Pricey **Antico Caffè Greco** (⌧ Via Condotti 86, near Piazza di Spagna ☎06/6791700) is a national landmark popular with tourists; its red-velvet chairs and marble tables have hosted the likes of Byron, Shelley, Keats, Goethe, and Casanova. **Rosati** (⌧ Piazza del Popolo 5, near Piazza di Spagna ☎ 06/3225859) is Piazza del Popolo's premier people-watching spot. Tables on the car-free square fill up quickly on weekends, when it seems the whole city is here. **Ciampini** (⌧ Piazza San Lorenzo in Lucina 29, near Piazza di Spagna ☎ 06/6876606), in a jewel of a piazza off Via del Corso, is a prime spot for a predinner aperitivo. Be sure to ask for the free assaggini.

Antico Caffè della Pace (⌧ Via della Pace 3, near Piazza Navona ☎ 06/6861216) is ornate and old-fashioned. Inside cozy candlelight is a treat, or you can sit outside by ivy-lined walls in warm weather. **Caffè Sant'Eustachio** (⌧ Piazza Sant'Eustachio 82, near Pantheon ☎ 06/6861309) makes one of the smoothest cappuccinos anywhere. The secret? *Crema di caffè* (coffee cream)—a rich, homemade addition slipped into each cup. If you want your *caffè* (espresso) without sugar, ask for it *amaro*. **Tazza d'Oro** (⌧ Via degli Orfani 84, near Pantheon ☎ 06/6789792) serves some of the best coffee in the city, as well as decadent *granita di caffè* (iced espresso) with a thick dallop of whipped cream mixed in.

Gelaterie & Pasticcerie

For Italians, gelato is more a snack than a serious dessert. Romans are not known for having a sweet tooth, but there are few *pasticcerie* (pastry shops) in town that distinguish themselves with particularly good examples of regional desserts.

Gelateria Duomo (⌧ Largo Arenula 27, near Campo de' Fiori ☎ 320/1633871) specializes in artisanal, all-natural gelato. **Il Gelato di San Crispino** (⌧ Via della Panetteria 42, near Piazza di Trevi ☎ 06/6793924), closed Tuesday, is perhaps the most celebrated gelato in all of Italy, made without artificial colors or flavors. It's worth crossing town for.

Giolitti (⌧ Via Uffici del Vicario 40, near Pantheon ☎ 06/6991243), off Via Campo Marzio, has a quaint tearoom and delicious fruit-flavored gelato. **Fiocco di Neve** (⌧ Via del Pantheon 51 ☎ 06/6786025) is renowned for its zabaglione and *riso bianco* (white rice) ice cream.

11

Fonte della Salute (✉ Via Cardinal Marmaggi 2, Trastevere ☎ 06/5897471), literally "fountain of health," serves frozen yogurt as well as traditional gelato. It's closed Tuesday in winter. **Forno del Ghetto** (✉ Via del Portico d'Ottavia 1, Ghetto ☎ 06/6878637) preserves a tradition of Italian-Jewish sweets that cannot be found anywhere else. The ricotta cake (with sour-cherry jam or chocolate) is unforgettable. This hole-in-the-wall—no sign, no tables, just a take-away counter—is a neighborhood fixture. It's closed Friday at sundown, Saturday, and Jewish holidays. The apple strudel and Sacher torte at **Dolceroma** (✉ Via del Portico d'Ottavia 20/b, Ghetto ☎ 06/6892196) may not be Italian, but this is a popular spot just the same. Prices have become a bit outrageous. It's closed Sunday afternoon, Monday, and four weeks July and August.

Dagnino (✉ Galleria Esedra, Via VE Orlando 75, near Termini ☎ 06/4818660) is an outpost of Sicilian sweets. The pastries, such as ricotta-filled cannoli and *cassata* (sponge cake with sheep's ricotta and candied fruit), as well as colorful marzipan candies, are exquisite. For decades, **Muse** (✉ Via Eleanora Duse 1E, Parioli ☎ 06/8079300), popularly known as da Giovanni (after the owner), has been a mecca for Romans in the know. Winter flavors include chestnut and almond. It's closed Sunday.

WHERE TO STAY

Updated by
Dana Klitzberg

Appearances can be misleading in Rome: crumbling stucco facades may promise little from the outside, but they often hide interiors of considerable elegance. By the same token, elaborate reception areas may lead to surprisingly plain rooms. Generally, rooms tend to be small by U.S. standards. Many of the lower-price hotels are actually old-fashioned *pensioni* (pensions) set on one or several floors of a large building. One disadvantage of staying in central hotels in lower categories is noise; you can ask for an inside room if you are a light sleeper, but you may end up looking out on a dark courtyard. The grand monuments to luxury and elegance are around the major piazzas and Via Veneto.

Rome is a year-round destination, so you should always try to make reservations, even if only a few days in advance. Always ask about special rates, often available in both winter and summer if occupancy is low. If you arrive in Rome without reservations, try **Hotel Reservation Service** (☎ 06/6991000), with an English-speaking operator available daily 7 AM–10 PM, and with desks at Aeroporto Fiumicino and Stazione Termini. A list of all the hotels in Rome, with prices and facilities, is available from the main **APT information office** (✉ Via Parigi 5, Termini ☎ 06/48899255 ⊕ www.romaturismo.it).

WHAT IT COSTS In euros					
	$$$$	**$$$**	**$$**	**$**	**¢**
FOR 2 PEOPLE	over €290	€210–€290	€140–€210	€80–€140	under €80

Prices are for a standard double room in high season.

Campo de' Fiori

$$$–$$$$ ⊞ **Hotel Ponte Sisto.** Staying near the pedestrian bridge that connects the Campo de' Fiori neighborhood to Trastevere provides the convenience of the city center and access to the trattorias and bars of Trastevere, an area popular with both Romans and expats. Once the palazzo of the noble Venetian Palottini family, the hotel now has clean and bright, if basic rooms. Wall-to-wall carpeting and green-marble bathrooms add refinement, but the real draw is the large internal courtyard, where you can get sun, read beneath the shade of the enormous palms, and sip cocktails under the stars. ⊠ *Off Ponte Sisto, Via dei Pettinari 64, Campo de' Fiori, 00186* ☎ *06/686310* 🖷 *06/68301712* ⊕ *www.hotelpontesisto. it* ⤴ *103 rooms, 4 suites* ♿ *Dining room, in-room safes, minibars, cable TV, bar, meeting rooms, parking (fee)* 🖃 *AE, DC, MC, V* ‖◯‖ *BP.*

★ $$–$$$ ⊞ **Residenza Farnese.** The Renaissance charm of this former priests' convent has been preserved—its landmark status prevents the owners from making too many changes. Room 309, believed to be a former chapel, has a ceiling fresco found during renovations; it's been professionally restored. Furnishings run from understated antiques and deep blue fabrics to more ornate hand-painted floral dressers and original artwork. All have hardwood floors and modern bathrooms with showers. There is a billiards room with a bar for socializing, and a large breakfast room where homemade breads and organic marmalades are served. ⊠ *Via del Mascherone 59, Campo de' Fiori, 00186* ☎ *06/68891388* 🖷 *06/ 68210980* ✉ *residenzafarnese@libero.it* ⤴ *31 rooms* ♿ *In-room safes, minibars, cable TV, billiards, bar, Internet, meeting room* 🖃 *AE, MC, V* ‖◯‖ *BP.*

$ ⊞ **Hotel In Parione.** Smeraldo's sister hotel shines with marble—cream in the staircases and hallways, deeper reddish tones in the guest room bathrooms. Celery green fabrics and cherry-stain wood decorate the rooms, which are smallish, but very neat. Five floors above one of the bustling *vicoli* (small side streets) near the Campo de' Fiori, the roof garden provides a peek into the residential side of Roman living. ⊠ *Via dei Chiavari 32, near Campo de' Fiori, 00186* ☎ *06/6892330* 🖷 *06/ 6834094* ⊕ *www.inparione.com* ♿ *In-room data ports, cable TV, minibars, bar* 🖃 *AE, DC, MC, V* ‖◯‖ *EP.*

$ ⊞ **Smeraldo.** The location, on a quiet side street a stone's throw from Campo de' Fiori, makes this an excellent choice in its price category. White marble floors, salmon-color bedding and curtains, and wooden bed frames and furniture decorate the guest rooms. Shiny new bathrooms in green marble have showers or a combination bath and shower. The roof terrace has a nice view of the surrounding neighborhood. ⊠ *Vicolo dei Chiodaroli 9, Campo de' Fiori, 00186* ☎ *06/6875929 or 06/ 6892121* 🖷 *06/68805495* ⊕ *www.smeraldoroma.com* ⤴ *25 rooms* ♿ *In-room safes, cable TV, bar* 🖃 *AE, DC, MC, V* ‖◯‖ *BP.*

Colosseo

$$$$ ⊞ **Hotel Capo d'Africa.** Designed on a boutique hotel model, the Capo d'Africa has '60s-style furnishings in bright purple and orange, commissioned artwork on the walls, and quirky light fixtures. The 1903 building was originally a school, and as a result rooms are different sizes; all are done in earth tones and saffron, with marble-and-tile bathrooms.

Two rooftop terraces, connected by the breakfast room, are a delightful bonus in warmer weather. ⊠ *Via Capo d'Africa 54, near Colosseo, 00184* ☎ *06/772801* 🖷 *06/77280801* ⊕ *www.hotelcapodafrica.com* 🛏 *64 rooms, 1 suite* ⚒ *In-room safes, minibars, cable TV, gym, bar, Internet, meeting rooms, parking (fee), no-smoking rooms* ⊟ *AE, DC, MC, V* ⦿ *BP.*

$$ 🏨 **Duca d'Alba.** This elegant hotel has made a stylish contribution to the ongoing gentrification of the Suburra neighborhood, near the Colosseum and the Roman Forum. The tasteful neoclassical decor includes custom furnishings such as inlaid wood headboards. All rooms are entirely soundproof. The breakfast buffet is ample. With its attentive staff and reasonable rates, Duca d'Alba is an exceptional value. ⊠ *Via Leonina 14, near Colosseo, 00184* ☎ *06/484471* 🖷 *06/4884840* ⊕ *www. hotelducadalba.com* 🛏 *27 rooms, 1 suite* ⚒ *In-room data ports, in-room safes, some kitchenettes, minibars, cable TV, bar* ⊟ *AE, DC, MC, V* ⦿ *BP.*

Piazza di Spagna

$$$$ 🏨 **D'Inghilterra.** Legendary names like Liszt, Mendelssohn, Hans Christian Andersen, Mark Twain, and Hemingway litter the guest book here. With a residential feel and a staff that is as warm as the surroundings are velvety, this hotel near the Spanish Steps was once the guesthouse of the fabulously rich Prince Torlonia. Rooms are so full of carpets, gilt-frame mirrors, and cozy bergères, you hardly notice the snug dimensions. The chic Café Romano, with ochre walls and vaulted ceilings, serves eclectic cuisine and has tables on Via Borgogna. ⊠ *Via Bocca di Leone 14, near Piazza di Spagna, 00187* ☎ *06/699811* 🖷 *06/69922243* ⊕ *www.hoteldinghilterraroma.it* 🛏 *90 rooms, 8 suites* ⚒ *Restaurant, in-room safes, minibars, cable TV, bar, laundry service, parking (fee), no-smoking rooms* ⊟ *AE, DC, MC, V* ⦿ *EP.*

$$$$ 🏨 **Hassler.** Enjoy sweeping views of Rome from the front rooms and the
Fodor'sChoice roof restaurant of the enchanting Hassler hotel, itself at the top of the
★ Spanish Steps; other rooms overlook the gardens of the Villa Medici. An extravagant 1950s elegance pervades the public spaces—especially the clubby winter bar and the summer garden bar. Luxe guest rooms are decorated in classic styles with rich fabrics and some ornate, hand-painted furniture; the fifth floor has stylized art deco rooms done in black and white. The penthouse suite, resplendent with antiques, has a huge terrace. ⊠ *Piazza Trinità dei Monti 6, near Piazza di Spagna, 00187* ☎ *06/699340* 🖷 *06/6789991* ⊕ *www.lhw.com* 🛏 *85 rooms, 15 suites* ⚒ *Restaurant, in-room safes, minibars, cable TV, gym, hair salon, bar, laundry service, concierge, parking (fee), no-smoking rooms* ⊟ *AE, DC, MC, V* ⦿ *EP.*

$$$$ 🏨 **Hotel Art.** Via Margutta has long been an artists' enclave, so it's fitting that this modern hotel is a favorite of creative types. In the futuristic lobby the check-in staff works within a glowing white, podlike fixture. Arches, vaults, and columns are painted in contrasting deep blue and white, defining the café-bar space. Each of the four floors has a corridor color (yellow, green, orange, and blue) that is mirrored in the guest rooms' bathroom tiles. Otherwise, the rooms—clean-line furnishings,

Where to Stay in Rome

high-quality linens, and sleek parquet floors—have a neutral palette. A central courtyard is a good lounging spot in warmer months. ⊠ *Via Margutta 56, near Piazza di Spagna, 00187* ☎ *06/328711* 🖷 *06/36003995* ⊕ *www.hotelart.it* ⤴ *46 rooms and suites* ⚭ *In-room safes, minibars, cable TV, gym, sauna, steam bath, bar* ⊟ *AE, DC, MC, V* ¶⊙¶ *EP.*

$$$$ 🏨 **Hotel de Russie.** In the 19th century this hotel counted Russian princes among its guests; later Picasso and Cocteau leaned out the windows to pick oranges from the trees in the lush terraced garden. Famed hotelier Sir Rocco Forte has brought the de Russie to a superlative standard of accommodations and service today. Rooms are chic Italian contemporary in style, with Roman mosaic motifs in bathrooms. Many have garden views, and several suites have panoramic terraces. The spa is luxurious, but be warned: you have to dole out an extra €11 for gym privileges, an absurdity given the room cost. ⊠ *Via del Babuino 9, off Piazza del Popolo, near Piazza di Spagna, 00187* ☎ *06/328881* 🖷 *06/32888888* ⊕ *www.rfhotels.com* ⤴ *130 rooms, 27 suites* ⚭ *Restaurant, in-room data ports, in-room safes, minibars, cable TV, health club, hair salon, spa, bar, Internet, meeting rooms* ⊟ *AE, DC, MC, V* ¶⊙¶ *EP.*

$$$$ 🏨 **The Inn at the Spanish Steps.** The name of this small, exclusive hotel tells it all. Staying here is like having your own little place on fabled Via Condotti, the elegant shopping street crowned by the Spanish Steps. The hotel occupies the upper floors of a centuries-old palazzo it shares with Caffè Greco. Rooms, all junior suites, are handsomely decorated with damask fabrics and antiques. ⊠ *Via Condotti 85, near Piazza di Spagna, 00187* ☎ *06/69925657* 🖷 *06/6786470* ⊕ *www.atspanishsteps.com* ⤴ *22 rooms* ⚭ *In-room safes, minibars, cable TV, airport shuttle, no-smoking rooms* ⊟ *AE, DC, MC, V* ¶⊙¶ *BP.*

★ **$$–$$$$** 🏨 **Locarno.** Art aficionados and people in the cinema have long appreciated this hotel's preserved fin de siècle charm, intimate feel, and central location off Piazza del Popolo. Wallpaper and fabric prints are coordinated in the rooms, and some rooms have antiques. Everything is lovingly supervised by the owners, a mother-daughter duo. The buffet breakfast is ample, there's bar service on the panoramic roof garden, and complimentary bicycles are available if you feel like braving the traffic. ⊠ *Via della Penna 22, near Piazza di Spagna, 00186* ☎ *06/3610841* 🖷 *06/3215249* ⤴ *64 rooms, 2 suites* ⚭ *Restaurant, in-room safes, minibars, cable TV, in-room data ports, bar, laundry service, no-smoking rooms* ⊟ *AE, DC, MC, V* ⊕ *www.hotellocarno.com* ¶⊙¶ *BP.*

$$$ 🏨 **Carriage.** The Carriage's location is its main appeal: it's two blocks from the Spanish Steps, in the heart of Rome. The decor of subdued baroque accents, richly colored wallpaper, and antique reproductions lends a touch of old-world charm. Some furniture has seen better days, and rooms can be pint-size, but several have small terraces. A roof garden adds to the appeal. ⊠ *Via delle Carrozze 36, near Piazza di Spagna, 00187* ☎ *06/6990124* 🖷 *06/6788279* ⊕ *www.hotelcarriage.net* ⤴ *24 rooms, 3 suites* ⊟ *AE, DC, MC, V* ¶⊙¶ *BP.*

$–$$ 🏨 **Margutta.** Looking for a decent value and friendly owner-managers? The Margutta's your place. The lobby and halls in this small hotel are unassuming, but rooms are a pleasant surprise, with tall windows, at-

11

tractive wrought-iron bedsteads, and modern baths. Three rooms have private terraces. Though it's in an old building, there's an elevator. The location is on a quiet side street between the Spanish Steps and Piazza del Popolo. ⊠ *Via Laurina 34, near Piazza di Spagna, 00187* ☎ *06/ 3223674* 🖷 *06/3200395* ⊕ *www.hotelmargutta.it* 🛏 *24 rooms* ✿ *Cable TV, Internet* ⊟ *AE, DC, MC, V* ⦿ *BP.*

$ 🛏 **Panda.** Via della Croce is one of Piazza di Spagna's chic shopping streets, so it's refreshing to find a budget option (with an old pensione feel) in this decidedly non-budget neighborhood. Guest rooms are outfitted in terra-cotta and wrought iron; they're smallish, but spotless and quiet, thanks to double-glaze windows. You can pay even less by sharing a bath—in low season, you may have it to yourself anyway. ⊠ *Via della Croce 35, Piazza di Spagna 00187* ☎ *06/6780179* 🖷 *06/69942151* ⊕ *www.hotelpanda.it* 🛏 *20 rooms, 14 with bath* ✿ *No a/c in some rooms, no room TVs* ⊟ *MC, V* ⦿ *BP.*

Trastevere

$$–$$$ 🛏 **Hotel Santa Maria.** All the ground-floor rooms at this lovely former convent surround a pebbled courtyard shaded by orange trees. Room furniture leans towards the standard American hotel style, with two double beds, but there are terra-cotta tile floors and a tub with shower in the bathrooms. In fair weather, breakfast or a drink in the courtyard is a real treat, with a backdrop of old Trastevere that seems more opera set than reality. ⊠ *Vicolo del Piede 2, behind Piazza Santa Maria, Trastevere, 00153* ☎ *06/5894626* 🖷 *06/5894815* ⊕ *www.htlsantamaria. com* 🛏 *18 rooms, 2 suites* ✿ *In-room safes, minibars, cable TV, bar* ⊟ *AE, DC, MC, V* ⦿ *BP.*

$$ 🛏 **Grand Hotel Gianicolo.** Atop Janiculum Hill, one of the famed seven **Fodor'sChoice** hills of Rome, the Grand Hotel feels removed from the urban chaos. ★ It's a bargain, with many of the trappings standard at higher prices: beautifully manicured gardens, a pool, and a rooftop terrace, conference rooms and a clubby bar. Comfortable guest rooms have patterned wallpaper and draperies. The viewpoint on the drive up has breathtaking, encompassing views of the Eternal City. ⊠ *Via delle Mura Gianicolensi 107, Trastevere, 00152* ☎ *06/58333405* 🖷 *06/58179434* ⊕ *www. grandhotelgianicolo.it* ✿ *Cafe, cable TV, in-room data ports, some in-room hot tubs, in-room safes, minibars, pool, bar, babysitting, laundry service, concierge, Internet, meeting rooms, free parking, some pets allowed, no-smoking rooms* ⊟ *AE, DC, MC, V* ⦿ *BP.*

$ 🛏 **Hotel Trastevere House.** Close to the pizzerias and bars of Viale Trastevere, yet off the beaten path in an 18th-century house tucked onto a tiny street, this bed-and-breakfast is a find. The cozy rooms are done in traditional dark wood and deep blue fabric, with wood-beam ceilings and terra-cotta floors. The owners have another hotel, Domus Tiberina, around the corner, complete with a suite with balcony. ⊠ *Vicolo del Buco 7, Trastevere, 00153* ☎🖷 *06/5883774* ⊕ *www.trasteverehouse.it* 🛏 *10 rooms, 7 with bath* ✿ *Cable TV; no a/c* ⊟ *MC, V* ⦿ *BP.*

Piazza Navona

$$$$ 🛏 **Raphaël.** Old-world European luxury is alive and well behind the vine-covered facade of Raphaël. An array of sculpture, hand-carved wood antiques, and original Picasso ceramics grace the lobby. Rooms—a few with minuscule proportions—are individually decorated, some with tapestries and columns. Bathrooms are finished with travertine marble or hand-painted tiles. A new Richard Meier–designed wing, under construction at this writing, will add modernized lodgings. Arrange to have your meal on the bi-level Bramante Terrace for great city views. ☒ *Largo Febo 2, near Piazza Navona, 00186* ☎ *06/682831* 🖷 *06/6878993* ⊕ *www.raphaelhotel.com* ↩ *51 rooms, 7 suites, 10 apartments* ♿ *Restaurant, cable TV, gym, sauna, bar, laundry service, Internet, parking (fee)* ▭ *AE, DC, MC, V* †⊙† *EP.*

\$\$ 🖵 **Abruzzi.** Look out from the windows of this little hostelry and the Pantheon is literally in your face. Though location is the main selling point, basic rooms are modern and now all have bathrooms with a shower or bathtub. At this writing, work on a rooftop terrace had begun. It should be completed by late 2005. ☒ *Piazza della Rotonda 69, near Pantheon, 00186* ☎ *06/6792021* 🖷 *06/69788076* ⊕ *www.hotelabruzzi.it* ↩ *26 rooms* ♿ *In-room safes, minibars, cable TV* ▭ *AE, MC, V* †⊙† *BP.*

★ \$\$ 🖵 **Cesàri.** The exterior of this 1787 hotel looks much as it did when Stendhal stayed here in the 1800s. Old prints of Rome embellish the cream-color guest room walls; soft-green drapes and bedspreads create comfort and serenity. Bathrooms are done in smart two-tone blue marble. Overall, Cesàri exudes a quiet elegance in a very central location on a traffic-free street. ☒ *Via di Pietra 89a, near Pantheon, 00186* ☎ *06/6749701* 🖷 *06/67497030* ⊕ *www.albergocesari.it* ↩ *47 rooms* ♿ *Some in-room safes, some minibars, cable TV, bar, laundry service, some pets allowed, parking (fee), no-smoking floor* ▭ *AE, DC, MC, V* †⊙† *BP.*

★ \$\$ 🖵 **Santa Chiara.** Three ancient buildings form a gracious hotel that has been in the same family for 200 years. The personal attention shows in meticulously decorated and maintained lounges and rooms. Each room has built-in oak headboards, a marble-top desk, and an elegant travertine bath. Double-glaze windows look out over the Piazza della Minerva. There are three apartments, for two to five people, with full kitchens. ☒ *Via Santa Chiara 21, near Pantheon, 00186* ☎ *06/6872979* 🖷 *06/6873144* ⊕ *www.albergosantachiara.com* ↩ *100 rooms, 4 suites, 3 apartments* ♿ *Some kitchens, cable TV, bar* ▭ *AE, DC, MC, V* †⊙† *BP.*

\$-\$\$ 🖵 **Coronet.** This small hotel occupies part of a floor in one wing of the vast Palazzo Doria Pamphilj; seven interior rooms overlook the family's lovely private garden court. Don't expect palatial ambience, but elaborate moldings in the carpeted halls and wood-beam ceilings in several rooms do lend a sense of age. The good-size rooms have oldish baths, some very small. Several rooms can accommodate three or four beds. ☒ *Piazza Grazioli 5, near Piazza Venezia, 00186* ☎ *06/6792341* 🖷 *06/69922705* ⊕ *www.hotelcoronet.com* ↩ *13 rooms, 10 with bath* ▭ *AE, MC, V* †⊙† *BP.*

¢ 🖵 **Fraterna Domus.** On a byway near Piazza Navona sits a guesthouse run by nuns, but you may not know it because they don't wear religious habits. Rooms are spare, with single beds, but they have small private bathrooms. Three hearty meals a day are served in the dining room (dinner €12), and the curfew is 11 PM. ☒ *Vicolo del Leonetto 16, Piazza*

Navona, 00186 ☎ *06/68802727* ✎ *domusrm@tin.it* 🖷 *06/6832691* ⇱ *20 rooms* ⚱ *Dining room; no a/c in some rooms, no room TVs* ▤ *DC, MC, V* ⦿⦿ *BP.*

San Pietro

$$$–$$$$ ⌧ **Giulio Cesare.** An aristocratic town house with a garden in the residential but central Prati district, the Giulio Cesare is a 10-minute walk across the Tiber from Piazza del Popolo. It's beautifully run, with a friendly staff and a quietly luxury. The rooms are elegant, with chandeliers, thick rugs, floor-length drapes, and rich damasks in soft colors. Public rooms have Oriental carpets, old prints and paintings, marble fireplaces, and a grand piano. The buffet breakfast is a veritable banquet. ⊠ *Via degli Scipioni 287, near San Pietro, 00192* ☎ *06/3210751* 🖷 *06/3211736* ⇱ *90 rooms* ⚱ *Dining room, in-room safes, minibars, cable TV, Internet* ▤ *AE, DC, MC, V* ⦿⦿ *BP.*

$$–$$$$ ⌧ **Atlante Star.** The lush rooftop-terrace garden café and the restaurant of this hotel have a knockout view of the basilica and the rest of Rome. The rooms in the distinguished 19th-century building are attractive, in striped silks and prints; many bathrooms have hot tubs. The friendly family management is attentive to your needs and takes pride in selling extra-virgin olive oil produced from their own trees in the country. A sister hotel around the corner, Atlante Garden, has larger rooms at slightly lower rates. ⊠ *Via Vitelleschi 34, near San Pietro, 00193* ☎ *06/ 6873233* 🖷 *06/6872300* ⊕ *www.atlantehotels.com* ⇱ *65 rooms, 10 suites* ⚱ *Restaurant, some in-room hot tubs, in-room safes, minibars, cable TV, bar, laundry service, concierge, parking (fee), no-smoking rooms* ▤ *AE, DC, MC, V* ⦿⦿ *BP.*

★ $$$ ⌧ **Hotel Farnese.** The intimate Farnese began life as a late-19th-century mansion. Today it's furnished with great attention to detail in belle epoque style: marble-top tables and curvaceous-wood or scrolled-iron headboards, for example. Fresco embellishments are lively; and the modern baths sparkle. A roof garden has tall hedges and umbrella-shaded tables for two. The hotel is not far from the metro. ⊠ *Via Alessandro Farnese 30, near San Pietro, 00192* ☎ *06/3212553* ⊕ *www.hotelfarnese.com* 🖷 *06/ 3215129* ⇱ *23 rooms, 2 suites* ⚱ *Minibars, cable TV, bar, laundry service, concierge, free parking* ▤ *AE, DC, MC, V* ⦿⦿ *EP.*

$$–$$$ ⌧ **Residenza Paolo VI.** The Paolo Sesto (Italian for Paul VI) is within the Vatican walls. Rooms in this former monastery are simple, with wood furniture, marble floors, and Persian rugs. The roof terrace, however, has a spectacular view of St. Peter's. Breakfast is an American-style buffet. ⊠ *Via Paolo VI 29, near San Pietro, 00193* ☎ *06/68134108* 🖷 *06/ 6867428* ⊕ *www.residenzapaolovi.com* ⇱ *29 rooms* ⚱ *In-room safes, minibars, cable TV, bar, laundry service, parking (fee), no-smoking rooms* ▤ *AE, D, MC, V* ⦿⦿ *BP.*

$$ ⌧ **Sant'Anna.** In the quiet Borgo neighborhood surrounding St. Peter's, this small hotel has much with its limited size: the spacious attic rooms have tiny terraces. Large bedrooms have carpeting and some coffered or slanted ceilings, with accents in navy, gold, and rose. Frescoes enliven the breakfast room, and the fountain in the courtyard is typically Roman. ⊠ *Borgo Pio 134, near San Pietro, 00193* ☎ *06/68801602* 🖷 *06/*

68308717 ⊕ *www.hotelsantanna.com* ☞ *20 rooms* ☼ *Minibars, cable TV, parking (fee)* ▤ *AE, DC, MC, V* ♔ *BP.*

¢ ▦ **San Giuseppe della Montagna.** This convent is right outside the Vatican walls, near the entrance to the Vatican Museums. It's run by Catalan nuns, so unless you speak Italian or Spanish, you may have to work at communicating with the staff. The rooms are immaculate (no pun intended), though spare; some have three beds. Unusual for a convent is that there's no curfew; you are given keys. ⊠ *Viale Vaticano 87, near San Pietro, 00165* ☎ *06/39723807* 🖷 *06/39721048* ☞ *15 rooms* ☼ *No a/c, no room TVs* ▤ *No credit cards* ♔ *BP.*

Termini & Via Nazionale

★ **$$$$** ▦ **Exedra.** The opening of the luxurious, stately Exedra in December 2002 transformed a dilapidated piazza into a vibrant meeting place. Construction also unearthed additional baths of Diocletian, on view under glass outside of the conference rooms on the lower floor. A red carpet leads to the arched entry; inside an attentive staff waits to attend your every need. Chandeliers hang from high ceilings that are detailed with stepped moldings or timbers, and king-size beds rest atop deep, soft carpets in neoclassical rooms. Marble adorns all bathrooms. A rooftop terrace contains the pool and a bar, and there's a world-class spa on-site. ⊠ *Piazza della Repubblica 47, near Via Nazionale, 00185* ☎ *06/489381* 🖷 *06/48938000* ⊕ *www.boscolohotels.com* ☞ *262 rooms 6 suites* ☼ *3 restaurants, in-room safes, minibars, cable TV, pool, health club, spa, 2 bars, babysitting, dry cleaning, laundry service, concierge, Internet, meeting rooms, parking (fee), no-smoking rooms* ▤ *AE, DC, MC, V.*

$$$-$$$$ ▦ **Mediterraneo.** Constructed in 1935—and operated as a hotel since 1940—the Mediterranneo is a service-oriented charmer. Though it lacks the slick modernities of a newly renovated hotel, it has clubby 1940s character. The lobby has a fireplace, and the breakfast room is done in green tile. Either parquet floors with Persian rugs or deep wall-to-wall carpeting lies underfoot in guest rooms, and velvet easy chairs wait for you to sink in. Double-glaze windows keep things surprisingly quiet. The rooftop terrace bar is open May–September. ⊠ *Via Cavour 15, near Termini, 00184* ☎ *06/4884051 or 800/2239832* 🖷 *06/4744105* ⊕ *www. romehotelmediterraneo.it* ☼ *Restaurant, room service, in-room safes, minibars, cable TV, bar, meeting rooms, laundry service* ▤ *AE, DC, MC, V* ♔ *BP.*

$$$ ▦ **Britannia.** Owner Pier Paolo Biorgi has created a very special small
Fodor'sChoice hotel. His influence is evident: the caring staff provides English-language
★ newspapers daily and local weather reports delivered to your room each morning. Planted palms and fluted columns adorn frescoed halls. Each guest room has a unique layout and is furnished with lush fabrics and original artwork. A heat lamp warms marble bathrooms. On the top floor, a light-filled suite opens onto a private terrace. ⊠ *Via Napoli 64, near Via Nazionale, 00184* ☎ *06/4883153* 🖷 *06/4882343* ⊕ *www. hotelbritannia.it* ☞ *32 rooms, 1 suite* ☼ *In-room safes, minibars, cable TV, babysitting, laundry service, free parking* ▤ *AE, DC, MC, V* ♔ *BP.*

$$ ▦ **Hotel Venezia.** Here's an old-fashioned, side-street hotel that's charming and, well, *pretty*—16th-century wood tables and sideboards set off by cozy matching armchairs and tapestries. Guest rooms are somewhat simpler but still a cut above many of the other hotels near the Termini station. There's even a "pillow menu" from which you can order the type of pillow you want to sleep on. ☒ *Via Varese 18, near Termini, 00185* ☎ *06/4457101* 🖷 *06/4957687* ⊕ *www.hotelvenezia.com* 🗗 *60 rooms* ♿ *In-room safes, minibars, cable TV; no a/c in some rooms* 🖃 *AE, D, MC, V* ○¶ *BP.*

$$ 🏨 **Morgana.** Apart from the fact it's near the central train station, nothing about this refurbished hotel screams Roman. Still, plaid wallcoverings, upholstered sofas, and soft chairs in the lobby reading room and the TV lounge are welcoming. The cozy public spaces belie the guest room decor, which could be mistaken for that of a boutique hotel—slick and modern, in gray, black, and burgundy. Everything about the place (including the elevator) is compact, except for the breakfast room, where there's a big, full buffet. ☒ *Via Filippo Turati 33, near Termini, 00185* ☎ *06/4467230* 🖷 *06/4469142* ⊕ *www.hotelmorgana.com* 🗗 *103 rooms, 2 suites* ♿ *In-room safes, minibars, cable TV, bar, laundry service, concierge, no-smoking rooms* 🖃 *AE, DC, MC, V* ○¶ *BP.*

$–$$ 🏨 **Des Artistes.** The three personable Riccioni brothers have transformed their hotel into one of the best for its price range in the Termini train station neighborhood. They've lavished rooms with paintings, mahogany furnishings, and marble baths. The breakfast room doubles as a TV lounge with Internet access. One floor has 10 dorm-style rooms (6–8 beds per room, €20 per bed). ☒ *Via Villafranca 20, near Termini, 00185* ☎ *06/4454365* 🖷 *06/4462368* ⊕ *www.hoteldesartistes.com* 🗗 *40 rooms, 27 with bath* ♿ *In-room safes, minibars, cable TV, in-room data ports, bar, concierge, parking (fee); no a/c in some rooms, no smoking* 🖃 *AE, DC, MC, V* ○¶ *BP.*

$–$$ 🏨 **Montreal.** On a central avenue, three blocks from Stazione Termini, the compact Montreal occupies three floors of an older building. It's been totally renovated and has fresh-looking, though small, rooms. The owner-managers are pleasant and helpful, and the neighborhood has plenty of reasonably priced restaurants. ☒ *Via Carlo Alberto 4, across from Santa Maria Maggiore, near Termini, 00185* ☎ *06/4457797* 🖷 *06/4465522* ⊕ *www.hotelmontrealroma.com* 🗗 *27 rooms* ♿ *In-room safes, minibars, cable TV, parking (fee)* 🖃 *AE, DC, MC, V* ○¶ *BP.*

$ 🏨 **Adler.** This tiny pension run by the same family for more than three decades provides a comfortable stay on a quiet street near the station for a very good price. Ideal for families, the Adler has six spacious rooms that sleep three, four, or five, as well as a single and a double. Rooms are basic but impeccably clean (owner Serena Biancalana sees to that). Worn but cozy chairs line the lobby, and in summer, breakfast can be taken on the leafy courtyard balcony. ☒ *Via Modena 5, near Termini, 00184* ☎ *06/484466* 🖷 *06/4880940* 🗗 *8 rooms* ♿ *Cable TV, bar* 🖃 *AE, DC, MC, V* ○¶ *BP.*

$ 🏨 **Tempio di Pallade.** This small hotel near Porta Maggiore is a good deal. Rooms are simple but elegant, done in blue and gold. The owners, Ranieri siblings, will be happy to make arrangements for you, from airport taxis to tours of the city to opera tickets. Triples and quads are available on request, as are group meals. ☒ *Via Giolitti 425–427 near Termini, 00185* ☎ *06/70451521* 🖷 *06/70452758* ⊕ *www.*

hoteltempiodipallade.com ↘ 50 rooms ☾ In-room safes, minibars, cable TV, concierge ☰ AE, DC, MC, V ⦶ BP.

★ ¢–$ ▥ **The Beehive.** Linda Martinez-Brenner and Steve Brenner are the friendly American couple who run this funky B&B—as well as apartment rentals. Bright, clean rooms have ultramodern furniture and colorful artwork. One hostel-style room with eight bunk beds costs a mere €20 euros per person. New for 2005 was a downstairs café-lounge that serves drinks, light meals, and snacks (the shared kitchen was removed.) There's free Internet access and concierge service; have them book you a dinner reservation while you sit in the lobby's Phillipe Starck chairs and wonder how something so good can cost so little. ⊠ *Via Marghera 8, near Termini, 00185* ☎ *06/44704553* ⊕ *www.the-beehive.com* ↘ *9 rooms without bath, 10 rooms apartments* ☾ *Fans, concierge, café, Internet; no a/c, no room TVs, no smoking* ☰ *No credit cards* ⦶ *EP.*

Via Veneto

★ $$$$ ▥ **Aleph.** Adam Tihany's upscale, boutique hotel design plays with the themes of heaven and hell: in the Paradiso spa, in the Angel lobby bar, in the flaming red Maremeto seafood restaurant. Guest rooms are done in a whimsical, modern Venetian style, with Murano-glass light fixtures, cream-and-deep blue color schemes, and black-and-white accents—including full-wall photo blow-ups. ⊠ *Via San Basilio 15, near Via Veneto, 00187* ☎ *06/422901* 🖷 *06/42290000* ⊕ *www.boscolohotels.com* ↘ *94 rooms, 2 suites* ☾ *Restaurant, in-room safes, minibars, cable TV, gym, spa, 2 bars, laundry service, concierge, Internet, no-smoking rooms* ☰ *AE, DC, MC, V* ⦶ *EP.*

★ $$$$ ▥ **Eden.** A superlative hotel combines dashing elegance and stunning vistas of Rome with the warmth of Italian hospitality. The Eden was once a preferred haunt of Hemingway, Ingrid Bergman, and Federico Fellini. Antiques, sumptuous Italian fabrics, linen sheets, and marble baths are the essence of good taste. Views from the rooftop bar and terrace can take your breath away (as can the bill). The hotel's top-floor restaurant, La Terrazza dell'Eden, is one of the city's best. ⊠ *Via Ludovisi 49, near Via Veneto, 00187* ☎ *06/478121* 🖷 *06/4821584* ⊕ *www. hotel-eden.it* ↘ *112 rooms, 14 suites* ☾ *Restaurant, in-room safes, minibars, cable TV, gym, bar, laundry service, concierge, parking (fee), no-smoking rooms* ☰ *AE, DC, MC, V* ⦶ *EP.*

$$$$ ▥ **Rose Garden Palace.** The elegant Rose Garden Palace is a marriage of the classic (marble floors, velvet sofas, patterned curtains) and the contemporary (clean lines, modern wood). Guest rooms are done in calming tones of beige, slate blue, and terra-cotta. A state-of-the-art fitness room, pool, and sauna and steam room below ground are small but ideal. Friday nights, jazz musicians play in the bar, and in warm weather the bar opens into the rose garden. The hotel is behind the American Embassy. ⊠ *Via Boncaompagni 19, near Via Veneto, 00187* ☎ *06/421741* 🖷 *06/4815608* ⊕ *www.rosegardenpalace.com* ↘ *59 rooms, 6 suites* ☾ *Restaurant, in-room safes, minibars, cable TV, indoor pool, gym, spa, bar, meeting rooms, parking (fee), no-smoking rooms* ☰ *AE, DC, MC, V* ⦶ *BP.*

$$$$ ▥ **Westin Excelsior.** Next door to the American Embassy, the Excelsior is the hotel of choice for visiting diplomats, American business confer-

ences, and celebrities. It's of the breed that put the *luxe* in deluxe: every corner is lavished with mirrors, moldings, Oriental rugs, crystal chandeliers, and huge, baroque floral arrangements. Guest rooms have elegant drapery, marble baths, top-quality linens, and big, firm beds. ⊠ *Via Veneto 125, 00187* ☎ *06/47081* 🖷 *06/4826205* ⊕ *www.westin.com* 🛏 *286 rooms, 35 suites* △ *Restaurant, in-room safes, minibars, cable TV, indoor pool, gym, bar, laundry service, concierge, no-smoking rooms* ⊟ *AE, DC, MC, V* ⊺◯⫯ *EP.*

$$ 🖭 **La Residenza.** Mainly Americans frequent this cozy hotel in a converted town house near Via Veneto. Rooms are basic and comfortable (although singles are windowless). The real charm is at the bar, on the terrace, and in the lounges (smoking and no-smoking), which have warm wallpaper and love seats, a big-screen TV, a piano, and card tables. Rates include a generous American-style buffet breakfast and an in-house movie every night. ⊠ *Via Emilia 22, near Via Veneto, 00187* ☎ *06/4880789* 🖷 *06/485721* ⊕ *www.thegiannettihotelsgroup.com* 🛏 *29 rooms* △ *In-room safes, minibars, cable TV, bar, laundry service, parking (fee)* ⊟ *AE, MC, V* ⊺◯⫯ *BP.*

Beyond the City Center

$$$$ 🖭 **Cavalieri Hilton.** Though the Cavalieri is outside the city center, distance has its advantages, including the magnificent view from the hotel's hilltop position (ask for a room facing the city). This hotel is an island of quiet good taste with a distinctive Italian flair. If you can tear yourself away from the gardens and pools, a courtesy shuttle bus to downtown Rome leaves every hour. Don't miss the acclaimed rooftop restaurant, La Pergola. ⊠ *Via Cadlolo 101, Monte Mario, 00136* ☎ *06/35091* 🖷 *06/35092241* ⊕ *www.cavalieri-hilton.com* 🛏 *357 rooms, 17 suites* △ *2 restaurants, cable TV, tennis court, 2 pools (1 indoor), health club, hair salon, spa, bar* ⊟ *AE, DC, MC, V* ⊺◯⫯ *EP.*

★ $$$–$$$$ 🖭 **Castello della Castelluccia.** Removed from the hustle and bustle of Rome's city center, this beautifully renovated 12th-century castle is surrounded by a small wooded park. The original structure has been preserved, complete with watchtower (now a three-level suite); all that's missing is a medieval knight clinking down the echoing stone halls. Guest rooms are luxuriously appointed, with inlaid-wood antiques and four-poster beds; a few have marble fireplaces, and two have giant, tiled hot-tub alcoves. There's shuttle-bus service to central Rome. ⊠ *Via Carlo Cavina, Località La Castelluccia, 00123, 16 km (10 mi) north of center* ☎ *06/30207041* 🖷 *06/30207110* ⊕ *www.lacastelluccia.com* 🛏 *18 rooms, 6 suites* △ *Restaurant, room service, minibars, cable TV, in-room data ports, some in-room hot tubs, pool, spa, horseback riding, bar, laundry service, meeting room, free parking, some pets allowed* ⊟ *AE, D, MC, V* ⊺◯⫯ *BP.*

$$ 🖭 **Crowne Plaza.** The sprawling, American-style Crowne Plaza has tons of facilities—for business conferences, for families, for sporting types. The luxurious Saturnia Spa has a long menu of services, a Turkish bath, a Jacuzzi, a modern gym, exercise classes, and indoor and outdoor pools. The rooms are comfortable and spacious, with two double beds in a double room, which is a breath of fresh air in often-cramped Eu-

ropean quarters. ✉ *Via Aurelia Antica 415, southeast of Vatican, 00165* ☎ *06/66420* 📠 *06/6637190* ⊕ *www.crowneplaza.com* ⇱ *321 rooms* ⚵ *2 restaurants, room service, in-room safes, minibars, cable TV with movies, 4 tennis courts, 2 pools (1 indoor), health club, hot tub, spa, bar, piano bar, shop, concierge, concierge floor, shops, babysitting, laundry service, Internet, business services, convention center, airport shuttle, car rental, free parking, no-smoking rooms* ☱ *AE, DC, MC, V* �託 *BP.*

NIGHTLIFE & THE ARTS

The Arts

Rome lacks the level of culture in some of Italy's other cities, but it is the capital, so performances from the worlds of music, dance, theater, and film are to be found. Consult one of the local publications for listings: in the back of the weekly *roma c'è* booklet (published Wednesday) there are comprehensive listings in English, along with handy bus and metro information. The monthly *Time Out Roma* gives event schedules, as well as editors' picks, that are mainly in Italian (with a small summary in English) but are easy to decipher. The monthly *Where* magazine is distributed free at hotels and restaurants. An English-language biweekly, *Wanted in Rome* (www.wantedinrome.com), is sold at central newsstands and has good listings of events and museum exhibitions. *Trovaroma* is the weekly entertainment guide published in Italian every Thursday as a supplement to the daily newspaper *La Repubblica.*

Concerts

Christmastime is especially busy classical concert season in Rome. Many small classical concert groups perform in cultural centers and churches year-round; all performances in Catholic churches are religious music and are free. Look for posters outside the churches. Pop, jazz, and world music concerts are frequent, especially in summer, although they may not be well advertised. Many of the bigger-name acts perform outside the center, so it's worth asking about transportation *before* you buy your tickets (about €8 to €30).

CLASSICAL A year-round classical concert series is organized by the **Accademia di Santa Cecilia** (Concert hall and box office ✉ Via della Conciliazione 4, near San Pietro ☎ 06/684391). The **Accademia Filarmonica Romana** (✉ Via Flaminia 118, near Stadio Olimpico ☎ 06/3201752, 06/3265991 tickets) has concerts at the Teatro Olimpico. **Istituzione Universitaria dei Concerti** (✉ Aula Magna, Piazzale Aldo Moro 5, near San Lorenzo ☎ 06/3610051 ⊕ www.concertiiuc.it) presents small concerts with music ranging from swing to Bach. The internationally respected **Oratorio del Gonfalone series** (✉ Via del Gonfalone 32/a, Campo de' Fiori ☎ 06/6875952) focuses on baroque music. **Il Tempietto** (☎ 06/87131590 ⊕ www.tempietto.it) organizes classical music concerts indoors in winter and in the atmospheric settings of Teatro Marcello and Villa Torlonia in summer.

Entertainment Alfresco

ROMAN NIGHTLIFE moves outdoors in summertime, and that goes not only for pubs and discos but for higher culture as well. Open-air opera in particular is a venerable Italian tradition; competing companies commandeer church courtyards, ancient villas, and soccer stadiums for performances that range from student-run mom-and-poperas to full-scale extravaganzas. The same goes for dance and for concerts covering the spectrum of pop, classical, and jazz. Look for performances at the Baths of Caracalla, site of the famous televised "Three Tenors" concert; regardless of the production quality, it's a breathtaking setting. In general, though, you can count on performances being quite good, even if small productions often resort to school-play scenery and folding chairs to cut costs. Tickets run from about €15 to €40. The more sophisticated productions may be listed in newspapers and magazines such as *roma c'e* and *Wanted in Rome*, but your best sources for information are old-fashioned posters plastered all over the city, advertising classics such as *Tosca* and *La Traviata*.

The church of **Sant'Ignazio** (⊠ Piazza Sant'Ignazio, near Pantheon ☎ 06/6794560) often hosts classical concerts in its spectacularly frescoed setting.

ROCK, POP & JAZZ

Tickets for major music events are usually handled by **Orbis** (⊠ Piazza Esquilino 37, near Santa Maria Maggiore ☎ 06/4744776). **Box Office** (⊠ Viale Giulio Cesare 88, near San Pietro ☎ 06/37500375 ⊕ www. ticket.it/boxoffice.htm) sells rock, pop, and jazz concert tickets from Monday to Saturday. **Hello Ticket** (⊠ At Termini train station ☎ 06/47825710 ⊕ www.helloticket.it) sells tickets to concerts as well as theater and other cultural events.

Dance

Modern dance and classical ballet companies from Russia, the United States, and Europe sporadically visit Rome; performances are at the Teatro dell'Opera, Teatro Olimpico, or one of the open-air venues in summer. Small dance companies from Italy and abroad perform in numerous venues.

The **Rome Opera Ballet** (☎ 06/48160255 tickets ⊕ www.opera.roma.it) performs at the Teatro dell'Opera, often with international guest stars.

Film

Movie tickets range in price from €4.50 for matinees and some weeknights up to €10 for reserved seats on weekend evenings. Check listings in *roma c'è* or *Trovaroma* (www.trovacinema.it). The three-screen **Pasquino** (⊠ Piazza Sant'Egidio 10, near Trastevere ☎ 06/5815208) shows exclusively original-language films, most in English.

Opera

The season for the **Opera Theater of Rome** (☎ *06/4817515* ⊕ *www.opera. roma.it.* runs from November or December to May. Main performances are staged at the Teatro dell'Opera in cooler weather and at outdoor locations, such as Piazza del Popolo in simmer. Ticket prices range from €16 to €120 for regular performances; they can go much higher for an opening night or an appearance by an internationally acclaimed guest singer. Standards may not always measure up to those set by Milan's fabled La Scala, but, despite strikes and shortages of funds, most performances are respectable.

Small, private companies, such as **New Mendelflor Music** (☎ 06/21707618) hold sporadic performances of the classics in venues ranging from school auditoriums to church courtyards.

Theater
Theater performances are staged throughout the year in Italian, English, and several other languages, depending on who is sponsoring the performance.

For comic theater in English, check out **The Miracle Players** (☎ 06/70393427 ⊕ www.miracleplayers.org), a group of English-speaking actors who write and produce free public performances every summer in the Roman Forum, presenting a perfectly balanced mix of the historical and the hilarious.

Venues
★ Rome's state-of-the-art **Auditorium-Parco della Musica** (✉ Via de Coubertin 15, Flaminio ☎ 06/80241350 ⊕ www.musicaperroma.it), a 10-minute tram ride from Piazza del Popolo, has three halls with excellent acoustics and a large courtyard used for concerts and other events—everything from chamber music to jazz to big-name pop, even film screenings and art exhibits.

Teatro Argentina (✉ Largo Argentina 52, near Campo de' Fiori ☎ 06/68804601), built in 1732 by the architect Theoldi, has been the home of the Teatro Sabile theater company since 1994. The theater has been renovated several times over the centuries, most recently in 2001. It's a beautiful, ornate structure, with velvet seats and chandeliers. The layout is more vertical than horizontal, creating a surprising number of seats, some at vertiginous heights. Teatro Argentina plays host to many plays, classical music performances, operas, and dance performances.

Both the city's ballet and opera companies, as well as visiting international performers, appear at the **Teatro dell'Opera** (✉ Piazza Beniamino Gigli 8, near Termini ☎ 06/481601, 06/48160255 tickets ⊕ www.opera.roma.it).

Teatro Valle (✉ Via del Teatro Valle 23A, near Pantheon ☎ 06/68803794) hosts dramatic performances of the same caliber as its neighbor, Teatro Argentina, but often with a more experimental bent, particularly during the fall season. Dance and classical music are also presented here.

The ancient **Terme di Caracalla** (✉ Via delle Terme di Caracalla 52, Aventino ☎ No phone) has one of the most spectacular and enchanting outdoor stages in the world.

Teatro Olimpico (✉ Piazza Gentile da Fabriano 17, Stadio Olimpico ☎ 06/3265991) hosts both concerts and dance performances.

Nightlife

Rome's nightlife is decidedly more happening for locals and insiders who know whose palms to grease and when to go where. The "flavor of the month" factor is at work here, and many places fade into oblivion after their 15 minutes of fame. Smoking has been banned in all public areas in Italy (that's right, it's actually happened); Roman aversion to clean air has meant a decrease in crowds at bars and clubs. The best sources for an up-to-date list of night spots are *roma c'è* and *Where*. Trastevere and the area around Piazza Navona are both filled with bars, restaurants, and people after dark. In summer, discos and many bars close to beat the heat (although some simply relocate to the beach, where many Romans spend their summer nights). The city-sponsored Estate Romana (Rome Summer) festival takes over, lighting up hot city nights with open-air concerts, bars, and discos. Pick up the event guide at newsstands.

Bars

So where do you go for a cocktail? **Bar della Pace** (✉ Via della Pace 5, near Piazza Navona ☎ 06/6861216) has been the chic people-watching cocktail bar of choice since time immemorial. **Acqua Negra** (✉ Largo Teatro Valle 9, Piazza Navona ☎ 06/97606025) packs in the twenty- to fortysomething crowd for aperitif, dinner, and postdinner drinks in a sexy, minimalist space. A hangout for scruffy-chic Romans sipping cocktails is **Société Lutéce** (✉ Piazza di Montevecchio 17, off Via dei Coronari, Piazza Navona ☎ 06/6832361).

Salotto 42 (✉ Piazza di Pietra 42, near Pantheon ☎ 06/6785804) is open morning until late; the cozy-sleek room reflects its owners' Roman–New York–Swedish pedigrees as it moves from daylight bar with smorgasbord to cocktail lounge–design den complete with art books and local sophisticates.

English- and Irish-style pubs have long been a prominent part of the bar scene in Rome, among Italians and foreigners alike. **Trinity College** (✉ Via del Collegio Romano 6, near Piazza Venezia ☎ 06/6786472) is one such drinking hall.

Following the modern design bar trend, **Fluid** (✉ Via Governo Vecchio 46/47, near Campo de'Fiori ☎ 06/6832361) serves drinks to cool patrons seated on glowing ice cubelike chairs, as water streams down the walls. **La Vineria** (✉ Campo de' Fiori 15 ☎ 06/68803268) is the original bar on a square that's now full of them. It remains the truest example of an old-school Roman enoteca, always in style and great for watching the "scenery." **Crudo** (✉ Via Degli Specchi 6, Campo de' Fiori ☎ 06/6838989 ⊕ www.crudoroma.it) is a spacious, modern, New York–style lounge serving cocktails and *crudo* (raw) nibbles such as sushi and carpaccio. **Sloppy Sam's** (✉ Campo de' Fiori 10 ☎ 06/68802637) is an American-run pub on one of the city's busiest piazzas. Look for happy-hour specials and student discounts. For that essential predinner aperitivo, head for the buzzing **Friends** (⊠ Piazza Trilussa 34, Trastevere ☎ 06/5816111) across the Tiber from the historic center. Late in the evening, head to **Stardust** (⊠ Vicolo de' Renzi 4, Trastevere ☎ 06/58320875) for cocktails mixed up by an international bar staff and an ambience provided by eclectic music and local characters.

Music Clubs

Jazz, folk, pop, and Latin-music clubs are flourishing in Rome, particularly in Trastevere and Testaccio. Jazz clubs are especially popular, and talented local groups may be joined by visiting musicians from other countries. As admission, many clubs require that you buy a membership card, often valid for a month, at a cost of €6 and up. On weekend nights it's a good idea to reserve a table in advance no matter where you're going.

Behind the Vatican Museums, **Alexanderplatz** (⊠ Via Ostia 9, near San Pietro ☎ 06/39742171), Rome's most famous jazz and blues club, has a bar and a restaurant. Local and internationally known musicians play nightly. **La Palma** (⊠ Via Giuseppe Mirri 35, Tiburtina ☎ 06/43599029) is the venue favored by experimental jazz musicians. It's near the Tiburtina metro stop. **Big Mama** (⊠ Vicolo San Francesco a Ripa 18, Trastevere ☎ 06/5812551) presents live blues, R&B, African, jazz, and rock. Latin rhythms are the specialty at **No Stress Brasil** (⊠ Via degli Stradivari 35, Trastevere ☎ 06/5813249), where there's a Brazilian orchestra from Tuesday to Saturday. Monday is karaoke night.

Il Locale (⊠ Vicolo del Fico 3, near Piazza Navona ☎ 06/6879075), closed Monday, pulls in a lively crowd for Italian rock. **The Place** (⊠ Via Alberico II 27–29, near San Pietro ☎ 06/68307137) has a mixture of live funk, Latin, and jazz sounds, accompanied by tasty fusion cuisine. In trendy Testaccio, **Caffè Latino** (⊠ Via Monte Testaccio 96 ☎ 06/57288556) is a vibrant Roman locale that has live music (mainly Latin) almost every night, followed by recorded soul, funk, and '70s and '80s revival; it's closed Monday.

Nightclubs

Most dance clubs open about 10:30 PM and charge an entrance fee of about €20, which may include the first drink (subsequent drinks cost

A GOOD WALK: TRASTEVERE BY NIGHT

For centuries home to Rome's artists and beggars, Trastevere has parlayed its bohemian appeal into a new life, as the place where all of Rome—and many of Rome's visitors—come out at night to play. After dark, you'll have your choice of restaurants, bars, street performances, and the best people-watching in town. But the quarter is more than just a place for town-painting. Here's a welcome to the neighborhood that mixes the sacred with the profane. You can follow this route in early evening, for gelato, dinner, and a stroll; or later

at night, for a pub crawl with a cultural chaser. It covers about three-quarters of a mile.

From Piazza Sonnino, enter Trastevere by walking past the pharmacy on your right down Via Lungaretta. This street is Trastevere's main artery, jammed after dark with restaurants, bars, jewelry shops, street vendors, and revelers partying until the early hours. Continue on Via Lungaretta until it ends in **Piazza Santa Maria in Trastevere** 69. Bordered by two cafés and the swanky Sabatini restaurant (at no. 13), the piazza has a fountain in the center ringed by steps on which passersby join neo-about €10). Clubs are usually closed Monday, and all those listed here close in summer, some opening instead at the beaches of Ostia or Fregene. The liveliest areas for clubs with a younger clientele are the grittier working-class districts of Testaccio and Ostiense.

The large **Art Café** (⊠ Via del Galoppatoio 33, near Piazza di Spagna ☎ 06/36006578) has multiple levels, and there are theme nights (Tuesday fashion night, Thursday live jazz and dinner, Friday hip-hop), and *privé* (private) areas with a wading pool. **Supperclub** (⊠ Via dei Nari 14, near Piazza di Spagna ☎ 06/68807207) is not only a place for reclined dining, but also a trendy club where DJs and live entertainment draw a sexy crowd. Most rooms are lined with big white beds and fluffy pillows, complete with roaming masseurs. Monday night is a laid-back hip-hop party organized by a former L.A. club promoter.

La Maison (⊠ Vicolo dei Granari 4, near Piazza Navona ☎ 06/6833312), bedecked in purple velvet and chandeliers, has two distinct spaces and one main dance floor, with DJs dishing up the latest dance tunes. **Bloom** (⊠ Via del Teatro Pace 29, near Piazza Navona ☎ 06/68802029) is a lounge-club in the city center, where Romans and visiting celebrities go to swill cocktails and dance in tight quarters. **Cabala** (⊠ Via dei Soldati 23c, Piazza Navona ☎ 06/68301192), a multilevel disco–piano bar inside a gorgeous palazzo, can be uncomfortably packed on weekends.

Alibi (⊠ Via di Monte Testaccio 39 ☎ 06/5743448) is a multilevel complex that caters to a mixed gay and straight crowd. **Goa** (⊠ Via Libetta 13, Testaccio ☎06/5748277) is among Rome's trendiest clubs. In a Southeast Asian–inspired space you can listen to hip-hop, tribal, and house music played by some of Europe's most touted DJs. The demographic is skewed toward the young.

One of Rome's first discos, **Piper** (⊠ Via Tagliamento 9, near Piazza Fiume ☎ 06/8414459) is still a magnet for young movers and shakers who favor disco and house beats and spectacular light effects. It's open Saturday and Sunday nights only. The **Ex Magazzini** (⊠ Via dei Magazzini Generali 8bis, Ostiense ☎ 06/5758040) is a happening disco bar that has a mix of live and DJ sets and hosts a vintage market on Sunday.

hippies, grimy punks, and fresh-faced tourists for a front-row seat. On summer nights and weekends, jugglers, flame-eaters, and magicians take turns wowing the crowds here. Bar del Marzio, next to Sabatini, has excellent gelato you can take with you out to the square. While you're there, stop into the church of Santa Maria in Trastevere, often open well into the evening in summer, for a look at the magnificent golden-tiled apse mosaic. Even if the church is closed, take a look at the fragments of ancient Roman graffiti salvaged from the city and plastered into the walls of the outer entryway.

Facing the church, follow the street leaving the piazza from the far right corner. It curves around to the right past several open-air restaurants, opening into Piazza Sant'Egidio. This lovely square is home to Rome's English-language Cinema Pasquino, a favorite with foreign residents. Next door are the outdoor tables of Ombre Rosse, where you'll find light meals, coffee, cocktails, the *International Herald Tribune*, and live music long, long into the night. Across the piazza, the Museo di Roma in Trastevere, open until 8, hosts Roman and international photography shows.

SPORTS & THE OUTDOORS

Biking

You can rent a bike at **Collalti** (⊠ Via del Pellegrino 82, Campo de' Fiori ☎ 06/68801084), which is also a reliable bike-repair shop; it's closed Monday. **St. Peter Moto** (⊠ Via di Porta Castello 43, near San Pietro ☎ 06/6875714) is a good place to rent scooters as well as bikes.

Running

The best bet for running in central Rome is the **Villa Borghese** park, with an ⅔-km (½-mi) circuit of the Pincio, among the marble statuary. A longer run in the park itself might include a loop around Piazza di Siena, a grass riding arena. Although most traffic is barred from Villa Borghese, government and police cars sometimes speed through. Be careful to stick to the sides of the roads. For a long run away from all traffic, try the hilly and majestic **Villa Ada** in northern Rome, in the upscale Parioli neighborhood. **Villa Doria Pamphilj** on Janiculum Hill is a beautiful spot for a run south of the city. History-loving runners should also do as the chariot horses did and run at the old **Circus Maximus**. A standard oval track (dubbed "il biscotto" as it's shaped like a cookie) is in the park flanked by the **Via delle Terme di Caracalla**.

Soccer

Italy's favorite spectator sport stirs passionate enthusiasm. Games are usually held on Sunday afternoons fall–spring and can be seen at many sports bars around the city: just follow the fans' screams.

The two city soccer teams, Roma and Lazio, are both in Series A (the top division); they play home games at the **Stadio Olimpico** (⊠ Viale dello Stadio Olimpico ☎ 06/3237333), part of the Foro Italico complex built by Mussolini on the banks of the Tiber. There's a chance of Lazio soccer tickets being on sale at the box office before game time, but it's a better idea to buy them in advance from **Lazio Point** (⊠ Via Farini 34, near Termini ☎ 06/4826688) to see the Lazio team play. Go to **Orbis** (⊠ Piazza Esquilino 37, near Termini ☎ 06/4744776) to buy tickets to see the Roma play.

Continue on Via della Scala (with your back to Ombre Rosse, the street leaving from the piazza's far right corner). This narrow, pedestrian-only street has more bars and restaurants, all with streetside seating. At the end of Via della Scala, you'll see the Porta Settimiana, one of the city's ancient gates. Turning right here, follow Via San Dorotea to No. 19, once the home of La Fornarina, Raphael's Trasteverina lover.

Continue on Via San Dorotea across Piazza San Giovanni Malva to Piazza Trilussa and have a look at the Ponte Sisto crossing the Tiber. The original bridge dates to the 2nd century BC, although most of what you see now dates from a 15th-century renovation (and a 1999 cleanup). Heading back through Piazza Trilussa, follow Vicolo del Cinque past more bars and restaurants. If it's after midnight, you can stop at No. 40, Daniela Orecchia, for *cornetti caldi*, hot, sweet pastries fresh out of the oven. Continue up Vicolo del Cinque, leading back to Piazza Sant'Egidio. Here you can have a nightcap and then retrace your steps across Piazza Santa Maria in Trastevere and down Via Lungaretta to Piazza Sonnino, where there's a taxi stand.

SHOPPING

Updated by
Dana Klitzberg

They say when in Rome to do as the Romans do—and the Romans love to shop. Stores are generally open from 9 or 9:30 to 1 and from 3:30 or 4 to 7 or 7:30. There's a tendency for shops in central districts to stay open all day, and hours are becoming more flexible throughout the city. Remember that many places close Sunday, though this is changing, too, especially in the city center. With the exception of food stores, many stores also close on Monday morning from September to mid-June and Saturday afternoon from mid-June through August. You can save some money taking advantage of the Tax-Free for Tourists V.A.T. tax refunds, available at most large stores for purchases over €155. Or hit Rome in January and early February or in late July, when stores clean house with the justly famous biannual sales. There are so many hole-in-the-wall boutiques selling top-quality merchandise in Rome's center that even just wandering you're sure to find something that catches your eye.

Shopping Districts

★ The city's most famous shopping district, **Piazza di Spagna,** is conveniently compact, fanning out at the foot of the Spanish Steps in a galaxy of boutiques selling gorgeous wares with glamorous labels. Here you can ricochet from Gucci to Prada to Valentino to Versace with less effort than it takes to pull out your credit card. If your budget is designed for lower altitudes, you also can find great clothes and accessories at less extravagant prices. But here, buying is not necessarily the point—window displays can be works of art, and dreaming may be satisfaction enough. Via Condotti is the neighborhood's central axis, but there are shops on every street in the area bordered by Piazza di Spagna on the east, Via del Corso on the west, between Piazza San Silvestro and Via della Croce, and extending along Via del Babuino to Piazza del Popolo.

Shops along **Via Campo Marzio,** and adjoining Piazza San Lorenzo in Lucina, stock eclectic, high-quality clothes and accessories—without the big names and at slightly lower prices. Running from Piazza Venezia to Piazza del Popolo lies **Via del Corso,** a main shopping avenue that has more than a mile of clothing, shoes, leather goods, and home furnishings from classic to cutting-edge. Running west from Piazza Navona, **Via del Governo Vecchio** has numerous women's boutiques and secondhand clothing stores. **Via Cola di Rienzo,** across the Tiber from Piazza del Popolo, is block after block of boutiques, shoe stores, and department stores, as well as street stalls and upscale food shops. **Via dei Coronari,** across the Tiber from Castel Sant'Angelo, has quirky antiques and home furnishings. Via Giulia and other surrounding streets are good bets for decorative arts. Should your gift list include religious souvenirs, look for everything from rosaries to Vatican golf balls at the shops between Piazza San Pietro and **Borgo Pio.** Liturgical vestments and statues of saints make for good window-shopping on **Via dei Cestari,** near the Pantheon. On **Via Cola di Rienzo,** near San Pietro, there are stands selling everything from CDs to handicrafts. **Via Nazionale** is a good bet for affordable stores of the Benetton ilk, and for shoes, bags, and gloves. The **Termini** train station has become a good one-stop place for many shopping needs. Its 60-plus shops are open until 10 PM and include a Nike store, the Body Shop, Sephora, Mango (women's clothes), a UPIM department store, and food stores.

Bargains

The market at **Via Sannio** (⊠ Near San Giovanni) has lots of designer shoes and stalls selling new and used clothing at bargain prices; hours are weekdays 8–2, Saturday 8–5. The **Borghetto Flaminio** (⊠ Piazza della Marina, Flaminio) market sells good-quality vintage clothing on Sunday 9–2. The morning market in **Piazza Testaccio**, in the heart of the neighborhood of the same name, is known for stands selling last season's designer shoes at a third of the original price or less.

Romans and visitors alike flock to the **McArthurGlen Designer Outlet** (⊠ Via Ponte di Piscina Cupa, Castel Romano ☎ 06/5050050 ⊕ www. mcarthurglen.it), 10 km (6 mi) east of the city. Housed in a mock ancient Roman setting, the complex has more than 90 stores that sell major labels at prices 30%–70% lower than normal. To get there, get on the Grande Raccordo Anulare ring road, take Exit 26 onto the Via Pontina (SS148) toward Pomezia, exit at Castel Romano, and follow the signs. The mall is open daily 10–10.

Department Stores & Malls

Italian department stores have little in common with their American cousins; most of them are much smaller and do not carry the same variety of merchandise, nor the recognizable brands. **Galleria Alberto Sordi** (⊠ Via del Corso and Viale Tritone, near Piazza di Spagna) is a mall with a café in the center of two corridors lined with shops. The star attractions are a large branch of Feltrinelli (a book and media store like Barnes & Noble), JAM (clothing and accessories, gifts and gadgets), and the women's affordable fashion mecca from Spain, Zara. **Rinascente** (⊠ Via del Corso 189, near Piazza di Trevi ☎ 06/6797691 ⊠ Piazza Fiume, Salario ☎ 06/8841231) sells only clothing and accessories in its main store. The Piazza Fiume branch also has furniture and housewares. Both stores are open seven days a week. **Oviesse** (⊠ Via Candia 74, near San Pietro ☎ 06/39743518) has moderately priced goods ranging from bathing suits to children's clothes.

Coin (⊠ Piazzale Appio 7, near San Giovanni ☎ 06/7080020 ⊠ Via Mantova 1/b, Salario ☎ 06/8416279) is somewhat trendier than other department stores; it carries a large collection of housewares as well as fashions for men and women. The midrange chain store **UPIM** (⊠ Piazza Santa Maria Maggiore ☎ 06/4465579) is an institution in Italy; it sells clothing, bed linen, and contemporary kitchenware at reasonable prices. **Cinecittà Due** (⊠ Viale Palmiro Togliatti 2 ☎ 06/7220910) was the first of Rome's several megamalls (100 stores); take Metro A to the Subaugusta or Cinecittà stops.

Markets

Outdoor markets are open Monday–Saturday from early morning to about 1 PM (a bit later on Saturday), but get there early for the best selection. Remember to keep an eye on your wallet—the money changing hands draws Rome's most skillful pickpockets. And don't go if you can't stand crowds. Downtown Rome's most colorful outdoor food market is at **Campo de' Fiori,** south of Piazza Navona. The **Trionfale market** (⊠ Via Andrea Doria, near San Pietro) is big and bustling; it's about a five-minute walk north of the entrance to the Vatican Museums. There's room for bargaining at the Sunday-morning flea market at **Porta Portese** (⊠ Via Ippolito Nievo, Trastevere). Seemingly endless rows of merchandise includes new and secondhand clothing, bootleg CDs, old furniture, car stereos of suspicious origin, and all manner of old junk and hidden treasures.

Specialty Stores

Antiques & Prints

For old prints and antiques, **Tanca** (⊠ Salita dei Crescenzi 12, near Pantheon ☏ 06/6875272) is a good hunting ground. Early photographs of Rome and views of Italy from **Alinari** (⊠ Via Alibert 16/a, near Piazza di Spagna ☏ 06/69941998) make memorable souvenirs. **Nardecchia** (⊠ Piazza Navona 25 ☏ 06/6869318) is reliable for prints. Stands in **Piazza della Fontanella Borghese** (⊠ Near Via del Corso) sell prints and old books.

Designer Clothing

All of Italy's top fashion houses and many international designers have stores near Piazza di Spagna. Buying clothes can be a bit tricky for American women, as sizes tend to be cut for a petite Italian frame. A size 12 (European 46) is not always easy to find, but the more expensive stores should carry it. Target less expensive stores for acessories if this is an issue.

D & G (⊠ Piazza di Spagna 82 ☏ 06/69924999), a spin-off of the top-of-the-line Dolce & Gabbana, shows trendy casual wear and accessories for men and women. If Valentino is the king of Roman fashion, the Fendi sisters are its queens. **Fendi** (⊠ Via Borgognona 40, near Piazza di Spagna ☏ 06/69666001) stocks an assortment of the fashion house's signature baguette bags, furs, and sexy separates. The **Giorgio Armani** (⊠ Via Condotti 77, near Piazza di Spagna ☏ 06/6991460) shop is as understated and elegant as its designs. **Gucci** (⊠ Via Condotti 8, near Piazza di Spagna ☏ 06/6783762) often has lines out the door of its two-story shop, testament to the continuing popularity of its colorful bags, wallets, and shoes in rich leathers. Edgy clothes designs are also available. Sleek, vaguely futuristic **Prada** (⊠ Via Condotti 92, near Piazza di Spagna ☏ 06/6790897) has two entrances: the one for the men's boutique is to the left of the women's.

Rome's leading local couturier, **Valentino** (Valentino Donna ⊠ Via Condotti 13, near Piazza di Spagna ☏ 06/6795862 ☐ Valentino Uomo ⊠ Via

Rome
Shopping

Bocca di Leone 15, near Piazza di Spagna ☎ 06/6783656), is recognized the world over by the "V" logo. The designer has shops for the *donna* (woman) and the *uomo* (man). **Gianni Versace** (✉ Versace Uomo ✉ Via Borgognona 24–25, near Piazza di Spagna ☎ 06/6795037 ✉ Versace Donna ✉ Via Bocca di Leone 26–27, near Piazza di Spagna ☎ 06/6780521) sells the rock-star styles that made the house's name: Versace Uomo for men, the Versace Donna for women.

Degli Effetti (✉ Piazza Capranica, near Pantheon ☎ 06/6791650) is a top-of-the-line boutique with men's and women's avant-garde fashion from the likes of Prada, Miu Miu, Jil Sander, and Helmut Lang.

MEN'S CLOTHING **Ermenegildo Zegna** (✉ Via Borgognona 7/e, near Piazza di Spagna ☎ 06/6789143) has the finest in men's elegant styles and accessories. **Il Portone** (✉ Via delle Carrozze 71, near Piazza di Spagna ☎ 06/69925170) embodies a tradition in custom shirtmaking. **Brioni** (✉ Via Condotti 21, near Piazza di Spagna ☎ 06/6783428 ✉ Via Barberini 79, near Piazza di Trevi ☎ 06/6783635) has a well-deserved reputation as one of Italy's top tailors. There are ready-to-wear garments in addition to impeccable custom-made apparel.

WOMEN'S CLOTHING Come to the **Dress Agency** (✉ 1B Via del Vantaggio, Piazza di Spagna ☎ 06/3210898) for designer label consignment shopping: finds have included Prada sweaters and Gucci dresses, some pieces as low as €20. Although you never know exactly when you'll hit pay dirt, try right after the season changes and Roman women have cleaned out their closets to make room for new goodies. **Galassia** (✉ Via Frattina 21, near Piazza di Spagna ☎ 06/6797896) has expensive, extreme, and extravagant women's styles by Gaultier, Westwood, and Yamamoto—this is the place for feather boas and hats with ostrich plumes. If you're in the market for luxurious lingerie, **La Perla** (✉ Via Condotti 79, near Piazza di Spagna ☎ 06/69941934) is the place to shop.

If you're feeling flush, **Nuyorica** (✉ Piazza Pollarolla 36, Campo de'Fiori ☎ 06/68891243) sells expensive, super-chic designer pieces from Balenciaga, Chloe, and American favorite Marc Jacobs, among others. **Josephine de Huertas & co** (✉ Via del Governo Vecchio 68, near Piazza Navona ☎ 06/6876586) is a precious little boutique with colorful, high-end stock from the likes of Paul Smith and lesser-known designers. **Ethic** (✉ Via del Pantheon 46/47 ☎ 06/68803167) is a great reasonably priced stop for funky fashions in this season's color palette, from knits to leather jackets.

The garments at **Luisa Spagnoli** (✉ Via del Tritone 30, near Piazza di Trevi ☎ 06/69202220) are elegant but contemporary, and they go to large sizes. **Leam Limited** (✉ Via Appia Nuova 30, San Giovanni ☎ 06/77207204) is a designer boutique selling the "greatest hits" from Italian designers like Marni, Missoni, and Prada; you can even find Ugg boots here.

Embroidery & Linens

Frette (✉ Piazza di Spagna 11 ☎ 06/6790673) is a Roman institution for luxurious linens. **Venier Colombo** (✉ Via Frattina 79, near Piazza di

Via Condotti
Shopping

Spagna ☎ 06/6787705) has a selection of exquisite lace goods, including lingerie and linens. **Lavori Artigianali Femminili** (✉ Via Capo le Case 6, near Piazza di Spagna ☎ 06/6781100) sells delicately embroidered household linens, infants' and children's clothing, and blouses.

Food

There are several hundred *salumerie* (gourmet food shops specializing in fresh and cured meats and cheeses) in town, but a few stand out for a particularly ample selection and items of rare, superior quality. Foodies should head straight for **Franchi** (✉ Via Cola di Rienzo 200, near San Pietro ☎ 06/6864576) to check out the sliced meats and cheeses that you can have vacuum-packed for safe transport home. They also sell the city's best take-out treats, including salmon mousse, roast beef, and vegetable fritters. **Castroni** (✉ Via Cola di Rienzo 196, near San Pietro ☎ 06/6864383) is a fine general food shop with lots of imported items. **Volpetti** (✉ Via Marmorata 47, Testaccio ☎ 06/5742352) has high-quality meats and aged cheeses from small producers. The men behind the counter will be happy to let you take a taste.

A bottle of liqueur, jar of marmalade, or bar of chocolate made by Cistercian monks at Italian monasteries makes an unusual and tasty treat to take home. Choose from the goodies at **Ai Monasteri** (✉ Corso Rinascimento 72, near Piazza Navona ☎ 06/68802783). Drop into **Panella** (⊠ Via Merulana 54, near Santa Maria Maggiore ☎ 06/4872344), one of Rome's most spectacular bakeries, for exquisite bread sculptures and a fine selection of pastas, oils, and preserves to take home.

Housewares

The kitchen shop at **'Gusto** (⊠ Piazza Augusto Imperatore 9, near Piazza di Spagna ☎ 06/3226273) has a great selection of cookbooks, including some in English. Pricey **C.u.c.i.n.a** (⊠ Via Mario de' Fiori 65, near Piazza di Spagna ☎ 06/6791275) is one of the best kitchen-supply stores in town. **D Cube** (⊠ Via della Pace 38, near Piazza Navona ☎ 06/6861218) is a kitschy boutique with colorful, architectural gadgets for the home. From within a striking frescoed 17th-century palazzo, **Spazio Sette** (⊠ Via dei Barbieri 7, near Campo de' Fiori ☎ 06/6869747) sells gadgets and furniture created by the biggest names in Italian and international design. **Leone Limentani** (⊠ Via Portico d'Ottavio 47, Ghetto ☎ 06/68806686) is a warehouse full of discounted kitchenware, by such names as Bernardaud, Reidel, andBaccarat.

Jewelry & Silver Objects

Fornari & Fornari (⊠ Via Frattina 133, Piazza di Spagna ☎ 06/6980105) has a vast selection of silver pieces, as well as fine crystal and china. What Cartier is to Paris, **Bulgari** (⊠ Via Condotti 10, near Piazza di Spagna ☎ 06/6793876) is to Rome; the shop's elegant display windows hint at what's beyond the guard at the door. **Buccellati** (⊠ Via Condotti 31, near Piazza di Spagna ☎ 06/6790329) is a tradition-rich Florentine jewelry house renowned for its silverwork; it ranks with Bulgari for quality and reliability.

At **Liliana Michilli** (⊠ Via Dei Banchi Vecchi 37, near Campo de' Fiori ☎ 06/68392154) you can buy convincing copies of Bulgari and Gucci rings for a fraction of the price. The craftswomen of **Danae** (⊠ Via della Maddalena 40, near Pantheon ☎ 06/6791881) make original jewelry pieces, working with metals and chunky stones like amber, milky aquamarine, and turquoise.

Shoes & Leather Accessories

It's the women's accessories—Luella bags to Marc Jacobs shoes—that bring shoppers back to the **Tad Concept Store** (⊠ Via del Babuino 155a, near Piazza di Spagna ☎ 06/32695131). Also sold are fabulous home decorating items and *the* music you should be listening to; there's even a café. For gloves as pretty as Holly Golightly's, shop at **Sermoneta** (⊠ Piazza di Spagna 61 ☎ 06/6791960). Any color or style one might desire, from elbow-length black leather to scallop-edged lace-cut lilac suede, is available at this glove institution. For the latest, Italian-made styles in mid-range handbags, shoes, scarves, and costume jewelry, go to **Furla** (⊠ Piazza di Spagna 22 ☎ 06/69200363), which has a number of downtown stores.

Ferragamo Uomo (⊠ Via Condotti 65, near Piazza di Spagna ☎ 06/6781130) sells classic shoes for men. **Di Cori** (⊠ Piazza di Spagna 53 ☎ 06/6784439) has gloves in every color of the spectrum. **Bruno Magli** (⊠ Via del Gambero 1, near Piazza di Spagna ☎ 06/6793802 ⊠ Via Veneto

70 ☎ 06/42011671) is known for well-made shoes and matching hand-bags at both moderate and high prices. **Campanile** (✉ Via Condotti 58, near Piazza di Spagna ☎ 06/6790731) has two floors of shoes in classic styles; they also sell other leather goods. **Tod's** (✉ Via Borgognona 45, near Piazza di Spagna ☎ 06/6786828) central boutique sells signature button-sole moccasins made by Italian shoe maestro Diego della Valle, as well as a line of handmade bags.

Federico Polidori (✉ Via Pie di Marmo 7, near Pantheon ☎ 06/6797191) crafts custom-made leather bags and briefcases complete with monograms. For original, handcrafted bags and purses (some based on styles from names like YSL), **Sirni** (✉ Via della Stelletta 33, near Pantheon ☎ 06/68805248) is worth seeking out.

For a vast selection of affordable, high-quality, Italian bags and accessories, head for **Regal** (✉ Via Nazionale 254, near Termini ☎ 06/4884893). **Calzature Fausto Santini** (✉ Via Santa Maria Maggiore 165, near Santa Maria Maggiore ☎ 06/6784114) is the place for colorful, offbeat Santini shoes at half price. (The flagship store is on upmarket Via Frattina.)

Silks & Fabrics
Fratelli Bassetti (✉ Corso Vittorio Emanuele II 73, near Campo de' Fiori ☎ 06/6892326) has a vast selection of world-famous Italian silks and fashion fabrics in a rambling palazzo. **Aston** (✉ Via Boncompagni 27, near Via Veneto ☎ 06/42871227) stocks couture-level fabrics for men and women. You can find some real bargains if there are *scampoli* (remnants).

Stationery & Gifts
Fabriano (✉ Via del Babuino 173, near Piazza di Spagna ☎ 06/6864268) sells stylish stationery, organized by color, as well as leather albums and pens of every description. Present your gifts with Italian flair: **Daniela Rosati** (✉ Via della Stelletta 27, Pantheon ☎ 06/68802053) has beautifully handmade gift boxes covered in colorful paper.

ROME ESSENTIALS

Transportation

BY AIR
Most international flights and all domestic flights arrive at Aeroporto Leonardo da Vinci, also known as Fiumicino, 30 km (19 mi) southwest of Rome. Some international and charter flights and most low-cost carriers land at Ciampino, a civil and military airport 15 km (9 mi) southeast of Rome. To get to the city from Fiumicino by car, follow the signs for Rome on the expressway from the airport, which links with the GRA, the beltway around Rome. The direction you take on the GRA depends on where your hotel is, so get directions from the car-rental people at the airport. A taxi from Fiumicino to the center of town costs about €50, including *supplementi* (extra charges) for airport service and luggage, and the ride takes 30–40 minutes, depending on traffic. Private limou-

Rome Metro &
Suburban Railway

sines can be hired at booths in the arrivals hall; they charge a little more
than taxis but can take more passengers. Ignore gypsy drivers who approach you inside the terminal; stick to the licensed cabs, yellow or white,
that wait by the curb. A booth inside the arrivals hall provides taxi information.

You have a choice of two trains to get to downtown Rome from Fiumicino Airport. Ask at the airport (at APT or train information counters) which train takes you closer to your hotel. The nonstop
Airport–Termini express takes you directly to Track 22 at Stazione Termini, Rome's main train station, which is well served by taxis and is the
hub of metro and bus lines. The ride to Termini takes 30 minutes; departures are every half hour beginning at 6:37 AM from the airport, with
a final departure at 11:37 PM. From Termini to the airport, trains leave
at 21 and 51 minutes past the hour. Tickets cost €8.80. FM1, the other
airport train, runs from the airport to Rome and beyond, terminating
in Monterotondo, a suburban town to the east. The main stops in Rome
are at Trastevere, Ostiense, and Tiburtina stations; at each you can find
taxis and bus and/or metro connections to other parts of Rome. This
train runs from Fiumicino from 6:35 AM to 12:15 AM, with departures
every 20 minutes, a little less frequently in off-hours. The ride to

Tiburtina takes 40 minutes. Tickets cost €5. For either train buy your ticket at automatic vending machines. There are ticket counters at some stations (at Termini/Track 22, Trastevere, Tiburtina). Date-stamp the ticket at the gate before you board.

🔲 Airport Information **Aeroporto Leonardo da Vinci** ☎ 06/65951, 06/65953640 English-language flight information ⊕ www.adr.it. **Ciampino** ✉ Via Appia Nuova ☎ 06/794941.

BY BUS, METRO & TRAM

There's no central bus terminal in Rome. COTRAL is the suburban bus company that connects Rome with outlying areas and other cities in the Lazio region. Long-distance and suburban buses terminate either near Tiburtina Station or near outlying metro stops such as Rebbibia and Anagnina. For COTRAL bus information, call weekdays 8 AM–6 PM.

Rome's metro (subway) is somewhat limited, but it's a quick, stress-free, and safe way to get around town if there's a stop where you're going. The public bus and tram system is the opposite—routes are extensive, but the city's narrow streets and chronic traffic can make street-level transport slow. Metro service begins at 5:30 AM, and the last trains leave the most distant station at 11:30 PM (on Saturday night, trains run until 12:30 AM). There are two lines—A and B—which intersect at Stazione Termini. Buses run day and night, although some routes change after 10 PM or midnight. Stops are marked by high white signs on yellow poles listing bus numbers and upcoming stops, but for serious exploring, a bus map (available at newsstands) is invaluable. The compact electric buses of Lines 117 and 119 take routes through the center of Rome that can save lots of walking. Routes change frequently, but you can plan itineraries and download maps before you go at ATAC's Web site.

FARES & SCHEDULES ATAC city buses and tram lines run from about 6 AM to midnight, with night buses (indicated N) on some lines. A ticket valid for 75 minutes on any combination of buses and trams and one entrance to the metro costs €1. You are expected to date-stamp your ticket when you board the first vehicle, stamping it again when boarding for the last time within 75 minutes (the important thing is to stamp it the first time). Tickets for the public transit system are sold at tobacconists, newsstands, some coffee bars, green machines positioned in metro stations and some bus stops, and at ATAC and COTRAL ticket booths (in some metro stations, on the lower concourse at Stazione Termini, and at a few main bus terminals). A BIG tourist ticket, valid for one day on all public transport, costs €4. A weekly ticket (Settimanale, also known as CIS) costs €15 and can be purchased only at ATAC booths.

🔲 Bus & Metro Information **ATAC** ☎ 800/431784 toll free ⊕ www.atac.roma.it. **CO-TRAL** ☎ 800/150008 toll-free.

BY CAR

The main access routes from the north are A1 (Autostrada del Sole) from Milan and Florence and the A12–E80 highway from Genoa. The principal route to or from points south, including Naples, is the A2. All highways connect with the Grande Raccordo Anulare (GRA), which channels traffic into the city center. As elsewhere in Italy, road signs for the center of town are marked with a bullseye. Signs on the GRA are confusing: take time to study the route you need.

Romans park wherever there is physically space, and double- and triple-parking is common. Parking spaces outlined in blue are paid by buying a ticket from a small gray machine, installed on the street nearby. Leave the ticket, showing the time up to which you've paid to park, visible on the dashboard. Parking spaces outlined in yellow are not parking spaces at all—stay away to avoid being towed. If you rent a car in the city, make sure the rental desk gives you specific directions for getting out of town, and invest in a detailed city map (available at most newsstands).

BY MOPED

Zipping and careening through traffic on a *motorino* (moped) in downtown Rome is an attractive way to visit the city for some, but if you're risk averse, pass on it. If your impulses—and reflexes—are fast, you can join the craziness of Roman traffic by renting a moped and the mandatory helmet at numerous rental spots throughout the city. Be extremely careful of pedestrians when riding: Romans are casual jaywalkers and pop out frequently from between parked cars.

🚩 Moped Rentals **Enjoy Rome** ✉ Via Marghera 8A, Termini, 00185 Rome ☎ 06/4451843 🌐 www.enjoyrome.com. **Happy Rent** ✉ Via Farini 3, Termini ☎ 06/4818185. **Scoot-a-Long** ✉ Via Cavour 302, Termini ☎ 06/6780206. **St. Peter Moto** ✉ Via di Porta Castello 43, San Pietro ☎ 06/6875714.

BY TAXI

Taxis in Rome do not cruise, but if empty (look for an illuminated TAXI sign on the roof) they will stop if you flag them down. Taxis wait at stands and can also be called by phone, in which case you're charged a bit more. The meter starts at €2.33 from 7 AM to 10 PM, at €3.36 on Sunday and holidays, and at €4.91 after 10 PM. Each piece of baggage will add an extra €2.03 to your fare. There are two different fare systems, one for outside the city and one for inside, shown on the LED meter display. Make sure your cab is charging you "tariffa uno"—the cheaper one—when you're in town. Use only licensed, metered yellow or white cabs, identified by a numbered shield on the side, an illuminated taxi sign on the roof, and a plaque next to the license plate reading SERVIZIO PUBBLICO. Avoid unmarked, unauthorized, unmetered gypsy cabs (numerous at airports and train stations), whose renegade drivers actively solicit your trade and may demand astronomical fares. Some taxis accept some credit cards, but you must specify when calling that you will pay that way.

🚩 Taxi Companies **Taxi** ☎ 06/5551, 06/3570, 06/4994, or 06/88177.

BY TRAIN

Stazione Termini is Rome's main train terminal; the Tiburtina and Ostiense stations serve some long-distance trains, many commuter trains, and the FM1 line to Fiumicino Airport. Some trains for Pisa and Genoa leave Rome from, or pass through, the Trastevere Station. You can find English-speaking staff at the information office at Stazione Termini, or ask for information at travel agencies. Purchase tickets up to two months in advance at the main stations or at most travel agencies.

Lines at station ticket windows may be very long: you can save time by using the electronic ticket machines, which have instructions in English, or by buying your ticket at a travel agency. You can reserve a seat up to one day in advance at a travel agency or up to an hour in advance at a train station. Tickets for train rides within a radius of 100 km (62 mi) of Rome can be purchased at tobacco shops and at some newsstands, as well as at ticket machines on the main concourse. All train tickets must be date-stamped before you board, at the machine near the track, or you may be fined.

🚂 Train Information **Trenitalia** ☎ 166/105050, 892021 from outside Rome—a small service charge applies ⊕ www.trenitalia.it.

Contacts & Resources

EMERGENCIES

Farmacia Internazionale Capranica, Farmacia Internazionale Barberini, and Farmacia Cola di Rienzo are pharmacies that have some English-speaking staff. Most pharmacies are open 8:30–1 and 4–8; some are open all night. A schedule posted outside each pharmacy indicates the nearest pharmacy open during off-hours (afternoons, through the night, and Sunday). Dial ☎ 1100 for an automated list of three open pharmacies closest to the telephone from which you call. The hospitals listed below have English-speaking doctors. Rome American Hospital is about 30 minutes by cab from the center of town.

🚑 Emergency Services **Ambulance** ☎ 118. **Police** ☎ 113. **Red Cross** ☎ 06/5510.

🏥 Hospitals **Rome American Hospital** ✉ Via Emilio Longoni 69, Via Prenestina ☎ 06/22551 ⊕ www.rah.it. **Salvator Mundi International Hospital** ✉ Viale delle Mura Gianicolensi 67, Trastevere ☎ 06/588961 ⊕ www.smih.pcn.net.

💊 Pharmacies **Farmacia Cola di Rienzo** ✉ Via Cola di Rienzo 213, San Pietro ☎ 06/3243130. **Farmacia Internazionale Barberini** ✉ Piazza Barberini 49, Via Veneto ☎ 06/4825456. **Farmacia Internazionale Capranica** ✉ Piazza Capranica 96, Pantheon ☎ 06/6794680.

ENGLISH-LANGUAGE MEDIA

BOOKS English-language books are expensive in Rome; most are imported from England, so prices in Rome reflect the strong pound and shipping costs. The Anglo-American Bookstore has the widest selection of genres. The English Bookshop has a smaller selection but better prices. Trastevere's Almost Corner Bookstore carries lots of offbeat new fiction and has a vast history section. For used books at lower prices, try the Open Door. At Feltrinelli International you can pick up novels and guidebooks in English as well.

📚 **Almost Corner Bookstore** ✉ Via del Moro 45, Trastevere ☎ 06/5836942. **Anglo-American Bookstore** ✉ Via della Vite 102, near Piazza di Spagna ☎ 06/6795222 ⊕ www.aab.it. **The English Bookshop** ✉ Via di Ripetta 24B, near Piazza di Spagna ☎ 06/3203301. **Feltrinelli International** ✉ Via Vittorio Emanuale Orlando 78/81, near Termini ☎ 06/4870171. **Lion Bookshop** ✉ Via dei Greci 33/36, near Piazza di Spagna ☎ 06/32654007. **Open Door** ✉ Via della Lungaretta 23, Trastevere ☎ 06/5896478.

NEWSPAPERS & MAGAZINES The *International Herald Tribune,* major English and American news-magazines and a few daily papers are available at some newsstands, including those on Via Veneto, Via del Corso (at Via del Tritone), and Campo de' Fiori. *Wanted in Rome,* a biweekly magazine for Rome's English-speaking community, has features, contact and event listings mixed in with expat classifieds.

MAIL & SHIPPING

Buy stamps at any tobacconist, and drop mail in red mailboxes, making sure to use the right-hand slot for service outside Rome. The Vatican has its own postal service, and stamps and mailboxes can be found at its two public post offices, one on each side of Piazza San Pietro.

◪ Post Offices **Main post office** ✉ Piazza San Silvestro 19, Piazza di Spagna ☏ 06/6798495.

OVERNIGHT SERVICES

Although DHL and UPS offices are far out of the city center, FedEx has walk-in service on Via Barberini; all three companies will pick up packages from anywhere in Rome.

◪ Major Services **DHL** (800/345345). **Federal Express** ✉ Via Barberini 115, Via Veneto ☏ 800/123800. **UPS** ☏ 800/877877.

TOURS

BIKE TOURS

Enjoy Rome organizes all-day bike tours of Rome for small groups covering major sights and some hidden ones. Remember, Rome is famous for its seven hills; be prepared for a workout.

◪ Fees & Schedules **Enjoy Rome** ✉ Via Marghera 8A, near Termini ☏ 06/4451843 ⊕ www.enjoyrome.com.

BUS TOURS

American Express and CIT offer general orientation tours of the city, as well as specialized tours of particular areas such as the Vatican or Ancient Rome. Stop-'n'-go City Tours has English-speaking guides and the option of getting off and on at 14 key sites in the city. A day pass costs €12.

◪ Fees & Schedules **American Express** ☏ 06/67641. **Appian Line** ☏ 06/487861. **CIT** ✉ Piazza della Repubblica 64, near Termini ☏ 06/4620311 ⊕ www.citonline.it. **Stop-'n'-go City Tours** ☏ 06/47826379 ⊕ romecitytours.com.

WALKING TOURS

All About Rome, American Express, Enjoy Rome, Context:Rome, Through Eternity, and Walks of Rome offer walking tours of the city and its sites.

◪ Fees & Schedules **All About Rome** ☏ 06/7100823 ⊕ www.allaboutromewalks.netfirms.com. **American Express** ☏ 06/67641. **Enjoy Rome** ✉ Via Marghera 8A, near Termini ☏ 06/4451843 ⊕ www.enjoyrome.com. **Context:Rome** ✉ Via Baccina 40, near Termini ☏ 06/4820911 or 888/4671986 ⊕ www.contextrome.com. **Through Eternity** ☏ 06/7009336 ⊕ www.througheternity.com. **Walks of Rome** ✉ Via Urbana 38 Quirinale ☏ 06/484853.

TRAVEL AGENCIES

◪ Local Agent Referrals **American Express** ☏ 06/67641. **Appian Line** ☏ 06/487861. **Carrani Tours** ✉ Via Vittorio Emanuele Orlando 95, near Termini ☏ 06/4880510. **CIT** ✉ Piazza della Repubblica 64, near Termini ☏ 06/4620311 ⊕ www.citonline.it.

VISITOR INFORMATION

◪ Tourist Information **Tourist office** (Azienda di Promozione Turistica di Roma/APT) ✉ Via Parigi 5, near Termini ☏ 06/488991 ⊙ Mon.–Sat. 9–7 ⊠ Aeroporto Leonardo da Vinci ☏ 06/65956074 ⊙ Daily 8:15–7.

Rome
Side Trips

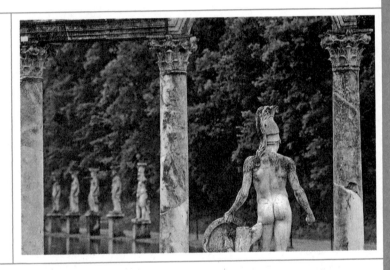

Villa Adriana, Tivoli

WORD OF MOUTH

"If you have a few extra days in Rome, northen Lazio, including
Viterbo and small jewels like Tuscania, is worth checking out.
If you'd like to see Etruscan tomb paintings in their original
underground state, Tarquinia is the place, and you can easily
drive to the airport from there and catch your flight home."

—alohatoall

WELCOME TO LAZIO

In Tuscia, the San Pellegrino district of **Viterbo** is a 13th-century time capsule, while at the gardens and palaces of nearby **Bagnaia, Caprarola,** and **Bomarzo** you can relive the Renaissance.

The ruins and tombs found along the Etruscan Seaboard in **Cerveteri, Tarquinia,** and **Tuscania** hold clues to the identity of the civilization that dominated central Italy prior to the Romans.

Aqua Claudia

Bomarzo

Bagnaia
Viterbo
Caprarola

Tuscania
Vetralla

Tarquinia

Civitavecchia

Lago di Bracciano

Cerveteri

Mare Tirreno

Rome

Ostia Antica
Lido di Ostia

Getting Oriented

All roads may indeed lead to Rome, but for thousands of years emperors, popes, and princes have been heading *fuori porta* (beyond the gates) for a change of pace from city life. To the west lies ancient Ostia Antica; as you work your way north you encounter the Etruscan seaboard and lava-rich Tuscia, with its Renaissance gardens. East of Rome is Tivoli, famed for retreats ranging from the noble—the Villa d'Este—to the imperial—Villa Adriana (Hadrian's Villa).

Ostia Antica, once ancient Rome's port, is now a parklike archaeological site.

Roman Theater, Ostia Antica   Sperlonga

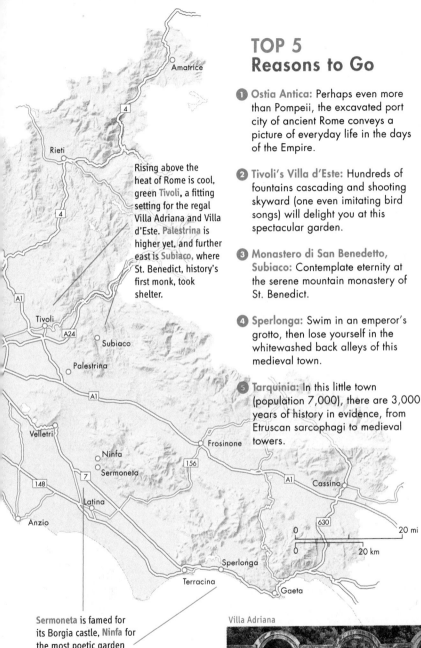

TOP 5
Reasons to Go

1. **Ostia Antica:** Perhaps even more than Pompeii, the excavated port city of ancient Rome conveys a picture of everyday life in the days of the Empire.

2. **Tivoli's Villa d'Este:** Hundreds of fountains cascading and shooting skyward (one even imitating bird songs) will delight you at this spectacular garden.

3. **Monastero di San Benedetto, Subiaco:** Contemplate eternity at the serene mountain monastery of St. Benedict.

4. **Sperlonga:** Swim in an emperor's grotto, then lose yourself in the whitewashed back alleys of this medieval town.

5. **Tarquinia:** In this little town (population 7,000), there are 3,000 years of history in evidence, from Etruscan sarcophagi to medieval towers.

Rising above the heat of Rome is cool, green Tivoli, a fitting setting for the regal Villa Adriana and Villa d'Este. Palestrina is higher yet, and further east is Subiaco, where St. Benedict, history's first monk, took shelter.

Sermoneta is famed for its Borgia castle, Ninfa for the most poetic garden in Italy, and Sperlonga—today an artists' idyll—as the original site of one of Emperor Tiberius's grandest villas.

Villa Adriana

ROME SIDE TRIPS PLANNER

Making the Most of Your Time

Ostia Antica is in many ways an ideal day trip from Rome: it's a fascinating sight, not far from the city, reachable by public transit, and takes about half a day to "do." Villa d'Este and Villa Adriana in Tivoli also make for a manageable, though fuller, day trip. Other destinations in Lazio can be visited in a day, but you'll get more out of them if you stay the night. A classic two-day itinerary would have you exploring Etruscan history in Cerveteri, Tarquinia, and Tuscania on Day 1, then visiting Viterbo's medieval borgo and hot springs or the gardens of Bomarzo, Bagnaia, and Caprarola on Day 2. An overnight to Sperlonga, Ninfa, and Sermoneta, is a summer trip —Ninfa is open only then, and in warm weather you can take advantage of Sperlonga's gorgeous beach.

Lazio, the Romans' Holiday

Foreign travelers aren't the only ones making day trips into the countryside of Lazio—on weekends, many Romans escape to the country, where they indulge in long, languorous meals. The good news is there are restaurants in the region that meet their standards. The bad news is on weekends when you'll be competing with natives for a table.

Getting Around

There's reliable public transit from Rome to Ostia Antica, Tivoli, and Viterbo. For other destinations in the region, a car is a big advantage—going by train or bus can add hours to your trip, and routes and schedules often seem like puzzles created by the Italian chapter of Mensa. For more about car, bus, and train travel, see "Essentials" at the end of this chapter.

Finding a Place to Stay

With relatively few exceptions (spas, beaches, and hill resorts such as Viterbo), accommodations in Lazio cater more to commercial travelers than to tourists. Public rooms and guest rooms tend to be functional and short on character, but they'll do the trick for an overnight.

Dining & Lodging Price Categories

WHAT IT COSTS in Euros					
	$$$$	$$$	$$	$	¢
Restaurants	over €22	€16–€22	€11–€16	€7–€11	under €7
Hotels	over €220	€160–€220	€110–€160	€70–€110	under €70

Restaurant prices are for a second course (un secondo). Hotel prices are for two people in a standard double room in high season, including tax and service.

Updated by
Valerie
Hamilton

A TRIP OUT OF ROME introduces you to a different kind of Italy: people are friendlier (although fewer of them speak English), schedules are looser, and it feels as though you've stepped a few years back in time. You'll find fewer lines, lower prices, and a tourism culture not so focused on the almighty euro. The monastery of San Benedetto at Subiaco is a good example—the monks and nuns there will take you in as a pilgrim, just as they've done for centuries.

Ostia Antica, Ancient Rome's seaport, is one of the region's top attractions—it rivals Pompeii in the quality of its preservation, and for evocativeness and natural beauty, it easily outshines the Roman forum. You'll also run across traces of the Etruscans in Lazio. The pre-Roman inhabitants of the area were wiped out in the city, but their remains—and some say, their bloodlines—persist in the rolling hills of Tuscia and the Etruscan seaboard north and northeast of Rome. So if the screeching traffic and long lines at the Colosseo start to wear on you, do as the Romans do—get out of town. There's plenty to see and do.

OSTIA ANTICA

Founded around the 4th century BC, Ostia served as Rome's port city for several centuries until the Tiber changed course, leaving the town high and dry. What has been excavated here is a remarkably intact Roman town in a pretty, parklike setting. Fair weather and good walking shoes are essential. On hot days, be here when the gates open or go late in the afternoon. A visit to the excavations takes two to three hours, including 20 minutes for the museum. Ostia Antica is 30 km (19 mi) southwest of Rome.

❶ Before exploring Ostia Antica's ruins, it's worthwhile to take a tour through the medieval *borgo* (town). The distinctive **Castello della Rovere,** easily spotted as you come off the footbridge from the train station, was built by Pope Julius II when he was the Cardinal Bishop of Ostia in 1483. Its triangular form is unusual for military architecture. Inside are (badly faded) frescoes by Michelangelo's pupil Baldassare Peruzzi. ✉ *Piazza della Rocca* ☎ *06/56358024* 🆓 *Free* 🕙 *Wed. and Fri.–Sun. 9–12:45, Tues. and Thurs. 9–12:45 and 2:30–4:15.*

FodorsChoice
★

Tidal mud and windblown sand covered the ancient port town, which lay buried until the beginning of the 20th century when it was extensively excavated. The **Scavi di Ostia Antica** (Ostia Antica excavations) continue to be well maintained today. A cosmopolitan population of rich businessmen, wily merchants, sailors, slaves, and their respective families once populated the city. The great warehouses were built in the 2nd century AD to handle huge shipments of grain from Africa; the *insulae* (forerunners of the modern apartment building) provided housing for the growing population. Under the combined assaults of the barbarians and the malaria-carrying mosquito, and after the Tiber changed course, the port was eventually abandoned. ✉ *Via dei Romagnoli* ☎ *06/ 56358099* 🌐 *www.itnw.roma.it/ostia/scavi* 💶 *€4, includes admission to Museo Ostiense* 🕙 *Tues.–Sun. 8:30–1 hr before sunset.*

Ostia Antica

Casa di Serapide **15**
Castello della Rovere **1**
Domus della
Fortuna Annonaria **8**
Domus di
Amore e Psiche **14**
Domus di Apuleio **6**
Forum **12**

Horrea **13**
Mithraeum **7**
Molino **9**
Museo Ostiense **11**
Porta Marina **17**
Porta Romana **2**
Sinagoga **18**

Teatro **4**
Tempio di Cerere **5**
Terme di Nettuno **3**
Termi dei
Sette Sapienti **16**
Thermopolium **10**

TO THE
BORGO

Romagnoli

TO ROME

Train
Station

1/8 mile

200 meters

V. d. del
Stazione

Via delle Tombe

Via del Mare

Viale

Fireman's
Barracks

Decumanus Maximus

Piazzale delle
Corporazioni

V. dei Molini

V. dei Dipinti

V. di Diana

Decumanus Maximus

Bivio del
Castrum

Cardine Massimo

Strada Panoramica

Pta.
Laurentina

Decumanus Maximus

Via degli Aurighi

V. della Foce

V. Epagathiana

Tiber

2 The **Porta Romana,** one of the city's three gates, is where you enter the Ostia Antica excavations. It opens onto the Decumanus Maximus, the main thoroughfare crossing the city from end to end. To your right, a staircase leads up to a platform—the remains of the upper floor of the

3 **Terme di Nettuno** (Baths of Neptune)—from which you get a good view of the black-and-white mosaic pavements representing a marine scene with Neptune and the sea goddess Amphitrite. Directly behind the baths is the barracks of the fire department, which played an important role in a town with warehouses full of valuable goods and foodstuffs.

12

4 On the north side of the Decumanus Maximus is the beautiful **Teatro** (Theater), built by Agrippa, remodeled by Septimius Severus in the 2nd century AD, and finally restored by the Rome City Council in the 20th century. In the vast Piazzale delle Corporazioni, where trade organiza-

5 tions similar to guilds had their offices, is the **Tempio di Cerere** (Temple of Ceres), which is only appropriate for a town dealing in grain imports—Ceres, who gave her name to cereal, was the goddess of agri-

6 culture. You can visit the **Domus di Apuleio** (House of Apuleius), built in Pompeian style, lower to the ground and with fewer windows than

7 was characteristic of Ostia. Next door, the **Mithraeum** has balconies and a hall decorated with symbols of the cult of Mithras. This male-only religion, imported from Persia, was especially popular with legionnaires.

8 On Via Semita dei Cippi, just off Via dei Molini, the **Domus della Fortuna Annonaria** (House of Fortuna Annonaria) is the richly decorated residence of a wealthy Ostian, which displays the skill of the mosaic artists of the period. One of the rooms opens onto a secluded garden.

9 On Via dei Molini you can see a **molino** (mill), where grain for the warehouses next door was ground with stones that are still here. Along Via

10 di Diana you come upon a **thermopolium** (bar) with a marble counter and a fresco depicting the fruit and foodstuffs that were sold here. At

11 the end of Via dei Dipinti is the **Museo Ostiense** (Ostia Museum), which displays sarcophagi, massive marble columns, and statuary too large to be shown anywhere else. A beautiful statue of Mithras slaying the bull that was taken from the underground Mithraeum and placed here. (The last entry to the museum is a half hour before the the Scavi closes.)

12 The **Forum,** on the south side of Decumanus Maximus, holds the monumental remains of the city's most important temple, dedicated to Jupiter, Juno, and Minerva; other ruins of baths; a basilica (which in Roman times was a secular hall of justice); and smaller temples.

13 Via Epagathiana leads toward the Tiber, where there are large **horrea** (warehouses) erected during the 2nd century AD to receive the enormous amounts of grain imported into Rome during that period, the height of the Empire.

14 West of Via Epagathiana, the **Domus di Amore e Psiche** (House of Cupid and Psyche), a residence, was named for a statue found there (now on display in the museum); you can see what remains of a large pool in an enclosed garden decorated with marble and mosaic motifs. Even in ancient times a premium was placed on water views: the house faces

the shore, which would have been only about ⅓ km (⅕ mi) away. The
⑮ **Casa di Serapide** (House of Serapis) on Via della Foce is a 2nd-century
multilevel dwelling; another apartment building stands one street over
⑯ on Via degli Aurighi. Nearby, the **Termi dei Sette Sapienti** (Baths of the
Seven Wise Men) are named for a group of bawdy frescoes found there.

⑰ The **Porta Marina** leads to what used to be the seashore. About 1,000
⑱ feet to the southeast are the ruins of the **sinagoga,** one of the oldest in
the Western world (from the 4th century AD).

Where to Eat

$–$$$ ✕ **Cipriani.** In the little medieval borgo near the excavations is an ele-
gant trattoria serving Roman specialties and seafood. A businesslike mood
at lunchtime contrasts with an upgrade in menu, style, and price in the
evening. The wine list is exquisite. ⊠ *Via del Forno 11* ☎ *06/56359560*
▤ *AE, DC, MC, V* ✆ *Closed Wed.*

THE ETRUSCAN SEABOARD

Northwest of Rome lie Etruscan sites on coastal hills that dominate ap-
proaches from all directions. The Etruscans held sway over a vast ter-
ritory mainly north of Rome from the 8th to the 4th century BC, before
the Roman Republic's gradual expansion northward. According to the
literary sources—mainly written by their Greek and Roman adver-
saries—Etruscans lived a fairly decadent life and had an unsurpassed
reputation in fields as diverse as bronze-working and soothsaying.
Though there are few remains of their settlements, they reserved some
of their finest construction skills for assuring comfort and style in the
afterlife: the Etruscan necropolis, or "city of the dead," was an agglom-
eration of tombs that most likely aimed to reproduce the homes and
lifestyles of the living.

As you make the trip north beyond Rome's city limits, you traverse green
countryside with pastures and endless fields of artichokes, a premium
crop in these parts. You catch glimpses of the sea to the west, where the
coast is dotted with suburban developments. Because the beaches in this
area are popular with today's Romans, highways (especially the coastal
Via Aurelia) and public transportation can be crowded on weekends from
spring to fall. Exploring the Etruscan sites requires some agility in
climbing up and down uneven stairs, and you need shoes suitable for
walking on rough dirt paths.

Cerveteri is the principal Etruscan site closest to Rome and features the
Necropoli della Banditaccia, a sylvan setting among mossy stones and
variously shaped monuments that are memorials to revered ancestors.
Tarquinia is farther north and has impressive painted tombs, as well as
an excellent museum full of objects recovered from tombs throughout
the region. On the way, you pass Civitavecchia, Rome's principal port.
From the highway or train you can see the port installations, which in-
clude a fort designed by Michelangelo. Northeast of Tarquinia is Tus-
cania, a finely preserved town brimming with cultural heritage and
medieval buildings.

Side Trips
from Rome

Orvieto

Lago di Bolsena

Montefiascone

Bomarzo ㉕

TUSCIA

Narni

Tuscania ㉑ **Bagnaia** ㉓
Viterbo ㉒

Orte

UMBRIA
LAZIO

Rieti

Norchia ◆

Lago di Vico

Caprarola ㉔

Civita Castellana

Tarquinia ⑳

Vetralla

Tivoli ㉖ A24 **Subiaco** ㉘

LAZIO

Monterosi

Palestrina ㉗

Frascati

Lago di Bracciano

Civitavecchia

Bracciano

Cerveteri ⑲

A12

Autostrada
Rome-L'Aquila

Mandela

Vicovaro

A24

Bagni di Tivoli ◆ ㉖ **Subiaco** ㉘

Rome ★

Tivoli

Villa Adriana ◆

Palestrina ㉗

S. Cesareo

0 — 10 miles
0 — 15 km

Fiumicino

Ciampino

Frascati

Ostia Antica ① - ⑱ see map page 628

Lido di Ostia

Lago di Albano

Velletri

Tyrrhenian Sea

Ninfa ㉚

Sermoneta ㉙

Latina

ITALY

Ninfa ㉚
Sermoneta ㉙

Anzio

Sperlonga ㉛

Latina

Terracina

Sperlonga ㉛

Uncovering the Etruscan Past

The countryside in northern Lazio is generously dotted with Etruscan ruins and tombs. For centuries these remnants offered the only insight into the mysterious civilization that dominated the area before the rise of Rome and set the precedent for many of Rome's accomplishments. In his 1920s travelogue *Etruscan Places,* D. H. Lawrence wrote, "We know nothing about the Etruscans except what we find in their tombs." Fortunately, modern scientific techniques have since delved much further, and museums in Cerveteri, Tarquinia, and Tuscania, along with the main Etruscan museum in Rome, the Villa Giulia, regularly offer new exhibits. Still, basic questions remain unanswered, such as where exactly the Etruscans came from, what family of languages Etruscan belongs to, and why they left no proper literature to posterity. But wherever you go in northern Lazio, the Etruscans are never far away: signs point to *Riva degli Etruschi* (Shore of the Etruscans), shops and businesses use imitation Etruscan lettering, and right in the middle of Tuscania, Etruscan sarcophagi are laid out by the main square.

Cerveteri

⑲ *42 km (26 mi) northwest of Rome.*

The nucleus of Cerveteri, in the shadow of a medieval castle, stands on a spur of tufa rock that was the site of the Etruscan city of Caere, a thriving commercial center in the 6th century BC.

In the **Necropoli della Banditaccia** the Etruscan residents of Caere left a monumental complex of tombs constructed during more than 500 years (from the 7th to the 1st century BC). Some are laid to rest in simple graves, others in burial chambers that are replicas of Etruscan dwellings. The round tumuli are prototypes of Rome's tombs of Augustus and Hadrian (in the Mausoleo di Augusto and Castel Sant'Angelo) and the Tomb of Cecilia Metella on the Via Appia. Look for the **Tomba dei Capitelli,** with carved capitals, and the **Tomba dei Rilievi,** its walls decorated with stucco reliefs of household objects. The **Tomba Moretti** has a little vestibule with columns. The necropolis is about 2 km (1 mi) northeast of Cerveteri's main piazza, a trip you can make on foot or by taxi. ⊠ *Piazza della Necropoli* ☎ *06/9940001* 💲 *€4* ☉ *Tues.–Sun. 9–1 hr before sunset.*

Where to Eat

$ ✕ **Tuchulcha.** Enjoy simple and satisfying home-style food at a country trattoria. Two of the specialties are handmade fettuccine and locally grown artichokes served in various ways. You can dine outside in good weather. Tuchulcha is about ½ km (⅓ mi) from the entrance to the Banditaccia Necropolis, on the road leading to the site. ⊠ *Via della Necropoli Etrusca 28* ☎ *06/9914075* 🚫 *No credit cards* ☉ *Closed Mon.*

Tarquinia

② *About 90 km (55 mi) northwest of Rome, 50 km (30 mi) northwest of Cerveteri.*

12

Fortified Tarquinia sprawls on a hill overlooking the sea. Once a powerful Etruscan city, it was also a major center in the Middle Ages. Though it is not as well preserved as some towns, there are unexpected pleasures, including the sight of the majestic 12th-century church of Santa Maria di Castello encircled by towers. Be sure to walk to the medieval wall at the inland edge of town for views over the Etruscan countryside. To explore Tarquinia's Etruscan heritage, visit the museum in Palazzo Vitelleschi, then see the frescoed underground tombs in the necropolis just east of the city.

The **Museo Nazionale Tarquiniense** contains a wealth of Etruscan treasures and is housed in **Palazzo Vitelleschi,** a splendid 15th-century building. The undisputed highlight is a terra-cotta relief of two marvelous winged horses that gleams against the gray-stone wall of the main hall. The horses once decorated an Etruscan temple and are vibrant proof of the degree of artistry attained in the 4th century BC. The rest of the museum and its courtyard are crowded with sarcophagi from the tombs found beneath the meadows surrounding the town: figures of the deceased recline on their stone couches, mouths curved in enigmatic smiles. ⊠ *Piazza Cavour 1* ☎ *0766/856036* ▭ *€4, €6.50 including necropolis* ☉ *Tues.–Sun. 8:30–7:30.*

The **Necropolis** tombs, painted with lively scenes of Etruscan life, date from the 6th to the 2nd century BC. The colors are amazingly fresh in some tombs, and the scenes show the vitality and highly civilized lifestyle of this ancient people. Apart from the wall paintings, the only evidence of the original function of the burial chambers is the stone platforms on which sarcophagi once rested. The tombs have been plundered by *tombaroli,* who dig illegally, usually at night. Of the thousands of tombs that exist throughout the territory of Etruria (there are 40,000 in the vicinity of Tarquinia alone), only a small percentage have been excavated scientifically. A thorough visit takes about 90 minutes, and good explanations in English are posted outside each tomb. The entrance is 1½ km (1 mi) southeast of the town walls, about a 20-minute walk from the main square, Piazza Matteotti. There's also infrequent bus service from Piazza Cavour. Ask at the Museo Nazionale Tarquiniense ticket counter or the tourist office for bus information. ⊠ *Monterozzi, on Strada Provinciale 1/b, Tarquinia–Viterbo* ☎ *0766/856308, 06/9941098 English-language tours* ▭ *€4, €6.50 including Museo Nazionale Tarquiniense* ☉ *Tues.–Sun. 8:30–1 hr before sunset.*

off the
beaten
path

NORCHIA – About 20 km (13 mi) northeast of Tarquinia on the road to Vetralla (S1bis) is the junction for the Etruscan necropolis of Norchia, which lies about 5 km (3 mi) farther to the north. From the far corner of the parking lot, a five-minute walk along a path between fields takes you to the edge of a thickly wooded gorge where Etruscan tombs are sculpted out of the cliff face. You're unlikely to see other visitors here, everything is covered in thick vegetation, *and* the site is unguarded. As you walk down to the bottom of the gorge—though it is not steep, good walking shoes and water bottles are recommended—look at the way parts of the rock face have been modeled to imitate architectural styles. To top it off, there are medieval ruins and a photogenic vantage point up the other side of the gorge (about 10 minutes away). As there is no site map on display and little by way of site information, stick to well-trodden paths.

Where to Stay & Eat

★ ¢–$ ✕ **Il Grappolo.** This central wine bar is the antidote to another pasta meal— a great place for a snack, a drink, or a light meal built around wine and good company. It's cold food only, but the menu includes such fresh creations as *insalata di pera, speck, e grana* (salad with pear, cured ham, and flakes of *grana,* aged granulated cheese), perhaps accompanied by Paterno wine, a local Sangiovese thoroughbred, considered Lazio's rival to fine Tuscan reds. The vibe is modern, youthful, and welcoming. ⊠ *Via Alberata Dante Alighieri 3* ☎ *0766/857321* ▤ *AE, DC, MC, V* ⊘ *Closed Mon. and Jan. 7–31. No lunch Nov.–Mar.*

$ ✕▥ **San Marco.** It would be impossible to find a better location for exploring the old center of Tarquinia than this ancient monastery, a huge, complex structure on the town's main square that's been operating as an inn since 1876. In the 1500s these hallowed halls housed the mysterious order of the Frati Neri (Black Monks)—an Augustinian sect whose cloisters remain intact in the hotel's courtyard. Rooms are simple, clean, and inviting; the bar hops with locals on weekend nights. The excellent restaurant ($–$$) uses recipes reconstructed from the brothers' 16th-century cookbooks (as well as pizza, for the less daring). ⊠ *Piazza Cavour 18, 01016* ☎ *0766/842234* ▤ *0766/842306* ⊕ *www.san-marco.com* ➷ *16 rooms* ⌂ *Restaurant, bar, dance club; no a/c* ▤ *AE, DC, MC, V* ✲⃝ *BP.*

Tuscania

★ ㉑   *24 km (15 mi) northeast of Tarquinia, 25 km (16 mi) west of Viterbo.*

Given its small size—a population of only 7,000—Tuscania seems to overflow with sites from a number of historical periods, much more so than neighboring Tarquinia and Viterbo. The medieval city walls were tastefully restored after a devastating earthquake in 1971, and the interior abutting the walls has been pleasingly landscaped with lawns and gardens. Narrow cobblestone streets dotted with medieval towers make for great walks. Piazza Basile, in front of the Palazzo Comunale, has a parapet with the sculpted lids of nine Etruscan sarcophagi; below is the Fontana di Sette Cannelle, the restored city fountain dating from Etrusco-Roman times. North of the city walls is the Museo Archeologico Tuscanese, housed in what was the convent of the adjacent 15th-century church, Santa Maria del Riposo. The long-abandoned ancient nucleus of the town, which includes the two outstanding Romanesque churches of Santa Maria Maggiore and San Pietro, is a 20-minute walk outside the city walls to the southeast.

The **Museo Archeologico Tuscanese** displays the necropolis material from two main Etruscan families, the Curunas and Vipinanas, dating from the 4th to 2nd century BC. The family members are depicted on the sarcophagi in typical banqueting position, looking far from undernourished. Also displayed are the grave goods, which would have been buried with them, as well as some helpful photographs showing what the tombs looked like when first excavated. The rooms above have finds stretching back to the 8th century BC, along with some information panels in English. ⊠ *Via della Madonna di Riposo 36* ☎ *0761/436209* ⊡ *Free* ⊘ *Tues.–Sun. 8:30–7:30.*

Where to Stay & Eat

★ $ ✕ **La Torre di Lavello.** Opposite the town's medieval tower, this trattoria-cum-pizzeria combines efficient service with stylish presentation at very reasonable prices. The menu is varied and imaginative. Highly recommended is the fettuccine *al ragù bianco* (a white sauce with beans), as well as the ricotta cheese *con miele* (with honey) for dessert. To be assured of a seat, arrive early or make a reservation. ⊠ *Via Torre di Lavello 27* ☎ *0761/434258* ☐ *DC, MC, V* ⊘ *Closed Wed.*

¢ ✕⌂ **Locanda di Mirandolina.** Rooms are distinguished by door color rather than number at a courteously run guesthouse in Tuscania's old town. Simple beds and side chairs furnish the immaculately kept spaces. The intimate restaurant ($$) is an excellent place to sample local recipes like *pappardelle al cinghiale* (wide, flat pasta with a wild boar sauce). Book well in advance as this is a popular choice, especially with northern Europeans. Locanda di Mirandolina makes a great base for visiting ancient Etruria. ⊠ *Via del Pozzo Bianco 40/42, 01017* ☎☎ *0761/436595* ⊕ *www.mirandolina.it* ⇆ *10 rooms* ☐ *MC, V* ⊙⫝̸ *BP* ⊘ *Closed Jan. 6–Feb. 12. Restaurant closed Tues.*

FodorsChoice ★

TUSCIA

The region of Tuscia (the modern name for the Etruscan domain of Etruria) is a landscape of dramatic beauty punctuated by deep, rocky gorges and thickly forested hills, with dappled light falling on wooded paths. This has long been a preferred locale for the retreats of wealthy Romans, a place where they could build grand villas and indulge their sometimes eccentric gardening tastes. The provincial capital, Viterbo, which overshadowed Rome as a center of papal power for a time during the Middle Ages, lies in the heart of Tuscia. The farmland east of Viterbo conceals small quarries of the dark, volcanic peperino stone, which shows up in the walls of many buildings here. Lake Bolsena is an extinct volcano, and the sulfur springs still bubbling up in Viterbo's spas were used by the ancient Romans. Bagnaia and Caprarola are home to palaces and gardens; the garden statuary at Bomarzo is in a league of its own—somewhere between the beautiful and the bizarre.

The ideal way to explore this region is by car. By train from Rome, you can start at Viterbo and get to Bagnaia by local bus. If you're traveling by train or bus, check schedules carefully; you may have to allow for an overnight if you want to see all four attractions.

Viterbo

㉒ *25 km (16 mi) east of Tuscania, 104 km (64 mi) northwest of Rome.*

Viterbo's moment of glory was in the 13th century, when it became the seat of the papal court. The medieval core of the city still sits within 12th-century walls. Its old buildings, with windows bright with geraniums, are made of dark peperino, the local stone that colors the medieval part of Viterbo a dark gray, contrasted here and there with the golden tufa rock of walls and towers. Peperino is also used in the characteristic and typically medieval exterior staircases that you see throughout the old town. More recently, Viterbo has blossomed into a regional commercial center, and much of the modern city is loud and industrial. However, Viterbo's San Pellegrino district is a place to get the feel of the Middle Ages, seeing how daily life is carried on in a setting that has remained practically unchanged over the centuries. The Palazzo Papale and the cathedral enhance the effect. The city has also remained a renowned spa center for its natural hot springs just outside of town, frequented by popes—and the laity—since medieval times.

The Gothic **Palazzo Papale** (Papal Palace) was built in the 13th century as a residence for popes looking to get away from the city. At that time Rome was a notoriously unhealthy place, ridden with malaria and plague and rampaging factions of rival barons. In 1271 the palace was the scene of a novel type of rebellion. A conclave held here to elect a new pope had dragged on for months, apparently making no progress. The people of Viterbo were exasperated by the delay, especially as custom decreed that they had to provide for the cardinals' board and lodging for the duration of the conclave. So they tore the roof off the great hall where the cardinals were meeting, and put them on bread and water. Sure enough, a new pope—Gregory X—was elected in short order. The interior of the Palazzo, which houses a museum of sacred art, is closed indefinitely for restoration, but you can climb the stairs to what was once the loggia. ⊠ *Piazza San Lorenzo* ☎ *0761/341124.*

The facade and interior of Viterbo's Duomo, **Chiesa di San Lorenzo,** date from the Middle Ages. On the ancient columns inside the cathedral you can see the chips that an exploding bomb took out of the stone during World War II. There's a small adjoining **museum** with a muddle of 18th-century reliquaries, Etruscan sarcophagi, and a crucifixion painting attributed to Michelangelo. ⊠ *Piazza San Lorenzo* ☎ *0761/ 309623* ✉ *Church free, museum €5* ☉ *Church 8–12:30 and 3:30–7, museum Fri.–Sun. 9:30–1 and 4–6.*

The medieval district of **San Pellegrino** is one of the best-preserved such neighborhoods in Italy. It has charming vistas of arches, vaults, towers, exterior staircases, worn wooden doors on great iron hinges, and tiny hanging gardens. You pass many antiques shops as you explore the little squares and byways. The **Fontana Grande** in the piazza of the same name is the largest and most extravagant of Viterbo's authentic Gothic fountains. ⌧ *Via San Pellegrino.*

⏱ Viterbo has been a spa town for centuries, and the **Terme dei Papi** continues the tradition. This excellent spa has the usual rundown of health and beauty treatments with an Etruscan twist: try a facial with local volcanic mud, or a steam bath in an ancient cave, where scalding hot mineral water direct from the Bullicam spring splashes down a waterfall to a pool under your feet. The Terme dei Papi's main draw, however, is the *terme* (baths) themselves: a 21,000-square-foot outdoor limestone pool into the shallow end of which Viterbo's famous hot water pours at 59°C (138°F)—and intoxicates with its sulfurous odor. Floats and deck chairs are for rent, but bring your own bathrobe and towel unless you're staying at the hotel. ⌧ *Strada Bagni 12, 5 km (3 mi) west of town center* ☎ *0761/3501* ⊕ *www.termedeipapi.it* ⌖ *Weekdays €12; weekends €15* ⊙ *Pool, daily 9–5:30; spa, daily 9–6.*

Where to Stay & Eat

★ **\$\$\$** ✕ **Enoteca La Torre.** One of the best wine cellars in Italy takes center stage at the elegant Enoteca La Torre. It's also a temple to good eating: in addition to an ever-changing menu there are lists for cheeses, mineral waters, oils, and vinegars. Chestnut fritters and rabbit stew are unusual delicacies, but whatever you choose will be local, traditional, and of the highest quality. ⌧ *Via della Torre 5* ☎ *0761/226467* ⊟ *AE, DC, MC, V* ⊙ *Closed Sun.*

★ **¢–\$\$** ✕ **Tre Re.** Viterbo's oldest restaurant—and one of the most ancient in Italy—has been operating in the *centro storico* (historic center) since 1622. The kitchen still focuses on nothing but traditional local cooking and the staff provides open, friendly service. A gregarious buzz of Viterbese businessmen and families fills the small, wood-paneled and white-walled room to overflowing at lunchtime, as diners enjoy the truest versions of specialties such as *acquacotta viterbese* (literally "cooked water," a hearty vegetable and hot-pepper soup that was the ancient sustenance of shepherds and stockmen. ⌧ *Via Macel Gattesco 3* ☎ *0761/304619* ⊟ *AE, MC, V* ⊙ *Closed Thurs.*

¢–\$ ✕ **Cantina Palazzo dei Mercanti.** Enjoy impeccably executed classics for
Fodor'sChoice pocket change at the casual Cantina, which shares a kitchen with the
★ elegant Enoteca La Torre—it's the best lunch value in town. Try whatever is listed as the daily rotating special, such as pappardelle with a tomato-and-meat sauce. You can select a glass or bottle from the Enoteca's epic wine list, which includes a complex matrix of ratings from Italy's foremost wine reviewers. ⌧ *Via della Torre 1* ☎ *0761/226467* ⊟ *AE, DC, MC, V* ⊙ *Closed Sun.*

\$\$\$ ⊞ **Hotel Niccolò V.** This upscale, airy hotel is connected to Viterbo's mineral baths and spa at Terme dei Papi. The complex is a surreal mix of doctors in scrubs, bathrobed bathers, and lost hotel guests wandering through an enormous mazelike lobby. In the guest rooms, though, marble baths and wooden floors provide a country-house elegance. Breakfast, a sumptuous buffet, is taken in a wood-beam gallery overlooking a small garden. Hotel guests have free use of the baths, as well as the option of dinner for a mere €8 extra per person. ⌧ *Strada Bagni 12, 01100, 5 km (3 mi)*

west of center ☎ 0761/350555 🖷 0761/350273 ⊕ www.termedeipapi.
it/soggiorni/ 🛏 20 rooms, 3 suites ᐸᐳ Restaurant, in-room safes, minibars,
pool, spa, bar, meeting rooms ⊟ AE, DC, MC, V ⎮◎⎮ BP.

Bagnaia

㉓ *5 km (3 mi) east of Viterbo.*

The village of Bagnaia is the site of 16th-century cardinal Alessandro
Montalto's summer retreat. Small twin residences are but an excuse for
the hillside garden and park that surround them, designed by virtuoso
architect Giacomo Barozzi (circa 1535–84), known as Vignola, who later
worked with Michelangelo on St. Peter's.

Villa Lante is a terraced extravaganza. On the lowest terrace a delightful Italian garden has a centerpiece fountain fed by water channeled down
the hillside. On another, higher terrace a stream of water runs through
a groove carved in a long stone table where the cardinal entertained his
friends alfresco, chilling wine in the running water. That's only one of
the most evident and innocent of the whimsical water games that were
devised for the cardinal. The symmetry of the formal gardens contrasts
with the wild, untamed park adjacent to it, reflecting the paradoxes of
nature and artifice that are the theme of this pleasure garden. ⊠ *Via G.
Baroni 71* ☎ *0761/288008* 🎫 *Park free, gardens and residences €2*
🕑 *Tues.–Sun. 8:30–1 hr before sunset.*

Caprarola

㉔ *21 km (16 mi) southeast of Bagnaia, 19 km (12 mi) southeast of Viterbo.*

The wealthy and powerful Farnese family took over this sleepy village
in the 1500s and had Vignola design a huge palace and gardens to rival
the great residences of Rome. The architect also rearranged the little town
of Caprarola, to enhance the palazzo's setting.

The massive, magnificent, 400-year-old **Palazzo Farnese,** built on an unusual pentagonal plan, has an ingenious system of ramps and terraces
that leads right up to the main portal. This nicety allowed carriages and
mounts to arrive directly in front of the door. Though the salons are un-
furnished, the palace's grandeur is still evident. An artificial grotto decorates one wall, the ceilings are covered with frescoes glorifying the Farnese
family, and an entire room is frescoed with maps of the world as it was
known to 16th-century cartographers. Weekdays you can only enter the
Palazzo with a tour—departing every half hour. From the windows you
can glimpse the garden, which can be visited only on weekdays, only
with a guided tour (at 10, 11, 12, and 3). ⊠ *Via Nicolai* ☎ *0761/
646052* 🎫 *€2* 🕑 *Tues.–Sun. 8:30–1 hr before sunset.*

Bomarzo

㉕ *15 km (9 mi) northeast of Viterbo.*

☾ The eerie 16th-century **Parco dei Mostri** (Monster Park) is populated by
weird and fantastic sculptures of mythical creatures and eccentric ar-

chitecture. It was created by Prince Vicino Orsini for his wife, Giulia Farnese, who is said to have taken one look at the park and died of heart failure. No one really knows why the prince had the sculptures carved in outcroppings of stone in a dusky wood on his estate, but it probably has something to do with the artifices that were an artistic conceit of his time. Children love it, and there are photo ops galore. However, be advised that the park's staff can be brusque. ✉ *1½ km (1 mi) west of town* ☎ *0761/924029* 🎟 *€8* ⊙ *Daily 8:30–1 hr before sunset.*

TIVOLI, PALESTRINA & SUBIACO

East of Rome are two of Lazio's star attractions—the Villa Adriana and the Villa d'Este in Tivoli—and in the mountains beyond them, the lesser-known and wonderfully peaceful Palestrina and Subiaco. The road from Rome to Tivoli passes through uninspiring industrial areas and burgeoning suburbs that used to be lush countryside. You know you're close to Tivoli when you see vast quarries of travertine marble and smell the sulfurous vapors from the not-so-interesting Bagni di Tivoli spa.

With a car you can continue your loop through the mountains east of Rome, taking in two very different sights that are both focused on religion. The ancient pagan sanctuary at Palestrina is set on the slopes of Mt. Ginestro, from which it commands a sweeping view of the green plain and distant mountains. Subiaco, the cradle of Western monasticism, is tucked away in the mountains above Tivoli and Palestrina. Unless you start out very early and have lots of energy, plan an overnight stop along the way if you want to take in all three.

Tivoli

❷❻ *36 km (22 mi) northeast of Rome.*

★ **Villa Adriana** (Hadrian's Villa) was an exclusive retreat, where the marvels of the classical world were reproduced for the ruler's pleasure. Hadrian, who succeeded Trajan as emperor in AD 117, was a man of genius and intellectual curiosity. From AD 118 to 130, architects, laborers, and artists worked on the villa below the ancient settlement of Tibur, periodically spurred on by the emperor himself when he returned from a voyage full of new design ideas. After his death in AD 138 the fortunes of his villa declined. It was sacked by barbarians and Romans alike; many of his statues and decorations ended up in the Vatican Museums, but the expansive ruins are nonetheless compelling.

It's not the single elements but the delightful effect of the whole that makes Hadrian's Villa a treat. Oleanders, pines, and cypresses growing among the ruins heighten the visual impact. To help you get your bearings, maps are issued free with the audio guides (€4). A visit here takes about two hours, more if you like to savor antiquity slowly. After sunset on Fridays, a one-hour tour under spotlights is available for €4.65. In summer there's a sound-and-light show at night; check with your hotel concierge or call the ticket office for the schedule. Otherwise, in summer visit early to take advantage of cool mornings. ✉ *Bivio di Villa Adri-*

ana, off Via Tiburtina, 6 km (4 mi) southwest of Tivoli ☎ *0774/530203* 🔳 *€6.50* ⊙ *Daily 9–1 hr before sunset.*

★ **Villa d'Este,** a late-Renaissance estate, is a playground of artistic whimsy, manifested in the 80-some fountains of all shapes and sizes that tumble down the vast, steep hillside garden. Cardinal Ippolito d'Este (1509–72), an active figure in the political intrigues of mid-16th-century Italy, set about proving his dominance over man and nature by commissioning this monument to

architectural excess. His builders tore down part of a Franciscan monastery to clear the site, then diverted the Aniene River to water the garden and feed the fountains. The musical **Fontana dell'Organo** and the animated **Fontana della Civetta** have been restored to working order: the organ plays a watery tune every two hours 10:30–6:30, and the mechanical *civetta* (owl) chases warbling sparrow figures out of the bath every two hours 10–6. On the other side of the garden the more timeworn **Fontana di Roma** is a scale model representing Rome's river network and mythology as well as some of its ancient buildings. Allow an hour for this visit, and bear in mind that there are a lot of stairs to climb. ⊠ *Piazza Trento 1* ☎ *0774/312070* ⊕ *www.villadestetivoli.info* 🔳 *€6.50* ⊙ *Tues.–Sun. 9–1 hr before sunset.*

Where to Stay & Eat

$–$$ ✕ **Del Falcone.** A central location—on Tivoli's main street leading off Largo Garibaldi—means that this restaurant is popular and often crowded. In the ample and rustic dining rooms you can try homemade *crespella* (a rolled pancake), flavored with nuts or ricotta cheese and spinach. Country-style grilled meats are excellent. ⊠ *Via Del Trevio 34* ☎ *0774/312358* ▤ *AE, DC, MC, V.*

$$ ✕▥ **Adriano.** The green surroundings here, at the entrance to Hadrian's Villa, provide a restful backdrop for the Adriano's 10 rooms, which are casually elegant and immaculately kept. Some have ironwork beds and some wood. The restaurant ($$–$$$) is sophisticated Italian, as in the risotto *ai fiori di zucchine* (with zucchini flowers). You can relax and dine at outdoor tables in summer. ⊠ *Via di Villa Adriana 194, 00010* ☎ *0774/382235* ▤ *0774/535122* ⊕ *www.hoteladriano.it* ⤴ *7 rooms, 3 suites* ⚹ *Restaurant, in-room safes, refrigerators, cable TV, tennis court, bar, Internet, meeting room, some pets allowed (fee); no smoking* ▤ *AE, DC, MC, V* ⊙ *No dinner Sun. Nov.–Mar.* ⏀❙ *BP.*

Palestrina

㉗ *27 km (17 mi) southeast of Tivoli, 37 km (23 mi) east of Rome.*

Except to students of ancient history and music lovers, Palestrina is surprisingly little known outside Italy. Its most famous native son, Giovanni Pierluigi da Palestrina, born here in 1525, was the renowned composer of 105 masses, as well as madrigals, magnificats, and motets. But the town was celebrated long before the composer's lifetime.

Ancient Praeneste (modern Palestrina) flourished much earlier than Rome. It was the site of the Temple of Fortuna Primigenia, which dates from the 2nd century BC. This was one of the largest, richest, most frequented temple complexes in all antiquity—people came from far and wide to consult its famous oracle. In modern times no one had any idea of the extent of the complex until World War II bombings exposed ancient foundations occupying huge artificial terraces stretching from the upper part of the town as far downhill as its central Duomo.

Large arches and terraces scale the hillside up to the imposing **Palazzo Barberini,** built in the 17th century along the semicircular lines of the original temple. It now contains the **Museo Nazionale Archeologico di Palestrina,** with material found on the site that dates from throughout the classical period. This well-labeled collection of Etruscan bronzes, pottery, and terra-cotta statuary as well as Roman artifacts takes second place to the chief attraction, a 1st-century BC mosaic representing the Nile in flood. This delightful work—a large-scale composition in which form, color, and innumerable details captivate the eye—is alone worth the trip to Palestrina. But there's more: a model of the temple as it was in ancient times helps you appreciate the immensity of the original construction. ⊠ *Piazza della Cortina 1* ☎ *06/9538100* 🎫 *€3* 🕙 *Museum, daily 9–7:30; archaeological temple zone, daily 9–1 hr before sunset.*

Where to Stay & Eat

¢ ✕🏨 **Hotel Stella.** Expect a cordial welcome at the restaurant ($–$$) of the central Hotel Stella in Palestrina's public garden. The menu lists local dishes such as light and freshly made fettuccine served with a choice of sauces, as well as unusual combinations such as *pasta e fagioli con frutti di mare* (pasta and bean soup with shellfish). Decor tends toward the bright and fanciful. The guest rooms are frilly and a bit worn, but clean and comfortable. ⊠ *Piazzale Liberazione 3, 00036* ☎ *06/9538172* 🖷 *06/9573360* ⊕ *www.hotelstella.it* 🛏 *30 rooms* ⚄ *Restaurant, cable TV, bar; no a/c in some rooms* ⊟ *AE, DC, MC, V* ⏏ *BP.*

Subiaco

28 *38 km (24 mi) northeast of Palestrina, 54 km (33 mi) northeast of Rome.*

Among wooded mountains in the deep and narrow valley of the Aniene River, Subiaco is a modern town built over World War II rubble. It is chiefly known (aside from being the birthplace of Gina Lollobrigida, whose family name is common in these parts) as the site of the cave where St. Benedict, history's first monk, retreated into meditation and prayer and later founded the Benedictine order in the monastery that still stands today. Even earlier, the place was a refuge of Nero, who built a villa here said to have rivaled that of Hadrian at Tivoli, damming the river to create three lakes and a series of waterfalls. The road to the monastery passes the ruins of the emperor's villa.

Convento di Santa Scolastica, between Subiaco and St. Benedict's hermitage on the mountainside, is the only hermitage founded by St. Benedict to have survived the Lombard invasion of Italy in the 9th century. It has three cloisters extant; the oldest dates from the end of the 12th century. The monastery was the site of the first print shop in Italy, set up in 1464, and the library houses priceless ancient manuscripts and extensive archives. The museum displays an interesting mix of archaeological, geological, and ethnological finds from the area in vaulted cellars beneath the monastery. ⊠ *Road to Jenne and Vallepietra, 3 km (2 mi) east of Subiaco* ☎ *0774/82421* 🖻 *Hermitage free, museum €2.50* ⊙ *Daily 9–12:15 and 3:30–6:30.*

The 6th-century **Monastero di San Benedetto**—still active—is a landmark of Western monasticism. It was built over the grotto where the saint lived and meditated. Clinging to the cliff on nine great arches, it has resisted assaults for almost 900 years. Over the little wooden veranda at the entrance, a Latin inscription wishes PEACE TO THOSE WHO ENTER. The upper church is covered with frescoes by Umbrian and Sienese artists of the 14th century. In front of the main altar a stairway leads to the lower church, carved out of the rock, with another stairway leading down to the grotto where Benedict lived as a hermit for three years. The frescoes here are even earlier than those above; look for the portrait of St. Francis of Assisi, painted from life in the early 13th century, in the **Cappella di San Gregorio** (Chapel of St. Gregory), and for the monastery's oldest fresco, painted in the Byzantine style in the 8th century, in the **Grotta dei Pastori** (Shepherds' Grotto). ⊠ *Subiaco* ☎ *0774/85039* ⊕ *www.benedettini-subiaco.it* 🖻 *Free* ⊙ *Daily 9–12:30 and 3–6.*

Where to Stay & Eat

¢–$ ✕ **Frà Diavolo.** About 5 km (3 mi) outside Subiaco on the road up to Cervara—right at the junction to Monte Livata—is this cheerful restaurant-cum-pizzeria. Choose between the sunny eating area inside or the fairly makeshift outdoor terrace. Brisk but courteous servers bring local specialties such as *strozzapreti alla Frà Diavolo* (homemade pasta with tomatoes, eggplant, mozzarella, and basil) to your table. ⊠ *Contrada Colle Perino 15* ☎ *0774/83850* ⊟ *AE, DC, MC, V* ⊙ *Closed Mon.*

¢ 🏨 **Foresteria del Monastero.** Part of the Santa Scolastica monastery complex has been tastefully renewed to create an efficient hotel. Doubles and triples have inexpensive modern furnishings. You have the option of half board for only €7 per person per day or full board for €12. Well-marked trails lead from the Foresteria up to the monastery of St. Benedict. The monastery's bells start ringing at 8 AM, so late sleepers might think twice. ⊠ *Monastero Santa Scolastica, Piazzale dei Monasteri, 00028* ☎ *0774/85569* 🖨 *0774/822862* ⊕ *www.benedettini-subiaco.it* 🛏 *46 rooms* ♨ *Restaurant, bar, 2 meeting rooms; no smoking* ⊟ *AE, DC, MC, V* ⑩ *BP.*

SERMONETA, NINFA & SPERLONGA

This trio of romantic places south of Rome, set in a landscape defined by low mountains and a broad coastal plain, lures you into a past that seems centuries away from the city's bustle. Sermoneta is a castle town. Ninfa, nearby, is a noble family's fairy-tale garden that is open to the public only at limited times. Both are on the eastern fringe of the Pontine Plain, once a malaria-infested marshland that was ultimately reclaimed for agriculture by one of the most successful projects of Mussolini's regime. Sperlonga is a medieval fishing village perched above the sea near one of emperor Tiberius's most fabulous villas. You need a car to see them all in a day or so, and to get to Ninfa. But Sermoneta and Sperlonga are accessible by public transit.

Sermoneta

29 *80 km (50 mi) southeast of Rome.*

In Sermoneta the town and castle are one. In medieval times concentric rings of walls protected the townspeople and provided shelter from marauders for nearby farmers. The lords—in this case the Caetani family—held a last line of defense in the tall tower, where if necessary they could cut themselves off by pulling up the drawbridge.

The **Castello Caetani** dates from the 1200s. In the 15th century, having won the castle by ruse from the Caetanis, Borgia Pope Alexander VI transformed it into a formidable fortress and handed it over to his son Cesare. The chiaroscuro of dark and light stone, the quiet of the narrow streets, and the bastions that hint at siege and battle take you back in time. Admission is by guided tour (in Italian) only; tours leave on the hour. ⊠ *Via della Fortezza* ☎ *0773/695404* ✉ *€5* ☉ *Apr.–Oct., Fri.–Wed. 10–noon and 3–6; Nov.–Mar., Fri.–Wed. 10–noon and 2–4.*

Ninfa

30 *5 km (3 mi) south of Ninfa, 75 km (47 mi) southeast of Rome.*

A place of rare beauty, a dream garden of romantic ruins and rushing waters, of exotic flora and fragrant blooms: Ninfa today is a preserve of the Worldwide Fund for Nature (WWF), managed in collaboration with Caetani heirs. In the Middle Ages, this was a thriving village, part of the Caetani family's vast landholdings around Sermoneta. It was abandoned when malaria-carrying mosquitoes infested the plain, and it fell into ruin. Over the course of the 20th century, generations of the Caetani family, including English and American spouses and gardening buffs, created the garden and brought Ninfa back to life. You can visit by guided tour only; call ahead for reservations. ⊠ *Via Ninfina, Doganella di Ninfa* ☎ *0773/632231, 0773/695404 APT Latina-Provincial Tourist Office* ✉ *€8* ☉ *Apr.–Oct, weekends 9:30–noon and 2:30–6.*

Sperlonga

31 *64 km (40 mi) southeast of Ninfa, 127 km (79 mi) southeast of Rome.*

Sperlonga is a labyrinth of whitewashed alleys, arches, and little houses, like a casbah wrapped around a hilltop overlooking the sea, with broad, sandy beaches on either side. Long a favorite haunt of artists and artisans in flight from Rome's quick pace, the town has ancient origins. The medieval town gates, twisting alleys, and watchtower were vital to its defense when pirate ships came in sight. Now they simply make this former fishing town even more pictorial.

Under a cliff on the shore only 1 km (½ mi) south of Sperlonga are the ruins of a grandiose villa built for Roman emperor Tiberius and known as the **Grotta di Tiberio.** The villa incorporated several natural grottoes, in one of which Tiberius dined with guests on an artificial island. The various courses were served on little boats that floated across the shallow seawater pool to the emperor's table. Showpieces of the villa were the colossal sculpture groups embellishing the grotto. The **Museo Nazionale** was built on the site especially to hold the fragments of

> **WORD OF MOUTH**
>
> "You can take a train from Rome's Termini to Sperlonga, then a local bus to the beach front. There are miles of unspoilt beaches, as well as the remains of Roman emperors' homes and a notable museum close by."   –Huitres

these sculptures, discovered by chance by an amateur archaeologist. The huge statues had been smashed to pieces centuries earlier by Byzantine monks unsympathetic to pagan images. For decades the subject and appearance of the originals remained a mystery, and the museum was a work in progress as scholars there tried to put together the 7,000 pieces of this giant puzzle. Their achievement, the immense Scylla group, largest of the sculptures, is on view here. ⊠ *Via Flacca (SS213), Km 16.5, 2 km (1 mi) southwest of Sperlonga* ☎ *0771/548028* ⬛ *€2* ⊙ *Daily 9–7.*

Where to Stay & Eat

$$–$$$ ✕ **Gli Archi.** On a landing of one of Sperlonga's myriad stairways, Gli Archi has a cute *piazzetta* with tables for fair-weather dining. Brick-arch interiors add a touch of refinement that puts this restaurant a cut above establishments closer to the beach. The owners take pride in serving high-quality ingredients with culinary simplicity. Seafood, including the house favorite *pennette alla seppiolina* (pasta with cuttlefish ink), predominates, but there are a few meat platters, too. ⊠ *Via Ottaviano 17* ☎ *0771/ 548300* ⊟ *AE, DC, MC, V* ⊙ *Closed Wed. and Jan.*

$$–$$$ ⬓ **La Sirenella.** Rest a night at a family-run hotel occupying a prime position on Sperlonga's sandy beach, which is short walk from the old town. Rooms are bright and airy with blue-and-white striped spreads and some French doors that open to small balconies. Ask for a room on one of the upper floors in the *ala mare* (sea wing) to enjoy views of the Circeo promontory and the lapping waves. ⊠ *Via Cristoforo Colombo 25, 01100* ☎ *0771/549186* ⬛ *0771/549189* ⊕ *www.lasirenella.com* ⬎ *40 rooms* ⬠ *Restaurant, cable TV, beach, bar* ⊟ *AE, MC, V* ¶⊙¶ *FAP.*

ROME SIDE TRIPS ESSENTIALS

Transportation

BY BUS

COTRAL buses leave Rome for Cerveteri from the Lepanto stop of Metro A, with service every 40 minutes or so during the day. The ride takes about 70 minutes. Tuscania has a regular bus connection with Viterbo.

Buses leave Rome for Tivoli every 15 minutes from the terminal at the Ponte Mammolo stop on Metro B, but not all take the route that passes near Hadrian's Villa. Inquire which bus passes closest to the villa and tell the driver to let you off there. The ride takes about one hour. From Rome to Palestrina, take the COTRAL bus from the Anagnina stop on Metro A. From Rome to Subiaco, take the COTRAL bus from the Ponte Mammolo stop on Metro B; buses leave every 40 minutes; the circuitous trip takes one hour and 45 minutes.

COTRAL buses for Viterbo depart from the Saxa Rubra stop of the Ferrovie COTRAL train. The *diretta* (direct) bus takes about 75 minutes. Bagnaia can be reached from Viterbo by local city bus. For Caprarola, COTRAL buses leave from the Saxa Rubra station on the Roma Nord line.

COTRAL buses for Sermoneta leave Rome from the EUR Fermi stop of Metro B. The ride takes about one hour.

🚌 Bus Information **COTRAL** ☎ 800/431784 toll-free ⊕ www.cotralspa.it.

BY CAR

To get from Rome to Ostia (a 30- to 40-minute trip), follow Via del Mare southwest, which leads directly there. If approaching from Rome's ring road, look for the Ostiense or Ostia Antica exit.

For Cerveteri, take either the A12 Rome–Civitavecchia toll highway to the Cerveteri-Ladispoli exit, or take the more scenic coastal route with stoplights, the Via Aurelia. The trip takes about 40 minutes on the autostrada, twice that on the slow road. To get to Tarquinia, take the A12 Rome–Civitavecchia highway all the way to the end, where you continue on the Via Aurelia to Tarquinia. The trip takes about one hour. From that point, Tuscania is inland another half hour.

For Tivoli, take the Rome–L'Aquila autostrada (A24). To get to Palestrina directly from Rome, take the Autostrada del Sole (A2) to the San Cesareo exit and follow signs for Palestrina; this trip takes about one hour. From Rome to Subiaco, take S155 east for about 40 km (25 mi) and the S411 for 25 km (15½ mi); the trip takes about 70 minutes.

For Viterbo, Bagnaia, and Bomarzo, head out of Rome on the A1 autostrada, exiting at Attigliano. Bomarzo is only 3 km (2 mi) from the autostrada. The trip takes one hour.

The fastest route to sites south of Rome is the Via Pontina, an expressway. For Sermoneta, turn northeast at Latina. The trip takes about 50 minutes. For out-of-the-way Ninfa, proceed as for Sermoneta, but before reaching Sermoneta follow the signs for Doganella/Ninfa. The trip takes about one hour. For Sperlonga, take the Via Pontina to Latina, then the Via Appia to Terracina and Sperlonga. The trip takes about 1½ hours.

EMERGENCY SERVICES Your car-rental company should be your first resource if you have automotive trouble, but it's good to know that ACI, the Italian auto club, offers 24-hour roadside assistance (free to members, for a fee to non members).

🚗 **ACI** ☎ 803/116.

BY TRAIN

Regular train service links the Ostia Antica station with Rome's Piramide Metro B Line station, near Porta San Paolo. Exit the Metro and go to the station called Ostia Lido adjacent to the Metro station. The ride takes about 35 minutes. Trains depart every half hour throughout the day.

For many destinations, you may need to take a combination of train and bus. From stations in Rome, FS and Metropolitana suburban trains take you to the Cerveteri-Ladispoli station, where you can get a bus for Cerveteri. The train takes 30 minutes; the bus ride then takes 15 minutes. To get to Tarquinia, take an FS train (Rome–Genoa line) from Rome or from Cerveteri to the Tarquinia station (this service is sometimes operated by bus between Civitavecchia and Tarquinia), then a local bus from the station up to the hilltop town. The trip takes about 75–90 minutes. There's a fast train service, the FM3, from Rome to Viterbo, which takes an hour and 40 minutes. Tuscania is accessible by bus from Viterbo. Trains also stop at Bagnaia, 10 minutes beyond Viterbo.

FS trains connect Rome's Termini and Tiburtina stations with Tivoli in about 30 minutes; Villa d'Este is about a 20-minute uphill walk from the station at Tivoli. The FS train from Stazione Termini to Palestrina takes about 40 minutes; you can then board a bus from the train station to the center of town.

FS trains on the Rome–Formia–Naples line stop at Latina Scalo, where you can get a local bus to Sermoneta, though service is erratic. Traveling time is about one hour. For Sperlonga, on the same line, get off at the Itri station, from which buses leave for Sperlonga. The trip takes about 1½ hours.

🚆 Train Information **FS–Trenitalia** ☎ 892021 ⊕ www.trenitalia.com.

Contacts & Resources

EMERGENCIES

Emergency numbers (listed below) are accessible from every phone, including cellular phones, all over Italy. If you have ongoing medical concerns, it's a good idea to make sure someone is on duty all night where you're staying—not a given in Lazio. As elsewhere in Italy, every pharmacy in Lazio bears a sign at the door listing area pharmacies open in off-hours, though in the countryside you may need a car to get to one.

🚑 **Ambulance** ☎ 118. **Carabinieri** (Military Police) ☎ 112. **Emergencies** ☎ 113. **Fire** ☎ 115.

TOURS

CIT has half-day excursions to Villa d'Este in Tivoli. American Express has tours to Hadrian's Villa. Appian Line has excursions to Hadrian's Villa. Carrani Tours has tours that include Hadrian's Villa. For Viterbo, authorized guides are available through the APT office.

🎫 Fees & Schedules **American Express** ☎ 06/67641. **Appian Line** ☎ 06/487861. **Carrani Tours** ☎06/4742501. **CIT** ☎06/478641. **Viterbo APT** ✉Piazza San Carluccio ☎0761/304795.

VISITOR INFORMATION

🚹 Tourist Information **Cerveteri** ⊠ Piazza Risorgimento 19 ☎ 06/99551971. **Palestrina** ⊠ Piazza Santa Maria degli Angeli ☎ 06/9573176. **Subiaco** ⊠ Via Cadorna 59 ☎ 0774/822013. **Tarquinia** ⊠ Piazza Cavour 1 ☎ 0766/856384 ⊕ www.tarquinia.net. **Tivoli** ⊠ Largo Garibaldi ☎ 0774/334522. **Tuscania** ⊠ Via del Comune 1 ☎ 0761/436371. **Viterbo** ⊠ Piazza Verdi 4/a ☎ 0761/226666.

12

Naples & Campania

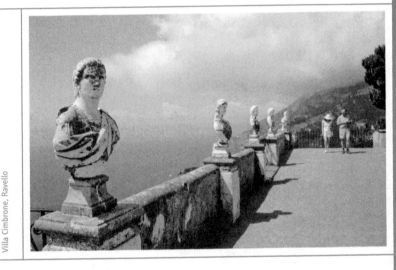

Villa Cimbrone, Ravello

WORD OF MOUTH

"Pompeii was everything I expected and more. I swear I could feel the spirits of the people going about their daily tasks, visiting the bar, the bakery, the spa, whisking down the street, being mindful to stay on the sidewalk and not step in the 'gutter.'"

—artstuff

"Napoli is a lively, vibrant and chaotic town. In short, it swings."

—ira

www.fodors.com/forums

WELCOME TO NAPLES & CAMPANIA

At Caserta, the Bourbons built a 1,200-room palace to rival Versailles.

The name Phlegrean Fields—*Campi Flegrei* in Italian, meaning the "fields of fire"—comes from the fact that the whole area floats on a mass of molten lava. The smoldering region helped define the Greek and Roman concept of the Underworld.

Naples, Italy's third-largest city, is densely packed with people, cafés, pizzerias, and an amazing number of Norman and baroque churches.

At Herculaneum and Pompeii you can see how ancient Romans defined the good life—until, one day in A.D. 79, Mt. Vesuvius covered the cities in volcanic ash.

The rocky island of Capri mixes natural beauty and *dolce vita* glamour. Procida and Ischia are Capri's more laid back sister islands.

A trip around the Sorrento peninsula takes you to the resort towns of **Sorrento, Positano, Ravello,** and **Amalfi.** The road between them is one of Italy's most gorgeous (and demanding) drives.

The city of Paestum contains remarkably well-preserved temples from the days of ancient Greek colonies in Italy.

Sorrento

Mare Tirreno

Getting Oriented

The Golfo di Napoli (Bay of Naples) holds most of Campania's attractions, including Italy's most famous resort towns, its greatest archaeological sites, and the city of Naples itself. Farther south are Greek ruins and the main draw inland is a monumental Bourbon palace.

Street, Pompeii

TOP 5
Reasons to Go

1. **Walking the streets of Naples:** Its energy, chaos, and bursts of beauty make Naples the most operatic of Italian cities.

2. **Exploring Pompeii:** The excavated ruins of Pompeii are a unique and occasionally spooky glimpse into everyday life—and sudden death—in Roman times.

3. **Ravello:** High above the Amalfi coast, two spectacular villas compete for the title of most beautiful spot in southern Italy.

4. **The gardens of the Reggia di Caserta:** The Reggia (royal palace) in Caserta was the Bourbon monarchs' attempt to outdo Versailles. With the splendid gardens, covering 296 acres, they almost succeeded.

5. **Fresh buffalo-milk mozzarella:** One of the region's unique culinary experiences, the softball-sized white cheese is served without unnecessary garnish (other than perhaps a slice of tomato and a sprig of basil) in practically any of Campania's restaurants.

PUGLIA

A16

BASILICATA

Polla

Teggiano

A3

18

| 0 | | 20 mi |
| 0 | | 20 km |

Plaster Cast, Pompeii   Royal Palace, Naples

NAPLES & CAMPANIA PLANNER

Making the Most of Your Time

In Campania, there are three primary travel experiences: Naples, with its restless exuberance; the resorts (Capri, Sorrento, the Amalfi Coast), dedicated to leisure and indulgence; and the archaeological sights (Pompeii, Herculaneum, Paestum), where the ancient world is frozen in time. Each is wonderful in its own way. If you have a week, you can get a good taste of all three, but with less time, you're better off choosing between them rather than stretching yourself thin.

Pompeii is the simplest to plan for: it's a day trip. You can easily spend the full day there, but moving at a fast clip you can see the highlights and head on to Herculaneum (if you're into archaeology) or back to your home base (if you're not). To get a feel for Naples, you should give it a couple of days at a minimum. The train station makes a harsh first impression, but the city grows on you as you take in the sights and interact with the locals.

That said, many people bypass Naples and head right for the resorts. More than anywhere else in Campania, you're rewarded here for slowing down and taking your time. These places are all about relaxing—you'll miss the point if you're in a rush. Sorrento isn't as spectacular as Positano or Capri, but it's a good base because of its central location.

Getting Around

You can get along fine without a car in Campania, and there are plenty of reasons not to have one: traffic in Naples is even worse than in Rome; you can't bring a car to Capri or Ischia (except in winter, when everything's closed); and parking in the towns of the Amalfi Coast is hard to come by.

The efficient (though slightly rundown) Circumvesuviana train travels around the bay from Naples to Sorrento, with stops at Pompeii and Herculaneum. Ferries and hydrofoils connect Naples with the islands and Sorrento, and there's ferry service between the islands, Sorrento, and the Amalfi Coast.

The SITA public bus system's Blue Line makes hourly runs along the spectacular coast road between Sorrento and Positano. It's inexpensive and efficient, and you're spared a white-knuckle driving experience. Aim for a seat on the side of the bus facing the water. For more about transportation throughout the region, see "Essentials" at the end of this chapter.

Pompeii Prep

Pompeii is impressive under any circumstances, but it comes alive if you do some preparation before your visit:

■ First, read up—there are piles of good books on the subject, including these engaging, jargon-free histories: *Pompeii: The Day a City Died* by Robert Etienne, *Pompeii: Public and Private Life* by Paul Zanker, and *The Lost World of Pompeii* by Colin Amery. For accurate historical information woven into the pages of a thriller, pick up *Pompeii: A Novel* by Robert Harris.

■ Second, be sure to visit the Museo Archeologico Nazionale in Naples. Most of the finest art from Pompeii now resides in the museum.

Safety Tips

Don't let fear of crime keep you away from Naples, but, just as in other large Italian cities, take common-sense precautions—look under "Safety" in the Smart Travel Tips section at the front of this book for pointers. The main risks in Naples are car break-ins, bag-snatching, pick-pocketing, and fraud. Give twosomes on scooters a wide berth—this is a favored method of bag-snatchers. Never make major purchases, such as digital cameras, from unlicensed dealers as goods can be artfully switched with worthless packages right under your nose. And be particularly vigilant around the central station area of Piazza Garibaldi.

Testing the Waters

Beaches here can be disappointing—most are patches of coarse sand. That doesn't mean you shouldn't pack your swim suit, but leave any Caribbean-inspired expectations behind. The area around Positano has the best beach options: Spaggia Grande (the main beach) is pleasant; a little further west, Spaggia di Fornillo gets better; and you can go by boat to the remote Spaggia di Laurito for a leisurely day of swimming and lunching on seafood. On Ischia, there's a half-mile stretch of fine sand at Ischia Ponte, and on Capri you can take a dip in the waters around the famous Faraglioni rock formation. You may not be won over by the sand, but the water itself is spectacular, with infinite varieties of blue shimmering in the sun, turning transparent in the coves.

Choosing a Place to Stay

Most parts of Campania have accommodations in all price categories, but they tend to fill up in high season, so reserve well in advance. High-season rates apply at all coastal resorts from April to September. In summer, hotels on the coast that serve meals almost always require you to take half board.

Dining & Lodging Price Categories

WHAT IT COSTS in Euros					
	$$$$	**$$$**	**$$**	**$**	**¢**
Restaurants	over €22	€16–f22	€11–€16	€7–€11	under €7
Hotels	over €220	€160–€220	€110–€160	€70–€110	under €70

Restaurant prices are for a second course (un secondo). Hotel prices are for two people in a standard double room in high season, including tax and service.

How's the Weather?

Campania is not at its best in summer, when Naples swelters and Vesuvius is obscured by haze. Optimum times are May–June and September–October. Visiting in winter can be an appealing choice–the temperature remains comfortable and rain is relatively rare. Be aware, though, that while a few hotels and restaurants in Sorrento and along the Amalfi Coast are open year-round, the islands of the bay shut down from November to March.

Amalfi Coast

TOP PASSEGGIATA

Chic Neapolitans take their evening stroll on and around Piazza dei Martiri, stopping at the boutiques, bookstores, and antiques shops of the neighboring streets, particularly the stretch between Via Carlo Poerio and Via dei Mille.

13

Updated by
Chris Rose

CAMPANIA IS A REGION OF EVOCATIVE NAMES—Capri, Sorrento, Pompeii, Herculaneum—that conjure up visions of cliff-shaded coves, sun-dappled waters, and mighty ruins. The area's unique geology has created a gorgeous landscape: a languid coastline stretching out along a deep blue sea, punctuated by islands. Heading inland, the hills at first roll gently, before suddenly transforming into mountains. Dense olive groves line the southern Cilento peninsula; vineyards flourish near Benevento and Avellino; and, spreading north toward Caserta and Rome, are the mozzarella and tomato producing plains.

Through the ages, the area's temperate climate, warm sea, fertile soil, and natural beauty have attracted Greek colonists, then Roman tourists—who gave the region the Campania Felix ("the happy land")—and later Saracen raiders and Spanish invaders. The result has been a rich and varied history, reflected in everything from architecture to mythology. The highlights span millennia: the near-intact Roman towns of Pompeii and Herculaneum, the amphitheaters of Pozzuoli and Capua, the Greek temples in Paestum and Cuma, the Norman and baroque churches in Naples, the white-dome fisherman's houses on the island of Procida. In the realm of myth, Cuma was home to the fortune-telling Sibyl, Herculaneum was built by Hercules, and Lake Averno was the gateway to the underworld.

Campania's complex identity is most intensely felt in its major city, Naples. It sprawls around its bay as though attempting to embrace the island of Capri, while behind it Mount Vesuvius glowers. Naples is lush, chaotic, scary, funny, confounding, intoxicating, and very beautiful. Few who visit remain ambivalent. You needn't participate in the mad whirl of the city, however. The best pastime in Campania is simply finding a spot with a stunning view and indulging in *"la dolce far niente"* ("the sweetness of doing nothing").

NAPLES

Before its decline after Italy's unification in 1860, Naples was a city that rivaled Paris as a brilliant and refined cultural capital, the ultimate destination for northern European travelers on their Grand Tour. A decade of farsighted city administration and a massive injection of European Union funds have kick-started the city back on course, though it is still a difficult place for the casual visitor to take a quick liking to: noise and air pollution levels are uncomfortably high, and unemployment protest marches and industrial disputes frequently disrupt public transportation and may even result in the temporary closure of major tourist attractions. Armed with the right attitude—"be prepared for the worst but hope for the best"—you will find that Napoli does not disappoint. Among other things, it's one of Italy's top *città d'arte,* with world-class museums and a staggering number of fine churches. The most important finds from Pompeii and Herculaneum are on display at the Museo Archeologico Nazionale—a cornucopia of sculpture, frescoes, and mosaics—and seeing them will add to the pleasure of trips to the ancient ruins. And Naples has a wonderful location: thanks to the backdrop of

CAMPANIA THROUGH THE AGES

Ancient History. Lying on Mediterranean trade routes plied by several pre-Hellenic civilizations, Campania was systematically settled by the ancient Greeks from approximately 800 BC onward. Here myth and legend blend confusingly with historical fact: the town of Herculaneum is said—rather improbably—to have been established by Hercules himself, and Naples in ancient times was called Parthenope, the name attributed to one of the Sirens who preyed on hapless sailors in antiquity. Thanks to archaeological research, some of the layers of myth have been stripped away to reveal an extensive pattern of occupation and settlement well before Rome became established. Greek civilization flourished for hundreds of years all along this coastline, but there was nothing in the way of centralized government until centuries later when the Roman Republic, uniting all Italy for the first time, absorbed the Greek colonies with little opposition. Generally, the peace of Campania was undisturbed during these centuries of Roman rule.

Foreign Influences. Naples and Campania, with the rest of Italy, decayed with the Roman Empire and collapsed into the abyss of the Middle Ages. Naples itself regained some importance under the rule of the Angevins in the latter part of the 13th century and continued its progress in the 1440s under Aragonese rule. The nobles who served under the Spanish viceroys in the 16th and 17th centuries enjoyed their pleasures, even as Spain milked the area with its taxes. After a short-lived Austrian occupation, Naples became the capital of the Kingdom of the Two Sicilies, which the Bourbon kings established in 1738. Their rule was generally benevolent as far as Campania was concerned, and their support of papal authority in Rome was an important factor in the development of the rest of Italy. Their rule was important artistically, too, for not only did it contribute greatly to the architectural beauty of the region, but it attracted great musicians, artists, and writers only too willing to enjoy the easy life at court. Finally, Giuseppe Garibaldi launched his famous expedition, and in 1860 Naples was united with the rest of Italy.

Modern Times. Things were relatively tranquil through the years that followed—with visitors thronging to Capri, to Sorrento, to Amalfi, and, of course, to Naples—until World War II. Allied bombings did considerable damage in Naples and the bay area. At the fall of the fascist government the sorely tried Neapolitans rose up against Nazi occupation troops and in four days of street fighting drove them out of the city. The war ended. Artists, tourists, writers, and other lovers of beauty began to flow again into the Campania region. As the years have gone by, some parts gained increased attention from knowing visitors, while others lost the cachet they once had. Though years of misgovernment have left an indelible mark, the tide appears to be turning: the region's immense cultural and natural heritage is finally being revalued as local authorities and inhabitants alike appreciate the importance of nurturing the area's largest industry—tourism.

Naples

Golfo di Napoli

KEY
Funicular
M Metro stop

0   300 yards
0   300 meters

Vesuvius and the islands in the bay, it's one of those few cities in the world that are instantly recognizable.

In Naples you need a good sense of humor and a firm grip on your pocketbook and camera. Expect to do a lot of walking (take care crossing the chaotic streets); buses are crowded, and taxis often get held up in traffic. Use the funiculars or the new metro (Line 1) to get up and down the hills, and take the quick—but erratic—metro Line 2 (the city's older subway system) when crossing the city between Piazza Garibaldi and Pozzuoli. For Pompeii, Herculaneum, and Sorrento, take the private Circumvesuviana Line, and the Cumana line from Piazza Montesanto takes in Pozzuoli and leads toward Baia and Cumae. The *artecard* allows you to combine public transport and entry to major museums: a three-day card (€25) includes free entry to two museums or archaeological sites, a 50% discount on other attractions, and free transport throughout the museum area—including return trips on fast craft across the bay from Pozzuoli as far afield as Salerno; a seven-day card (€28) gives free entry to all sights covered by the program but doesn't include a travel pass. You can purchase the artecard and find out more information on the sights covered at the airport stand (outside customs), at the train station at Piazza Garibaldi, and at the Web site ⊕ www.campaniartecard.it.

Royal Naples

Naples hasn't been a capital for more than 150 years, but it still prides itself on its royal heritage. Most of the modern center of the town owes its look and feel to various members of the Bourbon family, who built their palaces and castles in this area. Allow plenty of time for the museum visits, especially the Palazzo Reale and the Castel dell'Ovo. The views from the latter over the bay are good at any time, but are especially fine at sunset.

The Main Attractions

❹ **Castel dell'Ovo.** Dangling over the Porto Santa Lucia on a thin promontory, this 12th-century fortress built over the ruins of an ancient Roman villa overlooks the whole harbor—proof, if you need it, that the Romans knew a premium location when they saw one. For the same reason, some of the city's top hotels share the site. It's a peaceful spot for strolling and enjoying the views. ⊠ *Santa Lucia waterfront, Via Partenope, Santa Lucia* ☎ *081/2400055* 🎫 *Free* ⊗ *Mon.–Sat. 8.30–5, Sun. 8.30–2.*

❶ **Castel Nuovo.** Also known as the Maschio Angioino, this massive fortress was built by the Angevins (related to the French monarchy) in the 13th century and completely rebuilt by the Aragonese rulers (descendants of an illegitimate branch of Spain's ruling line) who succeeded them. The decorative marble triumphal arch that forms the entrance was erected during the Renaissance in honor of King Alfonso V of Aragon (1396–1458), and its rich bas-reliefs are credited to Francesco Laurana (circa 1430–1502). Set incongruously into the castle's heavy stone walls, the arch is one of the finest of its kind. Within the castle you can see sculptures and frescoes from the 14th and 15th centuries, as well as the city's **Museo Civico**, comprising mainly local artwork from the 15th to

19th centuries. It's hard to avoid the impression that these last were rejects from the much finer collection at the Museo di Capodimonte, though there are also regular exhibitions worth visiting. You can also visit the Palatine Chapel and the octagonal **Sala dei Baroni,** where Ferrante I disposed of a group of rebellious barons in 1485 by inviting them to a mock wedding party and then pouring boiling oil on their heads from the ceiling. The room is still regularly used for city council meetings. In the left corner of the courtyard is the **Sala dell'Armeria,** the Armory, where part of the flooring has been conveniently glassed over to reveal the remains of a Roman villa and a medieval necropolis. ⊠ *Piazza Municipio* ☎ *081/7955877* 🎫 *€5.* ⊗ *Mon.–Sat. 9–7, ticket office closes at 6; Sun. courtyard only 9–1.*

> **WORD OF MOUTH**
>
> "We spent three days in Naples and had a wonderful time. We visited the Archaeology Museum, the Palace, and wandered through Spaccanapoli and other neighborhoods. Also hired a cab to take us up to Lago d'Averno. No bad experiences to report. Very glad I got over my Fear-of-Naples syndrome." –Pausanias

❸ Palazzo Reale. Dominating Piazza del Plebiscito, the huge palace—best described as overblown imperial—dates from the early 1600s. It was renovated and redecorated by successive rulers, including Napoléon's sister Caroline and her ill-fated husband, Joachim Murat (1767–1815), who reigned briefly in Naples after the French emperor had sent the Bourbons packing and before they returned to reclaim their kingdom. Don't miss seeing the **royal apartments,** sumptuously furnished and full of precious paintings, tapestries, porcelains, and other objets d'art. The monumental marble staircase gives you an idea of the scale on which Neapolitan rulers lived. ⊠ *Piazza del Plebiscito* ☎ *081/400547* 🎫 *€4* ⊗ *Thurs.–Tues. 9–7:30.*

need a break?

Catercorner to the Palazzo Reale is the most famous coffeehouse in town, the **Caffè Gambrinus** (⊠ Piazza Trieste e Trento, near Piazza Plebiscito ☎ 081/417582). Founded in 1850, this 19th-century jewel functioned as a brilliant intellectual salon in its heyday but has fallen into a Sunset Boulevard–type existence, relying on past glamour, at the mercy of tourists and their pitiless cameras, and with often indifferent service. But the opening of some of its long-closed inside rooms with amazing mirrored walls and gilded ceilings makes this an essential stop for any visitor to the city.

Piazza del Plebiscito. The vast square next to the Palazzo Reale was laid out by order of Murat, whose architect was clearly inspired by the colonnades of St. Peter's in Rome. The large church of **San Francesco di Paola** in the middle of the colonnades was added as an offering of thanks for the Bourbon restoration by Ferdinand I, whose titles reflect the somewhat garbled history of the Kingdom of the Two Sicilies, which was made up of Naples (which included most of the southern Italian mainland) and Sicily. They were united in the Middle Ages, then separated, then unofficially reunited under Spanish domination during the

16th and 17th centuries. In 1816, with Napoléon out of the way on St. Helena, Ferdinand IV (1751–1825) of Naples, who also happened to be Ferdinand III of Sicily, officially merged the two kingdoms, proclaiming himself Ferdinand I of the Kingdom of Two Sicilies. His reactionary and repressive rule earned him a few more colorful titles among his rebellious subjects.

Via Toledo. Sooner or later you'll wind up at one of the busiest commercial arteries, also known as Via Roma, which has thankfully been closed to through traffic—at least along the stretch leading from the Palazzo Reale. Don't avoid dipping into this parade of shops and coffee bars where plump pastries are temptingly arranged.

Also Worth Seeing

Quartieri Spagnoli. The garrison for Spanish troops in the 17th century has become one of Naples most densely inhabited neighbourhoods. A tight grid of decaying tenements lining incredibly narrow alleys, the *Quartieri* lie between Via Toledo (downhill border) and Via Pasquale Scura (western leg of Spaccanapoli). The area is hectic, sometimes dangerous, and chock-full of local color. A five-minute walk west of Piazza Municipio, accessible from Via Toledo.

❷ Teatro San Carlo. This large theater was built in 1737, 40 years earlier than Milan's La Scala—though it was destroyed by fire and had to be rebuilt in 1816. You can visit the impressive interior, decorated in the white-and-gilt stucco of the neoclassical era, as part of a prearranged tour, and visitors are sometimes allowed in during morning rehearsals. ⊠ *Via San Carlo between Piazza Municipio and Piazza Plebiscito, Piazza Plebiscito* ☎ *081/7972331 or 081/7972412* ⊕ *www.teatrosancarlo. it* ⊠ *€5* ⊗ *Tours by appointment.*

> **need a break?** Across from the Teatro San Carlo towers the imposing entrance to the glass-roof neoclassical **Galleria Umberto** (⊠ Via San Carlo, near Piazza Plebiscito), a late-19th-century shopping arcade where you can sit at one of several cafés and watch the vivacious Neapolitans as they go about their business.

Vomero

Heart-stopping views of the Bay of Naples are framed by this gentrified neighborhood on a hill served by the Montesanto, Centrale, and Chiaia funiculars. Stops for all three are an easy walk from Piazza Vanvitelli, a good starting point for exploring this thriving district with no shortage of smart bars and trattorias.

The Main Attractions

★ **❻ Certosa di San Martino.** A Carthusian monastery restored in the 17th century in exuberant Neapolitan baroque style, this structure has now been transformed into a diverse museum. The gorgeous Chiostro Grande (great cloister) and the panoramic garden terraces—strangely quiet, with a view of the city sprawling below—are among the most impressive spots in the city. Popular exhibits include an anonymous painting

VOICES OF ITALY

Imma Marsella
architect, Naples

Imma Marsella is passionate about the buildings, art, landscape, and history of her native Naples. She's turned that passion into a career, overseeing restoration projects for the city architect's office. One afternoon she takes time out from work (restoring a 2,000-year-old Roman tunnel that runs under the Posillipo hill) to identify what she considers the most important buildings of Naples and the surrounding area. It's a question that sends her darting about her office, grabbing books from overburdened shelves; her reply is filled with tangents, as she recalls one fascinating building after another.

Fitting In. The best buildings, she feels, harmonize with the landscape. "A great starting point is the Castel del'Ovo, one of the city's oldest buildings, on the Borgo Marinaro. It looks like part of the island itself, rising up out of the sea. If you walk around the various levels of terraces, at each turn there's a new and unexpected view of the city and the bay. From there you can see the Castel Sant'Elmo up on the hill. It's made from tufa stone quarried from the hill it stands on. It was originally built in the 1200s but has been modified many times, like many buildings in this city where space is such a problem." The castle is connected to the San Martino monastery, another essential stop. "From its perch on the edge of the hill you get a series of views right around the bay."

Many of the finest buildings in the area date from the 18th century. "It was one of the largest and most important cities in Europe at the time. If the Bourbon royal family wanted a new Versailles, they got it!" The "new Versailles" was the Reggia palace in Caserta. "The gardens in particular are worth seeing. They're laid along a long avenue with an infinite vanishing point."

Imma mentions that Neapolitan buildings often have an interesting anthropological element to them. "In the San Gaudioso catacombs, for example, a cult of the dead grew up around the former cemetery. The majolica tiles in the cloister of Santa Chiara portray scenes of everyday life, so it's not just a beautiful space, but a historical record. The church of San Lorenzo encapsulates its own history—if you go underneath it you can see the remains of an old Roman street, then the church uses the Roman columns in its own construction."

Minimal Modernism. Imma laments the lack of great modern architecture in the city, but says a walk up Via Parco Margherita is worth making to see its art deco, or "Liberty style," palazzos. "At the top stands a building by the eccentric Scottish architect Lamont Young. He landed in Naples at the end of the 19th century and left behind fake castles, Renaissance palaces, and Swiss chalets." For a fine example of modernism, the Mostra d'Oltremare exhibition center in Fuorigrotta, with its Arena Flegrea, is a must—"though perhaps only for real enthusiasts," Imma concedes. "Otherwise, if you visit Capri, the Villa Malaparte is a great example of how modernism fits in with the landscape, the way the building stretches across the rocks, both part of it and different. Much like the Castel dell'Ovo—exactly where we started!"

13

that depicts the Naples waterfront in the 15th century and the return of the Aragonese fleet from the Battle of Ischia and the *presepi* (Christmas crèches). Take the funicular from Piazza Montesanto to Vomero. ⊠ *Museo Nazionale di San Martino, Vomero* ☎ *081/5585942* 🖃 *€6, includes admission to Castel Sant'Elmo* ☉ *Tues.–Thurs. 8:30–7.*

❺ Castel Sant'Elmo. Perched on the Vomero, this castle was built by the Angevins in the 14th century to dominate the port and the old city and remodeled by the Spanish in 1537. The stout fortifications are still in use today by the military, and occasionally there are performances, exhibitions, and fairs. ⊠ *Largo San Martino, Vomero* ☎ *081/5784030* 🖃 *€3* ☉ *Thurs.–Tues. 8:30–7:30.*

Spaccanapoli & Capodimonte

Nowhere embodies the spirit Naples better than the arrow-straight street informally known as Spaccanapoli (literally, "split Naples"). Gazing down it, you can sense where the name comes from—the street resembles a trench, running from the central station (where the old city walls stood) up to the San Martino hill, retracing one of the main arteries of the ancient Greek, and later Roman, settlements. At its western end, Spaccanapoli is officially named Via Benedetto Croce, in honor of the illustrious philosopher born there in 1866, in the building at No. 12. As it runs its course, the street name changes to Via San Biagio dei Librai and then Via San Gregorio Armeno. No matter the name, it's a place of vibrant street culture.

Capodimonte, to the north, was open countryside until the Bourbon kings built a hunting lodge there, after which it rapidly became part of the city proper. Between the two neighborhoods is the Museo Archeologico, Naples's finest museum. It's best to visit shortly after lunchtime, when the crowds have thinned out. Two hours will be just enough to get your bearings and cover the more important collections. The museum in Capodimonte—unlike many of the churches and the archaeological museum—is well lighted and can be viewed in fading daylight, so it's best left until last.

WALKING SPACCANAPOLI

V ibrant, chaotic Spaccanapoli is the essence of Naples. A walk along it takes you past peeling palaces, artisans' workshops, many churches and street shrines, stores of all sorts, bars, and people young and old. Start at **Piazza Gesù Nuovo,** the area's largest square. (At this point Spaccanapoli goes by the name Via Benedetto Croce.) The forbidding exterior of the church of **Gesù Nuovo ❼** dominates the piazza. For a complete contrast, cross the road and enter the church of **Santa Chiara ❽**. Originally built by Robert of Anjou in

the early 1300s and reconstructed after a direct hit from a bomb in 1943, the church is light, airy, and spacious. Look for the traces of Giotto frescoes behind the altar. A side entrance to the church leads into its delightful vine-laden cloister decorated with hundreds of hand-painted majolica tiles, an unexpected outbreak of peace in noisy Naples.

Back out on Spaccanapoli, heading east you cross **Via San Sebastiano,** a street filled with music shops frequented by students from the nearby conservatory; it can be a veritable symphony on the mornings. **Palazzo**

The Main Attractions

9 Cappella Sansevero. Off Spaccanapoli, the Cappella di Santa Maria della Pietà dei Sangro, better known as the Cappella Sansevero, holds the tombs of the noble Sangro di San Severo family. Much of it was designed in the 18th century by Giuseppe Sammartino, including the centerpiece, a striking *Veiled Christ* carved from a single block of alabaster. If you can stomach it, take a peek in the crypt, where some of the anatomical experiments conducted by Prince Raimondo, a scion of the family and noted 18th-century alchemist, are gruesomely displayed. ⊠ *Via de Sanctis 19, Spaccanapoli* ☎ *081/5518470* ⊕ *www.museosansevero.it* 🎫 *€5* ☉ *Oct.–Apr., Mon. and Wed.–Sat. 10–5:40, Sun. 10–1; May–Sept., Mon. and Wed.–Sat. 10–6:40, Sun. 10–1.*

11 Duomo. Though the Duomo was established in the 1200s, the building you see was erected a century later and has since undergone radical changes, especially during the baroque age. Inside the cathedral 110 ancient columns salvaged from pagan buildings are set into the piers that support the 350-year-old wooden ceiling. Off the left aisle you step down into the 4th-century church of **Santa Restituta,** which was incorporated into the cathedral; though Santa Restituta was redecorated in the late 1600s in the prevalent baroque style, a few very old mosaics remain in the **Battistero** (Baptistery). The chapel also gives access to an archaeological zone, a series of paleochristian rooms dating from the Roman era.

On the right aisle of the cathedral, in the **Cappella di San Gennaro,** are multicolor marbles and frescoes honoring St. Januarius, miracle-working patron saint of Naples, whose altar and relics are encased in silver. Three times a year—on September 19 (his feast day); on the Saturday preceding the first Sunday in May, which commemorates the transference of his relics to Naples; and on December 16—his dried blood, contained in two sealed vials, is believed to liquefy during rites in his honor. On these days large numbers of devout Neapolitans offer up prayers in his memory. The **Museo del tesoro di San Gennaro** houses a rich collection of treasures associated with the saint. Paintings by Solimena and Luca Giordano hang alongside statues, busts, candelabras, and tabernacles in gold, silver, and marble by Cosimo Fanzago and other 18th-

13

Filomarino, former home of philosopher Benedetto Croce and now the site of his library, is on the left as you continue. Next on your right is architect Cosimo Fanzago's **Palazzo Carafa della Spina;** coachmen once used the mouths of the gargoyles at the entrance to tamp out their torches.

Continuing on, **Piazza San Domenico Maggiore** opens up to your left. The rear of the church of San Domenico Maggiore, the Palazzo Corigliano (today part of the university), and a spire contribute to one of Naples's most charming urban set pieces. Various cafés (includ-

ing Scaturchio, one of Naples's most celebrated *pasticcerie*) give the square the feel of an open-air living room. Heading up the right-hand side of the piazza, swing right onto Via Francesco de Sanctis, where you find and the fascinating **Cappella Sansevero 9**, the tomb-chapel of the Sangro di San Severo family. Return to Spaccanapoli on Via Nilo, to the east of the chapel; where the two streets intersect you pass a statue of the Egyptian river god Nile reclining on a pedestal. (A few steps beyond, Spaccanapoli's street name changes to Via San Biagio dei Librai.) A little further century baroque masters. A guided visit is included in the ticket price. ✉ *Via Duomo 147, Spaccanapoli* ☎ *081/449097 or 081/294980* 💶 *Duomo and Cappella di San Gennaro free, Battistero and archaeological zone €3, museum €5.50* ⏱ *Duomo and Cappella di San Gennaro daily 8–12:30 and 4:30–7; Battistero and archaeological zone Mon.–Sat. 9–noon and 4:30–6:30, Sun. 9–noon; museum daily 9–5.*

7 Gesù Nuovo. The oddly faceted stone facade of the church was designed as part of a palace dating from between 1584 and 1601, but plans were changed as construction progressed, and it became the front of an elaborately decorated baroque church. Be sure not to miss the votive chapel dedicated to San Ciro (Saint Cyrus) in the far left corner of the church. Here hundreds of tiny silver ex-voto images have been hung on the walls to give thanks to the saint for his assistance in medical matters. You can buy ex-votos at any of the jewelers that line the street outside. ✉ *Piazza Gesù Nuovo, Spaccanapoli* ☎ *081/5518613* ⏱ *Mon.–Sun. 7–12:30 and 4:15–7:30.*

14 Museo Archeologico Nazionale. The National Archaeological Museum's huge red building, a cavalry barracks in the 16th century, is undergoing a massive restoration program that will include new galleries, a cafeteria, and a direct entrance from the Museo metro station. At any given time you may find several rooms closed to the public as the restoration progresses.

Fodor'sChoice ★

The museum holds one of the world's great collections of Greek and Roman antiquities, including such extraordinary sculptures as the *Hercules Farnese,* an exquisite Aphrodite attributed to the 4th-century BC Greek sculptor Praxiteles, and an equestrian statue of Roman emperor Nerva. Vividly colored mosaics and countless artistic and household objects from Pompeii and Herculaneum provide insight into the life and art of ancient Rome. For a free guided tour of the limited-access Gabinetto Segreto and its collection of erotic art, ask for information at the ticket office. Invest in an up-to-date printed museum guide or audio guide, because exhibits tend to be poorly labeled. ✉ *Piazza Museo 19, Spaccanapoli* ☎ *081/440166* ⊕ *www.archeona.arti.beniculturali.it* 💶 *€6.50* ⏱ *Wed.–Mon. 9–7.30.*

along is **Via San Gregorio Armeno,** a narrow street bridged by a tower linking two sections of a closed monastery. The street is filled with stalls selling the tiny *presepe* figures Neapolitans use to make nativity scenes at Christmas. Take San Gregorio Armeno north; turning right at Via Tribunali brings you to **San Lorenzo Maggiore** ⑩, whose 18th-century facade hides a Gothic-era nave and—surprise—one of the most interesting archaeological sites in the city, showing the streets of ancient Naples as they were 2,000 years ago. Continue along Via Tribunali, crossing Via Duomo (note the

Duomo ⑪ just to the left) as far as **Pio Monte della Misericordia** ⑫, whose church contains one of the greatest 17th-century altarpieces in Europe, Caravaggio's *Seven Acts of Mercy.*

Head back west along Via Tribunali, stopping to note the curious brass skulls outside the church of **Purgatorio ad Arco** on your right—touch them to bring good luck. At the end of Via Tribunali, turn right into **Piazza Bellini** and stop for a drink at one of the leafy square's many cafés. By now, you'll have earned it.

13

> **need a break?**

Timpani e Tempura (⊠ Vico della Quercia 17, Spaccanapoli ☏ 081/5512280) is a tiny shrine to local culinary culture. There are no tables; instead you perch yourself at the counter, but it's worth squeezing in for the *timballi di maccheroni* (baked pasta cakes) and the unique *mangiamaccheroni* (spaghetti in broth with *caciocavallo* cheese, butter, basil, and pepper). High-quality wines by the glass make this a place for a quick, delicious lunch. You can also buy cheese and salami to take home with you.

★ ⑮ **Museo di Capodimonte.** The grandiose 18th-century neoclassical Bourbon royal palace houses an impressive collection of fine and decorative art. Capodimonte's greatest treasure is the excellent collection of paintings well displayed in the **Galleria Nazionale**, on the palace's first and second floors. Besides the art collection, part of the **royal apartments** still has a complement of beautiful antique furniture, most of it on the splashy scale so dear to the Bourbons, and a staggering collection of porcelain and majolica from the various royal residences. The walls of the apartments are hung with numerous portraits, providing a close-up of the unmistakable Bourbon features, a challenge to any court painter. Most rooms have fairly comprehensive information cards in English, whereas the audio guide is overly selective and somewhat quirky. The main galleries on the first floor are devoted to work from the 13th to 18th century, including many pieces by Dutch and Spanish masters, as well as by the great Italians. On the second floor look out for stunning paintings by Simone Martini (circa 1284–1344), Titian (1488/90–1576), and Caravaggio (1573–1610). The palace is situated in the vast Bosco di Capodimonte (Capodimonte Park), which served as the royal hunting preserve and later as the site of the Capodimonte porcelain works. ⊠ *Via Miano 2, Porta Piccola, Via Capodimonte* ☏ *848/800288 information and bookings for special exhibitions* ⊡ *€7.50, €3.75 after 2 PM* ☉ *Thurs.–Tues. 8:30–7:30, ticket office closes 6:30 PM.*

> ### WORD OF MOUTH
>
> "The Naples Archaeological Museum has an incredible collection of real treasures, but the displays keep changing, and they close wings without notice or seeming reason." —mowmow

★ ⑫ **Pio Monte della Misericordia.** One of the defining landmarks of Spaccanapoli, this octagonal church was built around the corner from the Duomo for a charitable institution founded in 1601 by seven noblemen. The institution's aim was to carry out acts of Christian charity: feeding the hungry, clothing the poor, nursing the sick, sheltering pilgrims, visiting prisoners, ransoming Christian slaves, and burying the indigent dead—acts immortalized in the history of art by the famous altarpiece painted by Caravaggio (1571–1610) depicting the *Sette Opere della Misericordia* (*Seven Acts of Mercy*) and now the celebrated focus of the church. In this haunting work the artist has brought the Virgin, borne atop the shoulders of two angels, right down into the street—and not a rhetorical place, but a real street of Spaccanapoli (scholars have suggested a couple of plausible locations) populated by figures in whose spontaneous and passionate movements the people could see themselves. The original church was considered too small and destroyed in 1655 to make way for a new church, designed by Antonio Picchiatti and built between 1658 and 1678. Pride of place is given to the great Caravaggio above the altar, but there are other important Baroque-era paintings on view here; some hang in the church while others are in the adjoining *pinacoteca* (picture gallery). ⊠ *Via Tribunali 253, Spaccanapoli* ☎ *081/446944* ⊘ *Mon.–Sat. 9–1; pinacoteca, Tues., Thurs., Sat. 8:30–2.*

❽ Santa Chiara. This monastery church is a Neapolitan landmark and the subject of a famous old song. It was built in the 1300s in Provençal Gothic style, and it's best known for the quiet charm of its cloister garden, with columns and benches sheathed in 18th-century ceramic tiles painted with delicate floral motifs and vivid landscapes. An adjoining museum traces the history of the convent; the entrance is off the courtyard at the left of the church. ⊠ *Piazza Gesù Nuovo, Spaccanapoli* ☎ *081/5521597* 🏛 *Museum and cloister €4* ⊘ *Church Apr.–Sept., daily 8:30–noon and 4–7; Oct.–Mar., daily 8:30–noon and 4–6. Museum and cloister Mon.–Sat. 9:30–1 and 2:30–5:30, Sun. 9:30–1.*

> **need a break?** While you're exploring the old part of town, take a break at what the Neapolitans call "the best pastry shop in Italy"—**Scaturchio** (⊠ Piazza S. Domenico Maggiore 19, Spaccanapoli ☎ 081/5516944). The café was founded in 1918 by two brothers, one of whom, Francesco, invented the cakes called *ministeriali* to attract Anna Fouché, a famous actress of the time. You can still buy these cakes today, along with other Neapolitan specialties such as *babà*, *rafioli*, and *pastiera*, which you can eat there with a coffee or have gift-wrapped in the room at the back.

Also Worth Seeing

Napoli Sotteranea. From two different locations, Naples Underground explores the foundations of the city, some of which date back as much as 4,000 years. Forty meters underground, guides will show you ancient aqueducts built by the Greeks and Romans, which later served as a bomb shelter during World War II. The commentary is normally in Italian, though with advance notice an interpreter can be hired. ⊠ *Piazza San Gaetano 68, Spaccanapoli* ⊠ *Vico S. Anna di Palazzo 52, Piazza Plebiscito* ☎ *081/400256* ⊕ *www.napolisotterranea.org* 🏛 *€7* ⊘ *Tours Sat. at 10, noon, and 6, Sun. at 10, 11, noon, and 6, Thurs. at 9 PM; or call to arrange other times. Meet at Piazza Trieste e Trento, by Bar Gambrinus.*

⓭ Quadreria dei Girolamini. Off an improbably quiet cloister enclosing a prolific forest of lemon and loquat trees, the Girolamini art museum is attached to the restored Girolamini church. Its intimate, high-quality collection of 16th- and 17th-century paintings is one of the city's best-kept secrets, well worth a half-hour visit. ⊠ *Via Duomo 142, Spaccanapoli* ☎ *081/294444* 🏛 *Free* ⊘ *Daily 9:30–1.*

❿ San Lorenzo Maggiore. It's unusual to find French Gothic style in Naples, but it has survived to great effect in this church, which was built in the Middle Ages and decorated with 14th-century frescoes. Outside the 17th-century cloister is the entrance to **excavations** revealing what was once part of the Roman forum, and before that the Greek agora. You can walk among the streets, shops, and workshops of the ancient city and see a model of how the Greek Neapolis might have looked. ✉ *Via Tribunali 316, Spaccanapoli* ☎ *081/2110860* ⊕ *www.sanlorenzomaggiorenapoli.it* 🎟 *Excavations €4* ⊘ *Daily 9–1 and 3–6; excavations Mon.–Sat. 10–5, Sun. 10–1:30.*

Where to Stay & Eat

13

$$$–$$$$ ✕ **La Sacrestia.** Neapolitans flock to this upscale patrician villa for the restaurant's location—on the slopes of the Posillipo hill—and high culinary standards. The specialties include tasty antipasti, linguine in *salsa di scorfano* (scorpion-fish sauce), and fettuccine with small squid, black olives, and potatoes. ✉ *Via Orazio 116, Posillipo* ☎ *081/664186* ⌂ *Reservations essential* ▤ *AE, DC, MC, V* ⊘ *Closed Tues. and 2 wks mid-Aug.*

$$–$$$ ✕ **La Bersagliera.** You'll inevitably be drawn to eating at the Santa Lucia waterfront, in the shadow of the looming medieval Castel dell'Ovo. This spot is big and touristy but fun, with an irresistible combination of spaghetti and mandolins. The menu suggests uncomplicated, timeworn classics, such as spaghetti *alla pescatora* (with seafood sauce) and *tagliatelle alla bersagliera* with handmade pasta, cherry tomatoes, tiny octopi, and clams. ✉ *Borgo Marinaro 10, Santa Lucia* ☎ *081/7646016* ▤ *AE, DC, MC, V* ⊘ *Closed Tues. and 2 wks in Jan.*

★ $$–$$$ ✕ **Da Dora.** Despite its location up an unpromising-looking *vicolo* (alley) off the Riviera di Chiaia, this small restaurant has achieved cult status for its seafood platters. It's remarkable what owner-chef Giovanni can produce in his tiny kitchen. Start with the pasta dish *mezzanello*, which is laden with local seafood, and perhaps follow up with *pezzogna* (blue-spotted bream). Like many restaurants on the seafront, Da Dora has its own guitarist, who is often robustly accompanied by the kitchen staff. ✉ *Via Fernando Palasciano 30, Mergellina* ☎ *081/680519* ⌂ *Reservations essential* ▤ *AE, DC, MC, V* ⊘ *Closed Sun. and 2 wks in mid-Aug.*

$$–$$$ ✕ **Mimì alla Ferrovia.** Near the central station, this bustling fish restaurant is as close as you get in Naples to a Parisian brasserie. It's a local institution popular with lawyers from the nearby law courts and local business executives. The service is polite but not obsequious, the atmosphere relaxed but sometimes noisy. Try the *paccheri ai frutti di mare* (flat pasta with seafood), the *rigatoni fiori di zucca e gamberetti* (pasta tubes with zucchini flowers and shrimp), or the filling *pasta e patate con provola* (pasta, potatoes, and smoky provola cheese). ✉ *Via Alfonso D'Aragona 21, Piazza Garibaldi* ☎ *081/5538525* ▤ *AE, DC, MC, V* ⊘ *Closed Sun. and last 2 wks in Aug.*

★ $$–$$$ ✕ **La Stanza del Gusto.** The name means "The Room of Taste," and this restaurant lives up to the billing. A minute's walk from some of the city's busiest streets, up a flight of stairs opposite the Teatro Sannazzaro on Via Chiaia, it feels removed from the hectic world outside. Chef Mario Avallone mixes traditional, but often forgotten, Southern recipes with modern trends—hence the presence of the *tempura di verdura* (Japanese-style fried vegetables) alongside the *bomba savoia* (a savory cake of rice and potatoes). Save room for the delicious sweets. ⊠ *Vicoletto Sant'Arpino 21, Piazza Plebiscito* ☎ *081/401578* ⊟ *AE, DC, MC, V* ⚐ *Reservations essential* ⊘ *Closed Sun. and Mon., and Aug. Lunch by appointment only.*

★ **$$–$$$** ✕ **Vadinchenia.** Though it identifies itself as a cultural and gastronomic association, Vadinchenia has all the trimmings of a high-class restaurant. Husband-and-wife team Saverio and Silvana steer their guests through an innovative menu against a backdrop of refreshingly minimalist decor. Adventurous palates will enjoy such bold combinations as *paccheri alle alici e pecorino* (pasta with sardines and sheep's cheese), and meat eaters will delight in the *filletto al vino e sale grosso* (steak cooked in wine and rock salt). In winter round off the meal with the *purée di castagna* made from local chestnuts. ⊠ *Via Pontano 21, Chiaia* ☎ *081/660265* ⊟ *AE, DC, MC, V* ⚐ *Reservations essential* ⊘ *Closed Sun. and Aug. No lunch.*

$–$$ ✕ **Osteria Castello.** The walls are covered with shelves full of wine bottles, and there are red-check tablecloths with candles on them—it looks like the quintessential Italian restaurant, and it is, with simple dishes at excellent prices and friendly service. Start at the excellent antipasto buffet, followed by the essential *pasta e patate con la provola* (pasta and potatoes with smoked mozzarella—it sounds like carbohydrate overload, but it's actually divine) and then the grilled, flat *pleos* mushrooms. You can sip wine (preferably the local *aglianico* red) or a liqueur and sit for hours talking with friends. ⊠ *Via S. Teresa a Chiaia 38, Chiaia* ☎ *081/400486* ⊟ *AE, DC, MC, V* ⊘ *Closed Sun.*

$–$$ ✕ **Umberto.** Run by the Di Porzio family since 1916, Umberto is one of the city's classic restaurants. It's divided into a simple pizzeria and a more elegant restaurant, both of which offer the class of the Chiaia neighborhood and the friendliness of other parts of the city. Try the *tubettini 'do tre dita* ("three finger maccheroni" with a mixture of seafood), which bears the nickname of the original Umberto. Owner Massimo and sister Lorella (Umberto's grandchildren) are both wine experts and oversee a fantastically well-curated cellar. Umberto is also the only restaurant in the city that caters to those who have a gluten allergy. ⊠ *Via Alabardieri 30–31, Chiaia* ☎ *081/418555* ⊟ *AE, DC, MC, V* ⊘ *Closed Mon.*

¢–$ ✕ **Cantina della Tofa.** Located on one of the narrow alleys that lead off Via Toledo up into the Quartieri Spagnoli, this small, welcoming restaurant serves traditional Neapolitan fare that goes beyond standard pasta with seafood or tomatoes. Try the *vellutata di cicerchie,* a creamy soup made from beans that are a cross between chickpeas and fava beans. The orange-wall dining room has large wooden tables that seem more Tuscan than Campanian. The service is friendly and unhurried. ⊠ *Vico Tofa 71, Piazza Municipio* ☎ *081/406840* ⊟ *No credit cards* ⊘ *Closed Sun.*

¢–$ ✕ **L'Ebbrezza di Noè.** A small bar leads into a larger dining area decorated in the style of a very elegant farmhouse. Owner Luca has an enthusiasm for what he does that is quite moving—as you sip a recommended wine you can sense that he hopes you like it as much as he does. The attention paid to the quality of the wine carries over to the food—here

CLOSE UP

Folk Songs à la Carte

IF YOU WANT TO HEAR *canzoni napoletane*—the fabled Neapolitan folk songs—performed live, you can try to catch the city's top troupes, such as the Cantori di Posillipo and I Virtuosi di San Martino, in performances at venues like the Teatro Trianon. But an easier alternative is to head for one of the city's more traditional restaurants, such as La Bersagliera or Mimì alla Ferrovia, where most every night you can expect your meal to be interrupted by a *posteggiatore*. These singers aren't employed by the restaurants, but they're encouraged to come in, swan around the tables with a battered old guitar, and belt out classics such as "Santa Lucia," "O' Surdat' Innamurate," "Torna a Surriento" (Come Back to Sorrento), and, inevitably, "Funiculi Funiculà."

These songs are the most famous of a vast repertoire that found international fame with the mass exodus of southern Italians to the United States in the early 20th century. "Funiculi Funiculà" was written by Peppino Turco and Luigi Danza in 1880 to herald Naples's new funicular railways. "O Sole Mio," by Giovanni Capurro and Eduardo di Capua, has often been mistakenly taken for the Italian national anthem. "Torna a Surriento" was composed by Ernesto di Curtis in 1903 to help remind the current Italian prime minister how wonderful he thought Sorrento was (and how many government subsidies he had promised the township).

The singers are more than happy to do requests, even inserting the name of your *innamorato* or *innamorata* into the song. When they've finished they'll stand discreetly by your table. Give them a few euros and you'll have friends for life (or at least for the night).

13

---

you can taste delicate *carpaccio di chianina* (thinly sliced Tuscan steak), rare cheeses such as the Sicilian *ragusano di razza modicani,* and the local *caciocavallo podolico.* ⊠ *Vico Vetriera a Chiaia 8b/9, Chiaia* ☎ *081/400104* ⊟ *AE, DC, MC, V* ⊗ *Closed Mon. No lunch.*

¢–$ ✕ **Lombardi.** Lombardi is one of the city's most highly regarded old-style pizzerias. Simple decor and slightly cramped tables are more than compensated for by the excellent pizzas. The location is handy for a quick meal before or after a visit to the archaeological museum. ⊠ *Via Foria 12, near Museo* ☎ *081/456220* ⊟ *AE, DC, MC, V* ⊗ *Closed Mon.*

★ ¢–$ ✕ **Sorbillo.** Don't be put off by the lines—the locals know the wait is worth it. Take their advice and order a basic Neapolitan pizza (try the unique pizza al pesto or the stunningly simple marinara—just tomatoes and oregano). They're cooked to perfection by the third generation of pizza makers who run the place. Don't expect tablecloths: here you have the joy of eating on traditional white-marble tabletops. ⊠ *Via dei Tribunali 32, Spaccanapoli* ☎ *081/446643* ⊟ *AE, DC, MC, V* ⊗ *Closed Sun. (except Dec.), 2 wks in Aug.*

¢–$ ✕ **Vecchia Cantina.** The location is on a rather dark side street in the tattier section of the Spaccanapoli, but this place is well worth seeking out for its combination of old-style Neapolitan hospitality, high-quality food and wine, and excellent prices. It's a family affair, with Gianni out front and his mother, Nunzia, and wife, Maria, busy in the kitchen— much like in a typical Neapolitan household. The decorations are an accumulation of kitsch, and everyone who comes here seems to know everyone else. The pasta *e ceci* (with chickpeas) shouldn't be missed, and *baccalà fritto* (fried salt cod) is a specialty. The wine list includes selections from all over Italy. ⊠ *Via S. Nicola alla Carità 13–14, Spaccanapoli* ☎ *081/5520226* ⌂ *Reservations essential* ▭ *AE, DC, MC, V* ☉ *Closed Tues.*

¢   ✕ **Da Michele.** You have to love a place that has, for more than 130 years,
Fodor'sChoice   offered only two types of pizza—marinara and margherita—and a small
★   selection of drinks, and still manages to attract long lines. The prices have something to do with it, but the pizza itself suffers no rivals, and even those waiting in line are good-humored; the boisterous, joyous atmosphere wafts out with the smell of yeast and wood smoke onto the street. ⊠ *Via C. Sersale 1/3* ☎ *081/5539204* ▭ *No credit cards* ☉ *Closed Sun. and last 2 wks in Aug.*

$$$$ ☐ **Grand Hotel Vesuvio.** You'd never guess from the somewhat dull exterior that this is the oldest of Naples's great seafront hotels—the place where Enrico Caruso died, Oscar Wilde escaped with lover Lord Alfred Douglas, and Bill Clinton charmed the waitresses. Fortunately, the spacious, soothing interior compensates for what's lacking on the outside. Guest rooms are done in luxurious, traditional style with antique accents, vibrantly colored walls, and gleaming bathrooms; many overlooking the bay. You can pamper yourself at the spa, where there are myriad special services. The famous Caruso restaurant sits atop the hotel, affording wonderful views. ⊠ *Via Partenope 45, Santa Lucia, 80121* ☎ *081/ 7640044* ⬚ *081/7644483* ⊕ *www.vesuvio.it* ⬳ *163 rooms, 17 suites* ⌂ *Restaurant, in-room safes, minibars, cable TV, health club, bar, babysitting, meeting room, some pets allowed* ▭ *AE, DC, MC, V* �‖ *BP.*

★ $$$$ ☐ **Parker's.** This landmark hotel has been serving up doses of elegant, oldstyle atmosphere to visiting VIPs since 1870. The gilt-trimmed Empire bureaus, 19th-century paintings, shimmering chandeliers, fluted pilasters, and ornate ceilings all create a splendidly glittering environment. From the hotel's perch midway up the Vomero Hill (and convenient to funicular lines) you get fine views of the bay and Capri; if your room doesn't have one of these vistas, drink it all in from the excellent rooftop restaurant. There's also a day spa providing a full complement of health and beauty treatments. ⊠ *Corso Vittorio Emanuele 135, Chiaia, 80121* ☎ *081/7612474* ⬚ *081/ 663527* ⊕ *www.grandhotelparkers.it* ⬳ *73 rooms, 10 suites* ⌂ *Restaurant, in-room safes, minibars, cable TV, gym, massage, sauna, spa, bar, meeting rooms, parking (fee)* ▭ *AE, DC, MC, V* �‖ *BP.*

$$$–$$$$ ☐ **San Francesco al Monte.** This high-end hotel retains hints of its former life as a Franciscan monastery: the small lobby leads to narrow corridors lined with doors that look dauntingly cell-like, until you enter and find surprisingly spacious, simply decorated rooms, many with their own hot tubs, antique furnishings, majolica-tile floors, and stunning views of the city below and the bay beyond. The hotel's restaurant is equally upscale, its French chef adding a Gallic twist to Italian fare. ⊠ *Corso Vittorio Emanuele 328, 80135* ☎ *081/4239111* ⬚ *081/*

2512485 ⊕ *www.hotelsanfrancesco.it* ⤴ *50 rooms* ⚹ *Restaurant, in-room safes, minibars, cable TV, pool, bar, meeting rooms* ▤ *AE, DC, MC, V* ⧉ *BP.*

$$$ ⊞ **Caravaggio Hotel.** The old town's first luxury hotel, in a 17th-century palazzo on a tiny square behind the Duomo, takes its name from the painter of the amazing *Sette Opere della Misericordia,* which can be seen in the chapel opposite. The entrance hall is atmospherically furnished with blocks of volcanic stone, and the remains of the city's original Greek walls are visible. The guest rooms are all modern—each even has a power shower. Breakfast includes a selection of meats and cheeses from local Campanian farms. ⊠ *Via Riario Sforza 157, Spaccanapoli, 80139* ☎ *081/2110066* 🖷 *081/4421578* ⊕ *www.caravaggiohotel.it* ⤴ *16 rooms* ⚹ *Cable TV, bar, Internet, some pets allowed* ▤ *AE, DC, MC, V* ⧉ *BP.*

$$$ ⊞ **Il Convento.** In a 17th-century palazzo tucked away in the Quartieri Spagnoli, the Convent is conveniently close to Via Toledo. Rooms are small but elegant, with original architectural features such as arched or beamed ceilings. They are decorated in simple, modern Mediterranean style. Two junior suites have private roof gardens. ⊠ *Via Speranzella 137/A, Piazza Municipio, 80132* ☎ *081/403977* 🖷 *081/400332* ⊕ *www. hotelilconvento.it* ⤴ *12 rooms, 2 suites* ⚹ *Minibars, cable TV, bar, Internet* ▤ *AE, DC, MC, V* ⧉ *BP.*

$$$ ⊞ **Costantinopoli 104.** An oasis of what Italians call *stile liberty* (art deco style), this calm and elegant hotel sits in the bustling centro storico near the Museo Archeologico Nazionale. Each room is individually decorated. Ask for a room with a balcony in the warmer months and enjoy your breakfast alfresco, or opt for one of the garden rooms that open out onto the small swimming pool. ⊠ *Via Costantinopli 104, Spaccanapoli, 80139* ☎ *081/5571035* 🖷 *081/5571051* ⊕ *www.costantinopoli104.it* ⤴ *8 rooms* ⚹ *Cable TV, pool, bar, Internet, laundry service, parking* ▤ *AE, DC, MC, V* ⧉ *BP.*

$$$ ⊞ **Palazzo Albardieri.** One of the newest of the city's rapidly expanding list of luxury hotels, Palazzo Alabardieri welcomes guests into a small courtyard just behind the upmarket chic of the Piazza dei Martiri. A spacious marble-floor lobby makes the place feel bigger than it actually is, yet maintains a feeling of discretion and intimacy. The hotel prices itself on its marble bathrooms. ⊠ *Via Alabardieri 38, Chiaia, 80121* ☎ *081/ 415278* ⊕ *www.palazzoalabardieri.it* ⤴ *29 rooms* ⚹ *In-room safes, cable TV, bar, Internet, parking, some pets allowed* ▤ *AE, DC, MC, V* ⧉ *BP.*

$$–$$$ ⊞ **Hotel Toledo.** A centuries-old palazzo has been tastefully transformed into this boutique hotel a two-minute walk up from Via Toledo. Rooms are furnished in a pleasing rustic style, and the leafy rooftop terrace provides a quintessentially Neapolitan backdrop for your breakfast. ⊠ *Via Montecalvario 15, Quartieri Spagnoli, 80134* ☎🖷 *081/406800* ⊕ *www. hoteltoledo.com* ⤴ *18 rooms* ⚹ *Minibars, bar* ▤ *AE, DC, MC, V* ⧉ *BP.*

$$ ⊞ **Chiaja.** A two-minute walk from Piazza Plebiscito takes you to this hotel in a spruced up 18th-century palazzo, part of which was once a brothel. Above the fireplace in the homely entrance hall is a portrait of

13

the marchese Nicola Le Caldano Sasso III, original owner of the building; her granddaughter Mimi now runs the place. Rooms are small but comfortable; any sense of claustrophobia (a hazard with buildings in this old part of town) is offset by the opulent period furnishings. Vouchers for breakfast at nearby Gambrinus café are available. ⊠ *Via Chiaia 216, Chiaia, 80121* ☎ *081/415555* 🖷 *081/422344* ⊕ *www.hotelchiaia.it* 🛏 *27 rooms* ⚭ *Cable TV, minibars, bar, Internet* ▤ *AE, DC, MC, V* ⦿ *EP.*

$$ 🏨 **Neapolis.** Situated on a narrow alley just off the humming Via Tribunali and close to Piazza Bellini, this small hotel looks out over the 13th-century Pietrasanta bell tower. The mix of modern and traditional furnishings, the lovely terra-cotta floors, and data ports in every room make this a good base for exploring Napoli's medieval center. ⊠ *Via Francesco Del Giudice 13, Spaccanapoli 80138* ☎ *081/4420815* 🖷 *081/4420819* ⊕ *www.hotelneapolis.com* 🛏 *19 rooms* ⚭ *Minibars, in-room data ports, bar* ▤ *AE, DC, MC, V* ⦿ *BP.*

$$ 🏨 **Pinto Storey.** This fascinating old pensione overflows with warmth and charm. The simple and airy guest rooms are on the fourth floor of an elegant late-19th-century building off the chic Piazza Amedeo. Rooms here are always in demand, so book early. ⊠ *Via G. Martucci 72, Chiaia, 80121* ☎ *081/681260* 🖷 *081/667536* ⊕ *www.pintostorey.it* 🛏 *16 rooms* ⚭ *Minibars, bar* ▤ *AE, MC, V* ⦿ *EP.*

$ 🏨 **Soggiorno Sansevero.** In the heart of Spaccanapoli, this pensione occupies a floor in the former palace of the princes di Sangro di San Severo. Although Palazzo Sansevero overlooks the opera-set Piazza San Domenico, this tiny lodging is on a quiet inner courtyard. Rooms are simply furnished—linoleum floors, modern beds, great-grandmama's bureau—and may even come with ghosts: Renaissance composer Carlo Gesualdo murdered his wife and her lover on the palace's staircase. ⊠ *Piazza San Domenico 9, Spaccanapoli, 80131* ☎ *081/4201336* 🖷 *081/211698* ⊕ *www.albergosansevero.it* 🛏 *6 rooms, 4 with bath* ▤ *AE, DC, MC, V.*

Nightlife & the Arts

The Arts

Opera is a serious business in Naples—not in terms of the music so much as the costumes, the stage design, the players, and the politics. What's happening on stage can be secondary to the news of who's there, who they're with, and what they're wearing. Given the circumstances, it's hardly surprising that the city's famous San Carlo company doesn't offer a particularly innovative repertoire. Nonetheless, the company is usually of very high quality—and if they're not in form the audience lets them know it. Performances take place in the luxury liner of southern Italian opera houses, the historic **Teatro San Carlo** (⊠ Via San Carlo, Piazza Plebiscito ☎081/7972331 or 081/7972412 ⊕ www.teatrosancarlo.it). The hall still gleams with its mid-19th-century gilded furnishings and thick red-velvet drapes. For the opera and ballet seasons (generally December through June), many seats are presold by subscription, but there are often some available at the box office a few days before the performance. You can also book ahead by calling **Concerteria** (✉ Via Schipa 23, Chiaia ☎ 081/7611221). For an additional fee you can order tickets on the theater Web site.

Nightlife

Bars and clubs are found in many areas around Naples. The sophisticated crowd heads to Posillipo and the Vomero, Via Partenope along the seafront, and the Chiaia area (between Piazza dei Martiri and Via Dei Mille). A more bohemian crowd makes for the centro storico and the area around Piazza Bellini. The scene is relatively relaxed—you might even be able to sit down at a proper table. Keep in mind that clubs, and their clientele, may change rapidly, so do some investigating before you hit the town.

Caffè Intramoenia (✉ Piazza Bellini 70, Spaccanapoli ☎ 081/290720) is the granddaddy of all the bars in Piazza Bellini; it was set up as a bookshop in the late 1980s and still has its own small publishing house with a variety of the attractive titles. Seats in the heated veranda are at a premium in the winter, though many sit outside all year round. **Bere Vino** (✉ 62 Via San Sebastiano, Spaccanapoli ☎ 081/29313) looks like a shop from the outside, but inside you'll find long wooden tables and shelves of wine from all over Italy that are consumed on the premises. Peppery *taralli* biscuits, olives, and selections of cheeses and smoked meats can be used to *apoggiare* ("prop up") whatever you're drinking. Look for recommended wines by the glass on the chalkboard or spend ages perusing the encyclopedic list. **Aret' 'a Palm** (✉ Piazza S. Maria la Nova, Spaccanapoli) is Neapolitan for "behind the palm tree," and that's exactly where you'll find this agreeably dark bar on Piazza Santa Maria La Nova. Its long marble bar and mirrored walls suggest Paris more than Naples.

The **Enoteca Belledonne** (✉ Vico Belledonne a Chiaia 18, Chiaia ☎ 081/403162) is something of an institution among inhabitants of the more upscale Chiaia area. Between 8 and 9 in the evening it seems like the whole neighborhood has descended into the tiny space for an *aperitivo* (cocktail). The small tables and low stools are notably uncomfortable, but the cozy atmosphere and the pleasure of being surrounded by glass-fronted cabinets full of wine bottles with beautiful labels more than makes up for it. Excellent local wines are available by the glass at great prices. **66** (✉ Via Bisignano 66, Chiaia ☎ 081/5720269) is a good place to meet for an aperitivo; the range of snacks on the bar (several types of olives, fresh capers, spinach and ricotta pies, and even small helpings of spaghetti—virtually a meal in itself) makes the crowds of young professionals and steep drink prices worth it. **Siddharta** (✉ Via Vito Fornari 15, Chiaia ☎ 081/422334) has a slightly exotic touch, as it's one of the city's first sushi bars, though the stylish restaurant also offers excellent local fare. On the other side of the large underground space are a bar and disco that fill up with the area's bright young things on Friday and Saturday.

Sports & the Outdoors

Boating

Summer evening boat tours take in the Naples waterfront from the port at Mergellina to Cape Posillipo, with a view of Castel dell'Ovo on the way back. For bookings contact **Seafront Tours** (⊠ Galleria Umberto I 17, Piazza Plebiscito ☎ 081/5519188).

Bicycling

To rent a bike in town and for information on group excursions (including rides up Mount Vesuvius), contact **Napoli Bike** (⊠ Riviera di Chiaia 201 ☎ 081/411934 ⊕ www.napolibike.com), conveniently close to the Villa Comunale.

Shopping

Leather goods, jewelry, and cameos are some of the best items to buy in Campania. In Naples you'll generally find good deals on handbags, shoes, and clothing. If you want the real thing, make your purchases in shops, but if you don't mind imitations rummage around at the various street-vendor *bancherelle* (stalls). Most boutiques and department stores are open Monday 4:30–8, Tuesday–Saturday 9:15–1 and 4:30–8. Food shops are open Monday morning, but most close about 2 PM on Thursday afternoon.

Shopping Districts

The immediate area around **Piazza dei Martiri,** in the center of Chiaia, has the densest concentration of luxury shopping, with perfume shops, fashion outlets, and antiques on display. **Via dei Mille** and **Via Filangieri,** which lead off Piazza dei Martiri, are home to Bulgari, Mont Blanc, and Hermes stores. The small, pedestrian-only **Via Calabritto,** which leads down from Piazza dei Martiri toward the sea, is where you'll find high-end retailers such as Prada, Gucci, Versace, Vuitton, Cacharel, Damiani, and Cartier. **Via Chiaia** and **Via Toledo** are the two busiest shopping streets for most Neapolitans; there you'll find reasonably priced clothes and shoes, with a sprinkling of cafés and food shops. The **Vomero** district yields more commercial shops, especially along Via Scarlatti and Via Luca Giordano. **Via Santa Maria di Costantinopoli,** which runs from Piazza Bellini to the Archaeological Museum, is the street for antiques shops. You'll also find an antiques market on the third weekend of each month in the gardens of Villa Comunale and a flower market early every morning in the Castel Nuovo moat.

Specialty Stores

CHIAIA   **Gay Odin** (⊠ Via Toledo 214, Piazza Plebiscito ☎ 081/400063) produces handmade chocolates that you can find only in its Naples shops. Buy a delicious chocolate Mount Vesuvius, or try the famous *foresta* (flaked chocolate). **Lo Stock** (⊠ Via Fiorelli 7, Piazza dei Martiri ☎ 081/2405253) is a large basement in which designer-label remainders can be found at hugely reduced prices. Be prepared to rummage and hope they have your size. **Marinella** (⊠ Via Riviera di Chiaia 287/a, Chiaia ☎ 081/2451182) sells old-fashion made-to-measure ties that are favorites of the British royal family.

SPACCANAPOLI **Colonnese** (✉ Via San Pietro a Maiella 32/33, Spaccanapoli ☎ 081/ 459858) is an old-fashioned bookstore with antique wooden cabinets and tables laden with volumes on art, local history, and esoterica. **Melinoi** (✉ Via Benedetto Croce 34, Spaccanapoli ☎ 081/5521204) stands out from the many small boutiques in Naples for its originality; it stocks clothes and accessories by Romeo Gigli as well as a number of French designers. **Mario Raffone** (✉ Via Santa Maria di Costantinopoli 102, Spaccanapoli ☎ 081/459667) is a family printing business where they still use old presses. They sell prints of nativity figures and Vesuvius and have a catalog of old prints from the last century.

13

☉ The **Ospedale delle Bambole** (✉ Via San Biagio dei Librai 81, Spaccanapoli ☎ 081/203067), a tiny storefront operation, is a world-famous "hospital" for dolls. It's a wonderful place to take kids. **Nel Regno di Pulcinella** (✉ Vico San Domenico Maggiore 9, Spaccanapoli ☎ 081/ 5514171) is the workshop of famous Pulcinella maker Lello Esposito. The shop, a converted 16th-century stable, also has wonderful model volcanoes and the traditional good-luck symbol of the city, a red horn.

THE PHLEGREAN FIELDS

The name Campi Flegrei—the fields of fire—was once given to the entire region west of Naples, including the island of Ischia. The whole area floats freely on a mass of molten lava very close to the surface. The fires are still smoldering. Greek and Roman notions of the Underworld were not the blind imaginings of a primitive people; they were the creations of poets and writers who stood on this very ground and wrote down what they saw. Today it should take about half a day to assess it yourself.

Solfatara

16 *8 km (5 mi) west of Naples.*

At the sunken crater of Solfatara, a semiextinct volcano that last erupted in 1198, you can experience firsthand the volcanic nature of this otherworldly terrain. According to one legend, every crater in the Phlegrean Fields is one of the mouths of a hundred-headed dragon named Typhon that Zeus hurled down the crater of Epomeo on the island of Ischia. Another asserts that the sulfurous springs are poisonous discharges from the wounds the Titans received in their war with Zeus. The stark, scorched area, scattered with pools of boiling mud, exerts a strange fascination. The area has good visitor facilities, is well signposted, and is safe for walking if you stick to the path. ☎ *081/5262341* ⊕ *www. solfatara.it* ✉ *€5* ⊙ *Daily 8:30–1 hr before sunset.*

Pozzuoli

17 *2 km (1 mi) west of Solfatara, 8 km (5 mi) west of Naples.*

The small fishing town of Pozzuoli once boasted of its difference from nearby Naples, and though in recent years it has become a suburb of its neighbor, it still retains enough character and sights of interest to make

EATING WELL IN CAMPANIA

Campania's cuisine relies heavily on the bounty of the region's fertile farmland. Locally grown tomatoes are exported all over the world, but to try them here is another experience completely. Pasta is a staple, and spaghetti *al pomodoro* (with tomato sauce) and *alle vongole* (with clam sauce, either white or red) appear on most menus. Mozzarella—produced by Campania's thriving buffalo population—is used in many dishes; one of the most gratifying on a hot day is *insalata caprese* (salad with mozzarella, tomatoes, and basil). *Melanzane* (eggplant) and even zucchini are served *parmigiana* (fried and layered with tomato sauce and mozzarella).

Naples is the homeland of pizza, and you'll encounter it here in two classic forms: *alla margherita* (with tomato, mozzarella, and basil) and

marinara (with tomato, garlic, and oregano). Meat may be served *alla pizzaiola* (cooked in a tomato-and-garlic sauce). Fish and seafood in general can be expensive, though fried calamari and *totani* (cuttlefish) are usually reasonably priced. Lemons, grown locally, are widely used in cooking and for the sweet and heady liqueur *limoncello*, especially popular around Sorrento and on the Amalfi Coast. Among the region's grape varieties, Fiano, Greco di Tufo, and Falanghina make fine whites, and the Aglianico grape produces Campania's prestigious red, Taurasi. Wine production here has an impressive pedigree: Falerno wines (red and white) are mentioned by the Latin poet Horace, and Lacryma Christi (a blend of grape varieties) is produced from grapes grown around the slopes of Vesuvius.

it worth at least a half-day trip—or longer if you want to visit one of the town's famous fish restaurants. The **Anfiteatro Flavio** is the third-largest amphitheater in Italy, after the Colosseum and Santa Maria Capua Vetere, and once held 40,000 spectators. Judging from the underground network of *carceres* (cells), which definitely merit a visit, entertainment consisted mainly of *venationes* (fights), often involving exotic animals such as lions and tigers brought from far-flung corners of the Roman Empire. The *fossa*, the large ditch in the middle of the arena, may well have contained the stage, which could be raised when necessary. If visiting between June and September, ask at the ticket office about evening concerts. ☎ *081/5266007* ⊠ *€4 includes Cumae and museum and site of Baia* ⊙ *Daily 9–1 hr before sunset.*

You may want to make a short trip to Pozzuoli's **harbor** and imagine St. Paul landing here en route to Rome in AD 61, only 18 years before the eruption of Vesuvius. His own ship had been wrecked off Malta, and he was brought here on the *Castor and Pollux*, a grain ship from Alexandria.

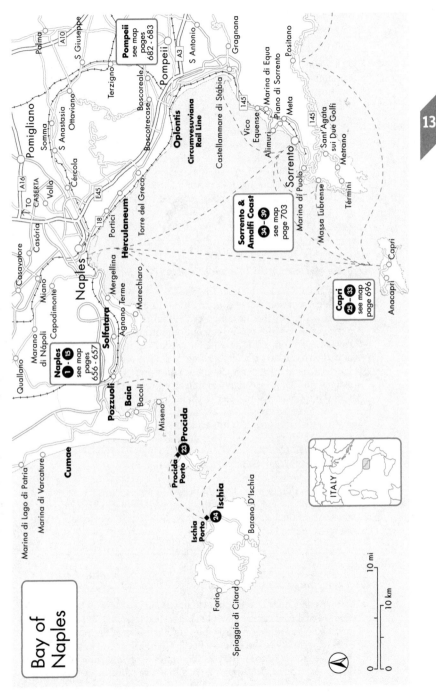

Bay of Naples

Pompeii see map pages 682-683

Sorrento & Amalfi Coast 34 - 39 see map page 703

Capri 25 - 33 see map page 696

Naples 1 - 15 see map pages 656 - 657

13

ITALY

Where to Eat

Pozzuoli is justly famed for its fish restaurants. On weekends in summer the town's narrow streets are packed with Neapolitans.

$ ✕ **Il Tritone.** You don't have to worry about what to order here—the waiters simply bring you the daily special. Meals begin with a rich supply of antipasti, after which you can either throw in the towel or continue with two types of pasta, a fish dish, and a dessert. If you stop after the antipasti there is a flat fee of €30. ⊠ *Via Vecchione 9/11* ☎ *081/ 5264307* ▭ *No credit cards* ⊘ *Closed Mon.*

$ ✕ **Ristorante Don Antonio.** Neapolitans flock to this restaurant in a *vicolo* (alley) one block from the waterfront for fresh seafood and unbeatable prices. Unlike other hostelries, which will happily serve well into the afternoon or late night, Don Antonio rolls down the shutters as soon as the day's catch has been consumed. ⊠ *Via Magazzini 20, off Piazza San Paolo* ☎ *081/5267941* ◿ *Reservations not accepted* ▭ *No credit cards* ⊘ *Closed Mon.*

Baia

🔟 *7 km (4½ mi) south of Pozzuoli, 12 km (7 mi) west of Naples.*

Now largely under the sea, this was once the most opulent and fashionable resort area of the Roman Empire, a place where Sulla, Pompey, Cicero, Caesar, Tiberius, and Nero all built holiday villas. Petronius's *Satyricon* is a satire on the corruption, intrigue, and wonderful licentiousness of Roman life at Baia. (Petronius was hired to arrange parties and entertainments for Nero, so he was in a position to know.) It was here at Baia that Emperor Claudius built a great villa for his wife, Messalina (who spent her nights indulging herself at public brothels); here that Agrippina poisoned her husband and was, in turn, murdered by her son Nero; and here that Cleopatra was staying when Julius Caesar was murdered on the Ides of March in 44 BC. You can visit the excavations of the famous *terme* (baths). ⊠ *Via Fusaro 35* ☎ *081/8687592* ▱ *€4 includes Cumae, the museum of Baia and the Pozzuoli amphitheater* ⊘ *Tues.–Sun. 9–2 hrs before sunset.*

en route   Follow the southern loop around Lago Miseno (a volcanic crater believed by the ancients to be the Styx, across which Charon ferried the souls of the dead) and Lago del Fusaro. You'll take in some fine views of the Golfo di Pozzuoli.

Cumae

🔟 *5 km (3 mi) north of Pozzuoli, 16 km (10 mi) west of Naples.*

Perhaps the oldest Greek colony in Italy, Cumae (Cuma in Italian) overshadowed the Phlegrean Fields, including Naples, in the 7th and 6th centuries BC. The **Antro della Sibilla** (Sibyl's Cave)—one of the most venerated sites in antiquity—is in Cumae. In the 6th or 5th century BC the Greeks hollowed the cave from the rock beneath the present ruins of Cumae's acropolis. You walk through a dark, massive stone tunnel that opens into a vaulted chamber where the Sibyl uttered her oracles. Standing here, the sense of mystery is overwhelming. "This is the most romantic classical site in Italy," wrote the English travel writer H. V. Morton (1892–1979). "I would rather come here than to Pompeii."

Virgil (70–19 BC) wrote in his epic *Aeneid* of the Trojan prince Aeneas's descent to the Underworld to speak to his father. To find his way Aeneas needed the guidance of the Cumaean Sibyl. Virgil did not dream up the Sibyl's cave—he must have stood here in her chamber. When he wrote *"Facilis descensus Averno"*—"The way to hell is easy"—it was because he knew the way. In Book VI of the *Aeneid* Virgil described how Aeneas, arriving at Cumae, sought Apollo's throne (remains of the **Tempio di Apollo** can still be seen) and "the deep hidden abode of the dread Sibyl / An enormous cave. . . ."

Little of ancient Cumae now stands aboveground—the Temple of Apollo has suffered woefully over the millennia—but the underground passages are virtually intact, though not entirely visitable. There are detailed information panels to guide you through the site, with extra information on flora and fauna supplied by the local Worldwide Fund for Nature. As you walk through, you'll soon appreciate why this was a good location: it was surrounded by fertile land, had relatively easy access to the sea (though no natural harbor), and an acropolis at the top providing an excellent vantage in all directions. Allow at least two hours for this visit to soak up the ambience, study the ruins, and reach the top level overlooking the Acherusia Palus—now Lago Fusaro—to the south and part of the Silva Gallinaria, the thick holm-oak ground cover to the north, once an immense forest stretching almost all the way to Rome. ☒ *Via Acropoli 39* ☎ *081/8543060* ☑ *€4 includes Pozzuoli amphitheater and museum and site of Baia* ☉ *Daily 9–2 hrs before sunset.*

Regarded by the ancients as the gateway to Hades, the fabled **Lago d'Averno** (Lake Avernus) was well known by the time Virgil settled here to write *The Aeneid*. Today the scene has changed a fair amount: in summer the area pulsates to the sound of disco music, and you would be more likely to come across members of the 21st-century underworld than meet the shades of the dead that Virgil so evocatively describes. As with Lago Lucrino (the Lucrine Lake) less than 1 km (½ mi) to the south, a tarmac road skirts much of the lake. However, some of the spell is restored by the backdrop: forested hills rise on three sides and the menacing cone of Monte Nuovo looms on the fourth. The smell of sulfur sometimes hangs over the landscape, and blocked-off passages lead into long-abandoned caves into which Virgil might well have ventured. ☒ *4 km (2½ mi) south of Cumae.*

HERCULANEUM, VESUVIUS & POMPEII

Volcanic ash and mud preserved the Roman towns of Herculaneum and Pompeii almost exactly as they were on the day Mt. Vesuvius erupted in AD 79, leaving them not just archaeological ruins but museums of daily life in the ancient world. The two cities and the volcano that buried them can be visited from either Naples or Sorrento, thanks to the Circumvesuviana, the suburban railway that provides fast, frequent, and economical service.

Herculaneum

★ ⑳ *10 km (6 mi) southeast of Naples.*

Lying more than 60 feet below the town of Ercolano, the ruins of Herculaneum are set among the acres of greenhouses that make this area one of Europe's principal flower-growing centers. About 5,000 people lived here when it was destroyed; many of them were fishermen, craftsmen, and artists. In AD 79 the gigantic eruption of Vesuvius (which also destroyed Pompeii) buried the town under a tide of volcanic mud. The semiliquid mass seeped into the

> ### WORD OF MOUTH
>
> "Herculaneum is definitely not to be missed. The buildings look as if you could move in with just a little restoration." —Juneisy

crevices and niches of every building, covering household objects and enveloping textiles and wood—sealing all in a compact, airtight tomb.

Casual excavation—and haphazard looting—began in the 18th century, but systematic digs were not initiated until the 1920s. Today less than half of Herculaneum has been excavated; with present-day Ercolano and the unlovely Resina Quarter (famous among bargain hunters for its secondhand-clothing market) sitting on top of the site, progress is limited. From the ramp leading down to Herculaneum's well-preserved edifices, you get a good overall view of the site, as well as an idea of the amount of volcanic debris that had to be removed to bring it to light.

Though Herculaneum had only one-fourth the population of Pompeii and has been only partially excavated, what has been found is generally better preserved. In some cases you can even see the original wooden beams, staircases, and furniture. Much excitement is presently focused on one excavation in a corner of the site, the Villa dei Papiri, built by Julius Caesar's father-in-law. The building is named for the 1,800 carbonized papyrus scrolls dug up here in the 18th century, leading scholars to believe that this may have been a study center or library. Given the right funds and political support, it is hoped that the villa can be properly excavated and ultimately opened to the public.

At the entrance to the archaeological park, pick up a map showing the gridlike layout of the dig. Splurge on an audio guide (€6 for one, €9 for two) and head down the tunnel to start the tour at the old shoreline. Though many of the houses are closed and some are in dire need of restoration, a fair cross section of domestic, commercial, and civic buildings is still accessible. Decorations are especially delicate in the **Casa del Nettuno ed Anfitrite** (House of Neptune and Amphitrite), named for the subjects of a still-bright mosaic on the wall of the nymphaeum (a recessed grotto with a fountain), and in the **Terme Femminili** (Women's Baths), where several delicate black-and-white mosaics embellished the rooms. Annexed to the former house is a remarkably preserved wineshop,

Continued on page 689

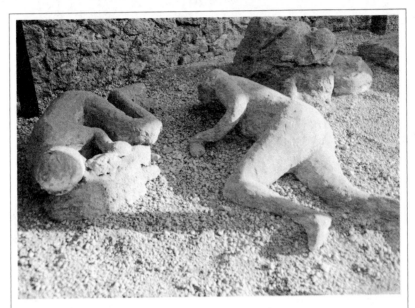

ANCIENT POMPEII
TOMB OF A CIVILIZATION

The Scavi di Pompeii, petrified memorial to Vesuvius's eruption on the morning of August 23, AD 79, is the largest, most accessible, and probably most famous of excavations anywhere.

A busy commercial center with a population of 10,000–20,000, ancient Pompeii covered about 160 acres on the seaward end of the fertile Sarno Plain. Today Pompeii is choked with both the dust of 25 centuries and more than 2 million visitors every year; only by escaping the hordes and lingering along its silent streets can you truly fall under the site's spell. On a quiet backstreet, all you need is a little imagination to sense the shadows palpably filling the dark corners, to hear the ancient pipe's falsetto and the tinny clash of cymbals, to envision a rain of rose petals gently covering a Roman senator's dinner guests. Come in the late afternoon when the site is nearly deserted and you will understand that the true pleasure of Pompeii is not in the seeing but in the feeling.

A FUNNY THING HAPPENS ON THE WAY TO THE FORUM as you walk through Pompeii. Covered with dust and decay as it is, the city seems to come alive. Perhaps it's the familiar signs of life observed along the ancient streets: the beer shops with tumblers' rings still fresh in the counter, the stanchion where horses were tethered outside the taverna, the tracks of chariot wheels cut in the pavement. Coming upon a *thermopolium* (drinking bar), you imagine natives calling out, "One for the road." But a glance up at Vesuvius, still brooding over the scene like an enormous headstone, reminds you that these folks—whether imagined in your head or actu-

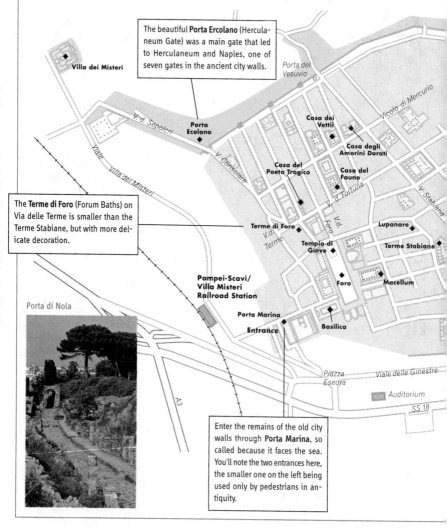

The beautiful **Porta Ercolano** (Herculaneum Gate) was a main gate that led to Herculaneum and Naples, one of seven gates in the ancient city walls.

Villa dei Misteri

Porta del Vesuvio

V. d. Sepolcri

Viale Villa dei Misteri

Porta Ecolano

V. Consolare

Vicolo di Mercurio

Casa dei Vettii

Casa degli Amorini Dorati

Casa del Poeta Tragico

Casa del Fauno

V. d. Fortuna

V. d. Stabiana

The **Terme di Foro** (Forum Baths) on Via delle Terme is smaller than the Terme Stabiane, but with more delicate decoration.

Terme di Foro

V. d. Terme

V. d. Foro

Lupanare

Tempio di Giove

Terme Stabiane

Pompei-Scavi/ Villa Misteri Railroad Station

Foro

Macellum

Porta di Nola

Porta Marina

Entrance

Basilica

A3

Piazza Esedra

Viale delle Ginestre

Auditorium

SS 18

Enter the remains of the old city walls through **Porta Marina**, so called because it faces the sea. You'll note the two entrances here, the smaller one on the left being used only by pedestrians in antiquity.

ally wearing a mantle of lava dust—have not taken a breath for centuries.

The town was laid out in a grid pattern, with two main intersecting streets. The wealthiest took a whole block for themselves;

Via dell'Abbondanza

those less fortunate built a house and rented out the front rooms, facing the street, as shops. There were good numbers of *tabernae* (taverns) and *thermopolia* on almost every corner, and frequent shows at the amphitheater.

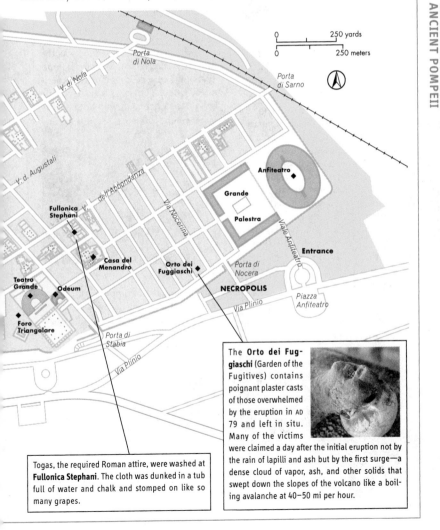

Togas, the required Roman attire, were washed at **Fullonica Stephani**. The cloth was dunked in a tub full of water and chalk and stomped on like so many grapes.

The **Orto dei Fuggiaschi** (Garden of the Fugitives) contains poignant plaster casts of those overwhelmed by the eruption in AD 79 and left in situ. Many of the victims were claimed a day after the initial eruption not by the rain of lapilli and ash but by the first surge—a dense cloud of vapor, ash, and other solids that swept down the slopes of the volcano like a boiling avalanche at 40–50 mi per hour.

PUBLIC LIFE IN ANCIENT POMPEII

Forum

THE CITY CENTER

As you enter the ruins at Porta Marina, make your way to the **Foro** (Forum), which served as Pompeii's cultural, political, and religious center. You can still see some of the two stories of colonnades that used to line the square. Like the ancient Greek *agora* in Athens, the Forum was a busy shopping area, complete with public officials to apply proper standards of weights and measures. Fronted by an elegant three-column portico on the eastern side of the forum is the **Macellum**, the covered meat and fish market dating to Augustan times; here vendors sold goods from their reserved spots in the central market. It was also in the Forum that elections were held, politicians let rhetoric fly, speeches and official announcements were made, and worshippers crowded the **Tempio di Giove** (Temple of Jupiter), at the northern end of the forum.

Basilica

On the southwestern corner is the **Basilica**, the city's law court and the economic center. These oblong buildings ending in a semicircular projection were the model for early Christian churches, which had a nave (central aisle) and two side aisles separated by rows of columns. Standing in the Basilica, you can recognize the continuity between Roman and Christian architecture.

THE GAMES

The **Anfiteatro** (Amphitheater) was the ultimate in entertainment for local Pompeians and offered a gamut of experiences, but essentially this was for gladiators rather than wild animals. By

Amphitheater

Roman standards, Pompeii's amphitheater was quite small (seating 20,000). Built in about 80 BC, it was oval and divided into three seating areas like a theater. There were two main entrances—at the north and south ends—and a narrow passage on the west called the Porta Libitinensis, through which the dead were most probably dragged out. A wall painting found in a house near the theater (now in the Naples Museum) depicts the riot in the amphitheater in AD 59 when several citizens from the nearby town of Nucera were killed. After Nucerian appeals to Nero, shows in the amphitheater were suspended for 10 years.

13

Fresco of Pyramus & Thisbe in the House of Loreius Tiburtinus

BATHS & BROTHELS

In its day, Pompeii was celebrated as the Côte d'Azur, the seaside Brighton, the Fire Island of the ancient Roman empire. Evidence of a Sybaritic bent is everywhere—in the town's grandest villas, in its baths, and especially in its rowdiest *lupanaria* (brothels), murals still reveal a worship of hedonism. Satyrs, bacchantes, hermaphrodites, and acrobatic couples are pictured indulging in hanky-panky.

The first buildings to the left after you've gone through the ticket turnstiles are the **Terme Suburbane** (Suburban Baths), built—by all accounts without planning permission—right up against the city walls. The baths have eyebrow-raising frescoes in the *apodyterium*

(changing room) that strongly suggest that more than just bathing and massaging went on here.

On the walls of **Lupanare** (brothel) are scenes of erotic games in which clients could engage. The **Terme Stabiane** (Stabian Baths) had underground furnaces, the heat from which circulated beneath the floor, rose through flues in the walls, and escaped through chimneys. The water temperature could be set for cold, lukewarm, or hot. Bathers took a lukewarm bath to prepare themselves for the hot room. A tepid bath came next, and then a plunge into cold water to tone up the skin. A vigorous massage with oil was followed by rest, reading, horseplay, and conversation.

GRAFFITI

Thanks to those deep layers of pyroclastic deposits from Vesuvius that protected the site from natural wear and tear over the centuries, graffiti found in Pompeii provide unique insights into the sort of things that the locals found important 2,000 years ago. A good many were personal and lend a human dimension to the disaster that not even the sights can equal.

At the baths: **"What is the use of having a Venus if she's made of marble?"**

At the entrance to the front lavatory at a private house: **"May I always and everywhere be as potent with women as I was here."**

On the Viale ai Teatri: **"A copper pot went missing from my shop. Anyone who returns it to me will be given 65 bronze coins."**

In the Basilica: **"A small problem gets larger if you ignore it."**

PRIVATE LIFE IN ANCIENT POMPEII

The facades of houses in Pompeii were relatively plain and seldom hinted at the care and attention lavished on the private rooms within. When visitors arrived they passed the shops and entered an open atrium, from which the occupants received air, sunlight, and rainwater, the latter caught by the *impluvium*, a Jacuzzi-shaped receptacle under the sloped roof. In the back was a receiving room, and behind was another open area, the *peristylum*. Life revolved around this uncovered inner courtyard, with rows of columns and perhaps a garden with a fountain. Only good friends ever saw this part of the house, which was surrounded by *cubiculae* (bedrooms) and the *triclinium* (dining area). Interior floors and walls usually were covered with colorful marble tiles, mosaics, and frescoes.

House of Paquius Proculus

Several homes were captured in various states by the eruption of Vesuvius, each representing a different slice of Pompeiian life.

Small Garden

Triclinium

Owner's Quarters

Kitchen

Servant's Quarters

Secondary Atrium

Entrance

Garden

Main Atrium

Impluvium

Peristyle

The **Casa del Fauno** (House of the Faun) displayed wonderful mosaics, now at the Museo Archeologico Nazionale in Naples. The **Casa del Poeta Tragico** (House of the Tragic Poet) is a typical middle-class house. On the floor is a mosaic of a chained dog and the inscription *cave canem* ("Beware of the dog"). The **Casa degli Amorini Dorati** (House of the Gilded Cupids) is an elegant, well-preserved home with original marble decorations in the garden. Many paintings and mosaics were executed at **Casa del Menandro** (House of Menander), a patrician's villa named for a fresco of the Greek playwright. Two blocks beyond the Stabian Baths you'll notice on the left the current digs at the **Casa dei Casti Amanti** (House of the Chaste Lovers). A team of plasterers and painters were at work here when Vesuvius erupted, redecorating one of the rooms and patching up the cracks in the bread oven near the entrance—caused by earth tremors a matter of days before.

CASA DEI VETTII

The **House of the Vettii** is the best example of a house owned by wealthy *mercatores* (merchants). It contains vivid murals—a magnificent *pinacoteca* (picture gallery) within the very heart of Pompeii. The scenes here—except for those in the two wings off the atrium—were all painted after the earthquake of AD 62. Once inside, cast an admiring glance at the delicate frieze around the wall of the *triclinium* (on the right of the peristyle garden as you enter from the atrium), depicting cupids engaged in various activities, such as selling oils and perfumes, working as goldsmiths and metalworkers, acting as wine merchants, or performing in chariot races. Another of the main attractions in the Casa dei Vettii is the small cubicle beyond the kitchen area (to the right of the atrium) with its faded erotic frescoes now protected by Perspex screens.

UNLOCKING THE VILLA DEI MISTERI

Villa dei Misteri

There is no more astounding, magnificently memorable evidence of Pompeii's devotion to the pleasures of the flesh than the frescoes on view at the **Villa dei Misteri** (Villa of the Mysteries), a palatial abode built at the far northwestern fringe of Pompeii. Unearthed in 1909, this villa had more than 60 rooms painted with frescoes; the finest are in the *triclinium*. Painted in the most glowing Pompeiian reds and oranges, the panels relate the saga of a young bride (Ariadne) and her initiation into the mysteries of the cult of Dionysus, who was a god imported to Italy from Greece and then given the Latin name of Bacchus. The god of wine and debauchery also represented the triumph of the irrational—of all those mysterious forces that no official state religion could fully suppress.

Pompeii's best frescoes, painted in glowing reds and oranges, retain an amazing vibrancy.

The Villa of the Mysteries frescoes were painted circa 50 BC, most art historians believe, and represent the peak of the Second Style of Pompeiian wall painting. The triclinium frescoes are thought to have been painted by a local artist, although the theme may well have been copied from an earlier cycle of paintings from the Hellenistic period. In all there are 10 scenes, depicting children and matrons, musicians and satyrs, phalluses and gods. There are no inscriptions (such as are found on Greek vases), and after 2,000 years historians remain puzzled by many aspects of the triclinium cycle. Scholars endlessly debate the meaning of these frescoes, but anyone can tell they are the most beautiful paintings left to us by antiquity. In several ways, the eruption of Vesuvius was a blessing in disguise, for without it, these masterworks of art would have perished long ago.

PLANNING FOR YOUR DAY IN POMPEII

GETTING THERE

The archaeological site of Pompeii has its own stop (Pompei–Villa dei Misteri) on the Circumvesuviana line to Sorrento, close to the main entrance at the Porta Marina, which is the best place from which to start a tour. If, like many potential visitors every year, you get the wrong train from Naples (stopping at the other station "Pompei"), all is not lost. There's another entrance to the excavations at the far end of the site, just a seven-minute walk to the Amphitheater.

ADMISSION

Single tickets cost €10 and are valid for one full day. The site is open Apr.–Oct., daily 8:30–7:30 (last admission at 6), and Nov.–Mar., daily 8:30–5 (last admission at 3:30). For more information, call 081/8575347 or visit www.pompeiisites.org.

WHAT TO BRING

The only restaurant inside the site is both overpriced and busy, so it makes sense to bring along water and snacks. If you come so equipped, there are some shady, underused picnic tables outside the Porta di Nola, to the northeast of the site.

MAKING THE MOST OF YOUR TIME

Visiting Pompeii does have its frustrating aspects: many buildings are blocked off by locked gates, and enormous group tours tend to clog up more popular attractions. But the site is so big that it's easy to lose yourself amid the quiet side streets. To really see the site, you'll need four or five hours.

Two buildings within Pompeii—Terme Suburbane (daily 10–2) and Casa del Menandro (weekends 2–4)—are open for restricted viewing on a first-come, first-served basis. Ask for a free coupon when you purchase your ticket and you will be assigned a visiting time.

TOURS

To get the most out of Pompeii, rent an audio guide (€6 for one, €9 for two; you'll need to leave an ID card) and opt for one of the three itineraries (2 hours, 4 hours, or 6 hours). If hiring a guide, make sure the guide is registered for an English tour and standing inside the gate; agree beforehand on the length of the tour and the price, and prepare yourself for soundbites of English mixed with dollops of hearsay.

MODERN POMPEI

Caught between the hammer and anvil of cultural and religious tourism, the modern town of Pompei (to use the modern-day Italian spelling, not the ancient Latin) is now endeavoring to polish up its act. In attempts to ease congestion and improve air quality at street level, parts of the town have been pedestrianized and parking restrictions tightened. Several hotels have filled the sizable niche in the market for excellent deals at affordable prices. As for recommendable restaurants, if you deviate from the archaeological site and make for the center of town, you will be spoiled for choice.

IF YOU LIKE POMPEII

If you intend to visit other archaeological sites nearby during your trip, you should buy the *biglietto cumulativo* pass, a combination ticket with access to five area sites (Herculaneum, Pompeii, Oplontis, Stabiae, Boscoreale). It costs €18 and is valid for three days. Unlike many archaeological sites in the Mediterranean region, those around Naples are almost all well served by public transport; ask about transportation options at the helpful Porta Marina information kiosk.

where amphorae still rest on carbonized wooden shelves. On the other side of the house is the **Casa del Bel Cortile** (House of the Beautiful Courtyard). In one of its inner rooms is the temporary display of a cast taken of some skeletons found in the storerooms down at the old seafront, where almost 300 inhabitants sought refuge from the eruption and were ultimately encapsulated for posterity. The sumptuously decorated **Terme Suburbane** (Suburban Baths)—open only mornings—and the **Casa dei Cervi** (House of the Stags), with an elegant garden open to the sea breezes, are all evocative relics of a lively and luxurious way of life. ⊠ *Corso Ercolano, a 5-min walk downhill from Ercolano Circumvesuviana station* ☎ *081/8575347* ⊕ *www.pompeiisites.org* ▧ *€10; €18 including Oplontis, Pompeii, and 2 other sites over 3 days* ⊘ *Apr.–Oct., daily 8:30–7:30, ticket office closes at 6; Nov.–Mar., daily 8:30–5, ticket office closes at 3:30.*

Vesuvius

㉑ *8 km (5 mi) northeast of Herculaneum, 16 km (10 mi) east of Naples.*

As you tour the cities that it destroyed, you may be overwhelmed by the urge to explore Vesuvius. In summer especially, the prospect of rising above the sticky heat of Naples is a heady one. The view when clear is magnificent, with the curve of the coast and the tiny white houses among the orange and lemon blossoms. If the summit is lost in mist you'll be lucky to see your hand in front of your face. When you see the summit clearing—it tends to be clearer in the afternoon—head for it. If possible, see Vesuvius after you've toured the ruins of buried Herculaneum to appreciate the magnitude of the volcano's power.

Reaching the crater takes some effort. From the Ercolano stop of the Circumvesuviana, take scheduled buses (trip takes one hour; there are four or five departures a day—check for the latest schedule at the bar just outside the train station) or your own car to Quota 1000 (the parking lot and cafeteria area near the top). From here you must make the 30-minute ascent up a soft, slippery cinder track by foot. The €6 admission includes compulsory guide service, usually young geologists with a smattering of English. At the bottom you'll be offered a stout walking stick (a small tip is appreciated on return). The climb can be tiring if you're not used to steep hikes. Wear nonskid shoes (not sandals). ☎ *081/ 7775720* ▧ *€6* ⊘ *Daily 9 AM–2 hrs before sunset.*

You can visit **Osservatorio Vesuviano** (Vesuvius Observatory)—2,000 feet up—and view instruments used to study the volcano, some dating back to the mid-19th century. ☎ *081/7777149 or 081/7777150* ⊕ *www. ov.ingv.it* ▧ *Free* ⊘ *Weekends 10–2.*

Oplontis

㉒ *20 km (12 mi) southeast of Naples, 5 km (3 mi) west of Pompeii.*

The spectacular archaeological site of Oplontis (surrounded by the fairly drab urban landscape of Torre Annunziata) is a villa complex that's been imaginatively ascribed—based on a mere inscription on an am-

13

phora—to Nero's second wife, Poppaea Sabina, whose family was well known among the landed gentry of neighboring Pompeii. As Roman villas go, Poppaea's Villa is truly exceptional. Excavation so far has uncovered an area of more than 100 by 75 meters (325 by 250 feet), and because the site is bound by a road to the west and a canal to the south, it may never be possible to gauge its full extent. What's been found includes porticoes, pools, baths, and extensive gardens, as well as the standard atria, triclinia, and a warren of *cubicula* (bedrooms).

Access is easiest from the Circumvesuviana station of Torre Annunziata, about 650 feet away. Outside the station turn left and then right downhill; the site is just after the crossroads on the left. If coming by car, take the Torre Annunziata turnoff from the Naples–Salerno autostrada, turn right, and then look for signs on the left for Oplontis at the first major crossroads. The main entrance to the site is from the north— you basically go into the villa through the gardens, with the atrium on the southern side lying under about 10 feet of pumice and pyroclastic material from Vesuvius.

✉ *Via Sepolcri 1, Torre Annunziata* ☎*081/8575347* ⊕*www.pompeiisites. org* ☞ *€5 including Boscoreale and Stabiae in 1 day; €18 including Herculaneum, Pompeii, and the 2 other sites over 3 days* ☉ *Apr.–Oct., daily 8:30–7:30, ticket office closes at 6; Nov.–Mar., daily 8:30–5, ticket office closes at 3:30.*

CASERTA & BENEVENTO

From Caserta, the Italian answer to Versailles, if you proceed to Benevento you'll view an almost perfectly preserved Roman arch. Benevento was badly damaged by World War II bombings, but among the modern structures there are some medieval and even older relics still standing in the old town. If you go by car, make a brief detour to the medieval hamlet of Caserta Vecchia on the hillside, where there are one or two good restaurants and a very old cathedral.

Caserta

★ *11 km (7 mi) northeast of Herculaneum, 25 km (16 mi) northeast of Naples.*

The palace known as the **Reggia** shows how Bourbon royals lived in the mid-18th century. Architect Luigi Vanvitelli devoted 20 years to its construction under Bourbon ruler Charles III, whose son, Ferdinand IV (1751–1825), moved in when it was completed in 1774. Both king and architect were inspired by Versailles, and the rectangular palace was conceived on a massive scale, with four interconnecting courtyards, 1,200 rooms, and a vast park. Though the palace is not as well maintained as its French counterpart, the main staircase puts the one at Versailles to shame, and the **royal apartments** are sumptuous. It was here, in what Eisenhower called "a castle near Naples," that the Allied High Command had its headquarters in World War II, and here German forces in Italy surrendered in April 1945. There's a museum of items relating to the palace and the region. Most enjoyable are the gardens and parks, particularly the Cascades, adorned with sculptures of the goddess Diana and her maidens. A minibus takes you along the 5-km (3-mi) path from the palace to the end of the gardens. ⊠ *Piazza Carlo III* ☎ *0823/448084* ⊕ *www. reggiadicaserta.org* ✒ *Royal apartments, Museo dell'Opera, park, and English garden* €6; *park only* €2; *minibus* €1 ۞ *Royal apartments Tues.–Sun. 8:30–7:30. Park Mar., Tues.–Sun. 8:30–5; Apr., Tues.–Sun. 8:30–6; May and Aug., Tues.–Sun. 8:30–6:30; June and July, Tues.– Sun. 8:30–7; Sept. and Oct., Tues.–Sun. 8:30–5:30; Nov.–Feb., Tues.–Sun. 8:30–3:30; ticket office closes 1 hr before closing.*

13

Benevento

35 km (22 mi) east of Caserta, 60 km (37 mi) northeast of Naples.

Benevento owes its importance to its establishment as the capital of the Lombards, a northern tribe that invaded and settled what is now Lombardy when they were forced to move south by Charlemagne's conquests in the 8th century. The tough and resourceful Lombards moved farther south and set up a new duchy in Benevento, later moving its seat to Salerno, where they saw the potential of the natural harbor. Under papal rule in the 13th century, Benevento built a fine cathedral and outfitted it with bronze doors that were a pinnacle of Romanesque art. The cathedral, doors, and a large part of the town were blasted by World War II bombs. The **Duomo** has been rebuilt, and the remaining panels of the original bronze doors are in the chapter library. Fortunately, the majes-★ tic 2nd-century AD **Arco di Traiano** (Trajan's Arch) was unscathed by the bombing. Roman emperor Trajan, who sorted out Rome's finances, extended the Appian Way through Benevento to the Adriatic. The ruins of the **Teatro Romano** (⊠ Take Via Carlo from Duomo ✇ €2 ۞ Daily 9–1 hr before sunset), which had a seating capacity of 20,000, have been extensively restored and host a summer music and theater season.

PROCIDA, ISCHIA & CAPRI

History's hedonists have long luxuriated on Campania's famous islands. The Roman emperor Tiberius built a dozen villas on Capri in which to indulge his sexual whims. Later residents have included dancer Rudolf Nureyev and droves of artists and writers. These days, day-trippers make up the majority of visitors. Ischia, less pretty and less chic than Capri, is still a popular destination on account of its spas, beaches, and hot springs. Procida, long the poor relation of the three, and the closest to Naples, is starting to capitalize on its chief natural asset, the unspoiled isle of Vivara. The pastel colors of Procida will be familiar to anyone who has seen the widely acclaimed film *Il Postino*.

Procida

㉓ *35 mins by hydrofoil, 1 hr by car ferry from Naples.*

Lying barely 3 km (2 mi) from the mainland and 10 km (6 mi) from the nearest port of Pozzuoli, Procida is an island of enormous contrasts. It is the most densely populated island in Europe—almost 11,000 people crammed into less than 3½ square km (2 square mi)—and yet there are oases such as Marina Corricella and Vivara that seem to have been by-passed by modern civilization. It's no surprise that picturesque Procida has strong artistic traditions and is widely considered a painters' paradise.

The sleepy fishing village of **Corricella,** used as the setting for the water-front scenes in the Oscar-winning film *Il Postino,* has been relatively im-mune to life in the limelight. Apart from the opening of an extra restaurant and bar there have been few changes. This is the type of place where even those with failing grades in art class feel like reaching for a paintbrush to record the delicate pinks and yellows of the buildings. The **Graziella** bar at the far end of the seafront offers the island's famous lemons squeezed over crushed ice to make an excellent granita.

Where to Eat

$–$$ ✕ **La Gorgonia.** This restaurant sits right on the waterfront, which draws in the crowds. The specialties here are combinations of seafood and lo-cally grown vegetables, such as pasta *con fagioli e cozze* (with beans and mussels). ⊠ *Marina Corricella 50* ☎ *081/8101060* ▤ *AE, DC, MC, V* ☉ *Closed Mon. and Nov.–Jan.*

Ischia

㉔ *45 mins by hydrofoil, 90 mins by car ferry from Naples, 60 mins by ferry from Pozzuoli.*

Whereas Capri wows you with its charm and beauty, Ischia takes time to cast its spell. In fact, an overnight stay is probably not long enough for the island to get into your blood. It does have its share of vine-grow-ing villages beneath the lush volcanic slopes of Monte Epomeo, and un-like Capri it enjoys a life of its own that survives when the tourists head home. But there are few signs of antiquity here, the architecture is un-remarkable, the traffic can be overwhelming, and hoteliers have yet to achieve a balanced mix of clientele—most are either German (off-sea-son) or Italian (in-season). But should you want to plunk down in the sun for a few days and tune out the world, this is an ideal spot; just don't expect an unspoiled, undiscovered Capri. When Augustus gave the Neapolitans Ischia for Capri, he knew what he was doing.

Ischia is volcanic in origin. From its hidden reservoir of seething molten matter come the thermal springs said to cure whatever ails you. As early as 1580 a doctor named Lasolino published a book about the mineral wells at Ischia. "If your eyebrows fall off," he wrote, "go and try the baths at Piaggia Romano. If you know anyone who is getting bald, any-one who suffers from elephantiasis, or another whose wife yearns for a child, take the three of them immediately to the Bagno di Vitara; they will bless you." Today the island is covered with thermal baths, often surrounded by tropical gardens.

A good 35-km (22-mi) road makes a circuit of the island; the ride takes most of a day if you stop along the way to enjoy the views and perhaps have lunch. You can book a boat tour around the island at the booths in various ports along the coast; there's a one-hour stop at Sant'Angelo. The information office is at the harbor. You may drive on Ischia year-round. There's also fairly good bus service, and you'll find plenty of taxis.

Ischia Porto is the largest town on the island and the usual point of de-barkation. It's no workaday port, however, but a lively resort with plenty of hotels, the island's best shopping area, and low flat-roof houses on terraced hillsides overlooking the water. Its narrow streets often become flights of steps that scale the hill, and its villas and gardens are framed by pines.

Most of the hotels are along the beach in the part of town called **Ischia Ponte,** which gets its name from the *ponte* (bridge) built by Alfonso of Aragon in 1438 to link the picturesque castle on a small islet offshore with the town and port. For a while the castle was the home of Vitto-ria Colonna, poetess, granddaughter of Renaissance Duke Federico da Montefeltro (1422–82), and platonic soul mate of Michelangelo, with whom she carried on a lengthy correspondence. You'll find a typical re-sort atmosphere: countless cafés, shops, and restaurants, and a 1-km (½-mi) stretch of fine-sand beach. **Casamicciola,** a popular beach resort, is 5 km (3 mi) west of Ischia Porto. Chic and upscale **Lacco Ameno,** next to Casamicciola, is distinguished by a mushroom-shape rock offshore and some of the island's best hotels. Here, too, you can enjoy the ben-efits of Ischia's therapeutic waters.

The far western and southern coasts of Ischia are more rugged and at-tractive. **Forio,** at the extreme west, has a waterfront church and is a good spot for lunch or dinner.

The sybaritic hot pools of the **Giardini Poseidon Terme** (Poseidon Gar-dens Spa) are on the Citara beach, south of Forio. You can sit like a Roman senator on a stone chair recessed in the rock and let the hot water cas-cade over you—all very campy, and fun.

Sant'Angelo, on the southern coast, is a charming village; the road does-n't reach all the way into town, so it's free of traffic, and it's a five-minute boat ride from the beach of Maronti, at the foot of cliffs.

The inland town of Fontana is the base for excursions to the top of **Monte Epomeo,** the long-dormant volcano that dominates the island landscape. You can reach its 2,585-foot peak in less than 1½ hours of relatively easy walking.

Where to Stay & Eat

★ $$$–$$$$ ✕ **Il Melograno.** A 10-minute walk south from the center of Forio takes you to the tranquil setting of one of Campania's finest restaurants. With antipasti such as *calamaretti crudi con pera* (raw squid with pears) and many tempting pasta dishes, you could be forgiven for skipping the main course. Try the very reasonably priced local wines (both white and red) from the Pietratorcia winery up the road. Dessert, appropriately called *dulcis in fundo* (the best for last), also merits attention. ✉ *Via G. Mazzella 110, Forio* ☎ *081/998450* ⊕ *www.ilmelogranoischia.it* ✍ *Reservations essential* ▤ *AE, DC, MC, V* ☯ *Closed Mon. and Tues. in Nov. and Dec., and Jan. 7–Mar. 15.*

13

$$ ✕ **Gennaro.** This small family restaurant on the seafront in Ischia Porto serves excellent fish in a convivial atmosphere. Specialties include spaghetti alle vongole and linguine *all'aragosta* (with lobster). ⊠ *Via Porto 66, Ischia Porto* ☎ *081/992917* ▤ *AE, DC, MC, V* ⊙ *Closed Nov.–mid-Mar.*

$$$$ ▦ **Grand Hotel Punta Molino.** Set in its own pine forest on the island's northeastern coastline, this hotel is still within walking distance of the best shopping. This pleasingly modern establishment provides privacy, relaxation, and low-key evening entertainment. Rooms are decorated in gentle Mediterranean hues—some of the best are in the villa annex. A crescent-shaped swimming pool wraps around part of the main building, and the gardens have walkways leading to shady pergolas. Rates include a buffet lunch or candlelight dinner. ⊠ *Lungomare C. Colombo 23, 80077* ☎ *081/991544* ▤ *081/9991562* ⊕ *www. puntamolino.it* ⇆ *90 rooms* ⌕ *2 restaurants, 3 pools, health club, spa, beach, piano bar, meeting rooms* ▤ *AE, DC, MC, V* ⊙ *Closed Oct.–Mar.* ⏐⊙⏐ *MAP.*

$$$–$$$$ ▦ **Hotel San Montano.** The modern San Montano is perched commandingly 300 feet up on Monte Vico. Nautical motifs are used in much of the hotel, so you'll find portholes in the lobby, brass finishings to the room furniture, and tiller-shaped headboards. With the full gamut of treatments available at the spa, you could be forgiven for not venturing down to sea level. Note that half board is required in high season. ⊠ *Via Montevico 20, 80076, Lacco Ameno* ☎ *081/994033* ▤ *081/ 980242* ⊕ *www.sanmontano.com* ⇆ *65 rooms, 12 suites* ⌕ *Restaurant, in-room safes, minibars, cable TV, tennis court, 2 pools, spa* ▤ *AE, DC, MC, V* ⊙ *Closed Nov.–Mar.* ⏐⊙⏐ *MAP.*

$$$ ▦ **Villarosa.** A highlight at this gracious family-run hotel—a villa with bright and airy rooms—is the thermal pool in the garden. In high season, half board is required, and you must reserve well in advance. It's in the heart of Ischia Porto and only a short walk from the beach. ⊠ *Via Giacinto Gigante 5, 80077, Ischia Porto* ☎ *081/991316* ▤ *081/ 992425* ⊕ *www.lavillarosa.it* ⇆ *37 rooms* ⌕ *Restaurant, pool* ▤ *AE, DC, MC, V* ⊙ *Closed Nov.–Mar.* ⏐⊙⏐ *MAP.*

$ ▦ **La Pergola.** The chance to stay on a working farm is the draw at La Pergola, a whitewashed villa perched on the slopes of Monte Epomeo. Surrounded by vineyards and olive and fruit trees, the villa has sweeping views westward over Citara Beach. Its dynamic young owners also operate a thriving restaurant serving local specialties including the fabled *coniglio all'ischitana* (rabbit simmered with tomatoes). ⊠ *Via San Giuseppe 8, 80077, Forio* ☎▤ *081/909483* ⊕ *www.agriturismolapergola. it* ⇆ *7 rooms* ⌕ *Restaurant; no a/c, no room phones, no room TVs* ▤ *No credit cards* ⏐⊙⏐ *MAP.*

Capri

75 mins by boat, 40 mins by hydrofoil from Naples.

Erstwhile pleasure dome to Roman emperors and now Italy's most glamorous seaside getaway, Capri (pronounced with an accent on the first syllable) is a craggy island at the southern approach to the Bay of Naples.

13

The summer scene on Capri calls to mind the stampeding of bulls through the narrow streets of Pamplona: if you can visit in spring or fall, do so. Yet even the crowds are not enough to destroy Capri's very special charm. The town is a Moorish opera set of shiny white houses, tiny squares, and narrow medieval alleyways hung with flowers. You can take a bus or the funicular to reach the town, which rests on top of rugged limestone cliffs hundreds of feet above the sea, and on which herds of *capre* (goats) once used to roam (giving the name to the island). Unlike the other islands in the Bay of Naples, Capri is not of volcanic origin; it may be a continuation of the limestone Sorrentine peninsula.

Limestone caves on Capri have yielded rich prehistoric and neolithic finds. The island is thought to have been settled by Greeks from Cumae in the 6th century BC and later by other Greeks from Neapolis, but it was the Romans in the early imperial period who really left their mark. Emperor Augustus vacationed here; Tiberius built a dozen villas around the island, and, in later years, he refused to return to Rome, even when he was near death. Capri was one of the strongholds of the 16th-century pirate Barbarossa, who first sacked it and then made it a fortress. In 1806 the British wanted to turn the island into another Gibraltar and were beginning to build fortifications until the French took it away from them in 1808. Over the next century, from the opening of its first hotel in 1826, Capri saw an influx of visitors that reads like a Who's Who of literature and politics, especially in the early decades of the 20th century.

Like much else about Capri, the island's rare and delicious white wine is sensuous and intoxicating. Note that most of the wine passed off as "local" on Capri comes from the much more extensive vineyards of Ischia.

On arrival at the port, pick up the excellent map of the island at the tourist office (€1). You may have to wait in

> ## WORD OF MOUTH
>
> "The Blue Grotto (Grotta Azzurra) really is worth it; the color is not to be believed. But . . . you have to sit in the little motor boat outside the grotto with all the other boats until it is your turn. Bad fumes, queasiness in everyone. . . . But I loved loved loved Capri. Not the main streets, but all the small byways."   –humanone

25 line for the cog railway (€2.60 round-trip) to **Capri Town,** perched some 450 feet above the harbor. If it's not operating, there's a bus and taxi service, as well as a network of steps leading all the way up. From the upper station, walk out into Piazza Umberto I, much better known as the Piazzetta, the island's social hub. You can window-shop in expensive boutiques and browse in souvenir shops along Via Vittorio

26 Emanuele, which leads south toward the many-domed **Certosa di San Giacomo.** You can visit the church and cloister of this much-restored monastery and also pause long enough to enjoy the breathtaking view of Punta Tragara and the Faraglioni, three towering crags, from the viewpoint at the edge of the cliff. ✉ *Via Certosa* ☎ *081/8376218* ☺ *Tues.–Sun. 9–2.*

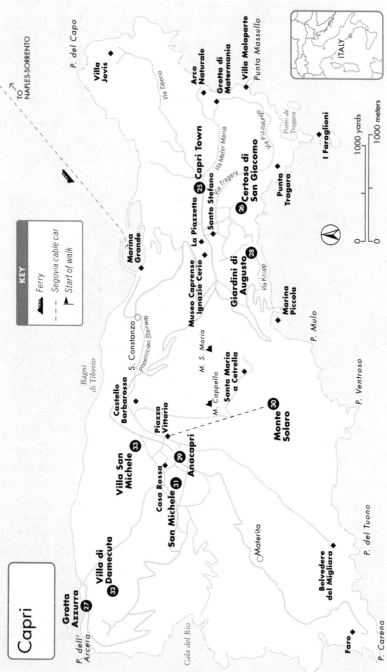

Capri

KEY

- Ferry
- --- Segovia cable car
- Start of walk

TO NAPLES-SORRENTO

P. del Capo

Villa Jovis

Via Tiberio

Arco Naturale

Grotta di Matermania

Villa Malaparte

Punta Massullo

I Faraglioni

Capri Town **25**

La Piazzetta **25**

Santo Stefano

Via Mater Mania

Certosa di San Giacomo **26**

Via Tragara

Via Pizzolungo

Punta Tragara

Porto de Tragara

1000 yards

1000 meters

Marina Grande

Museo Caprense Ignazio Cerio

Giardini di Augusto **28**

Via Krupp

Marina Piccola

P. Mulo

S. Constanzo

Phoenician Stairway

Bagni di Tiberio

M. S. Maria

M. Cappello

Santa Maria a Cetrella

Castello Barbarossa

Piazza Vittoria

Villa San Michele **33**

Anacapri **29**

Casa Rossa **31**

San Michele

Monte Solaro **30**

Materita

P. Ventroso

Villa di Damecuta **32**

Grotta Azzurra **27**

P. dell' Arcera

Cala del Rio

Belvedere del Migliara

Faro

P. del Tuono

P. Carena

ITALY

off the beaten path

VILLA JOVIS – From Capri Town, the 45-minute hike east to Villa Jovis, the grandest of those built by Tiberius, is strenuous but rewarding. Follow the signs for Villa Jovis, taking Via Le Botteghe from the Piazzetta, then continuing along Via Croce and Via Tiberio. At the end of a lane that climbs the steep hill, with pretty views all the way, you come to the precipice over which the emperor reputedly disposed of the victims of his perverse attentions. From a natural terrace above, near a chapel, are spectacular views of the entire Bay of Naples and, on clear days, part of the Gulf of Salerno. Below are the ruins of Tiberius's palace. Allow 45 minutes each way for the walk alone. ⊠ *Via Tiberio* ☎ *081/8370381* 💶 *€5* ⊙ *Daily 9–1 hr before sunset.*

13

㉗ Only when the **Grotta Azzurra** was "discovered" in 1826 by the Polish poet August Kopisch and Swiss artist Ernest Fries, did Capri become a tourist haven. The watery cave's blue beauty became a symbol of the return to nature and revolt from reason that marked the Romantic era, and it soon became a required stop on the Grand Tour. In fact, the grotto had long been a local landmark. During the Roman era—as testified by the extensive remains, primarily below sea level, and several large statues now at the Certosa di San Giacomo—it had been the elegant, mosaic-decorated nymphaeum of the adjoining villa of Gradola. Historians can't quite agree if it was simply a lovely little pavilion where rich patricians would cool themselves or truly a religious site where sacred mysteries were practiced. The water's extraordinary sapphire color is caused by a hidden opening in the rock that refracts the light. At highest illumination the very air inside seems tinted blue.

The Grotta Azzurra can be reached from Marina Grande or from the small embarkation point below Anacapri on the northwest side of the island, accessible by bus from Anacapri. If you're pressed for time, however, skip this sometimes frustrating and disappointing excursion. You board one boat to get to the grotto, then transfer to another smaller boat to take you inside. If there's a backup of boats waiting to get in, you'll be given precious little time to enjoy the gorgeous color of the water and its silvery reflections. ⊠ *Marina Grande* 💶 *About €15–€20, depending on boat company, including admission to grotto* ⊙ *Apr.–Sept., daily 9:30–2 hrs before sunset; Oct.–Mar., daily 10–noon.*

㉘ From the terraces of the **Giardini di Augusto** (Gardens of Augustus), a beautifully planted public garden with excellent views, you can see the village of Marina Piccola below—restaurants, cabanas, and swimming platforms huddle among the shoals—and admire the steep and winding Via Krupp, actually a staircase cut into the rock. Friedrich Krupp, the German arms manufacturer, loved Capri and became one of the island's most generous benefactors. The staircase has been closed for years, but you can reach the beach by taking a bus from the Via Roma terminus down to Marina Piccola. ⊠ *Via Matteotti, beyond monastery of San Giacomo* ⊙ *Daily dawn–dusk.*

㉙ A tortuous road leads up to **Anacapri,** the island's "second city," about 3 km (2 mi) from Capri Town. To get there you can take a bus either from Via Roma in Capri Town or from Marina Grande (both €1.30), or a taxi (about €15 one-way; agree on the fare before starting out). Crowds are thick down Via Capodimonte leading to Villa San Michele and around the square, Piazza Vittoria, which is the starting point of the chairlift to the top of Monte Solaro. Elsewhere, Anacapri is quietly appealing. It's a good starting point for walks, such as the 80-minute round-trip journey to the **Migliara Belvedere,** on the island's southern coast.

30 An impressive limestone formation and the highest point on Capri (1,932 feet), **Monte Solaro** affords gasp-inducing views toward the bays of both Naples and Salerno. A 12-minute chairlift ride will take you right to the top (refreshments available at bar), which is a starting point for a number of scenic trails on the western side of the island. Picnickers should note that even in summer it can get windy at this height, and there are few trees to provide shade or refuge. ⊠ *Piazza Vittoria, Anacapri* 🕾 *081/8371428* 🎫 *€4 one-way, €5.50 round-trip* ☉ *Daily 9–5:30.*

31 In the heart of Anacapri, the octagonal baroque church of **San Michele,** finished in 1719, is best known for its exquisite majolica pavement designed by Solimena and executed by the *mastro-riggiolaro* (master tiler) Chiaiese from Abruzzo. A walkway skirts the depiction of Adam and a duly contrite Eve being expelled from the Garden of Eden, but you can get a fine overview from the organ loft, reached by a winding staircase near the ticket booth (a privileged perch you have to pay for). Outside the church is the Via Finestrale, which leads to Anacapri's noted **Le Boffe quarter.** This section of town, centered on the Piazza Ficacciate, owes its name to the distinctive domestic architecture prevalent here, which uses vaults and sculpted groins instead of cross beams. ⊠ *Piazza Nicola, Anacapri* 🕾 *081/8372396* 🎫 *€2* ☉ *Nov.–Mar., daily 9:30–5; Apr.–Oct., daily 9–7.*

32 One of the best excursions from Anacapri is to the ruins of the Roman **Villa di Damecuta.** Sited strategically on a ridge with views sweeping across the Bay of Naples toward Procida and Ischia, the villa would have had its main access point at the landing stage right by the Blue Grotto at Gradola. This was probably one of the villas mentioned by Tacitus in his *Annals* as having been built by Tiberius: "Here on Capreae, in twelve spacious, separately named villas, Tiberius settled." Like Villa Jovis to the east, Villa di Damecuta was extensively plundered over the centuries prior to its proper excavation in 1937. Below the medieval tower (Torre Damecuta) there are two rooms (*domus* and *cubiculum*) that are thought to have been Tiberius's secret summer refuge. Affinities with Villa Jovis may be seen in the *ambulatio* (walkway) complete with seats and a stunning backdrop. To reach Villa Damecuta, get the bus from Anacapri to Grotta Azzurra and ask the driver to let you off at the proper stop. Alternatively, you can walk from the center of Anacapri down the bus route (about 30 minutes, but no sidewalks) or try your luck in the network of virtually traffic-free little alleyways running parallel to the main road. ⊠ *Via A. Maiuri* 🎫 *Free* ☉ *Daily 9–1 hr before sunset.*

From Anacapri's Piazza della Vittoria, picturesque Via Capodimonte leads
★ ㉝ to **Villa San Michele,** the charming former home of Swedish doctor and
philanthropist Axel Munthe (1857–1949) that Henry James called "the
most fantastic beauty, poetry, and inutility that one had ever seen clustered together." At the ancient entranceway to Anacapri at the top of the
Scala Fenicia, the villa is set around Roman-style courtyards, marble walkways, and atriums. Rooms display the doctor's varied collections, which
range from bric-a-brac to antiquities. Medieval choir stalls, Renaissance
lecterns, and gilded statues of saints are all part of the setting, with some
rooms preserving the doctor's personal memorabilia. A spectacular pergola path overlooking the entire Bay of Naples leads from the villa to
the famous Sphinx Parapet, where an ancient Egyptian sphinx looks out
toward Sorrento; you cannot see its face—on purpose. It is said that if
you touch the sphinx's hindquarters with your left hand while making
a wish, it will come true. The parapet is connected to the little Chapel
of San Michele, on the grounds of one of Tiberius's villas.

13

Besides hosting summer concerts, the Axel Munthe Foundation has an
ecomuseum that fittingly reflects Munthe's fondness for animals. There
you can learn about various bird species—accompanied by their songs—
found on Capri. Munthe bought up the hillside and made it a sanctuary for birds. ⊠ *Via Axel Munthe* ☎ *081/837401* ⊕ *www.sanmichele.
org* 💶 *€5* ☉ *May–Sept., daily 9–6; Mar., daily 9:30–4:30; Apr. and Oct.,
daily 9:30–5; Nov.–Feb., daily 10:30–3:30.*

Where to Stay & Eat

$–$$$$ ✕ **La Canzone del Mare.** This is the legendary spot at the Marina Pic-
cola, erstwhile haunt of Grace Fields, Emilio Pucci, Noël Coward, and
any number of '50s and '60s glitterati. The VIPs may have departed for
the beach at the Bagni di Tiberio, but the setting is as magical as ever.
Enjoy lunch (no dinner served) in the thatch-roof pavilion looking out
over the sea and I Faraglioni in the distance—this is Capri as picture-
perfect as it comes. ⊠ *Via Marina Piccola 93, Capri Town* ☎ *081/
8370104* ▤ *AE, DC, MC, V* ☉ *Closed Nov.–Mar. No dinner.*

$$$ ✕ **La Capannina.** One of Capri's finest restaurants, La Capannina is only
a few steps from the busy social hub of the Piazzetta. It has a discreet
covered veranda—open in summer—for dining by candlelight; most of
the regulars avoid the stuffy dining rooms. The specialties are homemade
ravioli and linguine *con lo scorfano* (with scorpion fish). Look for the
authentic Capri wine with the house label. ⊠ *Via Le Botteghe 12 bis and
14, Capri Town* ☎ *081/8370732* 🍴 *Reservations essential* ▤ *AE, DC,
MC, V* ☉ *Closed mid-Jan.–mid-Mar. and Wed. Mar. and Nov.*

$$–$$$ ✕ **Ristorante Pizzeria Aurora.** Though often frequented by celebrities—
their photographs adorn the walls—this restaurant offers *simpatia* to
all its patrons. Sit outside for maximum visibility or opt for extra pri-
vacy within. The cognoscenti start off by sharing a pizza *all'acqua,* a
thin pizza with mozzarella and a sprinkling of *peperoncino* (dried chili
peppers). If tiring of pasta, try the *sformatino alla Franco* (rice pie in a
prawn sauce). Reservations are essential for dinner. ⊠ *Via Fuorlovado
18–20, Capri Town* ☎ *081/8370181* ▤ *AE, DC, MC, V* ☉ *Closed Jan.
and Feb.*

★ $$ ✕ **Da Tonino.** It is well worth making a trip to the Arco Naturale, a rock formation east of Capri Town, to be pampered by creative chef Tonino. The emphasis here is on land-based dishes; try the *terrina di coniglio* (rabbit terrine) or ask for the pigeon dish with pesto, rosemary, and pine nuts, accompanied by wine from a well-stocked cellar. ⊠ *Via Dentecala 34, Capri Town* ☎ *081/8376718* ⊟ *AE, DC, MC, V* ⊘ *Closed Jan. 10–Mar. 15.*

$$ ✕ **I Faraglioni.** With shade provided by a 100-year-old wisteria plant, this popular restaurant is immersed in Mediterranean greenery. Meals in the fairly stylish dining room usually kick off with *uovo alla Monachina,* an egg-shaped dish stuffed with mystery ingredients. For the first course, try the *straccetti con gamberi e pomodorini* (fresh green pasta with shrimp and cherry tomatoes). ⊠ *Via Camerelle 75, Capri Town* ☎ *081/8370320* ⌂ *Reservations essential* ⊟ *AE, DC, MC, V* ⊘ *Closed Nov.–Mar.*

$–$$ ✕ **Al Grottino.** At this small and friendly family-run restaurant near the Piazzetta you'll find vaulted ceilings and autographed photos of celebrity customers hanging on the walls. House specialties include gnocchi with tomato sauce and mozzarella, and linguine *ai gamberetti* (with shrimp and tomatoes). ⊠ *Via Longano 27, Capri Town* ☎ *081/8370584* ⌂ *Reservations essential* ⊟ *AE, DC, MC, V* ⊘ *Closed Tues. and Nov. 3–Mar. 20.*

$–$$ ✕ **La Giara.** A two-minute walk from Anacapri's bustling Piazza Vittoria, this casual eatery has a variety of delicious dishes served briskly and courteously. For a change from seafood, try the *pennette aum aum,* pasta pleasingly garnished with eggplant, mozzarella, cherry tomatoes, and basil. ⊠ *Via Orlandi 67, Anacapri* ☎ *081/8373860* ⊟ *AE, DC, MC, V* ⊘ *Closed Wed., and Dec. and Jan.*

$$$$ ▦ **Punta Tragara.** Clinging to the Punta Tragara, this gorgeous hotel has
FodorsChoice a hold-your-breath perch directly over the rocks of I Faraglioni. Origi-
★ nally a villa visited by Churchill and Eisenhower, its exterior was renovated by Le Corbusier in traditional Capri style, then opened as a hotel in the 1970s. Baronial fireplaces, gilded antiques, and travertine marble set the style in the main salons, while guest rooms—no two are alike—are sumptuous. The garden area has two beautiful saltwater pools and an arbor-covered restaurant, La Bussola, which might be the prettiest spot on the island. To top it off, the staff seems to have been sent to the finest finishing schools. ⊠ *Via Tragara 57, 80073, Capri Town* ☎ *081/ 8370844* 🖷 *081/8377790* ⊕ *www.hoteltragara.com* ⇨ *48 rooms* ⌂ *Restaurant, 2 pools, bar* ⊟ *AE, DC, MC, V* ⦿ *BP.*

$$$$ ▦ **Quisisana.** This grand hotel, one of the island's most luxurious, sits in the center of Capri Town. The bright and spacious rooms have some antique accents. Many have arcaded balconies with views of the sea or the charming enclosed garden surrounding a swimming pool. The Quisisana is particularly popular with Americans. ⊠ *Via Camerelle 2, 80073, Capri Town* ☎ *081/8370788* 🖷 *081/8376080* ⊕ *www.quisi. com* ⇨ *149 rooms* ⌂ *2 restaurants, cable TV, tennis court, pool, gym, sauna, bar, Internet, convention center* ⊟ *AE, DC, MC, V* ⊘ *Closed Nov.–mid-Mar.* ⦿ *MAP.*

★ $$$$ ▦ **Scalinatella.** The name means "little stairway," and that's how this charming but modern small hotel is built, on terraces following the slope of the hill, overlooking the gardens, pool, and sea. The bedrooms are intimate, with alcoves and fresh, bright colors; the bathrooms have whirlpool baths. ⊠ *Via Tragara 8, 80073, Capri Town* ☎ *081/8370633* 🖷 *081/8378291* ⊕ *www.scalinatella.com* 🛏 *30 rooms* ⚖ *Restaurant, tennis court, pool, bar* ⊟ *AE, DC, MC, V* ⊗ *Closed Nov.–mid-Mar.* ¶⊘ *BP.*

$$$$ ╳🏠 **Villa Brunella.** This gem is in a garden just below the lane leading to the Faraglioni. Comfortable and tastefully furnished, the family-run hotel has spectacular views and a swimming pool overlooking the sea. The terrace restaurant ($$) also benefits from the superb panorama and is renowned for its seafood and other local dishes. ⊠ *Via Tragara 24, 80073, Capri Town* ☎ *081/8370122* 🖷 *081/8370430* ⊕ *www. villabrunella.it* 🛏 *20 rooms* ⚖ *Restaurant, cable TV, pool, bar* ⊟ *AE, DC, MC, V* ⊗ *Closed Nov.–Mar.* ¶⊘ *BP.*

$$–$$$ 🏠 **Villa Sarah.** This whitewashed Mediterranean building has a homey look and bright, simply furnished rooms. It's close enough to the Piazzetta (a 10-minute walk) to give easy access to the goings-on there, yet far enough away to ensure restful nights. There's a garden and a small bar. ⊠ *Via Tiberio 3/a, 80073, Capri Town* ☎ *081/8377817* 🖷 *081/8377215* ⊕ *www.villasarah.it* 🛏 *20 rooms* ⚖ *Cable TV, bar, Internet* ⊟ *AE, DC, MC, V* ⊗ *Closed Nov.–Mar.* ¶⊘ *BP.*

$$ 🏠 **Il Girasole.** A popular option for those on a budget, il Girasole is set in a grove of olive trees. It has small but bright rooms, which look out onto a flower-filled terrace. ⊠ *Via Linciano 47, 80071, Anacapri* ☎ *081/ 8372351* ⊕ *www.ilgirasole.com* 🛏 *18 rooms* ⚖ *No a/c* ⊟ *No credit cards* ⊗ *Closed Oct.–May* ¶⊘ *BP.*

$$ 🏠 **Villa Krupp.** Occupying a quiet location near the Gardens of Augustus, this historic hostelry was once the home of Maxim Gorky, whose guests included Vladimir Lenin. Rooms are plain but spacious. ⊠ *Viale Matteotti 12, 80073, Capri Town* ☎ *081/8370362* 🖷 *081/8376489* 🛏 *12 rooms* ⚖ *No a/c in some rooms, no room TVs* ⊟ *MC, V* ⊗ *Closed Nov.–Mar.* ¶⊘ *BP.*

$ 🏠 **Aida.** On a tiny lane that borders the Gardens of Augustus, the Aida offers a tranquil haven from the island's hustle and bustle. The staff is sociable, and the rooms, which look onto a small garden, are spacious, comfortably furnished, and immaculately clean. ⊠ *Via Birago, 80073, Capri Town* ☎ *081/8370366* 🛏 *4 rooms* ⚖ *No a/c* ⊟ *No credit cards* ⊗ *Closed Oct.–May* ¶⊘ *BP.*

SORRENTO & THE AMALFI COAST

As travelers journey down the fabled Amalfi Coast, their route takes them past rocky cliffs plunging into the sea and small boats lying in sandy coves like brightly colored fish. Erosion has contorted the rocks into shapes resembling figures from mythology and hollowed out fairy grottoes where the air is turquoise and the water an icy blue. In winter nativity scenes of moss and stone are created in the rocks. White villages dripping with flowers nestle in coves or climb like vines up the steep, terraced hills. Lemon trees abound, loaded with blossom or fruit—and netting in winter to protect the fruit. The inhabitants jest that they look after their lemons better than their children. The road must have a thousand turns, each with a different view, on its dizzying 69-km (43-mi) journey from Sorrento to Salerno.

Sorrento

㉞ *50 km (31 mi) south of Naples, 50 km (31 mi) west of Salerno.*

Sorrento is across the Bay of Naples from Naples itself, on autostrada A3 and SS145. The Circumvesuviana railway, which stops at Herculaneum and Pompeii, provides another connection. The coast between Naples and Castellammare, where road and railway turn off onto the Sorrento peninsula, seems at times depressingly overbuilt and industrialized. Yet Vesuvius looms to the left, you can make out the 3,000-foot-high mass of Monte Faito ahead, and on a clear day you can see Capri off the tip of the peninsula. The scenery improves considerably as you near Sorrento, where the coastal plain is carved into russet cliffs rising perpendicularly from the sea. This is the Sorrento (north) side of the peninsula; on the other side is the more dramatically scenic Amalfi Coast. But Sorrento has at least two advantages over Amalfi: the Circumvesuviana railway terminal and a fairly flat terrain. A stroll around town is a pleasure—you'll encounter narrow alleyways and interesting churches, and the views of the Bay of Naples from the Villa Comunale and the Museo Correale are priceless.

Until the mid-20th century Sorrento was a small, genteel resort favored by central European princes, English aristocrats, and American literati. During World War I American soldiers came to recuperate at the Hotel Vittoria. Now the town has grown and spread out along the crest of its famous cliffs, and apartments stand where citrus groves once bloomed. Like most resorts, Sorrento is best off-season, in spring, autumn, or even winter, when Campania's mild climate can make a stay pleasant anywhere along the coast.

A highlight of Sorrento is **Museo Correale di Terranova,** an 18th-century villa with a lovely garden on land given to the patrician Correale family by Queen Joan of Aragon in 1428. It has an excellent private collection amassed by the count of Terranova and his brother. The building itself is fairly charmless, with few period rooms, but the garden offers an allée of palm trees, citrus groves, floral nurseries, and an esplanade with a panoramic view of the Sorrento coast. The collection itself is one of the finest devoted to Neapolitan paintings, decorative arts, and porcelains, so for connoisseurs of the *seicento* (Italian 17th century), this museum is a must. Magnificent 18th-century inlaid tables by Giuseppe Gargiulo, Capodimonte porcelains, and rococo portrait miniatures are reminders of the age when pleasure and delight were all. Also on view are regional Greek and Roman archaeological finds, medieval marble work, glasswork, old master paintings, 17th-century majolicas—even Tasso's death mask. ⊠ *Via Correale* ☎ *081/8781846* ⊕ *www.sorrento-online.com/museocorreale* ⊠ €6 ⊙ *Wed.–Mon. 9–2.*

Worth checking out is the **Museo Bottega della Tarsialignea,** set up by local architects to ensure the continuity of the intarsia (wood inlay) tradition. It houses historical collections as well as exhibitions of modern work.

Sorrento &
Amalfi Coast

KEY

Ferry Lines

Guided tours, the only way to see the displays, depart every half hour. There's a shop where you can pick up an unusual souvenir. ✉ *Via San Nicola 28* ☎ *081/8771942* ⊕ *www.alessandrofiorentinocollection.it* 💰 *€8* ⊘ *Apr.–Oct., Tues.–Sun. 9:30–noon and 5–7; Nov.–Mar., Tues.–Sun. 9:30–noon and 3–5. Shop Tues.–Sun. 9:30–1 and 5–8 (Nov.–Mar. 3–6).*

Via Marina Grande turns into a pedestrian lane, then a stairway leading to Sorrento's only real beach at **Marina Grande,** where fishermen pull up their boats and there are some good seafood restaurants. A frequent bus also plies this route; tickets are sold at the *tabacchi* (tobacconist).

Where to Stay & Eat

★ $$$$ ✗ **Don Alfonso 1890.** The most heralded restaurant in Campania is the domain of Alfonso Iaccarino; *haute*-hungry pilgrims come here to feast on culinary rarities, often centuries-old recipes given a unique spin. The braciola of lamb with pine nuts and raisins is a recipe that dates back to the Renaissance, and the cannoli stuffed with foie gras pays homage to the Neapolitan Bourbon court. Nearly everything is homegrown, and the wine cellar is one of the finest in Europe. Those who want to make a night of it can stay in one of five apartments above the restaurant.

✉ *Corso Sant'Agata 13, Sant'Agata sui due Golfi, 7 km (4 mi) south of Sorrento* ☎ *081/8780026* 🖃 *AE, DC, MC, V* ⊙ *Closed Mon. and Jan. 10–Mar.; closed Tues. Oct.–May.*

\$\$\$–\$\$\$\$ ✗ **Antica Trattoria.** An old-fashioned dining room inside and garden tables in fair weather make this a pleasant place to enjoy the local cooking. The atmosphere is homey and the menu is voluminous; specialties include spaghetti alle vongole and *pappardelle all'antica trattoria* (fresh pasta with porcini mushrooms, prosciutto, tomatoes, and basil). You can also opt for one of four prix-fixe menus. ✉ *Via Giuliani 33* ☎*081/8071082* 🖃 *AE, DC, MC, V* ⊙ *Closed Mon. and 4 wks in Jan. and Feb.*

\$–\$\$\$\$ ✗ **Antico Francischiello da Peppino.** Overlooking rows of olive trees that seem to run into the sea, this eatery is away from the throng, halfway between Sorrento and Massa Lubrense. Two huge, beamed dining rooms with brick archways, old chandeliers, antique mirrored sideboards, hundreds of mounted plates, and tangerine-hued tablecloths make for quite a sight. Specialties at this fourth-generation establishment include ravioli filled with sea bass, baked bream in a potato crust with lemon, and limoncello ice cream. ✉ *Via Partenope 27, Massa Lubrense* ☎ *081/533–9780* 🖃 *AE, DC, MC, V* ⊙ *Closed Wed. in winter.*

★ **\$–\$\$** ✗ **La Favorita—O' Parrucchiano.** Set in a high-ceiling greenhouse, this sprawling eatery has enough tables and chairs amid enough tropical greenery to fill a Victorian conservatory. Opened in 1890 by a former priest (the name means "the priest's place" in the local dialect), La Favorita continues to serve classic Sorrentine cuisine. Though the white-bean soup, cheese baked in lemon leaves, ravioli caprese, lemon tart, and profiteroles are all excellent, they can't compete with the unique decor. ✉ *Corso Italia 71* ☎ *081/8781321* 🖃 *MC, V* ⊙ *Closed Wed. Nov.–Mar.*

\$ ✗ **Trattoria da Emilia.** You can sit outside at this trattoria on the Marina Grande and watch the life of the port go by. This simple, rustic restaurant with wooden tables has been run by Donna Emilia and her offspring since 1947 and provides typical Sorrento home cooking and a family atmosphere. Fried seafood is the specialty. Sofia Loren ate here while filming *Pane, amore . . ..* ✉ *Via Marina Grande 62* ☎ *081/8072720* 🖃 *No credit cards* ⊙ *Closed Tues. Oct.–Mar. No dinner Oct.–Mar.*

\$\$\$\$ 🏨 **Bellevue Syrene.** Set in a cliff-top garden close to the center of Sorrento, this exclusive hotel retains its old-fashioned comforts and sumptuous charm with Victorian nooks and alcoves, antique paintings, and exuberant frescoes. You can find interior-facing rooms at lower prices if you're willing to forgo the splendid views over the sea. Try breakfast on the sunny terrace in the summer. ✉ *Piazza della Vittoria 5, 80067* ☎ *081/8781024* 🖶 *081/8783963* ⊕ *www.bellevuesyrene.it* ➩ *73 rooms* ♢ *2 restaurants, minibars, gym, beach, dock, bar, meeting room, some pets allowed* 🖃 *AE, DC, MC, V* ⫴◉⫴ *BP.*

★ **\$\$\$\$** 🏨 **Cocumella.** A grand hotel in every sense, the Cocumella seems little changed since the days when Goethe and the Duke of Wellington stayed here. Overlooking the Bay of Naples, the hotel occupies a 17th-century monastery complete with frescoed ceilings and antique reliquaries. The amenities are hardly monastic: they include a spectacular pool area, a workout room, summer concerts in the hotel's baroque church, and Empire-style suites, some with fireplaces. For around €140 per person you can spend a day cruising in the hotel's 90-foot-long 19th-century yacht. Given the hotel's high standards, the restaurant is a disappointment. ⊠ *Via Cocumella 7, Sant'Agnello, 80065* ☎ *081/8782933* 🖷 *081/8783712* ⊕ *www.cocumella.com* ⤷ *50 rooms, 18 suites* ⚿ *Restaurant, cable TV, pool, gym, spa, bar, Internet, some pets allowed* ☰ *AE, DC, MC, V* ⊙ *Closed Nov.–Mar.* �|◎| *BP.*

★ **$$$$** 🏨 **Excelsior Vittoria.** Magnificently situated overlooking the Bay of Naples, this is a belle-epoque dream come true. Gilded salons, stunning gardens, and an impossibly romantic terrace where orchestras lull you twice a week with Neapolitan and modern music: in all, it's a truly intoxicating experience. Caruso stayed here and, more recently, Luciano Pavarotti. An outdoor swimming pool and gym add more modern comforts. ⊠ *Piazza Tasso 34, 80067* ☎ *081/8071044* 🖷 *081/8771206* ⊕ *www.exvitt.it* ⤷ *98 rooms, 20 suites* ⚿ *Restaurant, cable TV, pool, bar, Internet, meeting room, some pets allowed* ☰ *AE, DC, MC, V* �|◎| *BP.*

$$ 🏨 **Settimo Cielo.** Even if your wallet won't allow a stay at one of Sorrento's grand hotels, you can still find lodgings right on the water. This hotel, an excellent choice for budget travelers, is a few steps away from the beach. The grounds have pretty gardens and a swimming pool. The rooms, which all face the sea, are simple and modern. ⊠ *Via Capo 27, 80067* ☎ *081/8781012* 🖷 *081/8073290* ⊕ *www.hotelsettimocielo. com* ⤷ *20 rooms* ⚿ *Restaurant, pool, bar* ☰ *AE, DC, MC, V* ⊙ *Closed Nov.–mid-Dec., Jan.–Mar.* �|◎| *BP.*

$ 🏨 **Lorelei et Londres.** Once favored by room-with-a-view ladies on holiday, this amazing relic still looks like E. M. Forster's Lucy Honeychurch might pull up at any moment. In front is a beautiful terrace café, aflutter with red awnings and tablecloths. The welcoming lobby always seems to be filled with laughter, so apparently few guests mind that the linoleum-floored rooms upstairs are furnished with simple beds and creaking cupboards. Ask for sea-view rooms away from the noisy road. For luxe and modernity, go elsewhere; come here to take a trip back to the *bella* 19th century. ⊠ *Via Califano 2, 80067* ☎ *081/8073187* 🖷 *081/ 5329001* ⤷ *27 rooms* ☰ *AE, DC, MC, V* ⊙ *Closed mid-Nov.–mid-Mar.* �|◎| *BP.*

FodorśChoice ★

$ 🏨 **Mignon Meublé.** Spacious and simple yet stylish accommodations, a central location, friendly service, and bargain rates—with all this you'll understand why it's advisable to book well in advance. Breakfast is served in your room, but there's also a small sitting area where you can relax. ⊠ *Via Sersale 9, 80067* ☎ *081/8073824* 🖷 *081/5329001* ⤷ *23 rooms* ⚿ *No room phones* ☰ *AE, DC, MC, V* �|◎| *BP.*

Nightlife & the Arts

BAR At **Circolo dei Forestieri** (⊠ Via de Maio 35 ☎ 081/8773263) you'll get a memorable view of the Bay of Naples from the terrace. Drinks are moderately priced, and there's live music nightly in summer and every weekend the rest of the year. It's closed January and February.

Shopping

You may want to stop in one of the many shops selling limoncello, the famous lemon liqueur. Piemme and Villa Massa are recommended brands; the latter is exported to the United States.

Around **Piazza Tasso** are a number of shops selling embroidered goods and intarsia woodwork, a centuries-old tradition in Sorrento. **Fattoria Terranova** (✉ Piazza Tasso 161 ☎ 081/8781263) sells all kinds of foods ranging from cheeses to preserves, all made on a family-run farm in nearby Massa.

Along narrow **Via San Cesareo,** where the air is pungent with the perfumes of fruit and vegetable stands, there are shops selling local and Italian crafts—everything from jewelry boxes to trays and coffee tables with intarsia decoration. **Ferdinando Corcione,** in his shop on Via San Francesco, gives demonstrations of intarsia work, producing decorative plaques with classic or contemporary motifs.

Positano

★ ㉟ *14 km (9 mi) east of Sorrento, 57 km (34 mi) south of Naples.*

When John Steinbeck lived here in 1953, he wrote that it was difficult to consider tourism an industry because "there are not enough *tourists.*" Alas, Positano, a village of white Moorish-style houses clinging to slopes around a small sheltered bay, has since been discovered. The artists came first, and, as so often happens, the wealthy followed, and the artists fled. Another Steinbeck observation still applies, however: "Positano bites deep. It is a dream place that isn't quite real when you are there and becomes beckoningly real after you have gone. . . . The small curving bay of unbelievably blue and green water laps gently on a beach of small pebbles. There is only one narrow street and it does not come down to the water. Everything else is stairs, some of them as steep as ladders. You do not walk to visit a friend, you either climb or slide."

In the 10th century Positano was part of Amalfi's maritime republic, which rivaled Venice as an important mercantile power. Its heyday was in the 16th and 17th centuries, when its ships traded in the Near and Middle East carrying spices, silks, and precious woods. The coming of the steamship in the mid-19th century led to the town's decline; some three-fourths of its 8,000 citizens emigrated to America, most to New York.

What had been reduced to a forgotten fishing village is now the number one attraction on the coast. From here you can take hydrofoils to Capri in summer, escorted bus rides to Ravello, and tours of the Grotta dello Smeraldo. If you're staying in Positano, check whether your hotel has a parking area. If not, you will have to pay for space in a parking lot, which is almost impossible to find during the high season, from Easter to September. The best bet for day-trippers is to arrive by bus—there is a good, regular service—or else get to Positano early enough to find a parking space.

No matter how much time you spend in Positano, make sure you have some comfortable walking shoes (no heels) and that your back and legs are strong enough to negotiate those daunting *scalinatelle* (little stairways). Alternatively, you can ride the municipal bus, which frequently plies along the one-and-only-one-way Via Pasitea, hairpinning from Positano's central Piazza dei Mulini to the mountains and back, making a loop through the town every half hour. Heading down from the Sponda bus stop toward the beach, you pass Le Sirenuse, the hotel where John Steinbeck stayed in 1953. Its stepped terraces offer vistas over the town, so you might splurge on lunch or a drink here on the pool terrace, a favorite gathering place for Modigliani-sleek jet-setters. Continue to Piazza dei Mulini, and make a left turn onto Via dei Mulini.

> **WORD OF MOUTH**
>
> "For our honeymoon we went to Positano (and did day trips to Capri, Ravello, Sorrento, Amalfi and Pompeii). It was the most romantic place—so beautiful. Wonderful shops and restaurants were everywhere! The drive along the cliffs was scary, but exhilarating too!" —Gemini MBA

need a break? If you want to catch your breath after a bus ride to Positano, take a quick time-out for an espresso, a slice of Positanese (a delectable chocolate cake), or a fresh-fruit iced granita in the lemon-tree garden at **Bar-Pasticceria La Zagara** (⊠ Via Mulini 8 ☎ 089/875964).

Past a bevy of resort boutiques, head to Via dei Mulini 23 to view the prettiest garden in Positano—the 18th-century courtyard of the **Palazzo Murat,** named for Joachim Murat, who sensibly chose the palazzo as his summer residence. This was where Murat, designated by his brother-in-law Napoléon as King of Naples in 1808, came to forget the demands of power and lead the simple life. Since Murat was one of Europe's leading style setters, it couldn't be *too* simple, and he wound up building a grand abode (now a hotel) just steps from the main beach.

Beyond the Palazzo Murat is the Chiesa Madre, or parish church of **Santa Maria Assunta,** its green-and-yellow majolica dome topped by a perky cupola visible from just about anywhere in town. Built on the site of the former Benedictine abbey of St. Vito, the 13th-century Romanesque structure was almost completely rebuilt in 1700. The last piece of the ancient mosaic floor can be seen under glass near the apse. Note the carved wooden Christ, a masterpiece of devotional religious art, with its bathetic face and bloodied knees, on view before the altar. At the altar is a Byzantine 13th-century painting on wood of Madonna with Child, known as the Black Virgin, carried to the main beach every August 15 to celebrate the Feast of the Assumption. Legend claims that the painting was once stolen by Saracen pirates, who, fleeing in a raging storm, heard from a voice on high saying, "*Posa, posa*"—"Put it down, put it down." When they placed the image on the beach near the church, the storm calmed, as did the Saracens. Positano was saved, and the town's name was established (yet again). Embedded over the doorway of the church's bell tower, set across the tiny piazza, is a medieval bas-relief of fishes, a fox, and a pistrice, the mythical half-dragon, half-dog sea monster. This is one of the sole relics of the medieval abbey of St. Vito. ⊠ *Piazza Flavio Gioia above main beach* ☎ *089/875067* ⊙ *Daily 8:30–noon and 4:30–7.*

The walkway from the Piazza Flavio Gioia leads down to the **Spaggia Grande,** or main beach, bordered by an esplanade and some of Positano's best restaurants. Head over to the stone pier to the far right of the beach as you face the water. A staircase leads to the **Via Positanesi d'America,** a lovely seaside walkway. Halfway up the path you'll find the Torre Trasìta, the most distinctive of Positano's three coastline defense towers, which, in various states of repair, define the edges of Positano. The Trasìta— now a residence occasionally available for summer rental—was one of the defense towers used to warn of pirate raids. Continuing along the Via Positanesi d'America you pass tiny inlets and emerald coves until the large beach, Spaggia di Fornillo, comes into view.

If the Spaggia Grande is too orderly for you, take the small boat to the **Spaggia di Laurito.** (Look for the boat on the right side of the harbor as you approach the beach—it has a sign with a big red smiling fish on it.) You can spend an entire day in this little cove, taking the two steps up to the restaurant **Da Adolfo** when the exertion of swimming has worked up your appetite.

Where to Stay & Eat

$$–$$$ ✕ **Buca di Bacco.** After an aperitif at the town's most famous and fashionable café downstairs, you dine on a veranda overlooking the beach. The specialties include *zuppa di cozze* (mussel soup), fresh *spigola* (sea bass), and figs and oranges in caramel. ⊠ *Via Rampa Teglia 8* ☎ *089/ 875699* ▤ *AE, DC, MC, V* ⊘ *Closed Nov.–Mar.*

$$–$$$ ✕ **Donna Rosa.** This minimalist little hideaway in one-street Montepertuso, the hamlet high over Positano, is truly original. Everybody gets into the act: Mamma does the creative cooking to order, Pappa "makes noise," and the daughters rule out front. Homemade pasta is the house specialty, along with delectable desserts, which may include walnut or strawberry mousse and *crostata all'arancio* (orange tart). A wide selection of fine wines is on hand, and live music can be anything from jazz to Australian gospel, sweetly sung by one of the daughters. Reservations are essential at dinner. ⊠ *Via Montepertuso* ☎ *089/811806* ▤ *AE, DC, MC, V* ⊘ *Closed Mon.*

$$–$$$ ✕ **'O Capurale.** Even though *'o capurale* ("the corporal") himself no longer runs the place, his eponymous restaurant is still a great find in the crowded center of Positano. There's one large dining room with simple wooden tables, a marble floor, and a high coved ceiling with Fauvist-style frescoes. The space remains cool even in the height of summer when filled with diners digging into fresh pasta with mussels and pumpkin or rockfish *all'acqua pazza,* with a few tomatoes and garlic. ⊠ *Via Regina Giovanna 12* ☎ *089/875374* ▤ *AE, DC, MC, V* ⊘ *Closed Nov.–mid-Feb.*

$–$$$ ✕ **Il Ritrovo.** Stretching alongside the tiny town square of the mountain
Fodor'sChoice hamlet of Montepertuso is one of the finest restaurants in the area. Ta-
★ bles outside (heated in winter) provide a dizzying view of the coast, and inside, the wood-paneled dining room has the feel of a ship's cabin. The menu is a mix of sea and mountain food; try the *scialatielli ai frutti di mare* (thick spaghetti with all manner of things from the sea), accompanied by grilled vegetables or followed by *scamorza* (a mozzarella-like cheese) baked in lemon leaves. Save room for hazelnut *semifreddo* (soft ice cream) and a homemade liqueur. The wine list is excellent. ⊠ *Via Montepertuso 77* ☎ *089/812005* ✍ *Reservations essential* ▤ *AE, DC, MC, V.*

$$ ✕ **Da Adolfo.** At this completely informal spot on Spaggia di Laurito, most diners sit for hours in their swimsuits, whiling away the time reading or chatting over a jug of the light local wine (with peaches in summer) or a hefty plate of *totani con patate* (squid and potatoes with garlic and oil). The brusque but amusing waiters are part of the scene. ⊠ *Spaggia di Laurito* ☎ *089/875022* ⌨ *Reservations not accepted* ▭ *No credit cards* ⊘ *Closed Oct.–Apr.*

$$$$ 🏨 **Casa Albertina.** Clinging to the cliff, this little house is well loved for its Italian charm, its homey atmosphere, and its owners, the Cinque family. Rooms have high ceilings, bright fabrics, tile flooring, and sunny terraces or balconies overlooking the sea and coastline. Cars can't drive to the doorway, but porters will ferry your luggage. Note: it's 300 steps down to the main beach. Half or full board is required in summer. ⊠ *Via della Tavolozza 3, 84017* ☎ *089/875143* 🖷 *089/811540* ⊕ *www. casalbertina.it* 🗪 *21 rooms* ⌂ *Restaurant, minibars, cable TV, parking (fee), some pets allowed* ▭ *AE, DC, MC, V* ⦿ *MAP.*

$$$$ 🏨 **Palazzo Murat.** The location is perfect—in the heart of town, near the beachside promenade, but set inside a quiet, walled garden. The older wing is a historic palazzo with tall windows and wrought-iron balconies; the modern wing is a whitewashed Mediterranean building with arches and terraces. You can relax in antiques-accented lounges or in the charming vine-draped patio and enjoy gorgeous views from the comfortable bedrooms. ⊠ *Via dei Mulini 23, 84017* ☎ *089/875177* 🖷 *089/ 811419* ⊕ *www.palazzomurat.it* 🗪 *31 rooms* ⌂ *Restaurant, minibars, bar* ▭ *AE, DC, MC, V* ⊘ *Closed Nov.–Mar.* ⦿ *BP.*

$$$$ 🏨 **Il San Pietro.** An oasis for its affluent international clientele, the San Pietro lies a few bends outside the town and is set amid gardens high above the sea. The hotel has sumptuous Neapolitan baroque decor and masses of flowers in the lounges, elegantly understated rooms (most with terraces), and marvelous views. There's a pool on an upper level, and an elevator whisks you down to the private beach and beach bar. The proprietors organize boating excursions and provide car and minibus service into town. There is a three-night minimum stay. ⊠ *Via Laurito 2, 84017* ☎ *089/875455* 🖷 *089/811449* ⊕ *www.ilsanpietro.it* 🗪 *60 rooms* ⌂ *Restaurant, cable TV, tennis court, pool, gym, beach, dock, 2 bars* ▭ *AE, DC, MC, V* ⊘ *Closed mid-Nov.–mid-Mar.* ⦿ *BP.*

★ $$$$ 🏨 **Le Sirenuse.** A handsome 18th-century palazzo in the center of town has been transformed into this luxury hotel with bright tile floors, precious antiques, and tasteful furnishings. The bedrooms are spacious and comfortable; most have splendid views from balconies or terraces. The top-floor suites have huge bathrooms and whirlpool baths. One side of a large terrace has an inviting swimming pool; on the other is an excellent restaurant. ⊠ *Via Cristoforo Colombo 30, 84017* ☎ *089/875066* 🖷 *089/811798* ⊕ *www.sirenuse.it* 🗪 *60 rooms* ⌂ *Restaurant, cable TV, pool, gym, sauna, bar* ▭ *AE, DC, MC, V* ⦿ *BP.*

$$ 🏨 **La Fenice.** This tiny, friendly, unpretentious hotel on the peaceful outskirts of town beckons with bougainvillea-laden vistas, castaway cottages, and a turquoise pool, all perched over a private beach. Guest rooms—accented with coved ceilings, whitewashed walls, and native folk art—are simple and tranquil; book the best, those closest to the sea, only

13

if you can handle *very* steep walkways. ⊠ *Via G. Marconi 4, 84017* ☎ *089/875513* 🖷 *089/811309* ✍ *9 rooms, 6 cottages* ⚬ *Pool; no a/c, no room phones, no room TVs* ⊟ *No credit cards* ⎟◎⎟ *BP.*

$$ 🏠 **Villa Rosa.** Sharing almost the same views as hotels that go for twice the price, this family-run lodging has long been a favorite with independent travelers. It's centrally located but slightly set back from the road up the inevitable steps. Ask for one of the rooms on the first floor, which are quieter and have better views. Breakfast is served in your room. ⊠ *Via C. Colombo 127, 84017* ☎ *089/811955* 🖷 *089/812112* ⊕ *www. villarosapositano.it* ✍ *18 rooms* ⚬ *Laundry service* ⊟ *AE, DC, MC, V* ⎟◎⎟ *BP* ☯ *Closed Nov.–Feb.*

$ 🏠 **La Ginestra.** Set in hikers' paradise about 2,000 feet over Positano, the farming cooperative La Ginestra dominates the coastline with its converted 18th-century manor house. The peasants' quarters have been transformed into a thriving restaurant, and the guest rooms above are decorated in simple country style. Positano is reached via a network of footpaths—it's a good hour's slog up from the bottom. If arriving by train, get off the Circumvesuviana train at Vico Equense and take the local orange bus uphill to the village of Santa Maria del Castello, which is about 300 meters from the cooperative. Access by car is also easiest from Vico Equense. ⊠ *Via Tessa 2, 80069, Santa Maria Del Castello, Vico Equense* ☎☎ *081/8023211* ⊕ *www.laginestra.org* ✍ *7 rooms* ⚬ *Restaurant; no a/c, no room phones* ⊟ *MC, V* ⎟◎⎟ *MAP.*

Nightlife

L'Africana (⊠ Vettica Maggiore, Praiano, 10 km [6 mi] east of Positano on the coast road ☎ 089/874042) is the premier nightclub on the Amalfi Coast, built into a fantastic grotto above the sea.

Grotta dello Smeraldo

13 km (8 mi) east of Positano, 27 km (17 mi) east of Sorrento.

A peculiar green light that casts an eerie emerald glow over impressive formations of stalagmites and stalactites, many of them underwater, inspired the name of the Grotta dello Smeraldo (Emerald Grotto). You can park at the signposts for the grotto along the coast road and take an elevator down, or you can drive on to Amalfi and return to the grotto by more romantic means—via boat. Boat tours leave from the Amalfi seafront regularly, according to demand; the charge is €6 per person. Call ahead, as hours are subject to change. ☎ *089/871107* 🎫 *Grotto €5.50* ☯ *Apr.–Sept., daily 9–5; Oct.–Mar., daily 10–4.*

Amalfi

36   *17 km (11 mi) east of Positano, 35 km (22 mi) east of Sorrento.*

"The sun—the moon—the stars—and Amalfi," Amalfitans used to say. During the Middle Ages Amalfi was an independent maritime state with a population of 50,000. The Republic also brought the art of papermaking to Europe from Arabia. Before World War II there were 13 mills making paper by hand in the Valle Molini, but now only two small ones remain. The town is romantically situated at the mouth of a deep gorge and has some good-quality hotels and restaurants. It's also a convenient base for excursions to Capri and the Grotta dello Smeraldo. The parking problem here is as bad as that in Positano. The small lot in the center of town fills quickly; if you're willing to pay the steep prices, make a lunch reservation at one of the hotel restaurants and have your car parked for you.

★ Amalfi's main historical sight is its **Duomo** (also known as Cattedrale di Sant'Andrea), which shows an interesting mix of Moorish and early Gothic influences. You're channeled first into the adjoining **Chiostro del Paradiso** (Paradise Cloister), built around 1266 as a burial ground for Amalfi's elite and one of the architectural treasures of southern Italy. Its flower-and-palm-filled quadrangle has a series of exceptionally delicate intertwining arches on slender double columns in a combination of Byzantine and Arabian styles. Next stop is the 9th-century basilica, a **museum** housing sarcophagi, sculpture, Neapolitan goldsmithing, and other treasures from the cathedral complex.

Steps from the basilica lead down into the **Cripta di Sant'Andrea** (Crypt of St. Andrew). The cathedral above was built in the 13th century to house the saint's bones, which came from Constantinople and supposedly exuded a miraculous liquid believers call the "manna of St. Andrew." Following the one-way traffic up to the cathedral itself, you finally get to admire the elaborate polychrome marbles and painted, coffered ceilings from its 18th-century restoration; art historians shake their heads over this renovation, as the original decoration of the apse must have been one of the wonders of the Middle Ages. ☒ *Piazza del Duomo* ☎ *089/ 871059* ☐ *€2.50* ☉ *Daily: Mar.–June and Oct., 9–7; July–Sept., 9–9; Nov.–Feb., 10–1 and 2:30–5:30.*

The **Valle dei Mulini** (Valley of the Mills), uphill from town, was for centuries Amalfi's center for papermaking, an ancient trade learned from the Arabs (who learned it from the Chinese). Beginning in the 12th century former flour mills in the town were converted to produce paper made from cotton and linen, being among the first in Europe to do so. In 1211 Frederick II of Sicily prohibited this lighter, more readable paper for use in the preparation of official documents, favoring traditional sheepskin parchment, but by 1811 more than a dozen mills here, with more along the coast, were humming. Natural waterpower ensured that the handmade paper was cost-effective, but catastrophic flooding in 1954 closed most of the mills for good, and many of them have now been converted into private housing. The **Museo della Carta** (Museum of Paper) opened in 1971 in a 15th-century mill; paper samples, tools of the trade, old machinery, and the audiovisual presentation are all enlightening. ☒ *Via delle Cartiere 23* ☎ *089/8304561* ⊕ *www. museodellacarta.it* ☐ *€3.40* ☉ *Nov.–Mar., Tues.–Sun. 10–3; Apr.–June and Oct., daily 10–6; July–Sept., daily 10–8.*

Where to Stay & Eat

★ $$$–$$$$ ✕ **Da Gemma.** Since 1872 cognoscenti have sung the praises of this understated landmark, which has a terrace set above the main street. The menu, printed on local handmade paper, announces such favorites as oven-baked fish with lemon peel and the *tubettoni alla masaniello* (tiny pieces of pasta with capers, mussels, and prawns). Traces of Amalfi's Arabic roots can be found in the sweets made with almonds and citrus fruits that come from the glistening kitchen. ⊠ *Via Fratello Gerardo Sasso 9* ☎ *089/871345* ☰ *AE, DC, MC, V* ☺ *Closed mid-Jan.–mid-Feb. and Wed. Sept.–June.*

\$\$–\$\$\$ ✕ **Trattoria di Maria.** At this friendly establishment presided over by the convivial Enzo (son of Maria) you can dine with the locals on delicious pizza baked in a wood oven, local fish dishes, and lemon profiteroles. Ask for a glass of the limoncello or one of the other homemade liqueurs made from bay leaves, fennel, or bilberries (similar to blueberries). ⊠ *Piazza ad Amalfi* ☎ *089/871880* ☰ *AE, DC, MC, V* ☺ *Closed Mon. and Nov.*

\$–\$\$\$ ✕ **A Paranza.** Located in the hamlet of Atrani, a 15-minute walk from the center of Amalfi along the road to Salerno, this seafood restaurant is worth the walk. With coved ceilings and immaculate linen tablecloths, the two dining rooms are at once homey and quite formal. Each day's menu depends on the catch; the tasting menu (antipasti ranging from marinated tuna to fried rice balls, pasta, and risotto, and a choice of dessert) is a good option. If that sounds like too much, go for the scialatielli ai frutti di mare. Finish your meal with one of the divine cakes. ⊠ *Via Dragone 1/2* ☎ *089/871840* ☰ *AE, DC, MC, V* ☺ *Closed Dec. 8–26 and Tues. Oct.–May.*

★ \$\$\$\$ ⌂ **Santa Caterina.** A large mansion perched above a terraced and flowered hillside just outside Amalfi proper, the Santa Caterina is one of the top hotels on the coast. The rooms are tastefully decorated; most have small terraces or balconies with spectacular views. There are lovely lounges, gardens, and terraces for relaxing, and an elevator delivers you to the seaside saltwater pool, bar, and swimming area. On grounds lush with lemon and orange groves, there are two romantic villa annexes. ⊠ *Strada Amalfitana 9, 84011* ☎ *089/871012* 🖷 *089/871351* ⊕ *www. hotelsantacaterina.it* ⇌ *66 rooms* ⌂ *2 restaurants, cable TV, saltwater pool, gym, beach, 2 bars, Internet, meeting room, free parking* ☰ *AE, DC, MC, V* ⧖◯ *BP.*

\$\$ ⌂ **Piccolo Paradiso.** This upscale B&B, painted a sunny yellow with green shutters, is a special choice because of its location near the harbor. A small elevator deposits you in the cozy house, which has a casually furnished, sun-bright terrace. Guest rooms are smallish but comfortable, with wicker seating and wrought-iron headboards. Some rooms have private terraces. ⊠ *Via M. Camera 5, 84011* ☎ *089/873001* ⇌ *6 rooms* ☰ *AE, MC, V.*

\$–\$\$ ⌂ **Hotel dei Cavalieri.** This gleaming white Mediterranean-style hotel sits on the road outside Amalfi. Three villas across the road extend all the way to a beach below. Bright rooms are functionally furnished, with splashy majolica-tile floors. An ample buffet breakfast is served. ⊠ *Via M. Comite 32, 84011* ☎ *089/831333* 🖷 *089/831354* ⊕ *www. hotelideicavalieri.it* ⇌ *54 rooms* ⌂ *Restaurant, cable TV, bar* ☰ *AE, DC, MC, V* ⧖◯ *BP.*

Shopping

A must for lovers of art, vintage prints, and fine books is down by the waterfront: **Andrea de Luca** (✉ Largo Cesareo Console 8 ☎ 089/871954), a publisher of fine books and postcards, sells desk accessories, objets d'art, and art tomes. You'll find paper creations, maps, and other souvenirs near the Duomo at **Amalfi nelle Stampe Antiche** (✉ Piazza Duomo 10 ☎ 089/872368).

Ravello

37

Fodor'sChoice
★

5 km (3 mi) northeast of Amalfi, 40 km (25 mi) east of Sorrento.

Perched on a ridge high above Amalfi and the neighboring town of Atrani, the enchanting village of Ravello has stupendous views, quiet lanes, two important Romanesque churches, and several irresistibly romantic gardens. Set "closer to the sky than the sea," according to André Gide, the town has been the ultimate aerie ever since it was founded as a smart suburb for the richest families of Amalfi's 12th-century maritime republic. Rediscovered by English aristocrats a century ago, the town now hosts one of Italy's most famous music festivals.

The **Duomo,** dedicated to patron saint Pantaleone, was founded in 1086 by Orso Papiro, the town's first bishop. Rebuilt in the 12th and 17th centuries, it retains traces of medieval frescoes in the transept, an original mullioned window, a marble portal, and a three-story 13th-century bell tower playfully interwoven with mullioned windows and arches. The 12th-century bronze door has 54 embossed panels depicting Christ's life, and saints, prophets, plants, and animals, all narrating biblical lore. It was crafted by Barisano da Trani, who also fashioned the doors of the cathedrals of Trani and Monreale. The nave's three aisles are divided by ancient columns, and treasures include sarcophagi from Roman times and paintings by southern Renaissance artist Andrea da Salerno. Most impressive are the two medieval pulpits: the earlier one (on your left as you face the altar), used for reading the Epistles, is inset with a mosaic scene of Jonah and the whale, symbolizing death and redemption. The more famous one opposite, used for reading the Gospels, was commissioned by Nicola Rufolo in 1272 and created by Niccolò di Bartolomeo da Foggia. It seems almost Tuscan in style, with exquisite Cosmatesque mosaic work and bas-reliefs and six twisting columns sitting on lion pedestals. An eagle grandly tops the inlaid marble lectern.

A chapel to the left of the apse is dedicated to St. Pantaleone, a physician who was beheaded in the 3rd century in Nicomedia. Every July 27 devout believers gather in hope of witnessing a miracle (similar to that of San Gennaro in Naples), in which the saint's blood, collected in a vial and set out on an inlaid marble altar, appears to liquefy and come to a boil; it hasn't happened in recent years. In the crypt is the **Museo del Duomo,** which displays treasures from about the 13th century, during the reign of Frederick II of Sicily. ✉ *Piazza del Duomo* 🎟 €1.50 ☉ *Church: daily 9–1 and 3–7; museum: Apr.–Oct., daily 9:30–1 and 3–7; Nov.–Mar., weekends 9:30–1 and 3–7.*

13

Directly off Ravello's main piazza is the **Villa Rufolo**, which—if the master storyteller Boccaccio is to be believed—was built in the 13th century by Landolfo Rufolo, whose immense fortune stemmed from trade with Moors and Saracens. Within is a scene from the earliest days of the Crusades. Norman and Arab architecture mingle in profusion in a welter of color-filled gardens so lush that composer Richard Wagner used them as his inspiration for the home of the Flower Maidens in his opera *Parsifal.* Beyond the Arab-Sicilian cloister and the Norman tower are two flower-bedded terraces that offer a splendid vista of the Bay of Salerno; the lower "Wagner Terrace" is the site for the yearlong **Festival Musicale di Ravello** (☎089/858149 ⊕www. ravelloarts.org). ✉ *Piazza Duomo, 84010* ▣ *€4* ☉ *Daily 9–sunset.*

WORD OF MOUTH

"Ravello was absolutely the best part of our honeymoon. It had unbelievable views of the coast and sea; far better than Positano in my opinion."   –sam

From Ravello's main piazza, head west along Via San Francesco and Via Santa Chiara to the **Villa Cimbrone**, a medieval-style fantasy that sits 1,500 feet above the sea. Created in 1905 by England's Lord Grimthorpe and made world famous when Greta Garbo stayed here in 1937, the Gothic castle is set in fragrant rose gardens that lead to the **Belvedere dell'Infinità** (Belvedere of Infinity), a grand stone parapet that overlooks the impossibly blue Gulf of Salerno and frames a panorama that former Ravello resident Gore Vidal has called "the most beautiful in the world." The villa itself is now a hotel. ✉ *Via Santa Chiara 26* ☎ *089/ 857459* ▣ *€4.50* ☉ *Daily 9–sunset.*

Where to Stay & Eat

★ **$–$$$** ✕ **Cumpà Cosimo.** This family-run restaurant a few steps from the Piazza del Duomo offers a cordial welcome in two simple but attractive dining rooms. There's no view, but the food is excellent, most of it coming from owner Donna Netta's garden or her butcher shop next door. Among the specialties are cheese crepes, roast lamb, and a dish including seven types of homemade pasta. ✉ *Via Roma 44* ☎ *089/857156* ▤ *AE, DC, MC, V* ☉ *Closed Mon. and Jan. 10–Feb.*

$–$$ ✕ **Vittoria.** Down the bustling arcade of pottery shops adjacent to the Villa Rufolo, this is a good place to escape the crowds. Vittoria's thin-crust pizza with loads of fresh toppings is the star attraction, but also consider the pasta, maybe fusilli with tomatoes, zucchini, and mozzarella. The decor is extremely simple, with white walls and a few etchings of Ravello. ✉ *Via dei Rufolo 3* ☎ *089/857947* ▤ *AE, DC, MC, V* ☉ *Closed Tues. Nov.–Mar.*

$$$$ ▨ **Hotel Palumbo.** Occupying a 12th-century patrician palace outfitted with antiques and modern comforts, this elegant hotel has the feel of a private home. It has beautiful garden terraces, breathtaking views, and a sumptuous upstairs dining room. In summer you can descend to a villa and be pampered in the hotel's seaside retreat. Half board is compulsory except in winter, when the restaurant is closed. ✉ *Palazzo Confalone, Via San Giovanni del Toro 16, 84010* ☎ *089/857244* ▤ *089/ 858133* ⊕ *www.hotel-palumbo.it* ▭ *20 rooms* ⌂ *Restaurant, cable TV,* *bar, pool, conference room, private beach, laundry, parking* ▭ *AE, DC, MC, V* ❮❯❮ *MAP.*

★ **$$$$**   ▭ **Palazzo Sasso.** One of the finest hotels in southern Italy, this 12th-century palace dazzles you with a marble atrium and lofty coastal views. No less impressive is the courteous, attentive service. The Rossellini restaurant, open to the public only in the evenings, is also highly recommended. Every room has an ocean view, with high arched ceilings and tile floors that lend a Mediterranean feel. They are furnished with antiques. ✉ *Via San Giovanni del Toro 28, 84010* ☎ *089/818181* 🖷 *089/858900* ⊕ *www.palazzosasso.com* 🗲 *36 rooms, 8 suites* ⚓ *Restaurant, minibars, cable TV, pool, outdoor hot tub, bar, library, Internet, some pets allowed* ▭ *AE, DC, MC, V* ☯ *Closed Nov.–Mar* ❮❯❮ *BP.*

★ **$$$$**   ▭ **Villa Cimbrone.** Suspended over the azure sea and set amid rose-laden gardens, this magical place was once the home of Lord Grimthorpe and the holiday hideaway of Greta Garbo. Now the Gothic-style *castello* (castle) has guest rooms ranging from palatial to cozy (opt for the Peony Room, which has its own terrace). Tapestried armchairs, framed prints, vintage art books, and other antiques that belonged to Viscountess Frost, the lord's daughter, still grace the enchantingly elegant sitting room. Best of all, guests have the villa's famous gardens all to themselves once their gates are closed at sunset. The villa is a strenuous hike from the town center, but porters will carry your luggage and the distance helps keep this the most peaceful place on the Amalfi Coast. ✉ *Via Santa Chiara 26, 84010* ☎ *089/857459* 🖷 *089/857777* ⊕ *www.villacimbrone.it* 🗲 *13 rooms* ⚓ *Cable TV, minibars, library, hot tub, Internet* ▭ *AE, DC, MC, V* ☯ *Closed Nov.–Easter* ❮❯❮ *BP.*

$ ▭ **Villa Amore.** A 10-minute walk from the Piazza Duomo, this family-run hotel has a pretty garden and an exhilarating view of the sea from most of its bedrooms. If you're looking for tranquillity, you've found it, especially at dusk, when the valley is tinged with a glorious purple light. Rooms are small, with modest modern furnishings. One of the treats is delicious homemade jam at breakfast. Full board is available, and at least half board is required from July through September. Reserve ahead, and specify time of arrival if you need help with luggage from the parking lot or bus stop; you pay €4 per bag. ✉ *Via del Fusco 5, 84010* ☎🖷 *089/857135* 🗲 *12 rooms* ⚓ *Restaurant, bar, some pets allowed; no a/c, no room TVs* ▭ *DC, MC, V* ❮❯❮ *MAP.*

Salerno

㊳ *6 km (4 mi) east of Vietri sul Mare, 56 km (35 mi) southeast of Naples.*

Spread out along its bay, Salerno was long a sad testimony to years of neglect and overdevelopment, but the antique port is now reevaluating its artistic heritage. It's a well-connected base for exploring the Cilento area to the south, which has such lovely sea resorts as San Marco di Castellabate and Palinuro, and inland some fine mountain walks and spectacular gorges and caves, such as Castelcivita and Pertosa.

Salerno has an imposing Romanesque **Duomo** founded in the mid-9th century and substantially rebuilt by Robert Guiscard from 1076 to

1085. The scene is set by the doorway—see the marble lions at the base—which gives way to a spacious atrium. The Cosmatesque pulpits rival Ravello's for elegance, and ornately carved marbled sarcophagi reinforce the cathedral's stately pedigree. ✉ *Piazza Duomo* ☎ *089/231387* ☉ *Daily 10–1:30 and 3–6.*

The **Museo Archeologico Provincale,** in Salerno's medieval Benedictine abbey, has interesting displays of ancient artifacts from the region, with many of the higher-quality finds coming from the Greco-Etruscan necropolis in what is now the suburb of Fratte. Some fine Attic and Corinthian vases are on the upper floor, but the show-stealer is the 1st-century BC bronze head of Apollo fished out of the Gulf of Salerno in 1930. ✉ *Via San Benedetto 28* ☎ *089/231135* ✉ *Free* ☉ *Mon.–Sat. 9–7, Sun 9–1.*

Where to Stay

$ 🏨 **Plaza.** You can easily walk to the harbor, shops, and transportation from this clean, no-frills lodging across from the train station. The interior is decorated in warm, mellow tones, and guest rooms are spacious. When booking, ask for a room on one of the upper floors or in the back over the courtyard, as these tend to be quieter. ✉ *Piazza Vittorio Veneto 42, 84123* ☎ *089/224477* 🖷 *089/237311* ⊕ *www.plazasalerno.it* ⇆ *42 rooms* ☖ *Minibars, cable TV, lobby lounge; no a/c in some rooms* ⊟ *AE, DC, MC, V* ⦿ *BP.*

Paestum

★ ➌➒ *42 km (26 mi) southeast of Salerno, 99 km (62 mi) southeast of Naples.*

One of Italy's most majestic sights lies on the edge of a flat coastal plain: the remarkably well-preserved **Greek temples** of Paestum. SS18 from the north passes the train station (Stazione di Paestum), which is about 800 yards from the ruins through the perfectly preserved **Porta Sirena** archway. This is the site of the ancient city of Poseidonia, founded by Greek colonists probably in the 6th century BC. When the Romans took over the colony in 273 BC and the name was latinized to Paestum, they changed the layout of the settlement, adding an amphitheater and a forum. Much of the archaeological material found on the site is displayed in the well-labeled **Museo Nazionale,** and several rooms are devoted to the unique tomb paintings discovered in the area, rare examples of Greek and pre-Roman pictorial art.

At the northern end of the site opposite the ticket barrier is the **Tempio di Cerere** (Temple of Ceres). Built in about 500 BC, it's now thought to have been originally dedicated to the goddess Athena. Follow the road south past the **Foro Romano** (Roman forum) to the **Tempio di Nettuno** (Temple of Poseidon), a magnificent Doric edifice with 36 fluted columns and an extraordinarily well-preserved entablature (area above the capitals) that rivals those of the finest temples in Greece. Beyond is the so-called **Basilica,** the earliest of Paestum's standing edifices; it dates from early in the 6th century BC. The name is an 18th-century misnomer, for the structure was in fact a temple to Hera, the wife of Zeus. Try to see the temples in the late afternoon, when the light enhances the deep gold of the limestone and the temples are almost deserted. ☎ *0828/722654* ✍ *Excavations €4, museum €4, excavations and museum €6.50* ⊙ *Excavations July–Sept., daily 9 AM–10 PM; Oct.–June, daily 9–1 hr before sunset. Museum July–Sept., daily 9 AM–10 PM; Oct.–June, daily 9–6:30; closed 1st and 3rd Mon. of each month.*

Where to Stay & Eat

¢–$ ✕🏠 **Helios.** A few steps from the temples, the Helios has cottage-type rooms in a garden setting. Seven rooms have their own whirlpool baths. A pleasant restaurant serves local specialties that emphasize seafood. The ricotta and mozzarella made on the premises are especially good. The hotel also organizes visits to a local mozzarella producer and excursions around the area on horseback. ⊠ *Via Nettuno 7, 84063* ☎ *0828/ 811451* 🖷 *0828/811600* ➷ *27 rooms* ♻ *Restaurant, pool; no a/c in some rooms, no TV in some rooms* 🖃 *AE, DC, MC, V* ⦿ *MAP.*

NAPLES & CAMPANIA ESSENTIALS

Transportation

BY AIR

Aeroporto Capodichino, 8 km (5 mi) north of Naples, serves the Campania region. It handles domestic and international flights, including several daily between Naples and Rome (flight time 45 minutes). Throughout the year there is direct helicopter service with Cab Air between Aeroporto Capodichino and Capri, Ischia, or Positano. The cost is €1,400, regardless of the destination.

Taxis are available at the airport for the ride to downtown Naples (€15–€20). The transportation company ANM runs the Alibus service, which leaves the airport every 30 minutes with stops at Piazza Garibaldi and Piazza Muncipio (€2). The more frequent but slightly slower Bus 3S also goes to Piazza Garibaldi and to the port (Molo Beverello) beyond. Tickets can be bought from the newsstands inside the airport (€1).

🚹 Airport Information **Aeroporto Capodichino** ☎ 081/7896259. **ANM (Azienda Napoletana Mobilità)** ☎ 081/7631111. **Cab Air** ☎ 081/2587110.

BY BOAT & FERRY

A variety of fast craft and passenger and car ferries connect the islands of Capri and Ischia with Naples and Pozzuoli year-round. In summer Capri and Ischia are serviced by boats from the Amalfi Coast. Boats and hydrofoils for these islands and for Sorrento leave from Naples's Molo Beverello. Hydrofoils also leave from Mergellina. From June to September, the Metro del Mare runs a hydrofoil service from Bacoli as far as Sapri, with various stops inbetween. Ticket prices depend on the journey you make, but range from €2.50 to €10.

Information on departures is published every day in the local paper, *Il Mattino,* and in local editions of national dailies *Corriere della Sera* and *La Repubblica.* Alternatively, ask at the tourist office or at the port, or contact the companies—Caremar, Navigazione Libera del Golfo, SNAV,

and Alilauro—directly. Always double-check schedules in stormy weather.
🚢Boat & Ferry Information **Alilauro** ☎081/7614909 ⊕www.alilauro.it. **Caremar** ☎081/
5513882 ⊕ www.caremar.it. **Coop Sant'Andrea** ☎089/873190 ⊕ www.coopsantandrea.
it. **Mergellina** ✉ About 1½ km [1 mi] to west of Piazza Municipio. **Metro del Mare**
✉ ☎ 199/446644 ⊕ www.metrodelmare.com. **Molo Beverello** ✉ Southeast of Piazza
Municipio. **Navigazione Libera del Golfo** (NLG) ☎ 081/5527209 ⊕ www.navlib.it.
SNAV ☎ 081/7612348 ⊕ www.snavali.com.

BY BUS

Marozzi, a Rome-based line, runs direct air-conditioned buses from Rome
to Pompeii, Salerno, Sorrento, and Amalfi. Buses leave Rome's Stazione
Tiburtina weekdays at 3 PM, weekends at 7 AM. This service aside, trains
are a much better option for getting in and out of the region than buses.

Within Campania, there's an extensive network of local buses. ACTP
buses connect Naples with Caserta in one hour, leaving every 20 minutes from Piazza Garibaldi (every 40 minutes on Sunday). Buses to
Santa Maria Capua Vetere leave Piazza Garibaldi approximately every
30–40 minutes Monday to Saturday (travel time 45 minutes). There are
six buses a day Monday to Saturday from Piazza Garibaldi to Benevento.
The trip takes 90 minutes. SITA buses for Salerno leave every 30 minutes Monday to Saturday and every two hours on Sunday from the SITA
terminal on Via Pisanelli. SITA buses also serve the Amalfi Coast, connecting Sorrento with Salerno. Curreri operates a service (six runs daily)
between Sorrento and Aeroporto Capodichino.
🚌Bus Information **ACTP** ☎081/7001111. **Curreri** ☎081/8015420. **Marozzi** ☎06/4076140.
SITA ✉ Via Pisanelli, near Piazza Municipio ☎ 081/5522176 ⊕ www.sita-on-line.it.

BY CAR

Italy's main north–south route, the A2 (also known as the Autostrada
del Sole), connects Rome with Naples and Campania. In good traffic
the drive to Naples takes less than three hours. Autostrada A3, a continuation of the A2, runs south from Naples through Campania and into
Calabria. It also connects with the autostrada A16 to Bari, which passes
Avellino and is linked with Benevento by expressway.

Herculaneum (Ercolano), Pompeii (Pompei), and Oplontis all have
marked exits off the A3. For Vesuvius, take the Ercolano exit. For the
Sorrento peninsula and the Amalfi Coast, exit at Castellammare di
Stabia. To get to Paestum, take A3 to the Battipaglia exit and take the
road to Capaccio Scalo–Paestum.

The roads on the Sorrento peninsula and Amalfi Coast are narrow and
twisting, but they have outstanding views. In high season, from about
April through October, only residents' cars are allowed on Ischia and Capri.

GARAGES   If you come to Naples by car, park it in a garage, agree on the cost in
advance, and then keep it there for the duration of your stay. (If you
park on the street, you run the risk of being broken into.) Garage dei
Fiori (near Villa Pignatelli), Grilli (near Stazione Centrale), and Turistico (near the port) are all centrally located and safe.
🚗 **Garage dei Fiori** ✉ Via Colonna 21 ☎ 081/414190. **Grilli** ✉ Via Ferraris 40 ☎ 081/
264344. **Turistico** ✉ Via de Gasperi 14 ☎ 081/5525442.

BY PUBLIC TRANSIT IN NAPLES

Naples's rather old Metropolitana (subway system), also called Linea 2, provides frequent service and can be the fastest way to get across the traffic-clogged city. The other urban subway system, Metropolitana Collinare (or Linea 1), links the hill area of the Vomero and beyond with the National Archaeological Museum and Piazza Dante. An extension of the route to Piazza Garibaldi is expected to open in late 2005. Trains on both lines run from 5 AM until 10:30 PM.

For standard public transportation, including the subways, buses, and funiculars, a Giranapoli pass costs €1 and is valid for 90 minutes within the city boundaries; €2.32 buys a *biglietto giornaliero,* good for the whole day. Bus service has become viable over the last few years, especially with the introduction of larger buses and the regular R1, R2, and R3 routes.

BY TRAIN

There are trains every hour between Rome and Naples. Eurostar and Intercity, the fastest types of train service, make the trip in less than two hours. Trains take either the inland route (through Cassino) or go along the coast (via Formia). Almost all trains to Naples stop at Stazione Centrale.

A network of suburban trains connects Naples with several points of interest. The line used most by visitors is the Circumvesuviana, which runs from Corso Garibaldi Station and stops at Stazione Centrale before continuing to Ercolano (Herculaneum), Pompeii, and Sorrento. Frequent local trains connect Naples with Caserta and Salerno. Travel time between Naples and Sorrento on the Circumvesuviana line is about 75 minutes. Benevento is on the main line between Naples and Foggia. The Circumflegrea runs from Piazza Montesanto Station in Naples toward the archaeological zone of Cumae, with three departures in the morning. The Ferrovia Cumana runs from Piazza Montesanto Station to Pozzuoli and Lucrino. For the archaeological zone of Baia, get the shuttle bus outside Lucrino station.

A Fascia 1 ticket (€1.29 for 100 minutes) covers trips between Naples and a radius of about 10 km (6 mi), which includes Pozzuoli and Portici; Fascia 2 (€1.55 for 120 minutes) takes in Ercolano (Herculaneum), Baia, and Cumae; Fascia 3 (€2.01 for 140 minutes) includes Pompeii, Boscoreale, and Castellammare; Fascia 4 (€2.48 for 160 minutes) will take you as far as Vico Equense; and Fascia 5 (€2.84 for 180 minutes) covers trips to Sorrento and beyond.

Train Information Circumflegrea and Cumana ☎ 081/5513328 ⊕ www.sepsa.it. **Circumvesuviana** ☎ 081/7722444 ⊕ www.vesuviana.it. **Stazione Centrale** ⊠ Piazza Garibaldi ☎ 892021 ⊕ www.trenitalia.it.

Contacts & Resources

EMERGENCIES

Police ☎ 112. **Ambulance** ☎ 118.

Pharmacies Farmacia Helvethia ⊠ Piazza Garibaldi 11, opposite Stazione Centrale, Naples ☎ 081/5548894.

ENGLISH-LANGUAGE MEDIA

The monthly *Qui Napoli,* free from tourist offices, has useful information in English on museums, exhibitions, and transportation.

SAFETY

LOCAL SCAMS The main risks in Naples are car break-ins, bag-snatching, pickpocketing, and fraud. As a general rule, give twosomes on scooters a wide berth, and never make major purchases such as digital cameras from unlicensed dealers. Goods can be artfully switched with worthless packages right under your nose. Be particularly vigilant around the central station area of Piazza Garibaldi in Naples; make sure your valuables are carefully stowed away in an inside pocket.

TOURS

Fine Arts organizes made-to-measure guided tours and stays. The Associazione di Donnaregina, run by two Neapolitan artists, organizes small group tours (six to eight people) of Naples and surroundings, offering insights into the culture, traditions, and lesser-known places of the region. Other operators include Milleviaggi, Tourcar, and STS. A welcome center for visitors to Naples's old town, the Centro di Accoglienza Turistica Museo Aperto Napoli, offers a museum-style audio guide (€6) you can to listen to as you wander the area.

Associazione di Donnaregina ⊠ Via Luigi Settembrini 80, Naples ☎ 081/446799 or 338/6401301. **Centro di Accoglienza Turistica Museo Aperto Napoli** ⊠ Via Pietro Colletta 89 ☎ 081/5636062 ⊕ www.museoapertonapoli.com. **Fine Arts** ⊠ Via San Paolo 13, Naples ⊕ www.artifexgallery.it ☎ 081/291634. **Milleviaggi** ⊠ Riviera di Chiaia 252, Naples ☎ 081/7642064. **Tourcar** ⊠ Piazza Matteotti 1, Naples ☎ 081/5521938 ⊕ www.tourcar.it. **STS** ⊠ Via Bernini 90, Naples ☎ 081/5565164.

VISITOR INFORMATION

The EPT (Ente Provinciale per il Turismo) handles information for the province (Naples, Salerno, Caserta, Benevento or Avellino), whereas information offices run by the local tourist organizations are more ubiquitous, though they cover much the same ground.

Tourist Information EPT ⊠ Piazza dei Martiri 58, 80121 Naples ☎ 081/4107211 ⊠ Stazione Centrale, 80142 Naples ☎ 081/268779 ⊠ Stazione Mergellina, 80122 Naples ☎ 081/7612102.

Amalfi ⊠ Corso delle Repubbliche 27, 84011 ☎ 089/871107. **Benevento** ⊠ Piazza Roma 11, 82100 ☎ 0824/319938 ⊕ www.eptbenevento.it. **Capri** ⊠ Marina Grande pier, 80073 ☎ 081/8370634 ⊠ Piazza Umberto I, 80073 Capri Town ☎ 081/8370686 ⊕ www.capritourism.com. **Caserta** ⊠ Piazza Dante 35, 81100 ☎ 0823/321137. **Ercolano** ⊠ Via 4 Novembre 82, 80056 ☎ 081/7881243. **Naples** ⊠ Piazza del Gesù, 80135 ☎ 081/5523328. **Pompeii** ⊠ Via Sacra 1, 80045 ☎ 081/8507255. **Porto d'Ischia** ⊠ Via Iasolino, Porto Salvo, 80077 ☎ 081/5074231. **Ravello** ⊠ Piazza Duomo 1, 84010 ☎ 089/ 857096. **Salerno** ⊠ Piazza Vittorio Veneto, 84100 ☎ 089/231432, 800/213289 toll-free ⊕ www.crmpa.it/ept. **Sorrento** ⊠ Via de Maio 35, 80067 ☎ 081/8074033 ⊕ www. sorrentotourism.com.

The
Mezzogiorno

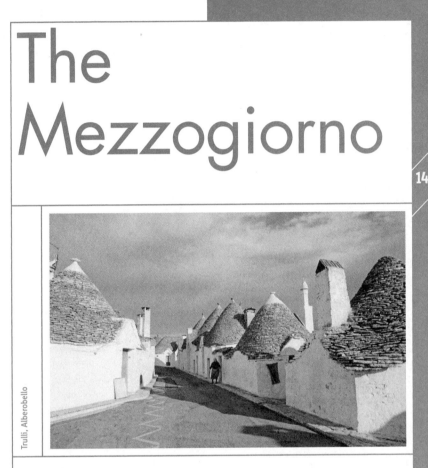

Trulli, Alberobello

WORD OF MOUTH

"I'd expected Puglia to be quaint, charming, but a little in need of some loving care. How wrong was I! Every town we visited had elegant centers with smart shops and restaurants. Puglia hasn't yet made it into the touring crowd's itinerary, but I feel this will change very soon, so go now! It's almost like someone mixed the best of Italy and Greece together: food, medieval towns, whitewashed houses, beaches, palm trees, endless olive groves, great local wine."

—Kate

WELCOME TO THE MEZZOGIORNO

Piazza del Duomo, Lecce

TOP 5
Reasons to Go

1 A wander through Matera's sassi: A complex network of ancient cave dwellings partially hewn from rock, some of which now house chic bars and restaurants, endow this simple Basilicata town with one of the most unique landscapes in Europe.

2 A trip to peasant-food heaven: Dine on Puglia's famous purée of fava beans with chicory and spicy olive oil in a humble country restaurant, and you'll be transported back to a golden culinary era.

3 A summer day on the beach of Puglia's Gargano Promontory: Some of Italy's most pristine coastline is still little known to foreign vacationers, so the beach culture on this peninsula remains unusually humble and relaxing.

4 Lecce and its baroque splendors: The beautiful, friendly city of Lecce might be known for its peculiar brand of fanciful baroque architecture, but it's not yet famous enough to have lost even an ounce of its Pugliese charm.

5 The trulli of Alberobello: Strange, conical homes—many of them still in use—dot the rolling countryside of Puglia, centering around Alberobello, a town still composed almost entirely of these trulli—they must be seen to be believed.

Caserta

Naples

Getting Oriented

The *mezzogiorno* ("midday") is the informal name for Italy's languid deep south, known for its sun-drenched olive groves, fertile hills, and time-frozen towns. The area includes the regions of Calabria, the toe of Italy's boot, on the Tyrrhenian Sea; Puglia, the heel, on the Adriatic; and between them, Basilicata, the instep. Along both coasts, stretches of pristine coastline are interspersed with rough-and-tumble fishing and shipping ports.

The **Gargano Promontory** juts into the Adriatic like a spur. It's full of summertime beaches, wooded campgrounds, and cliff-hanging hotels.

Bari, a lively, quirky, and sometimes seamy port city on Puglia's Adriatic Coast, is the biggest city in the mezzogiorno and home to its principal airport.

The **Trulli District**, named for its mysterious conical houses, is centered around **Alberobello**.

The ports of the heel include Casbah-like fishing villages such as **Gallipoli** and the gritty shipping centers of **Taranto** and **Brindisi**.

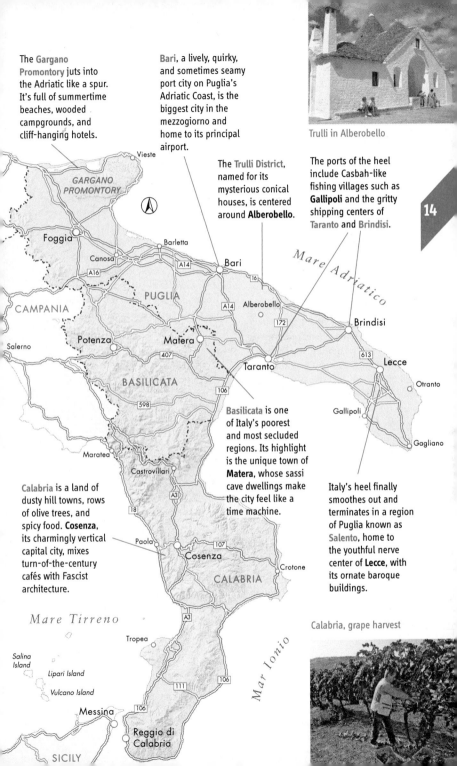

Trulli in Alberobello

14

Basilicata is one of Italy's poorest and most secluded regions. Its highlight is the unique town of **Matera**, whose sassi cave dwellings make the city feel like a time machine.

Calabria is a land of dusty hill towns, rows of olive trees, and spicy food. **Cosenza**, its charmingly vertical capital city, mixes turn-of-the-century cafés with Fascist architecture.

Italy's heel finally smoothes out and terminates in a region of Puglia known as **Salento**, home to the youthful nerve center of **Lecce**, with its ornate baroque buildings.

Calabria, grape harvest

Vieste

GARGANO PROMONTORY

Foggia

Barletta

Canosa

A16

A14

Bari

16

CAMPANIA

PUGLIA

A14

Alberobello

172

Mare Adriatico

Brindisi

Salerno

Potenza

Matera

407

613

Lecce

Taranto

Otranto

BASILICATA

106

598

Gallipoli

Gagliano

Maratea

Castrovillari

A3

18

Paola

107

Cosenza

Crotone

CALABRIA

Mare Tirreno

A3

Salina Island

Tropea

Lipari Island

Vulcano Island

111

106

Mar Ionio

106

Messina

Reggio di Calabria

SICILY

THE MEZZOGIORNO PLANNER

Making the Most of Your Time

If your priority is relaxing on the beach, plan on a few days in the Gargano Promontory's seaside fishing villages-cum-resorts, such as Peschici, Rodi Garganico, and Vieste; and perhaps a further stay at one of the Calabrian coastal resorts, such as Diamante, Pizzo, Tropea, or Bagnara or Maratea in Basilicata.

Otherwise, begin your jaunt in Bari, where you should spend a day or two exploring the atmospheric old town and bustling port. Take a day trip to touristy but interesting Alberobello and its conical trulli, then head east along the Adriatic route (SS16), stopping to see Polignano a Mare and idyllic hilltop Ostuni before continuing on to Lecce, where you'll want to spend at least two to three nights exploring the city's baroque wonders and taking a day trip down the coast to Otranto.

Next, take regional roads and Via Appia (SS7) to reach Matera, whose sassi cave dwellings are a mezzogiorno highlight; allow at least two nights there. Then it's back out to the SS106, stopping at Metaponto's ruins before moving on to Calabria and picturesque, time-frozen Cosenza. Reggio di Calabria is worthwhile only if you're an archeology buff and must see its museum.

Getting Around

Trains are reliable, but it's hard to get a good look at the countryside of Puglia and Calabria without wheels. This is particularly true if you want to hit the beaches along the coastline, or stay in agriturismi in the hill towns. Winding country roads are generally wide open and have little traffic, but allow plenty of time to get from place to place—slow trucks on two-lane roads abound. Fill up on gas whenever possible. In the towns of Bari, Brindisi, Lecce, Cosenza, and Matera, you'll want to leave your car and get around on foot.

Sasso Barisano, Matera

Speaking the Language

The dialects of Puglia, Basilicata, and Calabria, which vary from village to village, are impenetrable to anyone with knowledge of only textbook Italian. A further twist is the presence of *albanesi* (Albanian-speaking locals) in upland areas, especially around Bari and the Pollino massif. Everyone speaks Italian as well; English-speakers aren't as prevalent as in points north.

On the Beach

Italians and foreign visitors alike return summer after summer to the beaches of the mezzogiorno, where the relative lack of industry has preserved mile after mile of largely unpolluted coastline.

Southern Italy's most popular vacation destinations among domestic tourists is the Gargano Promontory, where safe, sandy shores and secluded coves are nestled between whitewashed coastal towns and craggy limestone cliffs, and the well-developed Tyrrhenian coast of Calabria. The beaches are visually stunning, and they fill up quickly in summertime.

Elsewhere in the mezzogiorno, the beach scene is more laid back. You won't find impeccably manicured sand lined with regiments of sunbathers, but you can pick and choose strands at whim and spread out.

Finding a Place to Stay

Hotels in the mezzogiorno range from grand, if slightly faded, high-class resorts to family-run rural *agriturismi* (country inns, often part of farms), which compensate for a lack of amenities with their famous southern hospitality. *Fattorie* and *masserie* (small farms and grander farm estates) offering accommodation are listed at local tourist offices. Children are welcome everywhere.

In beach areas such as the Gargano Promontory, campgrounds and bungalow lodgings are ubiquitous and popular with families and young budget travelers alike. Note that many seaside hotels open up just for the summer season, when they often require several-day stays with full or half board. And do remember that in a region like this—blazingly hot in summer and chilly in winter—air-conditioning and central heating can be important.

How's the Weather?

Summers are torrid this far south, and even the otherwise perfect villages of the mezzogiorno's interior are too dazzlingly white for easy comfort from July to early September. If you seek the sand in that season, keep in mind that during *ferragosto*, the period in mid-August during which all of Italy flocks to the shores, even relatively isolated resorts can be overrun by weeklong package tourists; reserve well in advance, and be prepared to pay extra.

In April, May and June, on the other hand, the weather is clear and warm, and you'll often have the beach to yourself. Swimming temperatures last through October. Wintertime in the mezzogiorno can see heavy rain and wind, but temperatures rarely fall below freezing.

14

Dining & Lodging Price Categories

WHAT IT COSTS in Euros					
	$$$$	**$$$**	**$$**	**$**	**¢**
Restaurants	over €22	€16–€22	€11–€16	€7–€11	under €7
Hotels	over €220	€160–€220	€110–€160	€70–€110	under €70

Restaurant prices are for a second course (un secondo). Hotel prices are for two people in a standard double room in high season, including tax and service.

TOP PASSEGGIATA

The walk along the ancient walls of Bari's old town reveals a new view with every turn: the castle, the port, the harbors, and the wide-open sea.

Updated by
Robin
Goldstein

MAKING UP THE HEEL AND TOE OF ITALY'S BOOT, the Puglia, Basilicata, and Calabria regions are known informally as the *mezzogiorno,* a name that translates literally as "midday." It's a curiously telling nickname, because midday is when it's quietest here. While the blazing sun bears down, cities, fishing ports, and sleepy hillside villages turn into ghost towns, as residents retreat to their homes for four or more hours. This is Italy's deep south, where whitewashed buildings stand silently over the turquoise Mediterranean, castles guard medieval alleyways, and grandmothers dry their handmade *orecchiette,* the most Puglian of pastas, in the mid-afternoon heat. The city-states of Magna Graecia (Greek colonies) once ruled here, and ancient names, such as Lucania and Salento, are still commonly used.

At every turn, these three regions boast unspoiled scenery, a wonderful country food tradition, and—especially in Puglia and Basilicata—an openness to outsiders that's unequaled elsewhere on the boot. It's here that the Italian language is at its lilting, hand-gesturing best, and it's here that a local you've met only minutes before is most likely to whisk you away to show you the delights of the region. When locals speak among themselves, though, their conversations revert to local dialects unintelligible to the student of textbook Italian.

Some of Italy's finest beaches grace the rugged Gargano peninsula and the coastline of Calabria, and there are cultural gems everywhere, from Alberobello's fairy-tale *trulli* (curious conical structures dating from the Middle Ages) to Matera's *sassi* (a network of ancient dwellings carved out of rock) to the baroque churches in vibrant Lecce, the town considered the jewel of the South. Beyond the cities, seaside resorts, and the few major sights lies a sparsely populated, sunbaked countryside where roadsigns are rare and expanses of silvery olive trees, vineyards of *primitivo* and *aglianico* grapes, and giant prickly pear cacti fight their way through the rocky soil in defiance of the relentless summer heat. Farmhouses, country trattorias, and weary low-lying factories sit among eternally half-built structures that tell a hard-luck story of economic stagnation. Organized crime, still a strong force in the region, poses no threat to tourists, but together with government neglect and archaic social patterns, it has long helped to prevent the development that other parts of the country have enjoyed—for better or for worse. As a result, the mezzogiorno still doesn't make it onto the itineraries of most visitors to Italy. This translates into an unusual opportunity to engage with a rich culture and landscape virtually untouched by mass tourism.

BARI & THE ADRIATIC COAST

The coast of Puglia has a strong flavor of the Norman presence in the south, embodied in the distinctive Puglian-Romanesque churches, the most atmospheric being in Trani. The busy commercial port of Bari offers architectural nuggets in its compact, labyrinthine Old Quarter abutting the sea, while Polignano a Mare combines accessibility to the major centers with the charm of a medieval town. For a unique excursion, drive inland to the imposing Castel del Monte, an enigmatic 13th-century octagonal fortification.

PUGLIA, PAST & PRESENT

Puglia has long been inhabited, conquered, and visited. On sea voyages to their colonies and trading posts in the west, the ancient Greeks invariably headed for Puglia first—it was the shortest crossing—before filtering southward into Sicily and westward to the Tyrrhenian coast. In turn, the Romans—often bound in the opposite direction—were quick to recognize the strategic importance of the peninsula. Later centuries were to see a procession of other empires raiding or colonizing Puglia: Byzantines, Saracens, Normans, Swabians, Turks, and Spaniards all swept through, each group leaving its mark. Romanesque churches and the powerful castles built by 13th-century Holy Roman Emperor Frederick II (who also served as king of Sicily and Jerusalem), are among the most impressive of the buildings in the region. Frederick II, dubbed *Stupor Mundi* (Wonder of the World) for his wide-ranging interests in literature, science, mathematics, and nature, was one of the foremost personalities of the Middle Ages.

The last 50 years have brought a huge economic revival after the centuries of neglect following Puglia's golden age under the Normans and Swabians. Having benefited from EU funding, state incentive programs, and subsidies for irrigation, Puglia is now Italy's second-biggest producer of wine, with most of the rest of the land devoted to olives, citrus fruits, and vegetables. The main ports of Bari, Brindisi, and Taranto are thriving centers, though there remain serious problems of unemployment and poverty. However, the much-publicized arrival of thousands of asylum seekers from Eastern Europe and beyond has not significantly destabilized these cities, as had been feared, and the economic and political refugees have dispersed throughout Italy. Compared with neighboring Albania a mere 70 km (44 mi) away across the Straits of Otranto, Puglia oozes with prosperity.

Bari

❶ *260 km (162 mi) southeast of Naples, 450 km (281 mi) southeast of Rome.*

The biggest city in the mezzogiorno, Bari is a major port and a transit point for travelers catching ferries across the Adriatic to Greece, but it's also a cosmopolitan city with one of the most interesting historic centers in the region. Most of Bari is set out in a logical 19th-century grid, following the designs of Joachim Murat (1767–1815), Napoléon's brother-in-law and King of the Two Sicilies. The heart of the modern town is **Piazza della Libertà,** but just beyond it, across Corso Vittorio Emanuele, is the *città vecchia* (old town), a maze of narrow streets on the promontory that juts out between Bari's old and new ports, circumscribed by Via Venezia, offering elevated views of the Adriatic in every direction. Stop for an outdoor drink at **Greta** (✉ Via Venezia 22) for a commanding view of the port and sea. By day, explore the old town's winding alleyways, where Bari's open-door policy offers a glimpse into the daily routine of southern Italy—matrons hand-rolling pasta with their grandchildren home from school for the midday meal, and handymen perched on rickety ladders, patching up centuries-old arches and doorways. Back in the new town, join the evening *passeggiata* (stroll) on pedestrian-only **Via Sparano,** then, when night falls, saunter among the exploding scene of outdoor bars and restaurants in Piazza Mercantile, past Piazza Ferrarese at the end of Corso Vittorio Emanuele.

In the città vecchia, overlooking the sea and just off Via Venezia, is the **Basilica di San Nicola,** built in the 11th century to house the bones of St. Nicholas, also known as St. Nick, or Santa Claus. His remains, buried in the crypt, are said to have been stolen by Bari sailors from Myra, where St. Nicholas was bishop, in what is now Turkey. The basilica, of solid and powerful construction, was the only building to survive the otherwise wholesale destruction of Bari by the Normans in 1152. ⊠ *Piazza San Nicola* ☎ *080/5737111* ☉ *Daily 7–1 and 4–7:45.*

Bari's 12th-century **Cattedrale** is the seat of the local bishop and was the scene of many significant political marriages between important families in the Middle Ages. The cathedral's solid architecture reflects the Romanesque style favored by the Normans of that period. ⊠ *Piazza dell'Odegitria* ☎ *080/5288215* ☐ *Free.*

Looming over Bari's cathedral is the huge **Castello Svevo.** The current building dates from the time of Holy Roman Emperor Frederick II (1194–1250), who rebuilt an existing Norman-Byzantine castle to his own exacting specifications. Designed more for power than beauty, it looks out beyond the cathedral to the small Porto Vecchio (Old Port). Inside are a haphazard collection of medieval Puglian art and archaeological artifacts and rotating exhibits of works by local artists. ⊠ *Piazza Federico II di Svevia* ☎ *080/5286218, 080/5286219 for tour reservations* ☐ *€2* ☉ *Thurs.–Tues. 8:30–7:30, ticket office closes at 7* PM. *Guided tours by appointment.*

Where to Stay & Eat

$–$$$ ✗ **Ristorante al Pescatore.** This is one of Bari's best fish restaurants, in the old town opposite the castle and just around the corner from the cathedral. Summer cooking is done outside, where you can sit amid a cheerful clamor of quaffing and dining. Try the grilled *céfalo* (mullet) if it is available, accompanied by crisp salad and a carafe of invigorating local wine. Reservations are essential in July and August. ⊠ *Piazza Federico II di Svevia 6* ☎ *080/5237039* ☐ *AE, DC, MC, V.*

★ **$$$** ☐ **Hotel Palace.** This downtown landmark is stationed steps away from Corso Vittorio Emanuele in the new city, but is also extremely convenient to the medieval center. The large, comfortable rooms are furnished lightly and tastefully. There are whimsical special pet rooms, children's rooms, and a room for music lovers, complete with stereo and classical CD collection. Other amenities include Smart Car rental service (€36 per day). The rooftop restaurant has great views outdoors in summer. ⊠ *Via Lombardi 13, 70122* ☎ *080/5216551* ☐ *080/5211499* ⊕ *www.palacehotelbari.it* ☞ *189 rooms* ☐ *Restaurant, bicycles, bar, convention center, meeting room, parking (fee), some pets allowed (fee)* ☐ *AE, DC, MC, V* ☉ *MAP.*

Puglia

ITALY

Adriatic Sea

50 miles
75 km

Bari ①
Molfetta
Corato
Trani ②
Andria
Barletta
Castel del Monte ④
Spinazzola
Gravina in Puglia
Altamura
Matera
Santeramo in Colle
Gioia del Colle
Polignano a Mare ③
Grotte di Castellana ⑫
Fasano
Alberobello ⑪
Trulli District ⑬
Locorotondo ⑬
Ostuni ⑭
Martina Franca ⑮
Massafra
Grottaglie
Taranto ⑯
Castellaneta Marina
Lido di Metaponto
Scanzano
Mare Piccolo
Mare Grande
Golfo di Taranto

Brindisi ⑰
Mesagne
VIA APPIA
Campi
Francavilla Fontana
Manduria
Lecce ⑱
Otranto ⑲
Santa Cesarea Terme
Castro
Maglie
Nardo
Gallipoli ⑳
SALENTO
Capo Santa Maria di Leuca
Leuca

PUGLIA
BASILICATA
CAMPANIA

Foggia ⑤
Cerignola
Lucera
San Severo
Peschici ⑧
Vieste ⑦
Foresta Umbra ⑨
Mattinata ⑥
Monte Sant'Angelo ⑩
Manfredonia
San Giovanni Rotondo
Rodi Garganico
L'Annunziata
Zapponeta
GARGANO PROMONTORY
Golfo di Manfredonia
Lago di Varano

TO THE ISOLE TREMITI
TO TERMOLI

Melfi
Potenza
Auletta
S. Angelo dei Lombardi
TO SALERNO NAPLES
Battipaglia

KEY
Ferry

VIA APPIA

EATING WELL IN THE MEZZOGIORNO

Southern cuisine is hearty and healthful, based around homemade pastas and cheeses, fresh vegetables, seafood, and olive oil. The best—and cheapest—meals are often found at a rustic family-run trattoria (sometimes referred to as a *casareccia* or *casalinga*), commonly located in the countryside or city outskirts. These barebones places usually don't offer printed menus—just flavors that rival those of any highbrow restaurant. Assent to the waiter's suggestions with a simple *va bene* (that's fine) and leave yourself in the chef's hands. Note that in many such restaurants you pay a set price for your meal, regardless of what you order.

Along the coastlines, the star attraction is fish, which can be grilled (*alla griglia*), baked (*al forno*), roasted (*arrosto*), or steamed (*al umido*). Among the highlights are delicate *orata* (sea bream), *branzino* (sea bass), swordfish, and calamari. But these are just a few of the wonderful options.

All over the mezzogiorno you find dishes unavailable elsewhere in Italy, such as *'ncapriata,* also called *favi e fogghi* (a fava-bean puree topped with vegetables and drizzled with olive oil; mix it all together before eating). Particularly at the more humble country restaurants, look for *pasta fatto in casa* or *pasta fatto a mano*—rolled out only hours before being served, and usually prepared with a thick tomato sauce or meat ragu. And don't miss the intensely flavorful and salty *ricotta forte*.

Each of the regions has its own specialties. In Puglia, look for focaccia *barese* (stuffed with onions, olives, anchovies, and ricotta), which makes a great snack or lunch; *strascenate* (rectangles of pasta with one rough side and one smooth side); and *orecchiette* (ear-shaped pasta) with *cime di rape* (bitter greens) and olive oil, a melodious preparation that's wondrous in its simplicity.

Basilicata is known for its excellent beef, various types of *funghi* (mushrooms) from the forest, antipasti of roasted vegetables soaked in olive oil, and hearty lamb stew. Calabria, meanwhile, is uniquely known for hot peppers. They pop up in *salame piccante* (spicy salami) and savory *salsiccia piccante* (hot Italian sausage), often sold by street vendors on a roll with peppers, onions, french fries, and mayonnaise. You'll also find dried *peperoncini* (hot peppers) or *olio piccante* (spicy olive oil) added to pasta dishes.

Puglia produces almost a fifth of Italy's wine. For a long time, most of it was *vino sfuso* (jug wine), but in the last 10 years quality has risen. The ancient primitivo grape (which purportedly was brought to California and renamed zinfandel), yields strong, heady wines. Look for primitivo di Manduria, as well as the robust Salice Salentino and the sweet red aleatico di Puglia. Top winemakers include Conti Zecca, Leone di Castris, Rubino, and Tormaresca. In Basilicata, several producers are using the aglianico grape variety to outstanding effect—try Paternoster's range of wines, and any Aglianico delle Vulture. In Calabria, producers such as Librandi have worked wonders with the local gaglioppo variety; their gravello is outstanding.

Nightlife & the Arts

While Bari's famous Teatro Petruzzelli awaits restoration from a 1991 fire, most drama and ballet have been diverted to the **Teatro Piccinni** (⊠ Corso Vittorio Emanuele 84 ☎ 080/5210878 ☉ Tickets on sale Mon.–Sat., 10:30–12:30 and 5–8). Italian rock and pop concerts can also be seen here. Ticket prices range from €15 to €35.

Caffè Borghese (⊠ Corso Vittorio Emanuele 122 ☎ 080/5242156) is a relaxing, traditional Belle Epoque café, wine bar, and light lunch spot in an old stone building; it's popular among young professionals. If you're feeling hipper than hip, try **Perini** (⊠ Via Sparano 13–15 ☎ 080/5244897). This is not your grandmother's Bari—it's a gleaming new place for cocktails and the requisite snacks that come with them; the high-concept setting comes with prices to match.

Trani

2 *43 km (27 mi) northwest of Bari.*

Smaller than the other ports along this coast, Trani has a quaint old town with polished stone streets and buildings, medieval churches, and a harbor filled with fishing boats. Trani is also justly famous for its sweet dessert wine, Moscato di Trani. The stunning, pinkish-white hued 11th-century **Duomo** (⊠ Piazza Duomo ☉ Daily 8–noon and 3:30–7), considered one of the finest in Puglia, is built on a spit of land jutting into the sea. The boxy, well-preserved **Castle** (☎ 0883/506603 ☉ Daily 8:30–7:30) was built by Frederick II in 1233. The Jewish community flourished here in medieval times, and on **Via Sinagoga** (Synagogue Street) two of the four synagogues still exist: **Santa Maria Scolanova** and **Santa Anna**, both built in the 13th century; the latter still bears a Hebrew inscription.

Where to Stay & Eat

★ $$ ✕⌂ **La Regia.** This small hotel-restaurant occupies a 17th-century palazzo superbly positioned in front of the Duomo, on a swath of land jutting out into the sea. Don't expect grand or spacious rooms, though they are perfectly adequate. The restaurant ($$–$$$) has attractive stonework, vaulted ceilings, and a terra-cotta tiled floor. Regional specialties are presented imaginatively: try the baked crepes (similar to cannelloni) or grilled fish. Reservations are essential for Sunday lunch and for dinner on summer weekends. ⊠ *Piazza Mons. Addazi 2, 70059* ☎ *0883/584444* 🖷 *0883/506595* ↳ *10 rooms* ⌂ *Restaurant, bar* ▤*AE, DC, MC, V* ☉ *Restaurant closed Mon. Hotel and restaurant closed 15 days in Jan.* ⦿⦿ *BP.*

Polignano a Mare

3 *40 km (24 mi) southeast of Bari, 14 km (9 mi) north of Castellana.*

With a well-preserved whitewashed old town perched on limestone cliffs overlooking the Adriatic, Polignano a Mare makes an atmospheric base for exploring the surrounding area. Bari is only a half hour's train ride up the coast. The town is virtually lifeless all winter, but becomes something of a weekend hot spot for city-dwellers in summer.

Where to Stay & Eat

$$ ✕🏠 **Grotta Palazzese.** Carved out of a cliff opening onto the Adriatic,
Fodor'sChoice   the Grotta Palazzese inhabits a stunning group of rocks and grottoes
★   that have wowed onlookers from time immemorial. Though all rooms but one have sea views, ask for one of the cave-apartments across the road rather than the more boxlike rooms in the main 1960s block. (Rooms 18, 25, and 139 are the most impressive.) The Grotta Palazzese's true tour de force is its summer restaurant ($$$–$$$$), serving impeccably prepared fish (try the assortment of raw Adriatic shellfish called *frutti di mare crudi*). The dramatic setting incorporates rock formations, with tables actually standing on an implausible bridge inside a jagged cave, while waves cast blue-green shadows on the grotto walls. It's one of the most romantic settings in all Italy. ⊠ *Via Narciso 59, 70059* ☎ *080/ 4240677* 🖷 *080/4240767* ⊕ *www.grottapalazzese.it* 🛏 *24 rooms* ♨ *2 restaurants, beach, bar, meeting room, parking (fee)* ▤ *AE, DC, MC, V* ☉ *Outdoor restaurant closed Oct.–Apr.* ⫿⊙⫾ *BP.*

Castel del Monte

★ ❹   *30 km (19 mi) south of Barletta, 56 km (35 mi) southwest of Bari.*

Built by Frederick II in the first half of the 13th century on an isolated hill, Castel del Monte is an imposing octagonal castle with eight austere towers. Very little is known about the structure, since virtually no records exist: the gift shop has many books that explore its mysterious past and posit fascinating theories based on its dimensions and Federico II's love of mathematics. It has none of the usual defense features associated with medieval castles, so it probably had little military significance. Some theories suggest it might have been built as a hunting lodge or may have served as an astronomical observatory, or even a stop for pilgrims on their quest for the Holy Grail. ⊠ *On signposted minor road 18 km (11 mi) south of Andria* 🎟 *€3* ☎ *0883/569997, 0339/1146908 tour reservations* ⊕ *www.castellipuglia.org* ☉ *Daily 10–1:30 and 2:30–7:30. Optional guided tours in English and Italian available every 1–2 hrs; call to reserve.*

Foggia

❺   *95 km (60 mi) west of Bari.*

Foggia, the chief city in Puglia's northernmost province, is not the most inspiring destination, though it makes a useful overnight stop for visitors to the Gargano. The old town is pleasant but fairly modern, having sustained significant war damage. On the main line from Rome and Naples, and easily accessible from the autostrada, Foggia has all the amenities you would expect from a major commercial center, hosting numerous fairs and conventions throughout the year. This means that, although it enjoys a decent selection of lodgings and restaurants, you'll need to reserve to ensure accommodations. This is the place to rent a car for excursions to the Gargano.

Where to Stay & Eat

★ **$$–$$$** ✕ **La Nuova Mangiatoia.** Set in an old farmhouse, this seafood restaurant looks like a medieval tavern, with arches and wood-beam ceilings. You can also dine in a large garden, where tables made from wagon wheels surround an old well. If you're lucky, game might be roasted on a spit right in the middle of the restaurant. The location is on the main road to Bari, near the Foggia Agricultural Fairgrounds. Reservations are essential on weekends. ✉ *Via Virgilio 2* ☎ *0881/634457* ▭ *AE, DC, MC, V* ⊘ *Closed Tues.*

$–$$ ✕ **Ambasciata Orsarese.** This hidden pizzeria and restaurant near Foggia's market, also referred to as "Trilussa," is very local, very good, and very small. In the tiny dining room the few tables are surrounded by rows of bottles of the region's best wines, which accompany pizza prepared in a 16th-century oven. Local antipasti and *primi* (first courses) are also available. Try their famed *pane divino,* a tasty and healthful bread that apparently aids digestion. ✉ *Via Tenente Iorio 50, corner of Rosati* ☎ *0881/709253* ▭ *No credit cards* ⊘ *Closed Wed.*

★ **$$$** ✕▥ **Cicolella.** Now part of the Mercure chain, this 1920s hotel near the station, on a tree-lined road, has tasteful rooms with floor-length curtains, regal wallpaper, and restful, discreet lighting. Some have balconies. The excellent restaurant ($$) serves international cuisine, but is at its best with local dishes. Service is impeccable, and a good regional wine list complements such country classics as puree of fava beans with chicory, drizzled with Puglian olive oil infused with hot peppers. Homemade *cavatelli neri* (dark pasta twists) are paired with a delectable tomato sauce made with pungent *ricotta dura* (hard ricotta). ✉ *Viale Ventiquattro Maggio 60, 71100* ☎ *0881/566111* 🖷 *0881/778984* ⊕ *www.hotelcicolella. isnet.it* ⇆ *91 rooms, 8 suites* ⚒ *Restaurant, meeting room* ▭ *AE, DC, MC, V* ⊘ *Restaurant closed weekends and Aug. 1–20* ⧆ *BP.*

GARGANO PROMONTORY

Forming the spur of Italy's boot, the Gargano Promontory (Promontorio del Gargano) is a striking contrast to the Adriatic's generally flat, unenthralling coastline. This is a land of whitewashed coastal towns, wide sandy beaches interspersed with secluded coves, and craggy limestone cliffs topped by deep-green pine and lush Mediterranean maquis. Not surprisingly, it pulls in the crowds in July and August, including many Germans and northern Italians. Prices are higher than elsewhere in Puglia as a result of its popularity. Camping is almost always an option, as plentiful and pretty campgrounds dot the Gargano's curvy, cliff-hugging roads. For the kids, the beaches and the Foresta Umbra national park are great places to let off steam, and many towns stage puppet shows in public gardens.

Mattinata

❻ *53 km (32 mi) northeast of Foggia, 138 km (86 mi) northwest of Bari.*

Just inland from a fine sandy beach, where you'll find most of the campsites and hotels, this is a generally quiet village that comes into its own in the summer season.

Where to Stay & Eat

$$–$$$ ✕ **Trattoria dalla Nonna.** The waves lapping at the shore just inches outside the picture windows of this elegant but unpretentious coastal restaurant, a few kilometers outside of Mattinata, are an indication of how fresh the fish will be. The memorable assorted raw seafood antipasto includes some shellfish you might not find anywhere else. *Cozze peruse* (an indigenous Puglian clam), hiding inside spiked-hair shells, are briny and buttery; tiny *noci* shellfish have a wonderful sweetness; and big, rich local oysters are all about texture. Try sweet grilled scampi with oil and lemon, and wash it all down with one of the great white wines on the extensive list. ⊠ *Mattinata Mare* ☎ *0884/559205* ⊕ *www.dallanonna. it* ⊟ *AE, DC, MC, V* ⊘ *Closed Mon. Oct.–Apr.*

$$$–$$$$ 🏨 **Baia delle Zagare.** This secluded, modern group of cottages overlooks an inlet and lies on the shore road around the Gargano Promontory, well north of Mattinata. An elevator built into the cliffs takes you down to a long private beach complete with limestone caves. The hotel restaurant is good enough to warrant staying on the premises all day. (You're expected to take half board in August.) Be careful when approaching on the road, as the gated entrance is easy to miss. ⊠ *Località Valle dei Mergoli, 17 km (10 mi) northeast of Mattinata, 71030* ☎ *0884/550155* 🖷 *0884/550884* ⊕ *www.hotelbaiadellezagare.it* ⊅ *150 rooms* ⚴ *Restaurant, minibars, tennis court, pool, health club, beach, dance club, theater* ⊟ *MC, V* ⊘ *Closed Sept. 15–May* ⵏⵔ *MAP.*

Vieste

➐ *93 km (58 mi) northeast of Foggia, 179 km (111 mi) northwest of Bari.*

This large whitewashed town jutting off the tip of the spur of Italy's boot is the Gargano's main commercial center and an attractive place to wander around. Though curvy mountain roads render it slightly less accessible from the autostrada and mainline rail stations than, say, Peschici and Mattinata, the range of accommodations (including camping) makes it a useful base for exploring Gargano. The resort attracts legions of tourists in summer, some bound for the Isole Tremiti, a tiny archipelago connected to Vieste by regular ferries. While in Vieste, make for the **castle.** Its interior is not open to the public, but there are good views from its high position overlooking the beaches and town.

Where to Stay & Eat

★ **$$–$$$$**   ✕ **San Michele.** Dine on exquisite Gargano fare at this charmingly intimate eatery on the town's main street. Their legendary antipasti include grilled eggplant and marinated anchovies. The porcini mushrooms picked from the region's Foresta Umbra are worth the visit alone. ⊠ *Viale XXIV Maggio 72* ☎ *0884/708143* ⊟ *AE, DC, MC, V* ⊘ *Closed Mon. and Jan.–mid-Mar.*

★ **$$$$**   🏨 **Pizzomunno.** Probably the most luxurious resort on the Gargano, Pizzomunno is right on the beach and surrounded by an extensive park. It is large, white, modern, air-conditioned, and well equipped. The rooms are ample and plush, all with terraces. Here you can unwind, or try your hand at tennis or archery. ⊠ *Spiaggia di Pizzomunno, 71019* ☎ *0884/ 708741* 🖷 *0884/707325* ⊕ *www.iqsnet.it/pizzomunno* ⊅ *210 rooms,*

10 suites ☼ 3 restaurants, 3 tennis courts, 2 pools, health club, sauna, archery, cinema, dance club, children's programs ▤ AE, DC, MC, V ☾ Closed mid-Oct.–early Apr. �†⊙⫯ BP.

$–$$ ▥ **Punta San Francesco.** After starting its life as an olive-oil factory, this hotel was tastefully refurbished in the mid-1990s. Thanks to its location near the waterfront in the heart of old Vieste, it is both quiet and close to the action. The owner is a warm, welcoming friend (and ardent promoter of local culture) to all who arrive, and the view from the rooftop is beautiful, especially at dawn. ⊠ Via San Francesco 2, 71019 ☎ 0884/701422 🖷 0884/701424 ⇗ 14 rooms ▤ MC, V †⊙⫯ EP.

Peschici

❽ 22 km (14 mi) northwest of Vieste, 199 km (124 mi) northwest of Bari.

Peschici is a pleasant resort on Gargano's north shore, a cascade of white-washed houses and streets with a beautiful view over a sweeping cove. Some surrounding areas are particularly popular with campers from northern Europe. Development has not wreaked too much havoc on the town: the mazelike center retains its characteristic low houses topped with little Byzantine cupolas.

off the beaten path

ISOLE TREMITI – A ferry service from Termoli, west of the Gargano (1¾ hours), and hydrofoil service from Vieste, Peschici, and Rodi Garganico (40 minutes to one hour) connect the mainland with these three small islands north of the Gargano. Although somewhat crowded with Italian tourists in summer, they are famed for their sea caves, pine forests, and craggy limestone formations. Interesting medieval churches and fortifications dot the islands. ☎ 199/123199 ferry reservations ⊕ www.adriatica.it/it/tremiti-orari.htm for ferry schedules.

Foresta Umbra

★ **❾** 25 km (16 mi) south of Rodi Garganico, 30 km (19 mi) southwest of Vieste.

In the middle of the Gargano Promontory is the majestic Foresta Umbra (Shady Forest), a dense growth of beech, maple, sycamore, and oak generally found in more northerly climates, thriving here because of the altitude, 3,200 feet above sea level. Between the trees in this national park are occasional dramatic vistas opening out over the Golfo di Manfredonia. From the north coast, take harrowingly curvy S528 (midway between Peschici and Rodi Garganico) south to head through the interior of the Gargano (do it during the day), or try the gentler ascent between Mattinata and Vieste on S89.

Monte Sant'Angelo

★ **❿** 16 km (10 mi) north of Manfredonia, 60 km (19 mi) southwest of Vieste.

Perched amid olive groves on the limestone cliffs overlooking the gulf is the town of Monte Sant'Angelo. Pilgrims have flocked here for nearly 1,500 years—among them, St. Francis of Assisi and crusaders setting

14

off for the Holy Land from the then-flourishing port of Manfredonia. Monte Sant'Angelo is centered on the **Santuario di San Michele** (Sanctuary of San Michele), built over the grotto where the archangel Michael is believed to have appeared before shepherds in the year 490. Walk down a long series of steps to get to the grotto itself; on its walls you can see the hand tracings left by pilgrims.

The **Tomba di Rotari** (Tomb of Rotari), believed to have been a medieval baptistery, has some remarkable 12th-century reliefs. It's reached by steps down and to the left from the Santuario di San Michele. Steep steps lead up to the large, ruined **Castello Normano** (Norman Castle) that dominates the town, with a view of the intricate pattern of the streets and steps winding their way up the side of the valley. Monte Sant'Angelo's medieval quarter, the **Rione Junno,** is a maze of little white houses squeezed into a corner of the narrow valley.

Where to Stay

$ ⊞ **Rotary Hotel.** This simple but welcoming modern hotel is set amid olive and almond groves just outside town. Most rooms have basic decor and terraces with views of the Golfo di Manfredonia. ⊠ *Via Pulsano, Km. 1, 71037* ☎ *0884/562147* 🖷 *0884/562146* ⊕ *www.hotelsantangelo.com/ rotary_hotel.htm* ⮧ *24 rooms* ⌂ *Restaurant; no a/c* ⊟ *AE, MC, V* ⎟◎⎟ *BP.*

THE TRULLI DISTRICT

The inland area to the southeast of Bari is one of Italy's oddest enclaves, mostly flat terrain given over to olive cultivation and interspersed with the idiosyncratic habitations that have lent their names to the district. The origins of the beehive-shaped trulli go back to the 13th century and maybe further. The trulli, found nowhere else in the world, are built of local limestone, without mortar, and with a hole in the top for escaping smoke. Some are painted with mystical or religious symbols; some are isolated, and others are joined together with roofs on various levels. Legends of varying credibility surround the trulli (for example, that they were originally built so that residents could quickly take apart their homes when the tax collectors came by). The center of trulli country is Alberobello in the enchanting Valle d'Itria: it has the greatest concentration of the buildings. You will spot them all over this region, some in the middle of desolate fields, and many in disrepair, but always adding a quirky charm to the landscape.

Alberobello

🅫 *59 km (37 mi) southeast of Bari, 45 km (28 mi) north of Taranto.*

Although Alberobello is something of a tourist trap, the amalgamation of more than 1,000 trulli huddled together along steep, narrow streets is nonetheless an unusual sight (as well as a national monument and a UNESCO World Heritage Site). As one of the most popular tourist destinations in Puglia, Alberobello has spawned some excellent restaurants (and some not-so-excellent trinket shops). Alberobello's largest trullo, the **Trullo Sovrano,** is up the hill through the trulli zone (head up Corso

Vittorio Emanuele past the obelisk and the Basilica). Though you can go inside, where you'll find a fairly conventional domestic dwelling, the real interest is the structure itself.

Where to Stay & Eat

$$$ ✕ **Il Poeta Contadino.** Proprietor Marco Leonardo serves "creative re-
Fodor'sChoice gional cooking" in this upscale country restaurant in the heart of the
★ attractive trulli zone. The room features ancient stone walls, candlelit tables, and a refined, understated ambience. Dishes might include *triglie vinaigrette alla menta* (red mullet with a mint vinaigrette) or *coda di rospo con pomodoro candito salsa al basilico* (monkfish in a tomato and basil sauce). In season, try anything with white truffle. ⊠ *Via Indipendenza 21* ☎ *080/4321917* ⟵ *Reservations essential* ▭ *AE, DC, MC, V* ⊙ *Closed Mon. and 3 wks in Jan. No dinner Sun.*

★ **$–$$$** ✕ **Trullo d'Oro.** This welcoming rustic restaurant set in five trulli houses has dark-wood beams, whitewashed walls, and an open hearth. Local country cooking includes dishes using lamb and veal, vegetable and cheese antipasti, pasta dishes with crisp raw vegetables on the side, and almond pastries. Among the specialties are roast lamb with *lampasciuni* (a type of wild onion) and spaghetti *al trullo*, made with tomatoes, *rughetta* (arugula), and four cheeses. ⊠ *Via F. Cavallotti 27* ☎ *080/4323909* ⟵ *Reservations essential* ▭ *AE, DC, MC, V* ⊙ *Closed Mon. (except in June–Aug.) and Jan. 10–31. No dinner Sun.*

$$$ ▣ **Dei Trulli.** Trulli-style cottages in a pine wood near the trulli zone make this a magical place to stay. It's decorated with rustic furnishings and folk-art rugs. The modestly priced restaurant serves local specialties. You're expected to take half or full board in high season. ⊠ *Via Cadore 32, 70011* ☎ *080/4323555* ⊟ *080/4323560* ⊕ *www.hoteldeitrulli.it* ⤶ *28 rooms* ⟜ *Restaurant, minibars, pool* ▭ *AE, MC, V* ❘⊙❘ *MAP.*

Grotte di Castellana

☼ ⑫ *20 km (12 mi) northwest of Alberobello, 63 km (52 mi) southeast of Bari.*

The Grotte di Castellana is a huge network of caves discovered in 1938. You can take one of the hour-long guided tours through the grottoes filled with fantastically shaped stalagmites and stalactites, part of the largest network of caves on the Italian mainland. A two-hour tour takes you on an extra 2-km (1½-mi) hike to another cave, Grotta Bianca. ⊠ *Piazzale Anelli* ☎ *080/4998211* ⊕ *www.grottedicastellana.it* ▱ *€9 1-hr tour, €14 2-hr tour* ⊙ *Apr.–Oct., daily 8:30–7, until 9 in Aug.; Nov.–Mar., daily 9:30–4. Last 2-hr tour leaves 1 hr before closing. English 1-hr tours at 1 and 6:30; English 2-hr tours at 11 and 4.*

Locorotondo

⑬ *9 km (5½ mi) southeast of Alberobello, 40 km (25 mi) north of Taranto.*

Locorotondo is an attractive hilltop town within the trulli district in the Itria Valley (take S172 from Alberobello). The *rotondo* in the town's name refers to the circular pattern of the houses, swirling down from the top. From the top of the town, on the road to Martina Franca, a verdant public garden gives way to lookout points over the entire Valle d'Itria, a landscape dotted with olive groves and trulli. Wander around the evocative alleyways of the *centro storico* (historic center) and look for the blazing yellow cathedral in Piazza Fra Giuseppe Andria Rolleo.

Where to Eat

$–$$ ✕ **Centro Storico.** The refined ambience and cuisine of this restaurant, set apart from the tourist haunts, make it a little pricier than its neighbors. But the food and service are worth it. Try such regional dishes as *sformato di verdura* (vegetable stew) and *agnello alla castellanese* (local lamb). ⊠ *Via Eroi di Dogali 6* ☎ *080/4315473* ⌕ *Reservations essential* ⊟ *AE, MC, V* ⊘ *Closed Wed. and 2 wks in Mar.*

Ostuni

⑭ *50 km (30 mi) west of Brindisi, 40 km (25 mi) northeast of Locorotondo.*

This sun-bleached, medieval town lies on three hills a short distance from the coast. From a distance, Ostuni is a jumble of blazingly white houses and churches spilling over a hilltop and overlooking the sea—thus earning it the nickname *la città bianca* (the White City). The **old town,** on the highest of the hills, has steep cobbled lanes, wrought-iron lanterns, some good local restaurants, and stupendous views out over the coast and the surrounding plain. **Piazza Libertà,** the city's main square, divides the new town to the west and the old town to the east.

Where to Stay & Eat

$$ ✕ **Osteria del Tempo Perso.** Buried in the side streets of the old town, this laid-back restaurant has rough-hewn stone interiors, with intriguing objects adorning the walls. It is open July–September nightly and October–June for Saturday dinner and Sunday lunch. Service is friendly and preparations focus on local cuisine such as delectable stuffed hot peppers and orecchiette with bitter greens and olive oil. ⊠ *Via G. Tanzarella Vitale 47* ☎ *0831/303320* ⊕ *www. osteriadeltempoperso.com* ⊟ *AE, MC, V* ⊘ *Closed Mon. and Dec. 27–Jan. 15. No Lunch July–Sept.; Oct.–June, Sat. dinner and Sun. lunch only.*

> **WORD OF MOUTH**
>
> "We spent a week in Puglia last fall. It's very worth the visit, but a car is almost mandatory to see the countryside and small cities like Alberobello, Lecce, Martina Franca (our favorite)." —DRJ

$–$$ ▦ **Incanto.** From the guest rooms of this large, modern hotel about a mile outside the old town, you can admire the expansive countryside, sea, and whitewashed hilltop city in the distance. It makes a convenient overnight base for visiting the area. ⊠ *Via dei Colli, 72017* ☎ *0831/ 301781* ⊟ *0831/338302* ⊕ *www.hotelincanto.it* ⇌ *75 rooms, 5 suites* ⌂ *2 restaurants, minibars, 2 bars* ⊟ *AE, DC, MC, V* ⦿ *BP.*

Nightlife

Especially in summer, Ostuni is livelier by night than you might expect. **Riccardo Cafè** (⊠ Via G. Tanzarello Vitale ☎ 0831/306046) is the hippest spot in town for a drink or a coffee before or after dinner. Grottoes, neon lighting, and contemporary sofas transport you to another Ostuni entirely.

Martina Franca

⑮ *6 km (4 mi) south of Locorotondo, 36 km (22 mi) north of Taranto.*

Martina Franca is a beguiling town with a dazzling mixture of medieval and baroque architecture in the light-color local stone. Ornate balconies hang above the twisting, narrow streets, with little alleys leading off into the hills. Martina Franca was developed as a military stronghold in the 14th century, when a surrounding wall with 24 towers was built, but now all that remains of the wall are the four gates that had once been the only entrances to the town. Each July and August, the town holds a music festival.

Where to Stay & Eat

$ ✕ **Da Gianni.** Sample the best pizzas in town at this welcoming wood-filled eatery replete with curious collages on the walls. Try their fabulous antipasti, including *scamorzine calde e speck* (small melting soft cheese balls and bacon) and bountiful plates of mozzarella served with roast potatoes. ✉ *Via Vittorio Emmanuelle 7* ☎ *080/4306323* 🖃 *MC, V* ۞ *Closed Mon.*

$ 🏠 **Park Hotel San Michele.** This garden hotel makes a pleasant base in the warm months, thanks to its pool. The two categories of single rooms have a small price difference; if alone, opt for the higher-priced ones. All rooms are spacious, some embellished with handsome furniture and including complimentary bowls of fruit. ✉ *Viale Carella 9, 74015* ☎ *080/4807053* 🖷 *080/4808895* ⊕ *www.parkhotelsm.it* ↜ *85 rooms* ♨ *Restaurant, pool, bar* 🖃 *AE, DC, MC, V* ۞ *BP.*

SALENTO & PORTS OF THE HEEL

This far south, the mountains run out of steam and the land is uniformly flat. The monotonous landscape, besides being agriculturally important, is redeemed by some of the region's best sandy coastline and a handful of small, alluring fishing towns, such as Otranto and Gallipoli. Taranto and Brindisi don't quite fit this description: both are big ports where historical importance is obscured by unsightly heavy industry. Nonetheless, Taranto has its archaeological museum, and Brindisi, an important ferry jumping-off point, marks the end of the Via Appia (the Imperial Roman road). Farther south, Salento (the Salentine Peninsula) is the local name for the part of Puglia that forms the end of the heel. Lecce is an unexpected oasis of grace and sophistication, and its swirling architecture will melt even the most uncompromising critic of the baroque.

Taranto

⑯ *100 km (62 mi) southeast of Bari, 40 km (25 mi) south of Martina Franca.*

Taranto (the stress is on the first syllable) was an important port even in Roman times. It lies toward the back of the instep of the boot on the broad Mare Grande bay, which is connected to a small internal Mare Piccolo basin by two narrow channels, one artificial and one natural. The old town is a series of old palazzos in varying states of decay and narrow cobblestone streets on an island between the larger and smaller bodies of water, linked by causeways; the modern city stretches inward along the mainland. Circumnavigate the old town and take in a dramatic panorama to the north, revealing Italy's shipping industry at its busiest: steel works, dockyards, a bay dotted with fishing boats, and a fish market teeming with pungent activity along the old town's western edge. Little remains of Taranto's past except the 14th-century church of **San Domenico** (⊠ Via Duomo 33) jutting into the sea at one end of the island, and its famous naval academy.

★ A compendium on the millennia of local history, Taranto's **Museo Nazionale** has a large collection of prehistoric, Greek, and Roman artifacts discovered mainly in the immediate vicinity, including Puglian tombs dating from before 1000 BC. The museum is just over the bridge from the old town, on the promontory. The collection is a testament to the importance of this ancient port, which has always taken full advantage of its unique trading position at the end of the Italian peninsula. Telephone ahead before visiting the museum, as hours can be irregular. ⊠ *Corso Umberto 41* ☎ *099/4532112* ☞ *€3* ⊙ *Daily 8:30–7:30.*

Where to Stay

$$ 🖭 **Grand Hotel Delfino.** This well-equipped hotel on the waterfront caters mainly to business clients, but it's a good, central place to unwind after exploring the city. There are sea views from the large modern lounge, the attractive terrace, and the airy rooms with balconies. The restaurant features regional seafood. ⊠ *Viale Virgilio 66, 74100* ☎ *099/7323232* 🖨 *099/7304654* ⊕ *www.grandhoteldelfino.it* ⇝ *200 rooms* ♲ *Restaurant, minibars, pool, bar, meeting room* ▤ *AE, DC, MC, V* ⊖ *BP.*

Brindisi

⑰ *114 km (71 mi) southeast of Bari, 72 km (45 mi) east of Taranto.*

Occupying the head of a deep inlet on the eastern Adriatic coast, Brindisi (the stress is on the first syllable) has long been one of Italy's most important ports. Today most travelers think of it only as a terminus for the ferry crossing that links Italy with Greece, and the seedy area around the port seems to confirm this. However, the impression fails to give credit to the broader importance of the city (which has a population of nearly 100,000) and to the assortment of interesting 13th- and 14th-century churches in the atmospheric old town. Brindisi has always played an important role as gateway to the eastern Mediterranean and beyond, and in the Middle Ages it was the departure point for several crusades to the Holy Land. That said, if you're looking for a place to spend the night in conjunction with a ferry departure or arrival, you'd be better served in nearby Lecce or Ostuni.

The core of Brindisi is at the head of a deep channel, which branches into two harbors, with the city between them. Look for the steeple of the cathedral to get your bearings, but go beyond it and down the steps to the water's edge. To the left is a tall **Roman column** and the base of another one next to it. These columns were built in the 2nd century AD and marked the end of the Via Appia (Appian Way), the Imperial Roman road that led from the capital to this important southeastern seaport. ⊠ *Viale Regina Margherita.*

The **Duomo,** a short walk from Brindisi's Roman column, has a mosaic floor in its apse that is worth the stop; the floor dates from the 12th century, although much of the rest of the cathedral was rebuilt in the 18th. ⊠ *Piazza Duomo* ۞ *Daily 7–1 and 4–8.*

The **Castello Svevo,** one of the defense fortifications built by the illustrious Frederick II in the 13th century, guards the larger of Brindisi's two inner harbors. It isn't accessible to the public. ⊠ *Piazza Castello.*

Where to Stay & Eat

★ **$–$$** ✕ **Lanterna.** An elegant dining experience awaits at this handsome, high-ceilinged 16th-century palazzo near the Duomo. Cool off in the equally enchanting courtyard under pergolas while sampling superb fish creations like *tubettini con frutti di mare* (small tubular pasta with seafood). ⊠ *Via Tarantini 14–16* ☎ *081/524950* 🖃 *AE, DC, MC, V* ۞ *Closed Mon. and Aug. No dinner Sun.*

$–$$ 🏨 **Mediterraneo.** Comfort and a central location are the advantages of this modern business-oriented Best Western hotel. Rooms have double-glazed windows and most have balconies. ⊠ *Viale Aldo Moro 70, 72100* ☎ *0831/582811* 🖷 *0831/587858* 🌐 *www.hotelmediterraneo.it* 🛏 *65 rooms* 🍴 *Restaurant* 🖃 *AE, DC, MC, V* ⊠ *BP.*

Lecce

18 *40 km (25 mi) southeast of Brindisi, 87 km (54 mi) east of Taranto.*

FodorsChoice
★

Lecce is the crown jewel of the mezzogiorno. The city is affectionately referred to as "the Florence of the south," but that sobriquet doesn't do justice to Lecce's uniqueness in the Italian landscape. Though its great shopping, modern bars, and the impossibly intricate baroque architecture draw comparisons to the Renaissance masterpieces of the north, Lecce's lively streets, laid-back student cafés, magical evening passeggiata (stroll), and openness to visitors are distinctively southern. The city is a cosmopolitan oasis two steps from the idyllic Otranto–Brindisi coastline and a hop from the olive-grove countryside of Puglia. Undiscovered by tourists, Lecce exudes an optimism and youthful joie de vivre unparalleled in any other baroque showcase. There is no Lecce of the north.

Although Lecce was founded before the time of the ancient Greeks, it's often associated with the term *Lecce baroque,* the result of a citywide impulse in the 17th century to redo the town in the baroque fashion. But this was baroque with a difference. Although such architecture is often heavy and monumental, here it took on a lighter, more fanciful air. Just look at the church of **Santa Croce,** with the **Palazzo della Prefettura** abutting it. Although every column, window, pediment, and balcony is given a curling baroque touch—and then an extra one for good measure—the overall effect is lighthearted. The buildings' proportions are unintimidating, and the local stone is a glowing honey color: it couldn't look menacing if it tried. ✉ *Via Umberto I* ☎ *0832/241927* ⊙ *Daily 8–1 and 5–8.*

Lecce's ornate **Duomo,** first built in 1114 but reconstructed in baroque style from 1659 to 1670, is uncharacteristically set in a solitary lateral square off a main street, rather than at a crossroads of pedestrian traffic. To the left of the Duomo, the more austere **bell tower,** reconstructed by master baroque architect Giuseppe Zimbalo in the 17th century, takes on a surreal golden hue at dusk. The facades of the adjoining 18th-century **Palazzo Vescovile,** farther past the right side of the Duomo, and the **Seminario** on the piazza's right edge, complement the rich ornamentation of the Duomo to create an effect almost as splendid as that of Santa Croce. The Seminario's tranquil **cloister** is also worth a visit. ✉ *Piazza Duomo, off Corso V. Emanuele* ☎ *0832/308884* ⊙ *Daily 8–1 and 5–8.*

In the middle of **Piazza Sant'Oronzo,** the city's putative center, surrounded by cafés, pastry shops, and newsstands, is a **Roman column** of the same era and style as the one in Brindisi, but imaginatively surmounted by an 18th-century statue of the city's patron saint, Orontius. Next to the column, the shallow rows of seats in the **Anfiteatro Romano** suggest Verona's arena or a small-scale Roman Colosseum.

Where to Stay & Eat

¢–$$ ✕ **Villa G. C. della Monica.** Set in a gracious 17th-century villa complete with palm trees, courtyard, and fountain, this restaurant comes into its own with summer alfresco dining in the garden. The menu focuses almost entirely on seafood, with the traditional Puglian *antipasto misto,* a generous spread of appetizers, followed by seasonal seafood dishes such as *maccheroni con vongole veraci, cozze tarantine, e fagioli bianchi* (macaroni with small Adriatic clams, mussels, and white beans) and fresh grilled fish. It's particularly suitable for families with young children, as there's lots of space to run around. ✉ *Via SS. Giacomo e Filippo 40* ☎ *0832/458432* ▱ *AE, MC, V* ⊙ *Closed Tues. and Jan.*

★ ¢–$$ ✕ **Wine Bar Corte dei Pandolfini.** At this wonderfully happening local spot you can choose from a vast list of Salento's best wines and feast on an unparalleled spread of artisanal *salumi* (cured meats) and local cheeses, accompanied by delicious local honey and *mostarda* (preserved fruit). It's all small plates here rather than the traditional *primi* and *secondi,* but you can easily make a meal of them. The location is on a little piazza is just off Via degli Ammirati, which starts on the backside of the Duomo. You can dine here until 1:30 AM. ✉ *Piazzetta Orsini* ☎ *328/ 0993709* ▱ *AE, MC, V* ⊙ *Closed Mon. No dinner Sun.*

¢–$ ✕ **Alle Due Corti.** Rosalba de Carlo, a local character, runs this traditional trattoria. The menu is printed in the ancient *leccese* language; the adventurous can try country dishes like *pezzetti te cavallu* (spicy horse-meat in tomato sauce) or *turcineddhi* (roasted baby goat entrails)—a crisp, gamy, fully flavored delight. The white-walled decor is stark, but character comes from the red-and-white checked tablecloths and the gregarious local families and groups of friends that inevitably fill the place. ✉ *Via Leonardo Prato 42* ☎ *0832/242223* ▤ *MC, V* ☾ *Closed Sun.*

★ ¢–$ ✕ **Trattoria Casareccia.** This is an excellent place to try traditional Pugliese cooking in a warm, casual setting of white walls and loud chatter. Don't expect a menu; choose from the daily specials, which might include home-made whole wheat pasta served with a delicate sauce of tomato and ricotta forte. The rustic *purè di fave e cicoria* (puree of fava bean with chicory) is topped with local olive oil and hot peppers; mix it together before eating. Service is informal and welcoming. ✉ *Via Costadura 19* ☎ *0832/245178* ▤ *AE, MC, V* ☾ *Closed Mon., Aug. 27–Sept. 11, 1 wk at Easter, and Dec. 23–Jan. 2. No dinner Sun.*

★ $$$–$$$$ ⬚ **Patria Palace.** It's convenient that the best hotel in Lecce also happens to be in one of the best possible locations, steps from all the action. This Starwood Luxury Collection property is impeccable, top to bottom, from the warm and elegant lobby with its recessed bar to the rooms, which are sumptuous without being over the top. For 50 well-spent euros more, you can reserve a room with a stunning private terrace overlooking Santa Croce, the crown jewel of Lecce baroque. If not, there's a beautiful rooftop gazebo for all. ✉ *Piazzetta Riccardi, 73100* ☎ *0832/245111* 🖷 *0832/245002* ⇨ *67 rooms* ⚐ *Restaurant, minibars, bar, lounge, meeting room, parking (fee)* ▤ *AE, DC, MC, V* ⦿⦿ *BP.*

$$ ⬚ **President.** Rub elbows with visiting dignitaries at this business hotel near Piazza Mazzini. The reception is expansive and furnishings are 1980s tasteful, with an emphasis on primary colors and modernist lamps. ✉ *Via Salandra 6, 73100* ☎ *0832/311881* 🖷 *0832/372283* ⊕ *www.hotelpresidentlecce.it* ⇨ *150 rooms, 4 suites* ⚐ *Restaurant, minibars, bar, lounge, meeting room, parking (fee)* ▤ *AE, DC, MC, V* ⦿⦿ *BP.*

$–$$ ⬚ **Risorgimento.** An old-fashioned Liberty-style hotel in an 18th-century palace, Risorgimento combines historic charm with modern comfort. For undisturbed sleep and summertime siestas during longer stays, ask for rooms overlooking the backstreets or the courtyard. The roof garden has great views. ✉ *Via Augusto Imperatore 19, Piazza S. Oronzo, 73100* ☎ *0832/242125* 🖷 *0832/245571* ⊕ *www.webshop.it/hotelrisorgimento* ⇨ *57 rooms* ⚐ *Restaurant, minibars, bar, lounge, meeting room, parking (fee)* ▤ *AE, DC, MC, V* ⦿⦿ *BP.*

Shopping

The best place in town to buy gastronomical delights from the Salento region, including olive oil, ricotta forte, hot pepper sauce, and an assortment of local baked goods, is **Golosità del Salento da Valentina** (✉ Via A. Petronelli 3 ☎ 0832/300549), a few steps from the Piazza del Duomo. The friendly and helpful owner presses his own olive oil and has infinite patience with—and interest in—visitors from abroad.

Nightlife & the Arts

The most popular hangout for the university crowd is **I Merli** (✉ Via Federico D'Aragona ☎ 0832/241874), a classy café where scores of locals gather each afternoon and evening for coffee, spirits, and gossip. Hours are 5:30 PM–2 AM (open earlier on weekends); closed Monday.

In July, courtyards and piazzas throughout the city are the settings for **drama productions** and, sometimes, opera. A **baroque music festival** is held in churches throughout the city in September. For details on forthcoming events call the **Tourist Information Office** (☎ 0832/248092).

Otranto

⑲ *36 km (22 mi) southeast of Lecce, 188 km (117 mi) southeast of Bari.*

In one of the first great Gothic novels, Horace Walpole's 1764 *The Castle of Otranto,* the English writer immortalized this city and its mysterious medieval fortress. Otranto (the stress is on the first syllable) has likewise had more than its share of dark thrills. As the easternmost point in Italy—and therefore closest to the Balkan peninsula—it's often borne the brunt of foreign invasions during its checkered history. A flourishing port from ancient Greek times, Otranto (*Hydruntum* to the Romans) has a history like most of southern Italy: after the fall of the western Roman Empire, centuries of Byzantine rule interspersed with Saracen incursions, followed by the arrival of the Normans. Modern Otranto's dank cobblestone alleyways alternatively reveal dusty, forgotten doorways and modern Italian fashion chains, and the spooky castle still looms above, between city and sea. On a clear day you can see across to Albania.

The historic city center nestles within impressive city walls and bastions, dominated by the famous **Castello,** which is attributed to the Spanish of the 16th century. ⊠ *Piazza Castello* ☎ *0832/930722* ⊘ *Tues.–Sun. 9–1* 🎟 *Free.*

The real jewel in Otranto is the **Cattedrale,** originally begun by the Normans and conserving an extraordinary 12th-century mosaic pavement in the nave and aisles. ⊠ *Piazza Basilica* ☎ *0836/802720* 🎟 *Free* ⊘ *Daily 8:30–noon and 5–7:30.*

off the beaten path

COASTLINE SOUTH TO LEUCA – The coastal road between Otranto and Leuca is one of the most beautiful in southern Italy. Sandy beaches are replaced by rocky outcrops and sheer cliffs watched over by scattered castles and seaside pleasure palaces. Along the way, **Santa Cesarea Terme,** with a pleasant shoreline and famous fanciful Moorish resort, and **Castro,** with another attractive marina, are worthwhile stops; this is land that few foreign tourists traverse. At the end of the journey, **Capo Santa Maria di Leuca** has a lighthouse at the southeasternmost point in Italy, the end of the Puglian Aqueduct, and the quiet, sparse basilica of **Santa Maria Finibus Terrae** (land's end). From here, you are only 70 km (44 mi) from Albania. The **Marina di Leuca,** below, is a little fishing village with excursion boats and a few summertime hotels and bars. If, after the drive, you're heading back to Lecce or points east, the inland highway is a faster route.

Gallipoli

⑳ *37 km (23 mi) south of Lecce, 190 km (118 mi) southeast of Bari.*

The fishing port of Gallipoli, on the Golfo di Taranto, is divided between a new town, on the mainland, and a beautiful fortified town, across a 17th-century bridge, crowded onto its own small island in the gulf. The Greeks called it Kallipolis, the Romans Anxa. Like the infamous Turkish town of the same name on the Dardanelles, the Italian Gallipoli occupies a strategic location and thus was repeatedly attacked through the centuries—by the Normans in 1071, the Venetians in 1484, the British in 1809. Today, life in Gallipoli revolves around its fishing trade. Bright fishing boats in primary colors breeze in and out of the bay during the day, and Gallipoli's fish market, below the bridge, throbs with activity all morning.

Gallipoli's historic quarter, a mix of narrow alleys and squares, is guarded by **Castello Aragonese,** a massive fortification that grew out of an earlier Byzantine fortress you can still see at the southeast corner. After being an operative base for the busy *Guardia di Finanza* (revenue police), it's now being renovated and adapted for future use as a public monument. Gallipoli's **Duomo** (✉ Via Antonietta de Pace ☎ 0833/ 261987), open daily 9–12:30 and 5–8, is a notable baroque church. The church of **La Purissima** (✉ Riviera Nazario Sauro ☎ 0833/261699) has a stuccoed interior as elaborate as a wedding cake, with an especially noteworthy tiled floor. You can visit daily 9–12:30 and 5–7:30.

Where to Stay & Eat

$$$–$$$$ ✕ **Marechiaro.** Unless you arrive by boat—as many do—you have to cross a little bridge to reach this simple port-side restaurant, not far from the town's historic center. It's built out onto the sea, replete with wood paneling, flowers, and terraces, with panoramic coastal views. Try the renowned *zuppa di pesce alla gallipolina* (a stew of fish, shrimp, clams, and mussels) and linguine with seafood. ✉ *Lungomare Marconi* ☎ *0833/ 266143* ▤ *AE, DC, MC, V.*

★ **$$$$** ▦ **Costa Brada.** The rooms all have terraces with sea views at this modern white beach hotel of classic Mediterranean design. The interiors are uncluttered and tasteful; rooms 110 through 114 are particularly spacious and overlook the beach. The hotel accepts only half- or full-board guests in summer. Room rates go down significantly at other times of year. ✉ *Baia Verde, Litoranea Santa Maria di Leuca, 73014* ☎ *0833/ 202551* 🖷 *0833/202555* ⊕ *www.grandhotelcostabrada.it* ⤴ *78 rooms* ⊙ *2 restaurants, snack bar, 2 pools (1 indoor), gym, sauna, shop* ▤ *AE, DC, MC, V* ⥮ *MAP.*

Sports & the Outdoors

BEACHES Ample swimming, water sports, and clean, fine sand make Gallipoli's
☺ **beaches** a good choice for families. The 5-km (3-mi) expanse of sand sweeping south from town has both public and private beaches, the latter equipped with changing rooms, sun beds, and umbrellas. Water sports equipment can be bought or rented at the waterfront shops in town.

BASILICATA

Occupying the instep of Italy's boot, Basilicata has long been one of Italy's poorest regions, memorably described by Carlo Levi in his *Christ Stopped at Eboli,* a book that brought home to the majority of the Italians the depths of deprivation to which this forgotten region was subject. (The tale of Levi's internment was poignantly filmed by Francesco Rosi in 1981.) Basilicata was not always so desolate, however. For the ancient Greeks, the area formed part of Magna Graecia, the loose collection of colonies founded along the coasts of southern Italy whose wealth and military prowess rivaled those of the city-states of Greece itself. Metaponto (formerly Metapontion or Metapontum) was one of the most important of these colonies; its remains are easily reached along the coastal S106. Farther inland, the city of Matera, the region's true highlight, is built on the side of an impressive ravine that is honeycombed with *sassi* (prehistoric dwellings), some of them still occupied, forming a separate enclave that contrasts vividly with the attractive baroque town above.

Matera

㉑ *45 km (28 mi) north of Metaponto, 62 km (39 mi) south of Bari.*

Matera is one of southern Italy's most unusual towns. On their own, the elegant baroque churches, palazzos, and broad piazzas—filled to bursting during the evening *passeggiata,* when the locals turn out to stroll the streets—as well as the outstanding modern cuisine, would make Matera stand out in Basilicata's impoverished landscape. But what really sets this town apart is its sassi.

Fodor'sChoice   Matera's **sassi** are rock-hewn dwellings piled chaotically atop one an-
★   other, strewn across the sides of a steep ravine. They date from Paleolithic times, when they were truly cave homes. In the years that followed, the grottoes were slowly adapted as houses only slightly more modern, with their exterior walls closed off and canals regulating rainwater and sewage. Until relatively recently, these troglodytic abodes presented a Dante-esque vision of squalor and poverty, graphically described in Carlo Levi's *Christ Stopped at Eboli,* but in the 1960s most of them were emptied of their inhabitants, who were largely consigned to the ugly block structures seen on the way into town. Today, having been designated a World Heritage Site, the area has been cleaned up and is gradually being populated once again—and even gentrified, as evidenced by the bars and restaurants that have moved in. (The filming here of Mel Gibson's controversial film *The Passion of the Christ* also raised the area's profile.) The wide Strada Panoramica leads you safely through this desolate region, which still retains its eerie atmosphere and panoramic views.

There are two areas of sassi, the **Sasso Caveoso** and the **Sasso Barisano,** and both can be seen from vantage points in the upper town. Follow the Strada Panoramica down into the sassi and feel free to ramble among the strange structures, which, in the words of H. V. Morton in his *A Traveller in Southern Italy,* "resemble the work of termites rather

than of man." Among them you will find several *chiese rupestri,* or rock-hewn churches, some of which have medieval frescoes, notably **Santa Maria de Idris,** right on the edge of the Sasso Caveoso, near the ravine. *Santa Maria de Idris:* ⊠ *Sasso Caveoso* 🔊 *€3* ⊙ *Oct.–Mar., daily 9–1 and 3:30–5:30; Apr.–Sept., daily 9–1 and 3:30–7.*

The **Duomo** in Matera was built in the late 13th century and occupies a prominent position between the two areas of sassi. It has a pungent Apulian-Romanesque flavor; inside, some of the columns came from Metaponto, and there's a recovered fresco, probably painted in the 14th century, showing scenes from the *Last Judgment.* On the Duomo's facade the figures of Sts. Peter and Paul stand on either side of a sculpture of Matera's patron, Madonna della Bruna. ⊠ *Via Duomo* 🕾 *0835/ 335201* ⊙ *Daily 8–12:30 and 3:30–7.*

In town you'll find the 13th-century Romanesque church of **San Giovanni Battista,** restored to its prebaroque simplicity in 1926. As you go in through a side door—the original end door and facade were incorporated into later buildings—note the interesting sculpted decorations in the porch. The interior still maintains its original cross vaulting, ogival arches, and curious capitals. ⊠ *Via San Biagio* ⊙ *Daily 8–noon and 3:30–7.*

need a break?

The distinguished, time-worn patina of downtown's elegant little **Caffè Tripoli** (⊠ Piazza Vittorio Veneto 17 🕾 0835/333991) only hints at the treasures that lie within: some of southern Italy's best coffee and gelato, including memorable versions of hazelnut and chocolate. They're also renowned for their unbelievably rich hot chocolate and other decadent drinks that blend coffees, creams, and gelatos. You can't go wrong.

Matera's excellent **Museo Ridola** is housed in the former monastery of Santa Chiara. Illustrating the human and geological history of the area, the museum includes an extensive selection of prehistoric and classical finds, notably Bronze Age weaponry and beautifully decorated Greek pottery. One room displays stolen art treasures recovered by a special department of the *carabinieri* (national police). ⊠ *Via Ridola 24* 🕾 *0835/ 310058* 🔊 *€2.50* ⊙ *Tues.–Sun. 9–8, Mon. 2–8.*

Where to Stay & Eat

$$
Fodor's Choice
★

✕ **Lucanerie.** Within the airy vaulted stone dining room of this casual restaurant you'll find some of southern Italy's most exciting food. A series of 17 or 18 small tasting plates, served at the beginning of the meal, steal the show. These creative antipasti might include bitter orange slices sprinkled with lemon zest and ground hot peppers, fried zucchini flowers, a memorable goat's ricotta with a sweet glaze of persimmon, and an herbaceous slice of rich *lardo* (lard) atop a crusty piece of bread whose texture approaches the apex of perfection. Other courses might include delectable hand-rolled pasta tubes or a fillet of local beef, though it takes a truly insatiable appetite to make it through both a primo and a secondo after such an opening spread. ⊠ *Via*

Santo Stefano ☎ *0835/332133* ⌀ *Reservations essential* ▤ *AE, DC, MC, V* ☺ *Closed Mon.*

★ **$–$$** ✕ **Le Botteghe.** This stylish restaurant is right in the heart of the sassi, occupying pleasingly restored vaulted premises. Carnivores will delight in the charcoal-grilled steak, which comes from the friendly owner's herd of grass-fed cows. Cooked wonderfully rare, this is one of the finest pieces of meat in the region. It's best washed down with local Aglianico del Vulture red wine. Solid renditions of local pasta dishes are also available. ⌂ *Piazza San Pietro Barisano 22* ☎ *0835/344072* ⌀ *Reservations essential* ▤ *DC, MC, V* ☺ *No dinner Sun. No lunch Oct.–Apr. Tues.–Fri.*

$–$$ 🏨 **Locanda di San Martino.** Combining good taste, an agreeable ambi-
Fodor'sChoice ence, and value, the Locanda is a prime place to stay among Matera's
★ sassi—and you can drive right up to it. The historic rooms—formerly cave dwellings—have been impeccably restored under the guidance of owner Antonio Panetto and American anthropologist Dorothy Zinn. Stepping out onto your terrace overlooking the old town is like being on a film set. ⌂ *Via San Martino 22, 75100* ☎🖷 *0835/256600* ⊕ *www. locandadisanmartino.it* 🛏 *15 rooms, 6 suites* ⌀ *Restaurant, minibars, bar, library, some free parking* ▤ *AE, DC, MC, V* ◎ *BP.*

$ 🏨 **Hotel Sassi.** Hotel Sassi lies right in the heart of the Sasso Barisano, directly across from the Duomo. It has a raw, cavelike design, with rough-hewn walls and stairs (making it inhospitable to people with limited mobility). Facilities are minimal; rooms are small and plain but clean, comfortable, and air-conditioned. Two rooms are set aside for hostel-type bunk accommodations at budget rates. Parking is a bit of a hike from the hotel, something to consider if you have heavy baggage. ⌂ *Via San Giovanni Vecchio 89, 75100* ☎ *0835/331009* 🖷 *0835/333733* ⊕ *www.hotelsassi.it* 🛏 *18 rooms, 4 suites* ⌀ *Minibars, bar* ▤ *AE, DC, MC, V* ◎ *BP.*

The Outdoors

WALKING TOURS The agency **SIC** (⌂ Via Casalnuovo 15, 75100 ☎ 0835/314244 ⊕ www.stoneincoming.it) arranges tours of the sassi area on request, charging around €10 per person for groups of four or more. Call ahead to request an English-speaking guide. Independent guides also offer their services on the spot, pricing by length of tour and the number in your party.

Metaponto

㉒ *48 km (30 mi) southwest of Taranto, 182 km (114 mi) south of Bari.*

Greek Metapontion was founded around 700 BC, most probably by Achaeans from the Greek mainland. The great mathematician and philosopher Pythagoras, banished from Kroton, established a school here in about 510 BC and eventually died in the city. Punished for its support of the Carthaginian general Hannibal (247–183 BC) after his victory over Rome at Cannae (216 BC), Metapontum, as it was known by the Romans, endured long years of decline—sacked by the slave-rebel Spartacus (died 71 BC) and subsequently ravaged both by malaria and Saracen raids. Most of what remained was used for building elsewhere in the region, but the *zona archeologica* (archaeological zone), which covers a vast area, retains enough interest to merit a visit. Nearby Lido di Metaponto has sandy, well-equipped beaches.

The modern **Museo Archeologico Nazionale** displays 4th- and 5th-century AD statuary, ceramics, jewelry, and coins. Perhaps most interesting are examples of coins stamped with ears of barley, symbolizing the cereal production to which Metapontion owed its prosperity. The museum lies about 2 km (1 mi) outside Lido di Metaponto—keep your eyes peeled for the scanty signs. ⊠ *Borgo Metaponto, Via Aristea 21* ☎ *0835/745327* 🖃 *€2.50* ☉ *Tues.–Sun. 9–8, Mon. 2–8.*

Highlights of Metaponto's sprawling **Parco Archeologico,** accessible to the east of the Museo Archeologico Nazionale, include the **Santuario di Apollo Licio** (Sanctuary of Apollo Lykaios), a 6th-century BC Doric temple, and the 4th-century BC **Teatro,** much restored. More compelling is the better-preserved Tempio di Hera (Temple of Hera), commonly known as **Tavole Palatine,** found 2–3 km (1–2 mi) north, where the main S106 crosses the Bradano River. With 15 of its fluted Doric columns surviving, it's the most evocative remnant of this once mighty state. ⊠ *Metaponto Borgo* ☎ *0835/745220* 🖃 *Free* ☉ *Daily 9 AM–1 hr before sunset.*

Aliano

❷❸ *127 km (79 mi) southwest of Matera, 102 km (63 mi) southeast of Potenza.*

This remote village off S598 in the center of Basilicata's empty interior was the site of Carlo Levi's internment during 1936 and 1937. After the war, Levi (1902–75) published his account of that time in his classic *Christ Stopped at Eboli,* later filmed by Francesco Rosi. Not significantly different from any of the countless villages scattered over the featureless clay gullies and outcrops stretching out on all sides, Aliano (called Gagliano by Levi) has not altered much, and readers can identify the church, the piazza where the Fascist mayor addressed the impassive peasants, and the timeless views. The house in Aliano where Carlo Levi stayed has been preserved as the **Museo Storico Carlo Levi,** displaying some personal artifacts as well as other articles of local interest. The old post office nearby in Piazza Garibaldi—where you will find the custodians to both buildings—has been converted into an art gallery. ⊠ *Palazzo Caporale* ☎ *0835/568315* 🖃 *€3 for both museum and art gallery* ☉ *Sept.–May, daily 10–12:30 and 4–6; June–Aug., daily 10–12:30 and 4–7. Closed Wed.*

Terranova di Pollino

❷❹ *70 km (43 mi) south of Aliano, 125 km (78 mi) east of Matera.*

Founded in the 16th century as part of the Duchy of Noja, Terranova is a quiet village—the end of the road for local buses—lying at the foothills of Italy's largest nature preserve, the Pollino National Park. It is base camp for hikes to sleepy Albanian hill communities and to the higher reaches of the spectacular Pollino massif. Thanks to a relatively low population density, wildlife thrives within the park, its best-known inhabitants being the golden eagle and the endangered wolf—there were 34 at the latest count, making up almost 10% of the population in all of Italy.

Where to Stay & Eat

★ ¢ ✕⌧ **Hotel Picchio Nero.** Situated just below the village of Terranova, this hotel combines rustic simplicity and excellent dining ($–$$). At the helm is the energetic Pino Golia, a welcoming, attentive host who has set up this first-class base for mountain hikers and dispenses copious information on local trails and history. The rooms are wood-paneled in Alpine style and look out onto soothing woods and valleys. The name *picchio nero* means "black woodpecker," one of the Pollino's conservation flagship species. ⌧ *Via Mulino 1, 85030* ☎ *0973/93170* 📠 *0973/ 93181* ⊕ *www.picchionero.com* ➫ *23 rooms, 2 family suites* ⚒ *Restaurant, bar; no a/c* ⊟ *AE, DC, MC, V* ⦿| *BP.*

Maratea

㉕ *103 km (64 mi) southwest of Aliano, 217 km (135 mi) south of Naples.*

When encountering Maratea for the first time, you can be forgiven for thinking you've somehow arrived at the French Riviera. The high, twisty road resembles nothing so much as a corniche, complete with glimpses of a turquoise sea below. Divided by the craggy rocks into various separate localities—Maratea, Maratea Porto, Maratea Marina—the sequence ends above the main inland village, a tumble of cobblestone streets where the ruins of a much older settlement (Maratea Antica) can be seen. At the summit of the hill stands a dramatic, gigantic Christ, a floating white ghost in the night sky reminiscent of the one in Rio de Janeiro. There's no shortage of secluded sandy strips in between the rocky headlands, which can get crowded in August. A summer minibus service connects all the different points once or twice an hour.

Where to Stay & Eat

$$ ✕ **Taverna Rovita.** Housed in a former convent with exposed beams, this restaurant in the heart of the old town offers a menu based on traditional recipes, but the food here is in a different league from that of Maratea's other eateries. The antipasti, for a start, are varied and abundant, and the homemade pasta comes with a selection of rich sauces that changes according to the season. Choose a locally caught fish for your second course. ⌧ *Via Rovita 13* ☎ *0973/876588* ⊟ *AE, DC, MC, V* ☾ *Closed Nov.–Feb., and Tues. in Mar.–May and Oct.*

$$$$ ✕⌧ **Villa Cheta Elite.** Immersed in Mediterranean greenery, this large historic villa in the seaside village of Acquafredda is strategically close to the beach (reached by elevator). Rooms are spruce and stylish without being overfurnished, while dining out on the restaurant's garden terrace ($$) against the backdrop of Basilicata's rugged coastline is simply fabulous. ⌧ *Via Nazionale, Loc. Acquafredda Maratea, 85041* ☎ *0973/*

878134 🖨 *0973/878135* ⊕ *www.villacheta.it* 🛏 *23 rooms* ♿ *Restaurant, minibars, beach, bar* 🖃 *AE, DC, MC, V* ⊘ *Closed Dec.–Mar. 15* †☉¶ *MAP.*

CALABRIA

Italy's southernmost mainland region has seen more than its fair share of oppression, poverty, and natural disaster, but this land of Magna Graecia, mountains, and *mare* (sea) also claims more than its share of fantastic scenery and great beaches. The accent here is on the landscape, the sea, and the constantly changing dialogue between the two. Don't expect much in the way of sophistication in this least trodden of regions, but do remain open to the simple pleasures to be found—the country food, the friendliness, the disarming hospitality of the people. Aside from coast and culture, there are also some sights worth going out of your way for, from the vividly colored murals of Diamante to the ruins of Magna Graecia at Locri. Inland, the mountainous Sila Massif, which includes a nature reserve, are a draw for hikers.

The drive on the southbound A3 highway alone is a breathtaking experience, the more so as you approach Sicily, whose image grows tantalizingly nearer as the road wraps around the coastline once challenged by Odysseus. This is the road you should take to get the big picture—but don't forget to stop for a bit to get a closer view of this fascinating land.

Diamante

❷❻ *51 km (32 mi) south of Maratea, 225 km (140 mi) south of Naples.*

One of the most fashionable of the string of small resorts lining Calabria's north Tyrrhenian coast, Diamante makes a good stop for its white-washed maze of narrow alleys, brightly adorned with a startling variety of large-scale murals. The work of local artists, the murals—which range from cartoons to poems to serious portraits, and from tasteful to downright ugly—give a sense of wandering through a huge open-air art gallery. Flanking the broad, palm-lined seaside promenade are sparkling beaches to the north and south.

Where to Stay

$$$ 🏨 **Grand Hotel San Michele.** A survivor from a vanishing age, the San Michele, operated by the illustrious Ana Maria Sinisalchi and her marine biologist son Andrea, occupies a belle epoque–style, cliff-top villa near the village of Cetraro, 20 km (12 mi) south of Diamante on SS18. Mingling Mediterranean charm with old-style elegance, the hotel is set within extensive gardens, and an elevator takes you down to the private beach at the base of the cliff. As with most hotels on Calabria's coast, substantial bargains are available on room rates outside July and August. ⊠ *Località Bosco 8/9, 87022 Cetraro* ☎ *0982/91012* 🖨 *0982/91430* ⊕ *www.sanmichele.it* 🛏 *84 rooms, 10 suites, 40 apartments* ♿ *Restaurant, 9-hole golf course, tennis court, beach (fee), bar, convention center, car rental* 🖃 *AE, DC, MC, V* ⊘ *Closed Nov.* †☉¶ *BP.*

VOICES OF ITALY

Andrea Peiser
hotel manager, Cetraro, Calabria

Andrea Peiser is an accomplished marine biologist, diver, and now hotel manager. He studied environmental science and zoology at the University of Hawaii, has been a member of the Italian civil defense as a forest-fire fighter, and has led an underwater search-and-rescue squad. He returned to the family business as general manager of the Hotel San Michele in Cetraro, Calabria, helping his mother, the illustrious Claudia Sinisalchi. Mrs. Sinisalchi once built dams in Nigeria and was a professor of hydrology and hydraulics in Rome, but eventually came back to Calabria to run the family hotel. Now it is Andrea's turn. He explains aspects of life in his native land.

The concept of time: "Sometimes is difficult to understand the way of living of some of my countrymen. They seem to have lost the concept of time. If you fix an appointment, it won't be at 10 AM sharp, but rather 'sometime in the morning or afternoon'—and which day is unknown. If you wait for someone the whole afternoon, the person might show up three days later in the morning. It's not too bad in the end; you have just to expect the unexpected."

The Ndragheta: "There are a lot of small fishing boats in Calabria, and most are run or controlled by people involved with Ndrangheta, the Calabrian version of the Mafia. This means that the whole fishing market is a sort of 'washing machine' for the dirty money coming from drugs, guns, and illegal aliens. With the Ndragheta, everything passes by, but nothing goes away. The organization has just changed a bit the way it makes money. Nowadays, they are more involved in the drug and gun trades, like organized crime everywhere. Still, the Ndragheta doesn't represent any threat to tourists—that's a common misconception."

Why his hotel won't serve swordfish: "Because in Calabria, they are caught with devices that are illegal, such as 'drifting nets,' which go through the water catching everything in sight. Although illegal, they're used by several fishing vessels departing from the small harbor of Cetraro and elsewhere. The coast guard organizes raids three or four times per year, confiscating boats and nets, but after a week everything is forgotten."

The pitfalls of running an old-world hotel: "A rich lady always requested breakfast in the bedroom and she ate it on the balcony facing the sea. The problem was that we had to evacuate the terrace below where the 'common' people ate because as the lady finished her breakfast she just tossed it off the balcony, bombarding our poor guests with dishes and empty teapots. We nicknamed her 'the throwing lady.'

"Another thing that happened last year was that a bat took up residence under a closed umbrella by the swimming pool. Early in the morning, an old lady from northern Italy would go to the pool and open the umbrella housing the bat—which would cause her to scream. Why she chose that particular umbrella each time is a mystery, but bats, foxes, and even snakes are realities of life in our part of Calabria when you run a hotel on wooded grounds."

14

Cosenza

㉗ *75 km (48 mi) south of Diamante, 185 km (115 mi) north of Reggio di Calabria.*

Cosenza, Calabria's biggest city, has a steep, stair-laden *centro storico* (historic city center) that truly hails from another age. Wrought-iron balconies overlook narrow alleyways with old-fashioned storefronts and bars that have barely been touched by centuries of development. Flung haphazardly—and beautifully—across the top and side of a steep hill ringed by mountains, and watched over by a great, crumbling medieval castle, Cosenza also provides the best gateway for the Sila, whose steep walls rear up to the town's eastern side. Though Cosenza's outskirts are largely modern and ugly, culinary and photographic gems await in the rolling farmland nearby and the mountains to the east.

Crowning the Pancrazio hill above the old city, with views across to the Sila mountains, **Castello Svevo** is largely in ruins, having suffered successive earthquakes and a lightning strike that ignited gunpowder stored within. The castle takes its name from the great Swabian emperor Frederick II (1194–1250), who added two octagonal towers, though it dates back originally to the Normans, who fortified the hill against their Saracen foes. Occasional exhibitions and concerts are staged here in summer. ⊠ *Porta Piana* ✉ *Free* ☉ *Daily 8 AM–8 PM.*

Cosenza's noblest square, **Piazza XV Marzo** (commonly called Piazza della Prefettura), houses government buildings as well as the elegant **Teatro Rendano.** From the square, the **Villa Comunale** (public garden) provides plenty of shaded benches for a rest.

need a break? In the heart of the centro storico, the charming and historic **Gran Caffè Renzelli** (⊠ Corso Telesio 46 ☎ 0984/46814) makes a fine spot for a pause. At tables inside or out (there is a no-smoking room as well as an outside terrace), you can enjoy *varchiglia* (a dry almond cake) along with a host of sweet and wonderful coffee-liqueur combinations, each served with cream in a tall glass. Join in the *chiacchiere al caffè* (talks over coffee), echoing the discussions of the literary salon that once met here.

Cosenza's original **Duomo** was probably built in the middle of the 11th century but was destroyed by the earthquake of 1184. A new cathedral was consecrated in the presence of Emperor Frederick II in 1222. After many baroque additions, later alterations have restored some of the Provençal Gothic style. Inside, look for the lovely tomb of Isabella of Aragon, who died after falling from her horse en route to France in 1271. ⊠ *Piazza del Duomo* ☎ *0984/77864* ☉ *Daily 8–noon and 3:30–7.*

Where to Stay & Eat

¢–$$ ✕ **L'Arco Vecchio.** This tavern-restaurant, right in the middle of the old town along the path up to the castle, appropriately under the famous Arch of Ciaccio, serves traditional Calabrian dishes in a warm, elegant vaulted room. Try the excellent *lagane e ceci* (homemade pasta with chickpeas). ✉ *Piazza Archi di Ciaccio 21* ☎ *0984/72564* ▭ *AE, DC, MC, V* ⊗ *Closed Sun. and 2 wks in Aug.*

¢–$$ ✕ **Da Giocondo.** In the new part of town, but near the centro storico, you can sample simple homemade dishes in a modern yet homey setting. Go for freshly picked mushrooms from the Sila as an antipasto, followed by *rigatoni alla silana* (pasta with tomato, basil, peppers, and local caciocavallo cheese), washed down with local Cirò wine. ✉ *Via Piave 53* ☎ *0984/29810* ▭ *AE, DC, MC, V* ⊗ *No dinner Sun.*

★ ¢–$$ ✕ **Wine Bar DOC.** Representing the contemporary edge of Cosenza, this postmodern feat of interior decorating oozes fusion, whimsically plopping spreads of tempting traditional Calabrian salumi and a superlative collection of wines amid a whirl of glass and exposed stone, all tucked into the cozy arches of an ancient palazzo. All the trendiest locals come out not just for the voluminous wine list, which showcases Calabria's absolute best, but also for the wonderful smoked meats, cheeses, and inventive pasta dishes. Come to eat or just to drink. ✉ *Vico San Tommaso 13, off Corso Telesio* ☎ *0984/73110* ▭ *AE, DC, MC, V* ⊗ *Closed Mon. No lunch.*

¢ 🏨 **Excelsior.** This 1900 building has been completely restored. The public areas are imposing, retaining their fin-de-siècle feel, while the spacious guest rooms are adequate if uninspiring. The location is close to the shops of Cosenza's main drag, Corso Mazzini, and an easy walk across the Busento river from the centro storico. ✉ *Piazza Matteotti 14, 87100* ☎ *0984/74383* 🖷 *0984/74384* ⊕ *www.italiaabc.it/a/excelsior* ⬐ *40 rooms* ⌂ *Restaurant, bar, meeting room* ▭ *AE, DC, MC, V* ⦿ *BP.*

Rende

28 *13 km (8 mi) northwest of Cosenza.*

Rende is a pleasing stop on the way to or from Cosenza. Leave your car in the parking lot at the base of a long and bizarre series of escalators and staircases, which will whisk you off to this pristine, cobblestoned hilltop town, whose winding streets and turrets preside over idyllic countryside views.

Where to Eat

★ $$–$$$ ✕ **Pantagruel.** You are completely in the hands of the chef at this prix-fixe-only temple to seafood. But they are good hands indeed, which is why Pantagruel is one of the most respected restaurants in Calabria. The set menu changes daily, but you'll surely encounter something memorable: for instance, a salad of octopus so thinly sliced and delicate that it's reminiscent of carpaccio, or a tender fillet of *spigola* (Mediterranean bass) with a sweet sauce of brandy, cream of licorice, and lemon rind. It's set in an elegant old house with sweeping views of hills dotted with little towns. ✉ *Corso Vittorio Emanuele 217* ☎ *0966/372260* ▭ *AE, DC, MC, V* ⊗ *Closed Mon. and Tues., Aug. 15–Sept. 15, and Dec. 21–Jan. 10.*

Camigliatello

㉙ *36 km (22 mi) east of Cosenza.*

Lined with chalets, Camigliatello, between Crotone and Cosenza, is one of the Sila Massif's major resort towns. Most of the Sila is not mountainous at all; it is, rather, an extensive, sparsely populated plateau with areas of thick forest. Unfortunately, the region has been exploited by construction and fuel industries, resulting in considerable deforestation. However, since 1968, when the area was designated a national park (Parco Nazionale della Calabria), strict rules have limited the felling of timber, and forests are now regenerating. There are well-marked trails through pine and beech woods, and ample opportunities for horseback riding. Fall and winter see droves of locals hunting mushrooms and gathering chestnuts, while ski slopes near Camigliatello also draw crowds. A couple of miles east of town, Lago Cecita makes a good starting point for exploring **La Fossiata,** a lovely wooded conservation area within the park.

Where to Stay

$ 🏨 **Tasso.** On the edge of Camigliatello, less than 1 km (½ mi) from the ski slopes, this hotel is in a peaceful, picturesque location. Don't be put off by its oddly futuristic 1970s look—it's well equipped, with plenty of space for evening entertainment, including live music, and relaxation after a day of hiking or skiing. The restaurant has a terrace shaded by a walnut tree, and all rooms have balconies. There are sometimes good full-board deals for seniors in summer. ⊠ *Via degli Impianti Sportivi, Spezzano della Sila, 87058* 🏨🏨*0984/578113* 🌐*www.hoteltasso.it* 🛏*82 rooms* 🍴 *Restaurant, bar, lounge, nightclub, recreation room, meeting room, free parking; no a/c* ▤ *AE, DC, MC, V* ⊗ *Closed Mar.–May and Nov.* 🍴*BP.*

Crotone

㉚ *105 km (65 mi) east of Cosenza, 150 km (94 mi) northeast of Locri.*

Occupying the main bulge along Calabria's Ionian coastline, Crotone was founded by Achaeans from the Greek mainland in about 708 BC and soon became one of the great cities in Magna Graecia. Though the drab modern town has obliterated most of the ancient settlement, a re-
★ markable gold hoard was found at the **Santuario di Hera Lacinia** on a promontory 11 km (7 mi) to the south, known as Capo Colonna for the single remaining column from the temple of Hera. The area has free access during daylight hours and is well worth a visit, especially in April and May, when it is awash with wildflowers. The **Museo Archeologico Nazionale,** close to the seafront castle in Crotone, features treasure from the Santuario di Hera Lacinia including Hera's gold crown with intertwined fig and myrtle leaves. ⊠ *Via Risorgimento 14* ☎ *096/ 223082* 💶 *€2* ⊗ *Sept. 16–June 14, daily 9–7:30; June 15–Sept. 15, Sun.–Fri. 9–7:30, Sat. 9 AM–11 PM. Closed 1st and 3rd Mon. of month.*

Pizzo

31 *148 km (92 mi) south of Diamante, 107 km (66 mi) north of Reggio di Calabria.*

Built up along the slope of a steep promontory overlooking the coast and a fishing port, Pizzo has a good selection of seafood restaurants and a small cliff-top Aragonese castle (built in 1486) near the center of town. Here the French general Joachim Murat (1767–1815) was imprisoned, tried, and shot in October 1815, after a bungled attempt to rouse the people against the Bourbons and reclaim the throne of Naples given him by his brother-in-law Napoléon.

While in Pizzo, sample the renowned *gelato di Pizzo,* a rich, creamy delight available in many flavors at any of the outdoor bars in the central Piazza della Repubblica.

The **Chiesetta di Piedigrotta,** a little over a mile north of Pizzo's castle, at the bottom of a flight of steps leading down to the beach, is a 17th-century church implausibly hewn out of rock by shipwrecked Neapolitan sailors in thanks for their rescue. They filled it with statues of biblical and historical figures, and the collection today includes a bizarre ensemble showing Fidel Castro kneeling before Pope John XXIII (1881–1963) and President John F. Kennedy (1917–63). ⊠ *Via Nazionale* ⊗ *Daily 9–1 and 3–7:30.*

Where to Stay

$ ⊡ **Hotel Murat.** Here's a good central choice for accommodation if you decide to overnight in Pizzo. Right on the town's main square, a stone's throw from the castle and perched overlooking the water, the Murat has comfortable rooms, of which the ones on the sides are biggest and have the best views (ask for 201 or 207). ⊠ *Piazza della Repubblica 41, 89812* ☎ *0963/534201* 🖷 *0963/534469* ⤶ *12 rooms* ⟡ *Restaurant, bar* ⊟ *AE, DC, MC, V* ⫶⊙⫶ *BP.*

Tropea

32 *28 km (17 mi) southwest of Pizzo, 107 km (66 mi) north of Reggio di Calabria.*

Ringed by cliffs and wonderful sandy beaches, the Tropea promontory is still undiscovered by the big tour operators. The main town, Tropea, easily wins the contest for prettiest town on Calabria's Tyrrhenian coast, its old palazzos built in simple golden stone on an elevation above the sea. On a clear day the seaward views from the waterfront promenade extend to embrace Stromboli's cone and at least four of the other Aeolians—the islands can be visited by motorboats that depart daily from Tropea in summer. Accommodations are good, and beach addicts will not be disappointed by the choice of magnificent sandy bays within easy reach of here. Some of the best are south at Capo Vaticano and north at Briatico.

In Tropea's harmonious warren of lanes, seek out the old Norman **Cattedrale,** whose interior displays a couple of unexploded U.S. bombs from

World War II, with a grateful prayer to the Madonna attached to each. ✉ *Piazza Sedile* ⊙ *Daily 7–noon and 4–7.*

From the belvedere at the bottom of the main square, Piazza Ercole, the church and Benedictine monastery of **Santa Maria della Isola** glisten on a rocky promontory above an aquamarine sea. Stroll out to visit the church on a path lined with fishermen's caves. Dating back to medieval times, the church was remodeled in the Gothic style, then given another face-lift after an earthquake in 1905. The interior has an 18th-century nativity and some fragments of medieval tombs. ✉ *Santa Maria della Isola* ⊙ *Daily 7–noon and 4–7.*

Where to Stay & Eat

$$–$$$ ✕ **Pimm's.** Since its glory days in the 1960s, this underground restaurant in Tropea's historic center has offered the town's top dining experience. Seafood is the best choice, with such specialties as pasta with sea urchins, smoked swordfish, and stuffed squid. The splendid sea views are an extra enticement. ✉ *Corso Vittorio Emanuele 2* ☎ *0963/666105* ▭ *AE, DC, MC, V* ⊙ *Closed Nov. 15–Dec. 15; closed Mon.*

$$$ ▥ **Rocca Nettuno.** Perched on the cliffs a 10-minute walk south of Tropea's town center, this deceptively large complex is one of the few hotels open throughout the year. Rooms are reasonably spacious and almost all have balconies. Some of the best—and quietest—are immersed in greenery near the cliff top. There is an all-inclusive package in summer months that includes a dine-around option so you can enjoy meals in town, too. ✉ *Via Annunziata* ☎ *0963/998111* 📠 *0963/603513* ⊕ *www.roccanettuno.com* ⇥ *264 rooms* ♿ *2 restaurants, pizzeria, minibars, tennis court, massage, sauna, beach, 2 bars, theater* ▭ *AE, DC, MC, V* ⧖ *FAP.*

Bagnara Calabra

㉝ *11 km (7 mi) south of Palmi, 36 km (22 mi) north of Reggio di Calabria.*

Fishing is in the blood of the local villagers in Bagnara Calabra, particularly when in pursuit of swordfish, for which the town has long enjoyed widespread fame. Casual trattorias make this a great lunch stop.

Where to Eat

$–$$ ✕ **Taverna Kerkira.** Centrally located on Bagnara's main street, this ca-
FodorsChoice sual restaurant emphasizes food above all else. The chef's mother hails
★ from Corfu, and as a result dishes represent creative Greek spins on Calabrian classics. Antipasti feature fish you'll encounter in few other places, such as delicately marinated, sashimilike *carpaccio di alalonga*

(raw Tyrrhenian tuna with olive oil and soy sauce). *Farfalle* pasta is prepared with Greek yogurt, lemon zest, cucumber, and a hint of mullet—a sublime creation. The chef also excels at *pesce spada* (swordfish)—try it breaded and baked with mint, vinegar, and Parmesan. ⊠ *Corso Vittorio Emanuele 217* ☎ *0966/372260* ⊟ *AE, DC, MC, V* ⊗ *Closed Mon. and Tues., Aug. 1–Sept. 10, and Dec. 20–Jan. 10.*

Reggio di Calabria

④ *26 km (16 mi) south of Scilla, 499 km (311 mi) south of Naples.*

Reggio di Calabria, the city on Italy's toe tip, is the jumping-off point for Messina- and Sicily-bound ferries, and was laid low by the same catastrophic earthquake that struck Messina in 1908. This raw city is one of Italy's most active ports, where you'll find every category of container ship and smokestack, but there's also a pleasant lido lined with palm fronds and urban beaches.

★ Reggio has one of southern Italy's most important archaeological museums, the **Museo Nazionale della Magna Grecia.** Prize exhibits here are two statues, known as the **Bronzi di Riace,** that were discovered by an amateur deep-sea diver off Calabria's Ionian coast in 1972. Flaunting physiques that gym enthusiasts would die for, the pair are thought to date from the 5th century BC and have been attributed to both Pheidias and Polykleitos. It's possible that they were taken by the Romans as trophies from the site of Delphi and then shipwrecked on their return to Italy. Coins and votive tablets are among the numerous other treasures from Magna Graecia contained in the museum. ⊠ *Piazza de Nava, Corso Garibaldi* ☎ *0965/812255* 🎟 *€5* ⊗ *Daily 9–7:30. Closed 1st and 3rd Mon. of month.*

Where to Stay

$$$ 🏨 **Miramare.** On the seafront midway between the port and the station, Miramare has one of the best locations in Reggio. It has been restored to evoke the charm of the early 20th century, yet has modern facilities. ⊠ *Via Fata Morgana 1, 89127* ☎ *0965/812444* 🖷 *0965/812450* ⊕ *www.reggiocalabriahotels.it* ⇌ *96 rooms* ⚴ *Restaurant, bar, parking (fee)* ⊟ *AE, DC, V* ⊗I *BP.*

Aspromonte

㉟ *Gambarie: 42 km (26 mi) northeast of Reggio di Calabria.*

Rising to the east of Reggio di Calabria, Aspromonte is the name of the sprawling massif that dominates mainland Italy's southern tip. Long the haunt of brigands, this thickly forested range reaches an elevation of nearly 6,560 feet. In summer it makes a cool respite from the heat of the coast, offering endless opportunities for hiking and shady picnicking. On a clear day you can see Mt. Etna. To get here going north from Reggio, turn inland off the autostrada or coast road at Gallico, 12 km (7 mi) north of town; driving east from Reggio on S184, turn left onto the S183 at Melito di Porto Salvo. Ask at **Reggio's tourist office** (⊠ Corso Garibaldi 329 ☎ 0965/892012) for Aspromonte walking itineraries.

> **en route**
>
> The fast S106 hugs Calabria's Ionian coast, leading south out of Reggio di Calabria and curving around Aspromonte to your left. Having rounded Capo Spartivento, the road proceeds north. If you don't want to continue farther north, turn left onto the S112dir, shortly before Bovalino and 14 km (9 mi) before reaching Locri. This winding mountain road takes you around the rugged northern slopes of Aspromonte, a highly scenic but rigorously winding route.

Locri

36 *100 km (62 mi) east of Reggio di Calabria.*

South of the seaside town of Locri are the excavations of **Locri Epizefiri,** where one of the most important of Magna Graecia's city-states stood. Founded around the 7th century BC, Locri became a regional power when—apparently assisted by Castor and Pollux—10,000 Locrians defeated an army of 130,000 from Kroton on the banks of the Sagra River, 25 km (16 mi) north. Founding colonies and gathering fame in the spheres of horse-breeding and music, Locri was responsible for the first written code of law in the Hellenic world. The walls of the city, parts of which are still visible, measured some 8 km (5 mi) in circumference, and the ruins within are scattered over a vast area. The museum is on the main coast road (S106) and the remains of a 5th-century BC Ionic temple are settled just behind it. ☎ *0964/390023* ✉ *Museum and site €2* ⊘ *Site daily 9 AM–1 hr before sunset, museum daily 9–7:30; museum and archaeological zone closed 1st and 3rd Mon. of month.*

Stilo

37 *50 km (31 mi) north of Locri, 138 km (86 mi) northeast of Reggio di Calabria.*

Grandly positioned on the side of the rugged Monte Consolino, the village of Stilo is known for being the birthplace and home of the philosopher Tommaso Campanella (1568–1639), whose magnum opus was the socialistic *La Città del Sole* (*The City of the Sun,* 1602)—for which he spent 26 years as prisoner of the Spanish Inquisition. A more tangible reason to visit the village is the tiny 10th-century Byzantine temple **La Cattólica.** Standing on a ledge above the town, this tiled and three-turreted building is believed to be the best preserved of its kind. ✉ *Via Cattólica* ✉ *Free* ⊘ *Daily 9–7.*

Where to Stay

$$ ⊞ **San Giorgio.** Tucked away off Stilo's main Via Campanella, this hotel is housed in a 17th-century cardinal's palace, Palazzo Lamberti, and decked out in the style of that period, with elegantly furnished guest rooms. There are exhilarating views seaward from the garden. Half or full board is required—the food is acceptable, and there's nowhere else in town to eat anyway. ✉ *Via Citarelli 8, 89049* ☎ *0964/775047* ✏ *10 rooms* ⚐ *Restaurant, pool, bar; no a/c in some rooms* ⊘ *Closed Oct. 20–Mar.* ⫧◯⫧ *MAP.*

en route

From Stilo you can take the S110 inland—a long twisty road that goes through the high Serra region, covered with a thick mantle of chestnut forest. There are terrific views to be enjoyed over the Ionian coast, and you can continue across the peninsula to Calabria's Tyrrhenian littoral, emerging at Pizzo. The total road distance between Stilo and Pizzo is around 80 km (50 mi).

MEZZOGIORNO ESSENTIALS

Transportation

BY AIR

14

Several airlines serve the cities of Bari and Brindisi in Puglia: Alitalia flies regularly between Bari and Brindisi and Rome and Milan; Volare-Air Europe connects Bari with Rome and Milan; Air One serves Bari with flights from Turin, Milan, Venice, and Trapani in Sicily, and operates one daily Brindisi–Milan flight; Ryanair operates service to Bari and Brindisi from London's Stansted; and Air Dolomiti, a Lufthansa partner, connects Bari with Verona, Turin, and Munich, Germany. Matera is most easily reached from Bari. In Calabria, Reggio di Calabria's Aeroporto Tito Minniti handles Alitalia domestic flights only, with five departures daily to Rome and two to Milan. Twenty-seven kilometers (17 mi) north of Pizzo, Aeroporto di Lamezia caters to international charters and domestic flights, with connections to Milan, Bologna, and Rome; airlines servicing the airport are Alitalia and Air One.

⏷ Airport Information Aeroporto di Lamezia ☎ 0968/51766 or 0968/51205 ⊕ www. sacal.it. **Aeroporto di Reggio di Calabria** ☎ 8488/65641 Alitalia ⊕ www.sogas.it. **Bari-Palese** ✉ Strada Provinciale Aeroporto ☎ 080/5835200 ⊕ www.seap-puglia.it. **Brindisi-Papola** ✉ Via de Simone Ruggero 1 ☎ 0831/4117208 ⊕ www.seap-puglia.it.

⏷ Airlines & Contacts Air Dolomiti ☎ 800/013366 ⊕ www.airdolomiti.it. **Air Europe** ☎ 848/848130, 080/5370495 in Bari ⊕ www.aireurope.it. **Air One** ☎ 199/207080 ⊕ www.flyairone.it. **Alitalia** ☎ 848/865641 ⊕ www.alitalia.com. **Ryanair** ☎ 199/ 114114, 0871/2460000 from U.K. ⊕ www.ryanair.com.

TRANSFERS
A regular bus service connects Bari-Palese (about 10 km [7 mi] northwest of the city center) and Brindisi-Papola (8 km [5 mi] to the north) with their respective cities. Alitalia buses provide service to and from both cities. Many hotels and taxis within other outlying cities provide service directly to and from the airports, which can be much simpler than public transport—call your hotel for details.

BY BOAT

Puglia and Calabria are major launching points for boat travel to other destinations. Ferries ply the waters from Bari and Brindisi to Greece (Corfu, Igoumenitsa, Patras, and Kephalonia), Turkey, Albania, and even Egypt and Croatia. Brindisi's connection to Patras is covered by some rail passes, thus immensely popular with backpackers.

In Calabria, ferries ply the Straits of Messina to Sicily every 15 minutes or so from Reggio di Calabria and from Villa San Giovanni, day and night (with reduced service in winter). Crossings take 20–40 minutes, and reservations are not needed. Villa is much preferable for car ferries, with more frequent service from Caronte and Tourist. Ferry entrances in Villa are well marked from the A3 autostrada. Allow extra time to sit in line waiting to get on the next boat, though. Hydrofoils also run from Reggio to Sicily's Aeolian Islands. In Reggio contact SNAV and FS; in Villa, FS and Caronte.

🚢 Boats & Ferries from Puglia **Adriatica di Navigazione** to Albania and the Tremiti islands; agents at A. Galli e Figlio ✉ Corso Manfredi 4, 71043 Manfredonia ☎ 199/123199 ✉ Gargano Viaggi Piazza Roma 7, 71019 Vieste ☎ 199/123199 ⊕ www.adriatica.it. **Blue Star Ferries** only Brindisi to Corfu and Igoumenitsa; agents at Il Globo ✉ Corso Garibaldi 65, 72100 Brindisi ☎ 0831/527684 ⊕ www.bluestarferries.com.

🚢 Boats & Ferries from Calabria **Caronte and Tourist** ☎ 0965/793111. **FS** ☎ 0965/863545. **SNAV** ☎ 0965/29568 ⊕ www.snav.it.

BY BUS

Compared with rail, travel times by bus into Puglia from Naples on the far side of the Apennines are substantially shorter. If traveling between Naples and Foggia, contact CLP. Miccolis runs a daily Naples–Lecce service, which takes five hours, about half as long as by train. For bus travel from Rome, contact Autolinee Marozzi, at their Rome office or in Bari. In Reggio di Calabria, contact Lirosi for buses to Rome, leaving three times daily.

Direct, if not always frequent, connections operate between most destinations within Puglia, Calabria, and Basilicata. SITA is the main bus company operating in the region. In many cases bus service is the backup when problems with train service arise. Matera is linked with Bari and Metaponto by frequent buses operated by Ferrovie Appulo-Lucane, and with Taranto by SITA buses. In Calabria various bus companies make the north–south run with stops along both coasts; Ferrovie della Calabria operates many of the local services. From Reggio di Calabria, Salzone runs to Scilla, and Federico to Locri and Stilo.

🚌 Bus Information **Autolinee Marozzi** ☎ 06/44249519 in Rome, 080/5562446 in Bari. **CLP** ☎ 081/5311706. **Federico** ☎ 0965/590212. **Ferrovie Appulo-Lucane** ☎ 0835/332861. **Ferrovie della Calabria** ☎ 0984/36851. **Lirosi** ☎ 0966/575552. **Miccolis** ☎ 081/200380. **Salzone** ☎ 0965/751586. **SITA** ✉ Piazza Aldo Moro 15/a, Bari ☎ 080/5213714.

BY CAR

The mezzogiorno is a fairly easy place to get around by car, and with erratic train and bus service, a car is often your best transportation option—it's the only way to see the more remote sights.

Coming from the Adriatic coast to the north, the A14 goes as far as Bari and Matera. Rome to Bari takes four or five hours by car. The A3, meanwhile, comes from Naples and Salerno on the west coast and continues all the way through Calabria to Reggio, meeting the Sicily ferries at Villa San Giovanni. As long as the construction continues (and it shows no signs of coming down), the trip from Naples to Reggio can take up to seven hours (three hours from Naples to Cosenza, and four hours from Cosenza to Reggio).

Roads are good, and major cities are linked by fast *autostrade*. In Calabria, Metaponto is a major road and rail junction for routes along the coast and inland. To get to Metaponto by car from Puglia's Taranto, take the S106 southwest for 45 km (28 mi). From Puglia's Bari, take the S96 south for 44 km (28 mi) to Altamura, then the S99 south 19 km (12 mi) to Matera. The A3 Autostrada del Sole runs between Salerno and Reggio di Calabria, with exits for Crotone (the Sila Massif), Pizzo, Rosarno (for Tropea), Palmi, and Scilla; it takes an inland route as far as Falerna, then tracks the Tyrrhenian coast south (except for the bulge of the Tropea promontory). A3 is toll-free, but you get what you pay for: it's under eternal construction, so factor in time for delays. Take the S18 for coastal destinations—or for a better view—on the Tyrrhenian side, and likewise the S106 (which is uncongested and fast) for the Ionian. To drive from Basilicata's Metaponto to Matera, take the S175 northwest for 45 km (28 mi). You can cross the Strait of Messina from Villa San Giovanni or Reggio.

14

Note that entering the historic centers of many towns requires a small car, folding side-view mirrors, and a bit of nerve; tentative drivers should park outside the center and venture in by foot. If you're squeamish about getting lost, don't plan on any night driving in the countryside—the roads can become confusing without the aid of landmarks or large towns. Bari, Brindisi, and Reggio di Calabria are notorious for car thefts and break-ins. If you are driving in these cities, do not leave valuables in the car or trunk, and find a guarded parking space if possible.

EMERGENCY SERVICES   ACI Emergency Service offers 24-hour roadside assistance.
🚗 **ACI dispatchers** ☎ 803/116.

BY TRAIN

Bari is a transit hub for train connections with northern Italy. Rome to Bari, with frequent service, takes about four hours. On the Calabria side, the main north–south FS (Italian State Railways) line has hourly services from Reggio north to Pizzo, Diamante, and Maratea, continuing on as far as Salerno, Naples, and Rome. There are nine daily Intercity or Eurostar trains linking Reggio di Calabria with Naples (4–5 hours) and Rome (6–7 hours). All FS trains also stop at Villa San Giovanni (for connections to Sicily), a 20-minute ride from Reggio. Two fast Eurostar trains run daily between Metaponto and Naples (3¾ hours) and Rome (5½–6 hours), and three others connect Metaponto and Salerno (2¾–3½ hours), from which there are frequent connections to Naples and Rome. There are two connections to Milan, fastest time 11½ hours.

Within the region, FS service links Bari to Brindisi, Lecce, and Taranto, but smaller destinations can often be reached only by completing the trip on a connecting bus operated by the railroad. The private Ferrovie Sud-Est (FSE) line connects the trulli area and Martina Franca with Bari and Taranto, and the fishing port of Gallipoli with Lecce. The main FS line from Taranto stops in Metaponto, from which there are regular departures to Matera on Ferrovie Appulo-Lucane (FAL) trains. The FAL rail line links Matera to Altamura in Puglia (for connections to Bari) and to Ferrandina (for connections to Metaponto or Potenza). South of Metaponto, FS trains run into Calabria, either following the Ionian coast as far as Reggio di Calabria or swerving inland to Cosenza and the Tyrrhenian coast at Paola. Main FS services run along both coasts but can be crowded along the Tyrrhenian.

🚆 Train Information FS ☎ 892021 ⊕ www.trenitalia.com. Ferrovie Appulo-Lucane ☎ 0835/332861 ⊕ www.fal-srl.it. Ferrovie Sud-Est (FSE) ☎ 080/5462111 or 0832/668111.

Contacts & Resources

EMERGENCIES

For general emergencies, dial 113. Pharmacies take turns staying open late and on Sunday. A list of hours is posted on each *farmacia* (pharmacy).

In Reggio di Calabria, the pharmacies Curia and Caridi are open at night. Elsewhere, late-night pharmacies are open on a rotating basis; information on current schedules is posted on any pharmacy door.

🚑 Ambulance, Fire, Police ☎ 113. Caridi ✉ Corso Garibaldi 327 ☎ 0965/24013. Curia ✉ Corso Garibaldi 455 ☎ 0965/332332. Hospital ☎ 0965/8501 in Reggio di Calabria, 0835/2431 in Matera.

VISITOR INFORMATION

🚆 Tourist Information Alberobello ✉ Piazza Ferdinando IV, 70011 ☎ 080/4325171. Bari ✉ Piazza Moro 32/a, 70122 ☎ 080/5242329 ⊕ www.pugliaturismo.it. Brindisi ✉ Lungomare R. Margherita, 72100 ☎ 0831/523072. Camigliatello ✉ Via Roma 5, 87052 ☎ 0984/578243. Cosenza ✉ Via P. Rossi, 87100 ☎ 0984/390595. Foggia ✉ Via Perrone 17, 71100 ☎ 0881/723141. Lecce ✉ Via Vittorio Emanuele 24, 73100 ☎ 0832/332463. Maratea ✉ Piazza del Gesù 32, 85046 ☎ 0973/876908. Matera ✉ Via Spine Bianche, 75100 ☎ 0835/331817. Ostuni ✉ Corso Mazzini 6, 72017 ☎ 0831/301268. Pizzo ✉ Piazza della Repubblica, 88026 ☎ 0963/531310. Reggio di Calabria ✉ Corso Garibaldi 329, 89100 ☎ 0965/892012. San Giovanni Rotondo ✉ Piazza Europa 104, 71013 ☎ 0882/456240. Taranto ✉ Corso Umberto 113, 74100 ☎ 099/4532392. Trani ✉ Piazza Trieste 10, 70059 ☎ 0883/585530. Tropea ✉ Piazza Ercole, 88038 ☎ 0963/61475. Vieste ✉ Piazza Kennedy, 71019 ☎ 0884/708806 ✉ Kiosk in Piazza della Repubblica, summer only ☎ 0883/43295.

Sicily

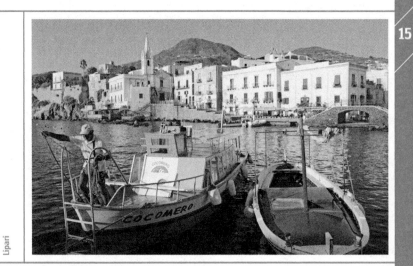

Lipari

WORD OF MOUTH

"Palermo/Monreale was our first stop. Come here for the monuments and churches . . . an endless array. If I had to pick a favorite place, it would be the Palatine Chapel in Palazzo Reale. It managed to be dazzlingly beautiful, while retaining a remarkable sense of warmth."

—Elizabeth S

WELCOME TO SICILY

Teatro Greco, Siracusa

TOP 5
Reasons to Go

1. **A walk on Siracusa's Ortygia Island:** Classical ruins rub elbows with faded seaside palaces and fish markets in Sicily's most beautiful port city, whose Duomo is literally built upon the columns of an ancient Greek temple.

2. **The palaces, churches, and crypts of Palermo:** Virtually every great European empire once ruled Sicily's strategically positioned capital, and it shows through most of all in the diverse architecture, from Roman to Byzantine to Arab-Norman.

3. **The Valley of the Temples, Agrigento:** This stunning set of ruins is proudly perched above the sea in a grove full of almond trees; not even in Athens will you find Greek temples this finely preserved.

4. **Taormina's Teatro Greco:** Watch a Greek tragedy in the very amphitheater where it was performed two millennia ago—in the shadow of smoking Mount Etna.

5. **Sicilian cuisine:** The quickest way to absorb Sicily's character is through a meal of pasta with sardines and raisins, a simply grilled whole fish, ricotta-stuffed cannoli, and a glass of deliciously sweet *passito*.

The **Western Coast** follows the island's northern edge west of Palermo, past **Monreale's** mosaics, **Segesta's** Doric temple, and the fairy-tale town of **Erice**.

Palermo, Sicily's capital and one of Italy's most hectic cities, conceals notes of extraordinary beauty amid the uncontained chaos of fish markets and impossible traffic.

To the south, Greek ruins stand sentinel in **Agrigento's Valley of the Temples**, blanketed in almond and juniper blossoms.

Cefalù

Getting Oriented

This splendid island is known as *trinacria* for its three corners. At the northeastern corner is Messina, connected by car and train ferry to the mainland. The eastern edge of Sicily is its Ionian Coast, which continues south to Catania, Siracusa, and the island's southeastern corner. Sicily's northern edge is the Tyrrhenian Coast, which includes Palermo and extends out to the island's third corner—the western one.

You may know the tranquil, wind-swept Aeolian Islands from the *Odyssey*, and some of them seem to have changed little since Homer.

The Tyrrhenian Coast is filled with summer beachgoers, but it also boasts the quaint town of Cefalù, with its famous cathedral.

For many, the Ionian Coast is all about touristy Taormina, spectacularly perched on a cliff near Mount Etna; but don't overlook lively Catania, Sicily's modern nerve center.

In hill towns such as Enna, the interior of Sicily reveals a slower pace of life than in the frenetic coastal cities. Piazza Armerina features the Villa Casale and its ancient Roman mosaics.

Seafaring Siracusa (Syracuse) was one of the great powers of the classical world. Today, full of fresh fish and remarkable ruins, it's content to be one of Italy's most charming cities.

15

Mare Tirreno

Mare Iónio

Stromboli

Panarea

Salina

Alicudi

Filicudi

Lipari

Vulcano

Milazzo

Messina

Reggio di Calabria

Capo d'Orlando

Cefalù

A20

A20

284

Mt. Etna

A18

Taormina

A19

Acireale

Enna

A19

Catania

Caltanissetta

189

640

417

194

Siracusa

Gela

115

Ragusa

Noto

0   20 mi

0   20 km

SICILY PLANNER

Making the Most of Your Time

You should plan a visit to Sicily around Palermo, Taormina, Siracusa, and Agrigento, four not-to-be-missed destinations. The best way to see them all is to travel in a circle. Start your circuit in the northeast in Taormina, worth at least a night or two. If you have time, stay also in Catania, a lively, fascinating city that's often overlooked. From there, connect to the regional SS114 toward the spectacular ancient Greek port of Siracusa, which merits at least two nights.

Next, backtrack north on the SS114, and take the A19 toward Palermo. Piazza Armerina's impressive mosaics and Enna, a sleepy mountaintop city, each make worthwhile stops in the interior. Take the SS640 until you reach Agrigento, whose valley of Greek temples is one of Sicily's most photographed sights. Stay there for a night before driving west along the coastal SS115, checking out Selinunte's ruins and stopping for a meal in Marsala before reaching magical Erice, a good base for one or two nights. You're now near some of Sicily's best summertime beaches at San Vito Lo Capo. Take the A19 to Palermo, Sicily's chaotic and wonderful capital city, to wrap up your Sicilian experience.

Getting Around

There are three ways to begin a trip through Sicily: flying into Palermo, flying into Catania, or coming down from the train or car ferry from Villa San Giovanni, near Reggio di Calabria. Renting a car is easily the best way to experience Sicily. Trains are unreliable, and roads are easy and scenic throughout most parts of the island. Note that triangular yield signs function as stop signs. If you pick up a car in Catania, you might want to drop it off in Palermo, or vice versa; one-way car rentals aren't prohibitively expensive. In Palermo and Catania, park in a garage as per instructions from your hotel, and don't touch your car until you leave town.

Snacking in Sicily

Sicily is famous for its bar snacks, from the ubiquitous *arancini* (fried balls of creamy rice stuffed with meat ragu or other fillings) to the wonderful pastries, marzipan creations, and ricotta-stuffed cannoli. Some of the island's best edibles are things that you'll never find at upscale restaurants. A coffee or almond *granita* (slush), for example, which is typically served with a brioche for dipping, is one of the world's most perfect midsummer snacks. So don't plan for a big meal every lunch and dinner. Instead, leave plenty of time and stomach space for frequent, spontaneous pit stops at small bars and *pasticcerie*, and don't be afraid to point; practically every town has its own trademark bar snack.

Safety Tips

Don't be paranoid about safety in Sicily, but do be careful. You have little to worry about in the smaller towns, but in the big cities, particularly Palermo and Catania, it's not recommended to wander around unpopulated streets, especially at night, and you should never flaunt expensive watches, jewelry, and the like. Women traveling alone should keep out of deserted areas at all times. Don't leave exposed luggage in the car. Take precautions; then enjoy the company of the Sicilians. You will find them friendly and often willing to go out of their way to help you.

The Mob Mentality

Though Sicily may conjure up images of Don Corleone and his Hollywood progeny, you won't come in contact with the Mafia during your time in Sicily anywhere other than in the newspapers. The "Cosa Nostra," as the Italians sometimes refer to it (don't use the term yourself) is focused on its own business and poses virtually no risk to tourists. Wandering through sleepy interior Sicilian hill towns like Corleone (yes, it's a real place) and Prizzi, you might be subject to some curious and guarded stares by the locals and feel the haze of a silent old-boy network, but nothing more than that.

Finding a Place to Stay

The good-quality hotels tend to be limited to the major cities and resorts of Palermo, Taormina, Siracusa, and Agrigento, along with the odd beach resort, but there has also recently been an explosion in the development of *agriturismo* lodgings (rural bed-and-breakfasts), many of them quite basic, but others providing the same facilities found in hotels. These country houses also offer all-inclusive, inexpensive full-board plans that can make for some of Sicily's most memorable meals.

How's the Weather?

Sicily comes into its own in spring, but you're not alone in knowing this. Taormina and Erice attract a flood of visitors around Easter, so avoid it or reserve early. Many sights like inland Segesta are at their best in the clear spring light. August is hot and crowded, and beaches are clogged with vacationers. Come in September or October and you'll find gentle, warm weather and acres of beach space. Reserve rooms well in advance for Easter, Christmas, New Year's, Agrigento's almond festival in February, and the Carnevale in Acireale.

15

TOP PASSEGGIATA

In Palermo, the area around the Politeama and adjacent shopping streets turn into an enormous party come early evening.

Dining & Lodging Price Categories

WHAT IT COSTS in Euros					
	$$$$	$$$	$$	$	¢
Restaurants	over €22	€16–f22	€11–€16	€7–€11	under €7
Hotels	over €220	€160–€220	€110–€160	€70–€110	under €70

Restaurant prices are for a second course (un secondo). Hotel prices are for two people in a standard double room in high season, including tax and service.

Updated by
Robin S.
Goldstein

SICILY HAS BECKONED SEAFARING WANDERERS since the trials of Odysseus were first sung in Homer's *Odyssey*—perhaps the world's first travel guide. Strategically poised between Europe and Africa, this mystical land of three corners and a fiery volcano once hosted two of the most enlightened capitals of the West—one Greek, in Siracusa, and one Arab-Norman, in Palermo. The island has been a melting pot of every great civilization on the Mediterranean: Greek and Roman; then Arab and Norman; and finally French, Spanish, and Italian. Today, the ancient ports of call peacefully fuse the remains of sackings past. Graceful Byzantine mosaics rubbing elbows with Greek temples, Roman amphitheaters, Romanesque cathedrals, and baroque flights of fancy.

The invaders through the ages weren't just attracted by the strategic location; they recognized a paradise in Sicily's deep blue skies and temperate climate, its lush vegetation and rich marine life—all of which prevail to this day. Factor in Sicily's unique cuisine—another harmony of elements, mingling Arab and Greek spices, Spanish and French techniques, and some of the world's finest seafood, all accompanied by big, fruity wines—and you can understand why visitors continue to be drawn here, and often find it hard to leave.

In modern times, the traditional graciousness and nobility of the Sicilian people have survived side by side with the destructive influences of the Mafia under Sicily's semi-autonomous government. Alongside some of the most exquisite architecture in the world lie the shabby, half-built results of some of the worst speculation imaginable. In recent years coastal Sicily, like much of the Mediterranean coast, has experienced a boom in tourism and a surge in condominium development. Chic boutiques selling lace and linen in resort towns give no clue of the lingering poverty in which their wares are produced. And yet, in Sicily's wind-swept heartland, a region that tourists have barely begun to explore, vineyards, olive groves, and lovingly kept dirt roads leading to family farmhouses still tie Sicilians to the land and to tradition, forming a happy connectedness that can't be defined by economic measures.

PALERMO

Once the intellectual capital of southern Europe, Palermo has always been at the crossroads of civilization. Favorably situated on a crescent-shape bay at the foot of Monte Pellegrino, it has attracted almost every people and culture touching the Mediterranean world. To Palermo's credit, it has absorbed these diverse cultures into a unique personality that is at once Arab and Christian, Byzantine and Roman, Norman and Italian. The city's heritage encompasses all of Sicily's varied ages, but its distinctive aspect is its Arab-Norman identity, an improbable marriage that, mixed in with Byzantine and Jewish elements, created some resplendent works of art. These are most notable in the churches, from small jewels such as San Giovanni degli Eremiti to larger-scale works such as the cathedral. No less noteworthy than the architecture is Palermo's chaotic vitality, on display at some of Italy's most vibrant outdoor markets, public squares, street bazaars, and food vendors, and above all in its grand,

PALERMO'S MULTICULTURAL PEDIGREE

Palermo was first colonized by Phoenician traders in the 6th century BC, but it was their descendants, the Carthaginians, who built the important fortress here that caught the covetous eye of the Romans. After the First Punic War the Romans took control of the city in the 3rd century BC. Following several invasions by the Vandals, Sicily was settled by Arabs, who made the country an emirate and established Palermo as a showpiece capital that rivaled both Cordoba and Cairo in the splendor of its architecture. Nestled in the fertile Conca d'Oro (Golden Conch) plain, full of orange, lemon, and carob groves and enclosed by limestone hills, Palermo became a magical world of palaces and mosques, minarets and palm trees.

It was so attractive and sophisticated a city that the Norman ruler Roger de Hauteville (1031–1101) decided to conquer it and make it his capital (1072). The Norman occupation of Sicily resulted in the Palermo's golden age (1072–1194), a remarkable period of enlightenment and learning in which the arts flourished. The city of Palermo, which in the 11th century counted more than 300,000 inhabitants, became the European center for the Norman court and one of the most important ports for trade between East and West. Eventually the Normans were replaced by the Swabian ruler Frederick II (1194–1250), the Holy Roman Emperor, and incorporated into the Kingdom of the Two Sicilies. You will also see plenty of evidence in Palermo of the baroque art and architecture of the long Spanish rule. The Aragonese viceroys also brought the Spanish Inquisition to Palermo, which some historians believe helped foster the protective secret societies that evolved into today's Mafia.

15

discordant symphony of motorists, motor bikers, and pedestrians that triumphantly climaxes in the new town center each evening with Italy's most spectacular *passeggiata* (the leisurely social stroll along the principal thoroughfare).

Exploring Palermo

Sicily's capital is a multilayered, vigorous metropolis; approach with an open mind when exploring the enriching city with a strong historical profile. You're likely to encounter some frustrating instances of inefficiency and, depending on the season, stifling heat. If you have a car, park it in a garage as soon as you can, and don't take it out until you are ready to depart.

Palermo is easily explored on foot, though you may choose to spend a morning taking a bus tour to help you get oriented. The Quattro Canti, or Four Corners, is the hub that separates the four sections of the old city: La Kalsa (the old Arab section) to the southeast, Albergheria to the southwest, Capo to the northwest, and Vucciria to the northeast. Each of these is a tumult of activity during the day, though at night the narrow alleys empty out and are best avoided altogether in favor of the more

Palermo

TO POTEAMA &
LIBERTA

VUCCIRIA

CAPO

ALBERGHERIA

LA KALSA

Train
Station

TO UNIVERSITY

300 yards
300 meters

KEY

🛈 Tourist information

Cattedrale **3**
Convento dei
Cappuccini **11**
La Martorana **6**
Museo Archeologico
Regionale Salinas **9**
Museo delle
Marionette **8**

Palazzo Abatellis **7**
Palazzo Reale **1**
Quattro Canti **4**
San Cataldo **5**
San Giovanni
degli Eremiti **2**
Teatro Massimo **10**

animated avenues of the new city north of Teatro Massimo. Sights to see by day are scattered along three major streets: Corso Vittorio Emanuele, Via Maqueda, and Via Roma. The tourist information office in Piazza Castelnuovo will give you a map and a valuable handout that lists opening and closing times, which sometimes change with the seasons.

The Main Attractions

★ ❸ **Cattedrale.** This church is a lesson in Palermitan eclecticism—originally Norman (1182), then Catalan Gothic (14th–15th century), then fitted out with a baroque and neoclassical interior (18th century). Its turrets, towers, dome, and arches come together in the kind of meeting of diverse elements that King Roger II (1095–1154), whose tomb is inside along with that of Frederick II, fostered during his reign. The back of the apse is gracefully decorated with interlacing Arab arches inlaid with limestone and black volcanic tufa. ⊠ *Corso Vittorio Emanuele, Capo* ☎ *091/334373* ⊕ *www.cattedrale.palermo.it* 🎫 *Church free, crypt €1* ⊙ *Church 7–7, crypt Mon.–Sat. 9–5.*

❶ **Convento dei Cappuccini.** Have you ever seen thousands of mummies hanging from the walls? The spookiest sight in all of Sicily, this 16th-century catacomb houses more than 8,000 corpses of men, women, and young children, many mummified and preserved, hanging in rows on the walls. Many of the fully clothed corpses wear priests' smocks (most of the dead were Capuchin monks). The Capuchins were founders and proprietors of the bizarre establishment from 1559 to 1880. It's memorable and not for the faint of heart; children (and adults) might be frightened or disturbed. ⊠ *Piazza Cappuccini, off Via Cappuccini, near Palazzo Reale* ☎ *091/212117* 🎫 *€1.50* ⊙ *Tues.–Sat. 9–noon and 3–5, Sun. 3–5.*

❻ **La Martorana.** Distinguished by an elegant Norman campanile, this church was erected in 1143 but had its interior altered considerably during the baroque period. High along the western wall, however, is some of the oldest and best-preserved mosaic artwork of the Norman period. Near the entrance is an interesting mosaic of King Roger II being crowned by Christ. In it Roger is dressed in a bejeweled Byzantine stole, reflecting the Norman court's penchant for all things Byzantine. Archangels along the ceiling wear the same stole wrapped around their shoulders and arms. The striking San Cataldo is adjacent; plan on visiting both churches in one outing. ⊠ *Piazza Bellini 3, Kalsa* ☎ *091/6161692* ⊙ *Mon.–Sat. 8–1 and 3:30–5:30, Sun. 8:30–1.*

❶ **Palazzo Reale** (Royal Palace). This historic palace, also called Palazzo dei Normanni (Norman Palace), was for centuries the seat of Sicily's semi-autonomous rulers. The building is an interesting mesh of abutting 10th-century Norman and 17th-century Spanish structures. Because it now houses the Sicilian Parliament, little is accessible to the public. The **Cappella Palatina** (Palatine Chapel) remains open, built by Roger II in 1132 it's a dazzling example of the harmony of artistic elements produced under the Normans. Here the skill of French and Sicilian masons was brought to bear on the decorative purity of Arab ornamentation and the splendor of 11th-century Greek Byzantine mosaics. The interior is covered with glittering mosaics and capped by a splendid 10th-century Arab honeycomb stalactite wooden ceiling. Biblical stories blend happily with scenes of Arab life—look for one showing a picnic in a harem—and Norman court pageantry.

Upstairs are the royal apartments, including the **Sala di Re Ruggero** (King Roger's Hall), decorated with medieval murals of hunting scenes—an earlier (1120) secular counterpoint to the religious themes seen elsewhere. Tour guides escort you around these halls once used by one of the most splendid courts in Europe. French, Latin, and Arabic were spoken here, and Arab astronomers and poets exchanged ideas with Latin and Greek scholars in one of the most interesting marriages of culture in the Western world. ⊠ *Piazza Indipendenza, Albergheria* ☎ *091/7056001* 🎟 *Free* 🕐 *Mon.–Sat. 8:30–noon and 2–5.*

★ ❺ **San Cataldo.** Three striking Saracenic scarlet domes mark this church, built in 1154 during the Norman occupation of Palermo. The church now belongs to the Knights of the Holy Sepulchre, and the spare but intense stone interior is rarely open to the public. Call ahead to arrange the requisite guided tour, or ask next door at La Martorana church. ⊠ *Piazza Bellini 3, Kalsa* ☎ *091/6375622* 🕐 *By tour Sept.–May, weekdays 9–1 and 3:30–5:30; June–Aug. 9–1 and 3:30–7.*

❷ **San Giovanni degli Eremiti.** Distinguished by its five reddish-orange domes and stripped-clean interior, this 12th-century church was built by the Normans on the site of an earlier mosque—one of 200 that once stood in Palermo. The emirs ruled Palermo for nearly two centuries and brought to it their passion for lush gardens and fountains. One is reminded of this while sitting in San Giovanni's delightful cloister of twin half columns, surrounded by palm trees, jasmine, oleander, and citrus trees. Last tickets sold a half hour before closing. ⊠ *Via dei Benedettini, Albergheria* ☎ *091/6515019* 🎟 *€4.50* 🕐 *Mon.–Sat. 9–7, Sun. 9–1:30.*

❿ **Teatro Massimo.** Construction of this formidable neoclassical theater was started in 1875 by Giovanni Battista Basile and completed by his son Ernesto in 1897. A fire in 1974 rendered the theater inoperable, but it reopened with great fanfare in 1997—its interior is as glorious as ever. *The Godfather Part III* ended with a famous shooting scene on the theater's steps. Visits are by 25-minute guided tour only; English-speaking guides are available 10–2 and 3–4. ⊠ *Piazza Verdi 9, at top of Via Maqueda, Olivella* ☎ *091/6090831* ⊕ *www.teatromassimo.it* 🎟 *€3* 🕐 *Tues.–Sun. 10–3:30, except during rehearsals.*

Also Worth Seeing

❾ **Museo Archeologico Regionale Salinas** (Salinas Regional Museum of Archaeology). Especially interesting pieces in this small but excellent collection are the examples of prehistoric cave drawings and a marvelously reconstructed Doric frieze from the Greek temple at Selinunte. The frieze reveals the high level of artistic culture attained by the Greek colonists in Sicily some 2,500 years ago. ⊠ *Piazza Olivella 24, Via Roma, Olivella* ☎ *091/6116805* 🎟 *€4.50* 🕐 *Tues.–Sat. 8:30–6:45, Sun. and Mon. 8:30–1:45.*

8 **Museo delle Marionette.** The traditional Sicilian *pupi* (puppets), with their glittering armor and fierce expressions, have become a symbol of Norman Sicily. Plots of the weekly performances center on the chivalric legends of the troubadours, who, before the puppet theater, kept alive tales of Norman heroes in Sicily such as Orlando Furioso and William the Bad (1120–66). ✉ *Piazzetta Niscemi 1, at Via Butera, Kalsa* ☎ *091/328060* ⊕ *www.museomarionettepalermo.it* 💶 *€3* ⊙ *Weekdays 9–1 and 4–7. Closed 2 wks in Aug.*

7 **Palazzo Abatellis.** Housed in this late-15th-century Catalan Gothic palace with Renaissance elements is the **Galleria Regionale.** Among its treasures are an *Annunciation* (1474) by Sicily's prominent Renaissance master Antonello da Messina (1430–79) and an arresting fresco by an unknown painter, titled *The Triumph of Death*, a macabre depiction of the plague years. ✉ *Via Alloro 4, Kalsa* ☎ *091/6230011* ⊕ *www.regione.sicilia.it/beniculturali/dirbenicult/PALAZZOABATELLIS/index.htm* 💶 *€4.50, additional €3.50 for guided tour* ⊙ *Mon.–Sat. 9–1 and 2:30–7, Sun. 9–1.*

Piazza Pretoria. The square's centerpiece, a lavishly decorated fountain with 500 separate pieces of sculpture and an abundance of nude figures, so shocked some Palermitans when it was unveiled in 1575 that it got the nickname "Fountain of Shame." Extensive renovation and cleaning were completed in December 2003. It's even more of a sight when illuminated at night.

4 **Quattro Canti.** The Four Corners is the intersection of Corso Vittorio Emanuele and Via Maqueda. Four rather exhaust-blackened baroque palaces from Spanish rule meet at concave corners, each with its own fountain and representations of a Spanish ruler, patron saint, and one of the four seasons.

Where to Stay & Eat

$$$ ✕ **Il Mulinazzo.** Palermitans drive the 45 minutes to savor modern and
Fodor'sChoice startling combinations in chef Nino Graziano's traditional country
★ house—probably Sicily's best restaurant. *Macco* (fava-bean puree), a staple of the rural poor, is playfully paired with scampi and finished with ricotta, *speck* (cured ham), peppercorns, and fried basil. Pistachios encrust a delicate pork fillet served with chocolate sauce, rice fritters, cinnamon applesauce, and swirls of raspberry. The wine list is excellent, and prices are reasonable—even for the spectacular tasting menu. Look for Il Mulinazzo on the right side of SS121, after a car dealership; the tiny sign is easy to miss. ✉ *SS121, Località Bolognetta Nord, 17 km (11 mi) southeast of Palermo, Villafrati* ☎ *091/8724870* �︎ *AE, DC, MC, V* ⊙ *Closed Mon., 2 wks in Jan., and 2 wks in July. No dinner Sun.*

$$–$$$ ✕ **Il Ristorantino.** Pippo Anastasio, one of the true personalities of Sicilian cooking, has created one of the most modern restaurants on the island. Here *pesce spada* (swordfish) reaches its loftiest heights, served simply marinated with olive oil, lemon, herb butter, and toast; meanwhile, Pippo's flights of fancy include *astice* (lobster) tortellini with cherry tomatoes, *bottarga* (cured tuna roe), and hot pepper. Dark wood con-

15

EATING WELL IN SICILY

Sicilian cuisine is one of the oldest in existence, going back to Siracusan cooking competitions in 600 BC. The Sicilians even have a reasonable claim to the invention of pasta; present-day *maccheroni* (long, thin pasta tubes) may bear the closest resemblance to the original. Today's cuisine represents Sicily's unique cultural mix, imaginatively combining fish, fruits, vegetables, and nuts with Italian pastas and Arab and North African ingredients such as *cus cus* (couscous).

In Sicily, naturally, you'll enjoy some of the freshest seafood in all of Italy. Pasta *con le sarde* (an emblematic dish that goes back to the Saracen conquerors, with fresh sardines, olive oil, raisins, pine nuts, and wild fennel) is different at every restaurant. Grilled *tonno* (tuna) and *orata* (daurade) are reliable coastal staples. King, however, is *pesce spada* (swordfish), best enjoyed marinated (*marinato*), smoked (*affumicato*), or

as the traditional *involtini di pesce spada* (swordfish roulades). Delicate *ricci* (sea urchins) are a specialty, as is spaghetti *alla Norma* (with a sauce of tomato, fried eggplant, ricotta, and basil). Meanwhile, the Sicilian bitter almond (*mandorla*), the pride of Agrigento, plays into everything from risotto alle mandorle to incomparable almond granita, an absolute must in summer.

Long neglected, Sicilian wines are some of the most up-and-coming in the world, but they're still the bargains of Italy. The earthy nero d'avola grape bolsters many of Sicily's traditionally sunny, expansive reds, but lately it's often cut with cabernet or merlot. The islands of Lipari and Pantelleria offer sweet, golden dessert wines, Malvasia and Passito. Marsala remains Sicily's most famous dessert wine. Look for anything from the world-renowned wine maker Planeta.

trasts with recessed lighting and stylized wall panels to create a design fusion that echoes the creativity of the menu. The suburban restaurant is an easy taxi ride from the center. ⊠ *Piazzale Alcide De Gasperi 19, Resuttana* ☎ *091/512861* ▭ *AE, DC, MC, V* ⊘ *Closed Mon. and 2 wks in Aug.*

★ **\$\$–\$\$\$** ✕ **Osteria dei Vespri.** A foodie paradise occupies a cozy-but-elegant space on an unheralded piazza in the historic city center. Try the superb antipasto *sei variazioni di crudo dal mare* (six variations of raw delicacies from the sea). Sheep's cheese ravioli with basil, fresh tomato, eggplant, and crispy onions adds creative depth to traditional preparation. Local fish is presented in dishes like a *tagliata di tonno al pepe nero e semi di papavero* (cut of tuna with black pepper and poppyseeds), which is served with herb-infused oil, sweet and sour Tropea onions, and steamed spinach. The wine list is one of the best in Palermo. ⊠ *Piazza Croce dei Vespri 6, Kalsa* ☎ *091/6171631* ▭ *AE, DC, MC, V* ⊘ *Closed Sun. and 1 wk in Aug.*

\$\$ ✕ **Strascinu.** The region's ubiquitous Arab-Sicilian dish, pasta *con sarde* (with sardines and *mollica tostata,* the trademark toasted bread crumbs), takes center stage at this informal and busy restaurant on the city outskirts. Amphoras, Sicilian ceramics, and even a miniature, electrically operated puppet theater enliven the rustic decor, and there's a large garden with gazebos. ⊠ *Viale Regione Sicilia 2286, Circunvallazione* ☎ *091/401292* ▭ *AE, DC, MC, V* ⊗ *Closed Aug. 9–24.*

$–$$ ✕ **Capricci di Sicilia.** Rumor has it that Capricci di Sicilia, in the heart of Palermo next to the Teatro Politeama, is the best place in town for *cassata siciliana* (sponge cake with sheep's ricotta and candied fruit). Only typical Sicilian specialties are served here, such as tuna with garlic and mint, sardine *polpette* (minced sardine balls), and spaghetti with sausage and fresh ricotta. The place is a bit impersonal. ⊠ *Via Pignatelli 6, Piazza Luigi Sturzo, Vucciria* ☎ *091/327777* ▭ *AE, DC, MC, V* ⊗ *Closed Mon.*

★ **$–$$** ✕ **Osteria Altri Tempi.** The "olden days" restaurant is a favorite among locals searching for the true rustic cooking of their Sicilian ancestors. Knickknacks fill the walls of the small friendly space. A meal begins with a carafe of the house red set down without asking and a superb spread of traditional antipasti. Dishes have old Palermitan names: *fave a cunigghiu* is fava beans prepared with olive oil, garlic, and remarkably flavorful oregano; and *vampaciucia c'anciova* is a lasagna-like pasta with a concentrated sauce of tomatoes, anchovies, and grapes. The meal ends well, too, with free house-made herb or fruit liquors and excellent cannoli. ⊠ *Via Sammartino 65/67, Libertà* ☎ *091/323480* ▭ *MC, V* ⊗ *Closed Aug. 15–Sept. 15. No dinner Sun.*

$ ✕ **Casa del Brodo.** On the edge of the Vucciria is a restaurant that dates to 1890, one of Palermo's oldest. In winter, tortellini *in brodo* (in beef broth), the restaurant's namesake, is the specialty of the house. Year round you can't go wrong with *carni bollite* (boiled meats) or the *fritella di fave, piselli, carciofi, e ricotta* (fried fava beans, peas, artichokes, and ricotta). A mix of tourists and locals crowd the two small rooms. ⊠ *Corso Vittorio Emanuele 175, Vucciria* ☎ *091/321655* ▭ *AE, DC, MC, V* ⊗ *Closed Tues. Nov.–Apr., Sun. May–Oct.*

★ **¢** ✕ **Antica Focacceria San Francesco.** Turn-of-the-20th-century wooden cabinets, marble-top tables, and cast-iron ovens characterize this neighborhood bakery. Come here for the snacks that locals love—and from which you can make an inexpensive meal. The big pot on the counter holds the delicious regional specialty *pani ca meusa* (boiled, sliced calf's spleen with Parmesan-like cacciocavallo cheese and salt). The squeamish can opt for the *panelle* (chickpea flour fritters), the fantastic *fritto misto* (assorted fried appetizers), or an enormous *arancino* (breaded, deep-fried ball of rice), with tomato and meat or vegetable filling. ⊠ *Via Paternostro 58, Kalsa* ☎ *091/320264* ▭ *AE, DC, MC, V* ⊗ *Closed Tues. and 2 wks in Jan.*

¢ ✕ **Pani Ca Meusa.** This supremely local institution facing Palermo's old fishing port has had only one item on the menu—and one legendary manager-cum–sandwich maker—for more than 50 years. Calf's spleen sandwich, the joint's namesake, is sprinkled with a bit of salt and some lemon and served with or without cheese to a buzzing crowd of Palermo's battle-wearied elders. In our book, their sandwich beats the Focacceria San Francesco for the title of best in town. There's no seating, though—only counters—and the overal menu is better at San Francesco. ⊠ *Porta Carbone, Via Cala 62, Kalsa* ☎ *No phone* ⌫ *Reservations not ac-*

cepted ▱ *No credit cards* ◷ *Closed Sun. and Mon., and unpredictable other days.*

★ **$$$$** 🏨 **Centrale Palace Hotel.** A stone's throw from Palermo's main historic sites, the Centrale is the only hotel in the heart of the *centro storico* (historic center) that was once a stately private palace. Built in 1717, the hotel weaves old-world charm with modern comfort like few establishments on the island. Salons are ornately furnished and "classic" rooms have antiques and reproductions. Forty "neoclassic" rooms (which are slightly pricier and done in a more modern elegance) were part of a 2003 expansion as were six spacious junior suites. The young, welcoming staff provides professional service. The rooftop restaurant serves creative Sicilian cuisine. ✉ *Corso Vittorio Emanuele 327, Vuccira, 90134* ☎ *091/336666* 🖷 *091/334881* ⊕ *www.centralepalacehotel.it* ⤶ *104 rooms* ♿ *Restaurant, minibars, some in-room safes, some in-room hot tubs, cable TV, Internet, bar, free parking* ▱ *AE, DC, MC, V* ﹒❙❖❙ *BP.*

$$$$ 🏨 **Villa Igiea.** Take a short taxi ride (through some rough-looking districts of Palermo) to a oasis of luxury and comfort in a private tropical garden at the edge of the bay. A meander through the grounds reveals such relics as an ancient Greek temple at the water's edge. Large rooms are furnished individually, the nicest with an Italian art nouveau flavor. Spacious lobbies and public rooms unfold onto a terrace and restaurant. There's infrequent shuttle service to the city center; a €12 taxi ride is more convenient. ✉ *Salita Belmonte 43, 90142 Acquasanta, 3 km (2 mi) north of Palermo* ☎ *091/6312111* 🖷 *091/547654* ⊕ *www.amthotels.it* ⤶ *110 rooms, 6 suites* ♿ *Restaurant, minibars, tennis court, pool, gym, bar, free parking* ▱ *AE, DC, MC, V* ﹒❙❖❙ *BP.*

$$$ 🏨 **Hotel Principe di Villafranca.** Fine Sicilian antiques, imperial striped silks, creamy marble floors, and vaulted ceilings evoke a luxurious private home not far from Palermo's glitzy shopping district. It's easy to get comfortable in the understated surroundings: relax in the library with an aperitif or savor an authentic meal in the rustic adjoining Ristorante Firriato, which drizzles its dishes with a sublime, homemade balsamic vinegar. Rooms are elegant, with fine linens and more antiques. Ask for a room on the street side; back rooms can actually be noisier. ✉ *Via G. Turrisi Colonna 4, Libertà, 90141* ☎ *091/6118523* 🖷 *091/588705* ⊕ *www.principedivillafranca.it* ⤶ *30 rooms, 4 suites* ♿ *Restaurant, café,*

A GOOD WALK: PALERMO PASSEGGIATA

It is surely one of Sicily's—and Italy's—greatest pleasures to take one's place in the procession of the evening's passeggiata. The passeggiata may be roughly translated as "a walk around," but it is more than that. The Sicilian passeggiata is a graceful dance of Italian pedestrians flirting with shop windows, with ice cream, and with each other, a nightly voyage whose provenance is also its only destination: the city street. Generally speaking, in Palermo, as elsewhere, the passeggiata begins somewhere around 7 PM on most nights, and continues until 9 PM or so. On Friday and Saturday, the pedestrians stay out later—until at least 10 PM, which is when many Italians go out for pizza on weekend evenings—and even past that hour, there is no let-up in the amount of foot traffic as the evening wears on, just a gradual replacement of the older crowd with younger carousers.

gym, library, Internet, meeting room, free parking ⊟ AE, DC, MC, V ⫢⊙⫢ BP.

$$$ ⊞ **Massimo Plaza Hotel.** This hotel has one of Palermo's best locations— opposite the renovated Teatro Massimo. It is small and select; the few rooms are spacious, comfortably furnished, and well insulated from the noise on Via Maqueda. Service is personal and polite, with continental breakfast served in your room with the newspaper of your choice. Book in advance for one of the seven rooms that have theater views. ⊠ *Via Maqueda 437, Vucciria, 90133* ☎ *091/325657* ⊞ *091/325711* ⊕ *www. massimoplazahotel.com* ⟿ *15 rooms* ⟁ *Minibars, cable TV, bar, Internet, parking (fee)* ⊟ *AE, DC, MC, V* ⫢⊙⫢ *BP.*

$$–$$$ ⊞ **Mondello Palace.** In summer Mondello Palace, the leading hotel at the Mondello resort, is indisputably the place to be. Making the best use of its private beach location just north of Palermo, there are cabins and changing rooms for the use of hotel patrons. The rooms are large, with luxury baths, and most have balconies. ⊠ *Viale Principe di Scalea, 90139 Mondello Lido* ☎ *091/450001* ⊕ *http://web.tiscali.it/ mondellopalace/* ⊞ *091/450657* ⟿ *83 rooms, 9 suites* ⟁ *Restaurant, minibars, pool, gym, beach, windsurfing, boating, bar, free parking, some pets allowed* ⊟ *AE, DC, MC, V* ⫢⊙⫢ *BP.*

¢ ⊞ **Hotel Moderno.** Right down to the 1930s technology at the reception desk, this third-floor hotel is a slice of slow old Palermo—perhaps the name is meant to be ironic. But the location and rates couldn't be better. (Singles are a particularly good deal, at not much more than half the double room rate.) A slightly shabby, mirrored reception area and bar give way to simple but clean and comfortable rooms, some with balconies overlooking Via Roma. ⊠ *Via Roma 276, corner of Via Napoli, Vucciria, 90139* ☎ *091/588683* ⊞ *091/588260* ⟿ *38 rooms* ⟁ *Bar, parking (fee)* ⊟ *AE, DC, MC, V* ⫢⊙⫢ *BP.*

Nightlife & the Arts

The Arts

CONCERTS & **Teatro Massimo** (⊠ Piazza Verdi, at the top of Via Maqueda, Capo
OPERA ☎ 091/6053111 ⊕ www.teatromassimo.it), modeled after the Pantheon in Rome, is truly larger than life—it's the biggest theater in Italy. Concerts and operas are presented throughout the year. Live out your

15

Palermo has one of Sicily's—and all of Italy's—most vibrant evening passeggiatas, and it's centered around Piazza Ruggero Settimo in front of the **Teatro Politeama.** Pedestrians stream in two different directions from the Politeama; to join in the passeggiata, you can take either route (or both). One streams up **Viale della Libertà,** where the most elegant boutiques lie; the other heads down **Via Ruggero Settimo** at least as far as the impressive **Teatro Massimo** ⑩, which will be on your right coming from the Politeama. There, you can stop for a moment to re-enact

the last scene of *The Godfather 3*. On either of those wide avenues you'll doubtless find yourself window shopping at the boutiques that deck out Palermo's most modern quarter, as the Italians do—it's perhaps the most characteristic aspect of the passeggiata.

Drinking a coffee, eating gelato, or taking an *aperitivo*—a short, lightly alcoholic drink such as Campari or Aperol that whets the appetite for dinner—is also an essential part of the passeggiata. However, in stark contrast to the café cultures in other parts of Europe such as France and Spain, don't expect to see many

Godfather fantasies; an opera at the Massimo is an unforgettable Sicilian experience. The shamelessly grandiose neoclassical **Teatro Politeama Garibaldi** (✉ Piazza Ruggero Settimo, Libertà ☎ 091/6053315) stages a season of opera and orchestral works from November through May.

FESTIVALS   The **Festa di Santa Rosalia** street fair is held July 10–15 in honor of the city's patron saint. Fireworks light up the evenings. **Epiphany** (January 6) is celebrated with Byzantine rites and a procession of townspeople in local costume through the streets of Piana degli Albanesi, 24 km (15 mi) south of Palermo. The village is named for the Albanian immigrants who first settled there, bringing with them the Byzantine Catholic rite.

PUPPET SHOWS   Palermo's tradition of puppet theater holds an appeal for children and adults alike. Street artists often perform outside the Teatro Massimo in summer. The **Figli d'Arte Cuticchio Association** (✉ Via Bara all'Olivella 95, Kalsa ☎ 091/323400 ⊕ www.figlidartecuticchio.com 🎫 €6) hosts performances September–May on most Saturdays and Sundays at 6:30, with the occasional morning performance scheduled as well.

Nightlife

Each night between 6 and 9 PM, Palermo's youth gather to shop, socialize, flirt, and plan the evening's affairs in an epic passeggiata along Via Ruggero Settimo (a northern extension of Via Maqueda) and filling Piazza Ruggero Settimo in front of Teatro Politeama. Some trendy bars also line Via Principe del Belmonte, intersecting with Via Roma and Via Ruggero Settimo.

BARS & CAFÉS   **Kursaal Kalhesa** (✉ Foro Umberto I 21, Kalsa ☎ 091/6161282) is one of the most fascinating places to drink or socialize down by the port and the Porta Felice. An energetic, eclectic crowd of Palermitan youth takes in lively jazz, coffee, and drinks inside an ancient city wall with spectacular 100-foot ceilings and an idyllic courtyard—it's truly representative of the New Palermo. There's live music (primarily jazz) Thursday night. Excellent, if pricey, Sicilian food with an Arab touch is served in the adjacent restaurant. Kursaal Kalhesa is closed Sunday night and Monday.

Parco Letterario Giuseppe Tomasi di Lampedusa (✉ Vicolo della Neve all'Alloro 25, near Piazza Marina, Kalsa ☎ 091/6160796 ⊕ www.

folks relaxing at tables and chairs with their libations, watching the world go by. This is a standing culture, not a sitting one, and if you want to do as the Italians do, you'll down your diminutive cup of coffee or little glass of bright red bitter liqueur in a few seconds, or get your ice cream to go, and continue on your way. There are scores of coffeeshops and ice-cream joints all along Viale Libertà and Via Ruggero Settimo, as well as around the Politeama; most are essentially similar, so you shouldn't worry too much about trying to find the best or most famous place for a refreshment. After all, the real experience is to be had outside.

parcotomasi.it) is a cultural center, wine bar, café, language school, and historic-tour operator. The center, open Tuesday–Sunday 9 AM–1 AM, runs courses in Italian for foreigners, has excellent local wines and a student social scene, and hosts art shows. The little library (and just about everything else) focuses not just on Palermitan history but on the life and times of the center's namesake, Lampedusa, author of the canonical *Il Gattopardo* (*The Leopard*).

NIGHTCLUBS Most nightclubs and discotheques are scattered around the northern, newer end of town. In summer the nightlife scene shifts to Mondello, Palermo's seaside satellite town on the other side of Monte Pellegrino. **Bar Costa** (✉ Via G. D'Annunzio 15, Libertà ☎ 091/334835) overflows with Italian bar-style treats, coffee, and so on; they also ship their famous delicacies abroad. **Mikalsa** (✉ Via Torremuzza 27, Kalsa ☎ 339/3146466) is a hip, coolly lighted nightspot with Sicily's best selection of Belgian beers. Try the interesting, unpasteurized Wild Spirit beer is the painstaking product of one of Sicily's first microbreweries (also available elsewhere around town). **Kandinsky Florio** (✉ Discesa Tonnara 4, Arenella suburbs ☎ 091/6375611) is a stiking disco-bar-restaurant in a restored tuna factory.

The Outdoors

At the sandy beach of Mondello, sailing and windsurfing facilities and instruction are available through **Albaria** (✉ Viale Regina Elena 89/a, Mondello ☎ 091/453595).

Sicily's most important center for scuba diving and other water sports is on the island of **Ustica**, north of Palermo. Its rugged coast is dotted with grottoes that are washed by crystal-clear waters and filled with an incredible variety of interesting marine life. In July Ustica hosts the International Meeting of Marine Fishing, which attracts sportsmen as well as marine biologists from all over the world. You depart from the Port of Palermo and the ferry ride takes two hours.

Shopping

North of Piazza Castelnuovo, Via della Libertà and the streets around it represent the luxury end of the shopping scale, with some of Palermo's best-known stores. A second nerve center for shoppers is the pair of parallel streets connecting modern Palermo with the train station, Via Roma, and Via Maqueda, where boutiques and shoe shops become increasingly upmarket as you move from the Quattro Canti past Teatro Massimo to Via Ruggero Settimo.

Most shops are open 9–1 and 4 or 4:30–7:30 or 8 and closed Sunday; in addition, most food shops close Wednesday afternoon, and other shops normally close Monday morning.

Ceramics & Gifts

Libreria Kalós (✉ Via XX Settembre 56B, Libertà ☎ 091/322380) publishes some of the finest books on Sicilian art and architecture. **Il Laboratorio Italiano** (✉ Via Principe di Villafranca 42, Libertà ☎ 091/320282) has a large selection of ceramics at reasonable prices. Quality ceramics, stoneware, and tiling can be found at **De Simone** (⊠ Via Gaetano Daiti 13B, Libertà ☎ 091/584876).

Clothing & Fabric

The classy **Carieri & Carieri** (⊠ Via E. Parisi 4, Libertà ☎ 091/321846) has an extensive selection of men's suits and shirts. For men's shirts and suits near the Quattro Canti, try the elegant but friendly **Barbisio** (⊠ Corso Vittorio Emanuele 284–298, Quattro Canti ☎ 091/329992).

Heavy fabric, fringe, and tassel seekers stop at **Giuseppe Gramuglia** (⊠ Via Roma 412–414, at Via Principe di Belmonte, Vucciria ☎ 091/583262).

Food & Wine

Enoteca Picone (⊠ Via Marconi 36, Libertà ☎ 091/331300) is the best wine shop in town, with a fantastic selection of Sicilian and national wines. You can taste a selection of wines by the glass in the front of the store; sometimes there's also table ser-vice in the back, where meats and cheeses are also served. **Pasticceria Alba** (⊠ Piazza Don Bosco 7/c, off Via della Libertà near La Favorita Park, Libertà ☎ 091/309016) is the place to find all the favorite Sicilian pastries such as cannoli and cassata siciliana.

The charming **I Peccatucci di Mamma Andrea** (Mamma Andrea's Small Sins; ⊠ Via Prinicipe di Scordia 67, near Piazza Florio, Vucciria ☎ 091/334835) sells a plethora of mouthwatering original creations, including jams, preserves, candies, liqueurs, honey, and Sicilian treats like su-perb *frutta di Martorana*, fruits, and other shapes made out of marzipan.

Markets

If you're interested in truly connect-ing with local life while searching for souvenirs, a visit to one of Palermo's many bustling markets is essential. Between Via Roma and Via Maqueda the many **bancherelle** (mar-ket stalls) on Via Bandiera sell every-thing from socks to imitation designer handbags.

★ It's easy to see how the **Vucciria Mar-ket** got its name, which translates in dialect as "voices" or "hubbub."

> **WORD OF MOUTH**
>
> "The Vucciria market: what a sight! Every kind of fresh meat (by fresh I mean the whole animal hanging by rope), fish, vegetables, etc. We bought several vacuum packed packages of olives and sun-dried tomatoes to bring back as gifts."
> –AP6380

Palermo's most established outdoor market in the heart of the *centro storico* (historic center) is a maze of side streets around Piazza San Domenico, where hawkers deliver incessant chants from behind stands brimming with mounds of olives, blood oranges, wild fennel, and long-stem arti-chokes. One of them will be going at the trunk of a swordfish with a cleaver while across the way another holds up a giant squid or dangles an octopus. Morning is the best time to see the market in full swing.

Wind your way through the Albergheria district and the historic **Ballarò Market**, where the Saracens did their shopping in the 11th century—joined by the Normans in the 12th. The market remains faithful to seasonal change as well as the original Arab commerce of fruit, vegetables, and grain. Go early; the action dies out by 4 PM most days.

THE WESTERN COAST TO AGRIGENTO

Western Sicily has a remote air, less developed than the eastern coast. Not far outside Palermo is Monreale with a cathedral that glittering mosaics among the finest in Italy. Traces of the North African culture that for centuries exerted a strong influence on this end of the island are most tangible in the coastal towns of Trapani and Marsala, and the outlying island of Pantelleria, nearer to the Tunisian coast than the Sicilian. In contrast, the cobbled streets of the hilltop town of Erice, outside Trapani, retain a strong medieval complexion, giving the town the air of a last outpost gazing out over the Mediterranean. The Greek presence is still strong, however, in the splendidly isolated site of Segesta and the cluster of cliffside ruined temples at Selinunte. The crowning glory of this region is the concentration of Greek temples at Agrigento, occupying a fabulous position on a height between the modern city and the sea.

15

Monreale

🏵 *10 km (6 mi) southwest of Palermo.*

★ Monreale's splendid **Duomo** is lavishly executed with mosaics depicting events from the Old and New Testaments. After the Norman conquest of Sicily the new princes showcased their ambitions through monumental building projects. William II (1154–89) built the church complex with a cloister and palace between 1174 and 1185, employing Byzantine craftsmen. The result was a glorious fusion of Eastern and Western influences, widely regarded as the finest example of Norman architecture in Sicily.

The major attraction is the 68,220 square feet of glittering gold mosaics decorating the cathedral interior. Christ Pantocrator dominates the apse area; the nave contains narratives of the Creation; and scenes from the life of Christ adorn the walls of the aisles and the transept. The painted wooden ceiling dates from 1816 to 1837. A small pair of binoculars will make it easier to read the Latin inscriptions. The roof commands a great view (a reward for climbing 172 stairs).

Bonnano Pisano's **bronze doors,** completed in 1186, depict 42 biblical scenes and are considered among the most important of medieval artifacts. Barisano da Trani's 42 panels on the north door, dating from 1179, present saints and evangelists. ✉ *Piazza del Duomo* ☎ *091/6404413* 🕑 *May–Sept., daily 8–6; Oct.–Apr., daily 8–12:30 and 3:30–6.*

The lovely **cloister** of the abbey adjacent to the Duomo was built at the same time as the church but enlarged in the 14th century. The beautiful enclosure is surrounded by 216 double columns, every other one decorated in a unique glass mosaic pattern. Note the intricate carvings on the bases and the capitals. Afterward, don't forget to walk behind the cloister to the **belvedere,** with stunning panoramic views over the Conca

d'Oro (Golden Conch) valley toward Palermo. The last tickets are sold a half hour before closing. ⊠ *Piazza del Duomo* ☎ *091/6404403* 🎫 *€4.50* ⊗ *Mon.–Sat. 9–7, Sun. 9–1:30.*

Where to Eat

\$–\$\$ ✕ **La Botte 1962.** It's worth the short drive or inexpensive taxi fare from Monreale to reach this restaurant, a good value for well-prepared local specialties. Dine alfresco on seafood-centered dishes such as *bavette don Carmelo,* a narrow version of tagliatelle with a swordfish *ragù* (a slow-cooking, tomato-base meat or seafood sauce), squid, shrimp, and pine nuts. Other regular favorites include *involtini alla Siciliana,* meat roulades stuffed with *salami* and cheese. Local wines are a good accompaniment. ⊠ *Contrada Lenzitti 20, S186* ☎ *091/414051* 🟰 *AE, DC, MC, V* ⊗ *Closed Mon. and June 1–Sept. 10. No dinner Sun.*

> ## WORD OF MOUTH
>
> "The Cathedral of Monreale dwarfs everything in Palermo, and I mean everything. It's the grandest and most spectacular church in all of southern Italy."   –GAC

Segesta

🕙 *59 km (37 mi) southwest of Monreale, 85 km (53 mi) southwest of Palermo.*

★ Segesta is the site of a **Tempio Dorico** (Doric temple) that's one of Sicily's most impressive, constructed on the side of a windswept barren hill overlooking a valley of wild fennel. Virtually intact today, the temple is considered by some to be finer in its proportions and setting than any other Doric temple left standing. The temple was actually started in the 5th century BC by the Elymian people, who some believe were refugees from Troy. At the very least, evidence indicates that they were non-Greeks; for example, they often sided with the Carthaginians. However, the style is in many ways Greek. The temple was never finished; the walls and roof never materialized, and the columns were never fluted. A little more than 1 km (½ mi) away, near the top of the hill, are the remains of a fine **amphitheater,** with impressive views, especially at sunset, of nearby Monte Erice and the sea. ☎ *0924/952356* 🎫 *€4.50* ⊗ *Oct.–Apr., daily 9–4; May–Sept., daily 9–6.*

Erice

🕙 *35 km (22 mi) west of Segesta.*

Erice is perched 2,450 feet above sea level, an enchanting medieval mountaintop aerie of castles and palaces, fountains, and cobblestone streets. Shaped like an equilateral triangle, the town was the ancient landmark Eryx, dedicated to the fertility goddess whom the Phoenicians called Astarte, the Greeks Aphrodite, and the Romans Venus. When the Normans arrived they built a castle on Monte San Giuliano, where today there's a lovely public park with benches and belvederes from which there are striking views of Trapani, the Egadi Islands off shore, and, on a *very* clear day, Cape Bon and the Tunisian coast. Because of Erice's elevation, clouds conceal much of the view for most of the winter. Sturdy shoes and something warm to wear are recommended.

Fans of Sicilian sweets make a beeline for **Pasticceria Grammatico** (✉ Via Vittorio Emanuele 14 ☎ 0923/869390). The place is run by Maria Grammatico, a former nun who gained international fame with *Bitter Almonds,* her life story cowritten with Mary Taylor Simeti. Her almond-paste creations are works of art, molded into striking shapes, including dolls and animals. The balcony from the tearoom upstairs has wonderful views. At **Pasticceria del Convento** (✉ Via Guarnotta 1 ☎ 0923/869777), Maria Grammatico's sister sells similar delectable treats.

Capo San Vito, 40 km (25 mi) from Erice, is a cape with a long sandy beach on a promontory overlooking a bay in the Gulf of Castellammare. The town there, San Vito Lo Capo, is famous for its North African couscous, made with fish instead of meat. In late September it hosts the five-day **Cus Cus Fest,** a serious international couscous competition and festival with live music and plenty of free tastings.

Where to Stay & Eat

$–$$ ✕ **Monte San Giuliano.** Sit out on the tree-lined stone patio and sample spicy Arab-influenced seafood couscous—served with a bowl of fish broth on the side to add as you wish—or delicious grilled tuna. Wash it all down with a good white Donnafugata, from the Rallo vineyards at Marsala. Monte San Giuliano is satisfyingly traditional. It's hidden within the labyrinth of lanes that makes up Erice, near the main piazza. ✉ *Vicolo San Rocco 7* ☎ *0923/869595* ▭ *AE, DC, MC, V* ☉ *Closed Mon., 2 wks mid-Jan., and 1st 2 wks Nov.*

$$ ✕▦ **Elimo.** Because it's on one of Erice's main cobblestone streets, the majority of the spacious rooms at this hotel have superb views overlooking the town's characteristic rooftops and the vast valley below (ask for one). The mix of antiques and plastic room doors adds a quirky dimension. Great views can also be had through the large picture window in Carmelo Tilotta's restaurant, where fresh local ingredients take center stage. (Tilotta and marzipan guru Maria Grammatico have appeared together at the James Beard Foundation House.) ✉ *Via Vittorio Emanuele 75, 91016* ☎ *0923/869377* ▨ *0923/869252* ↪ *21 rooms* ♤ *Restaurant, minibars, bar, lounge, library* ▭ *AE, DC, MC, V* ⊠◎ *BP.*

$$ ✕▦ **Moderno.** This modern, delightful hotel is decorated with local crafts and has a lovely terrace and a well-known restaurant ($–$$) serving seafood pasta and homemade desserts. In winter the lobby fireplace is always blazing. Some rooms, along with a large lounge and bar, are directly across the street from the main hotel. ✉ *Via Vittorio Emanuele 67, 91016* ☎ *0923/869300* ▨ *0923/869139* ⊕ *www.pippocatalano.it* ↪ *40 rooms* ♤ *Restaurant, minibars, bar* ▭ *AE, DC, MC, V* ⊠◎ *BP.*

$ ▦ **Ermione.** Nearly every room in this simple 1960s hilltop hotel provides lovely views of the Tyrrhenian Sea, although the tiled bathrooms and old-style Sicilian furniture are showing their age. The hotel is 1 km (½ mi) from the centro storico of Erice and has a restaurant serving well-executed basics to a healthy mix of locals and tourists. ✉ *Via Pineta Comunale 43, 91016* ☎ *0923/869138* ▨ *0923/869587* ⊕ *www.*

CLOSE UP

Prizzi's Honor

BURIED IN THE HEART of Mafia country (14 mi west of Lercara Friddi, which gave the world the mobster Lucky Luciano), Prizzi, population 6,000, is a fairy-tale aerie, a floating apparition of twisting stone alleyways and brown rooftops gently dusting the peak of a 3,267-foot mountain. Its medieval layout and architecture—surreally frozen in another age—and dreamy views of the surrounding countryside, perhaps best seen at sunset, make it well worth a stop along the way between Palermo and Agrigento. Prizzi was founded by the Greeks in about 480 BC, and was alternately conquered by the Byzantines (8th century AD) and Saracens (9th century AD), the latter of whom built three lofty castles and created a "cult of water" with an elaborate network of drinking troughs. Christian conquest came in the 11th century.

The name "Prizzi" became known to the outside world through 1985's wryly comic mobster movie *Prizzi's Honor*, but the town feels as far removed as imaginable from Hollywood glamour and glitz. There's little in the way of significant art or monuments, and the secrets of the Mafia presence lie out of reach to visitors, buried in inaccessible crevices of local culture. But you can spend hours wandering in and out of the maze of steeply sloped alleyways, with tiny, still-inhabited houses built into the rock, eventually giving way to the remains of the three castles and the mountain's dazzling peak, from which, on a clear day, you can view the sea of Sciacca to one side and the cone of Mt. Etna to the other.

Coming from Palermo, follow the signs to Sciacca; both Prizzi and Corleone—another name familiar to moviegoers—are on the way.

15

---

ermionehotel.com 🛏 *46 rooms* △ *Restaurant, bar, free parking* ▤ *AE, DC, MC, V* ⦿ *MAP.*

Trapani

⓯ *15 km (9 mi) southwest of Erice, 30 km (18 mi) west of Segesta.*

The modern town of Trapani, directly below Erice, is the departure point for ferries to Sardinia and to the island of Pantelleria, near the African coast. This rugged western end of Sicily is reminiscent of the many spaghetti Westerns that were filmed here.

The historic center is a well-kept secret. The lanes near Corso Italia hold a handful of churches worth wandering into. **Santa Maria di Gesù** (✉ Via San Pietro) has Gothic and Renaissance doors and a Madonna by Andrea della Robbia (1435–1525). **Sant'Agostino** (✉ Piazzetta Saturno), behind the town hall, has a 14th-century rose window.

off the beaten path

PANTELLERIA – Near the Tunisian coast is one of Sicily's most evocative islands, Pantelleria, although some find its starkness unappealing. The hilly terrain provides plenty to explore—volcanic formations, scant patches of forest, prehistoric tombs, and dramatic seascapes—either on foot or astride a rented moped. You can rent accommodations in the traditional *dammuso*, houses dug out of the earth with stout walls and dome roofs for maximum coolness in the fierce summer heat. Daily ferries and, in summer, hydrofoils, connect the island with Trapani. Contact the Trapani tourist office for more information.

Where to Stay & Eat

$$ ✕ **P&G.** Opposite the Villa Margherita public gardens near the train station, this small restaurant is quiet and dignified, with an attentive service. The local pasta, *busiate* (doughy handmade pasta), is cooked with swordfish and eggplant, and the couscous combines with fish in summer and meat in winter. A mixed grill of meats in a zesty orange sauce can revive any appetite suffering from fish fatigue. Reservations are a good idea on weekends. ⊠ *Via Spalti 1* ☎ *0923/547701* ⊟ *MC, V* ☾ *Closed Sun. and Aug.*

¢ ✕⊞ **Ai Lumi.** If you're still hungry after the abundance of the antipasto buffet, try the hearty traditional soups and a variety of tasty fish and meat dishes here. Salami hangs from the ceiling in this appealing and attentive *tavernetta* (cozy tavern) with a medieval door. The bed-and-breakfast upstairs has a variety of simple rooms with local Trapani ironwork beds, and inexpensive miniapartments with kitchens. The facilities are comfortable and the location couldn't be any more central. ⊠ *Corso Vittoria Emanuele 71/75, 91100* ☎ *0923/872418* ⊕ *www.ailumi.it* ↪ *14 rooms* ◔ *Restaurant, bar, some kitchens* ⊟ *DC, MC, V* ☾ *Closed 20 days in June.*

Marsala

16 *30 km (18 mi) south of Trapani*

The quiet seaside town of Marsala was once the main Carthaginian base in Sicily, from which Carthage fought for supremacy over the island against Greece and Rome. Nowadays it's more readily associated with the world-famous, richly colored sweet wine named after the town. In 1773 a British merchant named John Woodhouse happened upon Marsala and discovered that the wine here was as good as the port the British had long imported from Portugal. Two other wine merchants, Whitaker and Ingram, rushed in, and by 1800 Marsala was exporting its wine all over the British Empire.

A sense of Marsala's past as a Carthaginian stronghold is captured by the well-preserved Punic warship displayed in the town's **Museo Archeologico Baglio Anselmi,** along with some of the amphoras and other artifacts recovered from the wreck. The vessel, which was probably sunk during the great sea battle that ended the First Punic War in 241 BC, was dredged up from the mud near the Egadi Islands in the 1970s and is now installed under a climate-controlled plastic tent. ⊠ *Lungomare Boéo 30* ☎ *0923/952535* ⊡ *€2* ☾ *Mon., Tues., and Thurs. 9–2, Wed. and Fri.–Sun. 9–2 and 4–7.*

need a break? The spacious *enoteca* (wine bar) **Divino Rosso** (✉ Via XI Maggio (Largo A. Di Girolamo 1) ☎ 0923/711770) has a good selection of local wines, along with a brief but appealing food menu.

One of Sicily's foremost wine producers, the 150-year-old **Donnafugata Winery** is open for tours of their Cantina (reservations required) right in downtown Marsala. It's an interesting look at the winemaking process in Sicily, and it ends with a tasting of several whites and reds and a chance to buy; don't miss the delicious, full-bodied red Mille e Una Notte, and the famous Ben Ryè Passito di Pantelleria, a sweet dessert wine made from dried grapes. ✉ *Via Lipari 18* ☎ *0923/724200* ⊕ *www.donnafugata. it* 🎫 *Free* ⊗ *Mon.–Sat. 9–4, by appointment only.*

off the beaten path **MAZARA DEL VALLO –** Easily accessible at the end of the A29 highway, Mazara del Vallo is a typical time-frozen Sicilian port town with a beautiful baroque old center and pleasant palm-lined *lungomare* (promenade) running along the ocean. Some of the few tourists who venture to Mazara come seeking a glimpse of the Dancing Satyr, a precious Hellenistic bronze representing one of the mythological figures of the orgiastic group of Dionysus, Greek god of wine. Discovered in 1998 deep in the Mediterranean Sea by Mazara fishermen, the statue had probably been part of the cargo of a shipwrecked vessel sailing between Sicily and Cape Bon between the 3rd and 2nd century BC. It's on permanent display at **Museo Del Satiro** (☎ No phone ✉ Piazza Plebiscito, near the port). Besides the museum, Mazara buzzes with beachy activity in summer but is fairly sleepy in winter. It's a very relaxing place for a night's stopover or for lunch at one of the many seafood places and pizzerias lining the boardwalk or in the centro storico. The old port is a raw, colorful graveyard for rusty tugboats and fishing vessels.

Selinunte

🄗 *88 km (55 mi) southeast of Marsala, 114 km (71 mi) south of Palermo.*

Near the town of Castelvetrano, numerous **Greek temple ruins** perch on a plateau overlooking an expanse of the Mediterranean at Selinunte (or Selinus). The city was one of the most superb colonies of ancient Greece. Founded in the 7th century BC, Selinunte became the rich and prosperous rival of Segesta, which in 409 BC turned to the Carthaginians for help. The Carthaginians sent an army commanded by Hannibal to destroy the city. The temples were demolished, the city was razed, and 16,000 of Selinunte's inhabitants were slaughtered. The remains of Selinunte are in many ways unchanged from the day of its sacking—burn marks still scar the Greek columns, and much of the site still lies in rubble at its exact position of collapse at the hands of the Carthaginian attack. The original complex held seven temples scattered over two sites separated by a harbor. Of the seven, only one—reconstructed in 1958—is whole. Selinunte is named after a local variety of wild parsley (*Apium*

Continued on page 794

VALLE DEI TEMPLI

Built on a broad open field that slopes gently to the sun-simmered Mediterranean, Akragas (ancient Agrigento's Greek name) was a showpiece of temples erected to flaunt a victory over Carthage. Despite a later sack by the Carthaginians, mishandling by the Romans, and neglect by the Christians and Muslims, the eight or so monuments in the Valle dei Templi are considered to be, along with the Acropolis in Athens, the finest Greek ruins in all the world.

TIMING TIP

The temples are at their very best in February, when the valley is awash in the fragrant blossoms of thousands of almond trees.

Whether you first come upon the Valle dei Templi in the early morning light, or bathed by golden floodlights at night, it's easy to see why Akragas was celebrated by the Greek poet Pindar as "the most beautiful city built by mortal men."

MAKING THE MOST OF YOUR VISIT

GETTING AROUND

Though getting to, from, and around the dusty ruins of the Valle dei Templi is no great hassle, this important archaeological zone deserves several hours. The site, which opens at 8:30 AM, is divided into western and eastern sections. For instant aesthetic gratification, walk through the eastern zone; for a more comprehensive tour, start way out at the western end and work your way back uphill.

The temples are a bit spread out, but the valley is all completely walkable and generally toured on foot. However, note that there is only one hotel (Villa Athena) that is close enough to walk to the ruins, so you will most likely have to drive to reach the site; parking is at the entrance to the temple area.

WHAT TO BRING

It's a good idea to pack your own snacks and drinks, as there are hardly any restaurants in the temple area, and the handful of high-priced bars around the site cater mostly to tourists.

In summer the site can get extremely hot, so wear light clothing, a hat, and sun protection if possible.

15

VALLE DEI TEMPLI

A BRIEF HISTORY OF AGRIGENTO

Cornice
Frieze
Architrave
Capital
Shaft
Stylobate
Stereobate

KEY DATES	
750 BC	Greek city-states begin to colonize Sicily and southern Italy.
734 BC	Neighboring Siracusa founded.
582 BC	Akragas settled. The city grows wealthy through trade with Carthage, just across the Mediterranean.
ca. 450 BC–350 BC	Temples at Akragas erected over a period of about 100 years to celebrate the city's propserity.
413 BC	Battle of Siracusa vs. Athens.
406 BC	Fire from Carthaginian attack destroys much of Akragas. Despite this and future attacks, the city and its temples survive through the Roman era, the Middle Ages, and into the modern age.

The natural defenses of ancient Akragas depended on its secure and quite lovely position between two rivers on a floodplain a short distance from the sea. In Agrigento you will be treated to what many experts consider the world's best-preserved remains of classical Greece. All of the temples in the Valle dei Templi are examples of Doric architecture, the earliest and simplest of the Greek architectural orders (the others are Ionic and Corinthian). Some retain capitals in addition to their columns, while others are reduced to nothing more than fragments of stylobate.

THE TEMPLES

TEMPIO DI ERCOLE

The eight pillars of the **Temple of Hercules**, down the hill from the Temple of Concord, make up Agrigento's oldest temple complex (dating from the 6th century BC), dedicated to the favorite god of the often-warring citizens of Akragas. Partially reconstructed in 1922, it reveals the remains of a large Doric temple that originally had 38 columns. Like all the area temples, it faces east. The nearby Museo Archeologico Regionale contains some of the marble warrior figures that once decorated the temple's pediment.

Tempio di Ercole

TEMPIO DELLA CONCORDIA

The beautiful **Temple of Concord** is perhaps *the* best-preserved Greek temple in existence. The structure dates from about 430 BC, and owes its exceptional state of preservation to the fact that it was converted into a Christian church in the 6th century and was extensively restored in the 18th century. Thirty-two Doric columns surround its large interior, and everything but the roof and treasury are still standing. For preservation, this temple is blocked off to the public, but you can still get close enough to appreciate how well it's withstood the past 2,400 years.

TEMPIO DI GIUNONE

The **Temple of Juno**, east on the Via Sacra from the Temple of Concord, commands an exquisite view of the valley, especially at sunset. It's similar to but smaller than the Concordia and dates from about 450 BC. Traces of a fire that probably occurred during the Carthaginian attack in 406 BC,

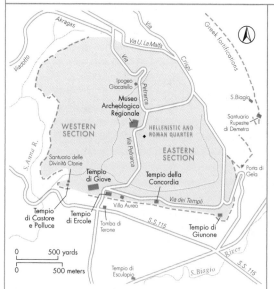

Valle dei Templi
Phone: 0922/497341
Admission: Site €4.50, with museum €6. One ticket covers all temples.
Open daily 8:30–7.

Museo Archeologico Regionale
Contrada San Nicola, 12
Phone: 0922/401565
Admission: €4.50, with temples site €6
Open Tues.–Sat. 9–7:30,
Sun.–Mon. 9–1:30

Agrigento tourist information
Via Cesare Battisti 15, 92100
Phone: 0922/20454

which destroyed the ancient town, can be seen on the walls of the cellar. Thirty of the original 34 columns still stand, of which 16 have retained their capitals.

TEMPIO DI GIOVE

Though never completed, the **Temple of Jupiter** was considered the eighth wonder of the world. With a length of more than 330 feet, it was once the biggest of the Akragas temples and one of the largest temples in the Greek world. The temple was probably built in gratitude for victory over Carthage and was constructed by prisoners captured in that war. Basically Doric in style, it did not have the usual colonnade of freestanding columns but rather a series of half columns attached to a solid wall. This design is unique among known Doric temples—alas, only the stereobate was left behind. Inside the excavation you can see a cast (not the original) of one of the 38 colossal Atlas-like figures, or telamones, that supported the temple's massive roof.

Tempio di Giove

TEMPIO DI CASTORE E POLLUCE

The **Temple of Castor and Pollux** is a troublesome reconstruction of a 5th-century BC temple. It was pieced together by some enthusiastic if misguided 19th-century romantics who, in 1836, haphazardly put together elements from diverse buildings. Ironically, the four gently crumbling columns supporting part of an entablature of the temple have become emblematic of Agrigento.

15

VALLE DEI TEMPLI

OTHER SITES OF INTEREST

To the left of the Temple of Concord is a Paleochristian **necropolis**. Early Christian tombs were both cut into the rock and dug into underground catacombs.

Right opposite the Temple of Castor and Pollux, facing north, the **Santuario delle Divinità Ctonie** (Sanctuary of the Chthonic Divinities) has cultic altars and eight small temples dedicated to Demeter, Persephone, and other Underworld deities. In the vicinity are two columns of a temple dedicated to Hephaestus (Vulcan).

At the end of Via dei Templi, where it turns left and becomes Via Petrarca, stands the **Museo Archeologico Regionale**. An impressive collection of antiquities from the site includes vases, votives, everyday objects, weapons,

statues (including one of the surviving original telamones from the Temple of Jupiter), and models of the temples.

The **Hellenistic and Roman Quarter**, across the road from the archaeological museum, consists of four parallel streets, running north–south, that have been uncovered, along with the foundations of some houses from the Roman settlement (2nd century BC). Some of these streets still have their original mosaic pavements, and the complex system of sidewalks and gutters is easy to make out—reminding you that the ancient world wasn't all temples and togas.

graveolens or *petroselinum*) that in spring grows in profusion among the ruined columns and overturned capitals. Although there aren't many places to stay right around Selinunte, it's an easy stop along the road to or from Agrigento and it only takes an hour or two to see—a richly rewarding stopover. ⊠ *SS115* ☏ *0924/46277* 🖃 *€4.50* ⊙ *Daily 9–5.*

Agrigento

⑱ *100 km (60 mi) southeast of Selinunte, 126 km (79 mi) south of Palermo.*

Agrigento owes its fame almost exclusively to its ancient Greek temples—though it was also the birthplace of playwright Luigi Pirandello (1867–1936). There's little reason to go up the hill from Valle dei Templi to the modern city except to ring the doorbell at the **Convento di Santo Spirito** and try the *kus-kus* (sweet cake), made of pistachio nuts and chocolate, that the nuns prepare. ⊠ *Salita di Santo Spirito, off Via Porcello* ☏ *No phone.*

Where to Stay & Eat

$$–$$$ ✕ **Trattoria dei Templi.** Along a road on the way up to Agrigento proper from the temple area, this simple vaulted restaurant can get very busy after it becomes too dark for temple exploring. The menu has all the classic Sicilian dishes, including satisfying homemade *maccheroni* (tubular pasta) and plenty of grilled fish. The antipasti, such as the carpaccio of *cernia* (grouper), are exceptional. ⊠ *Via Panoramica dei Templi 15* ☏ *0922/403110* 🖃 *AE, DC, MC, V* ⊙ *Closed June 30–July 10, Fri. Sept.–June, and Sun. July and Aug.*

$–$$$ ✕ **Kokalos.** On a hillside opposite the temple ridge, 6 km (4 mi) to the southeast, this large restaurant in an old village house has beautiful views over the temples. As well as serving local specialties, Kokalos has a pizzeria and enoteca—it hops on weekend nights. ⊠ *Via Cavaleri Magazzeni 3, Villagio Mosè* ☏ *0922/606427* 🖃 *AE, DC, MC, V.*

$$$$ ✕🖾 **Foresteria Baglio della Luna.** Fiery sunsets and moonlight cast a glow over a tower dating from the 8th century, which is central to the farmhouse hotel complex. Stone buildings surround around a peaceful geranium- and ivy-filled courtyard and a garden beyond. Standard rooms, some with views of the temples, are nothing fancy—mellow walls and wooden furniture. The intimate, rustic restaurant, Il Dehors ($$$–$$$$), serves pricey foodie fare that is ambitious and impressive. *Spigola* (Mediterranean bass) comes in a delicate potato crust with baby broccoli and asparagus. The hotel is in the valley below the temples: note that the dirt road up to the hotel is unmarked. ⊠ *Contrada Maddalusa, Valle dei Templi, 3 km (2 mi) southeast of old town, 92100* ☏ *0922/511061* 🖷 *0922/598802* ⊕ *www.bagliodellaluna.com* ➴ *22 rooms, 3 suites* ⌂ *Restaurant, minibars, bar* 🖃 *AE, DC, MC, V* ❄️ *BP.*

$$$–$$$$ 🖾 **Villa Athena.** The price here reflects the privileged position of the 18th-century Villa Athena, with a view over the Temple of Concordia. The lodging itself, although pleasant, is not outstanding. Many rooms have terraces overlooking the large gardens and the swimming pool. The temples are an easy walk away, and there's a convivial bar, where a multinational crowd swaps stories. The only hotel right in the midst of the archaeological zone is in much demand, so make reservations as early as possible. ⊠ *Via dei Templi 53, 92100* ☎*0922/596288* 🖷*0922/402180* ⊕ *www.athenahotels.com* ➯*40 rooms* ⚴ *Restaurant, minibars, indoor pool, bar, Internet* ▤ *AE, DC, MC, V* ⦶ *BP.*

\$\$ 🏨 **Tre Torri.** Stay here if you are sports-minded and bent on exploring the countryside around Agrigento. Bicycle tours, bicycle rental, and nature walks can be arranged or a boat booked for fishing trips and water sports. The pool is pleasant, public areas are spacious, and the modern rooms furnished with some veneer. The hotel's location, Villagio Mosè, 5 km (3 mi) southeast of town, is on a regular bus route. ⊠ *Villagio Mosè, 92100* ☎ *0922/606733* 🖷 *0922/607839* ⊕ *www.htretorri.com* ➯ *118 rooms* ⚴ *Restaurant, outdoor pool, gym, bicycles, sauna, bar, meeting room, travel services* ▤ *AE, DC, MC, V* ⦶ *BP.*

THE INTERIOR

Sicily's interior is for the most part underpopulated and untrammeled, though the Imperial Roman Villa at Casale, outside Piazza Armerina, gives precious evidence from an epoch gone by. Don't miss misty Enna, the Navel of Sicily, or Caltagirone, a ceramics center of renown.

15

Enna

⑲ *105 km (63 mi) northeast of Agrigento, 136 km (85 mi) southeast of Palermo.*

Deep in Sicily's interior, the fortress city of Enna (altitude 2,844 feet) commands exceptional views of the surrounding rolling plains, and, in the distance, Mt. Etna. Virtually unknown by tourists and relatively untouched by industrialization, this sleepy town charms and prospers in a distinctly old-fashioned, provincial, and Sicilian way. Enna makes a good stopover for the night or just for lunch, as it's right along the autostrada between Palermo and Catania (and thus Siracusa).

The narrow, winding streets are dominated at one end by the impressive cliff-hanging **Castello di Lombardia**, built by Frederick II, easily visible as you approach town. (The castle isn't open to the public.)

In town, head straight for Via Roma, which leads to **Piazza Vittorio Emanuele**, the center of Enna's shopping scene and evening passeggiata. The attached **Piazza Crispi**, dominated by the shell of the grand old Hotel Belvedere, affords breathtaking panoramas of the hillside and smoking Etna looming in the distance.

The mysterious **Torre di Federico II** stands above the lower part of town. This octagonal tower, of unknown purpose, has been celebrated for millennia as marking the exact geometric center of the island—thus the tower's, and city's, nickname, Umbilicus Siciliae (Navel of Sicily). The tower is not open to the public.

Where to Stay & Eat

\$–\$\$ ✕**Centrale.** This casual place has served meals since 1889. The bright walls of an old palazzo are adorned with Sicilian pottery, and an outdoor terrace soothes diners in summer. The varied menu includes local

East Sicily & the Aeolian Island

TO NAPLES

Stromboli 40

20 miles

30 km

TO TROPEA

Panarea 39

Alicudi 42 **Filicudi** 41

Salina 38

ISOLE EOLIE

37

Lipari

Vulcano 36

TO NAPLES

Tyrrhenian Sea

Golfo di Gioia

Mortelle

Milazzo

Messina 35

Patti

Reggio di Calabria

S113

Cefalù 44
Caldura

Capo d'Orlando

Santo Stefano di Camastra 43

S113

S117

A20

A18

Pizzo Carbonara

ITALY

Randazzo

Castelmola

Taormina 34

Giardini-Naxos

Bronte

Mt. Etna 33

Riposto

Giarre

Adrano

A19

Biancavilla

Nicolosi

Acireale 32

Enna 19

Paternò

S192

Catania 31

Caltanissetta

S288

Golfo di Catania

Ionian Sea

20 **Piazza Armerina**

Casale

21 **Caltagirone**

S124

S114

Gela

Palazzolo Acreide

Euryalus

Siracusa

Comiso

S124

Golfo di Gela

22 **Ragusa**

Avola

Ortygia Island
23 - 30
see map page 802

Noto

Modica

S115

Golfo di Noto

KEY

🚢 *Ferry Line*

⛷ *Ski Area*

Capo Passero

TO MALTA

preparation such as *coppole di cacchio* (peppers stuffed with spaghetti, potato, and basil) and grilled pork chops. Choose from a decent selection of Sicilian wines to accompany your meal. ⊠ *Piazza VI Dicembre 9* ☎ *0935/500963* ⊟ *AE, DC, MC, V* ⊙ *Closed Sat. Oct.–Mar.*

¢ ✕ **La Botte.** The menu pays homage to tradition—*orrecchiette alla Norma* (small, ear-shape pasta with an eggplant and tomato sauce) is a Sicilian classic—and has tasty dishes like the *papardelle alla botte,* wide noodles with a meat sauce. Order off the wine list or let the friendly staff fill your carafe with the good local table wine from *la botte* (the barrel). There's a fixed lunch menu on Monday and Wednesday. ⊠ *Via Roma 488* ☎ *0935/502331* ⊟ *AE, DC, MC, V* ⊙ *Closed Tues.*

$$ ▥ **Hotel Sicilia.** Sicily's interior has few decent accommodations, so if overnighting you have little choice but to stay at the central Hotel Sicilia. The place is institutional-feeling and monopoly-priced, but its bright rooms (some with excellent views) are reliably clean and adequate. Reserve ahead for one with a bathtub (number 10), air-conditioning, or a view over the town and hillside rather than onto the piazza. ⊠ *Piazza Napoleone Colajanni 7, 94100* ☎ *0935/500850* 🖷 *0935/500488* ⊕ *www.hotelsiciliaenna.it* ⇦ *60 rooms* ⟁ *Minibars, bar; no a/c in some rooms* ⊟ *AE, DC, MC, V* ⊺⃝⃒ *BP.*

Nightlife

After dark, **Wine Bar Up** (⊠ Piazza Garibaldi ☎ 0935/501111), upstairs from Caffè Italia, is a hip place to stop for a drink.

Piazza Armerina

㉚ *33 km (20 mi) south of Enna.*

A quick look around the fanciful town of Piazza Armerina is rewarding—it has a provincial warmth, and the crumbling yellow stone architecture with Sicily's trademark bulbous balconies creates quite an effect. The greatest draw, however, lies just down the road. The exceptionally well-preserved **Imperial Roman Villa,** 4 km (2½ mi) southwest of Piazza Armerina, is thought to have been a hunting lodge of the emperor Maximianus Heraclius (4th century AD). The excavations were not begun until 1950, and the wall decorations and vaulting have been lost. However, some of the best mosaics of the Roman world cover more than 12,000 square feet under a shelter that hints at the layout of the original buildings. The mosaics were probably made by North African artisans; they are similar to those in the Tunis Bardo Museum. The entrance was through a triumphal arch that led into an atrium surrounded by a portico of columns, after which the *thermae,* or bathhouse, is reached. It's colorfully decorated with mosaic nymphs, a Neptune, and slaves massaging bathers. The peristyle leads to the main villa, where in the Salone del Circo you look down on mosaics illustrating Roman circus sports. Room 38 even reveals a touch of eroticism—surely only scratching the surface of the bacchanalian festivities that Maximilian conjured up. ⊠*SP15, Casale* ☎*0935/680036* ⃞*€4.50* ⊙*Apr.–Sept., daily 8:30–5:30; Oct.–Mar., daily 8:30–4.*

FodorśChoice ★

Where to Eat

$$–$$$ ✕ **Al Fogher.** A beacon of culinary light shines in Sicily's interior, a region generally filled with good, but simple, places to eat. Ambitious—and successful—dishes include tuna tartare with potato puree and a fillet of baby pig crusted with black pepper and pistachio that's served with a sauce made from *bottarga* (cured tuna roe) and asparagus. Decor is simple and elegant. ⊠ *Contrada Bellia, near SS117 bis exit* ☏ *0935/ 684123* ▤ *AE, DC, MC, V* ☉ *Closed Mon. and 2 wks in July.*

Caltagirone

㉑ *30 km (18 mi) southeast of Piazza Armerina, 60 km (37 mi) southwest of Catania.*

Built over three hills, this charming baroque town is a center of Sicily's ceramics industry. Here you can find majolica balustrades, tile-decorated windowsills, and a monumental tile staircase of 142 steps—each decorated with a different pattern—leading up to the neglected **Santa Maria del Monte.** On the feast of San Giacomo (July 24), the staircase is illuminated with candles that form a tapestry design over the steps. It's the result of months of work preparing the 4,000 *coppi*, or cylinders of colored paper that hold oil lamps. At 9:30 PM on July 24, a squad of hundreds of boys springs into action to light the lamps, so that the staircase flares up all at once. ☉ *Daily 7–noon and 4–7.*

Shopping

Of the numerous ceramic shops in Caltagirone's old center, **Branciforti** (⊠ Scala Santa Maria del Monte 3 ☏ 0933/24427 ⊕ www. ceramichebranciforti.it), right on Caltagirone's fabled ceramic steps, is one of the best, selling eye-catching work with deep shades of blue and swirling arabesques.

Ragusa

㉒ *66 km (41 mi) southeast of Caltagirone.*

Ragusa and Modica are the two chief cities in Sicily's smallest and sleepiest province, and the centers of a region known as Iblea. The dry, rocky, gentle countryside filled with canyons and grassy knolls is a unique landscape in Sicily. Iblea's trademark squat stone walls divide swaths of land in a manner reminiscent of the high English countryside—but summers are decidedly Sicilian, with dry heat so intense that life grinds to a standstill for several hours each day. This remote province hums along to its own tune, clinging to local customs, cuisines, and traditions in aloof disregard even for the rest of Sicily.

> **WORD OF MOUTH**
>
> "Ragusa was probably the biggest surprise of any place in Sicily for me. The first view of the town built on what seem to be practically vertical walls is stunning. Then climbing up through the town's twisty stairways and alleys and through arches and narrow passageways . . . you feel transported clear out of the 21st century."   –RAR

Ragusa is known for some great local red wines and its wonderful Ragusano DOP cheese (a creamy, doughy, flavorful version of caciocavallo, made by hand every step of the way). It's a modern city with a beautiful old town called **Ibla,** which was completely rebuilt after the devastating earthquake of 1693. A tumble of buildings perched on a hilltop and suspended between a deep ravine and a sloping valley, Ibla's tiny squares and narrow lanes make for pleasant meandering. The **Basilica di San Giorgio,** designed by Rosario Gagliardi of Noto in 1738, is a fine example of Sicilian Baroque.

SIRACUSA

Siracusa (known to English-speakers as Syracuse), old and new, is a wonder to behold. One of the great ancient capitals of Western civilization, the city was founded in 734 BC by Greek colonists from Corinth and soon grew to rival, and even surpass, Athens in splendor and power; Siracusa became the largest, wealthiest city-state in the West and a bulwark of Greek civilization. Although the city lived under tyranny, rulers such as Dionysus filled their courts with Greeks of the highest artistic stature—among them Pindar, Aeschylus, and Archimedes. The Athenians did not welcome the rise of Siracusa and set out to conquer Sicily, but the natives outsmarted them in what was one of the greatest naval battles of ancient history (413 BC). Siracusa continued to prosper until it was conquered two centuries later by the Romans.

Siracusa still has some of the finest examples of baroque art and architecture; dramatic Greek and Roman ruins; and a Duomo that is the stuff of legend, a microcosm of the city's entire history in one building. The modern city also has a wonderful lively baroque old town worthy of extensive exploration, pleasant piazzas, outdoor cafés and bars, and a wide assortment of excellent seafood. There are essentially two areas to explore in Siracusa: the Parco Archeologico, on the mainland; and the island of Ortygia, the ancient city first inhabited by the Greeks, which juts out into the Ionian sea and is connected to the mainland by two small bridges.

Siracusa's old nucleus of Ortygia is a compact area, a pleasure to amble around without getting unduly tired. In contrast, mainland Siracusa is a grid of wider avenues. At the northern end of Corso Gelone, above Viale Paolo Orsi, the orderly grid gives way to the ancient quarter of Neapolis, where the sprawling Parco Archeologico is accessible from Viale Teracati (an extension of Corso Gelone). East of Viale Teracati, about a 10-minute walk from the Parco Archeologico, the district of Tyche holds the archaeological museum and the church and catacombs of San Giovanni, both off Viale Teocrito (drive or take a taxi or city bus from Ortygia). Coming from the train station, it's a 15-minute trudge to Ortygia along Via Francesco Crispi and Corso Umberto.

Archaeological Zone

The Main Attractions
Parco Archeologico. Siracusa is most famous for its dramatic set of Greek and Roman ruins. Though the various ruins can be visited separately,

see them all, along with the Museo Archeologico. If the park is closed, go up Viale G. Rizzo from Viale Teracati to the belvedere overlooking the ruins, which are floodlighted at night. The last tickets are sold one hour before closing.

Before the park's ticket booth is the gigantic **Ara di Ierone** (Altar of Hieron), which was once used by the Greeks for spectacular sacrifices involving hundreds of animals. The first attraction in the park is the **Latomia del Paradiso** (Quarry of Paradise), a lush tropical garden full of palm and citrus trees. This series of quarries served as prisons for the defeated Athenians, who were enslaved; the quarries once rang with the sound of their chisels and hammers. At one end is the famous **Orecchio di Dionisio** (Ear of Dionysus), with an ear-shaped entrance and unusual acoustics inside, as you can hear if you clap your hands. The legend is that Dionysius used to listen in at the top of the quarry to hear what the slaves were plotting below.

★ The **Teatro Greco** (Greek Theater) is the chief monument in the Archaeological Park—and indeed one of Sicily's greatest classical sites and the most complete Greek theater surviving from antiquity. Climb to the top of the seating area (which could accommodate 15,000) for a fine view: all the seats converge upon a single point—the stage—which has the natural scenery and the sky as its background. Hewn out of the hillside rock in the 5th century BC, the theater saw the premieres of the plays of Aeschylus. Greek tragedies are still performed here in May and June of even-number years. Above and behind the theater runs the Via dei Sepulcri, in which streams of running water flow through a series of Greek sepulchres.

The well-preserved and striking **Anfiteatro Romano** (Roman Amphitheater) reveals much about the differences between the Greek and Roman personalities. Where drama in the Greek theater was a kind of religious ritual, the Roman amphitheater emphasized the spectacle of combative sports and the circus. This arena is one of the largest of its kind and was built around the 2nd century AD. The corridor where gladiators and beasts entered the ring is still intact, and the seats, some of which still bear the occupants' names, were hauled in and constructed on the site from huge slabs of limestone. ✉ *Viale Teocrito* ☎ *0931/66206* 🖅 *Sites €4.50, with Museo Archeologico €6* ⊘ *Apr.–Sept., daily 9–7; Oct., daily 9–5; Nov.–Feb., daily 9–4; Mar., daily 9–6.*

> ┌─────────┐
> │ need a │ For some great Sicilian cakes and ice cream on your way to the
> │ break? │ Archaeological Park, visit **Leonardi** (✉ Viale Teocrito 123,
> └─────────┘ Archaeological Zone ☎ 0931/61411), a bar-cum-*pasticceria* (pastry
>   shop). It's popular with the locals, so you may have to line up for
>   your cakes in holiday times. It's closed Wednesday.

Also Worth Seeing

Catacombe di San Giovanni. Not far from the Archaeological Park, off Viale Teocrito, the catacombs below the church of San Giovanni are one of the earliest-known Christian sites in the city. Inside the crypt of San Marciano is an altar where St. Paul preached on his way through Sicily to Rome. The frescoes in this small chapel are mostly bright and fresh, though some dating from the 4th century AD show their age. Open hours may be extended in summer. ⊠ *Piazza San Giovanni, Archaeological Zone* ☎ *0931/66571* ✉ *€3.10* ⊗ *Tues.–Sun. 9–12:30 and 2:30–5:30.*

Museo Archeologico. The impressive collection of Siracusa's splendid archaeological museum is organized by region around a central atrium and ranges from Neolithic pottery to fine Greek statues and vases. Compare the *Landolina Venus*—a headless, stout goddess of love who rises out of the sea in measured modesty (a 1st-century AD Roman copy of the Greek original)—with the much earlier (300 BC) elegant Greek statue of Hercules in Section C. Of a completely different style is a marvelous fanged Gorgon, its tongue sticking out, that once adorned the cornice of the Temple of Athena to ward off evildoers. One exhibit depicts the Temple of Apollo, the oldest Doric temple in Sicily, on the island of Ortygia. Last tickets are sold an hour before closing. ⊠ *Viale Teocrito, Archaeological Zone* ☎ *0931/464022* ✉ *Museum €4.50, with archaeological park €6* ⊗ *Tues.–Sat. 9–7, Sun. 9–1.*

Museo del Papiro. Close to Siracusa's Museo Archeologico, the Papyrus Museum demonstrates how papyrii are prepared from reeds and then painted—an ancient tradition in the city. Siracusa, it seems, has the only climate outside the Nile Valley in which the papyrus plant—from which the word "paper" comes—thrives. ⊠ *Viale Teocrito 66, Archaeological Zone* ☎ *0931/61616* ✉ *Free* ⊗ *Tues.–Sun. 9–1.*

off the
beaten
path

PALAZZOLO ACREIDE – This small inland town is best known for its archaeological zone, the ancient Greek Akrai, founded by the Siracusans in 664 BC. The zone contains the foundations of a temple dedicated to Aphrodite and a well-preserved theater, whereas the town itself is unspectacularly baroque. ⊹ *40 km (25 mi) west of Siracusa.*

Ortygia Island

The Main Attractions

㉖ **Duomo.** Siracusa's Duomo is an archive of island history: the bottom-
FodorsChoice most excavations have unearthed remnants of Sicily's distant past, when
★ the Siculi inhabitants worshipped their deities here. During the 5th century BC (the same time as Agrigento's Temple of Concord was built), the Greeks built a temple to Athena over it, and in the 7th century Siracusa's first Christian cathedral was built on top of the Greek structure. The massive columns of the original Greek temple were incorporated into the present structure and are clearly visible, embedded in the exterior wall along Via Minerva. The Greek columns were also used to dramatic advantage inside, where on one side they form chapels connected by elegant wrought-iron gates. The baroque facade, added in 1700, displays a harmonious rhythm of concaves and convexes. In front, the piazza is encircled by pink and white oleanders and elegant buildings ornamented with filigree grillwork. ⊠ *Piazza del Duomo, Ortygia* ☎ *0931/65328* ⊗ *Daily 8–noon and 4–7:30.*

15

Ortygia
Island

Porto
Piccolo

Ionian Sea

C. Umberto

Via Malta

P.
Nuovo

Piazza
Pancali

ORTYGIA

Via Resalibera

Via Mirabella

Via Maestranza

Porto
Grande

Via Roma

Museo
Bellomo

Via Capodieci

KEY

i Tourist information

Mar Ionio

0   3/4 mile
0   1 km

㉙ Fonte Aretusa. A freshwater spring, the Fountain of Arethus, sits next to the sea, studded with Egyptian papyrus that is reportedly natural. This anomaly is explained by a Greek legend that tells how the nymph Arethusa was changed into a fountain by the goddess Artemis (Diana) when she tried to escape the advances of the river god Alpheus. She fled from Greece, into the sea, with Alpheus in close pursuit, and emerged in Sicily at this spring. It's said if you throw a cup into the Alpheus River in Greece it will emerge here at this fountain, which is home to a few tired ducks and some dull-colored carp—but no cups. If you want to stand right by the fountain, you need to gain admission through the aquarium; otherwise look down on it from Largo Aretusa. ✚ *Off the promenade along harbor.*

㉔ Piazza Archimede. The center of this piazza has a baroque fountain, the *Fontana di Diana,* festooned with fainting sea nymphs and dancing jets of water. Look for the Chiaramonte-style **Palazzo Montalto,** an arched-window gem just off the piazza on Via Montalto.

㉕ Piazza del Duomo. In the heart of Ortygia, this ranks as one of Italy's most beautiful piazzas, its elongated space lined with Sicilian baroque treasures and outdoor cafés.

㉓ Tempio di Apollo. Scattered through the piazza just across the bridge to Ortygia are the ruins of a temple dedicated to Apollo, a model of which is in the Museo Archeologico. In fact, little of this noble Doric temple still remains except for some crumbled walls and shattered columns; the window in the south wall belongs to a Norman church that was built much later on the same spot. ⊠ *Piazza Pancali, Ortygia.*

Also Worth Seeing

㉚ Castello Maniace. The southern tip of Ortygia island is occupied by a castle built by Frederick II (1194–1250), now an army barracks, from which there are fine views of the sea.

㉗ Palazzo Beneventano del Bosco. On a corner of the Piazza del Duomo, this elegant palazzo is a private residence, but you can take a peek at the impressive interior courtyard, ending in a grand winding staircase. ⊠ *Piazza del Duomo, Ortygia.*

㉘ Santa Lucia alla Badia. This baroque church stands at one end of Piazza del Duomo and has an engaging wrought-iron balcony and pleasant facade. It opens only for a week each year preceding Christmas. ⊠ *Piazza del Duomo, Ortygia* ⊘ *Closed Dec. 21–13.*

Where to Stay & Eat

$$–$$$ ✕ **Don Camillo.** A gracious series of delicately arched rooms, lined with wine bottles and sepia-tone images of Old Siracusa, overflows with locals in the know. Good local dishes include the sublime spaghetti *delle Sirene* (with delicate *ricci,* sea urchin, and shrimp in butter); and the bolder, sweeter *pennette alle pesce spada* (pasta tubes with swordfish, raisins, tomato, pine nuts, basil, and Marsala). End with a spicy cheese plate counterbalanced by Sicilian honey and sweet Marsala wine. ⊠ *Via*

15

Maestranza 96, Ortygia ☎ *0931/67133* ⊟ *AE, DC, MC, V* ⊘ *Closed Sun., 1st 15 days in Nov., and 1st 15 days in July.*

$–$$$ ✕ **Fermento.** This hip wine bar–restaurant–Internet café is graced with warm lighting, dark vaulted stone, candles everywhere, a dim buzz, and Sicilian wines served in huge, beautiful tasting glasses. The menu really revolves around wine, with a decent (if pricey) selection of local classics. Stick to the pasta dishes and creative salads rather than the meats. ✉ *Via Crocifisso 44/46, Ortygia* ☎ *0931/60762* ⊟ *AE, DC, MC, V* ⊘ *Closed Tues.*

$–$$ ✕ **Ionico.** Enjoy seaside dining in the coastal Santa Lucia district. The Ionico has a terrace and veranda for alfresco meals, and the interior is plastered with diverse historical relics and has a cheerful open hearth for the winter. Chef-proprietor Roberto Giudice cooks meals to order or will suggest a specialty from a selection of market-fresh ingredients. Try the pasta *con acciughe e il pan grattato* (in an anchovy sauce). ✉ *Riviera Dionisio il Grande 194, Santa Lucia* ☎ *0931/65540* ⊟ *AE, DC, MC, V* ⊘ *Closed Tues. and Nov.*

$ ✕ **Archimede.** The *antipasto misto* (mixed antipasto) should whet your appetite for the predominantly seafood menu of this small establishment. Risotto di mare and pesce spada are specialties. Sample the *involtini all'Archimede,* roulades stuffed with fish and bread crumbs, or the tagliatelli with sea urchin. ✉ *Via Gemmellaro 8, Ortygia* ☎ *0931/69701* ⊟ *AE, DC, MC, V* ⊘ *Closed Sun. and 2 wks in Nov. and Dec.*

¢–$ ✕ **La Siciliana.** More than 54 varieties of inexpensive pizza top the menu here. The traditional *Siciliana,* a crusty and flavorful fried calzone stuffed with *tuma* (fresh unsalted cheese) and anchovies, is served only in the evening. Other choices on the menu include pasta and fish. It's good place to enjoy a cold beer or a white wine. ✉ *Via Savoia 17, Ortygia* ☎ *0931/68944* ⊟ *DC, MC, V* ⊘ *Closed Mon.*

$$$$ ▥ **Grand Hotel Ortigia.** An elegant, fantasy-inspired design prevails at this venerable institution, which has enjoyed a prime position overlooking the Porto Grande since 1898. A surreal seascape painting and a whimsical chandelier set a dreamy tone in the lobby. Guest rooms have fine wood floors, inlaid wood furniture, and stained-glass windows. Spacious bi-level suites with staircases cost about €60 extra. Look out from roof-garden restaurant at superb views over the harbor and seafront,

A WALK THROUGH ORTYGIA ISLAND

The central part of Siracusa is a modern city, with Corso Gelone its main shopping street. At its southern end, Corso Umberto leads to the Ortygia Island bridge, which crosses a harbor lined with fish restaurants. Begin at Piazza Pancali, the square where you arrive after crossing the bridge. Behind the piazza stand the scanty remains of the **Tempio di**

Apollo ㉓. Proceed from here to **Piazza Archimede** ㉔, the beautiful city square with a fountain, from which it's a brief walk to **Piazza del Duomo** ㉕, the main square of the old town and site of Siracusa's ancient and splendid **Duomo** ㉖. Other impressive buildings to see in the piazza include the **Palazzo Beneventano del Bosco** ㉗ and the church of **Santa Lucia alla Badia** ㉘. After you've had your fill of this, stroll onto the waterfront where several bars cluster around the lovely **Fonte Aretusa** ㉙, with its inexplicable papyrus, a perfect spot for a break.

while you indulge in excellent food. A shuttle service is provided to the hotel's private beach nearby. ⊠ *Viale Mazzini 12, Porto Grande, 96100* ☎ *0931/464600* 🖷 *0931/464611* ⊕ *www.grandhotelsr.it* ⟿ *39 rooms, 19 suites* 🛆 *Restaurant, in-room safes, minibars, cable TV, beach, bar, meeting room, free parking* ⊟ *AE, DC, MC, V* ⵁ⎮ *BP.*

$$$ 🏨 **Grand Hotel Villa Politi.** European royalty, Winston Churchill, and various other VIPs have frequented the grand 18th-century Villa Politi. Now equipped with modern luxuries, it still retains its charm and elegance with rococo furnishings. High-quality service and all the trimmings are the standard. Set back from the road, the hotel is in the extensive, ancient gardens of the Latomie dei Cappuccini overlooking a small archaeological site. ⊠ *Via M. Politi Laudien 2, Archaeological Zone, 96100* ☎ *0931/412121* 🖷 *0931/36061* ⊕ *www.villapoliti.com* ⟿ *92 rooms, 4 suites, 4 deluxe suites* 🛆 *2 restaurants, in-room safes, minibars, cable TV, pool, bar, free parking* ⊟ *AE, DC, MC, V* ⵁ⎮ *BP.*

$$ 🏨 **Domus Mariae.** You can see the sea at the end of the corridor as you enter this hotel on Ortygia's eastern shore. In an unusual twist, it's run by nuns of the Ursuline order, who help to make the mood placid and peaceful. Don't expect monastic conditions, however: refined furnishings distinguish the public rooms. Guest rooms—six with sea views (an extra €15) and others with great Ortygia street balconies—are bright, modern, and comfortable. The hotel's small, modest restaurant downstairs also serves nice local food—walnut-radicchio risotto and the salad of citrus and seared eggplant both shine. ⊠ *Via Vittorio Veneto 76, Ortygia, 96100* ☎ *0931/24854 or 0931/24858* ⊕ *www.sistemia.it/domusmariae* ⟿ *12 rooms* 🛆 *Restaurant, bar, free parking* ⊟ *AE, DC, MC, V* ⵁ⎮ *BP.*

¢ 🏨 **Airone.** In a pretty old palazzo in the heart of Ortygia, this bed-and-breakfast (liberally interpreted—breakfast at a nearby bar is included) caters mostly to backpackers and those who have the stamina to brave the four-story climb. Service is friendly and hassle-free (you get your own keys to the building), and the price and location can't be beat. Rooms are aging but spotless and spacious, some overlooking the coastline. Bathrooms are shared. ⊠ *Via Maestranza 111, 96100* ☎ *0931/69005* ⊕ *www.bedandbreakfastsicily.com* ⟿ *9 rooms without bath* 🛆 *Lounge, parking (fee)* ⊟ *No credit cards* ⵁ⎮ *BP.*

15

Walking along the seafront promenade to the southern tip of Ortygia will bring you to the **Castello Maniace** 🟢. Ortygia's backstreets are largely composed of elegant baroque palazzi, whose uniformity is the result of the major reconstruction that took place following an earthquake in 1693, at a time when this style of baroque was de rigueur. Be sure to wander along **Via della Maestranza,** the main lateral street of the island, or **Via Veneto,** on the eastern side, where you'll notice the bulbous wrought-iron balconies said to have been fashioned to accommodate ladies' billowing skirts, and facades embellished with mermaids and gargoyles—and don't miss the stucco decoration on **Palazzo Lantieri,** on Via Roma (off Piazza Archimede). You'll need the better part of a day to do justice to Ortygia. Obviously, the more detours you make—and there are distractions aplenty here—the longer you'll spend. The Duomo alone can take an hour or so to see properly. Happily, there's no dearth of inviting bars and restaurants to break up your tour.

Nightlife & the Arts

The feast of the city's patron, Santa Lucia, is held on December 13 at **Santa Lucia alla Badia** (✉ Piazza del Duomo, near Catacombs of San Giovanni, Ortygia). A splendid silver statue of the saint is carried from the church to the Duomo: a torchlight procession and band music accompany the bearers, while local families watch from their balconies. If you're in search of holiday gifts, the city hosts the island's most colorful **Christmas market** in mid-December.

Every May and June, Siracusa's **Teatro Greco** (✉ Parco Archeologico ☎ 0931/465831 ⊕ www.indafondazione.org) stages performances of classical drama and comedy.

One of Sicily's best wine bars, **Peter Pan** (✉ Via Castello Maniace, Ortygia ☎ 0931/468937) remarkably serves absolutely any wine on its voluminous list by the glass. The place doubles as a smoky haunt of the city's far-left youth. On the edge of Ortygia, the **Ulysses Irish Pub** (✉ Vicolo al Forte Vigliena 3/15, Ortygia ☎ 0931/465615) is a raucous home base for expats, suburbanites, and locals. Popular and filled with locals, **Il Bagatto** (✉ Piazza S. Giuseppe 1, Ortygia ☎ 0931/464076) is a bar in the heart of Ortygia.

Shopping

Siracusa's specialty is papyrus paper. But beware—most of what you buy is commercially produced, hard, and of inferior quality to the handmade paper, which feels like fabric. One of the best of the few places to buy the genuine article is **Galleria Bellomo** (✉ Via Capodieci 15, Ortygia ☎ 0931/61340), opposite the Museo Bellomo. It's run by an artist who sells cards and paintings and may also give a demonstration of how to make the paper.

THE IONIAN COAST

Halfway up the eastern, Ionian coast, Catania has the vivacity of Palermo, if not the artistic wealth; the city makes a good base for exploring lofty Mt. Etna, as does Taormina. Messina's scant attractions include its unparalleled position opposite the mountains of Calabria and one of the island's best museum collections.

Catania

31 *60 km (37 mi) north of Siracusa, 94 km (59 mi) south of Messina.*

The chief wonder of Catania, Sicily's second city, is that it is there at all. Its successive populations were deported by one Greek tyrant, sold into slavery by another, and driven out by the Carthaginians. Every time the city got back on its feet it was struck by a new calamity: plague decimated the population in the Middle Ages, a mile-wide stream of lava from Mt. Etna swallowed most of the city in 1669, and 25 years later a disastrous earthquake forced the Catanese to begin again.

Today Catania is completing yet another resurrection—this time from crime, filth, and urban decay. Although the city remains loud and full of traffic, signs of gentrification are everywhere. The elimination of vehicles from the Piazza del Duomo and scrubbing of a lot of the historic buildings has added to Catania's newfound charm. Home to what is arguably Sicily's best university, Catania is full of exuberant youth, and it shows in the chic *osterie* (taverns) that serve wine, designer bistros, and trendy ethnic boutiques that have popped up all over town. Even more impressive is the vibrant nightlife—theater, dance, and live music—to which the town now sways. Every year Catania becomes more and more worthwhile as a stop on a tour of Sicily.

Catania's greatest native son was the composer Vincenzo Bellini (1801–35), whose operas have thrilled audiences since their premieres in the first half of the 19th century. Many of the town's buildings are constructed from three-century-old lava; the black lava-stone buildings combine with baroque architecture to give the city a singular appearance. Nowhere is this clearer than in the centro storico. Don't miss the stunning **Piazza Universitaria,** a nerve center made interesting by the facade of a majestic old university building, and the nearby Castello Ursino.

At the heart of **Piazza del Duomo,** which is closed to traffic, stands an elephant carved out of lava balancing an Egyptian obelisk—the city's informal mascot. The piazza shines from a 21st-century renovation. From here you can look way down the long, straight Via Garibaldi to see a black-and-white-striped fortress and entrance to the city, the Porta Garibaldi.

The Giovanni Vaccarini–designed facade of the **Cattedrale di Sant'Agata** dominates the Piazza del Duomo. Inside the church, composer Vincenzo Bellini is buried. Also of note are the three apses of lava that survive from the original Norman structure and a fresco from 1675 in the sacristy that portrays Catania's submission to Etna's attack. ⊠ *Piazza del Duomo, bottom end of Via Etnea* ☎ *095/320044* ⊗ *Mon.–Sat. 8–noon and 4–6:50, Sun. 4–6:50.*

Evenings **Via Etnea** is host to one of Sicily's most enthusiastic passeggiate, in which Catanese of all ages take part. The street is closed to traffic until 10:30 PM and is lined with cafés and clothing, jewelry, and shoe stores.

need a break? The lively **Savia** (⊠ Via Etnea and Via Umberto, near Villa Bellini) makes superlative *arancini* (fried risotto balls) with ragù. Or you could choose cannoli or other snacks to munch on while you rest.

An underground river, the Amenano, flows through much of Catania. You can glimpse it at the Fontana dell'Amenano, but the best place to experience the river is at the wine bar of the **Agorà Youth Hostel** (⊠ *Piazza Currò 6* ☎ *095/7233010* ⊗ *Daily 12:30 PM–2 AM.*). Here you can sit at a table near a grotto as swirls of water rush by.

Where to Stay & Eat

★ **$$–$$$** ✕ **Ambasciata del Mare.** When a seafood restaurant sits next door to the fish market, it bodes well for the food's freshness. Choose swordfish or *gamberoni* (large shrimp) from a display case in the front of the restaurant, for instance, and then enjoy it simply grilled with oil and lemon. This simple, bright, and cozy place could not be friendlier or more easily accessed—it's right on the corner of Piazza Duomo by the fountain. ⊠ *Viale Marco Polo 52* ☎ *095/376400* ⊟ *AE, DC, MC, V* ⊘ *Closed Mon. No dinner Sun.*

$–$$ ✕ **Costa Azzurra.** Reserve in advance for a table on the veranda, where you sit by the edge of the sea with good views of the harbor in the Ognina district. The fritto misto can be ordered as an antipasto or a main course, and the pesce spada steak is a classic, served grilled with a large slice of lemon. ⊠ *Via De Cristofaro 4, north of old town center on way to Taormina* ☎ *095/497889* ⊟ *AE, DC, MC, V* ⊘ *Closed Mon. and last 2 wks in Aug.*

★ **$–$$** ✕ **La Siciliana.** Salvo La Rosa and sons serve memorable seafood and meat dishes, exquisite homemade desserts, and a choice of more than 220 wines. The restaurant specializes in the ancient dish *ripiddu nivicatu* ("black" risotto with cuttlefish ink and fresh ricotta cheese), as well as *le sarde a beccafico* (stuffed sardines) and calamari *ripieni alla griglia* (stuffed and grilled). A meal at this fine eatery more than justifies the short taxi ride 3 km (2 mi) north of the center. ⊠ *Viale Marco Polo 52* ☎ *095/376400* ⊟ *AE, DC, MC, V* ⊘ *Closed Mon. No dinner Sun.*

$$$–$$$$ 🏨 **Excelsior Palace.** Ask for a room facing Piazza Verga, a neat tree-lined square in a quiet but central district of Catania. Sound-insulated windows add to the peace. Impeccably designed rooms have a careful balance of neoclassical and new furnishings. The American Bar should provide solace if you're feeling nostalgic for a Manhattan. ⊠ *Piazza Verga 39, 95129* ☎ *095/7476111* 🖷 *095/537015* ⊕ *www.excelsiorcatania. thi.it* ⤳ *158 rooms, 13 suites, 5 junior suites* ⚘ *Restaurant, gym, steam room, bar, no-smoking rooms* ⊟ *AE, DC, MC, V* †⊙† *BP.*

$$ 🏨 **Savona.** Stay just a stone's throw from Piazza del Duomo, where the receptionist can help arrange church tours—and provide parking suggestions. The high-ceiling rooms are solidly furnished with heavy wood beds and have patterned wall paper. The breakfast room–sitting area has soaring vaults and deep green leather couches ready to sink into. ⊠ *Via Vittorio Emanuele 210, 95124* ☎🖷 *095/326982* ⊕ *www. hotelsavona.it* ⤳ *30 rooms* ⚘ *In-room data ports, in-room safes, mini-bars, cable TV, bar, travel services* ⊟ *AE, MC, V* †⊙† *BP.*

Nightlife & the Arts

The opera season at the **Teatro Bellini** (⊠ Piazza Bellini, Catania ☎ 095/ 7150921 ⊕ www.teatromassimobellini.it), October to June, attracts top singers and productions to the birthplace of the great composer Vincenzo Bellini. Guided tours of the theater's lavish interior, built in 1890, run daily from 8:30 to 10:30.

International jazz acts bypass Palermo for Catania's live music scene, the best in Sicily. **La Bettola dei Cavalieri** (⊠ Piazza Federico di Svevia 20 ☎ 340/5977489) has great jazz with an Italian bent. **La Chiave** (⊠ Via

Sweet Sicily

SICILY IS FAMOUS for its desserts, none more than the wonderful cannoli (*cannolo* is the singular), whose delicate pastry shell and just-sweet-enough ricotta barely resemble their foreign impostors. They come in all sizes, from pinkie-size bites to holiday cannoli the size of a coffee table. Even your everyday bar will display a window piled high with dozens of varieties of ricotta-based dessert, including delicious fried balls of dough. The traditional cake at Easter (but available year-round) is the *cassata siciliana*, a rich chilled sponge cake with sheep's ricotta and candied fruit. It's the most popular dessert at many Sicilian restaurants,

and you shouldn't miss it. From behind bakery windows and glass cases beam tiny marzipan sweets, bizarrely fashioned into brightly colored apples, cherries, and even hamburgers and prosciutto.

Do as the locals do and dip your summer morning brioche—the best in Italy—into a cup of brilliantly refreshing coffee granita. The world's first ice cream is said to have been made by the Romans from the snow on the slopes of Mt. Etna, and the practice of producing top-quality gelato, and eating it in great quantities, is still prevalent throughout the island.

15

Landolina 64 ☎ 347/9480910 ⊕ www.lachiave.it) hosts blues on Thursday and jazz on Sunday.

Shopping

Catania is justly famous for its sweets and bar snacks. Of the numerous pastry shops along Via Etnea, **Al Caprice** (✉ Via Etnea 32, near Piazza Universitaria ☎ 095/320840) has the largest variety of homemade goodies and edible gifts, plus hot and cold snacks. The selection of almond-based delights from **I Dolci di Nonna Vincenza** (✉ Palazzo Biscari, Piazza San Placido 7 ☎ 095/7151844 ⊕ www.dolcinonnavincenza.it) may be slight, but everything is fresh and phenomenally good. In response to demand, Nonna Vincenza ships abroad and even has an outlet in the Catania airport.

The **outdoor fish and food market,** which begins on Via Zappala Gemelli and emanates in every direction from Piazza di Benedetto, is one of Italy's most memorable. It's a feast for the senses: thousands of specimens of impeccably fresh fish, some still wriggling, plus endless varieties of meats, ricotta, and fresh produce, and a symphony of vendor shouts to fill the ears. The market is open Monday–Saturday and is at its best in the morning.

Acireale

32 *16 km (10 mi) north of Catania.*

Acireale sits amid a clutter of rocky pinnacles and lush lemon groves. The craggy coast is known as the Riviera dei Ciclopi, after the legend narrated in the *Odyssey* in which the blinded cyclops Polyphemus hurled boulders at the retreating Ulysses, thus creating spires of rock, or *faraglioni* (pillars of rock rising dramatically out of the sea). Tourism has barely taken off here, so it's a good destination if you feel the need to put some distance between yourself and the busloads of tourists in Taormina. And though the beaches are rocky, there's good swimming here, too.

During Carnival celebrations, considered the best in Sicily, streets are jammed with thousands of fancy-dressed revelers and floats dripping with flowers and gaudy papier-mâché models. Acireale is an easy day trip from Catania.

Begin your visit to Acireale with a stroll down to the public gardens, **Villa Belvedere,** at the end of the main Corso Umberto, for superb coastal views.

With its cupola and twin turrets, Acireale's **Duomo** is an extravagant baroque construction dating back to the 17th century. In the chapel to the right of the altar, look for the 17th-century silver statue of Santa Venera, patron saint of Acireale, made by Mario D'Angelo, and the early-18th-century frescoes by Antonio Filocamo. ⊠ *Piazza Duomo* ☎ *095/ 601797* ⊙ *Daily 8–noon and 4–7.*

need a break?

El Dorado (⊠ Corso Umberto 5 ☎ 095/601464) serves delicious ice creams, and the *granita di mandorla* (almond granita), available in summer, invites a firsthand acquaintance.

The sulfur-rich volcanic waters from Mt. Etna found at **Terme di Acireale** were first enjoyed by the Greeks. In the 2nd century AD Acireale's patron saint, Venera, was martyred, after which the waters were accorded miraculous powers. After 1873, when the Santa Venera bathing establishment with its park was created, the baths attracted a stream of celebrated visitors, including Wagner. Book in advance to use the baths and have mud treatments and massages (multiday treatment packages are available). Nonpatrons can wander the gardens for free. ⊠ *Via delle Terme 47* ☎ *095/7686111* ⊕ *www.terme-acireale.com* 🖃 *€13 and up for baths, gardens free* ⊙ *Treatments by appointment, daily 7–1; gardens daily 9–8.*

Lord Byron (1788–1824) visited the **Belvedere di Santa Caterina** to lookout over the Ionian sea during his Italian wanderings. The Santa Caterina viewpoint is south of the old town, near the Terme di Acireale, off SS114.

Where to Eat

$$ ✕ **La Grotta.** A conventional looking trattoria entry fronts a dining room within a cave that has an actual rock-face wall. Try the *insalata di mare,* a selection of delicately steamed fish served with lemon and olive oil or fish grilled over charcoal. Chef-proprietor Carmelo Strano's menu is small, but there isn't a dud among the selections. ⊠ *Via Scalo Grande 46* ☎ *095/ 7648153* 🖘 *Reservations essential* 🖃 *AE, DC, MC, V* ⊙ *Closed Tues. and Oct.15–Nov. 5.*

Nightlife & the Arts

Puppet theater tradition carries on in Acireale, although it has all but died out in other parts of the island with the exception of Palermo. See shows at **Coop E. Macri** (⊠ Corso Umberto 11 ☎ 095/606272). The **Teatro dell'Opera dei Pupi** (⊠ Via Nazionale 95, Turi Grasso ☎ 095/7648035 ⊕ www.teatropupimacri.it) has puppet shows and a puppet exhibit.

Shopping

Acireale is renowned in Sicily for its marzipan, made into fruit shapes and delicious biscuits available at many pasticcerie around town. **Castorina** (⊠ Piazza del Duomo 20 ☎ 095/601546) sells marzipan candies (and cute gift boxes for them). A unique creation at **Belvedere** (⊠ Corso Umberto 230 ☎ 095/894164) is the *nucatole*, a large cookie made with heaping quantities of chocolate, Nutella, nuts, and other wholesome ingredients.

At **Bottega d'Arte** (⊠ Via Vittorio Emanuele 88 ☎ 095/606805 or 095/601987 ☉ Closed Sun.) you can see the local artist Salvatore Chiarenza at work carving wood statues and traditional carts, as his father and grandfather did before him. He also makes brass and wooden puppets.

15

Mount Etna

33 *30 km (19 mi) north of Catania.*

Fodor'sChoice
★

Mt. Etna is one of the world's major active volcanoes and is the largest and highest in Europe—the cone of the crater rises to 10,902 feet above sea level. Plato sailed in just to catch a glimpse in 387 BC; in the 9th century AD, the oldest gelato of all was shaved off of its snowy slopes; and in the 21st century the volcano still claims annual headlines. Etna has erupted 11 times in the past 30 or so years, most spectacularly in 1971, 1983, 2001, and 2002, when in each case rivers of molten lava destroyed the two highest stations of the cable car that rises from the town of Sapienza. Although each eruption is predictably declared a "tragedy" by the media owing to the economic losses, Etna almost never threatens human life. Travel in the proximity of the crater depends on Mt. Etna's temperament, but you can walk up and down the enormous lava dunes and wander over its moonlike surface of dead craters. The rings of vegetation change markedly as you rise, with vineyards and pine trees gradually giving way to growths of broom and lichen. Catania and Taormina are the departure points for excursions around—but not always to the top of—Mt. Etna. Buses leave from Catania's train station in early morning.

Although the 2002 eruptions destroyed the gondola, you can still climb Etna from Rifugio Sapienza, altitude 6,266 feet. The cost is approximately €40–€50 per person for the two- to three-hour round-trip, including jeep and guide.

Club Alpino Italiano in Catania is a great resource for guides up Mt. Etna. If you have some experience and don't like a lot of hand-holding, these are the guides for you. ⊠ *Piazza Scammacca* ☎ *095/77153515* ⊕ *www.cai.it.*

Call the **Gruppo Guide Alpine Etna** to arrange for a guide to meet you to climb Mt. Etna if you're a beginner. Their service is a little more personalized—and expensive—than others. Reserve ahead. ⊠ *Piazza Santa Caterina* ☎ *095/7914755.*

Instead of going up Mt. Etna, you can circle it on the **Circumetnea railroad,** which runs near the volcano's base. The private railway almost circles the volcano, running 114 km (71 mi) between Catania and Riposto—the towns are 30 km (19 mi) apart by the coast road. The line is small, slow, and only single-track, but has some dramatic vistas of the volcano and goes through lava fields. The round-trip takes about five hours, there are about 10 departures a day. ⊠ *Via Caronda 352, Catania* ☎ *095/541243* ⊕ *www.circumetnea.it* ✉ *€11 round-trip* ⊙ *Mon.–Sat. 6:30 AM–9 PM.*

For a bird's-eye view of Mt. Etna, you may be tempted to try paragliding or hang gliding; contact **No Limits Etna Center** (⊠ Via Milano 6/a, Catania ☎ 095/7212747 🖷 095/387313 ⊕ www.etnacenter.net). The company also organizes climbing, caving, and diving expeditions.

Where to Stay & Eat

★ **$$$$** ✕🏨 **Hotel Villa Paradiso Dell'Etna.** This 1920s hotel 10 km (6 mi) northeast of Catania was a haunt for artists before General Rommel took over during World War II. When the tide turned in the war, it became a military hospital. Today, after a painstaking renovation, Paradiso Dell'Etna resembles an elegant private villa housing mementos of a memorable past, the hotel has four exceptional suites and 30 sumptuous rooms, each filled with tasteful 19th-century Sicilian antiques and all the modern accessories befitting a four-star hotel—the pool is even heated. ⊠ *Via per Viagrande 37, exit A18 toward San Gregario, 95030 S.G. La Punta* ☎ *095/7512409* 🖷 *095/7413861* ⊕ *www.paradisoetna.it* 🛏 *30 rooms, 4 suites* ⚌ *Restaurant, room service, some in-room hot tubs, in-room safes, minibars, cable TV, tennis court, pool, gym, massage, sauna, bar, dance club, Internet, meeting room* ⊟ *AE, DC, MC, V* ⃢⃝ *BP.*

Taormina

❸❹ *64 km (40 mi) northeast of Mt. Etna, 50 km (31 mi) north of Catania.*

The medieval cliff-hanging town of Taormina is overrun with tourists and trinket shops, but its natural beauty is still hard to argue with. The view of the sea and Mt. Etna from its jagged cactus-covered cliffs is as close to perfection as a panorama can get, especially on clear days, when the snowcapped volcano's white puffs of smoke rise against the blue sky. Writers have extolled Taormina's beauty almost since its founding in the 6th century BC by Greeks from Naples; Goethe and D. H. Lawrence were among its more recent well-known enthusiasts.

The Greeks put a premium on finding impressive locations to stage their dramas, and the site of Taormina's hillside **Teatro Greco** is a fine one. Beyond the columns you can see the towns rooftops spilling down the hillside, the arc of the coastline, and Mt. Etna in the distance. The theater was built during the 3rd century BC and rebuilt by the Romans during the 2nd century AD. Its acoustics are exceptional: even today a stage whisper can be heard in the last rows. In summer Taormina hosts an arts festival of music and dance events and a film festival; many performances are held in the Teatro Greco. ⊠ *Via Teatro Greco* ☎*0942/232220* 🎫 *€4.50* ☉ *Daily 9–1 hr before sunset.*

Many of Taormina's 14th- and 15th-century palaces have been carefully preserved. Especially beautiful is the **Palazzo Corvaja,** with characteristic black-lava and white-limestone inlays. Today it houses the tourist office and the **Museo di Arte e Storia Popolare,** which has a collection of puppets and folk art, carts and cribs. ⊠*Largo Santa Caterina* 🎫*Museum €2.60* ☎*0942/610274 Palazzo* ☉*Museum Tues.–Sun. 9–1 and 4–8.*

15

need a break? A marzipan devotee should not leave Taormina without trying one of the gooey sweets—maybe in the guise of the ubiquitous *fico d'India* (prickly pear)—at **Pasticceria Etna** (⊠ Corso Umberto 112 ☎ 0942/24735 🖷 0942/21279). Locals also swear by the cannoli, and a block of almond paste makes a good souvenir—you can bring it home to make an almond latte or granita.

Stroll down Via Bagnoli Croce from the main Corso Umberto to the **Parco Duca di Cesarò,** the lovely public gardens designed by Florence Trevelyan Cacciola, a Scottish lady "invited" to leave England following a romantic liaison with the future Edward VII (1841–1910). Arriving in Taormina in 1889, she married a local professor and devoted herself to the gardens, filling them with Mediterranean plants, ornamental pavilions (known as the beehives), and fountains. Stop by the panoramic bar, which has stunning views.

By footpath or car you can approach the medieval **Castello Saraceno** (⊠ Monte Tauro), enticingly perched on an adjoining cliff above town, but you cannot continue all the way to the castle itself.

off the beaten path **CASTELMOLA –** If your passion for heights hasn't been quelled, visit Castelmola, the tiny town above Taormina with a spectacular 360-degree panorama. Local bars make their own refreshing almond wine. ⊕ *5 km (3 mi) west of Taormina.*

Where to Stay & Eat

$$$–$$$$ ✕ **La Giara.** Syracuse stone columns sculpted by local master stonecutters, and an open atrium in the back, enhance the elegant and classical in one of Taormina's oldest restaurants. The kitchen blends upscale modern techniques with the simple flavors of traditional specialties. Try scallops with *lardo di collonnata* (lard). You can extend your evening by taking an after-dinner drink at the popular piano bar. (The place is named after a giant Roman vase discovered underneath the bar.) ⊠ *Vico La Floresta 1* ☏ *0942/23360* ⊟ *AE, DC, MC, V* ⊘ *Closed Mon. and Nov.–Apr. No lunch.*

$–$$$$ ✕ **La Dracena.** Enjoy an ideal alfresco meal in the garden near the dragon tree that is this restaurant's namesake. The *mezzelune* (half-open ravioli) and dishes with zucchini are very good. La Dracena is just behind the castle. ⊠ *Via Michele Amari 4* ☏ *0942/23491* ⊟ *AE, DC, MC, V* ⊘ *Closed Mon. and Nov. 1–Mar. 1.*

$–$$ ✕ **La Piazzetta.** Reasonable prices bring in real Italian families to La Piazzetta. Classics such as *pasta con le sarde* (pasta with sardines and bread crumbs) are competently prepared, the grilled fish is extremely fresh, the menu is poorly translated (always a good sign), and the service is informal and friendly. The modest room has simple white walls—you're not paying for a view. ⊠ *Via Paladini 5, off Corso Umberto* ☏ *0942/626317* ⊟ *AE, DC, MC, V* ⊘ *Closed Mon.*

★ $–$$ ✕ **L'Arco dei Cappuccini.** Just off the radar screen of the main tourist strip lies this clean, diminutive restaurant with white tablecloths. Outdoor seating and an upstairs kitchen help make room for a few extra tables—necessary because the locals are well aware that both the price and the quality cannot be beat elsewhere in town. Indulge in *sopressa di polipo* (steamed octopus carpaccio), gnocchi *con pistacchi* (with pistachio cream sauce), or the fresh catch of the day. ⊠ *Via Cappuccini 7, off Via Costanino Patricio near Porta Messina* ☏ *0942/24893* ⟁ *Reservations essential* ⊟ *AE, DC, MC, V* ⊘ *Closed Wed. and Nov.–Easter.*

$$$$ ▥ **Grand Hotel Timeo and Villa Flora.** The deluxe Timeo—on a princely perch overlooking the town and below the Teatro Greco—wears a graceful patina that suggests the dolce vita. A splash of baroque mixes with the Mediterranean in the lobby, which has tile- and brickwork and vaulted ceilings. Wrought-iron and wicker chairs surround marble tables in the original bar from 1873 (made of gesso) and on the adjoining palatial patio. Exquisite moldings hang on butter-color walls. Fine earth-tone linens and drapes, Oriental rugs, and gilt-frame prints decorate the rooms, 30 of which are in the neighboring Villa Flora. ⊠ *Via Teatro Greco 59, 98039* ☏ *0942/23801* 🖷 *0942/628501* ⊕ *www.framonhotels.com* ↪ *70 rooms* ⚭ *Restaurant, room service, in-room safes, minibars, pool, gym, bar, convention center* ⊟ *AE, DC, MC, V* ⊕◎ *MAP.*

$$$$ ▥ **San Domenico Palace.** Sweeping views from this converted 15th-century Dominican monastery linger in your mind: the sensuous gardens—full of red trumpet flowers, bougainvillea, and lemons—afford a dramatic vista of the castle, the sea, and Mt. Etna. Expect luxury and ease at this extraordinarily expensive hotel, which is considered by some to be among the best in Europe. Rooms have hand-painted or hand-carved furnishings, exquisite linens, and ultramodern amenities. The San Domenico's Renaissance flavor is preserved by two exquisite cloisters, convent rooms, and the chapel, now a banquet and conference facility. ⊠ *Piazza San Domenico 5, 98039* ☏ *0942/613111* 🖷 *0942/625506* ⊕ *www.sandomenico.thi.it* ↪ *93 rooms, 15 suites* ⚭ *2 restaurants, room service, minibars, pool, gym, bar, Internet* ⊟ *AE, DC, MC, V* ⊕◎ *BP.*

FodorsChoice
★

$$$–$$$$ ▥ **Romantik Villa Ducale.** The former summer residence of a local aristocrat has been converted into a luxurious villa hotel a 10- to 15-minute walk from the center of Taormina. Individually styled rooms, furnished with antiques, each have their own balconies. An intimate wood-panel library is at once homelike and romantic, and the vast roof terrace, where a fantastic breakfast is served, takes full advantage of the wide panorama embracing Etna and the bay below. In summer a free shuttle bus connects the hotel with the area's best beaches. ⊠ *Via L. da Vinci 60, 98039* ☎ *0942/28153* 🖶 *0942/28710* ⊕ *www.hotelvilladucale.it* 🛏 *15 rooms, 1 suite* ⌂ *Minibars, bar* ☰ *AE, DC, MC, V* ⊘ *Closed Nov. 26–Feb. 27* ⍾⍾ *BP.*

$$$ 🏨 **Hotel Villa Paradiso.** On the edge of the old quarter, overlooking the lovely public gardens and facing the sea, this smaller hotel is not as well known as some of the blockbusters nearby, but with views of Etna from many rooms, delightful service, and a good restaurant, it's only a matter of time. Proprietor Salvatore Martorana will gladly share stories of Taormina in Goethe's day over an *aperitivo.* A regular hotel bus service runs to the beach. ⊠ *Via Roma 2, 98039* ☎ *0942/23921* 🖶 *0942/ 625800* ⊕ *www.hotelvillaparadisotaormina.com* 🛏 *20 rooms, 17 junior suites* ⌂ *Restaurant, minibars, cable TV, tennis court, bar, library* ☰ *AE, DC, MC, V* ⍾⍾ *BP.*

$$ 🏨 **Arathena Rocks Hotel.** Here's a good choice if you want to stay near the sea. The hotel stands at one end of the bay, right on the cape where Greek settlers first landed in Sicily. There's a large pool, around which Sicilian singers and musicians entertain you every other night in summer. A twice-daily free bus service links the hotel to Taormina. The town of Giardini Naxos, 8 km (5mi) south of Toarmina, makes a great base—in summer it's just as lively as Taormina, and the broad sandy beach is nearby. ⊠ *Via Calcide Eubea 55, 98035 Giardini Naxos* ☎ *0942/ 51349* 🖶 *0942/51690* 🛏 *49 rooms* ⊕ *www.hotelarathena.com* ⌂ *Restaurant, pool, bar, Internet; no a/c in some rooms* ☰ *AE, DC, MC, V* ⊘ *Closed Nov.–Easter* ⍾⍾ *BP.*

$$ 🏨 **Villa Fiorita.** This converted private home near the Teatro Greco has excellent northerly coastal views from nearly every room. Rooms vary in size and furnishings, but most are bright, breezy, and colorful, with large windows and balconies (do ask). Prices are reasonable considering the views, the compact swimming pool, and the garden. The elevator is at the top of 65 steps. ⊠ *Via Pirandello 39, 98039* ☎ *0942/24122* 🖶 *0942/625967* ⊕ *www.villafioritahotel.com* 🛏 *24 rooms, 1 suite* ⌂ *In-room safes, pool, bar, minibars* ☰ *AE, MC, V* ⍾⍾ *BP.*

Nightlife & The Arts

The Teatro Greco and the Palazzo dei Congressi, near the entrance to the theater, are the main venues for the summer festival dubbed **Taoarte** (☎ *0942/21142* ⊕ www.taormina-arte.com), held each year from May to September. Performances encompass classical music, ballet, and theater. The famous **film festival** (⊕ www.taorminafilmfest.it) in June is part of the Taoarte festival.

The **Teatro dei Due Mari** (⊠ Via Teatro Greco ☎ 0941/243176 ⊕ www. teatrodeiduemari.it) stages Greek tragedy at the Teatro Greco during the month of May.

en route | The 50-km (30-mi) stretch of road between Taormina and Messina is flanked by lush vegetation and seascapes. Inlets are punctuated by gigantic, oddly shaped rocks. It was along this coast, legend says, that the giant cyclops hurled his boulders down on Ulysses and his terrified men as they fled to the sea in Homer's *Odyssey*.

Messina

③ *43 km (27 mi) northeast of Taormina, 94 km (59 mi) northeast of Catania.*

Messina's ancient history lists a series of disasters, but the city nevertheless managed to develop a fine university and a thriving cultural environment. At 5 o'clock in the morning on December 28, 1908, Messina changed from a flourishing metropolis of 120,000 to a heap of rubble, shaken to pieces by an earthquake that turned into a tidal wave and left 80,000 dead and the city almost completely leveled. As you approach the sickle-shape bay, across which ferries connect Sicily to the mainland, you won't notice any outward indication of the disaster, except for the modern countenance of a 3,000-year-old city. The somewhat flat look is a precaution of seismic planning: tall buildings are not permitted.

The reconstruction of Messina's Norman and Romanesque **Duomo,** originally built by the Norman king Roger II in 1197, has retained much of the original plan, including a handsome crown of Norman battlements, an enormous apse, and a splendid wood-beam ceiling. The adjoining **bell tower** contains one of the largest and most complex mechanical clocks in the world, constructed in 1933 with a host of gilded automatons, including a roaring lion, that spring into action every day at the stroke of noon. ⊠ *Piazza del Duomo* ☎ *090/675175* ⊘ *Daily 8–12:30 and 4–7.*

Where to Stay & Eat

$-$$$ ✕ **Da Piero.** An institution in Messina for decades, this central restaurant (four blocks up from Piazza Cairoli) trades on its well-deserved reputation for classic Sicilian dishes, particularly seafood. Skip the smoked fish, shrimp cocktail, and risotto, but try the very good mussels *gratinate* (with cheese), the spaghetti *alle vongole* (with clams), or pleasing pasta *alla carrettiera* (with sliced tomatoes, garlic, and slightly spicy, aged pecorino cheese). Marsala sipped with one of the rich homemade desserts makes for a grand finale. ⊠ *Via Ghibellina 119* ☎ *090/718365* ☰ *AE, DC, MC, V* ⊘ *Closed Sun. and Aug.*

$$$ 🏨 **Grand Hotel Liberty.** Across the piazza from the train station, this hotel—at the top end of Messina's offerings—is a cool haven from the bustle of the surrounding streets. The entrance and public rooms are sumptuously fitted out in a white-marble neoclassical style with a meticulous attention to detail, whereas bedrooms are plainer but comfortably equipped. ⊠ *Via I Settembre 15, 98123* ☎ *090/6409436* 🖷 *090/6409340* ⊕ *www.framon-hotels.com* 🛏 *52 rooms* ♻ *Restaurant, minibars, bar, meeting rooms* ☰ *AE, DC, MC, V* ⎜⚬⎜ *BP.*

VOICES OF ITALY

Francesco Pensovecchio
wine critic, Palermo

Francesco Pensovecchio is a member of the elite corps of tasters who contribute to *Vini d'Italia*, Italy's definitive wine guide, published annually by the food and wine organization Gambero Rosso. Its Tre Bicchieri (three glasses) designation is the ultimate honor for Italian wine makers.

On Sicilian wine: "Sicily, between the 35th and 45th northern parallels, is quite simply one of the best places in the world for producing wine. Sicily also has diverse and interesting microclimates: volcanic soil that's moistened and chilled by Etna; the sun-soaked red sands of the Ragusa region; the salty marine microclimates of the Aeolian Islands and Pantelleria; and the strong, scorched clay of the interior.

"Right now, Sicily produces just under 20% of the wine in all of Italy. In the past few years, Sicily has been as successful with so-called 'international' varietals (e.g., Planeta's Chardonnay) as with the great native grape, Nero d'Avola, which has long been grown all over Sicily.

"Important Italian producers have begun to notice Sicily's abundance of cheap, high-quality land. And so mainland producers like Mezzocorona, Zonin, Marzotto, and Illva have bought big in Sicily—500 or 600 hectares. What they plan to do with all this wine is still unclear: blend it with the wines of the north? Make new lines of wine for sale abroad? Maybe both. If you know the story of Sicily, you know that colonization by foreign investors is nothing new . . ."

On Planeta, Sicily's biggest international success story: "People say that Planeta was born in 1995. This is partially true, but it's not the whole truth. The other part of the truth is that the Planeta family has been working in agriculture in Sicily since the 1600s. In 1985 a fire in the vineyards around Lake Arancio, in western Sicily, presented infinite possibilities of starting something completely new in the region. An institute whose president was named Diego Planeta began to plant Chardonnay, and the results were extraordinary.

"In 1995, the winery completed its first vintage. The Tre Bicchieri awards quickly followed, and in 1999 Planeta was selected Winery of the Year by Gambero Rosso. As it's grown, Planeta has begun producing Cerasuolo di Vittoria (a traditional southeastern wine) and expanded to Noto, a return to the origins of Nero d'Avola. The winery now produces over two million bottles per year."

On how to choose Sicilian wines: "The most important thing is to get a sense of the many styles. Among the wines of western Sicily, try Planeta's Chardonnay, Ceuso's Custera, Furat's Ajello, Duca di Salaparuta's Duca Enrico, Morgante's Nero d'Avola, and Donnafugata's Mille e Una Notte. Among the wines of the east, try Planeta's Santa Cecilia (a Nero d'Avola) and Gulfi's Nerojbleo (another Nero d'Avola). And be sure to try any Cerasuolo di Vittoria, the most characteristic wine from Iblea, bolstered by the fruity Frappato grapes. Great versions come from Planeta, Valle dell'Acate, and Avide."

15

THE AEOLIAN ISLANDS

Off Sicily's northeast coast lies an archipelago of seven spectacular islands of volcanic origin. The Isole Eolie (Aeolian Islands), also known as the Isole Lipari (Lipari Islands), were named after Aeolus, the Greek god of the winds, who is said to keep all the earth's winds stuffed in a bag in his cave here. The Aeolians are a world of grottoes and clear-water caves carved by waves through the centuries. Superb snorkeling and scuba diving abound in the clearest and cleanest of Italy's waters. The beautiful people of high society discovered the archipelago years ago—here Roberto Rossellini courted his star and future wife Ingrid Bergman in 1950—and you should not expect complete isolation, at least on the main islands. August, in particular, can get unpleasantly overcrowded, and lodging and travel should always be booked as early as possible.

Lipari provides the widest range of accommodations and is a good jumping-off point for day trips to the other islands. Most exclusive are Vulcano and Panarea, the former noted for its black sands and stupendous sunsets (and prices), as well as the acrid smell of its sulfur emissions, whereas the latter is, according to some, the prettiest. Most remarkable is Stromboli (pronounced with the accent on the first syllable) with its constant eruptions, and remotest are Filicudi and Alicudi, where electricity was introduced only in the 1980s. Access to the islands is via ferry and hydrofoil from Milazzo or from Naples. The bars in the Aeolian Islands, and especially those on Lipari, are known for their granitas of fresh strawberries, melon, peaches, and other fruits. Many Sicilians on the Aeolians (and in Messina, Taormina, and Catania) begin the hot summer days with a granita *di caffè* (a coffee ice topped with whipped cream), into which they dunk their breakfast rolls. You can get one any time of day.

Vulcano

36 *18 km (11 mi) south of Lipari, 25 mins by ferry, 10 mins by hydrofoil; 55 km (34 mi) northwest of Milazzo, 90 minutes by ferry.*

True to its name—and the origin of the term—Vulcano has a profusion of fumaroles sending up jets of hot vapor, but the volcano here has long been dormant. Many come to soak in the strong-smelling sulfur springs: when the wind is right, the odors greet you long before you disembark. The island has some of the archipelago's best beaches, though the volcanic black sand can be off-putting at first. You can ascend to the crater (1,266 feet above sea level) on muleback for a wonderful view or take boat rides into the grottoes around the base. From Capo Grillo there is a view of all the Aeolians.

Where to Stay

★ $$$-$$$$ Les Sables Noires. Named for the black sands of the private beach in front, this luxury hotel is superbly sited on the beautiful Porto di Ponente. The cool modern furnishings and inviting pool induce a sybaritic mood, and the white-wall guest rooms are tasteful and spacious. The restaurant, naturally, looks out over the bay: sunsets are framed by the towering faraglioni. Weeklong stays are required in high season. ⊠ *Porto di Ponente, 98050* ☎ *090/9850* 🖷 *090/9852454* ⊕ *www.framon-hotels.com* 🖛 *48 rooms* ♿ *Restaurant, pool, beach, bar* ⊟ *AE, DC, MC, V* ⊗ *Closed mid-Oct.–mid-Apr.* ¶◯| *BP.*

Lipari

③⑦ *37 km (23 mi) north of Milazzo, 2 hrs 10 mins by ferry, 1 hr by hydro-foil; Milazzo: 41 km (25 mi) west of Messina.*

The largest and most developed of the Aeolians, Lipari welcomes you with distinctive pastel-color houses. Fields of spiky agaves dot the northernmost tip of the island, Acquacalda, indented with pumice and obsidian quarries. In the west is San Calogero, where you can explore hot springs and mud baths. From the red lava base of the island rises a plateau crowned with a 16th-century castle and a 17th-century cathedral.

15

★ The vast, multibuilding **Museo Eoliano** is a terrific archaeological museum, with an intelligently arranged collection of prehistoric finds—some dating as far back as 4000 BC—from various sites in the archipelago. ⊠ *Via Castello* ☎ *090/9880174* 🖾 *€4.50* ⊗ *Daily 9–1 and 3–7.*

Where to Stay & Eat

★ $$–$$$ ✕▣ **Il Filippino.** The views from the flower-strewn outdoor terrace of this restaurant in the upper town are a fitting complement to the superb fare. Founded in 1910, the restaurant is rightly rated one of the archipelago's best. Top choice is seafood: the zuppa di pesce and the antipasto platter of smoked and marinated fish are absolute musts. Leave some room for the local version of cassata, accompanied by sweet Malvasia wine from Salina. The restaurant also runs Residence Albergo Mendolita, a comfortable B&B 300 yards away. The basic rooms are furnished in a style a bit reminiscent of a kids' rec room. ⊠ *Piazza Municipio* ☎ *090/9811002, 090/9812374 Mendolita* 🖷 *090/9814879* ⊕ *www.bernardigroup.it* 🖛 *18 rooms, 1 suite* ♿ *In-room safes, minibars* ⊟ *AE, DC, MC, V* ⊗ *Restaurant closed Mon. in Oct.–Mar. and Nov. 10–Dec. 20* ¶◯| *BP.*

$$$–$$$$ ▣ **Gattopardo Park Hotel.** Bright bougainvillea and fiery hibiscus set the tone at this grand villa, and its restaurant has sweeping views of the sea. Guest quarters are in the 19th-century main villa or in whitewashed bungalows in the surrounding tranquil parkland. Public rooms have wood-beam ceilings and rustic-style furnishings. A minibus shuttles between the hotel and Spiagge Bianche, one of Lipari's better beaches. There are also trips around the island, boat excursions to Vulcano and Stromboli, and folklore evenings. Half board is required in summer; weekly discounts are available. ⊠ *Via Diana, 98055* ☎ *090/9811035* 🖷 *090/9880207* ⊕ *www.netnet.it/hotel/gattopardo* 🖛 *53 rooms* ♿ *Restaurant, bar* ⊟ *MC, V* ⊗ *Closed Nov.–Mar.* ¶◯| *MAP.*

$$–$$$ ▣ **Villa Augustus.** A simple homey spirit prevails with friendly service and a discreet attention to detail at the peaceful Villa Augustus, which is on a side street in the center of Lipari's old town. In addition to a palm-shaded backyard garden, there's a roof-garden with good sea

views. Apartment-style rooms are bright and spacious. Arrive during daytime hours, as the hotel is managed by only one person. ⊠ *Vico Ausonia 16, 98055* ☎ *090/9811232* 🖷 *090/9812233* ⊕ *www.villaaugustus. it* 💤 *34 rooms* ⌂ *Gym, piano bar, meeting room* 🖃 *AE, DC, MC, V* ☉ *Closed Nov.–Feb.* ⦿| *BP.*

Salina

③⑧ *15 km (9 mi) north of Lipari, 50 mins by ferry, 20 mins by hydrofoil; 52 km (38 mi) northwest of Milazzo.*

The second largest of the Aeolian Islands, Salina is also the most fertile—which accounts for its excellent Malvasia dessert wine locally produced, unlike that found on other islands. Salina is also the highest of the islands, Mt. Fossa delle Felci rises to more than 3,000 feet, and the vineyards and fishing villages along its slopes add to its allure. Accommodations and restaurants are reasonable, and there are fewer crowds than Lipari.

Where to Stay

$–$$$ 🏨 **Bellavista.** This is a quiet hotel in a quiet location, even though it's right next to the port. Rooms are simply furnished and cheerfully decorated with bright materials and ceramic tiles. Almost all have sea views, which can be enjoyed from the balconies. The management provides a list of things to do while on Salina and can organize boat excursions and transport around the island, though you may well opt for the *dolce far niente* (idle life). ⊠ *Via Risorgimento, Santa Marina Salina, 98050* ☎🖷 *090/9843009; 090/9281558 in winter* 💤 *13 rooms* ⌂ *Bar, babysitting* 🖃 *No credit cards* ☉ *Closed Oct. 15–Mar.* ⦿| *BP.*

Panarea

③⑨ *18 km (11 mi) north of Lipari, 2 hrs by ferry, 25–50 mins by hydrofoil; 55 km (33 mi) north of Milazzo.*

Panarea has some of the most dramatic scenery of the islands: wild caves carved out of the rock and dazzling flora. The exceptionally clear water and the richness of life on the sea floor make Panarea especially suitable for underwater exploration, though there is little in the way of beaches. The outlying rocks and islets make a gorgeous sight, and you can enjoy the panorama on an easy excursion to the small Bronze Age village at Capo Milazzese.

Where to Stay

$$$$ 🏨 **La Raya.** This discreet, expensive hotel is perfectly in keeping with the elite style of Panarea, most exclusive of the Aeolian islands. Public rooms, including bars, a broad terrace, and an open-air restaurant, are built into a hillside right on the port; the residential area is a 10-minute walk inland, though the rooms still enjoy the serene prospect of the sea and Stromboli from their balconies. The decor is elegant and understated, with Moorish-type hangings and low divans helping to create a tone of serene luxury. Families with young children are asked to book elsewhere. ⊠ *San Pietro, 98050* ☎🖷 *090/983103* ⊕ *www.hotelraya.it* 💤 *30*

rooms ⚖ *Restaurant, minibars, bar, nightclub* 🖃 *AE, DC, MC, V*
🌣 *Closed Oct. 17–Mar. 25* ❘◎❘ *BP.*

Stromboli

40 *40 km (25 mi) north of Lipari, 3 hrs 45 mins by ferry, 65–90 mins by
hydrofoil; 63 km (40 mi) north of Milazzo.*

This northernmost of the Aeolians (also accessible from Naples) consists
entirely of the cone of an active volcano. The view from the sea—especially at night, as an endless stream of glowing red-hot lava flows into
the water—is unforgettable. Stromboli is in a constant state of mild dissatisfaction, and every now and then its anger flares up, so authorities
insist that you climb to the top (about 3,031 feet above sea level) only
with a guide. The round-trip—climb, pause, and descent—usually starting around 6 PM, takes about four hours; the lava is much more impressive after dark. Some choose to camp overnight atop the volcano—again,
a guide is essential. The main town has a small selection of reasonably
priced hotels and restaurants and a choice of lively clubs and cafés for
the younger set. In addition to the island tour, excursions might include
boat trips around the naturally battlemented isle of Strombolicchio.

Numerous tour operators have guides that can lead you up Stromboli,
among them **Società Navigazione Pippo** (☎090/986135 or 0338/9857883).
Rates are around €20 per person for four hours.

Filicudi

41 *30 km (16 mi) west of Salina, 30–60 mins by hydrofoil; 82 km (54 mi)
northwest of Milazzo.*

Just a dot in the sea, Filicudi is famous for its unusual volcanic rock formations and the enchanting *Grotta del Bue Marino* (Grotto of the Sea
Ox). The crumbled remains of a prehistoric village are at Capo Graziano.
The island, which is spectacular for walking and hiking and is still a truly
undiscovered, restful haven, has a handful of hotels and pensions, and
some families put up guests. Car ferries are available only in summer.

Where to Stay

★ **$$** 🏨 **La Canna.** Set on a height above the tiny port, this pension commands
fabulous views of sky and sea from its flower-filled terrace. It's won-
derful to wake up to the utter tranquillity that characterizes any stay
on this island. Rooms are small but adequate, kept clean and tidy by
the friendly family staff. The cooking is quite good, usually centered
around the day's catch (half or full board required in peak season). Arrange
ahead of time to be collected at the port. 🖂 *Via Rosa 43, 98050* ☎ *090/
9889956* 🖷*090/9889966* ⊕*www.lacannahotel.it* ⤴*10 rooms* ⚖*Restau-
rant, in-room safes, bar* 🖃 *MC, V* ❘◎❘ *MAP.*

Alicudi

42 *65 km (40 mi) west of Lipari, 3 hrs 25 mins–3 hrs 50 mins by ferry,
60–95 mins by hydrofoil; 102 km (68 mi) northwest of Milazzo.*

The farthest outpost of the Aeolians remains sparsely inhabited, wild, and at peace. Here and on Filicudi there is a tiny selection of accommodations, but you can rent rooms cheaply. Only the coming and going of hydrofoils (which run only occasionally, especially October–April) disturbs the rhythm of life here, and the only noise is the occasional braying of donkeys.

THE TYRRHENIAN COAST

Sicily's northern shore, the Tyrrhenian coast, is mostly a succession of small holiday towns interspersed with stretches of sand. It's often difficult to find a calm spot among the thousands of other tourists and locals in high summer, though the scene quiets down considerably after August. The biggest attraction is the old town of Cefalù, with one of Sicily's most remarkable medieval cathedrals, encrusted with mosaics. The coast on either side is dotted with ancient archaeological remains and Arab-Norman buildings. A couple of miles south of Cefalù, Pizzo Carbonara (6,500 feet) is the highest peak in Sicily after Mt. Etna. Piano della Battaglia has a fully equipped ski resort with lifts. The area has a very un-Sicilian aspect, with Swiss-type chalets, hiking paths, and even alpine churches.

Santo Stefano di Camastra

43 *128 km (80 mi) west of Messina, 104 km (65 mi) east of Palermo.*

When the original village of Santo Stefano di Camastra was destroyed in a landslide in 1682, the local duke, Giuseppe Lanza, rebuilt it on the coast according to strict military principles—a geometric street grid and artery roads connecting the center with the periphery. Today Santo Stefano is filled with the vividly colored pottery for which the town has an international reputation. For a comprehensive pottery education, drop in on the **Museo della Ceramica** in the center of town. ⊠ *Via Palazzo* ☎ *0921/331110* ᔕ *Free* ☉ *June–Sept., weekdays 9–1 and 4–8; Oct.–May, weekdays 9–1 and 3:30–7:30.*

Shopping
The Franco family has a long tradition of creating ceramic objets d'art by borrowing styles from past eras. Thus, Renaissance Madonnas rub shoulders with florid baroque vases, all richly colored and skillfully finished. Call ahead to visit their ceramic laboratory or the two outlets of **Ceramiche Franco** (⊠ *Via Nazionale 8* ☎ *0921/337222, 347/6004506 for reservations* ⊠ *Via Vittoria 4* ☎ *0921/339925*), as the stores don't have set hours.

Cefalù

★ **44** *33 km (20 mi) west of Santo Stefano di Camastra, 70 km (42 mi) east of Palermo.*

Cefalù is a classically appealing Sicilian old town built on a spur jutting out into the sea. It's dominated by a massive rock—*la rocca*—and a 12th-century Romanesque **Duomo**, one of the finest Norman cathedrals in Italy. Ruggero II began the church in 1131 as an offering of thanks for having been saved here from a shipwreck. Its mosaics rival those of Monreale; whereas Monreale's Byzantine Pantocratic Christ figure is an austere and powerful image, emphasizing Christ's divinity, the Cefalù Christ is softer, more compassionate, and more human. The traffic going in and out of Cefalù town can be heavy in summer; you may want to take the 50-minute train ride from Palermo instead of driving. At the Duomo you must be suitably attired—no shorts or beachwear are permitted. ⊠ *Piazza Duomo* ☎ *0921/922021* ⊘ *Daily 8–noon and 3:30–sunset.*

Where to Stay & Eat

$–$$$ ✕ **Al Porticciolo.** Nicola Mendolia's restaurant is comfortable, casual, and faithfully focused on the food. You might start with the *calamaretti piccoli fritti* (fried baby squid and octopus) and then follow with one of the chef's specials, which change weekly. Regardless, a refreshing *sgroppino* (whipped lemon sorbet with spumante) should end the meal. Dark, heavy, wooden tables create a comfortable environment filled with a mix of jovial locals and businesspeople. ⊠ *Via C. Ortolani di Bordonaro 66* ☎ *0921/921981* ▤ *AE, DC, MC, V* ⊘ *Closed Wed. Nov.–Apr. and 2 wks in Nov.*

$–$$ ✕ **Al Gabbiano.** Seagull is an appropriate name for a beachside seafood restaurant with a nautical theme. House specialties are *involtini di pesce spada* (swordfish roulades) and spaghetti marinara. ⊠ *Via Lungomare Giardina 17* ☎ *0921/421495* ▤ *AE, DC, MC, V* ⊘ *Closed Jan., weekdays Feb., and Wed. Sept.–June.*

★ **$$–$$$** ▦ **Baia del Capitano.** The whitewashed hotel with barrel-tile roofs blends into the rural surroundings of the peaceful area of Mazzaforno. The colorful gardens extending to the surrounding olive groves are an ideal setting for reading or an afternoon siesta in the shade. A good sandy beach is a short walk away. Large rooms have tile floors and some terraces. Half board is available. ⊠ *Contrada Mazzaforno, 90015 Mazzaforno, 5 km (3 mi) west of Cefalù* ☎ *0921/420003* 🖷 *0921/420163* ⊕ *www. baiadelcapitano.it* ⇆ *46 rooms* ⌂ *Restaurant, tennis court, pool, beach, Ping-Pong, bar, playground* ▤ *AE, DC, MC, V* ⊘ *Closed Nov.–Mar.* ⑩ *BP.*

$$–$$$ ▦ **Kalura.** Caldura, 2 km (1 mi) east along the coast, is the site of this modern hotel on a small promontory that's hard to reach without a car; it's only a few minutes by taxi from Cefalù, however. Sports facilities keep you from getting too sedentary, and the private beach is ideal for swimming. Rooms are bright and cheerful. Half board is required during July and August. ⊠ *Via V. Cavallaro 13, 90015 Località Caldura* ☎ *0921/ 421354* 🖷 *0921/423122* ⊕ *www.kalura.it* ⇆ *65 rooms* ⌂ *Restaurant, tennis court, pool, beach, bar* ▤ *AE, DC, MC, V* ⑩ *MAP.*

SICILY ESSENTIALS

Transportation

BY AIR

Sicily can be reached from all major international cities on flights connecting through Rome, Milan, or Naples on Alitalia. Meridiana, Air One, and Volare also connect Catania and Palermo to other cities all over Italy, and Alitalia operates periodic connections to Cagliari in Sardinia. There are also direct flights to Sicily from London on Meridiana and from Munich on Lufthansa. Note that domestic flights to and from Sicily, especially one-way flights, are much cheaper when purchased from travel agencies in Italy than internationally or through Web sites.

Planes to Palermo land at Aeroporto Falcone-Borsellino (named in memory of two anti-Mafia judges famously assassinated in 1992) in Punta Raisi, 32 km (19 mi) west of town. Catania's Aeroporto Fontanarossa, 5 km (3 mi) south of the city center, is the main airport on Sicily's eastern side.

🛫 Airport Information **Aeroporto Fontanarossa** ☎ 095/7239111 ⊕ www.aeroporto. catania.it. **Aeroporto Falcone-Borsellino** ☎ 091/591698 ⊕ www.gesap.it.

TRANSFERS Prestia & Comandè buses run every half hour between Palermo's Punta Raisi airport and the city center (Piazza Castelnuovo and the central station); tickets cost €4.80. Taxis charge around €35 for the same 45-minute trip. To get directly to the train station, take the hourly train leaving from the airport, Trinacria Express, which takes 40 minutes. There are also less frequent bus connections directly to and from Agrigento and Trapani on Sal and Segesta lines, respectively. Catania's Fontanarossa airport is served by Alibus, which leaves about every 20 minutes from the airport and the central train station, with stops at Piazza Stesicoro, on Via Etnea, the Duomo, etc. The journey takes around 25 minutes; tickets cost €1. Taxis cost around €20.

🚕 Taxis & Shuttles **Alibus** ☎ 095/7360450. **Prestia & Comandè** ☎ 091/580457 or 091/586351. **Sal Lines** ☎ 0922/401360 **Segesta Lines** ☎ 091/6167919 **Trinacria Express** ☎ 892021

BY BUS

Air-conditioned coaches connect major and minor cities and are often faster and more convenient than local trains but slightly more expensive. Various companies serve the different routes. SAIS runs frequently between Palermo and Catania, Messina, and Siracusa, in each case arriving at and departing from near the train stations. Cuffaro runs between Palermo and Agrigento. On the south and east coasts and in the interior, SAIS connects the main centers, including Catania, Agrigento, Enna, Taormina, and Siracusa. Etna Trasporti operates between Catania, Caltagirone, Piazza Armerina, and Taormina. Interbus serves the routes between Messina, Taormina, Catania, and Siracusa.

🚌 Bus Information **Cuffaro** ☎ 0922/403157 ⊕ www.cuffaro.it. **Etna Trasporti** ☎ 0935/ 532716 ⊕ www.etnatrasporti.it. **Interbus** ☎ 0935/565111 ⊕ www.interbus.it. **SAIS** ☎ 091/6166028 Palermo, 095/536168 Catania ⊕ www.saistrasporti.it.

BY BOAT & FERRY

Frequent car ferries cross the strait between Villa San Giovanni in Calabria and Messina on the island. The crossing usually takes about a half hour, but during the summer months there can be considerable delays. Overnight car ferries operated by Tirrenia run daily all year between Naples and Palermo. Tirrenia also runs regular service between Palermo and Cagliari, Sardinia, and between Trapani and Tunisia (in winter, frequency can be as low as once per week). SNAV has a daytime service (April–October) by faster catamarans, which also carry vehicles. Passenger-only hydrofoils also cross the strait from Reggio di Calabria to Messina in about 15 minutes. Grimaldi Lines' Grandi Navi Veloci run beautiful cruise ship–like ferries to Genoa (a 20-hour trip) year-round. The Aeolian Islands are reachable by hydrofoil from Naples, Messina, Palermo, and Milazzo. From Milazzo you can get ferry service to the islands. Call SNAV or Siremar, the other major ferry company serving the Aeolians.

Boat & Ferry Information **Grandi Navi Veloci** ☎ 091/587404 in Palermo ⊕ www1. gnv.it. **Siremar** ☎ 199123199 ⊕ www.siremar.it. **SNAV** ☎ 091/6317900 Palermo, 081/ 4285555 Naples ⊕ www.snav.it. **Tirrenia** ☎ 081/3172999 ⊕ www.gruppotirrenia.it.

BY CAR

This is the ideal way to explore Sicily. Modern highways circle and bisect the island, making all main cities easily reachable. A20 (supplemented by S113 at points) connects Messina and Palermo; Messina and Catania are linked by A18; running through the interior, from Catania to west of Cefalù, is A19; threading west from Palermo, A29 runs to Trapani and the airport, with a leg stretching down to Mazara del Vallo. The *superstrada* (highway) SS115 runs along the southern coast, and connecting superstrade lace the island.

You will likely hear stories about the dangers of driving in Sicily. Some are true, and others less so. In the big cities—especially Palermo, Catania, and Messina—streets are a honking mess, with lane markings and traffic lights taken as mere suggestions; you can avoid the chaos by leaving your car in a garage. However, once outside the urban areas, autostrade, superstrade, and regional state roads turn into a driving enthusiast's dream—they are winding, sparsely populated, and well paved and maintained, and they usually reveal a new, stunning view around every bend.

RULES OF THE ROAD Sicilians, especially in Palermo, are among the country's most aggressive drivers. Traffic lights are taken with a grain of salt, and many large intersections are just games of chicken—you'll sit all day if you don't lurch out at some point. Do keep your eye out for all-important yield signs, which can be easy to miss but often take the place of stop signs or stoplights. People within earshot routinely double-park—if you're blocked in, don't worry, just start honking and the owner will come move his car (and then, of course, take your space).

BY TRAIN

There are direct express trains from Milan and Rome to Palermo, Catania, and Siracusa. The Rome–Palermo and Rome–Siracusa trips take at least 10 hours. After Naples, the run is mostly along the coast, so try to book a window seat on the right if you're not on an overnight train. At Villa San Giovanni, in Calabria, the train is separated and loaded onto a ferryboat to cross the strait to Messina.

With Sicily, main lines connect Messina, Taormina, Siracusa, and Palermo. Secondary lines are generally very slow and unreliable. The Messina–Palermo run, along the northern coast, is especially scenic.

Train Information **FS (Italian State Railways)** ☎ 892021 ⊕ www.trenitalia.com.

Contacts & Resources

EMERGENCIES
🚑 **Ambulance, Police, Fire** ☎ 113. **Hospital** ☎ 091/288141 Palermo, 095/7591111 Catania.

INTERNET
🖥 Internet Shops **Internet Shop** ✉ Via Napoli 32/34, Kalsa, Palermo ☎ 091/320697). **Aboriginal Internet Cafe** ✉ Via S. Spinuzza 51, Teatro Massimo area, Palermo ☎ 091/6622229 ⊕ www.aboriginalcafe.com.

TOURS
Tours of Palermo and Monreale are provided by the Italian tour operator CST on Friday afternoon and Saturday morning, with pickups from your hotel or a central location such as outside the Politeama theater. Contact the agency to confirm details. CST also arranges tours of Taormina and Etna, bookable from their office in Taormina, as well as to Piazza Armerina, Agrigento, and western Sicily, or you can join a seven-day tour of all Sicily's major sights in a comfortable air-conditioned coach with an English-speaking guide, with weekly departures from either Palermo or Catania; the cost includes all meals and accommodations in luxury hotels.

🖥 Fees & Schedules **CST** ✉ Via E. Amari 124, Palermo ☎ 091/7439655 ⊕ www.compagniasicilianaturismo.it ✉ Corso Umberto 101, Taormina ☎ 0942/24189.

VISITOR INFORMATION
🖥 Tourist Information **Acireale** ✉ Via Oreste Scionti 15, 95024 ☎ 095/892129. **Agrigento** ✉ Viale della Vittoria 225, 92100 ☎ 0922/401352 ✉ Via Cesare Battisti 15, 92100 ☎ 0922/20454. **Caltagirone** ✉ Via Duomo 7, 95041 ☎ 0933/34191 ⊕ www.comune.caltagirone.ct.it/turismo2.htm. **Caltanissetta** ✉ Corso Vittorio Emanuele 109, 93100 ☎ 0934/530411 ⊕ www.aapit.cl.it. **Catania** ✉ Via Cimarosa 10, 95124 ☎ 095/7306211 ⊕ www.apt.catania.it ✉ Stazione Centrale, 95129 ☎ 095/7306255 ✉ Aeroporto Fontanarossa, 95121 ☎ 095/7306266. **Cefalù** ✉ Corso Ruggero 77, 90015 ☎ 0921/421050 ⊕ www.cefalu-tour.pa.it. **Enna** ✉ Via Roma 411, 94100 ☎ 0935/528228 ⊕ www.apt-enna.com. **Erice** ✉ Via Conte Pepoli 56, 91016 ☎ 0923/869388. **Lipari** ✉ Corso Vittorio Emanuele 202, 98055 ☎ 090/9880095. **Marsala** ✉ Via XI Maggio 100, 91025 ☎ 0923/714097. **Messina** ✉ Piazza della Repubblica, 98122 ☎ 090/672944 ✉ Via Calabria 301bis, 98123 ☎ 090/674236 ⊕ www.azienturismomessina.it. **Monreale** ✉ Piazza Duomo, 90046 ☎ 091/6564570. **Noto** ✉ Piazzale XVI Maggio, 96017 ☎ 0931/836744. **Palermo** ✉ Piazza Castelnuovo 34, 90141 ☎ 091/583847 ⊕ www.palermotourism.com ✉ Stazione Centrale, Piazza Giulio Cesare, 90141 ☎ 091/6165914 ✉ Aeroporto Falcone-Borsellino, 90045 ☎ 091/591698. **Piazza Armerina** ✉ Via Cavour 15, 94015 ☎ 0935/680201. **Siracusa** ✉ Via San Sebastiano 43, 96100 ☎ 0931/481200 ⊕ www.apt-siracusa.it ✉ Via Maestranza 33, 96100 ☎ 0931/464255. **Taormina** ✉ Palazzo Corvaja, Largo Santa Caterina, 98039 ☎ 0942/23243 ⊕ www.gate2taormina.com. **Trapani** ✉ Piazza Saturno, 91100 ☎ 0923/29000 ⊕ www.apt.trapani.it.

Sardinia

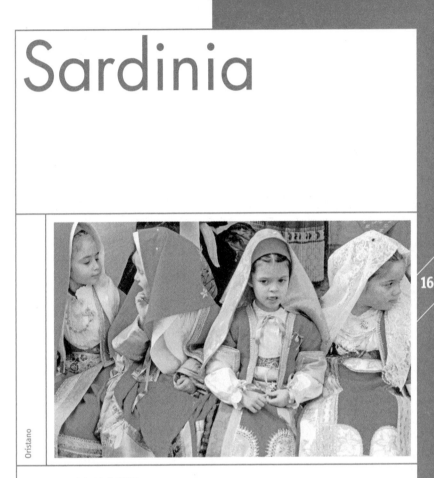

Oristano

WORD OF MOUTH

"All in all I loved Sardinia. It's a totally different experience from other areas I've been to in Italy. The itinerary wasn't so driven by historical sites as it was by beaches, towns, and just plain gorgeous scenery."

—AP6380

WELCOME TO SARDINIA

Alghero

TOP 5
Reasons to Go

1 **Su Nuraxi:** This UNESCO World Heritage Site is the most impressive of Sardinia's enigmatic *nuraghi* (bronze-age stone fortresses).

2 **Grotta di Nettuno:** Near Alghero, a wonderland of sea-soaked stalactites and stalagmites awaits visitors arriving by water or down an infamously steep stairway along the limestone cliffs.

3 **Cagliari's Museo Archeologico:** The artifacts here from the island's nuraghi are the only clues to the mysterious prehistoric people who built them.

4 **Nora:** These partially submerged (but otherwise well-preserved) ruins near Pula were first settled as a Phoenician port and later built up by the Carthaginians and Romans.

5 **Porto Cervo:** Even if you can't bring your own 100-foot yacht, you still may be able to splurge on one of the exclusive hotels here and sunbathe on some of Europe's most expensive sand.

Getting Oriented

Sardinia is a world apart from the rest of Italy. It's the second largest island in the Mediterranean—just smaller than Sicily—and its landscape closely resembles that of Corsica, 16 km (10 mi) to the north, with miles of untamed beaches and a rugged, mountainous inland. There's little sophistication in Sardinia, aside from the opulence of the Costa Smeralda, the island's outpost for the rich and famous.

Su Nuraxi   Cathedral, Cagliari   Ruins at Nora

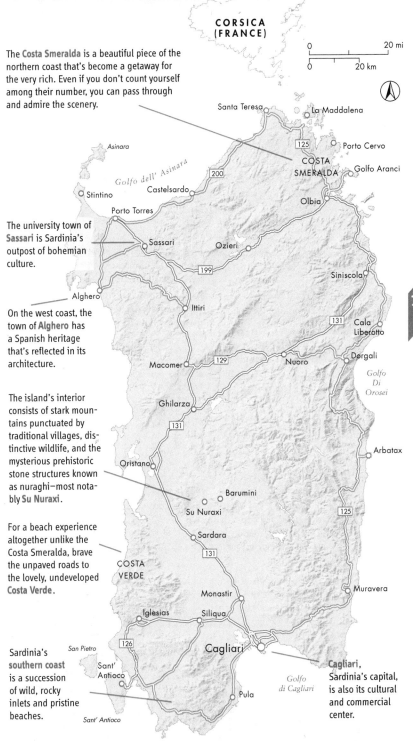

CORSICA (FRANCE)

0   20 mi
0   20 km

The **Costa Smeralda** is a beautiful piece of the northern coast that's become a getaway for the very rich. Even if you don't count yourself among their number, you can pass through and admire the scenery.

The university town of **Sassari** is Sardinia's outpost of bohemian culture.

On the west coast, the town of **Alghero** has a Spanish heritage that's reflected in its architecture.

The island's interior consists of stark mountains punctuated by traditional villages, distinctive wildlife, and the mysterious prehistoric stone structures known as nuraghi—most notably **Su Nuraxi**.

For a beach experience altogether unlike the Costa Smeralda, brave the unpaved roads to the lovely, undeveloped **Costa Verde**.

Sardinia's **southern coast** is a succession of wild, rocky inlets and pristine beaches.

Cagliari, Sardinia's capital, is also its cultural and commercial center.

Asinara

Golfo dell' Asinara

Santa Teresa   La Maddalena

125   Porto Cervo

COSTA SMERALDA   Golfo Aranci

Stintino

200

Castelsardo

Porto Torres

Olbia

Sassari   Ozieri

199

Siniscola

Alghero

Ittiri

131   Cala Liberotto

Macomer   129   Nuoro   Dorgali

Golfo Di Orosei

Ghilarza

131

Oristano

Arbatax

Barumini

Su Nuraxi

125

Sardara

131

COSTA VERDE

Monastir

Muravera

Iglesias   Siliqua

San Pietro

126

Sant' Antioco

Cagliari

Golfo di Cagliari

Pula

Sant' Antioco

16

SARDINIA PLANNER

Making the Most of Your Time

Cagliari is a popular point of entry for visitors to Sardinia and makes an excellent base for a general island tour. Its archaeological museum has the island's best antiquities collection, and both the ruins at Nora and the wild, deserted Costa Verde are nearby. Oristano is a good base for exploring the interior region's villages, wildlife, and ruins; the fortress at Su Nuraxi is an easy trip from either Cagliari or Oristano.

Though crowded in summer, the coastal beach and resort towns are ideal retreats in spring and fall; relax in luxury in Porto Cervo, or head to the southern coast for a less pricey alternative. On the western shoreline, near Alghero, the Grotto di Nettuno sits below the dramatic headlands of Capo Caccia, waiting to be explored.

Finding a Place to Stay

The Costa Smeralda has the most posh and costly hotels—not just on the island, but in all of Italy. Other resort areas are more affordable. Most lodgings on the coast shut down from October through April. Small-town hotels have basic accommodations, restrained but genuine hospitality, and low rates. Hotels of any vintage are hard to find inland.

Dining & Lodging Price Categories

WHAT IT COSTS in Euros					
	$$$$	$$$	$$	$	¢
Restaurants	over €22	€16–€22	€11–€16	€7–€11	under €7
Hotels	over €220	€160–€220	€110–€160	€70–€110	under €70

Restaurant prices are for a second course (un secondo). Hotel prices are for two people in a standard double room in high season, including tax and service.

Getting Around

You need a car if you want to explore the island. Smaller roads often provide better views and give you a better sense of place. Cagliari is the public transit hub, with bus or train service to most larger towns. For details about transportation, see "Essentials" at the end of this chapter.

Speaking the Language

The Sard language is incomprehensible to mainland Italians, let alone to foreigners, but most locals can switch from Sardinian to perfect Italian with ease. In the main tourist areas, most people you deal with will speak some English, though often less than elsewhere in Italy.

TOP PASSEGGIATA

Just off the western coast, the appealing town of Oristano has a vibrant predinner stroll with a family-friendly spirit.

How's the Weather?

Try to avoid the coastal resorts in steamy August, when they're swamped not only with tourists but also with locals on their annual break. May and September are much quieter and still temperate; the sea remains warm enough for swimming well into October. The mild spring and fall weather is also ideal for inland travel; from November through February the maestrale (winter winds) are fierce, and it snows most years in the Barbagia region. Quiet towns like Oristano and Sassari are pleasant stops any time of year.

Updated by
Ryan Bradley

AN UNCUT JEWEL OF AN ISLAND, Sardinia remains unique and enigmatic. Would-be conquerors from all directions—Phoenicians, Carthaginians, Romans, Catalans, Pisans, Piemontese—have left their marks, but no single outside culture has had a dominant impact. Pockets of foreign influence persist along the coasts (for example, the walled Catalan city of Alghero), but inland, a proud Sard culture and language flourish.

Sardinia's identity as a travel destination is split: the island has some of Europe's most expensive resorts, but it's also home to areas as rugged and undeveloped as anywhere on the continent. Fine sand, clean waters, and relative lack of crowds draw summer sun-seekers to beaches that are unquestionably among the best in the Mediterranean. Best known are those along the Costa Smeralda (Emerald Coast), where the super-rich have anchored their yachts since the 1960s. Less exclusive beach holidays can be found elsewhere on the island at La Maddalena, Villasimius, and Pula. There are also wonderfully undertouristed medieval towns—Cagliari, Oristano, Sassari—on or near the water.

But most of the coast is unsettled, a jagged series of wildly beautiful inlets accessible only by sea. And inland, Sardinia remains shepherd's country, silent and stark. Spaghetti Westerns were once filmed here, and it's not hard to imagine why: the desolate mountainous terrain seems the perfect frontier set, and the towns, such as Nuoro, have an air of deliberate provinciality. Against this landscape are the striking and mysterious stone *nuraghi* (ancient defensive structures), which provide clues to the lifestyles of the island's prehistoric peoples.

16

CAGLIARI & THE SOUTHERN COAST

Cagliari (pronounced *Cahl*-yah-ree) is Sardinia's capital and largest city; it contains the island's principal art and archaeology museums as well as an old cathedral and medieval towers that have lofty views of the surrounding sea, lagoons, and mountains. East of Cagliari the coast is no less scenic, but it's more built up; though blissfully uncommercialized for the most part, the coast does have pockets of development that have sprouted as tourism has found a niche. To the southwest, Pula is an inland town within easy reach of both good beaches and the excavated ruins at Nora. Swaths of eucalyptus and lush pine groves artfully conceal hotels at Santa Margherita di Pula, one of Sardinia's most luxurious holiday enclaves. South and west of Santa Margherita, the protected coast contains few beaches but does have jaw-dropping vistas unspoiled by construction.

Cagliari

❶ *268 km (166 mi) south of Olbia.*

The island's capital has steep streets and impressive Italianate architecture and churches in differing styles. Cagliari is characterized by its busy commercial center and waterfront with broad avenues, as well as by the typically narrow streets of the old hilltop citadel (called, simply, *Castello*). An ongoing revitalization effort has restored the nobility of several me-

SARDINIA, PAST & PRESENT

A Phoenician stronghold in ancient times and later a Spanish dominion, Sardinia doesn't seem typically Italian in its color and flavor. It was a bit too far from imperial and papal Rome, and from the palaces of the Savoy dynasty, to have been transformed by the events that forged the national character of the mainland. Yet Giuseppe Garibaldi, the charismatic national hero who led his troops in fervid campaigns to unify Italy in the mid-19th century, chose to spend his last years in relative isolation on the small island of Caprera, just off the coast of Sardinia. Later political leaders such as Antonio Gramsci and Francesco Cossiga, and such radical parties as the still-strong Partito Sardo d'Azione, have advocated Sardinian independence. It is one of the few regions that retains semi-autonomous political status.

Sardinians are courteous but remote, often favoring their forbidding regional language over Italian. In hamlets, women swathed in black shawls and long, full skirts look with suspicion upon strangers passing through. Like mainland Italians, the Sardinians are of varied origin. On the northwest coast, fine traceries of ironwork around balconies underscore the Spanish influence. In the northeast, the inhabitants have Genoese or Pisan ancestry, and the headlands display the ruined fortresses of the ancient Pisan duchy of Malaspina. As you explore the southern coast, you come upon the features, customs, dialects, place names, and holy buildings of the Turks, Moors, Phoenicians, Austrians, and mainland Italians. If there are any pure Sardinians—or Sards—left, perhaps they can be found in the south-central mountains, south of Nuoro, under the 6,000-foot crests of the Gennargentu Massif, in the rugged country still called, ironically, Barbagia, "Land of Strangers."

dieval landmarks, but has done little to alter the appealingly dilapidated feel of the old town. Medieval Spanish conquerors from Aragon as well as Pisans and Piemontese all left their marks, and grand, decaying castles, floodlit by night, overlook the old center's winding streets and bustling port from far above.

Begin your visit at the **Museo Archeologico,** within the walls of a castle erected by Pisans in the early 1300s to ward off the Aragonese and Catalans (attacking from what is now Spain). Among the intriguing artifacts are bronze statuettes from the tombs and dwellings of Sardinia's earliest inhabitants, who remain a prehistoric enigma. Ancient writers called them the nuraghic people, from the name of their curious stone dwellings, the nuraghi, which are unique to Sardinia. Archaeologists date most of the nuraghi to about 1300–1200 BC, the same time the ancient Israelites were establishing themselves in Canaan. ⊠ *Cittadella dei Musei, Piazza Arsenale* ☎ *070/684000* 🕮 *€4* 🕘 *Tues.–Sun. 9–7:15.*

The 1305 **Torre di San Pancrazio,** part of the imposing medieval Pisan defenses, is just outside Cagliari's archaeological museum, and it marks the edge of the Castello district. You can climb up the tower for a fabulous panorama of the city and its surroundings. Curiously enough, the tower's back wall is missing, which allows you to see the series of wooden stairs and landings inside without climbing a step. ⊠ *Piazza Indipendenza* ☎ *070/41108* ⊟ *€2* ⏱ *Tues.–Sun. 9–1 and 3:30–7:30.*

Torre dell'Elefante, twin to the tower of San Pancrazio, stands at the seaward end of Cagliari's bastions. Built in 1307, it was used as a prison in the 1800s. ⊠ *Via Università* ☎ *070/659674* ⊟ *€2* ⏱ *Apr.–Sept., Tues.–Sun. 9–1 and 3:30–7:30; Oct.–Mar., Tues.–Sun. 9–4:30.*

Cattedrale di Santa Maria, also known as the **Duomo,** was originally constructed in the 17th century, but the look was changed during construction in the mid-1930s. The tiers of columns on the facade resemble those of medieval Romanesque Pisan churches, but only the central portal is an authentic relic of that era. ⊠ *Piazza Palazzo, off Via Martini* ☎ *070/ 663837* ⏱ *Daily 8–noon and 4–8.*

On the narrow streets of the **Castello,** the quarter below the Duomo, humble dwellings still open directly onto the sidewalk and the wash is hung out to dry on elaborate wrought-iron balconies.

The **Terrazza Umberto I** is a monumental neoclassical staircase and arcade added in the 19th century to the Bastion of St. Remy (built by the Spaniards 400 years earlier). It has long been covered by graffiti, but a massive, years-long restoration is under way. ⊠ *Piazza Costituzione.*

The **Anfiteatro Romano** dates from the 2nd century AD. The well-preserved amphitheater arena—complete with underground passages and a beasts' pit—is evidence of the importance of this Roman outpost. ⊠ *Viale Fra' Ignazio* ☎ *070/652956* ⊟ *€3.30* ⏱ *Apr.–Oct., daily 10–1 and 3–6; Nov.–Mar., daily 10–4.*

off the beaten path	**SAN SPERATE –** Walls throughout this small town 20 km (12 mi) north of Cagliari have been brightened with *murales* (murals) by local artists and some well-known Italian painters. The murals were begun in 1968 and continue to be expanded upon today, transforming the entire town into an open-air art gallery.

Where to Stay & Eat

$$$–$$$$
Fodor's Choice
★

✕ **S'Apposentu.** Informed by his studies in Corsica and mainland France, young chef Roberto Petza has quietly created a new model of Sardinian cuisine, one deeply entrenched in the ingredients of his native island. Petza's otherworldly creations might include a stunning plate of *lasagnette* (thin, flat noodles) with San Gavino saffron, sausage, and local ricotta; spectacular Sardinian *agnellino* (baby lamb); or roast pigeon with a sauce made from white vernaccia wine and *mirto,* a local digestive. The stage is a soaring, ultramodern space—even the place settings are cutting-edge—that is lovingly set in Cagliari's opera house, the Teatro Lirico. ⊠ *Teatro Lirico di Cagliari, Via Sant'Alenixedda* ☎ *070/4082315* ⚐ *Reservations essential* ▤ *AE, DC, MC, V* ⏱ *Closed Mon. No dinner Sun.*

$$$
✕ **Dal Corsaro.** This formal restaurant near the port is one of the island's most recommended, so make reservations. The interior is refined, the welcome cordial. The menu includes fish and meat, with such dishes as

16

seafood antipasto and *porcheddu* (roast suckling pig). At various unpredictable times each year—always including August—the restaurant opens a branch at the seaside. ☒ *Viale Regina Margherita 28* ☎ *070/664318* ☒ *Marina Piccola* ☎ *070/370295* ⚓ *Reservations essential* ☰ *AE, DC, MC, V* ☉ *Closed Sun. and Dec. 23–Jan. 10.*

¢–$ ✗ **Antico Caffè** The gilded Antico Caffè has anchored the base of Terrazza Umberto I since 1855, serving as a social center from breakfast until well after midnight. A daily set menu (€12) lists local specialties like *burrida* (marinated dogfish) and the pastas and salads are reliable à la carte choices. Desserts are the real attraction here: try the flavorful *crema catalana* (crème caramel) or one of the elaborate ice cream conconctions. ☒ *Piazza Costituzione 10* ☎ *070/658206* ☰ *AE, MC, V* ☉ *Closed Tues.*

$$ ▦ **Panorama.** The exterior is nondescript, but this hotel just outside downtown Cagliari is geared to the business class—with high-speed Internet connections in the rooms and modern, functional furnishings. Rooms are spacious; try to reserve one on the higher of the nine floors to better enjoy the view over the harbor and bay. There's also a bar with—appropriately enough—a panoramic view on the top floor. ☒ *Viale Armando Diaz 231, 09126* ☎ *070/307691* 📠 *070/305413* ⊕ *www.hotelpanorama.it* ⇆ *64 rooms, 28 suites* ♨ *Restaurant, café, minibars, cable TV, pool, bar, Internet, meeting room* ☰ *AE, DC, MC, V* ¶◎¶ *BP.*

$ ▦ **AeR Bundes Jack.** Courtyard-facing rooms and simple furnishings make this central *secondo piano* (third-floor) pension cozy. Expect polite, friendly service. And yes, there's an elevator. The port is directly opposite the unprepossessing entrance under the arcades of Via Roma, with its entertaining parade of shops and sit-down bars. Bus and train stations are steps away. ☒ *Via Roma 75, 09100* ☎🖷 *070/657970* ✉ *hotel.aerbundesjack@libero.it* ⇆ *14 rooms, 7 with bath* ♨ *Bar* ☰ *No credit cards* ¶◎¶ *BP.*

Nightlife & the Arts

Cagliari's university stages concerts throughout the academic year; contact the tourist office for information.

Thousands of costumed villagers, many of them on horseback, parade through town during Sardinia's greatest annual festival, the **Festa di Sant'Efisio** (May 1–4). It's part of a four-day procession from Cagliari to Nora and back again, and it's a good chance to take part in a centuries-old event.

CAFÉS The **Libarium Nostrum** (☒ Bastioni di Santa Croce ☎ 070/650943) might well be the coolest café-bar in Sardinia: it's a dim, bohemian haunt full of nooks, crannies, wood beams, and castle walls. Contemporary art, electronic music, and a kitchen open until midnight attract university students to **Ritual's Cafe** (☒ Via Università 33 ☎ 070/652071). The central **Caffe dell'Elfo** (☒ Salita Santa Chiara 4/6 ☎ 070/682399) is favored by local professionals who linger over wine and conversation. The terrace of **Caffe de Candia** (☒ Via Maria de Candia ☎ 070/655884), built directly into the castle walls near Terrazzo Umberto I, catches the afternoon sun—it's a great place to enjoy wine or coffee after exploring the Castello quarter.

Sardinia

CORSICA
(FRANCE)

0   30 miles

0   45 km

TO GENOA

TO LIVORNO

TO TOULON
MARSEILLE

Bonifacio

**Santa Teresa
di Gallura**

La Maddalena

15   Costa Smeralda

Caprera

TO GENOA,
LIVORNO,
CIVITAVECCHIA

14   Palau

Baia Sardinia

16   **Porto Cervo**

Arzachena

Isola
Asinara

*Golfo dell'
Asinara*

Stintino

Porto Rotondo

18   **Golfo Aranci**

Castelsardo

Porto Torres

Sassari

13

Anghelu
Ruiu

Capo Caccia

12   **Alghero**

**Grotta di
Nettuno**

SS200

SS133

SS127

Oschiri

SS199

Olbia 17

Ozieri

SS597

SS125

Siniscola

ITALY

Bosa   Macomer

SS129

SS131

Mt. Ortobene

SS129

Nuoro 10

Dorgali

Cala
Gonone

Oliena

*Cala
di
Luna*

*Golfo
di
Orosei*

SS131 Dir

Orgosolo

Lago
Omodeo

Fonni 11

Cala Sisine

Mt. Spada

Sorgono

Tonara

Baunei

Bruncu Spina

San
Salvatore

*Monti del
Gennargentu*

Arbatax

**San Giovanni
di Sinis**

9

Cabras

Aritzo

Tharros

8   **Oristano**

**Giara di
Gesturi** 7

BARBAGIA

Arborea

Isili

Su Nuraxi 6

Barumini

Lago di
Flumendosa

**Costa
Verde** 5

SS126

Guspini

Mandas

Rio Flumendosa

SS125

Ingurtosu

CAMPIDANO PLAIN

**Grotta di
San Giovanni**

Iglesias

Carloforte

Capo
Sandalo

Portoscuso

Domusnovas

San Sperate

SS130

Mt. Sirai

Strada Carlo Felice

Carbonia

**San
Pietro**

4

Calasetta

SS196

3

Sant'Antioco

Pula

2

1   **Cagliari**

*Costa
Rei*

Villasimius

SS195

♦ **Nora**

*Golfo
di
Cagliari*

Capo
Boi

Capo
Carbonara

Teulada

Santa
Margherita
di Pula

TO CIVITAVECCHIA

TO NAPLES

TO GENOA, LIVORNO

TO GENOA

TO MALTA

TO TUNIS

TO PALERMO

Mediterranean   Sea

Shopping

Cagliari's two best shopping streets, full of boutiques, clothing stores, and such, are Via Manno and Via Garibaldi, just up from the port. **ISOLA** (✉ Via Bacaredda 176 ☎ 070/492756 ✉ Via Santa Croce 34 ☎ 070/651488) is a government-sponsored exhibition of artisan crafts; most of the work is for sale.

Sports

The **Lega Navale Italiana** (✉ Marina Piccola ☎ 070/370380 ⊕ www.leganavale.it) has information on the island's sailing facilities. Sardinia has some of the best windsurfing spots in Europe; the **Windsurfing Club Cagliari** (✉ Marina Piccola ☎ 070/380918) can provide advice to beginners and experts alike.

> **en route**   Driving east from Cagliari takes you through some dismal industrial suburbs on the road that leads to the scenic coast and beaches of Capo Boi and Capo Carbonara. **Villasimius,** 50 km (31 mi) east of Cagliari, is the chief resort here; the beautiful beaches lie a couple of miles north of the town center, on the golden sands of the Costa Rei.

Pula

❷ *29 km (18 mi) southwest of Cagliari, 314 km (195 mi) southwest of Olbia.*

Resort villages sprawl along the coast southwest of the capital, which has its share of fine scenery and good beaches. On the marshy shoreline between Cagliari's Aeroporto di Elmas and Pula, huge flocks of flamingos are a common sight. From Cagliari, first follow the S195 toward Teulada, then take the turnoff for Pula at Km 27. Nora is the headland south of Pula that has a rich Roman archeological site.

Beaches, and lodging catering to summer crowds, are concentrated 4 km (2½ mi) south of Pula, a little more than 1½ km (1 mi) south of Nora, in a conglomeration that makes up the town of Santa Margherita di Pula.

The small **Museo Archeologico Comunale** has archaeological finds from excavations of a site at Nora, including amphoras, anchors, and inscribed stones, mostly dredged up from the sea. ✉ *Corso Vittorio Emanuele 67* ☎ *070/92440315* ✍ *€2.50, €5.50 including archaeological site at Nora* ⊙ *Daily 9–8.*

★ The narrow promontory outside Pula, **Nora,** was the site of a Phoenician, then Carthaginian, and later a Roman settlement. An old Roman road passes the moss-covered ruins of temples, an amphitheater, and a small Roman theater. Nora was a prime location—the Phoenicians scouted for good harbors, cliffs to shelter their craft from the wind, and an elevation from which they could defend themselves against attack. Extensive excavations have shed light on life in this ancient city from the 8th century BC onward. You can make out the channels through which hot air rose to warm the Roman baths; note the difference between the Carthaginians' simple mosaic pavements and the Romans' more elaborate designs. If the sea is calm, look under the clear waters along the

EATING WELL IN SARDINIA

Sardinian cuisine is sharply divided between hearty, meat-based dishes from the interior and Mediterranean seafood fare with Catalan and North African influences along the coast. Meat dishes are most commonly veal, roast *agnello* (lamb) and *agnellino* (baby lamb), or *porcheddu* (roast suckling pig, most often available at Easter). *Cavallo*, or *carne equino* (horsemeat), is also a common specialty of Sardinia; it's generally served in the form of a *bistecca* (thin steak), which can be a bit chewy, but when properly grilled, also intensely flavored and delicious. Homemade pastas might be topped with a wild boar sauce. Finally, Italy's original, and best, pecorino cheese, made from sheep's milk, comes from the rugged slopes of the interior.

Langouste or *aragosta* (lobster) is a seafood specialty of the northern coast that can get pricey. Looking for the unusual? Try the *ricci* (sea urchins), which, unlike the Japanese

uni, are served atop pasta. *Bottarga,* another prized Sardinian product, is a dried, cured tuna roe that's best when shaved off a block directly onto spaghetti or with butter on *crostini* (thin slices of toasted bread). Foreign conquerors left their legacies of bouillabaisse (known here as *zimino*), paella, and *cuscus* (couscous), also called *cashkà*.

Native pastas include *malloreddus* (small shells of bran pasta sometimes flavored with saffron), *culurgiones* (the Sardinian version of ravioli), and *maccarones de busa* (thick pasta twists). And crispy bread called *pane carasau* (*carta di musica* in Italian) is typical island fare. Prized around Italy, and around the world, is Sardinia's *amaro di corbezzolo*, a honey with a bouquet and taste primordially foresty, slightly bitter, and dazzlingly complex. It's made by bees that suck nectar from a plant known as *arbutus*, the tree strawberry.

16

shore for more ruins of the ancient city, submerged by earthquakes, rough seas, and erosion. Guided tours begin on the hour. ✉ *3 km (2 mi) south of Pula* ☎ *070/9209138* 🎫 *€5.50, including Museo Archeologico Comunale* ⊘ *Daily 9–7:30.*

Sant'Efisio, the little Romanesque church at the base of the Nora promontory, plays a part in one of the island's most colorful annual events. A four-day procession during the Festa di Sant'Efisio accompanies a statue of the saint all the way from Cagliari and back again, culminating in a huge parade down Cagliari's main avenue. If you're in Sardinia from May 1 to May 4, don't miss it. ✉ *3 km (2 mi) south of Pula* ☎ *070/ 9208473* ⊘ *Apr.–Sept., Sat. 3–6 and Sun. 9:30–1 and 3–7:30; Oct.–Mar., Sun. 9:30–noon and 3–5.*

Where to Stay

$$$$ 🏨 **Flamingo.** Eucalyptus trees surround the main building and the six two-story cottages of this shady beachside resort hotel. Balconied rooms are light and airy, overlooking park or sea. Sports facilities abound, and the outdoor pool is open late into the night—a welcome treat in the balmy summer. ✉ *4 km (2½ mi) south of Pula, 09010 Santa Margherita di Pula*

☎ 070/9208361 🖷 070/9208359 ⊕ *www.hotelflamingo.it* 🖵 *134 rooms* ⬧ *Restaurant, minibars, miniature golf, tennis court, pool, beach, dive shop, windsurfing, piano bar, dance club* 🖃 *AE* ⊘ *Closed Nov.–Apr. 15* ⬧⬧ *BP.*

Sports
The 18-hole **Is Molas** (🖃 Santa Margherita di Pula ☎ 070/9241014 ⊕ www. ismolas.it) has won tributes from Tom Watson and Jack Nicklaus.

Sant'Antioco

❸ *75 km (47 mi) west of Pula, 100 km (62 mi) west of Cagliari.*

Off Sardinia's southwest coast is the sleepy island of Sant'Antioco—the most hectic activity seems to be the silent repairing of nets by local fishermen who have already pulled in their daily catch. It has become a popular holiday spot because of good beaches. The island has been connected to the mainland since Roman times by a still-standing causeway (the modern causeway that you traverse runs parallel).

Before leaving the main town, also called Sant'Antioco, take time to visit the **Zona Archeologica** at the top of the old section, which has terrific views of the Sardinian mainland. Here you can see a Punic necropolis and a burial site scattered with urns that contained the cremated remains of stillborn children. Admission includes a guided tour and entry to the onsite ethnographic and archaeological museums. 🖃 *Sant'Antioco* 🖃 *€5* ⊘ *Apr.–Sept., daily 9–1 and 3:30–7; Oct.–Mar., daily 9–1 and 3–6.*

Also of note on the island is the tiny fishing village of **Calasetta**. Its name literally means "silk cove," and it was from a villa outside this town that generations of an Armenian silk-trading family once supported much of the island's economy. 🖃 *10 km (6 mi) northeast of Sant'Antioco town.*

San Pietro

❹ *5 km (3 mi) northwest of Sant'Antioco.*

A ferry at the small northern port of Calasetta connects Sant'Antioco with Carloforte, the main town on the smaller island of San Pietro. This classic little Italian port village and its surrounding coastline are a favorite of wealthy Cagliarians, many of whom have built weekend cottages here. The best views are from Capo Sandalo, on San Pietro's rugged western coast, but head to the island's southern tip for the beaches. During daylight hours the ferry departs every 20 minutes in summer and every 30 in winter—the trip takes 20 minutes.

WORD OF MOUTH

"Unfortunately, too many travelers make the mistake of focusing on the Costa Smeralda area, which is *least* representative of Sardinia. By contrast, there are numerous interesting towns in the hinterland which are worth visiting, lovely medieval basilicas scattered about the lonely countryside, as well as beautiful Roman ruins along the coasts."   –gac

Where to Stay

$ ⊡ **Hieracon.** An art nouveau building with modern whitewashed rooms sits on the harbor in Carloforte. A few palm trees grow in the small courtyard garden near the bungalow-style apartments. Try to get a front-facing room for a harbor view, though there may be some traffic noise. Avoid rooms at the top, which have low ceilings and no view. The central location means that you're a short walk from some good restaurants. ⊠ *Via Cavour 63, 09014 Carloforte* ☎*0781/854028* 🖷*0781/854893* ✎*hotel-hieracon@tiscali.it* ➭ *17 rooms, 7 apartments* ♨ *Restaurant, some kitchenettes, minibars, bar* ▭ *AE, MC, V* ⭗❘ *BP.*

Costa Verde

❺ *35 km (22 mi) northwest of San Pietro, 80 km (50 mi) northwest of Cagliari.*

If you've come to Sardinia in search of untrammeled wilderness and sweeping sands as far as the eye can see, then this deserted coast is the place to find them. Hidden away in the forgotten southwest corner of Cagliari province, the Costa Verde is accessible only by a bumpy, unpaved track. The effort is worth it. The dune-backed sands shelter rare grasses and birdlife, as well as providing magnificent swimming.

You can approach the coast either from the town of Guspini, on the straggling S126, or from a turnoff a couple of miles farther south, which leads through the abandoned mining town of **Ingurtosu.** It's a strange, ghostly cluster of chimneys and workers' dwellings, forlorn amid the encroaching scrubland. Drive down the dirt track another 10 km (6 mi) or so, through woods of juniper, to reach the sea.

Where to Stay

★ $$$$ ⊡ **Hotel Le Dune.** A remote oasis on the beach, this hotel was formerly a depot for the minerals dug out from the surrounding hills; you can still see the remains of wagons, rails, and other mining bric-a-brac scattered about, which adds to the desolate allure. Bamboo furnishings give simple guest rooms a light, spacious feel. Eleven of the rooms have their own sitting areas. There's a good cocktail bar, where you can contemplate the limitless sands stretching out on either side. For exploring, guided tours are available on request. Half board is required year-round; rates drop to €180 for a double September–July. ⊠ *Via Bau 1, 09031 Ingurtosu* ☎ *0709/77130* 🖷 *0709/77230* ⊕ *www.leduneingurtosu.it* ➭ *27 rooms* ♨ *Restaurant, in-room safes, minibars, pool, bar, meeting room, travel services; no room TVs* ▭ *AE, DC, MC, V* ⭗❘ *MAP.*

SU NURAXI TO THE COSTA SMERALDA

A more traditional—and wild—Sardinia awaits the traveler who ventures into the island's mountainous interior. The Taviani brothers, noted Italian filmmakers, made the hinterland of the Barbagia region, where traditional Sardinian customs are maintained in remote hilltop villages, the subject of the extraordinary film *Padre Padrone* (1977). Inland Sardinians are hardy souls, used to living in a climate that is as unforgiving in winter as it is intolerable in summer. Old traditions, including the vendetta, are firmly rooted in the social fabric of this mountainous land, which is barren and beautiful. Here, rare species of wildlife share the rocky uplands with sturdy medieval churches and the mysterious *nuraghi* (ancient stone defensive structures) left by prehistoric people. The nuraghi were built beginning in the 16th century BC, and they vary from single defensive towers to multitower complexes sheltering whole communities—prehistoric versions of medieval walled towns. You may want to make your base Oristano, on the west coast and the medieval center of Sardinian nationalism.

As you move northward, the timeless beauty of the landscape begins to show greater signs of 20th-century development. The sunny resort of Alghero, the Spanish-influenced port on the west coast, is one of the island's premier holiday spots. Costa Smeralda, the luxury resort complex on the northeast corner of Sardinia, is as prestigious a summer getaway as any in Italy.

Su Nuraxi

6 64 km (40 mi) northeast of Ingurtosu on the Costa Verde, 60 km (37 mi) north of Cagliari.

Fodor'sChoice
★

It's definitely worth a detour to see the extraordinary stone fortress-village of Su Nuraxi, near the quiet town of Barumini. The most extensive of the island's 7,000 discovered nuraghi, Su Nuraxi's significance merits its inclusion on the UNESCO World Heritage List. Concentric rings of thick stone walls conceal dark chambers and narrow passages in a central, beehive-shape tower. The excellent guided tour (available in English) allows you to explore the interior. In the ruins of the surrounding village there are benches, ovens, wells, and other remnants of middle bronze–age society.

The specific functions of individual nuraghi remain a mystery, largely because their construction predates written or pictorial history. Though this particular type of construction is unique to Sardinia in Italy, similar buildings dating from the same era are found in other parts of the Mediterranean, such as Cyprus and the Balearic islands off Spain. If driving from SS131, don't be misled by other, lesser nuraghi—follow signs all the way to Barumini. ⊠ *Via Marini 11, 1 km (½ mi) west of Barumini* ☎ *070/9368128* 🎟 €*4.20* ☉ *Mar., daily 9–5; Apr., daily 9–6; May and June, daily 9–7; July and Aug., daily 9–7:30; Sept., daily 9–6:30; Oct., daily 9–5:30; Nov., daily 9–4:30; Dec.–Feb., daily 9–4.*

Giara di Gesturi

7 8 km (5 mi) north of Barumini, 68 km (42 mi) northwest of Cagliari.

On the 45-square-km (28-square-mi) basalt plateau of Giara di Gesturi roams some of the island's more exotic wildlife, including a species of wild dwarf horse. Another rare species in the Giara is the mouflon, a wild sheep distinguishable from its domesticated counterpart by its long, curving horns and skittishness. Long hunted for their horns, the mouflon are now an endangered species, with only a few surviving on Sardinia and Corsica. ✛ *Off S197, north of Gesturi.*

Oristano

8 *25 km (16 mi) north of Giara di Gesturi, 93 km (58 mi) northwest of Cagliari.*

The beautiful small colonial center exudes a distinct serenity. Oristano's evening *passeggiata* (predinner stroll) teems with vivacious young children and has an unambitious friendliness about it. The city's star shone most brightly in the Middle Ages, when it was capital of an independent duchy led by Sardinia's own Joan of Arc–type heroine, Eleanora di Arborea (circa 1340–1402). Oristano is now the scene of livestock fairs and a rousing series of horseback competitions, called Sa Sartiglia, marking the end of February's Carnival.

Where to Stay & Eat

★ **$$$** ✕ **Cocco e Dessì.** Chef Antonino Sanna's food is just as modern as his restaurant's bilevel interior and chrome bar. Try fusion flights of fancy such as crabs stuffed with sesame almond toffee and fish ravioli with escargot and scampi broth. There's an excellent tasting menu, and the prices are refreshingly reasonable, given that it's one of the most sophisticated restaurants in Sardinia. ⊠ *Via Tirso 31* ☎ *0783/300720* ⚲ *Reservations essential* ▭ *AE, DC, MC, V* ☾ *Closed Mon. No dinner Sun.*

$–$$ ✕ **Trattoria Gino.** The same family has run Trattoria Gino, under different names, for nearly a century. Authentic local seafood dishes include the *antipasto mare* (mixed seafood appetizer) and the delicious spaghetti *ai ricci* (with sea urchin). The lobster is a memorable splurge. Light walls lined with bottles of wine and simple rows of tables deck out the single room, and service is friendly and attentive. It's a popular spot for locals and an ideal lunch stop. ⊠ *Via Tirso 13* ☎ *0783/71428* ▭ *MC, V* ☾ *Closed Sun., 1 wk in Jan., and 3 wks in Aug.*

$ ▥ **I.S.A. Hotel.** This central downtown hotel has a clean and elegant (if a bit dated) lobby with chandeliers. Rooms, too, are well kept and comfortable, with simple white walls and wood furnishings, and excellent bathrooms. Nothing at the I.S.A. blows you away, but Oristano does everything in moderation, and the town's hotels are no exception. ⊠ *Piazza Mariano 50, 09170* ☎ *0783/360101* ⊷ *49 rooms* ♨ *Restaurant, minibars, bar, meeting room* ▭ *AE, DC, MC, V* ⑩ *BP.*

Nightlife & the Arts

☙ The **Sa Sartiglia** festival, on the last Sunday of February's Carnival season, includes rich costumes and ritual joustlike competitions on horseback. Each summer the town holds an **arts and crafts exhibition** (Tourist office ⊠ Via Cagliari 278 ☎ 0783/74191), with local foods and wines given prominence.

Tharros

9 *20 km (12 mi) west of Oristano, 113 km (70 mi) northwest of Cagliari.*

The site of the Carthaginian and Roman city of Tharros (Cabras in Italian), like Nora to the south, was chosen because it commanded the best views of the harbor and could provide an easy escape route if inland tribes threatened. Today the roadside ruins afford a scenic view over the

16

Sinis Peninsula. Four Corinthian columns still stand, and there are baths and fragments of mosaics from the Roman city. As at Nora, there is much more submerged under water. ⊠ *San Giovanni di Sinis* ☎ *0783/370019* 🎫 *€2* ⊙ *Daily 9–1 hr before sunset.*

At the **Museo Civico di Cabras** you can view many of the better-preserved urns and other artifacts that have been recovered from the ruins at Tharros. ⊠ *Via Tharros 121* ☎ *0783/290636* 🎫 *€1* ⊙ *June–Aug., daily 9–1 and 4–8, Sept.–May, daily 9–1 and 3–7.*

---

en route   On the way to Tharros you pass the ghost town of **San Salvatore**, revived briefly in the 1960s as a locale for spaghetti Westerns and since abandoned. The saloon from the movie set still stands. Among the dunes past San Salvatore are large rush huts formerly used by fishermen and now much in demand as back-to-nature vacation homes. The 5th-century church of **San Giovanni di Sinis**, on the Sinis Peninsula, is the oldest Christian church in Sardinia.

Nuoro

❿ *107 km (67 km) northeast of Tharros, 181 km (113 mi) north of Cagliari.*

The somewhat shabby provincial capital of Nuoro is on the edge of a gorge in the harsh mountainous area that culminates in Gennargentu, the island's highest massif (6,000 feet). Not much happens here; you can do some (relatively inexpensive) shopping amid strolling locals, or try the local Barbagia sausage, a sweet, fatty delight. The most interesting things in Nuoro are the views from the park on Sant'Onofrio Hill and the **Museo della Vita e delle Tradizioni Popolari Sarde** (Museum of Sardinian Life and Folklore), where you can see some domestic and agricultural implements, traditional jewelry, and local costumes worn by mannequins. ⊠ *Via Mereu 56* ☎ *0784/242900* 🎫 *€5* ⊙ *Mid-June–Sept., daily 9–8; Oct.–mid-June, daily 9–1 and 3–7.*

Make an excursion about 3 km (2 mi) east of Nuoro to **Monte Ortobene** (2,900 feet) for lofty views over the gulch below. Here you can also see up close the imposing statue of Christ the Redeemer overlooking the city. Picnic tables make this a handy spot for an alfresco lunch.

Where to Stay & Eat

$$$
Fodor'sChoice
★

✕🏨 **Su Gologone.** Rooms here are impeccable retreats, decked out with traditional Sardinian fabrics, wood chests, paintings, and wood beam ceilings. Staff members organize jeep and hiking expeditions. Stop in the rustic restaurant for an authentic Sardinian meal. Specialties include *maccarones de busa* (thick homemade pasta twists) and *culurgiones* (ravioli), *sebadas* (pockets of fried dough stuffed with cheese and lemon peel), and roast suckling pig. Much of the local Cannonau, a heady red wine, is made from grapes grown in the countryside around the inn. Su Gologone attracts droves, but for good reason. ⊠ *Località Su Gologone, 08025 Oliena, 20 km (12 mi) southeast of Nuoro* ☎ *0784/287512* 🖷 *0784/287668* ⊕ *www.sugologone.it* 🛏 *60 rooms, 8 suites* 🍴 *Restaurant, miniature golf, 2 ten-*

nis courts, pool, gym, massage, bicycles, bar, meeting rooms, some pets allowed ▭ AE, DC, MC, V ⊗ Closed Nov.–mid.-Mar. ⦾ MAP.

★ $ ▥ **Barbagia.** Rooms at this very simple, modern block-style hotel— more or less standard for provincial Nuoro—are quite comfortable, and those on the upper floor rooms have nice views out over the hills. Barbagia is out by the stadium on the fringes of downtown. ✉ Via Aosta, 08100 ☎ 0784/35585 🖷 0784/232782 ⇙ 42 rooms ♿ Restaurant, minibars, bar, lounge ▭ AE, DC, MC, V ⊗ Closed 1st 2 wks in Aug. and Dec. 22–Jan. 10 ⦾ BP.

Nightlife & the Arts
Nuoro's **Festa del Redentore** (Feast of the Redeemer) is held on the next-to-last Sunday in August. It's the best time to view the various traditional costumes of Sardinia's interior all in one place.

Shopping
Crafted for local festivals, wooden masks make unusual and festive souvenirs. The local shop of **ISOLA** (✉ Via Monsignor Bua 10 ☎ 0784/31507) is in the middle of the old town.

16

en route | **Orgosolo,** the old center of banditry halfway between Nuoro and Fonni, is still a poor and undeveloped village, but the houses have been painted with murals vividly depicting political and cultural issues. The effect is startling and lively. The forest and grassy plain above the village make fine walking country. ✉ 15 km (9 mi) south of Nuoro.

Fonni

⓫ 30 km (19 mi) south of Nuoro, 137 km (85 mi) south of Olbia.

In the heart of the Barbagia region, Fonni, with walls covered in murals, is the highest town on the island. This mountainous district, including Monte Spada and the Bruncu Spina refuge on the Gennargentu Massif, is Sardinia's most primitive. Life in some villages seems not to have changed much since the Middle Ages. Here a rigidly patriarchal society perpetuates the unrelenting practice of vendetta. Although as a tourist you may be looked at with curiosity, a smile goes a long way. High mountain roads wind and loop through the landscape; towns are small and undistinguished, their social fabric formed in complete isolation. On feast days elaborate regional costumes are taken out of mothballs and worn as an explicit statement of community identity.

Where to Eat
$ ✕ **Barbagia.** The best place downtown for a midday meal is also one of the most friendly to foreigners—a prize in this aloof village. The cheerful owners usher you into a rustic room full of nicely made-up tables, the obligatory TV in the corner, and not much else. Try the assortment of local *salumi* (cured meats), the maccarones de busa, and the typical grilled *bistecca di cavallo* (horsemeat steak), which is excellent. ✉ Via Umberto 106 ☎ 0784/58329 ▭ No credit cards ⊗ Closed Mon.

CLOSE UP

Sardinia by Rail

If you can stand a little agitation, consider taking a trip on the rickety old single-gauge railroad that runs between Cagliari and Arbatax, midway up the east coast (with a change at Mandas). The line has been operating since 1893; it takes about seven hours to cover the approximately 250 km (155 mi) of track. The train rattles up into the Barbagia district through some breathtaking mountain scenery, then eases down into desert inland landscape before arriving at Arbatax, where the trip ends on the dock next to the fishing boats. The daily (early-morning) departures are run by the **Trenino Verde della Sardegna** (☎ 070/342341 or 0800/460220 ⊕ www.treninoverde.com ☺ June–mid-Sept. ✉ €15 one-way). In Tortoli, just outside Arbatax, **Dolce Casa** (✉ Via Sarcidano 3 ☎ 0782/624235, 44/07803452748 off-season in Britain 🖶 0782/623484) is a modest hotel run by an English-speaking couple. It's the best lodging option in the area, but it's open only from June through September.

Nightlife & the Arts

You can see one of the most characteristic of the Barbagia's celebrations in local costume during the **Festa di San Giovanni**, held June 24.

Shopping

Special candies are made from honey and nougat and sold in hilltop **Tonara**, 15 km (9 mi) southwest of Fonni. In the mountain village of **Aritzo**, about 45 km (28 mi) south of Fonni, high up in the Barbagia, you can find handcrafted wooden utensils and furniture.

en route   Head back to Nuoro, and from there take the S129 west about 65 km (40 mi) to coastal Bosa, where you turn north into hilly and arid scrub country, with an abundance of cactus and juniper. Pines and olive trees shelter low buildings from the steady winds that make these parts ideal for sailing. About the only cash crop here is cork from the cork trees dotting the landscape. Yet in the low valleys and along the riverbeds, masses of oleanders bloom in June and July, creating avenues of color.

Alghero

⑫ *135 km (84 mi) northwest of Fonni, 137 km (85 mi) southwest of Olbia.*

A tourist-friendly town with a distinctly Spanish flavor, Alghero is also known as Barcelonetta (little Barcelona). Rich wrought-iron scrollwork decorates balconies and screened windows; a Spanish motif appears in stone portals and in bell towers. The town was built and inhabited in the 14th century by the Aragonese and Catalans, who constructed seaside ramparts and sturdy towers encompassing an inviting nucleus of narrow, winding streets with whitewashed palazzos. The native language spoken here is a version of Catalan, not Italian, although you probably have to attend one of the masses conducted in Algherese (or listen in on stories swapped by older fishermen) to hear it.

The **Museo Diocesano d'Arte Sacra** (Diocesan Museum of Sacred Art) is housed in a 13th-century church. The usual assortment of religious treasures—paintings, wooden sculptures, and bronzes—is on display; look for the masterful 16th-century Catalan silverware. ✉ *Via Maiorca 1* ☎ *079/9733041* 💳 *€2.50* ⏲ *Jan. and Feb. by appointment; Mar.–May and Oct., daily 10–12:30 and 5–8; June and Sept., daily 10–12:30 and 6–9; July and Aug., daily 10–12:30 and 7–11; Nov. and Dec., Thurs.–Tues. 10–12:30 and 5–8.*

West of Alghero are broad sandy beaches and the spectacular heights of **Capo Caccia**, an imposing limestone headland. At the base of a sheer cliff the pounding sea has carved an entrance to the vast **Grotta di Nettuno** (Neptune's Caves), a fantastic cavern filled with water pools, stalactites, and stalagmites. You must visit with a guide; tours start on the hour. ✉ *13 km (8 mi) west of Alghero* ☎ *079/946540* 💳 *€10* ⏲ *Apr.–Sept., daily 9–7; Oct., daily 9–6; Nov.–Mar., daily 9–2.*

★ ☙

16

By land you can reach the entrance to the Grotta di Nettuno by descending the 654 dizzying steps of the aptly named *escala del cabirol* (mountain goat's stairway). The trip to the top of the stairway takes about 50 minutes by **public bus**. ✉ *Via Catalogna* ☎ *079/950179* 💳 *€3.25 round-trip* ⏲ *From Alghero 9:15 year-round and 3:10 and 5:10 June–Sept. From Capo Caccia noon year-round and 4:05 and 6:05 June–Sept.*

Taking a **boat tour** from Alghero to see Neptune's caves takes 2½ hours and is much less exhausting than approaching on foot, but is not possible November–March and when seas are rough. The boat departs from docks near Bastione della Maddalena, on the northeast edge of the old town. ✉ *Navisarda* ☎ *079/950603* 💳 *€11, plus cave admission* ⏲ *Apr., May, and Oct., daily 9, 10, and 3; June–Sept., daily 9–5 on the hr.*

Where to Stay & Eat

★ $$–$$$ ✕ **Andreini.** Traverse the loftiest heights of Sardinian elegance at an expensive, opulent, ambitious—yet somehow cozy—restaurant. The place is set to the nines: candles, tablecloths, and waiters abound; the service and wine list are just so. The food is equally romantic; a great tasting menu highlights the Andreini brothers' artful use of local ingredients like pecorino cheese and wild fennel. Creations might include homemade cuttlefish-ink tagliatelle with asparagus or wild boar with Cannonau wine sauce. The weekday three-course "business lunch" is a good value. ✉ *Via Arduino 45* ☎ *079/982098* ⌂ *Reservations essential* 🟰 *AE, DC, MC, V* ⏲ *Closed Mon. Sept.–May.*

$–$$ ✕ **Da Pietro.** A menu that includes *bucatini all'algherese* (hollow, spaghetti-like pasta with a sauce of clams, capers, tomatoes, and olives) and baked fish with a white-wine sauce keeps this seafood restaurant bustling below its vaulted ceilings. Look for Da Pietro in the old town near Largo San Francesco. ✉ *Via Ambrogio Machin 20* ☎ *079/979645* 🟰 *AE, MC, V* ⏲ *Closed Wed. and Dec. 15–27.*

$$$$ 🏨 **Carlos V.** On the shore boulevard opposite the Villa Las Tronas, this modern hotel (pronounced Carlos Quinto) has an array of gardens and terraces, and a big pool overlooking the sea. Don't settle for a slightly cheaper room facing the back; the pleasure here is all in the magnificent view from your balcony. Low-season rates are a bargain. ⊠ *Lungomare Valencia 24, 07041* ☎ *079/9720600* 🖷 *079/980298* ⊕ *www. hotelcarlosv.it* 🛏 *110 rooms* ♢ *Restaurant, minibars, cable TV, miniature golf, 2 tennis courts, 2 saltwater pools, 2 bars, playground, business services, meeting rooms* ▭ *AE, DC, MC, V* ⋈ *BP.*

★ $$$$ 🏨 **Villa Las Tronas.** Gardens surround a narrow drive that separates this hotel's little island from the road, imparting a regal sense of seclusion to what was once a royal mansion. Belle epoque interiors have ornate gilt chairs or canopy-draped beds. The Villa is on a rocky promontory—above the sea but still near the center—and there are great views from most rooms. Service is elegant and impeccable, from the reception to the restaurant. It's open year-round, a rarity in these parts. ⊠ *Lungomare Valencia 1, 07041* ☎ *079/981818* 🖷 *079/981044* ⊕ *www.hvlt.com* 🛏 *22 rooms, 3 suites* ♢ *Restaurant, minibars, saltwater pool, gym, beach, bicycles, Internet, meeting room, some pets allowed* ▭ *AE, DC, MC, V* ⋈ *MAP.*

$ 🏨 **San Francesco.** The convent that was once attached to the church of San Francesco has been reinvented as a hotel. The rooms are grouped around the 14th-century cloister and, though somewhat cramped, are modern and quiet. It's quite central, in Alghero's Spanish quarter. ⊠ *Via Machin 2, 07041* ☎🖷 *079/980330* ⊕ *www.sanfrancescohotel.com* 🛏 *20 rooms* ♢ *Bar, meeting room* ▭ *MC, V* ⊗ *Closed Nov.–mid-Dec.* ⋈ *BP.*

Nightlife

The **Caffè Costantino** (⊠ Piazza Civica 30 ☎ 079/976154) is sumptuous and elegant, with yellow flowered walls, chandeliers, classical music, and a warm crowd of distinguished, well-dressed Algherese. Stop in for a glass of local wine or just a coffee; it's open until midnight.

Baraonda (⊠ Principe Umberto 75 ☎ 079/975922), a marvelous local wine bar, also carries specialty liqueurs and grappas from all over Sardinia.

The hip **Il Tunnel** (⊠ Via G. Ferret 37 ☎ 340/2476190) bar, inside an ancient tunnel, is striking and open late into the night.

Shopping

Jewelry purveyors dot Alghero's old quarter; **Via Carlo Alberto** is especially good for handmade coral products. A great place to buy wine is **Bacco e Tabacco** (⊠ Via Roma 91 ☎ 079/9735030 ⊕ www.baccoetabacco. it), which also ships all over the world.

Sassari

⑬ *34 km (21 mi) northeast of Alghero, 212 km (132 mi) north of Cagliari.*

Inland Sassari is an important university town and administrative center, notable for its history of intellectualism and bohemian student culture, an ornate old cathedral, and a good archaeological museum. Look for downtown vendors of *fainè*, a pizzalike chickpea-flour pancake glistening with olive oil, which is a Genovese and Sassarese specialty. Sassari is the hub of several highways and secondary roads leading to various coastal resorts, among them Stintino and Castelsardo.

Sassari's excellent **Museo Sanna** has the best archaeological collection outside Cagliari, spanning nuraghic, Carthaginian, and Roman histories, including well-preserved bronze statues and household objects from the second millennium BC. Summer hours vary from one year to the next. ⊠ *Via Roma 46* ☎ *079/272203* 🗐 €2 ☉ *Tues.–Sun. 9–7:30.*

Where to Eat

¢–$ ✕ **L'Assassino.** Get a true taste of great local Sassarese cooking—and many of the other obscure Sardinian specialties you might have been looking for but not yet found. Horse, donkey, and roast pig figure prominently on the menu; best of all is a *cena sarda,* a 10-dish tasting menu with *porcetto* (roast suckling pig), also spelled *porcheddu.* The service is friendly, and the room warm and cozy. Food is, unusually, served all afternoon long. ⊠ *Vicolo Ospizio Cappuccini 1, near Via Rosello* ☎ *079/ 235401* ▭ *AE, DC, MC, V* ☉ *Closed Sun.*

Shopping

Sassari has Sardinia's main **ISOLA** (⊠ Giardini Pubblici ☎ 079/230101), a craft exhibition center in the public gardens next to Viale Mancini built specifically as a showcase for gifts and souvenirs.

On the way to Santa Teresa di Gallura, the walled seaside citadel of **Castelsardo,** 32 km (20 mi) northeast of Sassari, is a delight for basket lovers. Roadside stands and shops in the old town sell woven baskets, as well as rugs and wrought iron. The appropriately shaped **Roccia dell'Elefante** (Elephant Rock) on the road into Castelsardo was hollowed out by primitive man to become a *domus de janas* (literally, "fairy house," in fact a Neolithic burial chamber).

Santa Teresa di Gallura

🔟 *100 km (62 mi) northeast of Sassari, 65 km (41 mi) northwest of Olbia.*

At the northern tip of Sardinia, Santa Teresa di Gallura retains the relaxed, carefree air of a former fishing village. Nearby beaches rival those farther down the coast but manage not to seem overtouristed.

Where to Stay & Eat

¢ ✕▥ **Canne al Vento.** Step into a family-run hotel and restaurant that is a quiet, cheerful haven in town. Despite a bland exterior, the place has a defiantly rustic feel, with a bamboo-roof restaurant and the odd ornamental wagon wheel. Rooms are sparsely furnished but cool and comfortable. The restaurant ($$$) specializes in authentic island cuisine, for example *zuppa cuata* (bread, cheese, and tomato soup), porcheddu, and seafood. ⊠ *Via Nazionale 23, 07028* ☎ *0789/754219* 🖶 *0789/754948* 🛏 *22 rooms* ᐸ *Restaurant, minibars; no a/c* ▭ *AE, DC, MC, V* ☉ *Closed Oct.–Mar. Restaurant closed Mon.* ◯⊙ *BP.*

$$$$ ▥ **Grand Hotel Corallaro.** This hotel has luxury accommodations in a panoramic spot right by the beach, a brief walk from the town center.

16

Rooms are functional and some have balconies. Public rooms are much grander, furnished with wicker chairs, and there are terraces and lawns on which to sip preprandial drinks. Half board and a seven-day minimum stay are required in August; the rest of the year, the minimum stay is three days (sizeable discounts are available). ✉ *Località Rena Bianca, 07028* ☎ *0789/755475* 🖶 *0789/755431* ⊕ *www.hotelcorallaro.it* ⌨ 82 *rooms* △ *Restaurant, beach, indoor pool, gym, Turkish baths* ▭ *MC, V* ⊗ *Closed mid-Oct.–Easter* ‖⊙‖ *MAP.*

La Maddalena

⑮ *30 km (19 mi) east of Santa Teresa di Gallura, 45 km (20 mi) north-west of Olbia.*

From the port of Palau you can visit the archipelago of La Maddalena, seven granite islands embellished with lush green scrub and wind-bent pines. Car ferries make the 3-km (2-mi) trip about every half hour.

Pilgrims pay homage to national hero **Giuseppe Garibaldi's tomb** (1807–82) on the grounds of his hideaway. Take the ferry to Isola Maddalena and then the bridge to Isola Caprera. ✉ *7 km (4½ mi) east of Isola Maddalena* ☎ *0789/727162* ✉ €2 ⊙ *Tues.–Sun. 9–6:30.*

Porto Cervo

★ **⑯** *35 km (22 mi) southeast of La Maddalena, 30 km (19 mi) north of Olbia.*

Sardinia's northeastern coast is fringed with low cliffs, inlets, and small bays. This has become an upscale vacationland, with glossy resorts such as Baia Sardinia and Porto Rotondo just outside the confines of the famed Costa Smeralda, developed by the Aga Khan (born 1936), who in 1965 accidentally discovered the coast's charms—and potential—when his yacht took shelter here from a storm. In the late '60s and '70s, the Costa Smeralda, with its heart in Porto Cervo, was *the* place to summer. The attractions remain geared to those who can measure themselves by the yardstick of Khan's fabled riches. Italian Prime Minister Silvio Berlusconi certainly does: a 40-room villa is owned by the man referred to by many Italians as the *distante signoria* (roughly translated as "distant lord of the manor"). Italy's most expensive hotels are here, and the world's most magnificent yachts anchor in the waters of Porto Cervo.

> **WORD OF MOUTH**
>
> "I love the Costa Smeralda, the ultimate Italian island experience."
> —m kingdom

All along the coast, carefully tended lush vegetation surrounds vacation villages and discreet villas that have sprung up over the past decade in spurious architectural styles best described as bogus Mediterranean. The trend has been to keep this an enclave of the very rich. Outside the peak season, however, prices plunge and the majesty of the natural surroundings shines through, justifying all the hype and the Emerald Coast's fame as one of the truly romantic corners of the Mediterranean.

Where to Stay

$$$$ 🏨 **Cala di Volpe.** Long a magnet for the beautiful people, this hyper-glamorous establishment, now part of the Starwood Luxury Collection, was built to resemble an ancient Sardinian village, albeit one with high-speed Internet access. The rustic-elegant interior has wood-beam ceilings, terra-cotta floors, Sar-

dinian arts-and-crafts decorations, and porticoes overlooking the sea. The Presidential Suite, in the highest tower, has a private pool. Summer prices, including the requisite half board, are so high (€1,900 and up) that you may think you've got the exchange rate wrong by a factor of 10—this is one of the most expensive hotels in the world (rates outside of July and August drop to just €1,000 and up). ⊠ *Cala di Volpe, 07020* ☎ *0789/976111* 🖷 *0789/976617* ⊕ *www.luxurycollection.com* 🛏 *107 rooms, 14 suites* ⚒ *2 restaurants, room service, in-room safes, cable TV with movies, in-room VCRs, in-room data ports, putting green, 3 tennis courts, saltwater pool, wading pool, spa, beach, boating, waterskiing, 3 bars, shops, babysitting, laundry service, concierge, Internet, business services, convention center, airport shuttle, car rental* ⊟ *AE, DC, MC, V* ⊗ *Closed mid-Oct.–mid-Apr.* �ⓞ *MAP.*

$$$$ 🏨 **Cervo Hotel.** Low Mediterranean buildings surround a large pool and garden in the heart of the Costa Smeralda's Porto Cervo. Colorful painted wood furniture and slipcovered pieces fill up the large rooms; most have a terrace. The five tennis courts are well-lighted at night. High-season prices (half board required) are through the roof, but in winter, prices fall to as low as one-tenth the summer rate. This Starwood Sheraton hotel complex is next to the marina and *piazzetta* (small piazza)—a popular spot to see and be seen. ⊠ *Waterfront, 07020* ☎ *0789/931111* 🖷 *0789/931613* ⊕ *www.sheraton.com* 🛏 *86 rooms, 6 suites* ⚒ *5 restaurants, room service, minibars, cable TV with movies, in-room data ports, 5 tennis courts, 3 pools (1 indoor), gym, beach, boating, waterskiing, squash, 4 bars, piano bar, babysitting, concierge, business services, convention center, travel services, no-smoking rooms* ⊟ *AE, DC, MC, V* �ⓞ *MAP.*

$$–$$$ 🏨 **Nibaru.** Pinkish-red brick buildings with tiled roofs stand on a secluded inlet amid lush gardens. Nibaru has all the best features of the Costa Smeralda at comparatively low rates: guest rooms are just a few yards from the sea and some superb swimming spots and Nibaru's lagoon-like pool. From here you have easy access of the Pevero Golf Club and the tennis courts of Porto Cervo. ⊠ *Località Cala di Volpe, 07020* ☎ *0789/96038* 🖷 *0789/96474* ⊕ *www.hotelnibaru.it* 🛏 *50 rooms, 2 suites* ⚒ *Minibars, pool, bar* ⊟ *AE, DC, MC, V* ⊗ *Closed mid-Oct.–mid-Apr.* �ⓞ *BP.*

Sports & the Outdoors

The world-class, 18-hole **Pevero Golf Course** (⊠ Bay of Pevero ☎ 0789/96210) was designed by Robert Trent Jones.

16

The **Yacht Club Costa Smeralda** (⊠ Via della Marina ☎ 0789/902200 ⊕ www.yccs.it) provides use of its pool, restaurant, bar, and guest rooms to those with memberships at other yacht clubs.

Olbia

🔟 *30 km (19 mi) south of Porto Cervo, 106 km (66 mi) north of Nuoro.*

Set amid the resorts of Sardinia's northeastern coast, Olbia is a lively little seaport and port of call for mainland ferries at the head of a long, wide bay. The little basilica of **San Simplicio,** a short walk behind the main Corso Umberto, is worth searching out if you have any spare time in Olbia. The simple granite structure dates from the 11th century, part of the great Pisan church-building program, using pillars and columns recycled from Roman buildings. ⊠ *Via San Simplicio* ☎ *0789/23358* ⊙ *Daily 6:30–12:30 and 4–7.*

Where to Stay & Eat

$–$$ ✕ **Barbagia.** Traditional dishes from Sardinia's wild interior fuse with local ingredients here. Antipasti might be a refreshing salad of sliced tomato and fresh cheese (called *sa t'amata chi sa frughe*). Then try maccarones de busa with a wild boar sauce; you might also find roast lamb and suckling pig in season. A good selection of pizza is served for dinner only. This is a classic downtown gathering place with a simple, bright array of tables. ⊠ *Via Galvani 94* ☎ *0789/51640* ▭ *AE, DC, MC, V* ⊙ *Closed Wed. Oct.–June.*

$$–$$$ 🏨 **Martini.** Plush, modern, and businesslike, Martini occupies an eye-catching site on the shore of a lagoon north of town. The hotel has lounge chairs on the roof with views of the port. Most of the classic bedrooms also benefit from the excellent vista. It's a 20-minute walk or easy taxi ride from the port and center, and is thankfully detached from the early-morning and late-night comings and goings of ferries. ⊠ *Via G. D'Annunzio 21, 07026* ☎ *0789/26066 or 0789/24545* 🖷 *0789/26418* ↳ *70 rooms* ↺ *Restaurant, in-room safes, minibars, bar, meeting room* ▭ *AE, DC, MC, V* ⭐ *BP.*

Golfo Aranci

🔟 *19 km (12 mi) northeast of Olbia.*

At the mouth of the Gulf of Olbia, Golfo Aranci is a small-scale resort and major arrival point for ferries from the mainland. The craggy headland west of town has been left undeveloped as a nature reserve, and there are some inviting beaches within an easy drive.

SARDINIA ESSENTIALS

Transportation

BY AIR

Flying is by far the fastest and easiest way to get to the island. Sardinia's major airport is in Cagliari, with smaller ones at Alghero and Olbia, the latter serving the Costa Smeralda. Cagliari's Aeroporto di Elmas is about 6 km (4 mi) west of town center, and there is regular bus service from the airport to Piazza Matteotti, in front of the train station. Alghero's Aeroporto Fertilia is 13 km (8 mi) from the city. A bus links the airport with the bus station in the center of town. Aeroporto Costa Smeralda is 4 km (2½ mi) southeast of Olbia, linked by local bus to Olbia.

Alitalia offers frequent direct flights between Cagliari and Rome's Fiumicino Airport; the trip takes about 40 minutes. Meridiana provides service between Cagliari and Bologna, Naples, Paris, Turin, and London's Gatwick; between Olbia and Bologna, Florence, Milan, and Rome; and between Cagliari and Olbia. Air One connects Cagliari with Milan, Pisa, and Turin; and Alghero with Milan and Rome. RyanAir has direct flights between Alghero and secondary airports of major Euopean cities: London's Stansted, Frankfurt's Hahn, Barcelona's Girona, and Rome's Ciampino. EasyJet provides service between Olbia and London's Gatwick and Berlin's Scho ⊙ nefeld, and between Cagliari and London's Luton.

🛫 Airport Information **Aeroporto Oblia Costa Smeralda (OLB)** ☎ 0789/563444 ⊕ www.geasar.com. **Aeroporto Cagliari-Elmas (CAG)** ☎ 070/211211 ⊕ www.sogaer. it. **Aeroporto Alghero-Fertilia (AHO)** ☎ 079/935282 ⊕ www.aeroportodialghero.it. 🛫 Airlines & Contacts **Air One** ☎ 199/207080 toll-free, 06/48880069 from outside Italy) ⊕ www.flyairone.it. **Alitalia** ☎ 800/223-5730 in U.S., 020/7602-7111 in London, 0990/ 448-259 in U.K., 06/65641 in Rome, 848/865641 elsewhere in Italy ⊕ www.alitalia.it. **easyJet** ⊕ www.easyjet.com. **Meridiana** ☎ 199/111333 toll-free, 0789/52682 from outside Italy ⊕ www.meridiana.it. **Ryanair** ☎ 0870/1-569-569 in U.K., 899/678910 in Italy, 353/12497700 from elsewhere to headquarters in Ireland ⊕ www.ryanair.com.

BY BOAT & FERRY

Large modern ferries run by Tirrenia Lines, Moby Lines, and the Ferrovie dello Stato (FS, Italian State Railways) connect Sardinian ports at Porto Torres, Olbia, Arbatax, and Cagliari with the mainland. These ferries are a popular mode of transport. Tirrenia connects Naples with Cagliari; Genoa with Porto Torres, Olbia, and Arbatax; Civitavecchia (near Rome) with Olbia, Arbatax, and Cagliari; Fiumicino (near Rome) with Golfo Aranci and Arbatax; and Cagliari with Palermo and Trapani. Vehicles can generally be transported on Tirrenia ferries. Moby Lines carries passengers and cars between Olbia and Civitavecchia, Genoa, and Livorno. FS ferries carry trains as well as passengers and cars; they sail from Civitavecchia to Golfo Aranci, near Olbia. Grandi Navi Veloci run comfortable ferries that resemble cruise ships between Genoa and Porto Torres (year-round) and Genoa and Olbia (June–September). French SNCM ferries transport passengers to and from Marseille, France.

FARES & SCHEDULES The ferry ride on Tirrenia from Naples to Cagliari takes about 17 hours and costs approximately €75 for first-class passage in mid- or high season with a berth (and €100 for automobile transport). The Civitavecchia–Olbia/Golfo Aranci run (€50) takes about eight hours, and there are overnight trips; or you can choose a high-speed ferry (summer only), which takes just four to six hours but costs more and gets booked up weeks ahead during the peak of the season in mid-August. Normal ferry service is scheduled two or three times a week, and high-speed ferries depart one to four times daily.

🚢 **Boat & Ferry Information** **FS** ☎ 1478/88088 ⊕ www.trenitalia.com. **Grandi Navi Veloci** ☎ 02/89012281 ⊕ www.gnv.it. **Moby Lines** ☎ 06/42011455 or 0586/826824 ⊕ www.mobylines.it. **SNCM** ☎ 33/0825888088 to France ⊕ www.sncm.fr. **Tirrenia** ☎ 199/123199, 081/3172999 from cellular phones and outside Italy ⊕ www.tirrenia.it.

BY BUS

Cagliari is linked with the other towns of Sardinia by a network of buses. Local destinations are served by ARST. Major cities, excluding Olbia, are served by PANI. The heart of the Sardinian bus system is the Stazione Autolinee, across the square from the main tourist office in Cagliari. City buses in Cagliari and Sassari operate on the same system as those on the mainland: buy your ticket first, at a tobacco shop or machine, and cancel it by punching it in the machine on the bus. Fares are €0.75 per ride.

🚌 **Bus Information** **ARST** ☎ 070/40981 ⊕ www.arst.sardegna.it. **PANI** ☎ 070/652326. **Stazione Autolinee** ✉ Piazza Matteotti, Cagliari ☎ 070/4098324.

BY CAR

Sardinia is about 260 km (162 mi) long from north to south and takes three to four hours to drive on the main roads; it's roughly 120 km (75 mi) across. Cars may be taken on board most of the ferry lines connecting Sardinia with the mainland.

The main highway linking Cagliari with Sassari was begun in 1820 by the Savoy ruler Carlo Felice; designated S131, but still referred to as the Strada Carlo Felice by the islanders, it runs through the fertile Campidano Plain, bordered by rhododendrons for virtually all of the 216 km (134 mi) between the two cities. The S131dir (not to be confused with the S131) and S129 connect the Strada Carlo Felice with Nuoro and the Barbagia. The S597 connects Sassari and Olbia.

Roads are generally in good condition, but bear in mind that roadside facilities are infrequent, especially in the east. Try to avoid driving at night, when mountain roads are particularly hazardous and slow; and especially in winter, beware the fog when traversing the mountains at night (or even by day).

BY TRAIN

The Stazione Centrale in Cagliari is next to the bus station on Piazza Matteotti. There are fairly good connections between Olbia, Cagliari, Sassari, and Oristano. You can reach Nuoro via Macomer; Alghero is reached via Sassari. Service on the few other local lines is infrequent and slow. The fastest train between Olbia and Cagliari takes more than four hours. Local trains connect Golfo Aranci, the Ferrovie dello Stato (Italian State Railways, or Trenitalia) port for the train ferry, with Olbia (20 minutes) and Sassari with Alghero (35 minutes).

🚆 **Train Information** **Ferrovie dello Stato** ☎ 892021 ⊕ www.trenitalia.com.

Contacts & Resources

EMERGENCIES

Late-night pharmacies are open on a rotating basis; information on current schedules is pinned up on any pharmacy door or can be obtained by calling 192.

ACI provides 24-hour roadside assistance for emergencies.

🖪 **ACI** ☎ 803/116. **Ambulance** ✉ Cagliari ☎ 070/4092901. **Hospital** Ospedale Civile San Michele ✉ Via Peretti, Cagliari ☎ 070/543266. **Police** ☎ 112 or 113.

TOURS

Cagliari travel agency conducts tours of Sardinia. The Associazione Nazionale di Turismo Equestre can provide information on horseback riding tours both along the coast and inland. The Centro Vacanze Ala Birdi organizes riding vacations.

🖪 Horseback Riding Tours **Associazione Nazionale di Turismo Equestre** ✉ Via Carso 35/a, Sassari ☎ 079/299889. **Cagliari** Viaggi Orrù ✉ Via Roma 95, Cagliari ☎ 070/659858 ⊕ www.viaggiorru.it. **Centro Vacanze Ala Birdi** ✉ Arborea, near Oristano ☎ 0783/80500 ⊕ www.alabirdi-arborea.it.

VISITOR INFORMATION

The official Sardinia Web site has information for many island towns.

🖪 Tourist Information **Sardinia** ✉ Viale Trieste 105 ☎ 070/606280 ⊕ www.regione.sardegna.it. **Alghero** ✉ Piazza Porta Terra 9, 07041 ☎ 079/979054. **Cagliari** ✉ Piazza Mateotti, 09100 ☎ 070/669255 ✉ Aeroporto di Elmas ☎ 070/240200. **Golfo Aranci** ✉ City Hall, 07026 ☎ 0789/21672 June–Aug. **Nuoro** ✉ Piazza Italia 19, 08100 ☎ 0784/30083. **Olbia** ✉ Via Catello Piro 1, 07026 ☎ 0789/21453 ✉ Aeroporto Costa Smeralda ☎ 0789/52634. **Oristano** ✉ Piazza Eleonora 19, 09170 ☎ 0783/36831. **Sassari** ✉ Viale Caprera 36, 07100 ☎ 079/299544.

16

ITALY AT A GLANCE

Fast Facts

Name in local language: Italia
Capital: Rome
National anthem: *Inno di Mameli*
Type of government: Republic
Administrative divisions: 20 regions; Abruzzo, Basilicata, Calabria, Campania, Emilia-Romagna, Friuli-Venezia Giulia, Lazio, Liguria, Lombardia, Marche, Molise, Piemonte, Puglia, Sardegna, Sicilia, Toscana, Trentino–Alto Adige, Umbria, Valle d'Aosta, Veneto
Independence: March 17, 1861
Constitution: January 1, 1948
Legal system: Based on civil law system; appeals treated as new trials; judicial review under certain conditions in Constitutional Court
Suffrage: 18 years of age, except in senatorial elections, where minimum age is 25
Legislature: Bicameral, Parliament of Senate (315 seats elected by popular vote of which 232 are directly elected and 83 are elected by regional proportional representation; in addition, there are a small number of senators-for-life including former presidents of the republic; members serve five-year terms) and Chamber of Deputies (630 seats; 475 are directly elected, 155 by regional proportional representation; members serve five-year terms)
Population: 58 million
Population density: 511 people per square mi
Median age: male: 39.4, female: 42.6
Life expectancy: male: 76.47, female: 82.52
Infant mortality rate: 6.2 deaths/1,000 live births
Literacy: 98.6%
Language: Italian (official), German (parts of Trentino–Alto Adige region), French (Valle d'Aosta region), Slovene (Trieste-Gorizia area)
Ethnic groups: Italian (includes small clusters of German-, French-, and Slovene-Italians in the north and Albanian-Italians and Greek-Italians in the south)
Religion: Predominately Roman Catholic, mature Protestant and Jewish communities, growing Muslim immigrant community
Discoveries & Inventions: First thermometer (1593), astronomical telescope (1609), barometer (1643), piano (1720), liposuction (1974)

Love and understand the Italians, for the people are more marvellous than the land.

—E.M. Forster

Geography & Environment

Land area: 294,020 square km (113,522 square mi), including Sardinia and Sicily, slightly larger than Arizona
Coastline: 7,600 km (2,934 mi) along Mediterranean Sea
Terrain: Mostly rugged and mountainous; some plains, coastal lowlands, highest point: Monte Bianco de Courmayeur (a secondary peak of Mont Blanc), 4,748 meters (15,577 feet)
Islands: Capri, Elba, Giglio, Lipari Islands, Montecristo, Pianosa, Sardinia, Sicily
Natural resources: Coal, crude oil reserves, fish, marble, mercury, natural gas, potash, sulfur
Natural hazards: Avalanches, earthquakes, flooding, landslides, land subsidence in Venice, mudflows, volcanic eruptions
Environmental issues: Waste from offshore oil production in

Mediterranean, remnants of 2002 Prestige tanker spill continue to be felt on Atlantic Coast, pollution from raw sewage outlets, water quality and quantity nationwide; air pollution; deforestation

Economy

Currency: euro
Exchange rate: €0.84 euro = $1
GDP: €1.2 trillion ($1.5 trillion)
Per capita income: €15,829 ($18,960)
Inflation: 2.2%
Unemployment: 8.5%
Work force: 23.6 million; services 63%, industry 32%, agriculture 5%
Debt: n/a
Economic aid: n/a
Major industries: Ceramics, chemicals, clothing, food processing, footwear, iron and steel, machinery, motor vehicles, textiles, tourism
Agricultural products: Beef, dairy products, fish, fruits, grain, grapes, olives, potatoes, sugar beets, soybeans, vegetables

Exports: €216.4 billion ($259.2 billion)
Major export products: Beverages and tobacco, chemicals, clothing, engineering products, food, machinery, minerals, motor vehicles, transport equipment
Export partners: Germany 14%, France 12%, U.S. 10%, U.K. 7%, Spain 6%
Imports: €198.9 billion ($238.2 billion)
Major import products: Beverages and tobacco, chemicals, energy products, engineering products, equipment, food, minerals and nonferrous metals, textiles and clothing, transport
Import partners: Germany 18%; France 11%; Netherlands 6%; U.K. 5%; U.S. 5%; Spain 5%; Belgium 4%

Did You Know?

• The longest salami in the history of the world was unveiled in Udine, Italy, in 2002. It was nearly 500 feet long and weighed 600 pounds.

• The Colosseum of Rome is the biggest amphitheater in the world, with a maximum capacity of 87,000 people.

• Italy produces more than 5 million liters of wine per year, more than twice the amount the United States makes.

• Italy is the only country in the world to have two other countries situated within its borders. Vatican City (population 770) is the smallest independent state on the globe and San Marino (population 25,000) is the fifth smallest.

• Italy has a higher rate of drug addiction than any other country in Europe.

• A mere 12% of Italian marriages end in divorce, the lowest percentage of any European country. The influence of Catholicism is a commonly cited explanation.

• Italy is the world's top exporter of leather. It imports more leather than any other European country, second in the world only to China and Hong Kong.

• Italy exports 43.5% of the world's couscous and pasta.

ITALIAN VOCABULARY

	English	Italian	Pronunciation
Basics			
	Yes/no	Sí/No	see/no
	Please	Per favore	pear fa-**vo**-ray
	Yes, please	Sí grazie	see **grah**-tsee-ay
	Thank you	Grazie	**grah**-tsee-ay
	You're welcome	Prego	**pray**-go
	Excuse me, sorry	Scusi	**skoo**-zee
	Sorry!	Mi dispiace!	mee dis-spee-**ah**-chay
	Good morning/ afternoon	Buongiorno	bwohn-**jor**-no
	Good evening	Buona sera	**bwoh**-na **say**-ra
	Good-bye	Arrivederci	a-ree-vah-**dare**-chee
	Mr. (Sir)	Signore	see-**nyo**-ray
	Mrs. (Ma'am)	Signora	see-**nyo**-ra
	Miss	Signorina	see-nyo-**ree**-na
	Pleased to meet you	Piacere	pee-ah-**chair**-ray
	How are you?	Come sta?	**ko**-may **stah**
	Very well, thanks	Bene, grazie	**ben**-ay **grah**-tsee-ay
	And you?	E lei?	ay **lay**-ee
	Hello (phone)	Pronto?	**proan**-to
Numbers			
	one	uno	**oo**-no
	two	due	**doo**-ay
	three	tre	tray
	four	quattro	**kwah**-tro
	five	cinque	**cheen**-kway
	six	sei	say
	seven	sette	**set**-ay
	eight	otto	**oh**-to
	nine	nove	**no**-vay
	ten	dieci	dee-**eh**-chee
	eleven	undici	**oon**-dee-chee
	twelve	dodici	**doe**-dee-chee
	thirteen	tredici	**tray**-dee-chee

fourteen	quattordici	kwa-**tore**-dee-chee
fifteen	quindici	**kwin**-dee-chee
sixteen	sedici	**say**-dee-chee
seventeen	diciassette	dee-cha-**set**-ay
eighteen	diciotto	dee-**cho**-to
nineteen	diciannove	dee-cha-**no**-vay
twenty	venti	**vain**-tee
twenty-one	ventuno	vain-**too**-no
twenty-two	ventidue	vain-tee-**doo**-ay
thirty	trenta	**train**-ta
forty	quaranta	kwa-**rahn**-ta
fifty	cinquanta	cheen-**kwahn**-ta
sixty	sessanta	seh-**sahn**-ta
seventy	settanta	seh-**tahn**-ta
eighty	ottanta	o-**tahn**-ta
ninety	novanta	no-**vahn**-ta
one hundred	cento	**chen**-to
one thousand	mille	**mee**-lay
ten thousand	diecimila	dee-eh-chee-**mee**-la

Useful Phrases

Do you speak English?	Parla inglese?	**par**-la een-**glay**-zay
I don't speak Italian	Non parlo italiano	non **par**-lo ee-tal-**yah**-no
I don't understand	Non capisco	non ka-**peess**-ko
Can you please repeat?	Può ripetere?	pwo ree-**pet**-ay-ray
Slowly!	Lentamente!	**len**-ta-men-tay
I don't know	Non lo so	non lo **so**
I'm American/ British	Sono americano(a)	**so**-no a-may-ree-**kah**-no(a)
	Sono inglese	**so**-no een-**glay**-zay
What's your name?	Come si chiama?	**ko**-may see kee-**ah**-ma
My name is . . .	Mi chiamo . . .	mee kee-**ah**-mo
What time is it?	Che ore sono?	kay **o**-ray **so**-no
How?	Come?	**ko**-may
When?	Quando?	**kwan**-doe
Yesterday/today/ tomorrow	Ieri/oggi/domani	**yer**-ee/**o**-jee/do-**mah**-nee

This morning/ afternoon	Stamattina/Oggi pomeriggio	sta-ma-**tee**-na/**o**-jee po-mer-**ee**-jo
Tonight	Stasera	sta-**ser**-a
What?	Che cosa?	kay **ko**-za
What is it?	Che cos'è?	kay ko-**zay**
Why?	Perché?	pear-**kay**
Who?	Chi?	kee
Where is . . .	Dov'è . . .	doe-**veh**
the bus stop?	la fermata dell'autobus?	la fer-**mah**-ta del ow-toe-**booss**
the train station?	la stazione?	la sta-tsee-**oh**-nay
the subway station?	la metropolitana?	la may-tro-po-lee-**tah**-na
the terminal?	il terminale?	eel ter-mee-**nah**-lay
the post office?	l'ufficio postale?	loo-**fee**-cho po-**stah**-lay
the bank?	la banca?	la **bahn**-ka
the . . . hotel?	l'hotel . . .?	lo-**tel**
the store?	il negozio?	eel nay-**go**-tsee-o
the cashier?	la cassa?	la **kah**-sa
the . . . museum?	il museo . . .?	eel moo-**zay**-o
the hospital?	l'ospedale?	lo-spay-**dah**-lay
the first-aid station?	il pronto soccorso?	eel **pron**-to so-**kor**-so
the elevator?	l'ascensore?	la-shen-**so**-ray
a telephone?	un telefono?	oon tay-**lay**-fo-no
Where are the restrooms?	Dov'è il bagno?	do-**vay** eel **bahn**-yo
Here/there	Qui/là	kwee/la
Left/right	A sinistra/a destra	a see-**neess**-tra/ a **des**-tra
Straight ahead	Avanti dritto	a-**vahn**-tee **dree**-to
Is it near/far?	È vicino/lontano?	ay vee-**chee**-no/ lon-**tah**-no
I'd like . . .	Vorrei . . .	vo-**ray**
a room	una camera	**oo**-na **kah**-may-ra
the key	la chiave	la kee-**ah**-vay
a newspaper	un giornale	oon jor-**nah**-lay
a stamp	un francobollo	oon frahn-ko-**bo**-lo
I'd like to buy . . .	Vorrei comprare . . .	vo-**ray** kom-**prah**-ray
a cigar	un sigaro	oon see-**gah**-ro
cigarettes	delle sigarette	**day**-lay see-ga-**ret**-ay
some matches	dei fiammiferi	**day**-ee **fee**-ah-**mee**-fer-ee
some soap	una saponetta	**oo**-na sa-po-**net**-a
a city plan	una pianta della città	**oo**-na **pyahn**-ta day-la chee-**tah**

a road map of . . .	una carta stradale di . . .	**oo**-na **cart**-a stra-**dah**-lay dee
a country map	una carta geografica	**oo**-na **cart**-a jay-o-**grah**-fee-ka
a magazine	una rivista	**oo**-na ree-**veess**-ta
envelopes	delle buste	**day**-lay **booss**-tay
writing paper	della carta da lettere	**day**-la **cart**-a da let-air-ay
a postcard	una cartolina	**oo**-na car-toe-**lee**-na
a guidebook	una guida turistica	**oo**-na **gwee**-da too-**reess**-tee-ka
How much is it?	Quanto costa?	**kwahn**-toe **coast**-a
It's expensive/cheap	È caro/economico	ay **car**-o/ay-ko-**no**-mee-ko
A little/a lot	Poco/tanto	**po**-ko/**tahn**-to
More/less	Più/meno	pee-**oo**/**may**-no
Enough/too (much)	Abbastanza/troppo	a-bas-**tahn**-sa/**tro**-po
I am sick	Sto male	sto **mah**-lay
Call a doctor	Chiama un dottore	kee-**ah**-mah oon doe-**toe**-ray
Help!	Aiuto!	a-**yoo**-toe
Stop!	Alt!	ahlt
Fire!	Al fuoco!	ahl **fwo**-ko
Caution/Look out!	Attenzione!	a-ten-**syon**-ay

Dining Out

A bottle of . . .	Una bottiglia di . . .	**oo**-na bo-**tee**-lee-ah dee
A cup of . . .	Una tazza di . . .	**oo**-na **tah**-tsa dee
A glass of . . .	Un bicchiere di . . .	oon bee-key-**air**-ay dee
Bill/check	Il conto	eel **cone**-toe
Bread	Il pane	eel **pah**-nay
Breakfast	La prima colazione	la **pree**-ma ko-la-**tsee**-oh-nay
Cocktail/aperitif	L'aperitivo	la-pay-ree-**tee**-vo
Dinner	La cena	la **chen**-a
Fixed-price menu	Menù a prezzo fisso	may-**noo** a **pret**-so **fee**-so
Fork	La forchetta	la for-**ket**-a
I am diabetic	Ho il diabete	o eel dee-a-**bay**-tay
I am vegetarian	Sono vegetariano/a	**so**-no vay-jay-ta-ree-**ah**-no/a
I'd like . . .	Vorrei . . .	vo-**ray**

I'd like to order	Vorrei ordinare	vo-**ray** or-dee-**nah**-ray
Is service included?	Il servizio è incluso?	eel ser-**vee**-tzee-o ay een-**kloo**-zo
It's good/bad	È buono/cattivo	ay **bwo**-no/ka-**tee**-vo
It's hot/cold	È caldo/freddo	ay **kahl**-doe/**fred**-o
Knife	Il coltello	eel kol-**tel**-o
Lunch	Il pranzo	eel **prahnt**-so
Menu	Il menù	eel may-**noo**
Napkin	Il tovagliolo	eel toe-va-lee-**oh**-lo
Please give me . . .	Mi dia . . .	mee **dee**-a
Salt	Il sale	eel **sah**-lay
Spoon	Il cucchiaio	eel koo-kee-**ah**-yo
Sugar	Lo zucchero	lo **tsoo**-ker-o
Waiter/Waitress	Cameriere/cameriera	ka-mare-**yer**-ay/ka-mare-**yer**-a
Wine list	La lista dei vini	la **lee**-sta **day**-ee **vee**-nee

MENU GUIDE

English	Italian
Set menu	Menù a prezzo fisso
Dish of the day	Piatto del giorno
Specialty of the house	Specialità della casa
Local specialties	Specialità locali
Extra charge	Extra . . .
In season	Di stagione
Cover charge/Service charge	Coperto/Servizio

Breakfast

Butter	Burro
Croissant	Cornetto
Eggs	Uova
Honey	Miele
Jam/Marmalade	Marmellata
Roll	Panino
Toast	Pane tostato

Starters

Assorted cold cuts	Affettati misti
Assorted seafood	Antipasto di pesce
Assorted appetizers	Antipasto misto
Toasted rounds of bread, fried or toasted in oil	Crostini/Crostoni
Diced-potato and vegetable salad with mayonnaise	Insalata russa
Eggplant parmigiana	Melanzane alla parmigiana
Fried mozzarella sandwich	Mozzarella in carrozza
Ham and melon	Prosciutto e melone
Cooked sausages and cured meats	Salumi cotti
Filled pastry shells	Vol-au-vents

Soups

"Angel hair," thin noodle soup	Capelli d'angelo
Cream of . . .	Crema di . . .
Pasta-and-bean soup	Pasta e fagioli
Egg-drop and Parmesan cheese soup	Stracciatella

Pasta, Rice, and Pizza

Filled pasta	Agnolotti/ravioli/tortellini
Potato dumplings	Gnocchi

Semolina dumplings	Gnocchi alla romana
Pasta	Pasta
with four cheeses	*al quattro formaggi*
with basil/cheese/pine nuts/ garlic sauce	*al pesto*
with tomato-based meat sauce	*al ragù*
with tomato sauce	*al sugo* or *al pomodoro*
with butter	*in bianco* or *al burro*
with egg, Parmesan cheese, and pepper	*alla carbonara*
green (spinach-based) pasta	*verde*
Rice	Riso
Rice dish	Risotto
with mushrooms	*ai funghi*
with saffron	*alla milanese*
Noodles	Tagliatelle
Pizza	Pizza
Pizza with seafood, cheese, artichokes, and ham in four different sections	Pizza quattro stagioni
Pizza with tomato and mozzarella	Pizza margherita
Pizza with oil, garlic, and oregano	Pizza marinara

Fish and Seafood

Anchovies	Acciughe
Bass	Persico
Carp	Carpa
Clams	Vongole
Cod	Merluzzo
Crab	Granchio
Eel	Anguilla
Lobster	Aragosta
Mackerel	Sgombro
Mullet	Triglia
Mussels	Cozze
Octopus	Polpo
Oysters	Ostriche
Pike	Luccio
Prawns	Gamberoni
Salmon	Salmone
Shrimp	Scampi
Shrimps	Gamberetti
Sole	Sogliola
Squid	Calamari
Swordfish	Pescespada

Trout	Trota
Tuna	Tonno

Methods of Preparation

Baked	Al forno
Cold, with vinegar sauce	In carpione
Fish stew	Zuppa di pesce
Fried	Fritto
Grilled (usually charcoal)	Alla griglia
Seafood salad	In insalata
Smoked	Affumicato
Stuffed	Ripieno

Meat

Boar	Cinghiale
Brain	Cervella
Braised meat with wine	Brasato
Chop	Costoletta
Duck	Anatra
Lamb	Agnello
Baby lamb	Abbacchio
Liver	Fegato
Pheasant	Fagiano
Pork roast	Arista
Rabbit	Coniglio
Steak	Bistecca
Sliced raw steak with sauce	Carpaccio
Mixed boiled meat	Bollito misto

Methods of Preparation

Battered with eggs and crumbs and fried	. . . alla milanese
Grilled	. . . ai ferri
Grilled (usually charcoal)	. . . alla griglia
Raw, with lemon/egg sauce	. . . alla tartara
Roasted	. . . arrosto
Very rare	. . . al sangue
Well done	. . . ben cotta
With ham and cheese	. . . alla valdostana
With Parmesan cheese and tomatoes	. . . alla parmigiana

Vegetables

Artichokes	Carciofi
Asparagus	Asparagi
Beans	Fagioli

Brussels sprouts	Cavolini di Bruxelles
Cabbage	Cavolo
Carrots	Carote
Cauliflower	Cavolfiore
Cucumber	Cetriolo
Eggplants	Melanzane
Green beans	Fagiolini
Leeks	Porri
Lentils	Lenticchie
Lettuce	Lattuga
Mushrooms	Funghi
Onions	Cipolle
Peas	Piselli
Peppers	Peperoni
Potatoes	Patate
Roasted potatoes	*Patate arroste*
Boiled potatoes	*Patate bollite*
Fried potatoes	*Patate fritte*
Small, roasted potatoes	*Patatine novelle*
Mashed potatoes	*Purè di patate*
Radishes	Rapanelli
Salad	Insalata
vegetable	*mista*
green	*verde*
Spinach	Spinaci
Tomatoes	Pomodori
Zucchini	Zucchini

Sauces, Herbs, and Spices

Basil	Basilico
Bay leaf	Lauro
Chervil	Cerfoglio
Dill	Aneto
Garlic	Aglio
Hot dip with anchovies (for vegetables)	Bagna cauda
Marjoram	Maggiorana
Mayonnaise	Maionese
Mustard	Mostarda *or* senape
Oil	Olio
Parsley-based sauce	Salsa verde
Pepper	Pepe
Rosemary	Rosmarino
Tartar sauce	Salsa tartara
Vinegar	Aceto
White sauce	Besciamella

Cheeses

Fresh:	Caprino fresco
	Mascarpone
	Mozzarella
	Ricotta
Mild:	Caciotta
	Caprino
	Fontina
	Grana
	Provola
	Provolone dolce
	Robiola
	Scamorza
Sharp:	Asiago
	Gorgonzola
	Groviera
	Pecorino
	Provolone piccante
	Taleggio
	Toma

Fruits and Nuts

Almonds	Mandorle
Apple	Mela
Apricot	Albicocca
Blackberries	More
Black currant	Ribes nero
Blueberries	Mirtilli
Cherries	Ciliege
Chestnuts	Castagne
Coconut	Noce di cocco
Dates	Datteri
Figs	Fichi
Green grapes	Uva bianca
Black grapes	Uva nera
Grapefruit	Pompelmo
Hazelnuts	Nocciole
Lemon	Limone
Melon	Melone
Nectarine	Nocepesca
Orange	Arancia
Pear	Pera
Peach	Pesca
Pineapple	Ananas
Plum	Prugna/Susina
Prune	Prugna secca

Raisins	Uva passa
Raspberries	Lamponi
Red currant	Ribes
Strawberries	Fragole
Tangerine	Mandarino
Walnuts	Noci
Watermelon	Anguria/Cocomero
Dried fruit	Frutta secca
Fresh fruit	Frutta fresca
Fruit salad	Macedonia di frutta

Desserts

Custard filed pastry, with candied fruit	Cannoli
Ricotta filled pastry shells with sugar glaze	Cannoli alla siciliana
Ice cream with candied fruit	Cassata
Ricotta filed cake with sugar glaze	Cassata siciliana
Chocolate	Cioccolato
Cup of ice cream	Coppa gelato
Caramel custard	Crème caramel
Pie	Crostata
Fruit pie	Crostata di frutta
Ice cream	Gelato
Flaked pastry	Millefoglie
Chestnuts and whipped-cream cake	Montebianco
Whipped cream	Panna montata
Pastries	Paste
Sherbet	Sorbetto
Chocolate-coated ice cream	Tartufo
Fruit tart	Torta di frutta
Apple tart	Torta di mele
Ice-cream cake	Torta gelata
Vanilla	Vaniglia
Egg-based cream with sugar and Marsala wine	Zabaione
Ice-cream filled cake	Zuccotto

Alcoholic Drinks

On the rocks	Con ghiaccio
Straight	Liscio
With soda	Con seltz
Beer	Birra
light/dark	*chiara/scura*

Bitter cordial	Amaro
Brandy	Cognac
Cordial	Liquore
Aniseed cordial	Sambuca
Martini	Cocktail Martini
Port	Porto
Vermouth	Vermut/Martini
Wine	Vino
blush	*rosé*
dry	*secco*
full-bodied	*corposo*
light	*leggero*
red	*rosso*
sparkling	*spumante*
sweet	*dolce*
very dry	*brut*
white	*bianco*
Light wine	Vinello
Bottle	Bottiglia
Carafe	Caraffa
Flask	Fiasco

Nonalcoholic Drinks

Mineral water	Acqua minerale
carbonated	*gassata*
still	*non gassata*
Tap water	Acqua naturale
Tonic water	Acqua tonica
Coffee with steamed milk	Cappuccino
Espresso	Caffè espresso
with milk	*macchiato*
decaffeinated	*decaffeinato*
lighter espresso	*lungo*
with cordial	*corretto*
Fruit juice	Succo di frutta
Lemonade	Limonata
Milk	Latte
Orangeade	Aranciata
Tea	Tè
with milk/lemon	*col latte/col limone*
iced	*freddo*

INDEX

PHOTO CREDITS

NOTES

NOTES

NOTES

NOTES

NOTES

ABOUT OUR WRITERS

After completing his master's degree in art history, Peter Blackman settled permanently in Italy in 1986. Since then he's worked as a biking- and walking-tour guide, managing to see more of Italy than most of his Italian friends. When he's not leading a trip, you'll find Peter at home in Chianti, listening to opera and planning his next journey.

While doing physics research in the same tower where Galileo once worked, Jeff Booth felt the gravitational pull of Venice. After two years of learning to row gondolas and raise a Venetian daughter, he hasn't fallen into the Grand Canal, yet. Jeff writes for *National Geographic Traveler* and *New York* magazine, among other publications.

Disinclined to stray far from superb wine and spectacular skiing, travel writer Ryan Bradley divides his days between northern Italy and northern California. Though the Dolomites are his part-time home, he's never quite prepared for the existential challenge of a face-to-face encounter with Bolzano's iceman.

Elaine Eliah has reported from African war zones and Asian mountaintops. Since settling in Venice in 1999, she's rowed nearly every canal and sailed many of the Venetian Republic's Adriatic trade routes. She currently writes, teaches English, and helps travelers discover the magic of her adopted home.

Although Robin S. Goldstein trained in philosophy at Harvard and in law at Yale, his heart has always been in his travel writing. His credits include not only his home base of Italy but also Spain, Mexico, Ecuador, and the Galapagos Islands. Once a resident of Genoa, he now spends most of his time in the *mezzogiorno* and along the Sicilian coast.

Cristina Gregorin has worked as a guide in Venice since 1991. She's the author of *Venice Master Artisans,* a study of the city's traditional arts and crafts.

In 1996 Valerie Hamilton transplanted from San Francisco to Rome, where she works as a journalist, TV producer, and freelance bon vivant. She holds a degrees in art history and archaeology, but travel is her first love.

Journalist and travel writer Roberta Kedzierski supplements life in Milan with time on the Italian lakes. Her areas of interest include the intriguing interplay between the English and Italian languages and other cross-cultural issues.

Dana Klitzberg studied at the Institute of Culinary Education and worked as a chef at the renowned Manhattan restaurant San Domenico. After a stint cooking in a restaurant in Rome, she decided to make the Eternal City her home. Now she runs her own company, through which she caters, gives cooking classes, and conducts culinary tours of the city.

Chris Rose arrived in Naples from Manchester, England, planning to stay for three months. Thirteen years later, he's still there, writing guidebooks, teaching English, and organizing events with writers and artists visiting from Britain. You can read his short story "The Shoemaker General of Naples" in *New Writing 10,* published by Picador.

Florence resident Patricia Rucidlo holds master's degrees in Italian Renaissance history and art history. When she's not extolling the virtues of a Pontormo masterpiece or angrily defending the Medici, she's leading wine tours in Chianti and catering private dinner parties.

California native Pamela Santini came to study art history 15 years ago at Venice's Ca' Foscari University, where she currently teaches. She's also a writer and translator and enjoys traveling with her husband and son.

A pediatrician by training, Maria Sophocles now writes from her home on Lake Como, where she and her family have lived for four years.

FODOR'S KEY TO THE GUIDES

AMERICA'S **GUIDEBOOK LEADER** PUBLISHES GUIDES FOR **EVERY KIND OF TRAVELER**. CHECK OUT OUR MANY SERIES AND FIND YOUR **PERFECT MATCH**.

FODOR'S GOLD GUIDES
America's favorite travel-guide series offers the most detailed insider reviews of hotels, restaurants, and attractions in all price ranges, plus great background information, smart tips, and useful maps.

COMPASS AMERICAN GUIDES
Stunning guides from top local writers and photographers, with gorgeous photos, literary excerpts, and colorful anecdotes. A must-have for culture mavens, history buffs, and new residents.

FODOR'S 25 BEST / CITYPACKS
Concise city coverage in a guide plus a foldout map. The right choice for urban travelers who want everything under one cover.

FODOR'S AROUND THE CITY WITH KIDS
Up to 68 great ideas for family days, recommended by resident parents. Perfect for exploring in your own backyard or on the road.

SEE IT GUIDES
Illustrated guidebooks that include the practical information travelers need, in gorgeous full color. Perfect for travelers who want the best value packed in a fresh, easy-to-use, colorful layout.

FODOR'S FLASHMAPS
Every resident's map guide, with 60 easy-to-follow maps of public transit, parks, museums, zip codes, and more.

FODOR'S LANGUAGES FOR TRAVELERS
Practice the local language before you hit the road. Available in phrase books, cassette sets, and CD sets.

THE COLLECTED TRAVELER
These collections of the best published essays and articles on various European destinations will give you a feel for the culture, cuisine, and way of life.

At bookstores everywhere.   www.fodors.com/books